Country
MUSIC

THE ENCYCLOPEDIA

Also by Irwin Stambler

The Encyclopedia of Pop, Rock and Soul

and forthcoming

Folk and Blues: The Encyclopedia
(with Lyndon Stambler)

Country MUSIC

THE ENCYCLOPEDIA

IRWIN STAMBLER
& GRELUN LANDON

*Contributors: Alice Seidman
and Lyndon Stambler*

ST. MARTIN'S PRESS

NEW YORK

Earlier editions of this book were published under the title *The Encyclopedia of Folk, Country and Western Music.*

Design by Ellen R. Sasahara

Library of Congress Cataloging-in-Publication Data

Stambler, Irwin.
  Country music: the encyclopedia

  Bibliography: p.
   1. Folk music—United States—Dictionaries.
2. Country music—United States—Dictionaries.
3. Musicians—United States—Biography.   4. Country musicians—United States—Biography. I. Title.
ML102.F66S7   1997   781.773'03'21   82–5702
ISBN 0–312–15121–7   642   AACR2

First edition: November 1997

10 9 8 7 6 5 4 3 2 1

CONTENTS

INTRODUCTION

S THIS THIRD EDITION of *Country Music: The Encyclopedia* goes to press, the field in many respects is in its best condition in its history—certainly from a financial standpoint—though concerns remain about whether it has strayed too far from its roots into the "pop" domain. Exactly what those roots include, however, is open to question. As introduced by the first white settlers, the origins of what eventually came to be considered American country music derived to a great extent from the folk ballads of the British Isles, typically played on the fiddle and related instruments. Yet other influences that have appeared since those early times have contributed equally notable characteristics to the sound of country.

Some of these influences stem from African rhythms and instruments. The banjo is generally accepted as having been brought to America by slaves who, though barred by slavers from bringing drums, still found percussion substitutes in their new homeland. And, of course, guitarists of the Spanish Empire in the New World are credited with introducing that instrument into the Western Hemisphere. More recently, German and Polish polka music had a great impact upon the work of country songwriters, particularly in Texas, and new folk and folk rock artists from Ireland, England, and Scotland have made their styles felt just as keenly as their ancestors had.

Today's country "mainstream" music represents an intermingling of a variety of elements from different cultures. The "father of modern country music," Jimmie Rodgers, "the Singing Brakeman," scored a major breakthrough with record buyers in the late 1920s and early 1930s with songs that added a strong leavening of black influences, including the blues, to traditional Appalachian-style music. Until recently, it appeared that Rodgers's approach sprang full-blown from his own experimentation. This view (which some veteran country artists were well aware was a little exaggerated) changed with the 1996 reissue of old recordings by a performer named Emmett Miller, whose initial career successes as a minstrel artist preceded that of Rodgers. Miller's recordings affected the careers of not only Rodgers, but such country legends as Hank Williams, Sr., and Bob Wills.

Of course, "purer" strains of mountain music, reflected by such Rodgers contemporaries as the Original Carter Family and various string bands like those featured on early Grand Ole Opry radio programs, coexisted for years with the new country music formats. Inevitably, though, there was an interaction between those segments that led to new blends in later decades. This helped bring about such categories as country rock (both rockabilly and straight-ahead rock and roll) and bluegrass, both of which are represented by artists covered in this volume. And, of course, there are other discernible musical strains in modern country music, including the Hispanic influence represented by Tex-Mex, tejano, conjunto, and the like and the Acadian French-derived Cajun genre.

The worry among many country music adherents in recent decades has been that the more earthy, rough-hewn aspects of country music would be sacrificed in favor of blander material calculated to compete for the mass market, noncountry audience. Bill Ivey, executive director of the Country Music Foundation, for instance, sounded this alarm in an article for the second edition of this encyclopedia. Referring to "country-pop" as the legacy of the 1960s and 1970s, he wrote that, "For many observers, the early 1970s foretold the demise of country music. It is a widely held theory that country music had begun as a form of folk-art; crude at times, but rich in excitement and honest poetic expression, which over the decades had been diluted by contact with other musical styles, and undermined by the demand of the commercial marketplace. Each decade seemed to produce a country style closer to the pop mainstream, as instrumentation, song, texts, and vocal style moved away from country music's Appalachian roots. Critics saw the early 1970s as the end of country music and many pundits predicted that country music would, by 1975, merge with pop music and lose its distinct identity."

Citing such best-sellers of those years as Lynn Anderson's "Rose Garden," Charlie Rich's "Behind Closed Doors," and Glen Campbell's "Rhinestone Cowboy," he noted that "None of those hits belonged to the country styles pioneered by Ernest Tubb, Hank Snow, Hank Williams, or Lefty Frizzell. To those connected with country music and Nashville in the 1970s, those crossover hits were proof that traditional country music was dying."

As it turned out, such obituaries were premature. In fact in the mid 1970s Waylon Jennings, Willie Nelson, Jessi Colter, and Tompall Glazer proved there was plenty of life in the so-called traditional country approach by turning out the best-selling *Outlaws* album. (The album was reissued on CD in 1996.) As Tompall told Deborah Evans Price of *Billboard* in 1996, "Waylon and I were disgusted with the way radio was handling country music. There was a logjam like it gets every once in a while where everything gets repetitious and labels are too much in charge. We were just trying anything we thought might break it."

The 1980s demonstrated there was room for both schools of thought. Thus artists like Willie Nelson and Merle Haggard had major successes in the first part of the decade, and traditional bluegrass star Ricky Skaggs found a sizable following. Record numbers of new artists began to appear on the scene, many meeting the country-pop concepts favored by the vast majority of country radio programmers, but quite a few also seeking to follow in the footsteps of people like Willie, Waylon, Johnny Cash, et al. In the late 1980s and into the 1990s, the audience for country/country rock and its subgroups seemed to expand exponentially as performers like Garth Brooks, Clint Black, and a resurgent Reba McEntire became familiar names on the highest positions in the pop charts as well as the country lists.

Country music has had its ups and downs over the decades of this century, drastically affected by the U.S. Depression of the 1930s, moving into relative boom times in the World War II years. Country music suffered a major decline in the late 1950s during the birth of rock and roll—ironically a genre whose first great stars, Jerry Lee Lewis, Elvis, and Johnny Cash among them—emerged from the country sector. As country star Bill Anderson recalled in the first edition of this encyclopedia, at the start of the 1960s major country entertainers looked back longingly on the "good ole days. . . . Backstage gab among the entertainers was often about the days when 'ole Webb [Pierce]' had twenty-one straight number one songs, the least of which sold a quarter of a million records . . . of the days when 'ole Hank [Williams, Sr.]' was packin' 'em in singing 'Lovesick Blues' [which he picked up from the aforementioned Emmett Miller] and the nights when souvenir book and picture sales totaled in the thousands of dollars. How many times did I hear from how many people in how many half-filled halls, in how many country musicless cities . . . 'Oh, those were the good ole days.'"

By the late 1960s, he stressed, country had rebounded thanks to the new insights provided by people like Buck Owens, George Jones, Tammy Wynette, and many other talented newcomers. The fortunes of this art form have generally improved since then, despite such temporary setbacks as the *Urban Cowboy* period; in fact, the late 1980s and the 1990s might be called the music's true golden years, both in monetary rewards and the expansion of the impact of country and its related forms to all parts of the world.

Reflecting on the field's status in the late 1990s, however, Ivey commented, "I think the country field is at a point in time in which it's far bigger than it's ever been, but the growth has flattened and may even begin to fall a little. On the artistic side it's a challenge to maintain the traditions of the music in terms of quality and talent. At this time we have a steadily expanding number of record labels, artists and larger [record and concert] sales than ever before, but we face artistic challenges. One problem is that while there are many more successful artists, there is a kind of sameness about everything. This is why I feel we are at a little bit of a turning point where we need to go back to basics and get to the roots of the music.

"Taking people like Mary Chapin Carpenter or Alison Krauss as examples, there's the question about whether some acts should be considered country or something else. A lot of acts also could fit into pop or rock. This is something argued about in Grammy Award discussions about which artists properly fit in which categories. As far as seeking ways to more traditional formats or alternatives to current best-sellers, I don't see it in terms of major industry labels or radio coverage. The question is, Where are the next big things coming from? We had the class of the 1990s, folks who came along over the last half decade like Garth Brooks, Clint Black, and Reba—she's been around longer, but really didn't become a big star until the end of the 1980s. In the early 1980s we had people like Ricky Skaggs and other bluegrass artists who went back to earlier forms and affected how the field developed. Now it seems we're at a sort of plateau waiting for the next breakthrough."

It is at least a profitable plateau, and one in which the top country stars can point to fan support far exceeding what even the greatest optimists could see possible a few decades ago. During the 1996 concert season, Garth Brooks finished second only to the veteran rock group Kiss, achieving a total gross of $34.5 million from 121 shows in 41 cities (versus $43.6 million from 92 shows in 75 cities for Kiss). Actually, Brooks outdrew Kiss, selling 1.9 million tickets compared to 1.2 million. The difference was that Brooks's ticket prices (called the bargain of the year by Gary Bongiovanni, editor of *Pollstar* magazine) were kept for the most part under $20, about half of the prices charged for rock and pop stars. Reba McEntire also made the concert top 10, grossing $26.1 million from 86 shows in 83 cities. The top 25 list for 1996 also included rewarding tour achievements for George Strait, Alan Jackson, Brooks & Dunn, Vince Gill, and Tim McGraw.

Ivey agreed that the status of country music has improved greatly in recent times. "It's pretty clear that the picture has stabilized. I've been looking at it for 25 years and today for the first time country music has become a real part of mainstream pop music and has penetrated the market to the extent that it wouldn't suffer depression times like what happened in the early 1960s or after the *Urban Cowboy* period. It might slip back a little, but I don't see it ever falling back to past lows. I have a feeling with the current standards of radio and records the U.S. country market will fluctuate between

12 and 17 percent of the market depending on public interest in some major acts at one time or another. For instance, someone like Alan Jackson may attract a big following one year, but much of that may turn in another direction the next. If we're going to move beyond that we need to get new sources of industry sales that will smooth out the situation."

One possibility is to make greater inroads into the international music sector. "There is more interaction with overseas fans," Ivey observes, "but while this has been talked about for six or seven years, it hasn't really become important. For a while a lot of country labels opened up international offices in their Nashville divisions, but most have been closed down. As the Country Music Television (CMT) network gets around the world, it may be the vehicle for getting country music out of the box for broader coverage. Right now, overseas fans associate it with a niche sector like cowboys, but CMT promises to extend our boundaries. It seems to be really catching on in Europe and they're working on Latin America. International growth has great potential; in fact, it's essential for country music to develop an international audience."

Of course, country rock always has found sizable interest around the world, as have folk-oriented artists like Nanci Griffith, Skaggs, and Emmylou Harris. In some cases, such performers do as well overseas as at home, but Ivey stresses this isn't true for most other artists in the country field. One possibility is that if the impact of CMT dramatically increase European interest, it might bring about the kind of feedback loop that occurred in rock in the 1960s, when the "British Invasion" resulted in new trends. (There are indigenous country artists working in other parts of the world, but thus far they essentially take their cue from U.S. styles.) Ivey's response: "I don't think that's near at hand. I think it needs a generation or two before something like that might happen. Such a scenario might be out there on the horizon, but I don't see it yet."

There is the fact, as well, that markets can vary in intensity internationally as well as in the U.S. For instance, in the 1970s, Japan was a hot market for country material, but that has cooled down considerably in recent years. The primary potential growth areas as seen from Nashville now are considered to be China, Brazil, and Europe.

An encouraging factor is continuing audience for country subgroups like grassroots bluegrass and western, aside from the burgeoning popularity of mainstream performers. Western music, in particular, has staged a comeback of sorts, spearheaded by people like Michael Martin Murphy, Red Steagall, and Riders in the Sky. Very respectable crowds are being drawn to events like Murphy's WestFest and Steagall's Ft. Worth–based Cowboy Gathering & Western Swing Festival, as well as to other gatherings spotlighting western music and poetry. Most of these feature not only country-western offerings, but ethnic Native American and Hispanic American artists. At the same time, Asleep at the Wheel and other such groups are keeping the flame of western swing burning.

As was the case in earlier editions, the entries in this book were chosen to reflect as much as possible the many facets of what has increasingly become a complex genre. Besides covering the careers of accepted superstars and creative influences, this also includes career entries of artists who haven't yet received the public acknowledgment they seem to deserve, such as Del McCoury and Bobbie Cryner, or who seem to have great potential for the future such as Gillian Welch. At the same time, we have chosen to focus this new edition on acts that, however loosely, can be grouped under the broad category of country music; coverage of the folk and blues acts we have expanded to create an entirely new volume, *Folk and Blues: The Encyclopedia*, to be published next year. Lastly, for this edition we have added a set of indexes that should make *Country Music: The Encyclopedia* easier than ever to use.

Completing a project of this kind, of course, called for the assistance and support of many people and organizations. Those to whom we are particularly indebted (including some cited in previous editions who are not listed here) include Bill Ivey, Don Burkhimer and Sony Music, Bob Merlis and Warner/Reprise Records, Stacey Studebaker and MCA Records, Glenn Dicker and Rounder Records, Chris Caravaggi and Wendy Pearl of Asylum Nashville, Megan Rubiner Zinn and Red House Records, Paula Batson, George Collier and Intersound Records, Karen De Marco of Myers media, Jacki Sallow (for original pictures of several major artists), Gary Glade, Peter Nash, John Mankiewicz, Michael Ochs (Michael Ochs Archives) Don and Irene Robertson, Mark Ford and the Nashville Songwriters Association International, Jeff Cohen, Academy of Country Music, Country Music Association, the trustees and directors of the Country Music Foundation, Recording Industry Association of America, McCabe's, Ed Pearl's Ash Grove, and such record companies besides those mentioned above as: Giant, Sony/Columbia/Epic, Curb, BNA, RCA, Arista, Capitol Nashville (Liberty), Elektra, Atlantic, Polydor, Polygram/Mercury, Rhino, A&M, EMI, American Recordings, and Geffen.

Appreciation also is due to the staff at St. Martin's Press, particularly editor Calvert Morgan, who performed yeoman service in shepherding a massive manuscript through all the preproduction phases.

Los Angeles, California, 1997
Irwin Stambler

$\mathcal{A}$

ACADEMY OF COUNTRY MUSIC: *Western-based country music industry organization, founded 1964. (Original name, Academy of Country & Western Music.)*

The concept of special awards for creativity in the entertainment field seems to have its strongest roots in California. Such events as the Academy Awards of the Academy of Motion Picture Arts and Sciences and the Grammy Awards of the National Academy of the Recording Arts and Sciences originated in the state. Thus the environment was right when a new series of awards for the country & western music field was established by the newly formed Academy of Country & Western Music in 1964.

The new organization grew out of discussions in 1964 between trade journal publisher Tommy Wiggins (*D.J.'s Digest*) and three other country music enthusiasts, Eddie Miller, Mickey Christiansen, and Chris Christiansen. Their original goal was to promote greater interest in country & western music in the western states and provide a framework for meetings and programs for the exchange of information about the field by interested parties. During initial organizational efforts, one goal was to provide forms of recognition for performers and executives in country & western music.

Interest was quickly forthcoming, leading to the holding of the first awards event in late 1964. Locale was the Red Barrel nightclub in the Los Angeles area. Wiggins's publication underwrote the evening and Tex Williams served as emcee. In 1965, a second awards dinner was held, sponsored by *V.I.P.* magazine.

As Academy membership increased, it was decided to form a continuing committee to handle future progress. A dues plan was instituted so that sponsorship of future awards affairs could be handled by the Academy itself. The first official awards show of the Academy was held at the Hollywood Palladium in February 1966.

By the time the second Annual Awards Dinner was held at the Beverly Hilton, Beverly Hills, California, on March 6, 1967, the Academy had elected its first officers: Tex Williams as president, Eddie Dean, vice president, Bettie Azevedo, secretary, and Herb Eiseman, treasurer.

Since that time, the Academy continued to expand its membership and activities. During the 1970s, it changed from a regionally oriented organization to a more national one in outlook. As part of the trend, the awards ceremonies became an annual feature of network TV, starting on ABC-TV in 1973 and switching to NBC-TV late in the decade. (For Award winners, see Appendix.)

ACUFF, ROY: *Singer, fiddler, band leader (Tennessee Crackerjacks, Crazy Tennesseans, Smoky Mountain Boys), emcee, songwriter, record and music industry executive. Born Maynardsville, Tennessee, September 15, 1903; died Nashville, Tennessee, November 23, 1992. First living member elected to the Country Music Hall of Fame; inducted 1962.*

Few would argue with Dizzy Dean's designation of Roy Acuff as "The King of Country Music." Embodying the soul and symbol of the *Grand Ole Opry* in the 1940s, Roy Claxton Acuff remained its most charismatic figure over the ensuing decades.

Giving little evidence of having much interest in a music career until he was in his late twenties, Roy, as a child, excelled in athletics. His talent was impressive: he won thirteen athletic letters in high school. While not starring on the playing field, he was holding the center of the stage. He recalled that he "acted in every play they [the high school] had."

After high school, Acuff played semipro baseball and had hopes of having a successful tryout for a major league baseball team when disaster struck. Playing in a game in Knoxville on July 7, 1929, he suffered a sunstroke and collapsed in the dugout. After a week, another fainting spell came and, following three months of rest, still another. When a fourth attack hit him during a round of golf, he was so ill he had to spend most of his time indoors for almost two years. Slowly he recovered his strength, and as he noted, "I had to pick me out a new career."

His father's collection of country records helped point the way. Roy spent many hours at home listening to the fiddling tunes of Fiddlin' John Carson and Gid Tanner and the Skillet Lickers, trying to emulate the masters.

By 1932, he seemed in excellent health again. But if it were not for a neighbor named Dr. Hauer, a patent medicine man, Roy might not have gone into music. He asked Roy to join his show, to sell something called "Moc-A-Tan." As Roy told Douglas B. Green of the Country Music Foundation, "There was three of us that got to do all the entertainment, and I got to play every type of character: the blackface, the little girl's part, the old woman's part, plus play the fiddle and sing. And I'd sing real loud on the med show, sing where they could hear me a long ways. Yes, I got a world of training."

The tour lasted from spring to early fall. When it was over, Roy formed a band, the Tennessee Crackerjacks. In a relatively short time, they had a following in the Knoxville region and soon were being featured on local stations KNOX and WROL. By the time they were approached by American Record Company to cut some sides, they were one of the most popular groups in Tennessee and had changed their name to the Crazy Tennesseans. Their first session, which included an odd type of gospel song called "The Great Speckled Bird," took place in Chicago on October 26, 1936.

Even prior to that, Acuff had yearned to join the *Grand Ole Opry*. Several inquiries had received little encouragement. But in early 1938, star *Opry* performer Arthur Smith, a favorite fiddler with program fans, got into an argument with the show and was suspended. A replacement was needed in a hurry. Someone thought of Acuff and, on the rainy night of February 19, 1938, he and the band set out for Nashville, arguing among themselves about what material to offer.

The matter still wasn't settled when Roy opened their set on the Dixie Tabernacle stage in East Nashville with the fiddle tune "The Old Hen Cackled and the Rooster's Going to Crow." He was so nervous, he told Green, "I did an awful poor job of fiddling. I played back of the bridge about as much as I played in front of it." Then he turned to dobro player Clell Summey and told him to start "The Great Speckled Bird," a number the band had urged him not to use. Again he felt he wasn't at his best. When the band left for their next engagement everyone thought they'd ruined their big chance.

Acuff recalled, "I didn't hear anything for two weeks after we returned to Knoxville. Out of the blue I received a telegram from David Stone asking me if I would come and take a regular job. The mail had come in tremendous—bushel baskets full—and they sent them on to me in Knoxville. That night 'The Great Speckled Bird' really changed my life."

Before 1938 was over, Acuff had begun to make his mark on the *Opry* and on country fans across the country. His single of the old Carter Family success, "Wabash Cannonball," was one of the most popular releases of 1938. He caught the fancy of *Opry* fans so rapidly that within a year's time he had replaced Uncle Dave Macon, the original superstar of the show, as the top performer. In the 1940 Republic film *Grand Ole Opry,* Acuff was considered the star of the movie, although Uncle Dave and other longtime luminaries were featured. Acuff also held center stage in 1940 on the "Prince Albert" broadcast, the most prestigious portion of the *Opry* program.

During 1939, at the urging of *Opry* management, the name of Roy's band was changed to the Smoky Mountain Boys, a name that stayed with the band. Although early members like Clell Summey and bassist Ed Jones departed to be replaced by other musicians as the 1940s went by, the band makeup in the mid-1940s remained together for many years: Howard "Howdy" Forrester, Jimmie Riddle on harmonica and accordion, Peter Kirby (better known as Bashful Brother Oswald) on dobro, banjo, and vocals. Other members in the

1940s were Lonnie "Pap" Wilson, Jess Easterday, and Tommy Magness. By the 1970s, Forrester, Kirby, and Riddle still were in the fold, along with Gene Martin, Charlie Collins, and Onie Wheeler.

Roy's records were top country sellers almost every month throughout the 1940s. His top sellers of the period included "Wreck on the Highway" and "Fireball Mail" in 1942, and "Night Train to Memphis," "Low and Lonely," and "Pins and Needles (In My Heart)" in 1943. Things were going so well for him in the early 1940s that he expanded his activities into the publishing field, joining forces with Fred Rose to form Acuff-Rose Publishing in 1942. The company became a major force in country music development over the decades, and its staff of contract writers provided not only some of the finest country songs but many of the top-ranked performers as well.

During the 1940s and early 1950s, Acuff made dozens of singles and albums that were issued on the Vocalion, Okeh, or Columbia labels (Columbia bought out the American Record Company). Some of his Vocalion singles were "Steamboat Whistle Blues," "New Greenback Dollar," "Steel Guitar Chimes," "Wabash Cannonball," "The Beautiful Picture," "The Great Shining Light," and "The Rising Sun." His output on Okeh included "Vagabond's Dream," "Haven of Dreams," "Beautiful Brown Eyes," "Living on the Mountain," "Baby Mine," "Ida Red," "Smoky Mountain Rag," "Will the Circle Be Unbroken," "When I Lay My Burden Down," "Streamline Cannonball," "Weary River," "Just to Ease My Worried Mind," "The Broken Heart," "The Precious Jewel," "Worried Mind," "Lyin' Women Blues," "Are You Thinking of Me Darling," "Wreck on the Highway," "Night Train to Memphis," "Don't Make Me Go to Bed and I'll Be Good," and "It's Too Late to Worry Anymore."

Roy's recordings for Columbia those years were even greater in number than his combined total on Vocalion and Okeh. His Columbia list included many of the songs listed above, plus such others as "Beneath That Precious Mound of Clay," "It Won't Be Long," "Branded Wherever I Go," "Do You Wonder Why," "The Devil's Train," "The Songbirds Are Singing in Heaven," "I Saw the Light," "Unloved and Unclaimed," "Mule Skinner Blues," "Not a Word from Home," "Waiting for My Call to Glory," "I Called and Nobody Answered," "Golden Treasure," "Heartaches and Flowers," "Tennessee Waltz," "Sweeter than the Flowers," "Polk County Breakdown," "I'll Always Care," and "Black Mountain Rag."

Since childhood, Roy had harbored thoughts of emulating his father's legal career. In the 1940s, he ran for governor of Tennessee on the Republican ticket, both in 1944 and in 1948. Had Tennessee been a state less dominated by the Democratic Party, things might have been different. As it was, though, Acuff lost both times and stuck to his musical career thereafter.

During the 1950s and first part of the 1960s, Roy was no longer able to penetrate the upper segments of the singles charts, but remained a fans' favorite on the *Opry* as well as on the county fair, rodeo, and concert circuits. Even if Roy himself wasn't dominating the charts, the output of Acuff-Rose was. Through 1967, that company's writers turned out 108 songs that made the top 10, including fifteen number-one records. That was more than twice as many top-10 successes as the next publisher, Hill and Range. During those years, Roy also diversified into other enterprises, operating Roy Acuff Hobby Exhibits, Dunbar Cave Park and Recreation Center near Clarksville, Tennessee. He also helped Fred Rose start Hickory Records and became a member of the Hickory recording roster in 1957. (His association with Columbia ended in 1952 and was followed by brief stays with Decca, MGM, and Capitol, before the Hickory alignment.)

Most of his album work from 1957 was for Hickory. Some earlier material was reissued on various labels in the 1960s, such as Capitol's *Best of Roy Acuff* in 1963, *Great Roy Acuff* in 1964, and *Voice of Roy Acuff* in 1965, and MGM's *Hymn Time* in 1962 and *Smoky Mountain Boys* in 1965. He was represented on Pickwick in the 1960s by the album *How Beautiful Heaven Must Be*. Decca also issued material by Roy in a series of seven albums titled *All Time Country & Western Hits* issued at intervals from July 1960 to August 1966. His name also graced several Harmony Record LPs, such as *Roy Acuff* (3/58), *That Glory Bound Train* (7/61), and *Great Roy Acuff* (7/65).

His Hickory LPs of the 1960s included *American Folk Songs, Gospel Songs, King of Country Music, Once More, Songs of the Grand Ole Opry, The World Is His Stage,* all issued or reissued in July 1964; *Great Train Songs, Hall of Fame, Sings Hank Williams* (1/67); *Treasury of Hits* (7/69). Harmony issued the LPs *Waiting for My Call* in August 1969 and *Night Train to Memphis* in July 1970. Hickory issued *Roy Acuff Time* in 1970. Also released about that time was the Columbia album *Roy Acuff's Greatest Hits,* and on Hilltop, *Roy Acuff Country.*

Like most country stars during their heyday, Roy was on the road hundreds of days each year. His schedules included long overseas trips to entertain the U.S. armed forces. His first such effort was to Berlin during the 1949 Russian blockade and continued with shows in Korea in the 1950s and the Dominican Republic and Vietnam in the 1960s. Roy and the Smoky Mountain Boys also were featured in concerts in many European countries. The intensive tour grind came to a halt, though, on July 10, 1965, in an automobile accident that injured Roy and several band members. He returned to action on the *Opry* three weeks later, but cut back sharply on the road work, pruning his schedule to almost nothing by 1972, when he was nearly seventy years old. Roy continued to be a mainstay of the *Opry,*

however, delighting countless fans throughout the decade of the 1970s. On the occasional *Opry* specials telecast on PBS, the show often included segments showing Roy happily presiding over impromptu jam sessions by *Opry* greats in his dressing room.

During the 1960s and 1970s, Roy's recorded output included a sizable number of remakes of earlier hits on Hickory. But he also included new numbers, such as his single "Back in the Country" in 1974. Many of those recordings, old and new, were included in the two-record *Roy Acuff's Greatest Hits, Volume 1,* issued by Elektra in 1978. In 1979, Elektra issued *Volume 2.*

Roy was nominated for the Country Music Hall of Fame in 1961 and his plaque was unveiled there the following year. It read, in part, "The Smoky Mountain Boy . . . fiddle[d] and sang his way into the hearts of millions the world over, often times bringing country music to areas where it had never been before. 'The King of Country Music' . . . has carried his troupe of performers overseas to entertain his country's armed forces at Christmas time for more than 20 years. Many successful artists credit their success to a helping hand and encouraging word from Roy Acuff."

In May 1982, Elektra issued the album *Back in the Country,* which included three songs previously released on Hickory in 1974: "Back in the Country," "Don't Worry 'Bout the Mule (Just Load the Wagon)," and "Smoky Mountain Memories." The rest of the tracks were newly recorded numbers by Roy and the Smoky Mountain Boys. Band members then included, besides Kirby, Riddle, Wheeler, Forrester and Collins, George "Leo" Jackson on guitar, Milton Huskey on bass, and Harold Weakley on drums.

A few months before the album came out, Roy was honored by a two-hour NBC-TV special, "Roy Acuff: 50 Years the King of Country Music," telecast on March 1. Among those taking part were President Ronald Reagan, Eddy Arnold, Chet Atkins, Emmylou Harris, Dolly Parton, and Kenny Rogers.

Asked about retirement in the early 1980s, Acuff replied, "I'll never quit. I love the roar of the crowd." True to his word, he continued to appear on the *Grand Ole Opry* year after year in the 1980s into the early 1990s. Almost every weekend he would walk up to the *Opry* mike, exhibiting his skills with a yo-yo as he did so, to start the show with the words, "This is the *Grand Ole Opry* from Nashville, Tennessee." As he once said about his *Opry* contributions, "I like to think I was the first person to bring voice to the *Opry.* I was one of the first fellows who reared back and hit a microphone with a strong voice."

From time to time he also toured with other *Opry* veterans in concerts that focused on country music's roots. He remained active almost up to his death in late 1992 at the age of 89. Among his recordings in print as of the mid-1990s was the early 1990s Columbia/Legacy collection, *The Essential Roy Acuff.* Total recording sales by his death were probably in excess of 30 million records; at the time of his entry into the Country Music Hall of Fame it was estimated he had accrued sales of over 25 million.

AKINS, RHETT: *Singer, guitarist, songwriter. Born Valdosta, Georgia, October 13, 1969.*

The surge of new talent that was a driving force in the worldwide expansion of country music audiences during the 1980s continued in the next decade when every year seemed to bring a new group of very talented performers to the fore. Nineteen ninety-five was no exception—the "Class of '95" included such promising new faces as Shania Twain and Rhett Akins, with more than a dozen other contenders on the horizon.

Akins was a somewhat unusual case in that, unlike most other aspirants, he hadn't been gaining experience in honky-tonks or other public places in his teens. In fact, it was almost as if he turned to seeking a professional music career on a whim. The time span from his first efforts in that direction to having recordings on the hit charts was only two or three years—not that unusual in pop genres, but more rare in country.

Rhett, who grew up in the small city of Valdosta, Georgia (population 50,000), didn't come from a family of entertainers, though there was musical interest in his family. His mother played the piano and one of his grandfathers led his church congregation in singing. He got his first guitar when he was fourteen and learned to play it, but restricted its use to picking and singing in his room and occasionally with friends or family. It wasn't something he thought much about, he recalled; his primary interest was sports and particularly football for which he earned quarterback letters at his high school. His dream, when he enrolled at the University of Georgia in the late 1980s, was to play someday in the National Football League.

However, after a year there he realized the NFL was beyond his reach and dropped out to go back to Valdosta where, in short order, he got married and started working for his father's oil and gas distributorship. The turning point came when he was asked to sing at his brother-in-law's wedding rehearsal dinner in 1991. His choices were "If Tomorrow Never Comes" and "As Long As I Have You." Hearing the applause inspired him to form a band with some friends, a step that later evolved into gigs at local hotel lounges and at parties and other events at places like Valdosta State College and the University of Georgia. The music they offered ranged from traditional country to hard driving rock 'n' roll.

Like many youngsters growing up in the 1970s, his tastes were shaped in part by the mainstream audience favorites of rock and soul. He recalled, "My mom and dad grew up in the sixties, so I was exposed to Jimi Hendrix, the Beatles, and the Stones. Once I got into junior high school, I started meeting people that came from all walks of life. That's when I got into Hank, Jr., and through him I wanted to know about his daddy. Then I got into George Jones and George Strait. I'd go to class wearing cowboy boots and a Van Halen World Tour T-shirt. Even though we were from a small town in Georgia, we had radios. I listened to Kiss and Van Halen, and then I listened to Jones and the Allman Brothers and Skynyrd. But the country lyrics—Hank, Jr., and his daddy—just nailed me to the wall.

"My voice, my accent, is country anyway, and when I started writing, my lyrics always turned out to be real rural and real life. I don't think of a hook and then try to write it; I write songs and then try to find a hook."

His mother was very impressed by his musical progress, he stated, and it was partly at her urging that he decided to move to Nashville in September 1992 to try for a full-time career as a songwriter or performer. But he also remembered another moment of insight that took place when he was listening to country programs while driving his father's fuel truck. The thought flashed through his mind, "I just can't sit here and sing to the radio anymore. I want to be on it," and he left for Nashville with a handful of originals in his pocket. He noted, "I started really seriously writing songs about '91. I wrote the first half of my first song sitting in a deer stand at a hunting camp and the other half pumping gas at this big concrete plant working for Daddy. So I came to Nashville with about three songs."

In a surprisingly short time he had gained the support of Jerry Smith of Sony Tree Publishing/Fire Hall Music, who helped line up cowriters for Rhett. Rhett made a series of demo tapes of his new compositions, some of which were given to record producer Mark Wright of Decca Records as possible vehicles for Mark Chesnutt. As has happened many times over the years, Wright liked Rhett's vocal work and signed him to the label. By then Rhett was mulling over other contract offers from smaller companies, but he jumped at the chance for major label affiliation.

It was a period when Rhett also started to get exposure as an artist. In 1992, for instance, he got the chance to a guest spot with Roy Acuff on the *Grand Ole Opry*. Singing one of his songs and Hank Williams's "Settin' the Woods on Fire." His second exposure on Nashville TV came in June 1994 when he appeared on the TV special "Music City Tonight Salutes Decca Records."

His debut album on Decca, *A Thousand Memories,* produced by Mark Wright, was released on January 17, 1995, with nine of the ten songs cowritten by Akins. The first single issued by Decca, "I Brake for Brunettes" (cowritten by Rhett and Sandy Ramos), spent several months on the *Billboard* charts, gaining the top 40 during March. The album made the *Billboard* list soon after it came out and stayed at mid- and lower positions into the summer months, when it was then given new impetus by the single "That Ain't My Truck" (cowritten by Akins, Tom Shapiro, and Chris Waters), which was moving toward top-chart locales in August. All in all, the signs suggested a new star in the country pantheon had been born.

By late 1995, he had recorded the first five songs for his second album, due out in the spring or summer of 1996. As he told Janet E. Williams of the CMA *Close Up,* he had high hopes for that year. "I want 1996 to be a year where I take the training wheels off and start doing some wheelies!"

ALABAMA: *Vocal and instrumental group. Personnel as of 1981: Randy Yeuell Owen, born Ft. Payne, Alabama, December 13, 1949; Jeffrey Alan Cook, born Ft. Payne, Alabama, August 27, 1949; Teddy Wayne Gentry, born Ft. Payne, Alabama, January 22, 1952; Mark Joel Herndon, born Springfield, Massachusetts, May 11, 1955.*

In the years following World War II, most of the names appearing on country music charts have belonged to solo artists, and to a lesser extent, duets. Very few bands have made the charts at all, and even fewer have reached the highest positions on the charts. Even those who have reached the top have failed to do so consistently. Alabama, in the early 1980s, seemed an exception to this trend, with a string of hit singles and albums, some of which also crossed over to the pop charts.

As its name implies, the band had its origins in Alabama. Randy Owen, Jeff Cook, and Teddy Gentry—the three cousins who are the band's primary members—were all born and grew up near Ft. Payne, Alabama, a locale where country music has strong roots. By the time the three cousins reached their teens, they were all interested in music and had learned to play various instruments. It would be a while, however, before they would perform together.

When the cousins first started jamming together around Christmas, 1969, it seemed doubtful that any of them would ever make music a career. At that time, Jeff was working for Western Electric, while Teddy was earning a living laying carpets, and Randy was still attending school. In their partnership, all three handled vocals with Randy singing most of the leads. Instrumentally, Randy and Jeff played guitar and Teddy bass guitar. Another cousin, Jackie Owen, was the group's first drummer. They formally became a band at the start of the 1970s, after getting a job offer to play at the nearby Canyonland tourist park. Each weekend, Canyonland brought in an established star like Bobby Bare, Narvel Felts, and Jerry Wallace, and the band would back them, then play a one-hour dance set.

After a while, when no new opportunities for the band opened up, Jeff became discouraged and took a government job in Anniston, Alabama. However, Randy (having finished high school) and Teddy remained hopeful and moved there also, both taking day jobs as carpet-layers. The cousins kept working days and picking up night and weekend band dates until March 1973, when they moved to Myrtle Beach, South Carolina, where they found work playing six nights a week in local clubs for tips. Without a record contract at the time, the group cut its own records and hawked them to audiences from the stage.

They sent demo tapes to record companies during the mid-1970s without success until they finally gained the attention of executives at GRT Records, which issued their single "I Want to Be With You" in 1977. The disc only made lower-chart levels, but helped bring a contract with MDJ Records of Dallas, which issued several Alabama recordings starting with "I Wanna Come Over" in late 1979, a tune that made the country singles top 40. By then a new drummer, Mike Herndon, had joined the group to complete the foursome, still intact in 1997. In early 1980, the MDJ release "My Home's in Alabama" (written by Randy and Teddy) rose to the top 20. *Cash Box* magazine named the band the New Vocal Group of the Year for both singles and albums, the first of dozens of awards and other honors Alabama was to receive during the 1980s and 1990s.

The band, which moved to the RCA label in 1980, continued its progress in 1981, beginning with the single "Old Flame," released January 23, which rose to number one on country lists in April. This was followed by "Feels So Right" (issued May 1, 1981) and "Love in the First Degree" (released September 4), which became a top-ten hit. Its 1980 debut LP was still on the charts during the year, where it was joined by the band's second RCA album, *Feels So Right,* issued in February. Eventually the debut album went double platinum, while *Feels So Right* stayed on the list several years to achieve quadruple platinum sales levels. Similar success was gained by the quadruple platinum *Mountain Music,* (issued in February 1982) and provided such chart singles as the title track (issued December 23, 1981), "Take Me Down" (issued May 6, 1982) and "Close Enough to Be Perfect" (issued August 19, 1982).

Meanwhile, the band was touring intensively, headlining in smaller clubs and opening for other, better-known acts in major venues. Alabama also gained a great deal of TV exposure, and was featured on Johnny Carson's *The Tonight Show* and the *The Merv Griffin Show,* among others. The band also performed on the 1981 Country Music Association Awards TV show, on which it was named Vocal Group of the Year and Instrumental Group of the Year. Earlier it had been voted Vocal Group of the Year by the Academy of Country Music, New Group of the Year by *Billboard,* and Group of the Year by *Radio & Records.* In the years that followed, Alabama was to receive many more trophies from all of those (not to speak of nominations). In the Grammy voting for 1982 (announced on the February 23, 1983, TV show), the *Mountain Music* album was named Best Country Performance by a Duo or Group with Vocal, an achievement repeated the following year by the band's fourth RCA album, *The Closer You Get* (released March 1983).

The last-named easily went past platinum, as did the next series of mid-1980s album releases. Those comprised *Roll On* (released January 1984), *40 Hour Week* (January 1985), *Alabama Christmas* (September 1985), *Greatest Hits* (January 1986), and *The Touch* (September 1986). The band also did well with its singles releases from 1983 through 1987, which encompassed "Dixieland Delight" (issued January 24, 1983), "The Closer You Get" (April 20, 1983), "Lady Down on Love" (August 8, 1983), "Roll On" (January 5, 1984), "When We Make Love" (June 12, 1984), "If You're Gonna Play in Texas" (July 16, 1984), "Fire in the Night" (October 22, 1984), "40 Hour Week" (April 17, 1985), "Can't Keep a Good Man Down" (August 9, 1985), "She and I" (December 30, 1985), "Touch Me When We're Dancing" (September 12, 1986), "(You've Got) The Touch" (January 16, 1987), "Tar Top" (August 3, 1987), and "Face to Face" (November 23, 1987).

In the last years of the decade, the band's sales impact "slowed down" a bit, to a point where their releases "only" tended to go gold. This perhaps reflected increasing competition from country bands who went through the door opened by Alabama's success. Many of those groups, as well as more than a few soloist newcomers to country stardom, paid tribute to Alabama as an important influence on their careers. The band continued to be as much a favorite with concertgoers as ever, and its performances seemed, if anything, to improve from the members' first years together.

The band closed out the decade with the albums *Just Us* (September 1987), *Alabama Live* (June 1988), and *Southern Star* (February 1989) and the singles "Fallin' Again" (issued March 28, 1988), "Song of the South" (November 17, 1988), "If I Had You" (February 13, 1989), "High Cotton" (July 28, 1989), and "Southern Star" (issued November 22, 1989 and number one in *R&R* the week of February 9, 1990). Among the band's 1989 honors were its selection by the Academy of Country Music as Artist of the Decade and by *Billboard* as Country Artist of the 1980s.

By the early 1990s, ACM Awards presented to the band included six times choice for Vocal Group of the Year, three times selection for Album of the Year, and five times Entertainer of the Year. Country Music Association honors included three times for Entertainer of the Year and two times each for Vocal Group of the Year and Instrumental Group of the Year. Between 1980 and 1994, the band was nominated for CMA Vocal Group of the Year every year except 1986 and 1990. The band also was nominated for Entertainer of the Year by the CMA six years in a row from 1980 to 1985. Besides that, its trophies included choice as Favorite Country Group in the American Music Awards eight times and

three times selection by *People* magazine readers as Favorite Group. Through the early 1990s, the group could also point to 26 *Billboard,* 27 *Cash Box,* and 16 *Radio & Records* awards.

Record buyers continued to look favorably on the band's singles, videos, and albums during the first half of the 1990s. The band received gold records for the albums *Pass It On Down* (May 1990 release), *Greatest Hits II* (October 1991), *American Pride* (August 1992), *Cheap Seats* (October 1993), and *Greatest Hits III* (October 1994). When *Cheap Seats* came out RCA reported the band had accumulated 37 number-one singles to that point and over 40 million album sales (including 4.5 million in other countries), while its *Greatest Hits Video Package* had achieved over 90,000 in sales.

From a singles standpoint, the band began the 1990s with a flourish, placing its first two releases high on the charts. "Pass It on Down" (issued May 25, 1990) reached number two in *R&R* the week of May 25 and "Juke Box on My Mind" (issued July 13) was number one for two weeks in September. The third single release of 1990, "Forever's As Far As I'll Go" (issued October 18), was a top-10 hit in November. In 1991, the band made the charts with "Down Home" (issued February 4), "Here We Are" (August 2), and "Then Again" (November 22). During 1992–93, all six singles releases by RCA made number one or two on the major charts. Those included "Born Country" (released March 2, 1992), "Take a Little Trip" (July 31, 1992), "I'm in a Hurry" (November 20, 1992), "Once Upon a Lifetime" (number one in *R&R* the week of March 5, 1993), "Hometown Honeymoon" (number one in *R&R* the week of June 4, 1993) and "Reckless" (number one in *R&R* the week of November 19, 1993). Alabama made *Billboard* and *R&R* singles charts in 1994 with "T.L.C. A.S.A.P." (number seven in *R&R* the week of March 4), "The Cheap Seats" (number thirteen in *R&R* the week of June 4), and "We Can't Love Like This Anymore" (number three in *R&R* the week of November 25).

Despite their fame and fortune, the band members continued to call Ft. Payne home and didn't let their achievements go to their heads. They helped out in charity events from time to time, and expressed support for preserving the environment. The video of "Pass It on Down," a song cowritten by bandsmen Randy Owens and Teddy Gentry with Ronnie Rogers and Will Robinson, was a plea for environmental awareness.

Owens told *Radio & Records,* "This is for the kids—everybody's kids. And for moms and dads who need to be aware of the chain of events that could happen—quicker than we think. Throughout this project, from the writing and recording of the song to the filming of the video [which contrasted the natural beauty of Los Angeles area Jordan Ranch with an abandoned steel mill], we've all felt like we've been part of something bigger than ourselves."

On September 27, 1994, RCA released the retrospective album *Greatest Hits, Volume III.* The disc, which peaked at number eight in *Billboard,* was still well inside the magazine's top 75 country album chart in mid 1996 with sales past R.I.A.A. platinum levels. (Its first *Greatest Hits* collection earned an R.I.A.A. 4 million copy multiplatinum award and *Greatest Hits, Volume II* a platinum award on July 31, 1995). The band's next new album, *In Pictures,* issued by RCA in mid 1995, peaked at number twelve and remained on the hit lists until the late spring of 1996, having earned the band another gold record award. That was the group's 18th gold album, more than the total for any other country act to that point. In early spring of 1996, the band had the top-20 single, "It Works." Later in the year it placed the single "Say I" on the charts. In the Country Music Association Awards poll for 1996, Alabama was one of the finalists in the Vocal Group of the Year category.

ALLEN, DEBORAH: *Singer, songwriter. Born Memphis, Tennessee, September 30, 1953.*

In a career that stretched from the 1970s into the 1990s, Deborah Allen was an artist whose musical accomplishments suggested she deserved greater recognition from the country audience than she received. Not that her efforts lacked highlights, but she never scored blockbuster sales despite turning out singles and albums of considerably more depth and vocal strength than the output of many performers whose names often topped the charts.

Her promise seemed evident from her debut album on Capitol in 1980, *Trouble in Paradise,* which drew praise from many reviewers including Dave Marsh and John Swenson, who compiled the *New Rolling Stone Record Guide.* They gave the album three stars, stating Deborah Allen is "A Nashville songstress with a voice eerily reminiscent of Stevie Nicks [of Fleetwood Mac and rock solo fame]. The way Allen employs that voice—full of loping raspiness but able to phrase like the flight of a bird—is what makes her so promising. Her equally intriguing songwriting capabilities (especially when working with Rafe VanHoy) assure her future."

Deborah's route to that milestone began in Memphis, Tennessee, where she was born and raised. (Her original name was Deborah Lynn Thurmond.) She had an interest in blues and country from an early age and applied her vocal skills to school events in her teens. In her twenties she moved to Nashville, where she did session work and polished her songwriting talents, eventually teaming up with husband-to-be, Rafe VanHoy. Her voice impressed recording industry executives enough that one got the idea of adding vocal tracks by her to songs taped decades earlier by the late Jim Reeves (who died in 1964). The updated versions of those numbers, when they were issued in 1979 by RCA Records, resulted in three top-10 singles.

Though she recorded the 1980 album for Capitol, she was signed to a long-term contract by RCA, for whom she achieved her most successful releases in the mid-1980s. The single "Baby I Lied," released in late 1983, provided a crossover hit on both pop and country charts. It stayed on the *Billboard* pop list for seven weeks during 1983–84, peaking at number twenty-five. It also reached the top 5 on both the country and adult-contemporary charts. During 1984 it earned her two Grammy nominations as well as a nomination for the Country Music Association's Horizon Award. Her releases also received sizable radio play in the mid-1980s, with "Baby I Lied" in good position on radio charts, being equaled by other singles such as the number one "I've Been Wrong Before" and the top 10 "I Hurt for You."

Husband-producer VanHoy helped her complete what was claimed to be the first digitally produced disc recorded in Nashville. The album *Let Me Be the First* won critical acclaim, adding to predictions of impending star or even superstar status. However, the record company was undergoing considerable turmoil at the executive level, and attention to her career suffered. Though offered a contract extension by RCA in 1988, she turned it down and sought another affiliation.

Unfortunately, no attractive deal was at hand, and for a while she concentrated on writing. Songs written solely by her or in collaboration with Rafe VanHoy or others provided hits for many performers in country and other music genres. Top-10 country hits based on her material included John Conlee's "I'm Only in It for the Love"; Janie Fricke's "Don't Worry 'Bout Me Baby"; Tanya Tucker's "Can I See You Tonight"; and Patty Loveless's "Hurt Me Bad (in a Real Good Way)." Others who recorded her songs were Diana Ross, Sheena Easton, Brenda Lee, Conway Twitty, and Loretta Lynn.

She took a positive view of the lull in her recording career, particularly since her songwriting output reflected imaginative progress. She said, "I just have a lot of faith. I know that all of the experiences we've had, and all the disappointment we've gone through will turn out in a positive way. I think if I'd been on top of the world and had hit after hit, maybe I wouldn't have had time to explore this part of my creative world."

In 1992 she signed a new contract, this time with the new label formed by former MCA Records top executive and longtime Eagles manager Irving Azoff. Her album debut on Giant Records, *Delta Dreamland,* focused on themes that drew on her Memphis rearing. She wrote or cowrote all the songs on the disc. (Her collaborators, besides her husband, included Billy Burnette, Mark Collie, and Bobby Braddock.) The tracks included "Chain Lightning," "Into My Life," "You Do All the Loving (and the Hurting Too)," and "Rock Me (in the Cradle of Love)." The last one, penned by the VanHoys, was issued in late 1992 and made upper-chart levels in early 1993.

In preparing the new collection, Deborah tried her hand at other elements of the project besides writing and singing. She bought a sophisticated camera system and learned how to edit film for her video products. The video of the debut single was filmed by Rafe and edited by Deborah. The VanHoys had also built and equipped their own recording studio, and all but two tracks of *Delta Dreamland* were made in that facility.

ALLEN, REX, SR.: *Singer, guitarist, fiddler, actor, songwriter. Born Willcox, Arizona, December 31, 1920 (or 1924).*

Through his narration of countless Walt Disney nature films, and his appearances at rodeos, Knott's Berry Farm, and Disneyland, Rex Allen seemed to epitomize the voice of the American cowboy from the 1950s through the 1970s. A ranch hand and rodeo contestant in his early years, he appropriately gained the nickname of "Mister Cowboy." Although his efforts tapered off, he was still turning out albums and occasional singles in the late 1960s and mid 1990s, adding to his many credits and chart successes over three decades.

Born and reared in Willcox, Arizona, Rex learned to rope and ride as a youngster and already was showing skills in local junior rodeos in his early teens. At eleven, he was given his first guitar and before long he was accomplished not only as a guitar player but as a fiddler. His fine voice began to be heard in western shows in his home state. His reputation grew rapidly, and, at thirteen, he was widely known as "that young cowboy with the amazing voice." Helping him to gain that designation was a series of engagements on radio, starting with his debut performance during the State Cattlemen's Convention. In high school, his music teacher also contributed to his career by entering him in a statewide singing contest, where Rex won first place.

For a while in his late teens in the early 1940s, Rex couldn't decide whether to concentrate on music or rodeo competition. He was above average at bulldogging and bronc riding and took part in a number of major rodeos. But in 1944, after he'd studied electronics for a time in California, he moved cross country to New Jersey, where he got his own show on station WTTM in Trenton. During part of 1944 and 1945, besides performing on that show, he also could be heard on station WCAU in Philadelphia. His activities included performing with the Sleepy Hollow Gang in Allentown, Pennsylvania. His ability attracted the attention of the *National Barn Dance* in Chicago, which lured him to the Midwest in 1945. He remained a featured artist on the nationally broadcast show until 1950.

Luring him farther west in 1949 was CBS's offer to do his own show. He finally made California his home base when Republic Pictures signed him in 1949 to start work on his debut film, *The Arizona Cowboy*. Throughout the 1950s, Allen fans were treated to a steady diet of new westerns that featured Rex and his horse, Koko. Before his association with Republic on the series ended, he was featured in thirty-five films. Meanwhile, Rex's CBS-TV show, *Frontier Doctor*, was a hit, ranked seventh nationally for the 1949–50 season, and remained a network favorite for a number of years.

His singing TV work in the 1950s included regular cast status on the *Town Hall Party* in Los Angeles and guest appearances on many network programs, including several on the *Red Skelton Show*.

His movie and TV activity continued in the 1960s and 1970s. Featured in the 20th Century-Fox film *For the Love of Mike* and Universal's *Tomboy and the Champ* in the 1960s, he also narrated more than 158 Disney Studios movies and TV programs from the early 1960s into the 1980s, for many years being the voice of the long-running Disney's Wonderful World of Color. His honors during that period included election to the Cowboy Hall of Fame in 1968.

Rex signed with Decca Records in the late 1940s and turned out many singles and albums for the label in the 1950s. In 1953, "Crying in the Chapel" was a top-10 single on country & western charts. Among the albums he completed for Decca were the 1958 releases *Under Western Skies* and *Mister Cowboy*. In the early 1960s, he moved from Decca to Mercury and scored a top-10 hit in 1961 with "Don't Go Near the Indians." He also recorded for Disney's Buena Vista label, which released his "16 Favorite Songs" in May 1962. His other LPs of the 1960s included Mercury's *Faith of a Man* and *Rex Allen Sings and Tells Tales* and, on Pickwick, *Western Ballads*. Though many of the songs on his various albums were traditional western ballads, such as "Old Faithful," "Streets of Laredo," "The Last Round-Up," and "On Top of Old Smoky," he often included some of his own compositions. By the end of the 1970s, his original songs numbered well over three hundred.

During the 1950s and 1960s, Rex played many engagements on the county fair and rodeo circuits. His contribution to modern rodeo in general was recognized by the Rodeo Producers of America and Canada in 1965 when it named him "Rodeo Man of the Year," the first entertainer to be given that award. In 1966, he was named Arizona Man of the Year and in 1968, he was elected to the Cowboy Hall of Fame, where he served as a member of the board of trustees in the late 1970s. As he said in 1973, "I love the personal appearance dates of a rodeo or fair more than anything else in my life. I love people and I love to be with people. I'm still a country boy at heart."

From the 1970s on, though, he followed a more leisurely pace than he had in earlier decades, "hunting, fishing, boating, and trying to climb every hill in California." It was a period, too, when one of his sons, Rex Allen, Jr., was establishing himself as a major name in modern country & western music.

While his son's career flourished, Allen, Sr., in effect entered semiretirement, though he still made a limited number of personal appearances and lent his voice to movies, TV documentaries, and commercials and made occasional new recordings in the late 1970s and 1980s.

Rex and his son performed together on relatively rare occasions, but they combined talents in 1995 to record an album for Warner Western Records called *The Singing Cowboys,* enlisting the support of other western artists on some tracks—including Roy Rogers, who joined the Allens on "Can You Hear Those Pioneers."

ALLEN, REX, JR.: *Singer, guitarist, songwriter. Born Chicago, Illinois, August 23, 1947.*

Although Rex Allen had four children, only his namesake has directly emulated him. Rex Allen, Jr., has shown himself to be a worthy recipient of the family heritage, and a performer likely to have a career marked with almost as many honors as his illustrious father.

Not surprisingly, Rex, Jr., was infatuated with the entertainment field from early childhood. Raised in Southern California, he was taken to some of the western movie sets his father was working on throughout the 1950s. When he was six, he began to travel as part of his father's act on the rodeo, fair, and theater circuit.

Young Rex quickly developed good stage presence and began to learn guitar chords before he was out of elementary school. In junior high school he formed his first group, the Townsmen, which performed at school and local events. Later, he assembled Saturday's Children, with whom he gave a number of shows and also headlined on several TV programs.

During the mid- and late-1960s, Rex, Jr., continued to pursue his music career with mixed results, taking time out from these efforts to serve in the U.S. military. Later he decided he would make better progress in country music by moving to Nashville. Once there, he managed to gain a spot on a CBS-TV summer replacement show called *CBS Newcomers.*

At the end of the 1960s and in the early 1970s, he made a little progress in his recording efforts. Represented by the album *Today's Generation* on the SSS label, he turned out other recordings that appeared on JMI Records. He also continued to add to his performing experience on various tours and TV programs around the country.

However, it was not until he joined Warner Brothers Records in 1973 that he began to attract a following. His first single release on the label, "The Great Mail Robbery," was issued at the end of 1973 and showed up on the lower levels of the country charts in January 1974. Several months later, he markedly improved on

that with his chart hit, "Goodbye." Both of those songs, as well as "The Same Old Way" and his version of the reggae song, "I Can See Clearly Now," were included in his debut LP, *Another Goodbye Song.* After much success in 1974, he had an equally impressive follow-up year with such charted singles as "Never Coming Back Again" and "Lying in My Arms." His second Warner's LP, *Ridin' High,* which came out in 1975, included his excellent baritone treatment of several songs associated with his father, such as "Streets of Laredo" and "San Antonio Rose," as well as an original composition, "I Gotta Remember to Forget You."

In 1976 Rex achieved his first major hit with the song "Can You Hear Those Pioneers," (cowritten with J. Maude). The song reached the top 20 in June. In September, he had another top-20 single, "Teardrops in My Heart." His third LP on Warner Brothers, *Rex,* didn't make the country top 50, but the sales total showed a steady gain compared to earlier LPs.

Allen, Jr.'s, 1977 offerings included the summer chart single "Don't Say Goodbye" and his fourth LP, *The Best of Rex,* issued in September. The album, he noted, "wasn't intended to be a 'greatest hits' collection," which would have been a bit premature, "but a collection of the songs that I've loved best or the people I respect or have liked." It did, though, include some of his more successful numbers, such as "Two Less Lonely People," "Can You Hear Those Pioneers," "I'm Getting Good at Missing You," and "Don't Say Goodbye." Accompanying them were tracks like "Tumbling Tumbleweeds," "Cool Water," Merle Haggard's "Silver Wings" and "Today I Started Loving You Again." In September 1978, one of Rex's best singles was issued, his own composition "With Love." It achieved top-10 levels, as did the single "It's Time We Talk Things Over" in early 1979, cowritten with J. Maude, and "Me and My Broken Heart" later in the year.

From the mid-1970s on Rex, Jr., was an increasingly important factor on the country & western concert circuit. As a featured artist, he often shared bills with the brightest names in the field, including Dolly Parton and Hank Williams, Jr. In many cases, he and his band were the headliners at rodeos, fairs, and in major auditoriums around the country. He also performed on almost all the important network country TV programs, including appearances on the *Grand Ole Opry.*

Rex began the 1980s in good style with such charted singles (on Warner Brothers) as "Yippi Cri Yi," "It's Over," and "Drink It Down, Lady" in 1980, and "Cup of Tea" and "Just a Country Boy" (the last written by him) in 1981. "Cup of Tea," a duet with Margo Smith, was in the top 20 nationwide in early 1981 and reached the top of some regional lists.

He placed other recordings on the chart as the 1980s went by, but tended to do better economically with his live performances in a period when record companies were focusing more on pop country than more traditional stylings. By the end of the decade, however, artists like Michael Martin Murphy and Red Steagall were beginning to spark a resurgence in western-based material that helped improve career opportunities for people like the Allens. In 1992, the Statler Brothers asked Rex, Jr., to become a regular cast member on their Nashville Network TV program. His segment, called "Yesteryear," became popular enough for TNN to make it a separate show. During that period, he signed with the Warner Western label and, with his father, prepared a new album, issued in mid-1995, titled *The Singing Cowboys,* which featured songs that had been hits for one or the other.

AMAZING RHYTHM ACES: *Vocal and instrumental group. Founding members, 1972, Russell Smith, born Nashville, Tennessee; Butch McDade; Jeff Davis; Billy Earhart III. Barry Burton, James Hooker added shortly after. Burton left 1977, replaced by Duncan Cameron. Group disbanded early 1980s.*

Like many of today's "country" bands, the Amazing Rhythm Aces were initially difficult to classify. Their main successes were in the country genre, but the Memphis-based group combined country, rhythm & blues, rock, and gospel sounds. This posed an image problem for the group with potential fans. An additional problem was the band's tendency, in concert, toward a harder-edged, more R&B–oriented musical format than on records.

Lead singer Russell Smith agreed that too much diversity was always a problem, although in 1979 he still felt optimistic about the situation. "It's been a problem for us just as it's been for groups like Asleep at the Wheel. But somebody likes us. They may not know exactly what to call us, but they're buying our records. Our last album [the 1978 ABC release *Burning the Ballroom Down*] sold the most of any of our LPs. It was over three hundred thousand the last time I looked. As long as somebody still likes us and comes to see us, that's all that counts. I don't care what they call us as long as they don't call us bad."

The unfettered approach to music of the group's members, he noted, was central in the band's formation in 1972. It was then that Smith and drummer/percussionist Butch McDade first got together over a shared interest in blues singer B.B. King. "The reason the band came into existence is probably the same reason nobody knows what kind of music we play. When Butch McDade and I got things started we were disaffected musicians. We didn't want to play heavy metal in bars; we didn't want to play disco; we wanted to play what we wanted to. So we kind of got together out of a dissatisfaction with other things going on and kept adding and dropping people until we got a group that fitted together with what we had in mind."

Among the initial additions who stuck with the band

were bassist Jeff "Sticks" Davis, who had played in Otis Rush's blues band, and keyboard-player Billy Earhart. By the time the band adopted the name Amazing Rhythm Aces in 1974, it had expanded to include engineer/multiinstrumentalist Barry "Byrd" Burton and pianist James Hooker. Burton came aboard to help engineer the band's recording of Smith's composition "Third Rate Romance." Smith, the group's principal songwriter, came from a musical family and was trying to write songs almost as soon as he learned to play guitar. One of his compositions of the early 1970s was "Third Rate Romance," which Jesse Winchester included on his *Learn to Love It* album. When a number of other artists began to pick up the song, Smith and his group decided they should make their own recording of it.

The single was on the band's debut album for ABC Records, *Stacked Deck*. It made upper-chart levels on country lists as well as national pop lists. The LP also spawned a second single that made country charts, "Amazing Grace (Used to Be Her Favorite Song)." The album won generally favorable reviews, as did the band's second album, *Too Stuffed to Jump*. Their third album, *Toucan Do It Too,* failed to attain the success of the first two, even though it contained some excellent original songs by Smith and McDade. In 1976, the Aces won a Grammy Award for Best Country Vocal Performance by a Group for Smith's composition "The End Is Not in Sight" from the third LP.

In the mid-1970s, the band maintained a busy touring schedule, often opening for noted country artists such as Willie Nelson and Waylon Jennings. The grind proved too much for Burton. Smith commented, " 'Byrd' just got tired. He got tired of touring. He didn't want to go out on the road as much as we do. He was older than the rest of us and all he wanted to do at this point was produce and play sessions. He finally got the chance to do that in Nashville and he took it. It [the split] was an amicable thing. We're still friends. He's in Nashville now playing a lot with Don Williams. We're satisfied with the present setup. He's going towards country and western and we're moving a little bit more rock 'n' roll, a little more blues and soul."

Burton was replaced by Duncan Cameron, who had been playing guitar and backing country bands since he was fifteen years old. He also had been a member of Dan Fogelberg's band, Fool's Gold. He made his first contributions to the group's fourth LP, *Burning the Ballroom Down,* on the charts in 1978.

For the next album, the Aces had a new producer. "We went to Jimmy Johnson of Muscle Shoals Studios," Smith noted. "Other things haven't changed. Actually, everything you hear on the new album is in the Amazing Rhythm Aces tradition. For instance, R and B and more rock-oriented music is stuff that we like to play on stage, but that hasn't been on our albums up to now."

The resulting 1979 ABC release, *Amazing Rhythm Aces,* had more R&B content, but also had a country-rock tune, "Lipstick Traces"; Cameron's country-rock ballad, "Homestead in My Heart"; and Smith's country-story song, "Rodrigo, Rita and Elaine." As good as any Aces collection, the album nonetheless failed to catch the public's fancy. In the early 1980s, Smith and Mc-Dade disbanded the group. Smith signed as a solo vocalist with Muscle Shoals Sound Records, with his debut LP due for distribution by Capitol Records in 1982.

Looking back at the group's rise and fall for Janet Williams of the Country Music Association's *Close Up* magazine, he noted, "I was a guy who sang and played rhythm guitar and wrote an occasional song. 'Third Rate Romance' was the first song I ever got published. I wrote the song and started doing it with my band. My drummer got an offer to go on the road with Jesse Winchester, and he went. He took a bunch of tapes with him and that song was on the tape. Jesse put that one and a couple of others in his show, and when it got time for him to do an album, he put them on his album. That's what really started it for the Amazing Rhythm Aces. We got signed and that was it. We hit the road and eventually quit because of the bottom line. We couldn't run a six-man band. We all had families that we didn't have when we started. The kind of schedule we had, we'd stay out all the time."

For his part, Smith also found it impossible to write new songs under the grind of constant touring. After a while, he noted, the novelty of it all wore off, particularly when each show was so similar to the last. He found he couldn't come up with new song ideas that might be turned into best-selling singles. "I just needed to escape," he noted, "to feel like I was living for myself again, instead of an organization."

It proved a wise move, for during the balance of the 1980s and into the 1990s, Smith developed into one of Nashville's most respected songsmiths. Working with such writers as Dave Loggins and Don Schlitz, among others, he wrote songs that were recorded by many internationally famous country artists. By the mid-1990s, besides such 1970s hits as "Third Rate Romance" and "Amazing Grace (Used to Be Her Favorite Song)," his output included such successful titles as "Honky Tonk Heart," "Don't Go to Strangers," "Heartbeat in the Darkness," "The End Is Not in Sight," and "The Old School." Many of his songs were recorded by more than one artist, and even the older ones still could connect with audiences. In 1994, for instance, Sammy Kershaw turned "Third Rate Romance" into a hit single once again for himself.

Smith never gave up performing completely, though he kept his number of appearances closely in check. (In 1989, though, he did have a new album on Epic Records, *This Little Town*.) One reason he gave to *Close Up* in the early 1990s was his role then as a single father. "With the boys, Jesse Lee and Matthew Miles, I can't tour extensively. So doing anything for giant mass ap-

peal, big budget, and so forth, wouldn't be fair. I'm just trying to have fun with it, have a good life."

When asked about what he believed was the best song he'd written, he responded, "I don't know. I hope I haven't written it yet."

Based in part on a 1979 phone interview with Russell Smith by Irwin Stambler.

ANDERSON, BILL: *Singer, guitarist, actor, songwriter, music industry executive, band leader (Po' Boys). Born Columbia, South Carolina, November 1, 1937.*

In an article Bill Anderson wrote for the first edition of the *Encyclopedia of Folk, Country, & Western Music,* he pointed out that the country music business was just recovering from the "rock 'n' roll depression" when he first entered it. "They talked in 1960 about the 'good ole days' of country music. Backstage gab sessions among the entertainers were often about the days when 'old Webb' had twenty-one straight number-one songs, the least of which sold a quarter of a million records . . . of the days when 'Old Hank' was packin' 'em in singing 'Lovesick Blues.'

"I notice today, however, that I don't hear too much of that anymore. Our people today are too busy talking about the new Country Music Hall of Fame and Museum in Nashville that's attracting tourists by the thousands, of the record crowds . . . at the *Grand Ole Opry* . . . of the full-time country radio stations in New York, Chicago, Philadelphia, Los Angeles, Dallas, Atlanta, and just about everywhere else. And they're talking about the attendance records broken nearly every week [by country stars], about the syndicated country music television shows pulling top ratings in just about every city. . . ."

That was written at the end of the 1960s, and perhaps is even more appropriate today. Country music has endured and prospered. So has Bill Anderson, who was as successful in the 1970s as he was in the 1960s, and who played a vital role in the rejuvenation of country music.

Born in South Carolina, Anderson grew up in Georgia, the heartland of country music. He was already working on his guitar chording by the time the Andersons moved from Commerce, Georgia, to the Atlanta suburb of Avondale, where he attended high school. In his teens, he had his own country band and won a high school talent contest for one of his original songs.

He earned his B.A. from the University of Georgia in the late 1950s in journalism. During his college years, not only did he play in country shows in Atlanta and other Georgia towns, he also had his own disc jockey program on local stations. Meanwhile, he kept writing country songs and tried to interest people in the country music field in performing them, even as he worked at newspaper jobs at the *Dekalb New Era* in Decatur and at the *Atlanta Constitution.*

In 1958, his first music breakthrough came with the hit single of "City Lights" by Ray Price. "That's What It's Like to Be Lonesome," another Anderson composition, made the national top 10 in 1959. At this point, Bill made a commitment to music and signed with Decca, the label for which he was still placing singles and albums on the country charts two decades later. (Decca merged with MCA, and the latter is the name found on his successes of later years.) In late 1959, Anderson started touring in support of his recording efforts, and, more than twenty years later, he remained a major concert attraction not only in the United States but in Canada and many other nations.

His credits as a performer and songwriter snowballed as the 1960s went by. In 1960, he made top-chart levels with "Tips of My Fingers," and the late Jim Reeves hit, "I Missed Me." In 1961, Hank Locklin hit the charts with Bill's "Happy Birthday to Me," and Bill made the lists himself with "Walk Out Backward" and "Po' Folks." (The latter song provided the name for Bill's famous backing band, the Po' Boys.) Among other songs that became hits for Bill or other artists in the 1960s were "My Name Is Mud," "Mama Sang a Song," "I've Enjoyed as Much of This as I Can Stand," "8 x 10," "I Love You Drops," "Nobody but a Fool," and "Still." While Bill wrote or cowrote much of his material, occasionally he recorded other writers' material, such as his 1964 hit single of Alex Zanetis's "Me."

In the years before the Country Music Association Awards, most honors came from trade magazines, DJ polls, or industry organizations such as Broadcast Music Inc. (BMI)—the music licensing agency to which Anderson belonged. Bill gained many honors from these, including Top Male Vocalist of the Year for 1963, Record of the Year for 1963, and Top Songwriter of the Year for C&W in 1963, 1964, and 1965. He was still winning or placing high in those competitions in the 1970s. As of 1979, for instance, he had been honored as Male Vocalist of the Year five times, Top Duet of the Year for his work with Jan Howard, with whom he worked in the late 1960s and part of the 1970s, and chosen in a 1970s *Billboard* magazine poll as one of the "Three All-Time Greatest Country Music Songwriters." As of 1977, he had received forty-nine BMI songwriter awards, more than any other country-music composer on the organization's roster. When the CMA Awards program got underway, Bill naturally took part in many of the events, either as a performer on the nationally televised TV shows or a nominee in various categories.

In 1961, he became a regular cast member of the *Grand Ole Opry* and was still on the show as the 1990s began. During the 1960s, he appeared on just about every important country TV show, as well as on his own syndicated program, which was still going strong at the end of the 1970s. Among those featured in the regular cast during that decade were Mary Lou Turner, his duet partner from 1973 to 1979, singer-instrumentalist Jimmy

Gately, and, naturally, the Po' Boys. The same cast plus (later renamed the Po' Folks) different guest stars was a major live concert attraction under the banner of the *Bill Anderson Show* throughout the United States and much of the world.

Anderson's other activities in the entertainment field ran the gamut from music publisher to film performer. Among his movie credits were *Country Music on Broadway, Forty Acre Feud, Las Vegas Hillbillies,* and *The Road to Nashville*. In the 1970s, he also owned his own radio station, KFTN in Provo, Utah, a full-time country-music channel.

In the 1970s there was no slowdown in Bill's recording accomplishments. He had a major hit in 1970 with his composition "Where Have All the Heroes Gone," also the title of a top-10 album. His other album releases of the late 1960s and early 1970s included *If It's All the Same to You* (with Jan Howard); *Love Is a Sometime Thing; Always Remember; Greatest Hits, Volume 2; That Casual Country Feeling.*

In the mid- and late 1970s, his chart hits included such original compositions as "I Still Feel the Same Way About You," "Country D.J.," "I Can't Wait Any Longer," and "Double S" (the last two cowritten with B. Killen). His single hits of other writers' songs in those years included "Thanks" in late 1975, "Peanuts and Diamonds" in mid-1976, "Head to Toe" in the summer of 1977, and "Still the One" in the fall of that year. He recorded duets with Mary Lou Turner, including the top-10 hits "That's What Made Me Love You" in May 1976 and "Where Are You Going, Billy Boy" in the late summer of 1977. Among his chart LPs in the late 1970s were *Sometimes* (with Mary Lou Turner) in 1976, *Scorpio* and *Billy Boy and Mary Lou* in 1977, and *Love . . . And Other Sad Stories* in 1978. For his 1979 LP, *Nashville Mirrors,* he wrote seven of the ten songs, including the chart hit "More Than a Bedroom Thing." At the end of the 1970s, after two decades of activity, Bill could point to a total of close to forty albums, over fifty hit singles, and tens of millions of records sold.

In 1980, he began a new phase of his career by signing up to emcee a new TV game show called *Funzapoppin*. The first shows were taped at Astroworld in Houston, with others planned to be taped at Opryland in Nashville. During the year, his charted singles for MCA included "Make Mine Night Time," "Get a Little Dirt on Your Hands" (written by Anderson, recorded as a duet with David Allan Coe), "Rock 'n' Roll to Rock of Ages," his composition "I Want That Feeling Again," and, in 1981, "Mister Peepers."

In the early 1980s, Bill Anderson had accomplished just about anything that one could do in the field of country music, except get elected to the Country Music Hall of Fame, and that seemed likely to come in due time. He continued his diverse activities in that decade, though as the years went by with decreasing success as a recording star. In mid decade he gained national attention as host of the *Fandango* game show on The Nashville Network. His TV credits also included hosting the ABC game show *The Better Sex* and the music news program *Backstage at the Grand Ole Opry*. In May 1989 Longstreet Press published his autobiography, *Whisperin' Bill*.

The 1990s found him continuing to ply his trade as a TV host, a performer on the concert network, and a veteran cast member on the *Grand Ole Opry*. One of his mid-1990s projects was performing with Jan Howard and Roy Clark on the longform video "Remembering Patsy," which paid tribute to the late, great Patsy Cline. In 1993, he had another book in print, *I Hope You're Eatin' As High on the Hog As the Pig You Turned Out to Be*. During 1995, the independent Varese Sarabande label prepared a reissue CD of some of Bill's most successful recordings. In 1996, he was one of the artists nominated for the Country Music Hall of Fame.

ANDERSON, JOHN: *singer, guitarist, songwriter. Born Apopka, Florida, December 13, 1955.*

With his rough-edged vocal style that combined elements of rockabilly, down-and-dirty honky-tonk, and blue-collar country, John Anderson seemed the rightful heir to such legendary artists as Willie Nelson, Waylon Jennings, and Merle Haggard. (He also cites Jimmie Rodgers, George Jones, and the Delmore Brothers as influences.) When he took the country field by storm in the late 1970s and early 1980s, he seemed on the way to deserved superstardom. But the tastes of the entertainment industry changed, and his career foundered in the mid-1980s—only to reemerge in what *Country America* magazine called the field's "most triumphant comeback of the nineties."

Born and raised in Florida, Anderson listened eagerly to the *Grand Ole Opry* and the country stars of the 1960s while he learned guitar and dreamed of future glory for himself. At 17, in 1972, he moved to Nashville, where he got into the familiar routine of Music City hopefuls—supporting himself with whatever work he could find, including putting shingles on the roof of the new home for the *Grand Ole Opry* in Opryland— while seeking opportunities in the music industry. During the mid-1970s that included playing various seedy bars in Nashville's Lower Broadway sector until he began to get the kind of wider attention that finally resulted in a major label recording contract.

His initial release didn't do much, but in 1978 he signaled his coming of age as an artist with his first top-40 single, "Girl at the End of the Bar." He placed some other recordings in lower chart levels until he scored his first top-10 single in 1980 with "1959." His talents did not escape the notice of his fellow performers, who nominated him in the Best New Artist category in the 1980 Academy of Country Music Awards voting.

He continued to be a favorite of country music fans in the early 1980s, scoring his first top-5 single with the

1981 "I'm Just an Old Chunk of Coal (But I'm Gonna Be a Diamond Someday)", and hitting number one on industry charts in 1982 with the single "Wild and Blue." In 1983, "Swingin'," which he cowrote with his friend and longtime collaborator, Lionel Delmore, hit the airwaves and blossomed into a runaway hit, selling over a million copies. That fall, the Country Music Association named "Swingin'" the Single of the Year, while also making Anderson its Horizon Award choice.

(Years later, the Association of Juke Box Operators voted "Swingin'" one of its all time top-40 jukebox hits, a category that included records like the Beatles' "Hey Jude" and releases by Elvis Presley, Frank Sinatra, and Patsy Cline.)

Anderson had another number-one single in 1983, "Black Sheep," which helped make that year his most successful yet. (Other 1983 honors included the *Music City News* Country Song of the Year award for "Swingin'.") Meanwhile he had progressed from opening act to headliner, as his concert tours took him to theaters, arenas, and country fairs throughout the U.S. At one appearance at the Beverly Theatre in Los Angeles, *Los Angeles Times* critic Robert Hilburn was "so enthralled by Anderson's performance" that he commented, "On any list of ten favorites at the moment, I'd have to find room for John Anderson" even though "there are so many commanding talents around that it's almost impossible to keep the list down to ten."

He noted that Anderson, who has the strongest Southern accent this side of Deputy Dawg, isn't a performer in the show-biz sense. "He planted his feet firmly in front of the microphone" and sang and played music that "mixes the energy of rock with the heartfelt desperation of the honky-tonk tradition."

Then, almost as suddenly, Anderson's career fell apart. His songs no longer made top-chart levels. Slowly he began to find his support among the broad spectrum of country fans diminishing. By the late 1980s, while retaining a cult following, he was back to playing the small venue circuits of the early years of his career.

Anderson persevered, continuing to write new songs and to seek a new label alignment. This finally bore fruit at the start of the 1990s when he was given a second chance at recording success by BNA Entertainment executives. The result was the album *Seminole Wind*. Anderson commented that the basic idea arose after a visit to his 95-year-old grandfather in Florida and a car trip around the state, which disclosed the drastic ecological and lifestyle changes that had taken place over the past decade. For the album's title song, an accompanying video was shot at a cypress preserve in the Florida Everglades "with assistance and participation of the region's native Seminole Indians."

The album won enthusiastic support from major reviewers across the nation, soon propelling it onto major charts. It peaked at number ten in *Billboard* and went even higher on other lists. It still was on the *Billboard* charts 120 weeks later and had earned a platinum award from the R.I.A.A. Both the single and video of the title track reached number one on various lists in the fall of 1992. Two other singles made top levels that year, "Straight Tequila Nights," number one in February, and "When It Comes to You" (which peaked at number seven in *Radio & Records* the week of July 10). With those blockbuster achievements, Anderson was once more in demand as a concert artist, doing some turns as a coheadliner with people like George Jones and Wynonna.

He added to his list of singles hits in 1993 with "Let Go of the Stone" (which peaked at number six in *Radio & Records* the week of January 29), "Money in the Bank" (number three in *R&R* the week of July 2), and "I Fell in the Water" (on hit lists from August 1993 into early 1994 while peaking in *R&R* at number nine the week of November 5, 1993). In mid-1993, his second BNA album, *Solid Ground* was released and proved a worthy follow-up to his BNA debut. It won strong critical backing. In *Rolling Stone* Peter Cronin stated that with Carlene Carter's new release (*Little Love Letters* on Giant Records), "Two hardcore survivors [of the 1970s period], that bygone era, manage to break the bland barrier with some of the best music of their careers. Both are 'follow-ups' to successful records that brought their careers back from the dead. And in both cases, the artists have opted not to mess with the formula and depend heavily on the team that brought 'em back."

He added that both artists in years past "have done a lot of kicking at their major-label stalls and God bless 'em for it. It's that stick to their guns stubborn streak that will keep them out of the rubber rooms of Branson, while contributing some much-needed musical depth to the mainstream."

Solid Ground was on *Billboard* and other lists from late summer of 1993 well into 1994. It did well with record buyers, though it proceeded at a somewhat slower pace than its predecessor. It just missed top 10 in *Billboard,* peaking at number twelve in 1993. Hit singles of 1994 drawn from it were "I've Got It Made" (cowritten with Max Barnes, which peaked at number three in *R&R* the week of February 25) and "I Wish I Could Have Been There" (cowritten with K. Robbins, which peaked at number three in *R&R* the week of July 8). Late in 1994, his third BNA album, *Country 'Til I Die,* came out and stayed on lower chart levels for a number of months in 1995. Early in 1995 that provided the hit single "Bend It Until It Breaks," cowritten with Lionel Delmore, which rose to number three in *Billboard* in March. Shortly after, the single "Mississippi Moon" was in upper *Billboard* positions.

Starting in 1993, Anderson began to collect a new set of awards to add to his early 1980s laurels. These included an Academy of Country Music nomination for "Straight Tequila Nights" for Single of the Year and the 1993 American Lung Association Blue Sky Award for the "Seminole Wind" video. That song, for which he provided both words and music, also earned John a 1993 CMA Awards nomination for Song of the Year. CMA voters also nominated him for 1993 Male Vocalist of the Year and included the "Seminole Wind" video among the finalists for Music Video of the Year. In the 1994 CMA voting, John again was nominated for Male Vocalist of the Year and was among a host of country stars who won trophies for their contributions to the album *Common Thread: The Songs of the Eagles* voted CMA 1994 Album of the Year.

In the title song from *Solid Ground,* one of two tracks he cowrote with Lionel Delmore, he sang of the importance of family tradition and parents who teach children right from wrong, something he told interviewers he stood by in his private life. He stressed he lived happily with his wife and two daughters on a 300-acre farm seventy miles from Nashville, where he grew his own tomatoes, sought to find Indian artifacts, and did some hunting and fishing in his time off between concerts and recording dates.

He commented in late 1993, "It feels good, believe me. The last fourteen or fifteen months have been incredible. It's been a pretty swift pace, but I'm here to tell ya, ol' Johnny loves it! It feels especially good [as a follow-up to] what I call 'The Honky Tonk Years.' I really do feel it's a just reward for all those years of hangin' in there. It just goes to show you gotta have faith in yourself and stay true to what you do."

Throughout the mid-1990s, Anderson continued to be a major attraction on the country concert circuit and also performed on a number of TV and radio shows. In early 1996, he had the single "Paradise" in upper chart positions.

ANDERSON, LIZ: *Singer, songwriter. Born Pine Creek, Minnesota, March 13, 1930.*

It was lucky for Liz Anderson that her husband was a car salesman. His contacts at the agency helped launch Liz on a songwriting career she might not otherwise have considered. And that, in turn, led to her becoming a singing star at a point in life when others might have thought more about behind-the-scenes work.

Liz grew up in a rural area of Minnesota near the Canadian border. Her birthplace, Pine Creek, she recalled as a "cross in the road" thirteen miles north of the town of Roseau, Minnesota. "I was born on a farm, though my father wasn't a farmer," she told *Music City News* (October 1967). "My folks were awfully poor and we were very, very religious. I can remember liking country music. We had a mandolin and when I was about eight years old we used to sing in church all the time. We also sang on street corners. I had a brother older than me and we used to harmonize, but he quit singing when he was about fifteen."

The family moved to Grand Forks, North Dakota, when Liz was thirteen. She attended high school there and met Casey Anderson. "He lived across the alley from me, but I didn't know him too well until he came home on leave one time while in the Navy. The only time I got to see him was when he was in the alley working on his cars—and I didn't like him because he was always so dirty looking. But he looked real handsome in that blue uniform."

The two were married on May 25, 1946, and within a few years had a young daughter named Lynn. In May 1951, they decided to head for California, where Casey meant to go to jet engine school. "But the way it worked out," he told *Music City News*, "is that we had a kid driving the truck and he busted an engine on us in Montana and when we hit California we were flat broke. So I started selling cars."

They first settled in Redwood City, but eventually moved to Sacramento, east of San Francisco, near members of Liz's family, and there, in 1957, Liz started writing original country songs. Sometimes when her sisters would come over to their house on weekends to socialize, everyone would sing songs, including some of Liz's.

Casey, impressed with his wife's writing skills, issued her a challenge a few years later that was to prove decisive. Being a member of the Sacramento Sheriff's Posse, which was planning to take part in the National Centennial Pony Express celebration, he suggested she write a song in honor of the Pony Express. She did, and her effort was named the official song for the event and earned her a Medal of Honor from the group.

These activities weren't lost on a friend Casey had made at work. Jack McFadden, then also on the sales force of the Chevrolet agency where Casey was employed, later became Buck Owens's manager. He spent time at the Andersons' home and heard some of Liz's country compositions. He liked "I Watched You Walking" and since he was dabbling in the country field on the side, asked if he could try to do something with it. He recommended it to Del Reeves, who recorded it for Slim Williamson's Peach Records label. The song achieved moderate regional success and encouraged Del to record more of Liz's work. He turned out another single on Peach, "I Don't Wonder," and when he was signed by Decca Records chose still another of her tunes, "Be Quiet Mind," for his initial sessions. The single became one of 1961's major hits, bringing both Del and Liz their first top-10 successes. The song also was the title number of Del's debut LP on Decca.

Interest in Liz's offerings naturally increased among country performers. In 1964 Ray Drusky made top-chart levels with her "Pick of the Week," which won a BMI award. A little later, Bonnie Owens came over to the Andersons' house, heard "Just Between the Two of Us," and recorded it with Merle Haggard. Haggard himself dropped by when he was appearing locally and became enthusiastic over a new song called "My Friends Are Gonna Be Strangers."

Liz recalled, "I remember telling Merle about some of the lines being so corny, like 'should be taken out, tarred and feathered,' but Merle said, 'No, leave it just like it is.' But it took him about a year to record the song and I thought he never was. He's a perfectionist, and he kept working until he thought we had it just right. . . . 'Strangers' opened the door for us in Nashville and we began to get more songs recorded. We made the 1965 disc jockey convention there and received a BMI award for the song."

The trip proved eventful in other ways. Chet Atkins of RCA Records had decided Liz had the potential to be a singing star, and she went into RCA's Nashville studios to work on her debut album. While the family was there, they also renewed acquaintances with Slim Williamson, who now headed Chart Records. Williamson expressed interest in signing the Andersons' pretty blonde teenage daughter, Lynn.

As country fans know, both Liz and Lynn since have made their mark on the field as top-rank vocalists. Liz's debut LP came out on RCA's Camden label in August 1966. Included in it was the song that became her first single release, "Go Now, Pay Later." In late 1967, Liz was represented with her first LP on the RCA label, *Cookin' Up Hits*. This was followed by a steady string of new singles and LPs throughout the late 1960s and the 1970s. Among her LP credits were *Game of Triangles* (recorded with Bobby Bare and Norma Jean), *Liz Anderson Sings Her Favorites, Like a Merry-Go-Round, Country Style, If the Creek Don't Rise* (12/69), and *Husband Hunting*. Lynn paid tribute to her mother in one of her albums, called *Songs My Mother Wrote*.

In the late 1960s, having gained enough rewards from country music to make it a full-time livelihood, Liz and Casey moved to Old Hickory Lake near Hendersonville, Tennessee. Casey took an increasing role in the music industry, helping to start the Andersons' own music publishing firm, Greenback Music. He also collaborated with Liz on a number of songs, including "The Fugitive," a charted single for Merle Haggard.

ANDERSON, LYNN: *Singer, guitarist, songwriter. Born Grand Forks, North Dakota, September 26, 1947.*

"Like mother, like daughter" is an expression that certainly tells the story of Liz and Lynn Anderson, who both became highly regarded country performers and songwriters. It's very likely, in fact, that if Liz hadn't started placing some of her original songs with country artists in the 1950s, her daughter Lynn might never have made country music her vocation, particularly since Lynn grew up far from the heartland of country music in an era when rock 'n' roll was the mainstay.

While Lynn was still a small child, the family left North Dakota and moved to Redwood City, near San Francisco, in May 1951. By the late 1950s they were living in Sacramento, California, where her father, Casey Anderson, worked as an automobile salesman.

There he met Jack McFadden, who dabbled in the country field in his spare time. Later McFadden helped Lynn's mother, Liz, place some of her songs with a variety of country performers.

Lynn enjoyed singing and dancing as a child, but her main passion was horseback riding. In high school, she was one of the top-ranked young horse-show competitors in California, winning over 100 trophies, 600 ribbons, two regional championships, a reserve championship at the Junior Grand National Horse Show at San Francisco's Cow Palace, and, in 1966, the title of California Horse Show Queen at the State Fair in Sacramento. Though she switched prime allegiance to music in the late 1960s, she never abandoned her interest in horses: living in Tennessee in the 1970s, she and her husband had their own ranch where they raised quarterhorses.

Lynn's early musical grounding (she learned guitar before she was in her teens) and home environment kept pulling her back towards a musical career in her late teens. At seventeen, she entered a singing contest sponsored by the *Country Corners* program on a Sacramento TV station. After her first year at American River Junior College, she got an offer to join the Lawrence Welk TV show in Hollywood—an opportunity too good to pass up.

She became a regular on the show in 1967 and also signed a recording contract with Chart Records, producing the album, *Ride, Ride, Ride* and a hit country single, "Too Much of You." Lynn received good responses from Welk show viewers, but her stay on the program was cut short by her marriage to R. Glenn Sutton on May 4, 1968. They set up housekeeping in Hendersonville, Tennessee, both to be closer to the "Country Music Capital," Nashville, and to Lynn's parents, who had earlier moved back East.

In the late 1960s, Lynn continued to turn out a steady series of well-received singles and albums for Chart, many of which became best sellers. Among her singles were "I've Been Everywhere," "That's a No-No," "Rocky Top," "Promises, Promises," and "Big Girls Don't Cry." Her Chart LPs included such titles as *Promises, Promises, At Home, Uptown Country Girl, Songs My Mother Wrote, I'm Alright, Greatest Hits, Lynn Anderson with Strings,* and *Songs That Made Country Girls Famous.*

At the start of the 1970s, Lynn signed a new contract with Columbia, which issued the LP *Stay There 'Til I Love You* in July 1970 and followed with *No Love at All* in September. But the real blockbuster arrived at year end with Lynn's single of Joe South's composition, "Rose Garden." It rose to the top of both country and pop charts and stayed there from the end of 1970 into early 1971. The album of the same title, released in February 1971, was equally successful, making Lynn a national celebrity. Besides earning her gold records from the Recording Industry Association of America

for both single and album, the song brought in thirteen more gold records from different countries around the world. (That album, as well as the ones that succeeded it, all were produced by her husband, Glenn Sutton.) "Rose Garden" also brought Lynn a Grammy for Best Country Vocal Performance of 1970.

Throughout the 1970s, Lynn continued to be a vocalist and recording artist of the first rank in the country field. During most of the decade, she spent a good part of every year on the road with her backing group, The Country Store, performing in concert halls, fairs, and rodeos throughout the United States and abroad. In the early 1970s, President Nixon invited her to attend the Celebrity Breakfast in the White House. She also was featured on almost every major network TV program, including Johnny Carson's *The Tonight Show, Kraft Music Hall, The Ed Sullivan Show, Johnny Cash, Merv Griffin, Mike Douglas,* and *Dean Martin's Music Country.* In addition, she was a guest on dozens of specials as well as returning a number of times to appear on *Hee Haw* and on some *Grand Ole Opry* telecasts.

In the early 1970s, one of Lynn's records was chosen as the national theme song for the Christmas Seal Campaign. At that time, Lynn and her daughter, Lisa, then twenty-one months old, were depicted on a national Christmas Seal poster.

Among Lynn's Columbia LPs after *Rose Garden* were such releases as *You're My Man, World of Lynn Anderson, I've Never Loved Anyone More* (a chart hit in the fall of 1975), and *I Love What Love Is Doing to Me/He Ain't You,* on country charts in late 1977. Her chart hit singles of the mid- and late-1970s included "Sing About Love" in late 1974, "Smile for Me," "I've Never Loved Anyone More" in the fall of 1975, "I Love What Love Is Doing to Me" in the summer of 1977, "He Ain't You," a top-20 hit in late 1977, and "Last Love of My Life" in the fall of 1978. Her 1980 Columbia chart hits included "Even Cowgirls Get the Blues" in the summer and "Blue Baby Blue" late in the year.

ARNOLD, EDDY: *Singer, guitarist, song writer. Born near Henderson, Tennessee, May 15, 1918. Elected to Country Music Hall of Fame in 1966.*

Eddy Arnold once said, "I'm a Heinz fifty-seven singer. I sing many different kinds of songs which mean something different to many different kinds of people." That facility, which included the ability to change his singing style and material to meet changing audience tastes, served him well in a long and eventful career. For decades he was a giant among country artists who was able to cross over into the general pop music field as well.

He rose to stardom from humble beginnings, hence his nickname, "The Tennessee Plowboy." His father was a sharecropper, and Eddy worked on the farm as soon as he was old enough to lend a hand. His parents enjoyed music; his father was an old-time fiddler and his mother was a guitarist and taught him the instrument when he was a boy. When he entered Pinson High School, he sang and played the guitar in school events. However, he had to leave high school in the early 1930s to help on the farm, and for a while, music was mainly a sideline. He still played for local functions, though, riding to and from the events on a mule with his guitar slung on his back. His income at the time came not only from music but from farming and a job as an assistant at a mortuary.

Gradually, his talent brought more and more chances to perform. In 1936, he made his radio debut on a Jackson, Tennessee, station. In the late 1930s, he performed for a while on station WMPS in Memphis, then went to St. Louis, where he worked in small night clubs and had a spot on a radio show. In 1942, he joined station WTJS in Jackson, Tennessee, and for six years was one of the audience's favorites. His growing reputation helped win him a contract with RCA Records in 1944, with whom, in 1946, he broke through with his first series of hits. (His first manager was Colonel Tom Parker, later Elvis Presley's manager.) His popularity snowballed from then on. From 1946 through 1952, it wasn't unusual for two or three of his records to be in the top 10 at the same time. He soon had star status on various country radio shows, including the *Grand Ole Opry*.

In 1948, he had no less than nine top-10 records, five of which ranked number one for several weeks each. Many of those he wrote or cowrote. His 1948 output included "I'll Hold You in My Heart" (cowritten with Horton and T. Dilbeck), number-one ranked "Just a Little Lovin' Will Go a Long Way" (cowritten with Zeke Clements), and "Then I Turned and Walked Slowly Away" (written with Fortner). Other 1948 hits included number-one songs "A Heart Full of Love," "Bouquet of Roses," "Any Time," "Texarkana Baby," and top-10 hits "My Daddy Is Only a Picture" and "What a Fool I Was to Cry Over You."

The 1949 hits included such Arnold coauthored songs as "C-H-R-I-S-T-M-A-S," "I'm Throwing Rice at the Girl I Love," "One Kiss Too Many," and "Will Santa Come to Shanty Town." Other 1949 hits included number-one ranked "Don't Rob Another Man's Castle," "Show Me the Way to Your Heart," "The Echo of Your Footsteps," and "There's Not a Thing I Wouldn't Do for You." His 1950 hit roster included "Cuddle Buggin' Baby," "Lovebug Itch," "Mama and Daddy Broke My Heart," "Take Me in Your Arms and Hold Me," "Why Should I Cry," and "Enclosed, One Broken Heart."

As the 1950s went by, Eddy added to his list of best sellers with every passing year. In 1951, he had such number-one ranked songs as "Kentucky Waltz," "There's Been a Change in Me," and "I Want to Play House with You." In top-10 ranks were "Heart Strings," "May the Good Lord Bless and Keep You," "Somebody's Been Beating My Time," and "Something New." The following year he scored with an original composition, "Easy

on the Eyes," and such others as "Bundle of Southern Sunshine," "Full Time Job," and "Older and Bolder." His other hits of the 1950s included number-one ranked "Eddy's Song," "Mama, Come Get Your Baby Boy" (1953); "Hep Cat Baby," "I Really Don't Want to Know," "My Everything," "This Is the Thanks I Get" (1954); number-one ranked "Cattle Call," "I've Been Thinking," "Richest Man," "That Do Make It Nice," "Two Kinds of Love" (1955); "Trouble in Mind," "You Don't Know Me" (1956); and "Tennessee Stud" (1959).

During the 1950s, Eddy appeared at one time or another in every state in the union and a number of foreign countries. He was a featured guest on such network TV shows as *Arthur Godfrey's Talent Scouts, Milton Berle, Perry Como,* and *Dinah Shore.* He had his own TV show for several years on NBC and ABC networks and also starred in a syndicated TV series, *Eddy Arnold Time.*

The Arnold magic did not wither in the 1960s. He continued to tour widely and appeared often on major TV shows. He also turned out several dozen chart hits during the decade. These included such top-10 hits as "A Little Heartache," "After Loving You," "Tears Broke Out on Me" (1962); "I Thank My Lucky Stars," "Molly" (1964); "Make the World Go Away," "What's He Doing in My World" (both number-one ranked hits) (1965); number-one ranked "I Want to Go with You," "The Last Word in Lonesome Is Me," "Tips of My Fingers," "Somebody Like Me" (1966); number-one ranked "Lonely Again" (1967); "Here Comes the Rain Baby," "It's Over," "Here Comes Heaven" (1968). Eddy was voted the number-one male vocalist in country music in country polls for several years and almost always was in the top 5 or 10 in year-end ratings of *Billboard, Cash Box,* and *Record World.* In 1968, for instance, he was neck and neck with Glen Campbell for number-one album artist.

His singles success was matched by enormous album sales as well. Among his RCA LPs of the late 1950s and 1960s, most of them top-10 hits, were *Any Time, All Time Favorites, Chapel on the Hill, Wanderin', Dozen Hits, Praise Him, Praise Him* (1958); *Eddy Arnold, Have Guitar, Will Travel, Thereby Hangs* (1959); *More of Eddy Arnold, Sings Them Again, You Gotta Have Love* (1960); *Memories* (1961); *One More Time* (1962); *Country Songs, Cattle Call, Our Man Down South* (1963); *Folk Song Book, Eddy's Songs, Sometimes I'm Happy, Pop Hits* (1964); *The Last Word in Lonesome, I Want to Go with You;* and *My World* (1966). In 1967, when *Billboard* ranked him number-one country album artist, he had five charted LPs, including *Somebody Like Me, Best of Eddy Arnold,* and *Lonely Again.* In 1968, his top-10 LPs included *Everlovin' World of Eddy Arnold, Turn the World Around,* and *Romantic World of Eddy Arnold.* His 1969 releases included the LP *Warmth* (12/69).

He had a steady stream of albums on RCA in the

early 1970s, though public interest seemed to slacken a bit. Among them were *Love and Guitars* (5/70), *Best of Eddy Arnold, Volume 2* (5/70), *Standing Alone* (9/70), *This Is Eddy Arnold* (two discs, 11/70), *Portrait of My Woman* (3/71), *Welcome to My World* (8/71), *Then You Can Tell Me Goodbye* (Camden, 9/71), *Loving Her Was Easier* (12/71), *Lonely People* (7/72), and *Chained to a Memory* (8/72).

Eddy's honors and milestones continued to multiply in the 1960s and early 1970s. In 1966 he was elected to the Country Music Hall of Fame. His bronze plaque in the Nashville museum reads in part, "He has been a powerful influence in setting musical tastes. His singing, warm personality, and infectious laugh have endeared Eddy to friends and fans everywhere." On February 23, 1970, during his New York night club debut in New York's Waldorf-Astoria, RCA records presented him with an award to commemorate his reaching the 60 million-plus-mark in record sales. (As of the end of the 1970s, the total went past 70,000,000). That, RCA stressed, placed him among the top recording artists of all time. (Earlier, Arnold's night club debut in Los Angeles took place in October 1967 at the Coconut Grove.)

From the late 1960s through the 1970s, he performed before millions of people in person and on TV, including two appearances at New York's Carnegie Hall and many performances with major symphony orchestras. He hosted more than twenty TV specials, including a *Kraft Music Hall* Christmas Special in 1970. Besides emceeing seventeen *Kraft Music Hall* shows, he headlined a summer *Kraft Music Hall* series titled *Country Fair*. Other credits included acting as a guest host for Johnny Carson on *The Tonight Show*, cohosting the *Mike Douglas Show*, and narrating an NBC-TV special that presented a history of country music, *Music from the Land*.

His recording career seemed to hit a dry spell the first part of the 1970s. At least it was a dry spell for Eddy, though many country artists would have been happy to trade with him. While almost all his singles still made the charts, they tended to linger in the mid- or lower-chart levels, as was the case, for example, with the 1972 RCA release, "Lonely People," which only made it to the top 30s. A similar situation occurred in the mid-1970s after his almost three-decade affiliation with RCA was severed and he moved to MGM. On that label he had a series of moderate hits that included "She's Got Everything I Need" and "Just for Old Time's Sake" in 1974 and "Butterfly," "Red Roses," and "Middle of a Memory" in 1975.

In 1976, Eddy returned to RCA and soon showed the old magic still could be rekindled. He made the top 15 in mid-summer with "Cowboy" and in September had a top-10 hit with "Rocky Mountain Music/Do You Right Tonight." In 1977, he had a moderate hit with "Freedom Ain't the Same as Being Free." Late in 1978, the single "If Everyone Had Someone Like You" ap-

peared on the lists and, in early 1979, rose to upper-chart levels. In early summer, he had another top-10 hit with "What in Her World Did I Do." Another 1979 hit single was "Goodbye," still on the charts in early 1980. He had another excellent year in 1980 with three more bestselling singles, "That's What I Get for Loving You," "Let's Get It While the Getting's Good," and "If I Ever Had to Say Goodbye to You."

Now in his sixties, Eddy began to taper off his activities in the early 1980s in a move toward early semiretirement. His lifelong contributions to country music were recognized in 1984 by the Academy of Country Music when it presented him with its Pioneer Award. Though he continued to make concert appearances, for a seven-year period, from the early 1980s to the start of the 1990s, Arnold made no new recordings. His track record was still very impressive, as shown by Joel Whitburn's compilation of the recording accomplishments of country artists through 1988. His data disclosed that Eddy was the number-one performer in terms of best-selling records, with ninety-one top-10 singles to his credit. His closest challenger at the time was George Jones with seventy-seven.

Toward the end of the decade, Eddy began discussing a return to the recording studio with RCA. Those plans were interrupted in the spring of 1990 when he underwent major heart surgery. Talking to Michael Bane of *Country Music* three months after the event, he said, "I'm doing very well. I'm being a very good patient. I didn't have a heart attack. I just went in for a physical and they worked up to it and found sixty to seventy percent blockage in the main artery. So I'm taking the whole summer off to get well. . . .

"I was working on a new album before I got detoured in the hospital. And I had some engagements booked that I had to cancel. Now I'm enjoying the warm weather, and I'm just beginning to be able to go boating again."

His main fear was that his rich baritone voice might not regain sufficient vigor for his concert work. He noted to Joe Edwards of the Associated Press ("Country Singer Eddy Arnold has reclaimed fine voice," May 1991), "It was frightening. I didn't say anything about it, but it really bothered me. . . . It [the voice] was the last thing to come back. So I started exercising and running the [musical] scale, working on it and singing every day. It gradually bounced back."

As a result, he was able to put the finishing touches on the 1990 album, *Hand Holdin' Songs,* which showcased his versions of sixteen pop songs, and record the country-based collection titled *You Don't Miss a Thing,* issued by RCA at the start of 1991. He also was able to go back to the in-person circuit in support of the latter. The album proved he was still a master of his trade, earning almost unanimous approval from reviewers. For instance, Jack Hurst of the *Chicago Tribune* wrote, "Led by an excellent title track, this is full of material aimed at Arnold's longtime fans, but is often worthy of wider hearing as well. The 72-year old still knows not only how to choose pretty and sensitive lyrics and melodies but also how to give them maximum effect." Indeed, the album demonstrated his baritone voice had come all the way back.

As of 1992, RCA reported Eddy was closing in on a total career sales mark of 85 million singles and albums. Those recordings, RCA added, embraced twenty-eight number-one singles that occupied that position for a total of 145 weeks—"far longer than those of any other performer."

During the summer of 1996, RCA released a retrospective package of Arnold's work on its Essential Series list.

ASLEEP AT THE WHEEL: *Vocal and instrumental group. Personnel as of late 1970s: Ray Benson, born Philadelphia, Pennsylvania, March 16, 1951; Lucky Oceans (Reuben Gosfield), born Philadelphia, Pennsylvania, April 22, 1951; Chris O'Connell, born Williamsport, Maryland, March 21, c. 1953; Danny Levin, born Philadelphia, Pennsylvania, 1949; Pat "Taco" Ryan, born Texas, July 14, 1953; Link Davis, Jr., born Port Arthur, Texas. Other bandsmen, Floyd Domino, LeRoy Preston, Tony Garnier, Chris York, Bill Mabry. Roster in 1982: Benson, Oceans, O'Connell, Levin, Ryan, Preston, Domino, Garnier, York, Mabry. Roster in mid-1990s: Benson, Tim Alexander, Cindy Cashdollar, Mike Francis, Ricky Turpin, David Earl Miller, Tommy Beavers.*

In the late 1950s and throughout the 1960s, the descriptive term "country music" was more fashionable than "country & western." But a rash of new bands came along in the late 1960s that brought the "western" back into "country," not the least of which was Asleep at the Wheel. The band considered Bob Wills and the Texas Playboys a major influence who, in turn, reciprocated with enthusiastic approval of the band's efforts to revitalize western swing.

Though the band's home base was centered in Austin in the mid-1970s, the Wheel's origins weren't in Texas. The founding members grew up in the Northeast, where the friendship between two Philadelphia suburban teenagers, guitarist-singer Ray Benson and pedal steel guitarist Reuben Gosfield (who took the stage name of Lucky Oceans) planted the seeds of the band. The two played in several local bands while attending high school in Springfield, Montgomery County, Pennsylvania. They kept in touch after going to college and later added a singer and drummer from Vermont named LeRoy Preston to their circle of friends. After finding another soulmate in Eastern-bred pianist Danny Levin, the foursome retired to a friend's ranch in West Virginia in 1970 to develop their blend of country, rock, and big-band swing. During the three months of rehearsals, Oceans came up with the group's name, reputedly while sitting in the outhouse.

Benson recalled, "We led a dual existence then—musically. Rather than a country-rock band, we were a country band and a rock band playing either hard-core country or genuine old-time fifties-style rock 'n' roll. We didn't mix the two."* The initial location was a 1500-acre ranch, but a run-in with the law required a move to a smaller forty-acre farm in Magnolia, West Virginia. From there the band went out to perform at local spots, including the Paw Paw Sportsmen's Lodge and the Moose Club. Typically the band makeup was rather fluid. Some musicians left and new members joined. One of the departees was Levin; one of the additions a high-school graduate named Chris O'Connell. Chris started as a backing singer and rhythm guitarist and in six months moved up front to share lead vocals with Benson and Preston.

As the band picked up skill and confidence, they began to perform in Washington, D.C., where they became almost a fixture in the city's music scene, usually as an opening act for groups like Poco and Joy of Cooking. Benson noted, "During 1970 and 1971, there was quite a little scene going on in the D.C. clubs. Emmylou Harris was getting her start there. So were Walter Egan and Bill and Taffy Danoff [cowriters of the John Denver hit "Country Roads" and later sparkplugs of the Starland Vocal Band]. We all played the same joints."*

One band that had musical tastes similar to Asleep at the Wheel was the Lost Planet Airmen, whose leader, George Frayne (stage name Commander Cody), suggested that San Francisco was a hotbed of activity. The Wheel decided to go there in late 1971. Chris O'Connell recalled that "except for the fact that we were starving it was really neat. There were fifteen hundred bands in the Bay Area and the Cody band helped out all they could, but we were still starving. We weren't even making a slight living. So we went on the road with country singer Stoney Edwards and made a worse living, except that we ate."

In 1972, keyboardist Floyd Domino was added, bringing considerable jazz and boogie woogie grounding to the dates the band headlined at the Longbranch Saloon in Berkeley, California. The group was slowly expanding its following and late in 1972 impressed United Artists executives enough to get a recording contract. The debut album, *Comin' Right At Ya,* was issued in March 1973, with little impact on the general public. Still experimenting with personnel, Benson and company welcomed another member—electric and standup bass player Tony Garnier.

Expanding its tour schedule during 1973, the group found a warm reception from Texas fans. This inspired it to shift headquarters again, this time to Austin, Texas, in February 1974. About the same time, the band gained a new contract from Epic, which led to release of its second LP, in September 1974, an album that, if it didn't make the charts, did expose a wider spectrum of people to the band's mixture of hardcore country, country rock, jazz, blues, and western swing. During 1974, Scott Hennige took over on drums while Preston concentrated on vocals and rhythm guitar. Danny Levin returned, this time stressing his fiddle and mandolin talents.

Still looking for a recording breakthrough, the group moved over to Capitol Records. This time Asleep at the Wheel hit paydirt. Its debut on Capitol, *Texas Gold,* which was released in August 1975, caught fire with country fans and rose into the top 10 on country LP lists while also showing up on national pop charts. The album spawned three singles that made hit charts in 1975–76: "The Letter That Johnny Walker Read," "Bump Bounce Boogie," and "Nothin' Takes the Place of You." The latter months of 1975 saw the addition of Bill Mabry on fiddle, allowing the band to emulate the famed twin-fiddle sound of the old Bob Wills group. Soon after, a third fiddle player, also adept on saxophone and accordion, came into the fold—Link Davis, Jr. From his father, Davis had inherited strong Cajun musical leanings, adding still another dimension to the Wheel's influences.

The Wheel's success proved to have an impact on the fortunes of the alumni of Bob Wills's Playboys. A number of the old Playboys band, including Leon McAuliff, assembled to make a joint appearance with Asleep at the Wheel on the *Austin City Limits* series on the Public Broadcasting System. That, in turn, led to the Playboys making several new albums on Capitol.

Capitol, meanwhile, had proven a good recording home for Asleep at the Wheel. The group's second LP on the label, *Wheelin' and Dealin',* came out in July 1976 and showed up on both country and pop charts. Handling drums by then was Chris York, born in Ft. Worth, Texas, who previously had worked in a band led by Leon Rausch. That album, like the one before, provided three chart singles, a country swing version of the old big band hit "Route 66," "Miles and Miles of Texas," and "The Trouble with Lovin' Today." "Route 66" received a Grammy nomination in 1976; it was the band's second, *Texas Gold* having earned a nomination the year before.

The band expanded to eleven members before work began on the third Capitol LP. Pat "Taco" Ryan, from Tulsa, Oklahoma, added his saxophone and clarinet skills. The next album, *The Wheel,* which came out in March 1977, contained almost all band-written material, including the title track, which received a Grammy nomination. The album included the traditional fiddle tune "Ragtime Annie," which provided a fourth Grammy nomination. Soon after the LP came out, the constantly moving group was in Europe making its debut appearance overseas on a tour with Emmylou Harris. Just before going abroad, the band recorded some of its work for the Smithsonian Institution's Americana archives. In early 1978, the Wheel was named "Best Touring Band" in the Academy of Country Music awards.

Despite the increasing trappings of success, Ray Benson still felt the group was falling far short of its potential with record buyers. He told Jack Lloyd of the *Philadelphia Enquirer* in late 1977, "We can and we do play Western swing, but we also play hard-core country and Cajun music and there's the strong jazz influences you find in Western swing. I call it all good music. But it seems the average person's musical taste is not eclectic enough to relate to both George Jones and Count Basie." What he felt was needed "is to translate our American country, western, blues, jazz and Cajun roots into our own thing."

There was strong indication the group was indeed going in that direction with release of the album *Collision Course* in July 1978. The album contained elements of most of the diverse styles the band embraced, but these were closely integrated into a consistent musical and rhythmic pattern. And it did contain still more singles chart candidates, such as "Me You and Texas." The album sold well, but there was no indication of any change in pattern from earlier Capitol releases.

Deciding that more adjustment was needed, Benson announced a reduction in size. "Our eleven-person lineup has been trimmed to a fighting weight of eight. And I don't mind telling you the newly reconstituted Asleep at the Wheel is the leanest, tightest, meanest, and most determined Asleep at the Wheel you've ever heard."*

The new alignment retained Benson, O'Connell, Oceans, Ryan, and Levin. Filling out the new cast was mutitalented musician John Nicholas (guitar, piano, harmonica, mandolin, lead vocals), who previously had his own band in Boston and also had backed notable blues harmonica player Big Walter Horton; stand-up bass player Spencer Starnes, who had worked with Michael Murphey; and drummer Fran Christina out of Nova Scotia. Though Link Davis, Jr., was no longer a full-time band member, he worked with the band from time to time as did saxophonist/fiddler Andy Stein.

A positive thing the band could point to for that period was receipt of their first Grammy Award, the 1978 trophy for Best Country Instrumental Performance for the album track "One O'Clock Jump." It closed out the decade with the 1979 Capitol album *Served Live.*

The group's album credits continued to increase in the 1980s starting off with the MCA release of 1980, *Framed,* followed by the Capitol collection *American Band 3.* Later in the decade, Benson moved his band to the Epic label, which paid off with more excellent collections that earned two more Grammys. In the voting for 1987, the group was named winner of Best Country Instrumental Performance for the "String of Pars" track from the album *Asleep at the Wheel.* It won in the same category the following year, this time for the "Sugar-

---

* *From an interview with Irwin Stambler in 1979.*

foot Rag" track from the album *Western Standard Time.* Throughout that decade and into the 1990s, the group continued to retain a loyal, if not enormous, following and drew respectable crowds to concerts across the U.S. and overseas. Some of its performances were taped for presentation on the U.S. Public Broadcasting System network, including several appearances on the *Austin City Limits* program.

In the mid-1990s, Benson and company returned to the old Capitol fold, signing with Liberty Records, formerly Capitol Nashville. In 1993, Benson recruited some of country music's brightest stars for a tribute album to the late Bob Wills. Among those performing with the band on the eighteen Wills standbys included in the album were Garth Brooks, Brooks & Dunn, Vince Gill, Merle Haggard, Johnny Rodriguez, Riders in the Sky, Marty Stuart, George Strait, Lyle Lovett, Dolly Parton, Suzy Bogguss, and Willie Nelson, plus rock star Huey Lewis. Also contributing were three Texas Playboys alumni: Leon Rausch, Johnny Gimble, and Eldon Shamblin.

By this time, outside of Benson, the Asleep at the Wheel band roster had changed completely from that of a decade earlier. The mid-1990s group comprised Tim Alexander on piano, accordion, and harmony vocals; Cindy Cashdollar on Hawaiian steel guitar; Mike Francis on saxophone; Ricky Turpin on fiddle, electric mandolin, and vocals; David Earl Miller on bass; and Tommy Beavers on drums. For the new album sessions, also taking part were former Asleep at the Wheel members Lucky Oceans, Floyd Domino, and Chris O'Connell. The album, *Asleep at the Wheel Tribute to the Music of Bob Wills and the Texas Playboys,* came out in mid-1993 and was a gesture of which Wills certainly would have been proud. It was voted one of the five final candidates for Album of the Year by Country Music Association members, and on the October 1994 CMA Award telecast Lyle Lovett (as well as some other contributing stars) joined the band to perform the album track "Blues for Dixie." In the Grammy voting for 1994, announced on the March 1, 1995, telecast, the song won Lovett and Benson's entourage the award for Best Country Performance by a Duo or Group with Vocal.

The band's concert and TV schedule for 1995–1996 revolved around its 25th anniversary celebration. In September 1995, the band and some alumni gave a special concert at the Bass Concert Hall in Austin. Meanwhile the mayor of Austin declared the date of September 22 "Asleep at the Wheel Day." Concert numbers included some songs from the band's new album, *The Wheel Keeps on Rollin'.* Later events included a January 27 show on the *Austin City Limits* TV program in which the band was joined by special guests Willie Nelson, Charlie Daniels, Delbert McClinton, Wade Hayes, Tracy Byrd, and Johnny Gimble. Also tak-

ing part were band alumni Chris O'Connell, Lucky Oceans, Johnny Nicholas, Floyd Domino, LeRoy Preston, and Larry Franklin.

ATKINS, CHET: *Guitarist, composer, singer, producer, record industry executive. Born Luttrell, Tennessee, June 20, 1924. Elected to Country Music Hall of Fame in 1973.*

It's hard to fit more than the highlights of Chet Atkins's illustrious career into a few pages—the many awards and honors presented him over the years alone could take up many lines of any encyclopedia entry. As an acknowledged all-time great guitarist, his instrumental technique has been studied and often copied, in part, by musicians in fields ranging from classical to rock. In the country field, besides having a hand in hundreds of important recordings—his own and those of the many others whose careers he helped to shape—he contributed to the growth of Nashville as the hub of that music. *Record World* editors noted, at one point, "No one person can honestly receive total credit for the phenomenal explosion of Nashville's music business. However, no individual has been more responsible for this growth than Chet Atkins."

He had the advantage of growing up in a home where music was almost a way of life, in the small town of Luttrell, twenty miles from Knoxville, in the Clinch Mountains of Tennessee. The son of a piano and voice teacher, Chet was only three years old when Jimmie Rodgers cut the first sides that were to revolutionize country music, but he soon fell in love with the Rodgers discs that were played on the family's old wind-up phonograph.

During that period, he already was interested in playing an instrument, but his brothers, Jimmy and Lowell, didn't want little Chet to play their guitar. Instead, he tried to master a fiddle. When he was nine, he traded an old pistol for a beat-up guitar, recalling, "I remember that deal well. It was one of the smartest I ever made. A lot of guitars have come and gone for me since then but it is the truth that I've been picking since I was nine."

By the time Chet finished high school he had acquired respectable proficiency on the guitar and got a job on station WNOK in Knoxville with the *Bill Carlisle Show.* He also filled in with a band called the Dixie Swingsters. He stayed in the Knoxville area for three years, then played jobs on the radio circuit as a solo act or sideman at WLW in Cincinnati, WPTF in Raleigh, North Carolina, WRVA in Richmond, Virginia, KWTO in Springfield, Missouri, and KOA in Denver.

His Missouri show started the chain of events that was to make him a Nashville legend. Steve Sholes, then RCA Victor's top country-music executive, heard Chet on a Mutual radio show that originated in Missouri. He liked Atkins's style, but couldn't find him for a time because of Chet's rapid changes in station affiliation.

Meanwhile, Si Siman of KWTO had forwarded a transcription of one show to Al Hindle, who ran the custom-records business for RCA from a Chicago office. Hindle sent it along to Sholes in New York, who realized, after listening to it, that Atkins was the man he was looking for. Sholes quickly followed up, as Atkins remembered:

"By that time I had been fired in Springfield and was working KOA in Denver with Shorty Thompson and his Rangers. Steve called me and asked me if I wanted to record for RCA and I said sure. He mailed me a contract. A couple of months later on I mortgaged my car, borrowed some money, and went to Chicago, where I met Steve and we recorded—two sessions in one day; one morning, one afternoon—eight sides."

Considering the fact that Atkins almost never uses his voice anymore, it's interesting to note that five of the eight numbers had vocals. The vocals included "I'm Gonna Get Tight," "Standing Room Only," and "Don't Hand Me That Line." Since then, Atkins has tried to locate and destroy all masters from those vocal efforts. The three instrumentals, "Canned Heat," "Bug Dance," and "Nashville Jump," found favor with disc jockeys and got considerable airplay even if they didn't make any bestseller lists. In 1949, though, releases like "Gallopin' Guitar," "Main St. Breakdown," and "Country Gentlemen" started to bring the first wave of public acceptance that was to bring him the nickname "Mr. Guitar."

His first appearance on the *Grand Ole Opry* was in 1946 with Red Foley, but he didn't become a regular until several years later. In the late 1940s, Chet started working with the Carter Family and, with his recordings starting to come off RCA presses, he decided to settle in Nashville. In 1949, Sholes made Chet studio guitarist for RCA Nashville sessions and noted that his suggestions often improved the overall work of the musicians concerned. His executive talents were recognized on a more formal basis in 1953 when he was designated a consultant to Victor's Nashville operations. By then he was a featured artist on the *Opry,* which added him to its regular cast in 1950.

In 1957, Sholes made Chet a part-time producer, and later that year, when Steve was named head of pop A&R in Victor's New York offices, Atkins moved up to full-time manager. In the decades after, Chet presided over the growth of the studios from a few people to a large, multifaceted organization. In 1968, he was named Division Vice President.

Sholes said, "The hit artists Chet found for us include Don Gibson, Floyd Cramer, Connie Smith, Dottie West, and many others. [Among those others were Waylon Jennings and Bobby Bare.] Although I was lucky enough to bring Jim Reeves in, Chet did all the successful recordings with him." In fact, very few of the RCA artists in the country field (plus some pop stars) didn't at one time or another profit from Atkins's tute-

lage. At any given time, he supervised recording efforts of twenty-five artists on a roster that included such names over the years as Elvis Presley, Al Hirt, Eddy Arnold, Homer and Jethro, Perry Como, and Floyd Cramer.

Atkins always tended to downplay his producing role. "You hear about the successes, but we try to keep the failures—the duds—a trade secret. There is no sure-fire system for hits. What I do is listen a lot during a recording session and try to pick up some little something from the musicians playing on the session that might make the record more commercial. A lot of us producers have picked up reputations as specialists with the help of some musician who tried just a little harder, or experimented with an unusual sound."

Sholes once pointed to the elements of Atkins's style that first gained his attention. "Chet plays finger-style guitar. He doesn't pick, he just *touches* the strings, pushes down on them and lets the fingers up—except for his thumb and that's generally for the bass strings. He can play other styles too—Spanish, classical, everything else. But the style that first got me intrigued was his finger-style playing. I had never heard it before. There are few people who play that way now."

Atkins never let his executive responsibilities take him away from his first love—performing—for any extended period of time. Year after year, from the 1950s into the 1990s, he turned out his share of recordings either as a soloist or in conjunction with other artists or groups. His recording partners over the years included Floyd Cramer, the Boston Pops, Ravi Shankar, Merle Travis, Jerry Reed, and, in the late 1970s, Les Paul, and an outfit called the Chet Atkins String Quartet.

Restlessly experimenting over the years, he donated his guitar artistry to all kinds of musical formats in many different settings. Besides performing as a soloist with symphonies in the United States, he appeared in concert with classical groups in Europe. He proved he could play jazz as well as anyone on occasion, including an acclaimed appearance at the 1960 Newport Jazz Festival. In March 1961, he played for the Press Photographers' Ball before an audience that included President Kennedy. His engagements with the Boston Pops in the 1960s helped pave the way for many other country stars guesting with Arthur Fiedler and Co. (He cut two Red Seal albums with the Pops.) Among his early 1970s musical activities were a series of country engagements called The Music Masters in which he joined forces with Boots Randolph and Floyd Cramer. Throughout the decades, besides his countless appearances on *Opry* radio programs, Chet was a regular visitor to all manner of radio and TV variety shows ranging from Johnny Carson to the Grammy Awards programs.

His name often appeared in the winner's circle at Grammy events. His first Grammy came when the RCA album *Chet Atkins Picks the Best* was named Best Contemporary Instrumental Performance of 1967. He added another one for 1970 when his duet LP with Jerry Reed, *Me and Jerry,* was named Best Country Instrumental Performance. In 1971, the National Academy of Recording Arts and Sciences voters chose his "Snowbird" as Best Country Instrumental Performance. In 1976, still another Grammy came his way, this time for his collaboration with another guitar legend, Les Paul, on the LP *Chester and Lester.* Some of his recordings made the final five even if they missed the award itself, an example being his *Solid Gold '69* album.

Atkins's name often topped the list in various polls for top guitarists. Year after year, from the early 1960s throughout the 1970s, for instance, *Cash Box* named him Outstanding Instrumentalist. He won the *Playboy* poll four times as Best Guitarist and was highly ranked in surveys in other magazines and in polls held in other parts of the world. In 1972, he was honored by the National Council of Christians and Jews, which gave him its Humanitarian Award.

In 1973, Atkins's preeminence in the country field was recognized by his fellow artists, who elected him to the Country Music Hall of Fame.

During his long career as a recording artist, Chet turned out dozens of albums. A partial list of his 1950s and 1960s LPs follows, all on RCA unless otherwise noted. Mid-1950s releases included *Sessions, In Three Dimensions, Stringin' Along,* and *Finger Style Guitar.* Late 1950s offerings included *Hi Fi in Focus,* issued in December 1957, *At Home* (7/58), *In Hollywood* (7/59), and *Hum & Strum Along.* Releases in the 1960s included *Mister Guitar* (1/60), *Teensville* (2/60), *Other Chet Atkins* (9/60), *Workshop* (2/61), *Guitar* (5/61-Camden), *Most Popular* (7/61), *Down Home* (3/62), *Caribbean Guitar* (9/62), *Back Home Hymns* (11/62), *Our Man in Nashville* (2/63), *Guitar Genius* (5/63-Camden), *Travelin'* (9/63), *Guitar Country* (2/64), *Best* (6/64), *Progressive Pickin'* (7/64), *Reminiscing* (12/64), *My Favorite Guitars* (5/65), *Guitar Country* (11/65), *Picks on the Beatles* (5/66), *Best* (7/66), *Music from Nashville,* (8/66-Camden), *From Nashville* (11/66), *Guitar World* (4/67), *Picks the Best* (6/67) *Class Guitar* (11/67), *Chet* (12/67-Camden), *Solid Gold '69, Warmth* (12/69).

In the 1970s, Chet's album output didn't taper off even though it was his third decade on RCA. His releases included *Best, Volume 2* (5/70), *Love and Guitars* (5/70), *Standing Alone* (9/70), *Me and Jerry* (10/70), *This Is Chet Atkins* (11/70), *Portrait of My Woman* (3/71), *For the Good Times* (4/71), *Welcome to My World* (8/71), *Then You Can Tell Me Goodbye* (9/71), *Pickin' My Way* (10/71), *Chet, Floyd & Boots* (11/71-Camden), *Lovin' Her Was Easier* (12/71), *Nashville Gold* (4/72-Camden), *Now & Then* (11/72), *Picks on the Hits* (11/72), *The Atkins-Travis Travelin' Show* (1974), *Atkins String Band* (1975), *Chester and Lester* (1976).

Following *Chester and Lester,* RCA album releases included *A Legendary Performer, Chester, Floyd and Danny,* and *Me and My Guitar* (all 1977); *American Salute* and *First Nashville Guitar Quartet* (1979); *Best of Chet Atkins/On the Road* and *Reflections* (1980); and *Country—After All These Years* (1981). Camden reissues included *Chet Atkins in Concert, Country Pickin'* and *Finger Pickin' Good.*

Though better known as an album artist, Atkins turned out many singles over the years, a number of which made the charts. Among his 1970s charted numbers, for instance, were "Snowbird" in 1971, "The Night Atlanta Burned" (1975, with the Atkins String Quartet), and the 1974 hit, "Fiddlin' Around." He was still placing singles on the charts at the start of the 1980s, one example being "Blind Willie" in 1980.

After making some seventy-five albums for RCA over a 36-year period, Chet left the label to sign with Columbia in 1982. His Columbia debut that year, *Stay Tuned,* featured guest guitarists from pop and jazz including George Benson, Larry Carlton, Mark Knopfler (of the rock group Dire Straits), and Earl Klugh. That project spawned a Cinemax special, "A Session with Chet Atkins, C.G.P." (where C.G.P. stands for certified guitar player). Before the 1980s were over, Chet had three more Columbia albums to his credit, *Street Dreams, Sails,* and *Chet Atkins, C.G.P.* His instrumental work on some of those was described by some reviewers as "New Age Jazz."

Atkins kept accruing more honors in the 1980s, adding to his three 1960s Country Music Association Instrumentalist of the Year selections with six more such trophies in the years from 1981 through 1985 and in 1988 (the year the category's name was changed to Musician of the Year). He picked up Grammy Awards in 1981 and 1985 for Best Country Instrumental Performance, the first for "After All These Years," the second a track from *Stay Tuned,* "Cosmic Square Dance." In the last-named, he was joined by Mark Knopfler. In 1988, he was the top vote-getter in the *Playboy* magazine jazz poll. In December 1989, the Nashville Symphony Orchestra supported his selection for the Harmony Award "in recognition of his contribution to the development and appreciation of American music culture."

Chet started off the 1990s with a schedule of activities as intensive as in previous decades. During the first part of 1990, he and Mark Knopfler recorded tracks for a joint album, *Neck and Neck,* in sessions in Nashville and London. They also performed together at the Amnesty International concert at the London Pavilion. During the year, Chet displayed his talents in a month of concerts with radio show notable (*Prairie Home Companion*) humorist Garrison Keillor. He also joined jazz star Stanley Jordan in concert at the annual Spoleto Festival in Charleston, South Carolina, and began work on a new album with longtime friend Jerry Reed.

The *Neck and Neck* album made hit charts in both pop and country categories in the U.S. and abroad.

Atkins and Knopfler earned two Grammy Awards for 1990, one for best Country Instrumental Performance based on the track "So Soft, Your Goodbye," the other for Best Country Vocal Collaboration on "Poor Boy Blues."

In May 1991, the section of South Street that passes through Nashville's Music Row was renamed Chet Atkins Place. Chet was included among "The 100 Greatest Musicians of the 20th Century" roster presented in *Musician* magazine's February 1993 issue. The editors wrote, "Back in the '50s, Atkins effortlessly combined flawless three-finger-style picking with perfectly executed, yakety string-bends to thrilling effect. Although some of the fire has gone out of his playing, he can still smoke when he wants to." The September 1994 special issue of *Life* magazine on "The Roots of Country Music" listed him in the top 10 of its choice of "The 100 Most Important People in the History of Country."

During 1993–94, Chet was one of the participants in two concept albums, one the *Asleep at the Wheel Tribute to the Music of Bob Wills and the Texas Playboys,* issued on Liberty Records, the other MCA's *Rhythm, Country & Blues.* Both albums did well on the charts and both were nominated by Country Music Association members for Album of the Year. During 1994, he recorded some songs with Suzy Bogguss and the two also appeared in a number of concerts together. Their single of "All My Loving" was nominated for a Grammy in the Best Country Collaboration with Vocals category for 1995.

In December 1994, country fans were startled to hear Chet's name reported among those artists who passed away during the year—a mistake that came about when someone had confused his name with that of actor Claude Akins. As Mark Twain had done under similar circumstances, Chet rushed to emphasize the reports of his demise had been greatly exaggerated.

In the spring of 1996, Columbia issued a primarily acoustic album by Chet titled *Almost Alone.* As part of the promotion for the disc, Chet signed 125 Gibson Epiphone guitars at the Hard Rock Café in Nashville. In one of the largest giveaways by the guitar manufacturer the signed guitars were distributed to retail outlets who then arranged for contests to determine the lucky winners.

In the summer of 1996, Atkins flew to New York for a performance at the Iridium Club with Les Paul, marking the 20th anniversary of their Grammy–winning *Chester and Lester* LP. It also was part of Chet's celebration of his 50th anniversary in the music business.

AUTRY, GENE: *Singer, guitarist, songwriter, actor, business executive. Born Tioga, Texas, September 29, 1907. Elected to Country Music Hall of Fame in 1969.*

Few performers can live up to the cliché "he did it all," but if anyone has come close to being the all-around entertainer, Gene Autry has. After enjoying an immensely successful career as a singer, guitarist, actor, and songwriter for more than four decades, he was able to turn most of his attention toward running the vast business empire he had been building, a rare talent of a different sort.

As a youngster growing up in Texas and Oklahoma, Gene naturally heard cowboy songs and country music, but the idea of a music career hardly occurred to him. Upon graduating from high school, he took a job as a railroad telegraph operator in Sepulpa, Oklahoma. It was a night job with long, lonely hours between messages, so he bought a guitar and learned to play it in order to keep himself awake. One night, a stranger came in to write a telegram while Gene was playing. The man waited until he finished the song, then said, "Young feller, all I can say is that you're wasting your time here. You ought to quit and try radio." The name on the telegram sheet was Will Rogers.

Autry took Rogers's advice and soon gained a job with station KVOO as "Oklahoma's Singing Cowboy." He became quite popular and his reputation spread to other states. In 1927, he went to Chicago to cut his first record for a small, independent record company. Nothing happened with that record, but Gene kept trying. He went to New York and in 1929 was signed by recording pioneer Art Satherly to make several cowboy records, among the first such songs ever recorded, for the old American Record Company. Out of the first six sides he recorded for Satherly, Autry had one hit, "That Silver Haired Daddy of Mine," a song he had written himself. In succeeding years that record sold over 5 million copies.

Following the success of "Silver Haired Daddy," Autry went to Chicago, where he was given his own singing program on radio station WLS. (The call letters stood for "World's Largest Store"—Sears, Roebuck and Co.) In the four years that he stayed at WLS, Autry became one of the best-known singers in the Midwest, through such top hits as "Mexicali Rose."

In 1934, Gene was signed to act in his first film, a bit singing role in a Ken Maynard western, *In Old Santa Fe.* The picture's box-office success led to a chance to star in a serial, *The Phantom Empire,* a thirteen-chapter cliff-hanger. When this, too, did well at the box office, Republic Pictures, a new movie company, signed Autry to a motion picture contract. It was for Republic Pictures that he made what came to be known as the world's first singing western, *Tumbling Tumble Weeds.* Around the same time, another newcomer to the movies, John Wayne, was also making a picture for Republic, entitled *Westward Ho.* These two films were the first to be made under the Republic banner.

Gene rapidly became one of the most popular film stars of that era, a status enhanced by personal appearances throughout the 1930s in all parts of the world. These included another first, the initial appearance of a movie cowboy as star of the World Championship

Rodeo in New York's Madison Square Garden. During the 1930s he was also honored by having the town of Gene Autry, Oklahoma, named for him. By the end of the 1950s he had been seen by untold millions in film audiences all over the world in eighty-two feature-length musical westerns; by 1968 the total exceeded one hundred.

At the same time that Autry was making one film after another, he also continued to write and record hit songs, such as "You're the Only Star in My Blue Heaven" and "Dust" in 1938, "Tears on My Pillow" and "Be Honest with Me" in 1941, and "Tweedle O Twill" in 1942.

On July 26, 1942, Autry enlisted in the Army Air Corps as a technical sergeant, thereby going from a salary of over $600,000 a year to one of around $135 a month. The wartime duties of the cowboy film star entailed serving as a flight commander and first pilot in the Far East and ferrying planes, cargo, and supplies to India, North Africa, and Burma. This occupation, however, did not stop him completely from writing songs or recording them; together with Fred Rose he wrote a song, "Mail Call Today," that sold over a million records during the war years.

After the war, Autry returned to Hollywood and resumed an even more dynamic career than before. For a time he continued to record for Okeh records and had hits such as "I'll Go Riding Down That Texas Trail," "The Yellow Rose of Texas," "Deep in the Heart of Texas," and "Maria Elena." He also continued to make motion pictures and started his own network radio show, *Melody Ranch,* which was to become the longest-running radio show for one sponsor (Wrigley's Gum). The television version of *Melody Ranch* remained on the air throughout the 1960s.

In the late 1940s, Autry signed with Columbia Records and proceeded to turn out dozens of records, many of which became all-time standards. Among these recordings were "Buttons and Bows," "Frosty the Snow Man," "Peter Cottontail," "South of the Border," "Back in the Saddle Again," "Tumbling Tumble Weeds," "You Are My Sunshine," and "Boots and Saddles." Among his largest hits were two Christmas records, "Here Comes Santa Claus" and "Rudolph the Red-Nosed Reindeer." As he told Claude Hall of *Claude Hall's International Radio Report:*

"After I came back here [from the war] I made a record that the first year sold a million and a half and that's after I'd been out of the record business five years. It was called 'Here Comes Santa Claus,' and I got the idea for the song—I wrote it with another guy. I was the Grand Marshal of the Hollywood Parade on Thanksgiving. I was riding down there, you know, the Grand Marshal and all the kids would say, 'Hey, here comes Santa Claus, here comes Santa Claus.' So I made a note of that and I got together with this guy and wrote the goddamned song 'Here Comes Santa Claus.'

"So the second year I was huntin' for another record, a Christmas record. And a guy from New York sent me a demonstration record, a demo, and I heard it. I played it several times but I didn't care a hell of a lot about it. So my wife said, 'I think that you ought to listen to that record you played called "Rudolph the Red-Nosed Reindeer." There's something about that thing that I like. It reminds me of the story of the ugly duckling—that line "They wouldn't let poor Rudolph join in any reindeer games." It's kind of cute.'

"I said, 'Well, what the hell.' I didn't have anything better so I recorded it. That thing sold two and a half million the first year. . . ." Over the years that record sold around 7 million copies.

Autry's other records continue to sell and he still gets royalties from many of them. In the 1960s he had some best-selling albums, including *Greatest Hits* (Columbia, 1961); *Golden Hits* (RCA Victor, 1962); and *Great Hits* (Harmony, 1965).

During the 1950s, while continuing his career as an entertainer, Autry began an additional vocation as an investor and business magnate. He had actually bought his first radio station in 1942 when he enlisted in the service. He realized that he might not be able to sing and perform forever but that he could continue to make money if he invested wisely. When he returned from the war he continued to buy radio stations and also had the foresight to purchase television stations when that medium was still in its infancy. By 1962 he owned a chain of TV and radio stations and also established his own record firm, Challenge Records, and his own television production company, Flying A Productions. (In the early 1960s, he performed in a series of fifty-two half-hour TV shows for Flying A.) He had by this time also branched out his investments to include a hotel chain, a music publishing firm, and more.

Autry had always been an avid sports fan and he was eager to get a contract to broadcast Los Angeles Dodgers games over his radio station, KMPC. However, he was unable to obtain this contract as the Dodgers had committed their coverage to another station. So Gene, along with sportsman Bob Reynolds, decided to try to put together their own Los Angeles baseball club. In 1962, their bid for an expansion franchise in the American League was accepted, and the Los Angeles Angels were born. In 1966, the team moved to nearby Anaheim and became known as the California Angels. At long last, in 1979, Autry saw his team have a winning season, as the California Angels became the Western Division American League champions.

In the 1980s and 1990s, essentially retired as a performer, Gene continued to look after his business affairs, spending many hours at Anaheim Stadium during the baseball season, hoping for a California Angels team able to make the World Series. As of 1997, though the team had seen some above-average seasons, that goal had not yet been achieved. In the 1980s, Gene established the Western Heritage Museum in Los Angeles's Griffith Park, featuring exhibits on the settling of the West and on cowboy-and-Indian lore. The museum was also the center for many special events over the years, celebrating western films, country & western music, and other appropriate subjects. C&W artists young and old took part in some of these shows, such as one in the 1990s that paired the venerable Roy Rogers with rising new country star Dwight Yoakam.

Although Gene was long past recording new material, some of his classic tracks were reissued by labels like Columbia/Legacy. In the mid-1990s, collections available from the Country Music Hall of Fame & Museum catalog were *The Essential Gene Autry 1933–1946* on Columbia Country Classics and *Columbia Historic Edition* on Columbia Records. In 1996, the group Riders in the Sky issued the album *Public Cowboy Number One* in tribute to Gene.

In the fall of 1996, a spotlight was cast upon a little-known phase of Gene's career when Columbia/Legacy released the CD reissue *Gene Autry—Blues Singer 1929–1931*. As pointed out in the liner notes, Gene had originally thought of forging a career for himself as a pop singer. While taking advantage of a railroad pass in the late 1920s to leave his job as a railroad telegrapher and visit New York, he took a friend's advice and approached recording companies as a potential competitor to blues yodel star Jimmie Rodgers. He got the attention of the American Record Company (forerunner of Columbia Records), a rival to Rodgers's RCA Victor recording home which had him perform a number of blues-type tracks of his own and other writers' songs. The CD demonstrates that Autry might have become a successful Rodgers-style blues artist if he hadn't scored a breakthrough with his single of "That Silver Haired Daddy of Mine," and followed up with the first of his cowboy musical films.

BALL, DAVID: *Singer, guitarist, string bass player, songwriter. Born Rock Hill, South Carolina, July 9, c. mid-1950s.*

In a decade of sudden breakthroughs in the country field, David Ball was a candidate for Best New Artist of 1994 in the Academy of Country Music poll when he earned a gold record the first time out with his debut on Warner Brothers Records, *Thinkin' Problem*. But while he was a newcomer to the national music scene, he had slowly honed his ability as performer and songwriter for some two decades. While one year's hits don't make a star, his talents and audience rapport—the latter indicated by excellent response when he was a last-minute

substitute in a Brooks & Dunn concert—augured well for continuing success.

He was born in Rock Hill, South Carolina, the son of a Baptist minister and a mother who liked to play piano for family sing-alongs. He recalled an early exposure to country music when his parents took him to see a concert by Fred Kirby in Charlotte, North Carolina. "I must have been five years old, but I can still see him in his cowboy suit singing 'Big Rock Candy Mountain.' This was the first time I heard somebody in concert and it left quite an impression on me."

Two years later, the family moved to Spartanburg, South Carolina. "A neighbor had a guitar and by Christmas I was begging for a guitar. Santa Claus almost came through and I wound up with a ukelele. By the time my birthday came around that July, the folks relented and I got a Stella guitar. There were lots of musicians in Spartanburg and by the time I was a teenager I began to hang out with them. Other than baseball, playing a guitar and singing was all I really wanted to do. I wrote my first song in the seventh grade and with a band I formed, played it in the school talent show. We called ourselves the Strangers, a knock-off of Merle Haggard's band."

Besides guitar, Ball also learned to play string bass. "It's the old story; a bass player was needed and I was elected. I was pretty serious about the instrument and even played it in the school orchestra for a year. But mostly, I just played the bluegrass stuff that I was comfortable with. Back then, we were just doing Doc Watson type stuff. I remember Don Reno and Red Smiley. That will always be some of the best music I ever heard. We traveled around a little bit while in high school, up to Durham, North Carolina, and down to Myrtle Beach, South Carolina, hitting different folk festivals or anyplace that would have us. Needless to say I loved it and was hooked on playing music."

By the time Ball finished high school, he was part of a country-bluegrass trio called Uncle Walt's Band, which moved to Austin, Texas, in the mid-1970s, since they felt there was more opportunity for their type of band than at home. In Austin, he recalled, "I first heard Texas dance hall music. I fell in love with the sound of Bob Wills and began incorporating it into my repertoire."

He was able to make a reasonable living working clubs and festivals in the Southwest while also getting married and starting a family. Like any creative musician, he longed to expand his horizons, and in the late 1980s he took the giant step to Nashville, where he began the typical routine of passing demo tapes around to publishing houses and record firms. He did get a publishing agreement, but his initial recording contract didn't lead anywhere. However, his recording efforts led to a friendship with record producer Blake Chancey.

That friendship really paid off, as Ball pointed out. "The Idle Hour was a place where Roger Miller and

Willie Nelson used to hang out. It's like a trailer with stucco stuck all over it, with a concrete floor, a pool table and a jukebox. Blake and I would go to the Idle Hour and occasionally I would pick and sing. One day Blake called Warner's A and R director Doug Grau, around late spring of '93, and said, 'You've got to come and hear this guy sing.'

"Grau came over and I just sat and sang, while a cab driver was in there trying to sell everybody tennis shoes he got from a tractor trailer wreck on the Interstate. Blake had already given me the nickname 'the human jukebox'—maybe I'll put that on my business cards. By the end of the night I'd played quite a collection of songs."

The audition paid off, and Grau soon signed Ball to the label. With Blake as producer, David assembled the tracks for his debut album, which was released in early December 1993. Most of the tracks were written or cowritten by David, but there were some others, including a remake of Webb Pierce's "The Wild Side of Life." It took some months before the album started to catch on with disc jockeys and the public, but by June, both the album, *Thinkin' Problem,* and the title song (cowritten by Ball, A. Shamblin, and S. Ziff) were moving up the charts. The album was in *Billboard*'s number six position in early June while the single made *Billboard*'s top 5 in August. *Thinkin' Problem* also showed up on the magazine's Hot 200 pop list, peaking at number fifty-three.

Major publication reviewers were generally quite enthusiastic about Ball's effort. For example, Don McLeese of *Rolling Stone* wrote, "You can hear in *Thinkin' Problem* exactly what David Ball has learned from George Jones, Lefty Frizzell and Hank Williams. What makes Ball such a fresh voice is a natural sense of swing and a sweetness in his upper register not often associated with honky tonk fare."

Ball acknowledged his debt to such artists in discussing the track of "The Wild Side of Life," a country classic covered by more than a few performers over the years. "When I really started getting into some serious singing, I was listening to country singers from what is sometimes called 'The Golden Era'—Ray Price, Don Gibson, Lefty Frizzell. I really loved the sound of it. I especially liked the fiddle playing on those Webb Pierce records. Anyway, I had sung 'Wild Side of Life' in bands forever and I thought I did it just like Webb, but after we cut it, I went back and listened to the original and I don't sing anything like him. I realized that over the years I had begun to sing my own way."

Doing it this way seemed to be paying off as 1994 went by. By mid-September, another single had debuted on *Billboard*'s list, "When the Thought of You Catches Up With Me" (words and music by Ball) and was moving toward the top 40. The week of November 27 it peaked at number seven in *Radio & Records*. In early 1995, the single "Look What Followed Me

Home" (cowritten by Ball and T. Polk) was heading for the top 10. His album was still on both country and pop charts in mid-1995, having gone past both gold and platinum R.I.A.A. certification levels. (The platinum record was presented to him on August 16, 1995.) In the spring of 1996, his single "Circle of Friends" (cowritten with B. Spencer) was moving toward upper chart levels. The album from which it was drawn, *Starlite Lounge,* was on the charts soon after.

BANDY, MOE: *Singer, guitarist, band leader. Born Meridian, Mississippi, February 12, 1944.*

Since Moe Bandy's birthplace, Meridian, Mississippi, was also the hometown of the great Jimmie Rodgers, the Singing Brakeman, and since his grandfather worked with Rodgers on the railroad, young Moe naturally listened to a lot of Jimmie Rodgers's records. Since his parents were musically oriented and, for a time, his father had his own country band, it might have been expected Moe would think of music as a career goal from the start. As it happened, for many years he was more interested in bronco-busting and bull-riding and, had he made the big time, rodeo's gain would have been country music's loss. But at least he knew what he was singing about when he placed recordings like the fall 1981 hit single "Rodeo Romeo" on the charts.

"My dad plays guitar and sings," he related in 1979, "and my mother plays piano and sings so that's where I got started. I learned guitar when I was a kid. My dad taught me. I dropped it for a long time, then took it up again when I was nineteen. He wanted me to be a fiddle player too, so I started, but I never did pick that up again.

"We moved to San Antonio, Texas, when I was six and I grew up there. I entered Burbank High School in 1959, then I switched to East Central. I graduated from there in 1962. I played very little music until I got out of high school. What I was doing was rodeoing. I started when I was about ten and by the time I was sixteen I was entering rodeos all over Texas. I broke a lot of bones and made a little money, but not much. My brother did better. He's been in the top ten for the last six years [as of 1979]."

Thus Moe, having little luck as a rodeo contestant, returned to picking guitar. He formed his first group, Moe and the Mavericks, in 1962. "I started playing local beer joints and honky tonks around Texas. It was a thrill. I just did it for fun at the start. I started in 1962 and did that for twelve years. I made several records on small labels—GP, Satin, Shannon, that didn't do any good." In order to survive, like so many other would-be musicians, he worked during the day (as a sheet-metal worker) and at night and on weekends he played as much as he could. His first single to come out during

Bandy quotes (except for Allen) from 1979 interview with Irwin Stambler.

that period was the 1964 release "Lonely Lady" on Satin. It got little attention, and Moe and the Mavericks continued to perform as the house band on a local TV show, *Country Corner,* and to back up national touring acts.

In 1972, Moe found out that record producer Ray Baker was in San Antonio on a hunting trip, so he knocked on his motel room door and persuaded Baker to listen to some of Moe's tapes. A few weeks later, Baker called Bandy and said he would like to try producing something for him. Moe hocked his furniture to pay for the studio time, but nothing much happened with the recordings.

Baker decided to wait until he found the right tune before trying again with Bandy. In 1973 he called Moe and told him to come to Nashville and bring some more money to pay studio expenses. This time Moe took out a loan, but the gamble paid off.

Bandy recalls, "Baker came up with 'I Just Started Hatin' Cheatin' Songs Today.' He made five hundred copies on Footprint Records and started promoting it. The record broke nationally and it was picked up by GRC Records in Atlanta, Georgia." Within five weeks after GRC took over, the song was in the national top 5 of the country charts and Moe was on his way. He followed with more singles hits on GRC: "Honky Tonk Amnesia" in 1973; "It Was Always Easy to Find An Unhappy Woman" and "Don't Anyone Make Love at Home Anymore" in 1974; and, in 1975, "Bandy the Rodeo Clown," which he co-wrote with Lefty Frizzell. That song, he noted, with its echoes of rodeo life and his brother Mike's bull-riding exploits, "is one of my favorites. I like all of them though. They've been good to me."

Although he co-wrote that tune and wrote some others, like the early "Lonely Lady," he stresses that writing isn't his forte. "I've written a couple of songs, but mostly I've done songs by other writers. I'm just gonna try to keep it the way it is. What I do is traditional type country music. It's what I do best and I think there definitely is a need for it. Other than performing, though, I like all kinds of music."

Moe's "hard country" songs follow in the tradition of Hank Williams—songs about cheating and heartache performed with a straightforward delivery. Will Hardesty of Rocky Mountain Music Express describes his impact in this way: "What he does best is enough to make a listener able to smell stale beer and stale cigarette smoke, enough to make the listener hear the clink of glassware, the buzz of conversation and laughter, the shuffle of slow-dancing feet. It's enough to make you want a beer."

In 1975, Moe left GRC and signed with Columbia, still his label in the early 1980s. By then, he also had three albums released on GRC, *I Just Started Hatin' Cheatin' Songs Today* (1973); *It Was Always Easy to Find an Unhappy Woman* (1974); and *Bandy the Rodeo Clown* (1975). On the new label, he picked right up

where he'd left off with a steady string of top-10 hits. In 1975, he started the new series with the single "Hank Williams You Wrote My Life" and followed, in the second half of the 1970s, with the chart hits "The Biggest Airport in the World," "Here I Am Drunk Again," "She Took More than Her Share" (all 1976); "I'm Sorry for You My Friend," "Cowboys Ain't Supposed to Cry," "She Just Loved the Cheatin' Out of Me" (1977); "Soft Lights and Hard Country Music," "That's What Makes the Jukebox Play," "Two Lonely People" (1978); "I Cheated Me Right Out of You," "Barstool Mountain," "It's a Cheatin' Situation" (duet with Janie Fricke) (1979).

During 1979, Moe joined forces with Joe Stampley to form a highly successful duo. About its origins, he said, "Joe and I was in Europe together and Joe came up with the idea and I talked to my producer [still Ray Baker] and got it all together." The first result of the new alignment was the single "Just Good Ol' Boys," which rose to number one on country charts. The song also served as the title track for a hit album from which two more hit singles (in 1980) were culled, "Tell Ole I Ain't Here, He Better Get on Home" and "Holding the Bag." The success of their teamwork was indicated by their May 1980 selection by the Academy of Country Music as Duo of the Year; a choice seconded in October by members of the Country Music Association, who voted them the Duet of the Year.

During 1980, Bandy continued his string of hit solo singles as well as his chart-makers with Stampley. Those included "One of a Kind," "The Champ," and "Yesterday Once More." He began 1981 with another duet top-10 hit, "Following the Feeling," this time with Judy Bailey. Soon after, he combined with Joe again for the top-10 single "Hey Joe, Hey Moe." Other 1981 successes included the solo "Rodeo Romeo" and the duet, with Stampley, "Honky Tonk Queen."

From the mid-1970s on, Moe also was represented on Columbia Records by albums that generally made upper-chart positions. His debut on the label in 1976, *Hank Williams You Wrote My Life,* was followed by such titles as *Here I Am Drunk Again* (1976); *I'm Sorry for You My Friend, Best of Moe Bandy, Volume I, Cowboys Ain't Supposed to Cry* (1977); *Soft Lights and Hard Country Music, Love Is What Life's All About* (1977); *It's a Cheatin' Situation* (1979); *One of a Kind, The Champ* (1980). With Joe Stampley he completed such LPs as *Just Good Ol' Boys* (1979); *Holding the Bag, Tell Ole I Ain't Here* (1980); *Hey Joe, Hey Moe* (1981).

After becoming well known to country fans across the United States in the early 1970s, Moe maintained a hectic in-person and TV schedule to maintain fan rapport. He didn't become a *Grand Ole Opry* regular, but did guest on it a few times. "I played the *Grand Ole Opry* twice as of 1979 and it was really a great thrill," he enthused. "I first played it in 1974 and played it again last year. I'm on the road two hundred and fifty to three hundred days a year. I've been overseas twice— England the year before last and this April [1979]. In April I also appeared in Sweden and Holland. We're doing real well overseas, especially in England. In the U.S. I've played every state. I've had a band for about four years—the Rodeo Clowns—it's a six-piece group. When I'm not on the road, I still live in San Antonio."

Though things still looked bright for Moe's career at the start of the 1980s, the emergence of new, strikingly handsome artists like George Strait changed the dynamics of the country music industry. Bandy's sales totals began to slip compared to his chart-topping 1970s heyday, and he suddenly became odd-man-out with major labels.

He recalled for Bob Allen for an early 1990s article ("After the Flood," *The Journal of Country Music,* vol. 15, no. 1, 1992), "My record sales slipped, and they just dropped me." It was the result of an industry realignment, he asserted, based on "lawyers, accountants, bean counters, and all that, and the minute your career starts droppin' off a little, you're gone."

The CBS decision to remove him from their roster, he said, "just scared the hell out of me, so I regrouped and got a new manager and a new producer and went back in and worked on an album [issued by MCA]. We put out 'Too Old to Die Young,' 'You Haven't Heard the Last of Me,' and 'Americana' [in the mid-1980s] and they hit. Then we put out one song that didn't, and everything went crazy. Nowadays, if you don't come out with a home run every time, you're gone." In his case, his stay with MCA was limited to one 1980s album release.

A temporary boost for his career came from presidential candidate George Bush's love for Moe's recordings. The single "Americana" was often played at Republican party events during the 1988 campaign, and after Bush became president, Bandy became a welcome guest at the White House. However, Bandy failed to find a new record label during Bush's tenure and his recording career languished.

Despite that, he retained a sizable if not massive following and could earn a living from club and concert dates. In the late 1980s, he took advantage of the burgeoning new country scene in Branson, Missouri, by settling there and opening his own 900-seat theater. Through the mid-1990s he continued to perform before typically sold-out houses twice a night in Branson for nine months of the year, restricting touring to the first three months.

He told Allen, "Man, this is like a dream out here. I love it. I've built a home out here on the golf course and I play golf every morning and do my two shows a day, and the crowds have been great. I don't have a manager. I don't have an agent, I don't have a label and I love it." But he had second thoughts about that label aspect, admitting he sorely missed having hit recordings that made radio playlists. During 1993–94, though, he got the chance to sign with Intersound Entertainment, joining a number of other veteran stars on the company's new record operation. In the spring of 1996, Razor & Tie Records released the reissue album, *Moe Bandy— Honky Tonk Amnesia.*

BANNON, R. C.: *Singer, guitarist, songwriter, disc jockey. Born Dallas, Texas, 1945.*

Over the years, musicians have been known to use the job of disc jockey as a stepping stone to performing success. Perhaps it's a sign of the times, though, that R. C. Bannon's first paid job in Nashville was as a discotheque DJ.

Bannon's road to Music City and eventual acceptance as an important part of the country music family was a circuitous one, beginning in Texas and wending its way through Seattle and Los Angeles. In his home town of Dallas, his father was active in local church affairs and R. C. sang in his family's Pentecostal church choir at the age of four. He continued to take part in gospel and hymn singing as he grew older, but increasingly his musical interests turned toward rock 'n' roll. By the time he got to high school, he was an above-average guitarist, and during his teens in the late 1950s and early 1960s, he organized several rock and soul bands.

After he moved to Seattle with his family in the mid-1960s, he not only performed in local night clubs but sang the "hymn of the hour" every morning on a local TV show. His main income, however, came from working as a disc jockey on a Seattle station.

After five years as a DJ, he decided to try for a full-time performing career again in Southern California and Las Vegas, opening for such country artists as Barbi Benton and Mayf Nutter. An important milestone was the chance to open for Marty Robbins during one of that *Grand Ole Opry* star's tours. Robbins was impressed enough with Bannon's singing and writing talents to suggest that R. C. move to Nashville. The latter demurred because "I knew the time wasn't right. I wasn't ready to compete with the 'big boys' in Music City."

Back in Los Angeles, Bannon kept honing his skills and seeking a recording contract from West Coast based record firms. In the mid-1970s he was signed by Capitol, but nothing much happened with the sides he made. In April 1976, Bannon belatedly took Robbins's advice and drove his Datsun pickup eastward to Tennessee. Musicians' jobs were hardly hanging from trees, so Bannon took what he could find—a record-spinning job at a Nashville discotheque for seventy-five dollars a week.

Meanwhile he kept seeking contacts in the country music industry, resulting in meetings with writer-performer Harlan Sanders. The two hit it off well. Sanders liked Bannon's songs and helped him get a job as a contract writer for Warner Brothers Music. From late 1976 on, an increasing number of artists included songs written or co-written by Bannon in their recording sessions. Among those who released singles of that material between 1977 and 1979 were Marty Robbins, Harlan Sanders, Ronnie Milsap, and Bobby G. Rice. During the summer of 1978, Milsap's "cover" of a song written by Bannon and John Bettis (included in Bannon's debut LP), "Only One Love in My Life," became one of the year's best sellers. In mid-July 1978, the Milsap disc stood at number one on the *Billboard* charts. At year end, Bobby G. Rice's recordings of another Bannon song (co-written with Sanders and K. Westbury), "The Softest Touch in Town," rose to upper-chart levels.

During 1977, Bannon was signed to a recording contract by Columbia Records. His debut LP, *R. C. Bannon Arrives,* was released in March 1978. The album included four songs co-written by Bannon and John Bettis (who was a coproducer of the LP), one co-written with Sanders, "Southbound," one entirely by Bannon, "Rainbows and Horseshoes," and a Paul Anka song, "It Doesn't Matter Anymore." The last three were on country charts in 1977–78. At the end of 1978, Bannon was represented on the charts by the single "Somebody's Gonna Do It Tonight."

His 1979 chart singles included duets recorded with Louise Mandrell, such as "We Love Each Other." (They met at Nashville's Fan Fair in 1977 and married in 1979.) In 1980 his chart singles were mainly solo efforts such as "Lovely Lonely Lady," "If You're Serious About Cheatin'," and "Never Be Anyone Else."

In 1982, R. C. moved to RCA Records with Louise. His debut LP on RCA, *Me and My RC,* featuring six duet tracks, came out in early 1982.

BARE, BOBBY: *Singer, guitarist, songwriter, actor. Born Ironton, Ohio, April 7, 1935.*

An outspoken advocate for trying new directions in country music, Bobby Bare sometimes raised the hackles of the traditionalists. But even the staunchest supporters of hewing to time-honored country-music formats had to admit Bobby was a tremendously talented performer and writer. As an innovator and a shrewd judge of talent who helped bring attention to a number of future superstars, he had a profound effect on his chosen field from the early 1960s into the 1980s.

Some of Bare's independence and toughness of spirit can be traced to the adversity of his early years. Born to a poor farm family in Ohio, he saw the death of his mother when he was five. Later, the family finances became so bad that his sister had to be given out for adoption. Bobby left school at fifteen to earn extra money for his family, toiling as a farm laborer and bundle-boy in a clothing factory for the next few years.

One of the few pleasures in his boyhood was music. He built a guitar for himself out of an old coffee can, a

stick, and some string. After a while, he obtained a regular instrument and by his mid-teens was performing with a country band in the Springfield-Portsmouth section of Ohio. In the mid-1950s, he was still at it—working at other jobs during the day while picking up whatever work he could in music, performing in small clubs in Ohio and Kentucky and occasionally on radio and TV. He was already writing original material, some of which he included in his club appearances.

Still, as the late 1950s drew on, his career wasn't progressing very quickly. He switched his singing and writing efforts to rock and moved to the Los Angeles area, leaving for California with only twenty-five dollars in his pocket. Shortly after arriving in Los Angeles, he was drafted. The day before he entered the service, he made some demonstration tapes and sent them to Ohio-based Fraternity Records. That label issued a single of one of Bare's songs, "All American Boy," in 1959, and it became a major pop hit.

As it happened, Bobby had recorded it under the name Bill Parsons, so its success didn't lift him from anonymity. In fact, the record company sent another performer out under the Parsons name since Bare wasn't available. (Bobby had no claim to the song by then anyway, having sold the rights for fifty dollars.)

After his discharge in the early 1960s, Bobby rushed back to the rock field with his excellent voice and good guitar style. Among the artists he toured with in that period were the Dave Clark Five, Jay and the Americans, Roy Orbison, and Bobby Darin. However, Bobby soon decided to return to his first love, country music, but with a perspective that was innovative, combining his stylings with an emphasis on modern themes. Some of his offerings of the first half of the 1960s were precursors of such later trends as folk-rock and progressive country.

RCA's Chet Atkins was quick to recognize Bobby's great potential and signed him to the label in the early 1960s, where Bare recorded such songs as "Shame on Me," on the charts in 1962, and "Detroit City," which rose to number one on all major charts in 1963. The latter won Bobby a Grammy in the 1964 National Academy of Recording Arts and Sciences competition. In 1963, he had another big hit in "500 Miles From Home" and in 1964 provided such top-10 successes as "Four Strong Winds" and "Miller's Cave." He also made his film debut that year with a leading role in the Warner Brothers movie *A Distant Trumpet.* That didn't interfere with his musical progress, though; he showed up with the 1965 top-10 hit "It's Alright" and, in 1966, another of his classics, "Streets of Baltimore."

Meanwhile, Bobby helped further the careers of promising new artists. In the early 1960s, after hearing a then unknown named Waylon Jennings in an Arizona club, he brought him to the attention of Chet Atkins. As he recalled for an RCA biographer, " 'Chet Atkins, you gotta sign that boy up,' I said. 'I listened to Waylon Jennings last night at the club in Phoenix and he's one of the best I've heard in ages.' And I said, 'Yeah, I know I'm cuttin' my own throat because he's gonna be doing the same thing I'm doing . . . but he deserves to be on a major label.' And I gave him Waylon's phone number and he called him up and signed him."

It was the same thing that happened almost a decade later to another aspiring artist named Billy Joe Shaver. Shaver told *Music City News* (December 1977), "I guess I'd been in and out of Nashville for about ten years with no luck. Then one day I walked into Bobby's publishing company. He told me flat out, he wasn't looking for any more writers, but I guess I musta looked kinda pathetic. He started to send me away, then he said I could leave a tape. But I didn't have any. My songs were all in my head. He said he'd listen to one song. By the time I was halfway through 'Restless Wind,' he'd signed me." In the mid-1970s, Bare was still working with Shaver, coproducing some of Billy Joe's albums on MGM.

Bobby also was an early supporter of other new writers and performers, including Mickey Newbury and Kris Kristofferson. One of his first singles released after he switched from RCA to Mercury Records at the start of the 1970s, for instance, was a Kristofferson composition, "Come Sundown." He also was quick to appreciate Shel Silverstein's writing skills, turning out his own version of the Dr. Hook hit, "Sylvia's Mother," on Mercury, reaching upper-country-chart levels in the fall of 1972. (Earlier that year his chart singles on Mercury included "What Am I Gonna Do.")

His enthusiasm for Shel's work led to a close collaboration between the two in the mid-1970s, sometimes as cowriters, other times with Shel providing songs especially for Bobby to record. For most of those years, Bobby once more had returned to the RCA fold. His chart hit singles of Silverstein's songs included "Daddy, What If" and "Marie Laveau" (the last named cowritten by Shel and B. Taylor) in 1974; "Alimony" in 1975; "The Winner" in 1976; and "Red Neck Hippie Romance" in 1977. The two worked closely on one of Bobby's more ambitious projects of the 1970s, a two-record "concept" album released in 1975 titled *Bobby Bare Sings Lullabies, Legends and Lies.* Bobby hardly restricted his output to material provided by Silverstein. His chart successes in the late-1970s included such songs by other writers as "Put a Little Lovin' on Me" and "Dropkick Me Jesus (Through the Goalposts of Life)."

During 1976, Bobby switched labels to Columbia, which released his debut LP, *Bare,* late in the year. Among those who made guest appearances on that Bare-produced LP were Waylon Jennings, Willie Nelson, Shel Silverstein, Dr. Hook, and Chet Atkins. In late 1978, he had his first major singles success on Columbia with "Sleep Tight Tonight, Goodnight Man" (by J. Silber and S. Lorber), which rose to number eleven on *Billboard* lists in early December.

Bare toured widely in support of his new Columbia releases as he had done for most of his illustrious career. By the end of the 1970s he had performed in all the states of the union and many other nations around the world. His European tours, in fact, went back to the early 1960s. In 1963, he was one of the first country artists to make a major swing through Germany and Scandinavia. His TV appearances in the 1960s and 1970s included most major country programs as well as such popular showcases as *American Bandstand, The Mike Douglas Show,* and *The Midnight Special.*

Though his own songwriting efforts slowed down somewhat in the 1970s, his total of original compositions numbered in the hundreds.

Bobby began the 1980s with the charted single "Numbers" in January 1980. Among his early 1980s discs that reached high-chart positions were "Have Another Tequila, Sheila" (a Shel Silverstein contribution) and "Food Blues" in 1980 and "Willie Jones" and "Dropping Out of Sight" in 1981.

Later in the 1980s, Bobby made some duet recordings with Rosanne Cash, which resulted in the top-10 single "No Memories Hangin' Round." He also devoted some of his time and energy during those years to charitable and community aid projects, including support of efforts to help missing and abused children. During the summer of 1986, for instance, he worked on a song and video called "America's Missing Children." Taking part in the taping was a chorus of youngsters that included his ten-year-old daughter, Angela.

In the mid- and late 1980s and in the first half of the 1990s, Bobby remained active on the concert circuit, though his output of hit records waned. Besides other appearances, in 1987 he signed a contract with Pinkerton Tobacco (whose products included Red Man Chewing Tobacco) to appear at trade shows and other events sponsored by the firm.

Among Bare's recordings in print in the mid-1990s were three CDs titled *Bobby Bare/Mercury Years, Parts 1, 2 and 3,* included in the Country Music Foundation catalog.

BELLAMY BROTHERS: *Vocal and instrumental duo, Howard Bellamy, born Darby, Florida, February 2, 1946 (vocals, guitar, songwriter); David Bellamy, born Darby, Florida, September 16, 1950 (vocals, accordian, keyboards, songwriter).*

Brothers David and Howard Bellamy picked up years of experience in the bubbling country rock circuit of Florida, a state that produced such stellar groups as the Allman Brothers and Lynyrd Skynyrd. The Bellamys' music contained elements of blues, soul, and rock, though it evolved more toward a slick pop-country sound that made their recordings cross over readily between the two fields.

Howard recalled, "My father influenced me a lot. He played dobro and fiddle in a bluegrass band. He was pretty good too. I really liked the country music, so when I was thirteen years old, I picked up the guitar. Actually I did it only to accompany myself as a singer."

David also was a role model. When he was nine he began learning the accordion and became reasonably proficient. Later on, though, his interest in blues and soul music caused him to concentrate on playing keyboards. Even before he picked up an accordion, David was doing some writing. "I began putting words down on paper when I was eight. Oddly enough, though, I only wrote short stories and poems until I was seventeen. That's when I wrote my first song."

The brothers grew up on a cattle ranch in west-central Florida that had been in the family since their great-great-grandfather Abraham Bellamy, after being wounded in the Civil War battle of Chickamauga, came from South Carolina to buy the property. (It remained in the family in the mid-1990s, by which time the Bellamy brothers had expanded it from the original 150 acres to some 2,500.)

David recalled, "Our father loved country music from Jimmie Rodgers to Webb Pierce and Hank, Sr. Dad would wake us up every morning with Merle Haggard. He put on the record player in the front room and just blasted it. He would have musician friends over to the house almost every weekend to play and sing. That's originally why we got involved—just for the fun of it."

But there were plenty of other influences. The brothers sang in church with their father, and their older sisters brought back pop records by 1950s stars like Elvis, Ricky Nelson, Buddy Holly, the Everly Brothers, and others. Howard also cited the songs they heard Jamaican migrant workers sing as they picked oranges in the area. "We'd pick with them, every year and when they worked they sang. It was so amazing to hear them sing across the treetops, high on those long wooden ladders, doing call and response things with great rhythms. It's funny now; we thought everyone heard beautiful island music as a child." In the 1960s, the Bellamys also paid heed to the British Invasion rock groups as well as R&B and soul music.

David was the first to play in a professional group when, in 1965, he became organ player for a soul group called the Accidents. "We played backup for people like Percy Sledge, Little Anthony and the Imperials, and various other black singers. Otis Redding was my favorite performer at that time. That's how I became involved in soul music. Those were fun days. I even had a go-go girl dancing on top of the organ."

In 1966, the Bellamys teamed up initially for an annual event in Tampa, Florida, called the "Rattlesnake Roundup," a popular festivity where "ranchers and farmers bring the rattlesnakes they've caught during the year and display them." For their part of the show, David held forth on accordion, Howard on guitar, and their father played the fiddle.

The brothers became members of a rock group called Jericho in 1968 that sometimes shared bills with such other performers as the Allman Brothers and Brewer & Shipley. "We played high school proms, assemblies, and small clubs," Howard noted. "When we worked with the Allmans, they also were starting out and we admired their music. We never dreamed that they would be as big as they became. After all, it's hard to imagine that kind of success when you're playing in a local coffee house called The Bottom of the Barrel." Major influences on their own developing sound, he stressed, included Paul McCartney and Brewer & Shipley.

The Bellamys were becoming interested in broader horizons as the 1960s came to a close. Howard had started writing original material "because I got tired of singing other people's songs." Their first recording efforts, however, in an Atlanta studio in 1969 proved disastrous. The results of the sessions were so poor, the group disbanded.

In the early 1970s, the brothers shifted their attention to studio work. They gained session assignments throughout the South, which helped them to polish their performing styles and increase their contacts. David recalled, "It gave us time to write. One day I wrote a song called 'Spiders and Snakes' and sent it to Phil Gernhard, who was producing Jim Stafford. Next thing I know, I'm on the phone with Stafford doing a rewrite." The Stafford single of the song became one of the top novelty successes of the mid-1970s, selling over two million copies.

That breakthrough brought a bid from Phil Gernhard and his associate, Tony Scotti, to handle the Bellamys as an act. The brothers moved their base of operations to Los Angeles, where they settled in to work on a new series of recordings. In early 1976, the single "Let Your Love Flow" was issued by Warner/Curb Records and quickly bcame a major hit on both country and pop charts. In the spring, their debut LP on Warner/Curb, titled *The Bellamy Bros.*, came out and also made upper-chart levels. Besides "Let Your Love Flow," which earned a gold-record award, it included another Bellamy offering that had been a regional hit, "Nothin' Heavy." For much of 1976, the duo and supporting bandmembers toured the United States and Canada to increase their name recognition. During the year, they were featured on many major network and syndicated TV shows.

Their second LP, *Plain and Fancy,* came out in 1977. Their 1977 tour schedule, in addition to dates all over the United States, included swings through Canada, England, the Scandinavian nations, and Germany. Their 1977 recording achievements, however, fell short of the previous year, which helped trigger a move to a new management alignment with former Loggins and Messina manager Todd Schiffman and to a new producer, Michael Lloyd. First fruit of that association was the May 1978 LP release *Beautiful Friends,* which provided several songs that made the charts—"Slippin' Away" and "Let's Give Love a Go." One of the elements that provided a thread between all three albums to that point was a series of songs written by David dealing with the early days in the American West. The songs were "Rodeo Road" in the first LP, "Livin' in the West" in album two, and "Tumbleweed and Rosalee" in the 1978 release.

At the end of 1978, the Bellamys had a new single, "Lovin' On," that promised to provide their first big hit since "Let Your Love Flow." By early 1979, it was in the country top 20 on the way to rarefied top-10 levels. In the spring, the brothers scored a major hit with Don's "If I Said You Had a Beautiful Body Would You Hold It Against Me," which made number one on country lists in May 1979. Later it received a Grammy nomination. The song was included in their fourth Warner/Curb LP, *The Two and Only.* Their fifth album on the label, *You Can Get Crazy,* came out in January 1980.

During 1980, they had such major hits as "Sugar Daddy," "Dancin' Cowboys," and "Lovers Live Longer," all written by David Bellamy. Also on the charts in early 1980 was a holdover from late 1979, "You Ain't Just Whistlin' Dixie." In March 1981, the brothers had the number-one hit single "Do You Love As Good As You Look." Another bestseller during the year was "You're My Favorite Star."

The Bellamys closed out 1981 with the Warner Brothers single "It's So Close to Christmas (And I'm So Far From Home)." They began 1982 with a number-one single on Elektra/Curb, "For All the Wrong Reasons." Before the year was over they had another Warner Brothers hit with "Redneck Girl." Other singles releases in the first half of the decade were "When I'm Away From You" (a number-one hit on Elektra/Curb); "I Love Her Mind," and "Strong Weakness" in 1983 (both on Warner Brothers); and, in 1984, "Forget About Me" and "World's Greatest Lover" on the Curb label. Album releases from mid-1980 to the end of 1984 were *Sons of the Sun* on Warner/Curb in 1980; *Greatest Hits, Volume 1* on Warner/Curb and *Strongest Weakness* on Elektra/Curb in 1982; and *Restless* on MCA/Curb in 1984.

The 1985–87 period also was an auspicious one for the brothers from the standpoint of hit records and capacity crowds for their shows at home and abroad. During those years five of their eight singles releases reached number one on the *Billboard* charts. Those were "I Need More of You" and "Feelin' the Feelin'" in 1985; "Too Much Is Not Enough" (with the Forester Sisters) and "Kids of the Baby Boom" in 1976; and "Crazy From the Heart" in 1987, all on MCA/Curb. The other three singles also made the charts. They were "Old Hippie" and "Lie to You for Your Love" in 1985 and "Country Rap" in 1987. Though the brothers' career was in excellent shape in that period, there was also the pain of the loss of their father in 1987.

While "Old Hippie" fell short of being a number-one hit, it remained the Bellamys' favorite song, and they found that typically it had the biggest effect on their concert audiences. That song and "Kids of the Baby Boom," they said, resonated with some of the feelings of the post–World War II generations.

David commented, "I actually wrote 'Old Hippie' and 'Baby Boom' the same day. 'Baby Boom' was sort of the lines left over from 'Old Hippie.' I studied Dylan a lot and in the early days he didn't care if there were fifteen verses if they were all good and served a purpose, and 'Old Hippie' ended up kind of being like that. It started as an autobiographical piece, but then I incorporated bits of people I knew, like a Vietnam vet from our home town. I just wrote it as long as I had ideas, and after seven or eight verses, I edited it to make more of a country song. It was actually harder to edit than it was to write, and what was left over, I decided to make another song.'

The brothers made their first music video in 1988 of their single "Santa Fe." Their next four releases on MCA/Curb had audio versions only: "I'll Give You All My Love Tonight" and "Rebels Without a Clue" in 1988 and "Big Love" and "Hillbilly Hell" in 1989. Their association with MCA/Curb, which lasted until 1990, included the singles "You'll Never Be Sorry" and "Center of My Universe" in 1989 and "Drive South" (with the Forester Sisters) and "I Could Be Persuaded" in 1990.

Their MCA/Curb album releases from 1985–1990 included *Howard and David* (1985); *Greatest Hits, Volume II* (1986); *Country Rap* and *Crazy from the Heart* (1987); *Rebels Without a Clue* (1988); *Greatest Hits, Volume III* (1989); and *Reality Check* (1990). In 1988, the brothers were nominated for Vocal Duo of the Year by Country Music Association voters, a nomination repeated every year through 1994. In October 1989, the Bellamys inaugurated an annual event called the Snake Rattle & Roll Jam with the concert proceeds to go to local and national charitable organizations.

In 1991 the duo had a brief affiliation with Atlantic Records, which released the album *Rollin' Thunder* along with the single and video "She Don't Know That She's Perfect" and the single "All in the Name of Love." In 1992, the brothers established their own label, Bellamy Brothers Records, distributed by Intersound Entertainment. In part this was inspired by the hardly unique feeling among artists that their recording careers had suffered from lack of creative freedom. Howard told an interviewer, "They call it the music business, but music and business mix like oil and water. There are a lot of shysters in this business. Everyone has had the screws stuck in them."

Their label debut single and video, "Cowboy Beat," was on both audio and video charts for a number of weeks in 1992, with the latter named Independent Video of the Year by CMT. Also released in 1992 were the albums *Best of the Best* and *The Latest and the Greatest* and the single and video of "Can I Come on Home to You." Their next album releases were *Rip Off the Knob* in 1993 and a special boxed set in 1994, *Let Your Love Flow—20 Years of Hits.* Singles for those years were "Hard Way to Make an Easy Livin'," "Rip Off the Knob," and a dance-mix version of "Get into Reggae Cowboy" in 1993 and "Not," "On a Summer Night," and "Dance Medley" in 1994. All the 1993–94 regular release singles were also offered in the video format.

The last-named single was released simultaneously in the U.S. and Germany, a first for the duo. The brothers had been popular outside U.S. boundaries for many years with several of their hits reaching number one on charts in other countries. As of 1995, Germany's Jupiter/BMC label had released three Bellamy Brothers CDs, including *Nobody's Perfect* in 1994, from which two singles, "On a Summer Night" and "Hemingway Hideaway," were drawn for European distribution.

The brothers had another busy year in 1996 with the release of the album *Sons of Beaches* (from which the summer single release "Shine Them Buckles" was drawn) and their first dance mix CD in July, *Dancin'.* (Both were distributed by Intersound). About the latter, David commented, "We have been tuned into the dance thing since we first started. The young college kids who are just getting turned onto country music have discovered our hits 'Redneck Girl' and 'Reggae Cowboy' and think they have just been released." The Bellamys also issued their first collection of holiday songs, *A Tropical Christmas,* recorded both in the U.S. and Germany.

BERLINE, BYRON: *Singer, fiddler, songwriter, band leader (Country Gazette, Sundance, L.A. Fiddle Band). Born Cornwell, Kansas, early 1940s.*

One of the finest fiddlers of modern times, Byron Berline has made his presence felt in everything from folk music to rock. The extent of his reputation can be assessed by the many first-rank artists who have enlisted his services for backing bands or session work: Bill Monroe, Doug Dillard, David Bromberg, Olivia Newton-John, Linda Ronstadt, Henry Mancini, Bob Dylan, the Rolling Stones, the Flying Burrito Brothers, and many others. Despite his backing of diverse artists, his first love remained bluegrass, an art form to which he contributed fine original compositions and inspired solo recordings.

Born in Kansas, but raised on a farm in Oklahoma, Byron took up fiddling as a child. As he told Michelle Pelick Kingsley for an article in *Frets* magazine (June 1979, pp. 34–36), "I guess I was five years old. My dad was a fiddle player and I had always heard music since the time I was born. I never played in any groups till I went to college, though. That was in the early 1960s. Folk music was popular back then and the local TV station was auditioning acts for a hootenanny program it

was going to do. . . . They said they needed a bluegrass band, so some of us put a group together. I didn't know what bluegrass was, but this banjo player knew 'Cripple Creek' so we got us a bass player and a guitar player and learned 'Cripple Creek' for that show. We called ourselves the Cleveland County Ramblers because Norman [Oklahoma], where the college is, was in Cleveland County. After that we played for fraternity parties around campus. Sometimes we'd make money, sometimes we wouldn't, but we really didn't care."

Next, he performed for two years on a TV program sponsored by Garrett Household Furniture of Oklahoma City. After receiving his B.A. from the University of Oklahoma in 1967, Byron joined Bill Monroe's famous Blue Grass Boys. He remained with Monroe into early 1968, when his career was interrupted by the military draft. He was stationed at Ft. Polk, Louisiana, performing at the officers' club and for special events as well as in nearby clubs with a local bluegrass band.

While attending the University of Oklahoma, Byron had made the acquaintance of Doug Dillard, and the two had worked on a show at the school. Dillard was enthusiastic about Berline's fiddle-playing and, years later, was only too happy to renew acquaintances when Berline moved to Los Angeles after leaving the army.

Byron arrived on the coast in July 1969 and became part of Doug's Dillard and Clark group, which gave way to Dillard and the Expedition. Berline was with the band until it broke up in 1971, and he still toured with Dillard on occasion in later years. Berline made a number of recordings with the Dillard organizations, including such LPs as *Pickin and Fiddling* and *Copperfields* on Elektra and *Duelin' Banjos* on 20th Century Fox.

In 1971, Berline was assembling a band of his own that was named Country Gazette when he was asked to tour with the Flying Burrito Brothers. Among the members of the Country Gazette were bass player Roger Bush, guitarist Kenny Wertz, and a long-time friend from Oklahoma days, banjoist Alan Munde. The first recruit was Wertz, followed by Roger Bush. As Berline told Michelle Kingsley, "When Alan Munde joined the group a little later, it became the Hot Burrito Revue. We went to Europe with the Burrito Brothers a couple of times. Kenny, Alan, Roger and I didn't really get going as Country Gazette until 1972 though. I stayed with the Gazette until 1975. The last gig I did with them was a trip to Europe." Berline lent his talents to a number of Burrito Brothers' LPs during those years, including *Burrito Deluxe* and *Last of the Red Hot Burritos* on A&M Records.

Tired of touring, Byron decided to stay home with his family in Los Angeles after that to concentrate on writing, session work, and movie assignments. Throughout the 1970s, he was in much demand for film scores. Among the movies he provided music for were *White Lightning, Bound for Glory* (the story of Woody Guthrie), *The Longest Yard,* Bob Dylan's *Pat Garrett and Billy the Kid, Sometimes a Great Notion* (the film version of the Ken Kesey novel), and many others. One of his favorite efforts, he told *Frets* magazine, was *Sometimes a Great Notion,* particularly since Henry Mancini was the one who invited him to provide fiddle music for the Mancini score.

Berline decided that if he formed another band he would get away from a straight bluegrass format. "I had known [guitarist] Dan Crary for a while and I had met [bassist] Jack Skinner in Las Vegas a few years before; the two of them and a couple of other people happened to call me up right around the same time, so I said, 'Let's get together and do some picking.' That's how Sundance got started: Dan, Jack [banjoist], John Hickman [guitarist], Allen Wald and myself. We got a record deal with MCA but that meant a big promotional tour right at the end of the summer and on into the fall. Dan [professor of speech at Cal State University at Fullerton] couldn't go because he had to start teaching again. We had to get another guitar player, somebody to play rhythm, so we took Skip Conover, who played dobro and guitar. He was kind of an honorary member. The record, *Byron Berline and Sundance,* was cut in 1976. That was our only album."

The group remained active until the end of 1978, playing folk clubs and festivals around the country. The band reorganized in the fall of 1976 when Skinner left and was replaced by Vince Gill (who became a member of Pure Prairie League in 1979). Also added were drummer Mark Cohen and bassist Joe Villegas. The last change before the group's final phase was John Hickman's departure in January 1977. However, he and Berline remained close friends and by 1979 they and Dan Crary joined in forming a production company called BCH.

Though Sundance had been shelved by 1979, Berline didn't lack projects. Besides session work, he completed a new solo album called *Barn Dance* in mid-April and also completed another LP with a group called the L.A. Fiddle Band, comprising three fiddles, dobro, banjo, guitar, and bass. A small label called Takoma also prepared an album based on Berline's solo appearance at the small McCabe's hall in Santa Monica (a well-known gathering place for local folk musicians and enthusiasts) called *Live at McCabe's.* During the summer of 1979, Berline was again on the road as part of Doug Dillard's new touring band.

In the 1980s and into the 1990s, Berline had plenty to keep him busy, ranging from session work to performances as soloist and band member at festivals at home and abroad. His studio work alone, he said in 1995, had averaged two or three sessions a week for 26 years. He also completed considerable soundtrack work for the movies and TV, from preparation of the music for Arnold Schwarzenegger's first film in 1976, *Stay Hungry,* to scoring the hit TV show of the 1990s, *Northern Exposure.*

He completed a number of new albums on smaller labels in the 1980s and 1990s which featured his phenomenal bluegrass fiddle playing. In August 1995, Sugar Hill issued a new album, *A Fiddle & a Song,* which, among other things, included a reunion with longtime friend Vince Gill, who sang Bill Monroe's bluegrass classic "Rose of Old Kentucky" and a Berline composition (with lyrics added by onetime Sundance member Jack Skinner), "Sweet Memory Waltz."

For the project, Byron also managed to reunite Bill Monroe and Earl Scruggs on "Sally Goodin" with backing from their sons James Monroe (bass) and Randy Scruggs (rhythm guitar). As Berline told Terri Horak of *Billboard* ("Fiddles, Songs and Friends on Berline's Sugar Hill Set," July 15, 1995), "The main thing I wanted to do was get just those two playing together, which I did. After that, I didn't care what I did. It was really a dream come true to get those two in there."

He also emphasized his continuing affection for his instrument. "I just love playing the fiddle, and it's fun to be able to play different styles of music. I remember years ago some old-time fiddlers heard me playing bluegrass and one of them said, 'You keep playing that bluegrass, it's going to ruin your fiddle playing,' and I said, 'Well, that's possible.'"

BERRY, JOHN: *Singer, guitarist, songwriter, band leader. Born Aiken, South Carolina, September 14, 1959.*

One of the most promising new faces on the country music scene in the mid-1990s, John Berry had to overcome problems few in his position encountered. His struggles to move from obscurity to the national spotlight were demanding, but not that different from what many successful performers had to endure. But most of the others never had to vie with life-threatening events, not once but twice, in the first stages of their careers.

Berry was born in South Carolina but grew up in Atlanta, Georgia, where he became enamored of country music at an early age. He started to play the guitar when he was twelve and, after working with local groups in his teens, also began spending many of his free hours writing original material by the time he was seventeen. He recalled, "I always knew music was where I should be, but it took a while for me to make a full-time commitment. When I got out of high school, I started working in manufacturing and playing music at night."

He loved entertaining, but hadn't yet decided whether or not to gamble on it as a full-time career option, when fate intervened. In 1981, he was injured so severely in a motorcycle accident that doctors told him there was a good chance he might never walk again. He resolved to prove them wrong and finally did. "I had some time to think about a lot of things while I was recovering," he said. "My mother died that year, on top of everything else. That was the same year I turned twenty-two, and when I finally got out of the hospital, I had a direction in my life. Music."

After he recuperated, he started to find work playing a college clubs, a routine that in the first part of the 1980s took him to many parts of the U.S., from Illinois to New Mexico, Oklahoma, Kansas, the Dakotas, the Carolinas, and points around and in between. By 1985 he was married, and he and his wife used money saved from concert work to buy a farm near Athens, Georgia, home of the University of Georgia. Once settled in, the Berrys (John's wife sang backing vocals in the act) found they could do reasonably well performing primarily in local Athens-area clubs.

Soon John established his own record label to produce albums he could sell at shows or in local stores. From the late 1980s through the early 1990s, he produced six albums of his own recordings, including many self-penned songs, the last of which, *Saddle the Wind,* became a best-seller for two years in an Athens store, amassing a sales total of over 12,000—a very impressive showing for such a project.

Finally, the Berrys decided it was time to seek a contract from a major label. "We figured the best thing to do was to play Nashville every forty-five days." The goal was to combine performances with showcases for local music industry executives. Berry noted, "I called ASCAP, and they sent me a list of people to invite, but I was nervous about the first show and was praying nobody would show up."

But some invitees or their contacts did show up, including music publisher Herky Williams. Williams was so impressed that as soon as he got home, he rousted Liberty Records' president Jimmy Bowen out of bed to rave about this new talent. An audition was arranged, and Bowen signed Berry to the label. In the fall of 1993, Berry's debut single, an original titled "She's Got a Mind of Her Own," came out and brought him some attention, though it wasn't a major hit. Then came another original, "Kiss Me in the Car," which provided both a single and video success in December 1993. This was followed by his first number-one single "Your Love Amazes Me" (number one in *Billboard* in mid-May and in *Radio & Records* the week of May 13). Berry's status was also buoyed in 1993–94 by an excellent set at the 1993 Gavin Convention, a challenging appearance on the nationally televised "A Day in the Life of Country Music," and a performance in the New Faces Show at the 1994 Country Radio Seminar.

It seemed nothing could stand in the way of a steady move to major stardom, but more dark days, unfortunately, were near at hand. That seemed unlikely in early 1994 when John's career was booming and he and his wife celebrated the birth of their second child, Shawn Thomas. (Their first child was daughter Taylor Marie. Berry emphasized that wife Robin's position as backup vocalist and the willingness of her mother to act as baby-sitter made it possible to keep his family together on the road.)

Yet soon after Shawn's birth, John had to enter the hospital for an operation to remove pressure on his brain. The emergency surgery worked, though it could just as well have ended his career or his life. He was still feeling the effects of it in the fall after his career continued to advance with the hit single "What's in It For Me" in October, and his debut album, *John Berry,* which went gold in early fall within weeks of its release. At a party hosted by the record company in honor of the album's success, he told Teresa George of the Country Music Association's *Close Up* magazine (October 1994) that before surgery "I knew exactly what I was going to do, and nobody was going to stand in my way. Now, I'm an emotional wreck. I can't watch *Little House on the Prairie.* There are certain things I have to be careful of. That's one of the reasons I'm so scared about [the party]. Just the emotional aspect of it."

Still, he was much better than he had been a few months earlier. "I wouldn't remember anything. If I had gotten up in the morning, by lunchtime I couldn't remember getting up. It was so frustrating. I remembered long-term things. I just couldn't remember having called my manager. I called the office twenty times a day, driving them crazy! They finally figured what was going on."

Physical problems aside, his career continued to prosper in 1995. He started off with the January hit single "You and Only You," and a few months later had "Standing on the Edge of Goodbye" (cowritten by Berry and S. Harris) moving toward top-chart position. That was the title track for his second Liberty album (on the company's new Patriot label) which entered the *Billboard* list in March and was inside its top 20 in May.

Berry's travails had given him insight into the truly important things in life. Asked about the most significant long-term event that had happened to him during 1994, he responded to a WSIX interviewer, "It has to be the birth of Shawn Thomas, because number-one songs will come and go, gold records will hang on the wall, you recover from surgery and go on with your life, but your children, you'll watch them grow and live forever and until you're gone. So that's the long-term."

At the end of 1995, Berry had the Christmas album *O Holy Night* within the *Billboard* top 30. And his *Standing on the Edge* album was still inside the magazine's top 40, having earned a gold record award from the R.I.A.A. In the summer of 1996, his album *Faces* was released; first single from the disc was "Change My Mind."

BLACK, CLINT: *Singer, guitarist, harmonica player, songwriter. Born Long Branch, New Jersey, February 6, 1962.*

As Clint Black wrote in his song, "No Time to Kill," "There's no time to kill between the cradle and the grave." Indeed, Black took his own advice, wasting little time in his own life, and becoming one of the most successful young country music singer-songwriters in the 1990s—combining the writing and performing of insightful songs with a charismatic, appealing persona.

Black was born in New Jersey, where his family was living temporarily while his father was working for an oil company. The family, which included Clint, his parents, and his three older brothers, moved back to Houston, Texas, soon after, and Clint spent the rest of his childhood there. His childhood was a happy one. Music was one of the things that kept the family close, and he was exposed to all sorts of music, from traditional country to rock, blues, and folk. When he was about thirteen, Clint borrowed one of his brother's harmonicas and taught himself to play. At fifteen he started playing guitar, and Clint joined with his brothers to play at family barbecues and other get-togethers. Clint also started writing songs around this time.

One thing that Clint did not enjoy was school, and he dropped out of high school before graduating, although he regrets that decision to this day. As he told Dick Sowienski in *Country America* ("Hollywood Is a Nine-Letter Word," April 1993), "Looking back, I wish I had made use of that time. I wish I would have gone on to college. I might not be doing what I am doing today, but I feel like information and knowledge are the most valuable and rewarding acquisitions. I think everybody is ignorant about something, but it is the abundance of it that frustrates me. The more I learn, the more I realize that I don't know."

After quitting school, Clint worked at some low-paying odd jobs, including work as a bait cutter and fishing guide. He kept singing and playing guitar, however, and performed in clubs and bars around the Houston area for the next six years. Around 1987, he met Hayden Nicholas, who was to become Clint's lead guitarist and cowriter of many of Black's songs. The two of them put together a demo tape and sent it to Bill Ham, who had been manager of the group ZZ Top. Within a few days, Ham called Black into his office, and after he sang a number of his songs, Ham agreed to manage him and was able to work out a contract with RCA Records.

Black's debut album, *Killin' Time,* was released in May 1989 and by September of that year was already certified gold; by October 1990 it had gone double platinum. The album spawned five number-one singles, "A Better Man," "Killin' Time," "Nobody's Home," "Walking Away," and "Nothing's News." According to *Radio & Records,* Black was the first artist to achieve five number-one singles from a debut album. All of these singles had been written or cowritten by Black.

Black's songs were tuneful and thoughtful, but fans also responded to his charm and good looks. He became identified by his trademark black hat and black T-shirt, exposing his well-muscled torso.

Not long after *Killin' Time* was released, Black garnered the first of many awards, the Horizon Award from the Country Music Association, in October 1989. In April 1990 he practically swept the Academy of Country Music awards, winning four, for Album of the Year (*Killin' Time*), Single of the Year ("A Better Man"), Best New Male Vocalist, and Best Male Vocalist. The Nashville Network/Music City News presented Black with the Star of Tomorrow and Album of the Year Awards in June 1990, and in October of that year he was named Male Vocalist of the Year by the Country Music Association.

Black's second album, *Put Yourself in My Shoes,* was released in November 1990, to mixed critical reviews. The album, however, was certified gold in January 1991, certified double platinum in October 1991, and yielded two number-one singles, "Loving Blind" and "Where Are You Now." Two other singles, "Put Yourself in My Shoes" and "One More Payment" went to number four and five, respectively.

As Clint told Dick Sowienski (*Country America,* April 1993), "It was really hard to make the second album. I wasn't prepared for going into the studio for five days and doing a press blitz in New York and then going back to the studio for three days and then hitting the road and doing twenty shows and then taking four days off and cutting three songs and then hitting the road again. Everybody told me this is the most important record of your career—I haven't made a record yet that wasn't the most important record of my career. It wasn't treated that way."

He decided to take his time with the next album to get it just the way he wanted, and his third album, *The Hard Way,* was released twenty months after the second. It was issued in July 1992, certified platinum by September. Three number-one singles resulted from that album, "We Tell Ourselves," "Burn One Down," and "When My Ship Comes In." Between those two albums, Black's life had changed both from a personal and business standpoint. In October 1991 he married actress Lisa Hartman, and in February 1992 he parted from his manager, Bill Ham. The breakup with Ham was a rocky one, with Black initiating a lawsuit against his former manager. Clint's life also came under public scrutiny on an episode of the TV show, *A Current Affair,* when an Arizona woman, Renee Bain, claimed that he was the father of her two-year-old daughter, Chelsea, and that he was paying her child support.

Nevertheless, Black's productivity continued unabated, and his fourth album, *No Time to Kill,* was released in July 1993 and certified platinum by January 1994. The single, "No Time to Kill," which played on the words of Black's previous hit single, "Killin' Time," went to number one on the country music charts. Also on that album was a duet with Wynonna (Judd), "A Bad Goodbye," which went to number two and was nominated for a Grammy Award in 1994. Other hit songs from that album were "A Good Run of Bad Luck," "State of Mind," and "Half the Man," about his wife. ("It's about my wife. That's her. She's made me better than I was. She's my right arm when my right arm won't work. . . . I don't think I could write a song that would really live up to my feelings—that would fully express how much I love her and what she means to me. This is a start.")

By the mid-1990s, if Black was not being nominated for as many awards as in the early part of his career, he was still placing singles at the top of the country charts. In June, 1995, for example, his single, "Summer's Comin'," (cowritten by Black and H. Nicholas) reached the number-one position. The impressive output of hit singles Black had produced in the six years since the release of his first album assured that he would be a constant presence on country radio stations. Many of them also played cuts from his holiday album, *Looking for Christmas*, released in the fall of 1995. In the fall his single "Life Gets Away" (cowritten by Black, Nicholas, and T. Schuyler) was on the charts, peaking at number 4, and remaining in the top 40 into early '96. In the fall of 1996, his *Greatest Hits* album was in the top 10 on the hit lists.

Black's impressive achievements as a songwriter was underlined by his being among the individuals who received a CMA "Triple Play Award." That award category was established by the organization to recognize composer members who had attained three or more number one songs over the previous 12-month period on country singles charts in *Billboard, Radio & Records* and *The Gavin Report*. Black's successes were "Wherever You Go," "Summer's Comin'," "One Emotion," "A Bad Goodbye," "No Time to Kill," and "Good Run of Bad Luck."

Clint Black appeals to country music fans both young and old. The songs he has written often have a literary quality, and Black, with his looks and easygoing, charming persona, wearing his black hat and smiling his dimpled smile, seems a throwback to the troubadours of renaissance times.—A. S.

BLACKHAWK: *Vocal and instrumental group. Henry Paul, born Tampa, Florida, c. mid-1950s (lead vocals, guitar, songwriter); Van Stephenson, born Ohio (vocals, guitar, songwriter); Dave Robbins, born Atlanta, Georgia (keyboards, songwriter).*

If the stylings of the power trio BlackHawk had some of the flavor of Restless Heart's successes that's understandable, since two of the three members had written some of that band's biggest-selling singles. And if there were touches of country rock that's not surprising, since lead singer Henry Paul had founded the country rock group the Outlaws and his BlackHawk mates has written gold-record hits for Poco and English rock superstar Eric Clapton. But the net result of the collaboration was a country band with its own sound that promised to place many recordings on top-chart levels from the mid-1990s onward.

Paul, born and raised in Tampa, Florida, organized the Outlaws in Tampa in 1974. (Other original members included Hughie Thomasson and Billy Jones on guitars, Frank O'Keefe on bass guitar, and Monte Yoho on drums.) The band signed with Arista Records soon after its formation and after its 1975 debut release, *The Outlaws,* which provided the top-40 single, "There Goes Another Love Song," turned out a stream of albums into the 1980s. The latter included *Lady in Waiting* (1976); *Hurry Sundown* (1977); *Bring It Back Alive* and *Playin' to Win* (both issued in 1978); *In the Eye of the Storm* (1979); and *Ghost Riders* (1980).

Paul emphasized that there was always a Southern edge to his performances, even though he had spent so many years with a rock band. His early influences, before he took his place in the professional musician ranks, included Johnny Cash and Flatt & Scruggs as well as artists like Poco, the Flying Burrito Brothers, and Gram Parsons. He was still involved with the Outlaws when he settled in Nashville in 1987 to cowrite some new Outlaws songs. He decided he felt more comfortable with modern country, so in 1989 he cut his ties to his old band and began seeking a solo opportunity.

He told Jack Hurst, country music critic for the *Chicago Tribune* ("Three Men and an Attitude," February 6, 1994), "Basically it was a question of leaving a comfortable job with a lot of demands and not a lot of returns. Good band: over with. So what're you gonna do now?"

As a musician and writer, he naturally knew other writers—including Robbins and Stephenson, who had risen to top songwriting ranks in Nashville during the 1980s. He told Hurst he wasn't thinking at first about joining another band, but exposure to the talents and lifestyles of those two helped change his mind. "Those guys were in place and working together and I was pretty darn impressed by the quality of what they were doing.

"I remember Van asked me for a ride home one day, and when I dropped him off at his house [I saw] he lives in a mansion. He's making this great living doing something he loves. I thought, 'Man, what could be wrong with this?' " So later when recording executive Tim DuBois came up with the idea of Paul being part of a threesome, he was very receptive.

Stephenson, born in Ohio, but a Pennsylvania resident for a number of years before his family moved to Nashville when he was ten, learned guitar by his teens and became involved in the country field via associations with bluegrass bands, including one with other young Nashvillites such as the son of Charlie Louvin of the *Grand Ole Opry* cast. He credited hearing Charlie Rich's early 1970s hit, "Behind Closed Doors," with helping focus his attention away from bluegrass toward more "mainstream" country material.

From his teens, Stephenson felt the urge to write original songs. "My goal was always to be a country music songwriter. Songwriting has always been the basis of my involvement in the music, and when Black-Hawk was formed, we knew it had to be the foundation of the group."

During the 1970s, besides playing gigs around Music City, he kept trying to find outlets for his songs, finally taking a major step upward when Crystal Gayle recorded his "Your Kisses Will" in 1979. Van continued to increase his songwriting credits in the 1980s, particularly after he teamed up with Robbins.

Robbins, growing up in Atlanta, naturally was aware of the country sound, but his early interest was in classical music, which was the basis for his initial piano training. As time went by and he paid more attention to pop in his teens, he began to turn from the classics to playing songs by groups like the Allman Brothers, Lynyrd Skynyrd, and even the Outlaws. His musical path eventually took him to Nashville, where the team of Robbins and Stephenson took form at the start of the 1980s. It was a time when many young writers flocked to Nashville, and creative cross-fertilization often occurred with songs being written not only by individual talents and two-person partnerships, but sometimes by whole teams of writers. Singers and band leaders were always coming to town to look for new songs or to collaborate with established writers on material to fit their needs.

Stephenson and Robbins were already gaining attention for their material from people like Kenny Rogers (who made the charts with their "All My Life"), Ronnie Milsap, and others when they struck up a close friendship with another writer—and soon to be producer and record executive—Tim DuBois. DuBois told Billboard's Peter Cronin ("Arista's BlackHawk Rises Through Ranks of Radio," January 15, 1994), "Actually, the inspiration for Restless Heart, which basically was a band I put together, came from a body of songs that Van, Dave and myself, along with Jeff Silber and Stan Lorber, were writing that people described as 'too pop to get cut country and too country to cut pop.' Out of the frustration of having this body of songs [I got the idea] to put Restless Heart together." Restless Heart's success arose to a great extent from that material, including a string of hit Robbins-Stephenson compositions such as "Let the Heartaches Ride" and "Bluest Eyes in Texas."

As it happened, at the beginning of the 1990s when Henry Paul was striving to become a solo artist, his top contact at Arista (the longtime Outlaws label) was DuBois, by then the head of Arista Nashville operations. DuBois was discussing possible plans with Henry when he became aware of the desires of his friends Stephenson and Robbins (with whom he had been staff writers at Nashville's House of Gold Music Publishing in the early 1980s) to pursue band possibilities. As with Restless Heart, he sensed the likely rapport of all three individuals and suggested during 1991 that they team up.

It took a while for their skills to mesh properly. Robbins recalled, "We sat down together and started from scratch. We all brought our influences to the table. We didn't start off by going and finding a song to see if we could sing together."

"We started by writing a song together," Stephenson told Hurst. In time, they came up with promising material and tried to make demos, but things just didn't seem to work. However, he noted, the three persevered and gradually a band style based on acoustic instruments emerged.

Paul said later, "This music is very Southern in its origin from the harmonies to the stringed instruments, with keyboards to broaden our music base and just enough of an electric edge to bring it into the nineties. . . . Most important has been that the collective effort has been fresh and different for all of us."

The debut album, BlackHawk, was released February 1, 1994, preceded by the first single, "Goodbye Says It All." The single made the charts late in 1993 and was in the top 40 in Billboard in early 1994. The album showed up in Billboard soon after it came out and, after peaking at number fifteen, went on to earn the trio a gold record. By late July the single "Every Once in a While," written by the trio, was at number three in Billboard. (It peaked at number one in Radio & Records the week of July 15.) The band added to its successful sales image with the top-10 single "I Sure Can Smell the Rain," written by Walt Aldridge and John Jarrard, which rose to number seven in R&R the week of November 4.

BlackHawk continued its red-hot pace in 1995. In March it had the top-10 single "Down in Flames" on Billboard and other charts. In June another single, "That's Just About Right" was receiving heavy airplay as it moved inside the Billboard top 15. Its debut album by then was still doing well on the Billboard list, having gone well past R.I.A.A. platinum requirements.

The debut album certainly was one of the more interesting collections of 1994–95, and the group also found good audience response in club and concert activities. Paul told Billboard, "We're having a good time without a lot of the pain and the problems. My mission in life as a musician and songwriter has been to create a country-rock sound and try to be on the cutting edge. The only thing that's different now is that I'm singing and writing with guys that are better."

In the summer of 1995, the group had a top-10 singles hit with "It's Just About Right" and in the fall had the album Strong Enough high on the charts. The disc peaked at number four in Billboard and by year-end had passed gold record levels on its way to platinum status in 1996. The group's single "I'm Not Strong Enough to Say No" peaked at number two in Billboard in the summer of 1995 and in the later fall the single "Like There Ain't No Yesterday" was in the top 40. In the spring of 1996, its single "Almost a Memory Now" (cowritten by Robbins, Stephenson, and D. Oliver) was a chart hit. In both the Academy of Country Music and Country Music Association Awards nominations announced during 1996, BlackHawk was a finalist in the Best Vocal Group category.

BOGGUSS, SUZY: *Singer, guitarist, songwriter, record producer. Born Aledo, Illinois, November 30, 1957.*

From the mid-1980s into the 1990s, there was an increase in folk music's influence in the country field, a force particularly noticeable among new female artists like Mary-Chapin Carpenter and Suzy Bogguss. Of course, historically country had evolved from folk roots; some hill-country ballads could be traced directly to Elizabethan antecedents, and performers in rural towns or Southern cities had obvious elements of such material in their offerings. In the case of midwesterner Suzy Bogguss, record executives wanted her to stress more of a pop sound in her early recordings, but she credited her return to her earlier folk interests with helping her gain a sizable country following in the 1990s.

She was born in a small Illinois town where country wasn't ignored, but rock and pop were daily bread. Interested in more folk-oriented material from her teen years, she sang in school and local events while gradually increasing her proficiency on the guitar. She earned money for expenses during her college years at Illinois State University through her entertaining skills. While earning a bachelor's degree in metalsmithing at the start of the 1980s, she managed to accrue performing experience at small venues, initially in the Rocky Mountain region and later in Chicago and some points east.

She built up a network of places she could play embracing what she referred to as "little pockets" of fans in sections of Colorado, Wyoming, and Montana. Most of those gigs were at clubs or hotels in resort areas of those states. The material she used tended to have more Western influence than contemporary country, a format she returned to to some extent a decade later. It was a style described by David Zimmerman of *USA Today* ("Bogguss' Varied 'Voices,'" November 4, 1992) as "more Western, sort of cowgirl folk-pop with contemporary themes." It's not surprising her first chart single was a version of Patsy Montana's 1935 recording, "I Want to Be a Cowboy's Sweetheart."

For the first part of the 1980s, Suzy continued to travel her mainly self-developed entertainment circuit mostly singing covers of other artists' songs, but with some experiments in original songwriting. It was an approach that often found her working as her own booker and publicist. Besides lining up appearances, she sent announcements to papers, even putting up posters for her own shows.

Naturally she wanted to seek more rewarding milestones and decided the logical destination had to be Nashville. She finally took up permanent residence there in 1985, after a lengthy self-booked tour of clubs in the U.S. and Mexico.

She told Dan Kening of the Chicago-based publication *Country Post* ("So Long Cinderella," January/February 1994), "I only knew two people when I moved to Nashville. One of them was performing at a rib joint called Tony Roma's and got me my first job there singing three nights a week. My other friend worked for a music publishing company and got me into singing demos for ten dollars a song, which allowed me to circulate my tapes around to different people."

(Her demo tape work also had another kind of impact. It brought her in contact with her husband-to-be, Doug Crider, when she taped his composition "Hopeless Romantic.")

"Every day I was in Nashville, something exciting happened and I learned something new. I remember singing 'Ain't Misbehaving' at Tony Roma's one night and I looked up and John Prine was sitting in the audience. He came up and gave me twenty dollars. That just about saved my life, because at that time twenty dollars would buy a whole new costume for me."

She continued to make new contacts and kept on the lookout for opportunities to move ahead in the country field. She auditioned and won a job to sing at Dolly Parton's theme park, Dollywood. To make some extra money and also hopefully increase her personal following, she had tapes of her material prepared, which she offered for sale to people at her performances. One of those came to the attention of executives from Liberty Records, who signed her to a recording contract. Her label album debut, *Something Between,* came out in 1987, and did well enough to attract interest among her musical peers as well as country fans. One result was her selection in 1988 voting by members of the Academy of Country Music as Top New Female Vocalist of the Year.

The album gave her career an initial boost, but because of her yodeling style on the Patsy Montana number she also found herself typecast as a yodeling cowgirl. She tried concentrating on writing new songs that were close to the current country mode as one way to broaden her horizons. Still, her second Liberty album, *Moment of Truth,* did poorly and suddenly she was faced with the possibility of having a career that ended almost before it began.

With Crider she pondered on how to turn things around. She decided she had to take firmer charge of what went into her next collection. For one thing, she fought for and obtained approval to coproduce that album. She told Kening, "People were trying to find a musical identity for me and it was really underneath their noses all the time. That's what happened with the *Aces* album. I said, 'The heck with it. I'm not doing anything that I don't absolutely want to do.' I had all kinds of new ideas for my music. I didn't want to make the same album over again."

Aces proved to be the turning point in her career. Released during 1991, it stayed on the charts for much of

1992. After peaking at number nineteen in *Billboard* it earned a gold record award from the R.I.A.A. while providing a series of hit singles. During 1991 she made top-chart levels with the singles "Hopelessly Yours" (a duet with Lee Greenwood that reached the top 5 on radio charts and earned a Grammy nomination) and a remake of the Ian Tyson 1960s tune "Someday Soon." The 1992 successes from *Aces* included Nanci Griffith's folk-flavored song, "Outbound Plane," which peaked at number six in *Radio & Records* the week of March 13, and the title track, which reached number seven in *R&R* the week of June 25. In October 1992, she picked up the Country Music Association's Horizon Award during the internationally telecast award show.

By year-end, the next album, *Voices in the Wind,* was rising on the charts, peaking at number thirty-one in *Billboard* in March 1993 and going on to win another R.I.A.A. gold record. The first hit single from the album was "Letting Go," written by Doug Crider and Matt Rollings, which peaked at number four in *R&R* the week of November 23, 1992. This was followed by her version of John Hiatt's folk-rock song "Drive South," which peaked at number three in *R&R* the week of February 19, 1993, and "Heartache" (written by Lowell George of Little Feat fame), which made *Billboard*'s top 20 in June 1993.

In late summer of 1993, her fifth Liberty album, *Something Up My Sleeve,* was released and remained on the charts well into 1994. It provided Suzy with two hit singles of songs she had cowritten, "Just Like the Weather" (written with Doug Crider), which peaked at number five in *R&R* the week of November 15, 1993, and "Hey Cinderella" (cowritten by Suzy with Matraca Berg and Gary Harrison), which made *Billboard*'s top 5 in February 1994. Two more chart singles accrued from that album, "You Wouldn't Say That to a Stranger" in the spring of 1994 and "Souvenirs," on lower-chart levels in September 1994. Also on the charts for a number of months in the spring and summer of 1994 was her first *Greatest Hits* album.

During 1993, Suzy was much in evidence on the concert circuit, where she opened for Dwight Yoakam during some eighty major venue dates, and on TV. (Her agenda for 1994 included a number of joint concerts with guitar great Chet Atkins.) Her TV work included guesting on a number of nationally televised shows and also serving as cohost of the TNN/Music City News Awards program. In the last-named, fan-based polls had made her a finalist in the Top Female Vocalist and Star of Tomorrow categories.

Besides her solo albums, Suzy also contributed her talents to two tribute albums, released in October 1993, that featured a panoply of country stars. One of these was *Common Thread: The Songs of the Eagles* whose proceeds were earmarked to help in the upkeep of nineteenth-century writer Thoreau's Walden Woods locale in Massachusetts. The other one was the *Asleep at the Wheel Tribute to the Music of Bob Wills and the Texas Playboys.* In the first project she performed "Take It to the Limit" while on the second she joined with the band to record the track "Old Fashioned Love." Both albums were among the finalists for Album of the Year in the CMA voting and the Eagles tribute won trophies for Suzy and her coparticipants.

Suzy also applied her creative skills in designing jewelry and clothes to prepare product lines that found commercial outlets. She told one fashion columnist, "Music gives me ideas for my jewelry and coats [the latter marketed through Nordstrom stores under the Baguda Wear label]. And when I'm working on designs I come up with some good song ideas."

Her 1995 credits included release of some duets that Suzy recorded with Chet Atkins. Their single of "All My Loving" was nominated for a Grammy in the Best Country Collaboration with Vocals category. During 1995, she received a platinum award from the R.I.A.A. for *Aces* on February 17 and a gold record trophy for *Something Up My Sleeve* on September 28. In midsummer 1996, Capitol Nashville released her album *Give Me Some Wheels.*

BOY HOWDY: *Vocal and instrumental group. Larry Park (vocals, guitar), born Stockton, California, March 14, c. late 1950s; Cary Park (guitar), born Stockton, California, June 3; Jeffrey Steele (lead vocals, bass guitar), born Burbank, California, August 27; Hugh Wright (drums), born Keokuk, Iowa, December 5 c. early 1960s.*

With the exception of the Bakersfield phenomenon, California hasn't been considered a spawning ground for country artists. But the state has always had its share of country fans and a network of small clubs where groups like Boy Howdy could sharpen their skills and even get a hearing from major labels' Nashville operations.

Boy Howdy evolved from the interaction of local musicians who performed in various bands in Southern California. Larry Park grew up in the area, but from an early age he was influenced by music played on local country music radio stations, which included a good helping of material by Bakersfield superstars like Merle Haggard and Buck Owens. He learned guitar and began picking out some of the traditional and new-style country rhythms but was also influenced by rock bands, including the English chart toppers the Beatles and the Kinks.

As time went by he formed his own country dance bands, which went through many personnel changes at the end of the 1970s and the early 1980s. His dates at local Los Angeles country night spots brought him in contact with a drummer whose style he admired, Iowa-born Hugh Wright. The two agreed to join forces in 1984 and Wright persuaded the leader of the group he'd worked with, Jeffrey Steele, to join. Steele first performed with the group as a substitute for Boy Howdy's bassist, who couldn't make one of the band's gigs at a chili cookoff in Long Beach, California. Steele felt so comfortable playing with the new alignment he agreed to become a permanent member two weeks later, bringing to Boy Howdy not only his bass skills, but talents as a lead vocalist. Soon after, Larry rounded out his new group by recruiting his guitar playing brother, Cary.

Larry recalled the foursome achieved almost instant rapport. Their vocal blend seemed almost instinctive. "We all knew what parts to sing. We never had to sit down and work them out. A lot of bands I've worked for, they sit around and rehearse harmonies. To me, that's something that you just don't really rehearse. We don't have to think about it. It's just a natural thing."

During the mid- and late 1980s, the band honed its skills through seemingly endless dance club dates, party and fair assignments, and any other engagements they could line up. As local fans got to know them, they were able to play return engagements at a number of nightclubs, including regular appearances at the Crazy Horse Steak House in the Orange County city of Santa Ana. In early 1994, the band had the satisfaction of returning to the venue as national headliners.

For most of its development period, the band had the name that eventually graced its recording successes. Larry Park commented, "To us our name's like a celebration of country music. Boy Howdy—in the old Western movies you'd see somebody riding off on a horse and they'd say, 'Boy, howdy, did you see that guy shoot that gun?' That kind of thing. It's a very western expression."

However, the band's music certainly wasn't reminiscent of Roy Rogers or the Sons of the Pioneers. It did incorporate elements of western swing with the raw country sounds of the Bakersfield scene and some country rock offerings, such as a bluegrass-tinged version of the Kinks' "You Really Got Me." In any case, the band's stylings finally found favor with Curb Record Company executives, who signed them in 1991. By 1992, the group was well along toward putting the finishing touches on its debut album, *Welcome to Howdywood,* when near-disaster struck.

In May 1992, the group was returning to Nashville to complete its debut video when drummer Hugh Wright suffered a near-fatal accident. He was attempting to help a roadside accident victim in the early morning of May 31 when another car hit him. With two broken legs and serious head injuries, he was unconscious when he was flown home for treatment in a Santa Monica, California, hospital. For a time it was touch-and-go whether he would recover sufficiently to resume normal activities or even live. He was in a coma for five months, then miraculously began to regain his senses. His prognosis improved from critical to serious to very hopeful.

His bandmates agonized over what course to take. Cary Park recalled, "We were deciding what we were going to do. We asked, 'Should we break this thing up

or continue?' We decided, 'No, we worked too hard. We're gonna keep it going for Hugh to have something to come back to.'"

In the interim the remaining threesome decided to focus on getting their new album material in front of disc jockeys nationwide. They lined up a stand-in drummer and took off to play wherever possible across the U.S., visiting 114 radio stations in twenty-six states during the first part of 1993. Larry Park told Mike Boehm of the *Los Angeles Times* ("The Skies Are Rosy Again for Country's Boy Howdy," January 31, 1994), "It was get up at six a.m. and get finished at eleven at night. It's the hardest thing I ever did in my life—just not getting any sleep and not knowing if it was going to do any good. But it sure paid off."

Their attention to the deejays won increased airplay for their material, which helped put both the album and some of its singles on national charts. The first two singles didn't do much, but the third release, "A Cowboy's Born With a Broken Heart," cowritten by Steele and record producer Chris Farren (as were many of the other album tracks) made the lists in early summer 1993 and made upper levels in a few months' time, including a number-eight peak in *Radio & Records* the week of September 3. By then Wright had returned, having left the hospital in November 1992 and mostly completed his rehabilitation in early 1993.

On March 6, 1993, Wright was back in action with the band. Larry Park told Boehm in January 1994, "He came back in playing stronger than ever. He did suffer a brain injury, which affected his speech, but he goes to a speech therapist and that gets better every day. I think he'll be back one hundred percent."

In late 1993, the Steele/Farren song "She'd Give Anything" began to receive extensive airplay and rose to number three in *R&R* the week of January 28. It served as the title song for a six-song extended play, discount-priced release that became a sales and multichart hit, staying on the *Billboard* list, for instance, for twenty-nine weeks from early in the year to mid-August. At the start of April 1994, the single "They Don't Make 'Em Like That Anymore" (another Steele-Farren product) hit the charts and rose to the top 10 in *Billboard* by early June while peaking at number two in *R&R* the same month.

Steele emphasized that what people heard on Boy Howdy records was what they got. "We really wanted to be a self-contained band and play, instead of hiring a bunch of session musicians. We're country to the bone, and we grew up with that whole Bakersfield sound and we knew that if we could play our own parts, we would make great records.

"When Chris and I finish a song I can already hear how the band's harmonies will work out and on uptempo songs I know Larry and Cary will come up with outrageous guitar parts. They always do. It's one of our trademarks."

The group's charted recordings during 1995 included "Bigger Fish to Fry" in the spring and "She Can't Love You" in the summer. The first was written by Steele, the second by Steele, Farren, and R. Sharp.

BOYD, BILL: *Singer, guitarist, band leader (Cowboy Ramblers), disc jockey, emcee, actor, songwriter. Born Fannin County, Texas, September 29, 1910; died December 7, 1977.*

An important figure in the "western" segment of country & western music, Bill Boyd sometimes suffered from a case of mistaken identity. He shared the same name as the famed cowboy film actor Hopalong Cassidy and, to add to the confusion, made a number of western films himself. However, if you added the descriptive "Cowboy Rambler" to his name, C&W fans immediately knew who was being referred to, though in truth his rambling never kept him away from his beloved home state of Texas very long.

Boyd had a legitimate cowboy background. Born and raised in ranching country, he learned to rope and ride at an early age on his father's stock farm and cattle ranch near Ladonia, Texas. As a boy, he often took part in family sings (he was one of thirteen children), initially accompanying himself on an old five-gallon paint drum; later his mother taught him the rudiments of guitar and banjo.

Bill performed for friends and at local functions in his teens, until he left for Dallas at nineteen to try to find work in the field. After a while, he joined a minstrel group called the Wolfe City Wanderers that got an audition on station WFAA (from which nothing much resulted).

In 1930, however, Boyd got a job on another Dallas station, WRR, as a performer and sometime disc spinner. The combination proved fruitful, as he built up a sizable following and remained WRR's most popular artist and DJ for twenty-five years. After that, he switched to station KSKY, where his show was broadcast regularly for twelve more years.

While maintaining his radio work, Boyd became one of the country & western field's best-known band leaders, beginning in 1931 when he and associate Cliff Wilkins put together the Cowboy Ramblers band. He billed himself on his live radio show as Bill Boyd and His Cowboy Ramblers, and he had a hand in almost every aspect of the show: singing, leading the band, functioning as master of ceremonies, as well as producing the program and providing many of his own compositions. Among his output of songs were "Blues," "David's Blues," and "New Fort Worth Rag." Besides starring on radio, Bill and his band played for fairs and dances throughout the Southwest.

In 1934, Bill signed a recording contract with RCA Victor, which quickly resulted in the single "Ridin' on a Humpback Mule." The following year, he and his band turned out the most famous of the three hundred-plus recordings they made for RCA, the instrumental "Under the Double Eagle," a track still available in the 1970s on RCA's "Gold Standard" series. Among Boyd's releases from 1934 through the early 1950s on RCA and Bluebird labels were such songs as "Oklahoma Bound," "Homecoming Waltz," "Shame on You," "Don't Turn My Picture to the Wall," "Get Aboard That Southbound Train," "Old Fashioned Love," "New Spanish Two-Step," "The Train Song," "Southern Steel Guitar," "Drifting Texas Sand," "Lone Star Rag," "Pass the Turnip Greens," "Over the Waves Waltz," and "Jim's Waltz" (written by his brother Jim).

By the start of the 1940s, Boyd and his group were nationally known to country & western music fans from their recordings and personal appearances. Producers Releasing Corporation signed him in 1941 to star in a series of musical westerns: *Texas Manhunt, Raiders of the West, Rolling Down the Great Divide, Tumbleweed Trail, Prairie Pals,* and *The Sundown Trail.*

After he finished the sixth opus, however, America's entry into World War II caused PRC to cut back on its output and Boyd's contract was one of the casualties. Boyd then answered the call from the U.S. Treasury Department to help the war effort by performing in shows for the armed forces and in bond drives. He became part of the group of cowboy actors that was called the Western Minute Men. Besides Bill, the group was composed of Art Davis (Boyd's movie costar), Hoot Gibson, Ken Maynard, Tex Ritter, Johnny Mack Brown, and Ray Whitley. Boyd kept up that series of appearances during 1942 and 1943 before returning to his regular recording and band-leading operations for the rest of the 1940s.

He kept up a fairly active schedule of radio work coupled with stage shows throughout the 1950s. In the 1960s, he started to taper off on his touring, restricting his in-person efforts to a scattering of concerts each year, a pattern he still held to in the early 1970s. In March 1969, he began a new disc jockey affiliation, signing to do an afternoon program on station KTER in Texas. The program continued on KTER into the 1970s, with the broadcast originating in a studio Boyd had built in his home. Boyd remained active in country & western music affairs almost to his death in late 1977.

BRADLEY, OWEN: *Pianist, band leader, record producer. Born Westmoreland, Tennessee, October 21, 1915. Elected to Country Music Hall of Fame in 1974.*

When the Country Music Association began its Legend Series of Membership Seminars, most of its emphasis was on current performers. But the trio selected for the honor in early 1989 included not only Chet Atkins and Brenda Lee, but also a man who had exerted tremendous behind the scenes influence on post–World War II country music— the preeminent Nashville record producer Owen Bradley. Still a powerful figure in the industry in the late 1980s and early 1990s, Bradley had been voted into the Country Music Hall of Fame almost fifteen years earlier.

Bradley, who spent his youth in the Nashville area, learned to play proficient piano by his teens and at fifteen found work as a pianist in local bars in and around the city. As he grew older, he became familiar with a wide range of people in the country music industry, which eventually led to his first opportunity to serve as a record producer at twenty-five in the early 1940s. His first project was to supervise preparation of recordings by Red Foley.

In 1947 he became chief record producer for Decca Records (later MCA), a position he held until 1977. However, that wasn't the only facet of a busy career. By the mid-1950s he had become the well-regarded leader of his own band and for a time was employed as music director for station WSM, home of the *Grand Ole Opry*. In 1955, with his brother Harold, he opened a studio on Sixteenth Street in Nashville, the first such facility on what was to become Music Row. Later they built an improved studio at the same location they called the Quonset Hut.

During Owen's 30 years as Decca's chief producer, he produced best-selling singles and albums for some of country's greatest stars, including Ernest Tubb, Kitty Wells, Loretta Lynn, Patsy Cline, Conway Twitty, and Brenda Lee. Many of those artists continued to seek Bradley out in the years after he gave up his Decca affiliation.

The Bradleys sold the Quonset Hut to Columbia Records in 1962 and not long after established a new recording operation called Bradley's Barn in an erstwhile farm building. The Barn quickly became one of Nashville's top recording centers and was still thriving in the 1990s.

As David Conrad, 1988 CMA President noted in helping to organize the Living Legends seminar that featured Bradley and Atkins, few people were better qualified to discuss the evolution of the Nashville music industry. "It's well known that Chet and Owen are two of Nashville's most important driving forces. They helped shape the Nashville recording community during its formative years in the fifties and sixties."

Bradley continued to produce new albums for many veteran country music stars throughout the 1980s and despite failing eyesight was still going strong in the first half of the 1990s. He also provided the master's touch for new performers as well, such as k.d. lang, whose best-selling *Shadowland* disc (which spent over two years on the charts at the end of the 1980s and start of the 1990s) was one of his projects. Whether or not he was involved in actual production, the studio that bore his name remained a favorite with recording artists in the mid-1990s as exemplified by the title of George Jones's 1994 chart-making album, *The Bradley Barn Sessions*.

BR5-49: *Vocal and instrumental group, Gary Bennett, born Las Vegas, Nevada, October 9, 1964 (lead and harmony vocals, acoustic guitar); Charles Lynn "Chuck" Mead, born Nevada, Missouri, December 22 (lead and harmony vocals, electric and acoustic guitar); Donald John Herron, Jr., born Steubenville, Ohio, September 23, 1962 (steel guitar, dobro, mandolin, fiddle, acoustic guitar); Jay Michael "Smilin' Jay" McDowell, born Bedford, Indiana, June 11, 1969 (upright bass); Randall Edward "Hawk" Shaw Wilson, born Topeka, Kansas, July 10, 1960 (background and harmony vocals, drums).*

In the mid-1990s, as many country traditionalists bemoaned the continuing trend toward a blander, mainstream-pop-oriented array of artists, a movement began among many young performers to combine modern sounds with the tougher approach of people like Hank Williams, Sr., Webb Pierce, and Merle Haggard—a kind of country underground. Performers like Wayne Hancock, the Derailers, the Dave & Deke Combo, Big Sandy, High Noon, Cowboys & Indians, and, in particular, the digitally named group BR5-49, began to gain attention from fans and media in small clubs around the United States, playing what was described by some adherents as "insurgent country" or "twang-core."

BR5-49 was in the vanguard, not because it was necessarily the first to make a major break with the dominant country approach of the 1990s, but because it came to the fore in the heart of Nashville and was the first of the new breed to win a recording contract with a major label. There were some elements of rockabilly in what the new groups played, but bands like BR5-49 hewed much more closely to the country stylings of the 1950s and 1960s, while adding all manner of other touches. Bass player McDowell pointed out to *Pollstar* magazine that all the members had been interested in the punk movement of the early 1980s, but also had loved the traditional-style country artists their parents had favored. He stressed, "We take our influences from everything from Bob Wills and Merle Haggard to Bob Marley and [the UK rock group] the Clash."

The genesis of the group was the meeting of Mead and Bennett at a songwriters' audition night at the Bluebird Cafe in Nashville in 1993. Both had come to Music City that year to try to carve out careers in the country field with music that would reflect their early influences. Bennett was born in Las Vegas, but spent his formative years in the small logging town of Cougar, Washington. Mead came originally from Nevada, Missouri, but later claimed Lawrence, Kansas, as home base.

Many of the people in Cougar, Bennett recalled, were relations, and most—including his parents—were devoted fans of country and gospel. As he said in 1996, "The era of music that we play now in BR5-49 is really our folks' generation of country music. They were buying these records when we were coming out, and we're lucky that they were. I think we all come by that honestly. There are songs that I sing every night that I've known since I was seven or eight years old." Cougar, he noted, "was kind of far away from everything, so you couldn't get a lot of TV or good radio reception. So we just sat around and listened to music a lot."

In his teens, he learned to sing harmony with a local country gospel group called the Carroll Family; at seventeen, he married the niece of the group's leaders. (The marriage broke up when he was 20.) But he also learned guitar and began to perform with country and punk rock bands while also starting to try his hand at songwriting. A song he completed just before leaving his home area for Nashville in 1993, "Even If It's Wrong," was included on the first full BR5-49 album.

Mead told Timothy White of *Billboard* ("BR5-49: Country's 'Call' of the Wild," July 27, 1996), "At twelve, I was playing hillbilly gospel with a group with my dad, Charles, and my mom, Lois, called the Family Tree. Back in the late forties and fifties, my uncle and grandpa and parents were known as the Wynes Family, after my mom's maiden name, and they sang on KNEM radio in Missouri." That phase ended, but in the 1970s his family started their musical activities anew and recruited their son for the band. "At twelve years old, they gave me a set of drums and said, you are now the drummer. I spent my formative years playing music on the weekend, earning money."

Much later, he told White, "in Kansas [where he attended the University of Kansas], I played in a country-flavored roots-rock outfit called the Homestead Grays, named for a Negro League baseball team, and we played the Bitter End in New York in the late 1980s." The group issued a vinyl extended play album, *Big Hits,* in 1988 and a CD called *El Supremo* in 1991 without making any great impact on the record-buying public.

He told *Country Music People* that his early idols included the Beatles, the Rolling Stones, Hank Williams, and Carl Perkins. Later influences included the Ramones and the Clash. "I was really into Gene Vincent and the Clash were like a modern version of that. I was really into the Jam, too. At one time I had a horrible little mod haircut, had a scooter and a parka. I still like that music. It eventually led me back to what we're doing now. I realized at one point I had more in common with Hank Williams than with Pete Townshend (of the UK rock band the Who).

"But, if you can use the same sort of aggression and the same sort of spirit that comes out of rock 'n' roll, which is what Hank had, which is what Bob Wills had, all those guys had that thing, it's an indefinable variable; that's what really counts and that's what I found out. This is what I truly love."

After Mead and Bennett met at the Bluebird, they both moved on to find band work at clubs in the once-flush, but now declining, Lower Broadway area near the old Ryman Auditorium. Mead found work at Tootsie's Orchid Lounge, while Bennett started leading a pickup band at Robert's Western World a few doors away—a place that sold boots and other western-type accessories during the day and turned into a beer joint at night. Needing a replacement for a sick guitarist one evening, Bennett asked Mead to sit in; they worked so well together, it was a natural decision to keep up the arrangement.

After a while, Mead and Bennett decided to form a regular band, asking McDowell to become a member. McDowell had been in the audience a number of times and liked what he heard. At the time he was playing guitar in a Nashville group called Hellbilly, but Mead and Bennett persuaded him to join up as an upright bassist, in hopes of emulating the string band sounds of early country music. Next addition was Don Herron, a talented multi-instrumentalist who had previously played in a band with Bennett in Portland, Oregon. Herron, born in Ohio but raised mainly in Moundsville, West Virgina, had been a great fan of Bob Wills's western swing style, but also brought to the group his love for jazz artists such as Stephane Grappelli and Django Reinhardt.

Mead and Bennett's interest in string band sounds didn't mean they would ignore the more modern elements of drums and percussion associated with contemporary country rock. To fill the fifth spot in the band they recruited "Hawk" Wilson, who had been a friend and fellow bandsman with Mead back in Lawrence, Kansas. He commented, "Chuck called me and said, 'We're making fifteen bucks a night playing music.' I said it sounds like a job to me."

As the band became a fixture at Robert's, where it played for tips, it hit upon the name BR5-49—inspired by a phone number that comic Junior Samples held up during a used-car salesman routine on the syndicated *Hee Haw* TV series. As the house band at Robert's during 1994 and 1995, the band's mixture of Webb Pierce-style ballads and frenetic versions of honky-tonk songs new and old—including excellent originals by Mead and Bennett—began to attract notice from average Nashvillites and music industry people. (Robert Moore, owner of Robert's, described the band's style for David Zimmerman of *USA Today* this way: "I don't think it's the fifties sound so much as the way they put an upbeat sound on it. It's crossover country rockabilly.") In 1995, the band's audience had grown steadily, mainly through word of mouth, and their arrival was heralded by the long lines that appeared wherever they played.

By mid-1995, the group began to get recording offers from many major labels. They finally decided on Arista Nashville because president Tim Dubois and his associates assured them they would not be subjected to pressure from the company to change their approach.

The first release by Arista, on April 30, 1996, was a six-song extended-play collection offered on CD, cassette, and vinyl titled *Live From Robert's*. Meanwhile, BR5-49 busied themselves recording some eighteen songs for a debut studio album. That collection was pared down to eleven tracks, including six originals by Mead or Bennett, and five numbers that band members considered to be country "classics"—including "Cherokee Boogie" by Moon Mullican and Chief William Redbird; "Honky Tonk Song" by Mel Tillis and Buck Peddy; "Crazy Arms" by Ralph Mooney and Chuck Seals; "I Ain't Never" by Tillis and Webb Pierce; and the Gram Parsons/Buck Buchanan composition "Hickory Wind."

The album, *BR5-49*, was released on September 17, 1996, a date chosen to coincide with Hank Williams, Sr.'s birthday. Certainly an above-average collection, it won unanimous approval from the print media, ranging from the *New York Times* to the country trade press.

Because label officials figured it would be difficult to get the band's material played on most country stations, they sent the band around to visit AM stations that favored traditional country, counting on that strategy, as well as intensive touring, to build a following. That included an early summer series in Europe that went over so well the band was booked to return in the fall to play the UK, Ireland, the Netherlands, and the Scandinavian countries.

McDowell noted to *Pollstar* in September 1996 that the band liked expanding its audience, though it had been satisfied just working at Robert's. And he commented that there were misconceptions after the Arista deal. After the signing, he observed, people said, "Wow, you got a record deal. You guys are rich." But to go on tour in a self-supported way, he added, "We make nothing like we made playing for tips at Robert's." In fact, BR5-49 still suggested tips would be welcome. "It's part of the show too. We canvass them for money. Hey, we're trying to make a living and we're trying to pay the bills. And it's not that *we* need the money so much as the people we *owe* really want the money. It's all kind of a little show bizzy. But people are really generous."

Mead argued getting a record contract hadn't been a key reason the musicians had come together. "The thing about it is, we didn't set out to get a record deal or anything. We just kinda set up and played there, and had fun. We were just doing it because that's what we do, as opposed to trying to do something and trying to create some context. We were just being ourselves."

BRITT, ELTON: *Singer, guitarist. Born Marshall, Arkansas, July 7, 1917; died McConnellsburg, Pennsylvania, June 23, 1972.*

One of the top stars of the country & western field during the 1940s and 1950s, Elton Britt (real name: James Britt Baker) literally sprang up from behind the plow to stardom. During World War II, his reputation was such that President Franklin D. Roosevelt sent Elton a personal invitation to perform at the White House.

Elton's half Cherokee Indian–half Irish background was symbolic of a country musical heritage. Though born in Arkansas, he was brought up in the Osage Hills of Oklahoma, where family sings were a tradition. His father was one of the top old-time fiddlers of Oklahoma and Arkansas. When Elton was still grade school age, his father bought him a five-dollar guitar from Sears Roebuck and taught him three chords. Elton continued to develop his singing and playing ability after that by listening to country & western records. Before he was in his teens, he occasionally entertained at local parties or dances.

In the early summer of 1932, some talent scouts came through the region looking for a real country boy who could sing and yodel. They were directed to Elton and found the fourteen-year-old plowing. They listened to him sing and promptly signed him to a year's contract with station KMPC in Los Angeles. Elton was rushed to California and in a few days was singing on his first radio program. Before the year was up, Elton had created quite a stir among local country & western fans and was soon featured on several network radio shows.

His following continued to grow, resulting in a recording contract with RCA Victor in 1937, where he turned out 672 single records and fifty-six albums in a relationship that lasted twenty-two years. In the 1960s he also recorded for several other labels, including Decca, ABC-Paramount, and Ampar.

During World War II, Elton became one of the nation's most popular recording artists, turning out a number of million-selling records: "There's a Star Spangled Banner Waving Somewhere," which he cowrote, sold more than 4 million copies through the early 1960s and was the first country music recording to receive a gold record award from the R.I.A.A. His other top-10 hits included "Chime Bells" in 1948, "Candy Kisses" in 1949, and, with Rosalie Allen, "Quicksilver" in 1950. Some of his other successful RCA records were "Detour," "Someday," "Blue Texas Moonlight," "I'd Trade All of My Tomorrows," "I Hung My Head and Cried," "Roses Have Thorns," "Born to Lose," "Cowboy Country," "Roses of Yesterday," "It Is No Secret," and "Oklahoma Hills Where I Was Born." His duets with Rosalie Allen included such songs as "Soft Lips," "Game of Broken Hearts," "Tennessee Yodel Polka," "Tell Her You Love Her," and "Cotton Candy and a Toy Balloon."

In 1948, Elton signed with Columbia Pictures for several films. His first one, in 1949, was *Laramie*. Later he also starred in such movies as *The Prodigal Son* for Universal International. During the 1950s and 1960s, Elton appeared on many network shows, including the *Grand Ole Opry*, WWVA *Wheeling Jamboree*, and the *George Hamilton IV* TV show. His LPs available in the 1960s included an RCA Victor album, *Yodel Songs,* and ABC-Paramount's *Wandering Cowboy, Beyond the Sunset,* and *I Heard a Cowboy Praying.* In 1968 he hit with the single "The Jimmie Rodgers Blues," released in April, the fortieth anniversary of Peer-Southern International Organization, publisher of Rodgers' songs.

In the years after his death in 1972, Britt made the final nomination slate for the Country Music Hall of Fame several times, but as of 1996 had not been elected. His albums were long out of print in the 1990s, though some of his recordings were included in country music compilations. His total album output over his career amounted to something over sixty releases.

BROOKS & DUNN: *Vocal and instrumental duo, songwriting team. Kix Brooks, born Louisiana, May 12, 1955; Ronnie Dunn, born Coleman, Texas, June 1, 1953.*

In the entertainment field, it sometimes takes an outside observer to perceive that two individual artists might achieve more as a team than as separate entities. This has happened in the movies, such as when Hal Roach brought Laurel and Hardy together—and, more recently, in the country field, where in the early 1990s a record company executive masterminded the association of Kix Brooks and Ronnie Dunn. Both had sought solo performing careers and each had achieved some success in placing original songs with other artists, but when they combined forces, they blossomed into one of the premiere country acts of the 1990s.

Brooks grew up in Louisiana, where country superstar Johnny Horton was a neighbor. Horton died in a car crash when Kix was a small boy, but his recording successes served as a beacon to the boy's interest in the field. Brooks learned guitar before he reached his teens and recalled playing in bands with schoolmates and friends before he was twelve. He kept up those pursuits in local clubs and honky-tonks while attending high school and college.

In the mid-1970s, at the urging of a friend, he moved to Nashville to seek opportunities as a songwriter and solo artist. He found performing gigs with various groups and did some session work, but his main progress came in writing, when some of his songs were recorded by artists like John Conlee ("I'm Only in It for the Love"), the Nitty Gritty Dirt Band ("Modern Day Romance"), and Highway 101 ("Who's Lonely Now"). He continued to work up new demo tapes in search of a record deal, but the years went by with little record company response.

He later told *Radio & Records,* "I waited my turn to become a recording artist—sometimes that turn never comes. I feel real fortunate that it has, but I would've kept writing songs no matter what."

Texan Dunn started playing bass guitar in high school and soon was performing in local night spots. For a time after high school he began studying to be a Baptist minister, but, as he said, "I got caught playing in honky-tonks and was kicked out." Later he settled in Tulsa, Oklahoma, where he got the chance to work with a rock band. "I was always the token hillbilly in the group—the country singing guy with the rock band behind me."

During the 1980s he managed to get a recording contract with Churchill Records that proved another dead end street. But he was building up music industry contacts—one of whom was drummer Jamie Oldecker, who toured with English rock guitar superstar Eric Clapton. Oldecker entered his friend's name in the 1989 Marlboro Talent Contest, and Dunn went on to take first place in his category. The victory entitled him to a recording session with highly regarded country producer Scott Hendricks in Nashville. Not much happened directly from that, but it brought Dunn in contact with Arista Nashville vice president and general manager Tim DuBois, who began keeping an eye on Brooks's efforts.

It was DuBois who introduced Brooks and Dunn, initially with the idea of improving their songwriting potential. Later, after hearing a demo they did together to promote one of their writing collaborations, he urged them to form a singing and instrumental team. DuBois signed them to the label and it wasn't long before their debut album, *Brand New Man,* which showcased a number of danceable, up-tempo honky-tonk originals, was on the charts. The album entered *Billboard* lists in late August 1991 and was still on them 145 weeks later in August 1994 after racking up sales of over 3 million copies. Meanwhile, the duo was scoring major singles hits on all major charts from late 1991 through 1994, and also gaining approval by country fans and musical peers alike as a major new force in the country spectrum.

No one was more surprised at this overnight stardom than the artists themselves. Brooks told Dennis Hunt of the *Los Angeles Times* (Calendar section, January 3, 1993), "We were real tentative with each other [at first]. We were trying to write together with no thought of singing together." After working through the initial awkwardness, Hunt was told, they became comfortable in both writing and singing collaborations. But both figured it might take a few years to really break through.

Dunn added, "It's real funny. Neither of us could work out a good solo deal, but when they heard us singing together on the songwriting demos, Arista offered us the duo deal. It bothered us some that they didn't want us as solo artists, but we figured it was worth a shot."

It certainly was worth it, as the duo placed single after single on the charts. Their first success was "My Next Broken Heart," which rose to number one in *Radio & Records* the week of December 12, 1991. This was followed in 1992 with "Neon Moon," issued in early 1992 and number one in *R&R* during May, "Boot Scootin'

Boogie," number one in *R&R* the week of July 31, and "Lost and Found," number five in *R&R* the week of November 20. Those records also made top-chart levels in *Billboard* and other publications. All of those songs were cowritten by Brooks, Dunn, and album coproducer Don Cook. Industry observers pointed out the fact that *Brand New Man* provided four straight singles hits, a debut feat never before achieved by a duo or group.

Their second album, *Hard Workin' Man,* was issued in early 1993 and soon was number two on the *Billboard* chart. It was still on over two years later having gone well past R.I.A.A. platinum record requirements. The title track was number four in *R&R* the week of April 9, 1993, and was followed later in the year by such hits as "We'll Burn That Bridge" (number one in *R&R* and number two in *Billboard* the end of July) and "She Used to be Mine" (number one in *R&R* the week of November 5).

In 1994, the twosome had a top hit with "Rock My Little World (Country Girl)" (number four in *Billboard* in late February), one of the rare releases they didn't write themselves, and followed it with *Billboard* chart toppers "That Ain't No Way to Go" (cowritten by the duo and Cook) in June and "She's Not the Cheatin' Kind" (written by Dunn) in late summer.

In the 1992 Country Music Association voting, the duo was nominated in three categories: Album of the Year for *Brand New Man,* Vocal Duo of the Year, and the Horizon Award. They won for Vocal Duo, a feat repeated in 1993. In the *Radio & Records* Country Radio Readers Poll for 1992 (reported in *R&R*'s March 4, 1994, issue) they won Best Duo for the second year in a row. *R&R* also named them Power Gold winner of 1993 in the twenty-five to fifty-four age bracket for having five songs over a year old receiving considerable airplay on country radio. *Hard Workin' Man* won two 1994 Grammy nominations for Best Country Album and Best Country Vocal Performance by a Duo or Group with Vocal. They continued to rank high with CMA voters in 1994, gaining two nominations for Entertainer of the Year and Vocal Duo of the Year.

When the 1994 Academy of Country Music selections were announced on ACM's May 10, 1995, telecast, Brooks & Dunn were named Vocal Duo of the Year. By then they had completed a third best-selling album, *Waitin' on Sundown,* released late in 1994 and recipient of an R.I.A.A. award for platinum sales by the end of May. On the *Billboard* chart the week of May 27, 1995, all three of the team's albums were still included. After 196 weeks, *Brand New Man* was at number fifty-one with sales of over 5 million copies. Right below it was *Hard Workin' Man,* having remained on the list for 116 weeks and sales of over 4 million. Meanwhile, on the singles list, Ronnie Dunn's song "Little Miss Honky Tonk" was slowly phasing out after having scored still another top-10 hit for the duo.

In the mid-1990s, the team became a major factor on the concert tour sector, first as opening acts and soon as headliners. Their fans crossed national boundaries, which encouraged them to record dialogue in several different languages to accompany their 1994 video of "Rock My World (Country Girl)." Arista stated the clips were sent to thirty foreign entertainment centers.

The reason for Brooks & Dunn's impact on the country scene, the country station program director for KZLA-FM told Dennis Hunt, was "their songs. They're just good songwriters, writing the kind of songs people want to hear. And they have a strong vocal presence that enhances their songs."

In the fall of 1995, the duo had a top-5 hit in *Billboard* with the single "Whiskey under the Bridge" (cowritten by Brooks, Dunn, and D. Cook). In March 1996, Arista issued their next album, *Borderline,* equal in quality to all of their past collections. The album rose to number one in *Billboard* and was still high on the list in 1997. They also scored a number one hit with their first single from the album, "My Maria," which reached that position in *Billboard* the week of May 18. At the Academy of Country Music Awards telecast on NBC on April 24, 1996, which Brooks & Dunn cohosted with Faith Hill, the duo was named Top Vocal Duet and Entertainer of the Year. They also earned Entertainer of the Year honors in the CMA voting, announced on that awards telecast in October 1996.

BROOKS, GARTH: *Singer, guitarist, songwriter, actor, band leader (Stillwater). Born Tulsa, Oklahoma, February 7, 1962.*

An extensive interview with Sir David Frost on the Public Broadcasting System; albums that typically debuted at number one on the *Billboard* pop charts and sold in the multimillions; a TV special on NBC that drew one of the largest audiences of the year—all that sounds more like the agenda of a rock superstar than that of a country performer. Yet, Garth Brooks achieved that and more, along the way making modern country music suddenly a challenger for mass audience attention the world over. He surged to the fore with a reedy tenor voice that certainly wasn't the greatest in country history and a guitar style that was good but not unusual. But he was an inspired interpreter of his own compositions as well as those by other top country writers, and gave concert performances that found everyone in the audience passionately involved in the proceedings.

Reviewing his 1993 album *In Pieces,* Holly Gleason commented in the *New York Times* ("A Megastar for Everyman," September 26, 1993), "Mr. Brooks's ability to be one of the boys, in addition to the man who fulfills his woman's needs, has propelled him to superstar status. Even at his most adventurous—for example, with the cowboy jazz of 'Kicking and Screaming,' a song that deals with life's ambiguities—he seems to be perpetually rooted in the Dust Bowl plains of his youth.

"In a world in which love can kill, in which nature is

polluted and poor children live at the margins, Mr. Brooks offers hope, respect and the values Middle America craves. He may not have all the answers, but his music says that sometimes the promise of possibility is more than enough."

Garth was a product of Middle America, growing up under comfortable circumstances in Oklahoma, the son of Troyal Raymond Brooks and Colleen Carroll Brooks. Colleen Carroll brought some music industry background to the family, having recorded for Capitol Records in the 1950s and also performed with Red Foley on the Ozark Jubilee. The Brooks family eventually embraced six children, two of whom later became part of Garth's entourage—Kelly as tour manager and Betsy as a member of his backing group.

Though Garth was interested in both pop and country music in his formative years, he gained more local attention from his athletic prowess, taking part in four sports in Yukon High School: football, basketball, baseball, and track. It was track that gained him a partial athletic scholarship at Oklahoma State University in Stillwater for his ability as a javelin thrower. His college major was advertising, but he exhibited a growing focus on the entertainment field, using his skills as a guitarist and singer, developed in his teen years, to gain work in bands at Stillwater clubs while also occasionally earning some extra income as a bouncer.

He graduated from OSU in December 1984 and kept up his musical activities rather than seek a regular nine-to-five job in the commercial area. His mid-1980s milestones included marrying his college sweetheart Sandy Mahl in 1986 and expanding his show dates with his band Santa Fe to other southwestern states besides Oklahoma. He finally decided the time was ripe to storm the citadel of country music and moved the group to Nashville. Soon after that move, the band broke up, but Garth persevered, striking up a writing and personal friendship with ASCAP songwriter Bob Doyle. Soon after they became acquainted, Doyle set up Major Bob Publishing to handle his own work as well as originals by Brooks. Besides making demo tapes of his work to pass around to record firms and other artists, Garth found work in the advertising sector, doing assignments like voice-overs on Lone Star Beer commercials.

Increasingly, Doyle felt his friend and protégé had major potential as a country artist and formed a new company with Pam Lewis, called Doyle Lewis Management, with the prime goal of promoting Garth's career. This paid off in 1988 with a contract for Brooks with Capitol Nashville (later renamed Liberty Records). His label debut, *Garth Brooks,* was released on April 12, 1989, and, supported by intensive touring by Garth and his band, Stillwater, and good coverage by country radio, soon began moving up not only country lists, but also the *Billboard* Top 200 pop chart. Before 1989 was over, the album had peaked at number thirteen on the top 200 and number two in *Billboard*'s country list.

The album spawned four hit singles, all of which, except for "The Dance," were written or cowritten by Garth. The first to make top-chart levels was "Much Too Young (To Feel This Damn Old)," top 10 in the fall of 1989. This was followed by three number-one successes, "If Tomorrow Never Comes" in late 1989 and "Not Counting You" and "The Dance" in 1990. "The Dance" stayed at number one for three weeks in *Radio & Records* in June. The album was still on the hit lists in 1993 with total sales of almost 5 million as of that August.

Brooks's second Capitol album, *No Fences,* came out on August 27, 1990, and showed he wasn't about to suffer any "sophomore jinx." The tracks were as good as or better than those on his debut collection, and the album quickly exceeded the early disc in popularity. It rose to number one on the country list in the fall and stayed there for months on end (forty straight weeks as of September 1991) while also peaking at number three in the top 200. Before year-end it had gone well past the R.I.A.A. requirements for a platinum award, and by late 1993 had gone past the 10 million mark. It provided four number-one singles, "Friends in Low Places" (which also was made into a hit video) and "Unanswered Prayers" in 1990 and "Two of a Kind, Workin' on a Full House," and "The Thunder Rolls" (also a hit video) in 1991. Garth wrote or cowrote the second and fourth of those. (In the Nashville Songwriters Association's Artist of the Year voting for 1992, Brooks and Alan Jackson tied for the award.)

By the end of 1990, Garth's name had shown up one or more times in just about all the major awards voting. The Academy of Country Music, Country Music Association, TNN/Music City News polls all acknowledged the arrival of a likely new superstar. His 1990 CMA nominations, for instance, included Single of the Year (for "If Tomorrow Never Comes"), Male Vocalist of the Year, Music Video of the Year (for "The Dance"), and the Horizon Award. He won two of those categories, the Horizon Award and Music Video Award. In 1991, the CMA voters nominated him in five categories, Entertainer of the Year, Single of the Year ("Friends in Low Places"), Album of the Year (*No Fences*), Male Vocalist of the Year, and Music Video of the Year ("The Thunder Rolls"); he won three of those, Entertainer, Music Video, and Album of the Year.

His third album, *Ropin' the Wind,* was released on September 2, 1991, and promptly made *Billboard* history on September 28 as the first album to enter both the top 200 and the country chart at the number-one position. It was also the first album by a country artist in eleven years to ever reach the top of the *Billboard* pop list. As was the case for its predecessor, it stayed at number one on the country chart for many months, easily passing platinum levels before 1991 was over. It provided five hit singles: "Rodeo" and "Shameless," both number one in late 1991, and "What's She Doing

Now," "Papa Loves Mama," and "The River" in 1992. Only "Papa Loves Mama" failed to reach number one, peaking at number two.

On January 17, 1992, Garth shook up the television world when his TV special on NBC, *This Is Garth Brooks,* drew astounding viewer attention, finishing number nine for the week and helping the network to its highest-rated Friday night in two years. The program propelled his first two albums back into the top levels of the *Billboard* Top 200, making him the first country performer to have three albums in the top-20 chart in the same week. Since Garth essentially had no exposure on pop radio or MTV, that achievement was attributed directly to the impact of the special. It caused some head-scratching among TV executives, who usually avoided music concerts because they didn't bring about the desired demographics of a large audience percentage of men and women in the eighteen to forty-nine age bracket. Paul Schulman, who analyzed such things for a major New York ad firm that placed around $175 million in commercials per year, told the *Los Angeles Times* that his data showed the program attracted some 16 million households—with 90 percent of the viewers between eighteen and forty-nine. He commented, "Garth got ratings that astounded everybody in the TV industry. When advertisers and networks see numbers like he pulled in you can bet they pay attention."

In late April 1992, Garth was on hand in Los Angeles for the Academy of Country Music telecast, where he had five nominations and won two, for Entertainer of the Year and Male Vocalist of the Year. (Some critics talked of this as a come-down since he had won six ACM trophies in 1991.) But Garth had a lot more things on his mind than new honors. His wife was expecting their first child (Taylor Mayne Pearl, born July 8, 1992) and there had been rumors he had been falling prey to the enticements of stardom. He had made mistakes, he indicated, but he loved his wife, and in the interest of preserving his family he considered whether the best thing would be for him to retire. After all, he had become a wealthy man and had proven himself from a creative standpoint. While that was discussed in the press area backstage, the city of Los Angeles beyond the building's walls was being wracked by the riots caused by the initial verdict in the Rodney King beating case. Riot coverage, in fact, preempted the entire NBC-TV ACM Awards coverage, which had to be presented on tape at a later date.

By year-end, Brooks announced plans for two concerts at the Inglewood Forum in late January 1993 to help raise $1 million for riot relief. (By then, thoughts of retirement had long faded away.) Manager Pam Lewis told reporters that during his stay in L.A. for the ACM Awards "he was deeply touched and that's why he wrote the song 'We Shall Be Free' and he wanted to come up with something to help the people of L.A." In 1992 he had made another charitable gesture by earmarking some of the income from his Christmas album, *Beyond the Season,* for the Feed the Children fund. The album, released on the Liberty label on August 25, 1992, peaked at number two in both the *Billboard* Top 200 and country charts and by late summer 1993 had raised over $2 million for the fund.

His second 1992 album release on Liberty, *The Chase,* became the second one to enter both the *Billboard* Top 200 and its country chart at number one. By the start of 1993 it had been certified platinum by the R.I.A.A., and at the end of the year had sold some 6 million copies. The disc spawned four more hit singles beginning with "We Shall Be Free," which peaked at number seven in October. It was followed by three number-one hits in 1993, "Somewhere Other Than The Night," "Learning to Live Again," and "That Summer." Besides those, the album included such diverse numbers as the old Patsy Cline hit "Walkin' After Midnight" and a rousing version of the Little Feat rock number "Dixie Chicken."

Sales figures showed the revolutionary impact of the new breed of country artists, and Brooks in particular, on the fortunes of the country field. In mid-1992, music analysts noted that during the first two years of the decade country was the fastest growing segment of music sold, accounting for some $1 billion of the industry's annual sales of $7.8 billion. Brooks's continued success in 1992 and the growing popularity of line-dancing was credited by the Country Music Association Index with achieving a 76 percent rise in industry sales from 1990 to 1992, including a jump in record sales from $6.6 million to $1.4 billion over that period. The data also showed concert revenues nearly doubled over that span from $64 million to $126 million.

Ranking at the top of country music attractions during the first half of the 1990s was the series of concerts headlined by Garth and his band, Stillwater. (Band members as of the mid-1990s included his sister Betsy Smittle on bass and background vocals, James Garver on lead guitar and backing vocals, Ty England on guitar and backing vocals, Steve McClure on steel and electric guitar, Mike Palmer on percussion, and Dave Gant on keyboards and fiddle.) People who attended his shows rarely felt they hadn't received their money's worth; furthermore, he was able to fill venues, like the Los Angeles Forum, that usually could only post the SRO sign for top rock acts.

After one Forum concert Richard Cromelin of the *Los Angeles Times* commented that Garth stuck to his concert basics—"but the Brooks basics are like no one else's. He still races all over the place with his mobile musicians, bringing a rock-show energy to country music. He grabbed a rope and swung out over the crowd. He drove the folks wild with a pumping arm and shouts of 'This is cool. . . . I like this!' His enthusiasm might embarrass Sammy Hager [of the rock band Van Halen] but the key is that he was having fun with it—

the roar of the crowd is another instrument for him, and he plays it like a virtuoso.

"He combined country with mainstream pop elements, and when he gets to the country roots, it's generally a brand of hard honky-tonk. . . ."

After his next album came out on Liberty, *In Pieces,* issued on August 31, 1993, its first single release, "Ain't Goin' Down (Til the Sun Comes Up)" made *Radio & Records* history by entering its country chart at number twenty-five "with 222 stations adding the song out-of-the-box." The album, of course, debuted at number one on the *Billboard* country charts and established residence there for many weeks. The debut single rose to number one in *R&R* the week of September 17, 1993, and was followed by another number-one hit in November, "American Honky-Tonk Bar Association." In March 1994 the single "Standing Outside the Fire" reached number three in *R&R* and the following July "One Night a Day" reached number five on that list. In the fall, Brooks had another number-one hit on both *R&R* and *Billboard* with "Callin' Baton Rouge."

At the end of 1994, Liberty put the finishing touches on Brooks's first greatest hits collection. Called *The Hits,* it quickly demonstrated Garth's continued rapport with a broad spectrum of American music fans. It entered the *Billboard* Top 200 at number one and sold well over 200,000 copies its first week in the stores. The album stayed number one for five weeks before being temporarily displaced by a Van Halen release—after which it returned to number one for many more weeks. At the same time, until mid-April of 1995, it remained at number one on the country chart, accumulating sales to that point of 5 million copies. As had been the case with his earlier albums, *The Hits* also was a best-seller in many other parts of the world.

By the start of 1995, Garth had earned many other honors both at home and abroad. In the Grammy voting for 1991 (announced on the February 25, 1992, Awards telecast), he was cited for Best Country Vocal Performance, Male, for the album *Ropin' the Wind.* In the 1993 CMA voting he was nominated for Entertainer of the Year, Male Vocalist of the Year, and a contributor, with other artists, to the George Jones recording "I Don't Need Your Rockin' Chair." The last named was chosen for Vocal Event of the Year. In 1993, he also performed on the album, *Asleep at the Wheel Tribute to Bob Wills and the Texas Playboys,* nominated for 1994 Album of the Year. (Besides those two CMA-nominated albums, Garth also sang on the albums by other artists, including Stephanie Davis, Chris LeDoux, Martina McBride, Buddy Mondlock, Eddie Murphy, and Trisha Yearwood, as well as on a Kiss tribute disc.) During those years, Garth also won five American Music Awards, a Juno Award from Canada, two German-American Country Music Federation Awards, a Dutch Country Music Award, and a top award from England's *Country Music Round-Up* publication. In addition, readers of

Rolling Stone magazine named him Favorite Country Artist for several years running, *Radio & Records* readers named him Country Performer of the Year for 1991 through 1993, and some 11 *Billboard* awards came his way during the first half of the 1990s, including Top Pop and Country Artist of the Year citations.

On December 9, 1995, Brooks's first studio album in two years, *Fresh Horses,* debuted at number one in *Billboard*'s country list and number two on the pop chart, achieving first week sales of an estimated 480,000 copies. No less than eight tracks from the collection showed up on national radio airplay lists, including "She's Every Woman," which peaked at number one in *Billboard* in the fall well in advance of the album's release and "The Fever," moving up the charts starting in November. In the spring of 1996, the single "The Change" was doing well on the charts. It had first shown up on the *Billboard* list the week of December 9, 1995, along with five other Brooks singles: "The Old Stuff," "The Beaches of Cheyenne," "It's Midnight Cinderella," "Rollin'," and "That Ol' Wind."

While his existing recordings continued to do well with record buyers, Brooks was largely inactive during 1995, though he did do benefit work to raise money for families affected by the bombing of the government building in Oklahoma City. His video of "The Change," which included searing images of the aftermath of the bombing, was a gripping moment at the 23rd American Music Awards on ABC-TV in late January 1996, Brooks shocked both the TV audience and telecast attendees by declining to accept the Favorite Artist of the Year trophy. He said, "I cannot agree with this [award]. Without any disrespect for the people who voted, for all the people who should be honored I'm gonna leave it right there." He did accept awards for Favorite Male Country Artist and Favorite Country Album (for *The Hits,* still on the charts and in the top 10 in the spring of 1996 after going past sales levels of 8 million copies).

Brooks expanded on his decision to turn down the award for journalists backstage. As the *Los Angeles Times* reported, he said, "It wasn't fair for me to walk away with that award. Maybe a year or two ago when we had a really good year. But I've been around [the U.S.] talking to retailers . . . and every one of them credits Hootie [and the Blowfish] for keeping them alive in 1995. And I couldn't agree more. So I thought that's who shoulda won."

The lack of touring, though, may have hurt prospects for *Fresh Horses* which, while going multiplatinum (over 2 million copies sold) in early 1996, didn't seem to have as good a track record as its predecessors. To try to reverse matters, Brooks scheduled a major tour starting in the spring. He told Robert Hilburn of the *Los Angeles Times* ("Coming Down to Earth," March 3, 1996), "I'm hoping the tour will make a difference, but if it doesn't we'll have to take a serious look at where we are in our career. If the record and ticket sales don't tell me that I'm stirring things up or changing people's lives then I think it's time to hang it up."

Pop and country fans both might be incredulous at that statement. But Brooks's reasoning was that, "I have respect for those artists who keep making music their entire life, but I don't want to ride that downside of the bell curve. You want to be remembered at your best. You don't want to be a trivia question on some cheesy game show in twenty years and see the [contestant] get it wrong."

BROTHER PHELPS: *Vocal and instrumental group headed by the Phelps brothers. Ricky Lee Phelps, born Paragould, Arkansas, October 8, 1953 (vocals, guitar, songwriter); Calvin Douglas Phelps, born Leachville, Arkansas, December 16, 1960 (vocals, guitar, songwriter).*

It takes a lot of gumption to leave a successful band like the Kentucky Headhunters, but the Phelps brothers decided the time had come to move into the spotlight as performers and writers in their own right in the mid-1990s. One of the prime reasons, they noted, was the desire to go beyond the musical boundaries the Headhunters had seemed to set up for their performances. Doug stated, "What we did in the Headhunters, the band did very well, but when it came time to do something a little more country, or a love song or ballad, something different from shuffle boogie-woogie, we kind of ran into a wall there."

Both Doug and older brother Ricky Lee were born in Arkansas, but grew up in Caldwell, Missouri, on the Missouri-Arkansas border. Their father, whom they sometimes called "the original Brother Phelps," was a minister at an Assembly of God church and their mother was an elementary school teacher. Music was an important part of their environment. Their father played guitar, their grandmothers wrote many gospel songs, and they often had musical sessions where uncles and aunts took part.

Ricky Lee was influenced, as was his brother after him, by both country and the burgeoning rock and pop field. Their parents saw to it that first Ricky and then Doug were members of the church choir. They grew up listening to hours of the *Grand Ole Opry,* which their father religiously tuned in every Saturday night.

The first time Ricky Lee performed in public was at an eighth grade talent show. He was learning to play guitar and polish his singing skills by the time he had his first paying music job at the Cardwell Community Center in 1967. When he finished high school, he decided to take a day job, starting as a worker in a shoe factory and later working as salvage yard and lumber yard worker and a hardware store employee. At times, though, he also earned money as a street performer. He also wasn't averse to the idea of being a sideman in a rock or pop band.

Eventually he moved to Arizona, where he worked with a number of bands. His musical influences over the years had extended beyond country to modern folk material and such rock groups as the Beatles and other 1960s headliners. From time to time he made some tapes of his own versions of current songs and sent them back to Doug. The latter recalled the tapes usually came at Christmas. "He'd be playing acoustic guitar, singing John Prine and Jimmy Buffett tunes. He came home for Christmas one year. We were sitting around the house, had guitars out and I started playing those songs. I learned them verbatim, but sang harmony. He was floored. We had been singing together, but it wasn't face to face."

Doug remembered his musical career starting at age seven, when he sang "Little Drummer Boy" in a church Christmas show. Like his brother, he first earned money from music at the Cardwell Community Center, though that came six years after Ricky Lee. The occasion was a Lion's Club affair. Later on, though Doug was active as a musician during his high school years, performing with friends in local groups, he enrolled in college after graduation, going on to complete two and a half years at Arkansas State University.

In the early 1980s, Doug decided he would emulate his brother and seek a career in music. By then he was a good bass guitarist, a capability which earned him a job performing with a band headed by Ronnie McDowell. The band also included guitarist Greg Martin. When not working with McDowell, Doug, Martin, and some of Martin's cousins began jamming together in their spare time, playing music that combined country with blues rock. After six months, they decided to focus on their separate group and called on Ricky Lee to come aboard as lead singer.

Ricky at the time was living in Nashville and working to set up a memorabilia museum incorporating beer and soda collectibles as well as such other things as clocks and playing cards. He left that for the new group, which became the Kentucky Headhunters. By the second half of the 1980s that band was gaining a reputation for exciting stage shows in Kentucky and nearby states. A key element in their future success was development of a radio program, "The Chitlin' Show," which was broadcast from a station in Mumfordville, Kentucky.

The band members felt they were ready to move onward and upward and spent $4,500 to make an eight-song demo tape. The tape eventually got them a recording contract with Mercury Records. The group added two songs to the original tape and soon found itself basking in unexpectedly early glory as the debut release became a best-selling album. The platinum debut was followed by a gold record certified follow-up plus a number of hit singles. While the Phelps brothers were with the Headhunters, the band accrued many awards, including four from the Country Music Association, one from the Academy of Country Music, an American Music Award trophy, and some Grammy Awards. Before the band started work on its next album, the Phelps brothers decided to leave. Ricky Lee explained, "For me, I was a country singer more than anything. I have a country voice. I wanted to sing ballads or really sing rather than scream or holler. I like to scream, holler and get down, too, but I wanted to sing something with a different flavor."

The brothers signed with Asylum Records in 1992 and their label debut, *Let Go,* came out in the second half of 1993. The title track, issued as a single, was a chart hit, rising to number six in *Radio & Records* the week of September 24, 1993. The single also was a top-40 entry on the *Billboard* chart. In November the single "Were You Really Livin' " (cowritten by the brothers) was on the charts, entering the *Billboard* top 40 by year-end. Another single drawn from the album, "Ever Changin' Woman," was on the charts from the late summer of 1994 into the fall months.

Another song on the album was a reminder of the recent past, "Everything Will Work Out Fine," a joint composition of the previous Kentucky Headhunters alignment. Doug commented, "We all wrote it before we split up. It has special meaning for us, sums it up, everybody going their own way. We had a good time; the good Lord blessed us, couldn't ask for anything better."

The brothers' initial releases had done reasonably well, but they hadn't achieved any blockbuster hits as of 1994. They had gained recognition from others in the field as demonstrated by their nomination for Vocal Duo of the Year in the Country Music Association 1994 poll. In early 1995 they had another single moving up the charts, "Anyway the Wind Blows."

BROWN, ANTHONY GRAHAM: *Singer, guitarist, songwriter. Born Atlanta, Georgia, October 30, 1954.*

Perhaps reflecting the increasing fickleness of the country music audiences after the 1960s, Anthony Brown, known professionally as T. Graham Brown, was a name often found on the hit lists in the latter half of the 1980s, but one that disappeared almost completely in the 1990s. Not that he was inactive during those years; he could often be seen on TV commercials and could still draw acceptable numbers to concerts, but he was unable to line up a new major label recording contract, at least through early 1995, after a number of years as a best-selling recording artist on Capitol.

Part of his problem was his loose identification with country music, since his repertory ranged from conventional country through rock and blues. At one point he defended his credentials in an interview, arguing, "I grew up in the rural South. I had a hog that I showed in a country fair. I am country by any definition of the word, yet I was not deaf to the music I grew up listening to and that included everyone from George Jones to Percy Sledge to Elvis and Johnny Cash, as well as the Beatles and Rolling Stones.

"There has always been a lot of hip country music if you know where to look for it. My generation has, to a great degree, switched over to country because conventional pop music seems to be undergoing what country did years ago, which is to become very restrictive in its sound. If you give the audience only one kind of music, they get bored and start looking for diversity. Country learned that expensive lesson during the *Urban Cowboy* craze and almost got destroyed by it. Nowadays, you can hear everyone from Randy Travis to the Kentucky Headhunters to Vince Gill and me on the same radio station and get a great cross-section of music."

Brown grew up in Georgia and, while he had some interest in music and learned to play guitar in his teen years, he was more interested in sports and, in particular, dreamed of someday making a career for himself as a professional baseball player. That certainly seemed a possibility during his high school years when he became a star pitcher and starting centerfielder on the school team. He had, though, worked with school friends on music projects, performing at dances and small clubs. The music he favored was more strongly influenced by music associated with the Motown Sound and Stax Memphis stylings than those of Nashville.

When he entered the University of Georgia in the early 1970s, he still had his hopes pinned on his baseball skills. He made the squad, but soon realized a lot of the other players were more talented. "I found out I'd be watching the game from the bench for my first year and that didn't sound like much fun, especially when a friend and I were being paid one hundred and fifty dollars a week to play music at the Holiday Inn."

The friend was Dirk Howell, and the music they performed was a blending of soul and blues called beach music. The duo began building a growing following in the Athens area over the next few years and Brown proposed they assemble a full-sized band. Howell was concerned that this might be too chancy a step and the two parted company, though they remained good friends. Another likely reason for the breakup was music content. Tony wanted to focus on more honky-tonk stylings than the blues-soul approach.

His new band, formed in 1976, he said, represented his "David Allan Coe" period. He had been known as Tony Brown in his duo phase and, since a lot of friends at school were calling him "T," he decided to use the name T. Graham Brown to avoid confusion between his new band and the duo. After working the honky-tonk and club circuit with that group for a while, he decided to incorporate his soul and blues influences in a new realignment called T. Graham Brown and the Rack of Spam. This was a nine-piece ensemble, which included horn players, that performed in many sections of the Southeast in the late 1970s and early 1980s.

In 1982, Brown decided it was time to try to move out of the regional music orbit and try for more wide-ranging milestones. He moved to Nashville and like many other hopefuls tried to keep his career alive through getting various minor gigs and singing on demo tapes for publishers and songwriters. He naturally also shopped tapes around to record companies for himself, and in 1984 this paid off with a contract from Capitol/EMI. His debut album, *T. Graham Brown,* came out soon after and spawned three chart singles. His debut single, "Drowning in Memories," which had been on one of the demos submitted to the record company, made the *Billboard* Top 40. It was followed on the hit lists in the mid 1980s by the top 10 "I Tell It Like It Has to Be" and the top 5 "I Wish That I Could Hurt That Way Again."

His career took an even sharper turn upward in early 1986 when he had two number-one hit singles, "Hell and High Water" (cowritten by Brown) and "Don't Go to Strangers." During that year he made album charts with his second Capitol release, *Brilliant Conversationalists,* which added three more chart singles, the title song, "She Couldn't Love Me Anymore," and "The Last Resort." His third album, *Come As You Are,* was issued in 1988 and provided the number-one single "Darlene." Also on the charts for a time was the single "Never Say Never."

The overall public response to his recorded output, though, did seem to be slowing down. That, coupled with management shifts at the label caused the artist and record company to go separate ways after the release of his fourth Capitol collection, *You Can't Take It With You,* in 1990. The album, coproduced by Brown and Muscle Shoals, Alabama–based expert, Barry Beckett, provided some charted singles, including "Moonshadow Road," a top-20 entrant in late 1990. In 1989 and 1990, he also recorded some duet material with Tanya Tucker, which brought a Country Music Association nomination in 1990 for Vocal Event of the Year.

While his recording career lagged in the first part of the 1990s, Brown kept busy with live performances, commercials, and film assignments. In the case of film, his credits went back to his years in Athens, Georgia, when he had a bit part in Richard Pryor's *Greased Lightning,* as well as *The Curse,* which starred John Schneider and David Keith. His recordings and live concerts in Europe helped bring him the opportunity to contribute to the soundtrack of a German movie, which also included material from Joe Cocker, Robbie Nevil, and Talk Talk. In 1988, he had a speaking part in the film *Heartbreak Hotel,* starring David Keith as Elvis Presley with Brown appearing as Elvis's musical right-hand man.

Brown's work on vocals for TV commercials went back to the early 1980s; over the years he worked on ads for firms like Kraft, Coca-Cola, and McDonald's. In the early 1990s he both sang and played a role in a series of "Run for the Border" Taco Bell commercials.

BROWN, JIM ED: *Singer, songwriter. Born Sparkman, Arkansas, April 1, 1934.*

When one of country fans' favorite singing groups, the Browns, broke up in 1967, it was feared the disbandment would leave a gaping hole in country ranks. However, in a short time, Jim Ed Brown showed he could do as well or better as a soloist than in the days he worked with his two talented sisters. Then, after close to a decade as a solo headliner, he added new luster to his career by teaming with Helen Cornelius in one of country music's most accomplished duos.

As a boy, Jim Ed was aware of country music from his early years, when listening to *Grand Ole Opry* broadcasts on Saturday nights was a family ritual. Jim and his older sister Maxine sometimes sang along with artists like Roy Acuff or Ernest Tubb and often daydreamed about holding the spotlight themselves. They formed a duo while in junior high school and began to sing at local events, school functions, and square dances. Later, they sang regularly on station KCLA in Pine Bluff, Arkansas. Still is wasn't certain that Jim would make show business his main interest in life, although his sister Maxine was enthusiastic about that prospect. Jim Ed worked regularly in his father's sawmill and thought seriously about taking over its operation later on.

That consideration prompted Jim to enroll as a forestry major at Arkansas A&M, but after a year, he decided that music interested him more and moved to Arkansas State. When he and Maxine won first place in a talent show on Little Rock's station KLRA in 1953, they became regular members on the station's *Barnyard Frolic* program. Soon after, the twosome got the chance to record for Abbott Records, owned by Fabor Robinson, and turned out several excellent sides, including "Draggin' Main Street" and "Looking Back to See." The latter, one of their own compositions, was recorded in a session in which the backing group included Jim Reeves (then on the Abbott label) on rhythm guitar and Floyd Cramer on piano.

They expanded their following with a highly successful guest appearance on the *Louisiana Hayride* show in Shreveport. In 1955, after younger sister Bonnie joined to complete the Browns trio, they became featured artists on Red Foley's *Ozark Jamboree* out of Springfield, Missouri. That same year Jim Reeves, who had moved to RCA, brought them to the attention of RCA executives Steve Sholes and Chet Atkins, who soon signed the Browns for the label. Over a quarter century later, Jim Ed still was an RCA recording star.

This steadily brightening outlook slowed down for a time when Jim Ed was drafted into the army. Another sister, Norma, filled in while he was away. Almost as soon as he returned, the tempo picked up. The trio recorded a song called "The Three Bells" that became one of the top country hits of 1959 and also crossed over into the pop charts. The single, which sold over a million copies, made the group nationally known. They consolidated their new-found star status with a series of hit recordings in the early 1960s. During those years, they became familiar to both concert-goers and TV viewers through constant touring and guest appearances. Among the network programs on which they were featured were *The Ed Sullivan Show* and Dick Clark's *American Bandstand*.

From 1960 to 1963, when not on tour, the trio tended to their business in the supper club and catering service fields in Pine Bluff, Arkansas. When they became regular cast members on the *Grand Ole Opry* during that period, the amount of touring they did was reduced, but Bonnie and Maxine wanted to spend still more time with their families and left the act in 1967.

Jim Ed set about developing his solo activities. From the start he showed he commanded a strong following in his own right. His initial releases on RCA in 1967 included "I Heard from a Memory" and the major hit "Regular on My Mind." Later on, he added such other 1960s best-sellers as "Pop-A-Top" and "The Enemy." He accepted a long engagement at the Sahara Tahoe's Juniper Lounge in Lake Tahoe, Nevada, in 1968, and from the late 1960s through the 1970s, Jim Ed remained a major headliner on the country music circuit.

His name rarely was off the singles or album charts for very long during the first half of the 1970s. His credits included the late 1970 top-10 success "Morning," which he reprised a few years later with the chart-making "Evening." Some of his other charted singles from 1970 through mid-1976 were "Sometime Sunshine" and "It's That Time of Night" in 1974; "Don Juanior" and "Fine Time to Get the Blues" in 1975; and "Another Morning" in 1976. His album releases included, on RCA, *Just for You* (8/70), *Morning* (3/71), *Angel's Sunday* (7/71), and *She's Leavin'* (12/71) and on Camden, *Gentle on My Mind* (8/71).

In 1976, he started singing with Helen Cornelius, and one of their initial collaborations, "I Don't Want to Have to Marry You" rose to the top of the charts in late 1976 after they earlier had reached top-charts levels with the single "Born Believer." They placed several songs on the charts, including "If It Ain't Love by Now," a top seller for many months in the fall. In 1978, they scored a top-10 hit with "If the World Ran Out of Love Tonight" in the fall and came out with their version of Neil Diamond's "You Don't Bring Me Flowers," which rose to top-chart levels in early 1979. In May 1979, their single "Lying in Love with You" soared to number one on the national country lists and in the fall they had another hit with "Fools."

Jim Ed and Helen were featured on many major radio and TV shows in the late 1970s, from the *Opry* to *Hee Haw, Pop Goes the Country* and Dolly Parton's *Dolly*. In addition, they were hosts of their own syndicated TV program, *Nashville on the Road*. Several times in the late 1970s they were among the five finalists in CMA voting for Vocal Duo of the Year.

Brown wound up 1979 with "You're the Part of Me" on the charts. The song remained on them into early 1980. During 1980, he teamed with Helen Cornelius on such charted singles as "Morning Comes Too Early" and "The Bedroom." (By 1981, the duet had broken up.)

Starting in the early 1980s, he focused more on his activities as host of the Nashville Network TV show *You Can Be a Star* than his recording efforts, though he still turned out new material from time to time. In the mid-1980s he also served as national spokesman for Dollar General Stores.

In early 1996, RCA issued the retrospective collection *Jim Ed Brown and the Browns* on its Essential Series label. During 1996, Jim Ed was active in helping to operate the reorganized Jim Reeves museum and its enterprises in Nashville. A long-time friend of the Reeves family, he agreed to help out since Jim's widow, Mary Reeves, who had guided the companies after her husband's death, was in poor health.

BROWN, JUNIOR: *Singer, instrumentalist (guitar, guit-steel), songwriter, record producer, music instructor. Born Kirksville, Indiana, June 12, 1953.*

A musician's musician, Junior Brown got high marks for his innovative instrumental stylings from performers across the musical spectrum from blues and rock to country. People like Ry Cooder, Chris Isaak, Nick Lowe, Jimmy Vaughn, Carlene Carter, and Neil Young sang his praises. As a soloist and session player, he provided a body of work that probed the boundaries of many pop genres, even if his name didn't challenge mass audience favorites for top-hit chart positions. *Musician* magazine commented, "Garth sells zillions, Wynonna's a household word, but Junior Brown is touched by genius."

Brown was born and raised in the Hoosier State. He recalled, "There was always music of some kind in the house when I was growing up. My dad was a piano player, so I started playing little melodies on the piano before I could talk. We lived in the woods outside of Kirksville, Indiana, and there's a lot of country people up there. I used to hear country music over the radio, Ernest Tubb and stuff. When we got a TV, I watched his show and I've always been a big fan of his."

As he grew older, Junior gravitated to guitar playing, and that was his favored instrument when he became a professional musician in the late 1960s. He played in various bands and made initial forays to Nashville in the 1970s. His activities brought him in touch with his idol, Ernest Tubb, who became something of a mentor. Perhaps a little anxious about a talented performer like Brown's exploration of a wide variety of musical formats, Tubb urged Junior to "Keep it country, son." Brown commented, "He was concerned about country music getting watered down. He wanted young people to get a hold on it and try to carry on. I was one of the young people he told and it kind of sunk in. He let his band get as wild as they wanted to as long as they brought it right back down to the country and remembered that they were in a country band."

Later he described his approach in concert from that perspective. "Just about the time they label me as some honky tonk singer, I throw something in there that surprises them. And then they'll appreciate the simplistic country stuff too. Do something to wow them without ruining the country stuff and they end up accepting the stuff they would have been prejudiced against."

In the mid-1980s, Brown settled in Oklahoma for a while where he taught guitar in a program organized by legendary steel guitarist Leon McAuliffe (famous for his own band work and his performances with the Texas Playboys) at the Hank Thompson School of Country Music, which was part of Rogers State College. While there he became acquainted with a promising artist named Tanya Rae. The two later married and Tanya joined Junior's act as rhythm guitarist and backup vocalist. Brown's guitar artistry had become known to many in the music industry, including English rock star Nick Lowe (who for a time was married to country star Carlene Carter). Nick took a demo tape of Brown's work to Elvis Costello's Demon Records, which resulted in Junior Brown's first album release, *12 Shades of Brown*. That album, issued in the U.K. and available as an import item in the U.S., included a song tribute by Brown to Ernest Tubb, "My Baby Don't Dance to Nothin' But Ernest Tubb."

After their marriage, the Browns decided to move to Austin, Texas, where, Junior stressed, "You can make a living playing this kind of music." They became regulars at Henry's Bar & Grill, where their audience soon included traditional country fans and rock adherents, including some normally interested in heavy metal.

While Austin remained home base in the late 1980s and the first half of the 1990s, the Browns found welcoming audiences in many other parts of the country. Junior's instrumental skills were featured on a number of major TV shows including *Saturday Night Live* on NBC and TNN's *American Music Shop*. Viewers were particularly enthralled by Brown's polished playing of an instrument he invented himself called the Guit-Steel, which combined features of both the standard six-string guitar and the steel guitar.

Brown explained, "I was playing both the steel and guitar, switching back and forth a lot, and it was kind of awkward. But then I had this dream, where they just kind of melted together. I thought, you know, that thing would work."

He called guitar maker Michael Stevens to explain his ideas and soon after was featuring the unusual double-neck design in concert. The odd looking instrument was shown in an artist's conception of "The All-Time, All-Star Country Band" presented in *Life* magazine's special 1994 issue on country music.

Brown's company in that dream group included, among others, Hank Williams, Sr., Bill Monroe, Jerry Douglas, and Leon McAuliffe.

In the mid-1990s, Junior signed with Curb Records. His initial release on the label was titled *Guit with It* in 1994. In 1995, his second release on the label came out, *Junior High,* from which the singles "Highway Patrol" and "My Wife Thinks You're Dead" were drawn. The album, produced by Brown, was nominated for a Grammy in the Best Country Album category.

In 1996, he shared the concert stage a number of times with the Mavericks, including a show at the Los Angeles Greek Theatre on May 31. His new album, *Semi-Crazy,* was released that month. During the summer he was a guest star on the George Jones video, "Honky Tonk Road."

BRYANT, BOUDLEAUX AND FELICE: *Fiddler (Boudleaux), songwriting team. Boudleaux born Shellman, Georgia, February 13, 1920, died June 25, 1987; Felice born Milwaukee, Wisconsin, August 7, 1925. Elected to Country Music Hall of Fame in 1991.*

Certainly one of the most successful and prolific husband-and-wife songwriting teams in popular music history, the Bryants contributed many standards both to rock 'n' roll and to country music. They had the pleasure of seeing their compositions both old and new show up on hit lists from the 1940s through the 1980s.

Boudleaux, born in Shellman but raised in Moultrie, Georgia, had an excellent classical background. He began to study violin when he was five and continued until he was eighteen, with the goal of becoming a concert violinist. In 1938, he played a season with the Atlanta Philharmonic.

Then, in a violin maker's shop, he met a man from Atlanta station WSB who needed a fiddle player for a country band. Having also played country music for his own enjoyment, Boudleaux took the job. He continued to perform as a country fiddler for several years, then joined a jazz band with which he toured much of the United States. In 1945, while playing in Milwaukee, he met Felice, an elevator starter at the Shrader Hotel, who was born and raised in Milwaukee.

Soon after that first meeting they were married, and after the wedding she traveled with him. Sometimes they made up country & western songs just for fun, and eventually decided to try to place some. In 1949, at the suggestion of a friend, performer Rome Johnson, they sent a song called "Country Boy" to Fred Rose of Acuff-Rose Publishing in Nashville. Rose bought it and Little Jimmie Dickens turned it into a hit. The next year, at Rose's suggestion, the Bryants moved to Nashville.

From then on, their songs rarely were absent from the hit charts. Many of the tunes made it on both country & western and popular charts. An example was "Hey Joe," a top-10 country hit for Carl Smith in 1953 and a million-seller for Frankie Laine in the pop domain. For some years the Bryants worked closely with Carl Smith. This resulted in such top-10 successes as "It's a Lovely, Lovely World," "Our Honeymoon," "Just Wait 'Til I Get You Alone," "Back Up Buddy," and "This Orchid Means Goodbye," the last named cowritten by Boudleaux and Carl.

In 1955, Eddy Arnold achieved hits with the Bryants' "I've Been Thinking" and "Richest Man." By the mid-1950s, the Bryants had begun to make their mark on the dynamic new field of rock 'n' roll. They were assigned to work with a rising young brother act, the Everlys. In 1957, this combination provided the Everlys with Bryant songs that made number one on both country and pop charts: "Bye Bye Love" and "Wake Up Little Susie." The following year, the Everlys were given two more number-one ranked songs, "All I Have to Do Is Dream" and "Bird Dog." In 1958, the Bryants were represented on country top-10 lists with Jim Reeves's version of "Blue Boy." From 1957 to 1960, the Bryants provided the Everlys with a number of other songs that made upper-chart levels, although not the very top.

In 1961, Boudleaux had a worldwide hit with an instrumental composition, "Mexico." The song won a gold record in Germany. After the Everlys signed with Warner Brothers Records and moved to Los Angeles in the early 1960s, the Bryants concentrated once again on country material. Some of their top-10 hits in the 1960s were the singles "Let's Think About Living" (performed by Bob Luman), "My Last Date" (Skeeter Davis, who cowrote the song with Boudleaux), "Baltimore" (Sonny James), "I Love to Dance with Annie" (Ernest Ashworth), and "Rocky Top" (Buck Owens). The Bryants published most of the material they wrote through their own firm, House of Bryant, which was still a thriving business in the 1990s.

A sampling of the charted singles in the 1970s written by one or both of the Bryants includes "We Could" (by Felice, a hit single for Charley Pride in 1974), "Take Me as I Am (Or Let Me Go)" (Mack White, 1976), "Sweet Deceiver" (Christy Lane, 1977), "Penny Arcade" (Christy Lane, 1978), and "Raining in My Heart" (Leo Sayer, 1978).

In late 1979, the Bryants tried a new tack by agreeing to record an album themselves for an English company. Called *Surfin' on a New Wave,* it was released in early 1980. Eight of the songs were new ones written for the LP. However, Boudleaux noted, "We were going to do nothing on the album but new songs, but our two sons [Dane and Del] suggested we record some of the older things for identification purposes." The four "oldies" chosen were "All I Have to Do Is Dream," "Bye Bye Love," "Raining in My Heart," and "Rocky Top."

In 1981, Boudleaux provided Joe Stampley and Moe Bandy with the top-10 single composition "Hey Moe, Hey Joe." While the Bryants continued to write new material in the 1980s prior to Boudleaux's death in 1987, much of their songwriting income came from the extensive catalog of hit songs from previous decades. As of the early 1990s it was estimated they had written over 1,500 recorded songs, versions of which have sold over 200 million copies. They were first nominated for the Country Music Hall of Fame in 1991 and inducted into it the same year.*

BUFFETT, JIMMY: *Singer, guitarist, songwriter, band leader (Coral Reefer Band). Born Mobile, Alabama, December 25, 1946.*

"Someone once asked me, 'How can you write those real sensitive songs and then write those real trashy songs?' Well, I told him, 'Sometimes I feel real sensitive and sometimes I feel real trashy!' " Those comments at a 1977 concert, typical of the offhand manner Buffett usually affected, had as much truth as comic content. Buffett always wrote songs as the mood struck him, and much of his output was in a light-hearted novelty vein, such as his 1978 single, "Cheeseburger in Paradise." Underlying his humor was a deadly serious creative bent that provided some of the best songs in the progressive country-folk-rock genre.

Although he was born and bred in the South and was later to achieve a high standing with country fans, for a long time the music Jimmy said he liked the least was country. In his youth Jimmy rebelled against many of the conventional things he saw around him. As he told an audience at a mid-1979 concert, "After I finished school I had to bust out and taste the many things that had been denied me while I was growing up. I spent eighteen years in the Catholic school systems and anyone who's been there knows what I mean." Later, when he was an established performer, he listed his occupation on a biography form as "Professional Misfit."

Jimmy could play the guitar reasonably well by the time he finished high school, but didn't yet think of music as a way of earning a living. He entered college in Mississippi to obtain a degree in journalism, but the delights of New Orleans proved too strong. Folk music was still popular in the mid-1960s, and Jimmy began performing at local folk clubs there and in other Gulf Coast locales. He sang many well-known folk or folk-flavored songs, but also began to work up original songs.

He got married and completed college in the second half of the 1960s and, now determined to stay in the music business, moved to Nashville late in the decade to further his career goals, though he had no desire to move into country & western music. Once there, he got a job as a reviewer for *Billboard* magazine, found some performing work on the side, and managed to get a recording contract from Barnaby Records. That label

* *Based in part on an interview with the Bryants by Irwin Stambler.*

issued two of his albums in the early 1970s, including *Down to Earth,* but neither of those made much of a dent in the marketplace.

After a while, he left *Billboard* and moved to Los Angeles, where he auditioned for the New Christy Minstrels. The management of that group had been interested in him since his first Barnaby release. Jimmy, more interested in drinking and toking with close friends, however, let the opportunity fall through.

From there he switched base to Key West, Florida, his favorite resting place from then on. In the late 1970s, when not on tour or in the recording studios, he was performing in local night clubs or sailing the Caribbean or Atlantic on his yacht *Euphoria II.*

However, for many months after he took up residence for the first time in Key West, he had to wage a continuing campaign to get a new record alignment. After a year of taking his demonstration material from company to company and talking to industry executives, ABC/Dunhill finally decided to take a chance on him. In mid-1973, his debut on the label, *A White Sport Coat and a Pink Crustacean,* came out. In his usual blunt way, he talked openly in one song of the supermarket raids he conducted to keep from starving: "Who's gonna steal the peanut butter/I'll get the can of sardines/Runnin' up and down the aisle of the Minimart/Stickin' food in our jeans." The album wasn't a smash hit, but it did gain enough attention for ABC to feel they might have a winner on their hands.

In 1974, Jimmy's live appearances in support of his new album, *Livin' and Dyin' in 3/4 Time,* brought growing approval from a still small but faithful group of fans. He also got the chance to write, score music, and act in the Frank Perry 1974 film *Rancho Deluxe.* Later he contributed to the 1978 film *FM* and to the preparation of the soundtrack for the Jack Nicholson vehicle *Goin' West.*

Jimmy continued to turn out new albums at a steady clip. In 1975, ABC issued *A1A* and in January 1976 released *Havana Daydreamin',* his most successful album to that point. The title song became one of his best-known numbers. In January 1977, the album that was to make him an international star, *Changes in Latitudes, Changes in Attitudes,* came out. In a few months it was well up on the charts, reaching top levels in both pop and country categories. The album was certified gold by R.I.A.A. in July and moved up to platinum by year end. During the summer of 1977, Jimmy also won a gold record for a single from the album "Margaritaville." By then he already had a growing catalogue of highly regarded songs, including such others as "Come Monday," "The Captain and the Kid," and "Door Number Three."

In March 1978, his sixth ABC LP, *Son of a Son of a Sailor,* came out and almost immediately showed up on the hit lists. In less than a month, on April 12, it was certified gold by R.I.A.A. Later in the year, a two-record live concert set, *You Had to Be There,* was issued. In mid-1979, he was represented by a new album, *Volcano,* one with a strong West Indies flavor, as befitted a collection recorded on the island of Montserrat, which was over gold-record levels by 1980. Other albums in his catalogue in the early 1980s included *Somewhere Over China* and *Coconut Telegraph.* Standing-room-only crowds greeting his 1979 and early 1980s concerts in all parts of the United States proved that Jimmy had arrived as a major artist.

Throughout the 1980s and into the 1990s, Jimmy's relaxed, easygoing style made him one of the most consistently successful live concert acts in the pop-country field. Much like the Grateful Dead's Deadhead acolytes, his legions of fans, dubbed "Parrot Heads," thronged his shows and roared approval at some of his longtime high-living party hits—though, as Jimmy emphasized in the 1990s, he had tapered off his own wild living and sought to appeal to his avid fans to avoid excesses.

Thus he modified the lyrics to his song, "Why Don't We Get Drunk," to include a reference to using condoms and getting a designated driver when occasions called for it. He told Robert Hilburn of the *Los Angeles Times* he originally wrote the song as a spoof of Conway Twitty's early 1970s offering, "Let's Go All the Way." He didn't think it would make it onto a record, but music industry associates and fans liked it so much he did include it on an album, and it became a regular part of his show.

His reason for adding the new lines was a sign of the times, he said. "It's a period of innocence and danger. By adding those lines, I'm warning against some of the dangers. It's my way of saying this is the nineties and that I don't want any of the fans to get drunk and drive, and to remind them about using a condom. By sticking the message in the song, it's a way to get the point across subtly, using some humor. I also slip in drunk-driving announcements before and after the show, and promote the ideas of [fans taking] 'tipsy taxis' to bars where they can take buses to the shows."

Year after year, new Buffett albums came out, on MCA in the 1980s (MCA bought out ABC in 1978). His albums from the 1978 gold record *You Had to Be There* to the 1990 gold-certified *Feeding Frenzy* were on that label, and his own Margaritaville Records in the 1990s was distributed by MCA. His albums usually showed up on the pop lists rather than country charts, though a good share of sales went to country enthusiasts. His 1980s offerings from 1983–1989 included *One Particular Harbour* (1983); *Riddles in the Sand* (1984); *Last Mango in Paris* and *Songs You Know By Heart* (1985, with *Songs You Know* going double platinum), *Floridays* (1986); *Hot Water* (1988); and *Off to See the Lizard* (1989). Among his charted singles during that period were "Hello Texas," "Stars Fell on Alabama," "I Don't Know (Spicoli's Theme)," and "Riddles in the Sand."

His 1990s Margaritaville releases included the platinum chart-hit *Boats, Beaches, Bars and Ballads* (1992); *Before the Beach* (1993—a reissue of the Barnaby records *Down to Earth* and *High Cumberland Jubilee*); *Fruitcakes* (1994); and, in mid-summer 1995, *Barometer Soup*. Buffett was also one of a number of performers featured on a 1993 Margaritaville compilation titled *Margaritaville Cafe Late Night*.

At the end of the 1980s, Buffett carved a new niche for himself as a best-selling author. In 1989, a collection of his short stories, *Tales from Margaritaville*, was published and spent twenty-seven weeks on the *New York Times* fiction best-seller list. In 1992, his novel *Where Is Joe Merchant?* also reached the top spot in that newspaper. Publicizing his work, Buffett became a familiar figure on many talk shows, including NBC-TV's *The Today Show*.

Unlike some artists who tire of concert work after years on the road, Jimmy seemed to thrive on it. He told a *USA Today* interviewer, even after two decades, "I don't think I ever really want to stop performing. It's a very demanding occupation, but it's also very rewarding. I think that the best feeling you get is never from drugs or liquor or traveling or anything like that. The best feeling ever is playing that stage and getting that adrenaline rush. If you can hang on to that through the trying times and the temptations and things, I think you have a real ability to survive."

BUTLER, CARL: *Singer, guitarist, songwriter. Born Knoxville, Tennessee, June 2, 1927; died Franklin, Tennessee, September 4, 1992.*

Carl Roberts Butler discovered how to cram two successful performing careers into a lifetime: add your wife to the act. For more than a decade, he had had star status as a solo performer and songwriter. Then in 1962, he was joined by his wife, Pearl, to form an act that won them the nod in a disc jockey poll as the number-one new vocal team in 1963.

Carl was born and raised in Knoxville, Tennessee, a hotbed of country music activity. He followed the *Opry* and other country & western programs eagerly as a boy and learned to play guitar before he reached high school age. In 1939, he was accomplished enough for his first show date, picking for a square dance and singing between the sets. By the time he was graduated from Stair Tech High School in the mid-1940s, he had a number of engagements at local clubs and dances to his credit.

During the next few years he appeared in shows in other parts of the Southwest. He also was featured on radio on such stations as WROL and WNOX, Knoxville, and WPTF, Raleigh, North Carolina. In 1948, he was asked to join the *Grand Ole Opry,* the start

of a long association with the show. He was featured on a number of TV shows in the 1950s, including appearances on WATE-TV and WBIR-TV in Knoxville.

In the 1950s, Carl moved ahead in the industry as both performer and songwriter. His own compositions were performed by such top artists as Roy Acuff, Carl Smith, Rosemary Clooney, Bill Monroe, and Flatt & Scruggs. He wrote some songs with Earl Scruggs, including "Building on Sand" and "Crying My Heart Out Over You." Some of Carl's other efforts included "If Teardrops Were Pennies," "My Tears Don't Show," "Crying Alone," "Grief in My Heart," "Loving Arms," "A White Rose," "I Like to Pretend," "So Close," "Hold Back the Dawn," "Guilty Conscience," and "Country Mile."

Carl's recording efforts began with a contract with Capitol in 1951. In 1953, he switched to Columbia Records. Among his recordings during the 1950s and early 1960s were "Borrowed Love," "Angel Band," "Walking in God's Sunshine," "Hallelujah," "We Shall Rise," "Only One Heart," "Through the Windows of Heaven," "Watching the Clock," "Cry You Fool, Cry," "If Teardrops Were Pennies," "Rivers of Tears," "I Know What It Means to Be Lonesome," "I Know Why I Cry," and "You Don't Steal Pennies from a Poor Man."

Close harmony had been long a private enjoyment of Carl and his wife, Pearl. In 1962, they decided to try their hand as a show business team. They soon had a top-10 hit of 1962, "Don't Let Me Cross Over." Now a hit act, they were featured on the Opry and such other network shows of the 1960s as Porter Wagoner's. They also appeared in a movie, *Second Fiddle to a Steel Guitar*. In 1964, they hit a new career high with another Carl Butler composition, "Too Late to Try Again." The song remained on the hit charts for many weeks, a good part of them in the number-one-ranked position.

Among Carl's LP total were such 1960s releases on Columbia as *Carl Butler* (1963), *Loving Arms* (1964), *Old and the New* (1960s), *Avenue of Prayer* (1967), and, on Harmony Records, *The Great Carl Butler Sings* (1966).

After the late 1960s, almost all of Carl's record releases were those made in conjunction with Pearl. Unfortunately, their 1970s and 1980s output was sharply limited, as younger artists gained the spotlight. Some of the newer performers included songs written or cowritten by Carl in their repertoire, one example being Ricky Skaggs's number-one singles hit with "Crying My Heart Out Over You" in 1982.

The Butlers still could count on the approval of concert audiences of their longtime fans into the 1980s, when their schedule included many tours with such *Opry* stars as Roy Acuff and Minnie Pearl. Pearl Butler died in 1989; Carl was found dead in their home in Franklin, Tennessee, on September 4, 1992, of an apparent heart attack.

BUTLER, PEARL: *Singer, guitarist, songwriter. Born Nashville, Tennessee, September 20, c. late 1920s; died March 1, 1988.*

A husband-and-wife team hailing from Knoxville and Nashville would seem a natural for country & western music success. The combined backgrounds helped move Mrs. Pearl Butler from the kitchen to front and center on the *Grand Ole Opry.*

Growing up in Nashville, young Pearl Dee Jones naturally had a youthful interest in country & western music. As a girl, she sang in school choruses but also enjoyed singing some of the *Grand Ole Opry* hits for her own pleasure. When she completed schooling in Nashville, she had both an excellent singing voice and a solid reputation as one of the best cooks in her class.

Later, she added to that reputation among country & western artists after her marriage to a young rising performer, Carl Butler. For a good many years she remained in the background as Carl won his spurs as a top songwriter and musician. When Carl had time away from his profession, he and Pearl often took a busman's holiday, singing together at home or at family get-togethers. In the early 1960s, after Carl completed a new song called "Don't Let Me Cross Over," they decided to record it as a duet for Carl's label, Columbia.

The song became a top-10 hit of 1962, and the new team of Carl Butler and Pearl was on its way to regular status on the *Grand Ole Opry.* Carl and Pearl recorded such other well-received songs as "Forbidden Street," "I'm Hanging Up the Phone," "Just Thought I'd Let You Know," "We'll Destroy Each Other," "Wrong Generation," "Little Mac," "Little Pedro," "Call 29," and "Same Old Me." In 1964, Carl wrote "Too Late to Try Again"; Carl and Pearl's recording became number one in the nation for several weeks in 1964.

The Butlers turned out a number of hit LPs during the mid-1960s, including *Don't Let Me Cross Over, Greatest Country and Western Hits,* and *Old and the New.* In nationwide demand for personal appearances, they performed in all fifty states between 1962 and 1967, as well as many parts of Canada and Europe. The Butlers also appeared in the movie *Second Fiddle to a Steel Guitar.*

Carl and Pearl were awarded the title of best new vocal team of 1963 in the annual disc jockey poll. In 1967, their many years of effort for the Salvation Army resulted in their receiving that organization's Meritorious Service Award.

Their record output dwindled in the 1970s, though they still had some active LPs such as the 1972 *Watch and Pray* on the Harmony label. They continued to make live performances throughout the decade and into the 1980s and, of course, continued their *Opry* appearances. Pearl's failing health brought the act to a close, culminating in her death in early 1988.

BYRD, TRACY: *Singer, guitarist, songwriter. Born Beaumont, Texas, December 18, 1966.*

When Tracy Byrd's second album, *No Ordinary Man,* came out in April 1994, he commented that the songs reflected to a great extent his family roots. " 'Lifestyles of the Not So Rich and Famous' and 'Pink Flamingos' are what I grew up in. My dad scrimped to make ends meet every month. He went to work at a plant, a blue collar worker for thirty years with DuPont. And my mom was a teacher's assistant and drove a school bus. They worked hard for a living and that's what the songs are all about."

Tracy was born in Beaumont, Texas, because although the family lived in Vidor, 15 miles away, Vidor didn't have a hospital. His parents both loved country music and, in fact, took Tracy when he was a baby to a *Grand Ole Opry* show in Nashville, a time, of course, of which he has no recollection. Most of the music he heard at home as he grew up was country style, though he naturally was aware of rock and soul. Unlike most country stars he didn't learn guitar at an early age or become deeply involved in amateur bands during his teens. But he did enjoy vocalizing. In his high school years, he recalled, "I was constantly singing. I would always sing when I was driving my truck, but I was shy about singing in front of anybody."

Among his influences were George Strait, Merle Haggard, and Bob Wills. He liked Strait, he said, because George "brought back the traditional sound to country." In fact, after finishing high school in the mid-1980s, he decided to enroll (as a business major) in the college Strait had attended, Southwest Texas University in San Marcos. However, as he told Shannon Heim for a profile in the Country Music Association's *Close Up* publication (October 1994), Merle Haggard was an even greater favorite.

"Haggard's my man. I get what the band calls 'Hag attacks,' and I've been getting them for years. I know every Haggard song that's ever been done. It's kind of a prerequisite—the band has to study up on Merle Haggard and know all the songs 'cause I might jump into any one of them [during a concert]. I've jumped out of a set before and done twelve Merle Haggard songs in a row. So that's a 'Hag attack.' Somethin' just comes over me."

After a year at Southwest Texas, Tracy transferred to Lamar University in Beaumont. During that time period, he also started to learn guitar. He still felt uptight about performing in public, but he decided to hear what he sounded like. He went to a shopping mall that contained a rudimentary recording operation and paid $7.95 to put his voice on a prerecorded track of "Your Cheatin' Heart." The saleslady who supervised the "session" liked his singing style and invited him to perform at a monthly amateur show. He recalled, "I did 'Folsom Prison Blues' and 'Weary Blues from Waiting,' an old Hank Williams song. I got a standing ovation. As soon as they stood up and started clapping I knew what I wanted to do."

The experience helped him overcome his reticence at appearing in public. He decided to drop out of college and seek a music career, something his folks weren't too happy about. "They were concerned because it wasn't a very rational decision." But he persevered, performing as a solo act to begin with and, after a while, with bands. He paid his living expenses with day jobs, first as a runner for a law firm and later as a house painter.

His first major breakthrough in the late 1980s came when he became a member of Mark Chesnutt's group, then the headline act at Beaumont's Cutter's Nightclub. When Chesnutt left to pursue a blossoming nationwide career, Byrd formed his own band and took Chesnutt's spot. Like most club performers, Mark's show mainly included covers of chart hits by country stars. As the months passed, he observed, "My voice just got stronger and stronger. When I was doing cover tunes I tried to let something inside of me, my own style, come out on those songs. I'm awful glad I did that now. I would rather try to create some kind of new style than sound like somebody else."

After ten months as the Cutter's headliner, he made his first foray to Nashville to seek a recording contract. Nothing happened and he returned to Beaumont empty-handed. But later, in the early 1990s, he tried again and this time made a showcase appearance at a local club set up by the management firm of Ritter-Carter. Showcase attendees included MCA executives Bruce Hinton and Tony Brown. After the show, they asked him to play some material for them in a private session, where he sang accompanied only by his acoustic guitar.

The result was a recording deal with MCA that led to release of his debut album, *Tracy Byrd,* in the late summer of 1992. For that collection, he said, "I wanted a Texas swing sound, which is what I do. And I wanted that sound with a little edge rather than a slick, polished sound." The first single, "That's the Thing About a Memory," was cowritten by Byrd, as was another album track, "She Loves Me, She Loves Me Not."

It took many months for Byrd to establish rapport with disc jockeys and record buyers, but in mid-1993 he had his first hit single moving up the charts. Titled "Holdin' Heaven," it debuted on *Billboard, Radio & Records,* and other charts in late spring and stayed on them for months, peaking at number one on some lists and number two in *R&R* the week of September 10, 1993. That song, like his other top hits of 1993–94, was written by others since, as Byrd told CMA's Heim, he felt he was still learning the writing trade.

"I started writing at the same time I started playin' guitar, just kinda dabblin' in stuff. I wrote some songs that were not so good and really didn't write a song I liked until I got to Nashville and started writing with

Frank Dycus who's a good friend of mine and taught me a lot about writing songs. That's something I still learn a lot about all the time. I still don't call myself a writer. I write, but I'm not like those guys who write songs for a living. I mean I sing and entertain, and thank goodness I can do that 'cause I don't think I could make a living as a writer. Not right now anyway."

Byrd ended 1993 with the single "Why Don't That Telephone Ring" moving toward *Billboard*'s Top 10. In April 1994, the album *No Ordinary Man* came out and the first single from it, "Lifestyles of the Not So Rich and Famous," moved to top *Billboard* chart positions in the summer, reaching the top 4 the end of July. (Byrd cowrote two album songs, the title track and "Redneck Roses.") The album charted in *Billboard* in mid-June, rose to number twenty-six in August, fell back a little, and then rose again, this time peaking at number twelve in September. That August he had another song moving rapidly upward in that publication, "Watermelon Crawl," which became a top-10 hit in October. (The song peaked at number five in *R&R* the week of October 10.) *No Ordinary Man* eventually rose to number three and was still in the top levels more than a year after its release. By the spring of 1995 it had passed R.I.A.A. platinum-record requirements. It was also a good spring for Byrd from a singles standpoint as his disc "The Keeper of the Stars" reached number two in *Billboard* in May and later gave him his second number one success. The song was nominated by CMA voters for 1995 Single of the Year. It didn't win the CMA trophy, but was selected as Song of the Year in Academy of Country Music voting. MCA also released a video of "Keeper of the Stars."

Meanwhile, Tracy was also working on his movie debut in a George Lucas film called *Radio Land Murders,* which starred such well-known professional actors as Corbin Bernsen, Harvey Korman, and Mary Stuart. Byrd's roll was limited, but fitting. He played a singing cowboy called Rex Rider who led a band called the Hoedown Boys and sang one song, the old Gene Autry tune, "Back in the Saddle Again."

His third album, *Love Lessons,* issued in late summer 1995, also found favor with his fans, peaking at number six in *Billboard* and becoming a recipient of a R.I.A.A. gold record award by the end of the year. He continued intensive touring in 1995, including accompanying Reba McEntire on her concert series. For 1996, Brooks & Dunn asked him to join their *Borderline* tour followed in the fall by the *TNT* tour with Tracy Lawrence. Chart makers from *Love Lessons* included the title track, "Walking to Jerusalem," "Heaven In My Woman's Eyes," and "4 to 11 in Atlanta." In September 1996, Tracy's fourth MCA album, *Big Love,* came out with the title track serving as the first single release. The disc, still on the charts in 1997, included one song by Byrd, "Tucson Too Soon," cowritten with Mark Nesler.

Tracy's achievements in music allowed him to indulge his love for fishing, including production of his own line of lures and sponsoring four Tracy Byrd Big Bass Tournaments in Beaumont, Texas; Little Rock, Arkansas; Charlotte, North Carolina; and Pigeon Forge, Tennessee. He arranged to donate $10 from each tournament entry fee and 10 cents from each lure to the Special Olympics International program for which he also served as a spokesperson.

C

CACTUS BROTHERS, THE: *Vocal and instrumental group. Paul Kirby, born Nashville, Tennessee (lead vocals, songwriter); Will Goleman, born Nashville, Tennessee (banjo, guitar); John Goleman, born Nashville, Tennessee (guitar); David Kennedy, born Nashville, Tennessee (drums); Tramp (fiddle, guitar); David Schnaufer (dulcimer); Sam Poland (lap steel guitar, dobro).*

Looking like reincarnations of 1960s San Francisco Haight-Ashbury flower children and providing a vocal and instrumental melange that melded rock, country—both traditional and avant garde—and folk, the seven-man group called the Cactus Brothers caused quite a commotion among fans and critics in the Nashville area in the early 1990s. No one knew quite what to make of them, but almost everyone agreed they put on a raucous audience-pleasing live act and certainly offered first-rate musicianship. Later in the decade, after the release of their debut album, the interest and conjecture about whether they represented one future direction for country expanded nationally and internationally.

Richard Ross of the *Los Angeles Reader* commented (October 1, 1993), "If a hard rock fan, a bluegrass aficionado, and someone who loved western swing were all living together, this is the one album that might be in all three of their collections. . . . the Cactus Brothers can trip on Hank Williams tunes, traditional hornpipes and reels, and original rockers alike. If you're ready for thrashing guitars, a fiddle and a mountain dulcimer in the same band, you're ready for the musical rollercoaster called the Cactus Brothers."

Miriam Longino wrote in the *Atlanta Journal-Constitution* that the group that "looks like Pearl Jam [of grunge-rock fame] meets the Kentucky Headhunters . . . do it with dulcimers instead of power guitars. Dig past the post-fab look and the trendy packaging and you'll find some kickin' country music. This band is tight . . . they mix rock, bluegrass and cry-in-your-beer country with sophisticated musical arrangements and humor to create an interesting sound that's a bit off the beaten radio track."

Nary a harsh word was aimed at the band by almost all other U.S. reviewers, and the paeans extended across the Atlantic to Ireland and the U.K. A writer for Ireland's *Kilmarnock Standard* commented (August 11, 1993), "If you've tagged Nashville's answer to [Irish folk rock group] the Pogues, then 'different' is definitely the term that applies. And the Cactus Brothers are just that, operating on the cutting edge between country, rock and folk itself and having a ball at the same time."

The band's core members were hardly newcomers to the Nashville scene, coming from Music City families in which their fathers were part of the country music industry. Paul Kirby's father, Dave, was one of Nashville's most esteemed session and road musicians and had placed original songs with many artists including the number-one hit by Charley Pride, "Is Anybody Going to San Antone." The father of the Goleman brothers, John Goleman, was a noted country songwriter, and some of the other bandsmen had family members involved in various facets of the country field.

Kirby and the Golemans' association went back to their grade school days when they formed a band in 1976. From early childhood they had been bathed in country music at home, but like all youngsters of the 1970s, they were influenced by the rock and soul numbers that dominated the hit lists and most radio outlets. So their band material had strong rock elements from preteen years, a flavor retained in the boys' music activities in high school.

The three friends later added another Nashville native, Dave Kennedy, on drums, and after various group lineups in the mid-1980s, they provided the nucleus of a five-piece rock group called Walk the West, which started to gain attention from local rock fans in the second half of the decade. After a while, Kirby decided to organize a spinoff from the band that could represent the country side of the band members. He told Brian Mansfield of *Request* magazine, "I had a bunch of country songs that I couldn't do with Walk the West."

He didn't intend to have the Cactus Brothers replace the rock operation, but thought of it as a creative release playing small Nashville area clubs. But audience interest in the new alignment's offerings grew so rapidly that it soon overshadowed the earlier format.

Members of the earlier band carried some notable honors into the new version. Dave Kennedy, for instance, had been named Best Rock Drummer by the music monthly published by Nashville station WRLT, *Metro*. He also was tabbed Best Drummer by the *Nashville Scene* publication. The *Scene* also had called dobro player Sam Poland, who joined the new band as lap steel-dobro performer, the city's Best Dobroist. David Schnaufer, recruited for the Cactus Brothers for his dulcimer skills, had recorded three well-regarded solo albums and also backed recordings by such country notables as the Judds, Johnny Cash, Hank Williams,

Jr., and fiddle champ Mark O'Connor. Rounding out the new seven-man lineup was Tramp, who played a number of instruments, but was best known for his fiddle playing with the Kendalls.

The band's first released product was a "plain pipe rack" video of their performance of a traditional song, "Fisher's Hornpipe." The number is an instrumental record live on a two-track system for a small independent label. The video was still impressive enough to gain inclusion on programs beamed out by The Nashville Network and Country Music TV and it soon became apparent it was also an audience favorite.

It spent many months in segments of both outlets and in late 1991 was chosen Best Independent Video by *Music Row* magazine. Later it also won a Bronze Award at Worldfest '92, the Houston International Film and Video Festival. The industry attention resulting from the video and word of mouth about their room-shaking live shows helped win them a spot in the Warner Brothers movie *Pure Country,* which featured George Strait and other country luminaries.

In their concerts, all the instruments were amplified, including the dulcimer. Kirby told Brian Mansfield that Schnaufer's customized electric instrument, dubbed the Goose, "can compete in volume with anything. The other day, our sound man told us, 'The dulcimer is the loudest thing on stage. Please turn it down.' And we were wailing."

The band's achievement in the early 1990s won a major label recording contract from Liberty. The debut album, *The Cactus Brothers,* released in the fall of 1993, contained twelve tracks, six written or cowritten by Kirby, Tramp, and Gary Scruggs. Non-Kirby-penned tracks included untempo versions of Merle Travis's "Sixteen Tons," the old Everly Brothers' number "The Price of Love," and, of course, "Fisher's Hornpipe" and another venerable instrumental, "Blackberry Blossom." In August 1995 the band's second album on Liberty, *24 hrs., 7 Days a Week,* was released. It featured some outstanding acoustic guitar contributions from another member of the Scruggs family, Randy, who also produced the collection.

Despite the group's typical blend of country and some rock elements, underneath a listener could discern similarities to traditional country string bands like those that were key parts of the *Grand Ole Opry* in its early years. Schnaufer commented, "If you take away the drums and bass, the Cactus Brothers are just like a country string band my grandfather would have felt comfortable playing music with."

CAMPBELL, GLEN: *Singer, guitarist, banjoist, actor, mandolin, and bagpipe player. Born Delight, Arkansas, April 10, 1938.*

Perhaps Glen Campbell was born lucky, for he was the seventh son of a farmer who had also been number seven in his family. In any case, Glen's talent (and perhaps luck) has won him nearly every major honor that a singer/musician could win and has brought him a long way from his hometown of Delight, Arkansas.

The world of music first opened up to Glen at the age of four when his father, sensing his interest in music, ordered him a five-dollar guitar from a Sears Roebuck catalog. By the time he was six, Glen had begun to receive regional acclaim for his guitar playing. Listening to Django Reinhart and Barney Kessel albums helped him to develop his guitar technique. Before he was fourteen, Glen dropped out of school and began playing with a western band led by his uncle, Dick Bills, in Albuquerque, New Mexico. Glen toured the Southwest with his own band for a few years before heading for California in 1960 to find work as a studio musician.

While Glen's reputation as a skilled musician was growing, he was able to interest a local label in his singing. That led to the single "Turn Around, Look at Me," which was a minor hit in 1961. The record attracted enough interest so that Capitol Records offered him a contract. The first LP issued under that agreement was called *Big Bluegrass Special.* It came out in November 1962 credited to "The Green River Boys Featuring Glen Campbell." His single "Too Late to Worry, Too Late to Cry," title song of his second LP (April 1963) made the charts, but he failed to follow up with more hits in the next few years. Still in demand as a backing musician, he supported many stars, including such top celebrities as Frank Sinatra and Elvis Presley. At one point he even stood in for Brian Wilson who was unable to travel on the Beach Boys' 1965 tour.

Meanwhile, Capitol still had faith in his singing potential, even though for a while his records didn't sell very well. In March 1964, the LP *The Astounding 12-String Guitar of Glen Campbell* was issued, followed in September 1965 by *Big Bad Rock Guitar of Glen Campbell.* Also issued were several singles, including "Universal Soldier" in 1965 which was a chart hit. Still, when his LP *Burning Bridges* came out in June 1967, he wasn't making much overall progress.

He finally achieved his big hit later in 1967 with "Gentle on My Mind," a John Hartford composition he had discovered when in Nashville. The song climbed to the top of the national charts and won Campbell Grammy Awards for Best Country and Western Performance and Best Country Vocal Performance, Male. He followed with another blockbuster hit, "By the Time I Get to Phoenix," for which he won Grammy Awards for Best Vocal Performer, Male and Best Contemporary Pop Vocal Performance, Male, bringing his total to four Grammies in 1967. In 1968, the Country Music Association named him Entertainer of the Year. He was also named Top Male Vocalist by the Academy of Country and Western Music, as well as being honored by that organization for Album of the Year and Single of the Year ("Gentle on My Mind").

In 1969, Glen won even more awards and honors than in the previous year. In addition, he was now beginning to appear on television shows and in movies. His television career began when he hosted the summer replacement for CBS-TV's *The Smothers Brothers Show.* In 1969, he won his own variety show, *The Glen Campbell Goodtime Hour,* which ran for four and a half years before he grew tired of the weekly grind and quit. The year 1969 also marked Glen's first motion picture appearance, with his boyhood idol, John Wayne, in *True Grit.* The following year he starred in the movie *Norwood.* Among his other movie credits was his 1974 appearance in *Range Homecoming,* a made-for-television movie, with Robert Culp and Barbara Anderson.

Meanwhile, Glen continued to turn out hits that tended to appeal not only to country-music fans but to a wider-based audience as well. His gentle country-rock style propelled such songs as "Galveston," "Dreams of the Everyday Housewife," "Wichita Lineman," "Manhattan Kansas," "I'll Never Pass This Way Again," "Oklahoma Sunday Morning," "Sweet Dream Baby," "It's Only Make Believe," and "Try a Little Kindness" to the top of the national music charts.

After a few years with some minor hits and no major successes, Glen again scored a smash hit in 1975 with "Rhinestone Cowboy." He followed up with more huge hits such as "Country Boy (You Got Your Feet in L.A.)," "Southern Nights," and "Sunflower." In late 1977, he had a hit with "God Must Have Blessed America" and in 1978 he scored with "Another Fine Mess" and "Can You Fool."

From the late 1960s on, Glen's name appeared many times on album charts as well as singles lists. During 1968, he was awarded gold records by the Recording Industry Association of America for the Capitol LPs *Gentle on My Mind* (issued 8/67); *By the Time I Get to Phoenix* (11/67); and *Wichita Lineman* (11/68). In 1969, he won gold records for *Hey Little One* (3/68); *Bobbie Gentry and Glen Campbell* (9/68); *That Christmas Feeling* (10/68); *Galveston* (3/69); and *Glen Campbell Live* (8/69). Other late 1960s LPs were *A New Place in the Sun* (5/68) and *True Grit* (7/69).

In 1970 he received a gold record for *Try A Little Kindness* (1/70). Also on the charts that year were *Oh Happy Day* (4/70); *Norwood* (6/70); and *The Glen Campbell Goodtime Album* (9/70). In 1971 he earned a gold record for *Glen Campbell's Greatest Hits* (2/71). Other 1971 charted albums were *The Last Time I Saw Her* (7/71) and a duet collection with Anne Murray, *Get It Together* (11/71). In late 1972 he had the LP *Glen Travis Campbell* (10/72) on the lists. His Capitol LP releases of the mid- and late-1970s included *Arkansas; I Knew Jesus (Before He Was a Star)* (5/73); *I Remember Hank Williams* (10/73); *Houston (I'm Comin' to See You)* (4/74); *Reunion* (10/74); *Ernie Sings and Glen*

Picks (5/75); *Rhinestone Cowboy* (7/75), a massive hit—like the title single, a gold record; *Bloodline* (4/76); *The Best of Glen Campbell* (10/76); *Southern Nights* (2/77) a number-one LP during 1977, bringing Glen his twelfth gold record album; *Glen Campbell Live at the Royal Festival Hall* (11/77); *Basic* (10/78); and *Highwayman* (10/79).

As of 1978, Glen had four gold singles, twelve gold albums, five platinum albums, and one double platinum album in the United States alone. He is also extremely popular in Great Britain and tours the United Kingdom regularly. In 1972 he gave a command performance for the Queen of England. He also hosted the Glen Campbell Los Angeles Open golf tournament, a major event on the PGA tour for a number of years.

Glen finished up 1979 with the single "My Prayer" on lower-chart levels. During 1980 he had duets on the charts with Rita Coolidge ("Somethin' 'Bout You Baby I Like") and Tanya Tucker ("Dream Lover," issued on MCA label). In June 1980, Capitol issued the LP *Somethin' 'Bout You Baby I Like,* his thirty-seventh for that company and the last released while he still was on the Capitol roster. In early 1981 he had his first top-10 hit single in some time as "Any Which Way You Can," title song of a Clint Eastwood movie, rose to the top-10 on the Warner/Viva label. Soon after, the Capitol single "I Don't Want to Know Your Name" was in mid-chart levels. Another duet single with Tanya Tucker (with whom his name was romantically linked), issued on Capitol, "Why Don't We Just Sleep on It Tonight," was on hit lists in the spring of 1981. In the fall, he had a single on his new record label, Mirage, "I Love My Truck," on the charts for several months.

As with most artists of today, Glen Campbell's style is difficult to categorize. Basically, he blends country, folk, and jazz into a style that is uniquely his own. He has often referred to his music as "crock," a blend of country and rock. His tenor voice is sweet, not at all gruff or angry. His relaxed, country personality and humor have also contributed to his on-stage performance and to his overall popularity.

In the 1980s, Glen continued to be a popular performer with plenty of opportunities to ply his skills in live performances or as a TV guest, but his chartmaking recordings were far and few between. In the mid-1980s, he recorded for Atlantic America and later in the decade he returned to his old label, Capitol. One of the projects he took part in during the summer of 1986 was preparation of a multistar album whose proceeds were earmarked to help in the renovation of the Statue of Liberty. He finished the decade in good style with a hit single on Capitol, "She's Gone, Gone, Gone," which rose high on both *Billboard* and *Radio & Records* charts, peaking at number five in R&R the week of December 15, 1989.

In the 1990s he was shifted to the Liberty label, which took over the country roster from sister label

Capitol. His work for Liberty included the early 1993 album *Somebody Like That*. Soon after, however, he left that label. Starting in May 1992, Glen took over as alternate host (with Louise Mandrell) at the new venue in Branson, Missouri, called The Grand Palace. The contract allowed him to have a "home base" for extensive concertizing while permitting open dates for performances elsewhere. In 1994, that gave him the chance to take part in some of the concerts in the Rhythm, Country & Blues Tour with many top stars in the country, soul, and rhythm and blues fields (though he did not perform on the album). By 1995 he had signed a new recording contract with Intersound Entertainment.

In 1995, he celebrated the 20th anniversary of the release of one of his classic hits, "Rhinestone Cowboy." He recalled for an interviewer from the CMA *Close Up* (February 1996) first hearing the song on station KNX-FM in Los Angeles in a recording by its writer, Larry Weiss. He phoned his secretary and asked her to follow up and she got a cassette of an album by Weiss on 20th Century Records called *Black and Blue Suite*. Campbell took the cassette on a tour of Australia and had it memorized by the time he got back to California. He particularly liked lines like "There's been a load of compromising on the road to my horizon."

Weiss had described the origins of the song for *American Songwriter*. "The idea for the song was a crying-out of myself. It was the spirit of a bunch of us on Broadway where I started out—Neil Diamond, Tony Orlando—we all had dreams of making it. I heard the phrase ('Rhinestone Cowboy') and thought, 'Boy, I like that title.' I put my own meaning to it and wrote the song. I'll always be a kid at heart, and 'Rhinestone Cowboy' was sort of a summation of all my childhood cowboy heroes—particularly Hopalong Cassidy."

The song, which rose to number one on *Billboard*'s pop charts the week of June 21, 1975, had sold an estimated 4 million copies worldwide as of early 1996.—A. S.

CARPENTER, MARY-CHAPIN: *Singer, guitarist, songwriter, record producer. Born Princeton, New Jersey, February 21, 1958.*

An Ivy League college graduate who grew up in the sophisticated urban environment of the American Northeast and Tokyo, Japan, whose initial musical background seemed more attuned to folk or folk rock might have appeared to be a longshot to make it in country music, much less become one of its most dominant figures of the 1990s. It seemed equally incongruous that the *Life* magazine editors who prepared the list of "The 100 Most Important People in the History of Country" for the September 1994 "Roots of Country Music" issue would include Mary-Chapin Carpenter on the list (albeit at number 99). Still, she had written and performed many songs that other, more "traditional" country artists wouldn't be afraid to be identified with

and, before her career is over, might indeed have proven a pivotal factor in shaping the field's future.

She was born into comfortable surroundings in the university town of Princeton, New Jersey, the third of four daughters born to *Life* magazine executive Chapin Carpenter and his wife, Bowie. She recalled the house was filled with music coming from records (or radio programs) spanning a range from opera to jazz, pop and show tunes, but no country. From her second grade in school on, she had started to pick out chords on an old guitar of her mother's, focusing on folk and pop material. Looking back, she said, "I remember being in the second grade and playing 'Cielito Lindo' in the school play."

In 1969, when she was ten, her father was transferred to Japan to work as publishing director for *Life*'s Asian edition. One later result was widespread interest among the Japanese public of her career achievements in the 1990s. After several years, the family moved again, ending up in Washington, D.C., in 1974, which remained its locale for some time and Mary-Chapin's home area into the 1990s.

Mary-Chapin completed her high school years at the prestigious Taft prep school in Connecticut, then enrolled in Brown University in Providence, Rhode Island. She began her freshman year there in the fall of 1976 after taking a year off for vagabond travel. She wasn't sure what her lifetime goals would be, but she continued to hone her skills as guitarist and singer. In the summer of 1977, back in Washington between semesters, she began to attend various open-mike sessions at local clubs. "One night I got my courage up and I walked up to the show host and asked if I could have a job," she said. "That's what I did every summer during my college years. I felt like I'd become part of a supportive community." Back at college, she added to her experience by performing at some of the local coffeehouses.

During those years, she began writing original songs, though she didn't include them in her act at first. Her repertoire typically included such varied stylings as songs made famous by jazz great Billie Holiday to work by avant garde country writer Townes Van Zandt. As time went by, she started to incorporate some of her own material into her sets.

After getting her B.A. from Brown in 1981, she went back to Washington, where she continued to find night jobs at local clubs (for a typical salary of $40 a night) while eventually supplementing her income with a day job as an administrative assistant at a Washington-based philanthropic organization.

It took a while for her to develop an assertive stage presence to go with her moving vocal interpretations. Gary Oelze, owner of the Birchmere Club in Alexandria, Virginia, where she became an audience favorite, told Margie Sellinger of *People* ("Mary-Chapin Carpenter Is Singing the Urbane Cowboy Blues," August

31, 1992), "She was very quiet and couldn't hardly look at an audience." Radio host Michael Demsey added, "She was so shy. She would do other people's songs. Gradually she got up enough courage to mix in a few of her own."

Slowly her self-confidence grew and she began to draw a sizable following of college students and other young music fans in the area. In 1986, she won the first of what would become a mantelpiece-sized collection of Wammie trophies from the annual Washington Area Music Awards. By then her act included accompaniment from guitarist and friend John Jennings, whom she'd met in 1982. The two began making tapes of some of her material in Jennings's basement studio. She told Jay Orr of *Request* magazine ("Home Town Girl Makes Good," August 1992), "I'd get a little money together and I'd cut a song and I'd get a little more money together and I'd cut another song. It was the ultimate labor of love. It had no commercial conscience."

The idea was to have a cassette album to sell at concerts that might also serve as a demo for record companies. Rounder Records offered her a contract, and she was on the verge of signing when her comanager Tom Carrico received another bid from Columbia Nashville. Oelze of Birchmere had extolled Carpenter's talents to Columbia executive Larry Hamby, who followed up with a call to Carrico. Mary-Chapin told Orr that Hamby was aware of the Rounder deal but wanted to hear the tape and promised a quick response. "The next afternoon Tom called me and said they wanted to sign a record deal, and I couldn't believe it."

A major label agreement promised considerably greater audience exposure than a smaller, specialty one, but Carpenter felt a little sad about it. "All my favorite records were on Rounder. That still would have been the happiest day of my life."

After signing with Columbia in 1986, Mary-Chapin began work on tracks for her debut, *Hometown Girl,* issued in 1987. Not much happened with the album, which initially sold about 20,000 copies—though later, when she began to get noticed for follow-up releases, sales picked up to the 100,000 mark. Columbia still had confidence in her, an attitude validated when her 1989 collection, *State of the Heart,* produced a series of chart-making singles starting with "How Do," whose lyrics covered things like cowboy boots, the Texas border, and Lone Star women. That was followed in 1989–90 by such successes as "Never Had It So Good," "Quittin' Time," "Something of a Dreamer," and the number-one video hit, "This Shirt. . . ." "Quittin' Time," which peaked at number five in *Radio & Records* the week of March 16, 1990, won a Grammy nomination for Best Country Vocal Performance, Female. In 1990, she gained her first major award when Academy of Country Music voters named her Top New Female Vocalist.

From the late 1980s into the 1990s, Carpenter enhanced her reputation with concert tours (typically as an opening act) that took her all over the U.S. and abroad. During 1990, besides playing clubs or arenas, she also demonstrated her talents at music festivals in the Texas hill country, Switzerland, and elsewhere while also winning attention at music industry showcases in New York, Nashville, and San Francisco. Her second album was on the charts a number of months during 1989–90, and later became a strong catalog item that appeared on the *Billboard* top-selling catalog list in 1993.

Mary-Chapin's third album, *Shooting Straight in the Dark,* issued in the fall of 1990, contained nine more originals solely penned by her and one jointly written with John Jennings, plus another track written by others. The album verified that here was indeed a superlative songwriter and performer. Soon after its release it was well inside the *Billboard* chart's upper levels, staying on the list for years and eventually passing multiplatinum levels. It spawned still more hit singles, including "You Win Again," which reached high positions on the *Billboard* list in late 1990, and the pulse-tingling Cajun-flavored song, "Down at the Twist and Shout," which rose to number two in *Billboard* the week of September 14, 1991, and became a number-one hit on almost every trade publication chart.

That song, which received widespread airplay as well as excellent country network coverage for its video, derived from an appearance with the Beausoleil Cajun band at a club in Bethesda, Maryland, since closed down. Beausoleil later worked with her on the recording. That experience, she told Orr, "was like going back to your high school cafeteria for a dance. I really can't believe, frankly, the song has become this special song. It's brought me so many special things. The thing I most treasure is my friendship with Beausoleil as a result of it, just musically being able to explore those tempos and those textures and everything about it."

That song won Carpenter her first Grammy (voted in 1991 and presented on the NARAS Awards telecast in February 1992) for Best Country Vocal Performance, Female. Other hit singles from that album included "Going Out Tonight" (number eleven in *R&R* the week of December 20, 1991) and "Right Now."

In the summer of 1992, Columbia released her fourth album, *Come On, Come On,* again mostly written or cowritten by her, which once more ranked among the best albums of the year. She gave an emotionally gripping rendition of one of that album's tracks, "I Am a Town," as part of the May 1992 CBS-TV special on the 25th Anniversary of the Country Music Hall of Fame. The album, which peaked at number six in *Billboard,* was gold before the end of 1992 and was still on the list in late summer 1994, by which time it had gone double platinum.

Its tracks included another group of hit singles, such as "I Feel Lucky," her first of several collaborations with veteran Nashville songsmith Don Schlitz, which peaked at number four in *R&R* the week of July 4, 1992. This was followed by "Not Too Much to Ask," a duet with country star Joe Diffie (number eleven in *R&R* the week of November 20, 1992); "Passionate Kisses (number four in *R&R* March 5, 1993, written by Lucinda Williams); "The Hard Way" (number nine in *R&R* June 18, 1993); and "The Bug" (written by Mark Knopfler of Dire Straits), number twelve in *R&R* the week of November 5, 1993.

Contributing support on some of the tracks were country and folk luminaries Rosanne Cash, Shawn Colvin, and the Indigo Girls. During the 1990s she often worked or toured with them as well as with other female stars like Nanci Griffith and Lucinda Williams. She told an interviewer, "We're all female, we play guitars and we all write songs, but we're all very different women." An all-women recording project she took part in prepared a collection of children's songs called *'Til Their Eyes Shine: The Lullaby Album,* issued by Columbia in the summer of 1992. Besides Carpenter and Rosanne Cash, other contributors were Dionne Warwick, Emmylou Harris, Gloria Estefan, Laura Nyro, Carole King, Deniece Williams, and Maura O'Connell.

Besides concert work and TV and radio performances (including appearances on *Austin City Limits* and *Grand Ole Opry* shows) Mary-Chapin also lent her talents to various causes such as Farm Aid and an Earth Day concert in Foxboro, Massachusetts. She commented, "It helps to feel like you're giving a little something back. It's corny, but it's the truth. It does feel like there is some sense of merging between art and belief and day-to-day life."

"I Feel Lucky" earned Mary-Chapin her second Grammy for Best Country Vocal Performance, Female, in the 1992 NARAS voting. (She won in the same category for 1993 and 1994, the 1994 win for "Shut Up and Kiss Me.") In the 1992 Country Music Association voting she was nominated for Single of the Year for "I Feel Lucky"; Song of the Year (songwriter's award) for "Down at the Twist and Shout"; and Female Vocalist of the Year. She won the last-named award, something she walked away with again in 1993. Besides that, her 1993 nominations included Album of the Year for *Come On, Come On.*

Nineteen ninety-four was another blockbuster year for Carpenter. (It also was the year she dropped the hyphen from her name.) She had three singles that made the highest levels in *Radio & Records, Billboard, The Gavin Report,* and so forth, capped off by her bestselling album to date. Her number-one placements in *R&R* began with "He Thinks He'll Keep Her" (March 19) followed by "I'll Take My Chances" (July 11), both cowritten with Don Schlitz, and "Shut Up and Kiss Me" (words and music by Carpenter) the week of No-

vember 18. Her new album, *Stones in the Road,* debuted at number one in *Billboard* the week of October 22 and stayed there four more weeks. Like several previous albums, it also made top positions on *Billboard*'s Top 200 pop chart, debuting at number ten. While the album nestled atop the country list, *Come On, Come On* was still in the top 30. By mid-January 1995, *Stones in the Road* already had been certified platinum by the R.I.A.A.

In the 1994 CMA voting, Carpenter again received multiple nominations. These were for Single of the Year ("He Thinks He'll Keep Her"); song of the year for that composition (by Carpenter and Schiltz); and Female Vocalist of the Year.

While emphasizing that much of her songs' contents didn't necessarily reflect actual events in her life, she did note some related to failed relationships. She began one West Coast concert, for instance, with a set of songs she referred to as "my recent ex-boyfriend trilogy." She told several interviewers in the mid-1990s about the tradeoff between the demands of an entertainment industry career and the possibilities of having a family of her own. It was something she sometimes agonized over as she observed her sisters' private lives with husbands and growing children.

Though Carpenter continued to make some concert and TV appearances during 1995 and 1996, she took her time about completing work on a new album. That disc, *My Place in the World,* her sixth Columbia album overall, finally reached store shelves in the fall. By the start of December it was a top-10 entry on the charts.

CARSON, FIDDLIN' JOHN: *Fiddler, singer, songwriter. Born Cobb County, Georgia, March 23, 1868(?); died Atlanta, Georgia, December 11, 1949.*

There is no doubt that John William "Fiddlin' John" Carson was an important figure in the history of country music, though the true nature of his talents and the details of his career are shrouded in the mists of history. He is credited with making the first hit record in country music, a disc recorded by Ralph Peer in 1923 when Carson was around fifty-five years old, but the quality of that release and other extant recordings by him are not good enough to determine if he was something other than an average instrumentalist.

Still, as Wayne W. Daniel wrote in *Bluegrass Unlimited,* "Whenever the history of country music in Atlanta is recounted, one name that appears over and over again is that of Fiddlin' John Carson, a man who became a prototype commercial country musician, establishing industry precedents and paving the way for the likes of Jimmie Rodgers, Roy Acuff, Johnny Cash, and a whole host of old-time and bluegrass fiddlers." (Carson was inducted into the Atlanta Country Music Hall of Fame in the 1920s.)

While Carson's birth date has been generally accepted as 1868 in Cobb County, Georgia, Gene Wiggins's biography of him, the most detailed to date (*Fiddlin' Georgia Crazy,* University of Illinois Press, 1987), notes there are three facts that cast that into dispute. One is that the marriage certificate of his parents, J. P. Carson and Mary Ann Beaty, in Cobb County, bears the date August 7, 1869 (though that certainly doesn't preclude a premarriage birth). The second is that the birthdate on his National Guard enlistment card of July 1914 gives his age as forty-one years, four months, which would predicate a birth year of 1873. Third, the year of his birth given on his tombstone is 1874. Wiggins also noted that some newspapers in the Fannin County, Georgia, region claimed that as his place of birth.

In any case, he did learn to play fiddle at a young age. Some accounts suggest he began playing as young as five years old, but the more generally accepted time is age ten, when he received a fiddle as a birthday present from his grandfather. When he was eleven, he made his first public appearance, playing at a political meeting in Copperhill, Tennessee, on March 23, 1879. (If his actual birth year was 1873, of course, he would only have been six.)

In the years that followed, John became a popular figure at many rural parties and dances, typically performing traditional fiddle tunes but sometimes including some of his own revisions or songs newly penned by him. Besides his performing work in the late 1880s, he earned some money as a railroad employee and at one time may have also served as a racehorse jockey.

He also continued to be in demand to provide musical support for political campaigns, a normal adjunct of many elections in the South in the late 1880s and right through most of the 1900s. Among his early credits was performing on speaking tours by Fiddlin' Bob Taylor, who eventually became governor of Tennessee, and Georgia politician Tom Watson. In the 1900s, he also contributed his fiddling abilities to campaigns of the Talmadge family, whose members included Georgia Governor Gene Talmadge and his son Herman, who also became governor (and later served in the U.S. Senate for many years).

By the early 1920s, Fiddlin' John was one of the best known country musicians in Georgia, but had little name recognition outside the South. When OKeh Records sent a team to Atlanta to try to expand its catalog to what had been an essentially unrepresented music form, Carson was a natural candidate for the sessions. Ralph Peer, who was part of the OKeh group, has long been quoted as calling John's vocals accompanying his fiddling as "pluperfect awful." That story is quoted in the *Life* magazine thumbnail sketch for his inclusion in the September 1994 list of "The 100 Most Important People in the History of Country."

Wiggins suggests that statement might have been taken out of context. "Peer was probably less than ravished by the live performances—'Little Old Log Cabin in the Lane,' and 'The Old Hen Cackled and the Rooster's Going to Crow'—but there is much to suggest that the technical results were what mainly bothered him. The engineers had never recorded a person who fiddled and sang into the same horn. Peer did not predict much success for John's record, but [OKeh Southeast sales representative] Polk Brockman insisted on a pressing of 500 copies for his own distribution."

With Carson's help, Brockman promoted the single and it quickly caught on, easily selling out the initial run. OKeh in New York soon ordered large-scale production and sales continued brisk in many parts of the South and elsewhere. Before long, John came to New York with his own backing band to record new material, including such songs as "The Baggage Coach Ahead," "The Orphan Child," "The Letter Edged in Black," and "My North Georgia Home." Other songs were recorded in Atlanta in the mid- and late 1920s and, increasingly, John was backed by his talented guitar-playing daughter Rosa Lee.

During those years, he also worked with many other country music pioneers including Gid Tanner and Clayton McMichen. Besides live shows, John also played on radio programs on a variety of Southern stations.

Among some of the things Wiggins discovered about Carson was his membership in the Ku Klux Klan, which might have been related to his fiddling support of politician Cliff Walker, an ardent Klansman. Wiggins commented, "John was a member of the Klan, but probably not an ardent one. Rosa Lee remembered him being a little more serious in his Klan membership than [son] Horace thought he was. John's only recorded comment on the Klan is less than worshipful: 'The night was dark and stormy/The air was full of sleet/The old man joined the Ku Klux/And Ma she lost her sheet.'"

Things in the entertaining field continued to be favorable for John through the end of the 1920s, but the onset of the Great Depression suddenly cast a pall over the recording field and also reduced chances for paid concert work. Opportunities for new record sessions dried up and, while Carson remained active as an itinerant musician, his income from music declined sharply.

From the early 1930s into the mid-1940s, some of his appearance work was in support of Gene Talmadge's races for the U.S. Senate and the governorship (followed by appearances on behalf of Gene's son Herman). His position as Talmadge's "minstrel," among other things, won him a patronage job as assistant doorkeeper for the state's House of Representatives. During those years, as had been true in the 1920s, Carson was a familiar figure at the various Fiddlers' Conventions, where he won more than a few fiddling contests. At many of the shows he was featured as Fiddlin' John Carson with "Moonshine Kate," the latter a pseudonym for daughter Rosa Lee.

In the late 1940s, John was highly regarded as an elder statesman in the Atlanta country music field. After he died of cancer in December 1949, he received a hero's funeral with the cortege escorted by members of the highway patrol and Governor Herman Talmadge on hand as an honorary pallbearer. More than a few of Carson's original songs continue to be performed by musicians around the world, including "Dixie Boll Weevil" and "The Farmer Is the Man That Feeds Them All." Some of his recordings were available in the mid-1990s as part of the Smithsonian Institution release, *Classic Country Music.*

CARTER, CARLENE: *Singer, guitarist, songwriter. Born Madison, Tennessee, September 26, c. 1955.*

Heir to the mantle of what truly could be considered country music royalty, Carlene Carter emulated many of the country stars of the post–Korean War era like Conway Twitty, Jerry Lee Lewis, and stepfather Johnny Cash by first gaining attention in the rock field before returning to her roots. Besides being a third-generation member of a country music dynasty that went back to the Original Carter Family, her life's progression involved contact with many of the prime influences on popular music from the mid-1950s on, including Elvis, Bob Dylan, Eric Clapton, Joni Mitchell, and most of the country superstars.

The granddaughter of Mother Maybelle Carter, she was born in Madison, Tennessee, to June Carter (later June Carter Cash) and country great Carl Smith. Though her parents divorced when she was two, she remained close to her father (she was named after him) as she grew up and followed her parents into the entertainment field. Later, of course, when Johnny Cash became her stepfather, that made her a stepsister of Rosanne Cash and a stepsister-in-law to Rosanne's husband, Rodney Crowell.

Long before that time, she recalled a childhood meeting with Elvis. "Mama was in New York at the same acting school as Elvis, and on Sunday afternoons he used to roll me around Central Park." She was a little over two when that occurred; she made her debut in public, she recalled, two years later. "I went on stage with my mother and sang 'Waterloo' and 'Charlie Brown.'"

She told writer Andy Wickham in 1978 she had fond memories of growing up with younger sister Rosie. "When Mama and Carl split up, Mama married Rip Nix and they had Rosie. We lived together in an old house in Madison, Tennessee, and Maybelle would come 'round to play cards. She really missed Ezra (Carter) since he passed away. He was her husband and A. P.'s brother. Things didn't last with Rip Nix. I hear he's now made millions in cement."

In the mid-1960s, her mother and Johnny Cash had begun performing together. She remembered her first meeting with Johnny, which came at her eleventh birthday party. "He bought me a pair of roller skates, so I figured he was okay."

She recalled going to country and state fairs with the Carter Family as a child, but when June began working with Johnny Cash, she told Janet Williams of the Country Music Association's *Close Up* magazine, "We didn't travel quite as much, because it wasn't her gig, so she couldn't bring her kids as easily. Up until Mom married Johnny, Rosie and I had no idea that she was well known. We were brought up with a lot of morals and values. We never had abundances of money or anything like that so it wasn't like we were spoiled in the sense that some kids get this big fat allowance. We got a dollar a week and that was a lot. We had fifteen acres, and Mama didn't have anybody to help her so Rosie and I mowed the grass. We worked real hard."

But soon after Johnny and June married (Carlene was twelve at the time), that changed. Johnny became the host of a nationally televised show, and soon all sorts of famous visitors came to their house—including Clapton, Dylan, James Taylor, the Monkees, and many others. "There were tourists lined up along the fence staring at us and we had to keep our curtains drawn. We'd go out in the car and they'd start taking pictures of us. Suddenly we couldn't mow the grass anymore."

During those years, Carlene was already building up her musical skills. She played piano and sang at five, took up guitar at eleven, and from preteen through teen years, studied classical piano. Those piano studies extended through some thirteen years. She also emulated her mother's past, in a way, by marrying and divorcing twice (the first time at age fifteen) before she was out of her teens. The marriages resulted in two children, a boy, John Jackson, and a girl, Tiffany.

Her nonclassical music interests turned away from country toward rock. When she began writing original songs at the end of her teens, though, they leaned in a country rock direction rather than toward hard rock. After completing high school, she attended Belmont College in Nashville for three years, a period when she continued to write new songs and sought to place them with publishers. It was a frustrating period, she recalled. Nashville publishers said her songs were too pop, while those in Los Angeles said they were too country. Her eventual publishing connection kept it all in the family—she signed with the House of Cash.

While in Los Angeles she met Rodney Crowell, then working as a writer and session guitarist for Emmylou Harris, who invited her to attend one of Emmylou's concerts. There she met Ed Tickner, Emmylou's manager, who soon agreed to add her to his roster and lined up a recording contract with Warner Brothers Records. She decided she wanted to record her debut material in England. "I wanted to record my first album somewhere where people didn't care where I came from." She went to London and, backed by rock star Graham Parker's band, cut the tracks in some ten days.

The debut album, *Carlene Carter,* came out in 1978 and proved to be an above-average country-flavored rock effort whose tracks included such originals as "Slow Dance" and "I Once Knew Love," the Rodney Crowell song "Never Together But Close Sometimes," and the Graham Parker rocker "Between You and Me."

Among those helping in the project was British producer-performer Nick Lowe, who became Carlene's third marriage partner in 1979 and who helped produce her second album, cut in New York, called *Two Sides to Every Woman*. That album had a much harder rock edge than her first collection. In 1980, backed by Lowe's Rockpile band, she returned to country-flavored material with the well-crafted *Musical Shapes*. By then she had achieved a reputation as a fine rock performer dubbed by some observers as the "Queen of Modern Rockabilly."

Her first releases, while not blockbusters, sold moderately well, but record buyers' response slowed down as the 1980s moved along, and a switch to another label didn't cause any sudden rebound. By the late 1980s, Carlene was starting to build a following with a more traditional country style repertoire, and she was seeking to find a creative opening in that area. She told Janet Williams, "There was always this 'thing' missing in what I was doing. I couldn't figure out what it was. I would do a record and say, 'Well, this is OK, but . . .'"

She credited producer Howie Epstein with helping bring some answers. "I met Howie when he joined Tom Petty and the Heartbreakers about nine years go. We didn't know each other real well, but we kept in contact over the years. I'd heard he was writing a lot of songs so I called him in October 1988 and asked him to write with me. We wrote 'Get Out of My Way' and made a tape. I thought, 'This is how I want to sound.' I decided to see if I could get a record deal. We were pretty sure we wanted to make a country record, but we didn't really have a foot in the door."

However, her background and contacts paid off in the long run with a new alignment with the Warner/Reprise label, which agreed to back a new album. The result was *I Fell in Love,* which reached the top 20 on the *Billboard* country chart in November 1990. It was preceded on the hit charts by the single of the title song, which reached number three in *Radio & Records* the week of September 14, 1990. Another single, "Come on Back" (written by Carlene) peaked at number eleven in *R&R* the week of November 30, 1990. She placed other singles on the charts in 1991, including "One Love" (cowritten by her, Epstein, and P. Lamex). During 1991 she received a Grammy nomination for Best Country Vocal Performance, Female, based on the *I Fell in Love* album. She also received an Academy of Country Music nomination for Best New Female Vocalist.

She was being well received on the concert circuit in the early 1990s, but 1992 turned out to be less than a banner year for her from an album sales standpoint. This inspired a shift from Warner/Reprise to Irving

Azoff's new Giant Records label, which issued her album debut (produced by Howie Epstein), *Little Love Letters*, in mid-1993. The album made the charts soon after that and remained on them until the beginning of 1994 after peaking at number thirty-five. The title song, written by her and Al Anderson, peaked at number four in *Radio & Records* the week of August 6, 1993. Another collaboration with Anderson provided her with the 1994 chart single, "Something Already Gone." During the summer of 1995, her next Giant Records album, *Little Acts of Treason,* coproduced by her and James Stroud, reached store shelves. In the fall of 1996, Giant issued a retrospective collection of her twenty-year recording career titled *Hindsight 20/20.*

CARTER, DEANA: *Singer, guitarist, pianist, songwriter, born Nashville, Tennessee, January 4, 1965.*

The old saying "blood is thicker than water" certainly seems appropriate for country music, where over the years more than a few musicians' offspring have gone on to establish successful careers of their own. It definitely applies to Deana Carter, a candidate for best new female artist of the late 1990s, who is the daughter of Fred Carter, Jr., one of the top-rated session guitarists of the post–Korean War years. (Carter, born Winnsboro, Louisiana, December 31, 1933, made major contributions to development of the "Nashville Sound;" in the mid-1960s, he played guitar on close to 90 percent of all Nashville recording sessions.)

As might be expected, Deana grew up in a household frequently visited by current or future stars of country or pop (her father's recording or concert credits included work with Conway Twitty, Willie Nelson, Roy Orbison, Waylon Jennings, Bob Dylan, Simon and Garfunkel, and Dean Martin, after whom she was named), a home where impromptu jam sessions were common. She recalled, "There was always music in our house. At family reunions, you either found a harmony part or washed dishes, so I chose the harmony part."

While attending high school in the Nashville suburb of Goodlettsville, Deana was a typical teenager. She enjoyed rock and roll as well as country and enjoyed TV (she told interviewers, "*Charlie's Angels* were my idols."). She became a member of the school's cheerleading squad and also served as class president. She had a good voice, and at seventeen, with her father's backing, decided to try for a career in music. "I went around with my dad, trying to get a record deal. I was young, and when it didn't happen for me right away, I thought I better do something else." Watching her grandmother suffer from a disabling illness gave her the idea of studying rehabilitation therapy, which became her major when she enrolled in the University of Tennessee. She didn't completely abandon music, though, she performed from time to time at clubs in the vicinity of the campus and also occasionally tried her hand at lyric writing.

After graduating in 1989, she entered the rehabilitation field for a time, working with stroke and head-injury patients. She soon decided it wasn't something she wanted to pursue as a lifetime occupation and left the field to focus on becoming an effective guitarist and songwriter. (As a youngster, she never tried to learn guitar, though her mother had arranged for piano lessons.) Despite her father's contacts, things didn't suddenly fall into place. Without any income from the music industry, she had to try to further her career while working at an assortment of jobs to help pay off the sizable loans she'd accrued to pay her college expenses. As she told David Zimmerman of *USA Today* ("True-to-life Tales Bear Fruit for Carter," December 17, 1996), at one point she held four positions at once, teaching preschool in the morning, working as a receptionist in the afternoon, waitressing at night, and "cleaning urinals and bathrooms for a couple hours after midnight."

She was determined to succeed and continued to try to hone her songwriting skills as a tool for gaining attention at various writer's nights at Nashville clubs. Her first attempts fell short of the mark, she said. "I wanted to write the kind of songs that could be taught in a poetry class. But I was trying too hard to be introspective. Then I learned to shut up and listen to what's going on in my head and my heart and not to try to force it out. I also learned to simply tell a story. Words have their own rhythm, their own melody. If you just listen it's in there. It's a matter of uncorking the bottle, realizing that you can sit down and write a crappy song, and it's okay. It's just a song. But it can get that bottleneck flowing."

One thing she was certain about, she added, was that she had to attain her goals on her own terms. As she told Bruce Feiler for a *New York Times* article ("This Impudent Ex-Cheerleader Has Something Different to Sing," Arts & Leisure section, February 9, 1997, p. 40), "Maybe it's just the will to succeed. And maybe it's dignity. I've never slept with an executive in this town, and believe me, they tried—for years."

In 1991, she managed to get an audition with the head of Liberty Records, Jimmy Bowen. He indicated he wasn't particularly impressed with her demo material, but, according to her, changed his mind after she said she thought he owed it to the Carters, in light of an event she remembered from her own childhood: Years before, apparently, Bowen had chosen to push a Dean Martin B-side recording of a song he'd written himself—to the detriment of the A-side, which Carter's father Fred had written. Feiler reported he contacted Bowen (by then retired and living in Hawaii) for confirmation, but the latter replied, "I don't remember what happened yesterday, no less five years ago." In any case, Bowen did produce what became Deana's debut album, released in 1992.

As it happened, the album was only released in Europe. Meanwhile, Bowen left and his successors couldn't make a decision on what to do about Deana's place on the label. She kept on writing new material and making demo tapes, one of which came to the attention of Willie Nelson. Nelson met with her and listened to her perform, after which he invited her to take part in 1994's Farm Aid VII concert, the show's only female soloist. Two years later, she joined Willie again on Farm Aid IX. While her record firm was trying to make up its mind on whether to keep her, she was shuttled around from label to label; after a stop at Patriot she landed at Capitol Nashville. Through it all she continued recording demos, which as of 1996 amounted to enough unreleased material for several more albums.

Capitol Nashville executives finally decided to revamp the 1992 album (retaining the title *Did I Shave My Legs for This?* after a track co-written by Deana and Rhonda Hart), dropping some songs and adding new ones, including "Strawberry Wine," a song about a teenage girl's "first taste of love" co-written by Matraca Berg and Gary Harrison. That one became the first single issued (on July 29, 1996), though the label had initially intended to start with "I've Loved Enough to Know" (co-written by Deana and Chuck Jones) for which there was already video. But when advance copies of the album were sent to radio stations, programmers and DJs favored "Strawberry Wine"—which proved a winner, climbing the charts in the fall to reach number one on November 11, 1996, displacing LeAnn Rimes' "Blue," which had been number one for twenty straight weeks. Happily, the date had a second significance for Deana, marking the first anniversary of her marriage to musician Chris DiCroce.

Aided by the strong public interest in the single, the album, issued on September 3, 1996, also soon was on its way to the top of the charts, reaching number one late in the year after passing gold record levels. By early 1997 it had gone past R.I.A.A. platinum requirements with sales of over two million copies. By the end of 1996, the second single, "We Danced Anyway" (by Matraca Berg and Randy Scruggs) was inside the *Billboard* country top 40 on its way to upper chart levels in early 1997. In the Grammy nominations for 1996, announced in January 1997, "Strawberry Wine" was cited in two categories, Best Female Country Vocal Performance and Best Country Song.

CARTER, WILF (MONTANA SLIM): *Singer, songwriter, guitarist. Born Guysboro, Nova Scotia, December 18, 1904.*

Wilf Carter was a pioneer western singer, but he was a true cowboy, no doubt about it. He has covered the rodeo circuit regularly and is in the Horsemen's Hall of Fame. He was brought up in Canadian ranch country, later shifting around from job to job, picking and singing.

After Merle Anderson hired him as a cowboy in 1924, Carter combined two professions into one. Anderson, who still entered a chuck wagon into the races at the Calgary Stampede each year into the early 1970s, was influential in encouraging Carter to entertain along the rodeo circuit.

Carter's radio experience started in Calgary (Ontario), Canada, in 1933, on CFCN. Shortly after another program for Radio Vancouver, he moved to New York for a CBS radio show. It was around this time that Bert Parks introduced him as "Montana Slim," which he adopted.

His recording career has been with Bluebird, Decca, and, in the mid-1960s, with Don Pierce's Starday label in Madison, Tennessee. His repertoire was predominantly campfire-and-round-up-flavored—plaintive ballads and yodels with overtones of Jimmie Rodgers's influence.

"I'm Hittin' the Trail" and "Swiss Moonlight Lullaby" are among the five hundred-plus songs written by Carter. In the late 1960s, Wilf was in professional semi-retirement, living in Winter Park, Florida. (As of 1996, his home base was in Arizona.) He kept his cowboy roots going with an interest in a Canadian ranching operation. A visit to New York to see Roy Horton of Peer-Southern Organization in 1967 resulted in a recording session that provided an LP, *Montana Slim-Wilf Carter*, released on Starday.

Carter was nominated in 1982 and a number of times afterward (including 1996) as one of the candidates for election to the Country Music Hall of Fame.

CARTER FAMILY, THE ORIGINAL: *Vocal and instrumental group. Alvin Pleasant "A.P." Carter, born Maces Spring, Virginia, December 15, 1891, died Maces Spring, November 7, 1960; Sara Carter, born Wise County, Virginia, July 21, 1899, died Lodi, California, January 8, 1979; Maybelle Carter, born Nickelsville, Virginia, May 10, 1909, died October 23, 1978.*

On August 1, 1927, a historic event took place in the border city of Bristol, Tennessee. In the upper story of a three-story house at 410 State Street on the Tennessee side (the state line between Virginia and Tennessee runs down the middle of the street), Ralph Peer, RCA Victor talent scout, supervised the first recordings of the soon-to-be famed Carter Family. That period was doubly important, for the first cuts of another legendary artist, Jimmie Rodgers, were also being made.

The Carter Family had come down from their home in Maces Spring, Virginia, near Clinch Mountain, in response to an advertisement in *The Bristol Herald* offering auditions to local musicians. Johnny Cash described their trip to Bristol in a booklet accompanying a commemorative album released in 1979: "With a hearty country breakfast under their belts, the four [A. P., his wife Sara, Maybelle, and her husband Ezra] loaded up into Ezra's old Hupmobile and headed for Bristol. Rains had swollen the Holsten River at a place where they were to ford it, and the Hupmobile stopped

right in the middle of the river and refused to go any further. Long dresses were hiked up over the ladies' knees, and guitars and autoharps carried on their shoulders to the dry bank, as the men pushed, struggled, and tugged until they finally got the old car moving. Up on the bank they discovered another problem; there was a flat on the right rear tire. A. P., being the flat-fixer, got out the hand patch kit and quickly repaired the flat, pumped the tire up, and, with the instruments and the ladies aboard again, they made their way on to Bristol."

When the trio came before Ralph Peer for the audition, Peer was immediately impressed with them, especially with Sara's strong, pure voice. On those first recordings, Sara sang lead, while A. P. sang the bass line, Maybelle and Sara played guitar and autoharp. The first six songs recorded that day, which were soon to make the Carter Family well known in many parts of the country, were "Bury Me Under the Weeping Willow," "Little Log Cabin by the Sea," "The Poor Orphan Child," "The Storms Are on the Ocean," "Single Girl, Married Girl," and "The Wandering Boy."

Long before this date, the Carter Family had been performing for church socials, school parties, and other local events. For A. P. and Sara, music was one of the prime pleasures they enjoyed together after their marriage on June 18, 1915.

Alvin Pleasant Delaney "Doc" Carter, or A. P., was the oldest of eight children born to Robert and Molly Bays Carter. Both of his parents came from musical backgrounds, but A. P.'s father gave up playing music when he got married because of his religious views. However, Molly Carter taught A. P. and his brothers and sisters the old ballads that had been handed down for years and years, many of which the Carter Family would later record.

When A. P. grew up, he left Virginia for Indiana, where he went to work for a railroad gang. However, after about a year, he missed his home on Clinch Mountain, and returned in 1911, selling fruit trees for a living. While he had been away from home, he had begun to write songs about his Clinch Mountain home and the life he had known there.

A. P. met Sara Dougherty on one of his many trips around the area selling fruit trees. According to family legend, she was singing "Engine One Forty-Three" and playing the autoharp when A. P. set eyes on her. Their romance blossomed and soon led to marriage.

Sara had learned to play the autoharp, a very popular instrument in those days, as a young girl and was quite skilled at it by the time she got married. A. P. played the fiddle although he was never confident of his ability. Both of them loved to sing and did so as often as they could, when A. P. was not busy working as a gardener or carpenter or farming or doing blacksmith work to supplement his income.

The third member of the group, Maybelle Addington, was added when she married A. P.'s brother Ezra in

1926. Like Sara, she had learned to play the autoharp as a child, and was well known in her hometown area of Scott County, Virginia, for her proficiency on the banjo and guitar. She had played with A. P. and Sara before her marriage to Ezra, but after their wedding she moved near Maces Spring, enabling her more time to practice with the now-complete group.

With the instrumental skill of Sara and Maybelle, the Carter Family was always in demand to perform at local events and get-togethers. Their vocal style was distinctive and innovative as well. As Johnny Cash wrote, "If you listen to the early hillbilly recordings, you find that, basically, the singers were barely singing over the instruments. The Carter style was built around the vocals and incorporated them into the instrumental background, usually made up of the basic three-chord structure. In essence, the Carter Family violated the main traditions of vocal and instrumental music, but in doing so created a whole new style and a whole new sound."

RCA apparently realized the innovative nature and potential for success of that new sound. A short time after Peer completed the first Carter cuts, RCA came back for more recordings. Those records sold well, so in May 1928 the Carter Family was asked to go to Camden, New Jersey, the recording center for the Victor Company at the time. They recorded eleven songs that May and twelve more in February 1929. Among the songs they recorded in those two sessions were some of the best-loved of Carter songs, "Wildwood Flower," "Diamonds in the Rough," and "The Foggy Mountain Top."

By the end of the 1920s, the music of the Carter Family was known from one end of the country to the other. In the 1930s, their fame continued to spread, resulting in many more record releases and personal appearances at country fairs and city auditoriums and on radio in many parts of the United States. Their popularity kept them together as a group even though increasing problems kept cropping up in the marriage of A. P. and Sara. They separated in 1933 and were finally divorced in 1939, but they continued to perform together until the early 1940s.

Among the many Carter recordings were such songs as "Keep on the Sunny Side," "Room in Heaven for Me," "Soldiers Beyond the Blue," "The Titanic," "Where the Sunset Turns," "False-Hearted Lover," "On the Rock Where Moses Stood," "The Homestead on the Farm," "On a Hill Lone and Gray," "Anchored in Love," "Meeting in the Air," "Pickin' in the Wildwood," "Worried Man Blues," "Gathering Flowers from the Hillside," "Forsaken Love," "You Are My Flower," "Western Hobo," "I Shall Not Be Moved," "Carter Blues," "Beyond the River," "The Wayworn Traveler," "Angel Band," "Dixie Darling," "Waves of the Sea," "Sunshine in the Shadows," "Bury Me Beneath the Weeping Willow," "Shall the Circle Be Unbroken," and

"My Clinch Mountain Home." From their first session in August 1927 to their last record date on October 14, 1941, the original Carters recorded more than 250 songs.

Typical Carter Family songs that became country standards were their versions of "Wabash Cannonball" and A. P. Carter's original compositions, "I'm Thinking Tonight of My Blue Eyes," "Lonesome Valley," and "Jimmy Brown the Newsboy."

In 1938, the Carters moved to Del Rio, Texas, to begin a series of broadcasts that lasted for three seasons over XERA, XEG, and XENT, Mexican border stations that broadcast 50,000 watts. Also taking part in some of the group singing by now were A. P. and Sara's children, Jeanette and Joe. In 1939, Maybelle's three daughters, Helen, June, and Anita, were added to the group. The Family stayed in Del Rio until 1941, when they moved to station WBT in Charlotte, North Carolina.

The Original Carter Family broke up in 1943, and the members went their separate ways. A. P. returned to Maces Spring, where he died in 1960. Sara moved to Angels Camp, California, with her second husband, Coy Bays, whom she had married in 1939. Maybelle formed a new act with her three daughters and moved to Richmond, Virginia, where they were featured performers on station WRVA from 1943 to 1948. Soon after this, they accepted an offer to join the *Grand Ole Opry*. In the 1950s, the girls went out in their own directions, but Maybelle remained a regular on the *Opry* for many more years and was later rejoined by daughters Helen and Anita.

The Original Carter Family was elected into the Country Music Hall of Fame in 1970, thus becoming the first group to be honored in this way. Maybelle and Sara were on hand to accept the award. Their commemorative plaque in the Hall of Fame building in Nashville, Tennessee, reads: "A. P. Carter, his wife, Sara, and his sister-in-law, Maybelle, played in one of the first commercial recording sessions at Bristol, Tennessee. For two decades they performed as an unbeatable team. Their songs became country standards, and some of A. P.'s original compositions are among the all-time greats. They are regarded by many as the epitome of country greatness and originators of a much-copied style."

Although the Carter Family ceased to exist as a group after 1943, some of their recordings always were in active record company catalogues in ensuing years. At the start of the 1980s, their available LPs included the following on RCA or its subsidiary label, Camden: *Fifty Years of Country Music, Happiest Days of All, Lonesome Pine Special, The Original and Great Carter Family, My Old Cottage Home, Smoky Mountain Ballads, Mid the Green Fields of Virginia,* and *More Golden Gems from the Original Carter Family Album.* Liberty Records offered *The Carter Family Album.* In the active Columbia catalogues in the early 1980s were *Three Generations, World's Favorite Hymns, Country's First Family,* and *Best of the Carter Family.* All Carter tracks were issued on CDs in the mid-1990s by Rounder.—A. S.

CARTER, MOTHER MAYBELLE: *Singer, autoharpist, guitarist, banjoist, songwriter. Born Nickelsville, Virginia, May 10, 1909; died October 23, 1978. Elected to Country Music Hall of Fame (as member of the Original Carter Family) in 1970.*

The artistry of the Carter Family had become a living legend in both folk and country music circles by the end of the 1930s. For nearly four more decades, until her death in 1978, the Carter sound was kept alive by an original member of the group, the redoubtable "Mother" Maybelle Carter.

Born and raised in southwestern Virginia, Maybelle Addington began to sing traditional hill-country ballads almost as soon as she could talk. She learned to play both the guitar and the autoharp before reaching her teens and won much applause from friends and relations at local sings. She was fairly accomplished on the banjo and fiddle also.

Maybelle's guitar and autoharp playing styles were unique. On the autoharp, she picked out the melody with her thumb and finger picks rather than merely strumming across the harp while barring a chord, as was generally done in those days. Her son-in-law, Johnny Cash, described her guitar-playing style as follows: "What she did was play the melody on the bass strings while maintaining a rhythm on the treble strings, fingering a partial chord. Later she developed some intricate melody runs on the bass strings. Of course, such runs were not new, but they were used differently by Maybelle; they were being used not only as a part of the lead instrument, but as fills and also for the 'bottom' of the song. Throughout it all, the strong emphasis on the bass was a must, and this was gained in part by the use of a thumb pick and two steel finger picks. Later, this style was to be imitated to the note by literally thousands of guitar players."

Before she was out of her teens, Maybelle married Ezra Carter on March 23, 1926, and set up housekeeping with him in Poor Valley, Virginia, about twenty-five miles from Bristol, Tennessee. Ezra also came from a musical family. His brother A. P. and A. P.'s wife, Sara, were particularly skilled musicians, and in the mid-1920s Maybelle joined them to perform at many local events. On August 1, 1927 (see Carter Family, the Original), A. P., Sara, and Maybelle (Ezra came along, too, but did not perform) traveled to Bristol to answer an RCA Victor ad for recording talent. The results of the first records soon made the Original Carter Family the royalty of American country music. In the years that followed, Maybelle joined A. P. and Sara in nationwide tours and many more recording sessions in such places

as Camden, New Jersey; Chicago, Illinois; New York City; Atlanta, Georgia; and Memphis, Tennessee,

In 1938, the Carter Family accepted a bid to broadcast a daily radio program on station XERA near Del Rio, Texas. Maybelle moved there with her family, which now included three daughters, Helen, June, and Anita. It was not long before all three were taking part in some of the programs, along with A. P. and Sara's children, Jeanette and Joe. The Carters stayed in Del Rio until 1941, when they all headed north again to a new show on station WBT in Charlotte, North Carolina.

The Original Carter Family broke up in 1943. A. P. and Sara had been divorced since 1939 and they now went their separate ways. Maybelle, however, formed a new Carter Family composed of herself and her daughters. Their first job together was with station WRVA in Richmond, Virginia. They broadcast a radio program there for five years, from 1943 to 1947. They then went to a station in Knoxville, Tennessee, in 1948, followed by a year in Springfield, Missouri, in 1949.

In 1950, Maybelle and the girls moved to Nashville, where they became featured stars on the *Grand Ole Opry.* Along the way they had discovered a bright young guitar player named Chet Atkins, and when they went to Nashville, he came with them. Later on in the 1950s Helen and Anita left to get married and raise their families and June pursued a career of her own as an actress and singer. Maybelle continued to star on the *Opry* until her death.

Among the songs Maybelle and her daughters recorded for Decca and Columbia Records were "Amazing Grace," "Wabash Cannonball," "Are You Afraid to Remember Me," "Wildwood Flower," "Gold Watch and Chain," "Blood That Stained the Old Rugged Cross," "Gethsemane," "How About You," and "Softly and Tenderly." They also treated *Opry* audiences to some of Maybelle's own compositions, such as "A Jilted Love," "Walk a Little Closer," and "Lonesome Homesick Blues." Their repertoire also included songs co-written by Maybelle, including "I've Got a Home in Glory," "The Kneeling Drunkard's Plea," "Don't Wait," and "A Rose-Covered Grave."

In the late 1960s and early 1970s, popular interest in country and traditional music increased. In 1967, Maybelle performed at the Country Music & Blues session of the Newport Folk Festival as well as many other concerts across the country, and she was always greeted with generous applause.

When Johnny Cash and his new wife, June Carter, became stars on their own television show at the end of the 1960s and in the early 1970s, Maybelle, Helen, and Anita got together once again and appeared on many of the weekly shows. From then on until her death in 1978, Maybelle enjoyed a period of acclaim that she well deserved as one of the artists who helped make country music what it has become today. In 1970 the Carter Family was elected into the Country Music Hall of Fame.

Maybelle was still a regular on the *Grand Ole Opry* during her last decade of life, performing with other artists and family members or exhibiting her solo vocal and instrumental talents. One of her notable recording contributions in the early 1970s was for the Nitty Gritty Dirt Band's *Will the Circle Be Unbroken.* The 1973 album, which was a chart hit, was designed as a tribute to early country music in general and the Carter Family in particular.

Starting in 1994, just about all her work as part of the Original Carter Family became available in CD as Rounder Records began releasing the initial volumes of a nine-CD set, which covered the group's entire recorded output on RCA from 1927 through 1941. The previous year, *Musician* magazine included her in its list of the 100 Greatest Guitarists of the 20th Century, placing her in the company of such performers as Jimi Hendrix, Muddy Waters, and Clarence White, to name a few. The magazine editors noted that her " 'thumb and brush' picking style (also known as the 'church lick'), where thumbpicked bass notes provide the melody while other fingers strum downward on the treble strings, was the rhythmic backbone of the Carter Family's sound and was massively influential among fledgling guitarists during the '30s, '40s and beyond."

Another album available in the mid-1990s was the German BCD collection *Sara and Maybelle Carter.*

CASH, JOHNNY: *Singer, guitarist, songwriter, band leader (Tennessee Three). Born Kingsland, Arkansas, February 26, 1932. Elected to Country Music Hall of Fame in 1980.*

When Johnny Cash reached his "Silver Anniversary" as a recording artist in 1979, he could look back on a career that had all the elements of a classic romance novel. He had reached the heights, then plunged to the depths of seeming self-destruction, from which he was saved, in effect, by a woman's love and his own inherent toughness. Almost at the gates of hell, defeated by drug addiction and despair, he rose to become one of the most respected figures in country and popular music of the post–World War II decades. After some occasional addictive backsliding in the 1980s and a tapering off of his solo recording success late in that decade and in the early 1990s, he regained his place as one of the legendary performers of his time with his superb 1994 album, *American Recordings.*

When Johnny was inducted into the Rock and Roll Hall of Fame in early 1992, he became only the second country artist (the first being Hank Williams, Sr.) to be voted into both the Country Music Hall of Fame and the rock 'n' roll pantheon. He also became the only living country artist to be elected to both of those as well as the Nashville Songwriters Association's Songwriters Hall of Fame, which welcomed him to its fold in 1977.

From the time his first recordings began to be played on radio and were available in record stores, his reputation with music fans extended far beyond the boundaries of the U.S. Achieving more than that, however, over his decades in the public eye he reflected an inner strength and strong religious faith that had an effect on millions of people the world over.

Some of the answers to the complex personality that for many years made him an erratic comet across the horizons of American music lay in the poverty and daily fight for survival of his youth. The Ray Cash family was proud, though bent by years of sharecropping, tragedy, and near tragedy. Johnny almost died of starvation in his infancy in Kingsland, Dyess County, Arkansas, a locale he called "just a wide place in the road." Life consisted of a dirt farmer's shack, five brothers and sisters, cotton patches to be hoed and weeded, and a fundamentalist bible rearing by a determined mother and a work-wearied father. Young John was hauling water for a road gang when he was ten and pulling a nine-foot cotton sack when he was twelve.

The family stayed together, but when Cash was in his early teens, another blow struck the sensitive boy. Sudden death claimed two brothers, leaving Johnny, Reba, Joann, and Tommy to work the fields with their parents. During those years Johnny already was showing signs of creative talent. He was writing songs by the time he was twelve, trying to emulate some of the country stars he sometimes heard on the radio. While attending high school he sang on radio station KLCN in Blytheville, Arkansas.

He seemed reluctant to break away from home, though. With the advent of the Korean War, Johnny enlisted in the air force and, after initial training, was assigned to Germany, where he worked as a military cryptographer. Since he found himself with a lot of time on his hands, he bought his first guitar; while learning to play it, he also wrote some new songs, including one of his future hits, "Folsom Prison Blues," inspired by the movie *Inside the Walls of Folsom Prison.* He recalled, "There wasn't much romance to the writing of 'Folsom Prison Blues.' I saw the movie, liked it and wrote the song. That's all there was to that."

After his discharge in the mid-1950s, Johnny settled in Memphis, Tennessee, where he scratched for a living as an appliance salesman and married his first wife, Vivian (they were to have a family of four girls). In his spare time, he took a radio announcing course as a gesture toward a more creative occupation. In Memphis, he met Luther Perkins, who played an amplified guitar, and bass player Marshall Grant. They got together and practiced with the ultimate objective of auditioning for Sam Phillips of Sun Records. The first material they brought to the record company was turned down as being too "country." But after Elvis Presley left for RCA, the label was more receptive to new talent. An audition with Phillips finally brought a contract, and the result of the first sessions of Johnny and the Tennessee Two was the hit single, released in June 1955, "Hey Porter," backed with "Cry, Cry, Cry." These were followed by "Folsom Prison Blues" and such top-10 hits in 1956 as "So Doggone Lonesome," "There You Go," and "I Walk the Line." All of those were Cash originals. He also made the charts with his version of the Rouse Brothers fiddle tune, "Orange Blossom Special."

Johnny by now was one of the most successful artists in Sun Records history. In 1957 he scored with such top-10 originals as "Train of Love" and "Next in Line" and a coauthored hit, "Home of the Blues." In 1958, Johnny had six top-10 hits, including two number-one ranked songs, "Guess Things Happen That Way" and "Ballad of a Teenage Queen." The other four records included songs he wrote or cowrote "You're the Nearest Thing to Heaven," "What Do I Care," "All Over Again," and "The Ways of a Woman in Love."

By now his first manager, Bob Neal, had booked Cash and the Tennessee Two into personal appearances throughout the country. (The band later became the Tennessee Three with the addition of drummer Bill Holland.) In 1958, Cash moved from Sun to the more affluent Columbia label, where his first release, his own song, "Don't Take Your Guns to Town," sold past the half-million mark and stayed in the number-one spot on both pop and country charts for many weeks. His first Columbia LP, *Johnny Cash* (issued in January 1959) sold an impressive 400,000 copies. Sun released more of his material and had another top-10 single in 1959 with "Luther Played the Boogie." Columbia hit pay dirt with "Frankie's Man Johnny" and "I Got Stripes."

The pressures of his growing success were beginning to tell on Cash, however. Adding to that was his depression when his friend Johnny Horton died in an auto accident in late 1960. Outwardly, as the 1960s began, things seemed about as bright as could be. Cash was an established national favorite. He was featured on both country & western and major network pop variety TV programs and was able to fill large concert halls in all corners of the land. As the 1960s went by, he also became a favorite with folk music audiences, starring at many major folk festivals and performing in folk music clubs around the United States, Canada, and overseas.

In his private life, however, things were far from serene. He had become increasingly dependent on amphetamines and barbiturates, going on wild binges that made some of his friends and associates despair for his future. Sometimes he failed to show up for concerts or if he did show up was in poor form or pleaded laryngitis. The strain told on his marriage, resulting in a separation from his first wife by the mid-1960s. At the same time, he could do an about face and show the world a blaze of boundless energy and a driving desire to work almost around the clock on his career.

Those spurts of energy resulted in a continued outpouring of new compositions and recordings that included some of his most notable successes. His top-10

hits of the period included "Seasons of My Heart" (1960); "In the Jailhouse Now" (1962); number-one ranked "Ring of Fire" (1963); "Bad News," "It Ain't Me Babe," "The Ballad of Ira Hayes," number-one ranked "Understand Your Man" (a Cash original) (1964); "Orange Blossom Special," "The Sons of Katie Elder" (1965); "Happy to Be With You," "The One on the Right Is on the Left" (1966); "Jackson" and "Guitar Pickin' Man" (1967). The last two were duets with June Carter, daughter of Mother Maybelle Carter of the Original Carter Family and the lady who helped change the course of Johnny's life.

June had been a member of Johnny's troupe since the early 1960s and performed with him in many memorable engagements, including the 1966 performance in Liverpool, England, that shattered the attendance record of no less a group than Liverpool's own Beatles.

June and Johnny became close and marriage seemed in the air, but June asked him to take steps to cure himself of his drug habit. Johnny agreed and, at June's urging, got together with Dr. Nat Winston, former head of the Tennessee Department for Mental Health, for an extended period of treatment. These sessions, coupled with Johnny's renewed interest in his Christian roots, succeeded. Cash no longer found it necessary to require chemical crutches to keep going, and his marriage to June in 1967 proved one of the happiest in the country music fellowship. From then on, they were almost inseparable in a family show that often featured June's sisters, Mother Maybelle, the Statler Brothers, the Tennessee Three, and a number of other excellent artists.

Johnny and June recorded such major hits in 1968 as "If I Were a Carpenter" and "Daddy Sang Bass." Johnny's TV appearances in 1967–68 won such fine response from critics and viewers that ABC gave him the chance to host his own summer replacement series in 1969. The show was hailed by sophisticated urban reviewers as well as "down-home" observers and resulted in a regular season version starting in January 1970.

The year 1969 was a halcyon one for Johnny. Not only was he "clean" of drug problems but happily married and recipient of all manner of awards. He received gold records for the LPs *Johnny Cash at Folsom Prison* and *At San Quentin* and the single "A Boy Named Sue." In the Country Music Awards, he won in every category in which he was nominated: Entertainer of the Year, Male Vocalist of the Year, Best Group (with June), Best Album *(San Quentin),* Best Single ("A Boy Named Sue").

The TV show was renewed for the 1970–71 season and continued to be very popular, though its ratings declined somewhat. It might have gone on further, but it was caught in the "prime-time squeeze" caused by new Federal Communications Commission restrictions on network programming for those hours and was cancelled.

Johnny and June continued to be favorites on the

concert circuit, both during and after their TV period. They filled major auditoriums in the United States, including shows at such places as the Los Angeles Forum and Madison Square Garden and Carnegie Hall in New York. They also performed before large crowds on several European tours and in other parts of the world as well. In November 1971, the Cashes fulfilled a longtime ambition by going to Israel to work on a film about Christianity and modern-day life in the Holy Land. Called *Gospel Road,* it originally was distributed by 20th Century Fox but later was acquired by Reverend Billy Graham's World Wide Pictures, of Burbank, California.

That was not the only movie credit of Johnny's career. He costarred with Kirk Douglas in *A Gunfight* for Paramount Pictures, among others. He also had a number of TV acting credits, including a role in *Columbo* opposite Peter Falk in March 1974 and in the 1978 CBS-TV movie (also featuring June) *Thaddeus Rose and Eddie.* He hosted the mid-1970s ABC-TV special on railroad history, *Ridin' the Rails,* and in 1976, filmed his first television Christmas special, a show that became an annual event the rest of the decade.

Johnny continued to turn out a steady stream of singles and albums over the decade from 1969 through 1979, many of which made top country (and sometimes pop) chart levels. His singles included the Shel Silverstein novelty song "A Boy Named Sue" in 1969, "See Ruby Fall," backed with "Blistered" (1969); "What Is Truth," "Sunday Morning Comin' Down," "Flesh and Blood" (1970); "Man in Black," "Singin' Vietnam Talking Blues," "Papa Was a Good Man," "A Thing Called Love" (1971); "Kate," "If I Had a Hammer" (with June); "Oney," "Any Old Wind That Blows," "The Loving Gift" (with June) (1972); "Children," "Praise the Lord and Pass the Soup," "Allegheny" (with June) (1973); "Orleans Parish Prison," "Ragged Old Flag," "The Junkie and the Juicehead (Minus Me)," "Father and Daughter" (with Rosie Nix), "The Lady Came from Baltimore" (1974); "One Piece at a Time" (1976); "After the Ball" (1977); "I Would Like to See You Again," "It'll Be Her" (1978); "There Ain't No Good Chain Gang" (a number-one hit with Waylon Jennings), "I Will Rock & Roll with You" and "Ghost Riders in the Sky" (1979).

During his decades with Columbia, Johnny recorded dozens of albums, both secular and spiritual. Among his releases were *Ride This Train* (9/60), *There Was a Song!* (12/60), *Johnny Cash Sound* (8/62), *Blood, Sweat & Tears* (2/63), *Ring of Fire* (8/63), *I Walk the Line* (7/64), *Bitter Tears* (12/64), *Orange Blossom Special* (4/65), *True West* (9/65), *Mean as Hell* (3/66), *Everybody Loves a Nut* (6/66), *Happiness Is You* (11/66), *Carryin' On* (9/67), *Greatest Hits, Volume 1* (9/67), *At Folsom Prison* ('68), *At San Quentin* (8/69), *Johnny Cash* (Harmony, 9/69), *Hello, I'm Johnny Cash* (6/70), *World of Johnny Cash* (two LPs, 7/70) *Jackson*

(with June Carter, 8/70), *Walls of a Prison* (11/70), *Johnny Cash Show* (1/71), *Man in Black* (8/71), *Greatest Hits, Volume 2* (two LPs, 12/71), *Thing Called Love* (6/73), *Give My Love to Rose* (with June, 7/72), *America* (9/72), *Any Old Wind That Blows* (1973), *Ragged Old Flag* (mid-1970s), *The Junkie and the Juicehead (Minus Me)* (mid-1970s), *I Would Like to See You Again* (4/78), *Gone Girl* (late 1978), and *Silver* (1979). His other Columbia albums included *Five Feet High and Rising, Johnny Cash's Children's Album, Johnny Cash Sings Precious Memories, Ballads of American Indians, Johnny Cash and His Woman, Sunday Mornin' Comin' Down, A Thing Called Love, Understand Your Man, Look at Them Beans, Strawberry Cake, One Piece at a Time, Last Gunfighter Ballad, The Rambler.*

During the late 1960s and in the 1970s, Sun Records also issued LPs of Johnny's earlier work on that label. Among these were *Get Rhythm, Living Legend, Johnny Cash—the Man, His World, His Music, Original Golden Hits, Volumes 1 and 2, Rough-Cut King of Country Music, Show Time, with the Tennessee Two, Singing Storyteller, Story Songs of Trains and Rivers,* and *Sunday Down South* (with Jerry Lee Lewis). Harmony Records also provided such albums as *Johnny Cash* (9/69) and *Johnny Cash Songbook* (10/72).

Cash recorded many religious albums over the years. Among these were *Hymns* (5/59). *Hymns from the Heart* (6/62), *Christmas, The Christmas Spirit, The Gospel Road* (1973), *The Holy Land and The Holy Road.* In 1979, he dedicated his two-LP release *A Believer Sings the Truth* (issued on Cachet Records) to his mother, Mrs. Ray Cash, "who inspired me at the age of seventeen when she said, 'God's got his hand on you, son. Keep on singing.'"

His singles continued to show up regularly on the charts in the early 1980s. He began 1980 with another Waylon Jennings duet, "I Wish I Was Crazy Again," in high-chart positions. Other charted releases that year were "Bull Rider," "Song of the Patriot," and "Cold, Lonesome Morning." His 1981 charted singles included "Without Love" and "The Baron."

Although he was a firm believer, Johnny wasn't obtrusive about his religious feelings, respecting the beliefs of others. He told writer Patrick Carr in 1978, "I don't impose myself on anybody in any way, including religion. When you're imposing, you're offending, I feel. Although I am evangelical and I'll give the message to anyone that wants to hear it, or anybody that is willing to listen. But if they let me know they don't want to hear it . . . [if] I think they don't want to hear it, then I will not bring it up."

His approach was not necessarily that of formal religion. He told Carr that while "the churches are full . . . the slums and the ghettos are still full, and for the most part, the church and the needy haven't gotten together yet. And until more people in the church realize the real needs of the people, and go out rather than going in . . .

I mean, to go into church is great, but to go out and put it all into action, that's where it's all at. And I haven't seen a lot of action."

Cash himself followed that approach whenever he could. Early in his career, he established a practice of singing before prison groups, and going into the 1980s, he still made ten to twelve such appearances a year. He also contributed his services to various charitable services over the years.

(Cash outlined his philosophy of life in his autobiography, *Man in Black,* published by Zondervan in 1975 and still in print in 1995. By then it had sold over 1.5 million copies worldwide.)

Columbia album releases of Cash's material in the early 1980s included *Rockabilly Blues* and *Classic Christmas* in 1980; *The Baron* (whose title track provided a hit video) and *Encore* in 1981; *The Adventures of Johnny Cash* and *The Big Hits* in 1982; and *Johnny 99* in 1983. The last named included Cash's versions of two Bruce Springsteen compositions, the title track and "Highway Patrol." In 1982, Time-Life Records issued a three-disc set titled *Johnny Cash,* which included the previously unissued CBS number "The Frozen Logger." A&M Records also issued the album *The Legend of Jessee James* in 1980 in which Johnny took the part of Frank James on several songs. Later he played that role with Kris Kristofferson portraying Jesse James on a made-for-TV movie. In addition to all those projects, Cash also was a guest artist on albums recorded by other country stars, such as Emmylou Harris's *Roses in the Snow* on Warner Bros., Marty Stuart's *Busy Bee Cafe* on Sugar Hill Records, and *Bill Monroe's Friends* on MCA.

In 1984, Charly Records in Europe issued a five-record set called *The Sun Years* that included Cash's original Sun releases along with some previously unissued songs. Several albums released in 1984 included guest work by Johnny, including Earl Scruggs's *Super Jammin'* and Ray Charles's *Friendship,* but there were no new albums by Cash himself. One reason was his continued battles with drugs that resulted in a 1984 stay at the Betty Ford Center in Rancho Mirage, California. He told reporters he had been fighting problems with amphetamines, barbiturates, and painkillers for years and he knew he had to take action to try to get rid of his dependency.

The cure seemed to take as Johnny quickly bounced back to record one of the highlight albums of 1985, *The Highwayman,* with Waylon Jennings, Kris Kristofferson, and Willie Nelson. He also joined with Jerry Lee Lewis, Roy Orbison, and Carl Perkins in recalling their pivotal Sun Records recording sessions for the *Class of '55* album issued on the Mercury/Polygram label in 1986. (That album won a Grammy in the 1986 Awards as the Best Spoken Word or Non-Musical Recording.) Some of Cash's original Sun material was included in two other 1986 releases, the European Bear Family

eleven-record box set, *The Sun Years,* and Rhino Records' *The Sun Story.* During 1986, Cash also recorded his final collection for Columbia, a joint effort with Waylon Jennings called *Heroes.* The album concluded a label relationship going back almost three decades, whose highlights were incorporated in the 1987 CBS two-disc retrospective, *Johnny Cash-Columbia Records 1958–1986.* Rhino Records in 1987 also issued *The Vintage Years, 1955–1963,* which incorporated previously unreleased tracks from Cash's years with both Sun and Columbia.

During 1987, Johnny signed with Mercury/Polygram, and his label debut, *Johnny Cash Is Coming to Town,* came out that April. The record company produced two videos from the album, "Six Tons" and "Let Him Roll." He also provided some backing vocals for the Carter Family collection *Wildwood Flower,* issued on the House of Cash label. In 1988, Johnny had two more albums on Mercury/Polygram, *Classic Cash-Hall of Fame Series* and *Water from the Wells of Home.* For the first of those, Cash rerecorded some of his classic songs from Sun and CBS. The original goal was to issue the disc in Europe only, but later it was released in the U.S. to coincide with a Country Music Hall of Fame exhibit dealing with Cash's career. In the other album, duet partners for Cash included Paul and Linda McCartney and his son, John Carter Cash. As the year came to a close, though, there were new worries for Johnny's family and friends as heart problems developed that required double-bypass surgery in December of 1988. But he seemed to recover in good fashion and was back working on new projects in early 1989.

Johnny's 1989 highlights included his contributions to the hit Nitty Gritty Dirt Band album *Will the Circle Be Unbroken, Volume 2* and, for the Thomas Nelson Organization's *Johnny Cash—The Spoken Word New Testament,* his reading of the newly revised King James version presented on fourteen cassettes. Late in the year, somber tones returned as he entered the Cumberland Heights, Tennessee, Alcohol and Drug Treatment Center for a two-week stay. It was nothing to worry about, his management said, but rather a preventive measure. During his heart-bypass incident, his doctors had given him strong painkilling medicine and later recommended he stay briefly at the treatment center to avoid any addictive relapse.

Johnny started his fifth decade as a performer by getting together with his Highwaymen friends to record *Highwayman 2* on Columbia. There had been no concert tour support for the 1985 album, but this time the four superstars combined their talents for intensive tour stages at home and abroad, still being pursued in 1992. The album, like its predecessor, was a best-seller, reaching multiplatinum sales levels. Besides the group effort, Johnny also was represented by a new Mercury/Polygram release in 1990, *Boom-Chicka-Boom.*

Though the Rock and Roll Hall of Fame had been

organized in 1985 and Cash had been regularly nominated, he hadn't gotten past that stage at the beginning of the 1990s. There was no doubt he had rock credentials, but some voters were a little hesitant to give someone so closely identified with country the rock OK. This finally changed in 1991. Cash could understand the situation. He told Robert Hilburn of the *Los Angeles Times* ("Johnny Cash Looks Back with a Smile," Calendar section, February 2, 1992), "When I kept getting nominated all those years, I thought, 'That's great, but it'll never happen to me.' I felt there are so many who deserve to be in the Rock and Roll Hall of Fame before I do.

"So when I got voted in this year, I figured there's got to be some people who resent me being here, but that's not the way it turned out. I got the biggest kick out of [the onstage jam session] when Keith Richards [of the Rolling Stones] saw that I was watching Fogerty to get the keys we were supposed to be playing in. Keith leaned over and said, 'Thank God you're watching him, because I sure don't know what the hell I'm doing either.' "

Later he remembered hearing someone singing "Loading Coal," "probably one of the most obscure songs I've ever recorded. I wondered who in the world could be singing that song and when I looked around I saw Keith and he had this big smile on his face. So I turned around and we sang the tune together. That's when I guess I knew everything was going to be OK."

For all of his honors and widespread respect from the music fraternity, it had been a long time since any of Cash's singles or albums had reached high chart positions. Of course, he remained a superstar with country fans in all parts of the world and he could count on good crowds if he went on tour, but many wondered if his peak creative days lay in the past. One person who believed Cash was as great a talent as ever was Rick Rubin, the young president of American Recordings. He had an excellent track record as a music industry executive, but in areas like rap and hard rock, so a few eyebrows were raised at the idea of his working with Cash.

But Rubin persevered and on June 1, 1993, it was announced that Johnny had left Mercury/Polygram to sign with a new label. (Polygram International, though, handles distribution of Rubin's company's products in all markets other than North America.) Cash was enthusiastic: "I'll be expanding my scope of activity while experiencing the excitement of today's contemporary music. I look forward to exploring the kind of artistic freedom, creativity and open-mindedness that I knew with the Memphis rockabilly sound."

(In truth, Cash had always shown great flexibility as a performer. The same year he signed with American Records he had an impressive input to the U2 hit rock album *Zooropa,* performing the lead vocals on a track called "The Wanderer," written for him by U2 lead singer Bono. The latter called Johnny's work "One of the best things we've ever recorded, and I'm not even on it.")

The decision was made by Rubin and Cash to prepare the new collection using only Johnny's vocals and his guitar accompaniment. To Robert Hilburn's queries about when Johnny first had the idea to do such a project, he replied something like thirty years earlier. "I always wanted to do an album like this. I even had a title for it, *Johnny Cash Alone.* I used to talk to Marty Robbins about it because Marty used to close the *Grand Ole Opry* by doing a song on his own, and it was my favorite part of the show. I just never got around to doing it."

Actually, he added, from time to time he had brought up the idea with other record companies and producers "but there was never an interest in doing it. We'd start out doing something simple, but they always thought it would be better—which means more commercial—if we had other instruments on there too, so I would go along."

When the album, *American Recordings,* came out in the spring of 1994 it was indeed a revelation, one of the best collections Cash had done in years and one of the most satisfying musical projects of the mid-1990s. It peaked at number twenty-three on the *Billboard* chart and stayed on the list for most of the year. Still, it suffered from a dearth of radio exposure of the type that would hardly have greeted Johnny's releases in his career heyday.

The new album's very warm reception from music critics the world over did seem to invigorate Cash's live act. (*Rolling Stone* magazine in a five-star review called it "a crowning achievement . . . at once monumental and viscerally intimate . . . unquestionably one of his best albums" and other major publications and newspapers echoed that evaluation.) Starting with a show at the Los Angeles Pantages theater on January 7, 1995, Johnny inaugurated a new series of acoustic concerts. Joining him was the enigmatic new pop performer named Beck; Cash's own four-piece backing band included his son on rhythm guitar while June Carter joined him on several duets.

American Recordings was Cash's 129th album, some 44 of which were still in print in the mid-1990s. By 1995, Cash alone or with June had sold 50 million records. As of the mid-1990s, he had recorded over 1,500 songs and had placed 48 singles on the *Billboard* singles charts, which the magazine noted "was about the same as the Rolling Stones and the Beach Boys." As John Lomax III pointed out as well, Cash was the youngest person ever chosen (as of 1995) to the Country Music Hall of Fame.

By the mid-1990s, Cash realized how fortunate he was to have survived the pressures of stardom, pressures that had brought drugs into his life for so long a time. He told Robert Hilburn, "In the early years, it was like I felt guilty about [stardom]. I had come from this real poor background and I didn't feel like I deserved all this money and attention. I kept thinking, 'I'm not what they think I am. I don't have all the answers. I'm not *magic.*'

"But then you grow with it, and you learn that it really doesn't matter what other people think of you. You're just one human being, and you're doing the best you can. But it's not easy. It almost destroyed me. There but for the grace of God . . . you know the line."

In the fall of 1996, Johnny's second album for American Recordings, *Unchained,* was introduced and again proved a unique, somewhat unorthodox (for Cash) collection. It was country, but with some unique rock flavoring reflected in musical arrangements and choice of material. Supporting him was Tom Petty and members of Petty's band, the Heartbreakers. In his vocals there were elements of the old Sun Sound and some gospel intonations and the disc's first two tracks were "Rowboat," written by Beck, and the Soundgarden tune, "Rusty Cage."

During the first week of December 1996, Cash was one of the recipients of the 19th Annual Kennedy Center Honors. Highlights of the weekend long event in Washington, D.C., included a series of dinners, brunches, and a gala on December 8 at the John F. Kennedy Center for the Performing Arts, preceded by a White House reception. At the reception, President Bill Clinton said of Cash, "[he] has made country music not just for our country but for the entire world." Kris Kristofferson, one of the many celebrities in attendance, commented, "Johnny Cash had a pretty wild reputation for a while. For him to get the respect he deserves has been very gratifying to me as a songwriter."

CASH, ROSANNE: *Singer, songwriter, actress. Born Memphis, Tennessee, May 24, 1955.*

If you want to break into the entertainment field, it helps to be the daughter of a superstar like Johnny Cash. That alone won't guarantee public favor, but Rosanne Cash proved by the early 1980s she had the ability to become a success in her own right.

A child of Johnny Cash's first marriage, she was born in Memphis, Tennessee, but moved to California in 1959 when Johnny settled the family near Ventura. In the early 1960s her parents separated, but her father kept in touch with the children. Rosanne attended grade and high school in Southern California; after getting her high school diploma, she joined her father's concert troupe. During her three years with the Johnny Cash show, she started as an assistant in the wardrobe department and later was promoted to backup singer and sometime soloist.

Wanting to figure out her own career goals, she went to England in 1976 and spent half a year in London before returning to the United States to enroll in drama classes at Vanderbilt University in Nashville, Tennessee. After a year there, she went back to the Los Angeles area to enroll in the famous Lee Strasberg Theatre Institute. She was still studying acting there when a 1978 demo tape she had made in Nashville (produced by Rodney Crowell) caught the attention of European-based Ariola Records. The company paid her way to Munich, Germany, to record an album slated only for European release.

That work, in turn, sparked interest in her by her father's record firm, Columbia. She signed a contract with Columbia in 1979. Assigned to produce the new LP was Rodney Crowell, whom she had married in early 1979. Titled *Right or Wrong,* that debut collection came out during 1980 and won both considerable favorable critical comment and audience interest. (Backing her on the album was a band called Cherry Bombs, whose members included Rodney Crowell, Emory Gordy, Frank Reckard, Hank Devito, John Ware and Tony Brown.) It spawned the 1980 hit singles "Couldn't Do Nothin' Right" and "Take Me, Take Me."

After that, Rosanne took some time off to have a baby before starting work on a second album the latter part of 1980. The new LP, *Seven Year Ache,* came out in February 1981. The title song was an original composition by Rosanne, as was another track, "Blue Moon with Heartache." The title song was issued as a single and moved to well within the top-20 by April. In the fall, another track from the album, Leroy Preston's "My Baby Thinks She's a Train," rose to number one on country lists. As she told interviewer Chet Filippo, it was a song almost left out of the sessions. "At first I didn't think I could sing that because of the octave changes. But I love it. Me and Rosemary [Butler] and Emmylou [Harris] did the harmonies like the Andrews Sisters going rockabilly."

Seven Year Ache's commercial success was followed by a disappointing (from a sales standpoint) album, *Somewhere in the Stars,* a rare miss as a producer for Rodney Crowell. Perhaps contributing to the setback were Rosanne's behind-the-scenes struggle to overcome drug addiction. It was a problem on the verge of shattering her marriage when she checked into the Ridge View Institute in Atlanta, Georgia, in January 1984 to try to shake a cocaine habit that had caused touchy emotions between the Crowells for much of the previous year.

Of her decision to go to Ridge View, she told Barbara Pepe ("Cash Regains Her Balance," *Los Angeles Times,* Calendar section, September 8, 1985), "I'd gotten to a point where I wanted to stop using drugs and found that I couldn't do it by myself. Though I thought it was degrading to ask for help, eventually I did. It changed my life completely."

After completing the treatment, Rosanne went back into the studio to record the album *Rhythm & Romance,* whose tracks included many lines she derived from her marital and substance abuse struggles. The collection seemed to restore her luster with fans and radio disc jockeys and provided in its contents the self-penned chart single, "I Don't Know Why You Don't Want Me," which earned a Grammy Award for Best Country Vocal Performance, Female.

The second half of the 1980s proved a rewarding time for Rosanne from a recording standpoint, providing her with a string of number-one hits produced for her by Rodney. They included "He Could Never Be You," "Hold On," "The Way We Make a Broken Heart," "Tennessee Flat Top Box" (a cover of an old Johnny Cash hit), "Runaway Train," "If You Change Your Mind," and "I Don't Want to Spoil the Party." Four of those came from her excellent 1987 hit album, *King's Record Shop.* Her 1980s output also included other singles that made top-10 ranks, such as "Ain't No Money," which peaked at number four, and a duet with Bobby Bare, "No Memories Hangin' Round," which reached number eight.

She began the 1990s with the album *Interiors* (accompanied by a new video, "Interiors Live") that was much darker in tone than the previous album and, indeed, most of her previous output. The songs involved a lot more soul-searching and bitter sounding comments on life and love. She told Chris Willman of the *Los Angeles Times* ("Interior Dialogue," Calendar section, March 31, 1991), "I don't know that I could ever make a record like *King's Record Shop* again. It's kind of, I don't know, innocent. No, I don't know that I could really make a really balanced record again."

The album did spend a number of months on the charts, moving for a time within *Billboard*'s Top 25, but sold only moderately. It did give her some chart singles, though none came close to top levels, such as "What We Really Want." The album's contents did show that Rosanne seemed to be making important creative strides even if the country establishment wasn't in her corner this time. She told Willman, "Country radio has resisted it, really. I guess it's not what they want to hear. . . . I really don't care, to tell you the truth. I knew the risk I was taking when I did it, and I was very comfortable taking that step." One group that approved her effort was the staff of the *Village Voice,* which voted the album one of the year's ten best.

Some people thought some of the lyrics indicated rumors of a final breakup with Rodney Crowell were true. She denied that during her national tour in support of the album, but in 1991 she and Rodney announced they had agreed on a divorce. That situation did inspire some career changes. Her 1993 album, *The Wheel,* like *Interiors,* indicated a move away from a solely country music focus at a time when she changed her physical surroundings, moving her family to New York's Greenwich Village.

She also headed in new creative directions, starting to write a series of short stories that resulted in the 1996 book, *Bodies of Water,* which the *Publishers Weekly* critic called an "impressive collection." She also won praise from the reviewing community for her new album, issued in early 1996, *10 Song Demo,* whose contents included such thoughtful tracks as "Bells and Roses" and "The Summer I Read Colette." About her writing efforts, she told Dana Andrew Jennings for an article in the *New York Times,* "I love writing short stories. I love the rhythm in them. You're not limited by three minutes and a rhyme scheme."

Asked by Richard Cromelin of the *Los Angeles Times* ("Finding Freedom Through Failure," July 16, 1996) whether she still considered herself a country artist, she replied, "It depends on which definition you're going by. If you're going by what's on radio, no, I'm not part of that. If you're going by something that's rooted in the past and something I wove into a hybrid kind of mix, then yeah, of course."

Queried about the impact of her father's legacy on her life, she said, "Probably not the role that people would think. People assume that he had some great influence on me becoming a singer. I don't see that so much as I see learning my respect for the English language and my love of literature from him. And also how he manages group energy, when he relates to an audience. What role he puts himself in, how timeless he is when he does that. Just seeing his back, his profile in the light, there's this kind of solitude and timelessness about him that's so profoundly moving to me. It's like he could be a medieval minstrel."

CHARLES, RAY: *Singer, pianist, songwriter, band leader, record-company executive. Born Albany, Georgia, September 23, 1930.*

"Soul is a way of life," Ray Charles once told a reporter, "but it is always the hard way." Ray should know, for he had a long, uphill fight to develop his talent and overcome the hindrances of racial prejudice and blindness. Despite those obstacles, he persevered and went on to become an acknowledged superstar, as gifted in capturing the essence of country & western songs as such other genres as R&B/soul, pop, rock, and jazz. And he also managed to remain singularly free from the bitterness and self-pity that might have accrued under the circumstances.

In general, Ray avoided social commentary about racial matters because, he once said: "My audiences have spent their hard-earned money to get a few minutes' entertainment. Everyone can see I'm black, so I guess I don't have to tell anyone about it."

But he didn't completely avoid the issue either. He took part in civil rights protests of the 1960s and recorded some pro–civil rights material, such as the 1980s LP *A Message from the People.* As he told Leonard Feather at the time, such a collection shouldn't have surprised anyone. "I was recording protest songs when it wasn't a popular thing to do. Back around 1961 I had one called 'Danger Zone' and there was another one called 'You're in for a Big Surprise.' Some of the words were: 'I call you mister, I shine your shoes/You go away laughin' while I sing the blues/You think I'm funny and you're so wise/But baby, you're in for a big surprise.' Now that was years before the black pride and black is beautiful songs came along, but it had the same sort of message."

He also recalled how his initial foray into country & western raised a few eyebrows. "But that first country & western album didn't indicate a change in direction," Hillburn noted, "any more than his new album *A Message from the People* does. These are all simply additional directions." Such efforts were significant not just for Ray, but for other artists. His success in country music, for instance, was a breakthrough of sorts against bigotry that made the path of the great black country singer Charley Pride a little easier later on.

Color, of course, was a strange concept for Ray to grasp, for his world was one of sound after the onset of blindness. Born in Albany, Georgia, Ray Charles Robinson lost his sight at age six from what was later conjectured to have been glaucoma. As a child he moved with his family to Greenville, Florida. His father, a handyman, died when Ray was ten. On a neighbor's piano, he picked out tunes, becoming aware of boogie-woogie and other pop styles he would later prefer to the classical piano he was taught at St. Augustine's School for the Deaf and Blind in Orlando. At fifteen, he became an orphan. Leaving school, he soon found work with a country & western band in Jacksonville. In his late teens, he wanted to try new musical directions and asked a friend to look at a map and tell him the farthest point away from Florida in the U.S. This led to his moving to Seattle, Washington, where he played piano at the Rockin' Chair club. Before long, Ray began seeking a record deal and got the chance to record the song "Confession Blues" for Los Angeles–based Swingtime Records. Unfortunately, the disc was made during a musician's strike and Ray was penalized by the union for strikebreaking. Other musicians had gotten around the ban by using assumed names, but the still-naive Charles had used his own.

Eventually, Ray moved his home base to Los Angeles and signed with Atlantic Records. (According to David Ritz, who helped write Ray's autobiography *Brother Ray*, Charles made his first recording when he was seventeen and already had recorded over forty singles by the time he signed with Atlantic. Ray went on to record thirty-four albums with Atlantic, twenty-four with ABC, three with Tangerine and four with Crossover before joining the Columbia roster in 1983, according to Ritz's data.) He achieved his first R&B singles hit, "It Should've Been Me," on Atlantic in 1954, and his first national chart hit, "I Got a Woman," the following year. From then on, Ray was rarely out of the spotlight as a concert artist, TV performer, and recording artist. His name was constantly on the R&B

and pop charts throughout the 1950s with such singles as "Blackjack," "Come Back," "Fool for You," "Greenbacks," "This Little Girl of Mine," "Drown in My Own Tears," "Hallelujah I Love Her So," "Lonely Avenue," "Mary Ann," "What Would I Do Without You," "Right Time," and "What'd I Say," all on Atlantic. Atlantic released many LPs of Ray's material during those years and continued to come out with albums of 1950s recordings in later decades. Among those still in print in the early 1980s were *The Great Ray Charles* (1957), *Soul Brother* (with Milt Jackson) (1959), *Genius of Ray Charles* (1960), *The Greatest Ray Charles* (1961), *Soul Meeting* (with Milt Jackson) (1962), *The Best of Ray Charles* (1971), and *Ray Charles Live* (1973). A *Twenty-fifth Anniversary in Show Business Salute to Ray Charles* (1973) was available as a Japanese import.

In 1960, Ray moved from Atlantic to ABC-Paramount and promptly had a hit single, "Sticks and Stones." Later in the year, he had his first number one national hit, a soul version of the pop classic "Georgia on My Mind," which was at the top of *Billboard*'s list the week of November 14, 1960. He followed with other hits, including "Them That's Got" and "Ruby." "Hit the Road Jack" hit number one on *Billboard*'s charts the weeks of October 9 and 16, 1961. He also made the charts with releases on ABC's jazz label, Impulse, scoring with "I've Got News for You" and top-10 instrumental "One Mint Julep." In 1962, he made his initial move into country, turning out three singles on ABC-Paramount that made both country and pop charts: "You Don't Know Me," "You Are My Sunshine," and "I Can't Stop Loving You." The last of those became his all-time best-seller, rising to number one in *Billboard* the week of June 2, 1962 and staying there for four more weeks. It easily earned a gold-record award from the R.I.A.A. From then on, country songs were a regular part of Ray's repertoire, with one or more often showing up on his albums throughout the 1970s and into the 1980s.

He continued to add to his list of charted singles throughout the 1960s and 1970s, though his pace slowed markedly after the 1960s. Among his top-10 hits on R&B and/or pop charts in the later 1960s were "Busted," "Don't Set Me Free," "No One," and "Take These Chains from My Heart" in 1963; "Crying Time," "Together Again," and "Let's Go Get Stoned" in 1966; and "Here We Go Again" in 1967. Among the ABC-Paramount LPs were *Live Concert, Together Again,* and *Cryin' Time* (1965); *Ray's Moods* (1966); *Man and His Soul* and *Listen* (1967); and, in the late 1960s and early 1970s, *I'm All Your Baby* and *All Time Great Performances*. His best-selling albums on the label in the 1960s included two completely devoted to country-based material, *Modern Sounds in Country & Western Music, Volumes 1 and 2.*

Ray's activities from the late 1960s through the late

1980s included worldwide touring and such ventures as operating his own record operation and music publishing firm. His home base remained Los Angeles, but he was constantly on the road backed by his band and female vocal group, the Raylettes. He continued to be a featured guest on almost every TV music show of consequence during those years, including more than a few country music shows. In the latter category he was even a featured artist of an episode of the Public Broadcasting System's *Austin City Limits* in the early 1980s.

During the 1970s and 1980s, Ray continued to be a prolific recording artist, adding dozens of new titles to his discography over that time, not to mention reissues of earlier material. In the mid-1970s, he put out a series of albums on his own Crossover label (he also had other label names of his own, such as Tangerine) including *Come Live with Me* (1974) and *My Kind of Jazz, Part 3* and *Renaissance* (1975). Ray then returned to Atlantic with the 1977 LP *True to Life.* (That same year, King Records issued a collection of his early recordings, *Fourteen Hits/The Early Years.*) He followed with *Love and Peace* (1978), *Ain't It So* (1979), and *Brother Ray Is at It Again* (1980). In 1980, the retrospective *The Right Time,* available on Atlantic as a Japanese import, was issued. Ray's new alignment with Atlantic came to an end at the start of the 1980s, but in 1982 Atlantic issued a four-disc boxed set. *A Life in Music,* covering much of his recording career.

In 1983, Ray became a member of the CBS Records roster. One of his initial projects was a country album recorded in Nashville, Tennessee. This album, *Wish You Were Here Tonight,* he told Kip Kirby of *Billboard,* represented still another new direction in his song interpretations. The album, he said "encompasses traditional country and I've never really done that before. In the sixties, I did a lot of country songs, but I always made them sound contemporary. I'd add strings, give them a pop feel, so that way I got a lot of people into country for the first time." The public response to the LP was strong enough to justify a follow-up album in a similar vein, *Do I Ever Cross Your Mind* (1984).

Ray's enormous contributions to all facets of pop music and to the American heritage was recognized in 1986, when he was one of a number of distinguished Americans honored with a special Kennedy Center Award medallion presented by President Reagan. The president and the award recipients were guests of honor on a nationally televised program from the Kennedy Center in Washington, D.C. In the segment of the program dedicated to Ray, he was serenaded by the teenage choir from his old school, St. Augustine's, and by fellow blind superstar Stevie Wonder. *(See The Whispers.)*

In the late 1980s and well into the 1990s, Ray's honors kept on growing as did his enormous list of recordings, concerts, and TV appearances. On TV, besides guesting on all kinds of musical program formats, he was the subject of a documentary telecast on the Public Broadcasting System. His series of TV commercials for Diet Coke, which also featured the Raylettes, won the attention of new generations of TV viewers.

Rock and Roll Hall of Fame voters recognized his major contributions to the field by inducting him into that pantheon in 1986. In 1987, the National Academy of the Recording Arts & Sciences during its Grammy Awards telecast announced the presentation to Ray of its Lifetime Achievement Award. Calling him "The Father of Soul," the award citation recognized his "unique and effervescent singing and piano-playing [that] have personified the true essence of soul music in all his recorded and personal performances of blues, pop ballads, jazz tunes and even country music."

Though Ray kept on turning out new albums and singles in the 1970s, 1980s, and 1990s, for almost two decades after his single "Booty Butt" (on Tangerine Records) made the *Billboard* Top 40 in May 1971, none of his releases rose that high until late 1989. That December "I'll Be Good to You" on Qwest (from a collection of Quincy Jones band arrangements featuring Ray and Chaka Kahn) reached number eighteen in *Billboard.* During the 1980s, Ray also coauthored his autobiography, *Brother Ray,* with David Ritz.

In the mid-1990s, Ray worked on new material with Warner Brothers Records, which issued the album *My World* in early 1993. For many years Ray had prepared new recordings in his home studio, but in this case he laid down most of the tracks in other places. To questions about whether he might consider retiring, he responded, "That's like asking me what keeps you coming back to food. Music to me is not a sidelight. It's my life . . . my bloodstream. Ever since I've come into the world, that's all I ever wanted to do. I never intended to do or be anything else. It's like breathing. If I can't play music, then what is there in this world for me? People ask me when I'm going to retire. Retire? What would I retire to? As long as I'm alive I want to be active. As long as there's breath in my body, if I'm able to play and sing my songs, that's all I care about.

"At the same time I do realize that I'm not twenty-five anymore, so I control my work schedule. I don't overextend myself. You're never going to read in the paper where I passed out from exhaustion. If you're self-employed like me, you learn to pace yourself. In my studio, I record my own music and do my own engineering and my own mixing. *My World* was an exception. I went outside to get a little different feel for things, open it up a bit."

Clips of Ray's performances of some of his classic hits were included in one segment of the *Time/Life History of Rock & Roll* series presented on TV stations around the U.S. in May 1995. (The series programs also were marketed for home video use.) Besides showcasing that material, the program also presented interviews with other artists, record producers, and so forth, who testified to Ray's great influence on the music and careers of many of the most notable performers who came after him.

Among the highlights of 1993 was induction of his 1960 rendition of "Georgia On My Mind" into the Grammy Hall of Fame. In October, he received the National Medal of the Arts, presented to him by President Bill Clinton in Washington, D.C. Early in the following year he received his twelfth Grammy in the Best R&B Vocal by a Male Performer category for "A Song For You" from *My World*. In May he was given the World Music Award for his "Lifelong Contribution to the Music Industry" in Monte Carlo, Monaco, while also being honored at home by the American Foundation for the blind with its Helen Keller Personal Achievement Award. In January 1996 his next album, *Strong Love Affair*, was issued on the Qwest label.

In the mid-1990s, despite Ray's assertion that he was careful to pace himself, he was still putting in some six months of concerts in all kinds of venues from the gaudy clubs of Las Vegas to Washington's Kennedy Center and the Hollywood Bowl, playing a repertoire ranging from country and soul to jazz. The year 1996 found him focusing more on jazz than other genres, including a summer concert in the Hollywood Bowl as part of the American Airlines Jazz at the Bowl series.

He told interviewer Don Heckman of the *Los Angeles Times* that his fall project was to record his first strongly jazz-oriented album in many years. But he told Heckman that the plan, plus his growing number of appearances at jazz festivals, didn't mean a return to his jazz roots. His goal for the album was "to bring together guys who, when they play one note on their horns, you know who they are. Guys like Milt Jackson, Louis Bellson, Johnny Griffin, Illinois Jacquet, David Newman. Guys who have a distinct sound. And I've got some arrangers working on charts for them like 'Just Friends,' things like that. . . . And I want to do the album now, because most of us are beginning to die out. When the album first came into my mind, I was planning to have Buddy Rich and Dizzy Gillespie, and the next thing I know they both died on me."

CHESNUTT, MARK: *Singer, guitarist, band leader. Born Beaumont, Texas, September 6, 1963.*

East Texas, whose favorite native son performer is the legendary George Jones, is honky-tonk country, and has been for many decades. To a child like Mark Chesnutt growing up in the area, honky-tonk music goes with the territory, particularly if your father is a singer and songwriter, and your mother a lifelong fan.

Country music, heavy on honky-tonky recordings, made its way into Mark Chesnutt's consciousness almost as soon as he was able to walk and talk. His father, Bob Chesnutt, was an aspiring musician and songwriter who recorded several singles released on an independent Nashville label in the late 1960s and early 1970s and was under contract to Cedarwood Publishing in Music City for five years before he decided he'd better start earning a regular salary in Beaumont to support his family. Looking back, Mark told Bob Millard for an article in *Country Music* ("Mark Chesnutt: Child of the Honky Tonks"), his father influenced his musical tastes from the beginning "'cause Daddy was the first singer I ever heard. As far back as I can remember, Daddy was singin', singin' Roy Acuff songs." Bob Chesnutt also was listening to, and sometimes singing along with radio and record numbers by other old-style artists like Hank Williams, Sr., George Jones, and Merle Haggard.

Young Mark's exposure didn't end there. From his very early years, he told Millard, "I remember going into those honky tonks with my parents and hearin' those songs and seein' those people dance. I still see that . . . I love to go to a bar now with a jukebox that has all those old songs. That's what I learned to sing on—songs like 'She Thinks I Still Care,' 'Swinging' Doors,' and 'The Bottle Let Me Down.' To me there's a mystique about that. I would rather listen to any old cryin' in your beer George Jones or Merle Haggard song than anything."

Mark started to pick out notes on a guitar when he was four or five years old and kept at it year after year until he was quite adept at playing in his teens. He also continued to listen closely to any country music he encountered whether on radio, records, or at clubs, memorizing lyrics and instrumental elements. He is said to know the lyrics by heart to some 1,000 songs, a capability that caused some people to dub him "the Human Jukebox."

Country music became an obsession when he went from grade school to high school. Whenever he could, he hung out in places in the area where singers and bands held forth and performed himself if the opportunity arose. He told Robert Oermann of *The Tennessean* ("Mark Chesnutt: A Country Classic," Living section, December 18, 1993), "I got so involved in music and that's when I started screwing up in school. My dad tried to talk me out of it. But back then I didn't care about proms and all that kind of stuff. I went straight to the clubs. I was singing in clubs and hanging out with people twice my age when I was sixteen, seventeen and eighteen years old."

He hastened to add he wasn't an advocate of other youngsters following his example. "Now I wish I had stayed in school, 'cause I missed out on all the fun, all the things that teenagers experience."

With his father's reluctant approval, he left school to work full-time on his career. He played, he recalled, "any place that would have me." A stumbling block was his refusal to compromise with his choice of songs. "Even then, whatever I'd sing had to mean something to me. The only songs I would learn were the ones that touched me in one way or another."

He noted to James Hunter of *LA Weekly* ("Beaumont Blues: Mark Chesnutt Hails Honky Tonk," April 24/30, 1992), "I tried to get jobs in Houston and Dallas, but they always told me I was too country. I would go listen to bands who played a Van Halen song, then a Michael Jackson song, and then a George Jones song. I would just sing country. I stuck to that, instead of changing to be a [pop-country] jukebox."

He also stressed that the style of country music from his home region had elements that tended to set it apart from sounds in other areas. "There's a certain type of music that comes from southeast Texas. I think it has to do with a fusion of Cajun, zydeco and just pure country. There's a little bit of Texas swing down there, but not much. There's more of a bluesy feel. And hardly any bluegrass." One reason for the form the music took there, he said at another time, was that "The people live to dance. There are folks who'll go out every night and hear live music if they have the money, and that's where I cut my teeth."

For a decade starting in 1981 he added to his experience performing at small clubs and honky-tonks in Texas and surrounding states. He expanded his contacts in the music field by finding work at George Jones's Jones Country venue, where at various times he opened for artists like Merle Haggard, Hank Williams, Jr., Willie Nelson, and Jones himself. During those years, Mark was constantly on the lookout for connections that could move him from a regional artist to a bigtime performer. He made a number of trips to Nashville to meet people in the music industry and look for new songs that might improve his prospects for a major record label deal.

While waiting for such an arrangement, he did manage to achieve some record releases on independent labels. From 1981 to the early 1990s, he made eight records, some for San Antonio–based AXBAR and some for Houston-based Cherry. None of them won much buyer response, but his Cherry single (one of the songs picked up during the Nashville visit) got the attention of MCA executives and got him signed to the label in 1990.

Mark Wright, who became Chesnutt's producer at MCA, recalled that after hearing the single, he and others at MCA had checked him out at a Beaumont club called Cutter's, where Mark fronted the house band. "I went to see him on a Wednesday night and there were five hundred people two-stepping and loving that wonderful [baritone] voice coming out of the speakers."

It was a bittersweet period. Mark's career was just starting to blossom when his father died. As he told Bob Millard, one consolation was that Bob Chesnutt lived long enough to see good things on the horizon for his son. "He always wanted to go with me [on tour], but he didn't want to leave my mother at home. And he still worked all the time. That's what got to me—now he wouldn't have to work. He wanted to be involved in

what I'm doin', and that's what I planned on. The way I look at it, he couldn't make it on the road with me and he wanted to go so bad, but this way he can. I believe he's always watchin' over me, still makin' sure I make the right moves."

His MCA debut certainly proved to be a right move, giving him a string of hit singles while doing well on trade-press charts itself to earn an R.I.A.A. gold record by the end of 1991. The album came out in late 1990, and five of the ten tracks on it made top-chart levels: the title song, "Brother Jukebox," "Blame It on Texas," "Your Love Is a Miracle," and "Broken Promise Land." In support of those releases, Mark was on tour almost constantly during 1991–92, opening for artists like the Judds, Reba McEntire, Alabama, and Kenny Rogers. Backed by a seven-piece band, he also headlined shows at small clubs and venues. During 1991 he was named Rising Star of the Year by members of the jukebox industry and was also nominated for the Country Music Association's Horizon Award. He didn't win the latter trophy that year, but was nominated again in 1993 and this time came in first in the voting. His debut album remained on the charts well into 1992 and eventually passed platinum sales levels.

His second MCA album, *Longnecks and Short Stories,* came out in early 1992 and quickly made the charts. After peaking at number nine in *Billboard,* it went on to pass gold-record awards in early 1993 and continued to accrue new sales until it was certified platinum by the R.I.A.A. It, too, spawned a string of hit singles that rose high on *Radio & Records, Billboard,* and *Gavin Report* lists. Those included "Old Flames Have New Names," number four in *R&R* the week of May 1, 1992; "I'll Think of Something," number one in *R&R* the week of August 14, 1992; "Bubba Shot the Jukebox," number five in *R&R* the week of November 5, 1992; and "Ol' Country," number five in *R&R* the week of March 19, 1993 (and also in *Billboard*'s Top 10 at the same time).

His third album, *Almost Goodbye,* released in the summer of 1993, peaked at number six in *Billboard,* and went past gold by the end of the year before garnering another R.I.A.A. certification in 1994. Hit singles from that collection included: "It Sure Is Monday," number one in *R&R* the week of August 6, 1993; the title track, number one in *R&R* the week of November 12, 1993; "I Just Wanted You To Know," at the top of the *Billboard* chart in March 1994; and "Woman Sensuous Woman," a chart hit some weeks later.

In his early days on the national scene, Mark seemed a bit shy and withdrawn in his live shows, but before long he relaxed and was able to energize the audience with strong singing and a boisterous stage presence. He credited the feedback from the crowd with inspiring him. "The only time I feel like a star is when I'm onstage, with all the lights in my eyes and all the people yelling." By 1993 he could say, "People who haven't seen us don't realize what kind of show we put on. It's not flashy, but a lot of fun, a lot of energy, a lot of movement. It's not choreographed. It's just a bunch of us having a good time."

The good times still seemed to roll for him as 1994 went by with the release of his new material on the historic Decca label, revived by MCA during the year. His debut Decca single, "She Dreams," was well inside the *Billboard* Top 10 in October. His first album on the Decca label, *What a Way to Live,* debuted at number fifteen in *Billboard* the week of October 1, 1994, with momentum that seemed likely to make it his best-selling effort to that point in time.

The album contents, as always, tended to shun the pop-country genre and demonstrated his objective of helping to preserve more traditional country roots. "As long as there are people like me who were brought up on that kind of music, as long as we're singing it, everything's going to be all right. . . . Hell, yeah, it's going to be just fine." The disc earned a gold record award from the R.I.A.A. on August 14, 1995. In the fall of 1995, Decca released his album *Wings* which fell short of his earlier efforts. It peaked at number twenty-four in *Billboard* then remained at lower chart levels for a number of months before dropping below the top 75 in the spring of 1996. In the fall of 1995, his single "Trouble" rose to number eighteen in *Billboard.* Later the single "It Wouldn't Hurt to Have Wings" found some favor with listeners, reaching the top 30 in February 1996.

CLARK, GUY: *Singer, guitarist, songwriter. Born Monahans, Texas, November 6, 1941.*

A painstaking poet songwriter of the so-called "Austin (Texas) School" of the 1960s and 1970s (whose members include Jerry Jeff Walker, Waylon Jennings, and Willie Nelson), Guy Clark has created a relatively small but significant body of classic songs. Rich in the imagery of people and places he's encountered from his youthful years in Texas to his slow progression along the way-places on the road to music industry success in Nashville, the heart of his repertoire is his own body of work.

One of his best-known tunes, "Texas—1947," harks back to the time when, as a six-year-old, Clark used to wait at the local railroad station to watch the first streamliner come through the small town he was living in. The boy puts a nickel on the track, old men leave games of dominoes or glasses of beer, and, the lyric goes, "You'd have thought that Jesus Christ himself/ Was coming down the line."

Clark was born in the small West Texas town of Monahans, located between Odessa and Pecos. He told Teresa George of the Country Music Association's *Close Up* publication, "You have a certain attitude growing up in Texas, a certain independence that you can do anything you say you can do. All the musical forms in Texas are a real inspiration too—Blues, Mexican, German, Czech, Polish—a potpourri of influence. The first year I played guitar, the only songs I knew were Mexican songs."

Another of his classic compositions dealt, as many Clark songs do, with one of the characters he knew in the bigger-than-life Texas environment. The song, "Desperados Waiting for a Train," deals with an oil-well driller, originally a Quaker from Pennsylvania, who decided to seek a permanent haven in his grandmother's West Texas hotel. Since the old-timer was down on his luck he wanted to pay for his keep by working as a handyman.

As Guy told Dale Adamson of the *Houston Chronicle,* "For some reason they just hit it off and said 'OK.' And he stayed there. When I was a kid, growing up, he was just like a grandfather, except not really because he was still who he was: 'He's a drifter and a driller of oil wells/He's an old school man of the world/Taught me how to drive his car/When he's too drunk to drive/He'd work and give me money for the girls.'

"I was around him a lot when I was a kid. Then we moved away from there—down to Houston, then to Rockport. The older I got, the less I saw him. So he seemed to change pretty drastically in later years.

"'One day I looked up and he's pushin' 80/Got brown tobacco stains all down his chin/To me he's one of the heroes of this country/So why's he all dressed up like them old men?'"

Clark learned to play guitar as a boy, initially playing Mexican songs rather than country or folk melodies on the instrument. The goal of making a career in music eventually took him to Los Angeles in the 1960s. While he sought outlets for his musical efforts, he earned his living by working in the Dopera Brothers guitar factory. The product made there is the famous dobro guitar widely used in both country and pop bands in recent decades. The paycheck put groceries on the table not only for him but for his equally talented wife, Susanna.

He didn't make much progress in placing his songs there, but the city proved the inspiration for one of his most important compositions, "L.A. Freeway." While he was fighting the battle of traffic jams and exhaust fumes one night, he thought, "If I can just get off this L.A. freeway without getting killed or caught. . . ." It became the chorus for a song that eventually was made a hit by Jerry Jeff Walker.

The Clarks moved to Nashville in 1971, where Guy made the rounds of studios and publishing firms and Susanna turned out a growing body of original paintings. The going was slow, but more and more artists became aware of Guy's ability as a writer from 1971 to the mid-1970s. Jerry Jeff Walker was a particularly strong supporter, using one or more Guy Clark songs in almost every album from the early 1970s on. *L.A. Freeway* was the title track on one of those, an LP that also included Guy's "That Old Time Feeling." Walker used "Desperados Waiting for a Train" in the album *Viva! Terlingua,* one of Walker's best releases of the 1970s. In *Ridin' High,* Walker sang Guy's "Like a Coat from the Cold," a song Guy wrote specifically for Jerry Jeff in honor of the latter's marriage.

Other artists have covered Guy Clark songs, including the Earl Scruggs Revue, the Everly Brothers, Jim Ed Brown, Rita Coolidge, Tom Rush, and David Allen Coe. In late 1975, Johnny Cash's version of "Texas—1947" made the country charts. Meanwhile, Susanna also was proving her prowess as a songwriter. At the same time the Cash single was gaining attention, good reaction was being voiced for Susanna's "I'll Be Your San Antone Rose," featured on an album by RCA singer Dottsy.

Though Guy Clark was signed to an RCA recording contract in the early 1970s, it took almost three years before that matured into an album. Clark, ever the perfectionist, didn't like some of the original recordings and insisted on reworking some of them. The album, *Old No. 1,* finally came out the end of 1975. It included his versions of already known songs like "Desperados," "Texas—1947," and "L.A. Freeway," as well as such other fine offerings as "Instant Coffee Blues" and "Rita Ballou." The album was one of the most impressive debuts in the country field of the 1970s, though it didn't do as well with the public as it deserved. In 1976, RCA issued the LP *Texas Cookin'*.

In 1977, Guy switched record labels, signing with Warner Bros. Again, he took his time in preparing the new release, which finally appeared in late 1978 under the title *Guy Clark*. He provided six originals of the ten songs in the album: "Fool on the Roof," "Fool on the Roof Blues" (despite the title, two different songs), "Fools for Each Other," the bluegrass track "The Houston Kid," "Comfort and Crazy," and "Shade of All Greens," the latter about "the late afternoon sun filterin' through the trees and the bushes out where I live. There's so many greens."

As Guy told Dale Adamson, "I write songs different every time. Sometimes the music comes first, sometimes the words come first. I don't have any set pattern to the way I write. I just try to get some sort of creative thing goin' and just follow it wherever it goes, whether it starts with the music or the lyrics or both at the same time.

"Sometimes I have to work at it really hard—like sit down and concentrate and work for days and days on a song. Sometimes it'll happen in thirty minutes, completely by surprise. There's just no real formula to it for me. But I do work at it. Both 'Texas—1947' and 'Desperados' are songs I worked on a lot, which may be obvious if you think they're well constructed. It took a long time to write those songs. But other songs, for example 'Old Time Feeling,' didn't take any time at all."

"When I write songs, I'm serious about writing them and I'm very self-critical. I don't just write a song to write a song. I really make sure I'm not just throwing away words or lines or something just to get a rhyme. It's got to make sense. It's got to hang together. . . . But I'm a singer, too. I write 'em to sing 'em. I don't write 'em specifically for other people. I really enjoy singin' and playin'. That's all part of it as far as I'm concerned."

Though a very entertaining concert artist, Clark continued to have his main impact on the music field as a songwriter. His albums, when they did come out, typically were finely crafted gems, but because of his personal high standards they didn't come out very often. For instance, from 1971 through 1984 only four original collections were released. When his albums did come out, he tended to keep a low profile rather than seek maximum exposure via intensive touring and public relations hype. For instance, when close friend Jerry Jeff Walker was touring almost 300 days a year and Guy could have been a featured member of the show, he usually stayed home working on new material.

In 1989 when he completed a new album, *Old Friends,* released on the Sugar Hill label, he paid the production expenses himself. By then, though still largely unknown to the mass country audience, he had a sizable following overseas who welcomed late 1980s live concert appearances by Guy in the U.K., Australia, and New Zealand. As a result, he didn't have to worry about overseas production and distribution costs which were handled by Mother Records (owned by the Irish rock group U2), which issued *Old Friends* in England and Ireland.

During the 1980s, other artists continued to do well with songs written or cowritten by Guy. Ricky Skaggs made the charts with a single of "Heartbroke," while Vince Gill recorded "Oklahoma Borderline," John Conlee recorded "The Carpenter," and Steve Wariner recorded "Baby I'm Yours." In 1986 his "Desperados Waiting for a Train" was included in the best-selling album *The Highwayman,* recorded by Johnny Cash, Waylon Jennings, Kris Kristofferson, and Willie Nelson. In the late 1980s, Rodney Crowell had a number-one hit with his single of "She's Crazy for Leaving," a song that had little impact when Clark released his own version in the early 1980s. In 1989, Jerry Jeff Walker also expressed interest in recording the first song Guy had written decades earlier, "Step Inside My House."

During the first half of the 1990s the pattern continued pretty much the same. Clark kept following his own path, spending much of his time at home painting or in his small Nashville Music Row office slowly developing new songs. Still, in the mid-1990s there were some positive signs for his recording status. He signed a contract to record new material for a major label, Asylum, and two of his early albums, *Old No. 1* and *Texas Cookin',* were reissued by the MCA Records' Texas

City Music catalog operation. In 1997, he was working on material for Sugar Hill Records again.

CLARK, ROY: *Singer, guitarist, banjoist, fiddler, songwriter, comedian. Born Meaherrin, Virginia, April 15, 1933.*

A multitalented individual, Roy Clark, with his corn-fed humor, would have the audience roaring with laughter and minutes later his superb instrumental artistry on guitar, banjo, or fiddle would have them rapt in attention. His instrumental skills proved adaptable to a variety of surroundings, from the madcap *Hee Haw* TV series to the concert halls of Russia or the stage of the Boston Pops.

He began his progress toward those accomplishments from his very early years in Virginia. His father, a sometime tobacco farmer, played in local groups, as did other relations, and his mother played piano. He recalled that "I was just a kid of about three when I discovered Dad's banjo and I naturally assumed it was a drum, something to pound on, which is exactly what I did. Well, I got straightened out pretty quick."

His father saw to it that the boy learned banjo techniques. An apt pupil, Roy began to impress those around him by his early teens. In the late 1940s, he entered the Country Music Banjo Championship and walked off with first prize. The next year he repeated, gaining an appearance on the *Grand Ole Opry.* By then he not only could play banjo, but the twelve-string acoustic guitar and fiddle as well.

At the start of the 1950s, he settled in Washington, D.C., where he worked as a sideman or soloist in country clubs. He became close friends with Jimmy Dean, who spotlighted Roy's talents when he had his own show in the early 1950s. Roy's growing reputation gained an additional boost when he guested on *Arthur Godfrey's Talent Scouts* in 1956, the first of several appearances with Godfrey. At the end of the decade, he joined forces with country star Wanda Jackson, working a number of engagements with her and also doing backing instruments on her recordings for Capitol. One of the places he worked with her was Las Vegas's Golden Nugget. It was the start of a loving relationship between Vegas hotels and Clark, who headlined many shows there from the mid-1960s on. In the 1970s, in fact, he had a long-term contract to play the main showroom of the Frontier Hotel twelve weeks a year.

Roy's backing work for Wanda Jackson helped bring a solo contract arrangement with Capitol. In 1962 his album *Lightning* won above-average attention from both critics and country fans. In January 1963, he made his debut on Johnny Carson's *The Tonight Show* on NBC-TV. As the decade went by, he returned a number of times to the show. Many times in the 1970s and at the start of the 1980s, besides appearing as a guest artist from time to time, he also served as Johnny's guest host. The year 1963 proved important in other ways;

Roy gained his first top-10 singles hit, "Tips of My Fingers," which became the title track for a hit LP issued in the fall. Throughout the mid-1960s, Capitol kept issuing new albums of his, including *Happy to Be Unhappy* in October 1964; *Guitar Spectacular* (12/65); *Lonesome Love Ballads* (3/66); *Stringin' Along* (6/66); *Roy Clark Live!* (on Tower Records).

Roy's activities continued along at a breakneck pace as the 1960s went by. Besides a steady diet of live engagements throughout the United States and in other countries, Roy often showed up on TV. Among his mid-1960s credits were the *Andy Williams Show, Jimmy Dean,* and a number of *Grand Ole Opry* radio and TV releases. In the mid- and late-1960s, he helped host the syndicated *Swingin' Country* show. At the end of the decade, he was asked to be cohost of a brand new series with Buck Owens called *Hee Haw,* a blend of corncob humor and contemporary country music. For its first two years of existence the show was presented on the CBS network. Though it got good ratings, CBS decided *Hee Haw* didn't fit its image and cancelled it.

But the show's producers decided to buck the odds and syndicate it themselves. Their gamble paid off, helped in part by the great rapport Clark had with viewers, and *Hee Haw* not only remained alive but prospered. In 1978, in fact, with Clark very much in evidence, the show celebrated its tenth anniversary. In the early 1980s, the program remained a staple on several hundred stations.

By the time Roy joined *Hee Haw* he'd changed record labels, going from Capitol to Dot (continuing on the Dot roster and the operation was absorbed by ABC Records, which in turn was acquired by MCA). In the late 1960s and early 1970s Roy's fans had plenty of new recordings to choose from, including such albums as *I Never Picked Cotton, Incredible Roy Clark, Magnificent Sanctuary Band, Best of Roy Clark,* and *Roy Clark Country.* He also had a number of hit singles, including the 1969 success "Yesterday When I Was Young," which sold over 250,000 copies and won him an Outstanding Country & Western Song Award from ASCAP. During the 1970s, he won more ASCAP Outstanding Country & Western Song Awards: "Then She's a Lover" (1970); "Riders in the Sky" (1973); "The Lawrence Welk Hee Haw Counter Revolution Polka" (1973); "Somewhere Between Love and Tomorrow" (1974); "Think Summer" (1976); "Heart to Heart" (1976); and "We Can't Build a Fire in the Rain" (1978).

During the 1970s, Roy added to his credentials with a bewildering array of TV specials including the *Mitzi Gaynor Special, Bell Telephone Hour* special, several Bob Hope specials, *The Captain & Tenille, Flip Wilson, Donnie and Marie* (Osmond), *Mac Davis, Merv Griffin, Dinah!, Sammy and Company,* and even a role on the *Odd Couple* comedy series. He was in evidence at many awards events and served as cohost of the nationally televised Country Music Association 1976 show and the American Music Awards.

Starting in the late 1960s, his superstar status was given increased recognition. The West Coast–based Academy of Country Music named him Top Country Comedy Act for 1969 and voted him similar awards in 1970 and 1971. The Academy also voted him TV Personality of the Year for 1972 and Entertainer of the Year for 1972 and 1973. During that period—from 1969 to 1972—the readers of *Music City News* voted him number-one Instrumentalist. The Country Music Association also honored him many times, starting with election as 1970 Comedian of the Year. Later the CMA named him Entertainer of the Year for 1973 and, with Buck Trent, Instrumental Group of the Year for 1975. In 1974 he was dubbed Country Music Star of the Year (for 1973) by the American Guild of Variety Artists. In 1975, a star with his name on it was embedded in the Walk of Fame on Hollywood Boulevard.

In 1976, Roy was given the opportunity to make a three-week concert tour of the Soviet Union. He performed before standing-room-only crowds in Riga, Moscow, and Leningrad, and his bravura performance led to standing ovations and an invitation for a future return engagement. In honor of that achievement, the CMA named him its International Friendship Ambassador. During the summer of 1976, Roy performed with Arthur Fiedler and the Boston Pops Orchestra, a show screened several times afterward on the Public Broadcasting System.

Additionally his ABC albums of the mid-1970s often showed up on the country charts and sometimes crossed over to the pop charts. In mid-1974, for instance, his LP *The Entertainer* was a top-10 hit, as was his mid-1975 duo with fellow banjo player Buck Trent, called *Pair of Fives (Banjos That Is)*. In the fall of 1975, his *Greatest Hits, Volume 1* was in the top 15 and his late 1975 release *Heart to Heart* was on the country lists in early 1976. In 1977, his ABC album release *Labor of Love* also appeared on country bestseller lists.

These discs helped bring new acclaim from his peers. In 1976, the CMA voted Roy and Buck Trent the Instrumental Duo of the Year for a second time and in 1977 and 1978 named Clark Instrumentalist of the Year.

Roy closed out the 1970s with his MCA single "Chain Gang of Love" rising on the hit lists, moving into upper brackets in early 1980. Several months later he had the charted single "If There Were Only Time for Love." In 1981, he made the charts with such singles as "I Ain't Got Nobody" and "She Can't Give It Away."

By the mid-1980s, Roy had been nominated twice more for his instrumental skills by the Country Music Association, reaching the final five for Instrumentalist of the Year in 1980 and 1984. In the 1982 Grammy voting he received the Best Country Instrumental Performance award for "Alabama Jubilee," a track from a Churchill Records album. In the mid-1980s he costarred with Mel Tillis in the film *Uphill All the Way.*

Throughout the 1980s, he continued to be a TV audience favorite for his work on the long-running *Hee Haw* syndicated series as cohost with Buck Owens to 1986 and primary host the rest of the decade and in the 1990s. Of course, he had plenty of other TV opportunities in the 1980s and 1990s time frame, guesting on many programs on the major country networks (like TNN) based in Nashville and sometimes serving as host or cohost of special events such as the 20th Annual *Music City News* Country Awards program.

He continued to record new material though he didn't place releases on upper-chart levels after the late 1980s. But he could always count on full houses for his live shows at Branson, Missouri, where he was one of the first major country stars to make the town a country performance center. He opened his own theater there in 1989 and remained one of the most popular Branson-based artists through the mid-1990s. Like many country stars, he found time for various charitable activities, such as his Nashville concert with the Hee Haw Gang in June 1990 to raise money for Dream Ship, Inc., an organization whose goal was to improve the quality of life for the mentally retarded.

In choosing him as one of its premiere candidates for *Life* magazine's September 1994 list of "The 100 Most Important People in the History of Country," the editors cited both his comic talents and great instrumental abilities. "Clark has long been an even greater entertainer than he is a picker—and he's an absolutely brilliant picker, whose many admirers include jazzmen like Joe Pass and Wynton Marsalis."

Among Roy's releases available in the mid-1990s was the MCA album, *Makin' Music,* recorded with Gatemouth Brown, as well as albums on several other labels. Some of his live performance work was included in multiartist videos like the *Country Gold* release. In the early 1990s, Roy signed with the Intersound organization, which issued his label debut, *Great Picks & New Tricks,* on the Branson Entertainment series in 1993. In mid-1995, some of Roy's earlier material was reissued by the independent label Varese Sarabande.

CLAYTON, LEE: *Singer, guitarist, songwriter. Born Russelville, Alabama, October 29, 1942.*

Border Affair by Lee Clayton (original name Billy Schatz), one of the best country albums of 1978, underscored the great talent of Clayton, one of the finest songwriters in Nashville in the 1970s. His contributions to the repertoires of artists like Waylon Jennings, Willie Nelson, and Jerry Jeff Walker earned him the designation of "the outlaw's outlaw."

Born in Alabama but raised in Oak Ridge, Tennessee, Clayton grew up in a household that played old Jimmie Rodgers songs and recordings of Red Foley like "Peace in the Valley." Lee inherited his father's love for country music and became addicted to listening to Saturday-night *Opry* programs featuring artists like Roy Acuff, Hank Snow, and a wonderful newcomer named Hank Williams. He recalled, "My father once took me to the *Opry* when I was six years old. To this day I still remember the entertainers signing autographs in the alley at the stage door and the smell of Tootsie's as we walked in the back entrance."

His father gave him the choice of learning accordion or guitar when he was nine. He chose guitar and was given a steel guitar. "I took lessons for about one and a half years on the Hawaiian guitar. I couldn't stand it. They started making me try to learn notes. My mind wasn't ready for it then, though I understand its importance now." Still, he progressed enough to debut "on the radio one Saturday playing Leon McAuliffe's 'Steel Guitar Rag' when I was ten.

"I picked up the guitar again when I was sixteen and the folk wave hit with the Kingston Trio. I married my high school sweetheart six months before I graduated from the University of Tennessee, put my guitar away again and proceeded to become 'Mr. Normal.' That lasted about one year.

"One morning I was sitting in bumper-to-bumper traffic on my way to work when an airplane flew over me on the way to landing. I looked up and said to myself, 'F it, I'm gonna fly!' I loved my wife, but she was working on a Ph.D. in mathematics and I was headed for a degree in hanging out. Within a year we were divorced and I was in the air force [in late 1965] taking pilot training."

As it turned out, flying was not well suited to Lee's personality. In fact, after he was discharged in 1969, he never flew again. But the change of environment made him concentrate on music more. He played whenever he could and also turned to songwriting in earnest. As he told the author of this book, "The first song I consider a song I wrote probably in 1966. That was a long time ago and I don't even recall its title. When I got into writing and hanging around Nashville after leaving the service, I'd written about twenty-five. Friends in country music told me, 'Well, when you're really a good writer you'll throw away the first one hundred.' I wrote 'Ladies Love Outlaws' right about that time. Waylon Jennings recorded it in early 1972 around March and it became my first writing success."

Lee began to get attention as a performer that year, which he considered another major turning point. "I got to go back to Griffith Springs, Texas, to the first big country-music concert there. I found myself performing on the same bill with people like Roy Acuff, Tex Ritter, Willie Nelson, and Waylon. Billy Joe Shaver and I went in there unknowns and came out with national publicity. It was luck. The first night before the concert began the concert people gave a party for everyone involved with the program. I met writer Arnie Lewis from *Rolling Stone* and Annie Leibowitz, a photographer from the magazine. We hung out together all three days. When they went back they wrote about me and Billy Joe."

That helped get him a contract with MCA Records, which released his debut LP in 1973. The album proved a failure. "After one of the most grueling years of my life, I realized that neither myself nor my music was together. I had absolutely no idea what to do except to stop and think about it." He did so for most of 1974. But meanwhile, other artists retained great interest in his songwriting abilities. The result was that an increasing number of recordings of his originals came out as the mid-1970s went by, including Jennings's versions of "If You Could Touch Her at All" and "Memory of You and I"; Jerry Jeff Walker's offering of "Won'tcha Give Me One More Chance"; "Silver Stallion" recorded by Bonnie Koloc; and Hoyt Axton's track of "Whisper on a Velvet Night."

After a sojourn in Joshua Springs, California, in 1974, Clayton returned to Nashville, where he settled down on a farm outside town to continue writing while seeking ways to rejuvenate his recording career. In 1977, he signed a new agreement with Capitol, which issued the LP *Border Affair* in late 1978. In 1979, with glowing reviews for the album in his file, he returned with full vigor to work on the follow up. He told us at that time, "On the new album I felt I went to a higher level of writing. The material is simpler in structure, closer to home in feeling—simple things are always harder, but I think it's the way to really express yourself musically."

One of the factors that had a negative effect on Lee's career was alcoholism, a demon he fought for many years. He once told an interviewer in the mid-1970s of a time when he spent most of the year in a motel room "just staring at the walls. I used to lock the doors and drink. One night I was at the point of death, and then I drank seven Dr Peppers and it saved my life."

His periodic binges and stretches of depression caused him to drop out of the music field for long periods of time. Nevertheless, he seemed to regain his control and, each time, begin trying to revive his career. However, his songs remained in high regard with other country artists who performed them in concerts or occasionally included them on albums, as was the case with "Silver Stallion." That was the leadoff track on the very successful *Highwayman 2* collection issued on Columbia in 1990. The song was performed by the superstar Highwaymen group on the record and during an extensive series of concerts in the early 1990s. (The Highwaymen comprised Johnny Cash, Willie Nelson, Waylon Jennings, and Kris Kristofferson.)

Clayton remained on the sidelines the latter part of the 1980s, but in the early 1990s he again was making the rounds of the Nashville country music establishment with demos of newly written songs.*

CLEMENT, JACK: *Singer, guitarist, songwriter, recording engineer, record producer, music industry entrepreneur. Born Whitehaven, near Memphis, Tennessee, April 5, 1931.*

One of the more colorful life stories in the annals of country music, Jack Clement's saga embraced occasions where he might be considered a character and others where his actions reflected true musical genius. Some of the wilder stories about his interaction with country music were probably apocryphal, but there's no doubting his enormous impact on modern country history—which involved providing some classic songs and, particularly, keen production guidance for a galaxy of stars ranging from Roy Orbison and Jerry Lee Lewis to the Irish rock group U2.

Growing up in the Memphis area, Jack was exposed to a variety of musical influences in his youth, including blues, country and gospel. Too young to serve during World War II, he later enlisted in the Marine Corps and ended up being stationed in a ceremonial detachment in Washington, D.C., in the early 1950s. He recalled writing his first song there, "Automatic Woman," and got enough favorable comments from fellow Marines to work on still more originals. Clement had learned to play above-average guitar in his teens and he began to demonstrate his ability on occasion at shows by promising newcomers like Roy Clark and Jimmy Dean. After a while he got together with Buzz Busby and Scotty Stoneman to form the group Buzz and the Bayou Boys, which found work in local clubs.

Finishing his service hitch, in 1954 Jack returned home to enroll in Memphis State University under the GI Bill. He added to his income with several sideline activities, including working as a dance instructor at an Arthur Murray studio, leading a big band, and doing gigs with a country group. The country band had a singer named Billy Lee Riley, who impressed him enough that he arranged to make demo tapes of two of her vocals. He took the tapes to Sam Phillips, owner of Sun Studios in Memphis. Phillips was more taken with the quality of the recordings than the singer, and asked Jack to join the operation as a recording engineer and record producer.

As Phillips told Jim Ridley and Collin Wade Monk for a *Nashville Scene* article ("Trapped in an Old Country Song—Jack Clement's Bodacious, Beleaguered Life," October 13, 1994), "Jack was open to what we were doing. I was looking for someone who had an intuitive feel for music and the type of demeanor to work with musicians and so-called artists. Jack was not what you call a quote-unquote demanding artist. Plus, he

Based partly on a 1979 phone interview with the authors.

picked a damn guitar pretty good, and he could really swing those vocals."

One of Clement's early chores was to record material by a twenty-one-year-old named Roy Orbison, who showed up at the studio in 1956. Over the next few years, Clement played a key role in jump-starting the careers of other superstars-to-be including Jerry Lee Lewis, Carl Perkins, and Johnny Cash. Besides taping classic songs like Lewis's "Great Balls of Fire," "Whole Lotta Shakin' Goin' On," and "Breathless" and several of Cash's signature numbers, he also provided more than a few hit numbers for them himself. The latter included "It'll Be Me" for Jerry Lee and "Guess Things Happen That Way" and "Ballad of a Teenage Queen" for Cash.

In 1959, his days at Sun ended abruptly when Phillips gave him his walking papers. Sam told Ridley and Monk, "There's no point in getting into what happened. I might've been wrong and he might've been right. It was something I felt I had to do. And I felt no bitterness toward him. Jack was, and is, one of my dearest friends. But I felt I was right at the time."

After working briefly with Chet Atkins at RCA, Clement teamed up with record producer Bill Hall to set up a joint recording operation in Beaumont, Texas, in 1961. Among the national hits that Clement helped bring about was the 1961 recording by Dickey Lee of his composition "Patches." In 1962, Goerge Jones recorded the Lee composition "She Thinks I Still Care" that made it to number one on the country charts. Jones also had another chart success with Clement's "A Girl I Used to Know." Among those who counted their asssociation with Clement in Beaumont as a vital learning experience were producer Allen Reynolds and songwriter Bob McDill. In 1965, because of disagreements between Clement and Hall about upgrading their studio, Jack left Texas and moved to Nashville, where he soon set up a new studio and music publishing firm.

Soon after, he became excited about a promising black country singer named Charley Pride. He made demo tapes of some of Pride's work and, after a number of turn-downs, convinced Chet Atkins of RCA Records that the label should sign the newcomer. The result, of course, was the start of a Hall of Fame career in which Jack helped produce many hit singles and thirteen gold albums of Pride's recordings. Working as a producer, arranger and songwriter, Jack affected the careers of many other artists from the mid-1960s into the 1970s, including those of Bobby Bare and Johnny Cash.

In the early 1970s, the outlook seemed bright for Clement as an important force in the country music field. Unfortunately, he decided to try his hand at movie production, choosing a horror film script by friend John Farris titled *Dear, Dead Delilah* as his first venture. Instead of seeking outside capital, he poured most of his savings into the venture and by the time the film flopped his finances were in such poor shape that he lost control of his various recording industry operations. To make matters worse, his association with Charley Pride fell apart at around the same time.

For the balance of the 1970s, he paid his bills with various production and other assignments. In the mid-1970s he signed a recording contract with Elektra that resulted in the 1978 LP *All I Want to Do in Life*. The album was not one of his better efforts, and had little impact on the country audience. But a positive result was his discovering a new friend and coworker in young rhythm guitarist Jim Rooney, who credited Clement with giving him an education in the basics of record production.

In the early 1980s, he became part of the production operation at the Jack Clement-organized Cowboy Arms studio in Nashville. Their clientele comprised mostly young, talented performers from the alternative country and folk sectors, including Townes Van Zandt and John Prine. Rooney and Clement coproduced two albums by Prine and Rooney got the chance to work with a promising new female artist from Texas, Nanci Griffith. His work with Nanci provided the fine mid-1980s album *Once in a Very Blue Moon*.

Things were slow in mainstream country in the early 1980s, but when it began to boom in the second half of the decade the rising group of country superstars overlooked the skills of Clement, who hadn't focused on country for a number of years. In the late 1980s, Jack found it difficult to find new production work, until he was offered the chance to produce tracks for the Irish rock band U2 in the old Sun Studios in Memphis. The 1989 sessions were the basis for the album *Rattle and Hum,* which became a best-seller in the U.S. and around the world. U2 would continue to seek out Clement through the following years for further work.

In the 1990s, Clement found new production opportunities, at his Cowboy Arms facility and other locations. He remained selective in which projects he accepted. As he told Jim Ridley and Collin Wade Monk for the *Nashville Scene,* "I just ain't into producing what I'm hearing on the radio at the moment. I don't feel like I'm mainstream. I'm just too experimental. I suppose I might make some people nervous. Most people don't know where I'm comin' from because I don't know myself. I want to hear something new."

In 1994, Clement began to work on new original songs with people like Don Robertson (with whom he had written a number of successes years before) and country star Marty Stuart. He also teamed with Robertson on several concert and TV dates. In April 1995, for instance, Clement, Robertson, and Joe Allen (writer of a number of country hits, particularly for Gene Watson) performed at the Tin Pan South show in Nashville. The friends also appeared three times at the mansion for Georgia Governor Zell Miller, and for members of the Georgia State Legislature. Those appearances included a July 1995 taping of songs for a Christmas TV special in which Clement and Robertson worked with Waylon Jennings and Jessi Colter.

CLEMENTS, VASSAR: *Fiddler, band leader (Vassar Clements Band). Born near Kinard, North Carolina, April 25, 1928.*

Vassar Clements, fiddler extraordinaire, likely could qualify as the greatest country instrumentalist never to win a Country Music Association or Academy of Country Music award. But he made up for that with the high regard in which he was held by other musicians and with the recognition he earned in lesser-known, but equally important, competitions.

The foreword to *Life* magazine's all-star country band selection in September 1994 included a description of Clements dragging his bow "slowly, slowly across the strings—as though each movement brought pain—and his listener dies with him, an agonizing, gloriously romantic death. Later, when Clements stomps the floorboards and his bow starts to whip and saw, no sorrow in the world can keep folks from kicking up their heels. It is this magical gift—to drive audiences from tears to two-steppin' and back again—that distinguishes *Life*'s Band of Dreams"—which included, among others, Bill Monroe and Earl Scruggs, with whom Clements had often shared concert stages.

Born in rural North Carolina, Vassar heard many excellent fiddle players as a boy and mastered the rudiments of the instrument by his teens. After playing with local bands he made the move to Nashville, where he joined Bill Monroe's band in 1949 and made his first recording as part of Monroe's group in 1950. He toured and recorded with Monroe for some years, then joined the Virginia Boys, backing group for bluegrass stars Jim and Jesse McReynolds. By the end of the 1960s, with Nashville as home base, he was eager to establish his own performing credentials, though he continued to be in demand as a session musician in the decades that followed. Over the years, his name appeared on albums recorded by many of the greatest stars in modern country history.

In the 1970s he headed his own group, the Vassar Clements Band, and was busy turning out a steady stream of albums on both small and major labels. His output included *Crossing the Catskills* on Rounder Records in 1973, *Hillbilly Jazz* on Flying Fish Records in 1974, *Vassar Clements and Superbow* in 1975 (both on Mercury), plus two more releases in 1977, *The Vassar Clements Band* on the MCA label and, on Flying Fish, *Vassar Clements: The Bluegrass Sessions*. Flying Fish continued to be one of his main recording producers in the 1980s, starting with the album *Vassar* in 1980. Also issued in 1980 was the album *More Hillbilly Jazz*. One of the highlights of his career was his appearance in the 1975 Robert Altman film *Nashville*.

His activities in the 1970s also included work with the late Jerry Garcia, noted guitarist of the rock band the Grateful Dead. Their association was called *Old and in the Way.* Rounder Records issued the all-acoustic album of that title in 1975; it was reissued on the Sugar Hill label in 1984, and later by Rykodisc on CD. In the early 1980s Vassar rejoined Jerry in the Jerry Garcia Band, whose other members were mandolinist David Grisman, guitarist Peter Rowan, and bass player John Kahn.

As that role suggests, Clements's activities remained essentially the same through the 1980s and into the 1990s: he sometimes took center stage as a soloist, while continuing to back various artists in live shows and on TV. He performed in many concerts with such people as Earl Scruggs and John Hartford. Vassar's album output in the decade included *Westport Drive* in 1984, *Hillbilly Jazz* and *Together at Last* in 1987 and *New Hillbilly Jazz* in 1988. *Together at Last* was a joint recording of performances with the great French jazz fiddler Stephane Grappelli (born Paris, January 26, 1908). His albums in print in the mid-1990s included two in the Rounder catalog, a bluegrass-jazz collection, *Vassar Clements, John Hartford, Dave Holland* (collection issued in 1988), and his bluegrass solo disc, *Grass Routes.*

CLINE, PATSY: *Singer, pianist. Born Winchester, Virginia, September 8, 1932; died Camden, Tennessee, March 5, 1963. Elected to Country Music Hall of Fame in 1973.*

"I remember the last time I saw Patsy alive. It was in Nashville on a Thursday. That Thursday night, I went over to Patsy's house because she had some tapes she wanted me to hear from a recording session. At that session she cut 'Sweet Dreams.'

"I remember that while we listened to the tapes, Patsy embroidered a tablecloth. She did that to relax. Her little boy Randy was on a rocking horse, rocking very hard. I was worried that he'd fall off and get hurt, but Patsy said not to worry. That night we made plans to go shopping when she returned from doing the benefit show in Kansas City for some disc jockey [Cactus Jack Call] who had gotten hurt in a wreck. . . ."

"On Sunday evening, March 6, 1963*, Patsy, Hawkshaw Hawkins, Cowboy Copas, and Randy Hughes, the pilot, were flying home from the Kansas City benefit in a twin-engine Comanche, when they ran into a storm near Dyersberg, near where I live today. On Monday morning I wondered why I didn't hear from Patsy. . . . Just then, I got a call from Patsy's booking agent, who told me she was dead. I said, 'Baloney, her and me is going shopping!' Then I realized it was true. . . . That just about broke me up to think that someone as good as that was gone."

Thus did Loretta Lynn recall the last days of Patsy

---

*The records show March 5 to be the correct date.

Cline in her autobiography, *Coal Miner's Daughter.* Her feelings of shock and loss were shared not only by Patsy's many friends and associates in country music but by the millions of people who had helped make her the logical choice not long before as "Top Female Singer."

Patsy, whose original name was Virginia Patterson Hensley, was often described as a child prodigy. When she was only four, she made her public debut by winning first prize in an amateur contest for her tap dancing skill in her home town of Winchester, Virginia. By the time she was in grade school, she was also exhibiting talent as a singer.

At eight, she started learning to play the piano. Knowledge of the basic patterns of music gained from her piano lessons helped improve her vocal efforts. While still in public school, she was a featured singer with her church choir and continued to sing with that group through her teens. She also sang in school plays and made some appearances in local clubs.

When she was sixteen, Wally Fowler of the *Grand Ole Opry* was starring in a touring show that played the Winchester Palace Theatre. Patsy managed to audition for him and won a guest spot on the bill. Through his intervention, her parents helped her to go to Nashville to try to carve out a career in the country field. Initially, she made little headway with agents or recording executives, and earned a precarious living mainly working as a dancer in small clubs. Discouraged, she finally returned home to Winchester.

However, still harboring hopes of scoring a breakthrough in the entertainment industry, she auditioned and won a chance to appear on *Arthur Godfrey's Talent Scouts.* The song she chose for her debut on the nationally televised program was "Walkin' After Midnight." Her rendition on January 21, 1957, won an ovation from the studio audience and approval from followers of the program. She won first prize and soon after was given a recording contract by Decca, which released her single of the song. The record became a hit on both pop and country charts and Patsy at twenty-five was embarked on the road to stardom.

For a time in the late 1950s, none of her follow-up recordings approached the success of "Walkin' After Midnight," particularly in the country field, but in the early 1960s, she started to turn out releases that found widespread favor with country fans. During those years, she became a headliner on the country concert circuit as well as a regular cast member of the *Grand Old Opry.* Her first banner year was 1961, when she had the top-10 hit "Crazy" and one of the top-selling singles of the year, "I Fall to Pieces," which went to number one on country charts. She turned out a number of excellent singles in 1962, including another number-one single, "She's Got You" and the top-10 "When I Get Through with You, You'll Love Me Too." In 1963, she had the top-10 singles "Faded Love," "Leavin' on Your

Mind," and "Sweet Dreams (Of You)," the last-named released after her death. Among her early 1960s album releases were *Patsy Cline* (1/62) and *Sentimentally Yours* (10/62).

Since that tragic plane crash in early 1963, Patsy's voice continues to this day to beam forth from radio stations and home turntables. Soon after the tragedy, Decca issued a two-record set titled *The Patsy Cline Story* in August 1963. This was followed in 1964 with *Patsy Cline Portrait;* in February 1965 with *How a Heartache Begins;* and in May 1967 with *Greatest Hits.* Several releases came out on the Evergreen label, including *Golden Hits* (1963); *In Memorium* (6/63); *Patsy Cline Legend* (3/64); and *Reflections* (2/65). Album releases on other labels included, on Vocalion, *Here's Patsy Cline* (8/65) and *Great Patsy Cline* (8/69); on Metronome, *Gotta Lot of Rhythm* (8/65); and on Pickwick, *I Can't Forget You, Stop the World, Today, Tomorrow, Forever,* and *In Care of the Blues.*

In 1977, Loretta Lynn paid tribute to her friend's memory with her album *I Remember Patsy.* The LP included Loretta's versions of nine of Patsy's major hits and a conversation between Loretta and veteran producer Owen Bradley (who had been Patsy's producer), reminiscing about the late, great vocalist.

Patsy was elected to the Country Music Hall of Fame in 1973. The bronze plaque in her honor reads, in part, "Patsy will live in country music annals as one of its outstanding vocalists. . . . Her heritage of recordings is testimony to her artistic capacity. [Her] biggest hit, 'I Fall to Pieces' . . . has become a standard. . . . Joined *Grand Ole Opry* 1960 . . . [which was the] realization of a lifelong ambition."

During the 1970s and into the 1980s, MCA Records, the successor to Decca, continued to maintain a number of Patsy's albums in its active catalogue and also issued repackaged collections of some of her work. As of late 1981, those comprised *Patsy Cline's Greatest Hits; Patsy Cline Showcase; Sentimentally Yours; A Portrait of Patsy Cline Always; Here's Patsy Cline; The Patsy Cline Story;* and *Country Great.* Occasionally, reissued or re-engineered versions of her recordings appeared on singles charts, such as the MCA release "Always" in 1980 and the 1981 duet with the late Jim Reeves (issued on RCA), "Have You Ever Been Lonely." Actually, Patsy never recorded with Reeves. The single resulted from an engineering merger of two separate recordings of the same song by the two artists.

Patsy's legend continued to grow throughout the 1980s and 1990s as more than a few country stars of the period paid tribute to her as a major inspiration for their careers. In the late 1980s, her life became the subject of the movie *Sweet Dreams,* starring Jessica Lange as Patsy. In early 1991 MCA released her *Greatest Hits* album, which became a runaway best-seller, almost immediately reaching the number-one position on *Billboard*'s Top Country Catalog Albums chart and remain-

ing there well into 1992. By late summer 1991, the album had gone double platinum; before leaving the top-chart section midway through 1992, it has sold more than three million copies. It soon returned, however, and for year after year remained on the list, usually at number one. In 1996 it went past the 7 million copy sales total and, already having a total of 261 weeks on the charts as of May 18, seemed likely to go past 300 weeks in early 1997.

In October 1991, MCA issued *The Patsy Cline Collection,* prepared in conjunction with the Country Music Foundation as part of the Country Music Hall of Fame series. The package contained some 100 songs comprising her entire catalog of Decca recordings as well as Four Star Records releases.

The editors of *Life* magazine's special edition in September 1994, "The Roots of Country Music," named Patsy as one of the 100 most important people in the history of the genre. She also was chosen by the *Life* staff as a member of the all-star country band.

A musical based on her career written by J. Ted Swindley, founder of the Stages Repertory theater in Houston, Texas, was first presented in that city in 1988. After several changes, it premiered at the Ryman Auditorium in Nashville in the mid-1990s showcasing many of her major song successes. The original Nashville cast recording of the show, titled *Always . . . Patsy Cline,* featuring Mandy Barnett in the title role, was issued by MCA Records in early 1995. It was a two-woman drama based on the true-life friendship of Cline and devoted fan Louise Seger, which took place during the last two years of Cline's life.

During the telecast of the National Academy of Recording Arts & Sciences' Grammy Award ceremonies in February 1995, it was announced that NARAS had chosen Patsy for one of the recipients of its Lifetime Achievement Award.

Meanwhile the show, which drew almost 250,000 fans during its run at the Ryman, by the end of 1995 had spawned three touring versions which drew capacity crowds to performances in major cities across the U.S. from Denver to Philadelphia.

CLOWER, JERRY: *Comic. Born Amite County, Mississippi, September 28, 1926.*

Rural humor always has been an integral part of the country music scene, sometimes in the form of comic sketches delivered by bandsmembers, other times handled by stand-up comics the likes of Minnie Pearl and the Duke of Paducah. Maintaining the latter tradition in the 1970s was burly Jerry Clower, "The Mouth of Mississippi," whose wild anecdotes of goings on in his home region of Amite County kept audiences howling with laughter, not only in the South but in all sections of the United States.

Clower depended for his impact on timing and historionics. As he said, "I tell stories funny, not funny stories." His approach was described by Lawrence Buser. "Clower talks. He bellows. He wails. He waves his arms. He contorts his face. Puckers his lips. Furrows his brow. And does the best imitation of a chain saw that you ever heard. (Although 'Wah-wa-wa-wa-wa-wa' does not look like much when you read it, listen to Clower bring it to life in one of his stories and then look around for that tavern screen door the notorious Marcel Ledbetter, in a fit of anger, reduced to a twisted pile of wire and splinters.)"

As a farm boy growing up in Mississippi in the 1930s and early 1940s, Jerry gave little thought to a show business career. In his teens, he already was a two-hundred pounder who liked sports of all kinds. In his late teens at the tail end of World War II, he entered the service for several years, then played football at a local junior college and gained a full scholarship to Mississippi State University, where he considered becoming a pro football player. But the competition was tough and he opted for a regular job as a fertilizer sales representative for Mississippi Chemical Corporation in Yazoo City, joining the firm in 1954.

Somewhat in the tradition of the first *Opry* star, Uncle Dave Macon, Jerry developed his comic touch as a sideline and didn't move on to the commercial entertainment arena until well along in years. In fact, he worked up his repertoire of funny stories mainly to help his sales pitch. Over a decade and a half of selling fertilizer, he unconsciously polished and refined his delivery until he was more a performer than huckster. After a while, he began to expand his scope by giving some of his routines at company sales meetings and in front of local groups. In time, people began to urge him to do more with his talent. On the advice of a friend, he taped a "raccoon" story and submitted it to Decca Records (now merged into MCA Records) in the early 1970s.

In 1971 Clower met his manager, Nashville-based agent Tandy Rice. "Ever since . . . my life's been boiling just like a great big Alka-Seltzer."

With those steps under his belt, things began to move for Clower. Decca recorded his first album, *Jerry Clower from Yazoo City, Mississippi Talkin'*, live (all his LPs through the late 1970s were recorded in that fashion, in line with his belief that he came across best that way). His appearances on the *David Frost Show* in New York and many other major TV programs helped to make the record a million seller. He quickly became a favorite with fans all over the country, and each succeeding album brought in new gold-record awards, including his second LP, *From the Mouth of the Mississippi*, followed by *Clower Power, Live in Picayune* (issued in 1975), and *The Ambassador of Good Will* (1976).

Clower soon was asked to become a regular on the *Grand Ole Opry*, where he still was a featured performer in the 1980s. His other activities included an appearance on a Walter Cronkite program on desegre-

gation in the South and a starring role on the syndicated country music show *Nashville on the Road*.

He was particularly proud of the Cronkite program because he felt it showed the real progress achieved in integration in his beloved home town of Yazoo City. He acknowledged to Buser that his views in favor of tolerance and equality made him anathema to the Ku Klux Klan. "I find I fought a war to give a man the right to be a bigot if he wants to, but those same people don't want to give me the right not to be one. I'm a redneck, but I'm an educated redneck. I was taught that you should never have your mind so made up that facts couldn't change it."

A Bible-reading Christian, he insisted to interviewers that he never drank, smoked, lied, cheated, or swore. As a lay minister and deacon of the First Baptist Church in Yazoo City, he often was called on to deliver sermons in his home church and elsewhere across the United States. His speaking engagements in the religious area included appearances with the Billy Graham Crusade and, on one occasion, serving as keynote speaker at the Southern Baptist National Convention in Miami, Florida.

At the start of the 1980s, Jerry continued to turn out new albums for MCA Records. In 1980, *Ledbetter Olympics* was released, followed in the fall of 1981 by *More Good 'Uns*.

From the early 1980s through 1996, Jerry's career followed the pattern established in previous years. He continued to perform comedy routines on the country concert circuit and as an after-dinner speaker at business and other functions. His albums weren't high volume sellers, but they did remain in print. For instance, his 1972 release *Mouth of the Mississippi* was certified gold by the R.I.A.A. on January 31, 1995 and his 1972 LP, *From Yazoo City (Mississippi Talkin')* earned a similar award on March 31, 1995.

COCHRAN, HANK: *Singer, guitarist, songwriter. Born Greenville, Mississippi, August 2, 1935.*

The name *Cochran* is familiar to both rock and country fans. To rock followers it brings to mind Eddie Cochran, a legendary figure whose "Summertime Blues" was almost an anthem for the teenagers of the 1950s. For country fans, the Cochran of note is Hank, writer of many classic songs and a talented performer in his own right. Oddly, both Hank and Eddie worked together for a time under the name the Cochran Brothers even though they were unrelated. Eddie died in 1960 after contributing some major rock hits; at the time, Hank was still unknown. Fortunately, he was active for decades afterward, still contributing to the country scene during the 1990s.

Hank (original name Garland Perry Cochran), born in Mississippi, spent many of his early years in Tennessee. His parents died when he was a child and he was placed in a Tennessee orphanage. At ten he ran away from there and somehow managed to keep from returning, eventually making his way to Hobbs, New Mexico, where he had some relatives. While there, he earned a living as an oil-field hand. He also took his first steps toward a music career when an uncle taught him to play guitar. Many of the first songs he picked out on the instrument were Hank Williams songs that he had listened to on the radio. After a while, though, Cochran felt the urge to write original material and he had a fair number under his belt by the time he headed for California in the mid-1950s.

Continuing to earn money from manual work, he spent much of his spare time at a place called the Riverside Rancho. Some of the time he just hung around listening to the regular country artists. On occasion he got to sit in with some of them. He also met other aspiring young musicians, including Eddie Cochran. The two teamed up and worked together for several years before Eddie decided to concentrate on rock in 1958. Hank by then was gaining a reputation as a good sideman and became a regular on a country TV show in Stockton, California, called the *California Hayride.*

Hank's career was interrupted for a time when he was drafted into the army and stationed at Ford Ord, California. His stay was fairly brief, and after his discharge he played for a time at the Fort Ord noncommissioned officers club. He was writing steadily by then and decided to try for a regular job. The result, at the end of the 1950s, was a job as staff writer with the California branch of Pamper Music Company at fifty dollars a week. His work was promising enough that within a year Pamper agreed to transfer him to its Nashville branch. He arrived there in October 1959. A few days after he reached Nashville, Skeets McDonald became the first Music City artist to record one of his numbers, "Where You Go I'll Follow." Another of the results of the move was a collaboration with Harlan Howard on a song called "I Fall to Pieces" that provided Patsy Cline with a number-one country hit.

In Nashville, Cochran hung out at a well-known club called Tootsie's Orchid Lounge, where he met other young hopefuls. One of them, with whom he forged a close friendship, was Willie Nelson. He thought so much of Willie's potential that when Joe Allison, then head of Liberty Records country-music division, offered Hank a recording contract, Hank urged them to sign Willie first. They did, but soon after added Cochran to the roster as well. Hank responded with several releases, the second of which, "Sally Was a Good Old Girl" (a Harlan Howard composition), remains a country classic.

But while Hank continued to perform in many major country spots as the 1960s went by, his main accomplishments were in the writing field. In 1961, he could point to his first number-one song on country lists, Patsy Cline's version of "I Fall to Pieces," which also peaked at number twelve on the *Billboard* pop chart the week of July 24, 1961. As he recalled for

Teresa George of the Country Music Association's *Close Up* magazine in September 1989, after he wrote the song he took it to every Nashville producer and was turned down until Owen Bradley heard it. "I don't know what Owen saw in the song, but I'm sure glad he did. He thought it was a hit. Patsy didn't like the song at first, but she respected Owen's opinion. He believed in the song and he believed in Patsy."

He followed that success with a banner year in 1962, with such hits as Burl Ives' recordings of "A Little Bitty Tear" and "A Funny Way of Laughin'"; Eddy Arnold's single of "Tears Broke Out on Me;" and Shirley Collie and Willie Nelson's release of "Willingly." In 1963, he provided Ray Price with the country standard "Make the World Go Away" (two years later a number-one hit for Eddy Arnold) and George Jones with "You Comb Her Hair." Arnold earned a number-one singles hit in 1965 with Hank's "I Want to Go with You." In 1966, Jeannie Seely scored a top-10 hit with his "Don't Touch Me," a recording that was rewarded with a Grammy as well.

In 1964, Hank left Liberty and signed with RCA, which released a number of his albums during the mid-1960s, including the collection *Hits from the Heart.* However, though many of the recordings were excellent, Hank never was able to achieve star status as a performer during those years. He continued to be on the Pamper Music staff up to the time the firm was sold to Tree International in 1969. Other than the ownership shift, nothing changed much. In the 1970s, Hank penned new material under the Tree banner.

For most of the 1970s, Hank kept a relatively low profile as a performer. In 1977, though, he signed a new contract with Capitol Records. His debut LP on the label was *Hank Cochran—With a Little Help from His Friends.* The friends referred to included Jeannie Seely, by then his wife, Merle Haggard, Jack Greene, and Willie Nelson. Nelson's contributions included working with Hank on Cochran's song "Ain't Life Hell." On another track, Haggard joined Cochran in a tribute to Nelson titled "Willie," written by the album's producer, Glenn Martin. In 1974, he was inducted into the Nashville-based Songwriter's Hall of Fame.

In 1979, Willie Nelson got Hank to appear in the movie *Honeysuckle Rose,* in which Cochran sang "Make the World Go Away." On the hit soundtrack LP from the film, Cochran's tracks comprised that song plus a later composition, "I Don't Do Windows." While Hank was working on the movie, he and Willie agreed to go to Austin, Texas, for one of the *Austin City Limits* shows. Cochran served as the program's host; the show was first telecast in 1979 and repeated several times in later years.

Another outgrowth of those activities was Cochran's agreement to assemble a band of his own as the opening act for a series of Willie Nelson concerts during the 1979–80 season. In late 1980, Willie and Ray Price placed a duet single of Hank's "Don't You Ever Get Tired of Hurting Me" on the top rungs of the country charts. By then Hank had a new recording contract of his own with Elektra/Aslyum Records; his first release with them was the November 1980 LP *Make the World Go Away.*

During the 1980s, Hank continued to focus on writing and producing more than performing. From 1969 to May 1989, his material was published by Tree International. After leaving that long-term association, he formed his own publishing firm, Co-Heart Music, with close friend and business partner Glenn Martin. Cochran also started his own record label, Gifted Few Records.

For most of his writing career, Cochran did all his work by himself except for occasional collaborations with former wife Jeannie Seely and longtime friends Glenn Martin and Willie Nelson. Starting in the mid-1980s, he became more open to joint efforts, cowriting George Strait hits (including "The Chair" and "Ocean Front Property") with Dean Dillon, for example, as well as a number of songs for Vern Gosdin albums. The latter included seven cowritten with Vern and/or Max Barnes for Gosdin's hit 1989 Columbia album, *Chiseled in Stone.* The latter included the charted singles "Set 'Em Up Joe" and "Who You Gonna Blame It On This Time?" Hank also cowrote five songs for Gosdin's next collection, *Alone.*

In the late 1980s, Cochran's credits also included serving as executive producer for preparation of an album and video by Johnny Paycheck, then serving time in Chillicothe Corrections Institution in Ohio for a firearms offense.

The 1990s situation stayed the course for Hank, as he wrote or cowrote new material and sought other outlets for his energies as a producer and entrepreneur.

COE, DAVID ALLAN: *Singer, guitarist, songwriter. Born Akron, Ohio, September 6, 1939.*

"From the time I was nine until just about three years ago," David Allan Coe said in 1970, "the longest I was 'free' at any one time was sixty days." It was, indeed, the truth that for twenty years of his life, Coe seemed an incorrigible jailbird and, in fact, toward the end of that period, it looked as though he might be put in the electric chair. He was one of those saved by the ending of capital punishment; his later achievements form a strong argument for a continuation of that trend.

Born in Akron, he was the product of an unhappy, broken home. He quickly developed an antisocial attitude, resulting in his initial experience with "rehabilitation." At nine, he was sent to a reform school in Albion, Michigan, the Starr Commonwealth for Boys. From then on, whenever he was released from reform school or prison, he always seemed to find some activity that would put him back behind penal walls. In his early years the offenses ranged from possession of burglary

tools to car theft and later for offenses related to membership in various motorcycle gangs (including the Headhunters Motorcycle Club in New York). At fourteen he was sent to Boys Industrial School, at sixteen to National Training School for Boys, at eighteen to Chillicothe Reformatory, at nineteen to Lima State Hospital (for observation), between twenty and twenty-five a series of remissions to Ohio State Penitentiary, and from twenty-five to twenty-seven, Marion Correctional Institution.

While he was in Ohio State Penitentiary, he killed an inmate who made a homosexual advance to him. To fight the man off, Coe grabbed the wringer from a mop bucket and struck out twice, killing his assailant. Though self-defense might have been indicated, a convict is limited in his resources. Coe was sent to death row, where he awaited execution for three months. Oddly enough, he was joined there by his foster father, also sent up for murder. While there, the two wrote songs and poems together. Coe, during his years in prison, had managed to learn to play guitar. After capital punishment was abolished, both of them had their sentences commuted to life.

Things looked a bit brighter, though still hardly encouraging, as Coe was beginning to have a different outlook on life. He continued to write and work on new material. He also became increasingly interested in performing and soon was headlining penitentiary shows. All of these activities apparently helped persuade the parole board to give him another chance. In 1967, he was released from prison, already aiming for a show business career. (His foster father was set free some seven years later.)

He headed for Nashville in an old car. When he got there, Edgar Bayer wrote, "He had exactly one dime. He slept in his car, picked his guitar and sang for meals. Spent days knocking on doors trying to peddle some of the jail-written songs that sang of pain, death, narcotics, prostitution, prison, and love—long before others were putting such stark realism into songs."

Finally, things began to turn his way a bit. Music executive Shelby Singleton took him in hand and soon Coe's debut LP, *Penitentiary Blues,* came out on the SSS label. The album received some attention, though it was hardly a major success. During those years he also had the satisfaction of seeing two singles reach the top 40, "Tobacco Road" and "Two Tone Brown." In the early 1970s, he recorded for Plantation, and a sardonic comment on the travails of the Nixon administration, "How High's the Watergate Martha?" was taken note of in a number of national publications. Coe also gained his first regional singles hit with "Keep Those Big Wheels Running."

His songwriting eventually provided the major turning point in his career. During the early 1970s, more and more country artists were including Coe compositions in their repertoire. Then Billy Sherrill selected the song "Would You Lay with Me (In a Field of Stone)" for a Tanya Tucker session. The single became one of her greatest hits, rising to number one on all trade magazine country charts during 1973. That achievement naturally attracted industry attention to Coe, and major record companies began to talk with him about his future plans. Ron Bledsoe, CBS vice president for operations in Nashville, was particularly impressed and asked Coe to prepare demonstration recordings of some songs. Satisfied with those efforts, Columbia signed Coe and Bledsoe produced his first album, *The Mysterious Rhinestone Cowboy.* Issued in 1974, the album caught fire with both critics and fans and soon Coe and Bledsoe completed a second album for 1974 release, *The Mysterious Rhinestone Cowboy Rides Again.*

David turned out two excellent singles on Columbia in 1974, "Sad Country Song" and "If I Could Climb the Walls of a Bottle." They weren't massive hits, but his version of Steve Goodman's "You Never Even Called Me by My Name" reached the top 10 in September 1975. By then Coe was starting to receive recognition from both the country audience and his musical peers as he guested on most major radio and TV shows. He also sometimes shared bills with such other members of the "progressive" country movement as Jerry Jeff Walker, Willie Nelson, and Waylon Jennings. During the mid-1970s, David also made a number of appearances on the *Grand Ole Opry.*

Throughout the mid- and late-1970s he continued to turn out a steady series of singles and albums on Columbia, many of which made the charts. Among his LPs were *Once Upon a Rhyme* (whose tracks included his version of "Would You Lay with Me in a Field of Stone)" and *Long-Haired Redneck,* both issued in 1976. The last-named album's title song included such lines as "My long hair can't cover up my red neck/I've won every fight I've ever fought/I don't need some turkey/Tellin' me that I ain't country/Sayin' I ain't worth the damned old ticket that he bought. . . ." In 1977, Coe completed his fifth Columbia LP, *David Allan Coe Rides Again,* as coproducer with Ron Bledsoe, and continued in that capacity for *Tattoo* in 1977 and *Family Album* in 1978. His second 1978 album, *Human Emotions* (which dealt in part with the break-up of his marriage), was produced by Billy Sherrill.

His singles releases in the mid- and late-1970s included "Would You Be My Lady" (1975); "When She's Got Me (Where She Wants Me)" (1976); "Willie, Waylon and Me," coproduced by Coe, Waylon Jennings, and Bledsoe (1976); "Lately I've Been Thinkin' Too Much," "Face to Face," "Just to Prove My Love for You" (1977); "Divers Do It Deeper," "You Can Count on Me," and "If This Is Just a Game" (1978), all produced by Billy Sherrill.

In 1978, Coe's songwriting talents again came to the fore as Johnny Paycheck scored a smash singles hit with "Take This Job and Shove It." The record was nominated for a Grammy for Best C&W Song of the Year. Paycheck's name joined a long list of others who recorded Coe's material in the 1970s, including Johnny Cash, George Jones, Charlie Louvin, Melba Montgomery, Billy Jo Spears, Del Reeves, Stoney Edwards, and Tammy Wynette.

Though now a celebrity in the 1970s, Coe didn't forget his earlier history. He gave concerts from time to time at prisons around the country. In addition, with two partners he set up a music publishing firm in the mid-1970s called Captive Music with the goal of providing a possible outlet for songs written by prison inmates.

In 1978, Coe's autobiography, called *Just for the Record,* was issued by Dream Enterprises with the credit line "written entirely by ex-convict David Allan Coe."

At the start of the 1980s, new Columbia singles by Coe continued to make the charts, such as the duet with Bill Anderson "Get a Little Dirt on Your Hands" in 1980 and "Stand by Your Man" in 1981.

In 1984, Coe celebrated his tenth anniversary with Columbia Records with a live benefit concert in Nashville dedicated to the memory of Steve Goodman. Goodman, of course, had written Coe's first hit, as well as others he had recorded over the years. In the mid-1980s, Columbia issued the *David Allan Coe's Greatest Hits* album, which proved a steady seller with his fans. On September 18, 1989, it was certified platinum by the R.I.A.A.

Throughout the 1980s in to the 1990s, Coe remained active as an important draw at fairs, nightclubs, and at major venues in many parts of the U.S. From time to time he guested on the major country music networks as well. By the second half of the 1980s, his record sales had begun to decline, and by the mid-1990s he was absent from the rosters of major record labels. He continued to lend his talent to benefit causes, joining the artists, for instance, appearing at the Farm Aid VII show at the New Orleans Superdome in September 1994.

COLLIE, MARK: *Singer, guitarist, pianist, songwriter. Born Waynesboro, Tennessee, January 18, 1956.*

It took a long time for Mark Collie's major label recording debut to become reality at the start of the 1990s, but his name was hardly unfamiliar to music industry figures. For much of the preceding decade he had established a reputation as one of the top Nashville songwriters, and his name graced the credits of releases by many country stars, a record that continued in the 1990s even as he gained attention for his own records and videos.

He grew up in the town of Waynesboro, Tennessee, roughly halfway between Memphis and Nashville. He was exposed to country music from his childhood, but didn't ignore such formats as rock and roll and rhythm and blues. As a boy he also enjoyed gospel music in the local church his family belonged to, and for a time sang in the church choir. The artist who had the greatest impact on him during that period, he said, wasn't a traditional performer, but country-influenced rock star Leon Russell.

In particular, he was entranced by Russell's country-style album, *Hank Wilson Is Back.* "I had the eight-track tape and wore that thing out. As much as I ever listened to, that album convinced me I could be a part of country music. Here was Leon Russell, one of the top pop-rock products of the sixties and seventies, yet his country interpretations were so pure. He was being more honest with country music than some of the artists that were on the country charts at that time. And that made me think, you know, that is what I want to be about."

In his preteens, Mark was already trying out his performing talents for his family, which included six other siblings. He learned to play piano and guitar, and by his teens was quite proficient on both instruments. When opportunities came along to perform at school events or to work with friends in bands, he took advantage of them.

Though he grew up relatively close to Nashville, his route to Music City was somewhat circuitous. Starting in the 1970s he pursued work in honky-tonks and clubs in many places outside his home state. He began to develop a following from appearances in many venues in the Southeast, and during one career phase he spent a year and a half performing in Hawaii. It was a demanding life, but as he paid his dues he honed his playing abilities and songwriting skills. He received a major shock in 1977 when he was diagnosed as a diabetic, but took the necessary steps to keep the disease at bay.

In 1982 he made the move to Nashville, where his demos were soon circulating among major recording artists; by the mid-1980s he began to make some inroads as a writer. (Among performers who recorded some of his songs in the 1980s and 1990s were Randy Travis, Aaron Tippin, Martina McBride, Collin Raye, and Marty Stuart.) After a while he got the opportunity to do some live performances at the Douglas Corner Cafe, not far from the city's main publishing and record company section of Music Row. In time this gained the attention of recording executives, which led to an MCA Records contract at the end of the 1980s.

His debut album, *Hardin County Line,* and second collection, *Born and Raised in Black and White,* spawned several singles and videos that won attention from radio and TV programmers in a number of locations. One of those singles that made the *Billboard* Top 30 (in September 1991) was "Callused Hands." The title track from the debut album was the first Mark cowrote with top-ranked Nashville writer and record producer Don Cook. It was a collaboration that was to pay off with a number of very successful recordings.

The first fruits came on Mark's third album, the Don Cook produced *Mark Collie,* which provided two major chart hit singles, "Even the Man in the Moon Is Crying"

and "Born to Love You." (The first of those rose to number three in *Radio & Records* the week of November 13, 1992, the second peaked at number five the week of April 23, 1993.)

Mark Collie's contents included the track "Is That Too Much to Ask?" which offered commentary on the recession, which had provoked hard times for ordinary people. Collie remarked, "The song was inspired by the realities of our social and economic situation. The American Dream has become a nightmare for so many honest, hardworking, deserving people."

Another album track issued as a single, "Shame, Shame, Shame, Shame" (written by Collie and J. Leap), made the *Billboard* Top 30 in July 1993. The song, Mark noted, had become a major part of his concert act. "I don't know why, but that song gets more response when we perform it live than any song I've ever written. It's just straightforward rock and roll sort of country and West Tennessee, I guess." At the end of 1993, Mark had another *Billboard* Top 30 single, "Something's Gonna Change Her Mind" (cowritten with Cook), that stayed on the charts until 1994.

Collie's fourth MCA album, *Unleashed,* came out in June 1994. The first single from the album, "It's No Secret" (cowritten by Collie and Mike Reid) was on the charts in May and made upper levels. It was followed on the singles lists by "Hard Lovin' Woman" (cowritten by Collie, Cook, and J. B. Jarvis), in upper positions in the fall.

In October 1994, Mark hosted the first annual "Mark Collie Celebrity Race for Diabetes Cure." The legendary NASCAR (National Association of Stock Car Racing) driver Richard Petty and other stock car greats agreed to take part, and Collie himself drove a Legend automobile. The goal was to raise funds for diabetes research. Collie commented, "There are some fascinating developments being made in treating diabetes, but the disease is not cured. I promised myself that if I was ever in position to assist in any way in finding a cure, I would do my part."

Mark's singles releases in 1995 included "Three Words, Two Hearts, One Night" (cowritten by Mark and G. House) on the charts in the summer. In the early part of 1996, Mark gave a series of concerts in Europe for U.S. forces stationed there. His shows included military bases in Croatia, Bosnia, Hungary, Germany, and France.

COLTER, JESSI: *Singer, pianist, songwriter. Born Phoenix, Arizona, May 25.*

Jessi Colter's stage name seems appropriate considering her association with the progressive country "outlaw" movement in the mid- and late 1970s. Her original name was Miriam Johnson, but when she became an entertainer she modified the name of a great-uncle of her father's, an outlaw and counterfeiter named Jesse Colter.

The sixth of a family of seven children, she grew up in Phoenix under strong gospel influence. "I started taking piano lessons when I was about six or seven. Because my mother was a minister and an evangelist, I grew up spending a lot of time in church and by the time I was eleven, I was playing piano in church." She recalls that by then she already had decided to make singing and writing her life's work. Five years later, she started singing professionally.

"When I was sixteen, I met Duane Eddy. I guess that's where it all started. My sister Sharon, who married Jack Clement [a major producer, performer, and songwriter], found out that Duane Eddy was looking for a singer to produce a record with. And she managed to set up an audition for me. Our family was strict, so my brother had to smuggle me out of the house because the audition was at a bar."

Duane liked her and "we recorded in Phoenix and Duane did some overdubbing in Los Angeles and finally the record came out on the Jamie label. . . . Nothing happened with the record." But Jessi toured with Eddy and married him several months later. The marriage brought her to Beverly Hills for a while and Jessi cut back on her music activities to raise a family. The marriage ended in divorce after seven years. Later she was to marry Waylon Jennings.

The two originally met in Phoenix while Waylon was starring at a club called JD's. She went over some of her songs with him and the two recorded a duet in a local studio. Waylon kept in touch with her and finally proposed. After the wedding, he got her a contract with RCA. She did an album and some singles were released, but again nothing resulted from it.

She continued to do some backing vocal work and write new songs while her career languished for a while. Then she got the chance to sign with Capitol Records, an alliance that resulted in the crossover national singles hit "I'm Not Lisa" and the gold-record album *I'm Jessi Colter* in 1975. The single actually was somewhat cloying, but other tracks on the album verified that Colter had a fine, flexible voice and the ability to project a range of emotions with strong impact. "I'm Not Lisa" was one of the five songs nominated for the 1975 Grammy for Best Country Vocal Performance, Female, and Jessi also was nominated for the songwriter's Grammy for Best Country Song.

Before 1975 was over, Colter could point to other songs on the country singles charts: "You Ain't Never Been Loved (Like I'm Gonna Love You)" and "What's Happened to Blue Eyes," the latter a top-10 success in October. She kept it up in 1976 with "I Thought I Heard You Calling My Name" early in the year (from her second Capitol LP, *Jessi*) followed by such other chartmakers as "Without You" and a duet with Waylon, "Suspicious Mind." Later in 1976, her album *Diamond in the Rough* not only made the country charts but, as

had been the case with her debut album, went well up in the pop top 100.

During that year, RCA released one of the landmark albums in recent country history, a collection of songs by Jessi, Waylon, Willie Nelson, and Tompall Glaser called *Wanted: The Outlaws.* The album was an exciting showcase of what progressive country is all about and caught the fancy of both country and non-country fans alike. As of the late 1970s, the album remained a steady seller and a country record seller, having earned R.I.A.A. certification for well over a million copies distributed. The extensive concert series that Waylon, Jessi, and Willie (sometimes with Glaser as well) offered in support of the album remains among the most memorable of the mid- and late 1970s.

In the late 1970s, Colter slowed down a bit; although her singles and albums still showed up on the charts, they tended to stay on country lists rather than cross over. Her fourth Capitol LP, *Miriam,* appeared on country lists in the summer of 1977. In the fall of 1978, her fifth album, *That's the Way a Cowboy Rocks and Rolls* (produced by Waylon and Richie Albright) suggested a change in musical direction. In her late 1978–early 1979 concert tour in support of the LP she was backed by her husband's band, The Waylors. Her next album effort was one for RCA with Waylon that was released in 1980. Called *Leather and Lace,* it passed R.I.A.A. gold record levels (in the fall of 1981). In 1981 she went into the studios to work on her first solo LP for Capitol since 1978. Called *Ridin' Shotgun,* it was scheduled for release in early 1982.

While not completely avoiding music, in the 1980s and 1990s Jessi spent more time on family matters than career activities. She could be found more often in the audience for one of husband Waylon's shows than onstage. At the start of the 1990s they still were close after twenty years of marriage.

While on tour with the Highwaymen in the early 1990s (a tour on which Jessi shared bus accommodations with Waylon), Jennings paid tribute to his wife. Discussing the lyrics of the song "Amanda," which at one point described the joys of playing with a hillbilly band, he told a *Los Angeles Times* reporter, "You know what other line hits me every time I sing it? The one about a gentleman's wife. I think of Jessi.

"She was what made me finally quit [drugs]. I looked at her face one day and I could see what I was doing to her, the pain I was causing. Nothing else had been enough. . . . The fact that I almost ruined my voice, that I couldn't even see straight some nights on stage."

CONFEDERATE RAILROAD: *Vocal and instrumental group headed by Danny Shirley (singer, songwriter), born Chattanooga, Tennessee, August 12, 1956. Other members as of 1995, Mark Dufresne , born Wisconsin, August 6, 1955 (drums), Chris McDaniel, born Atlanta,*

Georgia, February 4, 1965 (keyboards), Michael Lamb (guitar), Wayne Secrest, born Illinois, April 29, 1950 (bass guitar), Gates Nichols, born New York, May 26, 1944 (pedal steel guitar). Lamb replaced in 1996 by Jimmie Dormire, born Detroit, Michigan, March 8, 1960.

In an era of relatively bland, mass-audience-oriented country headliners, Confederate Railroad served as a reminder of the blue-collar roots of traditional country and the country raunch & roll groups of the rock era. As the band's lead singer, Danny Shirley emphasized, "I used to run with the boys in Lynyrd Skynyrd. What turned me on to country music was when Waylon and Willie hit, and I saw that the music I grew up around could have some balls to it. But Southern rock heroes—Skynyrd, the Allman Brothers and Marshall Tucker—became fans of my muse much earlier than my country music heroes."

Shirley grew up in Chattanooga and in his teens and twenties lived much of the rough and rowdy life blue-collar kids often passed through on their way to adulthood. As he told writer James Kelly in 1992, the band members, roadies, and other cast members looked as though they were members of Hell's Angels. "We were all Harley riders, long before the Yuppies knew what a Harley was." But, noting his ways in the 1990s weren't as wild as in the old days, he said that, on concert tours, the band typically was accompanied by nine families, including his own wife and son. "I guess we've all gotten old," he commented.

But the group's style, he emphasized in 1994, was no different from what it had been in 1981 when he first became leader of what evolved into Confederate Railroad. Their personal lives might be less tumultuous, but they performed with the same fervor and enthusiasm.

Starting in 1983, the band had its first bus, a 1958 Greyhound, and was on the road regularly backing other artists, playing one-nighters, or local bar dates wherever work could be lined up. Among the performers the band backed were such hard-bitten stars as David Allan Coe and Johnny Paycheck. On some of those tours, Shirley recalled, he was not only involved in providing band support, but also serving as combination booking agent, road manager, and publicist. All Paycheck and Coe had to do, he told a reporter, was get to a concert and sell their T-shirts; he would do the rest.

In 1985 the group moved headquarters to Kennesaw, Georgia, and got a job as house band for Miss Kitty's in Marietta. On some occasions, Travis Tritt, born and raised in Marietta, was on the bill at the club. The band continued its touring in between stints at Miss Kitty's, including performances in other locales, such as backing Coe for a gig at London's Wembley Stadium. For U.S. dates, Shirley retired the '58 Greyhound in 1991 in favor of leasing a 1982 bus and, after finally achieving a major record label pact in 1992, bought a brand-new '93 vehicle. He told John Wirt of the *Baton Rouge Morning Advocate* (Fun Section, December 11, 1992), "In a period of nine months we've gone from a '58 to a '93. This is a big deal around my house."

Shirley and his band mates naturally hoped to break through to bigger things via the recording route. During the 1980s he had recorded three solo albums on indy labels, but scored no notable successes. Finally, in 1991 the group came to Nashville for an all-out effort for a major label alignment "before old age really caught up with us." Their demos got the attention of Atlantic executives but initially they wanted to sign only Shirley as a solo artist.

Danny argued it made more sense to allow him to be part of a band. He told Dennis Hunt of the *Los Angeles Times* ("He Engineered Success of Confederate Railroad," May 21, 1994), "There were too many solo singles out there already. . . . I just didn't want to be just another clean-cut singer in a white hat or a black hat, singing some sad songs about losing your love, or other stuff like that. I'm a bar-band kind of a guy."

He convinced the record company officials who assigned them to work with Barry Beckett of Muscle Shoals fame (who produced important albums for artists like Hank Williams, Jr., Alabama, and Bob Dylan) on their debut album. That album, *Confederate Railroad,* came out in June 1992, and the blend of torrid raunch rock and country ballads soon won considerable critical praise and increasing radio airplay.

Accompanying this with intensive touring, the band saw results on the charts as the album moved as high as number seven on *Billboard* country lists, staying there into the summer of 1994, with sales of over 1.6 million copies. The debut single and video, "She Took It Like a Man," was a top-30 hit. Helping spur video sales were appearances by then–Atlanta Falcons head football coach Jerry Glanville, who told James Kelly, "There are at least five hit singles on this tape. These guys are so talented that they will rule the country music industry before long."

The achievement of the last of those predictions remains to be seen, but the band certainly appeared to have staying power. Its second single release, "Jesus and Mama Always Loved Me," was on the charts in late 1992, reaching number one on the *Gavin Report* list and hitting number two in *Radio & Records* the week of October 2. *R&R* later named the record one of the top country singles of 1992. "Queen of Memphis" from the debut album, also won major support in 1993, reaching number two in *Billboard* and peaking at number four in *R&R* the week of February 5. It was followed on the charts by "When You Leave That Way (You Can Never Go Back)" (which peaked at number nine in *R&R* the week of July 9, 1993) and "Trashy Women" (which peaked in *R&R* at number seven the week of October 15).

The band's second album, *Notorious,* came out in

early 1994 and by August has sold over 500,000 copies to surpass gold-record levels. The initial single, "She Never Cried," made the charts, as did the next release, "Elvis and Andy." The new single, "Daddy Never Was the Cadillac Kind," made the top-10 precincts, peaking at number seven in *R&R* the week of June 10. Other above-average album tracks were "Redneck Romeo" and "Move over Madonna."

Starting in 1993, the group began receiving recognition from its peers. It was one of the finalists in the Academy of Country Music Award in the category Best New Group or Duo. In 1994, Country Music Association members selected them as one of the finalists for the Vocal Group of the Year Award. The group also won nominations in other important music industry polls. Moving into 1995, it soon had another chart single, "When and Where," which made its way up the *Billboard* list in the late spring. Meanwhile the band prepared a new video titled "Bill's Laundromat, Bar and Grill."

The band's name and logo caused some observers to question whether its members might be encouraging the growth of old animosities. Shirley steadfastly rejected such suggestions. He told Kelly, "Everyone has their own opinion; to me it isn't racist. When I see the stars and bars, I don't think slavery, I think heritage. My forefathers fought for the Confederacy, but I don't think anyone, regardless of race, creed or color, should be for slavery. We study history to remind us what went right and what went wrong. If we ever forget our history, we're gonna make the same mistakes again."

To Hunt he commented, "We're not racists. I don't think we attract racists either—just people who like to drink beer and party and whoop it up. Being a redneck doesn't mean you're a racist. We were looking for a name that says we play Southeastern music. The name just helped us get some attention."

He also said there had been few problems in that regard. He did agree it might have some negative commercial impact. "I'm sure many companies would shy away from us because of our name. I don't think Coke or Pepsi or people like that would want us selling their products." In 1996, the band had the *Greatest Hits* album on the charts.

CONLEE, JOHN: *Singer, guitarist, songwriter. Born Versailles, Kentucky, August 11, 1946.*

In September 1978, with prospects for star status in the country field looking up, John Conlee played things close to the vest, driving his old 1973 Plymouth Fury and keeping his budget for stage outfits low. Having observed the pop field for years as a DJ, he thought he was on the right path. As he told Jack Hurst of the *Chicago Tribune,* "If somebody walked in right now and said 'I can make you a pop star,' I'd thank 'em and tell 'em to move along. You can't count on pop. It's nothing to

have two, three, or four hits in pop and never be heard of again. There's more longevity to country, and I want to establish myself there."

Of course, John's outlook was colored by his country roots. Born on a 300–400-acre farm in Versailles, Kentucky, he helped his father raise tobacco and tended the hogs, cattle, and other animals while growing up. Before he was nine, he was taking guitar lessons, and he kept up an interest in pop and country music in his teens. He didn't consider making a living at it, though, and instead took a 180-degree turn, becoming an embalmer and working at the trade for six years after finishing high school. In his mid-twenties the entertainment field still beckoned, so he quit the funeral home and sought work in radio. Having worked briefly on three stations in his home area, in Fort Knox, Elizabethtown, and Versailles, he then moved on to the country-music capital, Nashville, in 1971, where he joined station WLAC-FM (which later changed to WKQB). He remained there as a pop music DJ for most of the 1970s.

The Nashville environment seemed to revive his interest in country music. After a few years, he began trying his hand at songwriting with other station members, including fellow DJ Dick Kent, who later became his manager, and George Baber. Kent achieved the first milestone for John by bringing him together with ABC/Dot Records' head, Jim Foglesong, for whom John played some of his new material from time to time. In 1976, ABC/Dot was impressed enough by Conlee's progress to give him a recording contract. This led to some singles releases that brought in three regional hits during 1976–77, "Back Side of Thirty," "Let Your Love Fall Back on Me," and "The In Crowd." While having some minor hits is better than no success, it wasn't enough to induce John to give up his DJ efforts.

That changed in the spring of 1978 when he wrote a song called "Rose Colored Glasses" with George Baber, a song the Nashville *Banner* described as "hard core country about this poor guy who is in love with a two-timing girl and deludes himself into thinking she's true." The single of the song came out in late spring and by August had not only been on the charts most of the summer, but made it into the top 10.

In early June 1978, the record had already done so well that ABC was clamoring for an album and Conlee decided the time was ripe to depart the station. By September he was touring on weekends to booked engagements from Ohio to Texas and by mid-November had another single, "Lady Lay Down," in the country top 20 moving toward the topmost levels. Although things looked good, John shunned premature optimism. "To keep the ball rolling we have to keep having hit singles as strong or stronger than 'Rose Colored Glasses.' When we have a couple more of those, I guess we can throw a big celebration."

However, before long he had to agree there was good reason for optimism. "Lady Lay Down" remained on the best-seller lists in 1979 and by mid-January was number one in the United States. ABC came out with a reissue of "Back Side of Thirty" in the spring and it went into the top 5 in May. By the end of the year, on ABC's successor, MCA Records, he had another chart single, "Baby, You're Something," which made it to the national top-10 in February 1980. His other top-10 hits of the year were "Friday Night Blues," "Before My Time," and "She Can't Say That Anymore." His 1981 hits included "What I Had with You" and "Miss Emily's Picture."

He became a regular on the *Grand Ole Opry* during 1981 (debuting on February 7), which he always considered one of the high points of his musical life. Though he got to play in many cities other than Nashville in the 1980s and 1990s, including more than a few venues outside the U.S., he always looked forward to his *Opry* appearances—which, of course, also allowed him to spend time on the thirty-two-acre farm he shared with his wife, Gale, and their family near Goodlettsville, Tennessee. As he told Kelly Delaney of *Inside Country Music,* he had only fond memories of his childhood on his family's Kentucky farm.

"It's still the only way to grow up, as far as I'm concerned. It's the only way to raise a family. It's a good way to teach responsibility, a good way to teach nature. I wouldn't trade being raised that way for anything. I intend to raise my own kids that way."

His debut album on MCA was the November 1978 release *Rose Colored Glasses,* which was followed over the next few years by *Forever* (July 1979), *Friday Night Blues* (May 1980), *With Love* (July 1981), *Busted* (April 1982), *Greatest Hits, Volume I* (March 1983), and *In My Eyes* (August 1983). *Billboard* magazine listed the last two collections as among the top country albums of 1983–84 with *In My Eyes* ranked number nine and *Greatest Hits* number eighteen. His 1982–83 album output added still more singles hits to his repertoire, including "Busted" (January 1982), "I Don't Remember Loving You" (September 1982), "Common Man" (February 1983), "I'm Only in It for the Love" (June 1983), "In My Eyes" (September 1983), and "As Long As I'm Rocking With You" (February 1984).

His mid-1980s MCA releases included the albums *Blue Highway* (September 1984), *Greatest Hits, Volume II* (September 1985), *Songs for the Working Man* (January 1986), *Legends* (February 1986), *Conlee Country* (September 1986), and *Twenty Greatest Hits* (March 1987). Singles releases on the label during those years (besides "As Long As I'm Rocking") included "Way Back" and "Years After You" (issued, respectively, in June and September 1984), plus "Working Man," "Blue Highway," and "Old School" (respectively, February, June, and September 1985). By the

end of 1985, John had left MCA and signed with Columbia, which issued the albums *Harmony* (February 1986) and *American Faces* (March 1987), from which were drawn the singles "Harmony" (January 1986), "Got My Heart Set On You" (May 1986), "The Carpenter" (September 1986), "Domestic Life" (February 1987), and "Mama's Rockin' Chair" (June 1987). When the last was issued, Conlee could point to a total output of twenty-nine singles, twenty-six of which had made the top 20 or better, including eight that soared to number one.

Like many other country artists with farm roots, John became concerned about the future of family farms in the mid-1980s. In June 1985, he gave a benefit concert to help the cause at Omaha, Nebraska, and when he heard of Willie Nelson's plans for the Farm Aid show, he called to volunteer his services. "I certainly didn't help to organize the entertainers and the concerts for the publicity. I only wanted to help bring attention to the crisis affecting this nation's family farms. With the help of Willie and others, we brought the family problems to the forefront and some changes began to take place. I'm not a radical or a rebel, but I will stand up and speak my mind on issues that I feel affect me, my family and others, and the farm crisis was, and remains, one of those issues."

From the early 1980s on, Conlee continued to be a familiar figure on country music TV programs. To name a few, he served as cohost on *Nashville Alive* and guested on *Hee Haw, Pop Goes the Country, Austin City Limits, Opry 60th Anniversary Celebration, Music City Tonight/TNN, CMA Awards Show, Backstage at the Grand Ole Opry "Live"* (TNN), *Country Top 20, Canadian Country Music Awards* (as host), and CBS-TV's *65th Grand Ole Opry Celebration.*

At the end of the 1980s, Conlee signed with Opryland's 16th Avenue Records, which issued his label debut, *Fellow Travelers,* in April 1989. Four singles were released from the album, two of which, "Hit the Ground Running" and the title track, reached upper-chart levels. The other singles were "Hopelessly Yours" and "Don't Get Me Started."

One of the unusual audience reactions to one of his renditions came during a concert in the summer of 1990, when people came up to the stage as he sang "Busted" and threw down dollar bills. By the time that ended, over $60 was lying there. As Conlee told Jack Hurst of the *Chicago Tribune,* "It was funny at first, but when we added it up, we didn't know what to do with the money." He finally decided to give it to the Feed the Children organization. "I called Larry Jones at Feed the Children in Oklahoma City and told him about our dilemma. I also told him I'll keep doing the song as long as it makes money for the organization." The tradition continued, and by 1995, the amount raised that way had surpassed $87,000.

CONLEY, EARL THOMAS: *Singer, guitarist, songwriter, record producer. Born Portsmouth, Ohio, October 17, c. mid-1950s.*

Like many an aspiring talent, Earl Thomas Conley beat on Nashville doors for several years in the 1970s without making headway—not surprising in a town where hopeful new artists and songwriters are almost a dime a dozen. Finally he left town for Alabama, where he put his career in gear and eventually made Nashville executives take notice. When the opportunity came his way he quickly made record industry history in 1984, when he became the first performer in any segment of popular music to achieve four number-one singles from one album.

Conley, an Ohio native, was a proficient guitarist in his teens, and despite the dominance of rock and roll in the 1960s formed an early love for country music. In the mid-1970s he settled in Nashville, and made the round of publishers and record companies trying to take the first step toward success in the industry. After several years of turndowns, he gave up in frustration and found work as a musician in Alabama. Among the people he met there was Nelson Larkin, who was involved in a recording studio in Huntsville. Nelson took an interest in the young Ohioan and presented some of Conley's songs to his brother, recording artist Billy Larkin. Billy's recording of Conley's composition "Leave It Up to Me" charted in the country top 20 and gave Conley confidence he could make it either as a writer or entertainer.

During the late 1970s, Earl T. made enough money to keep body and soul together by playing nights in Alabama clubs while adding to his backlog of original songs during the day. Bobby G. Rice and Price Mitchell recorded some of them with little chart impact, but then Mel Street made top-chart positions with Conley's "Smoky Mountain Memories." That helped Earl get a recording contract with GRT Records, but the several singles he turned out on the label failed to find an audience. The first real turning point came when Conway Twitty's single of Conley's song "This Time I've Hurt Her More Than She Loves Me" reached number one on the country charts.

With that success, Conley could no longer be ignored by the country music publishing field; but he still wanted to make it as an entertainer. He got a new contract with Warner Brothers Records as the 1970s drew to a close, which released three singles, "Dreamin's All I Do," "Middle Aged Madness," and "Stranded on a Dead End Street." Those failed to do well enough to allow him to complete an album, but Nelson Larkin, who was working as Conley's record producer, got him another contract in the early 1980s with the small Sunbird label. His debut on the label, *Blue Pearl,* provided the singles hit "Silent Treatment," which remained on the charts for twenty weeks. The next single drawn from the album, "Fire and Smoke," became Conley's

first number-one hit on July 11, 1981. That brought major label interest, and before 1981 was over he signed with RCA.

His first RCA album, *Fire and Smoke,* produced by himself and Larkin, contained only songs he had written. Issued in the fall of 1981, it not only made the charts, but was picked by the reviewer of one major men's magazine as one of the five best recent country releases. The first single from the album, "Tell Me Why," was on the charts in late 1981, followed in early 1982 by "After the Love Slips Away."

With major label backing, Conley was able to plan extensive concert dates in support of his new releases, including a limited-engagement major market tour at the end of 1981 with label-mate Alabama. Now music journalists were interested in talking with him about his career development, and he told one of them, "I'm not a prolific songwriter. For me, that would be the key to instant plasticity. I have to go inside myself too far, and my songs contain emotions that are highly personal. I use a lot of intensity when I write, and it takes complete concentration and focus for me. There's an intuitive, inspirational side of me that guides my songwriting completely."

Over the next few years, Conley and Larkin collaborated on a series of new albums on RCA including *I Have Loved You Girl, Your Love's On the Line, Somewhere Between Right and Wrong,* and in 1984, *Don't Make It Easy On Me.* The last named provided the record-breaking four number-one singles, including "Angel in Disguise" and "Holding Her and Loving You." "Holding Her and Loving You" was nominated by Country Music Association voters for 1984 Single of the Year. Conley also was a finalist for the CMA's Horizon Award for 1984.

Once Conley achieved star status, he arranged to hold an annual "Homecoming Concert" at the country fairgrounds near Portsmouth, typically held every June. He was also in demand starting in the mid-1980s for guest appearances on major TV networks and as a headliner at fairs and major venues around the U.S. and abroad. His recorded output during those years included hit duets with such singers as Anita Pointer and Emmylou Harris. In its 1987 voting the CMA nominated Conley and Pointer for Vocal Duo of the Year, a feat he repeated the following year with Emmylou Harris. His work with Harris included the number-one hit "We Believe in Happy Endings," which reached that top position on October 1, 1988. He had another solo hit with "What'd I Say," which reached number one the week of February 3. Later on, the RCA album *Earl T. Conley's Greatest Hits* was certified gold by the R.I.A.A. on July 25, 1989.

Conley's name continued to show up on the charts in the 1990s with his first singles success of the new decade being "Bring Back Your Love to Me," which peaked at number six in *Radio & Records* the week of

April 20, 1990. In 1991 he had such chart singles as "Shadow of a Doubt," which made *Billboard*'s Top 10 in late summer, and "Brotherly Love," a duet with the late Keith Whitley. Also on the charts in the late summer was his RCA album *Yours Truly*. During the first part of 1992, he worked with Ricky Skaggs on the chart single "Hard Days and Honky Tonk Nights."

COOLEY, DONNELL CLYDE "SPADE": *Singer, fiddler, band leader. Born Pack Saddle Creek, Oklahoma, December 17, 1910; died Oakland, California, November 1969.*

When western swing got a new lease on life in the 1970s, two names tended to spring to mind from the past—Bob Wills and Spade Cooley. Thanks to the alumni of Wills's old band, the Texas Playboys, his memory remained alive. But Cooley's star had descended earlier and much more precipitously than his Texan contemporary and there was no band left to remind country fans of his one-time greatness.

For much of Cooley's life his story was one of an American Dream-like rise from rags to riches. He was born to an impoverished family in Oklahoma and was taken to Oregon when he was four, where his father, John, and mother, Emma, hoped for a better life. The change wasn't particularly successful—Spade once noted, "I was born poor and raised poor." However, it did bring about the boy's first exposure to music training. His father liked to play fiddle and made friends with a man who taught the instrument. One time when the two were playing together, the friend noted young Donnell imitating them and offered to give the boy lessons. The lessons were of classical, not country, music and later Cooley played violin and cello in his school orchestra.

As Spade grew older, when he wasn't helping on the farm, he earned spare money by playing country fiddle for local dances and parties. He still followed that routine when his family moved to a new farm near Modesto, California, when he was twenty. Longing to get away from farm work, Cooley went to Los Angeles and hung around small country-music clubs. Unsuccessful, he returned to Modesto and found a job performing for fifteen dollars a night at a local club. He was a sideman with several local bands in the early 1930s, but was down on his luck once more when he made a second foray to Los Angeles in 1934.

This time the pendulum swung his way. After scrounging a living as best he could for a time, he met Roy Rogers. Because Spade resembled Roy, this eventually led to a job as a stand-in when Roy became a featured actor in Republic Pictures' westerns. That gave him a reasonable income that he supplemented by working with various bands around the city.

At the start of the 1940s, he had established a reputation as an excellent fiddler with bands that played the Venice Pier Ballroom in Venice, California. The management suggested he form his own band and, when he did, he became a crowd favorite.

As the World War II years went by, things got better and better for Spade (a nickname he had earned many years before from his prowess as a card player). The exposure at the Venice Pier Ballroom led eventually to a recording contract with Okeh Records, signed on September 30, 1943. The recording sessions that got underway the following year resulted in the hit single "Shame, Shame on You," which remained on the country charts for some thirty-one weeks in 1945, including time in the number-one position. Spade adopted the song as his theme number. He continued to have chart singles on the label, most notably the 1946 hit, "Detour."

He and his orchestra made their film debut in the 1944 Bob Crosby film, *The Singing Sheriff,* the first of a number of movie credits that included *Chatterbox, The Singing Bandit, Outlaws of the Rockies,* and *Texas Panhandle.* Between recordings and films, the group became one of the best-known in Western swing. During that period, the band left the Venice Pier for a successful run at the Riverside Rancho, then moved to the highly regarded Santa Monica Ballroom. In 1946, Cooley left Okeh, going on to sign with RCA Records in 1947, an association that proved less rewarding from a chart hit standpoint.

Spade also was well positioned for the next entertainment revolution, the rise of television. He was given the opportunity to head his own show on station KTLA, the first commercially licensed TV station in Los Angeles. Called *The Hoffman Hayride,* after the sponsor, the Hoffman Company (which produced TV sets), it began in 1947 and quickly became the top-rated program in the area.

As Bruce Henstell noted in *Los Angeles* magazine ("How the King of Western Swing Reached the End of His Rope," June 1979), "Soon Cooley was calling himself 'the King of Western Swing,' and western swing became the name for the odd music he, and Bob Wills before him, played. Los Angeles loved Spade Cooley, and in the late 1940s, 75 percent of the receivers in Los Angeles were tuned each Saturday night to 'The Hoffman Hayride.' As the show's director recalled, 'Even Milton Berle couldn't compete with it on the coast.' "

However, the pressures of staying on top began to tell on Spade. In the early 1950s he was sidelined for a while by the first of a series of heart attacks. Competing programs also began to make inroads into his TV show's popularity. He tried various remedies, including replacing his old band with a new all-women aggregation. That didn't work, however, and he soon disappeared from the home video screen. He still was able to command a following as an artist, performing at various venues in and around California during the mid- and late-1950s.

Meanwhile, however, his performing frustrations

were aggravated by his personal ones. He had a drinking problem that tended to become worse as the years went by. He also had marital problems. During the 1950s, his second marriage disintegrated and he and his wife separated. But Spade couldn't stop seeing her, on the one hand talking of divorce but on the other hand harboring forlorn hopes of reconciliation. This dragged on for some years, then blew up in tragic fashion in July 1961 when an argument with his wife led to her death in a scene witnessed by their fourteen-year-old daughter.

After a trial sensationalized in the newspapers, Cooley was convicted of murder and sentenced to life in prison. During the trial he suffered another heart attack and afterward was sent to a medical detention center at Vacaville rather than a high-security prison. In prison, he seemed to find himself again. He calmed down and spent much of his time helping other inmates learn to play musical instruments or performing for them. The outlook was for a favorable response from the Parole Board when his case was due for review in 1970.

Before then, taking his excellent behavior into consideration, the Vacaville authorities gave him permission to go to Oakland, California, for a few days to take part in a benefit concert.

Henstell wrote in *Los Angeles* magazine, ". . . the fifty-nine-year old Cooley played before a crowd of 3,000 and was greeted warmly, at least by those who looked beyond the lingering memory of the murder. He thanked the crowd and the authorities 'for the chance to be free for a while.' Then he went backstage. There, speaking with friends, he slumped over from yet another heart attack. The show had been a triumph for Spade—but it was his last. The King of Western Swing was dead."

In the decades after Spade's death, Bob Wills went on to a legendary status in country & western music, while Cooley's name faded almost completely from public memory. An event that promised to restore some of the luster to his creative achievements was the 1994 release of the album *Spadella: The Essential Spade Cooley* on Legacy/Columbia Records. The release packaged essentially all of Cooley's single releases, including all his hits, in its twenty-nine tracks.

COOPER, STONEY: *Singer, fiddler, songwriter. Born Harman, West Virginia, October 16, 1918; died Nashville, Tennessee, March 22, 1977.*

The husband-and-wife team of Stoney and Wilma Lee Cooper for decades ranked as one of the best practitioners of traditional country music in the United States. They were held in high repute during a long career together both by country-music peers and by folk music experts. An example of the former was their long reign as featured members of the *Grand Ole Opry* cast and the latter, their selection in 1950 by the Music Library of Harvard University as the most authentic mountain singing group in the United States.

Dale T. "Stoney" Cooper was born and raised on a farm near Harman, Randolph County, West Virginia, in the famed Clinch Mountain region. He received considerable background in hill country music, music which in many cases could be traced back to Elizabethan folk music, from his own family. At an early age he learned to play the fiddle and, when he was twelve, taught himself the guitar as well. By the time he finished school, he was one of the more accomplished performers in his age group. For a time he was a member of a group called the Green Valley Boys.

One of the best-known local groups during those years was the singing Leary Family. At the end of the 1930s, Stoney joined that group and performed with them at church functions and on radio programs. He soon became fond of young Wilma Leary and she assented to his marriage proposal. They stayed with the family group for a time, then decided to strike out as a separate act.

They gained singing jobs on several stations in the late 1930s, starting in Fairmont, West Virginia, and continuing to Harrisonburg, Virginia, and Wheeling, West Virginia. However, income from performing wasn't enough to meet their bills, particularly after a daughter, Carol Lee, was born. To meet expenses, for a time Stoney had to work for a beverage company.

Things picked up in the early 1940s as the Coopers found jobs outside their area. They played on a variety of stations during those years, including ones in Grand Island, Nebraska; Indianapolis, Indiana; station WJJD in Chicago; Blytheville, Arkansas; and Asheville, North Carolina. Besides radio, the Coopers took part in whatever concert work they could line up. Still, while they lived in Chicago in the mid-1940s, Stoney worked in a defense plant in Gary, Indiana, for a time.

In 1947, the Coopers moved back to West Virginia as regular cast members on the famed *WWVA Jamboree* until 1957, starring on the Saturday-night show broadcast nationally from the Virginia Theatre several times a month on the CBS network. Backing the Coopers on those programs was their band, the Clinch Mountain Clan. In 1957, the Coopers and their band heeded the call to join the *Grand Ole Opry* and moved their home base to Nashville. Stoney remained an official member of the *Opry* for the rest of his life.

During the 1950s and 1960s, the Coopers spent a good part of every year on the road appearing at almost all major fairs and other country venues all over the United States one or more times over that period. Their live appearances included several overseas tours. Helping to increase their audiences was a series of successful recordings, including many that were original compositions. In 1959, they scored some of their biggest top-10 hits on the Hickory label, "Come Walk with Me," "There's a Big Wheel," and "Big Midnight

Special." In 1961, they had another top-10 hit with a revival of Dorsey Dixon's "Wreck on the Highway." Among their other successes were Wilma's singles "Legend of the Dogwood Tree" and "Walking My Lord Up Calvary's Hill."

Some of their other recordings included "The Golden Rocket," "West Virginia Polka," "Just for a While," "How It Hurts to Be Alone," "Please Help Me If I Am Wrong," "I Want to Be Loved," "Cheated Too," "Each Season Changes You," "Thirty Pieces of Silver," "This Crazy, Crazy World," "Tramp on the Street," "Rachel's Guitar," "Diamond Joe," "The White Rose," "Not Anymore," "We Make a Lovely Couple," "Row Two, Seat Three," "This Thing Called Man," "Is It Right?" and "Canadian Reel."

The Coopers' credits from the late 1960s to the mid-1970s included appearances on the network show *Anatomy of Music* and on a number of Canadian CBC network programs, including *This Is My Country* and the *Tommy Hunter Show*. They also appeared in the movies *Country Music on Broadway* and *W.W. and the Dixie Dance Kings*. In October 1976, Stoney received the honorary degree of Doctor of Christian Music from Victory Institute of Lewistown, Ohio. Stoney's last recordings with Wilma were for the Gusto Records LP *Wilma Lee and Stoney Cooper Sing The Carter Family's Greatest Hits*.

Stoney kept an intensive schedule of *Opry* work until the early 1970s, when failing health forced him to restrict his activities. He had a series of attacks that hospitalized him for various lengths of time over a period of four years. He had been in the hospital for some weeks when he passed away on March 22, 1977. Only a few days earlier, for the first time he heard his wife sing on the *Opry* when she dedicated the old A. P. Carter song "Little Darling Pal of Mine" to him on the Saturday-night broadcast.

COOPER, WILMA LEE: *Singer, guitarist, banjoist, organist, songwriter. Born Valley Head, West Virginia, February 7, 1921.*

Considered one of the finest traditional artists in post–World War II country music, Wilma Lee Cooper was heir to a family heritage in gospel and balladry that went back many generations. With her husband, Stoney Cooper, she continued to perform new and old songs in the folk style of the country idiom for decades and, after his retirement and death, went her own way as a solo artist.

Born Wilma Lee Leary in Valley Head, West Virginia, she was fated to join her musical parents in the Leary Family gospel group, one of the best known church-singing groups in the hill country. As soon as she was old enough to carry a tune, she joined the other members of the family, comprising several generations, in entertaining at church get-togethers and regional folk and country festivals. Her first public performance

came when she was five. From then on, she sang regularly with the Leary Family on many radio and church programs. In 1938, the group was featured at a national folk festival sponsored by the nation's first lady, Mrs. Eleanor Roosevelt. The group, not restricted to only immediate family members, included a boy from Harman, West Virginia, named Stoney Cooper. Not long after he joined the troupe, Wilma accepted his proposal of marriage.

Wilma had not been sure she would make music her life's work and completed high school and went on to earn a B.A. degree in banking from Davis & Elkins College in Elkins, West Virginia. But marriage to Stoney helped insure that music, not banking, would be her main concern. While she was completing her schooling, the Coopers stayed with the Leary Family. By the start of the 1940s, however, they started their own act. They performed at some local events and then got work singing on a station in Fairmont, West Virginia. From there they went on to perform on stations in Harrisonburg and Wheeling, West Virginia.

In the mid-1940s, with a growing family, they tried their luck outside their home region, doing some concert work and singing on a variety of stations, including Grand Island, Nebraska; Indianapolis, Indiana; station WJJD in Chicago; Blytheville, Arkansas; and Asheville, North Carolina. More often than not during those years, Stoney had to supplement family income with jobs in other fields. While staying in Chicago, he worked at a defense plant in nearby Gary, Indiana.

In 1947, the first important breakthrough came. They got the chance to join the regular cast of the *WWVA Jamboree* in Wheeling, West Virginia. It was a year in which they also got their first record contract with a major label. For a decade they were featured artists on various WWVA shows and were headliners from 1954 to 1957 on the prestigious Saturday-night *Jamboree* that was broadcast over many stations throughout the East and Midwest. In 1957, they moved to the highest rung on the country-music ladder, regular cast status with the *Grand Ole Opry*. (They had occasionally guested in previous years.) The Coopers moved to Nashville, remaining there the rest of their careers. From the late 1950s to the end of the 1960s, the Coopers were often away from home on extensive tours of the folk and country circuit. Their travels, accompanied by their band, the Clinch Mountain Clan, took them at one time or another to all fifty states, Canada, and many Western European nations.

During the Coopers' long career, they recorded for a number of labels, including Columbia, Hickory, Decca, and Gusto. Many of their songs were written by Wilma Lee or Wilma and Stoney. Among those were "Cheated Too" (1956); "I Tell My Heart," "Loving You," "My Heart Keeps Crying" (1957); "He Taught Them How" (1958); and "Heartbreak Street," "Tomorrow I'll Be Gone," and "Midnight Special" (1959), all on Hickory.

The last-named song was a top-10 hit for the Coopers in 1959, a banner year that also brought two other top-10 hits, "Come Walk with Me" and "There's a Big Wheel."

After another major hit in 1961 with their version of the old Dorsey Dixon classic, "Wreck on the Highway," the Coopers rarely had any releases that went past mid-chart levels. They retained a sizable following, though, and were warmly welcomed by crowds at state and county fairs and during their part of the *Opry* Saturday-night program. In the mid-1970s, failing health sidelined Stoney, but Wilma remained an *Opry* regular backed by the Clinch Mountain Clan. Just before Stoney's death, Wilma dedicated a song to him on an *Opry* show, the Carter Family's "Little Darlin' Pal of Mine."

Considered one of the finest country and bluegrass artists, Wilma was asked to provide material for a number of folk music collections over the years, initially with Stoney and later as a solo artist. Some of her recordings were made for the Library of Congress Archive of American Folk Music and Harvard University's Library of Music. In the 1970s, the Smithsonian Institution in Washington, D.C., asked her to appear at Baird Auditorium, where her live performance was recorded for the Institution's Archives of the Performing Arts Division. In July 1974, at the Institution-sponsored folk festival, she was honored as "First Lady of Bluegrass" as part of a series of "Women in Country Music." Over the years, she was named an honorary colonel by many state governors, including John J. McKeithen of Louisiana in 1961, George Wallace of Alabama in 1964, and Edwin W. Edwards of Louisiana in 1975.

She recorded on many labels in the 1970s, including Rounder and Gusto. Typically, these releases contained one of her favorite singles hits, "The Legend of the Dogwood Tree."

In 1979, Wilma, assisted by daughter Carol Lee and the Clinch Mountain Clan, was one of the featured acts of the *Bluegrass Spectacular* TV show telecast nationally over the U.S. Public Broadcasting System. Going into the 1980s, she remained an *Opry* star and continued to maintain a sizable touring schedule as well.

COUNTRY GAZETTE: *Vocal and instrumental group. Original members, 1971–72, Byron Berline, born Cornwell, Kansas, early 1940s, Roger Wertz, Roger Bush. Alan Munde joined 1972, Roland White, 1973. Reorganized group in early 1980s included Munde; White; Joe Carr, born Texas; Bill Smith, born Virginia. Band name later changed to Alan Munde and Country Gazette.*

The growth of the West Coast–based country genre at the end of the 1960s and start of the 1970s, which embraced bands like Poco, the Flying Burrito Brothers, and the Eagles, also helped spawn the bluegrass revival of the 1970s. One offshoot of the country rock movement, for instance, was the Country Gazette, a band that gained initial exposure as part of the Flying Burritos show and later went its own way on the folk circuit during the mid-1970s.

The first incarnation of Country Gazette comprised Byron Berline on vocals and fiddle, Kenny Wertz on vocals and guitar, and Roger Bush (earlier a member of the Kentucky Colonels bluegrass band) on bass and guitar. The threesome toured with the Burritos in 1971–72, performing as sidemen on some Burritos numbers and also doing their own set. After the Burritos disbanded, Berline sparked continued activity of the band (with various alignments of musicians) on the country and bluegrass circuit. Vocalist and banjo player Alan Munde, who joined in 1972, eventually took over leadership of a reorganized Gazette group. In 1973, another Kentucky Colonels alumnus, Roland White, became a member, providing his talents on vocals and mandolin.

The band got the chance to record for United Artists in 1972; the result was the fine LP *Traitor in Our Midst*, issued in 1972 and still in its catalog a decade later. Soon after, UA issued the album *Don't Give Up Your Day Job*. Later in the 1970s, Country Gazette was represented by the *Country Gazette Live* album on Antilles Records, and one titled *Out to Lunch* on Flying Fish. Other albums issued in the 1970s and start of the 1980s were *What a Way to Make a Living* and *All This And Money Too* on Ridge Runner Records, and, on Flying Fish, *Tellulive, 1979* and *American and Clean*.

By the end of the 1970s the three original members had departed, leaving Munde and Roland White still in the fold. The foursome Munde had assembled in the early 1980s added Joe Carr (vocals, guitar) and standup bass player Bill Smith. Munde took pains at the time to dissociate the band from its original "progressive bluegrass" image. "One of our goals is to appear at more of the traditional festivals. We always tailor our song selection to fit the type of event we're playing, and some of our best responses have come from traditional audiences."

It was a formula he continued to pursue during the balance of the 1980s and into the 1990s, by which time the group was called Alan Munde and Country Gazette. The band makeup changed a number of times during those years. (Roland White, for instance, left to work with a Nashville bluegrass group as well as to help supervise reissues of some of the Kentucky Colonels' recordings.) In the early 1980s, besides playing bluegrass venues and festivals, the group also took part in a four-part concert series presented on Alabama Public TV and played on a radio concert broadcast nationally over the National Public Radio Network. Some of the band's concert work in the mid- and late 1980s included performances in bluegrass concerts in other parts of the world.

All of the band members of the early 1980s also turned out solo albums. Among those in print at the time were three by Munde on Ridge Runner (*Banjo Sandwich, The Banjo Kid Picks Again,* and *Festival Favorites*), Joe Carr's *Other Nonsense* on Ridge Runner, Roland White's *I Wasn't Born to Rock 'N' Roll* on Ridge Runner, and Bill Smith's *The Nothin' Doin' Band* on Prime Time.

After Rounder Records acquired Flying Fish Records in the mid-1990s, it retained three Country Gazette albums in its catalog: *Hello Operator . . . This Is Country Gazette, Bluegrass Tonight,* and *Strictly Instrumental.*

COUNTRY GENTLEMEN, THE: *Vocal and instrumental group. Personnel in early 1960s: Charlie Waller, born Jointerville, Texas, January 19, 1935; John Duffey, born Washington, D.C., March 4, 1934; Eddie Adcock, born Scottsville, Virginia, June 17, 1938; Jim Cox, born Vansant, Virginia, April 3, 1930.*

From its inception in the late 1950s to the start of the 1980s, the Country Gentlemen ranked as one of the most popular bluegrass bands in the United States. Its concerts, featuring the group's trademark, "on-the-mark triple harmonies," were among the most consistently exciting in the field. The group attracted a following ranging from dyed-in-the-wool bluegrass fans to mainstream country and some soft-rock adherents.

Considering its many musical achievements, it may come as a surprise that the group was born by accident. Its genesis occurred when a mutual friend asked Charlie Waller, then working in Baltimore, and John Duffey, then at station WFMD, Frederick, Maryland, to fill in for a sick musician at a date in the Baltimore area on July 4, 1957. The two enjoyed playing together and decided to continue their musical association.

Before their paths crossed, Waller and Duffey had become proficient on guitar many years earlier. Waller, though born in Texas, went to Los Angeles with his family while still a child. When he was ten, he obtained a fifteen-dollar guitar and learned to play. By the time he met Duffey, he was an accomplished instrumentalist with a leaning toward bluegrass style.

Duffey grew up in the Washington, D.C. area, mainly in nearby Bethesda, Maryland. When Duffey was seventeen, a neighbor persuaded him it would be worthwhile to play guitar, and before long he was demonstrating his skills for friends and playing informally with other musicians.

After becoming friends, Waller and Duffey expanded the group to a trio by recruiting Jim Cox as banjoist and bassist in early 1958. Raised on a farm in Virginia, Cox began playing the banjo before he was in his teens. In June 1960, another Virginian, Eddie Adcock, was added, lending a stronger bluegrass tone to the group. Adcock learned to play the mandolin at twelve and became a regular on a gospel program on station WCHV, Charlottesville, Virginia, in his teens.

With the addition of Adcock, the group soon began to win attention from the burgeoning folk music audience of the early 1960s. The Country Gentlemen became familiar figures on the folk club, college auditorium, and folk festival circuit. Helping to move things along was their recording activities, initially on Folkways Records, which issued such early 1960s LPs as *Audience Participation* and the two-record *Country Gentlemen* (December 1960). Later in the 1960s, Folkways followed up with *Country Gentlemen, Volume 2, Volume 3,* and *Volume 4.* Some of their work also came out on Starday in the 1960s, including the LPs *Bluegrass* (July 1962) and *Country Gentlemen* (1965). Some of the group's LPs on other labels in the 1960s and 1970s were *The Country Gentlemen* and *Remembrances and Forecasts* on Vanguard and *Live at Roanoke* on Zap Records.

From the late 1960s on, the band's main record affiliation was with the Rebel label. Albums issued by Rebel in the late 1960s and early 1970s included *Bringin' Mary Home, The Traveler, Play It Like It Is, New Look, New Sound, One Wide River to Cross, Best of the Early Country Gentlemen,* and in 1972, *Sound Off* and *The Award Winning Country Gentlemen.* Another early 1970s release was *The Gospel Album,* which emphasized some fine vocal harmonies by the band members. Other mid- and late 1970s releases on Rebel were *Yesterday and Today, Volumes 1, 2* and *3,* and *Joe's Last Train.*

The Country Gentlemen persevered through the downturn in American interest in bluegrass during the latter part of the 1960s and were in a position to benefit from the rebirth of widespread activity in the 1970s. The group appeared at many of the annual festivals that thrived in the 1970s in places such as Telluride, Colorado, and Bean Blossom, Indiana, and often was featured at the bluegrass-week concerts in Nashville.

COUNTRY MUSIC ASSOCIATION: *Industry trade organization, based in Nashville, Tennessee.*

One of the important forces behind the growing popularity of country & western music from the start of the 1960s is the Country Music Association. The CMA was formed in 1958 by industry executives and artists to promote this form of music and try to combat the temporary depression caused by the rise of rock 'n' roll. In November 1958, a series of meetings led to the organization's formation with an original leadership of nine directors and five officers. Connie B. Gay was elected to the first two-year term as CMA president with Wesley Rose, president of Acuff-Rose, as CMA board chairman.

At the first annual meeting in November 1959, the board of directors was increased to eighteen and officers to nine. The meeting confirmed the continued work of Mrs. Jo Walker as executive secretary. The membership was divided into nine categories: Artist-

Musician, Artist-Manager, Booker, Promoter, Agent, Ballroom Operator, Composer, Disk Jockey, Music Publisher, Radio-TV and Record Company Personnel, Trade Publication Representative, and Non-Affiliated. Each category is entitled to elect two board members; the board, in turn, appoints the officers.

Functions of the CMA include promoting country & western music worldwide, conducting industry surveys to provide useful data to members, and informing members of industry news. The most ambitious project of the CMA was establishment of the Country Music Hall of Fame (see Country Music Hall of Fame), in which Country Music Foundation offices are now located. CMA offices are located in another building near Music Row in Nashville.

COUNTRY MUSIC HALL OF FAME AND MUSEUM: *Building in Nashville, Tennessee, housing plaques of members elected to Hall of Fame and collections of exhibits, historical data, and other items of interest.*

In 1967, an impressive monument to country music was opened to the public at 700 16th Avenue South, Nashville, Tennessee. The structure was the culmination of years of work by the Country Music Foundation toward a repository of information about the field. The idea for the center had been proposed by the Country Music Association in 1964. Funds had been collected from country artists, music fans, firms, and others.

The building, since expanded, consisted of a modernistic barn-shaped center section flanked by two flat wings. A "Walkway of Stars" led up to the center entrance, consisting of brass emblems with names of leading country artists on them embedded in concrete blocks. The right wing housed a fifty-seat theater in which films on the history of country music and videotapes of major artists are shown. The other wing includes the "Artists' Gallery," a series of pictures of famous performers below which are earphones for listening to some of their recordings.

The hall also housed other exhibits of importance: a library of tapes, books, films, recordings, and publications, and material from the John K. Edwards Memorial Foundation, a collection of information about country & western music considered one of the foremost of its kind in the world.

Each member elected to the Hall of Fame is represented in the center hall with a bronze plaque giving biographical data and including an image of the person. Selection of Hall of Fame members is by annual vote of a committee of approximately one hundred members selected by the Country Music Association.

The Foundation is administered by a full-time staff of scholars, educators, and museum and library professionals. More than 500,000 visitors a year from throughout the world pass through the exhibits, including nearby Studio B where all-time country greats recorded in the past.

The Foundation is the foremost organization in dealing specifically with country music, and in a larger sense speaks for the legitimacy and importance of all American folk and popular music forms through active participation in national museum, library, and arts associations. It has become the advocate for all forms of commercial, popular, and folk music and continues to argue in every forum for the equality of all artistic endeavors.

The first six members of the Hall of Fame included three living artists, Ernest Tubb, Roy Acuff, and Tex Ritter, and three deceased, Jimmie Rodgers, Hank Williams, and Fred Rose. (For complete list of Hall of Fame members, see Appendix.)

During 1996–1997, plans were drawn up to relocate the Hall of Fame and Museum to form an even larger complex in downtown Nashville by the end of the decade.

CRADDOCK, BILLY "CRASH": *Singer, guitarist, bandleader. Born Greensboro, North Carolina, June 16, 1939.*

When Billy "Crash" Craddock came onstage in baby-blue form-fitting slacks and matching sequined shirt, there was no mistaking the Elvis Presley-style touch of sensuality. Nor could you miss elements of rock, from Elvis through Charlie Daniels, in the arrangements offered by his brightly garbed band. But neither was there any doubt that Billy was, first and foremost, a country artist in basic form and content, albeit of the new breed that came to the fore in the 1970s.

Commenting on his approach, he told a reporter in 1977, "We country artists need the young audience. I love country music and I tried to record straight for fifteen years before I struck the fans with 'Knock Three Times.' I do country-rock now and it's because my fans won't accept me doing 'hard' country. It seems that after you get a hit record in one pattern, the fans sort of expect it."

Billy, one of ten children of a poor rural family, grew up on a farm near Greensboro, North Carolina, and recalls that Hank Williams was his first idol. He played a make-believe broomstick guitar as "accompaniment" before an older brother, Clarence, began giving him lessons on a real one when he was eleven. Soon after, he mowed an aunt's lawn for almost three months to earn the money to buy his own instrument from a local pawnshop.

When he was high school age, he and another brother, Ronald, were competent enough as "pickers" to win a local talent contest thirteen weeks in a row. Later they enlisted two friends for a rockabilly band called the Four Rebels. Taking a break from music, Billy was a running back on the high school football team, bringing him the nickname "Crash."

After a talent scout for Columbia Records caught the Rebels' act one night, Billy was signed and told to

The late, great Roy Acuff, whose tenure with the
Grand Ole Opry spanned seven decades

Alabama

John Anderson

The Amazing Rhythm Aces, 1970s. Russell Smith stands in the
center of the group

(RCA Victor Records)

Eddy Arnold

Asleep at the Wheel, mid-1970s:
(top) Ray Benson; *(middle row)*
Leroy Preston, Danny Levin, Chris
O'Connell, Scott Hennige, Floyd
Domino; *(bottom)* Lucky Oceans, Bill
Mabry, Link Davis, Jr., Tony Garnier

Chet Atkins, 1960s

(Lou Jacobs Jr./RCA Victor)

Bobby Bare

Suzy Bogguss

(Peter Nash)

(Peter Nash)

(Archive Photos/Darlene Hammond)

Garth Brooks

Brooks & Dunn

Junior Brown

The Buckaroos, Buck Owens's award-winning band, in the mid-1960s. Lead guitarist Don Ric *(left)* collaborated with Buck on many hit song before his untimely death in an accident

(Peter Nash)

Glen Campbell

Mary-Chapin Carpenter

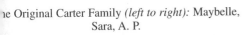

he Original Carter Family *(left to right):* Maybelle, Sara, A. P.

June and Johnny Cash

Johnny Cash

Rosanne Cash

Ray Charles

Mark Chesnutt

Guy Clark

Patsy Cline

Roy Clark

Hank Cochran

David Allan Coe

Jessi Colter

(RCA Victor)

Floyd Cramer

come to Nashville during 1959. He was naturally elated, but it proved a preface to a soul-searching letdown. "They tried to make another Fabian out of me. You've got to realize that back then there was pop and then there was country. There was no blend of the two like there is today. They wanted me to be a pop singer, but there was a great deal of country in my style. It just didn't work." The singles issued by Columbia fell flat at home, but strangely three songs became top-10 hits in Australia.

That wasn't enough to save the situation and Billy, discouraged, returned home. For most of the 1960s, he did shows in his spare time in North Carolina and neighboring states and worked in the construction field for his main income. At first fellow workers who heard of his Columbia contract gave him a hard time. "They would say, 'Hey, Crash! What the hell are you doing here? I thought you were some kind of big recording star.' I had to develop a pretty good sense of humor."

His luck finally turned again in 1969. A pharmaceutical salesman named Dale Morris caught a Craddock set in a local hall and was impressed. Still, it was hardly an overnight rise in fortune. It took almost two years for Morris and producer Ron Chancey to form a label called Cartwheel Records before Craddock got the call to Nashville once more. He cut the single "Knock Three Times," which amazingly gained enough exposure to reach number one on country charts in 1971. The team followed with two more hits, "Ain't Nothin' Shakin' " and "Dream Lover" (Craddock later named his band the Dream Lovers), after which ABC bought out Cartwheel to gain Billy's services.

Billy supported his recordings with concert tours that drew enthusiastic audiences representing almost every age group. From 1971 through 1977, he had seventeen singles that made the country top 10 on Cartwheel/ABC, including nine that reached number one. Among those were "Knock Three Times," "Dream Lover," "Ruby Baby," "Sweet Magnolia Blossoms," "Walk Softly," "Easy as Pie," and "Broken Down in Tiny Pieces." ABC released nine albums of his, all of which made the country charts. Some of his records also crossed over to the U.S. pop charts.

In the fall of 1977, Billy left ABC for Capitol Records. The first release from the new alignment was the album *Billy Crash Craddock*. With Dale Morris as producer, the album demonstrated again Billy's "hybrid" format, ranging from a version of Bobby Goldsboro's "Rock and Roll Madness" to the Lester Flatt arrangement of the country classic "Rollin' in My Sweet Baby's Arms." The debut Capitol single "I Cheated on a Good Woman's Love" found favor with country fans in 1978, bringing Billy his eighteenth top-10 country single. Also on the hit lists that year were "I've Been Too Long Lonely Baby," "Don Juan," and "Hubba Hubba." In 1979, he added such top-10 credits as "If I Could Write a Song as Beautiful as You," "Robinhood," "My Mama Never Heard Me Sing," and

the charted single "Til I Stop Shaking." His 1980 charted singles included "I Just Had You on My Mind" and "Sea Cruise."

As of the mid-1980s, the band comprised Charlie Waller on guitar, Robert Yates on bass (born Big Rock, Va., April 30, 1935), James Gondreaux, on mandolin (born Wakefield, R.I. on July 3, 1946) and Richard Smith on banjo (born Syracuse, N.Y., October 4, 1943).

CRAMER, FLOYD: *Pianist, organist, songwriter. Born Shreveport, Louisiana, October 17, 1933.*

During the 1960s and 1970s, while Chet Atkins held the unofficial Nashville title of "Mr. Guitar," his contemporary Floyd Cramer was regarded as "Mr. Keyboards." The similar designations to some extent reflected career interactions. It was Chet who first induced Floyd to come to Nashville, where the two often worked together on their own albums or on tour and backed recordings of other artists. And both contributed immeasurably to the post–World War II development of the Nashville sound.

Floyd showed countless young keyboard players how to achieve a characteristic country feel on piano and organ by adapting traditional guitar techniques used by people like Mother Maybelle Carter to keyboard playing. He described his approach, based on a method of slurring notes, in this way: "The style I use mainly is a whole-tone slur which gives more of a lonesome, cowboy sound. You hit a note and slide almost simultaneously to another. It is a sort of near-miss on the keyboard. You don't hit the note you intend to strike right off, but you 'recover' instantly and then hit it. It is an intentional error and actually involves two notes. The result is a melancholy sound."

Cramer was born in Shreveport, but his family moved to a small Arkansas sawmill town called Huttig where he grew up. He seemed to enjoy music almost as soon as he could walk and talk. "My parents told me that they saw in me an early love for music which was the reason they got a used piano when I was five. I was the only child and that old piano, which I learned to play by ear, became an inseparable companion."

When he was in high school, he played in school groups and also began to perform at dances and in local clubs. After finishing high school in 1951 he went to Shreveport to audition for the popular KWKH *Louisiana Hayride*. He got the job and soon was working on the show with people like Webb Pierce, Jim Reeves, and Faron Young. He toured with some of the *Hayride* stars, including Reeves and the immortal Hank Williams. Later, he was on the *Hayride* when a young performer from Mississippi made his debut—another musical giant, Elvis Presley. Floyd also backed Presley on concert dates in the early 1950s and later played for many Presley recording sessions as well as several of his movie soundtracks.

During his years in Shreveport, Floyd backed many

early recording efforts by future stars at Shreveport's Abbott Records. He also got the chance to cut his first solo record on Abbott and did a number of sides for the label in 1953–54.

On occasion, he went to Nashville for session work between 1952 and the end of 1954; while there he became acquainted with Chet Atkins. Chet was enthusiastic about Floyd's piano skills and urged him to move to Nashville to help out in sessions Chet supervised as part of his production duties at RCA and to cut original recordings on the label. In January 1955, Floyd complied and for decades after became what amounted to an institution on the country-music scene. During those years, not only was he the keyboards bellwether in that field, but like Chet Atkins, he demonstrated he was equally at home playing just about every kind of pop music and some classic material as well.

Starting in the 1950s, Floyd was constantly on the go, touring all over the United States and in many other nations. At the end of the 1970s, he still had a rugged schedule of appearances in concert halls, including many annual performances as a soloist with major symphony orchestras in pop concerts, clubs, and music theaters. During the 1970s, one of his notable series was called the Masters Festival of Music, where he headlined with Chet Atkins and Boots Randolph throughout the United States and Canada.

In the mid-1950s, he became a regular on the *Grand Ole Opry* and was often featured on nationwide *Opry* radio and TV programs for decades thereafter. Just a few of his network TV credits in the 1960s and 1970s were Johnny Carson's *The Tonight Show,* a Perry Como TV special, *Kraft Music Hall,* several appearances on *The Ed Sullivan Show, Jimmy Dean, Johnny Cash, Roger Miller, Merv Griffin,* and *Hee Haw.*

RCA began issuing albums and singles of Floyd's work in the mid-1950s, mostly recordings of songs written or made famous by others, but also a certain number of originals. In 1960, he scored his first major record success with his composition "Last Date," one of the top-selling country singles of the year. He followed up shortly after with another hit, "On the Rebound," and later in his career had a third major success with "Fancy Pants."

His albums remained a staple item in RCA's catalog. While few of them made rarefied top-chart levels, almost all found a steady market with Cramer's following, which cut across many of the arbitrary lines between pop music classifications. His yearly album output averaged two to three and covered all kinds of material, from country and pop songs to blues, jazz, ragtime, musical comedy, and movie themes. As of early 1979, his total of LP releases on RCA Records was forty.

Among them was an annual series called *Class of . . .* in which Cramer capsulized most of the top hits of the preceding year. The series began with the *Class

of '65,* issued in September 1965, and was followed regularly by collections generally released in September or October of each year. Besides those, his RCA list included such albums as *Blues,* issued in March 1960, *Late Date* (1/61); *On the Rebound* (5/61); *Pianist* (10/61); *Floyd Gets Organ-ized* (4/62); *Sing Along* (3/63); *Comin' On* (10/63); *Floyd Cramer* (3/64); *Best of Floyd Cramer* (8/64); *At the Console* (8/64); *Hits* (4/65); *Magic Touch* (5/65); *Big Ones* (3/66); *Here's What's Happening* (2/67); *Floyd Cramer Plays Monkees* (5/67); *Night Train* (8/67); *Country Piano/City Strings; Plays Country Classics* (2/68); *More Country Classics* (12/69); *Floyd Cramer with Music City Pops* (6/70); *This Is Floyd Cramer* (two records, 8/70); *Sounds of Sunday* (7/71); *Almost Persuaded* (8/71); *Floyd Cramer Date* (3/72); *Detours* (4/72); *Superhits* (1/79).

During his long career, Cramer received many awards and was nominated often in Country Music Association polls. He was among the five finalists for Instrumentalist of the Year nine times from 1967 through 1981. One of his more coveted awards was received in November 1974 while he was appearing in the Festival of Music at Opryland, USA. Chet Atkins was presenter of the Metronome Award, annually given to an individual who contributed most to the development of "Music City"—Nashville. Said Atkins, "This metronome serves a dual purpose, it marks your fifteenth year with RCA Records . . . and it'll help you keep time."

In the mid and late 1980s and the first part of the 1990s, Cramer remained active, but had little impact on the hit charts. In the 1990s, RCA issued several retrospective CDs of Cramer's earlier recordings on the label. During 1995, the independent label Ranwood Records issued *The Piano Magic of Floyd Cramer, Volume 1.* A second volume was issued by Ranwood in May 1996.

CROWELL, RODNEY: *Singer, guitarist, drummer, band leader, songwriter, record producer. Born Houston, Texas, August 7, 1950.*

One of the most promising of the new, creative individuals who started to have an impact on country music in the 1970s, Rodney Crowell had made his mark in several ways by the early 1980s. His original songs provided major hits for a number of artists; his production efforts brought new faces to the fore (including Rosanne Cash, who became his wife in 1979); and his potential as a performer and recording artist became evident.

Born and raised in Houston, Texas, Rodney gained considerable incentive toward a music career from his family environment. Both of his grandfathers were musically inclined—one was a church-choir leader and the other a bluegrass banjoist. One of his grandmothers played guitar and his father had performed in bars and honky-tonks as a sideline when the chance arose. The first instrument Rodney decided to play departed somewhat from family tradition. He took up drums at eleven and later, in his teens, worked with several local rock groups. However, he liked country music and became increasingly interested in the field as progressive country began to make its mark in the early 1970s. By then, he already was writing original material and also had developed skill as a guitarist in addition to his drum work.

At the start of the 1970s, he went to Nashville to try to further his songwriting efforts. He managed to gain the ear of Jerry Reed, who took him on as a writer. During that two-year association, Jerry recorded some of Rodney's songs. Meanwhile Rodney was making other contacts and friends, such as songwriter Guy Clark, whom he cited later as a major influence on his work, and producer Brian Ahern, who worked closely with Emmylou Harris.

When Ahern brought Crowell to Emmylou's attention she was strongly impressed with Crowell's writings. From the mid-1970s on, many of Crowell's songs showed up on her albums, including "Amarillo," "Til I Gain Control Again," "You're Supposed to Be Feeling Good," "Tulsa Queen," "Leaving Louisiana in the Broad Daylight" (cowritten with D. Cowart), and "I Ain't Livin' Long Like This." Rodney also became a member of her Hot Band, playing guitar with that group for two and a half years from 1975 to 1977.

In the fall of 1977, Rodney left that group to devote more time to his new record agreement with Warner Brothers and to do more production work. His debut LP on Warner Brothers, *I Ain't Livin' Long Like This,* came out in July 1978. It contained six originals and three by others, including an old Dallas Frazier song, "Elvira," which was the first single release.

Commenting on the project, Crowell said, "I'm not a pure country songwriter, but I think I'm a good country singer. On the album I tried to isolate different elements. For instance, there are straight-out country songs as well as straight-out rock songs. I've tried to stay close to my roots and at the same time give the songs a contemporary feel. Some of my own personal favorites are the title track and a tune Emmylou's recorded, 'Leavin' Louisiana in the Broad Daylight.' I'm also partial to 'Elvira.' "

His judgment couldn't be faulted. Although the songs didn't reach the top for him or Emmylou, all three became number-one hits for others. The Oak Ridge Boys had a number-one single with "Elvira" in 1981; before that they had gained a number-one hit with "Leavin' Louisiana in the Broad Daylight" in February 1980. In March 1980, Rodney could point to writing or cowriting two number-one hits in a span of two months as Waylon Jennings' version of "I Ain't Livin' Long Like This" made the top spot.

In the early 1980s, though, as Rodney's performing career moved forward it didn't seem far-fetched to see him singing his own way to a number-one record later in the decade. His second LP, *But What Will the Neighbors Think,* issued by Warner in February 1980, was a fine collection with such Crowell originals as "Here Come the '80s," "It's Only Rock 'n' Roll," and "The One About England." Equally impressive was his third LP on Warner Brothers, *Rodney Crowell,* released in the fall of 1981, which quickly moved onto the national country charts. At the same time, a single from the album, his composition "Stars on the Water" moved toward the top-20 on singles lists.

Rodney continued to add to his impressive production credits as well. In the early 1980s he helped his wife, Rosanne, achieve a major hit with the album *Seven Year Ache* and produced such other excellent collections as Bobby Bare's *As Is* and Guy Clark's *South Coast of Texas.*

Rodney could point to several songs of his that made the pop chart in the early 1980s, such as Bob Seger's hit single of Crowell's "Shame on the Moon," which stayed at number two on the *Billboard* list the end of 1982 and start of 1983. Before that the Dirt Band made the charts with Crowell's "An American Dream," which peaked at number six the week of January 12, 1980. That same year Rodney had a *Billboard* Top-40 pop hit of his own, "Ashes by Now."

From the end of the 1970s and throughout the 1980s, Rodney continued to write and/or produce a series of singles successes for Rosanne Cash. Number-one songs written by him and recorded by her were "It's a Small World" (a duet by Rodney and Rosanne) and "I Don't Know Why You Don't Want Me." Number-one singles he produced for Rosanne were "Seven Year Ache," "My Baby Thinks He's a Train," "Blue Moon with a Heartache," "He Could Never Be You," "Hold On," "The Way We Make a Broken Heart," "Tennessee Flat Top Box," "Runaway Train," "If You Change Your Mind," and "I Don't Want to Spoil the Party." Rosanne also had several top-10 hits with Crowell compositions: "Ain't No Money" and "No Memories Hangin' Round" (a duet with Bobby Bare).

Rodney didn't do badly during those years with his own recordings and self-productions. His number-one songs included "She's Crazy for Leaving," "I Couldn't Leave You If I Tried," "After All This Time," and the self-produced "Above and Beyond." The last named came out on Columbia Records, the label Rodney joined during the second half of the 1980s. He made the charts in 1988 with the Columbia album *Diamonds & Dirt,* which earned three Grammy nominations. One of those was for the album cut "After All This Time," which won him the trophy for Best Country Song in the 1989 voting. In some ways the end of the 1980s and the start of the 1990s proved a bittersweet period: his recording prospects were prospering, but he suffered the loss of his father, James Crowell, a one-time honky-tonk musician, in 1989 (at one time Rodney had played drums in his father's band) and his troubled marriage finally ended in divorce in 1991.

He took note of his father's death in two songs on

his 1989 album. One of them was "Many a Long and Lonesome Highway," which reached number two on the charts, the other "Things I Wish I'd Said." As he had said at one time, pain sometimes proved to be an incentive for new songs. "If I'm on the verge of tears and I'm close to the guitar, I think it's better to sit and cry with a guitar in my hand and turn the teardrops on a piece of paper into a song rather than to just sit in a corner and cry unproductively. Songwriting is my form of keeping a journal." Yet he acknowledged there are times when emotional pain is too deep for such an outlet.

Besides "Many a Long and Lonesome Highway," *Diamonds & Dirt* provided other chartmakers, including "If Looks Could Kill," which peaked at number two in *Radio & Records* the week of May 4, 1990, and "My Past Is Present," which reached number thirteen in *R&R* the week of August 11, 1990. By the time he began work on his next Columbia album, which also proved his last on the label, he had the newer pain of the end of his marriage to Rosanne, a situation reflected in the album's title song, "Life Is Messy." Getting ready for the project, he said, "I set out not to do anything in the same way. I took voyages into as many places as I could. I was digging for something deeper in myself in terms of how I dealt with realizing the potentials of the songs."

Some of his work was affected by the separation from his wife. It reflected, he said, "The eye-opening aspect of a 12 year relationship taking the final stages of the course it had run." The breakup, he commented, "brought challenges on all kinds of levels—physical and emotional. Man, to go through this, I've got to stretch."

But he stressed it wasn't the only influence. "My job as an artist is to dig, to find out something different about myself. I got some help from [coproducers] Bobby Colomby, Larry Klein and John Leventhal. We all knew what I do and we said, 'Let's experiment with this in a way that we find out something else about what I do.' So in each song, we looked for that extra something about the song that was way beyond the way I'd explored my songwriting before."

However, his personal problems may have had more of an adverse impact than he thought. The album was good and won generally favorable critical comments, but it didn't match the content of his previous hit collection. It did provide more chart singles, including "Lovin' All Night," number seven in *R&R* the week of May 25, 1992, and "What Kind of Love," number nine the week of August 28. The album, which was issued in the spring of 1992, even made the *Billboard* list and stayed on it until late in the year. But it never became a blockbuster, which played a role in Crowell's leaving Columbia and signing a new contract with MCA in 1993, which resulted in the release of his ninth album in March 1994.

Before finalizing the material for that collection, he did a two-week acoustic tour with guitarist John Jor-

gensen to try some new songs out on live audiences. But while the new album, *Let the Picture Paint Itself,* contained some excellent new originals, it failed to paint the hoped-for success with the record-buying public. In May 1995, MCA released his second album on the label, *Jewel of the South.*

CRYNER, BOBBIE: *Singer, guitarist, songwriter. Born Woodland, California, September 13, 1960.*

With a deep, soulful voice that could combine sultriness with compassion, Bobbie Cryner was a major discovery of mid-1990s country music. Yet her singing's very uniqueness was off-putting to some critics and radio programmers, who looked askance at her ultra-traditional country style—closer in tone to artists like Patsy Cline and George Jones than the blander pop-country formats of most 1990s stars. Of course, she did not lack for unstinting praise from knowledgeable critics, who also took note of her considerable promise as a songwriter.

Bobbie was the daughter of a truck-driving father and mother who supplemented family income for many years by working in a California tomato cannery. She was born and spent most of her early years in a town of about 50,000 in northern California "where everybody listened to traditional country music, music by people like Merle Haggard, George Jones, Tammy Wynette and Buck Owens. Maybe we weren't hearing it on the radio because that wasn't 'in,' but we were all still listening to that music [on records] because that's what we liked."

As a young girl, she was particularly attracted to the gospel side of country. She sang in church as a child and recalled always having an innate curiosity about the human condition. She told Valeria Hansen for *Country Post* magazine ("Bobbie Cryner Facing Her Fears," January/February 1994), "I grew up with a sense of humor [noting she had been the class clown through her elementary and high school years], but also an incredible yearning to find out why I'm here. I was a goof-off in school, but I was also a very serious child and pretty much of a loner."

In fact, her particular interest in evangelical religion caused her to join a strict fundamentalist Pentecostal church when only ten years old, a move in which she was not joined by her parents. Her views remained fairly consistent through her teens, she told Hansen, until she changed her emphasis in her early twenties. "I realized that religion is preparation for death, and spirituality is preparation for life. I decided to focus on life."

The condition of her family life changed when she was in her mid-teens, caused by a sudden decline in family fortunes. She told *Radio & Records* that growing up in northern California she experienced "just your regular suburban life. We weren't rich, we weren't extremely poor. But when I moved to Kansas [at age sixteen], everything changed. We became poor and didn't have a whole lot of everything. That's when I started writing a lot of my country [songs], because I could relate to how they felt, being in hard times."

She recalled, "When we moved to Kansas, I would get all these references from people I knew about, you know, being Dorothy [from the *Wizard of Oz*], but there's so much more to people out there. I remember driving through those little towns and you'd think, 'Gosh, there's people out there and they've got their own little soap operas going on and their own world,' but they worry on the same large scale you do about the very same things. Then you live in those towns and you find out it's exactly like the great big world."

Still, as she told Carrie Arolick of *Country Song Roundup* ("Bobbie Cryner—Hear Her Roar," December 1993), at sixteen in Flint Hills, Kansas, she felt she was "living in the middle of nowhere and there was no one around and nothing to do. I'd take this old guitar that this girl from Mexico gave me . . . and I'd just sit under a tree and sing and write.

"One time this lady (June Murphy) came through town. She was a real evangelist-type who played the piano and wrote her own songs. I worshipped her because of her strength in a place where we were considered nothing, and I thought, 'If she can do that, I can do that.' And I did. I never played those early songs for anybody, but it got me started. From there I just kept growing and believing."

After finishing high school, she entered junior college, paying her way through a variety of jobs. Among other things, she studied acting, taking part in four stage productions. Though she enjoyed singing, during her high school and college years she didn't try to perform in local nightspots, warned away from their dangers by her friends and fellow churchgoers.

But her lifestyle changed after she fell in love and got married at the start of the 1980s. She told Hansen, "I was never a partier in school, but I made up for that after I left the church, got married and went through the deterioration of the marriage. [She and her husband finally parted in 1991.] I was very confused. I just tried to numb everything out, pretending I didn't care. I got into bad relationships, got into drinking too much, got into all kinds of things that I'd never done in my life[,] all in a five year period."

She kept up her songwriting and, in the mid-1980s, began to have some thoughts of seeking a Nashville outlet. It was through her sister that opportunity finally arrived. She told Jack Hurst, *Chicago Tribune* country music critic ("Back to the Future: Bobbie Cryner's Fiery Sound Is Straight out of Yesterday," August 22, 1993), "My sister had met Sonny Lemaire, one of the lead singers of [the country group] Exile. We met him on vacation one year and they got together, and she wanted to be [in Nashville] to be near him.

"They eventually got married, and when we—my husband Bill and I—came out to see them one Christ-mas, Sonny introduced me to [successful country songwriter] Max D. Barnes and Max D. gave me some good advice. He told me, 'Nobody's going to come to Kansas to offer you a deal.'"

The fact that Barnes liked her work was encouraging, and in 1988, she moved in Nashville, where she cowrote some songs with him. But not much happened in that department, or in her initial efforts to gain a record company hearing, and she had to start working as a waitress in The Cooker restaurant to pay her living expenses. The hours were long and the work demanding, so for three years she found little time or energy to pursue recording work. (When she finally broke free to develop her debut album, it included a self-penned track called "I'm Through Waitin' on You.")

However, it was her job that proved the source of her creative breakthrough. "In that three years, I met a man named Carl Jackson. He came into the restaurant all the time, and I gave him a tape. I had never given my tape to anybody, but I got to know him to where I could trust him. He told me honestly what he thought of it. He liked it, and he gave it to his publisher, Susan Burns, who took it to Doug Johnson at Epic." By 1992 she was signed to the label, and Jackson and Johnson were coproducing her debut collection. The final tracks included a duet by Bobbie with Dwight Yoakam, and support on harmony vocals from Emmylou Harris.

Bobbie wrote or cowrote more than half the songs on the album (*Bobbie Cryner*, issued in the summer of 1993), including the excellent first single, "Daddy Laid the Blues on Me." The single made the charts in June 1993 and rose to mid-chart levels during the summer before fading from view. Hurst thought that reflected the key obstacle facing the artist. The situation, he wrote, "indeed could be construed as suggesting a paucity of demand for a rural-sounding woman in urban country markets. After starting off great, 'Daddy' has languished, rejected by many radio stations as sounding too 'different.'"

But many reviewers for major media outlets and many of her country music peers felt sure the tables would turn in time for so talented an artist. Among those were George Strait and his management, which had contracted to also represent her. A promising sign was the good audience reaction to her performance as opening act for Strait in his mid-1990s concert tours.

In the late spring of 1996, Bobbie had a new album out on the MCA label. Again it was a superb collection and again got little attention from country radio stations. An example of its contents was the fine single about the collapse of a marriage titled "You'd Think He'd Know Me Better." *Los Angeles Times* critics ranked it among the top-10 singles released during the first half of the year from any pop music sector. The *Times* writer noted, "You try to figure out what is going on in country radio when programmers ignore this record . . . which has much of the emotional pulse of

George Jones' classic, 'He Stopped Loving Her Today.' This may be the most striking country single since Garth Brooks' 'The Dance.' "

CYRUS, BILLY RAY: *Singer, guitarist, songwriter, band leader (Sly Dog). Born Flatwoods, Kentucky, August 25, 1961.*

Billy Ray Cyrus certainly was the phenomenon of the 1992 country music scene with his surprising monster hit, "Achy Breaky Heart," and the album that contained it, *Some Gave All.* He was severely downgraded by most major critics who considered his success an aberration and doubted he could sustain the momentum in years to come. But in the light of the major awards he collected in 1992–93 and the massive public support, even if he proved a temporary star he could laugh all the way to the bank.

He surely had the roots for an aspiring country artist. Raised in the small town of Flatwoods in eastern Kentucky, he heard many country stylings from his early years on. His father sang in the gospel group organized by Billy Ray's paternal grandfather, who was a Pentecostal minister, called the Crownsmen Quartet. His maternal grandfather was a hoedown fiddler, and Billy Ray's mother was part of her father's bluegrass group that played for local events on Saturday nights. Of course, those weren't his only influences; during his high school years Billy Ray and his friends also listened to rock 'n' roll, including country rockers like Lynyrd Skynyrd, and soul music.

By the time Cyrus reached his high school years, his parents had long parted (they divorced when he was five) and he was more into athletics than music. Baseball was a passion, and he recalled his earliest role model was all-star Cincinnati Reds catcher Johnny Bench.

During 1981, Cyrus took up guitar playing in earnest and formed a group called Sly Dog that soon found nightclub engagements in the tri-state region (Ohio, Kentucky, West Virginia). Convinced he could make it in the music business, Billy Ray moved to Los Angeles, where he played for a while in a band called the Breeze. In 1986, he decided L.A. wasn't his kind of environment and moved back to his home area where he found work playing five nights a week at the Ragtime Lounge in Huntington, West Virginia.

On most of his free days, he drove the six hours to Nashville to seek a recording contract. This routine ended his four-year marriage, which had started auspiciously in 1986 and then gone downhill due to repeated absences.

His perseverance finally paid off with a contract with Mercury Records in 1990 that gave him the chance to record material that included the song that was to provide his breakthrough single and video: "Achy Breaky Heart." Both were released in early 1992, and the video, issued in March, had particular impact thanks to a dance step that soon was being copied in clubs and country dance events across the nation.

When the album *Some Gave All* reached record stores (release date was May 19, 1992), it became an almost immediate success. It was still high on the charts in August 1994 after accumulating multiplatinum sales of over 7 million copies. Several other singles from the album made the hit lists, and Cyrus performed before enthusiastic crowds in many major venues. The other charted singles were "Could've Been Me," number one in *Radio & Records* the week of September 11, 1992, "Where Am I Gonna Live," and the title track.

In June 1993, Mercury issued Billy Ray's follow-up album, *It Won't Be the Last,* which included four songs written or cowritten by him. The album quickly made the charts and remained on them into mid-1994, racking up platinum recognition from the R.I.A.A. It fell far short of the total sales of Billy Ray's debut, but still ranked as a major hit by anyone's calculation. It provided three hit singles, "In the Heart of a Woman," which reached number one in *R&R* the week of September 10, 1993, and "Somebody Now," which peaked at number four in *R&R* the week of November 26, 1993, and "Words By Heart," which peaked at number ten the week of April 30, 1994. Other tracks reached lower-chart levels, including "Talk Some" in mid 1994.

Some observers had wondered how prophetic the title of his second album would be. The fact that it had gone past platinum levels, whatever its creative content, demonstrated it certainly would not be the last. Billy Ray's third album, *Storm in the Heartland,* came out in late 1994, peaked at number eleven in *Billboard,* and went on to gain R.I.A.A. gold-record certification in the spring of 1995. Its stay on the best-seller lists was significantly shorter than albums one and two. Nonetheless, it was a fact that Billy Ray's batting average, from the best-seller standpoint, stood at three for three. On August 20, 1996, his fourth album on Mercury Nashville, *Trail of Tears,* was issued. The video for the title track and first single release was filmed at Land Between the Lakes.

DALHART, VERNON: *Singer, songwriter. Born Jefferson, Texas, April 6, 1883; died September 18, 1948. Elected to the Country Music Hall of Fame in 1981.*

Though it remained for the original Jimmie Rodgers and the Carter Family to provide the impetus for the rise of country music to a major force in American popular music, some of the seeds already had been sown by Vernon Dalhart, the first country music "recording star." After recording his first country hits in 1924, he went on to record hundreds of country oriented numbers in the 1920s and 1930s on a variety of labels and with various pseudonyms.

Though born and raised in Texas (real name Marion Try Slaughter), he was not initially interested in "down home" music. He had a good voice and had some thoughts in his teens of an operatic career. Eventually, he went to New York to take professional vocal lessons and, while there, became impressed with the growing popularity of record discs. His first release appears to have been on the Columbia label in 1916 titled "Just a World of Sympathy." However, that disc received little public attention. Dalhart himself considered his first "real recording" as the result of a successful audition for Thomas A. Edison which led to the famed inventor's signing Dalhart as a recording artist for Edison Diamond Disc. His first Edison release, in August 1917, was "Cain't Yo Hea'h Me Calling Caroline."

From then until the early 1920s, Dalhart turned out many recordings of light opera or then-popular music stylings. That type of material did well for a time, then sales of his discs began to drop. Looking for something new to restore his fortune, he decided to try some "hillbilly" tunes. He initially selected a cover record of "The Wreck of the Old Southern 97," already released by another performer. For the other side of the single, he recorded (on August 13, 1924) an old poem, recently set to music, called "The Prisoner's Song." The latter, after the disc was issued by Victor Records (his label at the time) in November 1924, became a major hit and remained a favorite for many years with the record-buying public. At his death in 1948, an obituary in the *New York Daily News* claimed some 25 million copies of "The Prisoner's Song" had been sold.

"The Prisoner's Song" is considered to be the first million-selling country record; Dalhart is supposed to have earned $85,000 in royalties from it while it was in print. In the years that followed, Dalhart had great success with other country type recordings, such as "Molly Darlin'," "The Letter Edged in Black," "The Death of Floyd Collins," "Golden Slippers," and "My Blue Ridge Mountain Home." Though many of the records were issued under the name Vernon Dalhart (a name he formed from the names of two Texas towns), he employed more than one hundred pseudonyms. Among them were: Bob White, Jeff Calhoun, Tom Watson, and Mack Allen.

Dalhart, who early on saw the potential for "hillbilly" music, also was an early success on radio. During the 1930s, he was well known to many listeners for his radio work under still another pseudonym, "Sam, the Barbasol Man."

In 1981, Dalhart was elected to the Country Music Hall of Fame. Previously, in 1970, he had been elected to the Nashville Songwriters Hall of Fame, the selection based partly on his three best-selling compositions, "Prisoner's Song," "Wreck of the Old 97," and "The Death of Floyd Collins." In its September 1994 issue on *The Roots of Country Music, Life* magazine included Dalhart in its list of "The 100 Most Important People in

the History of Country"—though it's hard to see why, since the editorial comments were almost wholly negative, calling him "Country's first hack" and downplaying his vocal talents.

DANIELS, CHARLIE: CHARLIE DANIELS BAND: *Vocal and instrumental group. Personnel as of mid-1970s: Charlie Daniels, born Wilmington, North Carolina, October 28, 1936 (vocals, fiddle); Joel "Taz" Di-Gregorio, born Worcester, Massachusetts (keyboards); Tom "Bigfoot" Crain, born Tennessee (guitar); Charlie Hayward, born Alabama (bass); Fred Edwards, born California (drums); Don Murray, born Maryland (drums), Charlie Marshall replaced Murray on drums in 1978.*

The 1970s saw the rise of "raunch & roll," a blending of blues, country music, and rock made popular by bands with strong Southern roots. One of the bellwethers of that movement was the Charlie Daniels Band, organized and led by a good-natured, massive giant of a man (6 feet, 4 inches tall and built like a football tackle) who could play country fiddle (backing friends like Willie Nelson) or rock guitar with equal dexterity.

Charlie grew up in rural North Carolina and started playing music at a very early age. He recalled, "I don't know when the desire came to be a musician, but I had it since I can remember. My family wasn't musical. My father [who worked in a local lumber mill] played a little harmonica, that's all. When I was in my early teens [in the late 1940s] I got around with some guys who had experience with instruments. I started playing guitar when I was about fifteen, then learned mandolin and switched over to fiddle. The chords on a mandolin are about the same as those on a fiddle, so after a year and a half or so, I got into fiddle playing.

"We had a little bluegrass band in my home area around Wilmington, North Carolina. We called ourselves the Misty Mountain Boys. But there weren't any honky tonks. I lived in a dry county. We played square dances, school proms, things like that. There wasn't any rock 'n' roll when I began, but I got into that later about the time when Elvis came along. I never knew him, though he recorded a song of mine."

For a while, music was a sideline and Charlie worked days in the creosote plant where his father and grandfather were employed, while playing nights with a band in Jacksonville, North Carolina, near Camp Lejeune. "That's where I started playing professionally. When I decided to work in music full time [when he asked to be laid off at the creosote plant instead of a black employee who had a family to support] I drifted up the country to Washington, D.C. We'd switched to playing almost all rock and top-forty songs by then—Presley, Fats Domino, Bill Haley, Chuck Berry.

"It was the same band that turned into the Jaguars. We had two guitars, bass, and drums. Originally we called ourselves the Rockets. We went up there [to D.C.] in 1958 and 1959 and played about three years off and on. We made our first trip to California during that time and had jobs in Oklahoma, Kansas, Florida, Texas—all over the United States. In 1959 we went through Fort Worth, Texas, and cut our first record. Actually, the band got its name there. I met a guy named Bob Johnston who was a local record producer and we cut a tune called 'Jaguar' that came out on Epic. After we changed our name to Jaguars."

While Daniels wandered around the nation during the first part of the 1960s playing his mix of Southern rock, country, and blues, Johnston progressed along the Columbia Records ladder until he became one of its main producers working out of Nashville. "Bob brought me to Nashville. He said, 'Why don't you come down and see if you can do it as a studio musician, songwriter, what have you.' By then I had one song hit to my credit, 'It Hurts Me,' that Elvis recorded in 1963. I got seriously involved in songwriting in the late 1950s. The first one was 'Does Your Conscience Bother You?' Full of clichés. But it never got recorded. But since the CDB started I'm proud of everything we've got on record. In some of the earlier recordings, I'm prouder of the songs than the performance."

The move to Nashville proved rewarding. Daniels spent four years as a studio musician, earning a substantial living. He also was exposed to a wide variety of musical stylings. He supported such diverse artists as Bob Dylan, Al Kooper, Pete Seeger, Leonard Cohen, Ringo Starr, and Flatt and Scruggs. "I liked working with Dylan. He was always a gentleman to me. I contributed to albums like *Nashville Skyline, Self Portrait,* and *New Morning.*" Charlie also toured as part of Cohen's backup band in the late 1960s.

After a while, Charlie tried his hand as a producer. He was particularly involved with the Youngbloods and produced what is still considered that band's best LP, *Elephant Mountain.* When Jerry Corbitt left the group, Charlie produced two solo albums of Jerry's for Capitol. In turn Corbitt produced Daniels' debut album, also on Capitol.

"That first [and only] 1971 Capitol album was essentially a solo Charlie Daniels and we did it mostly with studio musicians. Then I put a band together and started doing concert business." He averaged 250 touring days a year for the rest of the 1970s and early 1980s.

By 1972, Daniels had changed labels to Buddah, a firm more closely associated with bubble gum or soul than Southern blues/country-rock. But his efforts on the five LPs issued on Buddah's Kama Sutra label, which began with the excellent *Te John, Grease and Wolfman* in 1972, helped establish the CDB as a first rank Southern country-rock group. The single "Uneasy Rider" from the *Honey in the Rock* album first placed the band on the charts. As he says, "That was perhaps the most unlikely hit song I've ever written or recorded."

It was Charlie's fourth Kama Sutra LP, *Fire on the Mountain* (LP three, *Way Down Yonder,* contained the CDB song "Whiskey"), that finally brought a full measure of success to the CDB. "When that came out in 1975 it was a turning point for me as important as the Presley song." The LP, which includes such tracks as "No Place to Go," Charlie's impassioned performance of the classic fiddle tune "Orange Blossom Special," and the CDB's signature song, "The South's Gonna Do It Again," brought the CDB its first gold record. Before moving to a new contract with Epic, Charlie made his *Night Rider* album (issued in 1976) for Buddah, which also showed up on the charts. The CDB roster at the time, besides Charlie, included Tom Crain on guitar and vocals, Charlie Hayward on bass, Joel DiGregorio on keyboards, and Fred Edwards and Don Murray on percussion. In 1978, Murray was replaced by Charlie Marshall.

The switch to Epic (which issued some of his old Buddah masters) didn't seem to hurt Charlie's reputation. His first two releases for Epic in 1976–77, *Saddle Tramp* and *High Lonesome,* both moved to upper levels of national charts. His third Epic LP, *Midnight Wind,* also made the charts, though it did better on country lists than pop ones.

One of Charlie's favored achievements was hosting the annual Volunteer Jam, which got underway in Nashville in 1974 with a concert featuring, besides his group, the Allman Brothers Band, Marshall Tucker Band, and several others. Charlie recalled, "We had such a good time, we decided we should do this once in a while." (The second Jam was held in April 1975 in Murfreesboro, Tennessee.) In 1978, Epic released a two-record set of the third and fourth events, *Volunteer Jam III and IV.* Before that, Epic issued two CDB albums in 1977, *High Lonesome* and *Midnight Wind.* During that period, Daniels was a strong supporter of Jimmy Carter's bid for the presidency, and his band played at the inaugural celebration in 1976.

Charlie and his band had one of their most productive periods during 1979–80. They turned out the album *Million Mile Reflections,* whose tracks contained the stirring fiddle tune "The Devil Went Down to Georgia." That combination provided the CDB with its biggest successes ever. Both single and album went over gold-record levels. The LP still was on the charts well into 1980 and had earned a platinum-record award. Charlie earned three awards in Country Music Association voting for 1979, announced on the network TV show in October 1979 and, when the Grammy winners were disclosed in February 1980 the CDB won the trophy for Best Country Vocal Performance by a Duo or Group for "The Devil Went Down to Georgia." On the nationally televised Grammy Awards show, the Daniels Band performed the song.

Charlie and his group closed out 1979 with another hit single, "Mississippi." In 1980 their charted singles included "Behind Your Eyes," "Long Haired Country

Boy," "In America," and "The Legend of Wooly Swamp." By then their credits included an appearance in the film *Urban Cowboy*. Their *Full Moon* album, which included "In America" (the single reached number eleven in *Billboard*), made top-chart levels. In the Country Music Association 1980 voting, "In America" was nominated for Song of the Year while the CDB also received nominations for Vocal Group of the Year and Instrumental Group of the Year. In early 1981, the band had the single "Carolina (I Remember You)" in upper-chart brackets. Epic also issued the album *Volunteer Jam VII* during that year.

As the 1980s went by, the group continued its touring and recording activities. Epic releases for the first half of the 1980s included the *Windows* album in 1981 (which spawned a CDB version of Dan Daley's "Still in Saigon" that rose to number twenty-two on the *Billboard* pop charts), *The Charlie Daniels Band—A Decade of Hits* in 1983 and *Me and the Boys* in 1985. The band received CMA nominations for Instrumental Group of the Year in 1982 and 1983.

In 1987, after completing the thirteenth straight Volunteer Jam, a combination of business and financial problems, plus complaints by the band's support staff of being overextended, caused Daniels to suspend the event for a while. Meanwhile, the CDB continued to add to its recordings list with *Powder Keg* in 1987, *Homesick Heroes* in 1988 (from which was drawn the top-10 country singles hit, "Boogie Woogie Fiddle Country Blues"), and *Simple Man* in 1990.

The album sold well and rose to number two on the *Billboard* country list, but the lyrics of the title song caused a furor that Daniels tried to calm in print interviews and as a guest on TV and radio programs. Those words, which Daniels asserted were those of a simple man "with simple attitude," called for the lynching of drug dealers and slow death by way of alligators and snakes for murderers, child abusers, and rapists. He wrote the song "out of frustration" after reading of a case where a child was killed by her stepfather.

He said, "I know how I feel about it; I know what I'd like to do. Some of it's kind of tongue-in-cheek; it's a knee-jerk reaction. I don't really want to take people out and leave them in the swamps. . . . But violent crimes—that's what that song's about."

He told Mandy Wilson of CMA's *Close Up* in July 1993, "I come from a long line of blue-collar folks, farmers and timber people. That's how my mind operates. When I write about things I always think about them from that perspective. I think about how it will affect the working class of people. I try to write to communicate to those kinds of people."

At the start of the 1990s, Charlie had an impact on the video charts with the long-form release *Charlie Daniels: Homefolks and Highways*. In the fall of 1990, Epic issued the band's first holiday album, *Christmas Time Down South*. In 1991, the album *Renegade* came

out, and Daniels announced a resumption of the Volunteer Jam. Held in May in Nashville, the guests included B. B. King, Steppenwolf, and Tanya Tucker.

In 1992, Charlie's long relationship with Epic ended and he signed with Liberty Records that issued his debut on the label, *America, I Believe in You,* in mid-1993. In 1994, CMA voters nominated Charlie and fiddler Mark O'Connor in the Vocal Event of the Year category for their single "The Devil Comes Back to Georgia" (which also featured Johnny Cash, Marty Stuart, and Travis Tritt). During that year, Charlie also had his debut gospel record, *The Door,* in print on the Sparrow label (a subsidiary of Liberty's parent company EMI). The album won a Gospel Music Association Dove Award and the Christian Country Music Association also presented him with the Video of the Year Award for "Two Out of Three." His second Sparrow album, *Steel Witness,* was released in the summer of 1996.

On February 10, 1995, his 1977 album *Midnight Wind* finally earned a gold record from the R.I.A.A. On August 18, 1995, R.I.A.A. presented him with a multi-platinum award after his *Million Mile Reflections* passed the three million miles mark. In early 1995, Epic issued the album *Super Hits,* which showed up on lower charts levels. Though it never reached the top positions, the album sold steadily and still hovered in the number sixty range more than a year later. An earlier retrospective of the CDB, *A Decade of Hits,* was still in the top 10 on *Billboard*'s Catalog Album list in mid-1996 having spent more than 250 weeks on the chart and received a platinum record award from the R.I.A.A.

Daniels's mid-1990s activities incuded starring with Chris LeDoux on the *Wrangler Cowboy Christmas* program on TNN on December 20, 1995, and appearing as a guest star in the January 27, 1996, *Austin City Limits* TV show that honored the 25th anniversary of Asleep at the Wheel. In October 1996, Sony/Legacy Epic Records issued a three disc, 45-song box set retrospective of his recordings for Epic titled *Charlie Daniels—The Roots Remain*.

About his band and his approach to music, Daniels said, "I think it's anybody's individuality that sets them off. I think the most important thing in any profession is being yourself and doing it your own way. We don't follow fads or trends, don't rush out to record disco or punk rock just because it's hot. We just record what we feel is best for us. I feel if the CDB is unique, that would be the reason why.

"The fact that there's no particular trend today is good for me. I can't just lock in on one style of music. I'd hate to think I'd never play another rock song, blues, jazz or what have you, because that's all of what we— the whole CDB—are. I don't think the genre is as important as the quality."

*Based partly on Daniels's interview with Irwin Stambler.

DAVIS, JIMMIE H.: *Singer, guitarist, songwriter, educator, public official. Born Quitman, Louisiana, September 11, 1902. Elected to the Country Music Hall of Fame in 1972.*

When TV viewers watched Senate majority leader Robert Byrd perform on the *Grand Ole Opry* in 1979, it seemed an unusual event. But Byrd, in truth, was following in a tradition of blending music and politics of long standing in country annals, a tradition that embraced such notable individuals as Roy Acuff, who ran for governor of Tennessee several times, Texas Governor W. Lee O'Daniel, and, of course, the two-time chief executive of Louisiana, as well as country superstar, Jimmie Davis.

Davis, born and raised in rural Louisiana, where his home town was Beech Springs, grew up in an environment where singing country music and gospels was an integral part of day-to-day living. He formed an early fondness for "the warm living songs of the cowboys and farmers and country folks." He learned to play guitar as a boy; by the time he began high school in Beech Springs he already had a considerable repertoire of songs, though at the time music seemed only a pleasant sideline.

He earned his B.A. degree from Louisiana College in Pineville in the early 1920s and from there completed a master's degree at Louisiana State University in Baton Rouge in the mid-1920s. Later in the decade, he was hired as a professor of history at Dodd College. In the meantime his musical efforts, particularly in the gospel field, continued and his reputation expanded well beyond his home state. By the late 1920s, he was giving gospel concerts at church meetings and at various religious centers all over the Southwest.

In the 1930s, he became more active both politically and musically. He was the holder of several public posts during the decade, including a year and a half as a public service commissioner and a period of time as a criminal court clerk. But it was as a performer of gospel and secular country material that he became well known. As the decade progressed, he spent more and more time on the road performing his country and gospel stylings before audiences all over the United States. Many of the songs he performed were original compositions, including "You Are My Sunshine" and "It Makes No Difference Now." Both songs became favorites of the Oklahoma Singing Cowboy, otherwise known as Gene Autry, who released singles of them that undoubtedly would have risen to number one on the charts—if there had been any hit charts in those years. As it was, they helped make Autry an international star. Both songs have been recorded by hundreds of artists over the decades since Davis wrote them and are among the classic songs of American music history.

By the end of the 1930s, though, Davis had acquired a national following that rivaled that of Autry's in size. He was a headliner on the country concert circuit and featured on national radio programs. He turned out dozens of records from the late 1930s through the 1940s on the RCA Victor label. He had a role in the movie *Louisiana*, released by Monogram Pictures in 1944.

During this time a yearning to make a name for himself in politics was in the back of Jimmie's mind. His musical achievements made his name familiar to almost everyone in his home state, which was no small help in his bid to gain the nomination for governor on the Louisiana Democratic ticket in 1944. He combined discussions of state problems with musical entertainment and won the post. He completed his first term as governor in 1948 and returned to the entertainment field, though the greater emphasis on gospel material than popular-style country songs. It was a pattern that continued throughout the 1950s, when his religious activities brought him many awards, including, in 1957, the American Youth Singers Award as Best Male Sacred Singer.

First for RCA and, in the 1950s and 1960s, for Decca Records, Jimmie turned out a great many sacred and secular recordings. Among his single releases were such songs as "Suppertime," "Lord, I'm Coming Home," "Get on Board," "Aunt Susan," "Honey in the Rock," "The Great Milky Way," "Alimony Blues," "You've Been Tom Cattin' Round," "Somewhere There's a Friend," "The Lord Has Been Good to Me," "Take My Hand, Precious Lord," "Worried Mind," "I'm Bound for the Kingdom," "Columbus Stockade Blues," "When I Prayed Last Night," "I Won't Have to Cross Jordan Alone," "There's a Chill on the Hill Tonight," "I Hung My Head and Cried," and "Down by the Riverside." He also recorded his own version of his classics "You Are My Sunshine" and "It Makes No Difference Now" as well as such other originals as "Doggone That Train" "Someone to Care," "When It's Roundup Time in Heaven," "When We All Get Together Up There," and "I Dreamed of an Old Love Affair" (the last two coauthored).

Among his 1950s albums on Decca were *Someone to Care* and *You Are My Sunshine*. He also recorded many gospel albums for that label, including *The Door Is Always Open* (issued in 1958), *Hail Him with a Song* (1959), *No One Stands Alone* (1960), *Watching Over You* (1961), *How Great Thou Art* (1962), *Beyond the Shadow* (1963), *Near the Cross, Highway to Heaven, Hymn Time, Songs of Faith, Suppertime, and Sweet Hour of Prayer.* In the early 1970s, he was represented in the Decca catalogue by such Christmas albums as *It's Christmas Time Again* and *Going Home for Christmas.*

Growing political upheaval in Louisiana at the end of the 1950s brought about another chance for Jimmie to enter the political arena. Amid cross-currents of racial strife and arguments about the Long family political machine, Davis entered the primary and won out over several adversaries. As Democratic nominee, he had no trouble in winning the governorship. Once again his music work came to a halt while he ran the affairs of the state from 1960 to 1964. As his term drew to a close, he was represented by a new release on Decca 1964 called *Jimmie Davis Sings*.

In the years after he stepped down from office for the second and last time, he maintained a relatively low profile. He was active in church endeavors but, in effect retired from any major country music involvement. Many performers, both veterans and newcomers, however, include some of his songs in their repertoire.

Jimmie's contributions to country music were recognized when he was nominated as a candidate for the Country Music Hall of Fame by Country Music Association members in 1968. In 1972, he receive the required number of votes for election. As the bronze plaque in his honor installed in the Hall of Fame in Nashville states, "His humility, deep felt responsibility to his audience and winning way with a song has brought much 'sunshine' to gospel and country music."

In 1996, then well into his nineties, Davis could lay claim to being the oldest living member of the Country Music Hall of Fame. Some of his recorded output was then available on the MCA *Country Music Hall of Fame Series* album.

DAVIS, LINDA: *Singer, pianist, Born Dotson, Texas, November 26, c. early 1960s.*

Up until 1993, when asked about Linda Davis people would respond, "Linda who?" Members of the country music industry in Nashville were aware of her as a lady with a powerful voice who made some very effective demos for other artists, and some in the advertising community valued her contributions to commercials for major products, but despite several solo recording attempts that provided some charted singles, she remained a face in the crowd. Then came a hit duet with superstar Reba McEntire called "Does He Love You," and suddenly she was a celebrity.

Linda was born in Dotson, Texas, a part of Pineola County that contributed superstars like Jim Reeves and Tex Ritter to the country & western pantheon. As a child she remembered listening mostly to country music, which was favored by her parents as well as by most adults in Pineola County. She told Marv Greifinger of *Country Fever* ("Linda Davis, No Overnight Sensation," August 1994) that her early female influences were Dolly Parton and Barbara Mandrell; she also recalled her male heroes: "Growing up, when we first got a record player for Christmas, the first albums in our house were Charley Pride and George Jones. So those were my first influences. And watching the Porter Wagoner Show I became a fan of the stylist.

"Of course, Willie Nelson became a great stylist, and I loved his work, and another one that I liked to listen to and sing harmony with, note for note, is Ronnie Milsap.

I had every eight track he ever made. You know, that's when I started developing my vocal ability and my style."

She had made her first public appearance at the age of six, singing on the East Texas Gary Jamboree and went on to start making her mark as a professional artist as a teenager on the *Louisiana Hayride* and *Texas Grapevine Opry*. Her parents encouraged her efforts, driving her to various jamborees and hayride events in which she would perform on weekends. Others in the family, a number of aunts and uncles, as well as friends, she recalled, would caravan to cheer her on at such places.

She spent a year in junior college, but decided she'd rather spend her time trying to make it as a performer. She tried to make contact with country music firms in Nashville on several occasions, ferried there at times by her parents. That didn't bring results, so she decided to move to Music City in 1982. The doors didn't open right away, but soon after settling in Nashville she met musician Lang Scott, who had moved there only two months before. Their relationship blossomed into a marriage that seemed to remain firm as Linda made her major breakthroughs in the mid-1990s. Before that, she told interviewers, his entertainment work had helped them through her lean career times of the mid- and late 1980s.

Soon after she moved to Nashville, it looked as though she might quickly find success with her vocal ability. She signed with a small independent label, MDJ Records, which at the time was promoting a band called Wild Country. That group, after a name change to Alabama, became a sensation with RCA Records. MDJ executives decided to have Linda perform with another roster artist, singer-songwriter Skip Eaton. As Skip and Linda, they recorded three singles, but their low-charting performance wasn't enough to justify MDJ investment in an album.

Linda remembered the emotional roller coaster in an interview with Jim Ridley of *New Country* ("Shooting for the Moon—Linda Davis Grabs the Spotlight," June 1994). "I had enough carrots waved in front of my nose as an artist that I thought, 'Oooh, this is going to happen—Skip and Linda's going to be the next big duet.' Well . . . it just wasn't meant to be. The music and our timing, I don't know—I don't question it. I just go forward. It was a little bit of a setback emotionally, though, to realize that putting a year and a half into something one hundred percent that it's really not going to work. . . . Our first big taste of rejection."

For a while she earned some spending money as a general purpose helper at MDJ, but lost that when the firm went out of business. Then she got a job with a Music Row public relations company, but that too failed. She and Lang had not yet married, and she realized she needed to find any kind of work—in the music field or not. She told Ridley, "I was a waitress and a hostess—and my heart wasn't in it. I just felt like I was going backward and didn't know what in the world I was going to do. I didn't have any extra money—my phone was cut off."

With marriage came a shoulder to lean on and more confidence in her potential as a singer. She could accompany herself on the piano, and in 1985 found a position singing nights at a hotel lounge, starting at a piano bar setup near an Interstate highway and then progressing to the role of regular performer at the Sheraton Music Row Lounge. In both spots, people from all walks of life, from show business figure to shop owner, were her audience. Sometimes, though, she noted, "It was just the tables and chairs and me. You really hear yourself like that, and you learn a lot. You find out how to get inside a song."

Among those dropping in to catch her act were songwriters and record producers, who finally brought her some opportunities in the industry. Among those who liked what they heard were songwriters Bobby David and Ray Kennedy, who set up her first demo sessions (at a time when she was eight months pregnant with daughter Hillary). Soon other writers gave her assignments that eventually led to work providing backing vocals for commercials for such national companies as Pepsi and Kentucky Fried Chicken.

Her hopes of escaping the lounge routine rose in 1987, when record producer Eric Montgomery recognized the quality of her singing at the Sheraton and got her a deal with Epic. The record company issued a video and three singles of her work from 1987–89, but the experience was similar to her time at MDJ: all three singles made the charts, but only the lower positions, and Epic dropped her from the roster. In 1990, the year she gave up the lounge work, she signed with another label, Capitol. By then she had made a crucial career move, though it would be a few years before it bore fruit: She signed with Starstruck Entertainment, the management and publishing company owned by Reba McEntire and her husband, Narvel Blackstock.

The roost of the association, she told Ridley, went back to a late 1980s performance by her at a fair in Missouri. "I was . . . on the free stage. Reba was in the big grandstand. By this time they'd heard me on tape a lot. Narvel heard I was across the midway, so he came and watched my show and invited me to watch Reba's that night. I accepted excitedly, because I'd never met her and I always loved her singing. So after the show, I went backstage and met her—and she was just as sweet and complimentary as everybody told me she was. And that's the beginning of what I call a dear, dear friendship."

Her singing under the Blackstock aegis in 1989 helped set up the Capitol deal that led to two early 1990s albums, one on the label and one under Capitol Nashville's new name, Liberty. Neither had any chart success, and Linda and Liberty parted company. Fortunately Blackstock helped her and Lang keep the wolf from the door by making them part of Reba's backing group on tour.

In April 1993, Reba asked Linda to record a duet with her on the song "Does He Love You." The session was held that month and, as Linda told Jerry C. Armor of *Country Song Roundup* ("Linda Davis," May 1994), "I knew it was magic when we did it. Reba was in one booth, I was in the other and the window between us. We were just looking at each other and just really getting into it. It was special."

The duet was featured on Reba's tour. Linda said, "It was a great learning experience. I've been content to stand in the shadows, soaking up everything I could on- and offstage. We'd sing that duet every night, and people would just go crazy."

Released as a single by MCA, the song became one of the top successes of 1993, rising to number one on all country lists, reaching that position, for instance, in *Radio & Records* the week of October 29, 1993. Enthusiastic public response was also given to the video.

All of this resulted in a flurry of awards in 1994, including a Grammy for Best Country Vocal Collaboration, a TNN/Music City News video trophy for Vocal Collaboration of the Year, and, sweetest of all, in October, Country Music Association recognition for Vocal Event of the Year. Linda expressed her thanks to the worldwide TV audience saying, in part, "Just think. This time last year, I wasn't here. I didn't even have a record deal."

But by then she had been on the Arista roster for many months, having completed her debut material for the album *Shoot for the Moon,* released on April 26, 1994. (It was preceded by the initial single from the collection, "Company Time.") The singles didn't have much chart impact (the second drawn from the album during the summer of 1994 was "Love Didn't Do It"), but the album made it into the *Billboard* Top 30 (peaking at number twenty-eight) and stayed on the list for a number of months.

In late 1995 her second Arista album came out, *Some Things Are Meant to Be.* The tracks included a cover of the Gladys Knight hit "Neither One of Us" and another duet with Reba McEntire, "If I Could Live Your Life." The title track was released as the first single and spent a number of weeks on the charts in late 1995 and early 1996, gaining the top 20 at one point. In the spring of 1996 she had another single on the hit lists, "A Love Story in the Making."

DAVIS, MAC *Singer, guitarist, songwriter, actor. Born Lubbock, Texas, January 21, 1942.*

Though most of Mac Davis's reputation was made in the pop music domain, there was no gainsaying his Texas roots. A good share of his popularity always lay with country fans and many of his recordings showed up on country charts over the years.

Davis's early upbringing in west Texas had many of

the basic elements of a country background. He spent much of his time on his uncle's ranch, and his early music experience was derived to a great extent from the church. His first public singing efforts were in a church choir as a boy. Later he sang in local choirs in high school. However, his teen years coincided with the rise of rock and he became increasingly interested in the kind of music typified by artists like Elvis, Jerry Lee Lewis, and Carl Perkins. By then Davis was playing guitar and working with teen groups in his home area.

Later he moved to Atlanta, Georgia, where he worked days for the Georgia State Board of Probation and attended night classes at Georgia State University. His thoughts turned strongly to music, though, and he spent his spare time hanging around clubs or recording studios picking up contacts and trying to further his songwriting efforts. At the start of the 1960s he formed his own rock band and worked at college dances and private parties in Atlanta and vicinity. In 1961, though, he gave that up because, he said, "I had this image of being a rock'n'roller at the age of thirty-five, trying to make a buck."

Management, he decided, was the way to go. He found work as Atlanta district and regional manager for Vee-Jay Records, which he held until 1965. He moved over to a wider ranging job at Liberty—setting up local offices for the label throughout the South. (Liberty later became United Artists Records.) He did well enough for the company to bring him to Hollywood to head its music publishing operation, Metric Music.

Since he had continued to build up a backlog of original songs during previous years, Davis began to show some of them to record company executives and performers. In 1967-68 two releases of his material made the charts: Lou Rawls's single of "You're Good to Me" and Glen Campbell's release of "Within My Memory."

Even more important, Davis's work caught the attention of his idol of his high school years, the King of Rock himself, Elvis Presley. Presley and his manager Colonel Tom Parker chose several Davis songs that Elvis sang in 1968, including one that made upper-chart levels, "A Little Less Conversation." Elvis next asked Mac to give him some new songs for his first recording session in many years in Tennessee. Among the material Davis turned over was a song about the deprivations of black life, "In the Ghetto." The song became a top-20 hit for Elvis in 1969 and, after Davis started his own singing career, a staple in his repertoire. Davis and Presley teamed up on still more hits in 1969–70: "Memories" and "Don't Cry Daddy."

Presley wasn't the only artist prospering with Mac's songs, some of which were published under such pseudonyms as Scott Davis and Mac Scott Davis. Hit releases of his material at the end of the 1960s and in the early 1970s included O. C. Smith's versions of "Friend, Lover, Woman, Wife" and "Daddy's Little Man"; Bobby Goldsboro's single "Watching Scotty Grow" (written about Davis's son from his first, brief marriage); and Kenny Rogers and the First Edition's rock hit, "Something's Burning." Other credits Davis achieved in those years were the preparation of music for the first Presley TV special and for two of Elvis's movies and the composition of five songs for the Glen Campbell film, *Norwood.*

At the start of the 1970s, Davis decided to come out from behind the scenes and make his way as a soloist. A series of appearances on Johnny Carson's *The Tonight Show* and the *David Frost Show* in 1970–71 got things rolling and from then on he was a frequent guest on all manner of major network shows. He also became a headliner at Las Vegas show spots and played major hotels and night clubs regularly in the United States and abroad throughout the 1970s.

He signed with Columbia Records in the early 1970s; his label debut, *Mac Davis: Song Painter,* came out in mid-1971. That same year he had two chart singles, both written by him, "Beginning to Feel the Pain" and "I Believe in Music." The latter did well in both pop and country markets. In 1972, he scored heavily with his single, "Baby, Don't Get Hooked on Me," number one on the U.S. pop charts in September and a gold-record award winner (September 20, 1972). The album of the same title was in upper-chart levels the last four months of 1972 and well into 1973, earning a gold record in May 1973. Earlier in 1972, he had made the charts with his second album, *I Believe in Music,* and the single "Everybody Loves a Love Song." In spring 1973, he again made album charts with the LP *Mac Davis.* Other hits of the mid-1970s were "Smell the Roses" and "One Hell of a Woman."

Most of his pop hits also did well on country lists. In fact, he was still placing songs on the country charts when his pop momentum seemed to be slowing down. Among his singles that made country lists in the mid-1970s were "Burning Thing" (co-written with M. James) and "I Still Love You (You Still Love Me)," both in 1975; "Forever Lovers," a top-20 hit in May 1976; and his composition "Picking Up the Pieces of My Life" in the summer of 1977.

During the mid- and late-1970s, Mac continued to be a popular in-person act and one of the more successful music industry hands at TV specials. For a while in the early part of the decade he had his own variety show, which gave way to a series of specials on NBC. His 1977 Christmas special, *I Believe in Christmas,* ranked sixth in the Nielsens and his first (of two) 1978 specials in May of that year also did well with viewers. During the year, he signed a new contract with the network for two specials a year for the next three years, bringing his association with NBC to nine years, the longest association of that kind for any artist.

His recording career languished somewhat in the

late 1970s. By the start of the 1980s he had moved from Columbia to Casablanca Records, accompanied by an upsurge of buying interest among country fans. In the spring of 1980 he had a top-10 hit single, "It's Hard to Be Humble," an original composition that provided the title track for the best-selling LP. Later in the year he added such top-10 singles hits as "Let's Keep It That Way" and his own composition, "Texas in My Rear View Mirror." In 1981 his singles successes included "Hooked on Music" and "You're My Bestest Friend."

Mac made his movie debut as a Don Meredith–style quarterback in the 1979 movie *North Dallas Forty.* The following year he played the male lead in the film *Cheaper to Keep Her.*

His 1980s credits included work on an ABC-TV sitcom called *Brothers-in-Law* at mid-decade.

For most of the 1980s, though Mac kept active as a performer in concerts and made occasional TV appearances, his achievements didn't match those of earlier decades. He did keep writing new material and in 1993 had the satisfaction of having his composition "Slow Dancing with the Moon" serve as the title track for an excellent solo album by Dolly Parton issued early that year. He commented, "I love this song and still can't believe Dolly didn't write it since it suits her so well."

During 1993, Mac got the chance to demonstrate his musical comedy skills for Broadway audiences when he took over the lead role in the long-running *Will Rogers Follies.* His association with the show extended into 1994. Meanwhile he could continue to count on royalties coming in from songs he had written for Elvis Presley (some of which, of course, were covered from time to time by other performers), considering that almost all of Presley's output remained constantly on the market.

DEAN, BILLY: *Singer, guitarist, fiddler, banjoist, songwriter. Born Quincy, Florida, April 2, 1962.*

While Billy Dean's signature song, "Billy the Kid," might have suggested he could be a new recruit to the "outlaw" breed of country artists, he seemed more a member of the mainstream contingent of 1990s country music. He certainly didn't have the gruff, rough-edged style of people like Waylon Jennings and Hank Williams, Jr., but in his own way as performer and songwriter he certainly had a strong impact on the improving fortunes of country music as a mass audience genre in the 1990s.

Some of his childhood escapades might seem to fit an outlaw description, though he told Sandy Lovejoy of *KNIX Country Spirit,* "I was just a real curious kid; I wasn't really destructive or anything. I'm really fortunate I grew up in a time where it was safe to let your kids go out and be adventurous and roam around the neighborhoods and different parts of the woods." Whether anyone would consider as childish fun the fact that young Billy once burned down the family home

while playing with matches—or, while emulating TV *Rifleman* star Chuck Connors, shot up the family gas station—is another matter.

Apart from those incidents, there seems to have been good rapport between Billy and his parents as he grew up in Florida. He was exposed to a variety of music styles as a youngster, particularly since his father, Bill Dean, Sr., whose day job was auto mechanic, moonlighted as a bandleader. He encouraged Billy to learn to play instruments as soon as the boy was old enough to focus on music, and by the time Billy was eight, he was playing guitar and able to make his debut in his father's band, the Country Rock.

Billy continued to work with his father's group and later, in high school, with other young musicians. In the mid-1970s, often singing some of his own original compositions, he found time outside school hours to perform in a number of towns on Florida's Gulf Coast, slowly building up a regional following.

But he also demonstrated promising athletic skills, particularly in basketball, which brought the offer of a scholarship from a small southern college. He didn't abandon music, though, and, in fact, always felt that was his main calling. He told Lovejoy, "Going to college was not my first choice out of high school. I would have like to have gone on to Nashville. But a lot of people worked real hard to send me to basketball camp and get that basketball scholarship for me. So I went to college, really, for them—out of respect to those people and my parents."

After a year, he dropped out of college and decided to pursue music full time. Among other things, he took part in the Wrangler Star Search competition and got an invitation to Nashville for the finals. There he performed on the stage of the *Grand Ole Opry* and impressed the judges, even if he didn't win first prize. Some of them urged him to move to Nashville, but he felt he needed more seasoning and spent more time on the road before moving to Music City in the late 1980s.

While seeking to place some of his songs with country publishers and performers, he paid his bills through occasional gigs and work as a commercial jingle singer and backup vocalist for established acts. He also took acting lessons and auditioned and won assignments in TV commercials for such companies as McDonald's, Valvoline Motor Oil, and Chevrolet. After a while, his song demos began to attract attention from country artists and some were recorded by the Oak Ridge Boys, Les Taylor, and Shelly West; one, "Somewhere in My Broken Heart," was a chart record for Randy Travis. His songwriting potential was aided by a publishing deal with EMI Music.

Looking back from the perspective of the 1990s—when, as an established artist himself, he had dozens of performing dates scheduled months in advance—he told Sheri O'Meara ("Billy the Kid Comes of Age," *Hot Country Headlines,* January 1994) that having a full schedule planned in advance was comforting "because for ten years in Nashville, I didn't know if I was going to work from one week to the next, and somehow the phone would ring on a Thursday or Friday and I'd know I'd have a gig on Friday or Saturday. But it drove me crazy for a long time because that was my only source of income—and I never knew from week to week if it was going to be there."

At the start of the 1990s, Billy finally made his breakthrough, signing a recording contract with SBK Records, a label distributed by Liberty Records. His debut album, *Young Man,* came out on Liberty/SBK during 1990, and the debut single, "Only Here for a Little While," soared to number two on one of the major charts. This was followed by a number-one hit, Billy's version of "Somewhere in My Broken Heart," cowritten by Billy and Richard Leigh. (Randy Travis's cut of the song had not yet been released.) The single stayed on the country charts for a notable nineteen weeks, and Billy also scored a hit video with the song. In the 1992 Academy of Country Music voting, the recording was named Song of the Year. The ACM members also named Billy New Male Vocalist of the Year. The song was also nominated for a Grammy Award. Besides all that, Country Music Association polling during 1992 made Dean a finalist for the Horizon Award.

During 1991, Billy's second album, *Billy Dean,* was released and did well on country charts. It also spawned another series of hit singles that rose high on *Billboard* and *Radio & Records* lists. Those comprised "You Don't Count the Cost," number nine in *R&R* the week of December 6, 1991; "Only the Wind," number three in *R&R* the week of March 13, 1992; "Billy the Kid," written by Dean, number two in *R&R* the week of July 24, 1992; and "If There Hadn't Been You," number one in *R&R* the week of November 13, 1992. By the end of 1992, Billy had built up his live appearance credits to include opening acts on major tours (The Judds' Farewell Tour in 1991, Wynonna Judd's 1992 solo tour, and the Clint Black 1992 Hard Way Tour) and headline status in clubs and small venues. Meanwhile, the second album had earned a gold-record award from the R.I.A.A.

Billy also had some other interesting 1992 credits. On TV he hosted VH-1's 1992 Top 21 Countdown, co-hosted on ABC-TV Disney "The Best of Country '92: Countdown at the Neon Armadillo," and cowrote and performed the theme song for the ABC-TV animated series, "Wild West C.O.W.—Boys of Moo Mesa."

Dean's third album, *Fire in the Dark,* came out in early 1993. The singles included two Dean originals, "Tryin' to Hide a Fire in the Dark," number five in *R&R* the week of February 26, 1993, and "I Wanna Take Care of You." A third chart-making single from the album was "We Just Disagree," which peaked at number seven in *R&R* the week of February 4, 1994. The album itself earned an R.I.A.A. gold-record plaque. Billy's concert

work during 1993 included supporting act on the Alan Jackson spring tour.

In early 1994, he had a *Greatest Hits* album released by Liberty/SBK, which was on the charts through the fall. In early June his single "Cowboy Band" debuted on the charts and, after making the *Billboard* Top 20, was also still on the list in the fall. His next collection, *Men'll Be Boys,* came out in May and appeared at mid- and lower levels of the *Billboard* Hot 75 through the summer months. The *Greatest Hits* album contained a track of the song "Once in Awhile," which Dean had written and performed on the soundtrack for the movie *8 Seconds to Glory.*

Some of the new songs Billy was beginning to add to his repertoire in the mid-1990s were inspired by his son, William Eli, born to him and wife Cathy in 1993. Cathy, he noted, took care of all the financial apsects of his career, while he took care of almost everything else. During part of 1992, in fact, he had tried his hand at doing *everything* else—acting as his own manager—but in 1993 he hired a comanager to relieve some of the burden. "It almost drove me crazy and I just had to train everybody to realize that I'm a person and not a slave to the business. . . . There are so many opportunities, it's hard to do all of them."

In early 1996, the title track from his new album on the Capitol Nashville label (the new name for Liberty country recordings), "It's What I Do," was on the charts followed a short time after by the album. The latter peaked at number eighteen in *Billboard* in the early spring. During the summer Dean helped Crystal Bernard (of TV's *Wings*) prepare her debut album on the River North label, issued in October. Besides contributing backing vocals on the disc, *The Girl Next Door,* Billy cowrote the song "Have We Forgotten What Love Is" with her and helped record it. The track was the first single released from the album.

DEAN, JIMMY RAY: *Singer, guitarist, accordionist, pianist, harmonica player, songwriter. Born near Plainview, Texas, August 10, 1928.*

From the 1970s on, Jimmy Dean probably was better known to most people for pork sausages and other food products than as an entertainer. Through the late 1970s he continued to keep his hand in with in-person appearances and TV work; by the start of the 1980s, however, he was devoting more and more of his time to his business activities and less and less to music.

His hectic pace during the 1960s, when he had been one of the stellar country artists with the ability to capture the attention of a broader popular audience with his recording and TV efforts, was a thing of the past by the 1970s. But he still demonstrated in that decade that he hadn't lost his touch by placing several more singles on the charts.

Dean sometimes recalled the straitened circumstances of his childhood when his mother, who was the family's sole support, ran a barber shop in their small Texas town to keep things going. As soon as Jimmy, who was born Seth Ward, was old enough to help, he had to pitch in and work on local farms. As he told Edith Efron of *TV Guide* (January 4, 1964), "Oh, I was a hardworkin' little boy. Pullin' cotton, shockin' grain, cuttin' wheat, loadin' wheat, choppin' cotton, cleanin' chicken houses, milkin' cows, plowin'. They used to laugh at my clothes, my bib overalls and galluses, because we were dirt poor. And I'd go home and tell mom how miserable I felt being laughed at. I dreamt of havin' a beautiful home, a nice car, an' nice clothes. I wanted to be somebody."

His mother wasn't able to provide him with material things but she taught Jimmy the piano when he was ten. Naturally talented, Jimmy not only picked up the piano rapidly, he soon taught himself to play a succession of other instruments—guitar, accordion, and harmonica.

Still, music seemed a sideline for a long time. When he was sixteen he went into irrigation engineering for a while, then gave that up in favor of a two-year enlistment in the Merchant Marine. After completing his seagoing hitch, he signed on with the Air Force. During those years, he used his musical skills as a source of spare-time income. Stationed at Bolling Air Force Base outside Washington, D.C. he formed a group called the Tennessee Haymakers with three friends and played in service clubs and local honky tonks. After he was discharged in 1948, he continued his musical routine.

Several years later, impresario Connie Gay agreed to represent Jimmy. In 1952 Gay sent him on a tour of U.S. bases in the Caribbean. Jimmy and his new group, the Texas Wildcats, then were placed on station WARL, Arlington, Virginia. In 1953 the group gained a national reputation with the singles hit, "Bummin' Around."

By 1955, Jimmy had his own TV show *Town and Country Time,* on WMAL-TV. It soon was expanded to *Town and Country Jamboree* and was syndicated to other parts of the country. The success of the show led to a CBS contract for a network morning spot called *The Jimmy Dean Show,* which debuted April 8, 1957. The show gained excellent audience response, but no sponsors. In 1958, an afternoon network show from New York was planned, but a dispute arose and Jimmy quit the project.

For the next few years, Dean concentrated on live appearances around the United States and on turning out records under a Columbia Records agreement. In 1961, while on a plane to Nashville for a recording session, he tried writing his first song. The result was the massive gold record winning hit, "Big Bad John." After that, he made the charts again with a variation of the theme, "Dear Ivan." In the Grammy voting for 1961, the single was named Best Country & Western Recording. Besides topping the country charts, the disc was number one on U.S. pop lists in the fall of 1961 for five straight weeks. In 1962 he followed with the hits "The

Cajun Queen," "P.T. 109," and "Gonna Raise a Ruckus Tonight." Also a chart hit that year was his LP titled *Big Bad John.*

His recording achievements helped him win a new TV show contract, this time from ABC. The show was a feature of afternoon TV from 1963 into 1966. An hour-long nighttime version aired from 1964 to 1966, attracting an audience of millions but still not enough for good Nielsen ratings. Besides hosting his own show, Jimmy was a frequent visitor on other major programs, including, *The Ed Sullivan Show, The Pat Boone Chevy Showroom, Hollywood Palace,* and many country syndicated programs. He toured widely, starring at such places as Harrah's Club in Reno, Valley Music Hall in Salt Lake City, Circle Star Theatre in the San Francisco Bay area, Shoreham Hotel, Washington, and many others. His mid-1960s activities also included a tour with the Icecapades. By then he had switched record affiliations from Columbia to RCA. Among his chartmakers in the mid-1960s for RCA were "Stand Beside Me" in 1966 and "I'm a Swinger" in 1967.

His album output on Columbia, besides *Big Bad John,* included *Hour of Prayer* and *Jimmy Dean Portrait* in 1962, *Everybody's Favorite* in 1963, the *Songs We Love* in 1964. Some of his material appeared on other labels, including *Favorites* on King in 1960 and *Television Favorites* on Mercury in 1965.

In 1967, he made his LP debut for RCA with *Jimmy Dean Is Here.* Also issued during the year was *Most Richly Blessed.* He continued to record for Victor through the early 1970s with such releases as *At Harrah's Club* (late 1960s); *Dean of Country* (6/70); *Country Boy & Country Girl* (12/70); *Everybody Knows* (7/71); and *These Hands* (12/71).

In the mid-1970s, Jimmy recorded on the GRT/ Casino label. One result of that affiliation was the best-selling single "I.O.U." which was awarded a gold record by the R.I.A.A. on May 20, 1976.

While Jimmy still performed occasionally in the 1980s and 1990s, his prime focus continued to be on his business interests, which included, along with the Jimmy Dean Meat Company of pork sausage fame, a chain of family-style restaurants.

DELMORE BROTHERS, THE: *Vocal and instrumental duo, songwriters. Alton Delmore, born Elkmont, Alabama, December 25, 1908; died Nashville, Tennessee, July 4, 1964. Rabon Delmore, born Elkmont, Alabama, December 3, 1910; died Athens, Alabama, December 4, 1952.*

Long-time favorites on the *Grand Ole Opry* and on country music programs on WLW, Cincinnati, and other stations, the Delmore Brothers provided some of the all-time standards in the country field, numbers like "Beautiful Brown Eyes" (cowritten by Alton and Arthur Smith) and "Blues Stay Away From Me," a joint composition of Alton and Rabon. The brothers also rank high in the bluegrass pantheon and formed the nucleus of one of the most famous quartets in country music history, the Brown's Ferry Four, a group whose members included, at various times, such notables as Grandpa Jones, Red Foley and Merle Travis.

Both brothers were farm bred and sang for pure enjoyment when their boyhood chores were through. They learned to play the fiddle at early ages and, in their teens, entered many fiddle contests in their local area. Later, they mastered guitar and became highly proficient on that instrument as well.

After playing for some years for local events, the boys auditioned for Columbia Records in 1931. It was their first time before a microphone and proved the start of an illustrious recording career. Soon after, they were signed by the *Grand Ole Opry* and they debuted on the program in 1932. They remained regulars on the *Opry* from 1932 to 1938. In the late 1930s and throughout the 1940s, the brothers were heard on many other stations, including WPTF, Raleigh, North Carolina; WFBC, Greenville, South Carolina; WAPI, Birmingham, Alabama; WIBC, Indianapolis, Indiana; WMC, Memphis, Tennessee; KWHN, Ft. Smith, Arkansas; and WLW, Cincinnati, Ohio. They became particular favorites of midwest audiences through their many years of association with WLW.

From the 1940s into the 1950s, the brothers were represented on King Records. Their output on the label included many original compositions; before Rabon's untimely death in 1952, they wrote a total of over 1,200 songs together or separately (some of the latter cowritten with other writers). Their King singles output included: "Prisoner's Farewell," "Sweet, Sweet Thing," "Midnight Special," "Why Did You Leave Me, Dear," "Don't Forget Me," "Midnight Train," "Freight Train Boogie," "Boogie Woogie Baby," "Harmonica Blues," "Barnyard Boogie," "Used Car Blues," "Peachtree Street Boogie," "Take It Out On the Captain," "Fifty Miles to Travel," "Shame On Me," "Calling to that Other Shore," "The Wrath of God," "Weary Day," "Blues Stay Away From Me" (a top-10 hit in 1949), "Pan American Boogie," "Trouble Ain't Nothin' But the Blues," "Blues You Never Lose," "I Swear by the Stars," "Sand Mountain Blues," "Life's Too Short," "I Let the Freight Train Carry Me On," "Please Be My Sunshine," "Field Hand Man," "Gotta Have Some Lovin'," "Everybody Loves Her," "Lonesome Day," "The Girl by the River," and "There's Something 'Bout Love." Their output included several sides with Grandpa Jones, including "Darby's Ram" and "Take It Out on the Door."

Besides "Blues Stay Away From Me" and "Beautiful Brown Eyes," their best known career successes included "Brown's Ferry Blues," "Freight Train Blues," and "Born to be Blue."

Before his death in 1964, Alton completed an autobiography, *Truth is Stranger Than Publicity,* which fi-

nally became available in book form from the Country Music Foundation in 1977 and was still in print as of 1997. The brothers were nominated for election to the Country Music Hall of Fame a number of times by the CMA selection committee in the 1980s and 1990s, but as of 1997 had not been voted in.

DEMENT, IRIS: *Singer, guitarist, songwriter. Born Paragould, Arkansas, 1961.*

With a voice and style somewhat reminiscent of Emmylou Harris (who contributed some of the backing vocals in Iris's debut album), Iris DeMent in a way represents a throwback to the folk roots of traditional country music. Melding elements of traditional country, bluegrass, and gospel in her performances with original songs that typically expressed heartfelt, yet up-to-date feelings about life and love, she held promise as one of the freshest new faces in 1990s folk-country music.

She was born in Paragould, Arkansas, the youngest of fourteen children born to Patric and Flora Mae DeMent. At that time, the DeMents were a farm family, but when its finances began failing they were forced to move to Southern California in 1964. Once there, Patric DeMent got a job as a gardener and janitor at the Movieland Wax Museum near Knotts Berry Farm in Orange County. The family took up residence in the city of Buena Park, where Iris attended elementary and high school.

As she told a *Los Angeles Times* reporter in October 1992, "My parents were very protective of us. We were discouraged from playing with kids outside the family. My life revolved very much around the church. I have serious doubts I'd be doing music today if it hadn't been for my upbringing in the church, which was reinforced at home." That reinforcement came partly from the focus of her parents and siblings on gospel music. Her mother sang religious songs around the house and was also a member of the church choir, while her father played fiddle and led song services. Some of her siblings eventually formed their own gospel group, the DeMent Sisters.

Iris said, "My parents pretty much stuck to gospel music. If Johnny Cash did a gospel album, they'd buy that." As Iris grew up she learned to play the piano, which she put to use in church services. She also joined her mother and other family members in the church choir.

However, Iris saw enough of the world outside church doors to have some nagging doubts about her world outlook. She knew she had grown up in a loving and warm environment. "But I felt very conflicted, because a lot of things they were saying (in church) didn't feel right to me, and I would have to sacrifice my own intelligence and my need to think for myself. But I couldn't walk away from it altogether."

She had vague ideas of doing things in music when

she graduated from high school in 1977, but she was shy and uncertain about what she might be able to do. In fact, she didn't begin to write songs, she said, until she was twenty-five. She told the *Los Angeles Times,* "I always wanted to (get into music), but never thought I could. I went through all these years thinking I wasn't talented enough or didn't have enough courage or wasn't pretty enough."

After completing high school, she moved to Topeka, Kansas, where she enrolled in a college creative writing class. "I was doing really well in the class, and it seemed a lot of things changed for me really quick. The writing and the music, the two things I loved the most, started coming together. I said, 'I'm just going to do what I do, singing the songs I love to sing, whatever way I wanted to sing them.' I became a much happier person."

It took a while for her to feel confident enough to begin composing her own songs. She recalled taking a trip from Topeka to Oklahoma that inspired her to write the song "Our Town," which became one of the most striking tracks on her debut album. From Topeka she moved to Kansas City, where she taught herself to play the guitar and began to perform from time to time on open mike nights at local nightclubs. (Her years in that city also brought marriage to a Kansas City fireman.)

After several years of this, she felt she was ready to try her luck in Nashville. Once there she found a number of places to showcase her talents and it wasn't long before many other performers, including Emmylou Harris and John Prine, were singing her praises. Prine told *Rolling Stone* magazine, "I can count on three fingers the number of people who impressed me much the first time I saw them live. . . . She sings quite a bit like Emmylou Harris, but her stage presence has a touch of Judy Holliday."

Her talents captured the attention of veteran record producer Jim Rooney, who suggested her to independent label Philo Records, a subsidiary of Rounder Records. When Philo executives signed her, Rooney was asked to produce her first sessions; the result was the album *Infamous Angel.* Many of Nashville's best session musicians were eager to take part, as were John Prine and Ms. Harris. Also providing some of the backing vocals was Iris's mother. Iris pointed out that several songs, such as "Mama's Opry" and "After You've Gone," reflected her deep feelings about her parents. "They have been the most important people in my life. I probably care about music the way I do because of them."

The album was a revelation, as was the series of performances she gave at small venues like McCabe's in Santa Monica, California. She moved back to Kansas City before setting out on her album-backing tour, a series of dates in which she proved herself a truly stunning newcomer. Billy Altman in *Entertainment Weekly* commented on her "unaffected snow-pure voice and a

batch of honesty, adult songs about love, home and family so good you'd swear you heard them before. She seems to be a single-bodied reincarnation of the entire Carter Family. I hear America singing—and it sounds like Iris DeMent."

Warner Brothers Records officials were equally impressed, and they bought the rights to *Infamous Angel* from Rounder while also signing Iris for the label. The company rereleased that album in early 1993 while making preparations for DeMent's second collection. By then the artist was mourning the death of her father, who passed away soon after her debut album had been issued.

She gave tribute to Patric while reminiscing about experiences with the emotions of growing up and the various aspects of love in a splendid album titled *My Life,* issued by Warner Brothers in the spring of 1994. Talking about it with Jim Caligiuri of the *CMJ New Music Report* (May 30, 1994), she said, "When I sat down to make this record, I didn't intentionally have any of it revolve around the death of my father. When my dad died, I told myself, on my next record I wanted to write something about him. But I never intended for it to be that long."

The last comment referred to an extensive story treatment she incorporated in album liner notes. "I was thinking of a paragraph or two. But somehow when I sat down and looked at the songs that I had, there was a certain feeling that seemed to tie them all together in some way. His death seemed to be a theme that tied all the songs together."

She agreed there was a certain somber, melancholy air about many of her compositions, including some written before her father's death. "Even though I have at times written songs that were lighter and more humorous, for some reason, during the past few years those kinds of songs haven't been coming that naturally to me. When I try to write songs like that I feel like I'm forcing it, so I just gave up. In general, I sit down to write when I'm feeling bad. It's a way for me to work something out. If I'm feeling good, I want to be out having a good time."

Iris continued to have a full schedule of concert dates along with occasional appearances on TV. Among her 1996 projects was singing the National Anthem at opening day for the Kansas City Royals baseball team in April. In the spring and summer she was in Randy Scruggs's Nashville studios developing tracks for a new album due out in the fall for which Scruggs was handling production. Making a guest appearance for that was guitarist/vocalist Mark Knopfler of rock music (Dire Straits) and Chet Atkins collaborations fame.

DESERT ROSE BAND: *Vocal and instrumental group founded by Chris Hillman, born Los Angeles, California, December 4, 1942 (singer, bass guitarist, mandolinist, songwriter) and Herb Pedersen, born Berkeley, California,*

April 27, 1944 (singer, guitarist, banjoist, songwriter). Other original members in 1986 included John Jorgenson (background vocals, guitars, mandolin, six-string bass); Steve Duncan (drums, percussion); Jay Dee Maness (pedal steel guitar); Bill Bryson (background vocals, bass). Maness replaced in 1991 by Tom Brumley. Jorgenson and Duncan replaced in 1992 by Jeff Ross and Tim Grogan. Group disbanded in 1994.

When folk-rock star Chris Hillman, who first gained fame as a key member of the original Byrds (with whom he was inducted into the Rock & Roll Hall of Fame in 1991) joined forces with banjo great Herb Pedersen in the mid-1980s to form the Desert Rose Band, the result was a dynamic version of country-style playing that incorporated elements of traditional country, bluegrass, blues, and rock. The upshot was a sound that won the allegiance of both country and folk adherents. The band, which took its name from a solo album Hillman turned out in the early 1980s, was one of the longer-lasting projects in Hillman's extensive career and one whose successes ranked it close to the Byrds' achievements.

Organization of the band helped turn around a decade for Hillman that began with doubts about his performing career. In fact, in 1981 he took the year off with thoughts of becoming a music teacher. But the lure of show business proved too strong and in a short time he was joining people like onetime Dillards stalwart Herb Pedersen and other bluegrass notables such as fiddler Byron Berline and steel guitarist Al Perkins in new musical combinations. In 1985, Hillman and Pedersen performed on a bluegrass album recorded by Dan Fogelberg, then joined him on a subsequent tour.

These efforts helped bring a request from organizers of the 1985 Los Angeles Street Festival for the Hillman-Pedersen combo to play some sets on an open-air stage in downtown L.A. For that, musician friends Steve Duncan and Jay Dee Maness were asked to sit in. Hillman recalled that the concert was so much fun he began booking the band into clubs in and around Los Angeles, including a show in February 1986 at the premiere country nightclub, the Palomino. The reaction of some record executives who caught the performance was favorable enough to bring a record contract from Curb Records (with MCA handling distribution).

Besides the many years of experience amassed by Hillman and Pedersen, a varied and well-regarded total of musical know-how was provided by the rest of the band. Multi-instrumentalist John Jorgenson, for instance, had played guitar with the Benny Goodman band as well as the Wyndham Hill Extravaganza and the Rose Maddox Band. The credits of bass player Bill Bryson and drummer Duncan included work with Buck Owens, Rick Nelson, and the Bluegrass Cardinals. Maness had been a featured pedal steel guitarist with many folk and bluegrass groups.

Before long the group had its debut album out on Curb/MCA, the Desert Rose Band, issued in 1987. Their first single, "Ashes of Love," a remake of the old Johnnie and Jack country hit, and the second single, "Love Reunited" (written by Chris Hillman and Steve Hill), caught the attention of some disc jockeys. Growing airplay backed by intensive dates in clubs and small venues began to draw an audience for the group. After a while, this resulted in two number-one hit singles, "One Step Forward" (cowritten by Hillman and Bill Wildes) and "He's Back and I'm Blue."

The band's second album, Running, came out in the late 1980s and spawned three more hit singles. Two of those, "Summer Wind" and "I Still Believe in You," rose to number one on country charts while "She Don't Love Nobody" peaked at number two. During 1989–90, Curb/MCA released two more albums, Pages of Life and A Dozen Roses/Greatest Hits. The new album provided three top-10 singles while two new singles were drawn from the Greatest Hits package. The top-10 hits were "Start All Over Again," which peaked at number four in Radio & Records the week of January 26, 1990; "In Another Lifetime," number nine in R&R the week of May 18, 1990; and "Story of Love," number seven in R&R the week of September 28, 1990. All of those also rose high on other charts, including Billboard's.

Meanwhile the band was drawing sizable crowds to its concert work, which kept it on the road most of the year. Its crowd rapport was recognized by members of the Academy of Country Music, which voted it Tour Band of the Year for three straight years, 1988 through 1990. Country Music Association members also nominated it for the 1989 Horizon Award and in 1990 made it a finalist for Vocal Group of the Year.

The grind caught up with Maness, who withdrew before the group started recording its next album. He was replaced in the studio work by veteran Nashville session musician Paul Franklin and in the concert lineup by Tom Brumley. Hillman commented, "Jay Dee just didn't want to tour anymore. We replaced him with an equally legendary guy, Tom Brumley. Tom, as everybody [in the industry] knows, was in Buck Owens and the Buckaroos and in Rick Nelson's bands, and he's just a great steel player. He was perfect to come in and Jay Dee's still our pal."

The new album, True Love, was released by Curb/MCA in late summer of 1991. While offering musical quality that seemed on a par with earlier collections, including a guest appearance by rising bluegrass star Alison Krauss, it didn't have the market impact of the earlier offerings. Some singles made the charts, but none got very far up. This was followed a year later by the band's sixth album, Life Goes On.

By the time album six was released, Jorgenson and Duncan had departed; their places were taken by guitarist Jeff Ross and drummer Tim Grogan. Hillman stated, "Jeff Ross is one of John Jorgenson's favorite guitar players. He plays in one of John's groups (the Guitar-slinging Hellecasters). He's a real unorthodox player and he takes chances, and I like him for that. He keeps the music spontaneous."

Grogan, from Dallas, Texas, was chosen after an audition. Hillman reported, "He once worked for Dizzy Gillespie, among others, and comes from a very musical family. He brings a new perspective as well as a love for country music. I like to see people come to country music from other pieces of the puzzle and see what they come up with."

But *Life Goes On* didn't seem to be the right piece of the puzzle for record buyers, perhaps in keeping with an apparent trend away from the days when country fans stood by their artists year in and year out to a more fickle environment resembling the workings of pop music. Another factor affecting the group's fortunes was the upsurge of country bands from a handful in the 1980s to many times that in the 1990s, all competing for a limited number of record buyers. In any case, by 1994, Hillman and Pedersen decided it was time to move on to other challenges, and the group was disbanded.

DEXTER, AL: *Singer, guitarist, organist, band leader (Texas Troopers, The Troopers), songwriter. Born Jacksonville, Texas, May 4, 1902; died January 28, 1984.*

One unique song sometimes can give a form of immortality to its creator, even after the writer's name has become dim in most people's memory. This is the case with "Pistol Packin' Mama," still familiar to millions of people who haven't the slightest idea that Al Dexter and his Texas Troopers once were among the best-known acts in the country & western field.

Dexter, born Albert Poindexter in Jacksonville, Cherokee County, Texas, was already acquiring musical experience before there was such a thing as the *Grand Ole Opry*. He learned to play guitar in his teens and was taking part in school events in 1917. Besides guitar, he learned the organ, which he sometimes played in local church services. As a result, his first efforts as a songwriter took the form of a series of hymns, the first titled "Going Home in Glory." As he reached adulthood, he became increasingly interested in playing with small local groups at square dances and parties and was already writing secular songs for some of those bands in the 1920s.

In the early 1930s, the impact of the Depression forced him to take a new look at his means of livelihood, which was house painting at the time. Because he loved writing and singing songs and because regular work was increasingly hard to find, he decided to focus on music as a full-time occupation and formed a band called the Texas Troopers. By then the impact of Jimmie Rodgers and the Carter Family had built more interest in the music industry for country & western musicians. The goal of any group, then as now, was to

break into the recording end of the field. In 1934, Dexter and his group managed to place some releases on a local label that won attention from East Texas fans. That success was a strong selling point for a contract from a major label, and before long the band's stylings were reaching wider audiences on the Vocalion and Okeh labels.

Some of the recordings were original compositions by Al. In a short speech in 1971 marking his induction into the Nashville Songwriters Hall of Fame, Dexter recalled trying to find satisfactory recording arrangements. "It was 1935 and times were not so good. The record company said they could not pay much royalty on records [that] sold for sixteen cents wholesale then, but I said I would take it as 'I'm not doing much anyway now.'"

During the 1940s, Dexter was considered one of Columbia Records' top artists thanks to such hit singles as "Honky Tonk Blues" and "Rosalita." The latter, written in 1942, became a favorite of audiences at his live appearances, but was kept off the air for a long time because of the contract dispute embroiling BMI, ASCAP, and the nation's radio stations. When the matter was settled, his record company advisors counseled Dexter to write a new song for the "B" side of "Rosalita." The song he came up with was "Pistol Packin' Mama," a recording that swept the country and made Dexter one of the best-known performers of the mid-1940s. Among the awards given him was one from the Juke Box Operators Association naming him the leading artist of 1946.

With "Pistol Packin' Mama" as the pièce de résistance, Dexter remained a favorite of country & western audiences in nightclubs, county fairs, and rodeos from the late 1940s through much of the 1950s. Though he made many other recordings during those years, some of which did quite well, none ever approached the impact of his one superhit. (Some of his other records were "Guitar Polka," "Car Hoppin' Mama," "One More Day in Prison," "Down at the Roadside Inn," "Triflin' Gal," "Little Sod Shanty," "Alimony Blues," and "Sundown Polka.")

During the 1950s, Al cut back on traveling and concentrated most of his entertainment efforts in his own nightspot, the Bridgeport Club in Dallas. Increasingly, as the years went by, he devoted more of his time to motel, real estate, and federal savings and loan operations than to music. After the 1950s, he essentially was retired from songwriting and recording, though an occasional album of his material came out. In 1962, Harmony Records issued an LP titled *Pistol Packin' Mama*, and in the early 1970s, a similarly titled album was available on the Hilltop label.

On October 11, 1971, he was officially named a member of the Songwriters Hall of Fame in Nashville. Estimating that the total number of songs he had written was somewhere around 300, he declared himself happy with his accomplishments: "I had my share of hits. I have had some dogs too."

As of the mid-1990s, little of Al's recorded material was available. In 1994, the Columbia Legacy label issued as part of its Country Classic Series an album titled *Hillbilly Boogie*. This included two songs by Al and the Troopers, "New Broom Boogie" (originally recorded by Columbia May 26, 1947) and "Saturday Night Boogie" (originally recorded November 15, 1947). Both songs were cowritten by Dexter.

DIAMOND RIO: *Vocal and instrumental group, Jimmy Olander, born Minneapolis, Minnesota, August 26 (lead guitar); Marty Roe, born Lebanon, Ohio, December 28 (lead vocals, guitar); Dan Truman, born Flagstaff, Arizona, August 29 (keyboards); Brian Prout, born Troy, New York, December 4 (drums); Gene Johnson, born Pennsylvania (vocals, guitar, fiddle, mandolin); Dana Williams, born Dayton, Ohio, May 22 (bass guitar).*

One of a growing number of talented, cohesive groups that earned the support of mainstream fans in pop as well as country, Diamond Rio's recordings and performances typically showcased many solidly written melodic originals. Drawn from musicians with years of experience with different kinds of country bands and considerable session work, the band prided itself on recordings free of engineered gimmicks.

Lead singer Marty Roe explained, "This is our sound. We don't do anything in the studio that we can't do on stage. These guys are some superpickers and that is exactly what we stand for."

The nucleus of the group, Roe, Jimmy Olander, and Dan Truman, were drawn from the Nashville Opryland theme park band called the Tennessee River Boys. Roe, who grew up in Ohio, recalled working as a country music professional when he was twelve years old. He became a Tennessee River Band member in 1984, shortly after moving to Nashville. Olander started taking banjo lessons at twelve in California and later added guitar skills as he began to play with local bands. He moved to Nashville in 1979 and joined the Opryland group in the early 1980s. Truman, from Utah, grew up in Mormon country and attended Brigham Young University. Classically trained, he took an interest in jazz as well and later went on tour with BYU's Young Ambassadors musical troupe.

Diamond Rio took shape in the mid-1980s, with some changes in band makeup until the 1990s organization was consolidated. Drummer Brian Prout joined in 1986, multi-instrumentalist Gene Johnson in 1987 and, during those years, bass guitarist Dana Williams. Prout performed with rock bands in upstate New York before joining a group called the Hot Walker Band in 1980. Later he played drums with the Nashville-based Heartbreak Mountain Band. Johnson for some years earned a living as a cabinet maker while gaining musical experience nights and weekends. He became particularly proficient on the mandolin, which paid off in work with folk artist David Bromberg, bluegrass exponent J. D. Crowe, and, after settling in Nashville, session and concert work with Keith Whitley.

Williams also remembered learning several instruments before his teens and participating in a Nashville bluegrass group when he was twelve. He had ready entry into the field as a nephew of the Osborne Brothers, members of the *Grand Ole Opry* and all-time greats in bluegrass music. In later years he became a top Nashville session player and one time or another performed in backing bands for Cal Smith, Vassar Clements, and Jimmy C. Newman.

After Diamond Rio was formed, the group started performing in local clubs and honky-tonks in and around Nashville. When possible, they also gained engagements as a supporting act for stars like George Jones. While opening a show for Jones in Alabama in 1989, their music caught the ear of Arista Records executive Tim DuBois, who asked for demo tapes to help get an OK from the company to sign them. The tapes did the job, and in 1990 the band was in the studio working on its debut album, whose initial single, "Meet in the Middle," was issued in the spring of 1991 and quickly moved up the charts to a number-one position.

Arista asserted that represented the first time a debut single by a country music group had achieved that feat. The debut album also did well. Titled *Diamond Rio*, it showed up on *Billboard* charts in the summer and peaked at number thirteen in August 1991. It was still in the top 40 in early April 1992 after forty-three weeks and receipt of a gold record award from the R.I.A.A.

The band continued to score with record and video buyers during 1992 with releases like "Mama Don't Forget to Pray for Me," number five in *Radio and Records* the week of February 7; "Norma Jean Riley," number five in *R&R* the week of June 19; and "Nowhere Bound," number four in *R&R* the week of September 18. The releases did well on other charts, too, including top spot in *Billboard*. Voters from the Academy of Country Music chose Diamond Rio as Vocal Group of the Year for 1992, an honor also bestowed the next year. In the Country Music Association voting in 1992, the band also was named the Vocal Group of the Year, a feat they repeated in 1993 and 1994. In 1995 the band again was a finalist, bidding for its fourth straight victory in the category.

The band opened 1993 with the single "A Week or Two" rising to number two on the *R&R* list the week of January 29, which was followed several months later with the single "Oh Me, Oh My, Sweet Baby," number four in *R&R* the week of June 11 and a top-level hit in *Billboard* at the same time. The band's second album, *Close to the Edge*, was issued by Arista in late 1992 and stayed on the *Billboard* list well into 1993, peaking at number twenty-four. Late in the year, the single "This Romeo Ain't Got Juliet Yet" was high on all hit lists, peaking at number nine in *R&R* the week of October 1, 1993.

In early 1994, the single "Sawmill Road" was a top-20 hit. Next on the singles charts was "Love a Little Stronger," which made the *Billboard* top three in mid-August and rose to number one in *R&R* the same month. That was the title track from the band's third Arista album, released in late May, which peaked at number thirteen in *Billboard* the week of August 13. It was still on the list in the summer of 1995, having earned a gold record from the R.I.A.A. In 1995, the band had still more singles hits such as "Bubba Hyde," in the *Billboard* top 20 in March, and "Finish What We Started," moving up the list in June. In February 1996, the group had the top 20 single "Walkin' Away" and in May had another single, "That's What I Get For Lovin' You" inside the top 40. Its fourth Arista album, *IV,* came out in the early spring and, after peaking at number fourteen in *Billboard,* didn't demonstrate the staying power of earlier releases, moving toward lower chart levels in following months.

Besides its other honors, the band received three nominations for the National Academy of Recording Arts & Sciences Grammy Awards in the first half of the 1990s.

DICKENS, LITTLE JIMMY: *Singer, guitarist, songwriter. Born Bolt, West Virginia, December 19, 1925. Elected to Country Music Hall of Fame in 1983.*

Nicknamed "little" for his four foot, eleven inch build, Little Jimmy Dickens was only diminutive in physical size. His energy and vocal skills galvanized country audiences year in and year out (including the hit song, "I'm Little but I'm Loud") and he remained a favorite for decades. In 1978, he celebrated thirty years as a regular cast member of the *Grand Ole Opry* with no indication of slowing down afterward.

Born and raised in rural West Virginia, he went on to enroll at West Virginia University. By the time he was in his teens he had learned to play guitar and entertain friends with country songs old and new. When he was seventeen he auditioned at station WJLS in Beckley, West Virginia, and won his first commercial job. He called himself Jimmy the Kid and worked with Johnny Bailes and His Happy Valley Boys. His early efforts included performing on another West Virginia station, WMNN in Fairmont.

After serving his apprenticeship locally, he moved further afield in the mid-1940s and began to sing on his own rather than as a member of a group. He toured many of the eastern and midwestern states and performed on several Midwest stations including WKNX, Saginaw, Michigan; WING, Dayton, Ohio; and WLW in Cincinnati. During the late 1940s, he signed with Columbia Records and began to turn out singles that showed up on country hit lists in various parts of the East, South, and Midwest. Coupled with personal ap-

pearances on the country fair and nightclub circuit, he began to build a growing reputation among country fans. In 1948, he was sufficiently well known for the *Grand Ole Opry* to ask him to become a regular cast member.

In 1949, he had his first top-10 country single with the Columbia release "Take an Old Cold Tater." His second major hit, "Country Boy," became one of his trademark songs ("I'm a country boy/A good old fashioned country boy/I'll be behind the ol' grey mule/When the sun comes up on Monday"). In 1950, he had two more top-10 singles with "A-Sleeping at the Foot of the Bed" and "Hillbilly Fever." Some of his other popular recordings were "Just When I Needed You," "My Heart's Bouquet," "Out Behind the Barn," "Conscience," "I Can't Help It," "Lovin' Lies," and "Salty Boogie." The original songs in his repertoire included "Sea of Broken Dreams" and "I Sure Would Like to Sit a Spell with You."

From the late 1940s through the 1960s he turned out a number of albums for Columbia. These included *Little Jimmy,* issued in December 1957, *Big Songs of Little Jimmy Dickens* (1/61), *Behind the Barn* (11/62), *Handle with Care* (4/65), *May the Bird of Happiness Fly Up Your Nose* (late 1965), and *Greatest Hits* (11/66). *May the Bird of Happiness* was his all-time bestseller on Columbia, rising to number one on country charts. He also had a number of LPs on the Harmony label, including *Old Country Church* (3/65), *Best of Little Jimmy Dickens* (5/64), *Little Jimmy Dickens* (3/65), and *Ain't It Fun* (6/67).

In the 1970s, the rise of "progressive" country and country rock tended to limit the audience of the more traditional artists like Jimmy. His long-time ties with Columbia ended by the end of the 1960s. However, he retained a sizable following in many parts of the United States and in other countries as well. Maintaining a busy schedule of in-person appearances from the 1970s on, two decades later he was still on the road some 150 to 200 days a year and still was a featured artist on the *Grand Ole Opry.* In 1983 he was elected to the Country Music Hall of Fame. From the 1970s through the mid-1990s his recordings appeared on various small labels. (Examples in the late 1970s included *Music to Park By* on Power; *Little Jimmy Dickens Picks on Big Johnny Cash* on Plantation; and *The Best of the Best of Little Jimmy Dickens* on Gusto.) In 1995 the album *Little Jimmy Dickens/Best of Country* on the NCD label was available from the Country Music Hall of Fame & Museum catalog. In 1994, the Columbia Legacy "Country Classics" series released the reissue collection *Hillbilly Boogie,* which included Little Jimmy's rendition of "Salty Boogie." Some of his vintage live performances also were included in Volumes 2, 4, 10, and 11 of the *Grand Ole Opry Stars of the Fifties* video series.

Jimmy was one of the artists who taped the November 30, 1995, program honoring the 70th anniversary of the Grand Ole Opry. The show was presented on CBS-TV in January 1996. On May 16, 1996, Jimmy was one of the performers featured on the CBS-TV tribute to the late Minnie Pearl. Others on the show included Marty Stuart, Pam Tillis, Trisha Yearwood, Wynonna, Barbara Mandrell, Lonestar, Vince Gill, and Chet Atkins.

DIFFIE, JOE: *Singer, guitarist, band leader (Heartbreak Highway), songwriter, Born Duncan, Oklahoma, December 28, c. 1960.*

If country music is truly "white man's blues," as many have described it, Joe Diffie has a legitimate claim to experiences that qualified him as a troubadour of such music. His life hasn't lacked for highs in the form of hit records and praise from many famous peers, but it had its downside as well. In one year in the mid-1980s he lost his job, his nine-year marriage (which produced two children) broke up, and he had to close his little recording studio in Duncan, Oklahoma; on top of all that, he became dangerously overweight. Rallying from that low point he became a rising star in the Nashville scene in the early 1990s—only to find that his second son by a second marriage had Down's Syndrome. All of that may have added conviction to his songwriting and singing by mid-decade, some critics were calling him heir to the mantle of country music greats like George Jones.

He told Janet E. Williams of the Country Music Association's *Close Up* that his family was always interested in music. His father played guitar, banjo, and "a little bit" of piano. He recalled his mother liked to sing, though the only song she'd sing on request was "Scarlet Ribbons." "As a kid we had an old pickup, and I remember the way my mom and dad kept my sisters and I entertained. We'd sing little kid songs, and I can remember that real vividly. I'd always like to sing 'Down in the Valley.'

"Mom and Dad claimed that I could sing harmony when I was three years old. I didn't realize what was happening so I guess it was kind of a God-given thing. I didn't always want to be a musician. I wanted to be a doctor. It sounds so weird, though. 'Dr. Diffie to the operating room!' "

Though Joe spent most of his formative years in Oklahoma, his family didn't stay there continuously. He recalled being in the first grade in San Antonio, Texas; fourth and fifth grades in Washington State; and from sixth grade through sophomore year in high school in Wisconsin.

His father, he told Bob Allen of *Country Music* magazine, always was a great country music fan and had a big record collection, including many albums of such favorites as George Jones, Merle Haggard, Johnny Cash, and Lefty Frizzell. "They were my favorites, too. When I got a little older, I was one of those guys who knew every dad-gum song on the radio and would run people crazy singing them all. I'd sing 'em all, whether they were men's or women's songs—whether I liked them or not. I didn't have any idea how good I was, but I could always match their licks."

As he got older, though, his focus turned to sport. In high school he was a multiletterman, playing football, baseball, and golf and running track. He told Williams one of the proudest moments of his life "was when I won the Best All-Around Male Athlete my senior year at Velma [Oklahoma] High." From high school he went on to Cameron University in Lawton, Oklahoma, intent on continuing his sports activities while earning credits toward medical school. When he looked at the brawny competition for the football team, though, he decided to give up his sports dreams. When he fell in love with the girl who became his first wife (in 1977), he also abandoned his medical ambitions and left school to start earning a living for the two of them and, soon after, their first child.

At first he did oil field work, then moved to Alice, Texas, where he got a job driving a truck used to pump cement out of oil wells. He told Allen, "The first week I worked about one hundred and eight hours. About two months of that was all I could stand. That's when I moved back to Oklahoma and went to work in the foundry."

The job at the casting plant took him and his wife back to the familiar surroundings of Duncan. While earning a reasonable income from his nine to five job, Joe became involved in music as a sideline; he didn't think he would make it a full-time avocation. His music activities in the late 1970s and early 1980s included singing with a gospel group (Higher Purpose) and, after that, working with a bluegrass group called Special Edition that played clubs in his home state as well as some dates further afield in Arkansas, Louisiana, and Kansas. Joe wrote some of the band's material, as well as more mainstream country-oriented numbers. His songwriting interests suggested it made sense for him to set up a little eight-track studio in Duncan to make demos of his own materials and also demos for other local musicians to help defray costs.

He told *Close Up,* "I didn't really start thinking about a career in music until I got into the bluegrass group and went out on the weekends and actually went away from home. It was just so much fun. Made a little extra money, and it was kinda nice being a minor celebrity." He and the band made some albums at their own expense, he recalled. "Terrible soundin' things now that I look back on it. Back in those days, I'd often have people tell me that I oughta go to Nashville. I'd just think to myself, 'Yeah, sure! Right!' "

Things were going along at a seemingly satisfying pace when his life was turned upside down in 1986. First the foundry operation shut down and he was out of a job; then, under financial stress, he lost his recording studio. Bankruptcy was followed by divorce, with the children going with their mother. He often said that if the foundry had stayed open, he might never have tried his luck in Nashville. Even then, it took a number of months of depression—during which he'd found solace in food, ballooning to some 264 pounds—before he finally decided it was time to move on to other surroundings. In December 1986 he borrowed some money from his parents and moved to Nashville in hopes of making his way as a songwriter.

He actually had some credits by then. While still working his foundry job, he had sent demos around to music companies and record firms in Music City and had one score and one near miss. The former was a single cut by Hank Thompson of a song cowritten by Joe, "Love on the Rocks"; the near miss came when Randy Travis asked a Nashville publisher to put a hold on a song titled "Love's Hurtin' Game" though, in the end Travis never recorded the number.

In Nashville he got a job working at Gibson Guitars and made more contacts in the music field. One was a neighbor, Johnny Neal, who was a published songwriter with Forest Hills Music. Joe began cowriting with Neal, and after a while became a contract writer with Forest Hills. Diffie's demo tapes helped the publisher place songs with a number of artists, including Doug Stone and the Forester Sisters. Word of his effectiveness as a demo singer got around, and by the late 1980s he was spending almost all of his free time preparing demos for other artists. In June 1989, he quit his day job and started earning a full-time living with his demo assignments. By then he had married again, having met Debbie, his bride-to-be, at the Nashville Stockyard Restaurant and Lounge.

The demos eventually opened the doors that led to a recording contract. He told Lisa Smith of The Gavin Report, "Bob Montgomery, who was then Vice President of A&R at Epic Records, heard some of the demos that I had done and met with me a couple of times. He said, 'I want to sign you, I can't right now, but I'm definitely going to do it if you'll just wait.' So I said, 'Okay, I'll wait.' In the meantime I continued writing, doing demos and preparing for my first album."

He waited a year, but Montgomery proved true to his word, and in 1990 Diffie was hard at work on his debut material, which included his first single. "Home," and the album A Thousand Winding Roads. In the fall of the year both made the charts, with the single reaching number one on major lists. That was the first of four straight number-one singles from the album, all cowritten by Diffie with various collaborators, the others being "If You Want Me To," "If the Devil Danced (in Empty Pockets)," and "New Way (to Light Up an Old Flame)," the last-named hitting top-chart levels in the early fall of 1991.

Joe, who had slimmed down by some eighty pounds since moving to Nashville, played his first big concert on New Year's Eve of 1990 as a supporting act for George Strait and Steve Wariner. By the mid-1990s, Diffie had accrued a steady string of hit recordings and

videos to make him a headline performer backed by his own seven-piece band, Heartbreak Highway.

His 1992 singles hits included "Is It Cold in Here," number three in Radio & Records the week of February 21, "Ships That Don't Come In," number one in R&R the week of July 3, and "Next Thing Smokin'," number twelve in R&R the week of October 10. His second album, Regular Joe, was issued by Epic in March 1992 and was on the Billboard chart soon after. His next album, Honky Tonk Attitude, came out on Epic in the early summer of 1993 and soon made Billboard and other hit charts. It was still on the Billboard list in late August 1994 after sixty-seven weeks and earned a gold record from the R.I.A.A. The title track provided a hit single that peaked at number three in R&R the week of June 11, 1993, and made the top spots in other charts. In the fall he had another singles hit, "Prop Me Up Beside the Jukebox," number two in R&R in October.

By early 1994 he had another top-5 single, "John Deere Greene," followed by "In My Own Backyard," in the Billboard Top 20 in May. In August he had another album on the way to hit status, Third Rock from the Sun, which debuted in Billboard at number fourteen and rose to number seven the following week. The album was still in top positions in Billboard the summer of 1995, having gone past R.I.A.A. platinum levels. The title track was also a hit, providing a single that peaked at number one in R&R the week of September 23. Later in the year the single "Pickup Man" peaked at number eight in R&R the week of November 25. In March 1995, Joe had the top-10 Billboard single, "So Help Me Girl," followed a few months after by the summer hit, "I'm in Love with Capital 'U.'"

But though Joe was now acknowledged as a major star, he still had to cope with setbacks in his private life. The second of two sons born to him and Debbie was a Down's Syndrome baby. He told Music City News ("Joe Diffie's New Look," January 1992), "That was really devastating when we first found out about (Tyler) having Down's Syndrome. My initial reaction was 'How can I have something imperfect?' But my producer, Johnny Slate, who also has a special child, told me that child will give me more joy than the other three combined because everything he does is a giant step. And it is.

"We've had a couple of small setbacks with him healthwise. He's been pretty sickly all his life with respiratory problems, but he doesn't have a care in the world. He's happy."

Joe could at least take consolation from his career progress. With a growing following, he was on the road 200 to 225 days a year, which put some pressure on both songwriting and family time. He told Music City News he had gradually changed his views about writing. "I used to think you had to wait for an inspiration to write a song, but you really don't. You set a schedule and you say, 'Now I'm going to write from ten o'clock to noon' or whatever. You try to come up with an idea or hope your co-writer has a good idea and you just base it off that. It's an acquired skill.

"It's something you have to work at. I feel confident after about three years of writing pretty steadily that I could go in with a good co-writer and come out with a pretty decent song. I'm not saying that it would be a hit, but at least it will be decent."

Though Diffie continued to add to his entertainment industry laurels through the rest of 1995 into 1996, he received more media attention for the breakup of his marriage. Articles discussed the divorce proceedings and some linked Diffie with Liz Allison, the widow of race car driver Davey Allison. For a cover article in the CMA *Close Up* of April 1996, he indicated to assistant editor Shannon Heim things finally were calming down. "Everything's cool. I think I was a little too open on that subject before, and I got burned a couple of times by people writing things that got taken out of context. I've just quieted myself down. It's not fair to the people that live around me."

Despite his personal travails, he remained a favorite with concert audiences and his recordings found good buyer response. In late 1995, his holiday album, *Mr. Christmas,* was in the top 40 and his new secular collection, *Life's So Funny,* was released at year end and showed up on the charts in early 1996, peaking at number twenty-eight in *Billboard.* The first single from the disc, "Bigger Than the Beatles," preceded it by a few weeks and moved to number one in February 1996. This was followed by another chart-maker from the album, "C-O-U-N-T-R-Y," which reached top chart positions in the late spring. While the album never made very top hit list rungs, it sold steadily and by the fall had earned a gold record from the R.I.A.A.

DIRT BAND, NITTY GRITTY DIRT BAND (name changed to Dirt Band in 1976, two names used interchangeably from late 1980s on): *Vocal and instrumental group. Original personnel, 1965, included Jeff Hanna, born Detroit, Michigan, July 11, 1947; and Bruce Kunkel, born Long Beach, California, circa 1948. Members as of late 1960s: Hanna, John McEuen, born Long Beach, California, December 19, 1945; Jimmie Fadden, born Long Beach, California, March 9, 1948; Ralph Taylor Barr, born Boston, Massachusetts; Leslie Steven Thompson, born Long Beach, California; Chris Darrow, born California. Barr replaced in 1972 by Jim Ibbotson, born Philadelphia, Pennsylvania, January 21, 1947. Band roster, 1974–75, reduced to Hanna, McEuen, Fadden, and Ibbotson. Ibbotson left in 1975; John Cable, Jackie Clark, and, later, Michael Buono added for 1976–77. For 1978–79, makeup changed to Hanna, Fadden, McEuen, Bob Carpenter, Al Garth, Richard Hathaway, Merle Brigante. The 1980–82 roster found Brigante gone with Vic Mastriani and Michael Gardner added. During 1983–86 period, Ibbotson had returned to join Hanna, Fadden, McEuen, and*

Carpenter. McEuen left by 1987, and Bernie Leadon joined for 1987–88 period. Leadon left by 1989 and the remaining foursome composed the roster through 1996.

The Nitty Gritty Dirt Band, which renamed itself the Dirt Band in 1976 and resumed its original name in the 1980s (though afterward both names were used) has gone through many changes over the years, but its core members Jeff Hanna, Jimmie Fadden, and John McEuen persevered and saw to it that the band's blend of folk, country, and rock continued to delight fans into the mid-1980s, when McEuen left. After that, Fadden and Hanna kept the group together and it still remained a major force in its chosen musical areas in the mid-1990s.

The band's origins were in Long Beach, California, where two high school students, Bruce Kunkel and Jeff Hanna, began getting together to play guitar and sing folk songs. After a while they brought in three other friends and formed a group called the Illegitimate Jug Band, the title reflecting the fact that it played jug band music without a jug player. After Kunkel and Hanna graduated from high school, the band reorganized into what was to soon be the Nitty Gritty Dirt Band. That group added four other Long Beach associates of Kunkel and Hanna: Jimmie Fadden (autoharp, harmonica, jug, washtub bass, trombone); John McEuen (five-string banjo, fiddle, accordion, guitar, steel guitar, vocals); Leslie Thompson (guitar, bass, mandolin, vocals); and Ralph Taylor Barr, born in Boston but who moved to Long Beach at eleven (guitar, vocals). Hanna, born in Detroit, but transplanted to Long Beach with his family in 1962, handled lead guitar and washboards and some writing. Kunkel handled vocals, guitar, and writing.

The band began its professional career in 1966 under the guidance of Bill McEuen, John's older brother, who had been a disc jockey and had established a good reputation as a producer of rock and R&B records by the mid-1960s. As manager, he helped gain initial dates in small clubs and coffee houses. Soon the group moved up to support roles in concerts featuring such stars as Nancy Wilson, Joan Baez, and Bob Newhart. At the same time, McEuen won a record contract from Liberty Records. The band stayed with the label after it was absorbed by United Artists and still was on the roster at the end of the 1970s.

The group's first single release, "Buy for Me the Rain," came out in 1967 and quickly became a major hit. When the band's debut LP *The Nitty Gritty Dirt Band* also rose high on the charts, the band was widely recognized as one of the 1967's most promising new groups. Besides the hit track, the album contained a potpourri of stylings, ranging from updated versions of folk songs like "Dismal Swamp" and "Candy Man" to Bruce Kunkel's folk-flavored composition "Song to Jutta" to such wild numbers as "Hard Hearted Hannah," "I Wish I Could Shimmy Like My Sister Kate," and "Crazy Words, Crazy Tune."

The follow-up LP, *Ricochet,* issued in November 1967, was arguably as good as the group's debut effort, but it didn't sell as well. The same held true for other albums issued by Liberty in 1968 and 1969. As the decade came to a close, U.S. audience interest tapered off, though a faithful core of fans remained.

Meanwhile, Kunkel left the band in 1968 and was replaced by Chris Darrow. In 1971, Barr moved on and Philadelphia-born Jim Ibbotson took over drums, bass guitar, accordion, and piano. Ibbotson, who earned a degree in economics from DePauw University in Indiana, previously had performed with such bands as the Arista-Tones, The Warf Rats, the Evergreen Blue Shows, and the Hagers.

The Liberty album *Uncle Charlie and His Dog Teddy* started getting major airplay in late 1970 and made the charts from November of that year until the following fall. A single from the album, the band's version of Jerry Jeff Walker's "Mr. Bojangles," began to gain attention, reaching the top 10 on the pop charts and doing well on country lists as well. By the spring of 1971 it had sold almost a million copies. Those new successes brought the group engagements in theaters and clubs all over the United States and a popularity that far exceeded that of its early years. Hanna said happily, "We're finally beginning to make a comfortable living, which is a nice change."

In mid-1971, the band had another singles hit with the Kenny Loggins song "House on Pooh Corner." In early 1972, United Artists released the LP *All the Good Times,* which featured sparkling renditions of Hank Williams' "Jambalaya" and the Cajun song "Diggy-Liggy-Lo." A single of "Jambalaya" made the charts in 1972, as did the singles "Some of Shelley's Blues" and "I Saw the Light." The latter record was a country hit in which the band was joined by Roy Acuff. There also was a strong country flavor to many of the tracks in the band's next album, *Will the Circle Be Unbroken,* issued in late 1972 and on the charts through mid-1973.

By the mid-1970s, the band had moved home base from California to Colorado, where much of its material was recorded throughout the decade. From there, the group sallied forth each year for extensive tours that took it to a wide range of venues, from college auditoriums and folk clubs to medium- and large-size halls across the United States and, on occasion, overseas. At times John McEuen worked as a solo performer, but always returned to the fold for band concerts and recording work.

Opening for a number of concerts of the band in the mid-1970s was a promising comedian named Steve Martin. Later, after Martin became a superstar, he still returned as a surprise guest from time to time to play banjo duets with McEuen. During a Dirt Band appearance at the Los Angeles Music Center in February 1978, Martin came on stage unannounced and delighted the audience by debuting his song "King Tut" with the band. Later in the year the song became a novelty hit.

In mid-1976, the band celebrated its tenth anniversary, shortening its name to Dirt Band and shifting from a quartet to a quintet. When Jim Ibbotson left he was replaced by two musicians, John Cable on guitar and vocals and Jackie Clark on guitar and keyboards. Both took part in the debut LP under the new name, issued in September 1976, titled *Dirt, Silver and Gold,* followed a year later by *Dirt Band.*

The group's landmark tour to the Soviet Union in early summer 1977 was hailed by some as the first break in the Russian "rock barrier." Talking about the origins of that unprecedented concert series, John McEuen told a reporter, "We were playing a concert in Washington, D.C. last year [1976] when there apparently were some representatives of the Soviet Union in the audience. Later we got a call that they would like for us to play the Soviet Union. After that it was up to the Soviets and the Americans to make the arrangements."

The tour extended from one end of the Soviet Union to the other, including concerts in Armenia and Riga, Latvia. One of the objections of the band members to arrangements was the tight security that insulated them from the ordinary people. What little contact they did have disclosed that most people had never heard of them until the tour began.

Although all concerts were sold out, audience response was relatively sedate until the band played Yerevan, Armenia. McEuen reported, "The Yerevan people were more like the ones back home. During our last performance, they packed fifty-seven hundred people into an outside stadium that was supposed to hold four thousand. We heard there were several thousand outside. Someone even threw in a tear gas canister which caused some excitement."

The group closed out the decade with the LP *Stars & Stripes Forever* in 1978 and *An American Dream,* released in mid-1979. The title song of the latter, issued as a single in early 1980, was on country charts for a number of weeks.

During 1980–82 the group, with its largest roster of eight musicians (Hanna, Fadden, McEuen, Bob Carpenter, Al Garth, Richard Hathaway, Vic Mastriani, and Michael Gardner), then had two more albums on the market, *Make a Little Magic* and *Jealousy.* The single of the title track from the first of those, featuring Nicolette Larson, made the pop charts top 20. In the 1983–86 timeframe, the band, now reduced to five members (Hanna, Fadden, McEuen, Carpenter, and a returned Jimmy Ibbotson) had such album releases as *Let's Go, Plain Dirt Fashion,* and *Partners, Brothers and Friends.* The single "Dance Little Jean" from *Let's Go* was a top-10 country hit. Besides that, the group scored its first number-one single with "Long Hard Road (The Sharecropper's Dream)," followed by a series of top-10 singles.

Among other credits, the band performed at the 1984 Olympic Games in Los Angeles and the Farm Aid benefit concert. It received nominations in both Academy of Country Music and Country Music Association awards voting, the CMA ones being for Instrumental Group of the Year in 1984 and 1985. During 1986, their album *Twenty Years of Dirt* was released to coincide with the 20th Anniversary of the NGDB's first performance at the Paradox in Orange, California, on May 13, 1966. The band celebrated with a sold-out concert at McNichols Arena in Denver, Colorado. Besides the band, others on the program included Ricky Skaggs, Emmylou Harris, Michael Martin Murphy, Doc Watson, John Prine, and Rodney Crowell.

The following year was marked by the departure of founding member John McEuen, the former Eagles star Bernie Leadon taking his place. The group kept right on going as a concert attraction and successful recording act. Its album *Hold On* provided the number-one single "Baby's Got a Hold on Me" (cowritten by Hanna, Carpenter, and Josh Leo). At one point, the band's TV exposure included appearances on NBC's *Today* and *Tonight* shows in the same week. The album *Workin' Band* also spawned two more top-10 singles. Meanwhile, the albums *Plain Dirt Fashion* and *Twenty Years of Dirt* received Canadian gold-record certification.

By 1989 the group had become a foursome of Hanna (vocals, guitar), Fadden (vocals, drums, harmonica), Ibbotson (vocals, bass, mandolin, guitar), and Carpenter (vocals, keyboards, accordion). The 1989 highlights included the hit MCA single "When She's Gone" (number fifteen in *Radio & Records* the week of December 15, 1989) and the charted albums *More Great Dirt* (the group's second authorized greatest hits collection) and *Will the Circle Be Unbroken, Volume II.*

The last-named album, issued by Universal Records, featured a list of guest artists that included Roy Acuff, Johnny Cash, Earl Scruggs, Bruce Hornsby, John Hiatt, Chris Hillman, Roger McGuinn, Emmylou Harris, and Levon Helm. In the Grammy Awards voting for 1989, announced on the February 21, 1990, telecast, it won in the Best Country Performance by a Duo or Group category, and the album track "The Valley Road," recorded with Bruce Hornsby, was voted Best Bluegrass Recording. The previous October the album had been chosen Album of the Year by CMA voters.

Besides that, the album earned a gold-record award from the R.I.A.A. and also spawned a long-form video, *The Making of "Will the Circle Be Unbroken, Vol. II."* The band's 1990 concert work included a return to the Soviet Union for three sold-out Moscow performances, and an appearance on the Soviet national TV network. Other places visited, besides major U.S. venues, in-

cluded Canada, Europe, and Japan. In June 1990, the band added another album to its growing list of releases, *The Rest of the Dream* on the Universal label.

In 1991, the group went to Red Deer in Alberta, Canada, to record a live CD to commemorate its twenty-fifth anniversary. The Universal release was titled *Live 25.* For the next album, the band returned to its original label, Liberty, with its album *Not Fade Away* coming out in 1992. One of the album singles, "Little Angel," was cowritten by Hanna and RCA recording artist Matraca Berg, who married in late 1993. During 1992, the Aspen School of Music in Colorado named a scholarship for the NGDB, the first time such an honor had been named for a pop group. By late 1993, the R.I.A.A. certified that *Twenty Years of Dirt* had achieved gold-record sales.

During 1994, the NGDB worked on its twenty-sixth album, on which, for the first time in years, no amplified instruments were used. The album, *Acoustic,* was issued by Liberty Records during the summer of 1994. Jeff Hanna told Robert K. Oermann of *The Tennessean* ("Dirt Band Gets Down to Nitty Gritty 'Acoustic,'" June 17, 1994), "We started putting an acoustic segment in our shows when we were on tour with Radney Foster in the spring of 1993 in Canada. We decided to do some of the material that we hadn't done in years—'House on Pooh Corner,' 'Home Again in My Heart,' 'Lovin' on the Side' and some other things—and audiences really responded to it, even in the big venues where it should have been harder to hold their attention."

He stressed he thought the whole "unplugged" idea was cool. "I like it. I love acoustic music. But think what all the great acts on the bluegrass and folk circuit must feel like. Some of them were never 'plugged' in the first place."

The band's 1996 concert series celebrated the group's 30th anniversary. It's recording work included contributing its version of "Maybe Baby" to the Decca Buddy Holly tribute album *Not Fade Away* and vocals on "You Believe in Me" for the MCA compilation *One Voice,* a country salute to the 1996 summer Olympics in Atlanta, Georgia.

DOUGLAS, JERRY: *Dobro player, composer, record producer. Born Warren, Ohio, May 28, 1956.*

Head and shoulders in performing skills above most players specializing in the dobro (a modified guitar invented by the instrument designers the Dopyera brothers), Jerry Douglas had a major impact on bluegrass music in particular and country music in general. From the mid-1970s on, his innovative instrumental work could be heard on dozens of albums both his own and as a backing musician for a Who's Who of country music artists.

He was born to the mantle of country music, as the

son of a bluegrass band leader. His father made certain that he learned the rudiments of several instruments as a child. He recalled, "I played mandolin at five; my father taught me guitar when I was seven and dobro when I was ten. I fell in love with the dobro after hearing early Flatt & Scruggs records and then after I got to see Josh Graves play I really was stuck on it from then on. I always loved the dobro sound on records, such a human sound, something so soulful."

By his early teens he was not only a regular band member, but had the chance to take solos during each set. "I started playing in bars with the band when I was about fourteen in the Warren, Ohio, area, which was my home area. I didn't move to Kentucky until 1975." In the early 1970s, when he was 16, the band performed at a summer festival, which had the highly regarded Country Gentlemen bluegrass group as a featured act. Members of that band were so impressed with the teenager's ability that they asked him to join them for the balance of their summer tour. When Jerry agreed, he found himself performing with such excellent instrumentalists as Don Laws and future superstar Ricky Skaggs.

He noted that he didn't play with the group full-time at first. "I was in high school then and I wanted to at least finish. I worked the summer of 1973 with them between my junior and senior years and then went back to school. I didn't know if I was going to do this for a living and I wanted at least a high school diploma. After that, I played another year with the Country Gentlemen before I joined J. D. Crowe."

His introduction to J. D. Crowe and the New South came in February 1975, when he took part in the sessions for the band's debut on Rounder Records, the acclaimed 1975 bluegrass release, *The New South*. His decision to join the group led to his moving to Lexington, Kentucky, in June 1975. That band, which amounted to an all-star group, comprised J. D. Crowe on banjo, Tony Rice on guitar and vocals, Ricky Skaggs on fiddle and mandolin, and Douglas on dobro. Soon after, when Skaggs formed his Boone Creek group, Douglas became a member. This was followed by a stint with David Grisman's band and, by the end of the 1970s, an association with the Whites, "The First Family of Bluegrass," that lasted until late 1985. His years with that band included a 1981 tour of China and Thailand sponsored by the U.S. Information Agency.

In mid-1978, Douglas said, "I moved back to Virginia and worked with the Gentlemen for about eight months, but my career didn't seem to be going anywhere. I said if something doesn't happen soon, I'm getting out of the business. Then Buck White called and I moved to Nashville in January 1979 and haven't ever looked back since."

Besides performing with the Whites, Douglas

Partly based on a phone interview with Irwin Stambler in May 1996.

worked as a session artist when time permitted and also worked to add to his own recording credits. He already had made his album debut with the Rounder Records collection (released in 1978), *Fluxology*. Backing him on that project were Rice, Skaggs, and Crowe. This remains one of the finest exhibitions of dobro playing and bluegrass harmonies ever issued. "There weren't too many dobro specialists in the field then and Rounder was interested in building its roster. They were influenced by my having played on the *New South* album which was the biggest selling bluegrass album back then." He followed in 1983 with his second Rounder release, *Fluxedo*. In the late 1980s, Rounder combined both of those albums on a new CD release.

During the years from 1979 through 1984, Jerry was named Best Dobro Player five consecutive years by *Frets* magazine. He was such a dominant figure in his chosen sector that in 1985 *Frets* "retired his name" to its Gallery of Greats.

By the start of 1986, Jerry had left the Whites' group. One reason for his decision to end his affiliation was his desire to find more leeway for the growing number of session requests and tour opportunities with a variety of pop, bluegrass, and country performers. He also wanted to seize the opportunity to work as a record producer; among his production credits in the 1980s was work with the Whitstein Brothers and many of the top names in modern bluegrass. His studio playing graced albums by such people as Ray Charles, Dan Fogelberg, Gail Davies, T-Bone Burnett, Hank Williams, Jr., the Dirt Band, Michael Martin Murphy, Gary Morris, Kathy Mattea, and Michael Johnson.

During the 1980s and into the 1990s, he continued to tour at home and abroad as a headliner or backing musician. Artists he toured with included Gary Morris, T-Bone Burnett, Mark O'Connor, Peter Rowan, and Maura O'Connell. In the spring of 1987 he was featured in concerts in Poland, Czechoslovakia, Turkey, and Portugal under the cosponsorship of the United Nations Information Agency and the Kentucky Center for the Arts. He went on several more tours of that kind in later years, the last one being a 1993 series in Asia that included concerts in Bangladesh, Sri Lanka, and Nepal.

In 1986, he was one of the first artists signed to the new MCA/Nashville Master Series roster. Douglas said, "Tony Brown started that label to go after the Windham Hill audience. A lot of people buy Windham Hill records because of its association with the New Age sound and he got the idea to record some instrumentalists he liked that might offer a style on the margins of New Age that could offer an alternative to people who liked that concept. The problem was that there was no staff to promote the label and the busier Tony got with other projects the less time he had for it. I got off the label before it wound up and went with Sugar Hill."

His first release on the MCA/Nashville Master Series, *Under the Wire,* was named number-two Album of the Year by *Frets.* His supporting musicians on that album included Mark O'Connor on fiddle, Bela Fleck on banjo, Russ Barenberg on guitar and mandolin, Glen Worf on bass, and Neil Work on drums. Those artists also backed him on his second Master Series album, *Changing Channels,* issued in September 1987. On one track of that collection, Ricky Skaggs and Buck White made guest appearances. The album, produced by Jerry, included six new original compositions by him. Before moving on, Jerry completed a third album on that series, *Plant Early.*

During that same period, Douglas pointed out, he completed another album with other major country/ bluegrass musicians including Bela Fleck, Mark O'Connor, and Edgar Meyer. "The album was titled *The Telluride Sessions* and we took the band name Strength in Numbers. The album still is in print [as of 1996] and selling."

Douglas was nominated in the Country Music Association's Instrumentalist of the Year awards category from 1986 through 1990, and during the first part of the 1980s had three Grammy nominations for Best Country Instrumental Performance, winning in 1983 for a track on a New South release on the Sugar Hill label called "Fireball." Sharing the award with him were Crowe, Skaggs, Rice, and Todd Phillips.

He continued his varied activities in the 1990s. In 1992, his debut disc on Sugar Hill, *Slide Rule,* was released, followed in 1993 by *Skip, Hop and Wobble,* the latter named after an old Jimmy Martin tune. Among the notable self-penned tracks on those collections were "Hide and Seek" and "Ankara to Ismire." During 1993–94, he coproduced the album *Great Dobro Sessions* with Tut Taylor, which was nominated for Best Bluegrass Album in the 1994 Grammy voting. In December 1995, Water Lily Records, Santa Barbara, California, released the album *Bourbon and Rose Water,* a collaboration between Douglas and Indian acoustic slide guitar player V. M. Bhatt. Bhatt had previously recorded an album with Ry Cooder that had earned a World Music Grammy.

In the spring of 1996, Jerry and Peter Rowan were on the concert circuit in support of a new duo album titled *Yonder.* Much of the album comprised either new arrangements of traditional songs by Douglas and Rowan such as "Cannonball Blues," "Texas Rangers," "Chicka-Li-Lee-O," and "Girl in the Blue Velvet Band," or originals by Rowan. Douglas still found time in the mid-1990s for session work, having added dozens of names to the list of major artists whom he'd backed since the mid-1980s. Those included James Taylor, Randy Travis, Garth Brooks, Patty Loveless, and Paul Simon. In Simon's case he had worked on the only new track ("Thelma") on the boxed retrospective set issued in 1995.

Discussing his writing approach, he noted, "I began writing my own stuff around 1975. My writings always have been instrumental. I write with the dobro, which makes it sort of unorthodox for a lot of other musicians. It makes the phrasing and fingering different for fiddlers and guitar players, but the professionals all can adapt to it."

As for career high points, he commented, "There have been a string of things that kept me going and made me feel I was doing the right thing with my life. One was to be picked up by a national band like the Country Gentlemen in 1973 when I was still a kid. And I've been fortunate to play with so many good musicians. Playing with James Taylor was always a big goal and when I did that it gave me a lot of satisfaction. I guess one of the biggest thrills is when you hear yourself played on the radio for the first time. That happened with the Whites in the early 1980s and then stations started doing all the Randy Travis stuff and now I can hear myself on the radio almost all the time."

In the Grammy nominations for 1996, announced in January 1997, Jerry and Peter Rowan's album *Yonder* was among the finalists in the Best Contemporary Folk Album category. The Del McCoury Band album *The Cold Hard Facts*, nominated for Best Bluegrass Album, was coproduced by Jerry and Ronnie McCoury; Jerry also played dobro on the album.

DRAKE, PETE: *Pedal steel guitarist, songwriter, producer, record industry executive. Born Atlanta, Georgia, October 8, 1932; died Brentwood, Tennessee, July 29, 1988.*

Pete Drake's innovativeness was a significant contribution to the resurgence in the use of the pedal steel guitar in bands and recordings in both pop and country music. It is difficult to believe that a few decades ago the instrument was almost unheard of.

Pete, born and raised in Georgia, initially learned to play acoustic guitar. An avid listener to the *Grand Ole Opry* radio program, he fell in love with the lap steel work of Jerry Byrd when he was eighteen. A used steel instrument at an Atlanta pawn shop cost him $33, and he essentially taught himself to play it. As he told Douglas Green in *Guitar Player* (September 1973), "I took one lesson, but I'd get records and sit around playing to them. That's how I really got started. This was around 1949 or 1950. Then when Bud Isaacs came out with a pedal guitar on 'Slowly' by Webb Pierce, that shocked everybody wondering how he got that sound. I guess I was the first one around Atlanta to get a pedal guitar. I had one pedal on a four-neck guitar. . . . I made it myself. . . . I was playing in clubs all around Atlanta, then right after that I formed my first band. . . . I had some pretty big stars working with me back then: Jerry Reed, Joe South, Doug Kershaw was playing fiddle, Roger Miller . . . and country singer Jack Greene was playing drums.

"And we got fired because we weren't any good. I

was on television for three and a half years, but we kind of wore ourselves out and I decided to move on to Nashville."

The Nashville move came in 1959; for a while Drake worked only sporadically. The style of pedal steel he'd developed in Atlanta didn't find favor at first, so he played conventional Nashville style. In mid-1960, Drake reverted to his old technique, using a C6th tuning on a session for Carl and Pearl Butler. Country artist Roy Drusky heard about it and asked Drake to use the same approach on a song he was doing for Decca. The result was the number-one hit "I Don't Believe You Love Me Any More." After Pete backed George Hamilton IV on another smash single, "Before This Day Ends," the "Pete Drake Style" became a Nashville trademark.

Later in the early 1960s, Drake gained new attention for his "talking guitar" efforts. The idea for the approach came to Pete from watching Alvino Ray do something similar in a Kay Kyser film. He told Douglas Green the way it works: "You play the notes on the guitar and it goes through the amplifier. I have a driver system so that you disconnect the speakers and the sound goes through the driver into a plastic tube. You put the tube in the side of your mouth then form the words with your mouth as you play them. You don't actually say a word. The guitar is your vocal cords and your mouth is the amplifier. It's amplified by a microphone."

The first record on which Pete applied the technique was Roger Miller's "Lock, Stock and Teardrops" on RCA. Although the single didn't do too well, Jim Reeves achieved a top-level hit when Pete used the talking guitar on "I've Enjoyed as Much of This as I Can Stand." By then Drake had done some solo recordings on the Starday label with regular pedal steel methods, including "For Pete's Sake." Mercury Records executives suggested he do some talking steel work, and the result was the smash hit single "Forever," which sold over a million copies in 1964. The album of that title, issued on the Smash label in June 1964, was a chart hit as was the follow-up *Talking Steel Guitar* (January 1965). Still another LP on the same theme was *Talking Steel Singing,* released in May 1965.

Throughout the 1960s and into the 1970s, Pete continued to be represented by new guitar albums, though he got away from the talking guitar emphasis after the mid-1960s. Some of his later LPs included *Fabulous Steel Guitar* on Starday and *Pete Drake Show* on Stop Records.

Though his solo work didn't often appear on bestseller lists after the mid-1960s, his instrumental talents continued to be in demand not only in the country field but in many other segments of pop musicals as well. As he noted in *Guitar Player,* "The steel wasn't accepted in pop music until I had cut with people like Elvis Presley and Joan Baez. But the kids themselves didn't accept it until I cut with Bob Dylan. After that I guess they figured it was all right. I did the *John Wesley Harding* album,

Nashville Skyline, and *Self Portrait.* Bob Dylan really helped me an awful lot. I mean, by having me play on those records he just opened the door for the pedal steel guitar, because then everybody wanted to use one."

Among the people who became enamored of pedal steel were the members of the Beatles. George Harrison brought Pete to London for a week to do session work on his album *All Things Must Pass.* Later Ringo Starr came to Nashville, where Drake performed and helped produce a number of country-rock and blues numbers by the Beatles drummer.

The interest in Pete's stellar musicianship never slackened as the 1970s went by. During his discussions with Green in 1973, for instance, he noted at one point that he contributed instrumental material on fifty-nine of the top seventy-five albums on the *Billboard* hit lists. In the mid- and late 1970s, he had his pick of countless recording sessions. His widening influence on the music field in general could be seen in the many top-rated pop and country bands in the 1970s that included a pedal steel player on their roster. Many of those musicians traced some of their performing techniques on the instrument to careful analysis of Drake's records or in-person efforts.

Drake received many honors over the years from various polls of top instrumentalists. His name often showed up on year-end lists in major music industry trades and he was nominated many times for various categories in both CMA and Grammy competitions.

Until his health failed, Drake continued to do sessions and tour work with many artists who were household names among country, pop, and rock fans. He also often held the spotlight for his solo or support work on many *Grand Ole Opry* programs. His 1980s honors included 1987 induction into the Steel Guitar Hall of Fame in St. Louis, Missouri, and receipt of the 1987 Master Award from the Nashville Entertainment Association. These were added to such previous honors as a Dove Award from Gospel Music Association voters, a National Academy of Recording Arts & Sciences Appreciation Award, and a *Cash Box* magazine instrumental award.

His career came to an untimely end in the summer of 1988 when he was felled by lung disease. After his passing, it was noted that he had played steel guitar on 118 albums that had earned gold and platinum certification from the R.I.A.A. Over the years, a number of songs published by his Drake Music Group had been given publishing awards by BMI and ASCAP.

DRIFTING COWBOYS: *Vocal and instrumental group, originally Hank Williams's band: Don Helms, born Alabama, Bob McNett, born Pennsylvania, Hillous Butram and Jerry Rivers, both from Nashville, Tennessee.*

To help him in what was to become his brief but creatively rich glory years, Hank Williams assembled a band called the Drifting Cowboys, a group that backed him on some of his most famous recordings. A quarter century after this death, the original members of the band reassembled and found a wide audience for their renditions of Williams's repertoire. Their live performances made many onlookers feel a palpable link to the career of one of the greatest innovators in country—and pop music—history.

The band assembled initially on July 14, 1949, Rivers told Kelly Delaney for an article in *Music City News* (June 1979, p. 23). "We met together for the first time up at WSM and ran through some songs with Hank. When Hank first began to hit on records, this brought him to Nashville and the *Grand Ole Opry.* As did most of the acts of that day, Hank decided to form a band around him to do everything—recording, tours, everything from that point on. He picked the name that he had used on some occasions previously, the Drifting Cowboys."

Steel guitarist Helms's association with Williams went back to 1943, when both lived in Alabama. "With the exception of two years I was in the service, I was with him off and on for eleven years until he died." For a while Helms joined another band during Hank's days with the *Louisiana Hayride* in Shreveport, Louisiana, because the pay was better. When Williams was invited to join the *Opry,* though, Helms agreed to go back with him.

McNett met Hank in Shreveport, where the Pennsylvania-born electric guitarist was a member of Patsy Montana's band. However, she broke up her group in time for him to accept a bid from Hank to come to Nashville. That city was home base for the other original bandmembers, Butram and Rivers.

At one point, fiddle player Rivers had turned down a bid to join Hank in Shreveport, preferring to stay in Music City. In the interim, he played with various *Opry* artists, including the Talking Blues Boys and Jam Up and Honey. He tried working as a duo with performer Benny Martin but that failed, and he was between jobs when Hank called to say he was forming a new band in line with his *Opry* affiliation. When Hank indicated he was looking for a bass player, Rivers recommended another Nashville sideman and session player, Hillous Butram.

Soon after the band got together, they and Hank could point to a number-one national hit, "Long Gone Lonesome Blues." In the short period of time left to Williams, the band basked in the glow of a series of hits, all now classics, including "Your Cheatin' Heart," "Cold, Cold Heart," "I'm So Lonesome I Could Cry," "Jambalaya," and "Hey Good Lookin'," as well as new recordings of some of Hank's earlier successes, including the 1949 number-one hit "Lovesick Blues."

But it was a trying period, during which Williams seemed intent on destroying himself. His unpredictability helped contribute to some changes in the group. In 1952, Butram left to take a job with the *Hank Snow Show* and was replaced by Cedric Rainwater Watts. Soon after McNett departed, going back to Pennsylvania to open a country-music park. Sammy Pruett took over on electric guitar.

Reminiscing, Rivers told Kelly Delaney, "None of us, including Hank, never even thought about thirty years from then—that Hank's impression on the business would be as much or more than Ernest Tubb, Cowboy Copas, Red Foley, all these people who were big before Hank. So none of us considered what he was accomplishing was any bigger than what they had done."

When they heard Hank had died on January 1, 1953, Rivers added, "It was a shock. It had to be [but] to me it wasn't a big, big surprise—like how in the world could this possibly happen. It wasn't that kind of shock. Personally, because of the way his life had turned, especially in the last six months of it, you didn't have to do a whole lot of wondering about how he could get into a situation like that. We had a lot more good experiences with Hank than we had bad, but we also had some real bad experiences with him."

Helms, who also stayed with Williams to the end, agreed. "The last several months before Hank died was the period where we were kind of thrown at a loss, because of the circumstances under which he left the *Opry.* It was a temporary leave of absence. He had some personal problems and his drinking had become more frequent. He needed to take some time off, get his head straight and come back. Well, we had all just bought homes and cars, and I just couldn't see under those circumstances pullin' up and goin' to Louisiana or Montgomery. I didn't know if he'd be back next week or next month."

The band members went separate ways until 1977, when Butram's involvement in a series of country movies made in Nashville sparked a reunion. Acting as talent coordinator for one of them, a film called *That's Country* that featured Lorne Greene, he brought the original Drifting Cowboys together to work in the project. One thing led to another and soon the group was working on many fronts, from radio to records.

One of the first efforts was a series of radio shows hosted by Grant Turner of WSM, an announcer long involved with the *Opry.* Soon the Drifting Cowboys got the chance to record an album on Epic, *A Song for Us All,* issued in 1978. During 1978, their single "Ragmop" made the country charts. The band was a natural choice for the first annual "Hank Williams Memorial Show" broadcast over station WWVA in Wheeling, West Virginia, in 1978. Before 1978 was over, their new credits included two appearances on Ronnie Prophet's TV country program telecast over the Canadian Broadcasting Company network and a set at Nashville's annual Fan Fair, which later was part of a TV presentation on the U.S. Public Broadcasting System. Some of the material from those performances was used to provide a 1979 live LP release, *The Best of the Drifting Cowboys.*

They continued to have a busy schedule in 1979. Besides appearing at a number of U.S. venues, the group went on a twenty-five-show tour of Britain during early summer. They also accepted an invitation to appear in a special performance honoring Hank Williams' contribution to American music sponsored by the Smithsonian Institution in Washington, D.C., in March 1980.

DRUSKY, ROY: *Singer, guitarist, songwriter, disc jockey, band leader (The Loners). Born Atlanta, Georgia, June 22, 1930.*

At the start of the 1980s, Roy Frank Drusky was in his third decade as one of the most respected regulars on the *Grand Ole Opry*. Considering his achievements in the music field, one would not expect that in his late teens he wanted to earn his living either as a professional athlete or in the veterinary field.

Not that he wasn't exposed to musical influences in his early years as a child in Atlanta. His mother was a church pianist for twenty years and tried to get him interested in piano lessons when he was a boy. But baseball and other sports caught his fancy early and he resisted her efforts successfully. As starting second baseman on the school baseball team, he dreamed of some day becoming a major leaguer.

After graduating from high school in the mid-1940s and attending the University of Georgia for a while, he signed for a two-year hitch in the U.S. Navy, which turned out to be the open-sesame to his future country music leanings. While aboard the cruiser U.S.S. *Toledo* in the Pacific, a number of his shipmates used to get together in the evening for some "pickin' and singin'." Roy was part of the audience to start with, but the more he heard, the more he wanted to be a participant. He recalled, "We were docked in Seattle, Washington, one day and I bought a seventeen-dollar guitar from a pawn shop. Each night when the fellows would perform on ship I would sit next to this guy who could really play and study how he moved his fingers. After they stopped playing, I'd go down to my bunk and practice making the same sound he did."

Still, after his discharge in 1950, he went back and enrolled in Emory University as a veterinary medicine major. He still loved sports, but had given up that idea after a four-day tryout at the Cleveland Indians training camp. Meanwhile he dropped by to visit an old friend who had a couple of guitars on hand and the two started jamming a bit. "It felt good," said Roy, "and we really had a ball. So we decided to get together the next weekend. Before long two other fellows joined our 'Sunday Afternoon Living Room Band.'"

In 1951, for a lark, the group entered a talent contest sponsored by station WEAS (now station WGUN) in Decatur, Georgia. The prize was a regular show on the station and Drusky's band walked off with the laurel. Under the name the *Southern Ranch Boys*, the program

became a favorite with WEAS's local listeners. The station asked him to become a featured announcer and disc jockey. Soon he also added two weekly TV shows on station WLWA in Atlanta to his activities and fronted a band in personal appearances throughout the local area.

After doing that for several years, Roy accepted an offer in 1955 to join station KEVE in Minnesota as a disc jockey. He also got the chance to headline at a major club in the area, the Flame Club. He already had shown signs of becoming a major recording artist. In 1953, he had a hit on Starday called "Such a Fool," which led to a contract with Columbia.

By then he was writing a lot of original material. Some of the great artists at the Flame Club brought word of Drusky's talents to Nashville. Before long, other artists were considering some of his songs for their own sessions and Roy was traveling between Minnesota and Nashville to try to further both writing and recording sides of his career. In the late 1950s, Webb Pierce suggested to executives of his record firm, Decca, that they issue a Drusky single of Roy's composition "Alone with You." Roy's version did well, but a Faron Young cover did even better, reaching the top 10 during 1958. Decca recommended he take up residence in Nashville and Roy complied. Before the 1950s were over, the move brought an invitation to join the *Grand Ole Opry* (1958). More than two decades later, that association was still going strong.

From the start of the 1960s into the 1980s, his reputation with country fans was equally firm as he racked up dozens of chart hits both with his own performances and as supplier of hit songs to other artists. In 1960, he made the top 10 with his releases of two original songs, "Another" and "Anymore." In 1961, he co-wrote two more hits for himself on Decca (with V. McAlin and J. Felrod), "I Went Out of My Way" and "I'd Rather Loan You Out." He also made top levels with his version of another writing team's song, "Three Hearts in a Tangle." In 1963, he had a hit with the single "Second Hand Rose." In 1964, he switched from Decca to Mercury and soon had another top-10 hit with Bill Anderson's "Peel Me a Nanner." In 1965, he scored his first number-one single, "Yes Mr. Peters," written by S. Karliski and L. Kolber, and recorded as a duet with Priscilla Mitchell. In 1966, he made upper-chart levels with "White Lightning Express" and added another top-10 feather to his cap with the single "World Is Round." In 1967, he had three singles on the charts for Mercury, though none gained the top 10.

The song "White Lightning Express" was the title song for a country & western film in which Roy appeared. He also starred in two other C&W films of the mid-1960s, *Forty Acre Feud* and *The Golden Guitar.*

Besides leading his band, the Loners, on extensive tours across the United States and in many other nations during the 1960s and 1970s, Drusky also worked at other aspects of the music business. Among other things, he handled production chores for a number of artists, including such people as the Coquettes, Brenda Byers, Bill Goodwin, and English performer Pete Sayers. In addition, he helped set up and, for a time, directed the Nashville office of the music licensing firm known as SESAC. He also headed his own music publishing firm, Funny Farm Music. Besides his regular *Opry* appearances, Drusky was a familiar figure on many TV country shows over the years. At times he hosted his own nationally telecast programs.

Roy had dozens of albums to his credit from the late 1950s into the 1980s. His late 1950s and early 1960s efforts were on Decca, including *Anymore,* issued in September 1961, and *It's My Way* (12/62). In 1964, he debuted on Mercury with the album *Songs of the Cities* (3/64), followed by such others as *All Time Hits* (7/64), *Yesterday's Gone* (10/64), *Pick of the Country* (1/65), *All Around the World* (6/65), *Love's Eternal Triangle* (9/65), *Great Roy Drusky Songs* (10/65), *Greatest Hits* (1/66), *Song Express* (3/66), *Roy Drusky with Priscilla Mitchell* (8/66), *In a New Dimension* (10/66), *If the World Stopped Livin'* (2/67), *Roy Drusky Now* (11/67), and *I Love the Way You've Been Lovin' Me* (late 1960s). Some of his recordings were issued by other labels, such as Vocalion (*Roy Drusky*—4/65—and *Country Special*) and Hilltop (*El Paso*).

He started the 1970s in fine style with a top-10 singles hit in late 1970, "All My Hard Times" and an equally successful LP of the same title on Mercury. However, the rest of the decade's records proved considerably less exciting than the previous ones. Changes in record companies failed to cause a reversal of the situation. As a recording artist for Capitol in the mid-1970s and Scorpion in the late 1970s, he placed songs on the charts, such as "Close to Home" on Capitol in early summer of 1974 and "Betty's Song" on Scorpion in mid-1977, but none made high chart levels. Still, he didn't lack for things to do. He remained one of the best regarded and most popular interpreters of country songs old and new through the 1970s and into the 1980s, whose concerts still drew sizable crowds in the United States and elsewhere.

DUDLEY, DAVE: *Singer, guitarist, songwriter. Born Spencer, Wisconsin, May 3, 1928.*

The truck driver as folk hero was one of the phenomena of the 1960s and 1970s and Dave Dudley was one of the first progenitors of the trend with his series of truck-driving songs. His material, related to both folk and country domains, was recognized by the organizers of the Newport Folk Festival of 1967, who invited Dudley as a featured performer.

Dave grew up in Stevens Point, Wisconsin, where, when he was eleven, his father bought him a guitar. Dave managed to learn to play the instrument by watching Saturday performances at the local Fox Theater.

Still, his main preoccupation was baseball. He was a star baseball pitcher in his teens with high hopes of a pro career. After the six foot, two inch Dudley completed high school he played semi-pro ball before he suffered an arm injury that invalided him home. While recovering he realized that the arm might never be good enough for him to make a success as a ball player.

So he was receptive when a neighbor who worked at station WTWT suggested he come down and spend some time there. One morning, Dave dropped in on disc jockey Vern Shepherd, who had just bought a new guitar. Dave picked it up and began to play along with the records Shepherd was spinning. The latter liked Dave's style and asked him to come down the next morning to sing live on the program—and a new career was born.

In the fall of 1950, Dave was given a morning show of his own on WTWT. His fan mail grew, and the next year he moved on to head a new DJ and singing show on station KOBK, Waterloo, Iowa. In 1952, he moved again, this time to KCHA in Charles City, Idaho.

In 1953, Dave went a step further by forming his own trio. For the next seven years, the Dave Dudley Trio played nightclubs and lounges in most of the Midwest states. Audience response generally was favorable, but nothing sensational happened. In 1960, Dave disbanded the group in Minneapolis and soon after, formed a new group, the Country Gentlemen, for a new nightspot called the Gay Nineties Club. The band, not to be confused with the bluegrass group of the same name, consisted of three other musicians and a woman vocalist. He gained enough of a following in the city to earn a disc jockey spot on station KEVE. He also was hired as master of ceremonies for a new country format featured at the Flame nightclub.

Dave's career seemed to be taking a turn for the better, but just at that point he was hit by a car after finishing work at the Flame on December 3, 1960. The injuries were serious; he was restricted to bed for six months. For another six months after that, he was only able to work a little each week. Other people had taken over the jobs he once held and it seemed Dave's musical career might go the same way as the athletic one.

But he decided to make one more try. He bought time at a local recording studio to cut a number called "Six Days on the Road," given to him by a friend from Decca Records. He took the dubbing to a friend named Jim Madison, who supplied records for jukeboxes. Madison recognized that the song might be a natural for placement in the many truck stops that dotted major highways. The song came out on Soma Records at a time when Dave was away from home on a trip to the Dakotas. It began to find favor both in jukeboxes and on country radio programs. When Dudley returned from the trip, he found that he suddenly was becoming known from coast to coast.

This time, he was ready to take advantage of his good fortune. He made the charts with several more songs on small labels, including a top-10 hit in 1963, "Cowboy Boots," on the Golden Wing label. In 1964, he moved up to the majors in the record field when he signed with Mercury Records and made top-chart levels with the singles "Mail" and "Last Day in the Mines." With a new four-piece backing band called The Roadrunners, he guested on most major national TV country shows and also was presented on the *Grand Ole Opry* radio program. In 1965, he added two more top-10 hits, "Truck Drivin' Son-of-a-Gun" and "What We're Fighting For." For the rest of the 1960s, he always had two or three singles on the charts during each year. In 1968, his singles credits included the top-10 hit "There Ain't No Easy Run" and two other chartmakers.

He was represented by a number of LPs on Mercury during the 1960s. His debut on the label, *Dave Dudley,* came out in June 1964, followed by *Travelin'* (10/64) and *Talk of the Town* (1/65). Other mid-1960s albums included *Dave Dudley* (9/65), *Star Spangled Banner* (3/66), *Greatest Hits* (1/66), *Lonelyville* (8/66), *Free & Easy* (1/67), *My Kind of Love* (6/67), and *Dave Dudley Country* (11/67). His Mercury LPs of the late 1960s and early 1970s included *Best of Dave Dudley, George & the North Woods* (1/70), *Pool Shark, Listen Betty,* and *Original Traveling Man* (1972).

Coming into the 1970s, Dave continued to place recordings on the country charts, but with declining frequency. In the mid-1970s, his long association with Mercury came to a close. With his many past hits to his credit, Dave retained a sizable following at home and abroad and continued to headline shows in nightclubs and on the state and country fair circuit throughout the decade.

In the late 1970s and early 1980s, Dudley recorded some songs for smaller labels. An example was the single "Rolaids, Doan's Pills and Preparation H" on Sun Records, which was on the charts for a number of weeks in the late summer and early fall of 1980.

DUNN, HOLLY: *Singer, songwriter, record producer. Born San Antonio, Texas, August 22, 1957.*

Perhaps reflecting the changing environment in country music, in which artists no longer can count on year-in and year-out support from devoted fans, Holly Dunn came to prominence in the second half of the 1980s but, after five years' success as a recording and concert artist, hit a dry spell in the mid-1990s. However, with her songwriting skills and excellent vocal talent, a strong comeback certainly was not out of the question.

She was born and raised in San Antonio, Texas, the daughter of a Church of Christ minister and a mother who had gained some national attention as a landscape painter. Gospel and country were the main kinds of music heard in her home, but she was not unaware of such elements of pop music as rock and soul. She recalled buying her first album in 1971, while she was

attending junior high school—*Mud Slide Slim,* by singer-songwriter James Taylor. She bought the LP with money she had been given for her lunch.

Her interest in a wide spectrum of music expanded during her teen years, when she also began to take some first halting steps toward songwriting. She still had no clear idea of what she wanted to do when she enrolled in Abilene Christian University in the mid-1970s. As a junior there in 1978, an advertising and public relations major, she had her first taste of songwriting success when gospel singer Christy Lane released a single of one of Holly's religious compositions.

After earning her B.A. in 1979, Holly decided to join her brother, Chris Wates, in Nashville to try to break into the country music field. She said, "Having a brother there with no real musical training who was very successful and writing platinum songs . . . it seemed real feasible."

For a time she had to try other things to earn spending money, including jobs as a book store sales clerk, travel agent, and waitress. She wasn't too excited about any of them. Referring to the travel agent position, she later joked, "I was terrible at it. I think I lost several businessmen who are still out there." But her brother was looking out for her and by early 1980 had found her a more acceptable position with the help of Charline Monk of CBS Songs. Holly recalled, "I was a receptionist at the office as well as being a full-time songwriter. It was a great place to go to school and learn the business."

Over the next few years she proved her worth as a writer. Louise Mandrell scored a top-10 hit with Holly's "I'm Not Through Loving You Yet," and a number of other performers also recorded her material including, among others, the Whites, and Silvia Gibbs, and Terri Gibbs. Of course, Holly wasn't giving up on hopes of making a name for herself as a performer. Some of her demos of new songs served double duty, showcasing both her songwriting skills and her singing style.

In 1984, she got her first opportunity as an artist when producer Tommy West selected her to be one of the first singers on the roster of a new label, MTM Records. Her MTM debut album, *Holly Dunn,* came out in 1986 and provided the hit single, "Daddy's Hands," for which her minister father was the inspiration. This was followed in 1987 by the album *Cornerstone* and the next year by *Across the Rio Grande.* Singles culled from those two albums resulted in four number-one hits and ten top-10 songs. Among those was "Only When I Love," the first one to be written by the threesome of Holly, her brother, and writer-producer Tom Shapiro. That triumvirate turned out many songs that made the charts in later years for Holly or other performers. Among Holly's chart successes of that period were "(It's Always Gonna Be) Someday" and "Love Someone Like Me."

Starting in 1987, she was constantly on the go as a concert artist, initially as an opening act and later as a headliner with her own band. During 1987, her talents were widely recognized by her peers. She received two Grammy nominations for Best Country Song ("Daddy's Hands") and Best Country Vocal Performance, Female. She also was named the Academy of Country Music's choice as Top New Female Vocalist and also won the Country Music Association's Horizon Award. In 1988, her duet with Michael Martin Murphy, "A Face in the Crowd," won her a third Grammy nomination.

Her writing skills also did not go without notice. In 1988 she shared the Broadcast Music Inc. Country Songwriter of the Year Award with Roger Miller, Paul Overstreet, and Dan Seals. She told Mandy Wilson of CMA's *Close Up* (September 1992) that her songwriting tended to suffer because of her busy performance schedule. "I would like to win [the BMI Award] again. I'm trying. The real problem is that I don't have time to write like I used to. I wish I could be the songwriter I was when I wrote things like 'Daddy's Hands' and 'Strangers Again' because at the time I was doing session work and I had the chance to read the trades and stay in touch with other writers. I miss that daily dose of the Music Row thing—the creative flow that is happening."

During 1988, MTM Records closed down and Holly signed with Warner Brothers. That company soon issued her label debut, *Blue Rose of Texas*, which featured a number of Dunn/Waters/Shapiro originals. That album was followed in 1990 by *Heart Full of Love* and in 1991 by *Milestones; Greatest Hits*. Besides earlier successes, *Milestones* included a new song, "Maybe I Mean Yes," which stirred up a hornet's nest of complaints from women's groups. The song's lyrics went, in part, "When I say 'no' I mean 'maybe' / or maybe I mean 'yes.' "

Issued by Warner Bros. Records in June 1991, the song rose rapidly up the charts, accompanied by a rising volume of protests. For example, Tammy Bruce, President of the Los Angeles chapter of the National Organization for Women, told Chuck Phillips of the *Los Angeles Times* ("Country Song Draws Ire of Feminists," July 26, 1991), "That lyric sends shivers up my spine. This kind of entertainment validates the ideas that women don't mean what they say." Similar comments came from others in the feminist movement.

Dunn told Phillips she believed the interpretation of her words wasn't correct. "The couple in the song never even get to the point where they go out. It's not about rape. All we're thinking about here is the funny little faux pas that have gone on between man and woman since the dawn of time.

"I think this song is a victim of timing. A few years ago, a record like this wouldn't have raised an eyebrow. But now everyone's sensitivities have been aroused by media coverage of the date rape subject. I think I just got caught in the cross fire."

In any case, Holly asked the record label to withdraw the disc from circulation, indicating she didn't want to profit from a possibly tainted hit.

The album overall didn't do as well as earlier releases, though it did peak at number twenty-five in the summer of 1991, nor did she reach top-chart levels with the 1992 Warner Brothers product (her seventh album to that time), *Getting It Dunn*. In part, it may have reflected the fact that in the first half of the 1990s, a veritable deluge of new faces tended to dilute the potential of even some of the stars from the 1980s. However, other artists such as John Anderson had rebounded from dry spells, and Holly hoped for a similar breakthrough when she signed with River North Records in mid-1994. By late spring of 1995 she had the single "I Am Who I Am" moving up the charts.

E

EAGLES, THE: *Vocal and instrumental group. Original personnel, 1971: Don Henley, born Gilmer, Texas, July 22, 1947; Glenn Frey, born Detroit, Michigan, November 6, 1948; Randy Meisner, born Scottsbluff, Nebraska, March 8, 1946; Bernie Leadon, born Minneapolis, Minnesota, July 19, 1947. Don Felder added early 1974, born Florida, 1948. Leadon replaced in 1976 by Joe Walsh, born Wichita, Kansas, November 20, 1947. Meisner replaced in 1979 by Timothy B. Schmit, born Sacramento, California. Group disbanded in 1982; reunited in 1993–94.*

From the mid-1970s to the start of the 1980s, the Eagles held sway as one of the great rock bands of the decade. But while rock was the group's forte, it blended elements of folk and country into many of its songs. While serving in some ways as heir to the mantle of such landmarks country-rock bands as Poco and the Flying Burrito Brothers, the Eagles achieved a rapport with the mass audience far beyond those groups' and turned out consistently high-quality recordings throughout the '70s.

In fact, as Glenn Frey, who teamed with Don Henley as the primary writers for the band, pointed out, they learned from the problems of pioneer country-rock groups. He told Cameron Crowe of *Rolling Stone*: "We had it all planned. We'd watched bands like Poco and the Burrito Brothers lose their initial momentum. We were determined not to make the same mistakes. This was gonna be our best shot. Everybody had to look good, sing good, play good, and write good. We wanted it all. Peer respect. AM and FM success. Number one singles and albums, great music, and a lot of money."

The Eagles evolved from the folk and country-rock movement that sprang up in Southern California in the late 1960s and early 1970s. None of the four founding members were native Californians, but all eventually settled in Los Angeles because of the musical environment. The closest to a native was Bernie Leadon, who was born in Minnesota, but moved to San Diego with his family at 10 and lived there until his father got a job in Gainesville, Florida, when Bernie was 17. An interest in folk music caused him to learn guitar and banjo before he reached his teens. Among the groups he played with in high school was the Scottsville Squirrel Barkers, headed by Chris Hillman, later of the Byrds, Burritos, and Desert Rose Band. Leadon played with local groups in Florida in the mid-1960s before heading back to Los Angeles in 1967, where he worked with a series of groups in the late 1960s, beginning with one called Hearts & Flowers and followed by a stint with the bluegrass-rock pioneers the Dillards and then the Burritos.

Meisner's career began in his teens with local groups in the Midwest. Later, in Los Angeles, he was a founding member of Poco with Richie Furay and Jim Messina. Besides performing with Poco and Rick Nelson's Stone Canyon Band, he did session work from time to time, which brought him in contact with people such as Leadon and Linda Ronstadt. Though he played a lot of country-oriented material, he had less of an interest in it than other original Eagles. He told Crowe: "No, I don't go along with everything they do. For example, I'm probably the only one who loves funky rock and roll, trashy music, and R and B. And I don't agree with some of our images either. But Don and Glenn have it covered. I guess I'm just very shy and nervous about putting myself on the line. They're used to doing that."

Glenn Frey grew up in the more frenetic pace of urban Detroit. After dropping out of college, he moved to Los Angeles. Hanging out at the Troubadour club, he became acquainted with another habitue, Don Henley. Henley liked to play drums, but wasn't sure of his career direction while attending college in Linden, Texas. He finally heeded the advice of an English teacher that music suited him best and he headed for the big time of Los Angeles.

He had formed a band in high school called Shiloh and he took that nucleus along with him to California. The band made some inroads in the L.A. music club scene, but nothing dramatic. He had more hours to kill in the Troubadour than he cared to remember. Frey meanwhile was trying to use some of his songs as a wedge for a solo career and got the chance to play some for David Geffen, then manager of Joni Mitchell and Crosby, Stills, Nash & Young and later president of Asylum Records before starting his own label. Geffen discouraged the solo approach and told Frey to join a band. Heeding this, Frey accepted a job with Linda Ronstadt. The band needed a drummer, which caused Frey to look up Henley. The two proved highly compat-

ible. "The first night of the Ronstadt tour," Frey recalled, "we agreed to start our own band."

The band, in effect, took shape around them. Ronstadt's manager, John Boylan, brought in Randy Meisner on bass guitar when Randy left Rick Nelson's group and also recruited Bernie Leadon on lead guitar. Much as the Band had gone on from being Bob Dylan's support group, the Eagles took shape and then left Ronstadt. As the Band has done with Dylan, the Eagles have appeared on joint concert bills with Linda over the years.

Henley points out that they didn't walk out on Ronstadt, but told manager Boyland of their goals. Both Boyland and Linda, while hating to lose them, he stressed, were sincere about not wanting to stand in their way.

Helped by a strong recommendation from Jackson Browne, the group got Geffen as their first manager. Geffen provided expense money so they could move to Aspen, Colorado, to rehearse, write songs, and polish their act in local clubs. Meanwhile, Geffen got Frey a release from Amos Records and lined up a recording contract with Asylum. In early 1972, he arranged for them to go to England to work on their debut LP under the direction of veteran producer Glyn Johns, who had supervised LPs by the Who, Rolling Stones, and Led Zeppelin. The first fruit of that was the hit single "Take It Easy," written by Browne and Frey and issued in early summer. In July 1972, the first album, *The Eagles,* came out. Critical response was mostly positive, although some reviewers from eastern U.S. centers tended to shrug it off as lacking in social commentary. And even though only a cursory listen showed the group could play a diverse array of musical styles, some critics bracketed it as another typical country-rock band. But concert audiences were the final judge. It also was the source of two more charted singles: "Peaceful Easy Feeling" and Henley and Leadon's composition "Witchy Woman."

In 1973, the band went back into London's Olympia Studios to work on album two. It was an ambitious project, a concept album with all the songs tied into the theme of the rise and fall of the Doolin-Dalton gang of Wild West fame. Called *Desperado,* it came out in the spring of 1973 and was only moderately successful. The lukewarm reception to the LP stirred unease among some admirers, fearing the Eagles might go the way of Poco and the Burritos. Adding to that were reports of internal dissension and, later, of arguments with Johns about the next LP.

In fact, after working with Johns on two songs, "You Never Cry Like a Lover" and "Best of My Love" in London, the Eagles decided to finish the album in L.A., returning in early 1974 to line up a new producer. Almost at the same time, the band switched from Geffen to Irving Azoff for management. But all ended well.

With Bill Szymczyk moving in as producer, the resumed album work went smoothly. In the process, the band found a fifth member, Florida-born session guitarist Don Felder, one of the best slide guitarists in pop music. Said Frey: "He just blew us all away. It was just about the best guitar work we'd ever heard." When the album, *On the Border,* was released by Asylum on March 22, 1974, it was announced that Felder had become the Eagles fifth member. The album easily went past gold-record levels. Turnaway crowds thronged Eagles concerts and the "Best of My Love," became the band's first number one *Billboard* single the week of March 1, 1975, followed by "One of These Nights" on August 2, 1975.

Rumors persisted about internal problems as the months went by and no follow-up LP appeared. However, there was some exaggeration, Azoff told the author at the time. "There was a lot of give and take on the fourth album just as there is on the next one and the one before that. But I wouldn't call it fighting. It's sort of like the president can veto a bill. It's a matter of rounding out, of finishing off the rough edges. Obviously, success has mellowed them some. They feel an obligation to the music field to maintain quality. Even more than before, they all want to take their time. To us, melodies, lyrics, and vocals all are really—and equally—important. And that's why we say the Eagles are the Beach Boys of the 1970s."

The new album bore him out. *One of These Nights* is arguably one of the finest pop collections of the decade. Released June 10, 1975, it went well past platinum levels not long afterward. The initial single, "Lyin' Eyes" by Henley and Frey, was a top-10 success hit and the LP produced such other singles successes as "Hollywood Waltz" (by Henley, Frey, and Bernie and Tom Leadon) and Meisner, Henley, and Frey's "Take It to the Limit."

By the end of 1975, though, Leadon indicated he had become tired of the touring grind and the pressures of band life and wanted out. His place was taken in early 1976 by Joe Walsh. Also managed by Azoff, Walsh was an excellent guitarist, singer, and songwriter, who had been a member of the James Gang and later a successful solo artist. His 1973 solo LP, *The Smoker You Drink, the Player You Get* on Dunhill, had gone gold.

Perhaps feeling a bit nervous about the shift, Asylum released the retrospective LP *The Eagles: Their Greatest Hits* on February 17, 1976. However, once Walsh took hold, the Eagles soared even higher. It took a while for that to become apparent, but his contributions helped make the next release as good or better than *One of These Nights.* The new LP, *Hotel California* (1977), combined unique insights with first-rate musicianship on every track. Among the singles hits culled from it were gems such as the title song and

"New Kid in Town," both number one in *Billboard* in 1977. The LP was number one for eight weeks on the pop charts.

But another personnel shift was on the agenda. Randy Meisner departed during 1979 to seek a solo career. His place was taken by bass guitarist Timothy B. Schmit. Schmit played with local bands in high school and while working on a degree in psychology at Sacramento State College. He opted for music, however, and became a long-time member of Poco prior to his Eagles affiliation.

The new lineup completed the next album in the fall of 1979. Issued by Elektra/Asylum in October, *The Long Run* had many tracks up to previous Eagles standards, but several that fell short. But the public was happy to have new Eagles songs. The LP went platinum and provided three top-10 singles, "Heartache Tonight" in 1979, the title song, and "I Can't Tell You Why." The group had another platinum album in 1980: *Eagles Live.* "Heartache Tonight" was number one in *Billboard* the week of November 10, 1979.

But the two prime writing forces, Frey and Henley, were eager for new challenges. In the early 1980s, they began work on solo albums. With their decisions to concentrate on those efforts, the group was disbanded in 1982 with the formal announcement made by manager Azoff in May. Soon after that, Don Felder also embarked on a solo career with his debut album, *Airborne* (1983, Asylum). He admitted he would have preferred to stay with the Eagles, but with Frey and Henley both doing well on their own in the late 1980s, the chance of an eventual reunion seemed remote.

A dozen years went by without any evidence of the band reforming, particularly since some members weren't on speaking terms. Then a project organized by one-time manager Irving Azoff's new Giant Records label to have top country stars record their versions of Eagles' hits unexpectedly also brought about the band reunion. The catalyst was Travis Tritt, who said he wouldn't take part unless Eagles members, among his early influences, also became involved. They agreed and, after helping complete the tribute in 1993, decided to get together for a new concert tour.

The tribute album, *Common Thread: The Songs of the Eagles,* included tracks from Tritt, John Anderson, Clint Black, Suzy Bogguss, Brooks & Dunn, Billy Dean, Diamond Rio, Vince Gill, Alan Jackson, Little Texas, Lorrie Morgan, Tanya Tucker, and Trisha Yearwood. Issued in 1993, the album showed up on both pop and country charts, passing the triple platinum R.I.A.A. level by the end of 1994. In the 1994 Country Music Association voting, whose results were announced on the October 1994 award telecast, the disc was named Album of the Year.

The new Eagles tour began in the spring of 1994 and drew sellout crowds across the U.S. By the end of 1994 it had amassed almost $100 million in gross receipts with more dates for the series (called "The Hell Freezes Over Tour") to be fulfilled. A live album, *Hell Freezes Over,* recorded early in the tour and including four new songs by band members, was released in the fall by Geffen Records and debuted on the *Billboard* Pop 200 chart at number one, where it stayed into early November. The new album was on the way to joining a catalog that was truly a goldmine for the band's recording firm. In a sense, as some observers noted, though the band was dormant from 1982 to the mid-1990s, it never left the scene, since its six original studio albums sold an average of 1.5 million copies per year during the hiatus.

That accomplishment was reflected in the stream of new record awards that continued to arrive from the R.I.A.A. through much of 1995. *Hell Freezes Over* brought a gold record plaque on January 13 and by April 8 earned a multiplatinum award for over 5 million copies sold. On June 5, the band received awards for 7 million copies sold of *Eagles Greatest Hits Volume II,* 22 million copies for *Eagles—Their Greatest Hits 1971–1975,* and a 14 million copy award for *Hotel California.*

EARLE, STEVE: *Singer, guitarist, band leader (the Dukes), songwriter. Born Fort Monroe, Virginia, January 17, 1955.*

Few artists like to be categorized, for fear that it will close creative doors as their careers progress or even prevent those doors from opening. Steve Earle is a case in point. A performer and gifted songwriter with a no-nonsense style, he seemed a throwback in some ways to people like Hank Williams, Sr., Ernest Tubb, and Johnny Cash. Yet in the rock era there could be no mistaking other elements in his musical personality that bore the stamp of rockabilly. This caused his recordings to tend to fall in the cracks as far as radio programmers were concerned; where he wasn't considered too country, he was too rock 'n' roll.

Helping to confuse matters further, his band, the Dukes, accepted engagements at both rock and country venues—which didn't seem to bother the fans, but did cause head-shaking among country music opinion makers. He told Don Winbush of *Time* ("The Color of Country," September 8, 1986), "I'm a country singer and I'm comfortable with that. But why does a country singer have to play only on country radio or a rock singer only on a rock station? I still don't understand why it's that big a deal."

Certainly Earle grew up in the heartland of country music. He was born in Virginia, but while still a child moved with his family to the Lone Star State. His parents put down roots in the town of Schertz, seventeen miles northeast of San Antonio. Schertz was a sleepy town, and as Steve approached his teens he began to wander farther afield to San Antonio, typically without

letting his parents know. He told Winbush, "I wasn't a bad kid. I wasn't gettin' in a lot of trouble. I just wanted to get away to walk the streets, mostly listening to all the songs I had in my head."

But he also acknowledged that the places where he stayed in San Antonio were hardly garden party locales. He recalled frequenting "a very dangerous part of San Antonio. I had to deal with death at a very early age. People in my neighborhood, you either graduated and went to college or you joined the bandidos. Then you die in a drug overdose or in a car or motorcycle accident or get cut or shot."

In 1971, when he was 16, he made Houston, Texas, his home for a time. "I slept on anybody's couch until I wore out my welcome." The person he spent the most time with was his uncle, Nick Fain, who helped Steve learn to play six-string guitar. Earle hung out at music spots where he met other young aspiring performers, including Townes Van Zandt, who helped get him gigs at small folk-oriented clubs and coffeehouses. He entered into the first of three unsuccessful marriages in 1974, but soon left his wife to move to Nashville in hopes of making a breakthrough as songwriter or musician. In 1975, he received word that Elvis planned to record one of his songs, but as often happens in the music field, the song never made it to session tape.

That was one of many disappointments Earle had to cope with as the 1970s went by and the 1980s began. During those years he kept writing songs, took on any performing dates he could get, and kept a roof over his head working various day jobs, including house construction and swimming pool installation. Some friends suggested he might be better off back in Texas, but he stayed put. As he said later, "It's disgusting how optimistic I am. I've been doing this a long time. The reason I stayed in this town, this Nashville, was that somehow I knew this was the place for me to be. If it didn't work, and if people weren't accepting what I was doing, well I felt my time would come if I hung in there. When the time came, I knew I would appreciate it more. I would be taken more seriously and I would be around for a lot longer."

His hopes rose in the early 1980s when he made some singles on the Epic label and eventually completed material for an album on Columbia, Epic's parent company. The tracks were recorded at various times from 1982 to 1984, but Columbia shelved the album. Meanwhile, other country artists were impressed by his songwriting and his live performance began to attract attention. Finally he got another chance, this time with MCA Records, and for once the timing was right. His debut album, *Guitar Town,* was enthusiastically received by critics and many influential country radio stations and, as Steve and his five-piece band the Dukes supported it with intensive coat-to-coast touring, made the hit lists. Before the year was out, the album rose to number one in *Billboard*. At year-end *Rolling Stone* editors voted him top country artist and similar acclaim came in other polls.

Based on that achievement, MCA signed him for seven more albums, the first of which was the 1987 release, *Exit 0*. By then, Columbia decided to issue the album he'd made before under the title *Early Tracks*. *Exit 0* proved a worthy successor to his MCA debut and again won extensive critical support. Stephen Holden of the *New York Times* named it his Pop Album of the Week (May 15, 1987), stating Earle and the Dukes projected "a vision of country music that transcends the conventional boundaries of Nashville—even those of the so-called new traditionalist movement. The music . . . runs from hard-driving contemporary rockabilly to open-road anthems reminiscent of Creedence Clearwater Revival to thorny country-rock songs whose attitude of defiance and frustration recall the young, cranky Bob Dylan." *Sounds* magazine that April lauded his recording of his self-penned "Fearless Heart," naming it Single of the Week while calling him a "heavyweight songwriter."

The Dukes were also singled out for praise in many reviews, with a number of critics calling attention to the steel guitar work of Bucky Baxter. Some of the members cowrote originals with Steve; drummer Harry Stinson was one of those making important contributions.

Yet the enthusiasm of Holden, *Village Voice* writers, and others more closely associated with rock and pop than country tended to cause a backlash among many segments of the country field. Comparing Earle's work to that of Springsteen and Mellencamp, as many mainstream publications did, caused confusion about whether Earle was truly a country artist. His recordings became much less prominent in the country radio spectrum, and his follow-up albums to *Guitar Town*, which included the 1988 *Copperhead Road*, suffered declining sales.

From the late 1980s into the 1990s, Steve continued to retain a loyal, if not massive, following and his live shows never lacked for high-voltage energy and attention-grabbing material. But he made few inroads onto country charts and the fact that he wasn't considered an all-out rocker hurt him in the pop sector. Other country artists appreciated his body of work and some castigated the country establishment for turning its back on him, and more than a few important performers covered some of his songs.

It didn't help matters any, however, that his personal life was a shambles by the start of the 1990s. He fell prey to drug addiction and other difficulties that at one juncture resulted in time in jail. His career disintegrated until he finally went into a treatment center which probably saved his life while giving him a second chance as a creative individual.

He had gone several years without new releases, before starting his comeback with the acoustic album, *Train a Comin'*, issued on the Winter Harvest label in the spring of 1995. The collection rivaled his superb MCA release of almost a decade earlier, *Guitar Town*, and confirmed anew he was one of country music's ablest performers and songwriters.

His concerts in support of his new album, his first tour in four years, focused on a less raucous folk/bluegrass oriented format in which he was capably backed by a band that included two of folk music's luminaries, Peter Rowan and Norman Blake. Though his voice reflected the ravages of his years of substance abuse, his ability to project feelings and emotions in his own and other writers' songs remained evident. In a set at the West Los Angeles *Troubadour* night club in January 1996, the sold-out audience paid rapt attention to such darkly flavored originals as "Ellis Unit One," written for the sound track of the film *Dead Man Walking*, while demonstrating word-for-word familiarity with many of his more upbeat songs by singing the choruses in response to his solo verse stylings.

The new songs Earle performed, including "Goodbye," which had been covered in an Emmylou Harris album, and other songs written for *Dead Man Walking*, but not included in the final soundtrack, verified he had not lost anything in his writing skills but, in fact, had surpassed much of his earlier work. Noting he had a new album due out in March 1996, he made a tongue in cheek reference to what might follow. "I've planned a concept album after that, one in which none of the songs have any reference to the devil in them" after which he sang a number of his best known material in which, of course, the devil was mentioned in one way or another.

A short time afterward his new album, *I Feel Alright*, was issued on the E-Squared/Warner Bros. label. It was another superb collection that surely merited the acclaim it received from critics across the U.S. The reviewing staff from the *Los Angeles Times*, for instance, gave it top rating in its "PopMeter" column for the week of March 10, 1996. Album tracks ranged from the exuberant rockabilly type number "Poor Boy" to the chilling "CCKMP" which stands for "Cocaine Cannot Kill My Pain" and deals with the gut-wrenching effects of heroin addiction.

EDWARDS, STONEY: *Singer, guitarist, pianist, fiddler, songwriter. Born Seminole, Oklahoma, December 24, circa 1930.*

Country music usually is thought of as white people's music, but the truth is there always has been a strong interaction between the rural music played in both black and white communities. Many of the elements Jimmie Rodgers, the father of modern country music, incorporated in his material derived from his association with black laborers on the railroad. There always have been black followers of country music; it's only been in recent years that black artists have found a forum for their country artistry. After Country Charley Pride blazed the initial trail, others have followed, most notably O. B. McClinton and Stoney Edwards.

Born and raised in a rural area of Oklahoma, Edwards came of a considerably mixed heritage. On his mother's side, his ancestry was Negro and Indian, on his father's a combination of Negro, Indian, and Irish. He had plenty of chores to do on the small farm he grew up on, especially after his father left and he had to help support his five brothers and two sisters. He did it until he was thirteen. As he told Glenn Hunter (*Country Music,* March 1976), "Runnin' corn liquor and helpin' to take care of them, I was only able to go up to the third grade. Later, I was too old. I was plum' shamed to go back to school. I still don't know how to read and write."

By the time he was thirteen, Stoney could play several instruments and had long been a country-music fan. He developed that liking during many childhood trips to relatives in North Carolina. He had a "bunch of uncles," he told Hunter, who would "sit around in a ring and pick, and I'd put right down in the middle of 'em. I had them to help steer my interest to Bob Wills and the *Grand Ole Opry.* I remember even back then I wanted to sing on the *Opry* so bad I could taste it."

For a time, in his teens, Stoney was reunited with his father in Oklahoma City, where he earned money working as a dishwasher. After a while he got restless and began to move around the country, going to Texas with an uncle, returning home for a time, leaving again, working at a variety of jobs ranging from janitor and truck driver to cowboy. In the mid-1950s, he made his way to California, where he met a girl named Rosemary, married her in 1954, and settled down to raise a family in the San Francisco Bay area. He found steady work for the next decade and a half, brought home a reasonably good paycheck, and kept at music only as a spare time activity.

That was the pattern until a near fatal mishap changed everything. It occurred in 1969 when he was working as a machinist in a shipyard in Richmond, California, and received a severe case of carbon dioxide poisoning. Though it was discovered in time, the after-effects were severe, requiring hospitalization. It affected his memory so that, for a time, he didn't even recognize his wife. He finally regained his strength and went back to the shipyard, only to suffer another accident that broke his back. This time, the doctors said he had to give up anything involving heavy physical labor.

At one point during those disasters, Stoney thought it might be best if he left so that his wife, at least, could go on welfare or find someone who could support the family better. He told Hunter, "I had my bag packed one night and was ready to leave when my little girl came in with this ole windup toy I'd bought her. She said, 'Daddy, if I can't go, how come you get to go?' Well, I just put my bag down and went to my room and wrote my first song, 'Two Dollar Toy,' before I went back to bed."

It was a harbinger of things to come. Stoney write more songs and played his guitar more in succeeding months. (Although he plays a number of instruments, he preferred not to use any of them on stage.) In 1970, he had an invitation to perform in a benefit show for Bob Wills in Oakland, California. He arrived a little late and almost wasn't allowed to take part, but a singer named Tony Rose insisted he take part of his set. After Stoney did "Mama's Hungry Eyes," an attorney in the audience was impressed enough to suggest he audition for Capitol. A week later he'd completed a demonstration recording and soon after was signed by the label.

His first album came out in March 1971, called *Stoney Edwards: A Country Singer,* and included such tracks as "Poor Folks Stick Together," "An Old Mule's Hip," "A Few of the Reasons," and his composition "The Cute Little Waitress." Stoney backed the album with an exhaustive concert tour, a pace of several hundred appearances a year at clubs, county fairs, and other country venues he kept up throughout the 1970s.

He was hardly an overnight success, but slowly he began to gain a following and his records started dotting the charts. Occasionally, as with "Hank and Lefty Raised My Soul" in 1973 and "Mississippi You're on My Mind" in the mid-1970s, he made the upper-chart levels. About "Hank and Lefty," a song by Dallas Frazier and A. L. Owens in praise of Hank Williams and Lefty Frizzell, Edwards told about going into a small bar in Nashville in 1973 to see Frizzell in a corner crying over the recording that was playing on the jukebox.

"Later this guy told me he'd overheard Lefty say, 'Why, that song's a tribute to me . . . and here I didn't think nobody cared a shit about me anymore. And wouldn't you know . . . it had to be a black man.'" Hunter noted that Stoney was asked whether he took offense. "Hell no," he roared, "that was a compliment."

Among the other singles by Edwards that made the charts in the 1970s were "She's My Rock," "Two Dollar Toy," "Daddy Bluegrass" (in early 1974), and "Love Still Makes the World Go Round" in the spring of 1976, all on Capitol. In 1978, Stoney was on a new label, JMI, for which he still provided a number of chart singles, including "If I Had to Do It All Over Again." By the start of the 1980s he was on a new label, Music America, for which he placed the single "No Way to Drown a Memory" on mid-chart levels during the summer of 1980 and "One Bar at a Time" in the fall of the year.

ELY, JOE: *Singer, guitarist, band leader, songwriter. Born Amarillo, Texas, February 9, 1947.*

From Joe Ely's appearance you can tell he's been through a lot of hardship, with a background of riding the rails and being stranded broke and alone in strange towns and cities. He wears old, beat-up cowboy boots and a large ranger-rider's hat, and he walks with the gait of someone used to the saddle.

"I was born in Amarillo, Texas," he says, sitting sprawled on a couch with his boots propped up on a motel room table, "about half a block from Route Sixty-six. I kinda grew up there and moved to Lubbock when I was about eleven. Not a whole lotta difference—one's a wheat town and one's a cotton town. My folks weren't interested in country music at all. There was always a piano, so there was a lotta music. Sorta church gathering music. My grandfather was always with the choir."

He was started out on the classics. "I started taking violin lessons in the second grade. Then I started taking steel guitar lessons around the fifth or sixth grade. A guy going door-to-door offered them. That didn't last too long. After a while the violin looked less and less appealing. So I turned to guitar. I found guitar was more of a total instrument. You could carry it around and use it to accompany yourself.

"Even though my folks weren't into country, growing up in the Panhandle of Texas I was kinda surrounded by it from the moment I popped out of the womb. I was also listening to some rock 'n' roll on the radio too. Guess that's why when I started writing there turned out to be a bit of rock in a lot of my songs. Of course I was influenced by all the early rockers like Bo Diddley and all, but I also was listening to country people like Jimmie Rodgers and bluesmen like Robert Johnson.

"I went to school in Lubbock. Not too long, but long enough to realize I didn't have any place in high school. I was playing in clubs when I was about fifteen or sixteen. There for a while I was playing solo and then got a little band together at the end of junior high school. We played wherever we could—mostly rock 'n' roll. By then I knew a lot of old country standards too, y'know.

"For a while I was washin' dishes in a fried chicken place and playin' in a band, tryin' to carve out somethin' between the two. I was about seventeen when I ended up playin' in clubs in ole Fort Worth and Houston and a little bit around Dallas. After that I turned up in Los Angeles, of all places."

The event that catapulted him on the way there was a brush with a Houston club manager. The latter got mad because Joe missed a performance and pulled a gun, threatening to have some club bully boys beat him up. "It scared the hell out of me. I ended up pooling all my money with another guy for a one-way plane ride to L.A. Someone had stolen my guitar before I left and I was broke and only had a few bucks to my name.

"When we got outta the L.A. airport we only had five or six dollars and we ended up walking to Venice Beach to save money. We didn't know where we was. Kind of spin-the-bottle kind of journey. All I had was this old amplifier. I had an extra shirt or two in the bottom of it. It was my only possession."

Out on the beach, Ely found a man with an old guitar and managed to buy it for five dollars. That, in effect, put him back in business. He still has the guitar. In fact, it is nestled in an old rundown case at one side of the motel room. For some years after that, Ely lived from hand to mouth, working odd jobs, playing for coins in the streets, picking up gigs here and there, knocking about.

"I started doin' a lot of hard travelin' goin' coast to coast with points in between. Those old freight yards in San Bernardino [California]—if you could find a brakeman who wouldn't pull the wool over your eyes you could get from L.A. to Amarillo in two to three days."

Riding the rods, besides getting him from one place to another, also gave him time to make up songs. "I guess I really started writing in the late 1960s and early 1970s. 'Cause more and more, that was the only thing I really had that moved me—playing, singing, and racking up songs. Along the way, no matter how I traveled, there was a lot of dead space in between some of those towns and music filled it in."

As the years went by, he kept "movin' on," even ending up in Europe at one point. "After a while, I kinda got burned out on California. I kept goin' back and forth between L.A. and Austin, Lubbock, and San Francisco. I kinda came back to Texas to be back home. I was workin' a little bit with a band in Austin when I just took off and went to New York with a friend.

"This friend of mine knew of a Texas bunch of people who were doing a thing with Joseph Papp's [New York] Shakespeare Theater. Sort of a Texas revue. My friend was a painter who was supposed to do a mural for the show and I was supposed to be his assistant. But he met Johnny Winter in our hotel and split back west with him, leavin' me at loose ends. I kind of asked the guys in the revue—like I had nowhere to go—so I said, 'I can do lights, a little guitar, anything.' They put me up and I had three squares.

"Right after I joined them, they got an offer to go around Europe to all the festivals. So that sounded like a good place to go. I took off with them. Stayed over there about five months. That was about 1970. When that finished I came back to Texas again and kept shuttlin' between there and New York. There was different groups I got together with, playing some, laying around waitin' for work other times."

During one of those early 1970s dry spells, he was in Albuquerque, New Mexico, and, on the spur of the moment, joined Ringling Brothers Circus. "It just happened to be there and I walked up and asked for a job. I ended up taking care of some animals. I had two horses, one called Omar, the other King. We went round and around with the world's smallest horse. I think it also was the world's meanest. I still got scars where he bit me. Then there were the llamas—they used to spit at me." Ely spent about three months with the circus before an injury sidelined him. "Finally I got kicked in the ribs and bid my farewell—enough is too much.

"I ended up pickin' pears and green chilis in New Mexico for a while. Knockin' around like that was beginning to get to me, though, I went back to Lubbock and got this band together. By then [in the mid-1970s] I had a lot of songs in my head. A lot written down, but a lot I just carried around in my memory."

Among the friends Ely renewed contact with was a West Texas songwriter-performer named Butch Hancock, whose material often is found on Joe's LPs. "Anyway, I got a band together with a guy named Jimmy Gilmore and we had a saw player named Steve Wesson and a mandolin player named Tony Pearson—an acoustic band. We just kinda got together and did some of my songs, and Butch's and Jimmy's. We went to Nashville—some guy on a radio station took the band there. We did a tape, but I didn't like the whole deal that was offered so I didn't sign. Turned out my hunch was right; nothing much ever happened to that material."

Back in Texas, though, word about Ely's potential was beginning to float around the music field, which eventually led to his signing with MCA Records. "I kinda got with them by accident. A new band kinda got together and we made a few tapes for our own satisfaction—just to have 'em because of the songs we worked up. The Gonzo Band—Jerry Jeff Walker's band—gave Jerry a copy of the tape. One of the MCA guys heard it and came out to Lubbock to hear us play at an old club [The Cotton Club] and he and some others were around again when we were in another town the next week. Things just started comin' together. Other music people began kickin' things around with us. But MCA just got together with us and worked out somethin' we both could live with."

Ely began recording material for MCA in late 1975; his debut LP, *Joe Ely,* came out January 10, 1976. The album created considerable excitement among pop music critics but fell far short of hit status. Although the signs were good, Ely's next LP didn't arrive until two years later, which caused a certain loss of momentum with the public. (Called *Honky Tonk Masquerade,* it was issued February 13, 1978.) Joe toured widely in support of it and his reputation grew, but hardly at a breakneck pace. In early 1979, his third LP, *Down on the Drag,* was released with suggestions that the time might be nearing for Joe to take his place with Willie, Waylon, and Jerry Jeff as a mainstay of the progressive country movement.

One of his problems was his unique, hard-to-categorize style, which combined often unusual lyric themes with varying blends of country, rock, and blues musical elements. This tended to confuse radio programmers; rock music selectors thought his material too "country," while country programmers had the reverse viewpoint. The resulting lack of airplay had the effect of making him a cult figure. This situation still held sway in 1981, when he came out with two more fine albums, the studio LP *Musta Notta Gotta Lotta,* issued by MCA in early 1981 and the live album *Live Shots,* released in the fall. The last-named album was recorded in England during 1980, a time when Ely became acquainted with the English punk group the Clash. Ely and the U.K. supergroup influenced each other, in Ely's case reflected in the more intense, urban flavor of his early 1980s material. Ely toured with the Clash in England and was later instrumental in setting up Texas dates for them. His concert work continued to excel. An example was his set at the California State University at Long Beach's Banjo, Fiddle & Guitar Festival in April 1981, where an audience of 7,000 initially unfamiliar with him ended up rewarding his performance with thunderous applause.

Still, it seemed that if the Goddess of Success were to claim Ely, she would have to do the pursuing. As he said, "I don't think about success. I never set success as a goal. I just set out to make music and that's what I've done. What I'm doin' now is all I can concern myself with. That in itself keeps me goin'. I woulda laid it down a long time ago without that. Music is my whole life. Sometimes I lay down the guitar for a while and take off, but I always come back to it.

"Of course, it's a lot different now than playin' at a truck stop on some highway for coffee and a hamburger. But when it comes down to it, it's about the same. I still drink coffee and I still eat hamburgers."

The departure of his guitar player and the death of the drummer in Ely's band caused a temporary hiatus in Joe's concert work. During 1982, he retired to his home, where he had his own recording studio rigged up to work on new material using a synthesizer and a computer system. This became the basis for his sixth MCA release, *Hi-Res.* In 1983–84, he was once again on the road in support of his new collection.

In the mid-1980s, Ely parted company with MCA when the company balked at releasing his next album, for which Ely had already completed the tapes. Part of the reason was likely that Joe, though continuing to be one of the most respected artists in his field, still could not attract mass market sales. Nonetheless, no one could argue with the quality of his work or his artistic integrity. In 1987, he debuted on a new label, Hightone, with the album *Lord of the Highway,* an album containing plenty of hard-driving, pulse-tingling cuts. He followed in 1990 with *Live at Liberty Lunch,* touring in support of that album with a band featuring guitarist David Grissom, who later left to join rock star John Mellencamp's backing group. Grissom continued to work Ely's new album sessions and in the mid-1990s was touring with him once more.

In the early 1990s, Tony Brown, head of Artists & Repertoire at MCA Records/Nashville, persuaded the company to re-sign Joe. Brown told an interviewer, "What can I say? He cast a spell on me. I went and saw him play with Grissom and all those guys, and it just blew me away. And then they played the demos he's been writing and, I don't know, we just hit it off. He had that live album, *Live at Liberty Lunch,* which I could buy automatically. We decided to buy that one and put it out, and then we'd cut an album."

The new MCA album, *Love and Danger,* was issued in 1992 and, like almost all his releases, was critically praised and purchased by a sizable number of longtime fans, but not my millions of record buyers. As usual, he assembled a first-rate backing band, which included Reese Wynans (previously with the late Stevie Ray Vaughn's group) on keyboards, Ian Moore on guitar (in place of Grissom), Davis McLarty on drums, and Jimmy Pettit on bass guitar.

In 1994, Ely demonstrated another facet of his talents by playing the male lead, with Jo Harvey Allen on the distaff side, in the country & western musical "Chippy Diaries of a West Texas Hooker." The show made its New York debut in July 1994 as part of the Lincoln Center's Serious Fun Festival.

By 1995, Ely was working on a new album, *Letter to Laredo,* released by MCA in July of that year. All the tracks except one featured highly regarded European flamenco guitarist Teye. The exception was Ely's composition "That Ain't Enough," about which Joe commented, "Me and my guitarist David Grissom got together on it. I had been writing that song for a couple of years on and off and it just all of a sudden felt right when we were sitting and playing it. It's kind of a moody song about breaking up and coming back together."

All of Ely's MCA albums were in print in the mid-1990s and available from the Texas City Music mail-order catalog. Reflecting on Texas traditions in the catalog (which offered recordings by many other past and present MCA C&W artists), he noted, "Where I grew up, up in Lubbock and Amarillo, the honky tonk was a big traditional thing. It went back to the dust bowl days, the hard times when people would work in the fields all week and then come to town on Saturday night. People would go out and hear a band, as opposed to going to the theater and seeing a movie. They go to dance halls. It's a physical thing, actually going to a spot and participating in it."

Based partly on a 1978 interview with Irwin Stambler.

EVANS, DALE (MRS. ROY ROGERS): *Singer, actress, songwriter. Born Uvalde, Texas, October 31, 1912.*

The first family in western entertainment in the decades just after World War II were Mr. and Mrs. Roy Rogers, Dale and Roy, both artists of the first rank, have contributed more than their share in humanitarian and religious activities.

The western outlook was natural to Dale, who was born and spent part of her girlhood in Texas. Later, her family moved to Osceola, Arkansas, where she attended high school and demonstrated a talent for

singing. After a brief marriage (1928–30) to Thomas Frederick Fox, she went on to concentrate on a career as a vocalist.

During the 1930s, she gradually worked her way to the top as a popular singer, and was featured on a number of radio stations in such cities as Memphis, Dallas, and Louisville. In the late 1930s, she became vocalist with Anson Weeks's band, then one of the top organization in Chicago. Her growing reputation resulted in a hit engagement at the Chez Paree Night Club in Chicago in 1940. That year she also was signed as a singer on a weekly CBS show called *News and Rhythm.* As the 1940s went by, she was a guest star on many major radio shows and vocalist on the *Edgar Bergen–Charlie McCarthy* network show.

Next came the chance to get started in films. In 1943, Dale made her Hollywood debut in *Swing Your Partner.* This was the first of her many movie roles over the next twenty years. Her picture credits from 1943 on included *West Side Kid, Here Comes Elmer, Hoosier Holiday, In Old Oklahoma, Yellow Rose of Texas, My Pal Trigger, Sunset in El Dorado, Bells of San Antonio, Bells of Coronado, Pals of the Golden West,* and *Don't Fence Me In.* Most of the films were with Roy Rogers, whom Dale had married in 1947.

In the 1950s, the team of Roy Rogers and Dale Evans had become number one in the western field. They were starred on the *Roy Rogers* show, which was one of the top-rated shows on NBC-TV for a number of years. In addition, they were featured at many rodeos and other major shows across the country, which continued into the 1980s, long after the show had ended. They often helped entertain New York audiences during the World's Championship Rodeo in Madison Square Garden. Their international popularity was well demonstrated by rousing receptions from audiences during their first tour of the British Isles in 1954.

Dale and Roy turned out many records during the 1950s for RCA Victor. Some were of songs composed by Dale, such as "The Bible Tells Me So," "Aha San Antone," and "Happy Birthday Gentle Savior." They were also represented in the 1960s by a long-time RCA Victor LP bestseller, *Dale Evans and Roy Rogers,* and a Capitol LP of religious songs. In addition to songwriting, Dale found time to write several books, including *Angel Unaware* and *Spiritual Diary.* She also turned out a number of articles for national magazines during the 1950s and 1960s.

The Rogerses won acclaim during the 1950s and 1960s for their charitable work and for their dedication to children. They adopted and raised a large family of their own. Over the years they received many awards for their efforts, including the Masquer's Club's George Spelvin Award for humanitarian service in 1956, the National Safety Council's public interest award, and citations from the American Red Cross, National Association for Retarded Children, Muscular Dystrophy

Association, National Nephrosis Foundation, and many religious denominations.

After Roy suffered a heart attack in the early 1970s, both he and Dale took a brief respite from the entertainment field. Before long, when Roy had recovered his strength, the two resumed a certain amount of career activity, but on a much reduced scale compared to earlier times. However, they picked up the pace somewhat as the decade drew to a close. In the early 1980s, their career had something of a renaissance, as they were featured guests on many network TV shows, both country and general variety. They also were asked to do a number of commercial endorsements of various products, so that their faces peered forth from billboards, magazine ads, and on TV spots. They continued to make their home in Apple Valley, where they continued to operate the Roy Rogers Museum.

For the balance of the 1980s through the first half of the 1990s, that pattern remained the same. The couple continued to make occasional appearances on TV and onstage and lent their names to charitable causes or projects that advanced the status of country and western music. In 1988, Dale was on hand for husband Roy's induction as a solo performer into the Country Music Hall of Fame. During 1994–96, Dale's activities were curtailed by health problems, including successful artery bypass surgery in May 1996. (*See also Roy Rogers*.)

EVERLY BROTHERS: *Vocal and instrumental team, solo artists after mid-1973. Both born Brownie, Kentucky; Don, February 1, 1937; Phil, January 19, 1939.*

Taking their cue from Elvis Presley, who was their early idol, the Everly Brothers had an impact on pop music in the late 1950s and early 1960s almost as great as Elvis'. Their country-rock recordings of those years affected the styles of many rock stars of the 1960s, both in the United States and abroad. Among their fans of the late 1950s in England, for instance, were future members of the Beatles and the Animals. Their performances also had an impact on young folk and country artists, which prompted Bob Dylan to say, at one point, "We owe those guys everything. They started it all." After the brothers parted company in 1973, their activities centered more and more on the straight country field rather than rock.

The boys had an impeccable country background. Their parents were Ike and Margaret Everly, country/gospel artists well known to Southern and Midwestern audiences from the 1930s into the 1950s. The boys learned to sing many country standards at an early age and learned the rudiments of guitar as soon as they could hold an instrument. When Don was eight and Phil six, they made their first public appearance on radio station KMA in Shenandoah, Iowa. After that, the boys regularly joined their parents on performing tours each summer.

After their parents retired just following the boys' graduation from high school, the brothers decided to keep going on their own. They moved to Nashville, playing the local clubs and waiting for their first break. It was the mid-1950s, and traditional country music was reeling from the success of rockabilly artists like Elvis and Jerry Lee Lewis. In 1956, the brothers got their first record contract with Columbia Records (but were dropped by that label within a year). In making the rounds of music publishers looking for new material, they met the songwriting team of Felice and Boudleux Bryant at Acuff–Rose (through music publisher, Wesley Rose). The Bryants played them a new composition, "Bye Bye Love," which the Everlys decided to record. A close association with the Bryants and Rose started that lasted many years and resulted in a series of hits, many of which have become standards and have since been recorded by many artists besides the Everlys in both the pop and country fields. The new disc was released on the Cadence label.

"Bye Bye Love" rose to number one on country and pop charts in 1957. The brothers then provided Cadence Records with another smash success with the Bryants' "Wake Up Little Susie." The brothers soon were featured on most American TV shows, including *The Ed Sullivan Show* and Dick Clark's *American Bandstand*. They had another excellent year in 1958 with such hits as "All I Have to Do Is Dream," "Bird Dog," and "Devoted to You," all by the Bryants and recorded on Cadence, and "Cathy's Clown," which marked a move to Warner Brothers Records. "Cathy's Clown" also signaled the brothers' emergence as songwriters, a talent they underlined in 1959 when they had a top-10 hit with their composition "Til I Kissed You." Their names continued to appear regularly at the top of the hit lists at the end of the 1950s and start of the 1960s, some of the releases material previously recorded on Cadence and some on Warner Bros. Their top-20 hits included, on Cadence, "Problems" in 1958; "Take a Message to Mary" in 1959; and "Let It Be Me" and "When Will I Be Loved" in 1960. On Warner Bros. their successes included "So Sad" in 1960; "Ebony Eyes," "Don't Blame Me," and "Walk Right Back" in 1961; and "Crying in the Rain" and "That's Old Fashioned" in 1962.

During those years, the duo also turned out a series of LPs, most of which made top-chart levels. On Cadence, their retrospective *Best of the Everly Bros.* was a bestseller. Their early 1960s albums on Warner Bros. included *It's Everly Time, Date with the Everly Brothers, Top Vocal Duet, Instant Party, Golden Hits,* and *Great Country Hits.*

The brothers moved to Los Angeles in the early 1960s, but their career slowed down soon after, partly because Don enlisted in the Marine Corps. While he was away in the mid-1960s, the Everlys still were represented in the music field by a series of LPs issued by

Warner Bros. Among them were *Rock 'n' Soul* (5/65), *Gone, Gone, Gone* (3/65), *Beat 'n' Soul* (10/65), *In Our Image* (5/66), *Hit Sound* (4/67), and *Everly Brothers Sing* (9/67).

The brothers began working together again in the late 1960s. They were guests on many shows, including the *Johnny Cash* show and *Glen Campbell Goodtime Hour,* and made a number of appearances on *The Smothers Brothers Comedy Hour.* Concert and club audiences welcomed them in many cities, although they were unable to regain the massive following that had been theirs a decade earlier. In both TV and live work, they demonstrated greater self-assurance and polish than ever before, showing a gift for comic repartee not evident in the past. Eventually they were invited to host their own CBS-TV summer replacement series in 1970.

Their albums sold well enough for companies to keep issuing new ones, though sales did not approach gold-record levels any more. Among their releases of the early 1970s were *Everly Brothers Greatest Hits* on Epic Records; *The Everly Brothers Show* on Warner Bros.; *Chained to a Memory* (Harmony Records, 5/70); and *End of an Era* (two discs, Barnaby Records, 5/71). In 1971, the Everlys' agreement with Warners ended and they signed with RCA. Their first RCA LP, *26,* was well received critically, but did not catch on with the public. The same held true for their *Stories We Could Tell* LP.

But the brothers retained a strong following, as indicated by the fact that they still could fill medium-size concert halls and pop and country clubs all over the world. However, there were increasing strains on the team—differences of opinion on creative directions and rising unhappiness about continuing to follow a well-trodden path. This feeling was indicated, for example, in Don Everly's early 1970s composition, "I'm Tired of Singing My Song in Las Vegas." Phil also showed a desire to go his own way by recording a solo album on RCA in 1973.

The brothers finally announced they were breaking up in mid-1973, announcing they would give their final concert together at Knott's Berry Farm's John Wayne Theater, Buena Park, California, on Saturday, July 14, 1973. As Don said at the time, "It's over. I've quit. I've been wanting to quit for three years now and it is finally time to just do it. I'm tired of being an Everly Brother. I still like to sing 'Bye Bye Love' sometimes, but I don't want to spend my life doing it. I've got to find something else." Later, he added, "The Everly Brothers died ten years ago."

Phil, who had stormed out of the first of three final shows that night, leaving Don to do the last two alone, noted in early 1974 that the decision to end the duo was his brother's, but it probably was inevitable. "It was simply a case of growing in different directions—musically, philosophically, politically—and add to that the normal, all-American brother-to-brother relationship,

compound that by being together almost constantly for fifteen years and you have a general idea of what went on. . . . There is some bitterness, yes. We do not see each other—but then you can't really say that we're on bad terms. That would seem to be a contradiction, but it's the only way to describe our relationship today."

Phil was the first to strike off on a new tack. In early 1974 he inaugurated a syndicated rock program called *In Session,* a combination talk and music program that he hosted. He also began touring as a solo artist, playing many major country music clubs, and was still doing so at the start of the 1980s. In mid-1975, one of his compositions, "When Will I Be Loved," provided a best-selling single for Linda Ronstadt. Other songs he wrote or cowrote showed up on the charts now and then, including one called "Better than Now" (cowritten with T. Slater) issued as a single by Dewayne Orender at the end of 1978. Phil continued to turn out new recordings of his own, including the 1979 LP *Living Alone.* In late 1980 and early 1981, his single of his composition "Dare to Dream Again" (issued on CBS/Curb Records) was on the country charts.

Don also continued doing stage shows and records from mid-1973 on, though with less intensity than Phil. Much of his activity took the form of behind-the-scenes work. As with Phil, he was represented on the hit charts from time to time with other artists' recordings of his songs. Among those were Connie Smith's chart-making singles of "Til I Kissed You" and "So Sad (To Watch Good Love Go Bad)" in 1976 and a new version of the latter made by Steve Wariner in mid-1978. In 1976, Don had the single "Yesterday Just Passed My Way Again" (on Hickory Records) on the country charts for a number of months.

The Everlys, who got back together in the 1980s, ended the decade with a recording project with Johnny Cash and Rosanne Cash that won a 1989 Country Music Association nomination for Vocal Event of the Year. In the 1990s, the brothers continued to perform at various venues around the U.S. and abroad but had no new chart-making record releases. Essentially all their recordings from their halcyon years were available in the mid-1990s on a series of releases by Rhino Records. As of 1995 those included reissues of their first two albums, *The Everly Brothers* (including a bonus track, "Poor Jenny") and *Songs Our Daddy Taught Us* plus such others as *The Best of the Everly Brothers* and *The Everly Brothers: Cadence Classics—Their 20 Greatest Hits.* Besides those, Rhino also offered *The Fabulous Style of the Everly Brothers,* which included, Rhino stated, "every Cadence era track not found on their first two albums" and *The Everly Brothers: All They Had to Do Was Dream,* which comprised a collection of previously unreleased alternate "and often drastically different" versions.

The brothers continued to appear in concerts through the mid-1990s and occasionally were featured on TV programs. In the spring of 1996, the Nashville Network presented *The Life and Times of the Everly Brothers,* part of TNN's documentary series about great names in country music history. The nominating committee of the National Academy of Recording Arts & Sciences voted to present the brothers with the organization's Lifetime Achievement Award during the February 1997 Grammy awards telecast.

$$\mathcal{F}$$

FARGO, DONNA: *Singer, guitarist, songwriter. Born Mt. Airy, North Carolina, November 10, 1949.*

It seemed ironic for a woman who became famous through a song titled "The Happiest Girl in the Whole U.S.A." and who seemed to personify that description for much of the 1970s to suddenly come face to face with crippling disease while she was still youthful and vigorous. But Donna Fargo faced up to multiple sclerosis in the late 1970s and learned to cope with it and carry on in the entertainment field with good grace.

It was a field she hadn't really thought of entering until well into her twenties. As a child growing up in Mt. Airy, North Carolina, she had sung some solos in the Baptist church her family attended, but that didn't suggest any career goals. Instead, after completing high school, she enrolled at High Point College, where she completed work on her teaching credentials. After graduation, she went to California, where she got a job as an English teacher.

The turning point in her life came when she met a man named Stan Silver, who was a musician and a hopeful music-industry executive. Stan, later to become her record producer and her husband, taught her to play guitar and, when Donna began composing her own songs, critiqued them as well as encouraged her to keep writing. While still teaching in high school, Fargo started performing as a country artist in local California clubs on weekends and during holidays. The response was usually quite favorable; eventually she decided to go into music full time, with the advice and assistance of Stan Silver.

She didn't become a star overnight. Indeed, she spent several years working in small clubs and perfecting her writing skills. She said later, "I wasn't ready for success and fate saw to it I didn't get the success right away. For that I'm actually glad."

In the early 1970s, she made a series of demonstration records, which finally caught the attention of Dot Records executives. Now success was almost overnight. Her 1972 single "The Happiest Girl in the U.S.A." was a smash, rising to number one on country charts and crossing over to become a pop hit too. Eventually the single went platinum and won a host of awards for her:

Academy of Country Music Award for Single Record of the Year, a Grammy for Best Country Vocal Performance, Female, and the Robert J. Burton Award from BMI for Most Performed Song of the Year (1972 and 1973).

She quickly proved it wasn't a fluke with a string of singles that rose to the top of the country charts: "Funny Face," "Superman," and "You Were Always There," with "Little Girl Gone" reaching the number-two slot.

After a few years of recording on the Dot label, Donna switched to Warner Brothers. Her first album for Warners, *On the Move* (issued in the spring of 1976), featured her hit song "It Do Feel Good" as well as other original compositions like "Sing for My Supper" and "Song with No Music" and an assortment of songs by other writers. Commenting on her writing approach at the time, she said, "I try to write all the time. I can never tell when an idea will strike me. When I have an album to do, though, I usually discipline myself. I lock myself in a room at home and start composing. I don't come out until I've got a handful of new songs. Most of the original songs for *On the Move* I've written over the last six months. 'Sing for My Supper' was co-written about two years ago, but I wrote new lyrics to it recently. I do that often: rewrite older songs. It's not that hard for me to write, but I'm kind of a perfectionist. I do think my songs convey a pretty consistent attitude."

Having established herself as a fine country artist when singing her own compositions (in "traditional" country style based on the twangy, relatively unpolished nature of her voice), she began to make hits out of other writers' songs. Her remake of the old standard "Mockingbird Hill," released in 1977, made it onto the top 10 on the country charts. Later that year, "Shame on Me," from the album of the same name, also entered the top 10. (The LP *Shame on Me* followed her second Warner Brothers LP, *Fargo Country,* issued in early 1977.) Donna also had a major hit in 1977 with an original composition, "That Was Yesterday." The song was entirely spoken, rather than sung, and it dealt with the conflicting emotions involved in daydreaming about a past love, a kind of "almost love" that never blossomed. During 1978, Fairchild had top country chart hits with "Do I Love You (Yes in Every Way)" and "Another Goodbye," both written by others.

In early 1978, everything seemed to be going extremely well for her. Her career was flourishing in every way. She was being featured on almost every major TV country variety show and some general talk/variety programs as well. In the mid-1970s she hosted her own syndicated TV variety show for several years. Her extensive tours and nightclub engagements (including an engagement in Las Vegas with Charlie Rich) won good audience response. But in the summer of 1978 she didn't feel quite right. She checked into a hospital in Santa Barbara, California, for a checkup. The tests showed her to have multiple sclerosis, a progressive, degenerative disease of the nervous system. Among possible symptoms are numbness, loss of coordination, pain-filled spasms, and paralysis.

She was despondent about the future for a time, then turned to religion for help. She said, "I always believed in God and went to church as a little girl, which I think is reflected in some of my songs. But I've gotten much more serious about it now. It's been a kind of gradual growth for me the past few years, though I certainly don't have it perfected yet. But I came to the realization through this disease that you eventually come to the end of yourself. You realize how helpless you are by yourself, that there has to be something in life bigger than you are. Now I read the Bible and I listen to faith-building tapes, especially tapes by Kenneth Hagin, a minister in Tulsa. I've found a lot of comfort in the reading and the tapes—in fact, they probably have saved my life." Later, after she resumed her career, she signed with MCA Records' Songbird label to record some religiously oriented albums.

After resting for some months, Donna felt ready to pick up the threads of her life. She was determined to follow her doctors' orders as much as possible, observing carefully regulated diet plans, finding out as much as she could about M.S. and its causes, and taking time for exercises to keep her body in as good condition as possible. With husband Stan she planned touring and TV schedules that would provide good audience exposure but without one-nighters requiring long bus rides between engagements.

Her recordings continued to show up on country lists, with 1979 providing such best-selling singles as "Somebody Special" and "Daddy." Her LP *Dark Eyed Lady*, on the charts the latter part of 1978, remained on them into 1979. In 1980 she made the lists with singles like "Walk on By" and "Seeing Is Believing." In the fall of 1981 her single "Jacamo" was moving up the charts.

FENDER, FREDDY: *Singer, guitarist. Born San Benito, Texas, June 4, 1937.*

"My real name is Baldemar G. Huerta. I was born in the south Texas valley border town of San Benito. I'm a Mexican-American, better yet, a Tex-Mex. I just picked my stage name, Freddy Fender, in the late fifties as a name that would help my music sell better with 'gringos.' Now I like the name.

"Music was part of me, even in my early childhood. I can still remember sitting on the street corner facing Pancho Dalvin's grocery store, plunking at my three-string guitar. It didn't have a back on it, but it sure sounded pretty good to me. Music kept a lot of us happy, even when it was hard for our mama to put beans on the table. We began migrating up north as farm workers when I was about ten. We worked beets in Michigan, pickles in Ohio, baled hay and picked tomatoes in Indiana. When that was over came cotton picking time in Arkansas. All we really had to look forward

to was making enough money to have a good Christmas in the 'valley,' where somehow I'd always manage to get my mother to buy me a guitar if the old one was worn out.

"When I was sixteen, I dropped out of high school and joined the Marines for three years. I got to see California, Japan, and Okinawa; but mainly I got my point of view from the time I spent in the brig. It seemed that I just couldn't adjust myself to such a disciplined way of life. I always liked to play the guitar in the barracks and to drink, so much so that sometimes I forgot where or who I was."

Thus the early saga of Freddy Fender in his own words. He wasn't much different from many other Chicano youngsters growing up in the difficult environment of the Anglo-Saxon–dominated United States. But there was opportunity for those with unusual talents. In Freddy's case, it took almost twenty years before he achieved stardom.

He had chosen music for a career when he returned home from the service in the 1950s. He played local beer joints and dances and began making a name for himself in the Mexican-American community with a series of all-Spanish discs that were top sellers in Texas and nearby Mexican regions. It was obvious to him, though, that the road to major success lay elsewhere, and he began to cut some Tex-Mex rockabilly songs. In 1959, this paid off with two songs, "Holy One" and "Wasted Days and Wasted Nights," which found an audience far beyond Texas borders and suggested that Freddy might be on the path to national acclaim. In 1960, he had another hit, "Crazy, Crazy Baby," but his hopes turned to ashes on May 13, 1960.

"I was busted for grass in Baton Rouge, Louisiana. I'm not bitter, but if friends ask, I still say that the three years I had to spend in Angola State Prison were a long time for a little mistake." He was released in July 1963 but found it wasn't possible to pick up where he'd left off. He got gigs, sang for most of the 1960s (to 1968) at Papa Joe's on Bourbon Street, in New Orleans, but he couldn't get his recording career back in gear. "I played music there with such cats as Joe Berry, Joey Long, Skip Easterling, and Aaron Neville."

In 1969, he went home to the San Benito Valley feeling it might be time to look elsewhere for his main vocation. He got a job as a mechanic "and played music on weekends, getting a dollar sixty an hour and twenty-eight dollars a night picking." He picked up his education again, taking the examination for a high school diploma, then taking college courses as a sociology major for two years.

In 1974, some musician friends suggested he contact producer Huey Meaux, who had a label in Houston called Crazy Cajun. His audition for Huey clicked and they cut a country song called "Before the Next Teardrop Falls." It became a local hit, and Dot Records, a subsidiary of ABC Records, bought national rights.

The song became a gold-record single, crossing over from country to pop charts in 1975, and Freddy's debut album of the same title did likewise. Before the year was over, Freddy had two more chart hits, the single "Secret Love" (a country remake of an old Doris Day vehicle) and his second album, *Are You Ready for Freddy.*

After all those years of obscurity, Fender was a national celebrity, starring on TV variety shows and singing one of the songs on the *Grand Ole Opry* stage during the Country Music Association awards telecast. In early 1976, at the Grammy Awards, Freddy received a nomination for Best Country Vocal Performance, Male, and "Before the Next Teardrop Falls" (written by Vivian Keith and Ben Peters) was nominated for Best Country Song.

Freddy remained a featured country artist for most of the years after that, though without the equivalent of the blockbuster year he had in 1975. His country following remained strong, as demonstrated by his appearance on hit charts regularly, including such top-10 singles as "You'll Lose a Good Thing" and "Living It Down" in 1976; "If You Don't Love Me (Why Don't You Leave Me Alone)" and "The Roses Came/Sugar Coated Love" in 1977 and "I'm Leaving It All Up to You" in 1978. Freddy's albums on ABC were *Freddy Fender, Before the Next Teardrop Falls, Are You Ready for Freddy, Rock 'n' Country, Since I Met You Baby, If You're Ever in Texas, Your Cheatin' Heart, If You Don't Love Me, The Best of Freddy Fender, Swamp-Gold,* and *Tex-Mex.*

In 1979, Freddy began recording for Huey Meaux's new record label, Starflite, distributed by Epic Records. His debut LP on Starflite, *Texas Balladeer,* was issued in June 1979. During 1980, he had such Starflite singles as "My Special Prayer" and "Please Talk to My Heart" on country hit lists.

Starting in the late 1970s, he also became interested in acting and screenwriting. His acting credits during those years included playing the role of General Pancho Villa in *She Came to the Valley* and a part in a show titled *Tijuana Donkey.*

Summing up the way things turned out overall, he said, "I always said the Old Man upstairs was shooting craps for me. Well, he finally rolled a seven."

By the early 1980s, however, Freddy's career was foundering as he increasingly fell prey to substance abuse. Things got progressively worse until his wife got a court order in 1985 to commit him to a treatment center. The treatment seemed to take hold, but trying to pick up the pieces of his performing life wasn't easy. He told the *Springfield* (Missouri) *News-Leader,* May 1989, "For the past three and a half years I've been hellbent . . . trying to catch up after ten years of drugs and alcohol."

By mid-1989, his first recording in eight years, "Spanish Harlem," was released and he also got the chance to play a role in a new NBC-TV miniseries, *Desperado.* A more significant step during the year,

though, was a new alignment with three other first-rank artists, Doug Sahm, Flaco Jimenez, and Augie Meyers, in a group called the Texas Tornados. The foursome completed the album *Texas Tornados* on Reprise Records, which proved one of the finest country music debuts of 1989.

The album was a chart hit and the track "Soyde San Luis" won the 1990 Grammy Award for Best Mexican/American Performance. The group toured widely the first half of the 1990s and completed several more albums before disbanding in 1994. (*See separate entry.*) The members had all done some solo work even while combining talents in the Tornados, and Freddy was able to transfer big energies performing solo with aplomb until the Tornados reformed in late 1995.

FLATT, LESTER: *Singer, guitarist, band leader (Foggy Mountain Boys, Nashville Grass), songwriter. Born Overton, Tennessee, June 28, 1914; died Nashville, Tennessee, May 11, 1979. Elected to Country Music Hall of Fame (as part of Flatt & Scruggs team) in 1985.*

The split of the long-time duo of Flatt & Scruggs into two separate units in the 1970s didn't bring either man the level of success achieved during their long association. However, both remained major figures in the country-music field, and Flatt continued to receive a warm welcome at concerts and festivals throughout the United States up to his death in 1979.

Tennessee remained his home for his entire life. He started learning the guitar as a boy, following the traditional "old-timey" style then popular in country music. For a long time, however, music was a sideline and Lester earned a livelihood working in textile mills. He steadily improved his guitar skills as the 1930s went by, performing with local groups when the opportunity arose.

Encouraged by friends to widen his horizons, he turned professional in 1939 and soon after made his radio debut on station WDBJ in Roanoke, West Virginia. In the early 1940s, he was increasingly interested in bluegrass-style music, working with many other young musicians who favored that style, including Mac Wiseman. In 1944, he was added to the roster of the most famous bluegrass group in the nation, Bill Monroe's Blue Grass Boys. He remained an important part of that band through the mid-1940s, touring all over the United States and appearing regularly on the *Grand Ole Opry.* In 1945, another talented instrumentalist joined Monroe, a superb banjo player named Earl Scruggs. The stage was set for the emergence of the most famous bluegrass act since the appearance of Monroe's band, a group that helped expand bluegrass from an essentially regional styling to a nationally recognized art form.

Flatt & Scruggs decided to join forces in 1948. In a short time they had a featured segment on Mac Wiseman's *Farm and Fun Time* show on station WCYB, Bristol, Virginia. Their popularity rose rapidly and they went on to star in bigger and bigger locales. They also signed their first recording contract with Mercury Records before the 1940s were over. Though they only stayed with Mercury for a few years, one of the songs they recorded was Earl's "Foggy Mountain Breakdown," one of their trademark hits, which was adopted for the name of their band, the Foggy Mountain Boys. In 1951, they switched from Mercury to Columbia, an association that provided big rewards both to the label and the group, even after the team disbanded in 1969.

During the more than twenty-year lifetime of the team of Flatt & Scruggs, the duo became what amounted to ambassadors of country music to the U.S. mass audience and to the world. Many of the dozens of albums and singles released by Columbia rose to upper levels of both country and pop charts. Among their massive hits were the theme song for *The Beverly Hillbillies,* "The Ballad of Jed Clampett," as well as the themes for *Petticoat Junction* and for the film *Bonnie and Clyde.* In 1953, they became regular members of the *Grand Ole Opry* and still were featured artists on the show when they came to the parting of the ways.

During their long association, both contributed not only important compositions and classic recordings but also innovations in bluegrass style. In Flatt's case, he popularized a guitar approach called the "Flatt Lick." As Lee Rector described it in *Music City News* (October 1973), "It consists of a run on the guitar that comes at the end of most every verse and chorus or however else it can be slipped in and can be adapted to almost every bluegrass song: boom, diddle, dum-di-dum-doom."

The breakup of Flatt & Scruggs was attributed to differences about future musical direction. Scruggs, influenced by his sons, preferred moving toward a blend of country and rock, while Flatt preferred staying with more traditional stylings. The announcement of the separation was made in early 1969, and that March, Flatt announced he would continue to appear at the head of the Foggy Mountain Boys on the *Martha White* TV show. (Martha White Flour was a long-time sponsor of Flatt & Scruggs.) However, objections from Scruggs at the use of that band name led to Flatt's adopting a new name, the Nashville Grass.

For the next decade, Flatt and his group had a regular segment on the *Grand Ole Opry,* which they opened and closed with the "Martha White Theme Song." Ensconced in his large tour bus, Flatt took his band all across the United States to solo concerts and as part of country and bluegrass festivals, typically covering 10,000 miles a month to keep engagements, some booked as much as a year in advance. The program usually included many of the songs made famous by Flatt & Scruggs.

The band lineup in 1973–74 included Charlie Nixon on dobro, Marty Stewart (then only fourteen) on mandolin and flat-top guitar, Johnny Johnson (previously with Ernest Tubb) on bass, Haskell McCormick on five-string banjo, and Paul Warren on fiddle. Warren's association with Flatt went back to the Foggy Mountain Boys band.

Flatt recorded steadily from 1969 to the late 1970s, initially on RCA and later for other labels. Many of his recordings in the early and mid-1970s were joint efforts with his old friend Mac Wiseman, with whom he also appeared on the *Opry* and in many concerts throughout the United States. His RCA LPs included *On Victor* (issued June 1971), *Lester 'n' Mac* (8/71), *Kentucky Ridgerunner* (3/72), and again with Wiseman, *On the South Bound* (8/72).

By the mid-1970s, Flatt could look with joy at a steady revival of interest in bluegrass music among young music fans, which he helped spark with an increasing number of concerts on college campuses. Throughout the 1970s, roughly two thirds of all his in-person appearances were on college campuses.

Lester remained in harness almost up to his last days. His health began to fail, though, when he underwent successful open heart surgery in 1975, then had to return to the hospital the next year for removal of his gallbladder. Stubbornly refusing to give up, he was back heading his band soon after. In November 1977, he again was sidelined by a brain hemorrhage, but rebounded once again to charm *Opry* fans in March 1979. It was a short-lived respite. On April 23 he fell ill once more and entered Baptist Hospital in Nashville, finally dying on Friday, May 11.

Commenting on Flatt's career afterward, Earl Scruggs told an Associated Press reporter, "His record speaks for itself as far as his playing and singing. He's going to be missed for a long time by a lot of people. He just had a talent that people enjoyed. He was blessed with a good following. We had a lot of good memories together."

The previous February, Flatt indicated he had had a fulfilling career. "We should be proud of being able to accomplish what we set out to do. We wanted to be in a field to ourself. We had a sound all our own. There always will be somebody to carry [bluegrass] on. It's been good for us since it started. They've quit playing it on radio and maybe this is good for us. This way, the festivals draw people to hear it." Bluegrass, he was sure, would never die.

After Flatt's death, the team of Flatt & Scruggs was nominated for the Country Music Hall of Fame a number of times before gaining induction in 1985. The recordings of both artists, together and separately, continued to captivate new generations of country and bluegrass fans in the 1980s and 1990s, with their joint work remaining particularly popular abroad.

As of the mid-1990s, an extensive number of Flatt & Scruggs CDs (with cassettes also available for some titles) were available at the Country Music Hall of Fame in Nashville or by mail-order from the Country Music

Foundation catalog. Multi-CD sets were available for two compilations, one titled *Flatt & Scruggs 1948–59* (4 CDs), the other *Flatt & Scruggs 1959–63* (5 CDs). Both bore the German Bear Family Records label. The first set contains all the recordings made by Flatt, Scruggs, and their band for Mercury and Columbia during those years. The second set includes their entire Carnegie Hall concert on one disc, as well as an album of fiddle tunes for square dancers and some songs that previously had only been issued as 45 rpm singles. Bear Family Records also offered a 6 CD boxed set covering Flatt & Scruggs recordings from 1964-1969.

Other Flatt & Scruggs albums available included, on Columbia, *Flatt & Scruggs/Songs of the Famous Carter Family, Lester Flatt & Earl Scruggs/Live at Vanderbilt University,* and *Flatt & Scruggs/Columbia Historic Edition;* on Deluxe, *Flatt & Scruggs/20 Greatest Hits;* on County CCS, *Flatt & Scruggs/Blue Ridge Mountain Home;* on Mercury, *Flatt & Scruggs/The Complete Mercury Sessions;* and, on Rounder, *Flatt & Scruggs/Don't Get Above Your Raisin'* and *Flatt & Scruggs/The Golden Era.* Rounder also offered *Bill Monroe with Lester Flatt and Earl Scruggs: The Original Bluegrass Band.* Also in print in the mid 1990s was the CMF album *Lester Flatt/Bluegrass Festival,* containing twenty live renditions by Flatt and his backing band.

FLYING BURRITO BROTHERS: *Vocal and instrumental group. Personnel as of 1968: Gram Parsons, born Winterhaven, Florida, November 5, 1946, died Joshua Tree, California, September 1973; Chris Hillman, born Los Angeles, California, December 4, 1942; Sneeky Pete Kleinow*, born South Bend, Indiana, circa 1935; Chris Ethridge; Popeye Phillips. Lineup as of late 1969: Parsons, Hillman, Kleinow; Bernie Leadon, born Minneapolis, Minnesota, July 19, circa 1947; Michael Clarke, born New York, New York, June 3, 1944. Sneeky Pete replaced by Al Perkins, 1971; Parsons by Rick Roberts, 1971. Other members during 1971–72 included Byron Berline, Kenny Wertz, and Roger Bush. Members in mid-1970s included Kleinow, Gene Parsons, Skip Batt (born Galipolis, Ohio), and Gib Gilbeau. Reorganized as Burrito Brothers in early 1980s with Gilbeau, Kleinow, and John Beland as core members. In late 1980s also used name Flying Burrito Brothers and Gib Gilbeau and Sneeky Pete.*

In the late 1960s, the idea of blending country with rock won many converts among veteran performers of the decade. However, the idea, which flowered in the mid-1970s with such bands as Asleep at the Wheel, Marshall Tucker Band, and the like, was ahead of its time in the 1960s. Bands that blazed the trail, such as Poco and the Flying Burrito Brothers, found little outlet for their recordings on major radio stations and, while they found an audience of sorts, never gained enough exposure to succeed. After the fact, many of the early recordings of groups like the Burritos have gained the reputation of classics.

The Burritos evolved in California with a strong flavor of the folk-rock pioneers. Two of the original Burritos in late 1967 had been Byrds members: songwriter/guitarist/bass player Chris Hillman and vocalist/songwriter/keyboard player/guitarist Gram Parsons influenced the group's move toward country-rock recordings. Joining them initially were Chris Ethridge (vocals, bass, piano, songwriter), Sneeky Peter Kleinow (pedal steel guitar), and Popeye Phillips (drums). The five members constituted the lineup on such early songs as "Hot Burrito #1" and "Hot Burrito #2," both included on the band's debut album on A&M Records, *The Gilded Palace of Sin.* Two of the LP tracks, "Sin City" and "My Uncle," were excellent examples of songs that, as one critic noted, "bridged the gap between country music and contemporary rock." Also notable from that period were such songs as "Wheels," "Christine's Song," and "Do Right Woman."

Almost from the start, the Burritos personnel kept shifting. A particular problem for a while was drums, when Phillips's spot was taken briefly by such others as Jon Corneal, Sam Goldstein, and Eddie Hoh. The situation was resolved to everyone's satisfaction in 1969 when original Byrds' drummer Michael Clarke, who had worked with a band called Dillard and Clark after leaving the Byrds, agreed to join up. Clarke remained as drummer until the group finally broke up in 1972. Another change in 1969 was the departure of Ethridge, whose place was taken by Bernie Leadon, who had worked with Clarke in Dillard and Clark and then was a backing musician for Linda Ronstadt. Leadon, of course, later was a founding member of the Eagles.

Despite lack of airplay and major concert exposure, the roster of Parsons, Hillman, Leadon, Kleinow, and Clarke did seem to make some progress with the music public during late 1969 and into 1970. The group completed a second LP, *Burrito Deluxe,* and added such songs as "God's Own Singer," "If You Gotta Go" (a Dylan song), "High Fashion Queen," "The Train Song," Merle Haggard's "Sing Me Back Home," John Loudermilk's "Break My Mind," and "Close Up the Honky Tonks." Things seemed to be picking up a little in 1970, when unfortunately Parsons, whose charismatic vocals formed a large part of the appeal at the time, was sidelined by injuries from a motorcycle accident.

The layoff seemed to dampen Parsons's ardor about the band. He returned for a while, then left for good in 1971. His place was taken by Rick Roberts, who had been added to the group in the summer of 1970 after Parsons' accident. Roberts also inherited Parsons's songwriting mantle, providing a number of originals featured by that group in its final phases, such as "Did You

---

*Kleinow's nickname has variously been spelled Sneeky and Sneaky.

See" and several tracks on the band's third album, *The Flying Burrito Brothers*. That album was supposed to include one of the relatively rare compositions by Kleinow, a showcase for his pedal steel talents called "Beat the Heat," but the song was omitted in the final mix. During 1971 and 1972, the band appeared in a series of concerts all over the United States, mostly on college campuses but with some engagements at places like Bill Graham's Fillmore theaters in New York and San Francisco and the Aquarius in Hollywood.

Before 1971 was out, the Burritos had a new pedal steel player, Al Perkins, who took over the seat from Sneeky Pete. Things were becoming increasingly desperate for the band as 1972 began. The group was not without some chart success, but the records that made it never went far enough up the ladder to make the band a household name. Bookings were slim and spirits tended to go down. However, the group reorganized with Perkins handling pedal steel and guitar. (Perkins, a fine musician who could play a number of different instruments, came to the Burritos from a group called Shiloh.) A trio of bluegrass artists from a band called Country Gazette were added: Kenny Wertz (vocals, guitar), Byron Berline (vocals, fiddle), and Roger Bush.

The 1972 edition of the Burritos naturally offered a blend of bluegrass, country, and rock that provided some new luster to its reputation. But that still wasn't enough to save the situation. In mid-1972, the group gave up the ghost. Ironically, there were already strong indications that the potential audience for the Burritos kind of music was increasing. The band's final album, *Last of the Red Hot Burritos*, had made inroads on the national charts.

The band's growing stature after the fact was demonstrated anew in 1974 when A&M issued a two-record set of their work titled *Close Up the Honky Tonks*. Besides containing tracks of many of the band's best-known previous recordings, the album presented many previously unreleased songs (but songs that the band played in live concerts), which, besides the title song, included "Beat the Heat," "Did You See," "Break My Mind," and Burritos versions of the Beatles' "Roll Over Beethoven," the Everlys' "Wake Up Little Susie," the Bee Gees' "To Love Somebody," and Gene Clark's "Here Tonight." That album set sold considerably better than some of the releases made when the band had been functioning.

Perhaps encouraged by that, some of the members of the earlier group brought it back to life in the mid-1970s. One such incarnation included original members Kleinow and Ethridge, ex-Byrd Gene Parsons, and newcomer (to the Burritos) vocalist/songwriter Gib Gilbeau. A contract with Columbia Records led to some new LPs: *Flying Again* and *Airborne* (the latter with another ex-Byrd, Skip Battin, among the band members). The new albums lacked the originality and spark of earlier releases, but the band did find it still had

fans out there during concert tours in the late 1970s. Gilbeau noted, "We found that we were real popular overseas, particularly in Europe and Japan."

Still, the rewards were too meager to justify keeping the band together. Once more, the Burritos were saved in the nick of time. Recalled Gilbeau, "We were about to give up the Flying Burrito Brothers as a group when I met John Beland [vocals, guitar, songwriter] at a Christmas party [in 1979]. We started talking about the group and how I really didn't want to see it fold. Somehow I believed that if it had taken a broader musical direction, or still could, we could keep it alive. John and I decided to get together and do some writing, and when we had put some tunes together, we presented them to the other members. They were agreeable to give our new direction a shot and a demo ensued which got us the deal with Epic/Curb Records."

The core of the 1980s incarnation was Gilbeau, Beland, and the sole remaining original Burrito, Kleinow. Under the new name of the Burrito Brothers, the band had the debut Epic/Curb LP *Hearts on the Line* in release in January 1981. It soon spawned several singles (of songs written by Gilbeau and Beland) that made the country charts: "She's a Friend of a Friend" in early 1981 and "She Belongs to Everyone but Me" in the fall.

Through the 1980s, the band called itself variously the Burrito Brothers or the Flying Burrito Brothers with Gib Gilbeau and Sneeky Pete. The latter was the name used, for instance, when the band was one of the featured acts at the second annual tribute concert in honor of Gram Parsons and Clarence White in September 1987 in Nashville. The group played at other concerts in that series which helped keep evergreen the memory of its most famous founding member.

FOLEY, CLYDE JULIAN "RED": *Singer, guitarist, harmonica player, songwriter, variety show host. Born Blue Lick, Kentucky, June 17, 1910; died Fort Wayne, Indiana, September 19, 1968. Elected to Country Music Hall of Fame in 1968.*

The words on the bronze plaque in the Hall of Fame in Nashville sum up Red Foley's career best: "One of the most versatile and moving performers of all time. He could make you pop your fingers to 'Chattanooga Shoeshine Boy' . . . choke back a tear with 'Old Shep' . . . or look to your God with 'Peace in the Valley.' A giant influence during the formative years of contemporary country music and today a timeless legend."

Indeed, Red Foley left a generous legacy to country-music enthusiasts in the form of the many recordings that are still highly regarded years after his death and still readily adapted by contemporary performers. His achievements as performer and writer bulk large in country music annals; at the time of his election to the Hall of Fame, for instance, he ranked fifth on the all-time list of country recording artists with thirty-one top-10 singles, including five that reached the number-one position.

As a boy in Blue Lick, Kentucky, Foley liked to go off by himself to his favorite blackberry patch and play the old battered guitar that his father bought him when he was six. Later, when his family moved to Berea, his father, who ran the general store, stocked harmonicas, which fascinated young Clyde. All of them were broken in before they were sold.

In high school, Foley excelled in track and basketball, winning several trophies and ribbons, but he felt a singing career was more promising than one in sports. His mother hired a vocal coach, which proved wearing for the boy; he decided to go along singing his own way.

Under the circumstances, his family was surprised when he won a local Atwater-Kent singing contest and was invited to Louisville to compete for state honors. When the seventeen-year-old came out on the "big city" stage to sing the hymn "Hold Thou My Hand, Dear Lord," he developed a case of the butterflies and had to start the song over three times, before he finally made it through. His excellent final treatment and unconscious showmanship so charmed the judges and audience that he won first prize.

In 1932, Foley entered Georgetown College, in Georgetown, Kentucky, where he continued to perform when he got the chance. During his first semester, a talent scout for WLS in Chicago spotted him and signed him for the fledgling *National Barn Dance* program.

In Chicago, Foley became enthralled by the blues and folk music often played on the radio. The thirties was a time when many unknown, talented black artists were flocking to the city and playing exciting new music in the streets and small clubs. Flat-top guitars played Hawaiian style with the neck of a broken bottle, washtub steel bands, the soul sounds of a population on the move—all of these sounds and sensations were absorbed by young Foley. Many of his major successes of future years were to reflect a blending of roots blues and the country and gospel heritage of his childhood.

Red's reputation in the country field developed rapidly in the mid-1930s, as did his ambitions to do bigger and better things in the genre. In 1937, he took a giant step forward when he originated the Renfro Valley radio show with John Lair. Two years later, he was the first country artist to have a network radio show, *Avalon Time,* which costarred comic Red Skelton. Strings of one-nighters, fair dates, theater engagements, and other personal appearances put Foley into gear for later recording success with Decca Records, which eventually signed him to a lifetime contract.

During the 1940s, such singles as "Foggy River" and "Old Shep" helped establish Red as one of the top country names. In 1948, he added the top-10 single "Tennessee Saturday Night" and finished the decade with a banner year in 1949, turning out such top-10

bestsellers as "Blues in My Heart" (co-written by Foley and Carson), "Candy Kisses," "Sunday Down in Tennessee," "Tennessee Border," and "Tennessee Polka." He then roared into the 1950s by dominating the country charts the first year of the new decade with no less than eight top-10 hits, including two number-one releases, "Birmingham Bounce" and "Chattanooga Shoe Shine Boy." The latter, one of his trademark songs thereafter, was recorded in Nashville in Owen Bradley's studios—a converted garage—and contributed to Red's total of 24 million records sold by the end of the 1960s. His other 1950 hit singles were "Choc'late Ice Cream Cone," "Cincinnati Dancing Pig," "Just a Closer Walk with Thee," "M-I-S-S-I-S-S-I-P-P-I," "Our Lady of Fatima," and his composition "Steal Away."

The pace slowed a bit after that, but it was a rare period through the mid-1950s when a Foley release wasn't on hit lists. His 1951 credits include the top-10 singles "Alabama Jubilee," "Hot Rod Race," and "Peace in the Valley." In 1952, he had the number-one hit "Midnight" and a top-10 single, "Too Old to Cut the Mustard," the latter with *Grand Ole Opry* sidekick Ernest Tubb. (Red became a regular on the *Grand Ole Opry* in 1946 and, for a long time in the 1940s and 1950s, hosted the *Opry's Prince Albert* national radio segment.) In 1953, his top-10 successes were "Don't Let the Stars Get in Your Eyes," "Hot Toddy," "No Help Wanted No. 2," and "Shake a Hand." In the mid-1950s, Red teamed with Kitty Wells as a featured duo, resulting in the 1954 top-10 single "One by One." In 1955, Red and Kitty scored with "As Long as I Live" and Red had solo hits with "Hearts of Stone" and "Satisfied Mind." In 1956, he and Kitty had the top-10 hit "You and Me." In the late 1950s, as rock music affected the country field and new performers came to the fore (some given a boost by Red himself on his country radio and TV programs), Red's string of chartbusters came to an end. Some of his releases still showed up on hit lists, but didn't rise to the very top rungs.

For quite some time Red was very active in television. For six years in the 1950s, his *Ozark Mountain Jubilee,* nationally telecast on ABC, was one of the major showcases of country music. Many future stars got their first exposure to large audiences on the Springfield, Missouri-based show. In 1962, Red was costarred with Fess Parker on an ABC-TV series, *Mr. Smith Goes to Washington.*

Throughout the 1960s, Red kept on the go making personal appearances across the United States and Canada. From his home base of Nashville in the 1960s, he handled the packaging of his own show for national distribution.

During his long career, Red recorded dozens of albums besides his extensive singles releases. Among them on Decca were *Red & Ernie Tubbs* (mid-1950s), *Souvenir Album* (mid-1950s), *Red Foley Story, Beyond the Sunset, He Walks with Thee* (10/58), *My Keepsake*

Album (3/59), *Let's All Sing* (4/59), *Let's All Sing to Him* (9/59), *Company's Comin'* (7/61), *Golden Favorites* (4/61), *Songs* (with the Jordanaires, 4/62), *Dear Hearts & Gentle People* (1962), *Red Foley Show* (3/63), *Songs Everybody Knows* (8/65), *Songs for the Soul* (4/67), and, posthumously, *Songs of Devotion.* A number of his LPs came out on Vocalion label, including *I'm Bound for the Kingdom* (6/65), *Red Foley* (11/66), and *Memories* and *I Believe* (with the Anita Kerr Singers, 8/69).

Foley remained a dedicated entertainer to the end of his life, a year after he had been elected to the Country Music Hall of Fame. He passed away of natural causes September 18, 1968, after taking part in two *Grand Ole Opry* shows.

Other members of his family continued the Foley heritage in country music in later years. His daughter Betty already had been a well-known country artist from the early 1950s. A decade after his death, one of his grandchildren, Debby Boone, established herself as a fine singer of both pop and country songs.

In including Foley on its September 1994 list of "The 100 Most Important People in the History of Country," *Life* magazine commented, "Although he was born in Blue Lick, Kentucky, Red's smooth vocal style (often compared to Bing Crosby's) had a citified ring. No matter . . . he was one of the most popular country entertainers of the '40s and '50s." The *Life* editors also stated that Red "was so hot in his time that he is often credited with helping make Nashville into Music City—simply by recording there."

Considering that in the 1950s Foley's name was mentioned in the same breath as artists like Hank Williams, Sr., and Roy Acuff, it is surprising how little of his extensive recorded material remained in print in the 1990s. An exception was the MCA Records' *Red Foley: Country Music Hall of Fame Series,* available from the Country Music Hall of Fame & Museum catalog.

FORD, TENNESSEE ERNIE: *Singer, songwriter, disc jockey, actor, emcee. Born Bristol, Tennessee, February 13, 1919, died Reston, Virginia, October 17, 1991. Elected to Country Music Hall of Fame in 1990.*

The trademark of Ernest Jennings "Tennessee Ernie" Ford was a relaxed air combined with the soothing tones of his deep bass voice. His portrayal made him one of the most popular performers first in country & western and then in the overall popular entertainment market. In the several instances when Ford left top-ranked TV programs to spend more time with his family, he found a national audience waiting to verify his star status on his return to the limelight.

Born and raised in Tennessee, Ernie spent many of his boyhood hours listening to country & western musicians, in person or on the radio. He was particularly interested in radio and, during his high school years in Bristol, spent many hours hanging around the local station. He won his first job as a staff announcer in 1937 at ten dollars a week, and, discovering that he had a first-rate voice, he went on to study at the Cincinnati Conservatory of Music in 1938. Returning to the announcing field in 1939, he worked for stations in Atlanta and Knoxville from 1939 to 1941.

Enlisting in the Air Corps soon after Pearl Harbor, he became a bombardier on heavy bombers and later spent two years as an instructor. Stationed in California, he met and married a girl named Betty Heminger and decided to settle there after the war. He found a job as a DJ on a San Bernardino station after his discharge.

He then moved on to an announcing spot with country & western station KXLA in Pasadena. There he struck up a warm friendship with veteran band leader Cliffie Stone, who had a show on the station. Ernie occasionally joined Cliffie's quartet in a hymn.

After a while, Cliffie asked Ernie to join his Saturday night program and also saw to it that Capitol Records auditioned Ernie. Capitol signed the newcomer and results were fast in coming. In 1949, Tennessee Ernie had two singles in the top-10 country & western charts, "Mule Train" and a song he wrote with Cliffie Stone, "Smokey Mountain Boogie." The following year things were even better, as Ernie recorded such top-10 hits as "Anticipation Blues," "I'll Never Be Free" (duet with Kay Starr), "The Cry of the Wild Goose," and "Shotgun Boogie." The last-named was an Ernie Ford original that remained number one nationally for many weeks.

In short order Ernie became a network radio figure, with his own shows on CBS and ABC from 1950 to 1955. During these years he continued to turn out top-10 hits, including "Mister and Mississippi" (1951); his own composition, "Blackberry Boogie" (1952); "River of No Return" (1954); and "Ballad of Davy Crockett" (1955). In 1955 he recorded a song by his friend Merle Travis that eclipsed anything he had done before, called "Sixteen Tons." This record became number one in both country & western and national polls and made Tennessee Ernie Ford an almost legendary figure. Through 1967, more than 4 million copies of the record had been sold.

By the end of 1955, Ernie was featured on his own daytime show on NBC-TV. This won such enthusiastic audience response that NBC started a new nighttime series in September 1957, starring Ernie. Sponsored by Ford Motor Company, the show was consistently among the top-rated during its five-year existence.

In 1961, Ford left TV to move to northern California and spend more time with his wife and sons on a ranch-style home in Portola Valley, forty-five miles from San Francisco. Ernie also spent much of his time in succeeding years building up his cattle ranch at Eagleville, California.

After a year away from TV, Ernie signed for a new

weekday show with ABC-TV, starting in April 1962. Ernie's personal magic quickly moved it to the top ranks of the polls, where it stayed until his three-year contract was up in 1965. Once again Ernie returned to Portola Valley and vicinity.

Continuing to give selected public appearances, in May 1965 he played to a sellout audience at the new Melodyland Theater near Disneyland. The following year, he signed for four more engagements at in-the-round theaters in the Los Angeles and San Francisco regions.

The pattern remained essentially the same from the late 1960s into the early 1980s. Ernie maintained a relatively low-key schedule, doing occasional club or stage appearances but having no intensive touring operations. He was a guest on many major TV programs during those years, including some work as a presenter or host on some of the awards shows, particularly those of the Country Music Association.

Ernie continued to turn out albums on Capitol Records until the mid-1970s. In 1974, his *25th Anniversary* album came out, a two-record set that later was reissued as two separate albums still in the Capitol catalogue at the end of 1981. His long association with the label came to an end in August 1976 with the release of his LP *For the 83rd Time.* After that, the only new titles on the Capitol lists were reissues of older material. Over the years, his religious albums were particularly well received, exceeding 10 million sales by the start of the 1970s. His only Grammy Award was for a gospel LP (*Great Gospel Songs*), which was named the Best Gospel or Religious Recording of 1964. He received six R.I.A.A. gold-record awards for gospel albums.

Among his album releases from the late 1950s into the early 1970s were *Hymns; Spirituals, Nearer the Cross* (1958); *Gather Round; Friend We Have* (1959); *Sing a Hymn, Sixteen Tons* (1960); *Come to the Fair, Civil War Songs South, Hymns at Home* (1961); *Sing a Hymn with Me, Sing a Spiritual with Me, I Love to Tell the Story, Favorite Hymns* (1962); *This Lusty Land, Tennessee Ernie Ford, We Gather Together, Long, Long Ago* (1963); *Great Gospel Songs, Country Hits* (1964); *World's Best Loved Hymns, Let Me Walk with Thee* (1965); *My Favorite Things, God Lives!, Wonderful Peace* (1966); *Aloha, Faith of Our Fathers* (1967); *Our Garden of Hymns* (1968); *Holy, Holy, Holy* (1969); *America the Beautiful, Everything Is Beautiful, Sweet Hour of Prayer/Let Me Walk with Thee* (two-record set), *Abide with Me,* and *Folk Album* (early 1970s). In the early 1970s, Ernie also was represented on the Pickwick label with the two-record reissue set, *Tennessee Ernie Ford.*

At the start of the 1980s, his LPs still in the active Capitol catalogue included *Spirituals, Hymns, Sweet Hour of Prayer, 25th Anniversary, America the Beautiful, Best of Tennessee Ernie Ford, Book of Favorite Hymns, Country Hits... Feelin' Blue, Great Gospel Songs, Nearer the Cross, Let Me Walk with Thee, Make a Joyful Noise, Precious Memories, Sing His Great Love, Star Carol,* and *Story of Christmas.* On Word Records, he also had the album *He Touched Me.*

In the 1980s, Ford certainly wasn't absent from the entertainment field, but compared to most artists he kept a relatively low profile. In the early 1980s he guested on a number of TV programs hosted by country stars, including Dolly Parton's *Dolly* series and *Barbara Mandrell and the Mandrell Sisters.* He also headlined some of his own TV shows during the 1980s.

He was also featured in several tours during those years. He told an interviewer, "The nicest thing that people say to me now wherever I go is 'I feel that I know you.' That's before they say anything about the show or about my singing." He told an Associated Press reporter in 1990 he also liked the idea of providing a relaxed environment for his TV audiences. He said he wanted viewers to feel "when the time came for my show they didn't have to change clothes or put sterling on the table."

As the years went by, the honors given him increased. In 1984, after the traditional gala performance, he was presented with the Medal of Freedom by President Ronald Reagan. In 1990 he was elected to the Country Music Hall of Fame. When the latter selection was announced during the CMA TV awards show that October, he put his head in his hands to hide the tears. Onstage he gave thanks "to all the pea-pickers who elected me."

In September 1991 he traveled from his home in Northern California to Washington, D.C., to attend a White House state dinner hosted by President George Bush. He was on his way home on September 28 at Dulles International Airport when he was stricken with what proved to be a fatal liver disease. He was rushed to a hospital in Reston, Virginia, where he died a few weeks later.

In the mid-1990s, a number of his albums were available in the Country Music Foundation catalog. These included the Capitol Records albums *Songs of the Civil War* and *All Time Greatest Hymns;* BCD Records' *Sixteen Tons;* Curb Records' *All Time Greatest Hymns;* and, on Rhino Records, *The Best of Tennessee Ernie Ford.*

During his career, he made over eighty albums, which sold many millions of copies. His gospel albums alone accounted for an estimated 25 million copies sold. His most noted career highlights were the gospel collections and his trademark version of "Sixteen Tons." The Merle Travis composition brought Ernie's name before people the world over. He recalled a concert tour of the former Soviet Union in 1974 where the audience didn't know who he was until he sang that song and the people started singing the words along with him.

FORD, WHITEY, "THE DUKE OF PADUCAH":
*Comedian, instrumentalist (banjo, mandolin, harmonica),
emcee. Born DeSoto, Missouri, May 12, 1901; died
Nashville, Tennessee, June 20, 1986. Elected to Country
Music Hall of Fame in 1986.*

"I'm goin' back to the wagon, these shoes are killin'
me!"

If any sentence can be said to be immortal in the
country field, it's this tag line of one of the greatest of
all rustic comedians, The Duke of Paducah. Although
he delighted audiences for decades on network shows
with his humor, his career covered many years as a pioneer musician in the country & western field.

Benjamin Francis "Whitey" Ford was born in Missouri, but when his mother died when he was only a
year old, he was sent to live with his grandmother in
Little Rock, Arkansas. He grew up in Little Rock and
was interested in music, though no more so than any
other boy growing up in an area where singing old
songs and playing the banjo or guitar was common.
With the country's entry into World War I, young Ford
ran away from home to enlist in the Navy in 1918. He
stayed in the service for four years.

While a sailor, he became more interested in music
and perfected his playing on the banjo. When he got out
in 1922, he decided to go into the music field, starting
his own Dixie Land Jazz Band. During the 1920s, he
toured widely with the band and with all kinds of other
organizations, including medicine shows, tab shows,
stage shows, burlesque shows, and dramatic tent shows.
Late in the decade, he teamed with Bob Van in a banjo
act on the national vaudeville circuit.

When vaudeville began to wane, Ford joined one of
the first major country & western bands, Otto Gray's
Oklahoma Cowboys. His experience with Gray led to a
bid from a young up-and-coming radio singer in
Chicago. The singer was Gene Autry, who asked Ford
to join his group on WLS, Chicago, as emcee, comic
(with Frankie Marvin), and banjoist. Once on WLS,
Ford also was one of the first cast members of the new
WLS Show Boat program, which later became the
famed network *WLS Barn Dance*. Ford teamed up with
Bob Van in a banjo duo on the *Show Boat* program.
During these years, he also acquired the nickname "The
Duke of Paducah" while performing on station KWK,
St. Louis, Missouri.

Ford left WLS before the *Barn Dance* went network. The reason was a chance to emcee on a new program called *Plantation Party* over the NBC network.
On the show, Ford was almost a one-man gang. As The
Duke of Paducah, he was the star comic. In addition, he
wrote the entire show and helped work out most of the
details of each performance. For nine years, he delighted audiences across the country with his stand-up
humor and deft handling of a show that featured many
of the top country artists in America. His work on *Plantation Party* started a personal gag library that eventu-

ally totaled over a half million jokes catalogued under
455 different subjects.

The Duke's association with *Plantation Party* came
to an end in 1942, when he left for an overseas trip entertaining the nation's armed forces. After his lengthy
tour, he came back to the United States to find that his
agent had booked him for three guest appearances on
the *Grand Ole Opry*. The audience at Nashville yelled
and thundered their approval, as did the radio listeners
with stacks of mail. The result was a long-term association between the *Opry* and The Duke that lasted for
sixteen years. During these years, he was featured in
personal appearances in major shows and theaters
throughout the United States. He also was often asked
to speak before church groups, college and high school
student groups, and at men's clubs.

At the end of the 1950s, The Duke decided to give
up the weekly routine of a network TV show. However,
he continued to tour, making from 150 to 200 personal
appearances a year. He also appeared on many TV
shows during the 1960s, including the *Opry,* the *Red
Foley Show, Gary Moore, The Jimmy Dean Show,* and
the *Porter Wagoner Show.* He also found time, in 1963,
to make his second movie, *Country Music on Broadway.* His first, some years earlier, was *Country Farm.*

Ford remained active in the entertainment field in
the 1970s, though by the early 1980s he lived in semiretirement. In failing health for several months in the
spring of 1986, he entered Nashville's St. Thomas Hospital in June, where he died on June 20. He was nominated to the Country Music Hall of Fame several times,
including a near miss as a finalist in 1982, before being
voted into the Hall in 1986.

FOSTER, RADNEY: *Singer, guitarist, songwriter.
Born Del Rio, Texas, 1959.*

As of the mid-1990s, Radney Foster really had been
involved in two careers in country music—one as part
of the Foster & Lloyd duo, which seemed on the verge
of wide success in the later 1980s, then a few years later
as a chart-making solo performer. Perhaps a third career could be cited, composing—his work as a songwriter who provided hits for people like T. Graham
Brown, Tanya Tucker, and Holly Dunn. In the 1990s,
his solo career looked as though it would really take off,
but he could remember earlier bright hopes that had
faded.

His years in Nashville had taught him not to take
anything for granted. He told Country Music Association's Teresa George, executive editor of the CMA
Close Up, that the hardest lesson he learned was to accept failures in both his private and his professional life.

"That's tough," he said, "and it's part of growing up.
This is a business that's not very good about making
people grow. It's kinda like high school with a lot of
money, you know. . . . There's this whole machine
that's designed to tell the public that that's what this

really is—a fantasy land, and if you buy that, you'll screw up most of the time. And we're human beings, and you've got to live like a human being like everybody else. And so I think that failure is a hard thing to deal with."

If his father had had his way, Radney would have followed in his footsteps and become a Texas-based lawyer. The family had deep roots in the area, going back four generations. His grandfather had been a cattleman, and while his father became an attorney, he never wandered far from home. But Radney had developed an interest in music in his preteen years, and could play guitar well by the time he finished high school and enrolled in the University of the South in Sewanee, Tennessee. Besides pursuing his college studies, he performed in local clubs when he could. He recalled in an interview that during one club performance a member of the audience approached him and said, "I've got a friend who is a producer in Nashville who really needs to hear your stuff." Radney replied, "Yeah, yeah, everybody knows a producer in Nashville."

Still, it made an impression on him and he went to Nashville to see what would happen if he tried his demo tapes out on people in the industry. There seemed to be enough interest for him to decide to take a year off from school and settle in Music City for awhile. Not too long after that he gained a writing contract with MTM Music Publishing, where in time he became acquainted with another MTM songsmith, Bill Lloyd.

Lloyd, nominally from Bowling Green, Kentucky, was a military child who rarely spent more than a few years in one place. As he told Kelly Gattis of *Close Up*, "At thirteen and fourteen your hormones start to rage and you have all these wild thoughts. That's when I started writing." He also took up guitar and became adept before he was out of his teens. He thought of music as a sideline activity when he matriculated at Western Kentucky University as a communications major, but it increasingly became his favorite occupation and, only half a year from getting a degree, he left school to try to make his fortune as a musician and/or songwriter.

In 1982 he moved to Nashville where in the mid-1980s he signed with MTM and soon joined forces with Foster. Before they teamed up, he had recorded a solo album for Throbbing Lobster Records in early 1987 called *Feeling the Elephant*. By then, Lloyd's reputation as an above-average guitarist had also made him a popular session musician.

The twosome started by writing songs together, which led to preparation of demo tapes that gained a hearing from record company executives and, in rapid succession, the chance to make their debut album in 1987. The initial single from the album, "Crazy Over You," soared to number one in both *Radio & Records* and *The Gavin Report* while also making the top 5 in *Billboard*. This was followed by two more singles hits in 1988, "Sure Things" and "Texas in the 1880s." They

made their first video for the latter song, which also scored well with the public.

During that period, the partners also could point to songwriting achievements for others. Their collaboration on "Since I Found You" proved a best-seller for Sweethearts of the Rodeo, while Foster helped Holly Dunn pen "Love Someone Like Me," which reached number one on major charts with Lloyd helping out with guitar support on her recording.

Reviewers from *Rolling Stone* to the country music press enthused about the initial Foster & Lloyd releases and, by mid-1988, the duo was in the running for the CMA Horizon Award. But the high hopes for the team faded by the start of the 1990s, and each artist went his own way. In Foster's case, he went back to stressing his songwriting skills while also picking up work as a guest act in shows headlined by other performers. In particular, he credited time spent opening for Mary-Chapin Carpenter with an increasing subtlety in his writing style.

He told Teresa George, "When I spent a year and a half out on the road after leaving Foster & Lloyd with just me and my acoustic guitar, most of the gigs I opened were for her. I rode the bus with her and her band for I'd say ninety percent of those gigs. . . . We've written three or four songs together. None of them have ever surfaced anywhere, but they're pretty good songs."

Foster kept looking for a new solo recording alignment, and Tim DuBois of Arista finally brought him on board. In 1992, his label debut, *Del Rio, Texas, 1958*, came out in the fall of 1992; and was on the *Billboard* list from last 1992 well into 1993. The album yielded a string of chart hits, including "Just Call Me Lonesome," which peaked at number eight in *Radio & Records* the week of November 6, 1992; "Hammer and Nails"; "Nobody Wins" (cowritten by Foster and K. Richey) which peaked at number two in *R&R* the week of April 9, 1993, and reached upper levels in *Billboard;* "Easier Said Than Done" (written by Foster) which peaked at number fifteen in *R&R* the week of August 20, 1993; and "Closing Time" (cowritten by Foster and M. Sager), which reached upper-chart levels in the spring of 1994. Late in 1994, Radney started what he hoped would be a new string of successes with the single "The Running Kind."

He indicated to *Close Up* in May 1994 that he hoped to pass on to his then-one-year-old son "faith and a sense of self-worth" without any preconceived notions of what the boy might do as a career. He recalled his father's hopes of his taking up law, but noted, "I would have made a lousy lawyer. . . . If I had wanted to make a living I'd'a moved back home to Del Rio. . . . But I didn't come here to do that. I came here to dream."

In the summer of 1995, his Arista single, "Willin' to Walk" was on the charts. It wasn't a top chart success, however and, by 1995, he was working on a new album for the Polygram label. During the summer of 1996, the Foster & Lloyd team reunited for a concert series.

FOXWORTHY, JEFF: *Comic, actor, author. Born Hapeville, Georgia, September 6, 1958.*

Historically, down-home humor has been an integral part of country music, whether in the stand-up antics of artists like Minnie Pearl or Jerry Clower or the musical satire of groups like Homer and Jethro or the Geezinslaw Brothers. For a time in the 1980s and 1990s, there seemed to be a dearth of new faces fulfilling this role, but then Jeff Foxworthy came along to add his own twist to the genre.

There weren't any major indications in his formative years that he would become a successful comedy performer. Growing up in Hapeville, a suburb of Atlanta, Georgia, in comfortable surroundings, he was more interested in technology than entertainment. He entered Georgia Institute of Technology in the mid-1970s and graduated with an engineering degree in 1979, after which he was hired as a computer engineer by IBM. But friends and fellow workers enjoyed his sense of humor, and after a while he began to think about trying to earn a living from making people laugh. In 1984, he quit his regular job and began to ply his comedic trade, first in small clubs and in a surprisingly short time in large venues, sometimes opening for major country acts.

Before long he was performing some 500 shows a year (including multiple sets on many evenings) with "redneck" humor being one of the mainstays of each appearance. He defined a redneck "as anyone with a glorious lack of sophistication. It doesn't matter where you live or how much money you make." He developed an endless series of one-liners defining what made someone a redneck. For example, he suggested, you might be a redneck if . . . "you've ever been too drunk to fish" or "you see a sign that says 'say no to crack' and it reminds you to pull your jeans up" or "you wear a dress that's strapless with a bra that isn't."

By 1990, he felt he was ready for bigger things, and he and wife, Peggy Gregg, moved from Georgia to the Los Angeles area, eventually settling in Beverly Hills. Two months after arriving, Jeff made his debut appearance on the *Tonight Show*, the first of eleven such spots through mid-1995. During that period he also starred in two *Showtime* specials and was nominated for two Cable ACE awards. However, he was unhappy that his efforts to expand his TV activities into more regular channels or to work his way into the movies met with rebuffs.

Just about when he and Peggy had decided to leave the Los Angeles area and return to Atlanta (where they bought a five-acre piece of land), ABC-TV gave him the green light for a sitcom called *The Jeff Foxworthy Show*. As he told Jon Matsumoto for an article in the *Los Angeles Times* ("You Might Be a TV Star If . . . ," Calendar section, December 23, 1995), "I was playing nine-thousand seaters and selling them out by myself. Yet people in Hollywood would tell me, 'You're not cool and you're not on the cutting edge.' I was like, 'Between New York and L.A. there are two hundred million people who aren't hip and they aren't cool and they don't want to be. This is who this show is for.'"

Those negative reactions changed abruptly when Foxworthy's mid-1990s albums on Warner Bros. became phenomenal successes, attracting country and non-country fans alike. The recording pact was one of the positive results of the Foxworthys' West Coast odyssey. Issued in early 1994, Jeff's Warners' debut album, *You Might Be a Redneck If . . .* rose to number three on the hit charts during the year and was still in the top 10 in the spring of 1995, by which time it had gone well past R.I.A.A. platinum requirements. During 1995, it also provided Jeff with a hit country single, "Redneck Stomp." Warner Bros. noted that Jeff became one of only two artists (The Jerky Boys were the other) to sell over a million copies of a spoken word album since Eddie Murphy in 1984. On July 18, 1995, his second Warners album, *Games Rednecks Play*, was released and went platinum in five weeks' time. Among the album's contents was his comment about his home state of Georgia hosting the Olympic Games in 1996, "Ain't no way we're gonna have a flame that big without a pig in it." He also joined with the group Little Texas in preparing a music video of the number "Party All Night."

Besides that, Foxworthy continued other activities, including writing. By the end of 1995 he had completed seven comedy books, and signed to pen his autobiography for publication during 1996. His ABC sitcom, which premiered in September 1995, didn't immediately gain top ratings, but it did well enough to be picked up for another season; in 1996 it moved from ABC to NBC.

He told Matsumoto he tried to keep everything in perspective. "I'm not so stupid to think that it's going to last forever, any of it. It's important to take it all in and smell it a little bit, so when it goes away you can remember what it felt like. Sometimes it's hard to do because once you get on a roll, once you get hot, it's almost like a blur."

Jeff maintained that he enjoyed his newfound celebrity, and didn't have the feeling of insecurity attributed to many jokesters. He told *People*, "I'm not one of those comedians laughing on the outside and crying in the middle. I'm laughing inside and out."

In the fall of 1996 he could smile again at the success of his album *Crank It Up*, in the *Billboard* top 3 the end of September.

FRAZIER, DALLAS: *Singer, guitarist, trumpeter, songwriter. Born Spiro, Oklahoma. October 27, 1939.*

Among his country-music peers, Dallas Frazier was known to be an extremely important force in the field. His name has shown up time and time again on the hit charts, but mainly in fine print. Though he is a polished singer and instrumentalist, his most important contributions have been behind the scenes as one of the top country songwriters of the 1960s and 1970s.

Dallas was born in Oklahoma but raised in a farming area near Bakersfield, California, then as now a hotbed of country-music activity. By the time Dallas was twelve he had learned to play several instruments. When he took first place in a talent concert sponsored by Ferlin Husky, Husky quickly offered the youngster a job with his touring troupe, traveling all over the United States. Ferlin brought Frazier's talents to the attention of Capitol Records and the company gave Dallas a recording contract.

Cliffie Stone, then heading the country operations at Capitol, was impressed with Frazier and soon brought him in as a regular cast member of his TV show, *Hometown Jamboree*. Frazier soon became a favorite with Los Angeles audiences, taking part in the show as a soloist and often teaming up to do duets with another young star of the *Jamboree*, Molly Bee. By this time Frazier was writing music steadily. He was still in his teens when he turned out his first smash hit, the novelty song "Alley Oop." The latter made the top 10 on the pop charts and also showed up on country lists during 1957. It has since been revived successfully several times by various pop and rock artists.

After Cliffie disbanded his show in the late 1950s, Dallas moved to Nashville. There he continued to work as a performer on radio and TV while steadily expanding his song output. Other artists gradually began to incorporate some of his compositions into their repertoires, though it took a while before Dallas really hit pay dirt. His first true banner year as a songwriter was 1966, when he provided three of the year's best-selling songs: Jack Greene's version of "There Goes My Everything" rose to number one on national country charts, while Connie Smith had a top-10 hit with "Ain't Had No Lovin'" and George Jones did likewise with "I'm a People." In 1967, George Jones made the top 10 with Dallas' "I Can't Get There from Here," and in 1968, Dallas' top-10 successes included George's single of "Say It's Not You" and Connie Smith's release of "Run Away Little Tears." Some of Frazier's other songs recorded by major artists in the 1960s were "Georgia," "Elvira," "Hawg Jaw," "Soakin' Up the Suds," and "Timber I'm Fallin'." By the end of the 1960s, Frazier had written over 300 songs.

He kept adding to his total throughout the 1970s. Among his chartmakers in 1974, for instance, were "Baptism of Jesse," cowritten with Sanger Shafer and recorded by Johnny Russell, "Ain't Love a Good Thing," a top-10 hit for Connie Smith, and "Freckles and Polliwag Days," cowritten with D. Owens and a success for Dallas' old mentor, Ferlin Husky. The following year proved another fine one for Dallas, starting off with charted singles such as "The Way I Lose My Mind" (cowritten with S.D. Shafer), recorded by Carl

Smith; "Champagne Ladies, and Blue Ribbon Babies" (cowritten with A. L. "Doodle" Owens), a moderate hit for Ferlin Husky; and "Then Who Am I" (cowritten with D. Owens), a number-one hit for Charley Pride. Later in the year, Dallas' name showed up in the writing credits for "The Fiddlin' of Jacques Pierre Bordeaux" (written with A. L. Owens), released by Frenchie Burke, and "Big Mable Murphy," recorded by Sue Thompson. In 1976, Frazier's charted songs included Roy Head's version of "The Door I Used to Close" (written with E. Montgomery) and Leon Rausch's recording of "That's the Trip I've Been On" (cowritten with S. D. Shafer).

In the early 1980s, Frazier's list of credits continued to grow. Gene Watson had a top-10 hit with "14 Karat Mind" (cowritten by Frazier and L. Lee) as one example. One of the best singles of 1980 was Emmylou Harris' version of his "Beneath Still Waters." In the spring of 1981, the Oak Ridge Boys made a new recording of one of Dallas' old compositions, "Elvira," and gained a number-one record on country charts as well as placing the single on pop charts.

During the 1970s, though Dallas did some concert and TV work, his main emphasis was on songwriting. In the early part of the decade, he was represented by a series of solo recordings on RCA Records, such as the LPs *Singing My Songs* (issued 7/70) and *My Baby Packed* (9/71). During the 1970s, more than a few artists released albums in which only songs written by Frazier were included.

FRICKE, JANIE: *Singer, guitarist. Born South Whitney, Indiana, December 18, 1950.*

For a time, Janie Fricke could have claimed the title of "Queen of the Country Session Singers." She backed so many major artists during one period in the mid-1970s it sometimes seemed that every other single released in the country field had her voice somewhere in the background. Between that and singing jingles for commercials and radio station announcements, she did so well financially that she hesitated to give it up in favor of a solo singing career. Fortunately for country fans, she decided to give up her anonymity, soon becoming one of the brightest new stars in the country music firmament in the late 1970s.

Janie was born into an Indiana farm family and grew up on her father's 400-acre farm near South Whitney. Her mother was a piano teacher who also played the organ. Janie recalled, "By the time I was eight years old I would sing while mama played the organ." Some of her early singing experience came from singing hymns solo or in duets with her older sister in the church the family attended. However, she said, "I would never sing hymns the straight way. I'd always kinda jazz them up or sing them in a folk style."

Janie was interested in secular music as well. In high school she liked the folk style of people like Joan

Baez and Judy Collins and the middle-of-the-road rock offerings of Neil Diamond. She sang at school events and local functions, accompanying herself on guitar after her father taught her how to chord when she was fifteen. When she went off to attend the University of Indiana in the late 1960s, she used her musical talents to earn money to help pay college expenses. Between her sophomore and junior years she spent some time in Memphis, Tennessee, where she made as much as $300 a week singing jingles and radio station call letters.

After receiving her degree and a teaching certificate in 1972, she headed for Dallas, where she again did commercial vocals. After a year there, she went to Los Angeles to try to get work as a session vocalist. However, the doors didn't open on the coast, so she returned briefly to Memphis, then continued on, in 1975, to Nashville. It proved a much more receptive environment for her talents than the other stopping places. In a short time she was providing anonymous vocals for commercials for such companies and products as United Airlines, 7Up, Coors Beer, and Pizza Hut. Her schedule of recording sessions also filled up rapidly. During 1976 and 1977, she backed many of the best-known artists in the country field, including Tanya Tucker, Ronnie Milsap, Billy "Crash" Craddock, Lynn Anderson, Mickey Gilley, Tommy Overstreet, Dolly Parton, Zella Lehr, Crystal Gayle, Barbara Mandrell, Donna Fargo, England Dan and John Ford Coley, and Johnny Duncan. With Duncan, she backed three straight number-one singles of 1976–77, "Stranger," "Thinkin' of a Rendezvous," and "It Couldn't Have Been Any Better."

The producer of those smash hits, Columbia vice president and top producer Billy Sherrill, didn't have to be hit with a brick to realize that Fricke had something special to offer creatively. He offered her a contract, an opportunity thousands of hopefuls would give their eyeteeth for, but Janie hesitated. She said, "I had to be coaxed to sign because I didn't want to give up the security of singing jingles and back-up for so many artists. But after a lot of discussion, plus the added incentive of getting to work with Billy Sherrill, I decided to give it a try."

The answer came almost immediately—and it was positive. Her first solo single on Columbia, "What're You Doin' Tonight," made the top 20 in late 1977. At the same time, she had another hit single with Johnny Duncan (this time with her name on the record), "Come a Little Bit Closer." She followed with three more hit solo singles in 1978, "Please Help Me (I'm Falling)," "Baby It's You," and "Playin' Hard to Get" (the last-named on the charts into early 1979). Those four initial solo hits plus "I'll Love Away Your Troubles for Awhile" all were culled from her first two LPs on Columbia, *Singer of Songs* (her debut LP) and *Love Notes*. In addition, in late 1978, she had a number-one hit single with Charlie Rich on Epic, "On My Knees."

Her accomplishments brought widespread recognition from the music industry as well as the public. Both *Billboard* and *Cash Box* magazines voted her the Top New Female Vocalist of 1978. In 1978 and 1979, the members of the Country Music Association nominated her for Female Vocalist of the Year. In 1979, the reader's poll of *Music City News* named her the Best New Vocalist of the Year.

Janie finished up 1979 with the single "But Love Me," from her third album, *From the Heart*, moving up the charts to reach upper levels in early 1980. Another song from the album, "Pass Me By (If You're Only Passing Through)," moved high on the charts in the early summer of 1980. Later in the year, she had a top-15 duet with Johnny Duncan, "He's Out of My Life." At year end, her single "Down to My Last Broken Heart," from her fourth album, *I'll Need Someone to Hold Me When I Cry* (issued October 1980), was on the charts, rising to number one on some lists in Jaunary 1981. In the spring of 1981, the single "Pride" was on the charts and in the fall the title song from album four was in the top 5. In September 1981, her fifth album, *Sleeping With Your Memory*, was released.

Other chart singles of that period included her version of the old Johnny Ray pop hit, "Cry"; "I'll Need Someone to Hold Me (When I Cry)"; "Do Me with Love"; and "Don't Worry 'Bout Me Baby." The last one was her first number one *Billboard* hit.

Starting in the late 1970s, Janie began to accrue a growing list of concert and TV credits. As an opening act, she appeared with stars like Ronnie Milsap, Kenny Rogers, Eddie Rabbitt, Charley Pride, and the Statler Brothers. By special request in the early 1980s, she also performed for President Ronald Reagan and his guest President Lopez Portillo of Mexico at Camp David. Her TV appearances through the early 1980s included *Dinah and Friends, The John Davidson Show, Mike Douglas, Merv Griffin, Dance Fever,* and a Showtime cable TV special, *Women in Music.*

In 1982 she scored another number one *Billboard* single with "It Ain't Easy Bein' Easy" and in early 1983 had the top-5 hit, "Your Heart's Not in It." Her accomplishments were recognized by members of the Country Music Association in 1982, when she was named Female Vocalist of the Year. She repeated the honor in 1983, a year in which she won the same award from the Academy of Country Music and the *Music City News* Awards poll. Her album *It Ain't Easy* was also nominated for the 1982 CMA Album of the Year.

In the mid-1980s she ranked as one of the top headliners on the country concert circuit, while she placed still more songs on the charts. Those included "He's a Heartache (Looking for a Place to Happen)," "Tell Me a Lie," and the top-10 hits "The First Word in Memory Is Me," "She's Single Again," "Somebody Else's Fire," and "Easy to Please." Whether accidentally or on purpose, the spelling of her last name suddenly became

Frickie and it was with that spelling it appeared on the 1986 CMA ballot of nominees for Female Vocalist of the Year. Her 1986 album, *Black and White,* yielded another number-one single, "Always Have Always Will." In 1987, Columbia issued a two-disc Janie Frickie "best of" set called *Celebration (1977–1987).*

Her recording career slowed down as the decade drew to a close. Though she was still active in the 1990s—in the early 1990s she was a regular on the Statler Brothers TV program—her name (again spelled Fricke) no longer appeared on top-chart rungs. During the 1990s, she also became one of the artists performing regularly at Branson, Missouri, which helped provide a new recording arrangement with Intersound Inc.'s Branson Entertainment label. Her first release was the 1993 *Janie Fricke/Now and Then.* In the spring of 1996, she began a new series of appearances in Branson, this time at the Charley Pride Theater.

FRIZZELL, LEFTY (WILLIAM ORVILLE): *Singer, guitarist, songwriter. Born Corsicana, Texas, March 31, 1928; died Nashville, Tennessee, July 19, 1975. Elected to Country Music Hall of Fame in 1982.*

When Lefty Frizzell died, people revered him as one of the grand old men of country music. Yet he was comparatively young, only forty-seven. His image, though, was one of a country-music traditionalist, whose biggest period of success had occurred two decades earlier.

He was only five years old when Jimmie Rodgers, the father of modern country music, died, but his family treasured the Rodgers recordings for years to come. As a boy in Texas, Lefty learned to play the guitar to the tunes of Rodgers and his immediate successors to country royalty, Ernest Tubb and Roy Acuff.

The Frizzell family was very transient. Lefty's father was an oil driller who moved from field to field in and around Texas. When the family was living in El Dorado, Arkansas, in the late 1930s, young William Orville auditioned and gained a featured spot on a children's program on station KELD. He kept up his musical activities as the Frizzells changed locales again and was playing country fairs and local dances by the time home was in Greenville, Texas, in 1943. A few years later, Frizzell was working the bar and club circuit in Waco and Dallas and winning a reputation as one of the better young country singers and pickers around.

Biographical information extant during his lifetime indicated he got his nickname from exploits as a Golden Gloves boxer. Later research determined his nickname actually came from a schoolyard fight in the early 1940s.

In the late 1940s, appearing for the most part in clubs in West Texas and New Mexico, Lefty had decided music would be his role in life. He worked up some demonstration recordings with Dallas agent Jim Beck, who took them to Nashville. Columbia producer

Don Law was impressed and asked Lefty, at the time appearing in clubs in Big Springs, Texas, to come to work on his debut releases on the label.

Those first releases, both written by Frizzell, were "I Love You a Thousand Ways" and "If You Got the Money, Honey, I've Got the Time." Issued as opposite sides of one single, both songs made the country top 10 in 1950. Both, of course, have since been recorded by many other artists as well. In 1951, Lefty achieved a banner year, mostly with songs he either wrote or cowrote. That year, two songs reached number one on country charts: "Always Late" (cowritten with B. Crawford) and "I Want to Be with You Always" (cowritten with J. Beck). Other 1951 top-10 hits were "Look What Thoughts Will Do," "Mom and Dad's Waltz" (both Frizzell compositions), and "Travelin' Blues." The last named was a track on one of Lefty's early album successes, *Songs of Jimmie Rodgers,* which was later reissued on the Harvard label in 1960.

In 1952, Lefty turned out four top-10 songs, "Don't Stay Away," "Forever," "Give Me More, More, More" (cowritten with Ray Price), and "I'm an Old, Old Man." At one point, those four songs provided him with the unusual achievement of having four of the top-10 country singles at the same time. Oddly, none of the four made it to the number-one position.

After 1952, though, things quieted down noticeably for Lefty. Though he recorded many singles that made the national country charts, some of which made the top levels regionally, he didn't have a single top-10 success until the end of the decade. In 1959, he broke the drought with the single (by Wilkin and Dill) "Long Black Veil." Part of the problem of course, was the onset of rock 'n' roll, which had severe repercussions on the country field in the mid- and late-1950s, particularly for artists who objected to changing their styles just to increase commercial appeal.

Frizzell, however, remained a major stage attraction on the country fair and package show circuit not only throughout the 1950s but the 1960s as well. Starting in the early 1950s, Frizzell began making appearances on the *Grand Ole Opry* and was a guest artist on many other country music radio and TV shows. Though a logical candidate for regular cast member of the *Opry,* the fact he chose to make his home on the U.S. West Coast mitigated against that. Some people believed that was one reason Lefty never received his due as a major artist during his lifetime. In 1964, Frizzell reminded the industry of his still strong rapport with the country audience when his single "Saginaw, Michigan" (by Don Wayne) rose to number one nationally, giving him a career total of thirteen top-10 songs and three number-one hits.

Columbia continued to release albums by him into the 1960s. These include *One & Only Lefty Frizzell,* issued October 1959; *Saginaw, Michigan* (5/64); *Sad Side of Love* (12/65); *Greatest Hits* (7/66); *Great Sound*

(10/66); and *Mom and Dad's Waltz* (7/67). In those recordings, as indeed in all his work right up the end, Frizzell maintained the same singing and picking style he always had used. It was a straightforward country approach with lyrical phrasing and delivery that has had considerable influence on new performers over the years.

In 1973, his long, mutually beneficial association with Columbia Records finally came to an end. A short time after, he signed a new recording agreement with ABC Records and went into the studios in Nashville to prepare new material. Before his debut album could come out on ABC, though, he suffered a massive stroke at his Nashville home on July 19, 1975. He was rushed to Memorial Hospital but failed to rally and died at 11:20 P.M. that night.

After Lefty's death, as his stature in country history began to assume legendary proportions, many wondered why his career had never flourished to the extent his talents suggested it should have. Don Law provided some insight in liner notes on an album issued after Frizzell's passing. "In his early years when I knew him best, he was happy-go-lucky and irresponsible. His motto could well have been the title of one of his hit songs—Always Late. He was never on time for a session and sometimes did not show up at all, having fallen by the wayside somewhere."

Law also recalled, "When I first heard about Lefty in that little tavern [the Ace of Clubs] in Big Springs, Texas, he was making forty dollars a week. Within a year or so he was being booked for as much as a thousand dollars a night. This was pretty strong medicine for a young country boy, and his reaction was predictable. He bought expensive cars, an airplane, hired a pilot and generally lived it up. At about this time the vultures started to move in."

As time went by, Frizzell suffered from an increasing drinking problem and a penchant for womanizing. Such distractions certainly didn't help his creative progress.

But artists who were influenced by Lefty's work, and there were more than a few who became major stars, suggested that with a little luck, Lefty could have been a global superstar. Robert Hilburn of the *Los Angeles Times* ("Hail to the Real King," Calendar Section, May 9, 1993) cited Merle Haggard's comments, "Hearing Lefty's voice was a turning point in my life. If Lefty had met Colonel Tom Parker back then, there probably would never have been an Elvis.

"Presley had definitely seen Lefty Frizzell by the time [he] went to Sun Records and met Colonel Parker. The sideburns, the overall look, the nervous energy on-stage—Lefty had all that too. And to my mind, he had a greater voice than Elvis. . . . He delivered every line in a song like Henry Fonda . . . absolutely unbelievable. . . . Every breath was authentic."

Country stars besides Haggard who drew on Frizzell's

legacy in shaping facets of their own careers ranged from veterans like Willie Nelson and George Jones to later arrivals like Garth Brooks and Randy Travis. Two years after Lefty's death, Nelson completed an album of his versions of Lefty's songs called *To Lefty from Willie*. Through the 1980s and into the 1990s some of Lefty's songs showed up on recordings by country, folk, and pop stars, including Haggard, Bob Dylan, John Fogerty, the Band, and John Prine. The Band, for instance, included Frizzell's "The Long Black Veil" in its first album, the 1968 *Music from Big Pink* and, in 1991, Prine sang Frizzell's "I Want to Be with You Always" on his album *The Missing Years*, which won a Grammy Award.

Both Columbia and ABC put out several albums of Lefty's recordings after his death, including the Columbia 1975 memorial collection, *Remembering Lefty Frizzell* and the 1977 ABC *Lefty Frizzell Collection*. As country music found a growing audience overseas, many European record fanciers became interested in Frizzell's work. The German Bear Family label released a boxed set of LPs of some of his repertory. In 1993 the company came out with a new all-inclusive twelve-CD edition called *Lefty Frizzell/Life's Like Poetry* that incorporated all of his Columbia and ABC recordings. Also available in the mid-1990s was Rhino Records' *The Best of Lefty Frizzell*. The last two were offered in the Country Music Foundation 1995 catalog along with the Columbia album *Lefty Frizzell/American Original*. A biography of Lefty published in 1996 won the Ralph J. Gleason Award.

Despite the high regard people like Haggard, Nelson, songwriting great Harlan Howard, and others had for Frizzell's contributions to country music, the unfamiliarity of many younger CMA members delayed his Hall of Fame entry for a number of years. Finally the campaign on his behalf by his industry supporters had its effect, and he was elected in 1982.

GATLIN, LARRY: *Singer, guitarist, songwriter, band leader (Gatlin Brothers Band). Born Seminole, Texas, May 2, 1948. Band members, both born Texas: Steve Gatlin, April 4, 1951; Rudy Gatlin, August 20, 1952.*

Larry Gatlin's name may be the best known of his family, but he is always quick to point out the contributions made by his younger brothers Steve and Rudy. Together they make up the Gatlin Brothers Band, from the mid-1970s on one of the most successful stage and recording acts in country music.

Music always had been a family affair for the brothers. They first performed together when Larry was six years old in a gospel group singing at family and church get-togethers. Their father worked as an oil driller and moved from job to job, taking his family with him wherever he went. One year the Gatlins lived in eight different towns.

Religion and music helped keep the family together during those rootless years. Finally the Gatlins settled in Odessa, Texas, and whenever gospel groups such as the Blackwood Brothers or the Statesmen came to town, the whole family would go to see them. Meanwhile the brothers kept singing together during their elementary and high school years, eventually performing on a weekly TV show in Abilene, Texas, for two years. Larry already was showing some interest in songwriting, writing religious lyrics to the melodies of popular songs. The brothers had other interests as well, including sports. Larry was an excellent athlete in high school and won a football scholarship to the University of Houston.

When he entered the university, it marked the first time he and his brothers went separate ways. When Steve and Rudy went to college, they enrolled in other schools. At the time, Larry harbored thoughts of eventually going into journalism or perhaps becoming a lawyer. The incident that changed his career direction was a 1971 job attempt that failed. While in school, he heard that the Imperials gospel group would be backing Elvis Presley and needed a baritone. He auditioned for the position and, although he didn't get it, the Imperials were sufficiently impressed with his singing to ask him to work with them for a month during a later Las Vegas engagement with Jimmy Dean. On the bill at the time was Dottie West.

Recalling that occasion, Larry said, "I started writing [songs] in 1971. I was out in Las Vegas trying for a job with the Imperials. I didn't get the job, but I sat around Dottie West's dressing room writing songs. She said, 'When you get home, why don't you send some to me,' because she had a publishing company. So I did and she liked them—rags to riches."

Larry's songs tend to take the form of short, short stories or vignettes, perhaps reflecting the fact that he was an English major at the University of Houston. He recalled, "I used to write short stories in college. I remember writing one titled 'I, a Handball,' that the teacher gave me an 'F' for. It was about a handball split up in a wastebasket talking enviously about its first cousin, the basketball, and second cousin, the football. Those cats were making a big splash and the handball was small, black, and discarded. I thought anyone could see it wasn't really about a handball at all and all the instructor could say was 'I don't understand it.' Maybe I'll try my hand at short stories again later on, but I think I'm really best suited to writing songs."

Dottie West certainly agreed about his songwriting

Larry Gatlin quotes from 1980 interview with Irwin Stambler.

skills. Of the eight songs he sent her, she recorded two, "Once You Were Mine" and "You're the Other Half of Me," and also helped get others recorded. She also furthered Larry's career by sending him plane fare to come to Nashville and continue his writing. When he got there, she also set about opening doors for him as a performer. She played one of his tapes for Kris Kristofferson, who in turn told Fred Foster, President of Monument Records, about the talented young writer-performer. By the time Foster offered a contract, Larry had influenced his brothers to come to Nashville so that all three, worked on the debut LP on Monument, *The Pilgrim*, which was released in January 1974. In preparation for that collection, Larry had written a hundred songs before he had ten which he felt were good enough for his first album. Among those was his first country hit, "Penny Annie," a song whose theme he hoped would provide the basis for a movie as of the early 1980s.

All of his subsequent albums contained one or more songs that became hit singles. His second LP, *Rain Rainbow*, featured the hit single "Delta Dirt." His third album, *Larry Gatlin with Family and Friends*, provided "Broken Lady," which reached number one on country charts in 1976 and also won a Grammy Award. Next came the album *High Time* from which came Larry's number-one single, "Statues Without Hearts."

Larry and the Gatlin Brothers Band's fourth Monument album, *Love Is Just a Game*, contained "I Don't Wanna Cry," which hit number one on the *Cash Box* country charts in August 1977. "I Just Wish You Were Someone I Love," from the same album, hit number one in early 1977. Their bestselling fifth album, *Oh! Brother*, was preceded by the number-one hit single "Night Time Magic" and also included the top-10 hit, "Do It Again Tonight." Larry and his brothers were represented on the charts in late 1978 and early 1979 with the single "I've Done Enough Dyin' Today." They continued their string of hits into 1980 with the number-one hit singles "Midnight Choir" and "I'm Taking Somebody with Me When I Fall." Also on the singles charts in 1980 were "All the Gold in California" and "We're Number One." All those 1980 discs were on a new label, Columbia, to which Larry and his brothers shifted in late 1979. Their album debut on the label, *Straight Ahead*, came out in late 1979 and made both country and pop charts, showing up on them in 1980 as well. In 1981, Larry and his brothers had several more Columbia singles on the charts, such as "It Don't Get Better than This" and "What Are We Doin' Lonesome."

From the mid-1970s on, the group performed across the United States and in many other countries. Their popularity was particularly high in England, where Larry was the subject of two BBC-TV specials. Their TV credits included almost every major country-music show as well as numerous network and syndicated talk shows. The Gatlins performed on several Country Music Association and Grammy Award TV programs and, over the years, their names appeared as finalists in several categories in those competitions as well as those of the Academy of Country Music, in which Larry and his brothers were big winners in 1980, walking off with awards for Top Male Vocalist, Best Single, and Best Album.

The secret to the Gatlin brothers' success lies in the consistent quality of the lyrics and music of their songs, almost all crafted by Larry, which often elicit response from listeners. For instance, Larry received mail objecting to the refrain of the song "Midnight Choir," which asks "Do they have Mogen David in heaven/Dear Lord, we'd all like to know/Do they have Mogen David in heaven, sweet Jesus/If they don't, who the hell wants to go?" Larry, whose own struggles with addiction caused him to be strongly against hard drugs and violence, does not believe in being sanctimonious about it. In this case, as he replied to critics, he was expressing the feelings of the people involved, not his own.

"When I write a song, I try to put myself in the position of the people I'm writing about. I try to look at it with compassion and hope that telling the truth will allow listeners to draw common sense conclusions. I had people condemn me for writing lines like not wanting to go to heaven, but that was the skid row derelicts talking, not me."

As it happens, the inspiration for the song was far removed from skid row. "We were eating in this Chinese restaurant in Saginaw, Michigan, and walked outside stuffed and happy. I said, 'Man, if they don't have Chinese food in heaven, I don't want to go.' It just stuck in my head. It was too good a line to lose. I couldn't get to sleep until I used it and the song just wrote itself."

Larry is quick to point out that the success of "Midnight Choir" indicates that most listeners did understand what he was trying to illustrate. He also expresses pride in responses describing the positive impact of some of his songs on people's lives. As an example, one girl wrote to tell him that listening to one of his songs on the radio snapped her out of a near-suicidal depression. In another case a mother wrote to say that "Penny Annie," about a girl whose life is destroyed by drug addiction, gave her daughter the strength to refuse to join others in her sorority in trying heroin. He called the family, who lived in Iowa, and asked how things were going. "I wanted to speak to her daughter, who wasn't there at first, but who came in while I was still on the phone. I talked to her and she told me all was going well."

One hint he has for aspiring songwriters is to listen as well as observe. "I try to be a very good listener. The ability to listen is a very important asset for someone who writes songs. I feel I'm maturing as a human being and a songwriter. I realize the same thing ties us all together—men and women, boys and girls—it's humanness. I try not to moralize, but I believe in caring and I hope it shows in my songs."

The album releases on the Columbia label by Larry Gatlin & the Gatlin Brothers continued to make the charts during the first half of the 1980s. These included *Help Yourself* in 1980; *Not Guilty* in 1981; *Sure Feels Like Love* and *A Gatlin Family Christmas*, both in 1982; *Greatest Hits, Volume II* in 1983; *Houston to Denver* in 1984; *Smile* in 1985; and *Partners* in 1986. These provided such singles hits as "Houston (Means I'm One Day Closer to You)" in 1982, "Denver" in 1984, and "She Used to be Somebody's Baby" in 1986. The last-named was from *Partners*, from which the singles "Talkin' to the Moon" (1986), "From Time to Time (It Feels Like Love Again)" (duet with Janie Fricke issued in spring 1987), and "Changin' Partners" (mid-1987) were drawn.

The Gatlins' association with Columbia came to an end in the late 1980s. Their final album releases on CBS were *Alive and Well . . . Livin' in the Land of Dreams* and *Biggest Hits*, both issued in 1988. *Alive and Well* provided their final CBS singles releases in 1988, "Love of a Lifetime" and "Alive and Well." The group moved on to complete an album for Universal, *Pure 'N Simple* (issued in March 1989) and two on Capitol, *Cooking Up a Storm* (July 1990) and *Christmas with the Gatlins* (October 1990, reissued on Branson, June 1994).

In the 1990s, the brothers reduced their emphasis on tour activities and focused attention on business opportunities. The group completed the album *Adios*, issued by Capitol's new country label, Liberty, in April 1992; its title also reflected the brothers' decision to abandon extensive touring. Steve noted, "The whole purpose for us getting off the road was to try to find an outlet, a way Larry, Rudy, and I could express ourselves and do some things creatively that we had always wanted to do."

In Larry's case it took the form of working in musical theater and films. In February 1993 he took over the lead role in the Broadway hit, *The Will Rogers Follies*, and stayed with the show for seven months. In the fall he began work on his feature film debut, costarring with Mickey Rooney and Randy Travis in *The Legend of O. B. Taggart*, released in early 1995. During the first half of 1994, he made a ten-city road tour with *The Will Rogers Follies*, taking time off in the spring to help launch a musical called *Alive and Well* in Bristol, Pennsylvania, a show he had written and scored. In mid-1994, he was in Nashville as a costar in a made-for-TV biography of his onetime mentor, the late Dottie West. That film, which featured Michelle Lee as Dottie, aired as the CBS Movie of the Week on January 22, 1995, and proved an excellent, insightful work.

During the first part of the 1990s, the brothers were also prominent members of the Branson, Missouri, scene. Rudy made his stage debut in the lead role of Curly in a Branson production of *Oklahoma!* in May 1993. Later he was featured in a Branson Christmas revue before joining a touring company of *Annie Get*

Your Gun in 1994. Besides that, he supervised the opening of a Gatlin Brothers Music City Grille in Bloomington, Minnesota, in August 1992, followed by a second Grille in Sacramento, California, that opened in November 1993.

Steve meanwhile worked on plans for a 2,000-seat Gatlin Brothers Theatre to be located in the Fantasy Harbor, Waccamaw, entertainment complex in Myrtle Beach, South Carolina. (He also found time to complete his first solo album, *Love Can Carry*, issued by Cheyenne Records in the fall of 1993.) The Gatlins were there for its opening in August 1994 with plans for them to appear together onstage for some six months a year.

Besides all that, they hadn't abandoned their Gatlin Brothers recording efforts, turning out a series of albums on the new Branson label. Those included *Moments to Remember* (1993); *Greatest Hits, Cool Water* and *Sincerely* (all released in 1994). During 1995, the brothers were named Entertainers of the Year by the South Carolina Music and Entertainment Commission.

In the spring of 1996, the brothers completed the gospel album *Gatlin Brothers Gospel* which included six songs written by Larry. It also was announced Larry would host an hour-long prime time TV special, *Beach Country*, in June 1996 to focus on the country stars and venues of Myrtle Beach, South Carolina.

GAYLE, CRYSTAL: *Singer, songwriter. Born Paintsville, Kentucky, January 9, 1951.*

Crystal Gayle hardly sounds like the typical country singer of several decades ago. Then again, the different musical styles of country and pop have increasingly faded into each other as country music has become accepted by a wider audience than ever before. By the same token, the influence of rock has become more acceptable in country circles. Indeed, Crystal has played an important role in the growing popularity of country music. Her dramatic, almost operatic, vocal style makes her more like an American version of the late French balladeer, Edith Piaf, than the more traditional country style of her older sister, Loretta Lynn.

Crystal's life, too, has been a blend of country and city influences. Born Brenda Gail Webb (later renamed Crystal Gayle when she started her recording career), she was the youngest of the eight children born to Ted and Clara Webb and spent much of her childhood in Wabash, Indiana. Loretta, the second eldest of the children, spent her entire youth in rural Butchers Hollow, Kentucky, only 400 miles away from Wabash, but an entirely different environment. Crystal's father, Ted Webb, an ex-coal miner, was a victim of black lung disease and had trouble finding work, so her mother, Clara, supported her children through a series of jobs. Ted died in 1959, and Clara eventually remarried; she and her husband lived in Wabash in the same house she bought before two of her daughters became famous singers.

Sister Loretta was married by the time Crystal was born, and while Gayle was growing up, Lynn was making her way up the rungs to country-music stardom. As a teenager, Crystal listened mainly to pop and folk music, yet she sang country songs with her family on weekends in church and for charity benefits. As she told one reporter, "Wabash just wasn't a country-music town. It was always a big thing in my life, but you know how some people used to think about country music: even if they liked it in the privacy of their homes, they were ashamed to admit it, because they didn't want to be looked down upon."

After Crystal graduated from high school, she started touring with Loretta, also signing on her sister's record label, Decca (now MCA). Crystal recorded a song written by Loretta, "I've Cried the Blues Right Out of My Eyes," which was a minor hit, making number 23 on the country charts. Loretta coined her new name, Crystal Gayle, so as not to duplicate the name of Brenda Lee, also on the same label. The name was derived from a hamburger chain, Krystal's, in business around Nashville. Despite her hit and her new name, Gayle was unhappy with MCA. She felt they didn't promote her enough and saw her only as Loretta Lynn's baby sister, so she signed with United Artists in 1972. By then she had also married her high school sweetheart, Bill Gatzimos.

At United Artists, Crystal teamed up with producer Allen Reynolds, who had also been responsible for refining Don Williams' laid-back country style. Reynolds helped Crystal to define her own taste and style, and soon after things began to happen for her. Her first United Artists single, "Restless," reached the top 40 on the charts.

Crystal's renown kept growing with each new album she recorded. Her first UA album, *Crystal Gayle*, contained three country hit singles, "Beyond You," "Wrong Road Again," and "This Is My Year for Mexico." Her second album, entitled *Somebody Loves You*, contained the hit single, "Somebody Loves You" and Crystal's first number-one hit, "I'll Get Over You." Her third album, *Crystal*, included "One More Time," "Do It All Over Again," and "Never Miss a Real Good Thing." This album was her first to show some pop crossover potential.

By this time, many country fans had taken note of Gayle's talent. She had already been named "Outstanding Female Vocalist" in 1976 by the Academy of Country Music. With the release of her fourth album, *We Must Believe in Magic*, in mid-1977, Crystal truly achieved nationwide recognition. Her single from that album, "Don't It Make My Brown Eyes Blue," climbed to number one on both country and pop music charts. The album reached platinum status in February 1978, the first recording by a female country artist to sell more than a million copies. Crystal was named Best Female Country Singer by the Grammy Awards, the

Academy of Country Music, and the Country Music Association.

Following these successes, some of Crystal's cuts from previous albums were re-released. In addition, she re-recorded a song from an earlier album, "Ready for the Times to Get Better," and earned herself another number-one country hit.

Crystal's fifth album, *When I Dream*, contained the hits "Talking in Your Sleep," "Someday Soon," and "Why Have You Left the One You Left Me For." The Country Music Association named her Best Female Vocalist in 1978, for the second year in a row. During 1979, she added to her list of top-10 singles on UA with releases like "Why Have You Left the One You Left Me For" and "When I Dream." At year end, "Your Old Cold Shoulder" was moving up the lists, reaching the top 10 in early 1980.

By 1979, the strikingly beautiful singer with knee-length hair had become an internationally known star. She appeared on all the major variety shows as well as on several specials, such as the Lou Rawls special, the Osmond Brothers special, and Bob Hope's "Road to China" television show, for which she went to the People's Republic of China during the summer of 1979. She also had her own special on CBS, the first for any female country vocalist.

In 1979, Crystal switched from the UA label to Columbia. When she moved, she took producer Allen Reynolds with her, who had been a major contributing factor to the continual success of her record releases. Her debut album on Columbia, *Miss the Mississippi*, came out during 1979 and went gold soon after its release. It provided such hit singles as "Half the Way," "It's Like We Never Said Goodbye," and "The Blue Side." "It's Like We Never Said Goodbye" became her first number-one single on Columbia, reaching that pinnacle in April 1980. Late in 1980, the single "If You Ever Change Your Mind" was in the top 10. Her 1981 hits included "Take It Easy" and "The Woman in Me." Her charted albums during 1980–81 included, on UA/Liberty, *Classic Crystal* and *A Woman's Heart* and, on Columbia, besides *Miss the Mississippi*, *These Days* and *Hollywood, Tennessee*. During 1981 she worked with Tom Waits on the soundtrack for the Francis Ford Coppola film *One from the Heart*, released in early 1982.

In an interview with Dennis Hunt of the *Los Angeles Times*, Gayle revealed that she consciously chose to record softer, more middle-of-the-road-type songs than her sister, Loretta Lynn. "If I sang real country like she does," Crystal said, "the country audience would never accept me. They'd all say I was trying to copy her. The kinds of songs she sings don't suit me, anyway. You have to be sort of hard to sing hardcore country. I wouldn't be convincing singing that stuff."

After her fifth album on Columbia, *True Love*, came out in 1983, Crystal signed with Warner Brothers Records. Her debut on that label was *Cage the Songbird*, which was followed over the rest of the decade by the albums *Nobody Wants to Be Alone, Straight to the Heart, A Crystal Christmas, Nobody's Angel*, and *What if We Fall in Love*. Some of her singles releases also did well as videos, which helped earn her the American Music Awards trophy for Favorite Female Country Video Artist of 1986. (Previously, in those awards, she had been voted Favorite Female Country Artist for 1979 and 1981.)

In the mid-1980s, she recorded several chart-making duets with Gary Morris which earned Country Music Association nominations for Vocal Duo of the Year in 1986 and 1987. On one of those CMA Awards telecasts the two sang their hit number "Making up for Lost Time." During the 1980s and into the 1990s she continued to perform before enthusiastic audiences throughout the U.S. and around the world. In the 1990s she often performed at Branson, Missouri. She also was a guest on a wide range of music and variety programs on the major networks and the Nashville-based country music TV programs. Among her TV credits at the start of the 1990s was an HBO concert special, a second special on CBS-TV, and contribution of the hit single "Another World" as the theme song for the soap opera of the same name.

Coming into the 1990s, Liberty Records issued two albums of her material, *Ain't Gonna Worry* and *Three Good Reasons*. In the mid-1990s she signed with her fifth label, Intersound, for which her debut album was titled *Best Always*. In 1995, Intersound released her first religious album, *Someday*, coproduced by Crystal and Bobby Wood. Crystal, who had hosted such TV programs over the years as the American Music Awards, Academy of Country Music Awards and Country Night of Stars, also applied her talents to various charitable events. For example, she served as co-host for the Arthritis Foundation Telecast in 1993, 1994 and 1995.

On September 20, 1996, Crystal returned to her home town of Paintsville, Kentucky, which city mayor Robin Cooper had proclaimed Crystal Gayle Day. At a special luncheon, Kentucky Lieutenant Governor Steve Henry officially proclaimed her a Kentucky Colonel. It also was announced that a section of U.S. Highway 23, known in Kentucky as the "Country Music Highway," had been dedicated to her and a sign with her name was unveiled on it. Afterward, Crystal went on to Ashland, Kentucky, for a concert at the Paramount Arts Center.

GENTRY, BOBBIE: *Singer, guitarist, songwriter. Born Chickasaw County, Mississippi, July 27, 1944.*

In early July 1967, six violin players, two cellists and a pretty, blue-jeaned guitar-carrying young woman entered Capitol Records' Studio C in Hollywood. The group recorded a song written by the woman and shown to Capitol artists & repertoire executive Kelly Gordon only a few days before. Within a few weeks after the session, the previously unknown woman had a worldwide reputation as the song, "Ode to Billy Joe," became number one on both pop and country charts in the United States and a worldwide sensation.

The song, which also became the theme for a motion picture of the same name in the 1970s, has become a classic. One of Bobbie Gentry's primary creative credits, the song was the first of many that were to have a marked impact on the pop and country field in the late 1960s and early 1970s.

Bobbie Gentry wrote the country/delta-blues melody to the song from memories of her childhood in Mississippi's delta region. She was born there and spent her early years in rural settings. When she was six she went to live with her grandparents in a farmhouse in Chickasaw County, Mississippi, without indoor plumbing or electricity. Her grandparents, sensing the child's musical interest, traded a cow for an old piano when Bobbie was seven.

She taught herself to play by imitating the methods of the local church pianist, who played mostly on the black keys. Bobbie remembers using those keys as the basis for her first composition, penned when she was seven and called "My Dog Sergeant Is a Good Dog," later to become part of her nightclub act.

When she was thirteen, Bobbie's family moved to Palm Springs, California, which was to become home. In her teens, she took up a number of other instruments, including guitar, vibraharp, banjo, and bass fiddle. She continued to spend time writing music and at one point got a job performing in a local country club.

After graduating from Palm Valley High School, she enrolled at the University of California at Los Angeles to major in philosophy and took on occasional club dates as an entertainer to help finance her education. After a while, she decided to focus on music, studying musical theory, composition, and counterpoint at the Los Angeles Conservatory of Music. During those years, she performed with several small theater groups and also worked as a dancer in Las Vegas, Nevada, for a time.

She built up a backlog of original songs and began to show them to record companies, finally achieving her 1967 Capitol session. When "Ode to Billy Joe" became a million-selling single, she incorporated many other songs based on the rhythms of her original home area into the debut LP, such as "Chickasaw County Child," "Lazy Willie," "Papa Won't Let Me Go into Town with You," and "Tuesday's Child." The album, *Ode to Billy Joe*, came out in November 1967 and made the charts soon after, remaining there into 1968 and bringing Gentry a second gold-record award. In the voting of the National Academy of Recording Arts & Sciences for 1967, Bobbie won three Grammy Awards: Best New Artist, Best Contemporary Female Solo Vocal Performance, and Best Vocal Performance, Female. The Academy of Country and Western Music also named her the Most Promising Female Vocalist of 1967.

For the rest of the 1960s, Bobbie established herself as an international star. Besides appearing in concerts all over the United States and Canada, she was featured in person and on TV in England, the Netherlands, France, Germany, and Australia. She was invited to appear at Italy's San Remo Song Festival and won the Italian Press Award for her performance of "La Siepa."

The same year, 1968, she was featured on *Tom Jones's Radio Special* on the BBC and was so well received there and as a guest on several TV shows that she was offered her own program. Beginning in 1968, she was hostess and star of the *Bobbie Gentry* TV series for BBC, an annual series that remained on the BBC through the early 1970s. The series was expanded to other overseas markets in 1971. At home, Bobbie also became a familiar TV figure, starring in three 20th Century-Fox specials and cohosting a CMA Awards show, a Grammy Awards show, and a number of other programs. In 1969, she was asked to host the weekly *Bobbie Gentry Show* on Armed Forces Radio, a program still featured during the first part of the 1970s.

In 1968, she recorded a duet LP with Glen Campbell, *Bobbie Gentry and Glen Campbell,* that caught the music public's fancy. It rose high on pop and country charts and earned both artists a gold-record award in 1969. Her work with Glen resulted in a number of successful singles, such as "Let It Be Me," which earned a Country Music Association Award in 1970, and a new version of an Everly Brothers' hit, "All I Have to Do Is Dream," which earned a silver disc as a bestseller in England in 1970. Among her other solo releases of the period were the LPs *Touch 'Em with Love* (8/69), *Bobbie Gentry's Greatest!* (12/69), *Fancy* (1970), *Sittin' Pretty/Tobacco Road* (1970), and *Patchwork* (4/71).

Bobbie continued to maintain a hectic schedule as performer, writer, and manager of several business enterprises, including her own production and publishing company, Gentry Ltd. However, she cut back on her work as public interest in her recordings appeared to fade and, by the late 1970s, her association with the music field mainly took the form of behind-the-scenes efforts.

GIBSON, DON: *Singer, guitarist, songwriter. Born Shelby, North Carolina, April 3, 1928.*

A common witticism in Nashville in the 1960s and 1970s was that if an artist badly needed a new hit record, the best approach was to listen to some old Don Gibson albums. A tribute to Don Gibson's songwriting ability, the approach worked for many performers—some who needed new hits and some who already were at the top of the heap. As for Gibson, though his career as a writer reached its zenith in the late 1950s and early 1960s, his efforts as a recording artist and sometime performer—using both original material and that crafted by others—continued along at a steady, if not spectacular pace throughout the 1960s, 1970s, and into the 1980s.

Growing up in North Carolina, Don showed an aptitude for music in his early years, learning to play guitar before he finished grade school and, before he was in his teens, singing at local events. At fourteen he turned professional and gained experience, during the mid-1940s, working on country shows at many radio stations in the South.

Just after World War II ended he moved to Knoxville, Tennessee, where he soon was featured on the WNOX *Tennessee Barn Dance* and the *Mid-day Merry-Go-Round*. By the mid-1950s, he was one of the best-known performers in the area and received the key to the city from the mayor in acknowledgement.

Don had expanded his audience somewhat in the early and mid-1950s with recordings that sometimes were local or regional hits. His major successes, however, came in the songwriting area. Increasingly, both Knoxville and Nashville artists looked to him for important new material. His first major credit came in 1956 when Faron Young gained a top-10 hit with Don's "Sweet Dreams," ever since one of the classic country songs. Kitty Wells had similar success in 1958 with "I Can't Stop Loving You"; the song was later a smash hit for Ray Charles, whose record spent five weeks at number one on the *Billboard* pop charts in the spring of 1962.

Meanwhile, Wesley Rose of Acuff-Rose Publishing Company had seen him perform at a Knoxville club and brought his talents to the attention of RCA Victor. The company signed Don to a long-term contract in 1957. The following year he scored three national country hits with his own compositions, a top-10 single "Give Myself a Party" and two number-one songs, "Blue, Blue Day" and "Oh Lonesome Me." Now a national celebrity with country fans, he was asked to join the *Grand Ole Opry* in 1958.

Gibson closed out the 1950s in style with two more top-10 hits, "Don't Tell Me Your Troubles" and "Who Cares." He moved into the 1960s with a top-10 original in 1960, "Just One Time," and in 1961, his own recorded hit of "Sweet Dreams." In 1961, he also made the top 10 with another writer's song, the H. David–P. Hampton "Sea of Heartbreak." In 1962, Kitty Wells made the top 10 with Don's "Day into Night" and Don also made it with two more of his own songs, "I Can Mend Your Broken Heart" and "Lonesome Number One." In 1963, he didn't have any top 10 releases, but Patsy Cline scored a top-10 hit with Don's "Sweet Dreams." After a rare year with no top-ranked songs or records in 1964, Don returned in 1965 with "Watch Where You're Going" and in 1966 with "(Yes) I'm Hurting." But the late 1960s proved disappointing, with only one or two chart-making releases and no major hits. This situation, in turn, ended his association with

RCA. He moved to Hickory Records, which helped spark a renewal of his career in the 1970s.

From the late 1950s to the start of the 1970s, Gibson provided material for several dozen albums on RCA or its subsidiary label, Camden, many of which made the album charts. Among those LPs were *Lonesome Me* (6/58), *No One Stands Alone* (2/59), *That Gibson Boy* (11/59), *Look Who's Blue* (6/60), *Sweet Dreams* (2/61), *Girls, Guitars* (9/61), *Some Favorites* (7/62), *I Wrote a Song* (10/63), *God Walks Hills* (6/64), *Blue Million Tears* (Camden, 3/65), *Best of Don Gibson* (8/65), *Too Much Hurt* (12/65), *Fabulous Don Gibson* (Harmony, 1/66), *Don Gibson with Spanish Guitars* (7/66), *Hurtin' Inside* (Camden, 11/66), *Great Songs* (12/66), *All My Love* (8/67), *King of Country Soul* (1968), *All Time Country Gold* (8/69), *Great Don Gibson* (with the Jordanaires, 10/70), *Best of Don Gibson, Volume 2* (3/70), *Lovin' Lies* (Camden, 5/70), *I Walk Alone* (Camden, 8/71).

Almost as soon as Don signed with Hickory (then part of the MGM organization), his name began to appear on the singles charts with regularity, for the most part with material written by others. Among his early 1970s chartmakers were "Someway" in late 1970; "Touch Your Woman," a top-10 hit in the spring of 1972; "I Think They Call It Love," a duet with Sue Thompson, in the summer of 1972; and the top-5 success that summer, "Woman (Sensuous Woman)." In the mid-1970s, his charted singles included "Snap Your Fingers" and "One Day at a Time" in 1974; "I'll Sing for You," "(There She Goes) I Wish Her Well" (written by Don), "Oh How Love Changes," sung with Sue Thompson, and "Don't Stop Loving Me" (by Gibson) in 1975; and, in 1976, "Doing My Time." In the late 1970s, he made the charts with releases like "If You Ever Get to Houston (Look Me Down)" and "When Do We Stop Starting Over" in 1977; "The Fool" and "Oh Such a Stranger/I Love You Because" in 1978; and "Any Day Now" in 1979. His releases from 1977 to 1979 were on the ABC/Hickory label.

Gibson also recorded many albums during the 1970s, including *Don Gibson on MGM* and, on Hickory, *Hits, Hits, Don Gibson Way*, *Perfect Mountain*, *Don Gibson Sings Hank Williams*, and *Country Green*.

During his long career, Gibson naturally traveled extensively, appearing at one time or another in all fifty of the United States and many foreign countries. Besides his many years on the *Opry*, he also was featured on countless radio and TV programs over the years. During the 1970s, he cut down on his travel schedule, though he still was making occasional swings across the United States at the end of the decade. In keeping with his low-key approach to performing, he refused to assemble his own band for such appearances, preferring to use various "house" bands. This approach indicated that he always valued his writing ability more highly than his entertaining efforts.

The lasting nature of his work was underscored by the way some of his 1950s compositions provided 1970s hits. In 1974, a then newcomer named Ronnie Milsap scored a number-one success with Don's 1959 song "Legend in My Time," an achievement that helped win him the CMA Award as Best Male Vocalist of that year. In 1975, Emmylou Harris earned a number-one country hit with the venerable "Sweet Dreams." In 1981, the hit single of his "One More Time" by Tompall and the Glazer Brothers played a role in making the reunion of the famous group successful.

In the early 1980s, Don formed a new recording affiliation with Warner/Curb Records. One of the first products of that was the 1980 charted single "Sweet Sensuous Sensations."

He continued to craft new songs and recordings in the 1980s, though not with the same success as in earlier decades. He was still warmly received by audiences both at home and in other countries. In 1984 he was given the Irish Hall of Fame Award after performing at the Carling Country Music Festival in Cork. During the 1980s and 1990s, remakes of his classic compositions (which had helped bring him election to the Nashville Songwriters Association Songwriters Hall of Fame in 1973) continued to grace new releases by new generations of performers. In 1990, for instance, the Kentucky HeadHunters had a top-10 hit with "Oh Lonesome Me" (the flip-side of Don's own 1958 single release of "I Can't Stop Loving You").

When Gibson was nominated for the Country Music Hall of Fame in mid-1992, his credits included over eighty charted recordings, nineteen of which made the top 10, including "Sea of Heartbreak," "Blue, Blue Day," "Just One Time," "Give Myself a Party," "Lonesome Number One," and "Woman (Sensuous Woman)," the last a top-10 hit in the mid-1990s for Mark Chesnutt. A survey of top country singles from 1944 through 1988 marked him the twenty-eighth best-selling artist in the country field during that time.

GIBSON/MILLER BAND: *Vocal and instrumental group, Dave Gibson, born Eldorado, Arkansas (lead vocals, guitar, songwriter); Blue Miller, born Detroit, Michigan, c. 1953 (vocals, guitar, songwriter); Bryan Grassmyer, born Nebraska (vocals, bass guitar); Mike Daly, born Cleveland, Ohio (steel guitar); Steve Grossman, born Islip, New York (drums).*

Country rock has been an influential part of the country music spectrum since rock came to the fore in the 1950s. Many of the pioneers of rock, of course, came from the country tradition, though it took a while for fans and peers in that field to accept artists like Elvis, Jerry Lee Lewis, and Carl Perkins as legitimate heirs to the musical form. The Gibson/Miller Band followed in the footsteps of groups like Lynyrd Skynyrd and Charlie Daniels, though with more of the elements of rock in its blend than earlier country rock groups.

It must have been a nervous Blue Miller (real name Bill Mueller), the founding band member, who sent an advance copy of the group's debut album to Levon Helm of the Band for an evaluation. Not to worry: Miller told Jay Orr of the *Nashville Banner* ("Gibson, Miller Hit It Off," January 12, 1993) that Helm said, "Man, you guys got the best damn band going in the United States right now, hands down. I know your headquarters are down there in Nashville, and they're calling you country, but if it's just about great American music, you guys got it."

The son of a pop guitarist, Miller began playing the instrument himself at an early age and could play reasonably well before he reached his teens. He also learned keyboards, and in his teens handled those instruments as well as lead vocals for his own band.

When he was eighteen, he joined the band of local favorite Bob Seger and worked with the latter (who had not yet gained national recognition) from 1971–73. During that time he played on four Seger LPs, *Brand New Morning, Smokin' OPs, Back in '72,* and *Bob Seger 7.* After leaving Seger, he worked for some years as a singer-songwriter in the Detroit area before moving down to Central Florida in 1979. At one point while in Detroit he earned a local Emmy for Best Original Music for a TV Documentary (written for a state-of-mass-transit special on Detroit's ABC-TV outlet). In Florida, he joined a country bar band based in Orlando that eventually became the house band at Orlando's Cheyenne Saloon.

The experience changed his musical outlook, he said. "Growing up in Detroit, my only exposure to country music was that twangy nasal stuff—and I thought that was country. When I got a gig playing in a Florida honky tonk, I realized, 'Hey, there's a lot going on here. This stuff is a whole lot different than what I heard growing up.' And so, as time goes by, I realize how much there is in the music."

His activities brought him in contact with recording enterpreneur Bill Lowery, who offered him work as a session player and sometime record producer at his Southern Tracks studio. His Detroit upbringing had made him a fan of sixties soul outlets such as Motown and Stax Records, so he welcomed the chance to work on two Isaac Hayes albums and also to tour with Hayes as the only white musician in the singer's band. Miller's hopes for a recording opportunity at Lowery's didn't pan out, but Miller became friends with Doug Johnson, the studio's chief recording engineer, which later became crucial to his career.

Miller made much of his income during those years from writing and singing commercial jingles. In 1987, he expanded his scope by renting a Chicago apartment and commuting between there and Atlanta. In Chicago, he was in demand for commercials work, turning out jingles for products like Frosted Flakes, NutraSweet, Bud Light, and Taco Bell. He also signed a songwriting contract with Chicago-based BMG Music Publishing, which in time resulted in his transferring to BMG Nashville in 1990, which in the past had turned down his demos as being too rock-oriented.

Gibson's roots were essentially country, though for a while his main association was with the folk field. Born in Arkansas, but raised for the most part in Odessa, Texas, he was influenced in his childhood years by artists like the Ventures, Elvis, Buddy Holly, the Everly Brothers, and Marty Robbins, whose music he heard on the local radio. When he told his father he wanted to learn guitar, he recalled for *Country Guitar* magazine, he was told no, it was a "sissy" thing. But his mother "ordered a three-pickup black Silvertone and a matching amp from the Sears catalogue, "which Gibson afterward traded for an acoustic guitar he later played in a high school trio called the Ramblers. Gibson told the magazine, "I learned to fingerpick from Joan Baez records."

When he finished high school, he enrolled at the University of Arkansas, and after graduating he settled in Chicago with the idea of finding work as a commercial artist. However, the booming local blues, R&B, and folk scene attracted him. He worked as a substitute teacher by day and kept up his music pursuits nights and weekends. He recalled becoming acquainted with such folk notables of the time as Steve Goodman and John Prine. He gravitated after a time to the country and country-rock format, which led to steady work performing at Nashville North, where he remained for five years. During those years, he was constantly writing country-oriented material. In 1982, ready for the next step, he moved to Nashville to try his luck as a writer and performer.

He arrived in Music City with introductions to several operations that soon resulted in a writing contract with the Oak Ridge Boys' organization. Before long he was placing songs with many artists, including the hit "Trouble" for Steve Wariner. The list of Gibson-penned successes by major country artists continued to grow as he moved from one music publisher to another, including Alabama's publishing firm, Maypop, in 1987 and, later, N.E.M. Entertainment. Among those who made top-chart levels with Gibson's songs were Tanya Tucker with "If It Don't Come Easy," Alabama with "Jukebox in My Mind," Joe Diffie with "Ships That Don't Come In," and Confederate Railroad with "Queen of Memphis."

While both Gibson and Miller were in Nashville at the start of the 1990s, it took a third party to bring them together. The person was Miller's Atlanta friend, Doug Johnson, who had begun managing a new country star, Doug Stone, and moved to Nashville. In his managerial capacity, he had come in contact with many creative people, including writers like Gibson. Miller told James Turano of the *Illinois Entertainer* ("Gibson/Miller Band: A Little Bit Country," April 1993), "It was really weird. I was in the lobby at Epic waiting to pitch a few songs and a friend of mine, Doug Johnson, saw me and said there was a guy here I had to meet. I don't think even Doug knew what to expect. We actually wrote a song that first day."

When Johnson heard demo tapes prepared by the writers as a performing team, he urged them to put an act together. "Doug just flipped out," Gibson recalled. "He said, 'Man, you guys got a great sound there.'"

Thus encouraged, the twosome organized what was to become the Gibson/Miller Band. After auditions and discussions, they added Bryan Grassmyer on bass, Michael Daly on steel, and Steve Grossman on drums. All had broad experience as session players and backing-band performers.

Nebraskan Grassmyer had lived in Los Angeles and Colorado before moving to Nashville in 1988. Besides session work, he had toured with artists like Vince Gill, Suzy Bogguss, and Sweethearts of the Rodeo. Grossman, who grew up in Long Island, New York, was another Sweethearts of the Rodeo alumnus. He had started gaining band experience at North Texas State University by working the Dallas nightclub circuit. His move to Nashville came in 1987. That was the same year Daly moved to Music City. By then he had honed his steel guitar skills in various local bands and quickly found work in demo sessions and backing groups for artists like Matraca Berg, Martina McBride, and Larry Boone. He had done some demo work for Gibson, which helped bring an invite for the new band.

The group refined their act in several places during 1992, including a week at the Dutch Treat Lounge in Franklin, Tennessee. Miller told Jay Orr, "We went in there and played two sets of original stuff. The first night we had a handful of people that couldn't quite figure out why we didn't do any Lynyrd Skynyrd.

"When we told them we were working on this new album and we were going to be out there touring and we really wanted to play our stuff in front of an audience, they were, 'OK, show us what you've got.' We went from a handful of people to packing the place by word of mouth."

By then the band had been working on its debut album for Epic Records, a signing (by label head Roy Wunsch) brought about at the urging of Doug Johnson, who had given up managerial work in 1991 in favor of becoming vice president for Artists & Repertoire at the label. The group's first Epic single, "Big Heart," was released on October 19, 1992, followed by the album in January 1993. The single and its video both made upper-chart levels by early 1993. This was followed by such *Billboard* Top 20 or Top 30 releases as "High Rollin'," top 20 in May 1993, "Texas Tattoo," top 20 in August, and "Stone Cold Country," top 40 in March 1994. In the Academy of Country Music Awards voting for 1993, the group was presented with the Best New Vocal Group or Duet trophy.

The album, *Where There's Smoke*, was on hit lists a number of months during 1993. The first four chart singles were all originals by Gibson and Miller. The band also showed it could give new insight into older material by other writers with its charted version in the summer of 1994 of "Mammas Don't Let Your Babies Grow Up to Be Cowboys."

GILL, VINCE: *Singer, guitarist, banjoist, fiddler, mandolinist, dobro player, band leader, songwriter. Born Oklahoma City, Oklahoma, April 12, 1957.*

Vince Gill might have been a rock star or bluegrass legend to rival Bill Monroe, or a professional golfer challenging for Masters or U.S. Open honors, or even a Hollywood matinee idol. . . . There are elements suggesting such possibilities in his background, but he chose to focus on more down-home country stylings and hence became one of mainstream country's new superstars of the 1990s. And he did it the hard way, paying his dues as a sideman with a variety of bands and as a solo performer who went years before achieving the great things people predicted for him.

For many of those years he stayed in the background while his wife, Janis, came to country prominence as a member of the hit duo Sweethearts of the Rodeo. He never seemed to begrudge her or other music friends their place in the sun, and persevered until his turn in the spotlight came in the early 1990s, a change in fortune that made him one of the major country figures of the decade.

English rock luminary Mark Knopfler, who at one point hoped Vince would join his band Dire Straits, testified to Gill's remarkable skills. He told Peter Cronin of *Musician* magazine ("Vince Gill: Pickin' and Grinnin'," September 1991), "Someone like Vince puts you in your place if you think you're hot stuff. Puts *me* in my place. He writes, sings on all the best records in Nashville, makes his own record and goes platinum, plays guitar like a god, of course, and then can do it on mandolin or something else! It's not enough to be a killer singer and musical genius, he's also got to play guitar like a professional. Of course! Nothing else would do, would it? I wouldn't be surprised if he's got a couple of Olympic medals."

Born and raised in Oklahoma City, Vince had a comfortable childhood; his parents projected a love of music—country music in particular—from his earliest years. His father, an attorney (and later a judge), was an amateur musician and in home songfests his mother sometimes joined in on harmonies. Before Vince reached his teens he had learned to play his dad's banjo and a four-string tenor guitar. His initial public appearances were at local events with his father and his friends.

In his formative years, Vince also was exposed to the rock music many of his friends favored, and he wasn't averse to playing some of that material. In high school, though, his prime interest was in the bluegrass domain, and he became a key member with his brother Bob in a bluegrass band called Mountain Smoke. He also was a good athlete and demonstrated particular proficiency in golf. In fact, his high school mentors and other friends suggested he pursue a career in that sport. But word of his bluegrass skills had begun to spread in music circles after people heard Mountain Smoke open for bands like Pure Prairie League. This eventually brought a call from Louisville, Kentucky, that caused him to set aside plans to concentrate on his golf talents.

The call was a request that he join a progressive bluegrass group called the Bluegrass Alliance, whose members at the time included highly respected performers Sam Bush and Dan Crary. As Vince recalled, he threw his belongings into his van and drove cross-country to join up. After a year, he seized the chance to gain more experience with a band called Sundance, organized by the top-ranked bluegrass fiddler Byron Berline. Vince moved to Los Angeles in 1976 to play with Sundance; it would remain his home for over seven years. He worked with Sundance for two years before moving on to join Pure Prairie League in 1979.

The Pure Prairie League alignment, he noted, resulted almost by accident. The group set up an audition as part of a reorganizing move, and one of Vince's friends decided to try out. Vince went along to see if the band members recalled him from his Mountain Smoke days. They did indeed, and asked him to become a member. The group's fortunes had declined in the late 1970s, but Vince's addition proved a lucky one. He recorded three albums with them that improved sales and provided a number of audience-pleasing new songs for their repertoire, including "I'm Almost Ready" and "Let Me Love You Tonight." Gill's expressive tenor lead vocal on the latter provided the band with its first chart hit in a number of years.

During those years, Vince kept in touch with the bluegrass and country music scene in the Los Angeles area, sometimes sitting in with other bands or just hanging out at various clubs. A visit to one called Sweetwater in Manhattan Beach in 1977 brought his first meetings with promising local artist Janis Oliver. Their paths crossed again in later months, and they eventually began dating; they married in 1980.

Gill said one of his most important musical influences in the mid-1970s was Emmylou Harris's *Pieces of the Sky* album, which included the song "Til I Gain Control," written by Rodney Crowell, who played guitar in her band. One evening at the Troubadour nightclub after Sundance played that song, Crowell came out of the audience after the show to compliment Gill on his work. In the early 1980s, when Crowell formed his own band, the Cherry Bombs, he persuaded Vince to join. Among the band members who were to go on to record industry success in later years were pianist Tony Brown and bass player Emory Gordy, Jr. "That was the best band I ever played with," Vince commented.

Not long after, Tony Brown accepted an A&R position at RCA Records in Nashville, the first step in a legendary career as a recording executive. To enhance prospects for both of the Gills' careers, the Gill family moved to Nashville in 1983. Brown signed Vince to RCA in 1984, but left for MCA Records before he could collaborate on Gill's recordings. That production task fell to another Cherry Bombs alumnus, Emory Gordy.

Gill's RCA debut album was the extended-play *Turn Me Loose,* whose title track was turned into a video. This was followed by his first full album, *The Things That Matter,* and a third and final RCA collection, *I Never Knew Lonely,* in the late 1980s. Those albums provided such top-10 singles as "If It Weren't for You" (a duet with Rosanne Cash), "Oklahoma Borderline," "Cinderella," and the 1988 chartmaker, "Everybody's Sweetheart." The last was a good-natured observation about the rising fame of Sweethearts of the Rodeo, which at that time far outstripped his audience reception.

He told Jane Sanderson of *People* magazine, "It was just an attempt at humor, saying 'She's everybody's sweetheart but mine.' It wasn't whining." There never was any real strain on their relationship, he always insisted. He told David Zimmerman of *USA Today* in 1993, "People were naturally looking for me to be upset. But she's my best pal in the world, and she was a singer and a guitar player long before I met her."

His RCA output was good, but not strong enough for major recognition. Richard Cromelin of the *Los Angeles Times* ("Dedicated to Just Plain Folks," Calendar section, September 25, 1994) wondered if the change in producers was a prime culprit. "I'm not saying Tony's leaving is the reason I didn't have hits when I was first signed over there," Gill said. "The timing of things was not right for me. It took a long time, but in hindsight now, it gave me a lot of time to watch, hang out and learn a lot of good things."

Not that Vince was ignored by the Nashville music community during those years. He continued to write new songs, which usually received close scrutiny from other artists looking for possible hits, and he was always in demand as a session musician, singing backing vocals on over 150 tracks for artists like Emmylou Harris and Reba McEntire and providing instrumental support for even more recordings.

His career might have taken a different tack if he'd accepted Mark Knopfler's suggestion that he join Dire Straits, but his heart was still in country. He told Cromelin, "I thought I was pretty good. I felt like I belonged. I knew I could play and I knew I could sing. I don't mean that egotistically. My ears tell me that. And

I have some talent. And I love it. I mean music is the greatest thing in my life."

The turning point came in 1989, when he signed with MCA Records and was reunited with Tony Brown. His debut album on the label, *When I Call Your Name,* exploded on the country scene, rapidly gaining critical acclaim in all major markets. The first single, "Never Alone," which he cowrote with Rosanne Cash, made the top 20 in 1989 and the next one, a duet with Reba McEntire titled "Oklahoma Swing," made the top 10. Then came "When I Call Your Name" (on which Patty Loveless sang harmony), which reached number one in both *Billboard* and *Radio & Records* in the summer (peaking at number one in *R&R* the week of August 3). Gill rounded out the year with another hit, "Never Knew Lonely," which peaked at number three in *R&R* the week of November 30.

By the end of 1990, the album had received R.I.A.A. gold-record certification, and in the 1990 Country Music Association voting "When I Call Your Name" was chosen as Single of the Year. That composition, cowritten by Vince and Tim DuBois, also was nominated for Song of the Year, a trophy it won in 1991. By 1991, Vince was becoming recognized as a major star with a steadily growing following among concertgoers and record buyers. His second MCA album, *Pocket Full of Gold,* rose to number five in *Billboard* in the spring of 1991, and had gone past gold-record levels by the end of summer. Meanwhile, RCA got some extra mileage from his success by issuing the album *Best of Vince Gill.*

In the 1991 CMA voting, *Pocket Full of Gold* was named Album of the Year, while Gill also was chosen as Male Vocalist of the Year, a trophy he picked up again for each of the next three years. During the 1991 CMA Awards telecast, Vince won another award as part of Mark O'Connor and the New Nashville Cats (the other Cats were Ricky Skaggs and Steve Wariner), which was selected as the Vocal Event of the Year. In 1991, Vince had another string of singles hits, topped off by "Look at Us," which peaked at number four in *R&R* the week of December 6.

By early 1992, *Pocket Full of Gold* had gone platinum, and in the fall it was joined on the charts by Vince's third MCA album, *I Still Believe in You.* His 1992 singles hits included "Take Your Memory with You" (number one in *R&R* the week of April 10); "I Still Believe in You" (number one in *R&R* the week of August 28); and "Don't Let Our Love Start Slippin' Away" (number two in *R&R* the week of December 18). In the Grammy Awards telecast in February 1992. Gill shared the award for Best Country Vocal Collaboration with Mark O'Connor and the New Nashville Cats for the single "Restless" from that Warner Brothers album. The previous year he had won a Grammy when "When I Call Your Name" was voted Best Country Vocal Performance, Male. In the 1992 voting, announced on the February 1993 telecast, Vince earned two more Grammys, one for Best Country Vocal Performance, Male, for the album *I Still Believe in You,* the other for Best Country Song for that album's title track, cowritten by Vince and John Barlow Jarvis.

The 1992 CMA Awards continued to underscore Vince's rising status. Nominated in four categories, he won three of them, for Entertainer of the Year, Male Vocalist of the Year, and Song of the Year (for "Look at Us," cowritten with Max D. Barnes). The last-named song also was nominated for Music Video of the Year. Gill, who had been inducted into the *Grand Ole Opry* in 1991, was asked to be cohost on the CMA's 1992 awards telecast. His laid-back persona and wry sense of humor impressed both TV viewers and show organizers, which guaranteed him the same role in the 1993 program.

In early 1993, Vince had another hit duet single with Reba McEntire, "The Heart Won't Lie." Later on he topped the charts with "No Future in the Past" (number one in *R&R* the week of July 2, 1993) and "One More Last Chance" (number one in *R&R* the week of October 1), both songs cowritten by him. He won nominations and trophies in polls ranging from the Academy of Country Music to TNN/Music City News competitions in that time period and extended his domination of the CMA Awards in 1993 by receiving nominations in no less than seven categories, winning in five of them: Entertainer of the Year, Male Vocalist of the Year, Song of the Year ("I Still Believe in You"), album of the year (*I Still Believe in You),* and as one of a number of artists on the track "I Don't Need Your Rockin' Chair" from the *George Jones & Friends* album, which was voted Vocal Event of the Year. In the latter category, he was also nominated with Reba McEntire for "The Heart Won't Lie." His other nominations were for Single of the Year and Music Video of the Year, both for "Don't Let Our Love Start Slippin' Away."

In late summer of 1993, Gill had still another album high on the charts, *Let There Be Peace on Earth,* well past gold-record levels by year-end. This was followed in 1994 by another best-selling MCA collection, *When Love Finds You,* which rose to number two in *Billboard* in the summer. His singles hits for the year included "Tryin to Get Over You" (number one for two weeks in *R&R* in February); "Whenever You Come Around" (number one in *R&R* the week of June 10); "What the Cowgirls Do" (number one in *R&R* the week of September 16); and "When Love Finds You" (number two in *R&R* the week of November 25). Again his name showed up on Grammy nominations, while he added new credits in many other competitions.

On the CMA Awards telecast in October 1994, he became the first solo host to emcee the entire three hour program. Once again he seemed the overall favorite of the voters, taking three trophies for Entertainer of the Year, Male Vocalist of the Year, and a share of Album of the Year honors for his part in the collection *Common Thread: Songs of the Eagles.* Those wins broke his old record as the all-time leading CMA Awards winner. In the Album of the Year category, he was also a contributor to two other nominees, the *Asleep at the Wheel Tribute to the Music of Bob Wills & The Texas Playboys* and *Rhythm, Country & Blues.*

By early 1995, *When Love Finds You* had gone platinum, and the title track (cowritten by Vince and Michael Omartian) had achieved top positions in just about all major music press charts overseas as well as in the U.S.

Throughout the first half of the 1990s, Vince had enhanced his career with intensive touring that took him to all parts of the U.S. and many other parts of the world. He drew capacity crowds to appearances at fairs and large arenas across the prime country-music regions, and could even fill places where rock and pop usually held sway such as Los Angeles's Greek Theatre. There also were featured appearances on major TV shows on ABC, NBC, and CBS, as well as the syndicated country programs.

He continued to set high performing standards for both himself and the members of his backing band. He told Cromelin, "I have drive and ambition. There are things I'm intense about. I get on the guys if they're not playing as good as they should. I want things to be the best. I'm a perfectionist. I want everyone else to be equally committed. I have a temper that shows up once in a while."

His band members agreed he was a strict taskmaster, but also fair and loyal. Martin Parker, who played drums for him, remarked that when he was forced to take months off for rotator cuff surgery, Gill assured him his job would still be waiting, when many other artists might have replaced him permanently.

Gill's prowess as an instrumentalist caused many young performers to examine his technique for hints on improving their own techniques. *Musician* magazine called attention to the way Vince played with a "stockstill right hand, combining pick and middle finger to get the speed and snap that mark his chicken-on-fire guitar solos."

Vince noted, "I keep the picking hand in place because I use my middle finger a lot to pop with. Playing the banjo helps because you work with three fingers in the Scruggs style." Peter Cronin elaborated: "Holding his pick between index finger and thumb and using his middle finger as a claw, Gill uses the pick for a series of upward bends on the G-string, answering with a trebly pop by pulling up on the B-string with his middle finger."

Gill emphasized, "I use the flesh of that finger to make the Tele [a 1955 Telecaster guitar] snap. Ricky

Skaggs uses his big fat fingernail. It's critical to him. If he lost it he'd be in trouble, but I'd have to lose the whole finger."

Vince continued to do well on the hit lists for the balance of 1995 and into 1996. During the summer of 1995 he had the top-10 single "You Better Think Twice" (cowritten with R. Nielsen) and his albums *When Love Finds You* and *I Still Believe In You* remained on the hit lists in 1996, with the former disc receiving a multiplatinum award for three million copies sold from the R.I.A.A. on December 13, 1995. He had two hit singles on the charts the latter part of 1995, his self-penned "Go Rest High on That Mountain" and a duet with Dolly Parton on her composition "I Will Always Love You." His MCA hit collection, *Souvenirs,* debuted on the *Billboard* chart at number three the week of December 9, 1995, and by May 1996 had already received a platinum R.I.A.A. award. In late November, Vince was among the stars who taped the *Grand Ole Opry* anniversary special (commemorating the debut show on November 28, 1925) that aired on CBS-TV in January 1996. In the spring of 1996, his tribute to bluegrass, "High Lonesome Sound," was doing well on the charts and it soon was joined in upper chart levels by Vince's album of the same name.

In October 1995, Vince again was host of the Country Music Association Awards telecast from the Grand Ole Opry House in Nashville, where he won the Male Vocalist of the Year trophy for a record fifth time. This brought his total of CMA awards to 15, still making him the top winner of all time in that competition. Though he wasn't an award winner in the Academy of Country Music Awards announced in April 1996, he had been a finalist for Top Male Vocalist and, with Dolly Parton, for Top Vocal Duet. In the 1996 CMA Awards voting, Vince once more was a finalist for Male Vocalist of the Year, but this time the honor went to George Strait. Other nominations he received were Vocal Event of the Year (Dolly Parton with Special Guest Vince Gill—"I Will Always Love You"); Music Video of the Year and Single of the Year ("Go Rest High on That Mountain"); and Album of the Year (*High Lonesome Sound*).

However, while his performing career prospered, his marriage did not as Janis Gill filed for divorce in the spring of 1997, requesting custody of their daughter.

GILLEY, MICKEY: *Singer, pianist, songwriter. Born Natchez, Mississippi, March 9, circa 1937.*

Entertainment history is full of stories about talented individuals who confront the problem of sounding almost exactly like someone already famous—Sinatra doubles, Presley sound-alikes, and so on. Some of those unfortunates make a precarious living mimicking the one lucky enough to come first; most sink without a trace. Mickey Gilley, however, beat the odds.

Gilley's problem was that both in vocal style and piano technique he seemed for a long time like a carbon copy of Jerry Lee Lewis. It wasn't all that surprising, since the two were first cousins. Gilley's mother, Irene, was the sister of Jerry Lee's father, Elmo. Jerry Lee was several years older, but the two were almost inseparable as children, along with a third cousin named Jimmy Swaggart, who went on to become a famous radio and TV minister. (Mickey was born in Natchez, Mississippi, but grew up in Jerry Lee's home area of Ferriday.) The three all became interested in playing the piano and, though they came from poor families, their parents managed to get them instruments. In Gilley's case, his mother saved money from the eighteen dollars a week she earned as a waitress to get her son a piano when he was ten or eleven.

It was the mid-1960s and blues and boogie-woogie were in vogue in the black community while country music was the staple of most white Southerners. The three boys fell in love with boogie-woogie, though, and crept into a place in the black section of town called Haney's Big House to listen to the music and pick up the infectious piano rhythms. By the time they were in their teens, all three could play pretty well, but only Jerry Lee thought of it as the basis for a career.

In 1954, Gilley had pretty well forgotten about the music field. He had gotten married and settled in Houston, where he worked in the parts department of an engineering firm. In 1956, he heard one of Jerry Lee's initial releases on Sun Records, "Crazy Arms," and after getting over his first excitement began to try to move in that direction himself. Soon he cut his first record at the Gold Star Studio in Houston amid dreams of glory. As he admitted later, the record was awful.

However, though success didn't smile on him, he had gotten the show business bug. He kept polishing his piano playing and began to get more session work in local studios, including one owned by Huey Meaux, the "Crazy Cajun," who later was instrumental in Freddy Fender's climb to fame. He began to work in clubs and bars in the latter 1950s, including stints in New Orleans, Biloxi, the Azalea Grille in Mobile, Alabama, and an extended stay at Ray's Lounge in Lake Charles, Louisiana. He cut more sides for a series of small labels and moved up a notch to Dot Records, where he gained some attention for the single "Call Me Shorty." However, by the time he decided to make Houston home base again in 1959, his recording efforts essentially were failures. Things took a slight upturn later in the year when he scored a local hit with his version of a Warner Mack success, "Is It Wrong?"

But that proved to be a flash in the pan. Audiences seemed to feel that one Jerry Lee Lewis was enough. In the meantime, Gilley developed into a personable live performer with a strong local following. He earned a reasonable salary working in a series of clubs, beginning with the Ranch House in 1959 and continuing in popular spots in an outlying area of Houston on the Spencer Highway. That was the way things went throughout the 1960s, despite another regional hit single, "Lonely Wine," in 1964. For most of the decade he was featured at Houston's Nesadel Club.

At the start of the 1970s, he changed his pattern, teaming up with a friend named Sherwood Cryer to open their own club, Gilley's, in Pasadena, Texas. The club prospered, featuring Mickey Gilley and his Rocking Piano. Mickey branched out some, hosting his own shows on local TV. Every now and then, he got restless, though, and made an effort to gain recognition outside the Houston area. His similarity to Jerry Lee didn't bother the Houston populace, who made Mickey one of their favorite entertainers, but it tended to work against him with record companies, disc jockeys, and the wider public. Thus when he got the chance to record an album for GRT in the early 1970s, he consciously tried to change his style. He went so far as to refuse to play the piano at all during the sessions.

As he told Peter Guralnick for a *Country Music* article, "I let it bug me to the point where it just about drove me nuts, man. I didn't want to sound anything like Jerry Lee at all, even though I knew that the type of music that he played was the type of music that I feel."

That effort came to naught too and, by 1974, Gilley had just about abandoned hope of national attention. Then a strange series of events catapulted him into the limelight almost before he knew what happened. The catalyst was the request by the ticket taker at Gilley's for Mickey to record a song she loved, 'She Calls Me Baby,' for local jukebox distribution. He agreed and, needing something for the "B" side, put in a song that had been a hit for George Morgan called "Room Full of Roses." In preparing the song, Mickey decided to overdub some steel guitar on his recording. But the engineer, in mixing the material, made the steel guitar much louder than Gilley thought proper.

As he told Guralnick, when he heard the final version of the single he had mixed emotions. "I liked 'She Calls Me Baby' and thought to myself, well, I finally got something. Then I flipped the record over. All I could hear was that damn steel guitar. The echo was just bounding off the walls. I called up the engineer. I said, 'Why's it so loud?' He said, 'Man, I just mixed it the way I felt it.' 'Well,' I said, 'I'm just going to have to remix it. This is terrible.' I went and got the tape. I actually cued the tape up, then I said, 'Hey, I don't want to take the time to mess with this. It's just a local record; it's only going to be played on the local jukeboxes.'"

Once the single came out, "Room Full of Roses" swept Houston. Smelling victory at last, Gilley flew to Nashville to try for a major record tie-up. Everyone turned him down and he was just about to give up again when he thought about one last possibility, the newly

established Playboy label. He took a plane to California, where the company's executives agreed to take a chance. The song turned out to have as powerful an influence on the national country audiences as on Houston. By early spring the single was on the national charts and before long Mickey had his first top-10 hit. This was only the beginning. He followed up with the single "City Lights," which came out at the end of 1974 and quickly zoomed to number one on the charts. Simultaneously, the album of the same title was making a similar move so that in February, Mickey's name dominated both the album and singles charts.

From then on, Mickey was on the move to the top echelons of the country field. He was featured on just about every major TV show, beginning with the *Grand Ole Opry* and extending to nationally telecast country and pop programs. Though Houston remained his main stomping ground, other pianists appeared at Gilley's while Mickey performed in the major stops on the country-music personal appearance circuit.

Meanwhile, Mickey's name rarely was missing from the charts in the mid- and late-1970s. Among his chart singles during that period were "Bouquet of Roses" and "Roll You Like a Wheel" (a duet with Barbi Benton) in 1975; "Don't the Girls All Get Prettier at Closing Time" and "Bring It on Home to Me," both top-10 hits in 1976; the number-one "Honky Tonk Memories" and "Chains of Love" in 1977; and "Here Comes the Hurt Again" and "The Song We Made Love To" in 1978. Mickey's Playboy chart albums included *Overnight Sensation* in early 1976; *Gilley's Greatest Hits, Volume 1,* in the top 10 in August 1976; and *First Class,* a top-10 hit in the summer of 1977. By the late 1970s, he signed with a new label, Epic.

Mickey still found time to appear at his own club in the late 1970s and into the 1980s, and Gilley's prospered whether he or some other country star headlined. The club was selected as the setting for John Travolta's film *Urban Cowboy,* released in 1980. Gilley and his band were given prominent parts in the film score and their contributions were included in the soundtrack LP that was released in April 1980.

His late 1970s and early 1980s chart singles on Epic included "Just Long Enough to Say Goodbye" and "My Silver Lining" in 1979; "A Little Getting Used To," on the lists from late 1979 to early 1980; "True Love Ways" and "That's All That Matters to Me" in 1980; and "A Headache Tomorrow (Or a Heartache Today)" and "Lonely Nights" in 1981. Also a bestseller was the single "Stand By Me," issued by Asylum Records during the summer of 1980. His 1980–81 chart hit Epic LPs included *Encore* and *That's All That Matters to Me.* Epic issued his LP *You Don't Know Me* in July 1981. The title track from that album provided him with another chart hit.

As the 1980s went by, Mickey remained a popular

figure in the country music field, though by the decade's end his ability to place recordings at the top of the charts tapered off. Still by then he had achieved a total of thirty-nine top-10 country singles, with seventeen of those going all the way to number one. Joel Whitburn's 1989 assessment of the most successful country artists in history cited Gilley among the top-50 country hitmakers. His extensive TV credits at the start of the 1990s included guest spots as a performer, actor, and awards show host. Dramatic programs in which he appeared included *Murder, She Wrote, Fantasy Island, The Fall Guy,* and *The Dukes of Hazzard.* He appeared as a panelist on the quiz show *Hollywood Squares.* Other features spots included appearances on *20/20, The Grammy Awards Show, American Music Awards, Solid Gold,* and *The Tonight Show.* He could even boast of having a star on the Hollywood Walk of Fame.

By the late 1980s, Mickey had decided to close down Gilley's Club, once billed as "The World's Largest Honkey Tonk," and shift his attention to the rising country music mecca of Branson, Missouri. He was one of the first country stars to open his own theater there. He commented, "Branson works because it provides the best conditions for both the fans and the entertainers. The fans get to see us under the best setting possible as far as seeing a singer. The theaters have good seats, and we have set up the best stage, the best sound and the best lights. We don't have to break down and set it back up day after day while we travel night after night, so everyone onstage is rested and ready to entertain. It's a quality situation for everyone."

Though he spent a good part of each year during the first part of the 1990s performing at Branson, he still found time on his schedule to work other venues, particularly in his long time habitats of Las Vegas, Reno, and Atlantic City. Though he bought a new home in Branson, as of the mid-1990s he still maintained a residence near Houston.

In 1991, Gilley signed with Warner Brothers Records, where he was reunited with old friend Jim Ed Norman, who had produced many of his chart successes. Later in the decade he moved to the Branson Entertainment records group. His debut on that label, the 1993 album *Make It Like the First Time,* included some of his best-sellers of the past, such as "Room Full of Roses," "True Love Ways," "Put Your Dreams Away," and "Fool for Your Love" as well as a number of new songs, including "You Need a Lady in Your Life," "Make It for the First Time," "The Last Dance with You," and "Object of My Affection."

Gilley's concert work in the 1994–1996 time frame included a number of concerts in Branson. He also had his Wild Bull Chili in food markets around the country and in early 1996 during a winter guest appearance on Conan O'Brien's *Late Show* on NBC-TV brought along enough of the product to treat the program crew and audience.

GILMORE, JIMMIE DALE: *Singer, guitarist, songwriter. Born Lubbock, Texas, 1945.*

Jimmie Dale Gilmore is an original, and as with any artist having a unique style, often difficult for radio programmers, and the music industry as a whole, to pigeonhole. Thus while he spent years building a cult following among music fans and earned the admiration of musicians across the pop-country-folk spectrum, he was still awaiting his first breakthrough to mainstream audiences as he neared the age of fifty. Even without blockbuster records and videos or prestigious awards, there's no doubt that he has made considerable creative contributions to country music, his primary love from his early years in West Texas.

Among the career contradictions Gilmore presented to music-industry executives was his twangy vocal style, which had the ring of traditional country (some observers described his style as a throwback to the presynthesizer era); at the same time, there were detectable elements of other musical genres (sometimes described as "Zen country") in the mix, and his original lyrics were often decidedly more complex than typical country material. His lyrics, in fact, while different in content, have an originality comparable to those of someone like Bob Dylan, a fact that has brought him the sobriquet of "the Sagebrush Poet."

Gilmore spent his earliest years in the small Texas town of Tulia; his father was a bacteriologist and sometime guitarist in a country band. When he was in grade school the family moved to Lubbock, a period when he started learning guitar and paid close attention to a wide range of musical formats. He told Cyndi Hoelzle of *The Gavin Report* ("The Father of Western Beat—Jimmie Dale Gilmore," September 27, 1991), "In the fifties and sixties there was really good radio in Lubbock, a huge selection. We had real good Country stations, and good rock and roll stations. And we also had those border stations that played the blues and gospel and old time hillbilly. And then there was the Tex-Mex influence." He attributed that environment as helping the development of the unique styles of such artists from the area as Buddy Holly, Butch Hancock, and Joe Ely.

While all that sank into his consciousness, he stressed that his first musical love was country. When his peer group in school first heard the country songs he played on his guitar, they laughed. "My friends made fun of me for liking country music. They just hated it, couldn't stomach it. But when I started playing, those same friends started listening and slowly became converts. I was a fluke in that I didn't learn to like country music because of Bob Dylan. I always liked it and I never rebelled against it."

As he told a *Los Angeles Times* reporter, his father's love for the music also was a key influence in his outlook. Country music was "just an ever present thing in our house and in our cars, and I loved it. But when Elvis came along and Little Richard and Chuck Berry, I just adopted that stuff along with it. I didn't stop liking the country music, which a lot of my friends did. I just adopted it."

Gilmore recalled that his early family years were happy despite an environment of extreme poverty caused in part by his father's alcoholism. During his high school years, though, conflicts arose which caused Jimmie to leave home once his high school years were over. Ironically, he left just about the time his father finally stopped drinking. He married schoolmate Jo Carol Pierce and, during a stormy three-year relationship, fathered a daughter. During the late-sixties period, Jimmie moved his family to Los Angeles, where he worked at various odd jobs while performing at small clubs in the area.

After the couple split up, Jimmie settled in West Texas again at the start of the 1970s, sharing a house with such other young music aspirants as Ely, Hancock, and Jesse Taylor. They organized an acoustic country string band called the Flatlanders that played at local clubs and honky-tonks, with Gilmore serving as lead vocalist. In 1972, the band went to Nashville and recorded the album *Jimmie Dale and the Flatlanders* for an independent label—an album that gained little attention at the time, but since then has assumed almost legendary proportions. The only single issued at the time was Gilmore's rendering of "Dallas." The album was reissued by Rounder Records in 1990, bearing the new title *More a Legend Than a Band.*

That band broke up in 1973, by which time Gilmore had become deeply involved in Eastern religions. For the rest of the decade he dropped out of the music industry whirl to live in Denver, Colorado, as a disciple of Indian teacher Guru Maharaj Gi. However, he emphasized to *Los Angeles Times* writer Richard Cromelin, "I never did truly leave the music. Sometimes it's been portrayed that I just blew off music entirely, but the thing is, I just wasn't pursuing a career. . . . The music was always a part of it."

At the end of the 1970s, he decided he needed to determine what to do with the rest of his life. He briefly thought about learning something like acupuncture and Chinese medicine, but the lure of the music field remained strong, and he chose to go back to Texas to see if he could make better progress in his first love. He settled in Austin, where many of his old friends now lived, and where people like Jerry Jeff Walker and Willie Nelson were spearheading a dynamic alternative country scene. But for a time it seemed as though Gilmore wouldn't make the most of new opportunities.

He recalled to Mike Boehm of the *Los Angeles Times,* "After I had been immersed in the spiritual discipline and surroundings, I came back into the music business and went hog wild to the other end of the pendulum. Over a period of years I just became completely crazed and drunk all the time.

"I backslid past the worst place I was before. Moderation in everything has to become a guiding principle. The coming out of a hard time and into a positive view, that was really the case. I reconnected with my spiritual discipline, I sort of was given a second chance."

In 1982, Gilmore got past that self-destructive phase and concentrated on moving his career forward. He began to renew old contacts and started finding good engagements at Austin venues while also expanding his audience to many other parts of the U.S. Getting a recording alignment was important and, aided by people like Ely, who were doing reasonably well as entertainers and recording artists, he got the chance to record new material on the independent Hightone label.

With Ely as producer, he completed the album *Fair Square,* an impressive collection that was hailed by many major reviewers after its 1988 release. He also received high praise for his follow-up, also produced by Ely, *Jimmie Dale Gilmore,* issued in 1989. Those certainly weren't best-sellers, but they won the attention of knowledgeable listeners and helped open new avenues for Jimmie to expand his performance credentials.

He got the chance to tour with a number of successful artists, including a notable performance at the Montreaux Jazz Festival in Switzerland on July 4, 1991. As part of an American music segment, Jimmie performed with Ely, Hancock, Kevin Welch, Jim Lauderdale, and the Texas Tornados in an enthusiastically received set that was described by one European writer as a showcase for "Western Beat."

By then Gilmore had been signed to a one-album deal for the Elektra/Nonesuch American Explorer label. The result was the album *After Awhile,* issued in 1991. The collection, which included such Gilmore concert favorites as "Treat Me Like a Saturday Night" and "I Think I'm Gonna Go Downtown," ended up on a number of Album of the Year lists. Dale got the opportunity to add more followers in 1992 when he went on a nationwide tour with country star Marty Brown.

After Awhile had no chance to show up on *Billboard* or other hit charts, but its critical reception and acceptable sales totals (of around 40,000 copies) encouraged Elektra to sign him on their major label roster. The new album, *Spinning Around the Sun,* once more confirmed his position as a major artist, one who would influence many other up-and-coming talents whether or not he ever broke through to stardom himself. Released in the fall of 1993, it followed its predecessor into many "Best-of" reviewer lists. During 1993–94, Jimmie got considerable TV exposure, including an appearance on the NBC *Tonight Show,* hosted by Jay Leno. He also was on the concert trail backed by a new band.

Jimmie, who always had the reputation of being a sweet-spirited and optimistic person, thought the success of hard-to-classify performers like Lyle Lovett might foretell better things ahead for himself. He told Richard Cromelin, "I think that public taste has moved, both in the country music world and the pop world, so there's more room for experimentation than five or ten years ago.... So it's beginning to look like now that being between the cracks is not only not an obstacle, but that it's an actual selling point for me."

In the summer and fall of 1996, Jimmie was touring in support of an excellent new album, *Braver Newer World.* The disc had a stronger rock flavor than earlier releases including support on some parts from the Seattle rock band Mudhoney. During a concert at the Coach House venue in San Juan Capistrano, California, in September 1996, he preceded performance of the Townes Van Zandt composition "Buckskin Stallion Blues" (played on the record with Mudhoney) with the comments, "This is a blues song and a rock song and a folk song and a grunge song. It's every song in one. It's mainly a beautiful song. Now it's a loud song. But you can hear the silence in it if you listen real closely."

GIMBLE, JOHNNY: *Singer, fiddler, mandolinist, banjo player, songwriter. Born near Tyler Texas, May 30, 1926.*

For decades most of Johnny Gimble's instrumental contemporaries knew that he was one of the greatest fiddle players Texas had ever produced. His name, however, wasn't very familiar to most followers of country & western music most of that time, though the sounds of his fiddle (and other instruments) could be heard on the hit records of many artists over the years. All that changed in the mid-1970s when Johnny, helped by a revival of interest in western swing bands, suddenly found himself in the spotlight as a solo performer.

Born and raised in Texas, Johnny showed ability as a musician at an early age and could play several instruments by the time he was in his teens. At the age of sixteen, he played banjo for a group headed by Bob and Joe Shelton. At the end of the decade, in 1949, he got the chance to join one of the foremost western swing bands in history, Bob Wills' Texas Playboys. Again he wasn't recruited as a fiddler but as a mandolinist.

In his years with Wills, which extended well into the 1950s, he established himself as a first-rank fiddler. Besides playing fiddle and other instruments, he also wrote a number of original songs, some of which were recorded by the Playboys. By the time Gimble's years with Wills came to an end, he had an impressive reputation with important artists in both country and pop music and with record producers. During the 1960s and 1970s, when he wasn't working as a sideman with various tour bands, he had a busy schedule of session work in major studios in Nashville and other major music industry centers. In his fiddle playing, he demonstrated amazing versatility on not just one type of fiddle but two. One of those was a four-string instrument he called "Ole Red," the other with five strings, he just referred to as his "Five."

This pattern might have continued throughout the 1970s except that Bob Wills, who had been semiretired for some years, conceived a new record project. He wanted to re-form his Playboys band for new versions of some of his most famous songs. But this wasn't to be just any band; he wanted to assemble what he considered the best of all those who had been in the band over the decades of its existence. The fiddle players he wanted were Keith Coleman and Johnny.

The project got under way, but only part of the sessions was completed when Wills was incapacitated by a stroke. The remaining members went on to finish the recordings, which later provided the basis for the multi-LP set *For the Last Time.* Meanwhile, Leon McAuliffe and Leon Rausch, who had taken over the band's reins after Wills was stricken, eventually agreed to some new stage work by the band. In October 1975 (by which time Wills had died), the group won a standing ovation when it made a guest appearance at Nashville's Exit-In club with Asleep at the Wheel. That, in turn, paved the way for further concert work in early 1976 and a decision to make some new band recordings for Capitol.

Gimble continued as a featured artist with the all-star group during those events and was a member of the band for its 1976 studio sessions for the new Capitol LP. Meanwhile, he had received additional notice for some of his solos in a Capitol release in August 1976 (*Bob Wills and His Texas Playboys in Concert*) prepared from tapes of old radio programs. This activity brought him renewed attention from members of the Country Music Association, who voted him Instrumentalist of the Year in the CMA Awards competition, results of which were announced on a network TV show in October 1976.

As a result, he began to get offers from recording executives to cut some solo albums of his own. By the time the new Playboys studio LP came out in August 1977, titled *The Late Bob Wills' Texas Playboys Today,* he had taken leave of the band to work on the new solo material. He turned out two LPs during the year, one on Capitol called *Fiddlin' Around* and another on Lone Star Records called *Johnny Gimble, Texas Dance Party.* Both albums still are considered prime examples of "old-timey" Texas fiddling.

In the late 1970s, Gimble headlined a number of shows of his own on the country-music circuit. He also continued to back some of the superstars of the period, such as Willie Nelson and Waylon Jennings. During 1979–81, for example, he was a member of Nelson's tour band, which played before large crowds in major venues all over the United States.

This pattern continued without much change for the rest of the 1980s into the 1990s. Johnny continued to be in demand as a session musician and supporting artist for veteran stars as well as some of the newcomers. In the span from 1980 through 1990, Gimble was nominated in Country Music Association voting for Instrumentalist/Musician of the Year ten of eleven years, missing out only in 1984 and winning the award four times: 1986, 1987, 1989, and 1990. In 1994 he was one of the artists contributing to the hit album *Asleep at the Wheel Tribute to the Music of Bob Wills & The Texas Playboys,* one of the CMA nominees for Album of the Year. He also took part in a number of events in honor of Asleep at the Wheel's 25th anniversary during 1995 and 1996 including the January 27, 1996 program on *Austin City Limits.*

GOSDIN, VERN: *Singer, guitarist, mandolinist, banjo player. Born Woodland, Alabama, August 5, 1934.*

One night in 1977 a nervous newcomer to country-music acclaim prepared to make his debut on the *Grand Ole Opry.* Vern Gosdin had first imagined himself on the *Opry* stage close to four decades earlier and had just about given up hope years before. But in the country field, there often is room for a second chance.

As he told writer Sanford Brokaw, "I used to listen to the *Opry* religiously every Saturday night down on our farm in Woodland, Alabama. There was no TV, so it was important. There were thirty-nine knobs and only two of them worked. The reception wasn't too good either. I had to go outside and jiggle the ground wire. Even then, I put one ear against the speaker so I could hear.

"There were many Saturday nights I went to sleep listening to the *Opry* and dreaming of being right there. By the time I was eight, I was a big fan of the Louvin Brothers. I really liked their harmonies. This, of course, has been a big influence on my singing."

Those harmonies were emulated by Vern and two brothers, who started singing gospel songs in their church and then became regulars on the Gosdin Family gospel show on WVOK radio in Birmingham, Alabama, in the early 1950s. Vern moved to Atlanta, Georgia in 1953, where he sold ice cream to support himself while he sought work as a country artist. His next move was north to Chicago in 1956, where he ran a country-music nightclub, the D&G Tap, for several years. During that time, he continued to hone his bluegrass oriented style as a multitalented musician and a strong-voiced singer.

The big time in country music or music in general obviously wasn't Chicago, so in 1960, Vern headed west to California to join brother Rex in a bluegrass group called the Golden State Boys. In the early 1960s, Vern and Rex switched to a group called the Hillmen, led by a young California-bred bluegrass musician, Chris Hillman. But the folk boom was fading and Chris moved into rock after a while as a founding member of the folk-rock supergroup, the Byrds. The friendship between Chris and the Gosdins remained, which later led to Chris and another ex-Byrd, Clarence White, recording Vern's song "Someone to Turn To" for the soundtrack of the film *Easy Rider.*

Meanwhile, Vern worked as a session musician in the mid-1960s and tried to break into the recording field. He was signed for short periods with a variety of labels, including Liberty, Capitol, Metromedia, Era, and Bakersfield International with varying degrees of success. Vern and Rex continued to stress their traditional bluegrass sound, which was favored by many Byrds, including Gene Clark. This led to Gene teaming with them for the 1966 album *Gene Clark with the Gosdin Brothers,* where the sidemen included such names as Chris Hillman and Michael Clarke from the Byrds, Leon Russell, Doug Dillard, and Glen Campbell.

The Gosdins recorded some sides for the small Bakersfield International label during that period, one of which, "Hangin' On," caught fire with country DJs and made it up to eighteen on the charts. (The song, like Vern, had a second time around.) The Gosdins seemed on the brink of country stardom, particularly when they moved over to Capitol in late 1967. They worked up an album called *Sounds of Goodbye* that included an excellent song by Vern's wife, Cathy (they since have divorced), called "Till the End." However, things slowed down for the brothers as the decade came to an end and they broke up the act.

Discouraged, Vern went back to Georgia and settled in Atlanta to raise his family. He opened a glass and mirror business that did reasonably well and relegated music to a spare-time avocation. That's the way things stood for close to a decade. Then, one day in 1976, producer Gary Paxton, a friend from Vern's years in Los Angeles, called from Nashville. "I ran into your brother Rex today," Gary said. "I told him I was looking for someone to record the old 'Hangin' On' as a single. Would you like to do it?"

Vern admits he was skeptical, but the pull of the music field was still too strong to refuse. He recorded several songs under a new pact with Elektra Records. The debut single wasn't "Hangin' On," but "Yesterday's Gone," which, with Emmylou Harris singing harmony, made the top 20. "Hangin' On" followed with equal success, finally making Vern begin to feel he might make it to the top after all those years. Still, for a while he refused to tour, staying in Atlanta to keep his business going. (Later he turned it over to his sons to operate.)

In June 1977, his debut LP came out on Elektra, named after the title track, "Till the End," which found the favor that had eluded it in 1969, making it into the country top five and helping the album to attain a similar position. Other songs from the album were issued as singles and showed up on the charts: "Mother Country Music" in October 1977 and "It Started All Over Again" in January 1978. In early 1978, Vern was back in the studios recording *Never My Love,* released in the spring and almost immediately a hit, as was the title track. In March, Rex rejoined Vern for a new round of concert dates. It was just like old times—only better.

Vern finished up the decade with several more chart hits on Elektra, including singles like "Break My

Mind," in the top 15 in late 1978, and, in 1979, "You've Got Somebody, I've Got Somebody" and "Sarah's Eyes." Vern's alignment with Elektra ended in 1979. His final albums issued on the label were *You've Got Somebody* and *The Best of Vern Gosdin,* both released in 1979.

At the start of the 1980s, he signed with Ovation Records, for whom he provided the 1981 chart single "Too Long Gone," During 1981 his Ovation debut album, *Passion,* was released and spent some months on the charts. Later in the decade he achieved his first number-one single, which made the top-chart position in 1984.

For a while, Vern continued to earn chart success with his new releases, but his recordings began to find decreasing fan response, and by the late 1980s he was without a record label. But he continued to write original material, collaborating with highly respected craftsmen like Max D. Barnes and Hank Cochran. After helping Vern prepare material for a new album for which Cochran cowrote seven songs with Barnes cowriting on some of those as well as several others, Cochran presented demos to Columbia and urged label executives to sign his friend.

Columbia agreed and the alliance resulted in the 1989 release *Chiseled in Stone.* Among the tracks of Gosdin/Cochran originals were such fine songs as "Set 'Em Up Joe," "Who You Gonna Blame It on This Time," and "That Just About Does It" (the last named was number seven in *Radio & Records* the week of December 22, 1989). The album was a chart hit, as was the title song, cowritten by Barnes and Gosdin. The Gosdin recording was one of the finalists for Country Music Association 1989 Single of the Year.

Gosdin recalled the origins of the song for the CMA *Close Up* magazine. "Max came to me with the title. His oldest boy was killed in a car wreck and he had been carrying around this line, 'You don't know about lonely 'til it's chiseled in stone.' It really touched me. I was coming from a totally different place, my divorce after eleven years. I was left all by myself with four walls and three empty closets. The song for me was symbolic of a love that was dead."

During 1990, Gosdin had a new album, *Alone,* in the stores, which included five songs he cowrote with Hank Cochran. His credits for the year included the hit singles "Right in the Wrong Direction" (number six in *R&R* the week of April 13) and "This Ain't My First Rodeo" (number ten in *R&R* the week of November 26), cowritten with Cochran and Barnes. In 1991 he made the *Billboard* list with his third Columbia album, *Out of My Heart,* and the single "The Garden."

GRAND OLE OPRY: *Weekly variety show, originating from station WSM, Nashville, Tennessee.*

In the days of vaudeville, the goal of all performers was to play the New York Palace Theater. During the years of Palace greatness, another institution was beginning to take hold in the South. An appearance on the *Grand Ole Opry*, a radio program broadcast from Nashville, Tennessee, was to become the goal of all hopefuls in the country & western field. Although the *Grand Old Opry* was a radio program, it bore a strong resemblance to the Palace shows. From its early years, the *Opry* was performed before live audiences and, after 1941, in its own auditorium, the Ryman Auditorium in downtown Nashville (where it remained until the early 1970s when it relocated to its present home, Opryland).

The show began under a different name on November 28, 1925. It was called the WSM *Barn Dance* and was founded by George D. Hay, known as the "Solemn Ol' Judge." (*See separate entry for Hay, George Dewey.*) The first performer on the program—broadcast for about an hour starting at 8 P.M., Saturdays, from Studio A of WSM in Nashville—was a bearded fiddler, Uncle Jimmy Thompson, accompanied by his niece, Mrs. Eva Thompson Jones. (Uncle Jimmy died at age 83 on February 17, 1931.) When the show later shifted to WSM's Studio B, it became known as the *Grand Ole Opry*.

Hay was credited with coining the new name. The *Barn Dance* followed a broadcast of the NBC Symphony Orchestra originating from New York City and, one evening, Hay introduced his show with the words: "From here on out folks, it will be nothing but realism of the realistic kind. You've been up in the clouds with grand opera, now get down to earth with us in a . . . shindig of *Grand Ole Opry!*"

During 1926, Uncle Dave Macon joined the cast, and soon became the first performer to achieve national stardom through the *Opry* broadcasts. He remained a featured artist with the show until his death in 1952, by which time the program had expanded to occupy most of the Saturday evening hours on WSM with the greatest names in country music taking part. Over the years, the *Opry* has continued to grow in stature while maintaining its position at the center of the country & western field. Since its inception, the program has showcased almost every country artist of any prominence as guests or regulars, including almost all the country performers listed in this encyclopedia.

The *Opry* can't claim the honor of being the first of its kind. Earlier examples of the same kind of format included a barn dance program broadcast on station WBAP, Ft. Worth, Texas, on January 4, 1923, and the *National Barn Dance*, which began its run on station WLS, Chicago, Illinois, in 1923. But long after the others had gone off the air, the *Opry* was still in existence as the acknowledged mecca of the major stars of the country & western field. After the rise of television, the *Opry* stage was used not only for *Opry* radio broadcasts, but also as the setting for countless country music specials and syndicated country TV shows. The first telecast of an *Opry* show took place on September 30, 1950.

The *Opry* had several temporary homes before it settled down to its many decades in the Ryman Auditorium. These includes the Hillsboro Theater, the East Nashville Tabernacle, WSM's Studio C, and the West Memorial Building. When the program moved to Ryman in 1941, long lines of people assembled every Saturday for the show that began at 7:30 P.M. and continued until midnight. By the 1960s, the outside of the theater had been turned into a replica of a big red barn with the words "Grand Ole Opry" spelled out in large white letters.

As the 1960s drew to a close, WSM management (the station has been owned by National Life and Accident Insurance Company throughout the *Opry's* history) decided the time had come to consider building a new home for the show. A study contract was issued to Research Associates, Los Angeles, the firm that had planned Disneyland, for a new combined auditorium (4,000 seats) and tourist center to be named Opryland. A site for the new theme park was chosen outside Nashville. Opryland opened officially on April 27, 1973. The last Saturday night *Opry* performance from the Ryman Auditorium took place on March 9, 1974, after which all performances were scheduled for the new Opryland.

GREENE, JACK: *Singer, guitarist, drummer, songwriter, band leader (The Jolly Giants). Born Maryville, Tennessee, January 7, 1930.*

A number of performers got their seasoning in Ernest Tubb's band, the Texas Troubadours. Perhaps the most notable is Jack Greene, called "The Jolly Giant" because of his height (over six feet) and personality, who sprang to stardom from the band.

Born and raised in Maryville, Tennessee, Jack started to learn guitar when he was eight and was still attending school when he was featured on two daily shows of his own on a home-town station. In his teens, he varied his musical routine by becoming proficient on drums.

By the late 1940s, he was living in Atlanta, Georgia, where he played guitar and sang with a group called the Cherokee Trio. The other members were standup bass player L. M. Bryant and fiddler Speedy Price. In 1950, he joined a group called the Rhythm Ranch Boys as a drummer and guitarist. The group started to pick up a following in the region, but that phase of Jack's career ended after a year when he entered the army. The army soon sent him to Alaska, where he spent much of 1951, and then back to Colorado the following year to be a member of the Special Drill Squad at Camp Carson.

In 1952, he received his discharge and returned to Atlanta, where he soon signed on with a group called the Peachtree Cowboys. For a decade, the band worked

the southern states, often serving as a house band for local clubs.

Jack's turning point came in June 1962, when Ernest Tubb had an opening for a skilled musician in his band. Tubb was impressed by Greene's versatility—the fact that he could perform on drums and guitar and also handle either lead or backing vocals with equal skill—and Greene won the job. The association with the Troubadours gave Jack exposure to Tubb's legion of fans and the chance to play regularly on the hallowed *Grand Ole Opry* radio program. The contacts he made on the *Opry* led to one of his first chances to take the spotlight. Dottie West had recorded a song with Jim Reeves a little before that superstar perished in a plane accident. She enlisted Greene's aid to take the male part on "Love Is No Excuse" on an *Opry* show in 1964.

During his stay with the Troubadours, Jack gradually received more and more opportunity to showcase his talents. Besides taking several solos on some show segments, he got the chance to sing lead on several recordings. In the mid-1960s, Decca released a band album titled *Ernest Tubb Presents the Texas Troubadours*, and one track, Jack's vocal of "The Last Letter," began to get airplay on country stations across the land. Public clamor for a single of the number became so great the record company released one. The single swiftly moved into the top-chart positions and Jack was catapulted from the band into stardom. Ensuring that status was the success of a string of hit singles from late 1966 into 1968.

The first of those was Hank Cochran's "Don't You Ever Get Tired of Hurting Me?" Next came his version of Marty Robbins' "Ever Since My Baby Went Away." But topping all of those was his single of Dallas Frazier's "There Goes My Everything," which became a number-one country hit. Jack noted that his wife, Barbara, had liked the song and tried several times to get him to record it. She commented, "It laid around the house for a couple of years and then one day he just decided to do it." During 1967, Greene had another number-one hit, "All the Time," to further solidify his reputation as a great new star.

At the end of 1967, on December 23, he received a special Christmas present—he was chosen as a regular cast member of the *Opry*. When he made his first appearance as a solo artist in front of *Opry* mikes, his introduction was given by long-time mentor Ernest Tubb. Jack's achievements were recognized by those voting in the Country Music Association's first annual awards competition that year. He was named Male Vocalist of 1967 and also awarded top spot for Single of the Year and Album of the Year (for *There Goes My Everything*). The song also was voted Song of the Year.

In addition to those honors, Jack also was given two Grammy nominations for 1967. Another highlight of the year for him was taking part in the Macy's Thanksgiving Day Parade. As part of that effort, he sang his hit song before NBC-TV cameras in front of the New York department store.

Jack continued to make top-chart levels in 1968 with such singles as "What Locks the Door" and "You Are My Treasure." Besides his *Opry* chores, he was on the road constantly in the late 1960s, headlining shows in major country venues all over the United States and Canada. At the end of the decade, he started doing a series of duets with Jeannie Seely that also caught the fancy of country audiences, Jeannie became a regular member of Greene's touring show, still one of the most popular on the country circuit over a decade later. That standing held true for the Greene and Seely segment of the *Opry*, which was still going strong at the start of the 1980s.

Greene continued to place songs on the charts in the early 1970s, though things slowed down for him after that. Among his charted singles were "Something Unseen/What's the Use," a top-20 hit in late 1971, "If You Ever Need My Love," in top-chart levels in the spring of 1972, and "What's Wrong with Our Love," a hit duet with Seely in the late summer of 1972.

Jack's debut album, *Jack Greene*, was issued by Decca in February 1967. Among his other LPs of the late 1960s were *All the Time* (8/67), *Jack Greene* (1/68), *I Am Not Alone*, and *Statue of a Fool* (8/69). Among his early 1970s album releases were *Lord Is That Me, Jack Greene with Jeannie Seely, Greatest Hits, There's a Whole Lot About a Woman*, and *Jack Greene Country*.

Jack and Decca/MCA parted company during the 1970s. In 1979 he signed with a new label, Frontline Records. His debut single for Frontline, "Yours for the Taking," was on country charts in early 1980 and was the title track for his debut album on the label. Later in the year he had such other charted singles as "Rock I'm Leaning On" and "Devil's Den."

GREENWOOD, LEE: *Singer, pianist, songwriter. Born Los Angeles, California, October 27, c. mid-1940s.*

As Lee Greenwood demonstrated, it's never too late to succeed as a performer in country music. He labored in obscurity for almost two decades before making it big as a writer and soloist. And, in a rare instance of an artist's role in national politics, one of his songs might be considered indirectly to have played an important role in electing a U.S. president.

He was born in Los Angeles, a hotbed of pop and rock, but his leanings early on were toward country. He became a proficient instrumentalist in his teens and found his initial opportunities in Las Vegas, Nevada, in the early 1960s. He found steady work as a lounge performer in Vegas casinos, where his rough-edged voice reminded some of the style of Ray Charles and others of the Doobie Brothers' Michael McDonald. He thought his Vegas stint (during which he worked as a music arranger, band leader, show tune writer, backup singer, and piano bar performer) would become a stepping-

stone to bigger things, but despite his efforts to enlist the aid of other artists who passed through that city's venues, for eighteen years he made little headway.

Toward the end of that period, his demos of original compositions did gain attention from some country entertainers, particularly Kenny Rogers, who had a chart hit with Lee's "A Love Song." At the start of the 1980s, Greenwood finally got a contract with a major label, MCA Nashville, and completed his debut album, *Inside Out*, by mid-1981. A single of the title track, "It Turns Me Inside Out," preceded the album and provided his first chart appearance on September 19, 1981. It became a chart hit as did succeeding singles from the album, which made the *Billboard* list and continued to sell steadily through the first half of the decade until it earned R.I.A.A. gold-record certification in late 1985.

Over the next few years he became a featured artist on the concert circuit while he placed two more solo albums and a string of singles on the charts. His output included two number-one successes, "Somebody's Gonna Love You" and "Going, Going, Gone."

By 1982, his name was showing up on nomination lists for all the major awards, including those of the Academy of Country Music, Country Music Association, and TNN/Music City News. CMA voters in the 1982 awards nominated "It Turns Me Inside Out" for Single of the Year and Lee for the Horizon Award. In 1983 he won a Grammy for his singles hit "I.O.U.," voted Best Country Vocal Performance, Male. The recording also was nominated for CMA Single of the Year with a nod to Greenwood for Male Vocalist of the Year. Greenwood received the trophy in the latter category on the CMA Awards telecast in October 1983.

In 1983, Lee struck a responsive chord with music fans from diverse genres with his composition "God Bless the U.S.A." That song, along with other number-one and top-10 releases were combined on his *Greatest Hits* album issued by MCA in 1984. "God Bless the U.S.A." quickly found wide use as a daily sign-off on many TV stations and as a supplement to "Take Me Out to the Ball Game" during the seventh-inning stretch at many baseball parks. It was also widely used by supporters of President Ronald Reagan during his successful reelection campaign in 1984. The song was nominated for CMA Song of the Year in 1984; Lee was also a finalist for Entertainer of the Year and Male Vocalist of the Year, winning the latter for the second year in a row. In 1985 CMA polling, "God Bless the U.S.A." was voted Song of the Year. (Greenwood also received another nomination for Male Vocalist of the Year.)

His career continued to prosper in the second half of the 1980s from a live performance standpoint, though not with the recording explosiveness of the first half. By the end of the decade he had signed with a new label, Capitol Records. His Capitol releases in the early 1990s included the solo singles chart hit in 1990, "Holdin' a Good Hand," and a duet with Suzy Bogguss, "Hopelessly Yours," which was inside the *Billboard Top* 15 in August 1991.

By the mid-1990s, Lee's association with Capitol had ended and he was looking for a new major label home. Meanwhile, he kept up an intensive touring schedule that took him to many important venues across the U.S. In the summer of 1995, Lee had a new album out on the Arrival Records label, *Totally Devoted to You.* He wound up 1995 by cohosting with Kathy Haas the December 31 TNN show *New Year's Eve at Sea World Live.* He stated that event would be his final tour date—at least for the time being—based on his plans to only perform at his new 1,770-seat Lee Greenwood Theater in Sevierville, Tennessee, which he opened in April 1996.

ℋ

HAGGARD, MERLE: *Singer, guitarist, band leader (The Strangers), songwriter. Born Bakersfield, California, April 6, 1937. Elected to Country Music Hall of Fame in 1994.*

When Bakersfield, California, gained the reputation of "Nashville West" in the 1960s a major reason was its native son, Merle Haggard. A rugged individualist, uncompromising in his creative efforts, he had an emotional flair that rarely failed to deeply affect his audiences. Though he became a superstar during the 1960s and 1970s, he always called Bakersfield home.

Merle's formative years, which formed the basis for many of his classic songs, were fraught with difficulties and traumas. The problems and poverty that beset his family at the time gave rise to an angry teenage rebellion that for a while seemed likely to destroy his life before it really got under way. It took a strong will for someone who, as Merle wrote in one song, "turned twenty-one in prison" to reverse his direction and set a positive example later on for his own children as well as millions of other young people.

His parents were victims of the Dust Bowl in Oklahoma during the Depression. Like thousands of other southwesterners in 1934, the Haggards en route to California found themselves mired in the so-called Hoover Camps so well depicted in John Steinbeck's *The Grapes of Wrath.* Merle's father finally found a low-echelon job on the Santa Fe Railroad and his mother milked cows. Still, it was a hand-to-mouth existence, and the family was living in a converted boxcar in Bakersfield when Merle was born in 1937.

The family's fortunes were improving in the 1940s until, when Merle was nine, his father died. The boy reacted bitterly, becoming increasingly wild as he approached his teens. Later, in the 1960s, he ruefully recalled the period with such moving songs as "Mama Tried" and "Hungry Eyes."

When he was fourteen, he ran away from home and spent much of the next half dozen years picking up odd jobs, wandering around California, occasionally resorting to petty crimes. Again, some of those activities turned up in songs such as "Workin' Man Blues," "Sing Me Back Home," and "The Bottle Let Me Down."

During all of this time his love for country music grew. At home he had listened to country programs on the radio, and, while he was on the road in his teens he continued to listen to the recordings of people like Jimmie Rodgers, Bob Wills, and Lefty Frizzell. After a while, he began to pick out some of these songs on the guitar.

His musical repertoire proved to be a sustaining force when, in 1957, he was convicted on a burglary charge and sent to San Quentin Prison for an extended period. Once in prison, exhorted by a brother to pull himself together, Merle slowly found a new path for himself. Part of the time he worked in the textile mill and took courses that promised the equivalent of a high school diploma. He also put his musical talents to work, first to entertain some of his cellmates, then as a member of the warden's country band. Merle began to think about trying to make a career in music once he returned to the outside world.

In 1960, after two years and nine months behind bars, having proved himself an exemplary prisoner, he was given his parole. He went home to Bakersfield to seek work as a musician. His auditions were impressive and he started working the many bars and nightclubs frequented by country fans in and around Bakersfield. Word of his talents started to circulate, leading to better assignments, including the opportunity to perform on local TV programs.

During the early 1960s, his contacts with the burgeoning Bakersfield country music operations expanded rapidly. He did some session work for established country artists and started looking for a recording alignment for himself. Among those he met was a fine female vocalist named Bonnie Owens, who originally came to Bakersfield as Buck Owens's wife (the two became estranged by the mid-1960s). Merle and Bonnie began to work together and, in 1964, had a moderate hit with the release "Just Between the Two of Us" on Tally Records.

That success caused Capitol Records to sign both of them in 1965, a pivotal year for Merle: he formed his own band, the Strangers, scored his first national top-10 hit, and married Bonnie Owens. Although he had already written quite a few original songs by then, either by himself or with Bonnie, his first breakthrough single was of a Bill Anderson song, "(From Now on All My Friends Are Gonna Be) Strangers." The title provided the name for his band.

His debut Capitol LP, also titled *Strangers,* issued in

October 1965, was a top country LP of the year. The album featured five of his own songs, including one that made upper-chart levels, "I'm Gonna Break Every Heart I Can." For Merle's follow-up LP, he was joined by his wife, Bonnie. Called *Just Between the Two of Us,* issued in May 1966, its title number was a remake of their earlier regional hit. His next solo LP, *Swingin' Doors* (November 1966), also was a bestseller as was the single of its title song, a Haggard composition. Besides that release, his singles output for 1966–67 included "The Girl Turned Ripe," "The Longer You Wait," "I'm a Lonesome Fugitive," "Someone Told My Story," "I Threw Away the Rose," "Loneliness Is Eating Me Alive," "You Don't Have Very Far to Go," "Branded Man," and "The Bottle Let Me Down." The last two, both written by Merle, were top-10 hits, as was "I Threw Away the Rose." "I'm a Lonesome Fugitive" did even better, rising to number one on national country lists and establishing Merle as a major new star with fans in all parts of the union. The song was the title tune of his third solo LP on Capitol, released in April 1967.

In recognition of his achievements, the western-based Academy of Country & Western Music named Merle and Bonnie the Best Vocal Group of 1965 and Merle the Most Promising Male Vocalist of 1965 and, in 1966, repeated the Top Vocal Group accolade. They won for a third time in a row in the 1967 voting.

To support their rising esteem with country fans, Merle, Bonnie, and the Strangers made many coast-to-coast swings of the United States from the mid-1960s on. They also starred on many top TV shows of the mid-1960s, including *The Jimmy Dean Show* and *Swingin' Country.*

In the late 1960s, Haggard's stature in the country field continued to increase rapidly as he turned out a stream of excellently crafted singles and albums. Among the LPs were *Branded Man* (10/67), *Sing Me Back Home* (2/69), *CloseUp* (7/69), *Portrait* (10/69), and *Okie from Muskogee.* The single "Okie from Muskogee," a litany in favor of old-time American virtues and against pot smokers and hippies, capped his 1960s efforts and made him a familiar figure to pop fans as well as country adherents. The song rose to number one on country charts, as did the album of that title, and was high on pop lists as well. The pro and con controversy that eddied around him for a while, he agreed, indicated "I had more than just a song on my hands." He also had a near sweep of the top awards announced at the 1970 Country Music Association festivities, winning the award for best single and album for "Okie . . ." and also being named Top Male Vocalist and Entertainer of the Year.

Taking the stir in stride, Haggard went his own way, turning out new albums and singles as the 1970s progressed and staying on the road with the Merle Haggard Show a good part of each year. Though he did occasional TV guest spots, he avoided attempts to have him front his own TV series, as he told Jack Hurst of the *Chicago Tribune* (June 7, 1979): "How many ways can you shoot a guy standing with a guitar? How many unique things can you find about a man singing?

"We do concerts. That's the way I support a band. And I have to have a band to make good records. If I sell out, so to speak, on a TV screen, people won't have any reason to come to the concerts. It starts a deterioration of the whole deal."

There seemed to be some proof of his concept in the consistency with which he made the charts throughout the 1970s. He began with such early 1970s singles hits as "Fightin' Side of Me" and "I Can't Be Myself/Sidewalks of Chicago" in 1970 and "Grandma Harp" and "It's Not Love (But It's Not Bad)" in 1972 and LPs like *Fightin' Side of Me, Hag,* a two-record set, *Sing a Sad Song/High on a Hilltop, Someday We'll Look Back, Tribute to the Best Damn Fiddle Player (Bob Wills), Let Me Tell You About a Song, Best of the Best,* and *Land of Many Churches.* The latter was a two-disc set recorded with the Carter Family and the Strangers.

His singles hits of the mid-1970s included the smash hit "If We Make It Through December," which rose to number one the end of 1973 and stayed there into early 1974, the top five "Things Aren't Funny Anymore" in the spring of 1974, and such top-10 or top-5 successes as "Kentucky Gambler," "Movin' On," "It's All in the Movies," and "The Roots of My Raising" in 1976. All of those were Haggard originals except for "Kentucky Gambler" (by Dolly Parton) and "The Roots of My Raising" (by Tom Collins). In 1977, Merle ended his long association with Capitol and joined MCA Records. There was little change in the pattern with record after record reaching the upper-chart levels, sometimes to be joined by Capitol releases of earlier material.

In mid-1977, he had a top-5 hit on MCA with a combination of his song "Ramblin' Fever" and an old standard, "When My Blues Moon Turns to Gold Again." Several months later he made topmost levels with his song "From Graceland to the Promised Land" on MCA and "A Working Man Can't Get Nowhere" on Capitol.

Although his career seemed to be going smoothly enough during that period, his personal life was in turmoil once more as his marriage to Bonnie came apart. By the end of the 1970s, the two were appearing on stage together, but the split, Haggard told Hurst, hadn't been easy. "No, it wasn't friendly. I don't think there's ever been a friendly divorce. But I think that everybody cooled off, seeing it wasn't something I was doing as a personal insult, I think she understood.

"We still have an obligation to the fans, I think, to appear together. You don't go out on the street corner and find a Bonnie Owens—someone who knows every song I ever wrote and is totally experienced in what I'm trying to do. We're talking about the right arm here."

So it was that when the bitterness had worn off, Owens was back on the road with Haggard in the late 1970s. The introduction ran, "This is my ex-wife and very dear friend, Bonnie Owens."

Typical songs on the program in the late 1970s were such hits as "It's Been a Great Afternoon," "The Way It Was in '51" (on Capitol, with the Strangers) and "The Bull and the Bear" from 1978 and "Red Bandana/I Must Have Done Something Bad" from 1979. "The Bull and the Bear" in record form was a duet with Leona Williams, who also co-wrote the tune with Merle. Leona, who had her own shows to give, had become the new Mrs. Haggard.

During 1979, a new facet of Haggard was revealed. He proved himself a fine actor in a number of segments of the NBC-TV multipart drama *Centennial* (a James Michener story). Haggard indicated he would probably do more acting in the future, but music remained his first love.

Merle closed out the 1970s and came into the 1980s with a steady stream of hits. The single "My Own Kind of Hat/Heaven Was a Drink of Wine" was on the lists at the end of 1979 and stayed there into 1980. During 1979 his charted LPs included *The Way It Was in '51* on Capitol and, on MCA, *Serving 190 Proof,* and *I'm Always on a Mountain When I Fall,* the latter originally issued in 1977. In 1980, he had the top-10 singles hit "The Way I Am" on the charts early in the year, followed by such others as "Bar Room Buddies" (a duet with film star Clint Eastwood), "Misery and Gin," and "I Think I'll Just Stay Here and Drink." "Bar Room Buddies" was on Elektra Records, the rest on MCA. His LP *Serving 190 Proof* stayed on the charts from 1979 into 1980. Late in the year he had another charted LP, *The Way I Am.* In early 1981, his composition "Leonard" on MCA provided one of the year's best selling country singles. Soon after he had another top-10 single, a duet with Johnny Paycheck of his composition "I Can't Hold Myself in Line," released on Merle's new record label, Epic. In the fall, he had the Epic release "My Favorite Memory" in the top 5 and moving toward number one.

His debut album on Epic was *Big City* in 1981, a year in which MCA issued three other albums, *Back to the Barrooms, Rainbow Stew/Live at Anaheim Stadium,* and *Songs for the Mama That Tried.* His first solo single on Epic, "My Favorite Memory," eventually reached number one on country charts, as did his second solo single, "Big City" in 1982. He also made top-chart levels with his third single, the 1983 "Are the Good Times Really Over for Good." He continued to make the album hit lists during 1982–83 with such Epic releases as *A Taste of Yesterday's Wine, Goin' Home for Christmas, Going Where the Lonely Go,* and *Pancho and Lefty,* all issued in 1982, and *That's the Way Love Goes* and *The Epic Collection* in 1983. *Pancho and Lefty,* a

duet album with Willie Nelson, was a best-seller, as was the single of the title track, and provided the incentive for a wide-ranging concert tour by the two artists that ranked among the best country series of the early 1980s. The title track from *That's the Way Love Goes* also was a major hit and earned Merle a Grammy as Best Country Vocal Performance, Male, of 1984.

After becoming one of the most honored artists in his field in the late 1960s and the first half of the 1970s, Merle went through an honors drought during the second half of that decade. But when the 1980s arrived, the recognition of his remarkable talents blossomed again, and he needed a new shelf for his trophies. For instance, the Academy of Country Music named him Top Male Vocalist of 1981 and in 1982 selected "Are the Good Times Really Over for Good" as Song of the Year. The Country Music Association's nominations for 1982 included a nod to his *Big City* for Album of the Year while also including his work with both George Jones and Willie Nelson as Vocal Duo of the Year finalists. In 1983, Merle and Willie were the winners in the Vocal Duo of the Year category and their single of "Pancho and Lefty" was voted Single of the Year. CMA also nominated *Pancho and Lefty* for Album of the Year. Merle also was nominated for Male Vocalist of the Year in both 1983 and 1984.

His 1983 CMA nominations also included one for Entertainer of the Year. His 1983 total of six nominations brought his total to thirty-nine, moving him past Loretta Lynn for the most nominated country music personality in CMA balloting to that point. In 1983, the voters in the first annual American Video Awards program selected his release of "Are the Good Times Really Over for Good" as the Best Country Video.

In the second half of the 1980s, Merle continued to turn out excellent new recordings, but he found it increasingly difficult to get his records into the top of the charts. This was true despite the fact that he remained one of the best draws with live concert audiences. In interviews he attributed this, with some bitterness, to the increasing trend in country radio to feature new artists to the exclusion of many of the older stars from program lists. He emphasized that he had the greatest respect for many of the new performers, but felt the country field should not abandon its traditional support of those who had helped make it a major art form.

He closed out the decade with several major projects for the TV market, including the special *Merle Haggard: Poet of the Common Man,* which was nominated in that category in the *Music City News* 1989 awards poll. During 1989, TNN Concert Specials featured Merle and Marie Osmond in two sixty-minute programs. As the 1990s began, he signed with a new record label, Curb. By then his total of number-one country hits was thirty-eight, and many artists had paid tribute to his abilities by covering many of his songs. As an example, his composition "Today I Started Loving You Again" had been recorded by more than 400 other artists by the end of 1989.

When his debut album on Curb, *Blue Jungle,* came out in the late summer of 1990, it contained several songs dealing with such problems as homelessness and the plight of disabled veterans ("Under the Bridge," "My Home Is on the Street," "Me and Crippled Soldiers"). He commented, "The songs talk about people who are homeless only by fate. It goes into different aspects of the current American situation, how living in America has changed in comparison with ten years ago. Every cut in some way relates to the same guy who's singing—if you sang these songs in concert you would not get a shift in mood." But he added, "I'm not in the music business for glamour. I'm in it to play music, to be in a band, to be around people I've admired for years. I just don't care about the fame. And I don't want my musical career to be based on my political views or religious beliefs or whatever. I'd like it to be based totally on my artistic ability, my talent."

During 1991, while touring in support of the new album, he discussed some of his views on what made a successful artist with Robert Hilburn of the *Los Angeles Times* ("This Guy Sounds Just Like Merle Haggard," Calendar section, February 10, 1991). He suggested there was more to it than the abilities one was born with. "People talk about singers being born. But if that were true, you'd have more great singers' kids turning out to be great singers. There may be something in the genes that gives you a particular voice, but you have to know what to do with it in order to be something special."

He went on, "The first thing is you've got to have this overpowering desire to sing. That usually means hearing someone else who excites you so much that you can't think of doing anything else. But you've got to be excited by the singing, not the stardom or the money. You've got to be excited enough so that you make singing a science . . . so that you become a historian of other singers.

"The idea isn't to imitate someone else, but to study and learn from them so that you can see what's possible. Then, you have to move past your heroes to find your own voice—and that sometimes is the hardest part.

"Your voice's deep inside you somewhere, but some people get satisfied with a little success and then give up before they reach deep enough. That's the real challenge. You just keep reaching down."

When Willie Nelson was inducted into the Country Music Hall of Fame in 1993, he suggested that there were many other great performers who were equally deserving, like Ray Price and Merle Haggard. Perhaps taking that to heart, the eligible voters in 1994 provided Haggard with the required number of approvals to fol-

low Willie and George Jones into the Hall. As it happened, Merle was able to savor not only that honor, but also his first CMA nomination in quite a few years. The latter was for his part (along with many other country stars) in the *Asleep at the Wheel Tribute to the Music of Bob Wills & the Texas Playboys,* nominated for Album of the Year. Bob Wills and his musicians had been among Merle's first influences, and he recalled that the Texas Playboys' vocalist, Tommy Duncan, had been one of his first heroes.

Coming to accept his Hall of Fame plaque during the October 1994 CMA Awards telecast, Haggard received a thunderous standing ovation. He turned that to peals of laughter as he drew out what he said was the list of those he wanted to thank—a long white roll that wound down to the floor. The first he wanted to thank, he said, was his plumber. After that he went on to express his gratitude for the honor.

A few weeks later, Arista Records released the album *Mama's Hungry Eyes: A Tribute to Merle Haggard,* which featured versions of Merle's classic songs by such performers as Brooks & Dunn, Emmylou Harris, Randy Travis, and Lorrie Morgan. The album showed up on the *Billboard* charts the first week of its release at the end of October. Almost simultaneously, Hightone Records released *Tulare Dust: A Songwriters' Tribute to Merle Haggard,* whose tracks were recorded by such singer-songwriters as Lucinda Williams, Dave Alvin, and Iris DeMent. At the same time, Haggard himself was represented on the *Billboard* catalog recurrents list with the old Epic *Merle Haggard's Super Hits* collection, a hat-trick of honors that Haggard well deserved.

In the spring of 1995, the independent label Razor & Tie issued a two-CD reissue set of Haggard material. During the year, Country Music Foundation Records worked on a comprehensive boxed set of Haggard's work. Koch Records also issued an album containing a number of long out-of-print tracks by Merle called *The Lonesome Fugitive: The Merle Haggard Anthology (1963–1977).* Also available as an import item from Germany's Bear Family records was a five-CD boxed set, *Merle Haggard: Untamed Hawk,* which contained his complete recordings on the Tally and Capitol labels from 1962–1968 (except for his Jimmie Rodgers tribute available separately from the company). The set includes many previously unreleased sides and alternate takes.

Haggard's concert work during 1995 included an appearance with Buck Owens at the second annual Bud Light Country Jam in Bakersfield, California, on June 16. It was the first time they shared the stage together in 25 years. In early 1996, he was featured on one of *Austin City Limits* TV programs. Soon after, he watched a terrazzo star in his honor installed on the Boot Walk of Fame at Country Star Hollywood restaurant in Universal City, California. Merle contributed a gold record of *Okie from Muskogee,* an autographed guitar, and "Hag" boots for the facility's memorabilia collection. At the time, MCG/Curb Records had released a new album, his 69th overall.

HALL, TOM T.: *Singer, guitarist, songwriter, author. Born Olive Hill, Kentucky, May 25, 1936.*

In the future, Tom T. Hall, whose career in the entertainment field got its initial impetus from his songwriting abilities, may be remembered most for the songs he penned. The unique quality of that body of work gave rise to his nickname, "The Storyteller." But he also has had a remarkable record as a singer, starting in the late 1960s, placing many singles and albums in the country top 10 and some in the number-one position.

He began life as the sixth child in a family of ten born to a Kentucky minister and his wife. He naturally listened to pop and country music during his formative years, but he didn't think of making music his profession at the time. When he attended Roanoke College in Virginia, his goal was a career in journalism. Among his favorite authors were Mark Twain, Sinclair Lewis, and Ernest Hemingway.

For a while, though, it looked as though he might opt for a military career. He spent eight years in the U.S. Army, stationed in Germany part of that time. When he returned to civilian life, he eventually made his first move into the music field by working as a disc jockey on a Roanoke radio station. He had become increasingly interested in writing songs by then and he soon started submitting them to Nashville publishers. One publishing executive, Jimmy Key, liked Tom's work and suggested he move to Music City. Once there, Tom settled in as a contract writer for a starting salary of fifty dollars a week. Before long artists were beginning to record some of his material. The first to release a recording of one of Tom's songs was Jimmy C. Newman with his version of "D.J. for a Day." From then on, new recordings of Hall's compositions came out regularly, either performed by other artists or by Tom himself. From the mid-1960s into the early 1980s, Tom earned one or more BMI songwriting awards each year, along the way being inducted into the Nashville Songwriters Hall of Fame.

At the outset, Tom T. was reluctant to become a recording artist; he never had thought of singing as his strong point. However, after he signed with Mercury Records in 1967, his viewpoint changed and his output of singles and LPs over the next decade and a half was one of the highest among country artists. Through early 1981, those efforts resulted in eleven singles that rose to number one. It was a song recorded by another that really brought him to prominence, though. The song, "Harper Valley P.T.A.," had lain dormant for a year before Jeannie C. Riley decided to put it on vinyl. When she did, in 1968, the result was phenomenal. The record sold over 6 million copies and, as evidence of its lasting popularity, was dramatized as a popular movie in 1978 and became the basis for a TV series in the early 1980s. The song's success also opened doors right away for its author. Within a few months after the record hit, songs written by him occupied as many as six spots on the country charts. It also helped pave the way for his success as a singer.

The songs he placed on the charts himself, or that made upper levels in versions by other performers, typically were based on incidents or observations drawn from his life. The story behind "Harper Valley P.T.A.," for instance, Tom T. said, was based on an actual event that had occurred in his home town during his youth. His "The Year That Clayton Delaney Died" was written about the man who helped inspire him to become a musician; and "Old Dogs, Children and Watermelon Wine" tells about an old black man he met while getting drunk in a Miami, Florida, bar during a Republican presidential convention.

Many of his songs deliver a message along with a story. This is the case with the above-mentioned songs as well as such hits as "The Ballad of 40 Dollars," which deals with hypocrisy, "Margie's at the Lincoln Park Inn," about temptation, and "Faster Horses," which suggests that the meaning of life is "faster horses, younger women, older whiskey and more money." More involved narratives are presented concisely yet evocatively in compositions like "Salute to a Switchblade," "Ravishing Ruby," and "Ode to a Ground Round." Still others are poems, in effect, ultimately simple yet touching, such as "I Love," a list of things the writer loves (such as "winners when they cry, losers when they try"). Other songs are just plain fun, such as "I Like Beer," in which he states over and over again that he likes to drink beer. In "Country Is," Tom T. defines the meaning of country through its conflicting images, and in "Sneaky Snake," he sings a children's story set to music.

During his stay with Mercury Records, from 1967 to 1977, Tom T. turned out one or more LPs every year. These include *Homecoming, Witness Life, One Hundred Children, In Search of a Song, We All Got Together, And . . . , The Storyteller, Tom T. Hall's Greatest Hits, For the People in the Last Hard Town, Songs of Fox Hollow, Rhymer and Other Five and Dimers, Country Is, I Wrote a Song About It, Tom T. Hall's Greatest Hits, Volume 2, Faster Horses, Magnificent Music Machine,* and *About Love.* A sampling of his chart hit singles on Mercury in the 1970s includes "Day Drinkin'" (with Dave Dudley, 1970); "Me & Jesus," "The Monkey That Became President" (1972); "Ravishing Ruby" (1973); "I Love," "This Song Is Driving Me Crazy," "Country Is" (1974); "I Care/Sneaky Snakes," "Deal," "I Like Beer" (1975); "Faster Horses (the Cowboy and the Poet)," "Negatory Romance" (1976); and "It's All in the Game" (1977).

In 1977, Tom T. left Mercury and signed with RCA, remaining with that label until 1981. His debut LP on RCA was *New Train . . . Same Rider.* It was followed by such others as *Places I've Done Time* (late 1978) and *Ol' T's in Town* (1980). His charted singles on RCA included "What Have You Got to Lose" (1978); "There Is a Miracle in You," "You Show Me Your Heart (and I'll Show You Mine)," "Son of Clayton Delaney" (1979); and "The Old Side of Town/Jesus on the Radio (Daddy on the Phone)," "Soldier of Fortune," "Back When Gas Was Thirty Cents a Gallon," "I'm Not Ready Yet" (1980).

During the 1970s, Tom T.'s face became quite familiar to TV viewers from his guest appearances on many country and pop shows as well as some specials of his own. He also made many concert appearances on the fair and rodeo circuit and in major venues, including a very successful show at New York's Carnegie Hall. His honors included nominations to various categories over the years in the Country Music Association awards competition and the receipt of a Grammy in the early 1970s for Best Album Notes (1972), written by him for his *Greatest Hits* LP. In the early 1980s, besides being a regular on the *Grand Ole Opry,* he was host of his own syndicated TV program, *Pop Goes the Country,* filmed at Nashville's Opryland.

His TV efforts continued to thrive through the 1980s into the mid-1990s, with his credits as of 1995 including spots on the *Today Show, Good Morning America, Hee Haw,* several PBS specials, many of the CMA Award telecasts, and appearances on most of the Nashville Network shows, including *Nashville Now, New Country,* and *Celebrity Outdoors.* Over the years he was also featured in commercials for such products as Chevy Trucks, Tyson Chicken, and Justin Boots. His association with the *Grand Ole Opry,* for which he served as a spokesperson at one time, continued strong with his regular appearances extending into the mid-1990s. His music-related ventures covered a spectrum that ranged from owning a radio station to operating his own recording studio. For some years he also served as a member of the Country Music Association Board of Directors.

In the mid-1990s, his diverse activities included serving on the board of directors of a bank, managing a farm, and working on behalf of various charities. Particularly close to his heart was his work helping raise money for a community animal shelter in Franklin, Tennessee, called Animaland.

His early interest in journalism was revived once he achieved success in music, with opportunities to do some prose work. During the 1970s he wrote two books, *How I Write Songs, How You Can* and *The Storyteller's Nashville,* the latter a combination of autobiography and a review of Nashville's development as a major force in pop music. In the early 1980s, Tom T. was at work on his first novel under contract to Double-

day. By the mid-1990s, his publishing credits, besides the novel, encompassed a second songwriting textbook and a collection of short stories. Besides writing those textbooks, he also taught the subject for two years at Middle Tennessee State University.

After Hall's recording affiliation with RCA came to a close in 1981, he signed with his old label, which reissued his *Greatest Hits ONE* album in 1981 and followed with *Greatest Hits 2* in 1982. Both remained in the company's catalog in 1995 and, Mercury reported, were still selling well. During the 1980s, new Mercury releases of Hall's work comprised *Natural Devices* in 1984; *Everything* and *Song in a Seashell* in 1985; and *The Essential Tom T. Hall 20th Anniversary Album,* a reference to his first signing with the label in the 1960s. Hall also wrote and recorded material for children, some of which was presented in the 1988 Mercury release *Country Songs for Kids.* At the end of 1994, he could point to a total output of thirty-two albums and the receipt of forty-six BMI songwriting awards.

In 1996, Tom had a new tome titled *What a Book* in print. In the summer he started work in recording studios in Florida on his first studio album in eight years. The Mercury disc, he said, would be called *Songs from Sopchoppy.* (Sopchoppy is a town in northern Florida.) In October 1996, the first single released by Alan Jackson from his new album, *Everything I Love,* was the Tom T. Hall composition "Little Bitty."

Hall emphasized that he tried to apply a consistent, humanistic philosophy to all of his creative efforts. "My goal is to establish a true voice not colored by prejudice, politics or preferences. If you're telling a story, you have to separate all that. You have to be careful not to make judgments and to be honest. That's the main thing. Just tell the tale."—A.S.

HAMILTON, GEORGE IV: *Singer, guitarist, songwriter. Born Matthews, North Carolina, July 19, 1937.*

George Hamilton IV, although his name was present on hit charts plenty of times in his long career, did not have as many top-10 hits as other major country artists. Instead he will be remembered as someone who helped make music fans all over the world aware of the delights of country music, an effort which earned him the unofficial title of the International Ambassador of Country Music.

Country, of course, was George's first love, a natural consequence of growing up in North Carolina. But it was rock and pop that first made his reputation when he sallied forth from college in 1956 to hit the national charts with "A Rose and a Baby Ruth," also the title song of his best-selling debut album on ABC that was released in March 1958. He followed with several other teenage favorites, such as "High School Romance" and "Why Don't They Understand."

By 1959, a combination of a slowdown in his pop career and a desire to concentrate on country stylings led to his moving to Nashville, where he started a new career phase as part of RCA Victor's country roster. In the early 1960s, he soon became a first-rank performer in the field, turning out such chart singles as "If You Don't Know I Ain't Gonna Tell You," "Before the Day Ends," "Ft. Worth, Dallas or Houston," "Truck Driving Man," and, in 1963, the number-one country hit "Abilene." RCA found cash registers clicked for his albums as well; LPs such as *Abilene* (released 10/63), *Ft. Worth, Dallas or Houston* (12/64), *Coast Country* (3/66), and *Steel Rail Blues* showing up on country charts. Asked to join the *Grand Ole Opry* early in the decade, he remained a cast member throughout the 1960s.

In the mid-1960s, George began to take increased interest in folk music, particularly the modern compositions being turned out by a gifted group of artists from Canada. As he told Jan Otteson of *Music City News* (January 1978), "For me . . . it started in 1965 when I was playing at the Horseshoe Tavern in Toronto. There I heard a record on the radio by Gordon Lightfoot. I wasn't aware of him then; I figured he was some Canadian Indian. But I really liked his sound. It seemed to be a perfect marriage of folk music and country music. When I met Gordon and we became good friends, he introduced me to people like Joni Mitchell, Leonard Cohen, and Ian and Sylvia and I found out how many great songs those people had written. I became infatuated with their music."

Hamilton's folk leanings became evident in his late 1960s releases. In March 1967, for instance, RCA issued his LP *Folk Classics,* followed by *Folksy* in September of that year. In 1969, his preoccupation with Canadian folk and country work culminated with the RCA release *Canadian Pacific,* a collection in which Hamilton performed only songs by Canadian writers, including a number by Lightfoot. The album wasn't a blockbuster with U.S. fans, but found favor with Canadians and people in England, Europe, and elsewhere and continued in the RCA catalogue in the 1970s. He dubbed his move in that direction as part of an attempt to expand the horizons of country music, a direction he described as "thinking man's country."

Hamilton's career took on its broad international flavor as the 1970s began. He had his start, he told Jan Otteson, in mid-1969, when he was invited to a concert in England. "That's when I attended the first Wembley Music Festival in England. And even though I didn't get paid for it, I liked it a lot and went back the following year. Then a guy from the BBC decided to put me in a BBC television series over there. From there, a Canadian TV producer named Mannie Pittson happened to see the show and asked if I would do a syndicated television show for him in Canada."

The idea made sense to George. He resigned from the *Opry* in 1971 and moved back home to Matthews, North Carolina. That shift allowed him to spend more time with his family and made it easier for him to organize his new international show. He and Pittson agreed that the program, which was to be taped mainly in Canada, would feature primarily north of the border talent. The concept, claimed to be the first internationally syndicated country-music show, rapidly found favor overseas. By the end of 1977, it was presented on outlets in the United Kingdom, Ireland, South Africa, New Zealand, Hong Kong, Canada, and, starting in 1978, Australia.

In 1974, Hamilton added another laurel to his international work, becoming the first country-music artist to perform in the Soviet Union and Czechoslovakia. The Russian authorities were pleased with his kind of music (which did not grate their political nerves the way rock tended to do) and later invited such others as Tennessee Ernie Ford and Roy Clark to tour.

Later on in the 1970s, though Hamilton didn't give up his foreign concerts and telecasts, he decided to reestablish his credentials with the home audience. He signed with ABC/Dot in the United States, the label he had originally gained fame with in his pop days, and Anchor Records in England. His first LP in this series, *Fine Lace and Homespun Cloth,* came out in early 1978. The songs chosen were by such writers as Larry Kingston and Shel Silverstein, and the treatment emphasized by Hamilton and his producer, Allen Reynolds, was in the folk-country vein. This Hamilton defined as meaning "lots of acoustic guitars and a strong rhythm section rather than the hard-core country music that's dependent upon steel guitars and fiddles. Allen, I feel, cuts a commercial country record . . . but they go beyond that. They're distinctive and always fresh sounding."

His frank goal was to stress "sounds with a M.O.R. [middle of the road] appeal," an approach at odds with the progressive country concept of grittier material. Hamilton, however, always stressed his belief there was nothing wrong with good M.O.R., since it promised to meet the tastes of a broad spectrum of tastes and age levels.

When ABC/Dot was merged into MCA Records, George signed a new agreement with them. The first album on the MCA label was *Forever Young,* issued in 1979. Meanwhile, Hamilton continued to add to his overseas credits. In 1976 he served as emcee of the first "International Festival of Country Music," held in Sweden, and served in the same capacity for subsequent events in Finland (1977), Norway and the Netherlands (1978), and Germany (1979). He continued his association with England's Wembley country music festival. From 1969 into the early 1980s, he was featured in the event all but three years. In 1979, he became the first American country singer to have a British summer season, appearing at the Winter Gardens Theatre in Blackpool.

The 1980s and 1990s saw Hamilton's career continue much as it had since the 1970s. His annual tour of England became a popular event with British country fans. In America, meanwhile, he continued to record new material when the opportunity arose; though his records failed to translate into hits, records like 1991's single "Good Old Days"—which registered on the lower reaches of some charts—testified to a continuing appetite for his music.

An example of Hamilton's intellectual approach to his profession was his analysis of the roots of country music and his understanding of its relation to centuries-old traditions in the British Isles. He stressed to *Music City News*, "I get a big kick out of taking the music that originally had its roots in places like England and Ireland back to the descendants of its originators. To me, I feel like I'm putting something back into my art form."

HANK THE DRIFTER: *Singer, guitarist, songwriter. Born Taunton, Massachusetts, September 2, 1929.*

One of New England's relatively few contributions to the country & western field, Hank the Drifter, as the pseudonym indicates, was a fan of the late Hank Williams from his early years. Since his voice turned out to closely resemble that of his idol, his career was based largely on that similarity.

His real name was Daniel Raye Andrade and he was born and raised in Massachusetts. He learned to play guitar by his teens and later joined a group called the Hayshakers. With Andrade as lead singer, the band entered amateur contests throughout New England and proved just about unbeatable. After the Hayshakers won fifteen straight first prizes, Andrade parlayed it into a fifteen-minute weekly show on station WPEP in Taunton. From there he moved on a somewhat bigger market, sponsored as Hank the Drifter by the *New Bedford Times* on station WNBH in that Massachusetts seacoast city.

After a while he wandered farther afield, ending up in Texas, where he struck roots in the 1950s and still resided (in Houston) in the 1970s. His appearances in the Lone Star State in the late 1950s and early 1960s included the *Corns a Poppin'* program on radio station KTRH, the *Big D Jamboree* in Dallas, and the *Cowtown Hoedown* in Ft. Worth. He continued to perform at county fairs, rodeos, and the like in Houston and other Texas cities throughout the 1960s and appeared on both radio and TV in the area.

During those years, he recorded for New England Records and also was featured on Canadian discs issued on the Sparton and Quality labels. Almost all the releases were original compositions, including such songs as "All These Things You Can't Erase," "I'll Never Say 'I Do' Again," "Hank Williams Is Singing Again," "Hank, You're Gone but Not Forgotten," "Cheaters Never Win," "Don't You Lock Your Daddy Out," "I'm Crying My Heart Out for You," "Bill Collector Blues," "Cold River Blues," "Why Did It Have to Be Me?" "You're Paying for It Now," "I'm Gonna Spin My Wheels," and "Painted Dolls."

HARRIS, EMMYLOU: *Singer, guitarist, songwriter, band leader (Hot Band, Nash Ramblers). Born Birmingham, Alabama, April 2, 1947.*

When Emmylou Harris was in high school, she wrote to her current idol, Pete Seeger, saying that she always wanted to sing folk songs but didn't know if she could because she hadn't suffered enough. As she told Robert Hilburn in an interview in the *Los Angeles Times,* "You know how it was in the folk era, you had to have had a real hard time to be valid." Seeger wrote back telling her not to worry about that. Her fans must be grateful that she did not get discouraged from pursuing success as a singer and musician.

But success, as usual, did not come easy. There was a time at the end of the sixties when rebuffs in New York and Nashville made her think about abandoning a musical career.

She was born and raised in the South, spending her early years in Birmingham, Alabama, and later moving to Virginia. (Her father was a Marine pilot who flew combat missions during World War II and the Korean War.) Coming from the South, she was certainly exposed to country stylings, but her first love was folk music, including roots blues. But she did recall "the first song I remember hearing on the radio . . . 'Cattle Call' by Eddy Arnold. That high lonesome yodel came drifting out a room in our house on Fifty-fourth Street in Birmingham, Alabama, about as far away as you can get from the Western plains Mr. Arnold was singing about. I was just four years old."

She told Brian Mansfield of *Request Magazine* ("Angel Eyes," October 1993), "I wasn't really raised on country music in the usual sense. My brother is a big country music fan, and he's older than me. He owned the record player. I heard a lot of Buck Owens, Kitty Wells, bluegrass, so I sort of absorbed it. But I didn't think of it in any serious way. I was into folk music pretty much, so it was Bob Dylan and Tom Rush. I listened to all the country blues and I was very much into that. I came to country music through Gram Parsons."

After finishing high school in the Washington, D.C., area, she entered the University of North Carolina as a drama major, but after a year and a half she dropped out and headed for New York.

In 1969, she was signed by Jubilee Records. She was pregnant when her first album was released (her marriage later ended in divorce). She didn't like the album, and when her daughter was born, retired temporarily to live with her parents in Washington, D.C. But by the following year, she had already begun singing in Washington, D.C., clubs, backed by a folk-country band. While she was appearing at the Cellar Door, the Flying Burrito Brothers saw her perform. They asked her to join their band, but a week later Emmylou discovered that they were breaking up.

However, it was through the Burrito Brothers that Emmylou met Gram Parsons, who was to have a lasting influence on her singing as well as, indirectly, a hand in the success she was later to enjoy. Harris was introduced to Parsons, an ex-Burrito member, by Burrito Chris Hillman late in 1971. Parsons had been looking for a female harmony singer, and he asked Emmylou to help him on his first album. She sang with him on that album, *GP*, later toured with him in the spring of 1973, and helped him on his last album, *Grievous Angel*.

Soon after, Gram Parsons died, a victim of drug abuse. Emmylou was saddened by his sudden demise and returned to Washington, D.C., for a time to play in small clubs, to write songs, and to organize her own band. Meanwhile, some people at Warner Bros. records had heard her on Parson's albums and had been impressed with her singing. She signed a record contract with them in mid-1974. Backed by several of Elvis Presley's musicians, she recorded an album, *Pieces of the Sky*, which was released in early 1975. As with all her future albums, this one contained a wide assortment of material. One cut from the album, a simple song previously recorded by the Louvin Brothers, "If I Could Only Win Your Love," became a number-one country hit. The album, too, reached number one on the country charts and also placed high on the pop charts.

During that period, she formed the first version of her backing group, initially depending mainly on musicians who had worked with Parsons. Over succeeding years that group, the Hot Band, included many artists who would make major names for themselves, including Rodney Crowell, Ricky Skaggs, and a keyboard player who was to become one of Nashville's most successful record producers, Tony Brown.

Emmylou proved that she could do it again with the release of her next album, *Elite Hotel*. The big hits from the album were "One of These Days" and "Sweet Dreams," an old Don Gibson composition. However, every song on the album was capable of becoming a hit, from the upbeat "Amarillo," co-written by Emmylou with Rodney Crowell, to a beautiful country version of the Beatles' "Here, There and Everywhere," to the three songs written by her mentor, Gram Parsons: "Wheels," "Sin City," and "Ooh Las Vegas." Her clear, high-timbred voice blended perfectly with her accompanying musicians, who often provided a bluegrass-sounding background, adding a new dimension to every song on the album. The album won Emmylou a Grammy Award for Best Country Vocal Performance, Female, for 1976.

Luxury Liner, her next LP, was of the same high caliber. The standouts were her chart hits, "You Never Can Tell," a Chuck Berry rock hit of the 1950s, "Making Believe," which had been a 1955 hit for Kitty Wells, and a more recent country tune, Susanna Clark's "I'll Be Your San Antone Rose." Her next album, *Quarter Moon in a Ten Cent Town*, continued to prove her remarkable consistency and quality. It provided her with two top hits, "To Daddy," written by Dolly Parton, about a woman, ignored by her husband and family,

who decides to leave home once her children are grown, and the poetic "Easy from Now On," written by Carlene Carter and Susanna Clark. *Quarter Moon* was one of five finalists in the Grammy competition for Best Country Vocal Performance, Female, of 1978.

Emmylou closed out the decade with still more chart-making singles in 1979: "Too Far Gone," "Save the Last Dance for Me," "Blue Kentucky Girl" and "Play Together Again, Again," the last named a duet with Buck Owens. She was represented on the album charts with two more LPs, *Blue Kentucky Girl* and *Profile/Best of Emmylou Harris*, both still on the lists at the start of the 1980s. *Blue Kentucky Girl* provided her with her third straight Grammy finalist nomination for the Best Country Vocal Performance, Female.

By the beginning of the 1980s she ranked as a superstar who appealed to audiences ranging the spectrum from folk and country to pop. Her concerts drew capacity crowds to college auditoriums and major venues in the United States and abroad. A program based on one of her concerts was presented several times on PBS-TV.

In the early 1980s, still recording for Warner Brothers (though there were reports of some strain in that relationship in 1981), she continued to have great rapport with record buyers and high respect from most critics. Among her 1980 offerings, all her singles made the country top 10 and most reached number one. The latter included her version of a Dallas Frazier song, "Beneath Still Waters," her haunting rendition of the old standard, "Wayfaring Stranger," and a duet with Roy Orbison, "That Loving You Feeling Again." Her 1979 single, "Blue Kentucky Girl," was still on the charts in 1980 and she also had a top-10 hit with Paul Simon's "The Boxer." Her early 1980 LP *Roses in the Snow* was on the country charts for most of 1980 and still on them in 1981, as was the case for the LP *Light of the Stable*, issued in late 1980 for the Christmas season. Her 1981 top-10 singles included "Mister Sandman" and a duet with Don Williams, "If I Needed You." In late 1981, her LP *Evangeline* was in the top 10.

In the late 1970s and early 1980s, her list of honors from her peers continued to grow. She often was one of the finalists in various categories not only on the Grammy Awards but also in voting for awards of the Academy of Country Music and the Country Music Association, and finished as top vote getter a number of times. In the October 1980 nationally telecast CMA Awards ceremony, at which she was one of the presenters, she was named the Female Vocalist of the Year for 1980. Her 1981 duet with Don Williams, "If I Needed You," was a finalist in the Grammies for Best Country Performance as a Duo or Group with Vocal.

As Robert Hilburn said of Harris in an article in the *Los Angeles Times*, ". . . the difficult thing in discussing Harris is fully describing her talent without stepping over the bounds of credibility. . . . [It's] hard to imagine how Harris can move through the various strains of country music—from traditional to progressive, ballad to honky-tonk, from heartbreak to celebration—with such purity and evocativeness."

Emmylou's album output during 1982 provided two more chartmakers, *Cimarron* and *Last Date. Cimarron* provided another hit duet with Don Williams, "If I Needed You." She was nominated by CMA voters for 1982 Female Vocalist of the Year; the same was true in 1983, when she was represented on album charts with a second greatest-hits album and a new collection, *White Shoes.* She placed both solo and duet singles on the hit lists during those years, the latter including "Wild Montana Skies" with John Denver and "All Fall Down" with George Jones. Her 1984 album, *The Ballad of Sally Rose,* spawned a Grammy-winning single, "In My Dreams," named Best Country Vocal Performance, Female, while the album was nominated for Album of the Year by both Grammy and ACM voters. She also demonstrated her vocal versatility by joining with the band Southern Pacific for a high-energy country rock version of Tom Petty's "Think About You" on Southern Pacific's first album release.

Among her mid-1980s recording credits were the albums *Thirteen* (released in 1986), *Angel Band* (1987), and *Bluebird* (1988). The performers backing her on *Angel Band* included such luminaries or soon-to-become luminaries as bassist Emory Gordy, Jr., Vince Gill, Carl Jackson, and Tony Brown. Those were all excellent creative units, but the last two albums did nowhere near as well with the record-buying public as her releases of the 1975–86 period. In fact, as of the mid-1990s, she has not had another top-10 solo album since 1986. It reflected a growing problem: that long-beloved country stars have been increasingly overlooked as country radio programmers gravitated toward what they considered dynamic newcomers. Emmylou still retained a strong following and certainly was as well-regarded by her peers as any country performer could be, but radio airplay in the 1980s and 1990s had become the arbiter of an artist's "star" status with the public at large.

This did not prevent a major hit with the album *Trio,* featuring Emmylou, Dolly Parton, and Linda Ronstadt. Issued in 1987, it actually evolved from sessions produced by Ricky Skaggs with the three vocalists in 1981. The album, which went on to achieve multiplatinum sales, was nominated by CMA voters in 1988 for Vocal Event of the Year. The voters also nominated Emmylou for Female Vocalist of the Year, as they had done every year since the start of the decade. During 1988, Emmylou and Earl Thomas Conley's duet of "We Believe in Happy Endings," which had risen to number one on the country charts, earned them a Vocal Duo of the Year nomination. That song was also included in Emmylou's 1989 Warner/Reprise album, *Duets.*

In the early 1990s, she had two more finely honed albums out on Warner Brothers, *Brand New Dance* and the 1992 *Emmylou Harris and the Nash Ramblers Live at the Ryman.* Strangely, Emmylou was not asked to become a regular cast member of the *Grand Ole Opry* until 1992, perhaps because some old-timers in the organization didn't consider her country enough. In any case, most cast members were happy to have her on board, and she was a featured performer from then on. Besides that affiliation, Emmylou served on the Board of Directors of the Country Music Foundation (which supervises the activities of the Country Music Hall of Fame) for a number of years in the 1990s, including a term as president.

In 1993, after eighteen years with Warner Brothers, Emmylou moved to the Asylum label (still a part of the Time-Warner conglomerate). Asylum, which had previously been mainly a rock label, set up its Nashville Division in the early 1990s to take advantage of country's growing popularity. One reason for the move, she indicated, was Warner's growing emphasis on economics rather than creativity. She told Brian Mansfield, "Warner Bros. did an incredible job for me, in the beginning especially. They were the only label that could understand us left-of-center artists. They still tend to do that in the pop department."

She added, "Country got so popular that I didn't fit anymore. I was always on the fringes anyway. The thing about Asylum is that they're sort of priding themselves on being a bit fringy."

Also having an impact on her career was her own self-imposed limitation on concert work. As she told a reviewer in the summer of 1993, "My priorities are that I tour in the summer so I can be home with my daughter during the school year." She was referring to her second daughter, Meghann, then fourteen, who spent most of the summer with her father, the second of Emmylou's three ex-husbands. Her other daughter, Hallie, then in her twenties, lived and worked in Nashville.

Her Asylum album debut, *Cowgirl's Prayer,* came out in mid-1993 and proved up to her considerable standards. Many reviewers in the print media suggested if it received the attention it deserved it could return her name once more to the top of the charts. Its contents included two original compositions by Emmylou, "The Light" and "Prayer in Open D," the latter perhaps the most compelling track in the collection. With the release of this album, she had twenty-two discs to her credit, eight of which had been certified gold by the R.I.A.A. Her hit singles by then totaled seven, her top-10 singles, twenty-seven.

Her backing band on the forthcoming concert tour in support of the album was the Nash Ramblers, whom she had first introduced on the Ryman stage. Its members included Sam Bush (who had founded the notable bluegrass group, the New Grass Revival) on mandolin, dobro expert Al Perkins, bassist Mark W. Winchester, guitarist Randy Stewart, and drummer Larry Atamanuil.

Its performance, combined with her sparkling vocals, provided audiences with live shows every bit as good as in her Hot Band days. The album made the charts and added two hit videos to Emmylou's long list of successes, her version of Tony Joe White's fast-paced "High Power Love" and the slower, gospel-flavored Jesse Winchester composition, "Thanks to You." The last named reached number one on CMT-TV in early 1994. Warner Brothers Records hadn't forgotten her, though. In August 1994, it issued her album *Emmylou Harris: Songs of the West* on its Warner Western label.

In the mid-1990s, Emmylou wasn't unhappy with her career and, on one level, appreciated country's new-found prominence with music fans. Asked about her evaluation by Robert Hilburn of the *Los Angeles Times*, she replied, "I have mixed feelings. I am pleased for the success, but it bothers me when so many talented people like Steve Earle have the door shut on them or when Nanci Griffith is sort of turned away. It seems anybody who has any rough edges is turned back, anyone who doesn't fit in some kind of mold. There is no way my first album would be played on country radio today."

During 1995 Emmylou worked with noted producer Daniel Lanois on her next Asylum album and the result was the superb *Wrecking Ball*, a collection which ranks among the best releases of the mid-1990s. In the fall of 1996, Reprise Records issued a boxed set called *Portraits,* a 3 disc package containing 61 songs Emmylou recorded for Warner Bros. from 1975–1992. The contents verified again the great range of material she had mastered and her artistic integrity, acknowledged by her musical peers if not by as large an audience as her work deserved.

—A. S.

HAY, GEORGE DEWEY: *Editor, reporter, announcer, radio station executive. Born Attica, Indiana, November 9, 1895; died Virginia Beach, Virginia, May 9, 1968.*

Few people have had a greater impact on the national development of country & western music than the man known as "The Solemn Ol' Judge." His insight into the potential of this form of entertainment led to the start of two of the landmark programs in the field, the *National Barn Dance* and the *Grand Ole Opry.*

In his teens, Hay began work in the real estate business. He worked for a number of firms in real estate and general sales until 1920. That year he gained a job as a reporter with the Memphis *Commercial Appeal*. The paper branched out into the infant field of radio, setting up station WMC, one of the pioneer stations of the South. Hay doubled in brass by spending part of his time as radio editor for WMC. In 1923, he suddenly gained a national reputation when he scooped the world with news of the death of President Warren Harding. Within a year, he moved north to Chicago as chief announcer for station WLS.

By now Hay was convinced of the bright future of the medium. He looked for other avenues for his talents, and eventually started a show called the *WLS Barn Dance,* later known as the *National Barn Dance*. Before long, the *Barn Dance* had a top national rating, and a country-wide poll by *Radio Digest* resulted in Hay's being named as the top announcer in the United States.

In the fall of 1925, Hay was invited to the dedication of a new 1,000-watt (75-mile range) station in Nashville, which went on the air on October 5, 1925. While in Nashville, Hay was offered the job of director of the new station, WSM, by its owners, the National Life and Accident Insurance Co. (The company still owns WSM.) A month later, he accepted and moved south again.

The continuing success of the *WLS Barn Dance* made Hay consider a similar show for WSM, but he took no action for a while. Part of his duties involved conducting studio tours; he became fascinated by the anecdotes on fiddle music related by one visitor, eighty-year-old Uncle Jimmy Thompson. This gave Hay the incentive to inaugurate the *WSM Barn Dance* with Thompson as the star. At 8 P.M., November 28, 1925, Thompson fiddled and Hay emceed a sixty-five-minute program. The *Barn Dance* was established as a regular WSM feature.

WSM, an NBC network affiliate, carried a number of programs originating in New York. One such was the *NBC Symphony Orchestra*. In the scheduling, the *Symphony* preceded the *Barn Dance*. One night not long after the *Barn Dance* began, Hay introduced the program with this historic bit of dialogue: ". . . From here on out folks, it will be nothing but realism of the realistic kind. You've been up in the clouds with grand opera; now get down to earth with us in a . . . shindig of Grand Ole Opry!" In January 1926, the show's name officially became the *Grand Ole Opry.*

Hay expanded the *Opry,* adding more performers, including Uncle Dave Macon in 1926. Macon, a singer-banjoist, added variety to the hoedown fiddles and jug and string bands. He was for many years the leading artist of the show. Other acts Hay introduced in the early years were Paul Warmack and his Gully Jumpers, George Wilkerson and his Fruit Jar Drinkers, the Dixie Dew Drop, Arthur Smith and his Dixie Liners, Sam and Kirk McGee, and the Delmore Brothers.

Before long, the *Opry* was extended to three hours of local programming. Hay, as emcee, brought the show to a close with a steamboat whistle. He literally "blew the whistle" indicating the end of another *Opry* radio segment in the middle of a rousing performance that went on for many minutes after the *Opry* was off the air.

Hay was instrumental in having the station designated a clear-channel station in 1929, and was successful in gaining approval for a maximum power jump to 50,000 watts in 1932. This signal strength permitted WSM to blanket the South and Midwest. Listeners were able to hear the *Opry* as far north as Canada.

Through the 1930s and 1940s, Hay continued to recruit new talent and encourage trends that resulted in the emergence of name performers from *Opry* bands, including such artists as Roy Acuff and Eddy Arnold. He evolved formats and types of entertainment now standard throughout the country-music field.

In 1951, he retired to live with a daughter, Margaret, in Virginia. In 1966, he made a triumphal return to Nashville to celebrate his election to the Country Music Hall of Fame. From retirement until his death in May 1968, in Virginia Beach, Virginia, he remained on call and on the WSM payroll.

HIGHWAYMEN: *Vocal and instrumental quartet comprising Johnny Cash, Waylon Jennings, Kris Kristofferson, and Willie Nelson. (See separate entries.)*

When this supergroup was formed in the mid-1980s, it wasn't realized that the name had been used some time before by a folk group. After threatened lawsuits, mutual agreement was reached to allow the new quartet to continue to use the name. The initial albums prepared by the foursome in the 1980s and 1990s were titled *Highwayman* after the Jimmy Webb song "The Highwayman" included in the first collection.

As of 1995, three discs had been issued, *Highwayman* and *Highwayman 2* on Columbia in 1985 and 1990, respectively, and *The Road Goes on Forever* in 1995 on Liberty.

HILL, FAITH: *Singer, songwriter. Born Star, Mississippi, September 21, 1967.*

She grew up, she recalled, hoping to be "the next Reba McEntire." Whether or not she ever realizes that dream, she certainly did get to be close to her idol, with whom she toured in the mid-1990s as the name Faith Hill made its inroads on the hit charts. It was not an overnight trip for this girl from the tiny town of Star, Mississippi, and it was not without paying dues on both personal and career levels.

She told Janet E. Williams of the Country Music Association's *Close Up* (June 1994, p. 8), "I'd say I'm blessed even if my career wasn't going good. I haven't always had a charmed life. I was married very young and got divorced. That was not easy at all. I was nineteen, trying to find out who I was and fell in love with this good-looking, smart, sweet guy. It just wasn't the right thing. That's the hardest thing I've had to live with in my life. It's really hard to leave a marriage because you're unhappy. It doesn't seem like a good enough reason. The biggest deal was admitting I'd made a mistake. I couldn't admit it to anybody, but my mom and friends saw I wasn't truly happy." Still the situation might have served to steel her for the uphill fight for singing success, which was set in motion when she and her family moved to Nashville after she decided to end the marriage.

Her love for music, she stressed, went back to her very early childhood. She first sang publicly in church when she was three. "My mother said that I held the hymnal upside-down and sang as loud as I could, pretending I could read the words off the book. We went to Star Baptist church where I spent a lot of time while I was growing up. My family still goes there."

Her mother encouraged her singing by starting to pay her twenty-five cents "to sing for the relatives at family reunions, or when we would have guests at our house. If it was a big family reunion it went up to fifty cents. I'd sing songs like 'Brand New Key,' 'Jesus Loves Me,' or 'Delta Dawn.' The truth is that I always wanted to sing and would have done it anyway. The first record I ever owned was Elvis's *A Legendary Performer, Volume Two,* which had songs like 'Can't Help Falling in Love,' 'Don't Be Cruel' and 'Peace in the Valley.'

"When I was in high school, I loved listening to Reba McEntire. I remember coming home after school and playing her records in my room over and over until it was time for supper. She was a big influence, as was Patsy Cline, who I think was one of the greatest singers. Emmylou Harris and Amy Grant were two other favorites.

"I had my first band when I was seventeen. We worked all of the time, singing at rodeos, fair dates, youth festivals, churches and wherever else." When she decided to take up residence in Nashville in 1987, some friends helped put her belongings into a small truck and followed Faith and her father to Music City. Her mother moved there, too, for a while to help her get settled.

"My first job in Nashville was selling T-shirts at the Country Music Fan Fair. I didn't know what Fan Fair was at the time, but I do now." In fact, Hill can look forward to performing regularly at the event now. When she sought a more permanent job, she noted, "Interviewers would always ask if I was a singer, writer or had anything to do with music. I would say, 'Yeah, as a matter of fact, do you have a band I can play in? Do you know somebody?'"

She soon realized that response was the wrong way to get hired. Professing no interest in show business, she eventually got a job as a receptionist at Gary Morris's publishing company, where she worked for a year and a half until, she claims, a writer named David Chase "heard me singing when I thought I was alone in the office and asked me to do a demo of a song called 'It Scares Me.'"

Chase played the tape for Gary Morris, who suggested Hill move on and focus on her career potential. She became acquainted soon after with performer-songwriter Gary Burr and became a backup singer in his shows at the Bluebird Cafe. Gary, she noted, played a major role in her odyssey by tutoring her on harmony singing, writing, and stage presence.

Her work at the Bluebird was monitored by Warner Brothers Artist & Repertoire executive Martha Sharp, which in time resulted in a recording contract. It had taken six years for her to reach that milestone after her departure from Star. Her album label debut, *Take Me As I Am,* was released in the fall of 1993 and made lower chart levels during the last two months of the year, its highest position number fifty-two on the *Billboard* list.

But singles from the CD began to gain increasing airplay. The initial single release, "Wild One," rose to number one on the *Billboard* Hot Country Singles chart the last week of 1993 and held that position into 1994. It peaked at number five in *Radio & Records* the week of January 7, 1994. Later her version of the Janis Joplin classic, "Piece of My Heart," was a major hit, reaching number one in April 1994. The album also contained one of Faith's songwriting efforts, "I've Got This Friend," cowritten with Bruce Burch and Vern Dant. Gary Burr also contributed "Just Around the Eye." In June 1994, she had the single "But I Will," moving up the charts. By then the album had become a chart hit, peaking at number seven in *Billboard* earlier in the year on the way to earning gold-record certification from the R.I.A.A. The album was still on the charts in 1995 after going past platinum-record totals.

Besides sparking growing interest in her concert appearances, her recording successes paved the way for exposure on major TV shows such as *Late Night with David Letterman* on CBS. She was also one of the finalists for the Country Music Association's Horizon Award in the fall of 1994. Soon after the CMA telecast the title track of her album was on the charts reaching the *Billboard* Top 10 late in the year and peaking at number six in *R&R* the week of November 25.

Looking back on reasons for the choice of "Wild One" in her initial recording sessions, she told Janet Williams it made her remember her headstrong teen years. "I was very independent and when I had my mind set on doing anything, I thought I was going to do it. I wasn't a problem child, but my mom and dad probably had a little problem keeping me under control. At the same time they understood it. They didn't let me go rambling wild and crazy. They let me explore different things and let me be who I am."

She might not have attained her early vision of being the next Reba, but she was certainly making inroads in country music annals as the first Faith Hill. By the start of 1995, though, her career suddenly seemed in jeopardy as she ran into problems with her vocal cords that required surgery in February. It was a traumatic period lightened slightly by receiving a platinum record award for her debut album on January 5, 1995. Fortunately, the surgery was successful and by April she was again in the concert circuit as an opening act for George Strait.

In late August, Warner Bros. issued her second album, *It Matters to Me,* which was preceded on the charts by the single "Let's Go to Vegas." The single, which peaked at number five in *Billboard* was still on the hit lists at year-end. The album peaked at number four and went gold by the end of 1995, moving on to platinum sales in 1996. The title track, issued as a single in late fall, rose to number one on the hit lists in January 1996. In the spring, Faith had another hit single with "Someone Else's Dream." Among her 1996 milestones were being included by *People* magazine editors among its list of the "50 Most Beautiful People" and cohosting the 1996 Academy of Country Music Awards telecast in April with Brooks & Dunn. In that voting, she was a finalist in the Single Record of the Year category (for "It Matters to Me") and Top Female Vocalist. On August 4, 1996, she joined Mark O'Connor as country music's Ambassadors to the World during the Southern Jamboree portion of the closing ceremonies at the Olympics in Atlanta, Georgia. Later in the year she was a finalist in the Female Vocalist category of the Country Music Association Awards voting.

HOLLY, BUDDY: *Singer, guitarist, violinist, songwriter, band leader (The Crickets, Buddy Holly Band). Born Lubbock, Texas, September 7, 1936; died near Ames, Iowa, February 3, 1959. The Crickets comprised Holly; Jerry Allison, born Hillsboro, Texas, August 31, 1939; Niki Sullivan; Joe Mauldin. Backup group, early 1959: Tommy Allsup, Waylon Jennings, Charlie Bunch. In early 1960s, Crickets comprised Allison; Sonny Curtis, born Meadow, Texas, May 9, 1937; Glen Hardin, born Wellington, Texas, April 18, 1939; Jerry Naylor, born Stephenville, Texas, March 6, 1939.*

In a life that lasted hardly more than twenty-two years, Buddy Holly gained the heights of popular music before he died in a plane crash. Like Elvis, he and his band, the Crickets, had a tremendous impact not only on American popular music, but the subsequent development of rock 'n' roll in England. The styles of the Beatles, Rolling Stones, and many other British supergroups were partly derived from Holly's arrangements and methods of guitar playing. His story didn't end with his death. He became a part of popular legend, memorialized in such famous songs as Don McLean's 1971 hit "American Pie," which described Buddy's death as "the day the music died." Buddy's life story was the subject of a hit movie in the late 1970s and reissues of his recordings still were appearing in the 1990s.

Born Charles Hardin Holley (the "e" in Holley was accidentally dropped on his first record contract, a change he let stand), he was initially influenced by country music and began as a country artist in his early teens.

As the youngest of four children, he grew up in a conservative Baptist family. His parents encouraged musical ambitions in their children and Buddy began to play the violin and piano at four and took up the guitar when he was only seven. There were country records in his home, including some old 78 rpm discs of such early stars as Jimmie Rodgers (the Singing Brakeman) and the Carter Family. He also picked up pointers on current country trends by listening to local west Texas radio shows and sometimes the *Grand Ole Opry* from Nashville, Tennessee.

In the early 1950s, he started singing in country groups while attending high school. By 1954, he was gaining a local reputation as a country artist and was playing in small clubs in the Southwest. As rock swept over the country in the mid-1950s, Holly, like many other young country-bred performers, was attracted to the new style. Though he developed his own method of doing rock music, he was an early admirer of Elvis Presley and R&B stars Little Richard and Chuck Berry, whose hits he often rerecorded.

In 1956, Decca released several rough-edged rockabilly solo singles Holly recorded in their Nashville studios, but they failed to sell, so Decca dropped his contract. Holly and some Lubbock friends then formed a band, naming themselves "the Crickets" after considering calling themselves "the Beetles." (Years later, England's Fab Four would choose the name "Beatles" as a tribute to the Crickets.) Buddy handled guitar and vocals; Jerry Allison, drums; Niki Sullivan, guitar; and Joe Mauldin, bass guitar. They became the protégés of Clovis, New Mexico–based record producer Norman Petty (born Clovis, May 25, 1927; died 1985), who used his connections to get their song "That'll Be the Day" released on Decca's Brunswick subsidiary in 1957. A number one success in *Billboard,* it led to a contract for the Crickets on Brunswick and for Holly as a solo on another Decca subsidiary, Coral. "They kicked us out the front door so we went in the back door," Buddy remarked.

Subsequent Crickets hits included "Oh, Boy!" (top 10, 1957) and "Maybe Baby" and "Think It Over" (1958). Holly's solo "Peggy Sue" made *Billboard*'s Top 10 in 1957. His lesser hits included "Early in the Morning" (1958, written by Bobby Darin and Woody Harris) and the posthumous "It Doesn't Matter Anymore" (1959, written by Paul Anka). "Peggy Sue" was originally titled "Cindy Lou," but Jerry Allison suggested substituting his girlfriend's name.

The Crickets' 1958 tour of England was one of the major pop events in that country to that time. Many of the aspiring young rock and blues musicians in England took careful note of Holly's guitar style. Called the brush-and-broom style, it was a technique derived from country music groups in Holly's home area. His technique was described in *Golden Guitars* by Irwin Stambler and Grelun Landon (Four Winds Press, 1971). "He would hit the note, which was the 'broom,' and then 'brush' his fingers across the chord. For example, a guitarist might pluck the G string, or the D string, then strum the G chord. (This type of playing is also used in many Johnny Cash arrangements.) This technique of note and strums is much simpler than the fancy runs of an artist like Jimmie Rodgers. Holly's material combined a Jimmie Rodgers–Leadbelly blues feeling with

heavy guitar sounds out front and a pronounced beat underneath."

Like most music stars, he maintained a hectic schedule of personal appearances that involved great amounts of travel from each one-night stand to the next. It was a wearing schedule that eventually cost him his life. Not long before his final, fatal tour, Holly had made a number of changes in his personal and music business life. For one thing, due to a feud with his mentor, Norman Petty, Holly and the Crickets became separate acts. Holly's role in the Crickets was taken over by an old Lubbock acquaintance, Earl Sinks, while Buddy set up a new backing band that eventually comprised Tommy Allsup on guitar, Charlie Bunch on drums, and future country star Waylon Jennings on bass guitar and backing vocals.

Buddy also had established New York as both recording and personal base. In the summer of 1958, he married Puerto Rican–born Marie Elena Santiago, whom he had met when she was working in his song publisher's office in New York. They took up living quarters in Greenwich Village, while he pursued his recording projects and studied acting. Among those projects were sessions backed by an orchestra led by Dick Jacobs, a far cry from his early rockabilly.

At the beginning of 1959, Holly and his backing group was booked for a Midwestern tour that also featured such best-selling artists as the Big Bopper (J.P. Richardson) and Ritchie Valens. They traveled between concert sites by bus, so the musicians had to spend long, grueling hours going from one small town to another under cold, crowded conditions. In Clear Lake, Iowa, faced with another trying journey to a date in Fargo, North Dakota, Holly, Allsup, and Jennings decided to hire a light plane so they could reach Fargo early enough to get some rest and have their stage outfits cleaned, as described in the authoritative biography, *Remembering Buddy* by John Goldrosen and John Beecher (Penguin Books, 1987).

Before they got on the plane, the passenger list changed. The Big Bopper wasn't feeling well and talked Jennings into giving him his seat. Valens challenged Allsup to a coin toss for the other place. Valens won. Allsup and Jennings stayed on the bus. Piloted by 21-year-old Roger Peterson, the plane took off from the Mason City, Iowa, airport in a blinding snowstorm. It quickly crashed, killing all occupants.

Holly's popularity remained strong decades after his death, fueled by periodic posthumous releases of his recordings. Immediately after the crash, Coral rushed into print *The Buddy Holly Story,* a gold-award-winning memorial album featuring his and the Crickets' major hits. Other Coral releases included *The Buddy Holly Story, Volume 2* (1960), the two-disc *Best of Buddy Holly* (1966), and *Buddy Holly's Greatest Hits* (1967). In 1962, Coral also reissued the 1957 LP *The Chirping Crickets* as *Buddy Holly and the Crickets.*

Reminiscing (1963), *Showcase* (1964), and *Holly in the Hills* (1965) mainly presented unpolished yet interesting studio tracks and home tapes never released as singles (including standards of his favorite R&B and C&W artists). His pre-Crickets Nashville sessions appeared on *That'll Be the Day* (Decca, 1958), reissued as *The Great Buddy Holly* (Vocalion, 1967).

As owner of Decca, Coral and Brunswick, MCA continued to release Holly reissues in the 1970s, 1980s and 1990s. The two-disc *Buddy Holly: A Rock & Roll Collection* (1972) was so clumsily assembled that it included a version of "Love's Made a Fool of You" the Crickets taped after Buddy left them. Originally released only in England, MCA's six-record *The Complete Buddy Holly* provided not only his professional recordings, but also interviews, tapes of a TV appearance on *The Ed Sullivan Show,* and sessions Holly produced for Waylon Jennings and Lou Giordano. *20 Golden Greats* was released to coincide with the first screenings of the fictionalized Columbia Pictures film biography, *The Buddy Holly Story,* starring Gary Busey as Holly. The soundtrack album, which presented the film's stars (Busey, Don Stroud, and Charles Martin) performing Holly's songs, was issued on American International Records, distributed by Epic Records.

In early 1983, MCA came out with *For the First Time Anywhere,* an impressive set of Holly recordings that had remained hidden in the vaults for almost twenty-seven years. These songs had been issued on many LPs over the years, MCA noted, but never in the form Holly originally had made them. Norman Petty had reworked the tapes by overdubbing them with instrumental backing by another of his protégé acts, the Fireballs. For decades, MCA didn't realize the original unretouched tapes were still in existence. They proved a new revelation of the raw excitement and urgency of Holly performances.

In 1985, MCA issued a CD of what it stated were remastered versions from original Coral, Brunswick and Decca tapes of Buddy's 20 most famous songs, titled *The Legend.* In mid-1986, it was released in LP (2 discs) and cassette formats.

In the decades following Holly's death, rerecordings of his songs by the Beatles, John Lennon, Blind Faith, Rolling Stones, Grateful Dead, Nitty Gritty Dirt Band, and Waylon Jennings further attest to Buddy's influence. Linda Ronstadt had hits with Holly's "That'll Be the Day" and "It's So Easy," as did Peter and Gordon with his "True Love Ways."

During 1995, Decca Records brought together artists from rock and country to record a tribute album, issued in late December, titled *Not Fade Away (Remembering Buddy Holly).* Contributors included the Band and the Crickets on the title song; Waylon Jennings on "Learning the Game"; Nanci Griffith on "Well . . . All Right"; The Mavericks on "True Love Ways"; and Marty Stuart and Steve Earle on "Crying, Waiting, Hoping." In late

1996, the National Academy of the Recording Arts & Sciences announced it would honor Holly posthumously with its Lifetime Achivement Award during its February 1997 Grammy Awards telecast.

HOMER AND JETHRO: *Vocal and instrumental duo, comedy team; Jethro (Kenneth C. Burns), born Knoxville, Tennessee, March 10, 1920; died February 4, 1989; Homer (Henry D. Haynes), born Knoxville, Tennessee, July 27, 1920; died Chicago, Illinois, August 7, 1971.*

For three decades, the team of Homer and Jethro reigned as the finest comedy duo in country music. Their humor was universal, as demonstrated by their ability to rouse gales of laughter in audiences ranging from rural country-fair crowds to sophisticated assemblages in Las Vegas, Chicago, and other major cities. Their flair for satirizing all kinds of pop music from pop ballads to Hank Williams's songs tended to hide the fact that both artists were accomplished instrumentalists as well.

Both Homer, whose real name was Henry D. Haynes, and Jethro, real name Kenneth C. Burns, were born and raised in Knoxville and started learning to play stringed instruments as boys. However, their association wasn't a planned step but an accidental byproduct of their early attempts to break into show business.

Jethro recalled the circumstances for an interviewer from the *Gibson Gazette* in 1971 (Volume 11, Number 1). "It all began in 1932 at Radio Station WNOX, Knoxville, Tennessee. We were contestants on an amateur program. I was doing a guitar and mandolin duet with my brother and Homer was working with a trio. We were twelve years old. And backstage before the show we had a little jam session goin'. The program director, Lowell Blanchard, heard us playing so he picked Homer, me, my brother and another kid and put the four of us together as a quartet. We appeared in the contest and he disqualified us before we started and gave us jobs on the radio station as staff musicians.

"We called ourselves The String Dusters. It was sort of a real pop, swinging group. Later the same guy that gave us the jobs gave us the names Homer and Jethro. Homer and Jethro was just kind of a thing we did for kicks."

By that he meant that the two boys used to clown around off-stage burlesquing popular songs, doing the lyrics "straight" but in a comedy bluegrass approach. Blanchard liked the routine so much he began to work it into the String Dusters set in WNOX's *Mid-day Merry-Go-Round.* The comedy worked so well, Homer noted, "We broke the group up in 1936 and started doing Homer and Jethro full time. That's when we started doing strictly comedy."

The boys remained on WNOX until 1939, when they decided it was time to seek new surroundings. They auditioned for the *Renfro Valley Barn Dance* in Renfro Valley, Kentucky, and quickly became cast regulars, appearing on both CBS and NBC network shows during their two years on the program. In 1941, they were considering an offer from the *Plantation Party* in Chicago to become cast regulars when both were drafted into the army and went off in different directions. Homer went into the medical corps and saw service in the Pacific while Jethro eventually ended up in Europe.

After their discharge, the duo reunited in Knoxville in 1945 and soon moved on to become part of the *Midwestern Hayride*. Homer told the *Gibson Gazette*, "We went to Cincy in 1945 to radio station WLW. We worked on the staff there with a lot of good guys: Chet Atkins, Rosemary Clooney, Merle Travis, and a number of other good musicians. We were there for about two and a half years and then we were fired." Jethro continued, "WLW was, at that time, owned by the Crosley Corporation and they had always gone heavy on country music because it was popular. Then they sold out to Avco. Well, the first thing Avco did was to bring in an efficiency expert and he just fired everybody he could find. In one week he fired Homer and Jethro, Rosemary Clooney, Chet Atkins, Merle Travis, and Roy Lanin."

The stay at WLW was valuable to the duo both for increased audience exposure and the team's first major record contract. They were signed by King Records, and during their work for the label from 1946–48, they turned out five albums and such hit burlesque singles of popular songs as "Five Minutes More," "Over the Rainbow," and "Symphony."

After leaving WLW, Homer and Jethro toured the United States with their own tent show for about six months, then returned to WNOX before going on to join the new Red Foley show on KWTO in Springfield, Missouri. They joined a cast that included Chet Atkins, Slim Wilson, and the Carter Family. Jethro recalled, "That was probably the most fun we ever had anywhere. It was very relaxed. Everybody went fishin'. We had a motto up there that 'We Never Let Work Interfere With Our Fishin'." During that period, the duo was sought out by Steve Sholes of RCA Records, which resulted in a recording contract that led to a long association and many major hit releases.

In 1949, the late orchestra leader Spike Jones persuaded the duo to join his management/booking company, Arena Stars. Homer noted, "We went on the road with Spike Jones in 1949. While we were in Chicago [in 1951] the *National Barn Dance* people came to us and asked us if we'd come down and perform at the *Barn Dance* in between shows. As a result of this, the Program Director offered us a job. Spike let us out of the contract with no problems. So we did the *Barn Dance* show every Saturday night and during the week we worked the *Don McNeil Breakfast Club*. We left the *Barn Dance* in 1958." The move to the *Barn Dance* also resulted in the team permanently relocating to the Chicago area. At Homer's death, he resided in Lansing

while Jethro still called Evanston home at the end of the 1970s.

Even before joining WLS, Homer and Jethro had made their mark on the national country and pop charts. In 1948, they made the top 10 with their side-splitting version of "Baby, It's Cold Outside," recorded with June Carter. They followed with more singles hits in the early 1950s, scoring their biggest success in 1953 with "Hound Dog in the Winter." Their RCA LPs of those years included such titles as *Worst of Homer & Jethro* (1958) and *Life Can Be Miserable* (1959). The year after they left the *Barn Dance*, they made the singles charts with "The Battle of Kookamonga." That effort won them a Grammy Award for the Best Comedy Performance of 1959.

At the end of the 1950s and throughout the 1960s, Homer and Jethro concentrated on personal appearances in major cities across the United States and Canada. They were a little hesitant about their debut in Las Vegas, and considered changing their act. Finally, noted Homer, "We went out there on opening night and our opening line was 'We are Homer and Jethro, we're not brothers . . . my brother is living.' And you would have thought it was the funniest thing that had ever been said." Jethro added, "We did these old things that we were doing back in the 1930s and just tore the place up. We did so well that the second night instead of being the supporting act, we were the headliners. The papers would say, 'The funniest material ever heard on the Strip was by two hillbillies over at the Thunderbird.'"

The team returned to Vegas many times as they did to many other entertainment centers. They also made repeat appearances on such major 1960s TV shows as Johnny Carson's *The Tonight Show, Dean Martin's Music Country,* and, in the late 1960s, the *Johnny Cash* program, where they guested eight different times.

During the mid-1960s, the team probably gained as much attention from the TV viewing public for its wild commercials for Kellogg's corn flakes as for its other activities. The duo was featured on both radio and TV in those commercials for four years.

Meanwhile, RCA continued to release a steady stream of new albums during the decade, including *At the Country Club* (1960); *Songs My Mother Never Sang* (4/61); *At the Convention* (5/62); *Playing Straight* (1962); *Zany Songs of the '30s* (1963); *Ooh! That's Corny* (1963); *Confucius Say* (1964); *Go West* (8/64); *Fractured Folk Songs* (12/64); *Tenderly* (6/65); *Old Crusty Minstrel* (1/66); *Best of Homer & Jethro* (2/66); *Any News* (7/68); *Wanted for Murder* (12/66); *Homer & Jethro* (3/67); *Songs for the 'Out' Crowd* (5/67); *Nashville Cats* (7/67); and *Somethin' Stupid* (11/67). Releases on the Camden label in the 1960s included *Strike Back* (6/62); *Humorous Side of Country Music* (9/63); *Songs to Tickle* (5/66).

The team continued to give concerts and turn out

new recordings into the early 1970s. Just before Homer died of a heart attack during the summer of 1971, the duo completed an album with its Nashville String Band called *Strung Up*. The emphasis with the String Band, of course, was to play the music straight rather than for laughs. However, the team didn't ignore comedy with 1971 takeoffs on such songs as "Help Me Make It Through the Night" and "The Good Times."

Asked about the reaction of writers to Homer and Jethro's antics, Homer told the *Gibson Gazette,* "People used to come to us and say, 'You shouldn't butcher a Hank Williams song because what would Hank think?' Well Hank, he told us one time, that he didn't think a song was a success until it had been butchered by Homer and Jethro. [They turned his "Jambalaya," for instance, into "Jam-Bowl-Liar."] And he gave us written permission to do any song he had ever written."

It took Jethro Burns a while to get over Homer's untimely passing, but by the mid-1970s he was working on a variety of projects. These included a close professional relationship with Chicage folk artist Steve Goodman, with whom he toured many major cities in the mid- and late 1970s, while also backing Steve on most of his recordings.

The work with Goodman showcased Burns's excellent musicianship, particularly as a mandolin virtuoso, which had tended to be downplayed during his madcap performances with his longtime comedy partner. The fact that both Homer and Jethro had fine singing voices and above-average instrumental skills was stressed in *Life* magazine's September 1994 selection of them as among "The 100 Most Important People in the History of Country."

Burns's work with Goodman became a closed chapter with the latter's passing in the early 1980s. However, Burns had plenty of other things with which to keep himself occupied. He taught mandolin and was also involved in a number of instrumental projects, including some with his brother-in-law Chet Atkins. He also demonstrated his musical versatility by making a fine series of jazz albums that earned considerable praise from critics in that field.

His health began failing in the mid-1980s and, after a long illness, he died on February 4, 1989.

HORTON, JOHNNY: *Singer, guitarist, songwriter. Born Tyler, Texas, April 3, 1929; died November 5, 1960.*

Most Americans have an affinity for the automobile and nowhere is this truer than in the Southern states. The bond has always been close for most country performers, indicated by many songs over the years about automobiles and truck driving, but also reflecting the fact that many have come from rural, poverty-stricken areas where the car represented an escape from a life of drudgery.

The relationship, though, has had some tragic overtones. Because country artists often perform in small towns that are out of the way of public transportation, such as airlines, the car became the transport system of choice. The combination of long rides and odd hours has resulted in the loss of many artists in automobile accidents, as was the case with Johnny Horton in late 1960. Of course, today major stars travel in well-appointed buses with professional drivers, but the dangers still exist for up-and-coming performers unable to afford such luxury.

In Horton's case, the fatal mishap cut short a career that might well have assumed superstar proportions in the 1960s. His untimely passing took place at what seemed the most important phase of his career, just after his recording of "Battle of New Orleans" had become a smash hit all over the world.

Horton was raised on a farm and had to work hard at chores as soon as he was old enough to help out his share-cropping parents. His mother had considerable talent and taught him to play the guitar when he was eleven. Johnny was also physically strong and a talented athlete. His prowess in high school and at Lon Morris Junior College in Jacksonville, Texas, and Kilgore Junior College in Kilgore, Texas, led to offers of athletic scholarships from many four-year colleges. He finally accepted a basketball bid from Baylor University in Waco, and went there for a while before transferring to the University of Seattle, Washington. Johnny had a lifetime interest in fishing and left Seattle for Alaska (without receiving his degree) to work as a fisherman.

In 1950, he went south to Los Angeles, where he also worked for a time in the fishing industry. His singing ability caused some of his friends to talk him into entering a contest at Harmony Park Corral in Anaheim. He won the contest and also the attention of such people as Cliffie Stone and Tennessee Ernie Ford. (His fishing background earned him the designation of "The Singing Fisherman.") He soon gained a spot on KXLA radio station in Pasadena and also was featured on Cliffie Stone's *Hometown Jamboree* TV show on KLAC for several years.

His growing reputation led to a bid from the *Louisiana Hayride* in Shreveport, which he accepted in 1955. He became the leading artist on the show in short order, and remained one of the Hayride's main attractions for the rest of his life. He also played engagements at county fairs, honky-tonks, and other country entertainment venues throughout the U.S. and also had guest shots on many major country shows, including the *Grand Ole Opry.* In addition, he had his own show Monday nights in the late 1950s over radio station KLIV, Tyler, Texas.

He had made several singles for independent labels in the mid-1950s before signing with Columbia Records in the latter part of the decade. His name started showing up on the hit charts in the late 1950s, starting with his 1957 single "I'm Just a One Woman Man." The following year he really began to move ahead with three top-10 hits, "Johnny Reb," "When It's Springtime in Alaska," and the number-one-ranked "Battle of New Orleans." It also was the year his debut album on Columbia was released, *The Spectacular Johnny Horton.* In November 1959, Johnny received the Grammy Award for Best Country & Western Performance for "Battle of New Orleans," a single that also had crossed over to the pop charts. Johnny continued on a roll in 1960 with the top-10 hit "Sink the Bismarck," cowritten with Frank Tillman. His single "North to Alaska" was number one for many weeks that year. Columbia also issued two more albums in 1960, *Johnny Horton Makes History* and *Johnny Horton's Greatest Hits.*

With his popularity at an all-time high, Johnny was in demand for an increasing number of personal appearances in widely separated parts of the country. On November 5, 1960, he finished a show in Louisiana and got in his car to drive to Nashville, where he was scheduled to be a headline act at a disc jockey convention. He never got there; in a jarring collision en route, he was killed instantly.

As happened with other stars, his voice remained widely popular on records for several years after his death. In 1961, he had a top-10 hit, "Sleepy Eyed John," and that was followed by perhaps his best recording, the top-10 "Honky Tonk Man." His albums continued to sell steadily during the first part of the 1960s as Columbia added to his catalog with *Johnny Horton on the Louisiana Hayride* and the 1962 release, *Honky Tonk Man.* In 1971, Columbia packaged almost all of Horton's recorded material on the two-disc set, *The World of Johnny Horton.* Years after his death, many country fans still had fond memories of his work and some of his releases, long out of print, could still be heard occasionally on country radio stations into the 1990s.

In print in the mid-1990s was a comprehensive package of Horton's recordings produced by Germany's Bear Family Records. Titled *Johnny Horton: 1956–1960*, the 4 CD set included all of Johnny's hits including "Springtime in Alaska," "Honky Tonk Hardwood Floor," "The Wild One" and "Battle of New Orleans." In addition, the compilation included a CD of demos that Horton completed just before his death.

HOWARD, HARLAN: *Songwriter, singer, publisher. Born Harlan County, Kentucky, September 8, 1929.*

Although born in fabled Harlan County, Kentucky, young Harlan was raised in and around Detroit, where his parents moved when he was two years old. Their background and the wattage power of WSM's *Grand Ole Opry* into Detroit provided the boy with country-music indoctrination.

His idol, Ernest Tubb, indirectly taught Howard how to write lyrics. Tubb would sing on the *Opry* and Howard would attempt to write down the lyrics, his quick ear retaining the melodies. There were gaps in the lyrics and he would fill them in, add new verses, and get a sort of Ernest Tubb song as a result. This led him to try writing his own songs, using the earthy three- and four-chord structures of his favorite writers, Tubb, Fred Rose, Floyd Tillman, and Rex Griffen.

Four years with the paratroopers followed his graduation from high school; it was at Fort Benning, Georgia, that his buddies taught him to pick the guitar. On Friday nights, he would head directly for Nashville with a buddy, hitchhiking both ways. Sometimes the luck of the thumb was sour and they would report back to the base late for Monday's roll call.

Following his army tour, Howard worked at various jobs in Michigan, Tucson, and finally Los Angeles. It was there that he met Johnny Bond and Tex Ritter, both of whom took an interest in his writing, and had their firms publish his songs. (In Los Angeles, he also met an aspiring young singer who soon became his wife. Jan Howard was to become an important country artist in the 1960s with many of her hit records Harlan's songs.) This was in the late 1950s, a period that saw Wynn Stewart, Buck Owens, Bobby Bare, Skeets McDonald, and others trying their luck on the California country nightclub and recording circuit.

Howard pointed out that he had tried to get his writing career started in Nashville but, as he told Robert Hilburn of the *Los Angeles Times* ("Heartaches by the Score," Calendar section, June 14, 1992), "Nothing really happened until I moved to California in 1955. I had been to Nashville a bunch of times to see if I could get anything going, but I was a factory worker and Nashville had no factory jobs so there was no way to support myself while I tried to write the songs. L.A., on the other hand, had jobs and there was a growing country music scene out there."

Stewart made the first recording of a Howard song, "You Took Her Off My Hands," for Capitol Records, under Ken Nelson's direction. Not long after, Columbia's Don Law recorded Charlie Walker with "Pick Me Up on Your Way Down," Howard's first recognized national hit. These were followed with Kitty Wells' "Mommy for a Day" and Ray Price's "Heartaches by the Number," which hit the pop charts with a cover record by Guy Mitchell.

"Heartaches" provided his major breakthrough. He had received some small checks for minor hits before, never for over $27, when he opened an envelope to discover a royalty check for $48,000 for that top-10 crossover success. He told Hilburn, "I thought that was all the money in the world. I was still driving a fork truck at a book bindery in Huntington Park out in California making two hundred dollars a week—two hundred and twenty-five dollars if I worked overtime. So what happens three days later? I get another check for fifty-two thousand dollars. Here I was all of a sudden with one-hundred thousand dollars, which must be like having a million dollars today, and I didn't even have a bank account."

With royalty money coming in nicely, Howard decided to go where the hits were being cut. In June 1960 he moved to Nashville. The first of his 400-plus recordings was made there, and in both 1961 and 1962 he was awarded *Billboard*'s top country & western songwriter award.

Howard kept up correspondence with country disc jockeys and artists, regularly covering recording sessions in the various Nashville studios, the *Grand Ole Opry*, and other pipelines of the business. In 1964 he started his own publishing firm, Wilderness Music Publishing Company.

His BMI award hits include: "Mommy for a Day," "Pick Me Up on Your Way Down," "Heartaches by the Number" (1959); "Above and Beyond (the Call of Love)," "Three Steps to the Phone," "I Don't Believe I'll Fall in Love Today," "Odds and Ends (Bits and Pieces)," "Under the Influence of Love," "I Fall to Pieces," "I Wish I Could Fall in Love Today," "Heartbreak USA," "The Blizzard," "Foolin' Around" (1960); "Don't Call Me from a Honky Tonk," "You Took Her Off My Hands," "Busted," "Second Hand Rose (Second Hand Heart)," "You Comb Her Hair" (1963); "Your Heart Turned Left" (1965); "I Won't Forget You," "I've Got a Tiger by the Tail" (1964); "Streets of Baltimore," "Evil on Your Mind," "It's All Over (But the Crying)" (1966).

During the 1960s, Harlan made some recordings of his own, such as the 1966 Monument Records album *Harlan Howard* and such RCA LPs as *Mr. Songwriter* (1967) and *Down to Earth* (1968). He also had an early 1970s release on Nugget Records, *Silent Majority*. However, his performing career remained secondary to his writing activities, particularly since he didn't like touring and was an avid fisherman. For many years he lived in Madison, Tennessee, with Jan and the couple's three sons, but Harlan and Jan separated during the 1970s.

From the 1970s through the mid-1990s, Harlan's name continued to appear on song credits of reissues or new recordings of his earlier work, and occasionally for recordings of new material. During those years, besides tending his own affairs, he also took time to encourage new talents in both the songwriting and performing areas. In 1973 he was voted into the Nashville Songwriters' Hall of Fame, and he took a major role in that organization's activities in the years that followed. In 1984, for instance, he organized the "Harlan Howard Birthday Bash and Guitar Pullin'" event, typically held in the BMI parking lot at 10 Music Square East in Nashville. That annual songfest, which featured top country performers and songwriters, was still going strong in the 1990s, with all proceeds from ticket sales earmarked for the Nashville Entertainment Association and the Nashville Songwriters Association's building fund for the Songwriters Hall of Fame.

While he continued to write new songs in the post-1970 years, including the Judds' 1980s best-seller "Why Not Me," he tended to focus more on administering his copyrights and opening doors for newcomers.

Though in some ways his private life could still be chaotic—by the mid-1990s he had been married five times, and endured four divorces—he remained one of the stones in the foundation of Nashville songwriting.

In 1996, the independent Koch Records reissued one of Howard's albums, *All Time Favorite Songwriter* (distributed by Sony Music Special Products). The disc contained his vocals of 12 of his best songs included "Busted" and "Heartaches by the Numbers."

HOWARD, JAN: *Singer. Born West Plains, Missouri, March 13, 1932.*

For decades after the late 1950s, the surname Howard often appeared on country charts. In bold face it was associated with singer Jan Howard, in fine print with songwriter Harlan Howard. Often both names appeared in connection with the same song, because many of Jan's hits were written by Harlan. For a long time it was a husband-and-wife partnership; although the two separated in the 1970s, for career purposes Jan retained her married name.

The idea of a music career seemed remote when Jan was growing up in West Plains, Missouri. However, she did enjoy listening to country & western music and sang along with records and radio programs as she reached her teens. She began to perform at local affairs, and in time moved to Los Angeles to try to further her musical background.

In California, she met an up-and-coming songwriter named Harlan Howard. It wasn't long before she became Mrs. Howard and settled down to raise a family that after several years of marriage consisted of three boys. Harlan made use of her singing ability on some demonstration records of new songs. There were plenty of listeners for these discs, for by this time Harlan was one of the most successful songwriters in the business.

One recording executive was as impressed with Jan Howard's voice as with the song. In short order, Jan had a part-time career as singer and recording artist. For Challenge Records, she turned out a number of hits, such as "Yankee Go Home," "The One You Slip Around With," and "A World I Can't Live In." Her ability was recognized by the jukebox operators of America, who selected her as the Most Promising Country & Western Female Vocalist for 1960. Shortly after, she received similar awards from *Billboard* and *Cash Box*. The year 1960 also was one in which the Howard family took up residence in the Nashville area, a region Jan still called home in the 1990s.

In the 1960s, she was featured on a number of network TV and radio shows, including appearances on the *Grand Ole Opry*. As her home schedule permitted, she also made personal appearances in many states and overseas. She made many recordings during the decade, including many releases that found favor with record buyers. One of her early-1960s credits was the Wrangler Records LP, *Jan Howard*. In the mid-1960s she signed with Decca Records. Among her successes on the label was the 1966 nationwide top-10 single, "Evil on Your Mind," (written by Harlan). It also served as the title song for a 1966 Decca LP. Among her chart singles in 1967 was the hit "Roll Over and Play Dead." During the year Decca released the LP *Bad Seed*. Her 1968 output included *This Is Jan Howard* and the chart hit LP *Count Your Blessings, Woman*. Her 1968 singles successes included a duet with Bill Anderson, "For Loving You," and her solo "Count Your Blessings, Woman." In 1969 she made singles charts with songs like "When We Tried" and "My Son." Her duet work with Bill Anderson at the end of the 1960s and start of the 1970s brought Country Music Association nominations for Best Vocal Duo in 1968 and 1970.

Her late 1960s and early 1970s albums on Decca included *For God and Country, If It's All the Same to You,* and *You Rock Me Back to Little Rock*. Among her early 1970s chart singles was the 1970 "The Soul You Never Had." By the mid-1970s, Jan's affiliation with Decca had ended. Later in the decade she recorded with the Con Brio label.

During the 1980s and into the 1990s, Jan remained active in industry affairs and continued to make concert and TV appearances, though she no longer had recordings that made the hit charts. Among her 1990s projects was taking part in the video *Remembering Patsy,* a tribute to Patsy Cline that also featured Roy Clark and Bill Anderson.

J

JACKSON, ALAN: *Singer, guitarist, band leader (the Strayhorns), songwriter. Born Newman, Georgia, October 17, 1958.*

In the 1980s and 1990s, country music veterans complained that the form's values had gone out the window in an era when it seemed more important for a performer to have a "heartthrob" appearance than a unique, creative point of view. Nonetheless, they had to agree there were artists like Alan Jackson who not only had matinee idol features, but were also in the blue-collar tradition of the genre. As Jackson himself commented after his career began to flourish, "It helps if you have good looks. But I'm not saying that's what sells records. There has to be talent in there too."

There's no doubt about his talent, but it wasn't something that was apparent to him in his youth growing up in Newman, Georgia, with his four sisters. While his family listened to music, there wasn't a tradition of performing or playing instruments to influence him. The son of a mechanic, he had a normal childhood and, thanks to his father's occupation, was more interested in tinkering with cars than thinking about a music career. He was already earning money from repairing old cars and selling them when he began dating the woman he would marry in 1979, Denise, who remained his wife and loving companion more than fifteen years and two children later.

She recalled for *People* magazine's special issue on country stars in the fall of 1994 that she was sixteen and entering her junior year at Newman High School when the recent school graduate (Class of '76) asked her out. At the time, Alan's pride and joy was a white 1965 Thunderbird that was the first car he'd owned and restored several years earlier. He told the interviewer, "That car was all I cared about. I drove it to high school, dated in it. It was like a member of the family." (He also used it for a time to drive to classes at the West Georgia Community College.)

Denise remembered being impressed by the car, too. "He had the T-bird, that was his biggest selling point. I think what attracted him to me was that I didn't go out with him the first time he asked me. But he called three or four months later, and I felt differently. We were just typical high school kids. We'd get mad at each other and break up. He'd go date somebody else to make me mad; I'd date the quarterback to make him mad. But we ended up back together." And, after they were married, Jackson sold his beloved T-bird to get the money for the down payment on their first home.

Alan had learned to play guitar and did some performing at local venues in his teens, but it was more a hobby or a way to make a little extra cash than what he considered a regular job. In fact, he didn't attend his first concert, he said, until he was twenty. He got his primary income from working in construction and driving a forklift. As he noted after winning a country music Favorite Album trophy in the 1992 American Music Awards, "I still feel like the same guy who was driving a forklift in the K-Mart warehouse ten years ago. Things have moved so fast, it's hard to see it all. But every now and then, you get a second where it hits you."

As the 1980s went by, he began receiving more local attention for his musical skills. He was also becoming more interested in writing original material. In 1985, he and Denise decided to sell their Georgia possessions and move to Nashville so that he could try to make the big time in the country field. Once there, Alan got a job in the mailroom at the Nashville Network while Denise augmented family finances by working as a flight attendant. Alan followed the usual route of making demos and passing them around to music publishers and record executives, while taking whatever club work he could get.

For four years he made little headway, receiving one

rejection after another. But he did acquire a manager, Barry Coburn, who worked with producer Keith Stegall (with whom Alan began cowriting a number of new songs) to get him a hearing with Arista Records' newly established Nashville operation. "They were new to country music," Jackson told an interviewer, "but they had a good track record for having a lot of faith and confidence in their artists."

His debut album, *Here in the Real World,* released in late 1989, contained ten songs, nine written or cowritten by Jackson. Buoyed by a number-one single, the album became a best-seller in 1990, earning a gold-record certification from the R.I.A.A. before year-end after peaking at number eight in *Billboard.* The album was still on the *Billboard* list in 1994 after passing multiplatinum levels. The 1990 singles successes included the title track, number one in *Radio & Records* the week of April 6; "Wanted," number one in *R&R* the week of August 24; and "Chasin' That Neon Rainbow," number one in *R&R* the week of November 23. Major honors swiftly came his way, such as the Top New Male Vocalist, 1990, from the Academy of Country Music and Star of Tomorrow in the TNN/Music City News Awards.

Besides those, *Radio & Records* cited him as the Best New Male Artist of 1990 in its Country Music Readers poll as well as in its Airplay Awards. "Here in the Real World" was named Song of the Year, 1990, in the Music City News Country Songwriters Awards, which also recognized "Chasin' That Neon Rainbow" and "I'd Love You All Over Again" among Top Ten Hits of the Year. TNN/MCN voters also chose *Here in the Real World* as Album of the Year.

Jackson soon demonstrated his 1990 breakthrough wasn't an aberration. He continued to add to his following with an extensive stint as opening act for Randy Travis in a tour that got underway in February 1991. His second album, *Don't Rock the Jukebox,* came out in the spring and proved as eye-opening a collection as his debut release. The album peaked at number two in *Billboard* and went platinum before the end of summer, reaching multiplatinum sales in 1992. The hit singles it provided included the title track (cowritten by Jackson, Keith Stegall, and R. Murrah) and "Someday" (cowritten by Jackson and J. McBride).

All of this resulted in still more keepsakes for his trophy collection. *Don't Rock the Jukebox* and its title track won TNN/MCN selections, respectively, for Album of the Year and Single of the Year while Alan was also declared Male Artist of the Year for 1991. That single was also named the Top Country Single in the *Billboard* Number One Awards and in the Academy of Country Music voting was chosen as Single Record of 1991 with the album cited as Album of the Year. Jackson was also chosen as Songwriter/Artist of the Year, 1991, by the Nashville Songwriters Association Intl. and, in the Country Music Association's Entertainment

Expo SRO Award polling he walked off with the award for New Touring Artist of the Year, 1991.

In 1991, Alan's star was rising not only in the U.S. but in other parts of the world; the Netherlands' *Country Gazette* chose him as Most Promising Country Act that year. Besides all those accolades, Jackson said one of hits greatest thrills came when he got the chance to perform on the 65th Anniversary TV program of the *Grand Ole Opry.* As he recalled, "The *Grand Ole Opry,* to a lot of people, is old-time, but to me, Nashville wouldn't be what it is if it weren't for the *Grand Ole Opry.* It's a very special organization for me, and it was an honor for me to go onstage and play there, and I think that'll be something that I'll always remember."

Jackson continued to build his reputation and performing and songwriting achievements in 1992, starting off with the single "Dallas" (cowritten with Keith Stegall), which hit number one both in *Billboard* and *R&R* the week of July 3, and the singles hits "Love's Got a Hold On You" (written by Jackson and C. Chamberlain), number one in *Billboard* for two weeks in September and "She's Got the Rhythm (and I've Got the Blues)" (cowritten by Jackson and Randy Travis), number one in *Billboard* in December.

His third Arista album, *A Lot About Livin' (and a Little About Love),* came out in the fall of 1992 and swiftly made the charts, eventually peaking at number one in *Billboard.* By the start of 1993 it had gone platinum and by early 1994 had passed triple-platinum levels. Like earlier albums, it made the pop as well as country charts. Alan's 1992 awards included one from ASCAP which named "Don't Rock the Jukebox" Country Song of the Year in its 1992 poll and selection by the CMA of his video of "Midnight in Montgomery" as Music Video of the Year.

During 1992 and 1993, Jackson and his backing band, the Strayhorns, progressed from opening act to headliners status. Commenting on an Atlanta concert, the *Atlanta Constitution* critic wrote that his performance, "which combined traditional lyrics with full-tilt crossover music . . . brought Mr. Jackson's admirers—an eclectic mix of young and old wearing everything from biker leather to business suits—to their feet. Most remained there, clapping, whistling and yelling for more, until the house lights went on several minutes later."

Despite his obvious appeal to a wide spectrum of fans, Jackson contended he was "a little bit shy in front of crowds. I'm not a ham. I just enjoy singing. As a songwriter it's a chance to get up there and give people a part of yourself. I like to go out and express myself through my music the best I can." He added that his writing approach in general was to stress positive things. "That may sound corny, but I'll leave it to the others to portray the down and out side. If I can add a positive note to the world, I'm satisfied."

Jackson's career certainly lost no momentum in 1993 and 1994 as his output was, if anything, more effective from both a writing and interpretation standpoint than before. His 1993 hit singles were "Tonight I Climbed the Wall" (words and lyrics by Jackson), number one in *R&R* the week of April 30; "Chattahoochee" (cowritten by Jackson and J. McBride), number one for two weeks in *Billboard* in July; "Mercury Blues" (by R. Geddins and K. C. Douglas), number two in *R&R* the week of November 26; and "Honky Tonk Christmas." In December 1993, he also made the charts with "Tequila Sunrise," a track from the Giant Records' Eagles tribute album. That album, *Common Thread: The Songs of the Eagles,* was a number-one *Billboard* hit and was also voted Album of the Year in the CMA 1994 voting.

Three more number-one hits were added to Jackson's achievements in 1994. Those included "Who Says You Can't Have It All" (cowritten by Jackson and J. McBride), number one in *R&R* the week of March 25; "Summertime Blues" (a remake of Eddie Cochran's 1950s rock classic), number one in *R&R* the week of July 22 and a multiweek stay at number one in *Billboard* in July and August; and "Livin' on Love" (written by Jackson), number one in *R&R* the week of October 28. Late in the year the single "Gone Country" (written by Bob McDill) appeared in lower *Billboard* chart levels, rising to higher positions in early 1995.

Jackson's *Honky Tonk Christmas* album was released in late 1993 and was in the *Billboard* Top 10 in December. It was still selling and on the charts in 1995 after receiving a gold-record certification from the R.I.A.A. His *Who I Am* album, issued in the summer of 1994 peaked at number one in *Billboard* and by early 1995 was on the way to multiplatinum sales totals. In the CMA voting for 1994, Jackson was nominated in a number of categories including Entertainer of the Year. He didn't win that one, which went to Vince Gill, but he shared Song of the Year honors with Jim McBride for "Chattahoochie." As he said at the October 1994 Award ceremonies, "I didn't come to Nashville to be a songwriter. People like Jim wrote with me in the early days when nobody else would." Alan also received a trophy for his part in the Eagles album project.

On the 30th Academy of Country Music Awards Presentation show in May 1995, Jackson was named Male Vocalist of the Year. When Johnny Cash opened the envelope for CMA Entertainer of the Year during the October 1995 telecast the name he announced was Alan Jackson. In his acceptance speech, Alan read a few lines from "Job Descriptions" which he had written for his daughters.

In the fall, his Arista album, *The Greatest Hits Collection,* topped major charts, reaching number one in *Billboard* in November. He added to his total of number one singles hits in the last half of the year with "I Don't Even Know Your Name" (number one in August) and "Tall Tall Trees" which reached number one in *Billboard* the week of December 9, 1995.

The plaques he'd received from the R.I.A.A. during 1995 included one for five million copies sold of *A Lot About Livin'* on April 5 and another for six million copies on July 14, a four million copy award for *Don't Rock the Jukebox* on April 5, and for *Who I Am,* a two million copy award on February 14, and a three million copy one on May 30.

Jackson still appeared to be a devoted family man in the mid-1990s despite the temptations celebrity brings. His wife told *People* his overwhelming success had worried her. "It's very unsettling to have been married ten years and just be a normal, private little couple—then all of a sudden he's this country hunk of America. You start having all these little insecurities like, 'How's this going to change him? Is he still going to want to be married?'"

Jackson, though, seemed to be taking it all in stride. He observed, "Everyday you sit and talk about yourself in interviews, and people tell you how great you are and they cheer you on stage. Nobody wants to make you mad. Every now and then I get grumpy and think I'm too good, but my wife will kick me in the rear."

His singles hits in 1996 included "I'll Try," in top chart levels early in the year and "Home," a best seller in the spring, both of which he wrote words and music. In the Academy of Country Music Awards announced in April 1996, Alan again was named Top Male Vocalist. In the 1996 CMA voting he was nominated for Entertainer of the Year, Male Vocalist of the Year, and in the Music Video of the Year category for "Redneck Games" in which he appeared as a special guest with Jeff Foxworthy. At the end of October 1996 his next album, *Everything I Love,* was released. First single from the disc was "Little Bitty" (written by Tom T. Hall). The album rose to number one on the charts before year-end.

JACKSON, STONEWALL: *Singer, guitarist, songwriter. Born Tabor City, North Carolina, November 6, 1932.*

"Stonewall" sounds like a nickname but in Stonewall Jackson's case it's his given name. His father named him after the famed Confederate general, though the latter's real name was Thomas Jonathan. Be that as it may, for a long time Stonewall lived up to his name by becoming a hard man to move from the hit charts from the late 1950s to the start of the 1970s. After that, new artists began to take over with record buyers, but Jackson was still a favorite of diehard fans into the 1990s.

Jackson's early road was not an easy one. His father died when he was two years old, and young Stonewall was brought up in the southern part of Georgia. When he was ten, he traded his five-dollar bike for an old guitar, one of the important steps in his life. Gradually he figured out the fingering for some of the chords and began to play. Before long he was singing some of the songs he heard on the radio and on records. In a few years, he went beyond this and started to make up his own songs. Some of these, such as "Don't Be Angry" and "Black Sheep," later became hits for him.

When he was seventeen, he signed up with the navy and entered the submarine service. One of his stations was Norfolk, Virginia, where he bought his first good guitar. He played whenever he could and was asked, on several occasions, to entertain the crews. In 1954, he was discharged and headed home to Georgia, determined to make a career in music.

He continued to write songs and began to figure out how to get started in show business. The obvious goal was the country-music capital, Nashville, but he needed a stake. For the next two years he worked on a farm in the summer and logged during the winter. Finally he had enough money saved for the trip to Nashville and headed there in 1956.

He quickly went to the studios of Acuff-Rose Publishing Company to make some sample records (dubs) of his songs. He intended to take these around to stars of the *Grand Ole Opry* in hopes that they would record them. While they were being prepared, Wesley Rose heard them being played and was quick to ask who had done them. Rose called Jackson and said he had arranged an audition with the talent directors. They listened to Jackson and signed him to a long-term contract. Shortly after, Jackson found himself putting his signature to a contract with Columbia Records.

Audiences took to the newcomer right away. Within a short time, he was known to people across the country from his TV appearances. In 1958, he scored his first top-10 hit, "Life to Go." He followed with the 1959 number-one-rated "Waterloo." The song not only became a top country & western hit but made the national pop charts as well. As a result, he was starred three times on Dick Clark's coast-to-coast *American Bandstand* program.

Jackson continued his winning ways in 1960 with "Why I'm Walkin'." In 1962, he had two bestsellers in "A Wound Time Can't Erase" and "Leona." In 1963, he hit with "Old Showboat" and in 1964 with his own composition, "Don't Be Angry," and the number-one best-selling "B.J. the D.J." Jackson's hits also included "Mary Don't You Weep" and "I Washed My Hands in Muddy Waters."

His early LPs on Columbia included his debut album, *Stonewall Jackson,* in 1959: *Sadness in a Song* (1962); *I Love a Song* (1963); *Trouble and Me* (1965); and *Stonewall Jackson's Greatest Hits* (1966). In 1966, he also was represented on Harmony Records with the LP *The Exciting Stonewall Jackson.* In 1967, he scored another top-10 success with "Stamp Out Loneliness." He also turned out a best-selling LP with this title that included such other songs as "Promises and Hearts," "You Can Check on Me," "The Wine Flowed Freely," and "A Man Must Hide to Cry." He scored another chart

hit in 1967 with his LP *All's Fair in Love 'n' War* (issued in 1966).

In the late 1960s Stonewall's recording successes tapered off. Though he placed singles on the charts (for example, two in 1968 and three in 1969), none reached the topmost levels. His album output on Columbia remained high into the early 1970s, including such titles as *Stonewall Jackson Country* (1967); *Tribute to Hank Williams* (1969); *Real Thing* (1970); *Stonewall Jackson at the Grand Ole Opry* and *Me and You and a Dog Named Boo* (1971); and *Stonewall Jackson's World* (1972). Though Stonewall kept active on the concert and TV circuit in the 1970s with his band, the Minutemen, for most of the decade he was not affiliated with a major record company.

In early 1981, First Generation records issued an album of his recordings as part of its new Opry Stars series. Much as in the seventies, Stonewall continued his appearances on the *Opry* and TV stations specializing in country music throughout the 1980s and the first half of the 1990s. His 1980s credits included a part in the 1986 film *Sweet Dreams* about the life of Patsy Cline.

JACKSON, WANDA: *Singer, guitarist, pianist, songwriter, band leader (the Party Timers). Born Maud, Oklahoma, October 20, 1937.*

"I was lucky. I made a decision. I chose a career and I was able to follow through with it. I've been performing since I was thirteen. I didn't have that agonizing, frustrating wait for the right place, the right time like so many performers."

That's the way Wanda Jackson summed up her early years for an interviewer in 1971. She also stressed she was fortunate in other ways, over the years. "My father always went on the road with me, driving, making all the arrangements, handling all the management. And then I married—well, I've never had to go it alone. I don't know that I could have done it myself. My parents actually made so much possible for me. My father, Tom Jackson, he probably could have been a pretty big star in country music. Somehow he just never had the chance. There was the Depression, then I was born. He never got a break, but he did so much for me. And my mother, she made my costumes, gave me encouragement, they really helped."

By the time Wanda was born in the small town of Maud, fifty miles southeast of Oklahoma City, her father earned a living by working at any odd jobs he could find. In his younger years he had played piano with small bands in Oklahoma. In 1941, like many others from the region, he put his family in their old car and headed to California for a better life, bucking a dust storm part of the way. In Los Angeles, he learned the trade of barbering and three months later moved north to Bakersfield. Once settled there, one of his early projects was to save enough money to buy his little daughter a guitar. He gave her the instrument in 1943 and soon spent many of his spare hours teaching her to play. He didn't have to urge her to practice; she loved the instrument. As her mother later recalled, "Wanda wasn't like other children after the guitar came into her life. Our problem was never to get her to practice—it was getting her to stop. She never wanted to quit practicing and as a result, we sometimes missed out on a full night's sleep."

When Wanda was nine, her father encouraged her newfound interest in the piano. He helped her learn to read music and pick out melodies on the keyboard. Even in those years, Wanda was beginning to make up songs of her own.

When Wanda was twelve, the Jacksons moved to Oklahoma City where Tom got a job selling used cars, a trade he followed many years later. Soon after, Wanda started attending classes at Capitol Hill High School. The school was only two blocks from station KLPR, which ran a weekly talent program. Wanda and her friends began to attend some of the shows until Wanda got up enough nerve to try out herself. She did so well the station gave her a fifteen-minute daily program of her own, quite a plum for a thirteen-year-old. Before long that gave way to a half-hour program that was one of the most popular country shows in Oklahoma City and remained so during most of Wanda's teenage years.

When she was in her junior year in high school, another major break occurred. She was leaving the station after finishing a show when she was called to the phone. A voice on the other end said, "Hello Wanda, this is Hank Thompson." After she recovered from the shock and responded, Hank continued, "I'm calling because I have a song I'd like for you to record with my band—if you're interested."

Thus, almost effortlessly, she was offered the first step to national recognition. She accepted the offer and recorded several songs, including a duet with the lead singer from Thompson's Brazos Valley Boys, Billy Gray, titled "You Can't Have My Love." The song soon became a major national country hit of 1954 on the Decca label, and Wanda was asked to sign with the label as well as join the band on a tour of the Northeast.

However, she demurred at becoming a full-time performer until she finished high school. She returned home, finished her senior year, and headed back onto the tour circuit for the 1955–56 season. The artist she toured with in those years was a young Mississippian, soon to set the world of entertainment on its ear—Elvis Presley.

Meanwhile, Hank Thompson had told one of the best talent agents in the country field, Jim Halsey, about her. Halsey listened to her records, watched her perform and agreed with Thompson's evaluation. In 1956, Jackson signed with Halsey's agency and he soon arranged for a new recording contract with Capitol Records, an association that was to last into the 1970s. He also set up her debut in one of the Las Vegas night

spots, the first of many such Nevada appearances. From the mid-1950s into the early 1970s, Wanda remained a favorite with Vegas audiences who watched her shows in places like the Golden Nugget, Silver Nugget, and Show Boat. She also was a headliner in Reno hotels over the years as well as country venues in major cities across the United States.

During the late 1950s and throughout the 1960s, she placed many singles and albums on national charts. Though not a prolific writer, she still wrote a number of her greatest hits herself. Some of her songs were written for other artists, an example being "Kicking Our Hearts Around," a major hit for Buck Owens that won her a BMI award and was a top-10 single for Hank Thompson as well. Two of her originals that she turned into top-10 singles in 1961 were "Right or Wrong" and "In the Middle of a Heartache." She actually had written "Right or Wrong" while "in a daydreaming mood" in 1959. She hadn't considered it anything special at the time, but two years later, artists and repertoire executive Ken Nelson of Capitol heard her humming it one day and asked her to record it. She told interviewer Ben Townsend in the mid-1960s, "It's likely to become a standard [at the time, version by various artists had brought total sales to over a million] and to think, I never had intentions of putting it on a record."

Among her other hits of the 1960s were such singles as "Let's Have a Party," "Little Charm Bracelet," "Happy, Happy Birthday," "Just Call Me Lonesome," "Candy Man," "Stupid Cupid," "There's a Party Going On," "Heartbreak Ahead," "Making Believe," "The Box He Came In," and "Fujiyama Mama." The last named became a major hit in Japan and brought large audiences out to hear her when she toured that country. In 1965, she had a major hit in Germany with a single she sang in Dutch called "Santo Domingo." The record edged the Beatles out of the number-one spot on German lists. All of that made her one of the first truly international country stars.

As she recalled, "You know, I've recorded in German, Dutch, and Japanese. I've had top hits in Germany and Japan, and I don't speak any of those languages. I've been told that I shouldn't try to learn them because it might ruin my natural accent and inflection—you know, if I'm trying to translate each word as I sing. I guess what it all comes down to is the feeling—the feeling, the mood of a song is the same no matter what the language."

Wanda married an IBM programmer named Wendall Goodman in October 1961 in Gainsville, Texas, and her new husband took over the management of her career. In the 1960s, besides accompanying Wanda on concert tours all over the world, Wendall also packaged her syndicated TV show called *Music Village*. Backing Wanda in all those efforts was her band, the Party Timers. In the mid-1960s, the band members were Mike Lane of Tyler, Texas, lead singer; Tex Wilburn of

Henderson, Texas, lead guitar; Al Flores of Liberal, Kansas, electric bass; and Don Bartlett of Liberal, Kansas, drums.

From the late 1950s into the early 1970s, Capitol released several dozen albums by Wanda, many of which made the country charts. Among those were *Day Dreaming,* issued in September 1958; *Rockin' with Wanda* (1960); *Right or Wrong* (12/61); *Lovin' Country Style* (6/62); *Wonderful Wanda* (10/62); *Love Me Forever* (7/61); *Two Sides of Wanda* (3/64), a major hit and nominee for a 1964 Grammy for best country LP; *Blues* (6/65); *Wanda Jackson Sings* (2/66); *Salutes the Country Music Hall of Fame* (11/66); *You're Always Here* (11/67); *Happy Side* (1968); *In Person* (12/69); *The Many Moods of Wanda Jackson* (1969); and in the early 1970s, *Country!, Woman Lives for Love, I've Gotta Sing,* and *I Wouldn't Want You Any Other Way.* Besides all those releases on Capitol, she had a few on the Hilltop label, including *Leave My Baby Alone* and *We'll Sing in the Sunshine.*

Though she spent major parts of most years on the road, Jackson and her husband still found time for family life. Home was in Oklahoma City, where they raised a son and a daughter in the 1960s and 1970s. From the mid-1970s on, Wanda shifted much of her attention to religious activities, including taking part as a performer in a number of evangelical tours. In the late 1970s she recorded on the Word label.

Wanda continued to be active as a performer in one way or another in the 1980s and into the 1990s, though her name no longer showed up on any hit lists. In the mid 1990s, Germany's Bear Family Records included an extensive collection of her 1950s and early 1960s recordings titled *Wanda Jackson: Right or Wrong.* The package comprised 4 CDs including early Decca and all her Capitol recordings up to 1962. The tracks covered both her pop and country stylings, with the latter including "Right or Wrong," "In the Middle of a Heartache," and "Silver Threads and Golden Needles." During 1996, Capitol Nashville Vintage collection released a retrospective of her work for the label. The CD contents included her self-penned "Right Or Wrong," her version of the Buddy Holly hit (written by Paul Anka) "It Doesn't Matter Anymore," plus such others as "Fujiyama Mama," "Kansas City," "Let's Have a Party," and "The Window Up Above."

JAMES, SONNY: *Singer, guitarist, songwriter. Born Hackleburg, Alabama, May 1, 1929.*

When somebody asked performer Hugh X. Lewis in 1976 whether he'd heard Sonny James's Columbia album set, *200 Years of Country Music* (a cavalcade of the nation's folk and country music from its birth to modern times), Lewis quipped, "No, I didn't realize he had been in the business that long." An observer might have responded that Sonny hadn't; it just seemed like it. From the standpoint of artistic longevity, "the Southern Gentleman" maintained a position as a major country star from the 1950s into the 1980s, ranking in the top 10 of best-selling album artists for much of that time.

Sonny, whose real name was Jimmie Loden, was born and raised in Hackleburg, Alabama. However, even as a small child he spent a lot of time on the road. Born into a show business family that toured throughout the South, he was only four years old when he made his stage debut with his parents and sister Thelma in a folk contest in Birmingham, Alabama. They won first prize before an audience that included singer Kate Smith, who, legend has it, gave little Sonny a silver dollar and predicted a great future career in the entertainment field. Before many more years had passed, he could play the guitar and sing occasional solos with the troupe. By the time he was in his teens, he had more hours of performing experience behind him than many artists in their twenties. He already had performed on a number of country radio shows before he reached high-school age.

In the early 1950s, his career was interrupted by fifteen months of military service during the Korean War. He kept his performing skills polished by singing before other servicemen or, on occasion, before Korean orphans. He had quite a few hours to kill when he was off duty and he put some of the time to good advantage by writing some original songs.

After his discharge in 1952, he returned to the United States fair and country nightclub circuit and began to look for ways to further his career. During his musical travels, he had become friends with Chet Atkins and visited Chet in Nashville for some advice. Chet introduced him to Capitol Records' producer Ken Nelson, for whom Sonny played some of his material. Nelson liked James's style as well as his compositions and recommended that Capitol sign him. As often happened with Nelson finds, it was the beginning of a long and rewarding relationship.

Sonny didn't achieve overnight stardom. His initial releases on Capitol had only moderate success, at best. In 1957, he scored his first big hit with his top-10 pop recording of "First Date, First Kiss, First Love." He followed with an even bigger success, his now classic "Young Love," which rose to number one on the pop charts and made the country top 10 as well. In 1962, Dot turned out a hit LP of Sonny's, also titled *First Love.* For a while, Sonny spent more time starring in pop and rock concerts than in the country field.

Then things slowed down for several years. He toured widely and remained a top favorite with audiences in the late 1950s and early 1960s, but didn't crack either the pop or country top 10 until the mid-1960s. By then he had settled down to a career as a country artist. And, from the mid-1960s on, he was a top country star with one release after another moving onto top-chart levels.

One of his first achievements in that period was a

song he coauthored with Bob Tubert, "You're the Only World I Know." The song reached number one on country lists and remained there for weeks. Since then it has been recognized as a country standard and has been recorded by many other artists. Sonny also had a second hit, in 1964, his top-10 version of Felice and Boudleaux Bryant's "Baltimore."

In 1965, Sonny again had a number-one hit, "Behind the Tear," and a top-10 success in "I'll Keep Holding On." The following year provided still another number-one song. "Take Good Care of Her," and the top-10 hit, "True Love's a Blessing" (cowritten with Carole Smith). In 1967, he added such number-one ranked singles as "I'll Never Find Another You" and "Need You." His other hits of those years included "The Minute You're Gone" and "Room in Your Heart." In 1968, he had one of the biggest country singles of the year, "A World of Our Own," and reached top-chart levels with "Heaven Says Hello." In 1969, he had the number-one hit "Only the Lonely." His other number-one singles of the late 1960s included "Running Bear" and "Since I Met You Baby." He started the 1970s with another number-one hit, "It's Just a Matter of Time."

Sonny duplicated his singles success with a number of album hits on Capitol. These included *The Minute You're Gone* (1/64), *You're the Only World I Know* (1/65), *Behind the Tear* (12/65), *True Love's a Blessing* (6/66), *Till the Last Leaf* (8/66), *Best of Sonny James* (11/66), *I'll Never Find Another You* (1967), *World of Our Own* (1968), *Best of Sonny James, Volume 2* (1/69), *Close-Up* (two discs, 8/69), and *Astrodome Presents Sonny James in Person* (10/69). Other LPs of the late 1960s–early 1970s period were *Bright Lights, Big City, Empty Arms, Here Comes Honey Again, My Love/Don't Keep Me Hanging On, #1*, and the double album *You're the Only World/I'll Never Find Another You.* Hilltop Records also issued one of his collections, titled *Timberline.*

From the late 1950s through the 1970s, Sonny's stage appearances took him to all fifty states several times over and to many other nations, backed by his own band, the Southern Gentlemen. During those years, he was featured on a wide variety of TV and radio shows, including a number of guest spots on the *Grand Ole Opry* plus such other shows as *The Jimmy Dean Show, The Ed Sullivan Show, Bob Hope, Tennessee Ernie Ford, The Pat Boone Chevy Showroom, Star Route, Music Scene,* and several 1970s appearances on *Hee Haw.*

During the 1960s, Sonny took part in several motion pictures. These included *Second Fiddle to a Steel Guitar, Las Vegas Hillbillies* (with Jayne Mansfield), and the 1967 *Hillbilly in a Haunted House,* which starred Basil Rathbone and Lon Chaney.

Sonny gathered a number of honors and awards, particularly in the 1960s. In the 1965 National Academy of Recording Arts and Sciences voting, he had

three Grammy nominations. He won the *Record World* magazine Record of the Year Award in 1965. In 1966, he won the Number One Artist rating from *Record World,* and *Billboard* ranked him in the top five country artists (male) for the year while *Cash Box* ranked him number three for 1966. He finished high in those polls the next few years and, in 1969, *Billboard*'s survey once again named him as number one artist.

Sonny's activities during the 1970s, besides his normal performing and recording routine, extended to music publishing and producing records of other artists. In that role, he supervised preparation of material for three albums by Marie Osmond, including the hit single "Paper Roses."

He continued to extend his list of chart-hit singles from the start of the 1970s to the end of the decade. His early 1970s successes on Capitol included "Endlessly," number one for weeks at the end of 1970, the top-10 "Only Love Can Break a Heart" in early 1972, the number-one ranked "When the Snow Is on the Roses" in September 1972, and "Surprise, Surprise" in early 1974. By the start of 1974, Sonny's long association with Capitol had ended and he had signed with Columbia Records. In short order he had a bestseller, "Is It Wrong (For Loving You)," number one on the country lists in May 1974. In 1975, he had such top-10 winners as "A Little Bit South of Saskatoon" (cowritten by Sonny and Carole Smith), "Little Band of Gold," and "What in the World's Come Over You?" In mid-1976, he had the top-10 single "When Something Is Wrong with My Baby" and, in the fall, the equally successful "Come on In" (cowritten by Sonny and Carole Smith). In mid-1977, his remake of the old Jimmie Rodgers classic "In the Jailhouse Now" rose to number fifteen and he also had a hit later in the year with "Caribbean." He closed out 1978 with the charted single "Building Memories" on Columbia, which made top-chart levels in early 1979.

During 1979, Sonny made another label change, leaving Columbia for Monument. His first charted single on that label was "Hold What You've Got," which was in the top 40 in the spring of 1979.

JENNINGS, WAYLON: *Singer, guitarist, songwriter, band leader (the Waylors). Born Littlefield, Texas, June 15, 1937.*

In the 1970s there was what amounted to a revolution in country music. In what was called "progressive country" by some and "outlaw music" by others, a new dimension was added to the field based on songs that more closely reflected the mores and trends of an urbanized, industrialized society. The leaders of the "revolt"—though they didn't consciously set about to organize a new movement—were two tough, talented Texans, Willie Nelson and Waylon Jennings. Though their careers developed in different ways, appropriately the two became close friends and joined forces for some of the pivotal developments that helped make the "new country" music a force whose impact extended far beyond conventional country & western audiences.

Though both Jennings and Nelson were bona fide superstars by the end of the 1970s, it had taken many years for them to achieve those reputations. Jennings's potential for stardom was agreed upon by many people in the country music industry when his initial RCA recordings came out in the mid-1960s. But for close to a decade he did not fulfill those predictions and seemed to almost fight the idea. He failed to show up for interviews, was hard to pin down on tour plans, and, at least in the view of promotion people trying to expose his name or new record for press or radio coverage, was unpredictable and erratic. Added to that was the fact that Waylon wrote or selected songs—and performed them—as he pleased without bending to the "establishment" ways of the Nashville hierarchy. In time, though, both audiences and the industry came around to his way of thinking and Jennings became more than a favorite; he became a legend.

Jennings grew up in Littlefield, Texas, where much of the population enjoyed country & western music. As a child, he showed a deep interest in music and already had begun to learn guitar chords before he was in his teens. At twelve, he began hosting his own disc jockey show on a home-town station, emphasizing pop records rather than country discs. Throughout his teens he spun records and occasionally sang for local audiences. He also hosted local talent shows and made personal appearances in towns in his part of Texas. By the time he was seventeen, he was paying more attention to country & western materials and he became a DJ on a country-music radio program.

By the time he moved to Lubbock, Texas, in 1958, to continue his DJ career in a more populous area, he had become a fan of Elvis Presley and the new rock movement. In Lubbock, he became acquainted with many of the young Southwest musicians eager to follow in Elvis's footsteps, sometimes playing backup guitar in local bands. Buddy Holly, already on the way to national stardom, liked Waylon's work and asked him to join his band as electric bass player. For the rest of 1958 and the beginning of 1959, Jennings toured with Holly. He was part of Holly's troupe the fateful day in early February 1959 when the group was to split up en route to an engagement, part taking a private plane, part going by bus. Jennings was supposed to take the plane, but he gave up his seat as a favor to another artist, J. P. Richardson (the Big Bopper). On February 3, 1959, the plane crashed in a field near Mason City, Iowa, killing all aboard.

Saddened and shaken, Jennings returned to Lubbock and resumed his career as a DJ and part-time musician. The Holly mystique contributed to an enhanced respect and helped to some extent in his efforts to upgrade his performing status. One result was that he

began to make records for small companies in the region. As time went by, he thought of himself more as a performer and less as a DJ.

In the early 1960s, Jennings went west, settling in Phoenix, Arizona. He formed his own band, called the Waylors—still his group's name at the start of the 1990s—and played a combination of country & western and rock 'n' roll, a blend that at the time sounded discordant to many musicians in both fields. But audiences seemed to like it, at least in Phoenix. The group won lengthy engagements at nightclubs in Phoenix and neighboring Scottsdale and Tempe. In a short period of time Waylon and the Waylors were being featured in one of the largest nightclubs in the region, J.D.'s in Phoenix. His first LP, on an independent label, *Waylon Jennings at J. D.'s,* came out in December 1964.

It was there that Bobby Bare, one of RCA Records' rising lights at the time, caught the show in 1964 and immediately sent word back to Chet Atkins in Nashville about Jennings's striking vocal sound. Atkins followed up, sought out Waylon, and signed him to an RCA contract in 1965. The first three recording sessions produced the singles "That's the Chance I'll Have to Take," "Stop the World and Let Me Off," and "Anita You're Dreaming," discs that made respectable showings on the charts and marked Jennings with country DJs as a promising new artist.

With his career seemingly on the way to the heights, Waylon moved to Nashville in April 1966. Once there, he and Johnny Cash, separated from his first wife and not yet married to June Carter, became roommates. As might be expected, some wild escapades resulted, but also some creative rapport that strengthened the innate individualism of both parties. Waylon, though he was a guest on the *Opry* in the mid-1960s and thrilled audiences in the Ryman Auditorium and in radioland with his gruff, powerful voice, was not the kind of artist most of the Nashville powers of the day were comfortable with. He didn't shrink from singing rock numbers if they pleased him—his version of the Beatles' "Norwegian Wood" was a mild hit in the mid-1960s—and he wore faded jeans and nondescript sports shirts rather than flamboyant rhinestone-studded pseudo-cowboy suits. If the country establishment looked askance at Waylon, the feeling was mutual, as he later took note of in compositions like "Nashville Bum."

He toured widely in the mid-1960s and found strong support from segments of local audiences across the United States. He also played engagements in many parts of Canada and even performed in Mexico. During those years, besides playing the *Opry* several times, he guested on a number of TV shows, including ABC-TVs *Anatomy of Pop,* the *Bobby Lord Show, American Swing Around,* and Carl Smith's *Country Music Hall.* He also found time to appear in a movie, *Nashville Rebel.*

And he continued to turn out a steady flow of

recordings. His singles of the period included "Dark Side of Fame," "Where I Went Wrong," "Look into My Tear Drops," "Norwegian Wood," "I Wonder Just Where I Went Wrong," "Time to Bum Again," and "That's What You Get for Loving Me," the last named a top-10 hit in 1966. He had reasonably good years in 1967 and 1968, making upper-chart levels in 1967 with the singles "Mental Revenge" and "Green River" and in 1968 with "Walk on Out of My Mind," "Only Daddy That'll Walk the Line," and a duet with Anita Carter, "I Got You." His debut album, *Waylon Jennings: Folk Country,* came out in March 1966 on RCA and was followed by titles like *Leavin' Town* (11/66), *Nashville Rebel* (1/67), *Ol' Harlan* (3/67) *Love of the Common People* (8/67), *One and Only* (11/67), *Country Folk* (with the Kimberleys, 9/69); and *Best of Waylon Jennings* (7/70). His work with the Kimberleys brought a 1969 Grammy Award for Best Country Performance by a Duo or Group for "MacArthur Park."

By the start of the 1970s, though, despite those and other credits, Waylon was not considered a first-rank star by most country industry people. He was still essentially a cult figure with an enthusiastic, but limited, following. His recordings often made the charts, but rarely the highest level and none had reached number one. (It was ironic that in mid-1975, when Jennings was on the verge of reaching superstar status, his wife, Jessi Colter, came out with her first single on Capitol, which rose to number one on country charts).

Doggedly, Waylon went on his own way and, in fact, went even further in what was to be known as "modern country" with his own writings and with presentation of the work of avant-garde country writers such as Kris Kristofferson, Billy Joe Shaver, and Mickey Newbury. His new repertoire of material began to take shape in his *Singer of Sad Songs* LP (11/70) and developed rapidly in such follow-ups as *The Taker/Tulsa* (2/71), *Cedartown, Georgia* (8/71), *Good Hearted Woman* (2/72), which first presented that Willie and Waylon classic title song, "Heartaches by the Numbers" (3/72), *Ladies Love Outlaws* (9/72). *Ruby, Don't Take Your Love to Town* (2/73).*Lonesome, On'ry and Mean* (3/73) and *Honky Tonk Heroes* (7/73). (All the songs but one on the last named were written by Billy Joe Shaver or by Jennings and Shaver). Some of those contained top-20 singles hits, such as "The Taker," in the top 15 in late 1970, and "You Ask Me To" (cowritten by Jennings and Shaver) in the top 15 in late 1973, early 1974.

More important, his new material found favor with young fans both in the country and pop fields. Waylon was received with riotous applause and cheers at a broad spectrum, such as the Bottom Line and Max's Kansas City in New York; a set presented at a Grateful Dead concert show at San Francisco's Kezar Stadium in May 1973 (where the 20,000 fans gave him a standing ovation); SRO concerts at Los Angeles' Troubadour in 1973 and 1974; a set at Willie Nelson's Dripping

Springs Festival in Texas on July 4; and many other country and pop nightspots around the United States.

The indications continued to multiply that Jennings's refusal to compromise musical principles was beginning to bear fruit. Sales of his albums, which had not been his strong point previously, began to rise. His early 1974 release, *This Time,* rose to upper country album chart levels in the spring and stayed there for many weeks. His *Ramblin' Man* LP (issued in late 1974) and *Dreaming My Dreams*—one of his finest collections (issued in the summer of 1975)—made the top 10. And then came *Wanted: The Outlaws* (issued at the start of 1976), one of the landmark albums in the entire pop/country field of the 1970s.

The LP was a combination of eleven previously released recordings by Waylon, Willie Nelson, Tompall Glaser, and Jessi Colter. (Jessi had married Waylon in 1974.) The album became a runaway hit, rising into the country top 10 in February 1976 and then moving into the number one position for many weeks. It also became a top 10 hit on the pop charts as well. It remained on country charts for years (occasionally slipping out of the top 50 only to return again) selling several million copies to become the all–time best selling country album to that point.

An RCA official speculated about the reasons to Bob Hilburn of the *Los Angeles Times* (April 6, 1976): "The only thing I can figure is there were a lot of people curious about all they had read or heard about the so-called 'outlaws' of country music—particularly Waylon and Willie—and they decided to take a chance on the package rather than buy a whole album by one of the artists. The important thing in this album is that it may then encourage people to go back into some of these artists' earlier works."

It did do that, but far more important, it focused wide attention on the artists' new work and consolidated the respect already building for Waylon. (Just before *The Outlaws* started to become a hit, Waylon was voted Best Male Vocalist for 1975 by the members of the Country Music Association.) Waylon's new albums almost routinely rose to top-chart levels. Thus *Mackintosh & T.J.* (soundtrack LP, issued early 1976) made the top 20, followed by two straight number-one solo album releases, *Are You Ready for the Country,* number one in September 1976, and *Ol' Waylon,* number one in mid-1977. Both albums held the number-one spot for a number of weeks each.

Waylon wasn't doing badly on singles charts either in the mid-1970s. He had a hit in early summer 1974 with his song "This Time" and made the top 10 in 1975 with "Rainy Day Woman/Help the Cowboy Sing the Blues", "Dreaming My Dreams with You," and "Are You Sure Hank Done It This Way/Bob Wills Is Still the King" (the latter three Jennings's compositions). In early 1976, his duet with Willie, "Good Hearted Woman" made number one and was followed by such

1976 top-10 hit singles as "Can't You See" and a duet with Jessi Colter, "Suspicious Minds."

At the start of 1978, RCA released the LP *Waylon & Willie,* arguably one of the best releases of 1978 and the 1970s as a whole. The album was number one on country charts for weeks and made the national pop charts top 10 in the United States and many other countries. Well over a year later, the album was still on the charts. Part of the time, it was joined on the charts by Waylon's solo LP, *I've Always Been Crazy,* issued in the fall of 1978 and number one from November into December. During much of 1979, a new *Greatest Hits* album of Waylon's was on the charts and was in the number-two spot in December. In late 1979, Waylon's next LP, *What Goes Around Comes Around,* was issued by RCA and already was number two on country charts in January 1980.

Jennings's name rarely was absent from singles lists either from the late 1970s into the 1980s. In the summer of 1977, he had the top-10 hit "Luckenbach, Texas" and late in the year had a major hit with "The Wurlitzer Prize," combining material by B. Emmons and Chips Moman with some by Jennings. In mid-1978 he had a number-one hit with Johnny Cash, "There Ain't No Good Chain Gang." That record was issued on Cash's Columbia label. In September 1978, he had a number-one single with his composition "I've Always Been Crazy." At year end, he had a single (of two of his songs) moving up from the number-five spot, "Don't You Think This Outlaw Bit's Done Got Out of Hand/Girl I Can Tell." His 1979 chart hits included "Amanda," "Come with Me," and another Johnny Cash duet (issued on Columbia), "I Wish I Was Crazy Again." He also helped Hank Williams, Jr., write and record a tribute to Hank's legendary father.

He began 1980 with another best-selling single, "I Ain't Living Long Like This" (written by Rodney Crowell) that reached number one in March. His other hit singles in 1980 were "Clyde," "Come with Me," and "Theme from *The Dukes of Hazzard.*" Waylon's rendition of the last-named song, which he wrote, always opened that hit TV comedy series. His charted albums in 1980, three of which had been on the lists for one to two years or more, were *What Goes Around Comes Around, Greatest Hits, Wanted: The Outlaws,* and *Music Man.* In early 1981 he teamed with wife Jessi for the hit single "Storms Never Last," written by her. Late in the year, another of his compositions, "Shine," was his vehicle for another best-selling release.

By the start of the 1980s, Jennings had made his mark not just on country but on pop music as well and seemed likely to have an influence on generations of writers and performers to come. And he had done it on his own terms, as is generally true for any pioneering artist. He expressed his pleasure at the breakthroughs of the 1970s to Robert Hilburn of the *Los Angeles Times* in this way, "There has been a big change in country music. At one time, it was considered too far out if you had a minor chord in a song. We've moved a long way since then." And he summarized his response to purists in another interview: "Instruments don't make country. We're entitled to a heavy rock beat if it complemented our songs. Or if we want to use a kazoo played through a sewer pipe, that's all right, too. Why should we lock ourselves in?"

For the first part of the 1980s, Waylon added many new singles and albums to his RCA credits. From 1980 through 1984 the albums included *Music Man* (May 1980), *Leather and Lace* (with Jessi Colter, February 1981), *Black on Black* (February 1982), *WW II* (with Willie Nelson, September 1982), *It's Only Rock and Roll* (March 1983), *Waylon and Company* (March 1983), *Take It to the Limit* (with Willie Nelson, April 1983), *Never Could Toe the Mark* (1984), and *Waylon's Greatest Hits, Volume 2* (October 1984). *Leather and Lace* and *WW II* both received R.I.A.A. gold-record awards. Those albums provided a number of charted singles, two of which, "Just to Satisfy You" (with Willie Nelson) in 1982 and "Lucille" in 1983 reached number one on the *Billboard* chart. Waylon's collaboration with Willie Nelson won them the 1983 Vocal Duo of the Year Award from the Country Music Association. *Never Could Toe the Mark* also had the distinction of being the first country album to premiere on Showtime's "Album Flash" program.

In May 1985, Columbia Records released an album called *Highwayman* recorded by a quartet calling themselves the Highwaymen. Besides Waylon, the other members were longtime compatriots Willie Nelson, Johnny Cash, and Kris Kristofferson. The album became a chart hit, peaking at number one in *Billboard* and eventually passing R.I.A.A. gold-record levels. The title track also became a number-one single. Simultaneously with that album's release, RCA issued *The Collector Series—Waylon Jennings,* and a month later a new studio album, *Turn the Page.*

By the end of 1985, Waylon had parted company with RCA, though that label issued two more of his albums in 1986, *Sweet Mother Texas* in March and *The Best of Waylon* in September. Jennings's debut on his new label, MCA, was *Hangin' Tough* (issued in January 1987). Next came *A Man Called Hoss* in October 1987, which Waylon referred to as his "audiography." Those were followed by *Full Circle* (September 1988) and *New Classic Waylon* (May 1989). Besides those, Waylon's recordings in the second half of the 1980s included a duet album with Johnny Cash on Columbia, *Heroes* (June 1986) and the RCA retrospective *The Early Years* (February 1989). *Heroes* also was Johnny Cash's swan song on Columbia as a solo artist.

In 1989, the Highwaymen were back in the studio working on *Highwayman 2,* which was released by Columbia in February 1990. The group hadn't toured in 1985, though they starred in a made-for-TV film, *Stage-*

coach (which aired May 18, 1986, with a phenomenal number-one Nielsen rating for the night and number five for the week), but this time a full-scale tour series was set up that lasted several years. By 1990, Waylon had left MCA, and his next solo album, *The Eagle,* came out on CBS in July 1990. His next two albums came out on Epic, *Clean Shirt* (with Willie Nelson, June 1991) and *Too Dumb for New York City, Too Ugly for L.A.* (August 1992).

Waylon, whose film credits included a role as a farmer in Sesame Street's *Follow That Bird* (he also sang a duet with Big Bird for the soundtrack album), began work on a children's album in the early 1990s. The disc, *Cowboys, Sisters, Rascals & Dirt,* came out on the BMG label in June 1993. Over the years, he had become increasingly concerned about the new generations and had on a number of occasions talked to schoolchildren about the importance of staying in school. In his case, he had been a tenth-grade dropout, but over the years had become increasingly concerned about the country's future and decided as well to work on his own high school equivalency (GED) diploma, which he earned in 1989. In contrast to his rough-hewn image, he strongly supported the idea of education by then and, indeed, became a spokesman for the GED program.

In the 1980s and 1990s, besides *Stagecoach* and *Follow That Bird,* he had many other credits in movies or TV as an actor or musician. Among others, he had a part in *Oklahoma City Dolls,* an ABC-TV movie with Eddie Albert and Susan Blakely; hosted the documentary *My Heroes Have Always Been Cowboys,* about an actual roundup in Texas, filmed by a British firm and televised over PBS and TNN in the U.S.; and played the role of a recluse, Ironhead Haynes, in a 1994 episode of the Fox-TV sitcom *Married with Children.* He also made a cameo appearance as a riverboat gambler in the 1994 film hit, *Maverick,* which starred Mel Gibson, Jodie Foster, and James Garner. His numerous guest appearances on TV included such programs as *Today, 20/20, Midnight Special, Austin City Limits, Good Morning America, Prime Time Live, Late Night with David Letterman, Dinah Shore Show, Entertainment Tonight,* and as a presenter or performer on the Academy of Country Music Awards and Country Music Association Awards.

Many of Waylon's original compositions were covered by other artists in addition to his own recordings, a fact recognized by a series of BMI million performance awards over the years. "Good Hearted Woman" passed the three million level in 1977 while his two million performance awards came for "Theme Song from the Dukes of Hazzard" in 1981, "Just to Satisfy You" and "Women Do Know How to Carry On" in 1983, "Never Could Toe the Mark" in 1985, and "Rough and Rowdy Days" in 1988. His million performance awards were for "You Asked Me To" in 1974, "This Time" in 1975, "Are You Sure Hank Done It This Way" and "Rainy Day Woman" in 1976, and "I've Always Been Crazy" in 1979.

In 1993, RCA assembled a forty-song double-CD boxed set called *Only Daddy That'll Walk the Line,* covering Waylon's major releases on the label over the twenty-year period from 1965 to 1985. The collaboration between the record company and Waylon worked so well RCA decided to re-sign him, which led to the 1994 release, *Waymore's Blues (Part II),* with all but two tracks composed solely by him and one of those two cowritten with Tony Joe White. Meanwhile, he got together with Willie, Johnny, and Kris for a new Highwaymen project, which resulted in the Liberty Records album *The Road Goes On Forever,* released in May 1995 and on the charts soon after. To support the new album, foursome appearances were lined up on *Late Night with David Letterman, The Tonight Show,* and *Saturday Night Live.* The debut single, "It Is What It Is," didn't get much attention from country radio, but in video form it got better response from the cable-TV sector. Along with concerts, guesting on albums by other artists like Travis Tritt, Hank Williams, Jr., and Mark Chesnutt and other activities in the mid-1990s, Waylon also began work on his autobiography *Waylon Jennings: The Autobiography,* with writer-musician Lenny Kaye, published by Warner Books during September 1996.

In early 1966 it was announced he had signed a new three record deal with the UK's Transatlantic Records. The first album issued under the pact was *Right for the Time* in May. Meanwhile RCA was putting finishing touches on a package commemorating the 20th anniversary of the release of *Wanted: The Outlaws.* The set combined the 11 songs on the 1976 LP with nine "lost tracks" recorded by Outlaws members in that same time period. The collection also included a song newly recorded by Waylon and Willie, "Nowhere Road," written by Steve Earle and Reno King.

Jennings, the original driving force in the effort, commented to Deborah Evans Price of *Billboard* ("RCA Believes 'Outlaws' Are Still Wanted 20 Years Later," May 18, 1996), he was very happy to see the original material, out of print for some five years, back in the current catalogue. "That [project] was something dear to my heart. I didn't know how it was going to come out [back when I first did it], because most of the songs were ten years old. I went in there and doctored them up and sweetened them up. Jessi came in and worked on hers and I went back and got a couple more of Willie's songs from the vault. . . . The music is forever."

JIM & JESSE: *Vocal and instrumental brother act, band leaders (the Virginia Boys). Both born Coeburn, Virginia; Jim McReynolds, February 13, 1927; Jesse McReynolds, July 9, 1929.*

For much of its history, bluegrass has tended to command the attention of an enthusiastic but relatively small segment of the music public, hence the descriptor bluegrass underground. The McReynolds brothers, Jim and Jesse, remaining true to their hill country roots, were part of the underground movement in its early stages and continued to play important roles through decades of changes of fortune. They were stalwarts through the boom times of the early and mid-1960s and remained so during the "recession" of the late 1960s and early 1970s and the bluegrass revival of the mid- and late 1970s still going strong in the mid-1990s.

The brothers and their group remained favorites of purists, who applauded the fact that their instrumental work always was acoustic, but the McReynoldses always moved with the times and their repertoire ranged from classic mountain ballads to bluegrass versions of all manner of modern pop music.

The brothers had been brought up in the bluegrass-country tradition. Their mother and father were talented musicians and often played for dances and get-togethers in their home in Virginia's Clinch Mountain region. Their grandfather was one of the best fiddlers in southwestern Virginia and made some early recordings for RCA Victor.

The boys learned to play stringed instruments in their early days on the family farm. When they reached their teens they began to sing at local gatherings, with Jesse playing mandolin and Jim the guitar. They made their radio debut in 1947 on station WNVA, Norton, Virginia, where they remained until 1952, when they moved to station WVLK, Lexington, Kentucky. They had made some records for Kentucky Records at the start of the 1950s, which helped bring a contract from Capitol Records in 1952.

With new recordings coming out on a major label and a growing reputation with country fans in general and bluegrass adherents in particular, the outlook seemed quite promising. However, the brothers suffered a dislocation when Jesse was called into service during the Korean War. He served for two years, including a year in Korea. While overseas, he met Charlie Louvin, and the two performed together for the troops in Korea.

After Jesse was discharged in 1954, the brothers set about making up for lost time. They became regulars on the *Tennessee Barn Dance* on station WNOX, Knoxville, and also were featured on CBS's *Saturday Night Country Style*. The following year they joined the *Swanee River Jamboree*, Live Oak, Florida, and also had a daily show on station WNER in Live Oak. In 1957, they moved again, this time to the *Lowndes County Jamboree* in Valdosta, Georgia, which remained home for many years. Their Virginia Boys, at the time, were Alfred Donald "Don" McHan, Robert Clark "Bobby" Thompson, and fiddling great Vassar Clements.

Because of the association of bluegrass with folk music, the boom times in the folk field in the late 1950s and early 1960s brought Jim & Jesse increasingly into the national spotlight. They were featured in a growing number of major folk festivals and headlined on their own on the folk club and college concert circuit. In 1963 they made their first appearance at the Newport Folk Festival in Rhode Island and returned again in 1966.

In 1962 the group changed record labels and signed with Columbia/Epic. Their debut on Epic, *Jim & Jesse*, was issued in April 1963. This was followed by a series of LPs over the years that included *Bluegrass* (11/63); *Country Church* (11/64); *Y'All Come* (6/65); *Berry Pickin in the Country,* a collection of bluegrass versions of Chuck Berry R&B/rock songs (1/66); *Sing unto Him* (10/66); *Diesel on My Tail* (8/67); *Sainting the Louvin Brothers* (7/69); *We Like Trains* (3/70). In the early 1970s, they had some releases on Capitol, such as *Freight Train* (4/71) and *20 Country Classics.*

In 1964, Jim & Jesse and the Virginia Boys were asked to become cast regulars on the *Grand Ole Opry* (they had been guests a few times before). This prompted a move to Nashville and the brothers and their families (the boys married sisters) settled on the Double JJ Ranch in Gallatin, Tennessee. Their 1965 credits included a guest spot on the *American Sing Along* TV show and their first appearance on a TV version of the *Opry* (taped in November 1965, but not shown nationally until January 1966). The group later appeared on other *Opry* TV programs, most presented on PBS, in the late 1960s and in the early 1970s.

In the mid-1960s, Jim & Jesse had one of their most productive periods in terms of chart hits. They hit the singles lists with such records as "Memphis" and "Johnny B. Goode" in 1965, the top-10 "Diesel on My Tail" in 1966, and "Thunder Road" and "Tijuana Taxi" in 1967.

In the late 1960s, the brothers worked on their own syndicated TV series, *Country Music Carousel*. In the early 1970s, they started turning out a second syndicated TV series, *The Jim & Jesse Show*. Although bluegrass record sales were shrinking, there was no lack of opportunities in the live performance field. The duo and their band were on the road over 200 days a year as the 1970s began, performing at bluegrass festivals, state and county fairs, and nightclubs around the country. They also made some overseas tours. The brothers had visited all of the states in the 1960s, and they repeated that cycle several more times in the 1970s. Among the festivals they performed at during the 1970s was the Bean Blossom, Indiana, event hosted by the Father of Bluegrass Music, Bill Monroe. During the decade they returned to Bean Blossom a number of times to play enthusiastically received sets.

In the late 1970s, the bluegrass field found new life, attracting a growing number of new adherents from both high school and college segments of the U.S. population. Many new festivals sprang up, such as the one in Telluride, Colorado, and the McReynoldses and their band at one time or another were featured in almost every one. In 1977, Jim & Jesse started their own annual bluegrass and country festival, generally held in early or mid-August, which was still going strong in the 1980s. In the fall of 1979, their group was featured on a special TV show called "Bluegrass Spectacular," telecast over PBS from the *Grand Ole Opry* auditorium in Opryland Park near Nashville, Tennessee. At one point, Jim, Jesse, and the Virginia Boys backed the renditions of Bill Monroe and his Blue Grass Boys.

The Virginia Boys in the late 1970s included Jesse's son Keith on bass, Joe Meadows on fiddle, and Garland Shuping on banjo. Jesse continued to excel both on his mid-range lead vocals and in demonstrating his special style of mandolin playing called "McReynolds cross-picking." He was supported by Jim's high, piercing tenor, though on occasion Jim sang lead, as did Keith McReynolds. Typically, the group offered several originals by the brothers, such as Jesse's "Dixie Hoedown" and "Cotton Mill Man" and Jim's "Cash on the Barrelhead." Other songs played in a late 1970s or early 1980s set might range from traditional ballads to spirituals, driving bluegrass instrumentals, or bluegrass versions of recent country hits.

Examples of songs played on late 1970s programs were "Better Times a-Comin'," "Then I'll Stop Goin' for You," "Sweet Little Miss Blue Eyes," "Little Old Log Cabin," "Blue Ridge Mountain Blues," "I Wish You Knew," "Heartbreak Mountain," "Last Train to Clarksville," "Border Ride," "Cumbanchero," "Iron Mule Special," "Mockingbird," "Lee Highway Blues," "Under the Double Eagle," "River of Jordan," "How Great Thou Art," "On the Wings of a Dove," "When the Wagon Was New," "Hard Hearted," "Ashes of Love," "Westphalia Waltz," "Dark as a Dungeon," "Knoxville Girl," "Old Slewfoot," and Hank Williams' "Mansion on the Hill." From the mid-1970s on, one of the band's most popular numbers was its version of John Prine's "Paradise," a song that told of the destruction of the hill country environment by the coal companies.

The Jim & Jesse saga continued along the same path throughout the 1980s and into the mid-1990s. They and their Virginia Boys continued to play the *Opry* and numerous folk and bluegrass festivals in all parts of the U.S. and abroad. They recorded new material for smaller labels during those years. In the mid-1990s, they had three albums available on Rounder Records: *In the Tradition* (1987), *Music Among Friends* (1991), and *Epic Bluegrass Hits*. Also in print in the 1990s was the extensive retrospective of their 1960s material compiled by Bear Family Records of Germany. This 5 CD set, *Jim & Jesse: Bluegrass and More*, contained all their recordings on Epic Records from 1960 to 1969 including the contents of two traditional gospel albums. Bear Family noted the packages included "surprisingly good

bluegrass versions of Chuck Berry tunes and some great truck driving songs like their hit 'Diesel On My Tail.'"

JONES, GEORGE: *Singer, guitarist, songwriter, band leader (The Jones Boys). Born Saratoga, Texas, September 12, 1931. Elected to the Country Music Hall of Fame in 1992.*

A performer's performer, George Jones was often cited as the favorite artist of many of the best-known names in country music. Equally appreciated by the public, he was a major star in the mid-1960s, and continued to be one of the most successful country entertainers into the 1990s. For much of the 1970s, when he wasn't reaching the top levels of hits charts as a soloist, he usually was teaming with Tammy Wynette on highly successful duet recordings, a pairing that lasted for over a decade after their relationship soured in the late 1970s.

He was born and raised in Texas and was a devotee of country and gospel music as a young boy. Both his parents were musically talented: his mother was a church pianist and his father liked to play the guitar as a form of relaxation from his work as a pipefitter. The Joneses encouraged their son's interest in music and gave him his first guitar when he was nine. In a few years George learned to play it well and entertained at church socials and other local functions.

In his late teens, George joined the Marines during the Korean War. After being discharged, he headed home to Texas, where he found a job as a house painter. Though at first he didn't think of music as a way of earning a living, word of his talent led to increasingly important professional engagements. The turning point came when veteran music executive H.W. "Pappy" Daily became interested in the young artist. Daily, then starting the Houston record firm of Starday, signed George for the label in 1954, starting a long and close association between the two men.

Soon after, George cut his first single for the label, "There Ain't No Money in This Deal." The record lived up to its name, but George and Daily persevered. In 1955, their persistence paid off when Jones scored his first major hit on Starday with the top-10 "Why Baby Why," a song he cowrote with D. Edwards. The song's success helped bring a bid for him to perform on the *Grand Ole Opry* in 1956. George was happy to accept, though he continued to call Texas rather than Nashville home. His new status was recognized by Starday with his debut album, *Grand Ole Opry's New Star,* which also was the record firm's first LP release.

George turned out a number of other chartmakers for the label, such as "You Gotta Be My Baby," before switching to Mercury Records. His first top-10 hit for the new label was "Treasure of Love," in 1958. In 1959, he scored with "Who Shot Sam," which he helped to write, and achieved his first number-one national hit with his version of Sheb Wooley's "White Lightning."

By 1961, he had moved on to his third record affiliation, United Artists, for whom he turned out a string of hits during the first part of the 1960s. The first of these was his original composition, "Window Up Above," in 1961. In 1962, he had a number-one hit, "She Thinks I Still Care," as well as the top-10 successes "Aching, Breaking Heart" and "A Girl I Used to Know." His 1963 hits for UA were "Not What I Had in Mind," a duet with Melba Montgomery, "We Must Have Been Out of Our Minds," and "You Comb Her Hair." He added more top-10 hits in 1964 with "The Race Is On," a song that also rose high on the pop charts, "Where Does a Little Tear Come From?" and "Your Heart Turned Left."

When Pappy Daily started his new company, Musicor, Jones signed with him and provided the label with a series of top-10-charted singles in the mid- and late 1960s. They included "Take Me," "Things Have Gone to Pieces," and "Love Bug" in 1965; "I'm a People" (1966); "You Can't Get There from Here" (1967); and "As Long as I Live" and "Say It's Not You" (1968). He also made upper-chart levels with "Flowers for Mama" and "4033."

During the late 1950s and throughout the 1960s, Jones was one of the major concert attractions on the country circuit, backed by his band, the Jones Boys. On the road for several hundred days a year, he appeared before audiences in all parts of the United States and Canada and made several overseas tours as well. Though he cut back a bit on his hectic stage work in the 1970s, he continued to be a major attraction wherever he went. His TV engagements included almost all of the major country shows of the 1960s and 1970s, such as *The Red Foley Show, The Jimmy Dean Show, Johnny Cash, Hee Haw,* and others. He was a guest on the *Grand Ole Opry* a number of times in the late 1950s and during the 1960s before he became a cast regular in 1969. He also found the time to take part in two movies in the 1960s.

For a long time Jones resisted the blandishments of Nashville and continued to live in a split-level ranch home in Vidor, Texas, with his second wife and two children (Jeffrey and Brian) during the 1960s. (His first marriage, in 1950, from which he has a daughter, Susan, ended in the early 1950s. He married his second wife in 1953.) In the 1970s, after that marriage broke up and he married Tammy Wynette (in 1968), he settled in Music City.

During the 1950s and 1960s, George completed a great many albums for the four labels he worked with during that period. The Starday catalogue included *Crown Prince of Country,* issued 10/61, *Fabulous Country Music Sound* (4/62), and *Greatest Hits* (4/62). Mercury LPs included *George Jones Sings* (1/60), *Country Church Time* (1960), *Country & Western Hits* (7/61), *Greatest Hits* (11/61), *Sings from the Heart* (9/62), *Ballad Side* (11/63), *Duets Country Style* (1/63),

Novelty Side (6/63), *Great George Jones* (3/64), *Blue and Lonesome* (7/64), *Salutes Hank Williams* (8/64), *Number 1 Male Singer* (11/64), and *Heartaches and Tears* (3/65). His United Artists releases during the 1960s included *Best of George Jones* (10/63), *Grand Ole Opry* (1/64), *More Favorites* (4/64), *Sings Bob Wills* (4/63), *What's in Our Heart* (1/64), *Sings Like the Dickens* (10/64), *I Get Lonely* (12/64), *Bluegrass Hootenanny* (5/64), *The Race Is On* (5/65), *King of Broken Hearts* (10/65), *Trouble in Mind* (4/65), *Blue Moon of Kentucky* (4/66), *Golden Hits* (10/66), *Golden Hits, Vol. 2* (5/67), and *Young George Jones* (10/67), plus such others as *Great George Jones, My Favorites, New Favorites, Hits of Country Cousins,* and *Homecoming in Heaven.* His releases on Musicor from 1966 through 1969 included *I'm a People, Old Brush Arbor, Love Bug, Mr. Music, New Hits with the Jones Boys, I'll Share My World with You, My Boys, Songs of Leon Payne, Where Grass Won't Grow, Will You Love Me on Sunday,* and *With Love.* In the early 1970s, Musicor issued *Best of George Jones* and *Double Gold George Jones.* He also had albums on various other labels, such as *Color of the Blues* and *Seasons of My Heart* on Nashville, *Country Memories* on Sun, *Heartaches by the Number* on Hilltop, and *Sixteen Greatest Hits* on Trip.

RCA Records issued a number of George's albums under a distribution arrangement in the early 1970s, but his singles and albums continued to come out on other previous labels. In 1970, Musicor had several hit singles of his, including the year-end success "A Good Year for the Roses." RCA released a string of Jones's LPs during 1972–73, such as *First in the Hearts of Country Music Lovers* (3/72); *I Made Leaving, Country Singer, George Jones and Friends,* and *Poor Man's Riches* (all 8/72); *Best, Volume 1* (7/72); *Four-O-Thirty Three, Take Me,* and *Tender Years* (11/72).

During 1971, by which time George was having great success teaming up with his wife, Tammy Wynette, as one of the foremost country duets, he signed a long-term contract with Tammy's record firm, Epic. His first duet single with Tammy was "Take Me" backed with "We Go Together," released in 1971; it also marked his first release on Epic. He was still on the Epic roster at the start of the 1980s and still turning out chart-making singles and LPs.

His Epic solo album debut was *George Jones,* issued in June 1972. However, he already was represented on the label with some of his duets with Tammy, included in their album *We Go Together,* a chart hit in early spring of 1972. In September, he and Tammy had another hit LP, *Me and the First Lady.* In late 1974, RCA issued the *Best of George Jones, Volume 2,* which was on the country album charts well into 1974. Later in the year, George had a top-20 hit with the Epic LP, *We're Gonna Hold On.* Among his other charted Epic albums of the 1970s were *Golden Ring* (with Tammy

Wynette) in 1976, *All the Greatest Hits, Volume 1,* in early 1977, *Bartender Blues* (1978), and *My Very Special Guests* (late 1979–early 1980).

His other Epic albums included such generally excellent offerings as *Grand Tour, Memories of Us, Picture of Me, The Battle, Alone Again,* and *I Wanta Sing.* A number of the latter were autobiographical or semi-autobiographical, dealing with the breakup of his marriage to Tammy Wynette; in particular, *The Battle,* one of his most impressive albums, dealt with the final stages of the relationship. After the separation, previously recorded duets by the two artists continued to be released, resulting in a number of hit singles. By the end of the 1970s, Jones's total of album releases on all labels was approaching 100.

George's rapport with the country-music audiences was proven again and again throughout the 1970s; his solo singles, as well as his duets with others, were constantly on the bestseller lists. In 1972, for instance, he had a top-10 solo hit with "We Can Make It" and a duet top-10 success, "The Ceremony," with Tammy Wynette. Both discs were on Epic as were almost all his other chartmakers from then on. Among those were "Once You've Had the Best" in 1974, "God's Gonna Getcha for That" (with Tammy Wynette) and "Memories of Us" in 1975; "The Battle," "You Always Look Best (Here in My Arms)," "Golden Key" (with Wynette). "Her Name Is . . ." (1976); the number-one ranked "Near You" (February 1977 with Wynette) and top-10 "Southern California" (with Wynette, August 1977); "Put 'Em All Together and I'd Have You" (1977); "I'll Just Take It Out in Love" (1978); and "Maybelline" (with Johnny Paycheck, late 1978, early 1979).

Despite his many achievements, by the late 1970s George's life was in a shambles. As do many entertainers, he had used alcohol regularly as a crutch to alleviate the tensions, frustrations, and boredom of the performing grind. As his private problems mounted, so did his drinking, until he had become an alcoholic. Things reached a climax as the decade came to a close. Not only had his marriage to Tammy ended in divorce, his financial status plummeted and he had to declare bankruptcy. Increasingly he became unreliable as a performer, often failing to appear for scheduled concerts. During 1979, his doctors warned him that if he didn't stop drinking not only his career but his life was in danger. Heeding the message, he checked into a clinic in Alabama for a month for an alcoholism cure.

The result was a new upsurge in his interest in living and in his musical reputation. After returning home from Alabama, he recorded a new album, *I Am What I Am,* which was one of his best collections. The LP became his best-selling album ever and was on the charts from 1980 into 1981. One song from the LP, "He Stopped Loving Her Today," released by Epic in the spring of 1980, rose to number-one in early summer. Later in the year, George had another number-one single with "I'm Not Ready." Meanwhile, the passions between George and Tammy had cooled. They announced in February 1980 that they would perform together again. Their first duet in several years had been recorded in January 1980 ("Two Story House") and released on February 12, by Epic. Jones and Wynette debuted the song on Johnny Carson's *The Tonight Show* and also took part in Johnny Cash's "25th Anniversary Special." In the fall, George and Tammy had another hit single, "A Pair of Old Sneakers."

Jones had received many honors during his long career. In 1956, all the major music trade magazines voted him Most Promising Artist of the Year. He was among the finalists a number of times in the voting for best male vocalist by the Country Music Association and the duet of Jones and Wynette was among the five finalists for vocal group of the year for most of the 1970s. Despite that, at the start of the 1980s, most of his entertainment industry peers felt he had never gained the recognition he merited. But all of that changed dramatically in the early 1980s.

In the CMA 1980 voting, he was a major winner, receiving the awards for Male Vocalist of the Year, Song of the Year, and Single of the Year (the last two for "He Stopped Loving Her Today"). At the Grammy Awards in early 1981, he won for Country Song of the Year ("He Stopped Loving Her Today") and similar approval was given by members of the Academy of Country Music, voting him Male Vocalist of the Year and naming "He Stopped Loving Her Today" Song of the Year and Single of the Year. In the annual *Music City News* Cover Awards in 1981, he was named Male Artist of the Year.

During 1981, his recording and concert work continued to prosper. Capacity audiences greeted him from coast to coast. (Members of his band, the Jones Boys, at this time were Rob Watkins, lead guitar and vocals; Mark Dunn, drums; Ron Gaddis, bass guitar and vocals; Tommy Keller, steel guitar; Steve Payne, keyboards; and Lorrie Morgan, backing vocals.) His album *I Am What I Am* earned a Recording Industry Association of America gold record, the first such in his career. In early 1981 he had the hit singles "You Better Move On" (a duet with Johnny Paycheck) and "If Drinkin' Don't Kill Me (Your Memory Will)" and later in the year made the top-10 with "Still Doin' Time." Also on the charts in late 1981 was his new album, *Still the Same Ole Me.* In October 1981, he won three more awards from the CMA, including being named Male Vocalist of the Year for the second straight time.

Reviewing the turnaround in his fortunes, George told Robert Hilburn of the *Los Angeles Times* (Calendar section, March 8, 1981), "When you're young, you take most things for granted—the money, the attention, the fans. But I can appreciate it all now. I'm older and I know what it is to have it all slip away. For a while, I didn't even know if I'd be alive much longer—much less be on stage. I'm a very lucky man."

Jones seemed to backslide soon after that, and concert promoters and fans once more started calling him "No Show Jones" for his failure either to make concert appearances on time, or at all. In 1982, when he was arrested after a high-speed chase, news cameras caught him being subdued by police in an apparently intoxicated condition, and the images were presented on national TV throughout the U.S. But in the mid-1980s, aided by his fourth wife, Nancy, he licked his demons again, this time apparently for good.

He told Cyndi Hoelzli of *The Gavin Report* ("George Jones," January 24, 1992), "I owe Nancy just about everything. She's really helped me and stuck by me through a lot of hard times. Of course we had a lot of fans and people praying for us and we did a couple of things right. We went into the hospital and got our thinking caps on. The low point was when I got so sick and messed up in the late '70s and very early '80s. I'm just glad to get out of all that mess and know there's a real world out there."

Despite his personal problems, Jones still could bask in the glow of being considered by his musical peers and fans alike as country's "greatest living singer." (He also acquired the nickname "Possum," based on the way he looked in a publicity photo taken for the *White Lightning* album, a side view of Jones with his crewcut hairstyle of those years.) His importance as an artist was reflected in two early 1980s biographies, one by Dolly Carlisle of *People* and the other by country writer Bob Allen.

For a while in the mid-1980s, to help insure that George had the chance to achieve a complete rehabilitation, he and Nancy moved from Nashville to Beaumont, Texas, where they opened a musical theme park. Jones commented, "It saved my life—and everything else." He wasn't completely absent from the recording field during those years. For instance, he won the 1986 Country Music Association Video of the Year for "Who's Gonna Fill Their Shoes." His 1980s output also included a duet album with Merle Haggard. At the end of the 1980s, after running the Beaumont park for five years, he sold it and moved back to Nashville with Nancy. In early 1989, he had a new album out on Epic, *One Woman Man.*

In 1990, George teamed with new country star Randy Travis for the single "A Few Ole Country Boys" on Randy's Warner Brothers label, which made the *Billboard* Top 10 in November. In 1991, after twenty years with Epic, Jones signed with MCA, which issued his label debut, *And Along Came Jones,* in September. The first single from the album, "You Couldn't Find the Picture," made the charts in the fall. (By then Epic had issued a retrospective album of Jones's work on the label. Titled *Super Hits,* the album stayed on the charts for some two years, earning gold-record certification from the R.I.A.A. along the way.)

During the October 1992 CMA TV Awards show, Jones received his long-deserved induction into the Country Music Hall of Fame. In his acceptance speech he took note of the virtual shutout of recordings by veteran country performers on radio, appealing to radio programmers to give older stars a fair chance with the younger entertainers. MCA at the time had released the single "I Don't Need Your Rockin' Chair" in both audio and video forms. The single, performed by George Jones and Friends (Alan Jackson, Mark Chesnutt, Joe Diffie, Patty Loveless, Vince Gill, Clint Black, Pam Tillis, Travis Tritt, Garth Brooks, and T. Graham Brown), hit high on the charts in early 1993 and later that year won the CMA's Vocal Event of the Year Award. His second MCA album, *Walls Can Fall,* came out in late 1992 and won mainstream acclaim, reaching upper *Billboard* chart levels in early 1993.

After relocating to Nashville, George resumed a tour schedule of over 100 dates per year, his tour bus bearing a front bumper sticker jokingly reading "No Show." However, George remained on the wagon and his own car had license plates that stated "IDOSHOW." On many tour dates he headlined with many new-generation stars. He noted in late 1993, "For the past year or so we worked with Tracy Lawrence, Mark Chesnutt, Confederate Railroad. We work a lot with the young artists. We just fit right in there. We have a ball."

In late 1993, the third MCA album, *High Tech Redneck,* was released and made the *Billboard* list soon after, staying on it into 1994. One of the tracks featured a duet with Sammy Kershaw on "Never Bit a Bullet Like This." In the spring, Jones began putting down tracks for a new album at the Bradley Barn studio in Mount Juliet, Tennessee. Backing him on the sessions was a group of Nashville's finest instrumentalists: Jerry Douglas, Vince Gill, Emmylou Harris, Mac McAnnally, Leon Russell, Ricky Skaggs, and Marty Stuart. Jones's singing partners on the album's songs included Mark Knopfler, Dolly Parton, Alan Jackson, Vince Gill, Trisha Yearwood, Keith Richards, and, for the first time in many years, Tammy Wynette. Rock superstar Richards cut short a mixing session for a new Rolling Stones album to fly to Nashville to work with Jones. The material taped by the two included a 1958 song written by Jones and Lester Blackwell, "I'm Gonna Burn Your Playhouse Down."

The *Bradley Barn Sessions* album was released by MCA in August 1994. (Earlier in the year, Legacy Columbia issued a multi-CD box set of Jones's best Epic recordings called *The Essential George Jones.*) Hardly had his fourth MCA album reached stores when it was announced that Jones had been hospitalized with heart problems. In mid-September a triple bypass operation was performed at Nashville's Baptist Hospital from which, as of 1996, he appeared to have recovered completely.

The September 1994 special edition of *Life* magazine on country music named Jones as one of "The 100 Most Important People in the History of Country." In his praise the editors wrote, "If your brew is hard-core country—not lush country or rocky country or jazzy country—then you probably figure ol' George has been our best singer for about four decades now. You probably also figure that he's better now than most of the dead ones once were.

"Thumper Jones (as George was first billed) grew up singing and living—all too enthusiastically—the honky tonk style. He could warble, slide up and down, accelerate and brake without losing his voice on the lyric. His phrasing, always good, seemed only to improve with age . . . and that's why we chant on, greatest living singer, greatest living singer, greatest living singer."

George's duet with Tammy on the *Bradley Barn Sessions* track, "Golden Ring," inspired a new collaboration that resulted in the mid-1995 album release, *One*. This had nothing to do with the old days, he stressed; he was still happily married to Nancy as was Tammy with George Richey. The two didn't spend a lot of time together, he noted; "But we are friends when we meet." A reminder of the old days, though, was the belated arrival at gold record status of the album *George Jones and Tammy Wynette's Greatest Hits*. That January 1977 LP finally received a gold record award from the R.I.A.A. on September 12, 1995.

In the CMA voting for the period from mid-1995 to mid-1996, *One* was nominated for Vocal Event of the Year. During the summer of 1996, George was recording tracks for another album, including preparation of a video of one number, "Honky Tonk Song," on which he was joined by singer/instrumentalist Junior Brown. He also was represented on the *Disney Country* album by a duet with Kathy Mattea of "You've Got a Friend in Me" from the computer generated film *Toy Story*. During the year, as if to confirm his permanent place in the pantheon, his autobiography became a best seller. Its perfect title: *I Lived to Tell It All*.

JONES, GRANDPA: *Singer, banjoist, guitarist, fiddler, comic. Born Niagra, Henderson County, Kentucky, October 20, 1913. Elected to Country Music Hall of Fame in 1978.*

When the new *Hee Haw* program debuted on CBS-TV the summer of 1969, the headliners were Roy Clark and Buck Owens, but contributing mightily to the success of the program was the inimitable Grandpa Jones with his relaxed down-home humor and driving banjo solos. When *Hee Haw* celebrated its tenth anniversary as one of the most successful syndicated country-music shows, Grandpa still was gracing each telecast with skill and exuberance, a favorite figure with country audiences as he had been for over forty years.

Born Louis Marshall Jones in Henderson County,

Kentucky, he started his music career at eleven when he surreptitiously practiced on a workman's old guitar on his family's farm. Enthralled by the experience, he persuaded his older brother to purchase a guitar, and then diligently tried to master it.

By the time the family moved to Akron, Ohio, in the late 1920s, he could play quite well. In 1929 he entered a talent contest promoted by Wendell Hall at the local Keith Albee theater. He won first prize, fifty dollars in gold pieces, and used it to buy a new guitar that he soon employed in a series of radio station jobs. From the end of the 1920s through 1935, he performed on radio stations in Akron and Cleveland. In 1935, he made a major step forward when he joined the group headed by veteran folk-country artist Bradley Kincaid to appear on the *National Barn Dance* over station WLS, Chicago. Besides that, he played on programs broadcast over station WBZ in Boston, Massachusetts, and WWVA, Wheeling, West Virginia, during 1935–36.

When Jones became associated with Kincaid, he sounded very old on the radio, though he was only twenty-three, and people started writing the *Barn Dance* about him, asking his age. As a result, he formed a new act as "Grandpa." He put on special makeup, used a false, bushy moustache (when he was older he was able to grow a grizzled one of his own), and affected old-time clothes, including large galluses and high boots. In addition, he now concentrated on banjo pickin' instead of the guitar. In 1937, with his own band, he debuted in Wheeling, West Virginia. The billing read "Grandpa Jones and His Grandchildren."

The audience went wild, as audiences still were doing many decades later. His style captured a rustic enthusiasm that conveyed the rural and pioneer spirit to people from all walks of life. It was described glowingly by Ed Badeaux, associate editor of *Sing Out!* in the December–January 1963–64 issue. "Grandpa plays the banjo not with just his hands and arms, but with his whole body. His footwork is as intricate as that of a prize fighter or ballet dancer, and is executed while he is both singing and playing the banjo. When he comes to a banjo solo, the neck of his banjo jets straight up in the air and he arches his body to get the drum as close to the microphone as possible. During his songs, he dances, does stationary road work, and takes frequent jumps and kicks to emphasize and reinforce the humor in his songs."

Grandpa took his new act to Cincinnati in 1938 as part of the cast of the new WLW *Boone County Jamboree*. He continued to delight radio listeners and live audiences from his WLW base until 1944, when he went into the Army. He ended up in Munich, Germany, after the war in Europe was over, where he played on the Armed Forces Network.

After his discharge in 1946, he returned to the States and soon accepted an offer to join the regular cast of the

Grand Ole Opry. Decades later he still was one of the *Opry's* most-loved artists. During the late 1940s and into the 1950s, he made many trips to entertain U.S. troops overseas. During one of those tours while the Korean War was raging, he took part in thirty-four shows in fourteen days before 38,000 soldiers. One performance was given within 200 yards of the front lines.

Through the 1950s and 1960s, Grandpa continued to tour widely. Most of his appearances—usually part of a package show—were on basically country-attraction circuits—theaters in the South and Southwest, county fairs, rodeos, etc. However, he also was well received in many major cities outside the South over the years. By the start of the 1970s, he had appeared in all fifty states and given concerts in many foreign nations as well. His wife, Ramona, accompanied him on his tours, adding her talents on fiddle and other instruments to the act.

During the 1950s and 1960s, Grandpa was an honored guest on almost every important country TV program, network or syndicated. His exposure on TV increased markedly when he became a regular on *Hee Haw* from 1969 on. His contributions included taking part in a variety of skits—such as the cornfield one-liners, the barber shop routine, and the hillbilly segment in which all the performers delivered their rural humor from supine positions. The spotlight often fell on one of his patented banjo solos during the program while at other times he joined Roy Clark and other pickers for banjo band performances.

During his long career, many songs became associated with Grandpa, including "Old Rattler," "Old Rattler Treed," "Old Rattler's Pup," "Good Ole Mountain Dew," "Eight More Miles to Louisville," "Going Down Town," and his version of the Lonzo and Oscar hit "I'm My Own Grandpa." All of those and many others were recorded by him over the years, sometimes more than once. His recordings were released on various labels, including King, Monument, Decca, Vocalion, and Nashville.

Grandpa was represented in record catalogues with dozens of releases from the start of the 1950s to the end of the 1970s. His LPs on the King label included such collections as *Gospel Songs* (issued 4/63), *Other Side of Grandpa Jones* and *Rollin' Along* (early 1960s), and *Do You Remember These Songs* (9/63). His Monument releases included *Rafters Ring* (4/62), *Yodeling Hits* (early 1960s), *Real Folk Songs* (9/64), *Grandpa Jones Remembers the Brown's Ferry Four,* (he was a member of that quartet during one phase of his career), *Everybody's Grandpa* (mid-1960s), and *Hits from Hee Haw* (1/70).

His LPs on other labels included *An Evening with Grandpa Jones* on Decca (8/63); *15¢ Is All I've Got* on Nashville (early 1970s); *Pickin' Time* on Vocalion (late 1960s), and *Grandpa Jones Lives* on Harmony (9/72).

One of the most memorable events for Grandpa occurred in October 1978. During the Country Music Association awards show telecast throughout the United States, he was called up on stage to watch the unveiling of the plaque commemorating his election that year to the Country Music Hall of Fame. In 1978 and 1979, he contributed part of his memorabilia, including some of his banjos, for use in his exhibit at the Hall of Fame museum in Nashville.

Through the 1980s and into the 1990s, Jones continued to perform on the *Grand Ole Opry* and *Hee Haw.* In 1985, his autobiography, cowritten with Charles Wolfe, was published as *Everybody's Grandpa—Fifty Years Behind the Mike.* In the mid-1990s, the Country Music Foundation catalogue offered two of his albums, the MCA Records' *Grandpa Jones: Country Music Hall of Fame Series* and Columbia Records' *Grandpa Jones/Live.* Some of his early *Opry* performances also were available on the *Grand Ole Opry Stars of the Fifties* video series, including clips in volumes 1, 3, 6 (a comedy package), and 10.

JUDDS, THE: *Vocal and instrumental duo, Naomi Judd, born Ashland, Kentucky, January 11, 1946; Wynonna Judd, born Ashland, Kentucky, May 31, 1964.*

If the cards had fallen differently Naomi Judd (born Diana Ellen Judd in Ashland, Kentucky) might have become known as an actress. She had started along that path, even winning a role in the movie *More American Graffiti.* But Hollywood's loss was country music's gain, as Naomi followed the lead of her daughter, Wynonna, more than a dozen years later, to enter country music. Their dynamic mother and daughter team, the Judds, won the affection of millions of concert goers and record buyers until a chronic illness forced Naomi to retire. It was a move that opened up still more entertainment possibilities for Wynonna in the 1990s.

Diana's father, who owned a gas station in Ashland, maintained his family in middle-class comfort as his daughter grew up to become a popular and attractive teenager. She was exposed to the traditional music of the region, including bluegrass, but as a high schooler in the early 1960s she was better attuned to rockers like Elvis and the Everly Brothers. However, she wasn't yet considering a music career; in fact, she was forced to think more about family values after learning she was pregnant by her high school sweetheart, Michael Ciminella. The two eloped, and a week before her high school graduation in 1964 she gave birth to Christina Claire Ciminella, the future Wynonna Judd.

Soon after, the Ciminellas moved to Lexington, Kentucky, where Michael finished work on a business management degree and then pursued movie-related activities that eventually led to work in video production. In 1968, Diana Ciminella gave birth to a second daughter, Ashley, who in her adult years became a successful actress. Her marriage, however, began to come apart in the early 1970s and ended in 1972. For a while Diana supported herself and her two girls with a variety of jobs that included clerking in a health-food store.

Her children, particularly young Christina, were troubled by the situation. Wynonna told an interviewer from the *Los Angeles Times* in 1992, "I think every kid who goes through a divorce is affected by it. You have to remember I was born in a very troubled time in Mom's life. Her brother died [of cancer] soon after I was born. Besides, I always felt I was the reason they got married and I was the reason they got divorced.

"Kids always blame themselves when their parents break apart I guess. I had asthma and was very emotional after their divorce. Music was my saving grace. When I sang, I just felt a sense of peace. I think to this day when I am singing, I am the happiest—period."

In the mid-1970s, Diana Ciminella decided it would be best if the children grew up in her hometown, and moved the family back to Ashland. She still had some thoughts of a movie career and, indeed, at one point moved everyone briefly back to California. But for the most part her daughters got their education in Ashland schools. To earn a more dependable income, Diana completed training in nursing; after a while, she also changed her first name to Naomi after the biblical figure. This inspired Christina to follow suit, choosing Wynonna from an Oklahoma town [Wynona] mentioned in the lyrics of the song "Route 66."

Wynonna spent much of her high school years in teenage rebellion against her mother, but as she reached her late teens a loving understanding began to arise between them. In particular, Wynonna brought her musical abilities to her mother's attention. Beginning to realize her daughter had true musical talent, Naomi started to think about entertainment as a way out of the workaday world. The two laid the groundwork for an act and, in the early 1980s, the Judds—much to the disapproval of Naomi's parents—moved to Nashville, where Naomi got a new nursing position in a local hospital. When she discovered that a patient's father was in the entertainment field, she gave the girl a demo tape to give to her father, Brent Maher. Maher liked it and started shopping it around until it was audited by a talent manager, Ken Stilts, who arranged for an audition at RCA.

The year was 1983 and the RCA executives were very favorably impressed. Producer Tony Brown, who worked with the Judds during their years on RCA and later accompanied Wynonna to MCA, recalled for the *Los Angeles Times*, "Naomi gave her little spiel about being from this small town and all and she was real charming, but when Wy strapped on her guitar she just knocked me out. Her voice blew me away. . . . That's why I couldn't understand when a lot of people around town seemed to have thought that Wynonna's career was all over after Naomi's illness."

Brown and executive Joe Galante quickly saw to it that the duo became an RCA act, and it didn't take long for the label to realize it had a potential new set of superstars on its roster. In their first major concert appearance as an opening act for the Statler Brothers in 1984, the Judds received a thunderous ovation after finishing their set from the 10,000 people in the hall. Their debut album became a best-seller and provided several chart singles including "Mama, He's Crazy," which won a Grammy in the 1984 voting for Best Country Performance by a Duo or Group with Vocal. That was the first of four Grammys won by the duo, the others being (all in the same category) the 1985 trophy for the album *Why Not Me,* the 1986 nod for the single "Grandpa, Tell Me 'Bout the Good Old Days," and the 1988 award for "Give a Little Love," a track from their *Greatest Hits* album.

In the 1984 voting of the Country Music Association the duo walked off with the Horizon Award for most promising newcomers, the first of eight CMA Awards given to them. During the 1980s they won many more honors from trade publications, video award competitions, the Academy of Country Music, and so forth. Over the period, the Judds placed some twenty songs in top-chart spots including many number-one hits. All of their album releases went gold or platinum and, in one case, double platinum.

At the end of the 1980s it was announced that Naomi would have to retire from the act, having contracted active hepatitis. Her doctors feared that the great strain of touring and performing could in time have a very severe impact on her health. The team decided to embark on a "farewell" tour starting in late 1989, a tour that drew capacity crowds to major arenas throughout the U.S. and in many other parts of the world. The demand for tickets was so great that the Judds extended the tour several times, causing some to joke that the farewell tour might not finish until it was time for Wynonna to retire. But the final concert was held the end of 1991 and Wynonna began working on her first solo album. As of 1993, their record company estimated their album sales total exceeded 11 million worldwide.

The duo continued to place new songs on the hit lists as their final tour unfolded in the early 1990s. Those included "One Man Woman," number five in *Radio & Records* the week of January 26, 1990; "Guardian Angels," number ten in *R&R* the week of June 1; and "Born to Be Blue," number four in *R&R* the week of October 5, 1990. Late that year their album *Love Can Build a Bridge* was at number twelve in *Billboard.* At the time their *Greatest Hits, Volume I* was still on the list, where it still could be found at the end of 1992. Still going well at the time was their *Greatest Hits, Volume II,* issued in the fall of 1991, and the "catalog" chart successes *Heartland* and *Collector's Series.*

As Wynonna's solo career took shape, her mother's health improved. With the hepatitis in remission, Naomi was able not only to give understanding and support for her daughter, but also to find energy for a variety of other projects. Those included writing an autobiography, collaborating with NBC on a miniseries about her life, and also working as a volunteer spokesperson for the American Liver Foundation. In the mid-1990s, a long-form video of highlights from their farewell concert tour was released and became a best-seller. Her 1996 activities included opening a restaurant called Trilogy in Nashville with husband Larry Strickland, serving as a presenter at the Academy of Country Music Awards TV show in April, and later appearing with Wynonna at a country music gala in New York City, called An Evening for Special Children, to raise funds for a variety of children's charities.

𝒦

KEITH, TOBY: *Singer, guitarist, songwriter. Born Clinton, Oklahoma, July 8, 1961.*

There's many a country artist who's sung about the cowboy's life without being closer to riding a horse than the merry-go-round. Toby Keith, whose single titled "Should've Been a Cowboy," marked him as a potential new star in the mid-1990s, didn't grow up on a ranch, but he did have some familiarity with rodeo events. Not, as he stressed, as a participant: "In high school I worked for a rodeo company, but I never thought about getting into professional rodeo. I was too tall to be a bull rider and I couldn't rope very good."

Nor was he really thinking of becoming a performer while growing up in the southwest. Still, he did have a good voice, and in his teens he did sometimes sit in with bands playing at his grandmother's supper club in Arkansas. His father worked in the oil fields, and though Toby spent some time in college, he dropped out when the chance to do similar work came along. It was a tough way to earn a living, but the money was good. As he told Radio 7 Records, "I jumped college and went straight to the money. Back then, a kid could make $40,000 straight out of school."

He spent four years in the oil industry, spending some of his time performing on weekends with a band he formed with some friends. The group played small clubs and local social events and at one point placed second in a statewide competition. Keith still wasn't sure what career path he wanted to follow. He had been a good athlete, having been a top-rated player with his high school team and a participant in semi-pro-football activities afterward. He decided to abandon oil field work to try for a football career.

He recalled, "Having passed up college ball to work in the oil fields, I felt that I made a mistake. So I tried out for, and made, an Oklahoma USTA squad that was trying to make it into the U.S. Football League." But when the league broke up, Keith decided to take music more seriously.

He assembled a band and sought gigs in the

Texas–Oklahoma–Arkansas region. After some false starts, the group found a niche on the dance-hall circuit and began to build up a good reputation with local fans. The natural next move was to seek national exposure through a recording contract. Toby and the band made a series of demo tapes, which were taken to Nashville from time to time to be put before record company officials.

Some of the material was written by Keith. He told *Radio & Records* in early 1993, "I've been writing for about 15 years. My sixth grade teacher would give us an hour each Friday to write a story. I always looked forward to that. My stories would be wild and crazy and psychedelic as a sixth grader could write. That may have been my early songwriting training."

Plenty of record labels passed on the band, but the tapes finally impressed Harold Shedd of Mercury Records. After flying out to see the band and Keith perform, he signed Toby in early 1992. By May of that year, Keith was working on the first candidates for his debut album. Eight of the ten numbers selected for the final collection were written by Keith.

The first single, "Should've Been a Cowboy," was issued the early part of 1993 and soon was moving up all the major hit charts. It reached number one in *Radio & Records* the week of May 28, 1993, and was number four and still rising in *Billboard*. The album, *Toby Keith*, showed up on the *Billboard* list that spring and was still on them seventy-one weeks later in September 1994, having surpassed R.I.A.A. gold-record levels along the way. The single "He Ain't Worth Missing," like the earlier one written by Keith, made it to number five in *Radio & Records* the week of October 8, 1993.

Toby continued his hot streak into 1994, supporting his records and videos with continuous touring throughout the country, mostly as an opening act for other artists. The week of February 19, 1994, his single "A Little Less Talk and a Lot More Action" rose to number two in *Billboard*. In late May the single "Wish I Didn't Know Now," released the previous February 28, also made it to number two, while gracing the number-one position in *Radio & Records* the week of May 20, 1994.

In early 1994, Mercury spun off its companion label, Polydor, as a separate entity with Harold Shedd, Keith's coproducer, as president. He brought Toby along with him as the label's centerpiece and started work with him on his second album. Called *Boomtown*, it was released September 27, preceded by the initial single "Who's That Man," words and lyrics by Keith. (Keith wrote or cowrote seven of the ten songs on the album.) The single quickly gained hit status, reaching number one in *R&R* the week of September 30 and in *Billboard* in early October. By year-end he had another single moving up the charts, "Upstairs Downtown" (cowritten with C. Cogg, Jr.). By then the album had been certified gold by the R.I.A.A.

In the spring of 1995, his Polydor single "You Ain't Much Fun" (cowritten by Toby and C. Goff, Jr.) made the charts and was in the number two position in *Billboard* for most of June. On June 10, 1995, it reached number one on the *Radio & Records* chart. On November 15 of that year he was one of the recipients of a CMA Triple Play Award presented to composer members who had attained three number-one songs during the previous twelve months in *Billboard, Radio & Records,* or *The Gavin Report.* Toby's successes were "Wish I Didn't Know Now," "Who's That Man," and "You Ain't Much Fun.") During the fall, Toby was represented by the video "Santa, I'm Right Here," about disadvantaged children, filmed at St. Patrick's Shelter in Nashville.

For a time Toby joined the roster of another label, A&M Nashville. His output for A&M included the album *Blue Moon,* which peaked at number six in *Billboard* the week of May 4, 1996. However, that record company closed its Nashville office and Toby moved over to the Mercury Nashville label.

KENTUCKY COLONELS: *Vocal and instrumental group, original members Roland White, born Maine (vocals, mandolin); Clarence White, born Maine, died July 14, 1973 (vocals, guitar); Billy Ray Latham (banjo); Roger Bush (guitar, bass). Group later added Bobby Slone (fiddle) and Leroy Mack (dobro).*

A resurgent interest in bluegrass music was one facet of the folk-music boom of the late 1950s and early 1960s. Though Bill Monroe, Flatt & Scruggs, and other veteran bluegrass musicians continued to thrive on both the folk and country scenes, their status was enhanced by the formation of innovative new groups by young musicians in all parts of the U.S. The ferment spread to California where Maine-born Roland White organized what was to become one of the most influential bands of the genre, the Kentucky Colonels. Though the band never achieved the mass audience success its exciting musicianship deserved, its stylings and instrumental skills had enormous impact on everything from country to rock 'n' roll.

The band began as a quartet comprising Roland, his enormously talented guitar playing brother, Clarence, banjoist Billy Ray Latham, and guitarist and bass player Roger Bush. Other musicians were added in the 1960s to form large ensembles. Playing fast-moving versions of traditional bluegrass, country, folk (including old-timey gospel music), the band became a favorite with country and bluegrass fans in the first part of the 1960s and as the decade went by widened its audience to other parts of the world. The band could often be heard at its home base in Southern California, particularly in dates at the Ash Grove on Melrose Avenue in Los Angeles. During the first half of the 1960s, it continued to be a featured act at festivals and on the college concert circuit.

The band made a number of recordings in the early 1960s including a notable all-instrumental collection, *The Kentucky Colonels,* issued by World Pacific Records in July 1964. While all the band members were very accomplished musicians, Clarence White in particular won the attention of his peer group. The late Jerry Garcia of the rock supergroup the Grateful Dead commented at one time in *Guitar Player* magazine, "Clarence was important in my life both as a friend and a player. He brought a kind of swing—a rhythmic openness—to bluegrass, and a unique syncopation. His feel has been incorporated by a lot of other players, but nobody has ever quite gotten the open quality of his rhythm. Clarence had a wonderful control over the guitar. He's the first guy I heard who knocked me out."

A combination of conflicting views on musical directions among members and the overshadowing of the folk-country sector by the overwhelming success of 1960s bands like the Beatles and Rolling Stones caused the group to disband in the mid-1960s. The members followed different career paths, working as sidemen with folk, country, or rock groups or doing session work. Ronald went to Nashville where, at various times, he was a member of both Bill Monroe's Blue Grass Boys and Lester Flatt's band (after the breakup of Flatt & Scruggs). Latham and Bush joined the band formed by Doug Dillard and Gene Clark in the late 1960s, the Dillard & Clark Expedition. Roland also worked for a time as the mainstay of Byron Berline's 1970 bluegrass band, The Country Gazette. Latham was with the Dillards from 1971 to 1977.

Clarence White played with other groups, such as Nashville West, before playing a key role in a rejuvenated Byrds operation, where his lead guitar work is an engrossing feature of the folk-rock band's later albums. He initially performed with the group as a session musician in early 1968 on the landmark country rock album *Sweetheart of the Rodeo.* That October, he took Gram Parsons's place when the latter resigned in protest over the Byrds' decision to perform in South Africa. He remained with the band through the early 1970s, contributing to a series of albums including the Byrds' final offering, *Farther Along.*

Some of those collections did not match Byrds releases in its heyday, but White's guitar work comprised some of his finest efforts in his all-too-short career. As *Rolling Stone* critic David Fricke commented in the booklet accompanying the four-CD Columbia 1990 release of the complete Byrds recordings, White continued to refine and innovate his sound. In albums like *Ballad of Easy Rider* and *Farther Along,* Fricke stated, White's "blazing solos and hairpin flourishes combined country-bluegrass facility with faultless melodic intuition and rock & roll spunk. With the Stringbender, a special guitar modification created with Gene Parsons . . . which enabled him to raise his string pitch as full tone, White developed a trademark sound that combined the scream of a pedal steel with the metallic stab of a Telecaster."

The Byrds saga was coming to an end. Founder Roger McGuinn broke up the group in the first part of 1973, but it looked as though promising new opportunities would arise for a new version of the Kentucky Colonels, organized by the White brothers for a highly successful Swedish tour. With the reviving interest in bluegrass in the seventies, the way seemed open for the Colonels to take their rightful place as a seminal music force. Unfortunately, it was a dream that was short-circuited by the untimely death of Clarence White, killed by a drunk driver on July 14, 1973.

The Swedish tour was the basis for a live album issued by Rounder Records titled *The White Brothers (The New Kentucky Colonels)*. Two other albums of the Colonels' work were issued in the 1970s, one on Takoma Records called *Livin' in the Past,* and one on Rounder, *The Kentucky Colonels.* In mid-1993, Rounder reissued the World Pacific 1964 material under the title *Appalachian Swing.* For those who had little exposure to the band's material it was a revelation, and critical comments without exception were ecstatic. The group's approach seemed in no way dated, and a listener could only mourn what further contributions to modern bluegrass and country might have been made had the timing only been right.

Carrying on the legacy, mandolinist Roland White was still an active musician in the mid-1990s as a member of the Nashville Bluegrass Band. He played a role in Rounder's preparation of its reissue, including help in detailing the 1964 sessions in album liner notes.

KENTUCKY HEADHUNTERS: *Vocal and instrumental group, members late 1980s to 1992: Richard Young (rhythm guitar); Fred Young; Greg Martin (guitar); Calvin Douglas "Doug" Phelps, born Leachville, Arkansas, December 16, 1960 (vocals, bass guitar); Ricky Lee Phelps, born Paragould, Arkansas, October 8, 1953 (lead vocals, guitar). Phelps brothers left in 1992, replaced by Mark Orr and Anthony Kenney.*

Cultivating a hayseed image and offering a musical style that combined country elements with blues-tinged rock, the Kentucky HeadHunters had a phenomenal impact on country music at the end of the 1980s and the start of the 1990s. However, with Nashville stalwarts questioning the band's country credentials and their rural-humor stance wearing a bit thin in the mid-1990s, it remained a question whether the reorganized band, following the departure of the Phelps brothers, could regain its momentum.

Impetus for the evolution of the HeadHunters came when veteran musician Doug Phelps from Missouri joined the backing band for country artist Ronnie McDowell as a bass guitarist and backing vocalist. There he became friends with lead guitarist Greg Martin, whose home base was Kentucky. In between engagements with McDowell, the two began performing with Greg's cousins Richard Young and Fred Young, where the emphasis was on country rock rather than straight country.

Martin's musical association with the Youngs went back much further than the early 1980s, however. Starting in high school, they and other friends played for school proms and other local events. In the late 1960s, Greg, the Youngs, and Anthony Kenney worked in a band called Itchy Brothers, which was still performing at local venues at the end of the 1970s. Another friend that sometimes joined in was vocalist Mark Orr.

Harking back to those days, Greg recalled for Mandy Wilson of the Country Music Association *Close Up* magazine that Itchy Brothers essentially covered music by well-known performers of the era. "I remember we played 'The Pusher' by Steppenwolf at the prom and got the PA [public address] system pulled on us. That was about 1970."

Richard Young noted that it was an anti-drug song, but school officials didn't realize it. Also, they played it because a slow song was desired for the introduction of the king and queen of the prom. "It was the only slow song we knew how to play. There was another band there, and of course they played appropriate music for a prom. We didn't want to play a slow song so we flipped a coin and lost. Mrs. Chambers, the wife of the assistant coach at the school, went over and jerked the PA out of the wall. The king and queen were out there dancing and they just looked at each other like, 'What happened?'"

Those days were far behind Greg and his cousins by the time they began working with Doug Phelps. After playing together for half a year, the need for a lead vocalist was apparent, and Doug brought his brother Ricky Lee aboard. The band got its own radio show, broadcast from Munfordville, Kentucky, in the mid-1980s and started to attract a local following. Encouraged by this, they put together $4,500 of their own money and bought studio time to prepare an eight-song demo. The demo eventually got them a contract from Mercury/Polygram.

The bandsmen added two more songs, and their label debut, *Pickin' on Nashville,* came out in 1989 and began to pick up airplay. It made the charts in late 1989, eventually peaking at number two in *Billboard,* and was still on the *Billboard* list in mid-1992, having gone past R.I.A.A. platinum-record levels.

Helping to bring the band to national attention was an intensive tour schedule, mostly as opening act for established artists, that totaled well over 200 days a year. In 1990, that exposure and TV and radio coverage helped provide three hit singles, "Dumas Walker" (number eleven in *Radio & Records* the week of May 4); "Oh Lonesome Me" (number seven in *R&R* the week of July 27); and "Rock 'n' Roll Angel" (number fourteen in *R&R* the week of November 30). In the 1990 Country Music Association voting, the band received awards for Vocal Group of the Year and Album of the Year (for *Pickin' on Nashville*) as well as a nomination for the Horizon Award. On the October 1990 CMA Awards telecast, the group was one of the featured acts. In April 1991, the Academy of Country Music named them Best New Vocal Group.

On the band's next Mercury album, *Electric Barnyard,* the band continued to emphasize its mythic hillbilly image which was at variance with the rock influences in its music and the non-hick background of the members. Four of the five had gone to college; Rick Young, for instance, had been a journalism major at Northwestern University. The new album made the charts, peaking at number three in *Billboard* in the spring of 1991. Though it stayed on the charts into 1992 and earned R.I.A.A. gold-record certification, it did not approach the debut record in fan appreciation. Only one single from the album made even lower chart levels, a remake of "The Ballad of Davy Crockett." The group, however, was voted Vocal Group of the Year for the second time in a row by the CMA.

The group started work on a third album, but disagreements about creative directions began to surface. The Phelps brothers wanted to get away from the back-country images in favor of more straight country renditions. Ricky Lee noted, "For me, I was a country singer more than anything; I have a country voice. I wanted to sing ballads or really sing rather than scream or holler. I like to scream, holler and get down, too, but I wanted to sing something with a different flavor."

Doug told an interviewer, "We made the decision to leave the band the night before we did it. There were no calls to record labels asking if we could have a deal. We left the band, the record label, the publicity company, everything. We were on our own."

The remaining HeadHunters regrouped by calling old friends Mark Orr and Anthony Kenney. There was no orientation problem, Kenney told Mandy Wilson. "It didn't feel strange at all. It was really natural because I've been with these guys since I was a kid."

The group completed its third album, *Rave On!,* during 1992 and it was issued by Mercury in early 1993. It made the *Billboard* Top 20 soon after, but made little progress beyond that. The group continued intensive touring during that period, playing a number of major venues as opening act for Billy Ray Cyrus. The sales of the new album, while not bad, were disappointing compared to the earlier discs, and the band left the Mercury roster by the end of 1993. It remained a concert attraction in 1994 while its representatives sought a new label alignment.

KERSHAW, DOUG: *Singer, fiddler, guitarist, songwriter. Born Louisiana, January 24, 1937.*

The Cajun sound developed by the descendants of French Canadians forcibly relocated from Canada to Louisiana centuries ago has become an important part of modern country music. Many artists have contributed to the growing influence of this music form, but no song has typified the genre better than Doug Kershaw's "Louisiana Man."

For Kershaw, who grew up in the bayou country in Louisiana, it was part of his natural heritage. The main language spoken in his house was French—he didn't start to learn English until he went to school—and the music played at family get-togethers mainly consisted of Cajun folk songs. As a child, Doug recalled going fishing and muskrat-trapping with his father in the back country of his home state.

Doug learned to play fiddle and guitar at an early age and helped introduce his younger brother Rusty (born February 2, 1940) to Cajun and country music when Rusty became old enough to pick it up. Although there were other children in the family, Rusty and Doug seemed to hit it off best musically. They practiced together and by their teens in the mid-1950s were good enough to become regular cast members on the *Louisiana Hayride* in Shreveport. They began turning out records that first made local charts and then began to gain wider attention. One result was the opportunity for the brothers to join the *Grand Ole Opry* in 1957.

That they moved to the *Opry* in a year with a seven in it seemed significant to Doug. He told La Wayne Satterfield of *Music City News* (October 1969), "It is really amazing how the number seven is constantly popping up in my life. You know I was on the Johnny Cash premier show [in the late 1960s] which was shown on television on June 7th. I recently taped a guest appearance on Hank Williams, Jr.'s television show and on the seventh take it was right. The first money I ever made was seven dollars."

Other events that fitted in included that he started school at seven, that his father killed himself that year, that Doug was the seventh child born in his family, that he signed a longterm writer's contract with BMI in 1967, that his solo recording contract was with Warner Bros. Seven Arts, and that "Louisiana Man" was the seventh song he wrote.

The two brothers interrupted their performing careers in 1958 when both volunteered for the Army at the same time. They reasoned that they were going to be drafted anyway and by enlisting together they insured they would get discharged together. That's what happened in the early 1960s and, for a time, the duo picked up as if nothing had intervened. In fact, they soon had their all-time biggest single with the release of "Louisiana Man" in 1961. The record made the top 10 in the country field and also won considerable favor from pop and folk fans too. The song, of course, has become Doug's signature song, one he has played countless times on almost every major TV show in the United States and in live concerts throughout the world.

The team of Rusty and Doug remained together for several more years after the success of "Louisiana Man" and for a while in the 1960s had several more hits on Hickory Records (which issued the LP *Rusty and Doug* in July 1964). In the mid-1960s, the brothers broke up the team after a career in which over 18 million of their records were sold.

As a solo artist, Doug continued to receive an enthusiastic welcome from pop and country fans throughout the late 1960s and into the early 1980s. However, though some of his releases made the charts he never was able to duplicate some of the recording achievements of his earlier years. His album releases on Warner Bros. sold steadily if not spectacularly. Among those LPs were *Cajun Way,* issued in late 1969, and such 1970s releases as *Spanish Moss, Doug Kershaw, Swamp Grass, Devil's Elbow, Douglas James Kershaw, Mama Kershaw's Boy, Alive and Pickin', The Ragin' Cajun,* and *Louisiana Man.* All of those still were in Warner Brothers' active catalogue at the start of the 1980s. While Doug also had a number of singles issued on the label during the 1970s, some of which made lower-chart levels, only "It Takes All Day (To Get Over Night)," from *The Ragin' Cajun* LP, became a major success.

In the mid- and late 1980s and into the 1990s, Doug remained active as a performer at Cajun and country festivals and other engagements, but did not have a major record-label affiliation. He also had many recording session opportunities. He continued to retain the high regard of his fellow instrumentalists, including fiddling star Mark O'Connor, who called Doug's playing a major influence on his career.

In the mid-1990s, Mark asked Doug to take part in his *Heroes* album project, which featured violinists who had been his childhood heroes. O'Connor noted, "I might not sound exactly like Doug Kershaw or Jean-Luc Ponty. I might not sound exactly like anybody on this album, but the spirit of their music and their playing and their technique and their emotion—everything about them has inspired and influenced me."

He recalled, "Johnny Cash was my favorite star, and I watched his TV show every week when I was eight years old. When Doug Kershaw took the stage, he had a very powerful impact on me—powerful enough for me to beg my parents for a fiddle for three years. I was already playing guitar, but the violin opened the door for me to be really inspired with music."

Commenting on the *Heroes* sessions, he said, "To see the 'Ragin' Cajun' play brought back my childhood memories. His bowing arm is so liquid that it moves like a snake. The rhythm he creates with the bow is deep into the groove and feel of the music. To see him bow both the melody and accompaniment, with his fiddle halfway down his arm, plus sing at the same time, is an incredible image. It is one that leaves a long-lasting impression."

KERSHAW, SAMMY: *Singer, guitarist. Born Kaplan, Louisiana, February 24, 1958.*

Anyone listening to Sammy Kershaw's records or watching him onstage can certainly discern a resemblance to the great George Jones. Sammy might be called a Cajun version of Jones, yet it would be hard to detect any Cajun inflections in his vocal style. At any rate, he took no offense at comparisons which noted, as in *CD Review,* that on Sammy's debut album his "soaring tenor . . . captures the George Jones ache better than any of his chart-topping peers." As *Pulse* suggested, "The man must be George Jones' illegitimate son."

Kershaw, who grew up in Kaplan, Louisiana, some twenty-five miles south of the Cajun-dominated city of Lafayette and forty miles north of the Gulf of Mexico, said his exposure to the music of Jones and other country luminaries essentially began in the cradle. "My mama used to rock me when I was a baby and sing Hank Williams. She had a real good voice and, oh man, did she love that music! She had stacks of records: Conway (Twitty), Hank Senior, Buck Owens. When I was about five, mama got her first George Jones records. I remember a little later I heard 'Things Have Gone to Pieces,' an old Jones hit. My mother bought the record, and I used to sit in the living room by myself and just play that song over and over. I've been hooked ever since."

In his preteen years, Sammy spent a lot of time outdoors roaming the nearby swamps, bayous, and woodlands of his home area. It was a satisfying life, though his family was far from affluent. But when he was eleven, tragedy struck. His father died of lung cancer and his mother had to take a job as a waitress to support him and his three siblings.

Luckily, Sammy had his grandfather as a male influence. He encouraged his grandson's musical interest, buying him a little Western Auto Tel electric guitar. Like many a future country star, he kept working until slowly he became able to play a few songs on it. He recalled making his public debut singing at a fourth-grade Christmas party in school.

When he was twelve, his mother in effect apprenticed him to a local musician named J. B. Perry. She saw it as an opportunity to have her paycheck stretch further while also keeping her son from the temptations of the teenager period. It turned out to be a good arrangement for both Sammy and Perry. Sammy was a combination gofer and supporting artist for Perry while learning firsthand what was involved in a show business career.

"It was a great experience," he remembered, one he remained involved in until he was almost twenty. "We got to open shows for just about all the Nashville stars, so I heard them all sing and I learned their songs—George Jones, B. J. Thomas, Charlie Rich . . . Cal Smith really impressed me, and Ray Charles was a big influence as well. And Mel Street—he was not one of the nicest people I ever met, but one of the hottest singers to ever hit country music. I still do songs of his like 'Borrowed Angel' and 'Lovin' on the Back Streets.'

"But I'd have to say George Jones was my biggest influence. I first met him when I was just a boy. I remember opening a show for him when I was 13 or 14. He walked onstage wearin' a pair of baby blue, handsome cowboy boots that probably cost him a thousand dollars. He was fantastic, and I got to say a few words to him. Five years later, I met him again and I was amazed that he remembered me. Then, still later on, we got to be friends and we hung out some together. I even got to sing with Lorrie Morgan [then part of Jones's band] now and then."

Given all Kershaw's contact and experience, one might have expected him to have little trouble in starting a solo career, but it didn't work out that way. From the late 1970s to the late 1980s, he had to scrounge a living with a variety of day jobs most of those years while seeking to improve his music prospects evenings and weekends. Adding to the pressures on him during that period was marriage and starting a family that numbered three children by the end of the 1980s.

Among the occupations he worked at in those years were welding, a position in a rice mill, store clerk, carpenter, and operator of a dry-cleaning business. He also tried some other show business avenues, including time as a standup comic and a stint as a disc jockey. His musical activities included singing in small clubs and honky-tonks and, for a while, as a member of a group called Blackwater, which performed wherever jobs could be found, including gigs in Wyoming and New Mexico.

Kershaw made a few independent records that won some attention from *Billboard* reviewers, but were flops otherwise. Despite setbacks, Sammy hated to give up. He noted, "I started singing in clubs when I was 12, and never really stopped. I did some hard livin' and lost everything I had a time or two in the process, but I always survived and I always came back. And I always knew music was what I wanted to do."

But finally, he had to admit he needed to pass up the sideline demands of a not too successful music effort. For one thing, there was the danger that he might lose his family. So he took a full-time job as a remodeling supervisor for Walmart Corp. at the end of the 1980s. For two years, he said, "I didn't even pick up a guitar or sing a note. It was just a sacrifice I had to make to get my life straight and my bills paid. For two years or so, I traveled all over the country remodeling Walmart stores. That first year I was only home 20 days or so. But the money was great, and it was a change I needed." One might wonder how his family ties held up when he was hardly more available at home than in previous years. But clearing money worries away was a positive act, and he stated he became closer to his family than before.

In 1990, the thought occurred to him he might do well starting his own remodeling firm. He was considering that while doing a job on a Walmart facility in Texas when the chance suddenly arose to achieve a breakthrough in his first love. A friend he knew through a Louisiana music business project had moved to Nashville and felt he could get Kershaw in some record company doors. He had Sammy send him a demo tape and an 8x10 photograph, and soon lined up an audition for Kershaw with Mercury Records.

This time the timing was right, and Kershaw was signed and given studio time to work on his first releases. This resulted in the album *Don't Go Near the Water,* which provided the debut single, "Cadillac Style." The album made the charts in 1991 and stayed on them for months. By early 1993, it was approaching platinum-sales levels, having passed R.I.A.A.'s gold-award threshold long before that. "Cadillac Style" also did very well, rising to number three in both *Billboard* and *Radio & Records.* The *R&R* peak position occurred during the week of January 10, 1992. The "Cadillac Style" video went to number one on both of the major country channels, CMT and TNN. Later that year, Sammy made the *R&R* top levels with the album title song, number eight the week of May 1, and "Yard Sale," number eight the week of August 28. He ended the year with the single "Anywhere But Here," number ten in *R&R* the week of December 18.

By then, of course, Sammy had assembled backing artists and had management people working to set up tour events around the U.S. Like any rising star, he was on the road most of the year, performing at some 220 concerts annually, concerts he was often headlining in the mid-1990s. His record and video credits kept on growing in 1993 and 1994. His single, "She Don't Know She's Beautiful," rose to number one in *Radio & Records* the week of April 15, 1993. In mid-July, the title track from his second Mercury album, *Haunted Heart,* hit number eight in *R&R* and in the fall, "Queen o' My Double Wide Trailer" was a top-10 hit in both *R&R* and *Billboard* in November and December. The album *Haunted Heart* was on the charts in the spring of 1993 and was still on the *Billboard* list seventy-three weeks later, the week of August 13, having earned a gold record award from the R.I.A.A.

His 1994 successes included the single "I Can't Reach Her Anymore," in upper levels in the spring, "National Working Woman's Holiday," which made number two in *Billboard* the week of August 6, and a remake of Pure Prairie League's "Third Rate Romance," in the *Billboard* Top 40 in September. Sammy's third album, *Feelin' Good Train,* came out in the summer, peaking at number nine in *Billboard* and with a good chance to add another gold and perhaps platinum award to his collection.

Kershaw said his dreams had finally come true, though he had begun to doubt they would be realized during his years of struggle. "Now that I've had the chance [to make it in country music] it's wonderful, and it's a relief. I don't have to wonder anymore. But every day I remind myself that if all this ended tomorrow, I could go right back to bein' a finish carpenter and I could build you one of the prettiest houses you've ever seen. It wouldn't be the end of the world if I had to go back to pouring concrete all day or doin' whatever it took to make a living. It wouldn't bother me at all, because I've already gotten to live a lot of dreams."

In early 1995, Sammy placed his Mercury Nashville single "If You're Gonna Walk, I'm Gonna Crawl" in the top 20. Late in the year, the single "Your Tattoo" was moving up the charts. In the fall the album *Sammy Kershaw—The Hits, Chapter 1* was on the hit lists, peaking at number 19 and staying on the *Billboard* list into the spring of 1996. In late spring of 1996, his single "Meant to Be" was in upper chart levels in *Billboard*. During the summer, Sammy provided the narration for a two and a half hour audio book based on the 1994 Ralph Gleason Music Book award-winning biography of Hank Williams. As Sammy detailed Hank's life for *The Legend of Hank Williams: Audio Book with Music,* he said he could feel an emotional rapport with his superstar subject since he had taken, but managed to survive, some of the destructive paths that caused Williams's early death.—A. S.

KETCHUM, HAL: *Singer, guitarist, drummer, band leader (the Alibis), songwriter. Born Greenwich, New York, April 9, 1953.*

Hal Ketchum rose to country music stardom via Austin, Texas, and his song styling seemed of a piece with the Austin movement of artists like Butch Hancock, Jerry Jeff Walker, and the like, which resulted in many articles early in his career describing him as a native of the Lone Star State. However, his route to music prominence was far more circuitous, starting in his hometown of Greenwich in upstate New York's Adirondack Mountains, with stops in Florida and Texas before he settled down as a Nashville celebrity.

His father and grandfather were both musicians, his father having played banjo in a local band and his grandfather a classically trained violinist "who moved to upstate New York and started playing square dances and had a little swing band." His father liked country music, which always has had a strong rapport with residents of rural areas in all parts of the U.S. and Canada. As Ketchum told *Radio & Records,* the only organization his father belonged to, "besides the printers' union, was the Buck Owens Fan Club."

Through his father, Hal was introduced not only to the music of Bakersfield artists like Owens and Merle Haggard, but such legendary Nashville performers as George Jones and Hank Williams. But Hal was well aware of the other elements of pop music of the 1960s and began learning to play drums. By fifteen he was part of a rhythm & blues trio that was able to get gigs in local clubs. Ketchum recalled, "My dad signed a per-

mission slip to let me play because I was underage. It was a great sociology lesson for me to sit back in a little beer joint behind a set of drums. I'd get four hours of the world going by." He observed that, "Being an R&B drummer is a very luxurious place to be. You're very protected and you get to play without any of the upfront risk."

After finishing school, he moved to Florida. He kept in touch with music in his spare time, but earned his living in other ways. He told *R&R,* "I started woodworking as a carpenter's helper when I was 17. I became real good at it—I built a lot of furniture in the '80s."

Next stop, in 1981, was Gruene, Texas, in the Austin area; again, he mainly had a 9-to-5 job in mind, but the excitement of the Austin music scene changed his plans. "The night I was moving into the house I'd bought there, I heard live music from somewhere in the distance. I got in my truck and drove into town and discovered this dance hall. I started going there regularly. On Sunday afternoons, they had great writers like Butch Hancock, Lyle Lovett, and Townes Van Zandt come in and play. It made me concentrate on playing guitar and writing songs—that place became a real school for me."

Picking up points from the Austin scene, Ketchum was soon feverishly writing new material and starting to perform in local clubs. This time he wasn't a "protected" drummer, but an upfront vocalist and guitarist. Soon he was taping some of his originals and taking trips to Nashville to seek an outlet for them. In 1986, he packaged ten of the songs on an album titled *Threadbare Alibis,* which was released on Watermelon Records in the U.S. and Line Records in Europe.

In the late 1980s, songwriter Pat Alger heard Ketchum sing at the Kerrville Folk Festival and was impressed enough to introduce Hal to an important Nashville producer, Jim Rooney. Hal noted, "I was already a fan of Rooney's. I knew he'd produced records I really respected on people like Nanci Griffith." With contacts like that, Hal felt he could move to Nashville and finally make his creative dreams come true. Once there he signed with Forerunner Music and began recording more professional demos to present his work to performers and record company executives. President Dick Whitehouse of Curb Records' country music operations heard some of the tapes and immediately knew he wanted Hal on the label. The pact was signed during 1989, and soon Ketchum was working with Jim Rooney and Allen Reynolds as coproducers on his label debut. Seven of the ten tracks were written or cowritten by Hal, but one of the other three was a country version of a song written by Reynolds, "Five O'Clock World," which had been a hit for the Vogues in the 1960s.

The album, *Past the Point of Rescue,* was released in April 1991 with the debut single "Smalltown Saturday Night." The single began climbing the charts during the summer and by September was at number two in *Bill-*

board and in upper levels on other lists, including *Radio & Records*. Aided by the single's success, the album entered lower-chart levels in late summer to begin a stay that extended well into the next year. It received a gold-record award from the R.I.A.A. in June 1992 and was still in the top 40 in *Billboard* on October 3 after fifty-eight weeks. The album spawned three more top-10 singles, "I Know Where Love Lives," number eight in *R&R* the week of January 17, 1992; the title track, number four in *R&R* April 24, 1992, and in *Billboard's* Top 10 as well; and "Five O'Clock World," number ten in *R&R* the week of July 31, 1992. All except the last provided number-one videos on TNN and CMT.

By 1991–92, Ketchum was on the tour circuit as an opener for established artists or headliners in small clubs like the Crazy Horse in Santa Ana. People who saw his shows could not fail but be impressed by the close-knit, expansive output of a band Hal called the Alibis. He organized it as a quartet, comprising himself on acoustic guitar, Scott Neubert on lead guitar and a lap slide mounted on a high-hat stand, Keith Carter on bass guitar, and Wes Starr on drums. Hal always favored smaller backing groups, whether for recording sessions or concerts. He noted, "The dynamic possibilities are more obvious with fewer players and I grew up listening to my dad's record collection which had a lot of the old quartets. So it was a natural musical move for me." When he sang, though, his voice had a commanding timbre and a quality one critic called "a subtle smokiness."

For his second Curb album, Hal again teamed up with Rooney and Reynolds and the album, *Sure Love,* and the single of its title track (cowritten by Ketchum and G. Burr) both came out in September 1992. The single reached top levels in both *Billboard* and *R&R* late in the year, peaking at number four in *R&R* the week of December 18. The album was on *Billboard* charts for many months in 1993 and 1994, peaking only at thirty-six. But more singles hits came from it, including "Hearts Are Gonna Roll" (cowritten by Ketchum and Ronnie Scaife), which reached number two in *R&R* the week of April 30, 1993, and top 5 in *Billboard,* and "Mama Knows the Highway," top 10 in both those publications and others as well during the summer of 1993.

Late in 1993, the single "Someplace Far Away (Careful What You're Dreaming)," written by Ketchum, was on the charts, moving to top levels in 1994. In the spring and summer of 1994, the single "(Tonight We Just Might) Fall in Love Again," cowritten by Ketchum and A. Anderson, was a chart hit. During those months, the album *Every Little Word* was on the mid-hit chart levels.

At one point during those years, Ketchum commented on his rationale in assembling a new album. Whatever is chosen, he commented, had to meet certain standards agreed upon by artist and producer. Typically,

the songs "come from a variety of experiences, some from within (in the case of an artist-written song), some from the simple viewpoint of a musician's love of a well-written song."

He commented to *Billboard* in late 1992 that he preferred to play small venues as a headliner than co-bill with others. But he agreed it was a valuable experience working with stars like Wynonna and Kathy Mattea. His prime hope, though, was not to rush things, to establish a slow growth pattern "that will ensure that I can do this for a long time and do it the way that I want to do it. My other professional goal is to never be a slave to this career."

Every Little Word, which peaked at thirty-one in *Billboard* in 1994, stayed on the list into the summer of 1995. For part of the time, his MCG/Curb single "Stay Forever," cowritten by Hal and B. Tench, was in upper chart positions, spending several weeks in the top 10 during May and June. Hal's activities during the year included joining other *Grand Ole Opry* stars on November 30 in taping a tribute to the *Opry's* 70th anniversary. The program was aired on CBS-TV in January 1996. In April, Hal was one of the artists featured at the *Merle Watson Memorial Festival* (hosted by Doc Watson) in Wilkesboro, North Carolina. During the summer of 1996, his MCG/Curb album *Hal Ketchum—The Hits* was issued, preceded by the single "Hang in There Superman" (cowritten by Ketchum and Roger Cook).—A. S.

KILGORE, MERLE: *Singer, guitarist, songwriter, disc jockey, actor, music industry executive. Born Chickasha, Oklahoma, August 9, 1934.*

As a performer, writer, and executive, Merle Kilgore had both direct and behind-the-scenes impact on the development of country music in the decades after World War II. He achieved a number of hits as a singer and contributed to the success of other artists by providing them with successful songs or, in some cases, with initial encouragement to move ahead in the country field.

He was born in Oklahoma, but his family soon moved to Shreveport, Louisiana, where he learned to play guitar at an early age and was awarded his first stint as a disc jockey on station KENT in Shreveport. This was the first of a number of DJ positions on such other Louisiana stations as KNOE, Monroe, and KZEA, Springhill. While in his teens, he also started to establish a reputation as a performer with Louisiana fans and already was writing original material that he included in his act. Before long, other artists were playing some of his songs, too.

During those years he also made his first acquaintance with the Hank Williams family. As he told Ray Waddell of *Billboard* in 1989, "I was about 14 years old at the time and they wanted me to ride around the courthouse square and ballyhoo the show while Hank and the others ate breakfast. We traveled in an old Packard limousine with a P.A. system mounted on the roof. I was scared to death because I didn't have a driver's license, and I didn't shift very well."

As he drove around he talked in a rapid, high-pitched voice, urging people to see "Hank Williams, in person, with the Drifting Cowboys." Then he saw Hank outside the diner waving him over. " 'Boy,' he said to me, 'Speak lower and slower.' That's why I speak with a low voice today." Later he became a gofer for Hank on the *Louisiana Hayride* program and recalled seeing Hank's three-week-old son, Hank, Jr., in 1949, a harbinger of things to come.

While still in high school, Merle was added to the *Louisiana Hayride* cast. The show, broadcast over station KWKH, Shreveport, at the time was almost as important as the *Grand Ole Opry* in the country field. An excellent guitarist by then, he accompanied many of the best-known performers on the show. In 1952, he also was featured on station KFAZ-TV in Monroe. He continued to perform on the *Hayride* while starring on KFAZ from 1952 to 1954. The year 1952 also brought his first guest spot on the *Grand Ole Opry* and on the *Big D Jamboree* in Dallas.

At first, after finishing high school, Merle decided to continue his education, entering Louisiana Tech in 1952. He stayed in college a year, then left in 1953 to work days for the American Optical Company while pursuing his musical career in the evening. In 1954, he achieved major success with his composition "More and More," a national hit for such disparate artists as Guy Lombardo and Webb Pierce. The response to that number encouraged him to concentrate all his efforts on the music field from then on.

Throughout the rest of the 1950s, he maintained a full schedule, appearing on the *Hayride* regularly, at country nightclubs throughout the region, doing his DJ chores, and writing steadily. Among the songs for which he wrote both words and music were "It Can't Rain All the Time" and "Seeing Double" (1954); "Funny Feeling" (1955); "I've Got a Good Thing Going" (1958); "Tom Dooley, Jr.," "Hang Doll" (1958); and "Baby Rocked Her Dolly," "It Will Be My First Time," and "Jimmie Bring Sunshine" (1959). In 1959, he had a singles hit with "Dear Mama" and also provided Johnny Horton with a best-selling song, "Johnny Reb."

Merle also cowrote songs with a number of others over the years. His 1950s collaborations included such songs as "Everybody Needs a Little Loving" (1955); "Take the Last Look," "The Wild One" (1957); "Swing Daddy Swing," "Little Pig," "Change of Heart," "You Don't Want to Hold Me," "Old Enough to Love," "We're Talking It Over" (1958); and "I Took a Trip to the Moon." One person he penned some numbers with in those years was a Springhill teenager named Joe Stampley, who hung around the studios where Kilgore was a DJ. He encouraged Stampley and helped line up his first record contract. Eventually, Stampley became one of country music's top stars of the 1970s.

Kilgore moved into the 1960s with a major hit, in the U.S. country top 10 during 1960, his composition "Love Has Made You Beautiful," on Starday Records. (During the 1950s, he recorded for D Records and Imperial.) Two years later he teamed with Claude King to write "Wolverton Mountain." King's single of the song was a number-one hit on Columbia Records in 1962 and the tune has since been recorded by dozens of other artists. In 1963, Merle cowrote another classic, this time with June Carter. Titled "Ring of Fire," the song was a smash hit for June's future husband, Johnny Cash, rising to number one on country charts and doing well on the pop charts, too.

Merle continued to perform widely on concerts and on TV as the 1960s went by. His engagements included appearances at the Hollywood Bowl in California, New York's Carnegie Hall, and as a headliner of a number of shows in Las Vegas and Reno. Although not placing his own recordings in the top 10 after 1960, he kept turning out discs that sometimes made lower-chart levels. Until the mid-1960s, he was associated with Starday, which issued the LP *Merle Kilgore,* in January 1964. He was represented on Mercury briefly, including the LP *Merle Kilgore* issued in January 1966. For a time, in the mid-1960s, he signed with Epic Records, then, in 1968, was affiliated with Ashley Records.

His association with the Williams family took a new turn in the mid-1960s, when Audrey Williams sought his services for her son's concerts. Merle recalled, "I started opening for Hank, Jr., in 1964 when he was 12 years old. For 21 years I was his opening act."

One of his first recordings for Epic was "Nevada Smith," the title song for a western film in which he starred. Before that, he had begun his acting career on film in *Country Music on Broadway.* His six foot, four inch frame lent itself well to western casting, and his mid-1960s credits included a leading role in *Five Card Stud,* in which Debbie Reynolds had the female lead.

Among Merle's other activities, he headed several music publishing firms during the 1960s and continued to spend much of his time in behind-the-scenes work in the 1970s. There were still occasional releases of his material in the early 1970s, such as the Hilltop LP *Ring of Fire.* By the latter part of the decade, though, he was without a recording contract, but had widened his responsibilities for Hank, Jr.'s, operations.

In the second half of 1975, Hank's career had been interrupted by his near-fatal fall on Ajax Mountain in Montana. Merle told Waddell, "I was out of work then, so George Jones gave me a job at [his Nashville nightclub] Possum Holler as the singing host. It was great for me because I got to keep in contact with everyone in the music business, and it also led to a lot of extra bookings from visiting club owners. It was a high profile gig."

After Williams recuperated, he almost immediately sought his friend Merle out. It was late 1976, Merle remembered, when Hank came into the Possum Holler club one night and told him, "Pack your bags, brother. You're moving to Alabama. Let's get the show on the road."

With Merle on board, Hank began to rebuild his career, and as time went by, Merle was asked to take over more and more of the backstage responsibilities. Finally, in the mid-1980s, Hank told Merle he wanted to consolidate his activities in Paris, Tennessee. Hank had also decided to replace his previous manager. "Hank said to me, 'Merle, I've been thinking, it's time you started making the big bucks. You're going to be my manager.'

"My new career began on April 6, 1986, when I took over as personal manager of Hank and executive VP of Hank Williams, Jr., Enterprises. We sold Hank's properties in Alabama, renovated the nightclub in Paris for offices, built the store [Kaw-Liga Korners] and the museum [Hank's Collectibles] and moved in on July 3, 1986."

At the time, Merle was on the roster of Warner Brothers Records, but from then into the 1990s he was inactive as a recording artist, devoting his energies to business and industry matters. The latter activities included election to the Country Music Association Board of Directors at the end of the 1980s, a post he still held into the 1990s.

KING, PEE WEE: *Singer, accordionist, band leader (Golden West Cowboys), songwriter, publisher, booking agent. Born Wisconsin, February 18, 1914. Elected to Country Music Hall of Fame in 1974.*

Raised in Wisconsin and later a permanent resident of Louisville, Kentucky, Pee Wee King probably will always be best known as cowriter of "Tennessee Waltz," though his activities and contributions to country and western music embrace a multitude of accomplishments. But his 1946 composition not only provided hit records for Patti Page and a number of other artists, it became the state song of the residence of the *Grand Ole Opry,* a show on which Pee Wee also starred for over a decade with his Golden West Cowboys.

King, whose original name was Frank Anthony Kuczynski, grew up in Milwaukee in a family that valued music. His father, who played ocarina and fiddle for dancers and parties in northern Wisconsin, encouraged him to play instruments. Before young Frank finished at Bay View High School in 1932, he already was playing public dates as a fiddler and accordionist. In 1932, he studied mechanical drafting at Vocational Trade School in Milwaukee, but music was too enticing. When the call came to join the cast of the WRJN *Badger State Barn Dance* in 1933, he jumped at the chance.

He formed his own band, which originally played some country and square dance material but began to add western-style music, particularly after Gene Autry asked him to bring his band to the *Gene Autry Show* in Louisville, Kentucky, in 1934, the city Pee Wee later chose as home. He recalled in the CMA *Country Music Close Up* in May 1976, "So I got into the Western end of the business. But I cut my eyeteeth on what they call country music by listening to a band led by Clayton McMichen."

By the mid-1930s, King had named his band the Golden West Cowboys, a famous name in country music annals, whose alumni include such greats as Ernest Tubb and Eddy Arnold. The band joined the *Midday Round Up* on station WNOX in Knoxville, a show Pee Wee (who at five feet seven inches was the shortest member of the group) headed for a number of years even while he and his band became regulars on the *Grand Ole Opry.* They were asked to perform on the *Opry* in 1936 and were regulars from 1937 until the late 1940s. Besides the band's *Opry* work, it was featured in country shows from one end of the United States to the other and, though the group was generally back in Nashville on weekends for the *Opry,* in between it was constantly on the move from one one-night-stand to another.

Pee Wee not only was building a national reputation with country fans with his group's sound, but was also steadily turning out a growing list of original songs, some of which became band standards in the 1940s. The song that was to become his prime trademark finally reached fruition in 1946, though it had been in the repertoire after a fashion for years before that.

The catalyst was Henry Ellis (Redd) Stewart, who had joined the group in the early 1940s as a multitalented sideman (guitar, fiddle, piano). As King recalled for the *Country Music Closeup,* it occurred while Stewart and Pee Wee were sitting in the band's luggage truck during a tour. "It was a Friday night in 1946 and the luggage truck was the easiest place to concentrate on listening to the radio. Bill Monroe's 'Kentucky Waltz' was playing on the radio. Redd said, 'You know, it's odd; we make a living in Tennessee, but nobody's ever written a Tennessee waltz that we know of.' And so we took the old melody that we were using as our theme— the 'No Name Waltz'—and Redd started writing the lyrics on the back of a matchbook cover. And we kept putting it together, putting it together."

But it wasn't until some time later, 1948, in fact, that "Tennessee Waltz" swept the nation. By then King had a show of his own on station WAVE and WAVE-TV in Louisville, which he began in 1947 and continued heading until 1957. The year was 1948 and singles of the song by King, for several years an RCA recording artist, and Cowboy Copas made the country top 10. But the version of the song by popular singer Patti Page did even better, reaching number one on the national pop charts.

He continued to add to his credits as the 1950s went along, making the charts with such singles as "Slow-Poke," one of his originals that reached number one in 1951, "Silver and Gold" in 1952, and "Bimbo" in 1954. Many more of his compositions showed up on country charts throughout the 1950s and in the 1960s, either recorded by him or other performers. In the early 1960s, for instance, Jo Stafford had a major pop hit with Pee Wee's song "You Belong to Me." In 1964, he had a top-10 country hit with another of his classic compositions, "Bonaparte's Retreat," a song that has served as a basis for hit singles for quite a few others since then.

As of the mid-1970s, his total compositions exceeded 400. From 1950 through 1955, his group had a stranglehold on the best country band title, being named to that spot throughout that period by both *Billboard* and *Cash Box* magazines.

King remained active on the movie scene, too, from the late 1930s into the 1950s. His initial appearance was in Gene Autry's *Gold Mine in the Sky*, and he took part in other films by Autry as well as working with such other western movie notables as Johnny Mack Brown and Charles Starrett.

Pee Wee's TV show was televised nationally from Louisville from 1955 to 1957 and later he had similar coverage from Cleveland on ABC. In fact, in the late 1950s and early 1960s, for a while King had four major television shows going at the same time. In 1962 he decided the grind was too rugged and gave up all of them, though he continued to make personal appearances. His recording activities also slowed down in the 1960s. His association with RCA had ended in 1959 when he moved to Todd Records. In the mid-1960s he made some recordings for Starday.

He formed a new band in 1967 as part of "Pee Wee King's Country-Western Hoedown," which performed on station WMAS-TV in Louisville. In 1969, he disbanded that group and essentially retired from the active performing side of things. He remained active on the business side, though, packaging country & western shows throughout the 1970s for engagements across the United States and Canada. The main emphasis was on providing shows for the county fair circuit.

In 1970, King was inducted into the Nashville Songwriters Association's Songwriters Hall of Fame. His contributions to country & western music for over four decades were further recognized by his peers in 1974, when he was elected to the Country Music Hall of Fame. King, a longtime supporter of industry organizations, was named to a two-year term as a member of the CMA Board of Directors in 1975 and later served on the board of the Country Music Foundation. His activities as a performer tapered off in the 1980s, and by the 1990s he essentially was in retirement as an enter-

tainer. He continued to play a behind-the-scenes-role as a participant in industry affairs, although in the mid-1990s his contributions were limited by health problems.

The editors of a special issue of *Life* magazine on country music in September 1994 included him on their list of "The 100 most Important People in the History of Country." Most of his recordings were out of print in the mid-1990s, but one exception was the Longhorn Records album *The Legendary Pee Wee King*. Another was the massive 6 CD collection prepared by Germany's Bear Family Records. This comprised 151 songs cut for RCA and Bullet Records between 1946 and 1948 including the original versions of "Tennessee Waltz," "Slow Poke," and "Bonaparte's Retreat."

KRAUSS, ALISON: *Singer, fiddler, band leader (Union Station), songwriter, record producer. Born Champaign, Illinois, July 23, 1971.*

With a wondrous touch on the fiddle, a voice that could give new expression to the high, lonesome sound of bluegrass, and a willingness to share the spotlight with her highly skilled band members, Alison Krauss set new standards for country, bluegrass, and folk music in the 1990s that dramatically expanded the audience for all of those art forms. At the same time she reflected a refreshing approach to the influence on creativity of massive entertainment conglomerates by resisting the blandishments of megabuck record firms in favor of less restrictive smaller organizations.

Growing up in the university town of Champaign, Illinois, where her father sold real estate (though he was a psychologist by training) and her mother an illustrator and painter, she demonstrated amazing skill on the violin when she was only five years old. Her parents saw to it that she continued taking lessons in classical music, amid expectations by instructors she might someday become one of the world's top violin prodigies. But she became interested in more popular ways of playing the instrument and, starting with a victory in a local fiddle contest when she was eight, went on to become state champion at eleven.

She recalled that until becoming exposed to bluegrass styles at twelve, she enjoyed competing "but not practicing." Bluegrass changed her outlook. Once she fell in love with it she didn't mind practicing; in fact, she enjoyed devoting as much time as possible to polishing her skills. At fourteen, she joined a local Champaign band called Union Station. Her addition brought rave notices from critics with greater opportunities for performing and, in a short time, the group became known as Union Station, featuring Alison Krauss.

After a sensational appearance at the Newport Folk Festival, the fifteen-year-old Krauss was signed to record a solo album for Rounder Records, *Too Late to Cry*, released in 1987. The sessions were held in Nashville where she was backed by such top studio musicians as Sam Bush and Jerry Douglas, who were amazed at her mastery of her instrument and other musical talents. Instead of pursuing her musical career full bore after that, she decided to keep it as a part-time activity while she attended the University of Illinois as a music education major. She was accepted as a freshman at the University at sixteen, after having completed only her first two years of high school.

After her solo debut, she wanted an album to showcase her band. The result was *Two Highways,* which featured Adam Steffey on mandolin, Barry Bales on standup bass, Ron Block on banjo, and Dan Tyminski on guitar and vocals. By the age of nineteen she had decided she was ready to take up performing as a full-time occupation, and had moved to Nashville where she completed a second solo album, *I've Got That Old Feeling.* Singles and videos of the title track (written by Sidney Cox) and "Steel Rails" received widespread radio and TV play, which helped put the album on *Billboard* charts in 1990. Meanwhile, Alison was increasingly asked to provide vocal and instrumental support on albums of many top names in the country field. Her personal credits included an acclaimed role in the opening segments of the 1991 Country Music Association Awards telecast and the first of many guest appearances on such major TV programs as TNN's *Nashville Now* and *American Music Shop.*

In the voting for the 1990 Grammy Awards (announced on the TV show of February 20, 1991), *I've Got That Old Feeling* was named Best Bluegrass Recording. The album's title-track video reached number one on Country Music Television and got heavy rotation on the Nashville Network. "Steel Rails" also won heavy rotation on both CMT and TNN. After those successes, she insisted on bringing Union Station in as an equal partner, not a backup band, stressing that the band members all contributed in creative decisions. For the next album by Alison and Union Station, *Every Time You Say Goodbye,* issued by Rounder in 1992, Steffey, Bales, and Block were joined by guitarist Tim Stafford. Another excellent collection, this did even better with record buyers than its predecessor while winning her a second Grammy as 1992 Best Bluegrass Recording. The first single and video from the album, "New Fool" (also written by Sidney Cox), won heavy rotation on CMT and TNN as did follow-up number, "Heartstrings."

While Alison downplayed her abilities, telling writer J. D. Considine, "I don't consider myself a virtuoso at all. There are plenty of people better than me," her country music peers typically sang her praises. Pam Tillis said, "You have your great stylists without great voices and you have great voices that aren't necessarily great singers. As far as I can tell God let Alison Krauss have it all in a big way." *Rolling Stone* editors concurred, dubbing her "a world class fiddle player whose haunting vocals recall the young Dolly Parton."

Fiddler par excellence Mark O'Connor told Tony Scherman for a feature article in the *New York Times* ("Once a 'Fiddlin' Teen,' She's Now in Demand," Arts & Leisure section, April 26, 1994), "Alison has created a beautiful style that is above all complementary—to her singing, to her band, to the songs she picks. Everything she plays—her rhythm, her tone, her notechoice—balances her band so great.

"The thing is, there's so much more to her than her fiddling. An amazing record producer, an angelic voice, a great bandleader, leading probably the best bluegrass band to come along in 20 years."

Alison continued to grow in stature as the 1990s went by. Her mid-1990s appearances included a program with Vince Gill on *Austin City Limits* and a featured spot on the ABC-TV *Women in Country* special as well as on the Country Music Hall of Fame 25th Anniversary show on CBS-TV. She also took part in *Grand Ole Opry* broadcasts, representing the first bluegrass performer to be made a cast member of the *Opry* in some thirty years. Her session credits as musician, backing vocalist, or guest performer included work with Vince Gill, Mark Chesnutt, Nanci Griffith, and Michelle Shocked. In early 1994, between tour dates in which she and her band opened for Garth Brooks in major venues around the U.S., she flew to support a new joint album being prepared as a follow-up to their 1987 *Trio* success by Dolly Parton, Emmylou Harris, and Linda Ronstadt. In late 1994, the band Shenandoah's debut on its new label, Liberty, featured a guest appearance by her on the title track, "In the Vicinity of the Heart," which became a hit single in early 1995.

Her own recording career continued to prosper with the gospel album, *I Know Who Holds Tomorrow,* made in conjunction with the Cox Family band rather than Union Station. Rounder reported in the spring of 1994 it had shipped over 100,000 copies of the album, compared to its typical "best-seller" total of around 20,000. During the year she started laying down tracks with Union Station for their next album project. In early 1995, Rounder issued the album *Now That I've Found You: A Collection,* which quickly rose to the top levels in *Billboard.* Nestled in the number-two spot in June for several weeks, it already had accumulated sales well past R.I.A.A. platinum requirements, making it the most successful album ever in the bluegrass field. At the same time, Alison and Union Station had a top-10 single in *Billboard,* "When You Say Nothing at All."

A young, wonderfully talented performer like Krauss brought big dollar signs to the eyes of executives in major record firms, who continually sought to draw her to their rosters. In countless instances, small companies like Rounder had seen potential superstars siphoned off by enticements from the majors; in Alison's case, at least as of 1997, this appeared the exception.

The reason, she indicated to Scherman, was artistic freedom. "I really like those guys at Rounder. I've got everything I want. A major label could sell a lot more records, make me a lot better known. But although these dates for Garth Brooks have been an incredible opportunity for us and for bluegrass, I'd never want the kind of fame Garth has. Because . . . it's not *music* anymore. I couldn't play on stages that big night after night. You can't hear, you don't know if you're singing in tune. When you get offstage, your ears are going *bop-bop-bop-bop*. Garth's whole thing is very appealing. But it's a show, it's totally different from what we do."

In Alison's first ever inclusion among nominees for Country Music Association Awards, she ended up a finalist in four categories. When the winners were announced on the October 1995 telecast, she turned out to score a sweep of all four entries. She was presented with the trophies for the Horizon Award, Female Vocalist of the Year, Single of the Year with her band Union Station for "When You Say Nothing at All," and Vocal Duet of the Year with Shenandoah for "Somewhere in the Vicinity of the Heart." She was less successful in the Academy of Country Music Voting announced in April 1996. She was a finalist for Top New Female Vocalist of the Year, but Shania Twain won that award.

She continued to be quite successful on the concert circuit, though, including a tour of the UK in the spring of 1996. During the summer she contributed to Dolly Parton's new album, *Treasures,* issued in the fall. The first single from the album was a duet with Dolly titled "Just When I Needed You." In the spring of 1997 her next album with Union Station, *So Long So Wrong,* was on hit lists.

KRISTOFFERSON, KRIS: *Singer, guitarist, songwriter, actor. Born Brownsville, Texas, June 22, 1937.*

A multitalented individual, Kris Kristofferson could achieve brilliant results in varied entertainment fields when he concentrated on his work. The problem was that at times he seemed to spread himself too thin and that, combined with some of his personal problems, caused phases of his career—particularly in songwriting and live concert work—to be distinctly erratic. But taken as a whole, his work in country music provided some of the finest original songs ever written.

The son of a two-star general, Kris moved to many different places during his childhood and youth, a pattern that contributed to a somewhat disjointed feeling at times. Born in Texas and having spent some of his childhood years in the South, he gained a natural affinity for country songs, though for a time he was more interested in pursuing a literary career than a musical one. He did learn guitar and could play quite well by the time he enrolled in Pomona College in Claremont, California. There he demonstrated considerable athletic ability, lettering in football and soccer, an achievement that helped make him a candidate for a Rhodes scholarship at Oxford University in England. The scholarship calls for both academic and athletic prowess and Kris was a fine student of literature, at one point winning the top four out of twenty prizes in the *Atlantic Monthly* collegiate short story contest. At Oxford, one of his major efforts was the study of the work of William Blake.

When he began his work there in the late 1950s, his primary aim was to become a novelist. However, by the time he completed his work, he felt depressed about his abilities. When he returned to the United States at the start of the 1960s, he had no real idea of what career to pursue. He had started to write songs, but was uncertain of their quality and soon took one way of dropping out: he enlisted in the U.S. Army and spent most of the first half of the decade in uniform. He became an officer, going through Ranger school, parachute jump school, and pilot training. He enjoyed flying and became an excellent pilot, specializing in helicopters.

However, in other ways, it was a destructive period for him. He told an interviewer in 1970, "For a time in the Army I quit writing. I nearly ended up destroying myself. I was drinking all the time, doing all kinds of reckless things. I totaled two cars and had four motorcycle accidents. But I had to write. I could no more not write than I could not breathe. It is a part of me." Unfortunately, a craving for alcohol also seemed to be a part of him and was to plague his career a number of times in the future.

After leaving the service in 1965, he toyed with the idea of accepting an appointment to teach English literature at West Point. But he had felt the pull of songwriting and decided to settle in Nashville and try to make the grade in that field. It was to prove a four-year, often desperate operation. He moved into a tenement and made the rounds of publishing houses, meeting with consistent turndowns. To stay alive and, by the end of the 1960s, support a wife and two children as well, he took any work he could find, including night janitor at Columbia Records Studios and day bartender at Nashville's Tally-Ho Tavern. Both jobs had the advantage of providing contacts with the country-music industry, the Tavern being a hangout for many established and aspiring songwriters. At times during those years he earned money by working as a laborer or flying helicopters to offshore oil rigs in the Gulf States area. Eventually, the strain proved too great for his marriage and a separation ensued.

Some of his experiences were reflected in his hit songs of later years. His loves and hitchhiking days are recalled in "Me and Bobby McGee": "Busted flat in Baton Rouge/Headin' for the trains/Feelin' just as faded as my jeans." The loneliness of the slum years appears in one of the songs from his 1971 hit LP, *The Silver Tongued Devil and I,* where, in "To Beat the Devil," he sings of the days when "Failure had me locked on the wrong side of the door . . . no one stood beside me but the shadow on the floor."

In 1969, Kris's persistence finally paid off. A long-time admirer of Johnny Cash, he practically lived outside the studio where Cash's network TV show was being taped. He pestered anyone of note who came there to look at his material, and finally Roger Miller gave in and agreed to consider it. Roger decided to record "Bobby McGee," which became a country hit and encouraged cover releases by many other artists from both pop and country genres.

Cash himself became a fan of Kristofferson's, featuring such songs as "Sunday Morning Comin' Down" on his show, referring to Kris as one of the new, great talents, and having Kris as a guest several times in 1969 and 1970. Johnny's single of "Sunday Morning" became a hit in 1969. Meanwhile, Janis Joplin decided to include her styling of "Bobby McGee" in her new and, as it turned out, last album. The single became one of the major pop hits in 1969, selling over a million copies and earning a gold record. It brought similar success to her LP *Pearl*.

By 1970, Kris was considered one of country music's most promising artists for the 1970s. That year the *New York Times* (July 26, 1970) ran an article noting that he was "the hottest thing in Nashville right now—and if you're hot in Nashville, man, you're hot everywhere." He had signed with Monument Records in 1969 and in 1970, his debut album, *Kris Kristofferson*, came out and was soon followed by *Me and Bobby McGee*. At the same time many artists eagerly checked out his new songs to turn out covers. Many of them recorded his "Help Me Make It Through the Night," but it was Sammi Smith who had the number-one selling version. The Nashville Songwriter's Association recognized his achievements by voting him Songwriter of the Year in 1970. In 1971, he got his first Grammy Award for "Help Me Make It Through the Night," voted Best Country Song.

During 1970, Kris worked on his first film score, for Dennis Hopper's *The Last Movie*. On June 23, 1970, he made his first professional appearance as a performer at a "name" club, the Los Angeles Troubadour. It was the first of countless live concerts which took him to every state in the union and many other parts of the world during the decade. From the early 1970s on, most of those shows also featured Rita Coolidge, who became Mrs. Kristofferson.

His concert work the first part of the 1970s was excellent, but for a time in the mid-1970s, he seemed to become dispirited, partly because of an increasing preoccupation with movie acting. Late in the decade, starting with his tours of 1977, he seemed to find renewed interest in working in front of an audience. Part of his problem, he told an interviewer in August 1977, had been the continued use of liquor as a crutch. He claimed

his resurgence was due to cutting back on that: "It feels weird out there. I mean I have to get used to singing sober again. It's like singing in the daylight or something. But it's coming."

Kris's own single of "Bobby McGee" finally became a chart hit in September 1971, helped by the success of a new LP, *The Silver Tongued Devil and I*, which made the charts in July 1971. Joining those favorites was a new single, "Loving Her Was Easier (Than Anything I'll Ever Do Again)," which became a bestseller during that summer. In 1972, he gained a gold record for "The Silver Tongued Devil" and had two new albums on the charts, *Border Lord* and *Jesus Was a Capricorn*, plus another chart single, "Josie." In 1973, he had another singles hit with "Why Me, Lord" (backed with "Help Me"), and he also released the single "Jesse Younger" backed with "Give It Time to Be Tender."

There was a gap of almost two years before he had a new solo album, but in 1973 he and Rita Coolidge joined for a dual-artist release on A&M Records, *Full Moon*. In 1974 he was represented on Monument by *Spooky Lady's Nightmare* and *Breakaway* (the latter another collection with Rita Coolidge), which contained some interesting material but seemed to indicate a creative slowdown from his earlier work. Things picked up a bit with his 1975 LP, *Who's to Bless and Who's to Blame*, but regressed once more in 1976 with *Surreal Things*. However, very little of his new work in the second half of the decade measured up to what he had done the previous five or six years. Among the albums were the soundtrack from his starring vehicle (with Barbra Streisand) *A Star Is Born* in 1976; a "best of" release, *Songs of Kristofferson* in 1977, *Easter Island* and *Natural Act* (with Rita Coolidge on A&M Records) in 1978; and *Shake Hands with the Devil* in 1979. *Easter Island* was the most disappointing of all his album releases, with little of his original work coming close to such earlier classics as "Bobby McGee," "The Pilgrim," "Chapter 33," or any of dozens of previous triumphs. Still, the quality improved markedly in his 1979 collection, bringing hopes for better things in the 1980s.

During the mid- and late 1970s, Kris recorded many duets with Rita Coolidge, including such singles as "Rain" backed with "What 'Cha Gonna Do" in 1974; "Lover Please" backed with "Slow Down," and "Sweet Susannah/We Must Have Been Out of Our Minds" in 1975. Kris and Rita won two Grammy Awards for Best Vocal Performance by a Duo, the first in 1973 for "From the Bottle to the Bottom" and the second in 1975 for "Lover Please."

One reason for the slump in songwriting was perhaps traceable to his movie work. There he had proven himself one of the finest new actors to come along in the 1970s. His initial major film breakthrough was in the movie *Pat Garrett and Billy the Kid*, released in mid-1973. He played Billy in the movie, which costarred Bob Dylan. From then on, a long series of movies came out featuring his talents as both a dramatic and comic actor. They included *Cisco Pike, Alice Doesn't Live Here Anymore, Bring Me the Head of Alfredo Garcia, Blume in Love, Vigilante Force, The Sailor Who Fell from Grace with the Sea, Semi-Tough* (costarring Burt Reynolds and giving some opportunity for Kris to use his athletic skills), *Convoy, A Star Is Born, North Dallas Forty, Heaven's Gate,* and in 1981, *Rollover,* with Jane Fonda. He won a number of awards for acting, including being named Best Actor by the Foreign Press Association for *A Star Is Born.*

By the end of the 1970s, his marriage to Rita Coolidge had gone sour and they separated. Late in 1979, Willie Nelson turned out an album of Kristofferson songs, and the two toured together during the 1979–80 winter concert season. At the start of 1980, Kris's single "Prove It to You Just One More Time" was on country charts. In the early 1980s, Columbia issued his LP *To the Bone.* In early 1982, after the drastic early 1980s recording industry recession caused most labels to reduce their backlists, only that LP, *Easter Island,* and *A Star Is Born* remained in print.

Things began to pick up again in Kris's career in the mid-1980s. With old friend Willie Nelson he appeared in the hit 1985 film *Songwriter,* and the two collaborated on the soundtrack album, released on the CBS label. It also was the gestation period for a new superstar group comprising Kris, Willie, Waylon Jennings, and Johnny Cash. They called themselves the Highwaymen after the Jimmy Webb composition that became the title track for their new album, *The Highwayman.* The album, issued by Columbia in 1985, became a smash hit and the title song was nominated by the Country Music Association voters for 1985 Single of the Year. Kris performed on five of the album tracks, "Highwayman," "The Last Cowboy Songs," "Desperados Waiting for a Train," "Big River," and "Welfare Line." Besides "Highwayman," Columbia issued "Desperados Waiting for a Train" as a single.

One reward of the group's rapport with country and pop fans for Kris took the form of a new recording contract with Polygram Records. His Polygram debut, *Repossessed,* came out in 1986, followed by three singles in 1987, "They Killed Him/Anthem 84," "Love Is the Way/This Old Road," and "El Coyote/They Killed Him."

At the start of the 1990s after settling a lawsuit over the Highwaymen name with an earlier folk group (whose members were asked to take part in the upcoming concert tour), the foursome reunited for the *Highwayman 2* album on CBS. Unlike the first project, it was decided to accompany the album release with an extensive tour, representing the first time all four stars took the stage together. The tour, which had dates extending into 1992, proved an enormous success, drawing large enthusiastic crowds to every venue the group played. Kris contributed to seven of the album tracks, "Silver Stallion," "Born and Raised in Black and White," "We're All in Your Corner," "American Remains," "Angels Love Bad Men," "Songs That Make a Difference," and "Living Legends."

While the Highwaymen tour proceeded in 1990, Kris's second solo album was issued by Polygram, *Third World Warrior.* In 1991, Columbia/Legacy issued a comprehensive retrospective of Kristofferson's career titled *Kris Kristofferson: Singer/Songwriter.* The set covered essentially all of his most important outputs with one half presenting seventeen renditions by Kristofferson and the other containing nineteen recordings of Kris's compositions by other artists.

In 1994 the foursome started work on another Highwaymen album, which was issued in the spring of 1995 on the Liberty Records label. Called *The Road Goes on Forever,* it made the *Billboard* list soon after its release, though it didn't rise as high as the two earlier ones had, both of which were best-sellers. In August 1995, Kris also had a new solo album out on Justice Records, *A Moment of Forever.* Returning to his acting activities, he agreed to play the role of a corrupt Texas sheriff in a new movie directed by John Sayles. The film, *Lone Star,* issued in mid-1996, won high praise from major U.S. movie critics.

The Highwaymen concerts caused many industry people to consider again what the contributions of the four stars to the evolution of country music had been. In Kristofferson's case, Bill Ivey, executive director of the Country Music Foundation, told Robert Hilburn of the *Los Angeles Times,* he had brought more of an urban outlook to what had been a predominantly rural art form. "Kris wrote about the everyday concerns of adults living in a kind of urban society and dealing with problems of relationships in really tough, hard-edged songs. As a writer, he probably had as great an impact on Nashville as Hank Williams did.

"That's the quality most needed in Nashville today—the hard-hitting kind of against-the-grain, never-say-die spirit that Kristofferson and Cash and the others had."

lang, k.d.: *Singer, guitarist, band leader (the reclines), songwriter. Born Consort, Alberta, Canada, November 2, 1961.*

In the 1980s and 1990s, there was no doubt that the boundaries of country music had expanded to include a wide range of innovative newcomers, but more than a few members of the industry, as well as the public, looked askance at some of the more unusual performers such as Lyle Lovett and k.d. lang (of lowercase fame). With her rich alto voice and highly skilled country-based backup group, the reclines, lang could deliver with fervor and/or humor material that undoubtedly met country guidelines, but was also equally at home with pop or jazz stylings.

Lovett, of course, fell into the same general classification and, like k.d., his appearance certainly wasn't what traditional country fans were used to. But he was a Texan, while lang came from north of the border and wasn't likely to be confused with Hank Snow. But new generations of fans weren't as hidebound as their elders, and they took lang's country offerings to heart in sizable numbers.

Kathy Dawn Lang, who later took k.d. lang as her professional name, was born in Alberta, but later claimed Vancouver, British Columbia, as home base. She was not, she acknowledged, a country fan in her youth, listening to the diverse mix of folk, rock, and pop typically dominant in an urban environment. Initially she was interested in the music she found in her sisters' record collections, which tended to stress folk and soft rock as presented by such artists as Maria Muldaur, Leon Russell, Delaney and Bonnie, and Joe Cocker. In her teens, she also included among her favorites Rickie Lee Jones, Kate Bush, and Joni Mitchell, and as time went by, major jazz artists.

During high school, she learned to play guitar and sometimes performed in school events. Country music, of course, was available in the Vancouver area at C&W clubs and on some radio stations, but lang didn't pay much attention to it until she was in her early twenties. Once she did begin following it, however, it became a passion and she began to think seriously about moving to Nashville to further a career in that field.

As she told Richard Cromelin of the *Los Angeles Times* ("For k.d. lang, It's Bye-Bye Patsy—Hello 'Ingenue,'" Calendar section, August 2, 1992), when she started performing country material, she had dreams of having a dramatic impact on the direction of that genre. "When I started, when I was 22, 23, I knew that I was odd, but I thought that I could somehow conquer or influence it. And as it progressed [her career], I realized that I was never gonna change it, but I still loved to sing it. The whole reason I was there was because I loved the form, the musical form as a root music. Because of its relationship with human emotions and its simplicity.

"And to be really honest, I think it's no surprise that I also understood and appreciated the kitsch in country music and used that as a part of humor too . . . I think that put [people in Nashville] on guard. But to me, humor and making fun of yourself, making fun of being a hillbilly or whatever, was always an integral part of country music. And I think that during this attempt to

urbanize country music it got shoved back in the closet and people were offended or afraid that I was trying to nullify its progression when actually I was trying to add to it."

Once lang began passing demo tapes around the music industry it became obvious she was a very talented individual. However, she was passed up by country music record firms and, after an early 1980s alignment with a small independent label, Bumstead Records, which issued the albums *Friday Dance Promenade* in 1983 and *A Truly Western Experience* in 1984, was signed instead by Sire Records (distributed by Warner Brothers Records), a label known for promoting avant garde rock groups rather than country performers. Signing with a no-country, somewhat offbeat record company somehow seemed to mesh with lang's general, odd-girl-out persona, but the association worked out well for both parties in spite of the cold shoulder given her recorded output by many country radio programmers.

Before gaining a record deal, lang had organized her band, the reclines, and gained attention for her emotionally charged stage performances. Their success led to the single "Friday Dance Promenade" which was a forerunner to lang's album debut, on the Bumstead label. This helped in her major label quest that resulted in the Sire agreement in 1984. Her Sire debut, *Angel with a Lariat*, was a very listenable and, in some ways, groundbreaking collection that went on to achieve R.I.A.A. gold record sales after its 1986 release. The follow-up album, *Shadowland* (issued in 1987), whose tracks, many cowritten by lang, provided strong reminders of Patsy Cline, ranked as one of the most creative country offerings of the late 1980s. The album made the country charts soon after its release and was still on the *Billboard* list in November 1990 after 114 weeks. Meanwhile, lang and her band were headlining shows in major venues across the U.S. and Canada while also performing on many network TV programs and in a film made for the Public Broadcasting System. Among other things, she took part in the 1988 Amnesty International Tour with such eminent companions as Sting, Bruce Springsteen, Peter Gabriel, and Tracy Chapman.

Shadowland helped earn lang the *Rolling Stone* magazine's Critic's Pick for Best Female Singer and Canada's Juno and CASBY Awards for Best Female Vocalist of the Year. She also recorded a duet with Roy Orbison of "Crying," issued on his label of the late 1980s, Virgin, which earned a Grammy Award for Best Country Vocal Collaboration of 1988.

In 1989, she turned out another compelling album, *Absolute Torch and Twang* ("torch and twang" was how lang described her country music style). Most of the songs were cowritten by lang and Ben Mink, such as "Wallflower Waltz," "Nowhere to Stand," and "Big

Boned Gal," but the most impressive track was her version of the old Willie Nelson/Faron Young honky tonker, "Three Days." Like the two previous Sire collections, this album spotlighted lang's exceptional creative and vocal abilities. Stephen Holden of *The New York Times* (May 28, 1989) said lang offered "one of the two or three most captivating voices to have emerged from country music in recent years. At once cool and impassioned, her singing strongly recalls Patsy Cline, while lacking her idol's gritty Southern edge. Ms. Lang is a more elegant stylist and also more of a crooner."

Absolute Torch and Twang provided lang with another chart hit, appearing on the *Billboard* list in mid 1989 and, after earning a gold record award from the R.I.A.A., staying on it into 1991. In the Grammy Awards voting for 1989, it was named the Best Country Vocal Performance, Female. She also was named the Top Selling Female Country Artist by the National Association of Record Merchandisers (NARM). During 1990, her performance of Orbison's "Crying" was a show-stopper at the memorial concert for that artist at the Universal Amphitheater in Los Angeles.

Despite the great success of all three of her Sire albums, lang took two years off from the recording field to pursue other interests. One such effort was playing a lead role in the movie *Salmonberries,* directed by Percy Adlon, who had previously earned critical acclaim for his film *Baghdad Cafe.* During this period, lang was also rethinking her music career goals; when she returned to the recording studio to prepare her next album she moved away from country to the determinedly pop material of her 1992 Sire release, *Ingenue,* also a best seller, reaching platinum levels in the U.S., double platinum in Canada as well as platinum in Britain and Australia. She won a third Grammy in the category Best Pop Vocal Performance, Female, for the single "Constant Craving" drawn from the album.

While signaling new musical directions with that album, lang also "came out" by addressing her sexual orientation (as well as her decision not to eat meat) in an interview for the gay magazine *Advocate* for June 16, 1992. She later told Richard Cromelin she discussed her homosexuality with *Advocate* because "I guess I was ready. I felt that my career always had this undercurrent of speculation, and people have been trying to ask me for years about the whole androgyny or why my hair's short.

"And, really, I felt quite strong now. And I kind of took the responsibility on because I didn't want to react defensively to some stupid tabloid story or something, and it seems like it would be the responsible thing to do for myself as a person and for the gay community."

She continued to command a large and devoted following who thronged her concerts in support of her fourth Sire release. Randy Clark of *Cash Box* commented on the ovations she received during standing-room-only concerts in the Southern California area.

"So what if the CMA hasn't embraced k.d. with the same warmth as mainstreamers Garth Brooks or Wynonna Judd? As great as lang's voice is, I think she can stand on her own quite well, thank you. So if country music fans have predominantly been meat-eating heterosexuals, who cares? Let all the straight women (or gay men) ogle over Alan Jackson and Clint Black, k.d. out-sings 'em all. And singing was what she showed up to do."

During the mid 1990s, lang continued to probe other areas of pop music (while not completely abandoning country elements). In 1993 she added to her album credits with work on the soundtrack Sire release *Even Cowgirls Get the Blues.* Her projects included duets with a number of non-country artists, Tony Bennett in particular, and finding new audiences for her avant garde activities. She shared the stage with Bennett for a duet of a nominated collaboration on the 1994 Grammy Awards telecast. In the fall of 1995, Warner Bros. issued her country/pop compilation, *All You Can Eat.* Unfortunately, though it had its high points it was not one of her best efforts. Some reviewers pointed out the album had sold disappointingly, but it still made the pop charts and had earned a gold record award from the R.I.A.A. by early 1996.

Her concert tour in support of the album, which ranged from the Universal Amphitheater in Los Angeles in February 1996 to New York's Radio City Music Hall in March of the year, was as audience-pleasing as ever. Robert Hilburn of the *Los Angeles Times* captioned his review article "lang Delivers Magic Moments with Borrowed Songs" (which referred to the fact that her songs by other writers were more pleasing than some of her own compositions) while Stephen Holden in *The New York Times* commented, that "letting out her full-throttle wails the . . . Canadian singer fuses Patsy Cline's earthy torchiness with Peggy Lee's smoky intensity and Liza Minelli's belting fervor." Her most effective number continued to be her impassioned version of Roy Orbison's "Crying" with Holden also casting a vote for "Barefoot," a pop ballad (with music by Bob Telson and lyrics by lang) used on the movie *Salmonberries'* soundtrack.

LAWRENCE, TRACY: *Singer, guitarist, songwriter. Born Atlanta, Texas, January 1968.*

When Tracy Lawrence's name began to show up on the hit charts in 1992 and 1993, he was categorized by many music journalists as a member of the new "Nashville youth movement" of the 1990s. But, as others noted, at age twenty-five he was one of the very few new names that really could be legitimately called a "young" artist. He was almost four years younger than Trisha Yearwood and Wynonna, while others like Garth Brooks, Clint Black, Doug Supernaw, and Pam Tillis were between thirty and thirty-six.

Discussing his second album, *Alibis,* in 1993, he

said that it was a little more progressive than his debut release: "'young country' I guess they call it. I had the opportunity to be a little more daring this time around. It's still very honky-tonk country, but it's much younger sounding. It's just where I'm at right now."

But he emphasized to Janet E. Williams for Country Music Association's *Close Up* (June 1993), that he wasn't ignoring his roots. "I wanted to keep it as traditional as possible, but still be able to give it a fresh, young sound. I wanted to have some similarities to the first time out as far as material and the quality of the music. But I didn't want to change the direction of my image, of what people perceive me as being. I don't want to be a rock 'n' roll singer. I don't want to be a pop singer. I just want to sing country music."

He spent his first four years in Atlanta, Texas, hardly a metropolis, but a little bigger than a place called Foreman, Arkansas, where his family moved next. His mother had remarried, and Tracy's stepfather was a banker. He had five siblings, but told Dixie Reid of the *Sacramento Bee* ("Wisdom Road," September 30, 1992) that he gave his mother the most trouble of all. "I was mean as a snake. I was very high-strung and rebellious and kind of kept to myself." But he wasn't so rebellious that he would refuse to join his family at the local Methodist Church, where in time he became a member of the choir.

He enjoyed listening to country artists on the radio and records, though like any youngster of the times, he could hardly ignore the dominance of rock and soul. By his fifteenth year, he had learned to play guitar and was performing in local music events. At seventeen he was working in honky-tonks and nightclubs. Still, he completed his high school education and went on to enroll as a mass communications and business major at Southern Arkansas University. But he kept up his music on weekend gigs, while sharpening his songwriting skills.

That brought opportunities for broader focus on the performing side and eventually he moved to Louisiana and became lead singer of a band that played three-day-weekend dates in many parts of the South. He stayed with the group for two years until, in 1990, the bass player, who owned most of the group's public address system, quit and broke up the operation. Lawrence got whatever money he could from his personal belongings and set off for Nashville in a ten-year-old Toyota Corolla that, he recalled, had expired license tags, no insurance, an inner tube adapted for a fan belt, and a mileage of over 250,000.

He arrived in Nashville on September 2, 1990, and set about seeking a place in the Music City pantheon. Though young, he emphasized to Dixie Reid, he wasn't wet behind the ears. "I was seasoned by the time I got here. A lot of people never play their music outside of Nashville and come here green. It is not a very forgiving town. Make your mistakes somewhere else—somewhere that's kinder."

He embellished that a bit for *Close Up.* "I've probably lived more life than most people my age should have because I started so young. I've seen some real good barroom brawls. A lot of it was because I was pursuing the music business and because of the places where I was hanging out and the things I was doing. Which is probably the reason my mom and dad didn't want me pursuing it in the beginning."

Once in Nashville, Lawrence took a remarkably short time to go from unknown to major-label recording artist. He got some of his subsistence money by entering and winning the many talent contests offered in Nashville, typically taking down $75 or $100 for first prize. He also got the chance to sing and play steadily at the local American Legion Hall and such blue-collar night spots as the Stagecoach, Gabe's Lounge, the Rose Room, and Broken Spoke. After a while, he became a cast member of the "Live at Libby's" radio show in Nashville while expanding his appearances to shows in other parts of the region. One date on Kentucky radio station WBVR-FM drew the attention of record industry executives in attendance, and cleared the way for a recording contract with Atlantic Records; by the spring of 1991 he was working on his debut collection in Nashville studios, which included several songs he wrote or cowrote.

He had just completed his vocal takes for the album when near-disaster struck. He and his date, country artist Sonja Wilkerson, had attended a concert by Alan Jackson when he was dropping her off at her motel in the early hours of the morning of May 31, 1991. They were in the parking lot of Shoney's on Semonbruen Street when they were confronted by a trio of armed robbers. Tracy told her to run while he confronted them as a shield. They shot him four times. Fortunately, he survived, but endured months of rehabilitation, particularly to a damaged hip, while the album release was put on hold.

Though still in pain from some of his injuries, by early 1992 he was on the road supporting his first album, *Sticks and Stones.* He was particularly concerned that any laurels he earned were for his material, not the notoriety from the incident. At the time *Alibis* came out, he said, "I was so aggressive when I first got to town. I knew what I wanted and worked very hard to get where I am now. The problem I have at this point is trying to overcome being known as 'the kid who got shot on Music Row,' and have people know me because of my music. I want to be remembered for why I came here, and not for some fluke accident."

He needn't have worried. His career blossomed both on the record/video front and in his live appearances. The title track, issued the end of 1991, made top-chart levels, including a number-one position in *Radio & Records* the week of January 10, 1992. *Sticks and Stones,* the album, peaked at number ten in *Billboard* the week of April 4, 1992, and was still on the list in the summer of 1993 after earning an R.I.A.A. gold record. This was followed by two more singles hits in 1992, "Today's Lonely Fool," number one in *R&R* the week of April 24, and "Runnin' Behind," number one in *R&R* the week of August 21. Those singles also were top-level hits in *Billboard*. At year-end, another single, "Somebody Points the Wall," was number six in *R&R*. Meanwhile, Tracy was racking up 289 performance dates, opening for the likes of Vince Gill, George Jones, and Shenandoah. At the end of 1992, *Billboard* named him country music's Best New Male Artist.

He continued to add to his laurels the following year. His second album, *Alibis,* came out in the spring and went gold seventeen days after reaching the stores. It was still on the *Billboard* list at year-end, having passed R.I.A.A. platinum-award levels, and stayed on it into 1994. The title track reached top-chart levels in all major publications following the country field, including number four in *Billboard* in May. In July, he had another top-5 *Billboard* hit with "Can't Break It to My Heart" (cowritten by Lawrence with K. Roth, E. Clark, and E. West). In December 1993, the single "My Second Home" (cowritten by Lawrence, L. Beard, and P. Nelson) was number one in *Billboard.*

During 1993, Lawrence began to make his mark as a headliner, typically earning marks of excellence from fans and critics. One example was the review by Michael Corcoran, country music critic of the *Dallas Morning News* ("No Trace of Doubt, Tracy Lawrence Makes It Clear That He's Star Material," May 31, 1993), of Tracy's show before 6,000 people at Six Flags. "Ricky Van Shelton and Randy Travis are better pure singers. George Strait and Hank Williams, Jr., have better bands. Dwight Yoakam writes better songs. Travis Tritt can kick harder and Garth Brooks is a better showman, but nobody at his age could put it all together like Tracy Lawrence. For the past two years, he's almost singlehandedly kept country radio from drowning in a sea of sap. And as he proved at Six Flags, he's ready to enrich the concert schedule for many years to come. Make no mistake about it, a superstar was born in that man-made mist at Six Flags on Sunday night."

By mid-1993 Lawrence could also bask in the glow of the award from the Academy of Country Music for Best New Male Artist. By early 1994, he could look back on two years of hard-earned achievements. His career seemed poised to move still higher as he opened 1994 with the singles hit "If the Good Die Young." But while his career continued to prosper, there were dark entries in his private life. This took the form of an odd occurrence in April that brought unwanted attention from the trade and general media.

As reported in *Cashbox* of April 16, 1994, he was charged "with two counts of aggravated assault on April 4 after allegedly firing a gun into the air in the driveway of a Leesville Pike (Tennessee) home and fleeing the scene just after midnight. He was charged with carrying a prohibited weapon because he lacked a handgun permit for what investigators said was a .357 magnum." *Cashbox* noted Lawrence also was charged with impersonating a police officer when officers found a badge with an identification card in the truck for "Capt. Tracy Lawrence," naming a nonexistent police department.

Through his attorney, Lawrence responded a group of youths had initiated the situation by firing shots at the truck driven by his brother, Stewart, on Route 40. (Police stated they had found no evidence of such firing.) That occurrence, the brothers claimed, caused them to follow the other vehicle and fire warning shots where it ended up.

Though court hearings went on, Lawrence's recording career didn't seem to suffer. In mid-August 1994, he had a single, "Renegades, Rebels and Rogues," in the *Billboard* Top 10. In the fall he had the hit album *I See It Now,* which peaked at number three in *Billboard,* doing well on all the charts on its way to earning a gold record from the R.I.A.A. by year end and a platinum award on August 8, 1995. The title track, issued as a single, was in the *Billboard* Top 10 in November 1994. Another track from the disc, "Texas Tornado," provided a number one single for Tracy in late June 1995. In the fall his single "If the World Had a Front Porch" earned good fan response and rose high on both the singles (peaking at number two in *Billboard)* and video lists. Joining the high tech parade of the music field, on midnight November 28, 1995, he had his first single release, "If I Loved You," that was delivered directly to some 2,000 radio stations via Digital Generation Systems.

He began 1996 in good style when his new album, *Time Marches On,* debuted at number six in *Billboard* and seemed certain to earn another platinum award in due time. The title track also won good airplay, entering the top 10 in *Billboard* in May 1996.

LEDOUX, CHRIS: *Singer, guitarist, songwriter. Born Wyoming, October 2, c. early 1950s.*

The singing cowboy has been a familiar enough presence in the American musical consciousness ever since motion pictures began to talk, but few of those performers could claim firsthand experience with ranching and rodeoing. A modern exception to this is Chris LeDoux, who came to country music success from years as a champion rodeo competitor.

He grew up around horses and true life cowhands in the state of Wyoming where, in the mid-1990s, he still returned to his ranch in Kayce in between concert tours. He began working as a cowboy and riding in rodeos when he was fourteen years old and for some three decades earned most of his living from prize money for bullriding and bareback horse riding. He did well enough in his teens and early twenties to achieve a reputation as a top-level performer on the rodeo circuit, using some of his earnings to buy a sizable ranch in his home state.

As he told Earl Dittman for an article in *Tune In* magazine ("A Cowboy's Heart," January 1994), "Being a rodeo rider is a state of mind. It is for yourself—your self-esteem, pride and ego. You're brainwashed at an early age to want to emulate your heroes. You always want to be like them. For a lot of kids, myself included, cowboys are the last real heroes. You always want to take yourself to their level. That's probably why I got into it."

Probably the pinnacle of his rodeo career came in 1976 when he won the world championship title in bareback bronc riding at the National Finals Rodeo, which some describe as the Superbowl of Rodeo. It was an unexpected victory, since serious injuries he suffered in 1975 caused many observers to doubt he could even take part. But he had settled in at his ranch and worked hour after hour to prepare himself physically and mentally for a return to his first love, including rugged workouts on a mechanical bucking horse. It paid off handsomely when he won the first-place prize money and the gold buckle in the finals, emblematic of one of the highest achievements in the sport.

Chris had been interested in music as well since childhood, and learned to accompany himself on the guitar. He often played and sang for pleasure at home or while away at rodeo events. After a while he also began to write original songs, which he tried out on other riders and rodeo personnel. Eventually he set up a small record company staffed essentially by his mother and father, who took care of assembling their son's recorded material in a series of albums he sold to other rodeo participants or anyone else who'd buy them. Before he gave up the rodeo circuit he had completed twenty-two such albums.

It was a surprisingly large collection, since, as he told Richard McVey of *Cash Box* ("Chris LeDoux Goes Haywire over His New Album," September 17, 1994), writing was a demanding task. "I'm the kind of guy that needs about four months of nothing to be able to write and get into this sort of 'songwriting twilight zone.' The songs that I really feel good about that I've written take 6–8 months. I really work hard at them. I have an idea, or maybe a melody line, and then try to find out what would be the most appropriate subject to go along with the melody and hammer out the words—just like building a house. It seems like everything I do just takes a long time."

Music became more important during lean times in the rodeo business, when bills began to pile up. He told Dittman, "For awhile it looked like we were going to lose the ranch. That went on for 12 years. It looked like there was no light at the end of the tunnel. It looked real bad. That was one of the motivating factors in pursuing the music so hard and heavy. At the time I was thinking, 'Maybe this will help.' Originally, though, I got into the

music because I loved it. I still love it. Once that wolf starts howling and scratching at your door, you start looking at the music a little more as something that'll help you get what you want."

More than a few people were impressed by the cowboy's recordings, among them a young country artist named Garth Brooks. Brooks's debut album included a track called "Much Too Young (to Feel This Damn Old)" that had a line that referred to "a worn-out tape of Chris LeDoux." LeDoux recalled hearing it with astonishment on his car radio. He told Janet Williams for Country Music Association's *Close Up,* "To be driving along and hear that on a mainstream Country station . . . it was kind of a touching moment. After all the years I've been doing this, wondering if what I'm doing is worthwhile . . . this song says, 'Yeah, you've helped somebody out.' It touched people."

Chris retired from rodeoing in 1984 to work on ranching and furthering his musical career. His earlier exploits were documented in his 1987 book, *Gold Buckle Dreams: The Rodeo Life of Chris LeDoux.* Aided by people like Brooks, Chris began seeking an alignment with a major record label. In 1991 this finally brought him a contract with Liberty Records. As part of the agreement, Liberty obtained the rights to all twenty-two of his independent albums. As of the mid-1990s, the label had reissued twelve of the latter for its own catalog: *Rodeo Songs Old and New; Songs of Rodeo Life; Rodeo and Living Free; Life As a Rodeo Man; Sing Me a Song, Mr. Rodeo Man; Used to Want to Be a Cowboy; Old Cowboy Classics; Melodies and Memories; Gold Buckle Dreams; Chris LeDoux and the Saddle Boogie Band; Powder River;* and *Radio and Rodeo Hits.*

His Liberty debut album, *Western Underground,* came out in mid-1991 and spent a number of months on the *Billboard* chart, at one point making it inside the top 40 to a peak position of number thirty-six. This was followed in 1992 by the album *Whatcha Gonna Do with a Cowboy,* whose title track was a duet with Garth Brooks. The single of the song became a chart hit in late summer, peaking at number seven in *Radio & Records* the week of September 4, 1992. The album also made top-chart levels in the summer and fall of 1992, peaking at number nine in *Billboard.* It was still on that list for much of 1993, having earned an R.I.A.A. gold-record award. That was a busy time for LeDoux on the concert circuit, as he won enthusiastic audience approval as a supporting or headline act in large arenas and small clubs throughout the U.S. and Canada.

During late 1992 and early 1993, he had another single that did well on the charts, "Cadillac Ranch," which peaked at number fifteen in *R&R* the week of January 15, 1993. In the summer of 1993, his next Liberty album, *Under This Old Hat,* debuted in *Billboard* at number twenty-nine the week of July 29. The single of the title track also spent some time on various hit lists.

In early 1994, he had the single of a Joe Ely composition, "For Your Love," on lower-chart levels and later in the year was represented on hit lists by the album *Best of Chris LeDoux* and the single "Honky Tonk World."

LeDoux's name turned up among the finalists for a variety of awards for either records, videos, or overall talent in 1992 and 1993. Among those so naming him were voters from the Country Music Association, Academy of Country Music, TNN/Music City News, and the Grammys. Among other milestones of that period was the opportunity to be featured in his first TV special.

During the summer of 1995 he had the single "Dallas Days and Fort Worth Nights" on the charts. In the fall of that year he placed his handprints in cement on the Nashville "Sidewalk of the Stars" near the Music Valley Wax Museum of the Stars and not far from Opryland. He closed out the year by starring with Charlie Daniels in a TNN program on December 20 called *A Wrangler Cowboy Christmas*. In early spring 1996, his twenty-seventh album, *Stampede*, reached the record stores and spent several months on the hit lists. "Gravitational Pull" from the album spent some months on lower chart levels in the spring.

LEE, BRENDA: *Singer. Born Lithonia, Georgia, December 11, 1944. (Press sources in the 1960s gave place of birth as Conyers, Georgia.)*

For someone whose management indignantly denied that she was a country singer in the 1960s, diminutive Brenda Lee (born Brenda Mae Tarpley) hasn't done badly at all in the "down home" field since that decade. At the time, of course, Brenda had been a rock star for years even though only in her early twenties. But it would have been surprising if, coming from Georgia, she didn't have a strong feel for country music; in fact, a look at her career shows she first made major inroads into her music career as a protégé of the great Red Foley.

Her interest in music began very early. When Brenda was only three, her mother recalled, she could hear a song twice and start singing it almost letter perfect. When Brenda was five she sang "Take Me out to the Ball Game" at a local spring festival and won a first-prize trophy. Her singing ability continued to progress rapidly. Her mother took her to auditions for show business engagements while Brenda was in the beginning grades in elementary school. When the girl was only seven, she won a regular slot on the *Starmakers' Revue* radio show in Atlanta. That exposure caused the producers of *TV Ranch* on Atlanta's WAGA-TV to offer some guest spots on that program.

In early 1956, Red Foley's manager, Dub Albritton, took over direction of her career. She started sharing bills with Foley and was so well received that Dub soon lined up appearances for her on such nationally televised shows as *The Steve Allen Show, The Ed Sullivan Show, Bob Hope, Red Skelton Show,* and *Danny Thomas*. Record executives quickly began clamoring for her services and she soon signed with Decca Records. On July 30, 1956, she began her first recording session in a Nashville studio. A decade later, at twenty-one, she had completed a total of 256 sides for that company. Recalling that first encounter, producer Owen Bradley said, "She was so small. But I remember when we started on the first take all of a sudden she yelled, 'Stop, stop, he missed a note,' and she pointed straight at the bass player. The bass player had missed a note and no one else had caught it."

Songs recorded in her initial 1956 sessions included "Jambalaya" and "Bigelow 6-200." Those didn't provide chart hits, but later sessions did, with her first chart entry being "One Step at a Time" in 1957. In 1958, she recorded "Rockin' Around the Christmas Tree," which made upper-chart levels two years later and went on to become a seasonal classic. The success of that single at the end of 1960 rounded out a year that began with her first major hit, "Sweet Nothin's" (in the top 5 in February), and her first number-one *Billboard* single, "I'm Sorry." Her other 1960 successes were "That's All You Gotta Do" (peaked at number six) and the number-one ranked "I Want to Be Wanted."

By the fall of 1960, her 1958 recording of "Rockin' Around the Christmas Tree" proved to be a major hit. It was only the beginning. In short order she turned out such pop hits as "Sweet Nothin's" and "I'm Sorry."

She already was considered a pop star at the end of the 1950s, a position she maintained well into the 1960s when, for five consecutive years, both *Billboard* and *Cash Box* named her the Most Programmed Female Vocalist. From the late 1950s through mid-1960s she performed in night clubs, major auditoriums, and concert halls the length and breadth of the United States and also was a favorite of overseas audiences. Her European engagements began soon after she started recording for Decca with a long series of concerts at the Olympia Music Hall in Paris. Naturally, she also was featured on almost every major TV show at home and abroad.

Among the many albums released by Decca were *Grandma, What Great Songs,* issued in September 1959, *Brenda Lee* (8/60), *This Is Brenda Lee* (1/61), *All the Way* (9/61), *Emotions* (5/61), *Sincerely* (4/62), *Brenda, That's All* (12/62), *All Alone Am I* (4/63), *Let Me Sing* (1/64), *By Request* (7/64), *Versatile* (7/65), *Top 10 Hits* (4/65), *Too Many Rivers* (11/65), *Bye Bye Blues* (5/66), *10 Golden Years* (7/66), *Coming on Strong* (1/67), *Reflections in Blue* (12/67), *Memphis Portrait* (late 1960s).

After her marriage to Ronald Shacklett in 1963, she cut back on her music activity in favor of having a family. Her first child, a daughter named Julie Leann, was born in 1964 and a second daughter, Jolie, in 1969. Although Brenda was maintaining a relatively low profile in the latter 1960s, she showed that her performing skills still were formidable with the chart-making "Johnny One Time," a Grammy Awards nominee in 1969.

Starting in the early 1970s, Lee began to shift her musical focus away from pop and toward country. Most of her pop releases had made country charts in years past and country fans proved even more enthusiastic about her new material. In 1971 she placed "Is This Our Last Time" on country charts and followed in 1973 with "Nobody Wins" and "Sunday Sunrise." In 1974, she had a series of top-5 hits: "Wrong Ideas," "Big Four Poster Bed," and "Rock on, Baby." In 1975 she placed two more singles on country charts, "Bringing It Back" and "He's My Rock," and in 1976 added two more credits, "Find Yourself Another Puppet" and "Takin' What I Can Get."

In January 1978, Brenda switched to the Elektra/ Asylum Records label; her first single for that company was issued in May. The songs on it were "Could It Be I Found Love Tonight" backed with "Leftover Love."

Brenda's association with Elektra proved a brief one; by late 1979 she was recording for MCA Records. By year end her single "Tell Me What It's Like" was on the charts and in January 1980 it moved into the top 10. In April of that year, another single, "The Cowboy and the Dandy," was in the top 15. Also on the bestseller lists during the year were "Don't Promise Me Anything" and "Broken Trust," the latter in the top 10 in late fall. In 1981, Lee had still more charted singles on MCA, such as "Every Now and Then" and "Only When I Laugh."

In 1984, after Brenda's duet with George Jones on "Hallelujah, I Love You So," made the charts, she began what turned out to be a five-year absence from the recording studios. In 1989, however, she signed with Warner Brothers Records, which issued her label debut, *Brenda Lee,* in early 1991. Accompanying that was a new single and video of the album track "One and Only." At the time of the release of the new recordings, her total album sales worldwide were claimed to have exceeded 100 million.

Though Brenda headlined many concerts in the mid-1990s and was a guest on many network TV programs, she had relatively little impact on the hit charts over that period. She continued to be highly regarded among many knowledgeable country observers for her talent and her contributions to country music, a fact recognized by the editors who compiled *Life* magazine's "Roots of Country Music" special edition in September 1994, which included her in its list of the 100 most important people in evolution of the genre. The album cited as best defining her musical achievements was MCA's *Brenda Lee Anthology.* Another notable retrospective of the early phase of her career available in the mid-1990s (as an import item from Germany) was Bear Family Records' *Brenda Lee: Little Miss Dynamite.* The four CD boxed set contains all of her recordings from 1956 until 1963.

LEWIS, JERRY LEE: *Singer, pianist, songwriter. Born Ferriday, Louisiana, September 29, 1935.*

One evening in early 1979 at the Palomino Club in Los Angeles, the m.c. was singing the praise of the headliner, a relatively new female performer. He barely got out the words "I'm going to present one of the great country performers of the day" when Jerry Lee Lewis stood up in the audience and shouted "I'm the greatest." To the consternation of the host, he rushed on stage, sat down at the piano, and quickly worked the audience into frenzied excitement. It could never be said "the Killer" lacked confidence. And not without reason—in more than four decades as a performer, he cut a wide swath as a superstar, first in rock 'n' roll, then in his original proving ground, country music.

Jerry Lee was born and raised in the small town of Ferriday, Louisiana, where gospel and country music were part of the environment. (Blues were sometimes considered off limits, but Jerry and his childhood friends—including his cousins, future country star Mickey Gilley and future evangelist Jimmy Swaggart—sometimes snuck into honky-tonks to hear some of that music too.) He showed such an early aptitude for the piano that his father, Elmo, took the boy around to perform in small shows in neighboring towns, playing the keyboards from the back of a flatbed truck. As he grew older, Jerry Lee also performed in gospel meetings and church programs.

But his early love of the blues helped inspire an interest in the mid-1950s outburst of rockabilly. In 1956, he moved to Memphis and became a session pianist at Sun Records, backing rockabilly founders such as Carl Perkins and Billy Lee Riley. In the wake of selling Elvis Presley's contract to RCA, Sun was in the market for new talent and Jerry was quick to seize the opportunity. With his free-wheeling adaptations of Irving Berlin's "End of the Road" and Ray Price's country hit "Crazy Arms," Jerry Lee made his record debut in 1956 and soon was out on the road gaining rising attention in touring rock shows. Kicking the piano bench across the stage, waving the microphone with vigor as he played piano with the other hand, and jumping on top of the piano, he set off shock waves of enthusiasm among young onlookers.

In 1957, he hit his peak with the smash single "Whole Lotta Shakin' Goin' On," a worldwide hit which earned him his first gold record. Late in the year, he came out with the gold blockbuster, "Great Balls of Fire," an anthem of rock. After that he placed other songs in top-chart levels, including "Breathless" and "High School Confidential" (the title song of his first movie, which he sang from the back of a flatbed truck).

In 1958, though, his soaring fortunes plummeted abruptly when word came around that he had married his thirteen-year-old second cousin, Myra. (The marriage lasted thirteen years.) That wasn't startling to many in the rural South, where early unions often occur. In fact, Jerry Lee had married the first of his two previous wives when he was only fourteen. But it shocked the rest of the nation and the world. The story broke amid a concert tour of England. The condemnation there was so great that concerts were canceled. The situation was only a little less bleak for him back home.

For the next half-dozen years, he fought to keep his career afloat. He had some minor successes on Sun during that period, including the singles "John Henry," "Carry Me Back to Old Virginny," and a remake of Ray Charles's "What'd I Say." But the Killer seemed relegated to a minor role in pop music from then on.

However, national morals were changing and the events of six years ago were ancient history to most fans. In 1964, with things at Sun in the doldrums, Jerry Lee switched to Smash Records (a subsidiary of Mercury) and suddenly found his career rejuvenated. His first releases in March 1964 and January 1965 (both titled *Jerry Lee Lewis*) and *Rock Songs* in June 1965 all were aimed at rock fans. But the albums sold much better in the country field. Of course, country always was one of the elements in Lewis's stylings and by the mid-1960s, many youngsters in the South had adopted country-rock as part of their own culture. So without changing his approach too much, Jerry Lee set his cap in that direction and soon was doing quite well, thank you.

His new direction was indicated by the title of his January 1966 smash LP, *Country Songs*. After that album, his LPs did steadily better over the last half of the decade. He followed with such releases as *By Request* and *Return of Rock* (1967), *Soul My Way* (1968), and one of the best-selling country LPs of 1968, *Another Place, Another Time*. His singles sales also moved along nicely. The title song of the latter album moved high on the charts and he achieved another top-10 hit in 1968 with "What's Made Milwaukee Famous (Has Made a Loser out of Me)." Other hit singles of the late sixties were "She Even Woke Me Up to Say Goodbye," "To Make Love Sweeter for You," and "She Still Comes Around (to Love What's Left of Me)."

Jerry Lee's in-person success moved right along with his recording achievements. He starred in such diverse places as plush Las Vegas hotels, college campuses, county fairs, and large auditoriums. In 1969 and into the early 1970s, he was a prime drawing card in the rash of rock 'n' roll revival shows. Another milestone occurred in 1968, when he starred in the role of Iago in "Catch My Soul," a rock version of Shakespeare's *Othello* presented at the Los Angeles Music Center.

In the 1970s, his albums kept coming out on several labels. When he still was on Smash in the late 1960s, some of his earlier work was reissued by Sun. In 1970, Mercury Records absorbed its subsidiary, Smash. Among his Sun releases of the late sixties and early seventies were *Ole Tyme Country Music, Volume 1, 2 and 3; Monsters: Rockin' Rhythm & Blues; Taste of Coun-*

try; and *Original Golden Hits, Volumes 1, 2, and 3.* Sun's *Golden Cream of the Country* made the country top 10 in May 1970. Two Sun singles also brought him top 10 laurels in 1970: "One Minute past Eternity" and "I Can't Seem to Say Goodbye." At year-end, another Sun single, "Waiting for a Train," was high on the lists.

Smash LP releases of 1969 and the early seventies were *Together* (with Linda Gail Lewis, 1969), *Hall of Fame Hits, Volumes 1 and 2* (1969), *She Even Woke Me Up to Say Goodbye,* and *Best of Jerry Lee Lewis* (1970).

In the early 1970s, his material came out on Mercury Records, starting with his first release on the label, *Live at the International, Las Vegas.* Also well received were such 1971 releases as *There Must Be More to Love than This, Touching Home,* and *Would You Take Another Chance on Me.* He also had a series of top-10 singles country hits: "There Must Be More to Love than This," "Touching Home," "Would You Take Another Chance on Me"/"Me and Bobby McGee" (1971) and "Chantilly Lace"/"Think About It Darlin'" (1972). 1972–73 Mercury album hits included *The Killer Rocks On* and *The Session.* Among the singles he placed on the country charts were "Lonely Weekends," "Turn on Your Love Light," "When He Walks on You," and "Who's Gonna Play This Old Piano."

In the middle and late seventies, Jerry Lee continued to make the country charts with Mercury singles "Drinking Wine Spo-Dee-O-Dee" (1973); "Boogie Woogie Country Man" (1975), "Don't Boogie Woogie" (1976), "Let's Put It Back Together Again" (top 20, 1976), "Middle Age Crazy" (top 10, 1977), and "I'll Find It Where I Can" (top 15, 1978).

Besides a breakneck series of concert dates numbering in the hundreds each year, Jerry Lee still found time for other tasks, including playing himself in *American Hot Wax* (1978), a film biography of rock impresario Alan Freed.

Early in 1979, Jerry made another record company move, switching to Elektra. His March 1979 debut on the label, *Jerry Lee Lewis,* was recorded in Los Angeles, the first LP he had cut outside Nashville in some time. It offered a combination of rock and country songs, including a previously unrecorded Bob Dylan song, "Rita May," that Dylan had offered to Jerry.

He began the 1980s with two excellent new Elektra albums: *When Two Worlds Collide* and *Killer Country,* both released in 1980. In 1981, however, his career almost came to an abrupt end when he was hospitalized with an ulcerated stomach. The physicians told reporters it was a life-threatening illness, but Lewis recovered and by late 1982 was back on the concert trail again. Through the mid-1980s, despite various health and personal problems, Jerry Lee persevered and thrilled audiences with his musical antics. As reporter Kristine McKenna of the *Los Angeles Times* enthused, even at that stage of his career: "He still pulsates with arrogant leering life, and packs more sex and rhythm into a sideways glance than most bands can muster operating at full steam."

In the 1980s, Rhino Records issued the excellently annotated two-LP *Milestones,* featuring 1956-77 tracks, plus the CD *18 Original Sun Greatest Hits.* Books concerning Jerry Lee included ex-wife Myra Lewis's *Great Balls of Fire* (Quill, 1982), Nick Tosches's *Hellfire* (Delacorte, 1982), Robert Palmer's *Jerry Lee Lewis Rocks* (Deliha, 1981), and Robert Cain's *Whole Lotta Shakin' Goin' On* (Dial, 1981).

As might be expected, when the new Rock 'n' Roll Hall of Fame was organized in Cleveland, Ohio, in the mid-1980s, Jerry Lee was one of the first names proposed for entry and one of the first voted in.

During 1987, two extensive reissues of Jerry Lee's work became available. One of those was a twelve-record boxed set of recordings Jerry made on Sun Records from 1956 to 1963, issued by England's Charly Records and distributed in the U.S. by Street Level Records, Gardena, California. The other was a series of three boxed sets issued by the German record firm Bear Family, covering material Lewis recorded on Mercury from 1963 to 1977. The series, collectively titled *Jerry Lee Lewis: The Killer,* was offered to U.S. record buyers by mail order from Down Home Music in El Cerrito, California.

In 1989, a movie on Lewis's life, *Great Balls of Fire,* starring Dennis Quaid as the Killer, came out. It had been a rocky journey from inception to completion, producer Adam Fields told the *Los Angeles Times* in February 1989. "In the eight years I've been trying to make this film, Jerry had one of his wives die, a son die, he'd declared bankruptcy twice, been arrested all over the place and he's been in and out of the hospital who knows how many times, once with a hole the size of a tennis ball in the middle of his stomach."

After lining up the necessary approvals, Fields had been able to bring in ABC Films as a backer in the early 1980s when the 1983 death of Jerry's fifth wife, a twenty-five-year-old former barmaid named Shawn, derailed the project. The death, which occurred under mysterious circumstances, spawned press and TV coverage, including an investigative article in *Rolling Stone* and a Geraldo Rivera TV special. No charges ever were filed against Lewis, but the unseemly publicity caused ABC and other potential studios to back off.

After things quieted down, Fields sold the idea to Dino De Laurentis based on having Mickey Rourke portray Lewis, as had been the case in the ABC deal. In keeping with the oddities of the Jerry Lee Lewis saga, the arrangement turned out to be one of mistaken identity. Field told the *Los Angeles Times,* "I couldn't figure out why Dino kept complaining that Mickey wasn't funny. Until it turned out that Dino thought he'd bought the rights to 'The Jerry Lewis Story.'"

Finally, in 1989, Fields got support from Orion Pictures, which resulted in the film's completion with Quaid as star by the start of 1989. Fields heaved a sigh of relief. He said, "Keeping Jerry Lee Lewis happy is a full time job. Every day it's something new. Whenever Jerry Lee thinks you need him, he holds you up for something." If it wasn't Lewis, Fields indicated, it was his managers who wanted more favors for their client.

Both Lewis and his managers indicated those statements were, at the very least, exaggerations. And those years had been traumatic ones for Jerry Lee, even more so than the wild times of previous decades. Lewis told an interviewer at his home that he recalled standing at the nearby wet bar "when my son, Jerry Lee, Jr., who was 19, was driving down the road out here and turned over his Jeep and died.

"I came close to questioning God then. I asked, 'Lord, why did this happen to me?' And I finally said, 'Jerry Lee, you've got no right to do that. The Lord giveth and the Lord taketh away.' I've been tested, but I've still got my music and now I've got this movie. . . . You can look at it lots of different ways, but I think my blessings far outweigh my woe."

Certainly Jerry Lee's music sustained him throughout the 1980s and into the 1990s, as he continued to star in venues large and small, from Vegas to the country circuit. The movie wasn't a blockbuster, but it did focus renewed attention on the performer, which increased his status as a concert draw during the first half of the 1990s. During the summer of 1993, Rhino Records came out with a new retrospective, *The Jerry Lee Lewis Anthology—All Killer No Filler!* which included forty-two tracks on two CDs covering his career from early Sun rock hits to his Mercury Records country chart successes.

Jimmy Guterman, who wrote the liner notes for the Rhino package, had previously written the book *Jerry Lee Lewis: Rockin' My Life Away,* published by Rutledge Press, Nashville, in 1991. While interesting, the book was less a biography than a song-by-song treatment of his music.

In September 1994, the compilers of the list of "The 100 Most Important People in the History of Country" for a special *Life* magazine issue on that art form, properly included Jerry Lee's name. Like the other "originals" to whom he compared himself (Al Jolson, Jimmie Rodgers, and Hank Williams, Sr.), *Life* noted, he was an artist who "blended seemingly discordant strains of music into a single riveting sound. Jerry Lee did it at Sun Records in the 1950s and early '60s, creating the wildest rockabilly the world has ever heard."

From the mid-1980s into the first part of the 1990s, Lewis made no new studio recordings (except for his overlooked soundtrack to *Great Balls of Fire).* This hiatus came to an end in the mid-1990s when producer Andy Paley managed to arrange for new sessions under the Sire Records banner. The result was the album *young blood,* issued in April 1995 (with distribution by Elektra Entertainment). The contents ranged from boogie woogie and rockabilly to country ballads, including a Jimmie Rodgers–inspired version of the old song "Miss the Mississippi and You," complete with yodels; a fast-paced cover of Huey "Piano" Smith's "High Blood Pressure"; and his take on Pete Seeger and the Weavers' folk hit "Gotta Travel On." The performance was vintage Jerry Lee, but the song selection might have been more adventuresome. In 1996, Lewis mounted a 40th anniversary tour that signaled a higher concert profile than the sixty-year-old performer had seen for some time.

Objectively, it would seem apparent to an outside observer that Lewis should have been a member of the Country Music Hall of Fame by 1996. His notoriety and initial association with the birth pangs of rock had mitigated against that, but it would be surprising if in the fullness of time his claim to that additional honor wasn't recognized.

Those wanting vintage packages of Jerry Lee's seminal recordings could do worse than seek out the boxed sets assembled by Bear Family Records of Germany. As of 1996 there were two such sets. One titled *Jerry Lee Lewis: Classics!* consists of 8 CDs encompassing all of his Sun Records releases including many previously unissued takes. The other, called *Jerry Lee Lewis: The Locust Years,* also was presented on 8 CDs, this time covering the period from 1963–1969. Besides covering many rock or rock-oriented songs that were generally ignored by radio programmers, the collection includes his career-reviving country hits of 1968 and 1969 such as "Another Place, Another Time," "What's Made Milwaukee Famous," and "She Even Woke Me Up to Say Goodbye." The set also includes an extensive 1976 interview with Lewis.

LIGHT CRUST DOUGHBOYS, THE: *Vocal and instrumental group, formed early 1930s with many different alignments of musicians during its decades of existence. Early members, 1931–32: Bob Wills, Milton Brown, Durwood Brown, Clifton "Sleepy" Johnson, and Herman Arnspiger.*

One of the legendary names in country & western history, the Light Crust Doughboys, claims so many different alumni it almost could provide material for an encyclopedia of its own. The two individuals most closely associated with its initial phases, Bob Wills and W. Lee "Pappy" O'Daniel, went on to carve national reputations for themselves, Wills as leader of the famed Texas Playboys and O'Daniel as the politician who used his country & western background to help win him the governorship of Texas.

Recalling the origins of the group, Texas Playboy alumnus Leon McAuliffe said, "Bob Wills in about 1931 came to Ft. Worth, just himself and a guitar player [Herman Arnspiger]. He met a fiddler named Milton Brown [1903–1936]. Brown and his brother, Durwood, were the central figures in a landmark western swing

band called Milton Brown and His Musical Brownies and they went on radio station KFJZ as the Wills Fiddle Band. They first got their show sponsored by the Aladdin Lamp Co. Called themselves the Aladdin Laddies. They were so popular they got themselves sponsored on a network of radio stations called the Texas Quality Network, whose members included WBAP in Ft. Worth, KPRC in Houston, and WOI in San Antonio. The company that sponsored them was the Burris Mill and Elevator Company that manufactured Light Crust Flour. That's where the Light Crust Doughboys name came from."*

In getting that sponsorship, Wills approached O'Daniel, who then was on the sales staff of Burris. O'Daniel was born in Malta, Ohio, on March 11, 1890. His family later moved to Kingman, Kansas, where he finished his schooling and began working as a flour seller for local firms in the early 1920s. In 1925, he moved to Ft. Worth and got a job with Burris Mills. After Wills approached him in 1932, O'Daniel was receptive to the idea and initially sponsored the newly named group on KFJZ. In 1933, the group, by then already a favorite with Ft. Worth audiences, moved to WBAP, performing daily at 12:30 P.M.

Wills didn't stay with the band too long after that move. McAuliffe noted, "Milton and Bob went separate ways. Bob went to Waco and started the band he called Bob Wills and the Playboys. In the summer of 1933 he moved to Oklahoma for a short stay and then on to Tulsa where, in 1934, the group finally took the name Bob Wills and the Texas Playboys."

Meanwhile the Light Crust Doughboys kept going, with O'Daniel taking the helm as master of ceremonies. Brown's place was taken by fiddler Clifford Graves from Kentucky, and others were added to round out the band. The Doughboys made several recordings for RCA Victor before Wills left, but the bulk of the group's output came afterward when O'Daniel arranged a recording contract with Vocalion. Among the songs recorded for that label from 1933 to 1935 were "Beautiful Texas," "On to Victory Mr. Roosevelt," "Bluebonnet Waltz," "Texas Breakdown," "Memories of Jimmie Rodgers," "Doughboys' Rag," "Texas Rose," "Saturday Night Rag," "Gangster's Moll," "When It's Roundup Time in Heaven," "Alamo Waltz," "My Pretty Quadroon," "Carry Me Back to the Lone Prairie," "Milenburg Joys," "Old Rugged Cross," "The Cowboy's Dream," "Kelly Waltz," and "She's That Old Sweetheart of Mine."

O'Daniel's association with the group ended in 1935 when he resigned from Burris to form his own firm, Hillbilly Flour Company. Later on, when he entered politics, he and the Doughboys performed during his speeches and rallies, a move that helped win him the election and a technique later used by another country

---

Interview with Irwin Stambler, 1979.

entertainer turned politician, Jimmie Davis, to score a similar victory in neighboring Louisiana.

Eddie Dunn took over from O'Daniel as emcee. He previously had a group of his own whose members soon took on Doughboys raiment: Marvin Montgomery, Dick Reinhart, Bert Dodson, and Muryel Campbell. His tenure was short, though. In 1936, the leadership of the group went to Cecil Brower.

Despite the personnel shifts, the band continued to be a mainstay of station WBAP programming into the 1940s. The situation changed in 1942 when Burris Mills canceled its advertising support. A new sponsor, Duncan Coffee Company, came aboard, and the Doughboys became the Coffee Grinders. Under that name the band kept going through the World War II period, but after the war was over it was decided to go back to the original name even without Burris's sponsorship since the Doughboys name had become famous in its own right.

The band of that name continued to survive in one form or another for over two decades afterward. Besides doing radio and TV work in the 1950s and 1960s, the group also continued to give live sets at various clubs around the United States and on the fair and rodeo circuit. None of those efforts, though, ever returned the group to the position it held in its heyday from the early 1930s through the early 1940s.

LITTLE TEXAS: *Vocal and instrumental group, Del Gray, born Hamilton, Ohio, May 5 (drums); Porter Howell, born Longview, Texas, June 21 (vocals, lead guitar, electric sitar); Dwayne O'Brien, born Ada, Oklahoma, June 30 (vocals, guitar); Duane Propes, born Longview, Texas, December 17 (vocals, bass guitar); Tim Rushlow, born Arlington, Texas, October 6 (lead vocals, guitar, mandolin); Brady Seals, born Fairfield, Ohio, March 29 (vocals, keyboards).*

With a name taken from a street and an instrument mix that extended from guitars and pianos to sitars, Little Texas found the right path to country music success in the first half of the 1990s. Blending elements of country rock, honky-tonk, R&B, and bluegrass, the group took advantage of the burgeoning opportunities for new artists in the 1980s and 1990s, when country suddenly became competitive with mass-audience formats like rock and soul.

Tim Rushlow stressed his group was part of the new wave of country artists (a development country traditionalists weren't too happy about). "I feel like we're the first country band that was influenced by 'Young Country.' Sure, we love bands like the Eagles and Poco [interestingly, bands considered part of mainstream rock, but with country elements], but our real influences were Alabama, Restless Heart—country's new sound."

The origins of the band went back to 1984, when Oklahoman Dwayne O'Brien met Texan Tim Rushlow. Rushlow had been interested in music since his childhood years as the son of Tom Rushlow, lead singer of the 1960s rock group Moby Dick and the Whalers. Tim learned guitar and polished his vocal talents, which he put to use in small gigs in the Arlington area before he and O'Brien joined forces for a time.

O'Brien, still a student at East Central State University, returned to earn a degree in chemistry, after which he moved to Nashville to resume his music career with Rushlow, who had taken up residence there in 1986. Deciding to form a band, they brought in two young musicians from Longview, Texas, Duane Propes and Porter Howell, who were then attending Belmont University in Nashville. The new band, not yet called Little Texas, fronted by Rushlow, practiced for awhile, then found jobs playing in bars and county fairs across the U.S. While playing at a fair in Massachusetts, the band members struck up a friendship with keyboard players Brady Seals and Del Gray, who were then working, respectively, with country artists Sandi Powell and Josh Logan.

Later on, Seals and Gray agreed to round out the roster to a six-member operation. Both of them had grown up in Ohio, and Seals in particular had good contacts in the music field as nephew of hit country songwriter Troy Seals and country star Dan Seals.

By the fall of 1988, the band had come under the wing of manager Christy DiNapoli, who began to set up showcase performances for record industry executives. At a show in Birmingham, Alabama, DiNapoli brought Warner Bros. A&R man Doug Grau to see them. Grau liked what he heard and agreed to set up a development deal with the band, which took the name Little Texas in 1989.

O'Brien said, "We worked for eight months without finding a name we liked. Then we had a showcase performance coming up in June 1989 and really needed one. We had been rehearsing out at Doug's farm, south of Nashville—it was way out in this holler, and the last paved road leading to it was Little Texas Lane. This area had a real tough reputation from the '20s through the '50s as a hideout from the law. So we became Little Texas."

He recalled the band members felt they still needed intensive work, including writing and publishing some of their own compositions, before they would be ready to start making a name for themselves with country fans. O'Brien said, "We had the ability and the enthusiasm, but we weren't seasoned yet. We took three years to develop individually, and as we each matured, so did the band overall."

Rushlow added that their management lined up almost nonstop club dates in all parts of the U.S. "We would roll into town and play five or six nights at a place. We'd write a song, put it in our show and see how people liked it. It gave us a chance to experiment and see just what our little niche was."

O'Brien said, "It was difficult at first. People had no

idea who we were. But by working our tails off, we got our name out there and it got easier as things went along. But that came from working like crazy and never slacking off."

In December 1990, Warner Brothers okayed the first recording session. A product of that was the cut "Some Guys Have All the Love," issued as a single in July 1991. It made lower-chart rungs and, backed by effective marketing to radio stations and the band's continued touring, slowly began to move up. O'Brien recalled, "We called it 'the little song that could.' It crawled up the charts so slowly, but it kept making progress." The band hoped it would just make top 40, but it hit that and kept going, finally peaking at number eight in *Billboard* that November and reaching the *Radio & Records* Top 15 the same month. The group had also made a video of the song, which eventually reached number one on TNN.

With those laurels, the band got the chance to record its debut album in the Ardent Studios in Memphis, Tennessee. Released in February 1992, *First Time for Everything* made the charts late in the year, eventually earning a gold record from the R.I.A.A. while spawning more hit singles. The title track reached number nine in *R&R* in May 1992, "You and Forever and Me" rose to number five that September, and "What Were You Thinkin'" made the top 15 in December. All of those singles did well on other hit lists, including those in *Billboard*.

During 1993, the band continued to see its name on hit lists with new singles releases while also keeping more impressive company on tour. The band was on the concert bills in 1992–93 of such artists as Clint Black, Kenny Rogers, and Dwight Yoakam. They were also a lead-in act for stars Travis Tritt and Trisha Yearwood on the 1993 Budweiser 'N' Country tour. At a Budweiser date near Austin, Texas, Governor Ann Richards was so enthralled with their song "God Blessed Texas" (which peaked at number three in *R&R* that November) that she later named the group "Honorary World Ambassadors of the Great State of Texas." The band's other hit singles in 1993 were "What Might Have Been," number one in *R&R* in August, and the top-10 success, "I'd Rather Miss You" in April. The band's 1993 credits included a spot on the nationally televised 35th Anniversary Show of the Country Music Association.

The whirlwind rise of Little Texas in 1992–93 earned them two nominations for the 1993 Academy of Country Music Award. The band was one of five finalists for Top New Vocal Group or Duo and Top Vocal Group of the Year.

In the current country music environment, it isn't unusual for an artist or group to become famous one year and fall from view the next. (In that sense, the country field has become more like the pop-rock world.) However, the content and fan response to the band's second album, *Big Time*, issued by Warner Brothers in April 1993 (containing the hit singles for 1993 noted above), suggested this wouldn't be the case for this group. The album made the charts soon after release and, after peaking at number six in *Billboard*, still was on the lists in mid-1995, having earned a platinum record award from the R.I.A.A. Nineteen ninety-four hit singles drawn from it were "My Love," which reached number one in *R&R* the week of April 1, and "Stop on a Dime" (cowritten by Howell, O'Brien, and Seals), top 10 in both *Billboard* and *R&R* in August.

In the Country Music Association voting in 1994, Little Texas was nominated in two categories, Vocal Group of the Year and Music Video of the Year (for "God Blessed Texas"). The group finished the year with a new album on the charts, *Kick a Little*. The album rose to number ten in *Billboard* and earned a gold record award from the R.I.A.A. by early 1995. The single "Amy's Back in Austin," issued in late 1995, stayed on the charts well into the following spring. Next came "Southern Grace" (cowritten by Howell, Seals, and S. Harris) which was in top chart levels by late summer of 1995. During the summer, the group was honored at the ASCAP Pop Music Awards for writing two songs that were among the 50 most played ASCAP registered numbers in 1994, "What Might Have Been" and "God Blessed Texas."

In the fall of 1995, the band had another singles hit, "Life Goes On" which peaked at number five in *Billboard*. In early 1996, it placed "Country Crazy" on singles charts. The retrospective album from Warner Bros., *Little Texas' Greatest Hits*, came out in the fall of 1995, peaked at number seventeen in *Billboard*, and remained on the hit lists well into 1996. This was followed by the 1997 album, *Little Texas*.

LOCKLIN, HANK: *Singer, guitarist, songwriter, public official. Born McLellan, Florida, February 15, 1918.*

To go from a farm boy chopping cotton to a star of the *Grand Ole Opry* is not unusual in country-music lore. To do this and then return and win an election as mayor of one's home town, though, is much rarer.

Henry Locklin had little idea of becoming mayor of McLellan, Florida, when he hoed and chopped cotton on his family's farm in the 1920s. He did like to sing country songs, though, and, when he was ten, gathered enough small change for a down payment on a guitar from the local pawnshop. Although the monthly charges were only $1.50, he found this sum hard to come by and the guitar was repossessed.

Managing to learn a lot about playing the instrument before returning it, Hank persevered and finally got another one, on which he worked out some of his early compositions. He began to take part in local dances and sings, moving on to win a number of local contests when he was in his teens. In the 1930s, he performed as often as he could, but times were tough in those Depression years, and he ended up earning his keep working on road projects of the government Works Project Administration.

Locklin refused to give up his hopes for a successful musical career. This stubbornness finally paid off with more important dates and his first radio engagements, on Florida stations WCOA, Pensacola, and WDLP, Panama City. His star continued to rise with appearances in other cities in the South and air shots on such stations as WALA, Mobile, Alabama; KLEE, Houston, Texas; and KTHS, Hot Springs, Arkansas.

Hank really began to move after World War II. He joined the cast of KWKH *Louisiana Hayride* in Shreveport soon after that show began. By the early 1950s, he was one of the audience favorites and had signed a record contract with Decca. He moved for a time to Four Star, the label of his first major record hit, the 1953 "Let Me Be the One." Soon after, Hank became a regular on the *Grand Ole Opry* in Nashville and signed a long-term contract with RCA Victor.

From the mid-1950s on, Locklin rapidly became one of the top artists in country music. He scored a top-10 hit in 1957 with "Geisha Girl" and followed up in 1958 with "It's a Little More like Heaven" and his own composition, "Send Me the Pillow You Dream On." In 1960, his version of Don Robertson's standard, "Please Help Me, I'm Falling," was number one nationally for many weeks. His other best-sellers of the early 1960s were "Happy Birthday to Me" (1961) and "Happy Journal" (1962).

During the 1950s and 1960s, Hank was represented by many successful LPs. These included two King LPs, *Best of Hank Locklin* and *Encores, Hank Locklin* on Metro (1965), *Born to Ramble* and *Sings Hank Locklin* on Pickwick, and the Wrangler label's *Hank Locklin Favorites*. His RCA Victor output included *Foreign Love* (1958); *Please Help Me* (1960); *Happy Journey, Hank Locklin, Tribute to Roy Acuff* (1962); *This Song Is for You* (Camden), *Ways of Life* (1963); *Irish Songs, Sings Hank Williams* (1964); *Sings Eddy Arnold* and *My Kind of Music* (Camden) (1965); *Once Over Lightly, The Girls Get Prettier, Best of Hank Locklin, Gloryland Ways* (1966); *Bummin' Around* (Camden), *Nashville Women, Send Me the Pillow* (1967); *Bless Her Heart* (late 1960s); *Country Music Hall of Fame* (1968).

Among the songs Locklin recorded in addition to those above are: "Living Alone," "Foreign Car," "Border of the Blues," "I'm a Fool," "Goin' Home All by Myself," "The Rich and the Poor," "How Much," "She's Better than Most," "The Same Sweet Girl," "Born to Ramble," "Fraulein," "Hiding in My Heart," "Anna Marie," "Blues in Advance," "My Old Home Town," "Seven Days," and the 1968 hit "Country Music Hall of Fame."

Over the years, Hank's personal appearances took him to all fifty states, Canada, and Europe. He guested on many major TV shows in the 1950s and 1960s, in-cluding ABC's *Jamboree U.S.A.* In the early 1960s, Hank returned to his home town of McLellan to live, and soon was elected mayor. To complete a boyhood dream, he established his residence on the rambling "Singin' I. Ranch," which incorporated the cotton field in which he'd once worked as a child.

Hank continued to be affiliated with RCA in the early 1970s. His LPs included: *Hank Locklin with Danny Davis and the Nashville Brass* and *Candy Kisses* (Camden) (1970); and *First 15 Years* (1971).

The most complete selection of Locklin's recorded contributions to country music available in the mid-1990s was the 4 CD boxed set, *Hank Locklin: Please Help Me I'm Falling*, produced by Bear Family Records in Germany. The discs contained all of his major hits from 1955 to 1964 including the contents of such classic albums as *Foreign Love, Irish Songs, Country Style*, and *A Tribute to Roy Acuff*. Among the tracks were such hit releases as "Geisha Girl," "Send Me the Pillow You Dream On," and "Please Help Me I'm Falling." Locklin, in the meantime, was not absent from performing ranks. In the early 1990s, for instance, he sang "Please Help Me I'm Falling" twice on the *Grand Ole Opry* backed on piano by the song's composer, Don Robertson.

LONESTAR: *Vocal and instrumental group. Personnel: Michael Britt, born June 16, 1965, Dallas, Texas (guitar, background vocals); Richie McDonald, born February 2, 1962, Lubbock, Texas (lead vocals, guitar); Keech Rainwater, born January 24, 1963, Plano, Texas (drums); John Rich, born January 7, 1974, Amarillo, Texas (lead vocals, bass), Dean Sams, born August 3, 1966, Garland, Texas (keyboards, background vocals).*

A line from one of Dolly Parton's songs goes, "Sometimes you have to go away just to find what you left behind." This line could apply to the formation of the group Lonestar, since all the members of the group were born and raised in Texas, but the band actually formed in Nashville. Of course Texas is a big place, and while three of the band members came from the Dallas-Fort Worth area two others came from the West Texas panhandle. Once assembled, however, the group was cohesive and quickly rose to become one of the most successful country groups of the late 1990s.

The core of the band had its origin when Dean Sams and Richie McDonald were both auditioning in Dallas for spots at the Opryland amusement park. Sams had worked there the summer before, and McDonald took time off his job at the Coca-Cola bottling plant to audition. Each was impressed with the other's vocal skills. Sams got the job and McDonald went back to Coca-Cola, but kept singing. A job singing jingles for Miller Lite enabled him to save enough money to move to Nashville around 1992. One day he was at Opryland with his wife when he recognized Sams performing in the show "Country USA." McDonald went backstage, and the two exchanged phone numbers; they got together soon after and started singing together and decided to form a band. Sams started calling everyone he knew who could play an instrument. He persuaded John Rich, a fellow performer at Opryland, to join with them. Other Opryland cast members included future stars Chely Wright, Ken Mellons, and James Bonamy.

After John Rich joined the group, Sams persuaded Michael Britt to join. At that time, Britt was working at a pizza joint after having kicked around with a country music group called Canyon, which had issued ten singles between 1988 and 1992 but had never had a major hit. Britt called former Canyon drummer Keech Rainwater and asked him to join them. At first, Rainwater was not interested in coming to Nashville to join a new group. He was happy in Dallas, and he was burned-out on the music scene after his experience with Canyon. But after Britt called, Sams and McDonald both called, and Britt told Rainwater, "just get here or I'm going to kill you." Once Rainwater started playing with the band, he knew he had made the right move. When he joined the other four on the Eagles' "Best of My Love," he was impressed by the vocal harmonies that were already in place.

At first calling themselves Texassee, the band played their first gig at Nashville's Backstage Pass. A booking agent saw them, liked what he saw, and booked them on the road. For the next two years, the group traveled around the country and played over 500 shows. Those few years were tough, with the band on the road constantly, traveling in a Jeep pulling a trailer with their instruments and gear. Several times they had their things stolen. But life on the road did not pull them apart. During a month-long stop in Reno, Nevada, the group started working up original material written by McDonald, Britt, and Rich. They also changed their name to Lonestar.

Along the way, Lonestar picked up fans, so that when they recorded their own independent live mini-album, Wal-Mart bought about 40,000 copies to sell in its stores. Some of the management at Wal-Mart wanted to market Lonestar's albums, not realizing that Lonestar did not have a record deal yet.

Getting a record deal was not that simple for the group. Nearly every major record company in Nashville turned them down, including BNA, which eventually reversed its position to sign the band to its first contract. Among the arguments given against signing Lonestar was that there were two lead singers, John Rich and Richie McDonald, and they had very different vocal styles, with Rich, a former bluegrass musician considered a twangy uptempo singer and McDonald stronger on slow ballads. This was considered a disadvantage by most record labels, although as Rich later pointed out, "The Eagles did it and the Beatles did it." The group, of course, did not consider this a disadvantage, and persisted trying to get a contract. Rich and

McDonald were versatile singers and able to switch styles if needed. In addition, unlike many prominent country music groups of the 1990s, Lonestar started with its focus on vocals, as all five members were talented singers and less proficient musicians, though with all their touring, their instrumental proficiency improved as well. On their debut album, in fact, five of the songs featured John Rich as the lead singer and five of them featured Richie McDonald.

As often happens in the music industry, a change in personnel led to Lonestar's record contract with BNA. Joe Galante had returned to Nashville from New York to take over management of BNA. By this time, Lonestar had teamed up with producer Don Cook, who had helped produce albums for Brooks & Dunn, Shenandoah, and The Mavericks, and Grammy-winning songwriter and producer Wally Wilson. Cook knew Galante and told him that he had a band he wanted him to sign. Lonestar thus became the first record act Galante hired for the BNA label upon his return to Nashville.

The group's first album, Lonestar, came out in the fall of 1995 and the first single release, "Tequila Talkin'," soon moved up the charts to become a top-10 country hit. Reminiscent of some of The Eagles' best work, the song did stand out for its pure vocal style. In the spring of 1996, Lonestar was named Top New Vocal Group by the Academy of Country Music.

The group's next singles release proved to be an even bigger hit, "No News." The upbeat song about a relationship, in which the woman leaves to find herself and never comes back, spent several weeks at the number-one spot on the country charts and was one of the biggest hits in 1996. The video that went with the song was Lonestar's first commercial video, and it was extremely successful. It featured a young woman in glasses with her hair up who leaves her man, then gets on a bus, takes off her glasses, takes down her hair, and puts on makeup and becomes instantly glamorous. The video also showed the band playing and singing.

Heading into 1997, the news seemed to be all good news for Lonestar, whose star looked bright for the group to continue to be one of country music's strongest bands in the late 1990s and possibly into the next millennium.—A.S.

LONZO AND OSCAR: *Vocal and instrumental comedy duo. Original members: Ken Marvin, born Haleyville, Alabama, June 27, 1924, and Rollin Sullivan, born Edmonton, Kentucky, January 19, 1919. Marvin replaced in mid-1940s by Johnny Sullivan, born Edmonton, Kentucky, July 7, 1917, died Nashville, Tennessee, June 5, 1967. Sullivan replaced in 1967 by Dave Hooten, born St. Claire, Missouri, February 4.*

Down-home humor always has been an important part of country music; one of the most famous teams in that tradition is that of Lonzo and Oscar. From the 1940s to the end of the 1970s, there always was a duo of that name on the *Grand Ole Opry,* though with several changes in personnel over the years.

For much of Lonzo and Oscar's history, the duo was a brother act—John Sullivan taking the part of Lonzo and Rollin Sullivan that of Oscar. The team didn't start as a brother act, though, nor did it end as one.

The Sullivan brothers, oddly enough, were working together prior to the birth of Lonzo and Oscar. Both born in Edmonton, Kentucky, to a poor rural family, the boys were working at family chores and then odd jobs from their early years. Country music was a prime form of relaxation and both Sullivans took to playing and singing such material when still quite young. By the time they were in their teens, Johnny could play both bass fiddle and guitar and Rollin was a fine mandolinist. They already were performing in small clubs in their home area by the end of the 1930s.

Just before the United States entered World War II, the Sullivans made their radio debut on station WTJS, Jackson, Tennessee. There were a lot of other excellent country artists performing on WTJS programs, including Ken Marvin and Eddy Arnold. Marvin and Rollin Sullivan got together to form the original duo, with strong encouragement from Arnold. It was Eddy, indeed, who suggested they call themselves Lonzo and Oscar, with Marvin serving as Lonzo. Ken and Rollin made the first recordings under that title, though Johnny contributed by writing some of the original material with Rollin. It was one such collaboration, a comic number called "I'm My Own Grandpa," that made the duo's reputation in the mid-1940s. Marvin and Rollin made the original single, though later on Rollin and Johnny did their own version.

Things were moving quite well for the duo—they were invited to become cast regulars on the *Grand Ole Opry* in 1942—when the Sullivan brothers both entered the armed forces. By the mid-1940s, they were mustered out and Rollin and Marvin resumed their association. For a time, the comic act plus Johnny was part of a band that was featured on station WAVE, Louisville, Kentucky. In 1945, Ken Marvin retired from the music field and Johnny Sullivan took over as Lonzo. For a time, the brothers were part of the Eddy Arnold group, an association they ended in 1947, the year they also became full *Opry* cast members under the Lonzo and Oscar banner.

During the late 1940s and through the 1950s and most of the 1960s, the Sullivans toured widely with their own show. Among the members of the show over the years were many *Opry* stars, including Cousin Jody, Cousin Luther, Smokey Pleacher, and Tommy Warren. Besides personal appearances in all fifty states and in many other nations, Lonzo and Oscar had many TV credits. These included twenty-four films of their own show for TV, guest spots on *Kate Smith, The Ed Sullivan Show,* and *Dave Garroway,* and featured spots on most major country syndicated network TV programs.

The team recorded on many labels over the years, including RCA, Decca, Starday, their own label, Nugget, and starting in 1967, Columbia. Their singles included such songs as "If Texas Knew What Arkansas," "My Dreams Turned into a Nightmare," "I'll Go Chasin' Wimmun," "Ole Buttermilk Sky," "My Adobe Hacienda," "Julie," "Hearts Are Lonely," and "Movin' On." Among the many originals they recorded or included in their act were "You Blacked My Blue Eyes Once Too Often," "Last Old Dollar," "There's a Hole in the Bottom of the Sea," "I Don't Forgive No More," "Take Them Cold Feet Out of My Back," "Cornbread, Lasses and Sassafras Tea," and "She's the Best I Ever Saw."

Their LPs included *Country Comedy Time* on Decca; *Lonzo and Oscar* (1961) and *Country Music Time* (1963) on Starday; and *Country Comedy* on Pickwick. The original Ken Marvin and Rollin Sullivan recording of "I'm My Own Grandpa" was included in the RCA mid-1960s collection *Stars of the Grand Ole Opry.*

The team temporarily was dissolved when Johnny Sullivan died in June 1967. Several months later, it was reactivated when Dave Hooten took over the part of Lonzo. The new team went back into action on the *Grand Ole Opry* and on the concert circuit and was still finding a sizable country following for its satirical offerings over a decade later.

LOUDERMILK, JOHN D.: *Singer, banjoist, bass fiddle player, mandolinist, trombonist, cornet player, organist, fiddler, songwriter, record producer. Born Durham, North Carolina, March 31, 1934.*

There's no doubt that John D. Loudermilk ranks among the most prolific and creative of country-music writers, with over 700 original compositions to his credit at the start of the 1980s. Many of those songs paved the way to stardom for a number of performers. A look at his career shows that he might well have become a superstar of stage and TV had he wanted to.

His parents were hard-working, family-oriented people who saw to it that their son got a better educational grounding than they'd received. His father, a carpenter who helped build the chapel at Duke University in Durham, John's birthplace, couldn't read or write. As soon as John mastered those fundamentals in school, his father started taking the boy down to the grocery store on Saturday afternoon to endorse his paychecks.

While John grew up, his family had to move constantly, though always staying in the same general area. He recalled the many times his mother had to pack up pasteboard cartons that the moving van took to a new locale. In all, there were nineteen such moves within the same school district before John finished high school and entered junior college.

By then he already had considerable experience as an entertainer. As a child he had enjoyed singing in church, where the accompaniments ranged from stringed instruments, horns, tambourines, and a bass drum to hand clapping. He remembered, too, the pleasure he got as a boy while taking his Saturday night bath in a galvanized wash tub placed next to the kitchen stove within listening distance of the radio, which carried the *Grand Ole Opry* show. When he grew older he became a member of the Salvation Army Band, where he learned to play just about every instrument imaginable, from fiddle to horns to banjo and guitar. It was in church as a youngster that he made his first public appearance, joining his mother to play and sing "Life's Railway to Heaven."

He already had considerable stage presence before he was in his teens. When he was eleven, he made his singing debut on radio and soon had his own show on a Durham station. When he was twelve, he entered and won a place on the Capitol Records Talent Contest in Charlotte, North Carolina, a show whose host was the now legendary Tex Ritter.

John continued his interest in music in his high school years, a period when he was expanding his purview to include not only country but many other categories, from the classics to rhythm & blues. Among the artists whose work he admired during those years were Eddy Arnold, Jimmy Reed, Andrés Segovia, Ivory Joe Hunter, Fats Domino, and Lloyd Price. He also was strongly influence by the writings of the philosopher-poet Kahlil Gibran, which inspired him to write a number of poems of his own.

John got a job on TV station WTVD in Durham, where his activities included painting sets and also working as a part-time bass fiddler in the *Noon Show* band at the station. By then he already was experimenting with not only poetry but original melodies. He came to the *Noon Show* one day in 1955 with a poem he'd set to music and played it on the air. Not only did the song, "A Rose and a Baby Ruth," elicit delighted letters and phone calls from viewers, it also brought a call from a local record producer named Orville Campbell who wanted to have another young singer, named George Hamilton IV, record it. The result was a smash hit that rose to number one in the United States in 1956 and became a springboard to industry renown for both Hamilton and Loudermilk.

At the time, Loudermilk had not considered music as a career. In fact, he left to study at Campbell University in Buies Creek, North Carolina. While there he wrote a second landmark song called "Sitting in the Balcony," which became his debut effort as a recording artist. The single gained some attention but, more importantly, it was picked up by a previously unknown rock artist named Eddie Cochran, whose version of the song in 1957 became his first massive hit. Loudermilk's main concern now was what to do about a spate of contract offers from New York and Nashville publishers. His life was changing in many other ways as well. While back in Durham he met a Duke University music major named Gwen Cooke who in time agreed to marry him. They were, in fact, married in 1959 in the same Duke chapel his father had helped to build.

Loudermilk eventually aligned himself with Jim Denny and Cedarwood Music, Inc., and moved to Nashville, where, besides writing a steady flow of fine songs, he also recorded a number of albums for RCA in the 1960s under Chet Atkins's guidance. (During these years, he also shifted his writing efforts from Cedarwood to Acuff-Rose Publications.) Some of his songs helped George Hamilton IV's transition from the pop field to country stardom in the 1960s, including such often covered numbers as "Break My Mind" (also a major hit later for Anne Murray), "Blue Train," and "Abilene." From the early 1960s into the 1990s, those or other Loudermilk compositions were recorded by just about every famous or near-famous artist in the country & western field and often became hits for pop performers as well. Among his oft-recorded songs are "Talk Back Trembling Lips," "Waterloo," "Sad Movies," "Norman," "Paper Tiger," "From Nashville with Love," "Thou Shalt Not Steal," "Bad News," "I Wanna Live," "Ma Baker's Little Acre," "Torture," "Big Daddy," "Tobacco Road," "Then You Can Tell Me Goodbye," "Ebony Eyes," "The Little Bird," "It's My Time," "Indian Reservation," "Googie Eye," and "Windy and Warm."

During the 1970s, Loudermilk became interested in the field of ethnomusicology and its relationship to contemporary record production. As a result of his studies, he gave many lectures at folklore society meetings and at colleges on the contributions of people like Pete Seeger and Jimmie Driftwood to all phases of music. Most of his limited amount of personal performances in that decade were at various folk and country music festivals in the United States and Europe.

Besides writing and recording, he also did a certain amount of production work in the 1960s and 1970s. One of his credits included handling production on the first recordings of the Allman Brothers Band at the end of the 1960s.

Among his honors are a Grammy Award, a Manny Award from the National Songwriters Association International, dozens of gold records for hit versions of his songs by various artists, and a similar large number of BMI citations for top-rated compositions. At one point, his career also was the basis for a series of TV specials telecast on the British Broadcasting Corporation. He also served on the board of directors of the National Academy of Recording Arts & Sciences (sponsoring organization for the Grammy Awards) and was elected to the board of directors of the Country Music Association of America for two different terms, the second one for the years of 1979 and 1980. He also was inducted into the Nashville Songwriters Association's International Hall of Fame.

The Charlie Daniels Band

Desert Rose members Chris Hillman *(left)* and Herb Pedersen

Diamond Rio

Don Felder of the Eagles

(Jacqueline Sallow)

(Peter Nash)

Joe Diffie

(Jacqueline Sallow)

Eagles members stir up a country rock storm
in the late 1970s

(Jacqueline Sallow)

Steve Earle *(left)* and Mike Martt

Freddy Fender

The Flatt & Scruggs Band

Tennessee Ernie Ford in the mid-1960s

Jimmie Dale Gilmore

Jim & Jesse as they appeared on the Grand Ole Opry
in the 1960s

Merle Haggard

Faith Hill

(Peter Nash)

Buddy Holly

(Peter Nash)

(RCA Victor)

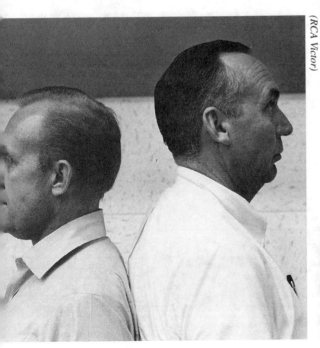

Homer & Jethro

Alan Jackson

Waylon Jennings

The Judds

Jerry Lee Lewis

Alison Krauss

Jerry Lee Lewis at Country Fest in Irwindale, California, May 1988

Little Texas

Charlie Louvin

Lyle Lovett

Lynyrd Skynyrd, 1978: Ronnie Van Zant *(with hat),* Leon Wilkeson *(bottom),* and *(left to right)* Billy Powell, Allen Collins, Artimus Pyle, Steve Gaines, and Garry Rossington

LOUVIN, CHARLIE: *Singer, guitarist, songwriter. Born Rainesville, Alabama, July 7, 1927.*

The Louvin Brothers were one of the premier acts of country music for more than a decade and a half; when they split up in 1963, some wondered whether they could achieve equal success as soloists. For Charlie, still a *Grand Ole Opry* star in the mid-1990s, the answer was a resounding *yes!* and the same probably would have proven true for Ira had he not died in a tragic accident.

The brothers grew up as members of a farm family in Henegar, Alabama, and spent many a backbreaking day as boys working in the cotton fields and doing other farm chores. Country music naturally was one of their interests as they grew up and both started picking out chords on guitars before they reached their teens. Charlie, the younger of the brothers by three years, recalled that their entry into the music business occurred "sort of accidentally" when he was sixteen. The duo won an amateur contest in Chattanooga, Tennessee; first prize was a radio program on station WDEF broadcast daily at 4 A.M. To make the show, the brothers worked first shift in a cotton mill, their mill earnings being their major revenue at the time. During the mid-1940s, they began to find additional jobs playing small clubs, country fairs, and the like, finally reaching the point where they could concentrate on performing alone.

As their reputation increased with local fans, the brothers began to look further afield, with a record contract a primary goal. Their first association was with Decca, which only released one recording; then in 1949 they signed with MGM. The MGM effort seemed promising at first, but later releases failed to continue the momentum and the contract lapsed in 1951.

One event that contributed to that downturn was the Korean War, which claimed Charlie's services in the Army for a time at the start of the 1950s, leaving Ira behind to try to keep things going as a single. In 1951, Charlie was back in Tennessee, trying to revive his career with Ira. The team's mentor, Fred Rose of Acuff-Rose Publishing, who had set up the MGM deal for them, sent some of their material to Capitol (the brothers had been writing original songs for some years), where producer Ken Nelson agreed that they had great potential. When he sought them out, their careers had slid to the point that they were working in a Memphis, Tennessee, post office and only playing an occasional weekend date.

The Louvins soon turned out the first of the more than 100 singles they made for Capitol, a label Charlie remained with into the 1970s and that Ira recorded for until his death in 1965. As the early and mid-1950s went by, the team became steadily better known to country audiences and disc jockeys through intensive live and radio performances and the release of a series of well-regarded singles and albums. In 1955, they were asked to become cast regulars on the *Grand Ole Opry* and the Nashville area became home.

Among the duo's hits were three top-10 singles in 1956, "Hoping That You're Hoping," "I Don't Believe You've Met My Baby," and "You're Running Wild." In 1959, they had a top-10 single with "My Baby's Gone." Some of their original compositions that made upper-chart levels, if not the top 10, were "When I Stop Dreaming," "The Weapon of Prayer," and "I Take the Chance." The brothers had twenty albums in the late 1950s and early 1960s of which about half were sacred. The team received many honors and topped many polls, during one period being voted Most Programmed Sacred Group and Most Programmed Duet by the nation's country & western disc jockeys for five straight years.

In 1963, Charlie decided he wanted to see if he could make it as a solo act. As he recalled, "You know how it is. After so much time you get too close, can't accept criticism anymore."

Charlie expanded on that to Jimmy Guterman in 1987 for an article in *The Journal of Country Music* ("Songs That Tell a Story," Volume XII, no. 2, 1989). "My brother and I broke up in 1963 because the business had gotten rotten. When the business gets bad, it disturbs some people and they become lesser artists than they were when the business was good. They put more moves in the act and less talent because of the fading popularity of whatever they're doing. Some people think you can cure a disturbed situation with a bottle."

The move soon proved wise for him; one of his first releases, "I Don't Love You Anymore," became a major hit, reaching the top 10 in 1964. He followed with many other singles that made the top 20 or better, including "Less and Less," "Think I'll Go Somewhere and Cry Myself to Sleep," "You Finally Said Something Good," "Off and On," and a major hit of 1965, "See the Big Man Cry, Mama." (Of his philosophy on hits, he once said, "I've never strived to be number one, but I sure do love being in the top twenty. There's not as many people shooting at you if you're not number one. It's more comfortable.") However, he never disdained a top-10 hit, and "See the Big Man Cry" not only rose high on the lists, it also was nominated for a Grammy.

Charlie's debut solo LP on Capitol, *Charlie Louvin,* was issued in March 1965, followed soon after by *Many Moods of Charlie Louvin* (2/66); *Lonesome Is Me* (7/66); *I'll Remember Always* (3/67), a tribute to his brother; *I Forget to Cry* (10/67), and several more late 1960s LPs, including *Will You Visit Me on Sundays, The Kind of Man I Am,* and *Here's a Toast to Mama.* In September 1970, Capitol issued his tenth solo album, *Ten Times Charlie.* At the end of the 1960s and in the early 1970s, Charlie teamed with Melba Montgomery for a series of duet recordings, including the albums *Something to Brag About* and *Baby, You've Got What It Takes.*

Over the years Charlie continued to add to his catalogue of original compositions, many of which provided chart-making recordings for other artists besides himself. At the end of the 1970s, artists like Emmylou Harris were including some of the songs written jointly by Charlie and Ira or by Charlie alone in best-selling albums. Reviewing his writing efforts in the early 1970s, Charlie noted, "I've written forty or fifty since Ira died; must have done over 500 together."

Among the albums that focused on Louvin-type material, Guterman noted, were two recorded for Rounder Records by Charles and Robert Whitstein. Charles Whitstein recalled hearing the Louvins when he and his brother were five and six and being attracted to "the harmonies, the way they would go up and down, the unisons. It was just beautiful to us. The Delmores are more of a straight harmony and the Louvins came along with high and low . . . We don't have quite as nasal a sound as Ira Louvin, it's not as coarse a sound. We try to do about the same type of harmony. But it always goes back to the Louvins."

Charlie remained a major attraction on the country music circuit from the mid-1960s throughout the 1980s, appearing in shows all over the United States. He also gave a number of concerts in Canada and other countries of the world over the years. Besides that, he was featured on many TV and radio programs, including guest spots on such 1960s programs as *Porter Wagoner Show, Bill Anderson Show, Bobby Lord Show, Wilburn Brothers Show, Flatt & Scruggs,* and *American Swing Around* and such 1970s shows as *Hee Haw* and some of the PBS telecasts of the *Grand Ole Opry.*

Charlie pointed out that people remembered the brothers' music even in the 1980s. He told Guterman, "I stayed with Capitol for twelve years, the same amount of time as the Louvin Brothers recorded for them. I sold more records than the Louvin Brothers did. Yet when I tour today, people don't come up to me and say they loved one of my songs. They say, 'I used to love the Louvin Brothers.' That music did last."

He ended his long affiliation with Capitol in the mid-1970s and signed a new contract with United Artists. Among the UA singles he placed on the charts were "You're My Wife, She's My Woman" and "It Almost Felt like Love." In 1980, he celebrated twenty-five years as a regular on the *Grand Ole Opry* and continued to appear on the show into the 1990s.

By the mid-1980s, Charlie commuted to his *Opry* appearances from his original home near Henegar, Alabama. He established the Louvin Brothers Music Park there where, among other things, he sponsored an annual spring bluegrass festival. The park also included an unobtrusive Louvin Brothers museum.

He continued to record new material in the 1980s, though it was an uphill battle to reach the main country audience against the preference of country radio for young new artists like Randy Travis and his peer group. Reissues of Louvin Brothers recordings continued to appear from time to time. These included a reissue by

Stetson Records of a 1960 Capitol LP, *My Baby's Gone,* and one from Canada's Rebel Records label, *The Best of the Early Louvin Brothers.* Rounder released such albums as *The Louvin Brothers* (from an original 1951 release on the MGM label), *Tragic Songs of Life* (Capitol 1956), and *Songs That Tell a Story* (from 1952 Capitol sessions). As of 1995, only the last-named remained in Rounder's catalog. Also available was the Country Music Foundation's *Louvin Brothers/Radio Favorites '51–'57.* Still in print in the mid–1990s was the extensive 8 CD boxed set produced by Germany's Bear Family Records titled *The Louvin Brothers: Close Harmony.* The set's 219 cuts cover all of the brothers' releases on Apollo, Decca, MGM, and Capitol.

The Louvins were finalists several times in the Country Music Hall of Fame selection process, but as of 1996 had not yet gained enough votes for induction. In late 1996, Charlie was in the studios working on a new album.

LOUVIN, IRA: *Singer, guitarist, songwriter. Born Rainesville, Alabama, April 21, 1924; died near Jefferson City, Missouri, June 20, 1965.*

The Louvin Brothers were so closely associated with each other for so many years in the minds of country fans that as the past faded into history many assumed their breakup was due to the untimely death of Ira in a car accident. Actually, the brothers had agreed to go their separate ways sometime before, though there's no doubt that Ira's passing had a near-shattering impact on Charlie.

The brothers grew up together on the family farm in Alabama, where they both worked long hours in the fields as boys. By the time they were in their teens, they had moved to Tennessee with their family, where they still helped do chores and sang and played guitars and other stringed instruments in their spare time. By his late teens, Ira had married and was working in a cotton mill with Charlie to help support his wife when the first chance to go into music came along. The brothers won a talent contest in Chattanooga, Tennessee, in 1943, which brought the opportunity to have their own daily program on station WDEF in the early morning.

That effort came to a halt when both entered the service in the mid-1940s. After being discharged, they got back together and won regular cast work on the WNOX, Knoxville, *Mid-day Merry-Go-Round.*

Their recording career began with one release on Decca, which didn't do much. In 1949, Fred Rose of Acuff-Rose Publishing brought them to the attention of MGM Records. Their material on MGM got off to a promising start, but that was interrupted when Charlie was called back to the Army during the Korean War. When he returned home in 1951, the brothers had to start almost from scratch. Both worked in the U.S. Post Office in Memphis and moonlighted as entertainers. They were following that routine when the chance came to sign with Capitol in 1951. Before long, some of their singles began to make lower-chart levels and jobs opened up on country network radio shows. By 1955, they had established their talents to the point that the *Grand Ole Opry* asked them to come on as regular cast members.

By the late 1950s, the brothers had a number of albums to their credit, including *Tragic Songs of Life, Nearer My God to Thee, Ira and Charlie* (released 2/58), *Family Who Prays* (2/59), and *Satan Is Real* (10/59). Their early 1960s LPs included *My Baby's Gone* (7/60), *Encore* (8/61), *Weapon of Prayer* (7/62), *Keep Your Eyes on Jesus* (1/63), and *Current Hits* (6/64).

The duo had four top-10 singles hits in the 1950s: "Hoping That You're Hoping," "I Don't Believe You've Met My Baby," and "You're Running Wild" in 1956, and "My Baby's Gone" in 1959. In the early 1960s, they placed a number of singles on the charts, but none approached the success of those earlier releases. That situation was one element in the increasing disagreements between the brothers that finally made them decide to split up in 1963, but an even more decisive factor was Ira's alcoholism.

Ira developed his own show and began playing road dates as a soloist in 1963. Also part of the show was his fourth wife, Florence, who sang under the professional name of Anne Young. It was while Ira and Florence were on the way back to Nashville from an engagement in Jefferson City, Missouri, on Father's Day 1965 that they were killed in a head-on collision on a Missouri highway. Ira was buried at Harpeth Memory Gardens on Route 100, fifteen miles west of Nashville.

Ira had been working on a solo album before his death that was issued posthumously by Capitol under the title *Ira Louvin* in December 1965. Several Louvin Brothers' albums were issued or reissued by Capitol in later times, including *Thank God* (7/65) and *Great Roy Acuff Songs* (12/67). The LP *Ira and Charles* also came out on the Metro label in February 1967.

Ira's memory was kept alive by his brother, who often devoted part of his concerts to some of the songs he and Ira had been known for. Many of the over 500 songs Ira and Charlie wrote together were included in albums or singles issued by other country artists in the late 1960s and on through the 1970s into the 1990s.

Starting in the late 1980s, the Louvin heritage took another turn with the efforts of Ira's daughter Kathy as a songwriter. The daughter of his first wife, from whom he separated when Kathy had just started elementary school, she had some bittersweet memories of her father and shed some light on the trauma of country artists in the post–World War II period.

She told Mandy Wilson of CMA's *Close Up* magazine (March 1992), "There were a lot of good times. I want to make that clear. In the old days, people would come to live with you when they were first trying to make it with their music. This was really special looking back, but there were a lot of unpleasant things for me as well."

These included increasingly divisive actions by her parents, though she emphasized they were never abusive or unkind to her. Some of the problems undoubtedly resulted from the pressures and fears of trying to succeed in a difficult industry. She told Wilson, "There was a lot of drinking and raising hell. My dad and his buddies were younger than I am when they were doing that. They'd travel on the road and never see the kind of money they were making. It's funny because they really didn't have anybody to look up to. In a way, they were making the history. It was a whole new thing and they were afraid that at any moment it was all going to fall out from under them. You know, that the *Opry* was going to close, and nobody would listen to Country Music anymore."

But it was also an exciting time, she recalled. "There were very few lazy Saturday or Sunday afternoons with people napping in the house, bread baking and Benny Goodman on the radio. We had a steel guitar that stayed in our living room. It belonged to Shot Jackson and it was there for whoever wanted to play it. There were things all over the place. I guess our house was kind of like a studio."

Kathy avoided the country field for a long time, but in November 1988 she began a writing partnership with Russell Smith, an Amazing Rhythm Aces alumnus. Over the next few years she had songs recorded by Dwight Yoakam, Patty Loveless, and Randy Travis, culminating in the breakthrough composition "Keep It Between the Lines" that provided Ricky Van Shelton with a number-one single in the early 1990s.

The Louvin Brothers were nominated several times for membership in the Country Music Hall of Fame, but as of the late 1990s had not gained enough total votes for induction. Ira's collaborations with his brother were recaptured in the extensive retrospective available from Bear Family Records of Germany in the 1990s. That firm compiled an 8 CD boxed set titled *The Louvin Brothers: Close Harmony*. It contained 219 songs comprising all of the Louvins' recordings on Apollo, Decca, MGM, and Capitol. In 1995, the independent Razor & Tie label produced a CD reissue of Louvin Brothers material.

LOVELESS, PATTY: *Singer, songwriter. Born Pikeville, Kentucky, January 4, 1957.*

Patty Loveless is certainly one of the most traditional of modern country singers. Her straight-from-the-heart, strong yet vulnerable vocal style is descended from the old-time mountain singers, down through the Carter family, Kitty Wells, and Loretta Lynn.

Like Loretta Lynn, Patty Ramey was a coal miner's daughter from Kentucky, the seventh of eight children. Her father later died of black lung disease. According to

Patty, she was a shy child and she liked to be alone. Her mother would ask her to sing for guests, and she would comply, but only when she could go into another room where she could be heard but not seen. Patty also starting writing songs.

When she was fourteen, Patty and her older brother, Roger, started performing as a duo in Nashville on weekends; there she was introduced to Porter Wagoner and Dolly Parton. In fact, Loveless recalls that "Dolly used to take me into the bathroom at the Ryman and show me how to put on make-up between shows—and that really reinforced what a country star was! . . . Of course, then I'd have to go back to school on Monday, so it was a pretty different way to grow up."

School notwithstanding, Patty stayed involved in the music scene. While still in her teens, she landed a publishing deal with the Wilburn Brothers' Surefire Music, the company that had originally promoted the career of Loretta Lynn. At the age of nineteen, Patty married Wilburn Brothers drummer Perry Lovelace. For a time, she sang rock and roll and worked as a waitress.

In 1985, with her marriage foundering, Patty decided to return to Nashville to try her hand at country music once again. She had changed her name from Lovelace to Loveless. With her brother, Roger, acting as her manager, Patty was ready for her career to take off. She signed her first record contract with MCA in 1985 and had her first single in 1986. Her first album, *Patty Loveless,* also came out that year. This was followed by *On Down the Line, Up Against My Heart, Greatest Hits, If My Heart Had Windows,* and *Honky Tonk Angel,* all on the MCA label under the aegis of record producer Tony Brown.

Patty slowly began to taste the success she had worked so long and hard for. In 1988, she had her first top-10 hit, "Blue Side of Town." Other hits that year were "If My Heart Had Windows" and "A Little Bit in Love." Her album, *Honky Tonk Angel,* went gold, indicating sales of more than 500,000 copies. She also became a member of the *Grand Ole Opry* in 1988. The next year, she hit the charts with "Don't Toss Us Away," "Timber I'm Falling in Love," and "The Lonely Side of Love." On the personal side, she got a divorce from Perry Lovelace in 1987. In February 1989 she married producer and bass player Emory Gordy, Jr., but they kept their marriage a secret from the public until the following year.

In the next few years, Patty kept up a rigorous touring schedule and continued to place hits on the country charts, such as "Chains" and "On Down the Line" in 1990 and "I'm That Kind of Girl" and "Hurt Me Bad (in a Real Good Way)" in 1991. However, her sixth album for MCA, *Up Against My Heart,* was not a commercial success, and her career seemed to stagnate. At this point, Patty made a difficult decision to change her record label and her business manager, a decision made

even more difficult because her business manager was her brother. She had made six records with MCA, but with such other country female stars as Wynonna, Trisha Yearwood, and Reba McEntire all on that label, Patty felt that she was getting lost in the shuffle. She asked for, and was granted, a release from her contract with MCA, and she signed with Epic Records. In the meantime, the single, "Jealous Bone," from her last record with MCA, rose to number nine on the *Radio and Records* charts in March 1992.

But in 1992, just when Patty was about to begin recording her first record for Epic, she came up against one of the biggest trials of her career. Although she had noticed problems with her voice as far back as 1989 or 1990, the problem kept getting worse. In October 1992, she received the diagnosis of an aneurysm, or an enlarged blood vessel, on one of her vocal cords. At first she did not want to cancel any of her appearances, but her doctor and her new business manager, Larry Fitzgerald, told her that she had no choice and would have to undergo surgery immediately. The surgery was a success, and after a month of being unable to talk at all, followed by several months of vocal therapy, Patty was ready to go back into the recording studio and then resume her touring schedule.

Patty's first effort for Epic, *Only What I Feel,* gave evidence that she was coming back stronger than ever. The single, "Blame It on Your Heart" rose to number one on the *Radio and Records* chart in June 1993. The same album yielded other hit singles, "Nothin' But the Wheel" and "You Will." The touching ballad "How Can I Help You Say Goodbye" was not only a number one single, it was also nominated for Song of the Year by the Country Music Association and also for a Grammy Award for Country Single of the Year. The album stayed on *Billboard* charts from spring of 1993 until early 1994 and went gold in 1994.

Patty's second Epic album, *When Fallen Angels Fly,* was released in 1994 and featured a mix of songs from the upbeat "I Try to Think About Elvis," which was a country hit in late 1994, to the haunting "Here I Am," which was a top-10 country hit in early 1995. The album entered the *Billboard* at number nine during September 1994 and by year-end had earned her a gold record award from the R.I.A.A. The single "You Don't Even Know Who I Am," also from that album, was a chart hit in 1995, making the hit lists in the spring and peaking at number five in *Billboard* in June. In the 1995 CMA voting she was nominated for Female Vocalist of the Year and for Album of the Year (for *When Fallen Angels Fly*). When the winners were announced on the October 1995 telecast from the Grand Ole Opry House stage, the latter trophy went to her as well as her husband, Emory Gordy, Jr., who produced it. She accepted the award in an emotional moment on the program when, tears in her eyes, she thanked husband Gordy for his help, noting he couldn't be there because he was working on an album. She commented, "I'm sure he's about to fall over, too."

The following month, Patty was among the performers who taped a program honoring the 70th anniversary of the *Grand Ole Opry*. The program was prepared on November 30, 1995, and telecast on CBS in January 1996. At the beginning of 1996 she had another single on the charts, "You Can Feel Bad," which moved rapidly upward until it reached number one in *Billboard, Radio & Records,* and *Country Network.* In February her third Epic album and ninth overall, *The Trouble with the Truth,* again produced by Emory Gordy, Jr., debuted at number fifteen in *Billboard* and continued on the list, after peaking at number ten, for the rest of the year. *When Fallen Angels Fly* continued to meet with buyer favor and by early 1996 was past platinum record levels. In May she had another single moving up the hit lists, "A Thousand Times a Day."

Academy of Country Music voters nominated her for Female Vocalist of the Year and *When Fallen Angels Fly* for Album of the Year for 1995. On the NBC-TV awards telecast on April 24, 1996, she received the top prize in the first of those categories.

Talking about how she and her husband combined their efforts in selecting material, she told Janet E. Williams, editor of CMA's *Close Up* (February 1996), "Emory and I listen to the songs and get together for pre-production. He sits down with a guitar and puts my voice down on tape, just to see what it's going to sound like on tape. Sometimes you sound differently than if you just sung off a microphone. I wish we didn't have to use microphones. I love the sound without them and without monitors. But it's a necessity, you have to. We try to see what I can do with a song in order to make it my own. I know that I am becoming more comfortable with what I am doing, but boy! There are times when I listen to some of the other girls out there singing like Trisha Yearwood, Wynonna and Martina McBride. I hear their voices and go, 'Wow! I wish my voice had a little bit of that in it.' But it doesn't, and that's what makes me different from them."

In the CMA 1996 voting, she was nominated in the Album of the Year (for *The Trouble with the Truth*) and Female Vocalist of the Year categories. When the results were announced on the October telecast, she won out in the latter category.

That Patty Loveless is able to sing, with absolute sincerity, both upbeat dance numbers and thought- or tear-provoking ballads, is the reason she is one of the most successful female country singers in the mid-1990s. Just as a good actor or actress may disappear into the roles they play, Patty tends to disappear into her songs. She may not be one of the more flashy personalities around; nevertheless, the songs she chooses to sing and the way she sings them are some of the best of what modern "traditional" country music is all about.—A. S.

LOVETT, LYLE: *Singer, guitarist, band leader (Large Band), songwriter, actor. Born Klein, Texas, November 1, c. 1959.*

In the 1990s, Lyle Lovett was known for a time more for his courtship and marriage of film star Julia Roberts than for his far-reaching creative efforts, which ranged from songwriting, touring and recording with his Large Band, and displaying unsuspected acting talent in a series of Robert Altman movies. But once the press moved on to other entertainment figure topics, he quietly resumed his position as an artist and performer who expanded the boundaries of whatever musical genre interested him at the time. He first made his mark in country, though with a unique style that confused radio programmers who couldn't decide if his urban-flavored styling properly belonged in their sector. In the 1990s, his following went far beyond traditional country ranks to embrace a growing number of people who took pleasure in his often quirky-seeming blends of rock, jazz, blues, and what might be called sophisticated country.

As a native Texan, a member of a family that had kept Houston as home base since 1840, he certainly could claim deep country roots. However, he emphasized that he grew up in an urban environment, not a rural one. He told Chris Willman of the *Los Angeles Times* ("Lovett Country," Calendar section, May 31, 1992, pp. 3, 54), "The people that are really successful in country music, they're the real thing. If to have been really successful at country music I would have to pretend to have been from somewhere out in the country and only listened to the *Grand Ole Opry* on Saturday nights and never gone to town, I wouldn't have enjoyed it very much."

Growing up in Houston, of course, he was exposed to plenty of country music as well as rock, pop, and other formats. He could play reasonably good guitar in his teens and did play with various kinds of groups in his high school and college years.

He enrolled in Texas A&M at College Station in 1975 as a journalism major. He recalled, "I was supposed to graduate in '79, but I played music a lot [at local clubs]," which delayed graduation until 1980. "I don't think I had what it takes to be a journalist. For one thing, journalists have to tell the truth. For another, I don't know if I could've worked that hard. What I do mostly is have fun. I get to do something for a living that I would do for fun, even if I couldn't do it for a living. I get to travel to interesting places; I get to meet interesting people; I get to eat out in great restaurants; and I get to sing and play my guitar. I get to think about life and turn it into music. What could be more fun than that?"

Of course, he said those words in the early 1990s, when his career had gone past the years of low-paying gigs and initial obscurity. His statements often couldn't be taken at face value, since in his low-key way he possessed a wry sense of humor; critics sometimes called some of his lyrics "quirky" and "bent." To which he replied, "I really don't consider myself quirky or bent. I enjoy having a sense of humor in my songs. In that, I owe a lot, in terms of influence, to songwriters like Randy Newman and Tom Waits and John Prine . . . but I don't really try to write quirky songs. I try to write songs that express a feeling or an emotion or an idea in a way that someone hasn't done before."

After getting his college degree he began to pursue his musical interests in earnest. He wrote and sang country-style material, though with strong pop-rock undertones. In the mid-1980s this won him a contract from MCA/Curb Records, which released his debut album, *Lyle Lovett,* soon afterward and followed that with the album *Pontiac* and *Lyle Lovett and His Large Band,* all of those recorded in Nashville. Considering his limited airplay on country stations (whose programmers, he whispered to Willman, felt "he's not quite right"), he managed to do surprisingly well through his engrossing concerts, which resulted in excellent word-of-mouth among younger country fans. His initial albums spawned a string of top-20 singles and the *Lyle Lovett and His Large Band* release earned a Grammy for Best Country Vocal Performance, Male.

He did it his way, eschewing cowboy boots or ten-gallon hats. While he wasn't averse to wearing T-shirts and jeans offstage, his typical concert pose made him look like a businessman in blue suit and conservative tie. From the start of his MCA/Curb affiliation he downplayed his country side. Karen Schoemer of the *New York Times* ("Straying from Country's Straight and Narrow," April 12, 1992) wrote, "Neither [k.d. lang nor Lovett] looks the part of a country singer. Put a cowboy hat atop Mr. Lovett's tall, sculpted do, and it would sit a few inches above his head . . . 'I ain't never been no cowboy,' sings Mr. Lovett in 'Cowboy Man' [from his debut album]. 'Heaven knows I've tried.' "

It took three years between Lovett's third and fourth albums, and the latter, *Joshua Judges Ruth,* signaled a move away from heavy emphasis on country and country rock to a melange that included elements of gospel, pop, jazz, folk, and, in particular, new emphasis on rhythm & blues stylings. Lovett was hardly retired in the interim. He kept writing new songs and touring with his impressive array of musicians, produced an album for MCA Master Series singer-songwriter Walter Hyatt, worked with the Grateful Dead on material for their *Deadicated* album, cut tracks for the *Switch* movie soundtrack, and made his acting debut in Altman's *The Player.*

The road to acting came with the help of Altman's daughter, who took her father to a Lovett show at Los Angeles's Greek Theatre in 1990. Altman thought there was something about the musician's style that made him right for a film he was considering called *Short*

Cuts. He talked to Lyle about that, but when that film was delayed in favor of *The Player,* he found a role for Lyle in the new movie as a Pasadena police officer. (Lovett later was cast as a baker when *Short Cuts* was filmed.)

Lovett, never having considered the acting profession before, was somewhat nonplussed. He told Chris Willman, "I said, 'Should I take some acting lessons? I've never done this. I want to do a good job.' [Altman] said, 'Nah, that'll just screw you up. Just come and hang out and get to know everybody. Besides, this guy you're playing, he's not from Hollywood, but he's hanging around these Hollywood people and trying to act cool, and he's not a very good actor.' " Lovett proved he was, in fact, an excellent actor both in that movie and Altman's next project. When *Short Cuts* came out in 1993, Altman had already penciled Lyle in for his follow-on film cast.

When the *Joshua Judges Ruth* album came out in early 1992, it won considerable praise in the non-country press. Reviewers at *FMOB,* an industry magazine that focused on rock formats from middle of the road to heavy metal and grunge, chose the track "You've Never Been So Good Up to Now" as one of its premier picks for radio play. "Though critics have heralded his talent for years, programmers have looked askance at Lyle, perceiving him as either too Rock for Country radio or too Country for Rock radio. . . . In concert, he lets his 'large band' of accomplished virtuosos solo and improvise frequently for a music spectacle that keeps the rest rooms in the hall empty at all times. [On this song] backed by L.A.'s finest studio rats . . . Lyle pours on a stinkin' blues groove that nets his most AOR (Album Oriented Rock) suited track yet."

Lovett's Large Band roster changed considerably over the years. Among members of the group in the late 1980s and early 1990s were guitarist Ray Herndon, pianist Matt Rollings (nominated for CMA Instrumentalist of the Year a number of times), bass guitarists Leland Sklar and Edgar Meyer, cellist John Hagen, and vocalist Francine Reed.

Since both Julia Roberts and Lovett had roles in *The Player,* some conjectured that's where their first meeting took place. He had wanted to make her acquaintance, he told Robert Hilburn of the *Los Angeles Times* ("I Couldn't Be Happier," Calendar section, July 22, 1993, p. F1), but he had concert dates while her movie takes were made. "I was looking forward to meeting her because someone called me a couple of years ago and said they had seen her on some movie premiere or other event on one of the Nashville Network shows. They asked her who her favorite country singer was and she said me."

His interest was further whetted in early 1993, when he was interviewed by Susan Sarandon's brother, who is on the *St. Petersburg (Florida) Times* staff. He told Lovett "he had just gotten back from Costa Rica with

Susan and Julia and that Julia had all my albums. So this time I decided I should call her and I did."

The two married soon after, and his concert audiences were abuzz constantly about whether she'd make an appearance, which she did on some occasions. Lovett had written several songs in past years that made fun of marriage, and he took note of that in some of his concerts. In a summer 1993 appearance at Los Angeles's Universal Amphitheater, he introduced a song by saying, "This song is proof that, uh, anything I ever wrote about marriage or about, er, the opposite sex— that all was out of, er, ignorance." The song was titled "She's No Lady (She's My Wife)." Unfortunately, his idyll was not to last.

By the time Lyle's sixth album, *I Love Everybody,* was released on Curb/MCA on September 27, 1994, *Joshua Judges Ruth* had been certified gold by the R.I.A.A. The first video from the new album, "Penguins," was shot in Paris while Lovett was there for the filming of his role in the new Robert Altman film *Pret-a-Porter* (in which Lyle played a Texas millionaire boot manufacturer). For that video project, Lovett and collaborator Billy Williams (who coproduced the album) directed an extended version featuring many of the performers in *Pret-a-Porter* that included Lauren Bacall, Stephen Rea, Teri Garr, and Danny Aiello.

On October 5, 1994, Lovett was back in Nashville to take part in the 28th Annual Country Music Association TV Awards program. He performed with Asleep at the Wheel, doing one of the numbers from that band's album, *Tribute to the Music of Bob Wills and His Texas Playboys,* which was nominated for Album of the Year. There was the usual contrast between Lyle's accountant-like appearance and the spangled cowboy costume of band leader Ray Benson.

Lyle recalled the evolution of his personal fashion for Bob Hilburn. "Well, I guess the haircut is a trademark, but it was unintentional. The reason for it originally was I went on this tour with Bonnie Raitt for about two months and I didn't get a haircut and all of a sudden people were writing about my hair—and I thought this is a pretty easy way to [get attention]. So I sort of left it.

"But the rest of what you see is me. I never had the kind of personality where I just sort of walk into a room and take over. I have always been quieter. But I feel real comfortable with the audiences. They seem to know my songs better than ever and it's like visiting with old friends."

Like so many show business marriages, Lyle's and Julia's didn't survive the long separations and different job requirements. By the time the Grammy Awards telecast came along in early 1995, the two had separated. They divorced soon after. (The marriage lasted 21 months.) The Asleep at the Wheel Bob Wills tribute album and the track "Blues for Dixie" from it were nominated, respectively, for Best Country Album and

Best Country Performance by a Duo or Group with Vocal. The album didn't win, but "Blues for Dixie," the song that featured Lyle and the band, earned a Grammy. Lyle, however, was unable to be on hand, because of injuries suffered in a motorcycle accident.

By summer he had recovered and was pursuing his concerts and other entertainment field activities. In the summer of 1996, Lyle's first new album since the breakup of his marriage to Julia was released, *The Road to Esmeralda.* The tracks covered the gamut from high spirited or humorous numbers like "Her First Mistake" and "Don't Touch My Hat" to less cheerful ones that outlined failed relationships ("I Can't Love You Anymore," "It Ought to Be Easier"), but Lovett emphasized to interviewers that they shouldn't necessarily draw parallels between lyric content and his personal life. Among the album's high spots was "Long Tall Texan" in which Randy Newman sang backup. When Lyle embarked on his concert tour in support of the album (which included an appearance on September 7, 1996, at the Theater at Madison Square Garden in New York) he sported a curly hairstyle rather than his high pompadour. The album quickly demonstrated he still had rapport with country fans, showing up on the *Billboard* country list soon after its release and gaining the top 10 in September.

LULU BELLE AND SCOTTY: *Vocal and instrumental duo, songwriters. Myrtle Eleanor Cooper Wiseman (Lulu Belle), born Boone, North Carolina, December 24, 1913; Scotty Wiseman, born Spruce Pine, North Carolina, November 8, 1909; died Gainesville, Florida, February 1, 1981.*

The comedy and singing of the husband and wife team of Lulu Belle and Scotty was one of the highlights of the country-music scene from the early 1930s to the 1950s. At one stage of their careers, they vied with stars of the *Grand Ole Opry* for national attention as headliners of the rival *National Barn Dance* show broadcast nationally for decades from station WLS in Chicago. Apart from their performing efforts, some of the songs written by Scotty or cowritten by Scotty and Lulu Belle rank as classics in country and folk music and have been recorded and re-recorded over the years by many other artists.

Both were natives of North Carolina. Scotty grew up in the Spruce Pine region, where he learned many traditional songs from his friends and family. During his years at Altamont High School, Crossmore, North Carolina, he perfected his instrumental style on guitar and banjo. Although he performed in his spare time, his goal was a teaching career. With that in mind, he attended Duke University during 1927–1928, then entered Fairmont State College in West Virginia in 1929, earning his B.A. in 1932.

Meanwhile, Wiseman added to his performing experience. In 1927 he made his radio debut on station

WRVA in Richmond, Virginia. During his college years in Fairmont, he sang and played as a regular performer on station WMMN. That brought the opportunity to join the cast of the *National Barn Dance* in Chicago. It was too good to pass up, so he accepted the offer in 1933 and moved to the Windy City. There he met another North Carolinian named Myrtle Eleanor Cooper who soon became Mrs. Wiseman. Myrtle was born in Boone and also enjoyed singing the traditional country songs of her home area from her girlhood. By the time she was a teenager, she had learned to play guitar and progressed from performing for friends or in school events to more extensive musical efforts in the late 1920s. For a while, she earned her primary living as a shoe clerk, her entertainment work essentially a sideline. In 1932 she auditioned and made the *National Barn Dance* and was a regular cast member the year before Scott Wiseman joined the show.

It wasn't too long after the team of Lulu Belle and Scotty debuted on the *Barn Dance* that they were on the way to becoming favorites of the program's nationwide audience. In 1933, Scotty wrote a song called "Home Coming Time" that became one of their first big hits the following year. It was the forerunner of many major hits on such labels as Conqueror, Vocalion, Bluebird, Brunswick, Vogue, Mercury, and KaHill. In the 1930s and 1940s, their best-known singles included "Whipperwill Time," "Mountain Dew," "Empty Christmas Stockings," "Time Will Tell," "In the Doghouse Now," "My Heart Cries for You," and "Have I Told You Lately That I Love You."

"Mountain Dew," a great country comedy classic, was cowritten by Scotty and Bascom Lunsford in 1935. Other songs that he wrote or cowrote (some with Lulu Belle) included "Empty Christmas Stocking" (1938); "Remember Me" (1940); "Time Will Tell" (1945); "You Don't Love Me like You Used to Do," "Tell Her You Love Her," "That New Vitamin E" (1946); "Don'tcha" (1947); "That Old Bible" (1953); "Tender He Watches over Me" (1954); "Between You and Me" (1955); and "Come as You Are" (1957). His most famous song was "Have I Told You Lately That I Love You," recorded by well over a hundred artists over the years.

During the 1930s and throughout the 1940s, the fame of the team (who became known as "The Sweethearts of Country Music") spread far beyond Chicago as network broadcasts of the *Barn Dance,* personal appearance tours, and records made them national figures. For many years, besides performing on the *Barn Dance,* where they were regular cast members from 1933 to 1958, they had their own highly rated radio show on WLS, *Breakfast in the Blue Ridge.* For a while in the early 1940s, they starred on the *Boone County Jamboree* on station WLW, Cincinnati, which later became the *Midwestern Hayride.* In 1949, back in Chicago, they were featured on station WNBQ-TV, an association that lasted until 1957.

The duo were guest stars on many major shows in the 1950s, including the *Grand Ole Opry* in 1950 and 1952 and Red Foley's *Ozark Jamboree* in 1957–58. They also were guests on many major variety TV programs over those years, including an appearance on *The Steve Allen Show* in 1955. The team also made several movies over the years, including *Harvest Moon* (1938), *Country Fair* (1939), *Village Barn Dance* (1940), *Swing Your Partner* (1942), *Hi Ya Neighbor* (1943), *National Barn Dance* (1943).

The Wisemans were beginning to tire of the performing grind in the mid-1950s. Scotty began taking courses at Northwestern University, Evanston, Illinois, for an advanced teaching degree. He received his master's in 1958 and he and Lulu Belle moved back to North Carolina soon after, settling in Spruce Pine, where Scotty taught speech at Spruce Pine College. They announced they were in semiretirement from the entertainment field. They still did some concertizing, particularly during college vacation periods. It was not until the 1960s that they sharply curtailed those endeavors and made only occasional appearances. They were still represented on records as of the mid-1960s, when Starday issued such LPs as *Lulu Belle and Scotty* (1963) and *Down Memory Lane* (1964).

In the 1970s, the Wisemans were drawn out of show business retirement from time to time for special occasions, such as the annual Fan Fair Reunion in Nashville, sponsored by the Country Music Association and *Grand Ole Opry.* From their set at the 1975 event, their performance of "Have I Told You Lately That I Love You" was included in the album of the show issued by CMA's Foundation Records.

During the 1970s, Scotty continued with his teaching activities while Lulu Belle became interested in politics. She and Scotty were essentially retired from show business when she decided to pursue a political career, but they used their act as part of her 1974 campaign efforts. She served two terms in the state legislature, one starting in 1975 and the second in 1977. She ran as a Democrat, becoming the first of that party to serve in a normally Republican district since 1922.

In 1980, Lulu Belle and Scotty were nominated for the Country Music Hall of Fame. Sadly, not long afterward, in February 1981, Scotty died of a heart attack in Gainesville, Florida.

Some years later, in discussing her early years in show business with William Lightfoot for an article in *The Journal of Country Music* ("Belle of the Barn Dance: Reminiscing with Lulu Belle Wiseman Stamey," Volume XII, no. 1, 1987), Lulu Belle stressed that if it hadn't been for Scotty's love for performing she would have been happy to be a homebody. With income from his teaching, she said, "we could've gone back up to Fairmont. That's what I wanted to do—have five or six kids, and just be 'Mrs. Wiseman.' That's all I wanted to be." (They did have two children, Linda and Steve Wiseman.)

But Scotty at the time loved entertainment. "I don't know what I didn't like about it. One thing I didn't like about it: my mother gave me all kinds of advice about the boys, you know, all the fellows, and these men on the show were always trying to get around you, you know, young girl, free, trying to get you somewhere in a bed."

After she and Scotty decided to get married, she told Lightfoot, they almost decided to tie the knot on a *Barn Dance* program. (They didn't appear as a team until their marriage.) But they worried that when the ceremony came to the part asking "'if there's anyone here who . . . ' Scott had a couple of girlfriends before me, and they were pretty jealous. So he was afraid they might come up with something when they asked if there were any reason that this wedding shouldn't be, why these two shouldn't be married. Scott said, 'What if one of those girls walked out and said something on the air?' So we were afraid of it and just went ahead and did it (in Naperville, Illinois).

"And then we became the Hayloft Sweethearts," she added. "And I never liked it, that my name was before Scotty's. He didn't mind, but I minded. I thought it should be 'Scotty and Lulu Belle,' because you always refer to the man first. The reason they did that was I [was on the show] first, and I'd already gotten myself a little name before he and I got together." She suggested to the program manager that their names be reversed, "and he said that it was because I was there first. It didn't bother Scott, so it stayed that way."

Lulu mourned the loss of her husband for many months before marrying a longtime friend and neighbor of the Wisemans, Ernest Stamey, a retired lawyer and Christmas tree farmer. In the mid-1980s, many of the Lulu Belle and Scotty early recordings became available on a reissue on the Old Homestead label, *Lulu Belle and Scotty: Early and Great, Volume 1*. In 1986, she ended her long absence from the recording studio by working on a new album for Homestead, *Snickers and Tender Memories with Lulu Belle*.

LYNN, LORETTA: *Singer, guitarist, band leader, songwriter. Born Butcher Holler, Kentucky, April 14, 1935. Elected to Country Music Hall of Fame in 1988.*

Starting from an unlikely place called Butcher Holler, Loretta Lynn went on to become a reigning queen not only of country music, but popular music as well. By the start of the 1980s, with the success of her autobiography and the movie based on that book, she was the most famous "Coal Miner's Daughter" in the world, a heady achievement for a girl from humble origins whose main goal as a teenaged bride was to make a good home for a husband and growing family.

As a young girl growing up in a log cabin in the Kentucky mountains, she was known to her friends and family as Loretta Webb. Her parents named her after movie star Loretta Young. The actress's picture had been one of several clipped from fan magazines by Mrs. Webb to help brighten up the cabin walls. Though the comforts were few, as Loretta Lynn recalled, there was a lot of warmth and love during her childhood years, particularly in the close rapport she had with her coal miner father.

As Loretta approached her teen years, she helped with household chores and got what education she could from a mountain grade school that she attended through eighth grade. She was still only thirteen when she met a boy named O. V. Lynn—usually called by one of two nicknames, "Mooney" or "Doolittle"—at a school social. He was attracted to her and they started dating. Within a month, he managed to get her father's approval for them to marry.

When they married, Mooney had a job with the Consolidated Coal Company, but before a year had passed, he lost it. With other work scarce, Mooney and Loretta's brother Jay Lee (Junior) Webb decided to hitchhike cross-country to look for jobs in the state of Washington. After finding work on a farm, Mooney sent travel money to his fourteen-year-old wife, by then pregnant with their first child. Though Loretta went to join him in Custer, Washington, it was a wrenching experience to leave her home and, particularly, her beloved father. Later, as she noted in her autobiography, one of her greatest sorrows was to be far from her family when her father died.

For about four years, Loretta's occupation was taking care of their living quarters—three little rooms and an outhouse, and no running water—and ministering to a growing family. (She had four of their six children before she was twenty-one.) She was good at housework, she stressed, as evidenced by her winning all the blue ribbons awarded for food canning one year at the Washington State Fair. Meanwhile, her husband was the breadwinner, first as a farm worker, later as a logger.

Around the house, Loretta sometimes sang to the children just to keep her mind occupied. Taking note of that, her husband began to mull over the possibilities of turning her talents to economic use. On her eighteenth birthday, he bought her an inexpensive guitar and urged her to learn to play it.

Loretta managed to pick up the rudiments of guitar playing and Mooney kept trying to figure out ways of getting her career underway. Bolstered by a number of drinks one Saturday night, he took her to the local Grange hall in Custer and talked the country band playing there to let her try out for the radio show they taped on Wednesdays. Though the band was counting on their not showing up, Mooney and Loretta appeared at the designated time and Loretta sang so well she was asked to become a member of the Saturday night show. By the end of the 1950s, she had formed her own band, with brother Jay Lee Webb (on guitar) backing her at shows in clubs in Custer and other towns in the Northwest.

Both Lynns were now excited by Loretta's prospects, blissfully unaware of the tremendous gap between where they were and what usually was required for success in country music. As Loretta became more confident about her singing, they looked for some way of breaking into the record business. They managed to get the backing of a Vancouver, British Columbia, businessman for her to make her first recording. Called "I'm a Honky Tonk Girl," it was pressed on the Zero Records label. Mooney somehow got a list of country radio stations and soon was mailing off review copies of the 45 rpm disc to D.J.s across the country. Many of them, surprisingly, took the time to listen to it and quite a few began to play it even though, as it turned out, there were no copies in the stores that fans could buy.

Loretta and Mooney were nothing if not resourceful. As soon as they heard the record was getting some airplay, they decided to do their own promotional tour. She later told an interviewer about their reaction after hearing it was on the charts: "We didn't even know what the charts was. But, by golly, me and Doolittle loaded up in that old car, and Shirley and Jay Lee Webb—my brother and his wife—kept all four kids, and we took out to hit ever' radio station that was country. Zero Records give us money to buy gas—but not food—and we went all the way across the country one way and come back another way, eatin' bologna and cheese and crackers and sleepin' in the car."

Hugh Cherry, long a major country disc jockey in Los Angeles, remembered the day his station was a stop on that early 1960s trip. "I was working as a late night jock on KFOX in Long Beach, California. One evening, the buzzer rang downstairs and a voice said, 'Hello, I'm Loretta Lynn, and a disc jockey in Seattle, Washington, said I should come to Los Angeles and see Hugh Cherry. I've got a record for you.' So I let her in and she comes up very talkative and animated.

"'I understand that if somebody wants to get a hillbilly record to break in California that you are the man to see. Well, I've got one right here—"Honky Tonk Girl." It's mine!'"

"I put it on the turntable and the record was really good. Loretta said she was going to Nashville to get the record played there and to be on the *Grand Ole Opry*. I said to her, 'But honey, don't you know that it sometimes take three or four years to get on the *Opry*?" Loretta replied, 'I can't wait that long.'

"Well, a few months later I began to hear some rumblings out of Nashville about her. 'Honky Tonk Girl' became a hit, and soon Loretta was on the Decca label. And sure enough she got on the *Grand Ole Opry* . . . a bit sooner than I expected."

By any yardstick, Loretta's rise qualifies as meteoric. Just an unknown in 1961 with one single to her credit on an obscure label, by 1962 she was on her way to stardom. It was a year in which she had her first top 10 single for Decca, appropriately named "Success,"

and was asked to become a regular on the *Opry*. As she and her family settled in to their new Nashville surroundings, her name was becoming known to country fans the length and breadth of the States. In fact, for 1962, *Cash Box* magazine named her the Most Programmed Female Country Star.

She was beginning to experience the excitement and exhilaration of success—as well as its pitfalls, among them, resentment among some of her country music peers at her swift rise, the strain of constant touring, and the natural nervousness of a newcomer on the scene. Luckily, at this point she was greatly helped by a newfound close friend, established country star Patsy Cline. As Loretta wrote in her autobiography, Patsy's warmth and understanding had an impact on her life almost as great as her father's. Not surprisingly, Loretta experienced a tremendous sense of loss after Patsy's untimely death in a plane crash in March 1963.

Loretta continued her career, however, and met with steadily growing approval from fans and critics. Throughout the mid- and late 1960s she kept adding to her list of hit singles and albums, including a number of songs she wrote herself. In 1963, she had the top-10 single "Before I'm Over You," and in 1964, "Wine, Women and Song." In 1965, she had the top-10 singles "Blue Kentucky Girl," "Happy Birthday," and "The Home You're Tearing Down," and in 1966, "Dear Uncle Sam," "You Ain't Woman Enough to Take My Man Away," and the number-one-ranked "Don't Come Home a Drinkin'" (the first two written by her and the third a collaboration). "Don't Come Home a Drinkin'" stayed on the lists into 1967, when Loretta had another top-10 hit, "If You're Not Gone Too Long." In late 1967, *Billboard* magazine named her the Top Country Female Vocalist of the year. In 1968, she made the top 10 with the singles "Fist City" and "You've Just Stepped In (From Stepping Out on Me)."

She also established herself as a major album artist during those years, with most of her releases on Decca making the charts and many achieving top 10 status. Her debut LP on the label, *Loretta Lynn*, came out in early 1964. Among the other albums that followed during the decade were: *Before I'm over You* (1964); *Songs from My Heart, Blue Kentucky Girl* (1965); *I Like 'Em Country* (1966); *Don't Come Home a Drinkin', Singin' with Feelin'* (1967); *Fist City* (1968); and *Woman of the World,* (1969). Other albums released at the end of the 1960s and in the early 1970s were: *Wings upon Your Horns, Coal Miner's Daughter, Hymns, I Wanna Be Free, Loretta Lynn Writes 'Em and Sings 'Em,* and *We Only Make Believe.* The last named was a duet album with Conway Twitty, also a Decca (later MCA) Records superstar. The Lynn/Twitty duo became one of the most successful in country music history, achieving dozens of top-10 hit singles and albums during the 1970s and early 1980s. One of their early collaborations, "After the Fire Is Gone," won the

1971 Grammy Award for Best Country Vocal Performance by a Duo or Group.

From the mid-1960s on, Loretta accrued many nominations and awards in every poll covering the field of country music. In the very first Country Music Association annual awards voting in 1967, she was named Female Vocalist of the Year, and in 1972, she won the highest award given out by the CMA, Entertainer of the Year. She and Conway Twitty were nominated many times for CMA Vocal Duo of the Year and won the award several times. Loretta won the Academy of Country Music Female Vocalist of the Year award a number of times and in 1975 she was voted ACM Entertainer of the Year. (In fact, in the 1975 ACM awards, Loretta won in three categories: Female Vocalist of the Year, Album of the Year for *Feelin's,* with Conway, and Top Vocal Group, with Conway.) All in all, as of the early 1980s, Loretta had received more awards from the CMA and ACM than any other performer.

During the 1970s and early 1980s, Loretta could almost always be found on the country singles and album charts. In some cases, her recordings crossed over onto the pop charts. In 1970, she had one of the year's best-selling singles with her rendition of her own composition, "Coal Miner's Daughter." (Later in the decade it served as the title for her autobiography and the movie based on the book.) Loretta's best-selling singles of the first half of the 1970s included "Here I Am Again" (1972); "Love Is the Foundation" (1973); "They Don't Make 'Em Like My Daddy" and "Trouble in Paradise" (1974); and "Home" (1975). With Conway Twitty, she had such hits as "Mississippi Woman—Louisiana Man," "Before I Hang Up the Phone," and "Feelin's."

In the second half of the 1970s, her chart makers included the MCA releases: "When the Tingle Becomes a Chill" and "Red, White and Blue" (1976); "Why Can't He Be You" (1977); "Spring Fever," "We've Come a Long Way Baby" (1978); and "I Can't Feel You Anymore" and "I've Got a Picture of You on My Mind" (1979). With Conway Twitty, her successes included "The Letter" (1976); "I Can't Love You Enough" (1977); "From Seven Till Ten/You're the Reason My Kids Are Ugly" (1978); and "You Know Just What I'd Do/The Sadness of It All" (1979).

Her charted albums during the 1970s included: *Lead Me On* (with Twitty, 1972); *One's on the Way* (1972); *They Don't Make 'Em Like My Daddy, Country Partners* (with Twitty) (1974–1975); *Back to the Country, Home, Feelin's* (with Twitty) (1975); *When the Chill Becomes a Tingle* (1976); *Unlimited Talent* (with Twitty, number one, August 1976); *I Remember Patsy, Dynamic Duo* (with Twitty) (1977); *Honky Tonk Heroes* (with Twitty) (1978); *Diamond Duet,* (with Twitty); *The Very Best of Loretta Lynn and Conway Twitty* (1979).

Throughout the 1970s Loretta kept up a whirlwind schedule of concerts and TV appearances, sometimes performing with Conway Twitty. Her shows totaled about 125 a year and usually involved 150,000 miles of travel per year in her specially outfitted bus. Her TV credits included three regular-season Dean Martin TV shows in 1973 and two in his summer series, as well as guest spots on a Frank Sinatra special, *The Ed Sullivan Show, The Kraft Music Hall,* Dick Cavett, David Frost, Merv Griffin, Dinah Shore, *The Mac Davis Show, The Flip Wilson Special—Travels with Flip, The 50th Anniversary of the Grand Ole Opry,* a Bill Cosby special, and *The Tonight Show.* She also was spotlighted on the CBS documentary program *Magazine* and was cohost twice in the mid-1970s of the NBC-TV *Midnight Special* program. To top off her impressive list of television credits, President Jimmy Carter invited her to perform on the CBS preinaugural special.

One of her major projects in the mid-1970s was the writing of an autobiography in collaboration with *New York Times* correspondent George Vecsey that spanned the period of her life from the ages of thirteen to twenty-five. Released in hard cover by Henry Regnery Company, *Coal Miner's Daughter* became one of the best-selling books of 1976. Issued as a paperback by Warner Books in April 1977, it climbed past the 1.2 million sales mark during the summer. The movie rights were purchased by Universal Studios and by the fall of 1979, the production had neared completion with Sissy Spacek starring as Loretta, Tommy Lee Jones playing the part of Loretta's husband, Mooney Lynn, and Beverly D'Angelo taking the role of Patsy Cline.

Coal Miner's Daughter was previewed in the Kennedy Center in Washington, DC, in early 1980, where it received excellent reviews, and soon had enthusiastic support from critics in other major cities. The film became one of the year's hits and the soundtrack album on MCA was in the country top 10 by April, where it stayed for months.

The movie naturally spawned still more requests for interviews from TV, newspapers, and magazines. Loretta continued with business as usual in the early 1980s, turning out new recordings and touring. Her chart singles included "Pregnant Again" (she never hesitated writing or singing about "controversial" aspects of modern life, as indicated previously by releases like "The Pill"), "Naked in the Rain," and "Cheatin' on a Cheater" (1980); and "Somebody Led Me Away" (1981). Her duet hits with Conway Twitty in the early 1980s included "It's True Love" (1980) and "Love What Your Lovin' Does to Me" (1981). Early 1980s charted LPs by Loretta included *Loretta* and *Lookin' Good.*

Her continued emphasis on personal appearances related to her philosophy about the relationship between a performer and audiences. "If you're gonna record," she told an interviewer, "you gotta be out there with the people that buy your records. That's the way I feel about it." People who couldn't get tickets to her standing room only shows could still see her perform on TV. Among the specials that featured her talents in the early 1980s was the spring 1982 show on NBC, *Loretta Lynn—the Lady, the Legend.*

Besides the other recognition gained in the early 1980s, Loretta received Country Music Association nominations for Female Vocalist of the Year in 1980 and 1981 and she and Conway Twitty were nominated for Vocal Duo of the Year in those years as well as 1982. In the mid- and late 1980s she remained a featured artist on the *Opry* and an audience favorite on the concert circuit. She continued to place recordings on the charts, though not with the regularity or impact of years past due in part to the industry focus on new competitors for country glory. But her tremendous contributions to the field were recognized by her peers, who elected her to the Country Music Hall of Fame in 1988.

In the mid-1990s the Country Music Foundation offered a number of her recordings in its catalog. Those included (all on MCA Records); *Loretta Lynn: Country Music Hall of Fame Series; Loretta Lynn's Greatest Hits* and *Greatest Hits, Volume 2; Loretta Lynn/20 Greatest Hits; Loretta Lynn/Remember Patsy;* and *Loretta Lynn/Coal Miner's Daughter.* Also available were video presentations of a variety of Loretta's performances such as the sixty-minute *Honky Tonk Girl* compilation (including home movies) chronicling her life from her first *Grand Ole Opry* appearances to her selection as Country Music's Entertainer of the Decade; *An Evening with Loretta Lynn,* offering live concert footage of eighteen of her most notable song successes; and *Loretta Lynn in Concert,* filmed at Harrah's in Reno, Nevada.

At the start of the 1990s, her husband, Mooney's, heart problems caused her to cut back on her musical activities, particularly reducing tour commitments, though she certainly didn't move into retirement or even semiretirement. In 1992 she was asked to take part in a new recording project with two other superstars, Dolly Parton and Tammy Wynette. The three put together a list of some sixty song candidates which, after discussions with coproducers Parton and Steve Buckingham, were reduced to twenty-two recordings, then pared down to twelve for the final version, titled *Honky Tonk Angels,* issued by Columbia in the fall of 1993. The twelve tracks contained nine stylings of country "standards" plus one original each from the ladies. Loretta's contribution was "Wouldn't It Be Great," a song in which a woman fantasizes about her husband's giving up drinking and making her his only true love.

Almost simultaneously with the album's release, the threesome performed their version of "Silver Threads and Golden Needles" from the disc on the October 1993 CMA Awards telecast. The album made both the country and pop charts and had passed R.I.A.A. gold-record levels by early 1994.

In interviews promoting the record, Loretta emphasized the challenges facing any new artist trying to make it in country music, a situation particularly severe for female performers. To achieve stardom, she said, a performer couldn't go halfway. An aspiring artist "had to jump in head first and never look back." And, as she stressed to writer Howard Dee, "You have to be specially strong in country music. As a woman you have to fight doubly hard in what is a male dominated industry. I haven't taken any 'male crap' over the years. I've simply remained in touch with myself as much as I could. When I've lost touch with me, and there have been times when that's happened, they are the times when I've made career mistakes."

In late 1994, MCA released a boxed set of Loretta's work on three CDs or cassettes called *Loretta Lynn: Honky Tonk Girl.* As might be expected, the collection contained most of her career recording highlights including her key self-penned compositions. On June 11, 1996, at the Entertainment Radio Networks Inc.'s third annual Country Music Radio Awards held at the Tennessee Performing Arts Center she was presented with the Legends Award. (Previous honorees were Johnny Cash in 1994 and Merle Haggard in 1995.) Up to that time this was the only awards show created for radio.

LYNYRD SKYNYRD: *Vocal and instrumental group. Members (mid-1970s): Ronnie Van Zant, born Jacksonville, Florida, 1949, died near McComb, Mississippi, October 20, 1977; Allen Collins, born Jacksonville, Florida, c. 1949, died January 23, 1990; Gary Rossington, born Jacksonville, Florida, c. 1949; Steve Gaines, born Florida, c. early 1950s, died near McComb, Mississippi, October 20, 1977; Artimus Pyle, born Spartanburg, South Carolina; Billy Powell, born Florida, c. early 1950s; Leon Wilkeson, born Florida, c. early 1950s. Group disbanded in late 1977, reorganized in 1987 with Rossington, Collins, Powell, Wilkerson, Pyle, Ed King, Randall Hall, Johnny Van Zant.*

It's possible to find all sorts of strange portents and symbols in the events leading up to the tragic plane crash in October 1977 that wrote "finis" to the original Lynyrd Skynyrd band. The band had just released an album, *Street Survivors,* whose cover showed the seven musicians seemingly engulfed in flames (achieved by setting fire to an old set on the Universal Studios back lot). Some of the songs in the album reflected on what appeared to be self-destructive urges among many of the members from which they always previously managed to escape.

Even so, five of the seven bandsmen survived when an aging Convair 240 plowed into swampy ground near McComb, Mississippi. Unfortunately, the two who failed to come through were perhaps the key members of that group: lead singer/songwriter Ronnie Van Zant (whose younger brother, Donnie, starred in another successful band, .38 Special) and guitarist/songwriter Steve Gaines. Gaines's sister, Cassie (a singer with the band), also perished. Van Zant on several occasions commented on knowing success could be ephemeral, but his untimely passing occurred just when things seemed brightest for his band and when the mantle of number-one country-blues-rock group in the South had shifted from the Allman Brothers to his boogie band from Jacksonville.

Van Zant was one of a trio of Jacksonville high schoolers who decided to form a band at a time when the Allmans, also Floridians, had been playing professionally for close to a half decade. The other two were Gary Rossington and Allen Collins, who met in 1965, Gary recalled, when he was in eighth grade. A year later, they met Ronnie at a time when sports was the prime interest, not music. The three played Pop Warner baseball together and, Ronnie later recalled, he in particular dreamt of a sports career. "I went as far as playing [American] Legion ball. The next step would have been AA [minor league ball]. I played center field. I had the highest batting average in the league one year and a good arm—you've gotta have a good arm to play center field. Gary was good too, but he gave it all up when he got to like the Rolling Stones."

Gary's enthusiasm for rock music, he told interviewer John Swenson, came from seeing the Stones perform on the *Ed Sullivan Show*. Soon he was spending hours practicing guitars while urging Collins and Van Zant to join him in a band. "It happened slow at first. It took a long time to learn how. We were trying to learn from people, no lessons or anything, just watch. After about four years playin' at parties, playin' anywhere we could, we were makin' about $20 a week.

"We'd play anything on the radio, 'Satisfaction,' 'Day Tripper'—we were into Yardbirds, Blues Magoos. We used to play at clubs at night and go to school during the day. They called us a psychedelic band and it was hard for us to get work at dances because people wanted top 40."

During those years the three friends and whomever they got to play with them changed band names almost as fast as they changed socks. Their titles included the Noble Five, Wildcats, Sons of Satan, Pretty Ones, and One Per Cent. The last one stuck the longest before the band became Lynyrd Skynyrd. (Lynyrd Skynyrd was a takeoff on the name of their high school gym teacher, Leonard Skinner, who had them expelled from school for having long hair. Later on, when Skinner was working in real estate and the band was a success, everyone let bygones be bygones and Skinner introduced the group at one concert.)

In those early years, Gary reminisced to Swenson: "We used to practice after school until the cops would run us off every night, then on the weekends, early in the morning, all day, all night. Then every once in a while we'd play. Ronnie had a car and we'd load his car up about five times to run the equipment over there. Sometimes we'd do it all ourselves, get our parents to drop us off with our amps. All our parents helped us

out. We were lucky enough; even though they gave us a hard time, they gave us a pull too, findin' places for us to practice, they'd sign for our amps and stuff."

At the start of the 1970s, the band finally began to make some headway, partly through acquisition of an Atlanta-based manager, Alan Walden. At that time, under the name One Per Cent, it was a quintet comprising Van Zant on lead vocals, Collins and Rossington on guitars, Larry Junstrom on bass guitar, and Bob Burns on drums. By then, Van Zant and other band members were writing original songs, some of which were laid down on a rough demonstration tape that Walden asked his partners in Muscle Shoals Sound Productions in Muscle Shoals, Alabama, to consider as a basis for recording an album at Muscle Shoals Sound Studios.

Jimmy Johnson (a co-owner of the studio part of the organization along with Barry Beckett) was impressed. "I like Ronnie's voice," he said, "and I liked the guitars I heard on their demo tape. So I agreed to produce them without even meeting the band, just because I liked the demo. Ronnie had a very unique voice."

The group signed with the production company and got ready to record an album in September 1971. Just before that, Burns announced he was leaving. The others frantically sought a replacement, finally choosing Rickey Medlow, a guitarist turned drummer.

Johnson said: "We cut 'Freebird,' 'Preacher's Daughter,' and about one or two other things the first week. They made periodic visits back over the next six months, going back to Jacksonville to play clubs and one-nighters, anything that Alan could get for them.

"They were very inexperienced and insecure in the studio. In fact, the first time Skynyrd ever recorded [professionally] was in our studio. They didn't know much about recording at the time, so we basically taught them the ropes. They worked very hard and ended up writing 'Sweet Home Alabama' about their feelings from working in Muscle Shoals."

After the first of those sessions, Junstrom moved to Miami with his parents and was replaced on bass by Greg Walker. Those early sessions resulted in eleven tracks that were submitted to almost every major label, with no takers. Undaunted, Johnson arranged for the band to record six more songs, including another due to become one of Lynyrd Skynyrd's best-liked numbers, "Simple Man."

Johnson remembered: "I felt a big improvement the second time around. They had a new drummer [actually their old drummer, Bob Burns, who had returned] and a new bass player [Leon Wilkeson, who replaced Walker] and a batch of fresh songs. Musically they were getting better. The guitars—Rossington and Collins—were really getting together, and the group was better acquainted with how to play in the studio. We cut what I considered better stuff on this next go-round."

For various reasons, including misplaying of the tape by one potential label, the material fared little better. But the tracks were to resurface later when Lynyrd Skynyrd existed only on recordings.

The experience gained from those efforts and increased exposure in concerts outside the Jacksonville area helped give band members greater confidence in their future. One result of the broader touring was acquisition of a new guitarist, Ed King, whom band members came to know while opening for the band he was with, Strawberry Alarm Clock. With King on board, Lynyrd Skynyrd developed a unique style based on playing driving country-blues-rock with a three-guitar attack, an approach that varied, Van Zant noted, only for a short period in 1975, when the band experimented with the use of two lead guitarists.

In 1973, after rock producer-performer Al Kooper agreed to handle the band through his Sounds of the South label, Lynyrd Skynyrd at long last gained a major label affiliation, MCA. The band's debut on MCA, *Pronounced Leh-Nerd Skin-Nerd,* came out that year. Backed by extensive touring, mostly as an opening act, the gold album helped establish the band as a strong contender for southern blues-rock honors. This was given increased momentum by an equally exciting second MCA collection, the gold *Second Helping,* with the top-10 single "Sweet Home Alabama." The band began to get widespread publicity both for its hard-driving rock performance and its off-stage hell-for-leather antics.

During those years, the band continued to change, though Van Zant, Collins, and Rossington remained at their posts. Burns left again and was replaced on drums by Artimus Pyle. The band became a seven-man group with the addition of Billy Powell on keyboards. Wilkeson continued as bass guitarist, though, until the band's flame was snuffed out in 1977.

Though increasingly popular as a headliner, the band seemed to slip a notch or two creatively. Its third LP on MCA, the gold 1975 *Nuthin' Fancy,* though it contained a rip-roaring track called "Saturday Night Special," seemed much tamer than its two predecessors. The gold *Gimme Back My Bullets* (1976) was even weaker, perhaps reflecting the loss of Ed King, who left in 1975, pleading exhaustion from the band's frenetic tour schedule. His place was taken by Steve Gaines, brother of a woman backup singer, Cassie Gaines, who toured with the band. Once Gaines settled in, he proved to have not only good guitar skills, but first-rate songwriting talents that promised to give a new thrust to the group's future repertoire.

The band's first live album, the platinum double-disc *One More (for) from the Road* (1976), seemed to set the group back on track.

But then came a setback that could have ended the band's history in 1976. On Labor Day weekend, Rossington and Collins made headlines with separate car crashes. After the incident was over, it was agreed that the band needed to "grow up."

Ronnie Van Zant later told Cameron Crowe of the *Los Angeles Times* (October 24, 1976) that he was determined to bring hijinks to an end. The two friends were assessed heavy fines by other members. Van Zant said: "It's a terrible thing when you get behind the wheel and you're so drunk that you can't drive a car to begin with. Those boys will pay for it. Allen hit a parked Volkswagen and knocked it across an empty parking lot. That was just a fender bender compared to Gary.

"I can't tell you how mad I got at him for that. We're glad he's gonna make it, he's tremendously lucky to be alive . . . but it was his fault. He passed out at the wheel of his brand new Ford Torino, with his foot on the gas. He knocked down a telephone pole, split an oak tree, and did $7,000 worth of damage to a house. That's being just plain stupid. I told him that on his hospital bed." The accidents also cost the band a lucrative concert date with Aerosmith that weekend at Anaheim Stadium in Anaheim, California.

Some of those events came in for comment in the Collins-Van Zant song "Oooh That Smell," on the next LP: "Whiskey bottles and brand new cars . . . There's too much coke and too much smoke/Too much going on inside you." When the band members got to work on that next album in 1976, of course, there was no inkling of what was in store. The tracks of that LP reflected newfound exuberance and writing skills that built on the fine work in the first two MCA studio collections. Called *Street Survivors,* the LP was dynamic and up-tempo from the throbbing initial comments on groupies ("What's Your Name," written by Rossington and Van Zant) to the hard-rocking arrangement of Merle Haggard's "Honky Tonk Night Time Man." The impact of Steve Gaines is felt in such songs as the boogie-woogie rocker "I Know a Little" and his country-blues collaborations with Van Zant, "You Got That Right" and "I Never Dreamed." Gaines also contributed the one relatively slow track, the blues-rock "Aint No Good Life."

The platinum album undoubtedly would have been a best-seller even without the tragic events that ended Van Zant's and the Gaines's lives and made headlines throughout the U.S. and Europe. To some, the shattering blow of the plane crash might have seemed symbolic of the band's reputed devil-may-care lifestyle. But there was evidence that the group was committed to a less destructive approach.

Van Zant had told Crowe in late 1976: "You know, the biggest change in myself that I've noticed is that for the first time I'm really thinking about the future. I'm 27 now and I've got a baby girl and I plan to stick around and watch her grow up. I also plan to collect for the last 10 years of self-abuse."

Though Collins and Rossington survived, they initially said they did not intend to re-create the old band without Van Zant. They instead formed a new group, the Rossington-Collins band. It continued to record on MCA, but couldn't recapture the dynamism of the original group and broke up in 1982. Both Collins and Rossington organized separate bands, but again without reclaiming the old Lynyrd Skynyrd audience.

For its part, MCA continued to release albums of earlier material. The first of those, the platinum *Skynyrd's First . . . and Last,* was drawn from the material Jimmy Johnson had labored over in 1972–73. In 1979, MCA issued a two-disc retrospective of the band's hits, *Gold and Platinum,* which went gold and then platinum.

During the summer of 1987, plans were completed for a reorganized Lynyrd Skynyrd group to conduct a memorial concert tour starting with a September 6 appearance at Charlie Daniels's *Volunteer Jam* in Nashville. The proposed lineup included original band alumni Collins, Rossington, Powell, Wilkerson, and Pyle plus Ed King on guitar and vocals (King had performed with some of the original band's groupings), Randall Hall on guitar and, on lead vocals, Ronnie Van Zant's brother, Johnny. By 1987, however, Allan Collins (born 1953) was sidelined by injuries suffered in a 1986 accident. (On January 23, 1990, he died of pneumonia.)

Coinciding with the group's reemergence was the release by MCA of a new album, *Legend.* That album contained songs selected by 1987 band members from MCA archives. All those featured Ronnie Van Zant's vocals and some spotlighted the late Steve Gaines and had been overdubbed and/or remixed for release. Other Lynyrd Skynyrd albums released by MCA in the 1980s and early 1990s included *Southern by the Grace of God, Lynyrd Skynrd Box Set,* and *Skynyrd's Innyrds.*

The original band had a great impact on the evolution of country music in the 1980s and 1990s. More than a few artists who reached stardom during those years listed them as a key influence. Even established performers from pre-Skynyrd times said the band's style had changed their approach to country music in some ways.

That regard was demonstrated in the 1994 MCA release, *Skynyrd Frynds,* where many country mainstays gave their versions of Skynyrd songs. Thus Alabama performed "Sweet Home Alabama"; Travis Tritt sang "Don't Ask Me No Questions"; Confederate Railroad cut "Simple Man"; Sammy Kershaw did "I Know a Little"; Hank Williams, Jr., covered "Tuesday's Gone"; and Charlie Daniels did the same for "One More Time." Other contributors were The Mavericks ("Call Me the Breeze"), Steve Earle ("What's Your Name"), Terry McBride & The Ride ("Saturday Night Special"), and Wynonna ("Freebird").

In the liner notes, Michael McCall commented, "To be young and Southern in the 1970s meant that Lynyrd Skynyrd was an irrefutable part of your life. Like the scent of magnolias in the morning and the buzz of mosquitoes at night, the band's music was in the air, and everyone felt its bite."

The album participants strongly agreed. For instance, Mark Herndon of Alabama observed, "When I was hanging out, learning to play drums and dreaming those dreams back in South Carolina in the early 1970s, I had only two records to practice with. One was Charlie Daniels's *Fire on the Mountain.* The other was Lynyrd Skynyrd's *Second Helping.*" Hank Williams, Jr., said Ronnie Van Zant's vocal style was one of his favorites and he had used several of the band's numbers in his *Wild Streak* album including "Tuesday's Gone."

M

MACON, UNCLE DAVE: *Singer, banjoist, songwriter, band leader (Fruit Jar Drinkers, Dixie Sacred Singers). Born Smart Station, Cannon County, Tennessee, October 7, 1870; died Readyville, Tennessee, March 22, 1952. Elected to Country Music Hall of Fame in 1966.*

If the old saying "when they made him, they broke the mold" applies to anyone, it certainly is Uncle Dave Macon, one of the most flamboyant and endearing individuals in the history of folk and country music. The first "name" artist on the *Grand Ole Opry,* Uncle Dave delighted audiences for decades, yet didn't turn "professional" until he was forty-eight and didn't achieve stardom until he was close to sixty. Although he died in 1952, stories about his career continued to be told years afterward and reissues of some of his recordings were still coming out in the 1990s.

Macon was born and spent his early years on a Tennessee farm, but while he was a boy his family bought a hotel in Nashville frequented by show people. From some of the lodgers, he learned the basic techniques involved in playing the five-string banjo. As he grew older, he mastered the instrument, adding innovations of his own until he became one of the most influential banjo players of all time. He also kept on the watch for interesting songs to add to his repertoire and, in time, became almost a walking repository of what is now considered traditional folk and country music.

Still, he came close to being a complete unknown. During Macon's early years, he often entertained friends and relatives or performed at local functions, but only as a sideline and until he was almost fifty, never for pay. He worked as a hired hand on local farms for some years, then bought his own farm near Readyville, Tennessee. As the decades went by, although he often took center stage at square dances or other events, it seemed that farming would be his main occupation until the end of his days.

A chance event in 1916, material in the John Edwards Memorial Foundation at UCLA indicated, changed all that. It occurred when another farmer asked him to play for a party and Dave, who was "busy and tired," tried to put him off by saying he'd only do it if he was paid fifteen dollars. However, "to his surprise, the farmer accepted. At the party, among the many guests, was a talent scout for Loew's Theaters and he was impressed by Uncle Dave, so he offered to book his 'new find' at a leading theater in Birmingham, Alabama, for several hundred dollars per week."

Uncle Dave's freewheeling style, his driving banjo playing, sometimes done to the accompaniment of clog dance steps, high kicks, and other eye-catching action, "wowed 'em" not only in Birmingham but soon in cities and towns all over the South. While never completely divorcing himself from the rural home he loved so much, Dave increasingly found himself on the road for longer and longer periods of time. With the onset of the 1920s and the rise of radio and recordings, the stage was set for his move to prominence.

While his best-known recordings came out after he was an *Opry* member, he began cutting sides some years earlier. Ralph Rinzler, in liner notes prepared for a Decca commemorative album released in 1966 (in honor of his posthumous election to the Country Music Hall of Fame), stated, "In 1923, Uncle Dave was playing his banjo in Melton's Barber Shop in Nashville when a young fiddler named Sid Harkreader happened to walk in with his fiddle case under his arm. Shortly after that they were playing at Loew's Theater in Nashville for a three-week run. They went on to travel the circuit of Loew's Theaters throughout the South as part of a five-act vaudeville show going as far west as Dallas, Texas.

"The following year, Mr. Ed Holt of the Harley-Holt Furniture Company, sent Uncle Dave and Sid to Chattanooga to play at a furniture convention. They went on to Knoxville for another such gathering. There, a Mr. C. C. Rutherford of Sterchi Brothers Furniture Company offered to pay their expenses if they would go to New York and record for the Aeolian Company. They accepted the offer and 14 sides featuring Uncle Dave, with assistance from Sid on some songs, were issued from these sessions which took place in the summer of 1924."

Apparently the results were satisfactory because Macon returned to New York in April 1925 and April 1926, turning out many more songs each time. In the latter instance, he brought along guitarist Sam McGee who with his brother Kirk also became a featured *Opry* act later on. Among the songs recorded in 1926 were "Whoop 'Em Up Cindy," "Way Down the Old Plank Road," "The Death of John Henry," and "Late Last Night When My Willie Came Home."

In 1926, knowing that Macon not only was a superlative performer but also was increasingly well known to country fans, George Hay and the *Opry* made him a cast regular. Hay recalled in his book *A Story of the Grand Ole Opry* (issued in 1945): "During the first two or three months of the year 1926 we acquired about 25 people on the *Opry*. When Uncle Dave came on, we

moved him back so that he would have plenty of room to kick when he played. He has always been an actor who thought the microphone was just a nuisance. It took a long time to 'hitch' him to it."

Within a short time Uncle Dave was the *Opry* headliner. He worked both as a soloist and with various bands, one named the Fruit Jar Drinkers. Deeply religious and a regular Bible reader (and sometime preacher), he often sang hymns and gospels. For those efforts he had a group called the Dixie Sacred Singers. From the mid-1920s until the late 1940s, he continued to command a wide following of *Opry* listeners and country concert-goers who often sang the praises of the artist variously nicknamed "The Dixie Dewdrop," "King of the Banjo Players," and "King of the Hillbillies."

He continued to record steadily throughout the late 1920s. The pace slowed somewhat in the 1930s because of the Depression, but Macon made a number of recordings in that decade. During those sessions, he was accompanied at various times by the McGee Brothers, "Fiddlin' Sid" Harkreader, fiddler Jasper Aaron "Mazy" Todd, and, beginning in the 1930s, by his son Dorris. The recordings were made in either New York or Chicago and were issued on Brunswick or Vocalion labels.

Rinzler writes of those late 1920s sessions that, "surely the most interesting from a musical standpoint were those held May 7–11, 1927, in New York City. Those not only produced some of the finest recorded performances of Uncle Dave's career (including 'Tom and Jerry,' 'Tell Her to Come Back Home,' 'Sleepy Lou,' and 'Shall We Gather at the River'), but they provide us with some of the best examples of string band ensemble playing ever recorded. Uncle Dave seemed to revel in the sound of the reedy, yet excellent, fiddling of Mazy Todd and Kirk McGee. He crows and hollers with joy when Sam momentarily abandons his guitar bass line to beat out a clog rhythm on the top of his then new Martin. The ensemble singing is unique on the secular songs: Uncle Dave sticks to the melody, Kirk departs from singing unison and moves to tenor at the end of each line, and Sam barks out his own distinctive bass line which includes a winning combination of unison and bass harmony notes. Uncle Dave weaves his banjo syncopations and double-time back-up rhythms around the extraordinary subtle fiddle lead of Mazy Todd, while shouting exuberantly above the din his verses, square dance calls or just an expression of joy: 'Shout if you are happy! Kill yo'self.'

"A total of 50 songs (both sacred and secular) were made during that four-day period. The sessions preserved 'Rock About My Saro Jane,' 'Sail Away Ladies,' and 'Jordan Is a Hard Road to Travel,' and through these memorable performances, these songs reached the (1960s) folk song revival where they underwent considerable arranging . . . almost succumbing in the process. 'Sail Away Ladies' even made a rock and roll record."

Another notable session took place in Chicago on July 25–26, 1927, with Sam McGee using an unusual banjo-guitar. In those sessions, notes Rinzler, "'From Earth to Heaven,' 'Buddy Won't You Roll Down the Line,' 'I'm the Child to Fight' were recorded as five- and six-string banjo duets, probably the only examples of this instrumental combination recorded in country music."

Many of Uncle Dave's most popular songs were those he had either written himself or discovered in his travels. These included "All In, Down and Out Blues," "The Dixie Bee Line," "From Earth to Heaven," "Cumberland Mountain Deer Race," "They're After Me," "Rock About My Saro Jane," "Ain't It a Shame to Keep Your Honey out in the Rain," "When the Train Comes Along," and his special banjo solos, dubbed "Uncle Dave's Beloved Solos."

Macon still was at the top of *Opry's* fans' lists in the early 1940s, though new young artists were beginning to take over the limelight. Thus he was featured in the 1940 Republic Pictures movie *Grand Ole Opry*. The film also focused on his son Dorris and such others as emcee Hay, Roy Acuff, and Little Rachel.

By the late 1940s, while still welcomed warmly by *Opry* crowds, he no longer ranked as a reigning superstar. Still he could get onlookers cheering and applauding such well-known numbers as "Two-in-One Chewin' Gum," "11-Cent Cotton, 40 Cent Meat," "Give Me the Gal with the Red Dress On," "Bully of the Town," "Rabbit in the Pea Patch," and his many other classics.

He was still basking in *Opry* listeners' applause three weeks before his death in 1952. Fourteen years later, in October 1966, he was voted into the Country Music Hall of Fame at the same time as his longtime friend and associate, George Hay. His bronze plaque on the Hall of Fame wall in Nashville reads, in part, "The Dixie Dewdrop . . . was a man whose delightful sense of humor and sterling character endeared him to millions. A professional performer on the *Grand Ole Opry* for 26 years, he was a 'minstrel of the countryside' prior to that. He was a country man who loved humanity and enjoyed helping others. A proficient banjoist, he was a singer of old-time ballads and was, during his time, the most popular country music artist in America."

In the 1960s and 1970s, occasional reissues of some of his recordings were released. In some of the folk collections of RCA Victor (for whom he did some sessions in the 1930s), some of the tracks were of his material. In the 1970s, three albums of his recordings were available from small companies, two on the RBF label and one on Country.

MADDOX, ROSE: *Singer, guitarist, band leader (Rose Maddux band). Born Boaz, Arizona, December 15, 1926.*

The family group is a recurring feature in the history of folk and country & western music. One of the most popular acts of post–World War II decades was the Maddox Brothers and Rose. The team comprised the four Maddox brothers, Cal, Henry, Fred, and Don and their sister, Rose. In time, Rose went her own way to gain recognition as one of the top female vocalists of the 1960s.

The Maddox family grew up in the heartland of country music, Alabama. Their mother, in particular, encouraged their interest in music. Her strong influence was reflected for many years in the selection of songs and the engagements the Maddoxes played. However, the Depression weighed heavily on the family in the early 1930s. Finally, it seemed wise to leave Alabama. Mrs. Maddox bundled her family, then ranging in age from seven to sixteen, into a freight car for the long journey to central California. Once settled in the Bakersfield area, the Maddox children helped repair family finances by performing at local events. Their act became more polished as the 1930s progressed and, by the end of the decade, they were well regarded by country & western fans in many parts of the state.

In the early 1950s, the Maddox Brothers and Rose graduated from local appearances in California to regular cast status on the *Louisiana Hayride* in Shreveport. The combination of Cal on guitar and harmonica, Henry on mandolin, Fred on stand-up bass, Don in comic roles, and Rose as lead voice resulted in many song stylings that had audiences asking for more. As their popularity grew from *Hayride* network exposure, the Maddox Brothers and Rose became one of the most popular groups for one-nighters in the business. In addition to personal appearances, they also performed on most major country & western network shows, including the *Grand Ole Opry*.

The Brothers and Rose turned out many best-selling records for Columbia, King, and Capitol Records during the 1950s and early 1960s. These included such successes as "Philadelphia Lawyer," "Whoa, Sailor," "Tall Man," and the famous "Tramp on the Street." "Tramp on the Street" was one of many sacred and gospel-type recordings featuring a combination of western beat and country material. Their other standards of this kind included "Gathering Flowers for the Master's Bouquet" and "Will There Be Any Stars in My Crown?" Their LP credits included *I'll Write Your Name* on King and *Maddox Brothers and Rose* (1962) on Wrangler.

In the late 1950s, the Maddoxes again moved their base of operations to California. Their appearances ranged from station KTRB in Modesto to *Town Hall Party* in Compton. At the start of the 1960s, however, the group disbanded and Rose decided to go out on her own as a single act.

She soon had many notable recordings to her credit on Capitol Records, including the LPs *One Rose*

(1960), *Bluegrass* (1962), and *Along with You* (1963). Her 1963 recording of "Sing a Little Song of Heartaches" was second only to Skeeter Davis's for most record sales by a female vocalist. She also teamed with Buck Owens on "We're the Talk of the Town," a recording that was third highest bestseller in the duet and vocal group category for the year. The result was selection in the *Cash Box* poll as the top country female artist of 1963. Similar awards were given to her in Europe and New Zealand.

The year 1964 saw continued success for Rose. She again teamed with Buck Owens on such hits as "Loose Talk" and "Mental Cruelty." At year's end, she and Buck won the top duet award in national disc jockey polls. Also during 1964, Harmony Records issued the LP *Best of Rose Maddox.*

After the mid-1960s, Rose's success as a recording artist tapered off, though she and others in her family remained active as stage performers into the early 1990s. After leaving Capitol, she recorded some material for Carthay Records, and at the end of the 1960s she was on the UNI label. In the early and late 1970s, she had releases out on Starday Records, including the early seventies album *Rose.* For many concerts she was backed by her own group, the Rose Maddox Band.

In the late summer of 1985, Columbia Records as part of its Columbia Historic Edition series released some of the early career recordings by Rose and her siblings as an album titled *Maddox Brothers and Rose,* which also contained some previously unissued performances. Her in-person work was temporarily interrupted in July 1988 when she suffered a heart attack while singing in a Bakersfield nightclub. Fortunately, she recovered and was able to resume some entertainment activities by the start of the 1990s.

During the 1980s and early 1990s, Rose made occasional local TV appearances with one or more of her siblings. Rose was featured on several Public Broadcasting System documentaries dealing with the California contributions to country music, particularly the development of the Bakersfield Sound. Rose was also one of several veteran country singers spotlighted in the 1993 CBS-TV special, "Women in Country Music," which paid tribute to the trailblazers like herself while showcasing many of the new young female stars gaining widespread attention as country soloists.

In the mid-1990s, many of her best renditions were collected in the Bear Family Records of Germany box set *Rose Maddox: The One Rose.* The 4 CD package, which like other Bear Family releases, was available in the U.S. only as an import item, contained most of the Maddox Brothers and Rose recordings for Capitol between 1959 and 1965. The set included 15 previously unissued tracks. Voters for the 38th annual Grammy Awards (for 1995) nominated the new Arhoolie Productions album by Rose, *$35 and a Dream,* in the Best Bluegrass Album category.

MAINER, J. E.: *Banjoist, fiddler, band leader. Born Weaversville, North Carolina, July 20, 1898; died Concord, North Carolina, June 12, 1971.*

Though Jimmie Rodgers was called the "Father of Country Music," his stylings derived from a country-music tradition that had been strong for a long time before him. People like Gid Tanner, Eck Robertson, and J. E. Mainer and his band had been well known to southern and rural audiences years before Rodgers; Mainer, indeed, continued to perform and lead his own band right up to the time of his death in 1971.

Mainer summed up many of the details of his life in a letter to John Edwards, founder of the Edwards Foundation, some of which was reprinted with permission in the 1969 edition of *The Encyclopedia of Folk, Country, & Western Music,* and parts of which are presented in the quotations below.

Mainer wrote that he was born in a one-room log house in Buncombe County in the Blue Ridge mountains of North Carolina. "Started to play a five-string banjo when I were nine years old going to square dances. Me and my brother-in-law, he played the fiddle, he played left-handed. I stayed around home until I were fifteen years old then I left home and went to work in a cotton mill at Noceville [Knoxville], Tennessee. Worked there for seven years then I come to Concord, N.C. [which remained his home the rest of his life]: . . . Got me a job in the cotton mill here. In 1923 Wade come to Concord. I still had my banjo with me and Wade began to learn to play it. He were seventeen years old and he got to where he could play it pretty good by me showing him how to play it. Then I thought I would get me a fiddle, so I sold some seed and sent the money to the seed company and they sent me a little old tin fiddle. But I got to where I could play 'John Henry' on it then I went and got me a good fiddle then we would play two hours ever' night. In about one year we could play most anything we wanted to. Then we met John Love who played a guitar. We got to going to fiddle conventions and we met Claud Moris [Claude Morris] in Old Port, N.C., who played guitar and we all four of us sure did love to play. Then we got to winning about all the prizes wherever we went. Then the Crazy Water Crystals Co. heard about us and sent for me to come to their office in Charlotte, N.C. and they gave us a job playing for them, advertising for them. We worked over WBT Charlotte for four years when they sent us to WWL, New Orleans, Louisiana. We stayed there for a while then they sent for us to come back to Charlotte, then they sent us to Raleigh, N.C.—WPTF—there for four years. In this time, John Love had married and had a baby then I nicknamed him Daddy John Love and I had nicknamed Claude Morris, Zeke, and the boys is still carrying their nicknames today."

During those years, the band was called the Crazy Mountaineers after the sponsor. During the time J. E. and Wade, his brother, were together the band was called the Mainer Mountaineers, a name J. E. returned to after his years with the Crazy Water Crystal Company were over. Among the early recorded successes of the group were "Maple on the Hill," "Take Me in the Life Boat," and "Drunkard's Hic-Ups." During the heyday of the Crazy Mountaineers, Wade Mainer had his own group, though Wade and J. E. joined forces again later and made a number of recordings.

Continuing J. E.'s note to John Edwards, "We made records for the Victor Recording Co. [starting in the 1920s]. We made some records that were on top for about 4 years, then I left them [went to] Raleigh, N.C., and I got me another bunch and went back to Charlotte on another radio station, WSOC. I had Leonard Stokes and George Morris, Zeke's brother, and my banjo player but the first ones we made were in 1935 in Atlanta, Georgia. We made records for them ever' 6 months for 5 years. [Some of those were reissued in a number of RCA/Camden collections of early mountain music in the 1960s and 1970s.] I got married here in Concord the same year I come here. We had 6 children—2 girls and 4 boys. 2 of the boys and 2 girls were guitar players. Their names were Carolin, and the other were Mary. My old'st boys were J. E. Jr. and Glenn Mainer.

"I took them and went to Johnson City, Tennessee, in 1939. Went to work over radio station WSIS and we went to recording records for the King Recording Co. Worked for them for two years."

The pace slowed down for J. E. and his band after the start of the 1950s, but he remained active, sallying forth from his home in Concord to play at folk and country festivals while also working radio and TV whenever possible. In the post–World War II decades, Mainer and his group made recordings for the folk music archive of the Library of Congress. In the 1960s and at the start of the 1970s, he made a series of recordings of classic hill-country tunes for Rural Rhythm.

In the 1960s and up to Mainer's death, the group often was invited to take part in bluegrass festivals. At the time J. E. died of an apparent heart attack at his home in Concord on June 12, 1971, the group was getting ready to leave for such an event in Culpepper, Virginia. The makeup of the Mainer Mountaineers at the time was Mainer on fiddle, Bill Beaton on guitar, Morris Herbert on banjo, Earl Cheek on bass, and, on that time-honored but almost extinct instrument, the washboard, Jerry Cheek.

MANDRELL, BARBARA: *Singer, guitarist, steel guitarist, banjoist, saxophone player, accordionist, bass guitarist, band leader (the Do-Rites). Born Houston, Texas, December 25, 1948.*

At a very early age, Barbara showed that she had musical talent and, what may be even more remarkable, that she had the desire to pursue that talent, to work at it, to stay with it and turn it into a career. In that goal,

she always had the strong support of her parents, who both were musically inclined (father Irby was a singer and guitarist and mother Mary a music teacher and pianist), and she, in turn, helped encourage other children in the family to follow similar paths.

When she was five years old, she gave the first indication of her ambition by asking her mother to teach her to play the twenty-four-bars accordion; thus she learned to read music before she could read English. She recalled for Douglas A. Green of *Pickin'* magazine (September 1978) that she made her public debut at five in a Houston, Texas, church. "I went to church with my parents, and dragged the accordion on up to perform, nobody knowing how I'd react. I only knew one song called, believe it or not, 'Guitar Boogie,' and I played it through. Everybody seemed to love it and gave me a lot of applause and eventually asked for an encore. The trouble was, I only knew one song—so I played it again! If I'd known more tunes I might have played all night."

Soon after that, the Mandrells moved from Texas to Oceanside, California, where her father bought a music store. Some years later, Barbara added skills on a very different instrument to her repertoire. One of her father's acquaintances was steel guitar player Norman Hamlet, and eleven-year-old Barbara decided to take lessons on the instrument from him. She told Green, "There wasn't a better teacher in the world. I started off on a little Fender eight-string, but I had pedals even then. This was the era that Bud Isaacs and Ralph Mooney were revolutionizing the use of the steel guitar with all the pedal work and that's of course what I wanted to learn. Still, Norm made sure I knew all the western swing things like 'Boot Heel Drag,' giving me a good historical foundation as well as the latest licks. I spent countless hours with Norm."

Her pedal steel ability soon paid dividends. After she'd been studying for half a year, her father took her with him to a music trade show in Chicago, Illinois, where she was hired to demonstrate steel guitar work as part of the Standel Amplifiers display. By then, she also knew how to play saxophone and, after country star Joe Maphis heard her steel guitar work in Chicago, Mandrell got the chance to join his show in Las Vegas for a while playing pedal steel and sax.

Back in California, Joe helped her become a regular cast member (still at age eleven) of the local Southern California TV program *Town Hall Party*. When she was twelve, Mandrell made her network TV debut on ABC's *Five Star Jubilee*, telecast from Springfield, Missouri. All this attention inspired Irby Mandrell to form a family group comprising Barbara, himself, his wife, and two young men on guitar and drums. The drummer, then working his way through college, was named Ken Dudney. When Barbara was fourteen, she and Ken dated for a while, but they broke up for several years when she was in her mid-teens. Later, though, they reconciled and married in 1967, a union (graced by then with two children) considered one of the happiest in the country field as of the early 1980s.

Remembering the days of the Mandrell Family band, Barbara told Jack Hurst of the *Chicago Tribune* (*Chicago Tribune Magazine,* April 22, 1979), "We had a tight group, good music, and we'd incorporate Beatle tunes and old stuff like 'Up a Lazy River' and the 'Beverly Hillbillies' theme. I'd play sax, banjo, steel. [Inspired by the folk boom of the early 1960s, she learned banjo in her mid-teens, helped at one point by top banjoist Dale Sledd of the Osborne Brothers band.] We worked Camp Pendleton; we worked San Diego for the Navy; the El Toro [California] airbase. . . . There was lots of work to be had."

Mandrell kept trying out new instruments, among them the guitar and bass guitar. She told Green she was only a fair guitarist, no better "than the average Joe on the street—a few chords is all. I learned enough to play a boogie with the Mandrells' guitar player, you know, two of us playing the same guitar. . . . I love the bass and I always have. I can play it, but I don't really get down. I'm not the bass player my sister Louise is."

After marrying Ken Dudney, Barbara gave up professional music for a while in favor of staying home. But when Ken became an Air Force pilot and was sent overseas soon after the nuptials, she went to stay with her parents, a step fated to change her life around. The Mandrells moved to Nashville because Irby had decided to leave music and go into the contracting business with a brother who lived in the country-music capital. One Friday night in 1968 Barbara suggested Irby take her to watch the *Grand Ole Opry* because neither she nor he ever had seen a live *Opry* show.

Irby told Hurst, "We went, and halfway through the show she turned to me and said, 'Daddy, if you've got any faith in me, I'd like to try to get on the other side of the microphone again. I wasn't cut out to be in the audience.' "

It was her instrumental aptitude that gave her the initial boost. She got the chance to play with the Curly Chalker Trio at the Printer's Alley in Nashville. She was featured on steel but also did some vocals, and word got back to Columbia producer Billy Sherrill that he would be wise to visit the show. This resulted in her first recording contract, signed on March 1, 1969. Although traditional country always has been her first love, she has enjoyed other music formats as well, particularly rhythm & blues, to the point that some of her records became hits with black audiences. Her R&B efforts went back to the start of her recording career. She told Jack Hurst (*Chicago Tribune,* January 3, 1979), "My first record was an Otis Redding song. I've also done Joe Tex's 'Show Me' and Aretha Franklin's 'Do Right Woman, Do Right Man.' I've always dabbled in all areas of music."

However, the majority of Mandrell's record releases were unmistakably country and brought enough favorable response from fans and industry peers for her to be asked to become a regular *Grand Ole Opry* cast member in 1972, an association still maintained in the early 1990s. Among her chartmakers during her five-year stay with Columbia were "After Closing Time," a top-10 duet in late 1970 (with David Houston—all Mandrell-Houston recordings were on Columbia's Epic label); "Show Me" in 1972; "Give a Little, Take a Little" in 1973; "I Love You, I Love You" (with Houston), "Ten Commandments of Love" (with Houston), "This Time I Almost Made It," all 1974. Her albums of those years included *Treat Him Right* and, with David Houston, *A Perfect Match.*

In 1975, Barbara left Columbia for ABC/Dot, a switch that seemed to give her career new momentum. Her first single on the new label, "Standing Room Only," made the charts in late 1975 and entered the top 10 in early 1976. As the year progressed, she had such other chartmakers as "That's What Friends Are For" and "Love Is Thin Ice." She followed with even more popular songs, such as "Woman to Woman" and "Married but Not to Each Other," that went to number two on country charts and rose high on R&B lists as well. In late 1977 she had the top-10 hit "Hold Me" and more successes the following year, such as "Tonight," in the top five during the summer.

Those increasingly impressive credits had won some notice from the country-music industry. In October 1978, for instance, she was one of the five finalists for the Country Music Association's coveted Female Vocalist of the Year Award, but, as had occurred twice before, she was an also-ran. But the groundwork had been laid and her move from star to superstar got under way almost as the echoes from the 1978 awards died away. In November 1978, Barbara had her first number-one single, "Sleeping Single in a Double Bed," on country charts in that position three weeks in a row and a major pop hit besides. In early 1979, she soon had a second number-one hit, "(If Loving You Is Wrong) I Don't Want to Be Right," which rose even higher on pop lists than "Sleeping Single." Also a major hit for her (by now ABC had been acquired by MCA Records) was "Fooled by a Feeling."

Her popularity indeed was soaring, and she kept up a hectic schedule of concert work and TV appearances. Among Mandrell's 1979 TV credits were cohosting the Academy of Country Music Awards in May, a special with Charo and Priscilla Mitchell, and appearances on Dick Clark's *American Bandstand* and the ShaNaNa's syndicated rock show. Among her other TV appearances of the mid- and late-1970s were guest spots on the *Merv Griffin* show, the *Mike Douglas* show, ABC's *Wide World of Sports* (with the Harlem Globetrotters), CBS's *Third Annual Collegiate Cheerleading Championship,* cohost of some segments of the *Mike Douglas* show, NBC's *77th Birthday Salute to Bob Hope,* NBC's

Elvis Presley Remembered—Nashville to Hollywood,
The Rockford Files, and cohost of Home Box Office's
Nashville Country Pop Festival.

In 1979, Mandrell not only cohosted the Academy
of Country Music show but also was named the organization's Female Vocalist of the Year. This was echoed
throughout the year when she won the same category in
voting by the readers of *Music City News* and *Radio &
Records* and by members of the Country Music Association. In 1979, both *Cash Box* and the American Music
Awards voted "Sleeping Single in a Double Bed" Single of the Year. With continued recording and performing achievements in the early 1980s, Barbara added
more trophies to her collection, including the 1980 Entertainer of the Year Award from the Country Music
Association and the 1981 Entertainer of the Year Award
from the Academy of Country Music. In the 1981 poll
of the *Music City News,* she came out first for both Musician of the Year and Female Artist of the Year.

Mandrell's singles hits of the early 1980s included
"Years," "Crackers," and "The Best of Strangers" in
1980, and "Love Is Fair/Sometimes, Somewhere/Somehow," "Wish You Were Here," and "I Was Country
(When Country Wasn't Cool)" in 1981. In the Country
Music Awards voting, "I Was Country" was nominated
for Single of the Year for 1981. Her charted albums during 1979–80 included *Moods, The Best of Barbara
Mandrell* and *Just for the Record,* which was still on the
lists in 1981. As for 1982, all of the albums Barbara
recorded for ABC/Dot-MCA were still in print. They
included *This Is Barbara Mandrell* (her debut LP),
*Midnight Angel, Lovers, Friends and Strangers, Ups
and Downs of Love, Love Is Fair,* and the three noted
above. In 1982, MCA issued the LP *Barbara Mandrell
Live.*

During the 1980–81 season, Barbara inaugurated
her own TV show on NBC, an hour-long Saturday night
program titled *Barbara Mandrell and the Mandrell Sisters.* Joining with her on the variety format were
younger sisters Irlene and Louise. Although the show's
ratings hardly were overwhelming, the program was
one of the better music offerings on the air and was renewed for the 1981–82 season. Both her TV and personal appearance work continued to be an extended
family affair in the early 1980s, with father Irby acting
as manager and Ken Dudney serving as financial manager. (When not on the road, the Dudneys usually called
home, where they resided with children Matt and
Jamie, a large house fronting on Old Hickory Lake near
Gallatin, Tennessee. However, they also could escape to
a condominium in Aspen, Colorado, or another lakeside
home in Dadeville, Alabama.)

One of the ironies of Mandrell's career was the fact
that many of her hits were "cheatin' songs," though she
herself favored the traditional idea of marriage. She
told Hurst, "I think of myself as an actress. I try to make
people believe what I'm singing. I'm a very sentimental, emotional person, and maybe a little of that comes
out in my voice. For the few moments I'm singing "If
Loving You Is Wrong, I Don't Wanta Be Right,' I really
want to be with this married man that I have no right to.
And if I'm singing 'I love you and the kids, and home
is great,' then I live that too."

The requirements of doing a weekly TV series plus
all her other activities proved draining, and on doctors'
orders she gave up both TV and touring for a time at the
start of the 1980s. Refreshed by mid-1982, she resumed
her concert work. During the year she received
R.I.A.A. gold records for the MCA albums *The Best of
Barbara Mandrell* and *Barbara Mandrell Live.* Highlights for 1983 included presentation of her stage show,
"The Lady Is a Champ," in Las Vegas, which was then
performed at the Tennessee Performing Arts Center in
Nashville where it was taped for her first Home Box
Office cable TV offering. (It didn't screen on HBO until
May 1986.)

From 1979 through 1984, Barbara continued to accrue honors in major awards competitions. She was
nominated as Female Vocalist of the Year by the CMA
in every year between 1979 and 1984, winning in 1979
and 1981. She was nominated for CMA Entertainer of
the Year from 1980 through 1984 and won in 1980 and
1981. The Academy of Country Music also named her
Entertainer of the Year in 1980 followed by the Top Female Vocalist of the Year Award in 1981. In the first half
of the 1980s, she also won in various categories in such
other polls as the American Music Awards, *Music City
News* Awards, and People's Choice Awards. One of the
honors she most treasured, though, was the Outstanding
Mother Award presented her in New York City in April
1983 by the National Mother's Day Committee.

Her gospel recordings also won recognition over
those years, resulting in two Grammy Awards. In the
National Academy of Recording Arts & Sciences voting for 1982, her Songbird/MCA album, *He Set My Life
to Music,* was named Best Inspirational Performance.
For the following year, a duet track with Bobby Jones
on Myrrh/Word, "I'm So Glad I'm Standing Here
Today," was voted Best Soul Gospel Performance by a
Duo or Group. She also had chart success in secular
duet recordings with Lee Greenwood, which won them
CMA nominations in 1984 and 1985 for Vocal Duo of
the Year.

Things seemed to be moving along for Barbara in
fine fashion when her career was interrupted, and almost ended, by a nerve-shattering traffic accident. This
occurred on the night of September 11, 1984, when a
young driver let his car drift over the center line to crash
head-on into Barbara's vehicle. As she recalled later,
for some reason, only minutes before she had fastened
her seat belt and told her two children to do the same.
Both cars were demolished and the other driver was
killed, but all in her car survived. Before that, she had
not always worn her seat belt, but afterward it was a

must. While Barbara escaped with her life, she did not go unscathed, suffering injuries that took many months and much pain to heal. It was not until 1986 that she was able to resume her full scale of activities. Though her activities were limited for a while, she was still represented on records and TV. In January 1985 her program "Barbara Mandrell—Something Special" appeared on CBS-TV. Later in the year her *Greatest Hits* album was issued, providing a chart hit single "There's No Love in Tennessee." During January 1985 she was unable to appear in person to accept the *Music City News* "Living Legend" award, recognizing her twenty-five years of achievement in the country field, but by the next year she was able to host the awards telecast. In the fall of 1985, CBS-TV screened the drama "Burning Rage," in which Barbara made her acting debut, having filmed the show in the spring of 1984.

In March 1986, Barbara finally had put her injuries behind her and was able to give her first concert in eighteen months. The venue was the Universal Amphitheatre in Los Angeles, and helping celebrate her return were longtime friends Dolly Parton and Lee Greenwood. Dolly gave the opening set, and Greenwood joined Barbara for several duet numbers. (By then she had added a third child to her family.) The crash apparently had done nothing to impair Mandrell's talents as singer or instrumentalist, and she continued to tour regularly from then on into the 1990s. It has, as she noted on a Barbara Walters Special and a syndicated "Mandrell Sisters and Family" show, made her appreciate more the need to enjoy life and take nothing for granted. Her fans greeted her return with some new honors, an example being her choice in voting for the American Music Awards as 1987 Favorite Female Country Vocalist.

For some reason, the mishap seemed to mark a dividing line between continuous top-chart hits and a much lower recording profile for her. She continued to draw well in live stage appearances in the late 1980s and in the 1990s and remained a star on the *Grand Ole Opry,* but she had no major new hit singles during that period. Like many other country stars, Barbara became one of the regulars performing at venues in Branson, Missouri. In 1993, she was one of the artists featured on the initial *Star Spangled Branson* program presented on the Family Channel that Labor Day. The program organizers planned this as the opening show of a series of programs sometimes focusing on a single artist or group, other times on a variety format. Barbara's was also a familiar face on TV screens throughout the first part of the 1990s as the featured personage in various commercials for food products. In 1996, she changed the pattern a little by appearing as a featured performer in an episode of the CBS-TV program *Dr. Quinn, Medicine Woman.*

In including Mandrell as one of "The 100 Most Important People in the History of Country" in the *Life*

magazine special issue in September 1994 on country music, the editors paid tribute to her amazing instrumental versatility and "her jaw-dropping athleticism as a dancer." But they also asserted that "like Red Foley before her, she is basically a pop singer who uses country as her milieu. . . . She's got style, but it ain't all country style."

MAPHIS, JOE AND ROSE LEE: *Vocal and instrumental duo, songwriters. Joe, born Suffolk, Virginia, May 12, 1921, died Nashville, Tennessee, June 27, 1986; Rose Lee, born Baltimore, Maryland, December 29, 1922.*

One of the most talented and popular husband and wife teams in country music, Joe and Rose Lee Maphis, at one time or another, were cast members of almost every major "barn dance" program in the heyday of that format. In addition, in more than three decades of show business work, they guested on almost every other country show from the *Grand Ole Opry* to *Hee Haw.* Over the years, Joe maintained his reputation as one of "the fastest guitarists alive," both as a featured performer and a session musician backing many well-known country stars. Many aspiring guitar players tried to emulate Joe's "flash" style, which he developed while trying to transfer complex fiddle leads to the guitar.

The meeting place for Joe and Rose Lee was the *Old Dominion Barn Dance* on station WRVA in Richmond, Virginia. Before their paths crossed there in 1948, both had been professional artists while still in their teens. Otis W. "Joe" Maphis, born and raised near Harpers Ferry, Virginia, learned to play fiddle from his father and entertained at local square dances by the time he was ten. At sixteen, he was featured on station WBRA in Richmond. Beside fiddle, he also learned to play guitar, mandolin, and bass. Rose Lee started singing and playing guitar before she reached high school age. At fifteen, she had her own program on a Hagerstown, Maryland, station, billed as "Rose of the Mountains."

For a number of years in the 1940s, Joe was featured on many of the top shows emanating from the Midwest, including the *Boone County Jamboree, Midwestern Hayride,* and Chicago's *National Barn Dance.* In 1952, Joe met and married Rose Lee while working with the group Sunshine Sue and Her Rangers. Soon after, they moved across the country to California. There they appeared on Cliffie Stone's Los Angeles *Hometown Jamboree* TV show for several years and later in the 1950s were featured on the *Hollywood Barn Dance* and the *Town Hall Party* telecast from Compton, California. Besides his duets with Rose Lee, Joe often teamed with Merle Travis on many songs.

Joe and his wife signed with Capitol Records in the 1950s, but also did considerable session work backing other performers. Some of those with whom they worked were Merle Travis, Ricky Nelson, Stuart Hamblen, and Tex Ritter. Among the many songs recorded by Joe and Rose Lee, which included some originals, were "Twin Banjo Special," "Katy Warren Break-down," "Your Old Love Letters," "Flying Fingers," "Randy Lynn Rag," "Guitar Rock and Roll," "Tuning Up for the Blues," and "Honky Tonk Down Town." Joe also provided the sound track for such TV shows as *FBI Story* and *Thunder Road*.

From the 1950s through the 1970s, the Maphis show maintained a busy touring schedule. Their personal appearances over those three decades took them to all fifty states as well as France, Germany, Spain, the Philippines, Okinawa, Taiwan, and Vietnam. Over the years, they headlined at almost every country-music club in the United States and Canada and at almost every major state and county fair. Even in the late 1970s, they typically covered an average of 100,000 miles a year traveling to live dates. During the 1960s, Joe and Rose Lee left California to make Nashville their home.

They recorded a number of albums over the years either as a duo or with Joe in the spotlight. Among them were the Capitol LPs *Fire on the Strings* and *Joe Maphis* (June 1964). In the mid-1960s, they signed with Starday, which issued a series of albums including *Joe and Rose Lee Maphis* (November 1964), *King of the Strings* (mid-1960s), *Golden Gospel Guitar* (mid-1960s), and *Fastest Guitar Goes to the Jimmy Dean Show*. LPs of their material issued at the end of the 1960s and in the early 1970s included *Gospel Guitar* and *Volume 2* on Word Records and *Guitaration Gap* on Chart Records.

During the 1970s, Joe and Rose Lee took part in several of the annual Fan Fair Reunion Shows in Nashville, sponsored by the Country Music Association to focus on veteran artists. They were represented on the live album of the 1975 event, produced by CMA's own Foundation Records, with the track "Hot Time in Nashville Tonight."

The Maphises continued to be active in the country music field in the 1980s until Joe was stricken with cancer, from which he died in 1986 after a long struggle. His obituaries cited some of his other achievements, including his performance on a number of movie soundtracks such as *Thunder Road* and *God's Little Acre*. It was also noted that he provided theme music for such hit TV shows as *Bonanza* and *The FBI*. During his performing years, he also gave a boost to the careers of other artists, the most successful of whom was Barbara Mandrell. In the mid-1990s, some of his recorded material was included in the CMA compilation *50 Years of Bluegrass Hits*.

MARSHALL TUCKER BAND: *Vocal and instrumental group from Spartanburg, South Carolina. Tommy Caldwell, born Spartanburg, November 9, 1950, died Spartanburg, April 28, 1980; Toy Caldwell, born Spartanburg, November 13, 1947, died Spartanburg, February 25, 1993; George McCorkle; Paul Riddle; Jerry Eubanks; Doug Gray, born Spartanburg, circa 1948. Tommy Caldwell replaced by Franklin Wilkie, 1980.*

After the Allman Brothers Band lost momentum in the mid-1970s following the untimely death of Duane Allman, a number of groups vied for the title of number-one Southern country-rock band. A major contender was the Marshall Tucker Band from Spartanburg, South Carolina, which seemed fitting since that talented six-person group had first drawn attention to itself in the early 1970s as the opening act for an Allman tour. Ironically, the Tucker band's position was threatened in 1980 by the death of one of its founders, bassist-vocalist Tommy Caldwell.

While the Tucker band was generally classified with the Allmans, the two groups actually were far from carbon copies. The Allmans strongly stressed blues elements in their music, whereas Marshall Tucker demonstrated much more diverse influences. In fact, the members themselves had a hard time finding a consensus about their main style, with lead guitarist (and major songwriter) Toy Caldwell stating they played "progressive country," his brother, bass guitarist Tommy Caldwell, and drummer Paul Riddle considering country-jazz the best description, lead singer Doug Gray favoring "bluesy rock 'n' roll," and rhythm guitarist George McCorkle opting for "an American rock 'n' roll band which plays traditional American music." Anyone familiar with the band's material knows there is validity to all those definitions. In fact, it is perhaps the way the band melded so many diverse influences into its repertoire that made it popular with audiences throughout the United States and overseas as well. As Doug Gray told an interviewer in 1977, "Sure we're popular in parts of the South, but we're really big in places like New York and New Jersey. And our western market is really coming on strong. People tend to think southern bands have most of their appeal in the South, but that isn't necessarily true." The group proved this on many of its concert tours of the 1970s when it drew massive crowds in all parts of the country from Seattle to Miami. In late 1978, the band made its debut at New York's Madison Square Garden before an equally large and enthusiastic audience.

All of the band members grew up in Spartanburg, South Carolina, where most of them were as interested in blues and rock as country music. In fact, at one point in the late 1960s, some of the founding members were in a group called the Toy Factory that played mainly soul music. Some of that early experience is carried over in the blues and jazz elements in many of the group's arrangements.

As might be expected in a small town environment (Spartanburg has a population of about 45,000), the original members of the group knew each other from childhood and some had been in bands together during high school. The military call interrupted the musical activities of some of the men, but when they were discharged at the start of the 1970s, they soon were involved in the local rock and pop scene. In 1971, the

Caldwell brothers joined with their four friends to form what was to become Marshall Tucker, and at the beginning of the 1980s, the same six artists were still together.

The name Marshall Tucker is mysteriously missing from the roster of the founding members. The name is a fictitious one. When the men were rehearsing in an old warehouse one of them found an old key with the name Marshall Tucker on it. They promptly adopted it as their band designation.

The group began to play locally at first, then gained dates in neighboring states as their reputation spread. One of the bands they worked with was Wet Willie, whose members brought word to the executives of Capricorn Records in Georgia that Marshall Tucker was a group with promise. The band auditioned for the label and, in May 1972, was signed.

The band's debut LP, *The Marshall Tucker Band,* was issued in 1973, a year that saw the band begin to expand its reputation well beyond South Carolina on tour with the Allmans. The exposure didn't make the first album a smash success at the time, but it encouraged Capricorn and band members to look toward future progress. In 1974, the group provided two new albums, *A New Life* and *Where We All Belong,* and supported them with a back-breaking schedule of tours that kept them on the road most of the year. During the mid-1970s, the band typically gave 250–300 concerts a year, a schedule it cut back on once its reputation had been established. The intensive touring plus the quality of the original songs by band members began to pay dividends during 1974–1975 as each succeeding album rose a little higher on the charts, and maintained steady sales patterns. By the end of 1975, the group had its first gold-record awards, finally going over the top with its debut LP on August 14, 1975, and later gaining one for *Where We All Belong* on November 7, 1975.

The gap between release and gold-record levels began to narrow. The band's fourth LP, *Searchin' for a Rainbow,* was issued in 1975 and earned a gold record on February 4, 1976. Meanwhile, other artists in country and pop were recording songs by some of the band members. During 1976, for instance, Waylon Jennings gained a top-5 hit with Toy Caldwell's "Can't You See." Other performers who recorded material by the Caldwells and other Marshall Tucker members were Kitty Wells, Hank Williams, Jr., and Gary Stewart. By 1977, *Searchin' for a Rainbow* became the band's first platinum album.

The group continued its series of hit LPs with *Long Hard Ride* in 1976 and *Carolina Dreams* in 1977. The latter also went platinum. *Carolina Dreams* was the most consistently well-written album to that point, demonstrating that all the members were becoming increasingly proficient as writers. Toy Caldwell remained the main contributor with the excellent songs "Fly Like an Eagle" (which became a massive hit for Steve Miller), "Heard It in a Love Song," "Desert Skies," and "Tell It to the Devil." Tommy Caldwell provided a western-style number, "Never Trust a Stranger," and cowrote the R&B-flavored "I Should Have Never Started Lovin' You" with George McCorkle and Doug Gray. McCorkle and Jerry Eubanks penned "Life in a Song."

Up to then, the band had almost exclusively succeeded as album artists, with none of its singles making top-chart levels. That changed with "Heard It in a Love Song," however, one of the better-selling singles of 1977. In 1978, the group expanded its LP achievements when its seventh LP on Capricorn, *Together Forever,* made the national charts and later was certified gold, making a full sweep—all seven LPs up to then had earned the coveted award.

In 1978, the group's contract with Capricorn ran out. They decided to move to Warner Bros. Records, which for a number of years had distributed Marshall Tucker releases for Capricorn. The debut on the new label, *Running like the Wind,* came out in March 1979 and in short order was moving up the national hit lists.

In early 1980, the band's future seemed in jeopardy when Tommy Caldwell died from injuries in an auto accident in Spartanburg in April. There were thoughts of disbanding, but the group decided it would be more fitting for Tommy's memory to keep going. To take Tommy's place on bass, Franklin Wilkie, a longtime friend of the group members, was recruited.

Wilkie had played in a group called the Rants with Toy Caldwell and George McCorkle during 1964–66, leaving the group to enter college, where he worked with a band called Puzzle (1966–68). He then spent several years with the Air Force before returning to Spartanburg in the early 1970s. There he played for a time with Toy, Doug Gray, and Jerry Eubanks in Toy Factory, a group that later evolved into Marshall Tucker. When Tommy returned from the Marines to take over on bass, Wilkie moved to Atlanta to do studio work, then joined Garfeel Ruff, with whom he worked for six years.

By mid-1980, the reorganized band was touring again. Among its concert offerings were songs from its second Warner Bros. album and tenth overall called, simply, *Tenth.* In April 1981, Warner Brothers released the band's eleventh album, *Dedicated.* As the title indicates, it was dedicated to the memory of Tommy Caldwell. In the fall of 1981 the retrospective album *Best of Marshall Tucker* was on the pop charts.

The group continued to have a sizable following for its live performances throughout the 1980s and into the 1990s, though its recordings didn't do as well as in past years. The band makeup as of the start of the 1990s included Doug Gray on lead vocals, Toy Caldwell on lead guitar, Franklin Wilkie on bass guitar, George McCorkle on rhythm guitar, Paul Riddle on drums, and Jerry Eubanks on saxophone and flute.

By the end of the 1980s the group's association with Warner Brothers Records had been over for some time, and in the early 1990s the band recorded for the Cabin Fever label. One of the group's releases for that record firm was the 1992 album *Still Smokin'*, from which the videos "Driving You out of My Mind" and "Ten Yard Road" were drawn.

The second founding member from the Caldwell family, Toy, died in February 1993. Band spokespersons said he died in his sleep after having been ill for several days with influenza and bronchitis. In late 1993 Cabin Fever issued the single and video "Down We Go." During that year, the label also posthumously released Toy Caldwell's self-produced solo label debut. The band's extensive concert series in 1993 was billed as its "20th Anniversary Tour," a reference to the release of its first album in 1973. For much of 1994, the group was on the road in support of its new Cabin Fever album, *Walk Outside the Lines*.

MARTIN, GRADY: *Fiddler, guitarist, vibraphonist, band leader (the Slewfoot Five). Born near Chappel Hill, Tennessee, January 17, 1929.*

One of the multitalented musicians who helped make the "Nashville Sound" famous in the post–World War II decades, Grady Martin backed a virtual pantheon of artists from all facets of country and pop music in addition to making his own contributions as a soloist and band leader. Along the way, he pioneered or was among the outstanding exponents of such instrumental innovations as fuzztone, gut-string fills, straight-neck dobro, Echoplex, and double-neck guitar.

Born on a farm near Chappel Hill, Tennessee, Martin spent his boyhood years taking in the sights and sounds of rural life. When he was old enough, he helped in the chores and, after his father brought home a battery-operated Zenith radio, spent some of his leisure time listening to country music on the radio. On weekends, like countless Tennessee families, the Martins listened to the *Grand Ole Opry*. After hearing the great guitar playing on some of those programs, Martin recalled, "Right then I decided I didn't want to milk any more cows."

He began to seek ways of learning music himself, concentrating on the fiddle, though he started picking up some guitar chords as well. He began to frequent the country shows that, in those years, used to travel from town to town playing early evening dates at local school houses, observing the various fiddlers and practicing some of their techniques at home. In his teens, he played with local groups and sometimes asked to sit in with visiting bands.

"One night when I was fifteen, Big Jeff Bess heard me play fiddle and he went to my parents and asked them to let him take me to Nashville to play on the radio. Mom didn't want to let me, but Dad said I might as well go since I wasn't gonna be happy on the farm."

In Nashville, Grady steadily built up a reputation as a sideman and before long he was sought out for both group and session work. As a member of the Bailes Brothers band, he debuted on the *Opry* in 1946 and remained a regular performer on the show for many years, moving from the Bailes Brothers to backing groups for people like Curley Fox and Texas Ruby. By the time he was on the *Opry* a few years, he had become as well known for his guitar work as for his fiddling.

Over the years from the late 1940s to the early 1980s, he worked as a session musician on hundreds of recordings. The first major success he contributed to began in a session in the converted garage studio of Owen Bradley, with Red Foley as featured artist. The effort produced Foley's best-selling single, "Chattanooga Shoe-Shine Boy." Among other milestones for Grady was his vibraphone work on Floyd Cramer's first massive hit of 1960–61, "Last Date." Martin also is credited with the first performance of the electric guitar technique known as fuzztone in his work on the Marty Robbins single "Don't Worry." Among others whom Martin backed over the years were Hank Williams, Henry Mancini, Bing Crosby, Johnny Cash, Kris Kristofferson, and Larry Gatlin, to name just a few.

During the 1960s and 1970s, Martin often headed his own band, the Slewfoot Five, on TV, live shows, and a number of albums. In the mid- and late-1970s, his efforts included leading the TV band on the Nashville based T. Tommy Cutler show. During that period he also was active as a producer for Monument Records and made a number of recordings for the label as well. Among the acts he worked with on the production side was Brush Arbor, one of the best "progressive" country bands of the 1970s.

Martin's activities as a record producer, session musician, and bandsman continued through the 1980s into the 1990s. He often worked with Willie Nelson, and from the late 1970s on was a regular in the "Willie Nelson Family," touring worldwide with Willie's troupe and backing Nelson on most of his hit records of the period. As a record producer through the mid-1990s he worked with many of the most successful artists in the country field, and his name could be found among the credits on more than a few best-selling singles and albums.

MATTEA, KATHY: *Singer, guitarist, songwriter. Born Cross Lanes, West Virginia, June 21, c. 1959.*

With a clear, liquid alto voice and a passion for country music's folk and bluegrass roots, Kathy Mattea was one of the freshest new additions to country music in the 1980s and continued to be an important force in the 1990s. Her desire to expand the horizons of the genre came at a time when, as she said, a new generation of writers and performers had shown that "Country music can cover so much ground now without losing its identity as country music." She proved an innovator on the social level as well, spearheading country music's efforts to benefit AIDS victims and research efforts to seek a cure. In the early 1990s, it seemed her career might be cut short by vocal problems, but she refused to give up, and by the mid-1990s was again achieving new recording successes.

She was born and raised in West Virginia, growing to adulthood in a suburb of Charleston. As a child, she sang in her family's local church, but also paid attention to the diverse music broadcast on radio and TV in the latter part of the 1960s and the early 1970s, which included country, rock, soul, and one of the country subsets, bluegrass. By the time Kathy was in high school, she had learned to play acoustic guitar and accompanied herself as she sang at local get-togethers and school shows. Later she recalled the pleasures and learning experiences of sitting in living rooms with friends or family and playing guitars while singing one-on-one.

It was a pattern that continued when she spent her college years at West Virginia University. She remembered, "I was a folkie. Folk and bluegrass formed my roots. Yet it was always a quirky, earthy kind of thing. A lot of bluegrass I played, for example, was that music given a progressive treatment, what people call 'New Grass.' That's what Southeastern college kids were listening to then. When the Grateful Dead made a bluegrass album, we knew the whole thing from cover to cover."

After finishing college, Kathy had decided she could make her way as a professional musician in the country field and soon transferred her efforts to Nashville, which in the early 1980s was not as open to new country formats as it was to become later in the decade. She did manage to gain the attention of some record company executives, but they sought to change her style from emphasis on folk-bluegrass fusion to more country-pop-oriented material. She said, "I couldn't make that work. I couldn't make that believable on record."

She decided she had to stand firm on her creative approach, and luckily encountered a similar frame of mind in record producer Allen Reynolds. "I hooked up [with him]. The *Urban Cowboy* style music happening all around us at the time disturbed him greatly, and he had even contemplated a return to songwriting. It was a time when watered-down country aimed at the pop audience was in vogue.

"We found each other. Every day in the afternoon, I'd stop over at his studio. It was just Allen, the engineer Mark Miller, and me. There wouldn't even be a receptionist out front. We'd talk a couple of hours, drink a couple of beers. We'd discuss the business, why we make records, just what might ever artistically sustain us for years to come. All of that gave me so much a sense of belonging. It has formed the core of what's kept me going."

A series of demo tapes grew out of that cooperative approach, which eventually brought her a recording contract with Mercury Records, an association that reached its tenth anniversary in 1994. With Reynolds as producer, the first album was completed and released in 1984, the first of five albums turned out by Reynolds and Mattea by the end of the decade. The albums rapidly built up Kathy's status as a budding country superstar, providing a long list of hit singles and videos that included "Love at the Five and Dime" and "Eighteen Wheels and a Dozen Roses."

During those years, Kathy rose to headliner status on the concert and county fair circuit and was also featured on many TV programs and the *Grand Ole Opry*. Besides a series of best-selling albums and singles, her performances won acclaim from her industry peers. She was voted Female Vocalist of the Year in 1989 by the Country Music Association, an honor given her again in 1990. Her 1990 output included a best-of album titled *A Collection of Hits* and the chart singles hits "Where've You Been," number six in *Radio & Records* the week of January 26, "She Came from Fort Worth," number one in *R&R* the week of June 1, and "The Battle Hymn of Love" (duet with Tim O'Brien), number nine in *R&R* the week of September 3, 1990. She also received a Grammy Award in 1990 for Best Country Vocal Performance, Female (for "Where've You Been").

Her early 1990s activities included recording some material for the soundtrack that accompanied Ken Burns's monumental Public Broadcasting System *Civil War* program. Her recording was later used as a track on the *Songs of the Civil War* album. It was one more undertaking in addition to almost ceaseless work on new projects, a situation she said later, that reflected emotional difficulties in dealing with stardom.

She told Janet E. Williams of the Country Music Association's *Close Up* magazine, "My manager [Bob Titley] has a theory that you spend your whole life preparing, dealing with rejection, dealing with failure in this business, and then when you get successful, you have no skills to cope with it. I just kept working and working and working. 'I just have to do everything,' I told myself, 'and that way I won't have to think about it.'"

In the late 1980s and early 1990s, she told another interviewer, "The light shone on me, and it was bright. I had some trouble with it emotionally. I wrestled with how I might be thrilled by success while at the same time not be completely motivated by it in the future."

After her album *Time Passes By* came out in 1991, she decided she needed a change of environment to grapple with those problems and decided also to take a change of pace from a musical standpoint. She took the step of going to Scotland for a while to work on a folk-based collection with Scottish folk artist Dougie MacLean. Released at the end of 1992, that album,

Lonesome Standard Time, was on the country charts for much of 1993. The title track peaked at number eight in *Radio & Records* the week of November 27, 1992.

That wasn't her only project of 1992–93, however. She completed a Christmas album, *Good News,* and also sang and appeared in Dolly Parton's video, *Romeo.* Both the album and video received Grammy nominations.

But Kathy's frenetic pace was catching up with her. Her voice increasingly would not respond to her commands and her doctors finally recommended surgery to repair years of overuse. The medical treatment was to keep her out of action for a year and a half before she resumed her career in late 1993. However, it was not at all certain when the initial diagnosis was made that she could ever take up professional singing again.

She told Janet Williams, "They give you the big scary talk—'Every once in a while it doesn't take. You have to be prepared for that possibility.' In many ways that was a really peaceful time in my life because I had one mission—to take care of my body and be in tip-top shape for the operation. I would just go for long runs, walk in the woods, get long massages, read a lot. I spent a lot of time being quiet, and every once in awhile I'd get out my laptop computer and have a long conversation with somebody about the meaning of life.

"And I thought, 'I've had a hell of a run, and every career has a beginning, middle, and an end. Maybe this was what was meant for me. There are all kinds of things to do in this life, and maybe it's time for me to move on to the next chapter.' All I tried to do was not resist it and just let it happen the way it was supposed to happen."

During 1993, Kathy was represented on the charts with several releases (of previously recorded material) which didn't fare badly, though they might have done better if she'd been able to support them in live appearances. One single was "Standing Knee Deep in a River (and Dying of Thirst)," which rose to number twelve in *R&R* the week of March 26 and also spent a number of months on other charts. Later the single "Seeds" was on the lists, debuting in *Billboard* in May and staying on the chart into the summer.

Before 1993 was over, Kathy was given the go-ahead to resume her career activities. Besides preparing to work on a new album, she was represented by two interesting radio and TV programs. In one she joined Willie Nelson and other top-flight country artists on National Public Radio's *Long Gone Lonesome Blues: The Story of Hank Williams.* In the other, she took part in *The Beatles' Songbook* segment of the Public Broadcasting System's *In the Spotlight* series.

In the summer of 1994, Kathy's first studio album since her vocal surgery, *Walking Away a Winner,* came out. It proved an event worth waiting for. While not without its flaws, in general it was a very satisfying effort that ranked in quality with the best of her previous releases. The title song was well inside *Billboard*'s Top 10 by June, and in September she had another hit single in "Nobody's Gonna Rain on Our Parade," which peaked at number nine in *R&R* the week of October 7. The album also did well, staying on the *Billboard* list for many months after peaking at number twelve.

Her concern about the AIDS crisis increased in intensity over those years, culminating in her efforts with others in the country field to do something about the epidemic. In the 1990s, one overall music industry idea was to put out a series of albums featuring stars from various sectors of the music field, with the proceeds earmarked for research on the disease. Through 1994, four such albums were released, starting with *Red Hot + Blue,* followed by *Red Hot + Dance, No Alternative,* and *Red Hot + Country.* The last-named project, which Kathy helped spearhead, was issued in the late summer of 1994. Mattea's contribution was her duet with Jackson Browne on his song, "Rock Me on the Water."

Commenting on possible pitfalls confronting a veteran performer like herself, she said, "I think there's a danger, when you've been doing this for awhile, of listening to your voice instead of the song. I believe that when you do that, you become a caricature of yourself, a puppet of the voice. An honest reading of the song is the best thing I think I can bring to music. In the past, sometimes I've worried it wouldn't be enough. But that's what I do."

In the spring of 1995, Kathy's single, "Clown in Your Rodeo," was a top 20 entrant in *Cash Box.* Her 1995 credits, aside from a number of concerts around the U.S., included appearing on Kathie Lee Gifford's Christmas special on CBS-TV on December 19. In 1996, her duet with George Jones of "You've Got a Friend in Me" (from the computer generated film *Toy Story*) was included in the *Disney Country* album issued mid-year.

MAVERICKS, THE: *Vocal and instrumental group. Raul Malo, born Miami, Florida, August 7, 1965 (lead vocals, guitar, songwriting), Robert Reynolds, born Kansas City, Missouri, April 30, 1962 (bass), Paul Deakin, born Painesville, Ohio, September 2, 1959 (drums), and Nick Kane, born Camden, New Jersey, August 21, 1954 (guitar).*

The popularity of the Mavericks in the early and mid-1990s is proof of one of the most exciting aspects of country music of this era: the broadening base of listeners along with an acceptance of a wider variety of country music styles. A country band from Miami with a Cuban-American lead singer-songwriter: It seems unlikely that such a diverse combo could have found success in any previous decade. Yet by 1995, the Mavericks were mainstream enough to be voted Top Vocal Group and Top New Vocal Group by the Academy of Country Music, and nominated for both of those honors by the Country Music Association.

Despite the novelty of the Mavericks' background,

however, in many ways their music fits directly into the 1950s countrified rock 'n' roll tradition of Elvis Presley and Johnny Cash. In fact, lead singer Raul Malo's voice has often been compared to that of the late, great country-rock singer Roy Orbison.

The band formed in the late 1980s in Miami with Malo, Reynolds, and Deakin. Malo had grown up in that city's Little Havana, the son of Cuban immigrants. When he was a child, he fell in love with the rockabilly music of Buddy Holly and began to sing, play guitar, and write songs. In the 1980s, he was playing with a band at local clubs and bars, when he met Robert Reynolds, who was also playing gigs in the Miami area. As Reynolds told Gene Harbrecht of the *Orange County Register*, July 14, 1995 ("Mavericks, Hottest Item in Country"), "The only reason the [Mavericks] formed was because we had a couple of things in common and that was a love for honky-tonk, rockabilly and some of the rock 'n' roll from that time. We got together essentially over 'Folsom Prison Blues.' "

As Reynolds describes it, he was playing that song with his combo in a small room in Miami when Malo saw him and they started to talk about music. The group eventually formed when Reynolds brought along former jazz drummer Paul Deakin and joined Malo for their first rehearsal in a warehouse in November 1989. The fourth member, Nick Kane, was added in 1994.

As far as the group's name was concerned, as Reynolds told Gene Harbrecht, "There's not a ton of story to it. A talent manager who Raul knew said, 'You guys wanna do this [country music] here in Miami. You should call that the Mavericks because you will definitely be doing something different.' So when we got together in the warehouse on that first day, we kind of already were what we are today in terms of name."

The group produced its own first album, which brought them to the attention of MCA in Nashville, who signed them to their first record contract in 1991. Their first MCA album, *From Hell to Paradise*, mixed their rockabilly-Cuban flavor with songs about politics and society, including one with an anti-Castro theme. It was a jarring juxtaposition, and the album was not a commercial success.

Their second MCA album, *What a Crying Shame*, retained the raw flavor, but the subject matter of most of the songs, many of them cowritten by Malo, was more in keeping with popular tastes. The title track climbed the country charts in 1994, reaching as high as the number-eight slot on *Billboard*. Other hits from that album included "O What a Thrill" and "There Goes My Heart." None of the remaining singles hit the top 10 on the charts, but the album went platinum, selling over one million copies. The freshness and drive of their music, harkening back to the fifties and sixties, when music was sheer fun and energy, won the Mavericks many fans and led the way for the success of other groups, such as the Tractors.

On the personal side, Robert Reynolds married one of the most successful country female singers, Trisha Yearwood. In fact, on the Mavericks' third album for MCA, *Music for All Occasions,* Yearwood and Malo team up for a duet of the old Frank and Nancy Sinatra song, "Somethin' Stupid."

By September 1995, a single from their new album, "Here Comes the Rain," was climbing the country music charts, the group was opening for Mary-Chapin Carpenter on an extensive touring schedule, and the future looked bright indeed for the Mavericks.

As producer Tony Brown, MCA/Nashville president, told Richard Cromelin of the *Los Angeles Times,* "They're a contemporary country band unlike anybody else. They look like U2 and they sound like Buck Owens and Roy Orbison. . . . Their chemistry is so cool, but Raul's voice comin' out of those speakers, man, how can you deny that? I think it's one of the greatest voices to come down the pike in Nashville in years."

On the Country Music Association Awards telecast on CBS in October 1995, the band performed "Here Comes the Rain." It also picked up its first CMA trophy for Vocal Group of the Year. In late 1995, its next album, *Music for All Occasions,* appeared on the charts, peaking at number twelve in *Billboard* and staying at upper chart levels well into 1996. During early 1996, the Mavericks appeared on the Country Music Television Network Showcase Artists program. Later CMT reported it as one of its highest rated episodes, something reflected in a 41% jump in sales of the group's new disc. In the Academy of Country Music Awards announced on the NBC-TV show on April 24, 1996, the band was named the Top Vocal Group of 1995. Later in 1996 at the CMA October Awards program, the group was named Vocal Group of the Year for the second consecutive time.—A.S.

McAULIFFE, LEON: *Singer, steel guitarist, band leader (Western Swing Band, Cimmaron Boys), songwriter. Born Houston, Texas, January 3, 1917; died Tulsa, Oklahoma, August 20, 1988.*

An integral part of the Texas Playboys legend almost from the beginning, Leon McAuliffe fittingly became front man for the new Playboys revival in the mid-1970s. It was McAuliffe, of course, whose steel guitar playing was a central element of Bob Wills's group from 1935 to 1942 and whose name was immortalized every time Wills would shout, "Take it away, Leon," for the next steel guitar break.

McAuliffe, like Wills, was a native Texan, born and raised in Houston. When he was fourteen years old, he was given a seven-dollar Stella guitar for a Christmas present and in a short time he was a proficient player. Actually he started to learn under the guidance of an instructor, but he quit when he mastered new material faster than his teacher could provide him with additional music. He became enamored of the steel guitar and, though he could play other instruments as time went by, it remained his forte throughout his career.

In 1932, he got a summer job on the staff of station KPRC in Houston. In 1933, he became a member of a station group called the *Swift Jewel Cowboys*. Meanwhile, Bob Wills and W. Lee "Pappy" O'Daniel had inaugurated the *Light Crust Doughboys* program on a Ft. Worth station. McAuliffe recalls, "The band was being reorganized in 1933 and O'Daniel liked the sound of the steel guitar but couldn't find anyone he liked in Ft. Worth. He contacted me and I went up and auditioned and got hired." Leon stayed with the Doughboys for close to two years while Wills was off on his own with the new band that became known as the Texas Playboys.

"After a while, Bob began to make changes, dropping some people and adding new ones—and new instruments. In 1935, for instance, he added a small piano and drums. His bass player, Kermit Whelan, could play steel guitar a little, but not full time. When he left in early 1935, Bob sent for me to play the steel guitar full time and I joined in March 1935." McAuliffe moved to Tulsa, Oklahoma, with the band, which became his home for many years. He played a major role in the band's rise to prominence not only with country fans, but for others who responded to their "western swing" stylings.

One of Leon's first contributions was his instrumental composition "Steel Guitar Rag," which became a staple of the Playboys' repertoire and remained so in the new phase of the mid- and late-1970s. He also coauthored another song that became a country & western classic, "San Antonio Rose." "When that song became a major hit for us in the early 1940s, it really established us as a nationally known band. Actually the song started as an instrumental, then we came back with it with lyrics in 1940–41."

Leon's career with the Playboys was interrupted by World War II. "My time with him ended in December 1942. Up to then we'd recorded several times a year and made ten western movies. When World War II came along, everybody began to get draft notices or left to take a defense job. Both Bob and I went into the service, but he didn't stay in very long. Actually he shouldn't have gone in the first place because he was thirty-eight years old when he entered."

McAuliffe joined the Navy and became a flight instructor before leaving in 1946. After he got out, he continued his flying, buying his own plane that he often used to travel to various performing dates. He didn't ignore his music while in uniform, though, serving as a band member for many engagements with the Glenn Miller dance band led by Tex Beneke.

Based primarily on a 1979 interview with Irwin Stambler.

By the time Leon left the Navy, Wills had moved his operation to California. Leon opted to stay in Tulsa. "I didn't go back to him when I got out of the Navy. I started my own band [called the Western Swing Band]. I happened to appear on a couple of shows he was on, but that was the extent of our involvement until we got together for *The Last Time* album in 1973." Leon did well with his new group, though. The band won a wide following in the late 1940s and the early 1950s with their own radio shows on station KVOO and KRMG in Tulsa. McAuliffe then became owner and operator of his own facility, the Cimmaron Ballroom in Tulsa, and changed the band's name to the Cimmaron Boys. Under that designation, besides playing in their home club, they also traveled extensively during the late 1950s and much of the 1960s, performing throughout the United States and in European venues as well. During that period, McAuliffe also had his own TV show originating from Tulsa.

In the 1960s, the band was featured on many TV and radio shows, including the *Grand Ole Opry, Lawrence Welk, Jubilee U.S.A., Country America Show, Town Hall Party,* and the *Buddy Deane Show.* From 1956 into the mid-1960s, the Cimmaron Boys were voted one of the top three country & western bands in major trade magazine polls.

Despite all that, Leon notes he and his band had to work extremely hard to make ends meet during those years. "Young people began to go for Bill Haley and then Elvis came along. It was rough to keep going. We had to travel longer and play more nights, but it was the only way to survive. Our schedule got rougher and rougher and the only way we could make it was with the airplane. Typically five of us took the plane for one date to the next and three drove.

"We had a complete show—not just one singer. Everybody in the band was a vocalist. Some could do comedy. We had little acts and comic bits we used. We could sustain a two-hour show easily with the kind of talent we had."

McAuliffe recorded many numbers with his various bands from the late 1940s into the mid-1960s. Most of these were written by others. "I've written some songs that are good, but not many. I can't manufacture 'em, they have to come to me. I wrote 'Steel Guitar Rag' and the bridge to 'San Antonio Rose'—the trumpeter wrote the words—but Bob has total credit. But I'm happy to trade that for 'Take It Away, Leon' any time. I wrote 'Panhandle Rag,' which was a hit for my band in 1948 and that's the last song I've written."

With his Western Swing Band, he had forty records for Columbia from the late 1940s to mid-fifties. During 1957–59, his Cimmaron Boys' releases came out on Dot Records and from the mid-1950s to mid-1960s, his recordings were issued by various labels including ABC-Paramount, Starday, Cimmaron, and Capitol. His LPs of these years included *Take Off* on Dot, *Cozy Inn* on ABC-Paramount, *Mister Western Swing* on Starday, *Swingin' Western Strings* on Cimmaron, and *Dancinest Band Around* on Capitol. Capitol, with whom he signed a long-term contract in the early 1960s, was his recording home for that decade and, as it happened, was the label for which he turned out the new Original Texas Playboy LPs in the mid- and late 1970s.

Steadily declining interest in western swing influenced Leon to break up his group and go into retirement by the late 1960s. He was living in Missouri doing some occasional session work when the call came from Bob Wills to do a retrospective album in 1973. "The Texas Playboys are back together because Bob wanted us to do a final album. He picked eight people to do it, all of whom had been in the band over its thirty or forty years of existence."

Wills suffered a stroke before the new album was finished, but Leon and the other seven hand-picked musicians completed it, and the album came out under the title *For the Last Time* in 1975. The response to the album was so good that Capitol asked McAuliffe and Leon Rausch to keep things going even after Wills's death. The result was a series of new LPs beginning with the March 1977 release *The Late Bob Wills Original Texas Playboys Today.*

Harking back to the Wills inspired album, Leon stresses, "Because the old man wanted us to do it, we agreed to do it. I credit Asleep at the Wheel [a new band that stressed western swing in its repertoire] with being a key in the Playboys' resurgence. Like everything turned out right. Waylon and Willie started singing 'Bob Wills Is Still the King' and all of a sudden all these kids who'd been ignoring their parents' comments on what had been done musically in the past said, 'Hey, it's not too bad.'

"As for the new Playboys, musically we're doing the same thing we've done forty years ago. We still play the same style and if we play a new tune we adapt it to our style. But it's not a full-scale revival for most of us. We may play some key places if Capitol wants us to, but outside of Leon Rausch, who makes his living playing music, the rest of us go other ways. Some are retired, some have businesses, some have jobs, and one teaches school. We hold 'em down. We don't want to work too much and we're very dedicated to preserving the Bob Wills sound."

That sound, McAuliffe agreed in 1979, included his ringing steel guitar work and the memories it evoked of the famous Bob Wills "holler." "When Wills started his holler, I don't know, 'cause he was doin' it the first time I knew. Bob would play fiddle up to the time Tommy [Duncan] was to sing and he'd say 'Come in Tommy.' When we recorded 'Steel Guitar Rag,' before we cut it he said, 'You hit a chord and let me talk.' That's what I did—I hit a slide chord and he said, 'Lookout! Here comes Leon. Take it away, boy, take it away!'"

In the 1980s, Leon called Tulsa, Oklahoma, home and he focused most of his efforts on helping pass along country music skills to new generations, setting up classes with various instructors at the Hank Thompson School of Country Music, part of Rogers State College. His awesome instrumental skills continued to be recalled by many country artists and fans years after his death in 1988. Not surprisingly, he was included in the "All-Time All-Star Country Band" dreamed up by *Life* magazine for its special issue on the country field in September 1994. During that year, two of his recordings were reissued in the Columbia/Legacy *Hillbilly Boogie* album, both performed with his Western Swing Band. One was "Take It Away, Leon" (recorded July 30, 1950), the other "Blue Guitar Stomp" (recorded January 29, 1951). Some of his instrumental work could also be heard on the many Bob Wills & the Texas Playboys albums still in print in the mid-1990s.

McBRIDE, MARTINA: *Singer. Born Sharon, Kansas, c. 1966.*

Winsome, gray-eyed Martina McBride, a stunningly attractive brunette, appeared to epitomize K. T. Oslin's comment that to succeed in modern country music an artist had to be "a hunk or a babe." But once she began singing, her high-powered, throbbing vocals and her choice of often socially meaningful material—such as the song "Independence Day," which described a woman's escape from spousal abuse—indicated she was indeed much more than just a pretty face.

She spent her formative years on her father's wheat farm in Kansas, where, as is true in most rural areas, country music was the favorite of local residents. She remembers those days with a certain nostalgia. As she told Holly Gleason of *Bone* magazine ("Martina McBride—Beautiful Woman, Beautiful Music," January 1994), "When I was little, my sister and I used to go down to the pasture and bring the cows in for milking. And when it was the fall, we'd go out and help with the harvest, fix lunch and take it down to the people working. That's how it is, and you don't think about it.

"Sometimes the music business gets a little scary and you want to go back to the farm, because it's been in the family for generations. I grew up thinking it was something that was solid that I'd always be a part of and I know if I go back there in 40 years, it will always be there. . . . That solid background gave me a sense of myself and that's been the thing that's probably made a difference for me."

As a child, Martina liked to sing, sometimes vocalizing with songs on the radio or record player. Her first identification was with country music, but like most teenagers she enjoyed the hits of the reigning rock stars. In high school she teamed up with some of the teenage bands and by the mid-1980s was finding work as a professional vocalist in venues in and around Wichita, Kansas.

Even then, she was beginning to attract attention from the music scene observers outside her home area. Writer Jeff Shibley recalled in *The Note* publication ("Kansas Gal Martina McBride," November 1993) visiting a small Wichita club in 1986 to hear his cousin Winston Blair's group, "I don't remember the name of the band (or the club for that matter), but Winston is always in great bands. I do remember having my socks knocked off by a stunning female singer. She belted out the blues and got in your face when she sang rock 'n' roll. That was the first time my path crossed with Martina. For the next four years she continued to play rock and R&B in other Wichita bands."

Her music field endeavors brought her in contact with her future husband, John, a sound engineer who set up his own company, MD Systems. In 1990, the couple decided to move to Nashville so John could expand his business and Martina could seek a major label recording contract. John's fortunes were the first to improve as he gained work with several country stars, including Ricky Van Shelton and Garth Brooks. John signed on as production manager for Brooks's 1991 tour and, to keep him company, Martina spent nine months selling Garth Brooks T-shirts.

Martina made a number of demo tapes of country renditions, which were passed on to Nashville executives. This finally brought a contract from RCA Records that cleared the way for her to work on her debut album, *The Time Has Come*. She also took a step that eventually proved a major help in career progress by lining up manager Bruce Allen. Unusual for a homegrown U.S. artist, her choice was a Canadian. (Allen was already the manager of the Canadian rock star Bryan Adams.) The contact came about through her husband's brother-in-law, a Canadian-based photographer who had once done work for Allen.

The debut album, which focused on traditional country material, won praise from a number of reviewers, but flopped with record buyers. Three tracks from the album, the title song, "Cheap Whiskey," and "That's Me," made video and record charts, but none made top levels and each one peaked lower than the previous release. But Martina slowly built up her reputation, aided by Garth Brooks's invitation to be the opening act on his seventy-five concert schedule from the summer to late December of 1992.

For her second album, Martina—with advice from Bruce Allen and other advisers—decided she should be more adventurous both in her material selection and her vocal arrangements. While no one was counting her out, everyone was aware this could be a vital career turning point. She told *Country Song Roundup,* "I think the pressure was there, but I never let myself think that way. For one thing, I love to make records. It's such a

creative outlet for me. I don't write songs, so that's where my creative outlet is. I dive in and have a lot of fun. This album was easier than the first one for me. I didn't wonder if I was doing the right thing. The first time, you really don't have anything to judge it by, you don't have any mark to try to better. So the second album was easier for me."

Released in late summer of 1993, *The Way That I Am* appeared on various charts in September and over the next few months accumulated good responses from fans and reviewers. *CD Review* commented, "Unlike singers who find a song they like, then try to imagine what the songwriter was feeling, McBride has a knack for singing songs that reflect her emotions and attitudes—giving you a glimpse into her soul." The *Houston Chronicle's* critic noted (October 31, 1993), while her 1992 debut album "got lost in the shuffle of new artists, it would be a shame if the same thing happened to *The Way That I Am,* because McBride has a vision to go with her voice and image."

The title song, it was noted, "paints a balanced portrait of a modern woman's romantic concerns. The first single (released in June 1993), 'My Baby Loves Me,' is an upbeat tune sung from the point of view of a woman who's finally found someone who loves her for who she is. 'Independence Day,' on the other hand, is about a woman who burns her house down, with her abusive husband inside. Both songs were written by Gretchen Peters." (McBride commented, "If I could write like anybody, I'd like to write like her.")

Similar glowing comments were made in dozens of other reviews in the U.S. and Canada. This time the encomiums didn't go unnoticed by radio programmers or fans. The album made *Billboard* in September and was still on the chart in the summer of 1995 (having peaked earlier at number fourteen) with sales totals past R.I.A.A. platinum-record levels. In the fall of 1993, the single "My Baby Loves Me" made top-chart levels, rising to number two in *Billboard* (behind a Garth Brooks number-one hit, "American Honky Tonk Bar Association"). The video of the song was a sensation at home and abroad, hitting number one on Country Music TV in the U.S. two weeks in a row and also soaring to number one in 1993 on CMT Europe, TNN, and VH-1's country video program. The single "Life #9," issued in late 1993, was a top-6 hit in *R&R* in April 1994 and during the summer of 1994, "Independence Day" was a top-10 success.

Of the latter, the most searing track of the album, Martina said, "I love to sing story songs, which is what this is all about. It's a song about overcoming abuse. This woman really did the most extreme thing, but she saw this as her only way out. I think that a lot of women in this world can identify with that. I don't think that her way of getting out is necessarily the right way, but I think she was a desperate woman in a desperate situation. It has a wonderful anthem-like chorus that really evokes the emotions of freedom and independence felt after leaving a life filled with emotional and physical oppression."

During 1993, Martina gained increasing exposure on various TV and radio shows and also toured with Ricky Van Shelton and other country stars. For 1994, Garth Brooks asked her to open for him a second time, this time on a European tour starting in April. With her growing acceptance in Europe, RCA rush-released a European album titled *The Way That I Am* that also included some cuts from her first album. Earlier that year, Martina made her acting debut, performing a guest role as a country singer in the syndicated TV series *Baywatch* that aired in May.

For her performances in late 1993 and throughout 1994, Martina cut her hair short, giving her a gaminlike look. She told Holly Gleason, "This is a business and a society where we place too much importance on how people look. To me, it's what's inside people that counts—maybe subconsciously that's one of the reasons I cut my hair."

In the Country Music Association 1994 voting, she was nominated for the Horizon Award and Music Video of the Year (for the Gretchen Peters composition "Independence Day"). She was presented with one of those on the October 1994 awards telecast. "Independence Day" also earned Martina a 1994 Grammy nomination for Best Country Vocal Performance, Female. Her achievements also were recognized with nominations in several categories in the Academy of Country Music voting, whose results were telecast in the spring of 1995.

Her album *The Way That I Am* was still on the charts in the summer of 1995, having earned a platinum award from the R.I.A.A. Her singles releases in 1995 included "Safe in the Arms of Love" on all the major charts (it peaked at number four in *Billboard*) in the summer. On November 30, 1995, she was one of the artists who taped a TV program (shown on CBS-TV in January 1996) in honor of the *Grand Ole Opry*'s 70th anniversary. On the program it was noted that she had become the newest member of the *Opry*.

During the fall of 1995, the album *Wild Angels* was issued and it remained on the charts into 1996 after peaking at number seventeen in *Billboard*. The title track, issued as a single, made the top 10 on major hit lists as did the next release in the spring of 1996, "Phones Are Ringin' All Over Town."

McBRIDE, TERRY, McBRIDE AND THE RIDE:
Singer, guitarist, songwriter, band leader (the Ride). Born Austin, Texas, December 16.

Like many country artists, Terry McBride was a second-generation performer. His interest in the field came naturally, inspired by the career of his father, Dale McBride, who had eleven singles that made hit charts

on various independent labels. Terry was fortunate to reach maturity when country music was entering a boom period, which gave him the opportunity to gain a national reputation on a major record label.

He was born in Austin, Texas, but grew up sixty miles away in the small ranching community of Lampasas. He started to learn guitar at nine, helped along by some hints from his father, and by high school was involved in musical projects with friends and associates. After completing high school, he toured for three years with his father. By then in his early twenties, he spent the next two years as a bass guitarist and backing vocalist with Delbert McClinton.

During those years, he said, he thought his eventual career activities would be as a songwriter and solo vocalist rather than as a band leader. He said, "Growing up with my dad as an entertainer, I always took for granted that I'd be a singer and do what my dad did, but I really didn't know what it took to get there. When I got out of high school, I really wanted to be just a great player, that's what I concentrated on. I always played in bands where they'd feature me, even Delbert featured me, but I was never working to get that band of my own. Then I set my sights on writing. I guess in the back of my mind I always hoped someday to be able to perform these tunes, but when I came to Nashville I was in search of getting songs cut more than trying to be the artist. [But] it just fell into place."

Following typical songwriting-selling practice, once in Nashville Terry recorded demos of his material, which he shopped around to publishers and record companies. He also took part in competitions and also got the chance to sing at local clubs. Eventually, Terry's talents caught the attention of Tony Brown, who decided that with a backing group McBride would be a good addition to the label. For a performance at the annual Fan Fair event in Nashville in June 1989, Brown lined up guitarist Ray Herndon and drummer Billy Thomas as the first version of the Ride. Those three, together with other musicians, later went into the studio to record their debut album. Called *Burnin' Up the Road,* the album came out in early 1991, backed by intensive touring by a group—of which McBride, Herndon, and Thomas were the nucleus—called McBride and the Ride, as opening acts in larger venues or headliners in small bars and night spots. The album showed up on the *Billboard* list in May and stayed there into the fall after peaking at number twenty-seven. It provided the hit single "Can I Count on You," which went to number thirteen on radio charts and also was the basis for a video hit that was the longest-running release on the CMT channel during 1991. The single, "Same Old Star," cowritten by McBride with several others, was on the *Billboard* chart from late summer through several fall months. The band's achievements won them Top Vocal Group nominations from both the Academy of Country Music and the

Country Music Association. *Cash Box* also named them New Group of the Year for 1991. CMA members also nominated the group for Vocal Group of the Year in its 1992 voting.

In 1992, the group had two major singles hits, "Sacred Ground," title track of the band's second album, which reached number one on several lists, including *Radio & Records* the week of June 5. The other success was "Going out of My Mind," number three in *R&R* the week of October 2. The band opened 1993 with the single "Just One Night," appearing on *R&R, Billboard,* and other charts, moving to top levels in February when it was number five in *R&R* the week of February 19. A few months later the single "Love on the Loose, Heart on the Run" won fans' attention, rising eventually to number three in *R&R* the week of June 18. The band's album *Hurry Sundown* made the *Billboard* list in May 1993 and stayed there for some months, providing a top-15 hit of the title track in the fall.

In the fall of 1993, McBride was asked to provide a soundtrack song for the movie *8 Seconds,* about the life of rodeo star Lane Frost. McBride teamed up with producer-writer Josh Leo on the song "No More Cryin'." By the time the song made the charts in November, the original group had been disbanded with the departure of Herndon and Thomas. A new group, now called Terry McBride and the Ride, was assembled, which made its debut opening a New Year's concert by Wynonna. The new group comprised Gary Morse on steel (a holdover from the earlier roster), Rick Gerken on keyboards, Keith Edwards on drums, Bob Britt on guitar and Randy Frazier on bass. Of those, only Morse did the studio work on McBride's 1994 album release.

While plans were under way for that new album, titled *Terry McBride & the Ride,* Terry focused particular attention on cowriting a new song called "I'll See You Again Someday." It was written in memory of his father, who died during 1993. He recalled, about a month after his dad's passing, "I wanted to write about what I was feeling at the time. I knew Tim Mensy had written a real sensitive song about his grandfather when he passed away. Tim and I spent two days writing that song. It's really just a song of hope for anybody who's lost a loved one."

The debut single from the new album, "Been There," was issued in early summer of 1994 and made mid-chart levels in *Billboard* and other music industry publications. Besides the song for his father, McBride's writing contributions for the new album included "Teardrops," "I'd Be Lying," and "He's Living My Dreams."

McCLAIN, CHARLY: *Singer, Born Memphis, Tennessee, March 26, circa 1956.*

Though she uses a masculine first name (derived from her given name, Charlotte Denise McClain), there's nothing macho about Charly McClain. Indeed,

with her flashing smile, dark brown eyes, flowing brown hair, and well-proportioned five-foot-one-inch figure, she was among the more eye-pleasing additions to country music's new wave of promising young singers in the late 1970s.

The middle child of three in a Memphis, Tennessee, electrician's family (she has a younger sister and older brother), she became interested in country music at an early age. After watching the first Country Music Association Awards TV show in the late 1960s, she reputedly told her family she expected to win the Female Vocalist Award in 1981. As she grew up, she began to take steps to make that prediction come true—or at least achieve a close approximation. Still, she could just as well have become an electrician, since she aided her father on his rounds at times and learned the basics of the craft.

It was because her father became seriously ill, McClain told Dolly Carlisle of *Country Music* magazine (April 1979), that she took a major step toward a singing career. "He was in the hospital for over a year with tuberculosis. During that time the children couldn't see him and our only means of communication was through taped messages. In the beginning we sent him talking tapes, but eventually they turned musical. Shortly afterwards, my brother and I formed a band and kept right on singing."

The two McClains helped assemble a band that worked at local functions in the early 1970s. But the group broke up when several members received draft notices. Charly then successfully auditioned for the Memphis-based *Mid-South Jamboree* program and became a cast member for a while until the show was phased out. In the mid-1970s, she added to her experience by joining the O. B. McClinton show, with whom she toured many places in the United States.

All of those jobs helped improve her stage presence and polish her performing style. They also increased her friends and contacts in the music field. Among the people McClain came to know were members of the Memphis band Shylo. She was watching them perform at the Mid-South Fair in Memphis in 1977 when she was asked to sing a few numbers with the group.

She told Dolly Carlisle, "They just called me up on stage." Soon after, she got a call from Larry Rogers, Shylo producer, to make a demo tape. "Larry took the tape to Billy Sherrill. I got a contract with Epic a few weeks later. It sounds like I had an easy way of it, but I had pushed tapes for years on Nashville's Music Row with no success. . . . It really hasn't been easy. There were a lot of promises made that never came through."

However, once Charly's voice became available on commercial records, it was easy for many country fans to become enamored of her singing style. Her debut LP on Epic, *Here's Charly McClain,* spawned her first chart single, "Lay Down." She did even better with the material recorded for her second album, *Let Me Be Your*

Baby, issued in late 1978. First the track "Let Me Be Your Baby" reached upper-chart levels and, in November 1978, a second track, "That's What You Do to Me," made the country top 10.

Through much of 1978 she toured on her own, but by the end of the year, things were rolling along well enough for her to assemble her own traveling band, Bluff City. It was a psychological breakthrough, she admitted to Carlisle. "[Before] it was depressing to appear in a city never knowing what the circumstances were going to be or if the band that was to accompany me was going to be good. I was very tired. My new band has made all the difference in road work. Now I feel very proud of our act. It's polished, professional and I feel good."

She had reason to feel even better about her musical efforts over the next few years, particularly in the early 1980s when her popularity reached new heights. She finished the 1970s with additional recording credits, including the 1979 charted single "When a Love Ain't Right" and a duet with Johnny Rodriguez, "I Hate the Way I Love It," but started off the 1980s in even better style with the early 1980 bestseller, "Men." Later in the year she had such audience favorites as "Let's Put Our Love in Motion" and "Women Get Lonely." In early 1981, she had what was to prove her most successful release to that point, the single "Who's Cheatin' Who," which reached number one on country charts in February. Before the year was over, she had other top-10 hits such as "Surround Me with Love" and "Sleepin' with the Radio On."

Charly made the country album charts in 1981 with *Surround Me with Love* and followed with such early 1980s releases as *Too Good to Hurry* in 1982 and *Paradise* and *The Woman in Me* (both 1983). In addition to appearing on the concert circuit, she also found time for roles on TV programs. Her credits during the 1980s included appearances on *Hart to Hart* and *Fantasy Island.* Her mid-1980s albums included *It Takes Believers* (with Mickey Gilley) in 1984, *Radio Heart* in 1985, and *Still I Stay* in 1987. Her releases in the late 1980s included the 1988 album *Charly McClain.*

McCLINTON, DELBERT: *Singer, harmonica player, guitarist, songwriter. Born Lubbock, Texas, November 4, 1940.*

He was known for years among fans of country blues and rhythm & blues as the "King of the White Texas Bluesmen." His style was respected and sometimes copied by many famous artists, from the Beatles to Waylon Jennings. His original songs were covered by many performers, in fields ranging from rock and R&B to country, providing major hits for some artists in the 1970s. Despite that, until the start of the 1980s he was virtually unknown to most of the music public outside Texas. Fortunately, the long overdue discovery of

his great creative abilities finally came after decades of dues paying. As Jack McDonough headlined in *Billboard* (January 17, 1981): "20-Year Triumph: McClinton Charts."

The long road to that recognition began in Lubbock, Texas, where Delbert was born and lived until his family moved to Ft. Worth, Texas, when he was eleven. Considering his later affinity for the blues, he didn't emerge from the typical background of early poverty or broken family. He recalled having had a happy childhood and traced his interest in music and songwriting as something that just evolved naturally. "I started singing while I helped wash the dishes. It's one of those things you do, then someone starts paying you to do it." After a while he found himself making up some songs on his own, a task that came easily because of a habit of talking to himself. In his teens, he got his first guitar, a used Kay he bought for about $3.50, and soon was playing for friends and classmates at his Ft. Worth high school.

He quickly expanded his efforts outside school. He told Suzan Crane of *Hit Parader,* "I was playing clubs probably when I was sixteen . . . no, before that . . . fifteen." He also was moving in and out of a series of bands—the Mellow Fellows, the Losers, the Bright Side, the Acme Music Company. Finally he formed one called the Straitjackets, which became the house band at a blues club south of Ft. Worth called Jack's Place.

He told Crane, "The blues was real popular in the Texas area. People like Howlin' Wolf and Jimmy Reed, Bobby Bland and Junior Parker, and Sonny Boy Williamson. Being the house band out there, and that being the club they usually came to, we backed 'em up. We also liked it, so we already knew all the songs.

"One night we were playing a song called 'Fanny Mae' by Buster Brown. We were backing him up and Jimmy Reed in the same night, and I had just bought me a harmonica because they were two of the best, ya know, and I was ready to learn. Well, we were sittin' in the dressing room before the snow—I didn't drink at the time—but they were both passing a quart of Old Grand-Dad, and I was sittin' in the middle helping 'em drink it—I never did see the show!"

That might have been the starting point for McClinton's later "two fisted he-man" image. But it didn't keep him from pursuing his romance with the harmonica. He picked up tips from the greatest blues harp players he could find and added touches of his own that made him a premiere exponent of that instrumental style. He included some blues harp licks on his first record, a cover of Sonny Boy Williamson's "Wake Up Baby" on the Le Cam label. He used the pseudonym Mac Linton on the disc, which was the first by a white singer ever played on the Ft. Worth black station KNOK. Over the years, many of his other recordings found play-time on black stations.

In 1962, his harmonica backing helped bring rock

artist Bruce Channel a chart hit single, "Hey Baby." Delbert was asked to tour with Channel, a job that took him all over the United States and, among other places, to England. British musicians quickly took note of Mc-Clinton's harmonica skills.

He recalled for Suzan Crane, "From the first night I was there, somebody in every band had a harmonica [and] come down to the dressing room and wanted to learn something. And this went on every night. . . . Well, one night we worked with the Beatles. They were the opening act for the Bruce Channel show and the only thing I knew about them was this girl had said 'I want you to hear this band; they're the hottest band in the North of England,' and they were. They had on these nice-looking lightweight black leather suits and whichever one I taught to play something on harp, I asked him where he got the suit, and I went into London the next day and got me a coat."

Later, when Delbert was back in Texas, he heard the results of his tutelage. It took the form of the harmonica work on the Beatles "Love Me Do."

In 1964, McClinton formed a group called the Ron-Dels that had some success with Texas fans. The group recorded some songs for three different labels, two of which were local hits, "Crying over You" and "If You Really Want Me to I'll Go." The last named, written by Delbert, was covered by a number of artists and Waylon Jennings's version made the national country charts.

For the balance of the 1960s, McClinton continued to play the blues clubs, beer joints, and honky tonks in and around Texas without gaining much attention beyond his home borders. In 1970, though, a woman he was involved with, recently divorced and with settlement money in her purse, provided the incentive for a move to Los Angeles. The romance failed to last, which inspired some of McClinton's 1970s songs, but once in California he teamed with a friend named Glen Clark to make some recordings for the now long-defunct Clean Records. The team of Delbert and Glen had two album releases on Clean during the early 1970s that, he said, "not enough people know about yet." Discouraged at the state of the music industry in California ("We weren't speaking their language and they weren't speaking ours"), he returned to Texas in the summer of 1974 to try to put the pieces of his career together again.

He soon was receiving grateful applause from crowds at his old honky tonk haunts and negotiating a new record deal with ABC. The first of the new solo LPs, featuring all original songs, *Victim of Life's Circumstances,* was released in the spring of 1975. This was followed by *Genuine Cowhide* in 1976 and *Love Rustler* in 1977. The latter showcased McClinton's varied musical tastes, ranging from the R&B-tinged "Under Suspicion" to a southern rock version of Laura Lee's "Long as I Got You." Most of the tracks, including the excellent "Some People," were written by Delbert.

The ABC releases impressed many critics, but didn't have much impact on fans, R&B, country, or otherwise. In fact, it looked as though McClinton might achieve whatever success that would come to him from his writing rather than performing efforts. Artists had been including some of his material in albums and some singles right along; in 1978, Emmylou Harris had a number one country hit with his "Two More Bottles of Wine." At the end of the decade, the late John Belushi and Dan Ayckroyd included his composition "B Movie Boxcar Blues" in their hit *Blues Brothers* LP. Belushi and Ayckroyd, like many of McClinton's entertainment industry peers, were long-time fans of his, and when Delbert played the Lone Star Cafe in New York in the late 1970s, they went onstage to join his act. They were soon followed by such other luminaries as Jimmy Buffett, Leon Redbone, and Joe Ely.

In 1978, McClinton contracted for new albums with Capricorn Records. This resulted in two excellent collections, *Second Wind* (recorded with the Muscle Shoals Rhythm Section in Alabama), issued in 1978, and *Keeper of the Flame,* released in 1979. Unfortunately, Capricorn had gotten into financial difficulties and its demise dimmed the prospects for the new albums. In addition, the company's collapse also washed out negotiations McClinton was involved in for doing the soundtrack for the film *Middle Age Crazy.*

It was just another setback to join a long list of frustrations. McClinton always had a reputation for artistic integrity, but while he had high standards that didn't mean he enjoyed living a relatively hand-to-mouth existence (and he had a wife and two sons to support). He told a reporter he was proud of his work, but wanted something more. "When you're in this business, you want to make money. You need a national hit . . . that's how you make money."

He was beginning to think such a hit was just wishful thinking. However, he kept on hoping. In 1980 he signed with the newly established Muscle Shoals Sound Records. His first album under the new agreement was *The Jealous Kind,* released in October 1980 and distributed by Capitol Records. Strangely, it was his first LP without a single original song by him. He explained, "This time I just didn't have any songs I considered high energy enough." The album quickly made the charts, as did the single from it, "Giving It Up for Your Love." Both recordings showed up on both country and pop lists and the single made the top 10 on pop charts in early 1981.

One reason he finally had such a breakthrough, he told Pete Oppel of the *Dallas Morning News* (March 24, 1981), was the support the record company had provided. "Because all the other record companies I've been with have folded . . . these companies never put any money into the albums. If you've got something to sell, you've got to put money into it to make people aware of it. I can name you three record companies right off the bat that didn't do that. But this one [Capitol Records] is and it's making quite a noticeable difference."

Looking back, he said, "Actually I'm proud of all the records I've made, so that, in itself, is successful. Of course, I wanted them to sell, but the fact that they haven't doesn't mean they're not good records."

By mid-1981, McClinton was in Muscle Shoals putting the finishing touches on a new album. This one included some of his own songs, such as "I Wanna Thank You Baby" and "Sandy Beaches," the latter the first single from the album. The LP was released by Capitol in November 1981, titled *Plain from the Heart.*

Plain from the Heart was not a blockbuster and turned out to be Delbert's last collection on the Muscle Shoals Sound/Capitol label. While other artists continued to record some of his songs, McClinton himself had no new recordings out for some seven years. He likely could have found another home label, but he didn't push hard for it. As he later told an interviewer, he didn't go all out "because getting a record deal was on the back burner. I had so many other things going on in my life."

One reason he was always glad to have songs from many writers in his repertoire, McClinton said, was that he was never a prolific writer. This was due to "my pride in my music. I work hard to perfect my songs. I've taken as long as two years to finish one simply because it needed a line and I don't want to pad. I know when it can be better and if it can be better I want it to be. I want people to hear my songs, but I want them to hear their honesty."

In the late 1980s, he left Texas for Nashville, intent on returning to the recording wars. His decision to settle in Music City, he said, reflected a friend's advice: "If you want to pick cotton, you should go to the cotton field." By then he had completed material for a new album, released by Alligator Records in 1988, called *Live from Austin.* As was usually the case with McClinton, it was a quality album that won a 1989 Grammy nomination for Best Contemporary Blues Album.

During 1989, he signed with Curb Records/Nashville, which issued his label debut, *I'm with You,* in 1990. McClinton had a hand in writing five of the ten songs in the album, presenting a number of them in the some 250 concert dates he had lined up each year of the new decade. Response to the album suggested that the 1990s finally might be the period when McClinton could gain mass audience appreciation of his creative talents. The album did reasonably well domestically, but won him many fans overseas, particularly in Scandinavia where it became a top-10 hit.

In 1991 he teamed up with Bonnie Raitt, also beginning to come into her own, for the duet "Good Man, Good Woman." She included this in her album *Luck of the Draw.* Their single of the song won them a 1992 Grammy for Best Rock Vocal Duo. As that underscored, categorizing Delbert always has been difficult since his stylings in each album typically cover a musical spectrum from country (with folk elements) to blues and jazz. Thus while he always had a country following (which increased greatly in the 1990s), in 1989 the state of South Carolina issued a proclamation citing his "outstanding contribution to rhythm and blues."

In 1992, Curb released a new studio album, *Never Been Rocked Enough,* on which backing artists included Bonnie Raitt, Tom Petty, and Melissa Etheridge. The album, he said, reflected his long-held goal of making "the kind of music that makes you want to forget all your troubles and have a good time, get up and dance even if you can't. If it wasn't for a few people, the flame of this particular kind of music might have died. I like to think I'm helping to keep it alive."

Delbert achieved another chart duet hit in 1993 when his voice was teamed with Tanya Tucker's on the single "Tell Me About It." The release made upper country-chart levels in the late spring. Later it resulted in Delbert and Tanya receiving a Country Music Association nomination for 1993 Vocal Event of the Year.

McCLINTON, OBIE BURNETT "O. B.": *Singer, songwriter. Born Gravel Springs Community near Senatobia, Mississippi, April 25, 1940 (year of birth has also been given as 1942); died September 23, 1987.*

In the early 1970s, O. B. McClinton wrote a song called "The Only One," which referred to a case of mistaken identity: when he performed in country shows and clubs, people thought he was Charley Pride. It wasn't that his traditionally oriented country style was a carbon copy of Charley's, simply that they had the same skin color. But as the 1970s went by, if O. B. didn't achieve the same massive success as Charley, he did gain a strong following that admired him for his own approach to music and for the many excellent original songs that were part of his repertoire.

Obie Burnett McClinton became interested in music at an early age in his home state of Mississippi. He recalled to LaWayne Satterfield of the *Music City News* (October 1973) that he often daydreamed about show business as a boy growing up on his father's (Reverend G. A. McClinton) farm. "This wasn't hard to do if you're a kid of ten or eleven and put to doing a chore you don't want to do—hoeing crops, rounding up livestock, and 'following' a mule—and especially if your dad's farm is a big, 700-acre place, a most unusually sizeable thing for a black man to own in Mississippi, and you are next to the youngest of seven (three boys and four girls) with plenty of secret places in which to hide."

Then and during his teenage years, his interest in singing grew stronger. One of his favorite artists was

Hank Williams, much of whose style wore off, with the result that later on people sometimes told him, "Why, you sound just like Hank Williams."

He was still doing chores on the farm at seventeen when he decided to run off and make his mark in entertainment. He wanted to go to San Francisco, but he only had a small amount of money and when he got to Memphis the sight of a guitar in a store window so enthralled him that he bought it with his travel money. He returned home, finished high school, and spent a lot of his spare time experimenting on the guitar.

Upon graduating, he returned to Memphis and earned a living at a variety of odd jobs. Still unsure of how to proceed, he applied to college and gained a choir scholarship from Rust College in Holly Springs, Mississippi. He spent four years there, singing in the A Cappella Choir, and was graduated in 1966. He moved to Memphis once more, this time getting a DJ job with station WDIA, but that was cut short in December 1966 when, to avoid being drafted into the Army, O. B. enlisted in the Air Force. He spent four years in the service, stationed at various Air Force bases from Lakeland and Amarillo in Texas to Shaw in South Carolina. While in uniform, he polished his skills as a singer, winning a number of talent shows, and also began to turn out promising original songs. Most of his writing emphasis then was on R&B material, which got him a writing contract from Fame Publishing Co. in Muscle Shoals, Alabama.

After his discharge at the start of the 1970s, O. B.'s activities centered for a while in Muscle Shoals. His songs were reaping big rewards for many R&B artists. Among his credits were "Baby, You Got My Mind Messed Up" and "A Man Needs a Woman," recorded by James Carr; "You Can't Miss What You Can't Measure," a hit for Clarence Carter; and "Keep Your Arms Around Me," released by the great Otis Redding.

O. B. had made some relatively unsuccessful efforts to work as an R&B singer. He loved country but was doubtful a black man could succeed in the field. However, Charley Pride's breakthrough plus the way people responded to O. B.'s Hank Williams phrasing gave him confidence he might do it.

He told Satterfield, "I was in Muscle Shoals and staying at the Holiday Inn writing a tune for Willie Hightower called 'The Back Road to Town,' and I learned I was staying next door to Al Bell." Bell, a top Stax Records executive, had been an acquaintance when both were Memphis DJs in 1966. McClinton sought him out and played some of his country tapes without telling Bell who was doing it.

"After listening to them for a while, Al asked, 'Who is he? Is he signed?' When I wouldn't tell, Al kept after me until I admitted it was me. He told me I was joking and the only way I could convince him that was really me singing on them tapes was to sing along with the tapes. He put me under contract on January 12, 1971." O. B. was assigned to the Stax country label, Enterprise.

After several releases received regional attention, O. B. made the national country charts with the single "Don't Let the Green Grass Fool You." O. B. not only sang but produced the record. During the 1970s, McClinton produced other artists' material as well. As the 1970s went by, he turned out a steady series of singles and albums, including his debut LP, *Country McClinton,* in 1972 and *Live at Randy's Rodeo* in 1973. Among his mid-1970s chart singles were "Yours and Mine" in early 1975, "Hello, This Is Anna" in mid-1978, and "Natural Love" in late 1978. The last two were on Epic Records, to which O. B. switched after Stax Records went out of business in the mid-1970s. In the early 1980s, he had some releases on Sunbird Records, including the single "Not Exactly Free," on the charts in the fall of 1980.

In the early 1980s, O. B. found it difficult to line up new recording assignments, so he kept his career going writing songs for other artists and by touring and appearing on TV shows like *Nashville Now.* The TV exposure helped him retain a sizable following that made it possible for him to line up live dates almost every weekend. His TV experience made him believe he might gain new recording success by marketing his material via TV commercials rather than through stores. This led to release of the album *O. B. McClinton* by Suffolk Marketing in the fall of 1986, which combined his versions of hits by other country artists with tracks of his self-penned songs.

Just when it looked as though this approach finally might bring him the respect he deserved from the country audience, O. B. was diagnosed with a cancerous tumor. An operation was performed in September 1986, but the doctors told him the outlook for survival was grim.

The respect he had earned from other performers was underscored on November 11, 1986, when many stars got together to hold a benefit performance to help him pay his medical bills. Those taking part included Exile, Kathy Mattea, Rex Allen, Jr., Waylon Jennings, Tom T. Hall, Rodney McDowell, Reba McEntire, Ricky Skaggs, and Steve Wariner. O. B. closed the proceedings, held at Nashville's Stockyard Restaurant, by singing three of his songs including, "The Only One." Afterward Epic Records agreed to assemble a new album of his material. For the new collection, called *The Only One,* O. B. recorded ten of his originals. The album was issued in the fall of 1987, but its release was overshadowed by his death in September.

His body of work, including the many songs he had created, lived on in the years that followed, with more than a few included in new forms by artists who respected him as a person and talent. Rob Bowman pointed out in an article in *The Journal of Country Music* ("O. B. McClinton: Country Music, That's My Thing," Volume 14, no. 2, 1992) how odd it was that O. B. achieved so much as a writer when he couldn't play any instrument in even a rudimentary fashion. He recalled McClinton's description of his technique: "I hear melodies. It's really weird to musicians in Nashville all the time and they can't believe that I write a song 100 percent melody and lyric and don't play an instrument. I hear a melody and I start humming this melody on my mind and then I will write lyrics to go with this melody and everything is in meter. I can go down with a good session player who knows the number system and sing this melody."

McClinton went on, "Maybe I might sing it over three or four times and they'll keep playing. They'll play one chord and if it's not right they'll say, 'What about this?' But I know when they play the right chord—it feels right."

McCOURY, DEL: *Singer, guitarist, banjoist, songwriter, band leader (Dixie Pals, the Del McCoury Band). Born North Carolina, 1937. Band members in mid-1990s besides Del included Rob McCoury (banjo); Ron McCoury (lead and tenor vocals, mandolin); Jason Carter (baritone vocals, fiddle); Mike Bub (baritone vocals, bass).*

Internationally recognized by bluegrass fans as one of the giants of the genre, named Male Vocalist of the Year three out of four years by the International Bluegrass Music Association (IBMA) during the first part of the 1990s, Del McCoury nonetheless had little or no name recognition among the vast expanse of country music fans. He was, in fact, as the *New York Times* described him, "The best country singer you've never heard of." It was a strange position for a performer whose fans included legendary Bill Monroe and such stars of the 1980s and 1990s as Alison Krauss and Ricky Skaggs. It could be traced to the fact that the vast majority of bluegrass artists labored in obscurity as far as the mass market was concerned, but as the millennium neared, the signs suggested that at long last McCoury finally might get the attention his superb musicianship deserved.

Del was born in North Carolina in 1937, one of a family that was eventually to comprise six children, three boys and three girls. When he was two, the McCourys moved to Pennsylvania, which remained home base for most of his life until he settled in Nashville in the 1990s. The instrument he first tried to use was a guitar given him by his older brother when he was nine. Later, when he was fourteen, his brother brought home Flatt & Scruggs's recording of "Rolling in My Sweet Baby's Arms," and Del fell in love with the banjo. After his father gave him an old Vega banjo, he taught himself to play it by listening to records of Scruggs and other top-flight banjo pickers. By the mid-1950s he was demonstrating his skills by playing in local events.

In 1957, he met fiddler Keith Daniels, who brought Del in as a banjoist with the Stevens Brothers band. Later Keith formed his own group, the Blue Ridge Ramblers, and enlisted Del as a sideman. That association ended when McCoury was drafted into the army in early 1962, but Del was in the service only a short time before he was given a medical discharge. After that, he joined a Baltimore-based group called the Virginia Playboys, with whom he was performing when Bill Monroe came by to listen to them perform at a local club.

Monroe was very impressed with Del's banjo skills and, since he then needed a banjo player for his Bluegrass Boys, asked Del to come to Nashville and join them. Del hesitated, and in the interim, Monroe filled the banjo slot with Bill Keith. When Del told Monroe he had decided to accept his offer, Monroe said the position he now needed to fill was that of guitarist and lead singer.

McCoury hadn't played guitar since his boyhood and wasn't sure he could meet Monroe's demanding creative standards. As he told Jan Jerrold of *British Bluegrass News* ("The Del McCoury Band," May 1993), "Up until that time I had never really seriously tried to do anything with a guitar because I wasn't that much interested in it. But Bill said, 'Now I'll tell you what. If you can make the grade in two weeks, I'll hire you.' I knew I was on a trial basis so I really had to work at it. I had played with plenty of guitar players that played behind the beat—they just couldn't get on top of it. So I think the biggest thing on my mind was to play on top of the beat and play to Bill's mandolin, to his rhythm lead."

Del passed the test and joined the Bluegrass Boys full time in February 1963. A year later, McCoury got what sounded like a lucrative offer to join a California-based group, the Golden State Boys. That didn't work out too well, and Del and another Bluegrass Boys alumnus, Billy Baker, started their own bluegrass group, the Shady Valley Boys. After a number of months, the leaders left the Golden State in favor of Pennsylvania, where a reorganized Shady Valley Boys started appearing at local clubs and festivals. In 1966, Baker and McCoury parted company amicably. They kept in touch and, in 1967, Baker helped Del complete tracks for his first album, the Arhoolie Records release *Del McCoury Sings Bluegrass*. That disc stayed in print into the 1970s and in the 1990s was reissued under the title *I Wonder Where You Are Tonight*.

Del played pickup dates with different groups until a new band, organized with fiddler Bobby Diamond, evolved. This soon took the name Dixie Pals. That remained the name of Del's group from the late 1960s to the late 1980s, though with many changes in personnel over those decades. Among the performers at various times was Del's bass-playing brother, Jerry. The first album issued by Del McCoury and his Dixie Pals was the 1972 Rounder release, *High on the Mountain.* Although McCoury and his various aggregations had albums on a number of labels, in time Rounder became his primary recording affiliation.

The record labels on which Dixie Pals' tracks appeared in the 1970s and early 1980s included Revonah, Rebel, Grass Sound, and Leather. The Grass Sound release of 1976 had actually been recorded in 1971. Del and his band built up a small but loyal following at home and, in some ways, had even better audience success in other parts of the world. During 1979, the band won a warm welcome in Japan, where it recorded a live album issued only overseas and not available in the U.S. until a reissue came out many years later called *Live in Japan.* Group members at the time included brother Jerry on bass, Dick Smith on banjo, Sonny Miller on fiddle, and Hershel Sizemore on mandolin.

In the early 1980s, bluegrass fans almost lost the opportunity to add the excellent album *Take Me to the Mountains* to their collections. Soon after issuing it, the record company, Leather Records, folded, but fortunately Rebel Records took over distribution. With a somewhat different band makeup, McCoury's next album, *Sawmill,* also came out on Rebel. Among the members of the band from about 1981 was Del's son Ron, initially as a mandolinist and later showing himself a chip off the old block as a "high lonesome" lead singer.

In the mid-1980s, Del's younger son, Rob, was ready to join. Teenager Ron first took over on bass and soon became the band's banjo player. Del told Jerrold, "When he first picked up the banjo, he was pretty small [nine]. He seemed to take an interest in it, so I showed him the roll. And then all through school he'd play and I'd show him things." Rob turned out to be not only a fine banjo player, but an extraordinary one, as did Ron on the mandolin.

In 1987, with the group now becoming a family affair, Del renamed it the Del McCoury Band. The new roster proved to have an even tighter sound than before, and the instrumental treatments gave even more impact to Del's unique vocal abilities. As Dana Andrew Jennings raved in the *New York Times* ("Bluegrass, Straight and Pure, Even if the Money's No Good," Spring 1995), Del McCoury sings "in a mountain tenor so high, so blue, so lonesome that it seems he, or the audience, could swoon for lack of oxygen. It's a midnight voice, a voice to make you hit the bottle one moment, then drop to your knees and pray the next."

The new band quickly became a favorite with audiences at bluegrass clubs and festivals, including events sponsored by the International Bluegrass Music Association. Still, as Jennings indicated, that didn't make them candidates for the millionaire entertainers rosters. In the late 1980s and into the 1990s they continued to play mainly before small, if appreciative, audiences for blue-collar pay. Their new albums on Rounder all made

top-chart levels on lists like Bluegrass Unlimited's National Bluegrass Survey, but a bluegrass hit album typically sold in the 10,000–15,000-copy range, hardly a blip on the gold-record scorecard. They began the 1990s with the 1990 Rounder release *Don't Stop the Music,* one of the finest bluegrass releases of the year, whose tracks included "I Feel the Blues Moving In" which became one of their concert staples. This was followed by another album likely to become a bluegrass classic, *Blue Side of Town.*

During 1993, the McCourys moved to Nashville and changed the band roster to include, besides the three family members, Mike Bub (born Los Angeles, 1964) on guitar and Jason Carter on fiddle. The first efforts of the new group resulted in the acclaimed 1994 Rounder release, *A Deeper Shade of Blue,* which included the Del McCoury–penned song "I'm Lonely for My Only" and "Quicksburg Rendezvous," composed by his sons.

Even as those releases caught bluegrass and country listeners' fancy, Del and his sons weren't restricting themselves to McCoury Band projects. Among the early 1990s releases was a Rounder album prepared by Del and brother Jerry called *The McCoury Brothers.* Another release, *Families of Tradition,* combined the talents of Del, Rob, and Ron with those of David and Don Parmley of the Bluegrass Cardinals. Del also was featured on six songs on David Grisman's double album, *Home Is Where the Heart Is,* in which other bluegrass stars besides Del guested. Ron and Rob also began working on separate projects in the mid-1990s.

Both McCoury sons were nominated or won in their instrumental categories in IBMA voting. *Families of Tradition* also won a Bluegrass Album of the Year Award. At the IBMA Awards show in Owensboro, Kentucky, on September 22, 1994, Del and his cohorts dominated the proceedings. Besides performing on the program, they also won the Entertainer of the Year and Album of the Year (for *A Deeper Shade of Blue*) trophies, while Ron was named Best Mandolin Player and shared credit with Jerry Douglas for producing the winning album. When Del came to the microphone to accept his honor, he observed, wryly, "I always thought I could sing a little. But I didn't know I could entertain people. I can't dance. Bill Monroe can dance." In the Grammy Awards voting for 1994, announced in January 1995, *A Deeper Shade of Blue* was nominated in the Best Bluegrass Album category. In 1996, Rounder issued another fine collection, *The Cold Hard Facts.* Two years later, the band had another Grammy nomination for the Rounder release *The Cold Hard Facts,* coproduced by Ron McCoury and dobro star Jerry Douglas. The spirited playing of the group included two Del McCoury originals, "The First Time She Left" and "Loggin' Man," as well as Ron McCoury's composition "Baltimore Jonny." Ron was also nominated in the Best Country Instrumental Performance category (along with David Grier, Stuart Duncan, Todd Phillips, and Craig Smith) for *Rawhide.*

In all but widespread public acceptance, it seemed as though Del and his band deserved to be considered superstars. Still, it appeared their steadfast focus on their own creative interests might yet pay off. With each passing year bluegrass seemed to be gaining momentum as indicated by the mid-1990s best-selling releases by label-mate Alison Krauss and the increasing inclusion of bluegrass-based material in albums issued by mainstream country stars. Those trends, plus the accolades increasingly given the McCoury Band by major publications, suggested there might be a bright future ahead for "the best country singer you've never heard of."

McCOY, NEAL: *Singer, guitarist, band leader. Born Jacksonville, Texas, July 30, c. 1960.*

There are more than a few performers who first became enamored of show business after seeing and hearing a boy named Michael Jackson star on records and TV, but almost none of them were moved to become country artists. An exception was Neal McCoy, who bids fair to achieve Charley Pride–style stardom in the 1990s and beyond.

McCoy told Mandy Wilson of the Country Music Association's *Close Up* magazine that he got tremendous pleasure watching Jackson, then eight years old, on TV. "I was taken in by the fact that there was someone my age singing and dancing on television. I thought, 'Boy, what a neat thing. He probably doesn't even have to go to school. He's just hanging out and having fun.' But being from a small town like Jacksonville, I came back to reality. I knew that I would never have the opportunity to get into show business."

Fortunately for country fans, as he got older his views about that changed. Of course, growing up in Texas, Neal was in an environment heavy on country songs despite the seductive allure of rock and soul. His excellent vocal ability in his preteen and teen years was honed partly in church choirs and school choruses, but he also sought other performance avenues, singing in school and community center musicals and in various vocal and band groups organized among school friends and local musicians.

As he entered his twenties, his musical career continued on a part-time basis as he earned most of his income from various day jobs, including working at a shoe store in a local mall. That job paid off in an unexpected way when, in 1981, he met his future wife, Melinda, who was a store customer. Later, when she got a job in the same mall, they started dating and soon married. He later indicated that the stability and encouragement of his marriage afforded him a strong foundation for his subsequent achievements.

The year 1981 proved propitious for McCoy in another way. He got his first major career break when he won a talent contest at Dallas's Belle Star nightclub. Charley Pride was in the audience, and later sought McCoy out as a good candidate for his management and booking operation. McCoy signed and was soon working as an opening act for Pride's concerts, appearing in major concert venues, country fairs, and festivals across the U.S. and Canada.

Neal credits the chance to watch superstar Pride organize and perform his stage shows with preparing him to move ahead as a solo artist when the opportunity came along. He told Mandy Wilson, "I watched him. He was so great at making people feel at ease. It's not a secret. Everybody knows that, but there are only a few people that are naturals at it. Some people are natural singers and natural writers. Some are natural entertainers. I think that's what I am. I hope I am."

One of things he learned from that apprenticeship was the way a free and easy approach to developing a show could help energize an audience. "I let my band decide a lot of times what the first song is going to be. I just ask them what they want to do, and we do it. It's spontaneous from there. We don't have a list, we just wing it. It gives you the opportunity to feel the crowd out. It keeps it fun for the band."

For much of the 1980s, McCoy continued to open shows for Pride. But this work helped him build up contacts with many other people in the country music industry. When not working with Charley, he accumulated experience as a solo performer in small clubs and honky-tonks while also taking the first steps toward expanding that aspect of his career. It was a slow process, but at the start of the 1990s he signed with a major record label, Atlantic.

Atlantic issued his debut album in 1991. The collection didn't become a best-seller, but it did provide singles that made lower chart levels, such as "There Ain't Nothin' I Don't Like About You," on the *Billboard* list for several months in the fall of 1992. His second album provided singles releases that did even better, suggesting to country fans that a major newcomer was gaining a place in the country spotlight. Among his 1993 singles was "Now I Pray for Rain," a *Billboard* Top 40 entrant in March.

His third Atlantic album, *No Doubt About It,* issued in late 1993, put his career in overdrive. The album rose to number thirteen in *Billboard* in early 1994 and by August had earned a gold-record award from the R.I.A.A. This time, besides a best-selling album, Neal could point to major successes in the video and singles area after the title track rose to number one in *Radio & Records* the week of March 11. During the summer the single "Wink" had similar success, reaching number one in *R&R* the week of June 17. Later he made top-chart levels with the single "The City Put the Country Back in Me," which came out in late summer and remained on the lists through the fall. At one point (August 27), the last two singles were right next to each other in *Billboard's* Top 40.

By that time, McCoy was a full-fledged headliner who could fill sizable venues in many parts of the U.S. and was gaining a reputation with overseas fans as well. Those fans, as well as the many millions of watchers in North America, got the chance to see him sing one of his hits on the Country Music Association Awards program on CBS-TV in October 1994.

In early 1995, Neal's next album, *You Gotta Love That,* was issued and, after peaking at number ten in *Billboard,* spent many more months on the list. The single "For a Change" from that album was in *Billboard's* Top 3 in March. His next album releases were *Neal McCoy* in 1996 and *Greatest Hits* in 1997. In the late spring of 1995, Neal had another album on the charts, *They're Playin' Our Song.* By July the album was in the *Billboard* top 3. The single of the title track also reached top-10 levels in *Radio & Records* and *Billboard* during June. CMT chose him as its Showcase Artist of the month, featuring him on TV segments each Friday. In the fall, McCoy placed another single on the charts, "If I Was a Drinkin' Man," which peaked at number 16 in *Billboard.* He maintained his momentum into 1996 with the single of "You Gotta Love That" on the charts for the first half-year after reaching number three in the trades; he followed that in mid-May with the John Loudermilk song "Then You Can Tell Me Goodbye," which remained on the hit lists into the summer.

McDANIEL, MEL: *Singer, guitarist, trumpeter, songwriter, band leader (A Little More Country, Oklahoma Wind). Born Checotah, Oklahoma, September 6, c. mid-1940s.*

Even though pop musicians usually have to wait a while before their talents are recognized, the typical country or blues artist usually has to wait even longer. In Mel McDaniel's case the experience of waiting was manifest in his many songs that dealt with the joys and problems of everyday living.

Mel was born in Checotah, but grew up in the towns of Okmulgee and Tulsa, Oklahoma. He showed a youthful interest in music when he took up the trumpet in the fourth grade and then started to learn guitar soon after. In his teens he played in local bands and, by the time his high school years were through, was working as a musician in Tulsa clubs. He managed to record several singles for some local labels, and then decided to try his luck in other locales, first in Ohio, then in Nashville, in the late 1960s.

His primary goal in Music City was to succeed as a songwriter. He worked in a gas station to earn a living while he tried to gain the attention of music publishers and performers. That didn't work out, so his next move was to far-off Alaska, where he became a favored country performer in Anchorage. Still, he knew stardom re-quired being based in the lower forty-eight, and he jumped at the chance to return to Nashville in 1973, where he became a fixture for nine months playing at the Holiday Inn.

The quality of his deep voice for bringing out the shadings in country songs soon brought other work recording demonstration records for songwriters and publishers. He also formed an association with record producer Johnny MacRae, who finally got him the much sought-after contract with a major label, Capitol, in 1976. One of his first recordings for that firm made the country singles charts in May 1976 and Mel was on his way. Later in the year, he placed still another single on the charts, "I Thank God She Isn't Mine." This was followed by still more chart singles in 1977, "All the Sweet" early in the year and "Gentle to Your Senses (Easy on Your Mind)," a top-20 chartmaker in August.

Thus Mel had four hit singles to his credit in just over a year without being represented with an album. That was rectified in late summer of 1977 with his LP debut, *Gentle on Your Senses,* which not only made the country hit lists but spawned two more chart songs, "Soul of a Honky Tonk Woman" and "God Made Love." McDaniel added to his growing following with in-person appearances across the country and on TV backed by his band, called A Little More Country. His achievements were recognized by members of the California-based Academy of Country Music, who nominated him for Most Promising Male Vocalist of 1977.

In July 1978, his second Capitol album, *Mello,* was released. The first single from the album, "Border Town Woman," was on the charts during the summer of 1978. In 1979, Mel had such charted singles as "Love Lies" and "Lovin' Starts Where Friendship Ends." In late 1980, his single "Countryfied," title track from his third Capitol album, *I'm Countryfied Mel McDaniel,* showed up on the lists and rose into the top 20 in early 1981. Later in the year he had the charted singles "Louisiana Saturday Night," "Right in the Palm of Your Hand," and "Preaching Up a Storm."

His 1982–83 albums, *Take Me to the Country* and *Naturally Country* provided such singles releases as "Take Me to the Country," "Big Ole Brew," and "I Wish I Was in Nashville" in 1982 and "Old Man River (I've Come to Talk Again)," "Hot Time in the Old Town Tonight," and "I Call It Love" in 1983. His 1984 output included the album *Mel McDaniel with Oklahoma Wind* and the singles "Where'd That Woman Go," "Most of All I Remember You," "All Around the Water Tank," a reissue single of "Louisiana Saturday Night," and "Baby's Got Her Blue Jeans On." The last named became a major hit of 1984–85, reaching upper levels on all country charts. In the Country Music Association voting for 1985, the single was nominated for Single of the Year (also bringing writer Bob McDill a Song of the Year nomination) and McDaniel was a finalist for the Horizon Award.

Throughout the 1980s and into the 1990s, Mel maintained an intensive live concert schedule of 200 or more shows a year. From the mid-1980s on his backing band was a six-piece group named Oklahoma Wind. He also signed on as a regular on the *Grand Ole Opry,* something he told interviewers in the mid-1990s was the honor he was most proud of.

His mid-1980s album releases were *Let It Roll* and *Stand Up* in 1985, *Just Can't Sit Down Music* in 1986, and *Mel McDaniels' Greatest Hits* in 1987. His singles during those years were "Stand Up" and "Let It Roll (Let It Rock)" in 1985, "Shoe String," "Doctor's Orders," and "Stand on It" in 1986, and "Oh What a Night," "Anger & Tears," "Love Is Everywhere," and "Now You're Talkin'" in 1987. He closed out the decade with the albums *Now You're Talkin'* in 1988 and *Rock-a-Billy Boy* in 1989 and the singles "Ride This Train," "Real Good Feel Good Song," and "Henrietta" in 1988 and "Walk That Way," "Blue Suede Shoes," and "You Can't Play the Blues (in an Air-Conditioned Room)" in 1989.

Mel's first album release in the 1990s was the 1991 *Country Pride,* from which were drawn the singles "Turtles and Rabbits" and "My Ex-Life." Like many country stars of the late 1980s and the first half of the 1990s, Mel often performed at theaters in Branson, Missouri. In 1992 he signed a new recording contract with the Branson Entertainment label, which spawned his 1993 label debut, *Baby's Got Her Blue Jeans On.* The album contained some new songs, along with new versions of his previous best-selling singles.

By the mid-1990s, Mel could point to a good collection of songwriting awards from ASCAP and, in addition, a star in the Country Music Hall of Fame's Walkway of Stars. Home base in the 1990s was near Nashville, a residence he shared with Mary, his wife of over thirty years. He also had access to a lake where in the mid-1990s he kept a new boat called the BassCat to serve his hobby of angling. He said, "Although there's nothing like making a living doing what you love, there's not a thing that can top being out on that lake."

McENTIRE, REBA: *Singer, songwriter, actress, record producer. Born Chockie, Oklahoma, March 28, 1954.*

"My Mama—they used to say she coulda been as big as Patsy Cline if she'd had any breaks, but she was teachin' school by the time she was sixteen or seventeen. So she didn't have much of a chance. My father was a world champion steer roper. He rodeoed an awful lot, so Mama, she taught us how to sing three-part harmony. That was a way she had to pass the time away with us kids. There was my sister Alice, and my brother, Pake, and my little sister Susie. . . . We've always lived right here in southeastern Oklahoma. It's a real small town, little bitty nothin' but people's houses. Daddy owns a 7,000 acre ranch—but we weren't no wealthy West Texas people or nothin'. It's mostly

rocky, mountain country, but enough to run a few steers on."

That's the way Reba McEntire described her home region and early upbringing to Jack Hurst of the *Chicago Tribune* (June 14, 1979). The singing lessons she received from her mother often took place on the road when the family traveled from town to town with their father on the rodeo circuit. The first time Reba performed for a wider audience than her family, she recalled, was in the first grade Christmas program in Oklahoma, when she sang "Away in a Manger."

Throughout grade and high school, she continued to add to her performing credits, initially for amateur functions and later on for pay. While she was in the ninth grade, she was part of a country band led by one of her teachers. At other times she was part of an act with her brother and sisters. She told Hurst, "In high school we'd play over at Ardmore in them old clubs. For thirteen dollars apiece, we'd sing from nine 'til three o'clock in the morning."

As might be expected, Reba learned to ride a horse at an early age and later showed promise as a rodeo performer. In her teens, she did some rodeo riding, though many of her visits to various rodeos involved vocalizing. Still, after graduating from high school, she thought she might follow her mother into the teaching profession, enrolling in Southeastern Oklahoma State University as an elementary education major. She was a student there when the rodeo connection changed her career plans.

In 1974, McEntire got the chance to sing the national anthem at the National Rodeo Finals in Oklahoma City. She told Hurst, "At one of the performances a friend of mine who owns a dance place there called me over and said, 'Reba, I'd like you to meet this red-headed guy here: Red Steagall.' Well, about the next month—I was back in school down at Southeastern State at Durant, Oklahoma—Mama got a call from Red. He said, 'Do you think you could get Reba down here to cut a demonstration tape?' Pake had already decided he'd rather rodeo and Susie wasn't even out of high school. So I was the guinea pig."

In time, the demo tapes got Reba's singing activities rolling. During 1975, she was signed by Mercury Records, whose producers and recording engineers were greatly impressed by the range and power of the voice of the lithe five-foot-six-inch-tall girl. For some of her initial recordings, producer Jerry Kennedy reported, he had to use two "limiters"—devices employed to prevent the sound input from causing distortions in the electronic signals—to capture her vocal quality. In most cases, not even one is needed for an artist's voice.

By 1976, McEntire's early singles were starting to show up on lower-chart levels, an example being "I Don't Want to Be a One Night Stand," in the 80s range in May. In 1977, Mercury issued her debut album, *Reba*

McEntire, and, soon after, the respect she already had generated among her musical peers was indicated by a chance to debut on the *Grand Ole Opry.*

She had several more modest hits in late 1977 and early 1978, then teamed with Jacky Ward for a series of duets. The first single released by them was "Three Sheets in the Wind/I'd Really Love to See You Tonight," which reached the top 20 in July 1978. Late in 1978, Reba had a solo hit with her single "Last Night, Ev'ry Night." In early 1979, she had another single in upper-chart levels, "Runaway Heart." In August 1979, her second LP, *Out of a Dream,* was issued by Mercury. Included in the LP was a duet with Jacky Ward titled "That Makes Two of Us," which was issued as a single during the summer. At the end of 1979 McEntire's single of "Sweet Dreams" was a chart hit.

In the early 1980s, Reba's name showed up regularly on the bestseller lists. In 1980, her charted Mercury singles included "(I Still Long to Hold You) Now and Then," "(You Lift Me) Up to Heaven," and "I Can See Forever in Your Eyes." In 1981, her successes included "I Don't Think Love Ought to Be That Way" and "Today All Over Again."

Rodeoing continued to be a major interest of McEntire's life. In 1976 she married a member of the Professional Rodeo Cowboy Association, Charlie Battles, whom she helped run a cattle-ranching operation in their Oklahoma home when they weren't away on their respective tour circuits. "Charlie's always backed me," she told Hurst. "He rodeos, and he knows how hard it is to go off by yourself and have to put up in a hotel. It's rough, but it's worth it. I always thought that if I didn't do it, my talent'd be taken away from me. And the money's good. It's got its bad days, but it pays more than waitin' tables.

"What do I want out of it? Oh, I don't know. I don't wanta do it the rest of my life, to get big and then go downhill just straggling along. I'd like to get popular enough to win a few awards, maybe be the best in the business for a while. Then if somebody came along and took my place, that'd be fine. I'd step aside and let some other person have a turn."

That philosophy might have seemed logical at the start of the 1980s, when her career was moving along at a moderate, but not spectacular, pace. But over the span of the decade, she certainly did become "the best in the business"—and, in fact, a superstar who was considered by the country field to have taken over the title of queen of country music.

One of the steps taken in 1980 that was to have important future consequences was the addition of steel-guitar player Narvel Blackstock to her backing group. Before long he progressed to being her band leader and important adviser, then road manager, tour manager, full manager (in 1988) and, soon after, her second husband. With his support, she decided to switch labels in 1983, leaving Mercury after seven albums to sign with

MCA. (Her 1980s albums on Mercury/PolyGram were *Feel the Fire* in 1980, *Heart to Heart* in 1981, *Unlimited* in 1982, *Behind the Scenes* in 1983, and *Just a Little Love* in 1984.) She was already considered a fine performer by other country artists, as indicated by Country Music Association voters nominating her for the 1983 Horizon Award, but after her MCA album debut, *My Kind of Country,* came out in 1984, she started to attract major attention from the country music audience. The album became a best-seller, eventually earning Reba's first gold-record award from the R.I.A.A., and provided a series of singles that made top-chart positions.

In the CMA voting of 1984, she was named the Female Vocalist of the Year, an honor she would earn for an unprecedented four years in a row. The *Music City News* poll named her Female Artist of the Year in 1985 and repeated that award every year through 1989. The Academy of Country Music followed suit, naming her Top Female Vocalist four years in a row from 1985 through 1988. Other mid-1980s acknowledgments included appearing in *Rolling Stone*'s Critic's Choice Poll: Top Five Country Artists and CMA's naming her 1986 Entertainer of the Year.

Her mid-1980s album releases included *Have I Got a Deal for You* in 1985, *Whoever's in New England* and *What Am I Gonna Do About You* in 1986, and three 1987 albums, *Reba McEntire's Greatest Hits, The Last One to Know,* and *Merry Christmas to You.* Supported by intensive touring, including working as an opening act on occasion for artists like Alabama, and appearances on many major TV programs, all those albums made the charts and, except for the 1985 release, passed gold-record-award levels. *Whoever's in New England,* one of the most influential country collections of the mid-1980s, and *Greatest Hits* both went past R.I.A.A. platinum-record requirements. The single "Whoever's in New England" became a number-one hit and won Reba a Grammy for Best Country Vocal Performance, Female, in the 1986 voting (announced on the awards telecast in February 1987). The number also became a best-selling video, earning awards for Video of the Year in both ACM and *Music City News* polls for 1987, as did her next video release, "What Am I Gonna Do About You." In 1987 she had another video doing well on the charts, "The Last One to Know."

During 1987, Reba shocked many fans by divorcing Charlie Battles. She didn't talk too much about the event, when she did stating she just felt the close relationship had ended and it was time to move on. There were some protesting letters, she told the *Ladies Home Journal.* One woman wrote, "How dare you get divorced. I was patterning my life after you." "I wrote back, 'Don't you dare put me on a pedestal. I'm just a regular old human being.'"

At one time, such an event would have ended a country artist's career, but in this case there was little lasting effect. For one thing, she told Jack Hurst of the *Chicago Tribune* ("Arriba Reba!" September 26, 1993), "I think what the divorce did was show women I was a strong person, and I sing songs that relate to that subject: being strong and overcoming problems. Since I didn't have a perfect life, when I sing a sad song, they know I've been through it." Some of her feelings at the time were reflected in the tracks on her 1987 album, *The Last One to Know.*

She closed out the 1980s with three more hit albums she helped produce, *Reba* in 1988, *Sweet Sixteen* and *Reba Live!* in 1989. All earned R.I.A.A. gold-record awards and the first two passed platinum levels. Her singles releases included the number-one hit (in March 1988) "Love Will Find Its Way to You." More honors came her way, such as the American Music Awards selection as Favorite Female Country Vocalist in 1988 and 1989, TNN Viewer's Choice selection as Favorite Female Vocalist in 1988 and 1989, Gallup 1988 Youth Survey selection among the Top 10 Female Vocalists, and *People* magazine inclusion in the Top Three Female Vocalists.

Still she felt the best rewards of those years were her marriage to Narvel Blackstock in 1989 and the birth of their son, Shelby, in February 1990. It had not been an easy pregnancy. She had to stay in bed the final three months to avoid going into labor prematurely. But she emphasized that it was worth the struggle and pain, as she told Marjie McGraw of *Country Music:* "Shelby is the first thing I think of every morning. I just want to go see Shelby. . . . At first I didn't want to be away from him a minute. I felt that his growing up years were very, very important; the first two years are very crucial for me to be there. But I wanted my career, and I didn't want ever to slow down—I still wonder what else we can do. It's the challenge, it's not the money."

Certainly she didn't become a homebody, and her career in the 1990s prospered as never before. She began the new decade with another hit album, *Rumor Has It,* which stayed in the charts for several years and easily exceeded platinum sales totals. She had four hit singles that year: "Little Girl," number three in *Radio & Records* the week of February 23, "Walk On," number three in *R&R* the week of June 8, and "You Lie," number one in *R&R* the week of October 12. She also made her film debut in *Tremors* and let it be known she hoped to pursue acting with intensity in years to come, hoping someday to qualify for an Oscar nomination.

Everything seemed to be going well when tragedy struck people she had been very close to. After concert performances on the U.S. West Coast, her manager and band boarded a private aircraft to return to Nashville. Fortunately, neither Reba nor her husband planned to go along. On March 16, 1991, the plane crashed, killing her tour manager and seven band members including the leader, Kirk P. Capello. (Two bandsmen survived.) She told *Ladies Home Journal,* "The divorce was

tough, but it was nothing compared with the crash. It was the worst time of my life. It still causes a knot in my throat just to think of it."

Still, some criticized her for resuming her music activities only a short time after the disaster. She argued it was something her late band members would understand, keeping the music going. And not only did she refuse to stop flying, she and Narvel set up their own Nashville-based jet charter service, Starstruck Jet. She reasoned, "People have car accidents and then get in an ambulance and drive to the hospital. Why shouldn't I fly?"

Again she let some of her sorrow and sympathy for the loss be reflected in some of the songs on her 1991 album, *For My Broken Heart.* She told *Woman's Day* ("Reba Rising," November 3, 1992), "It has been a very healing album for me. I was in the middle of choosing songs for it when the accident happened. Tony [coproducer Tony Brown] kept bringing me songs that were up-tempo and happy and I couldn't even listen to them. I needed to hear—and sing—songs that dealt with misery and heartache. The songs have helped me tremendously because they've made me talk about what happened. The crew and the two band members who survived couldn't talk about it at first . . . but we had to talk. We had to get back on the road. . . ."

The album became another platinum release. The title song provided a number-one single in November. (It had been preceded in top-chart levels by "Rumor Has It," number one in January 1991, and "Fancy," number four in July 1991.) In 1992 she scored such singles hits as "Is There Life out There," number-one in *R&R* the week of March 20, "The Night the Lights Went out in December" (number eight July 3), and "The Greatest Man I Ever Knew," the last named, a number-one hit in *R&R* the week of October 15, a tribute to her father, who still actively ran his Oklahoma ranch in his mid-sixties. Meanwhile she expanded her film credits by costarring with Kenny Rogers in the made-for-TV movie, *The Gambler IV,* telecast in two parts on NBC on March 1991.

Her 1992 MCA album, *It's Your Call,* was one of her weaker creative efforts, but it still found favor with record buyers who soon brought its sales totals past double platinum. In the fall of 1993, her *Greatest Hits, Volume Two,* came out, which included two new cuts, one of them a duet with Linda Davis titled "Does He Love You." (The other new song was "They Asked About You.") The Davis duet became a number one hit in October (peaking at number one in *R&R* the week of October 29). Before the album had been issued, she had scored three other hits in 1993, "Take It Back" (number four in *R&R* the week of January 29), "The Heart Won't Lie" (duet with Vince Gill, number one in *R&R* the week of April 9), and "It's Your Call" (number one in *R&R* the week of July 23). On October 15, 1993, her next film assignment appeared on TV, *The Man from*

Left Field, in which she costarred with Burt Reynolds. In the CMA 1993 awards voting she received three nominations, for Entertainer of the Year, Female Vocalist of the Year, and Vocal Event of the Year (the latter for her duet with Vince Gill on "The Heart Won't Lie"). She didn't win any of those in 1993, but in 1994 her duet song with Linda Davis, which they performed on the awards telecast in October, was named Single of the Year.

In early 1994, she was featured in the new Rob Reiner film, *North,* which unfortunately wasn't up to his earlier creative efforts. But Reba continued to show herself at the top of her form as a performer, drawing record crowds in the U.S. and other parts of the world. Narvel Blackstock recalled the differences in touring from the days Reba was just starting to develop her stage skills for Jack Hurst. "I remember when there were just four of us out here on the road. We were in a van pulling a horse trailer then. Sometimes Reba would have to dress in the trailer. When we started opening for Alabama, we'd try to get to all the venues early and park way in the back of the parking lot, so people wouldn't see us coming in. Now we have nine drivers, six trucks, three buses. A total of 50 people."

Reba's 1994 chart singles included "They Asked About You" in March, "Why Haven't I Heard From You" in June, "She Thinks His Name Was John" in September, and "Till You Love Me" in November. By year-end her second *Greatest Hits* had gone well past double platinum, and the first one was still on the charts after more than 180 weeks. In September 1994, her twenty-second album, *Read My Mind,* was issued and, after peaking at number two in *Billboard,* remained high on the charts into 1995, earning another multiplatinum award. At the same time that album came out, her autobiography, *Reba: My Story,* was published.

During the first half of the 1990s, it was rare that she didn't receive nominations and awards in major competitions. American Music Awards voters named her Favorite Female Country Vocalist year after year while citing her for Album of the Year in 1991 and 1993. ACM awards included Top Female Vocalist of the Year in 1992, Video of the Year ("Is There Life Out There") in 1993, and Female Vocalist of the Year and Entertainer of the Year in 1995. In the TNN *Music City News* poll announced in early 1995, she was nominated in the Entertainer of the Year, Video of the Year ("Why Haven't I Heard From You"), and Female Artist of the Year categories and won in the last of those.

Though she had accomplished much by the mid-1990s, she usually told interviewers she had no plans to give up her harried career pace. As she stressed, she had been brought up to enjoy taking on challenges, and one of them was to keep trying to beat the competition. "I have to have competition," she said. "I thrive on it."

In the fall of 1995 her album *Starting Over* came out and peaked at number one on the *Billboard* country chart and number five on the pop list. It provided such singles as "On My Own" (recorded with Trisha Yearwood, Linda Davis, and Martina McBride), "Ring on Her Finger, Time on Her Hands" (in top chart levels in late 1995 and early 1996), the title track, and "You Keep Me Hanging On" (a dance remix single).

Her 1996 projects included hosting a benefit rodeo competition and tribute for the late actor Ben Johnson, which screened on TNN on June 2. Many top artists participated, including Billy Dean, Lynn Anderson, and Red Steagall.

Reba's next collection, *What's If It's You,* came out on MCA in October 1996 and seemed likely to be a chart resident through 1997. It peaked at number one on the hit lists soon after it came out. Up to its release, it was estimated she had sold over 35 million records and no other female country artist could point to receiving five triple platinum certifications from the R.I.A.A. The initial single was "The Fear of Being Alone."

Perhaps responding to suggestions by some critics that *Starting Over* seemed overly pop-oriented rather than country, she emphasized the arrangements were a lot simpler this time. "Everything feels different about this record. We've made changes in every aspect—the songs, the attitude, the excitement of the new [Starstruck] studio, the band, new microphones, new production, everything.

"My last album, *Starting Over,* was so heavy with instrumentation, so thick in production. This time, I want a crisp mountain stream, not an ocean. Sometimes when you hear somebody on the radio, it sounds like they're right there on the dash of your car. I wanted that sound too! John Guess has been working with me as an engineer for more than ten years. We know each other so well; and he co-produced the record. We did a lot of pre-production together. He and I went in and experimented with six different microphones and he picked the one that gave me the fullest, richest sound. I'd just come back from vacation before we went into the studio and I was really ready to sing."

McGEE BROTHERS: *Singers, instrumentalists. Both born Franklin, Tennessee; Sam McGee, May 1, 1894; Kirk McGee, November 4, 1899. Sam McGee died Franklin, Tennessee, August 21, 1975.*

At the Fourth Annual Country Music Fan Fair Reunion Show in Nashville, Tennessee, on June 14, 1975, one of the acts that awoke fond memories in many old-time fans was the Fruit Jar Drinkers. The group harked back to the very early days of the *Grand Ole Opry* and two of its four members, Sam and Kirk McGee (the others were guitarist Hubert Gregory and Golden Stewart on bass), were closely linked with the work of the first great *Opry* star, Uncle Dave Macon. In their own right, guitarist Sam and fiddler Kirk represented some of the finest instrumental ability ever to grace the country field.

Like many country artists, they were born and raised on a family farm, in this case near Franklin, Tennessee. In fact, they continued to work on that farm throughout their lives, despite the demands of performing careers, and it was there that Sam died soon after the 1975 Fan Fair appearance. Their father was an accomplished fiddler and they were exposed to music almost from the time they were born. As soon as they could hold banjos, they were working with their father at local gatherings, though later they were to choose other instruments.

In their teens they played banjos at dances for as little as ten cents apiece. As Jon Pankake wrote in *Sing Out!* (November 1964, p. 47), they expanded their string abilities at this time to include the effects of Negro syncopated music. The boys had the chance to observe this style when the family moved for a short period of time to the central Tennessee town of Perry. As Sam told Pankake, the Negro rhythms "would just ring in my head."

A turning point in the brothers' lives came in 1923, when they heard Uncle Dave Macon perform in the first professional show they had ever seen. They were so enthusiastic about his flamboyant singing and playing that they determined to try to join his troupe. After persevering, they finally gained his approval in 1924 and accompanied him on the first of many tours on the country-music circuit. When Uncle Dave joined the *Opry* in 1926, the McGees were part of his first band on the radio show. Among the other names Macon called his group, the Fruit Jar Drinkers gained the most renown. (There is a certain amount of confusion here because for a time there was another group on the *Opry* also called Fruit Jar Drinkers.)

The career of the McGee Brothers, whose traditional style of playing made folk experts as well as country enthusiasts lay claim to them, flourished for many decades, both in concert with the career of Uncle Dave and on a solo level. Over the years, when they were making recordings with Macon they usually made some as a separate act, sometimes with Uncle Dave acting as their backing musician rather than the other way around.

The first recording session of Sam McGee with Macon took place in New York from April 14 to 17, 1926. Among the songs they placed on vinyl were such favorite numbers as "Whoop 'Em Up Cindy," "Way Down the Old Plank Road," "The Death of John Henry," and "Late Last Night When My Willie Came Home."

During May 7–11, 1927, both Sam and Kirk worked with Macon and another legendary performer, fiddler Mazy Todd, in what Ralph Rinzler describes "as some of the best examples of string band ensemble playing ever recorded. Uncle Dave seems to revel in the reedy, yet elegant fiddling of Mazy Todd and Kirk McGee. He crows and hollers with joy when Sam momentarily abandons his guitar bass line to beat out a clog-rhythm

on the top of his then new Martin. The ensemble singing is unique on the secular songs. Uncle Dave sticks to the melody, Kirk departs from unison and moves to tenor at the end of each line, and Sam barks out his own distinctive bass line which includes a winning combination of unison and bass harmony notes."

During these sessions, the McGee Brothers and Todd recorded three songs, one with Uncle Dave playing supporting banjo. Kirk and Sam's own output in those 1927 sessions also included nine duets.

One of the more notable late 1920s sessions took place in Chicago on July 25–26, 1928. For those recordings, Sam used a very unusual instrument called a banjo-guitar he had picked up in the mid-1920s in Birmingham, Alabama. Discussing the sessions in liner notes for the 1966 Decca *Uncle Dave Macon* memorial album, Ralph Rinzler wrote, " 'From Earth to Heaven,' 'Buddy Won't You Roll Down the Line,' and 'I'm the Child to Fight,' among others, were recorded as five- and six-string banjo duets ... probably the only examples of this instrumental combination recorded in country music. Sam also recorded 'Easy Rider' and 'Chevrolet Car' as solos on the six-string banjo."

The McGees, who often had solo spots on the *Opry* from the late 1920s on, in 1930 formed a new alignment called the Dixieliners in which they joined forces with fiddler Arthur Smith. The act became one of the most popular on the *Opry* in the 1930s and made the team a favorite with country fans when it played local venues and country fairs throughout the South. Smith left in the late 1930s, but later rejoined the McGees for several appearances in the mid-1960s, including a 1965 appearance at the Newport Folk Festival in Rhode Island that won a standing ovation.

The McGees for a time teamed up with a comedy act called "Sara and Sally" at the end of the 1930s and in the early 1940s. After that, they became a featured part of Bill Monroe's show, performing with the Blue Grass Boys and also doing their own separate segment. They traveled throughout the United States with the Father of Bluegrass, typically finishing each Monroe stage appearance with a twenty-minute old-time country-music songfest.

In the 1950s, the McGees worked primarily as a separate brother act, as headliners on the country-music circuit. They remained *Opry* standbys, mainly as members of the Fruit Jar Drinkers. As the folk movement gathered momentum in the late 1950s, interest in the McGees arose among younger elements of the pop audience. The brothers were asked to appear in folk festivals around the nation and to play before audiences on many college campuses. That pattern continued into the mid-1960s, when rock once more pushed folk music to a subsidiary role.

The McGees, though, had remained charter members of the country field and held forth on many *Opry* programs as they had been doing for decades. In the

1970s, the brothers were still active in country music, but on a much less hectic level than in times past. Their musical ability, as audiences at the 1975 Fan Fair discovered, remained exceptional despite their advanced years. Unfortunately, their long association was ended when Sam was killed while working on his farm at the age of eighty-one.

Though the McGees made many recordings during their long career, little or nothing was available in the 1960s and 1970s other than individual tracks on "old time country" retrospective albums. The folk boom resulted in some releases, such as the 1965 Folkways LP, *McGee Brothers and Arthur Smith,* but those too were discontinued by the 1970s.

McGRAW, TIM: *Singer, guitarist. Born Delhi, Louisiana, May 1, 1967.*

In a way, Tim McGraw emulated his baseball pitcher father, Tug McGraw, whose widely repeated motto, "You gotta believe," played an important psychological role in the saga of the Miracle Mets' World Series triumph of 1969. Tim decided early to make his mark in country music, and he finally did that in 1994 when the twenty-seven-year-old's album *Not a Moment Too Soon* and a series of hit singles dominated country charts almost the entire year.

Actually, while Tim eventually assumed his natural father's name, for a good many years he didn't know there was any relationship. While the older McGraw was with a Mets farm team in Jacksonville, Florida, Tim's mother and Tug had a brief liaison that led to Tim's birth. Soon after the romance had ended, his mother moved to Louisiana, where Tim was born. With her husband, she settled in the small town of Start in Northern Louisiana where Tim grew up. It was an environment where sports and country music were poles of attraction for youngsters and adults alike.

Tim recalled that he didn't find out who his natural father was until he was eleven and didn't really get to know him until he was in college in Northeast Louisiana University. "I never knew my dad until I was 18. I was raised by my mother and stepfather. There's a preconceived notion that I grew up this rich kid, the son of a baseball player. It wasn't like that at all. I had a great childhood. If you have great parents it doesn't matter if you're wealthy or on welfare. It's not like I've been handed a silver spoon. I grew up in rural Louisiana and my music reflects that."

Tim did show prowess as a baseball player before he was old enough to join Little League. He developed steadily and was good enough in his teen years in baseball and other sports to receive an athletic scholarship to Northeast Louisiana. He was interested in music, but didn't take it seriously as a future career although, as he said, "I grew up listening to music. I was always fascinated with it. I always wanted to be a singer." He recalled taking a cue from his mother to sing along with all kinds of radio music, from rock and soul to Merle Haggard. When he was fifteen, he thought it would be wise to learn guitar, but didn't follow up on that idea right away.

When he accepted the scholarship from NLU, which he selected over several other offers because it was close to home and relatively inexpensive, he figured he'd work toward a law degree. But his grades weren't exceptional and he finally learned to play guitar. "It was a big commuter school. In the summer, everybody left town. I got bored, bought a guitar and taught myself to play." By that fall he could start making a little money from music.

At first, he worked solo in local clubs for tips, then made contact with other young musicians in the area. During the late 1980s he found work with country and rock bands for gigs in Louisiana, and the Jacksonville, Florida, region. Meantime he was spending more time with his father. Since then, they have grown quite close.

He told Richard Cromelin of the *Los Angeles Times* ("Look Out for the Turbo-Tonker," Calendar section, June 5, 1994), that the stories of Tug's quirky character weren't inaccurate. "He's a nut and fortunately I didn't inherit any of that—well—you might get conflicting reports, but I'll say I didn't.

"A lot of our mannerisms and stuff are alike. We think different because we grew up in different areas, but we also think alike on some things. I'm a big believer in genetics. It's amazing sometimes how much we're alike. It scares the hell out of me. We have a great relationship. He likes to tell everybody I'm his older brother. What's scary is sometimes it works."

In 1989, believing he could make it in country music big time, McGraw left college after finishing his third year and moved to Nashville. It took awhile, but he finally signed a recording contract with Curb Records. His debut album, *Tim McGraw,* came out in 1993. It didn't gain too much attention, but one track, "Welcome to the Club," did gain a spot for some weeks on singles charts. One result was that *Country Music* magazine picked him as one of "Country's most likely to succeed."

The ink was hardly dry on those pages when McGraw became an overnight sensation with the success of his second album, *Not a Moment Too Soon.* Released by Curb in March 1994, it was on the charts soon after, hitting number one on the *Billboard* lists on April 9, where it stayed for more than eighteen straight weeks. In mid-1995 it was still in the top 5. The album crossed over to reach number one at one point on the *Billboard* 200 pop chart. It also scored number one successes on just about every major list including *Hits* and *The Gavin Report.* By the summer of 1994 the album had sold over two million copies and a year later had doubled that total.

McGraw also did very well with singles releases. "Indian Outlaw" rose to number eleven in *Radio &*

Records the week of March 25, 1994, and the next one, "Don't Take the Girl," hit number one the week of May 27. Later in the year "Down on the Farm" reached number two in *R&R* (September 16) and "Not a Moment Too Soon," number twelve (November 25). Helping the groundswell of interest in McGraw was a public relations ploy characterizing his musical style as "turbo-tonk," sort of honky-tonk in overdrive.

During the summer of 1994, Tim was voted one of the five finalists for two Country Music Association Awards, Single of the Year (for "Don't Take the Girl") and the Horizon Award. In the Academy of Country Music's 30th Annual Poll (results announced on the May 10, 1995, telecast), Tim was named New Male Vocalist of the Year.

Tim received some flak over "Indian Outlaw" by some who felt it represented racial stereotyping. He responded by stating he always had been a Native American advocate. He told Cromelin, "So it hurts my feelings that somebody would take it that way. But at the same time you understand that interpretation is interpretation and you can't please everybody."

McGraw maintained that his sudden success wasn't unexpected. He pointed out how often as a child he would lie in bed and dream of making the great catch or the key putout. "You go through it in your head over and over and over. Then when the situation comes, you're ready. It's the same thing in music. I've never had a doubt. I always pictured myself doing this and being successful at it. I've never thought any differently."

In October 1995, his second album, *All I Want,* was released and debuted on the *Billboard* chart the week of October 7, remaining there for several weeks. In mid-1996 it was still in the top 10, having gone past double platinum levels in December. (On December 7, 1995, R.I.A.A. presented him with plaques for gold, platinum, and multiplatinum sales totals for the album.) In the spring of 1996, his album *Not a Moment Too Soon* remained a best seller, having already received an R.I.A.A. award on April 5, 1995, for four million copies sold. His singles hits included "Refried Dreams" (which peaked at number five in *Billboard* in the spring); "I Like It, I Love It" (which peaked at number one in the fall of 1995); "Can't Be Really Gone," on the charts in late 1995 and early 1996, having peaked at number two in *Billboard;* and "All I Want Is a Life," in upper chart levels the first half of 1996 (having reached number five in *Billboard* early in the year).

In the Academy of Country Music voting for its 1995 awards, McGraw was nominated in four categories. These were for Top Male vocalist, Entertainer of the Year, Single of the Year (for "I Like It, I Love It"), and Album of the Year (for *All I Want*). As it happened, he was shut out from winning any of those trophies, but he was a featured performer on the Awards telecast on April 24, 1996. He continued to be a major draw on the concert circuit while also finding time to do some record production work for other artists.

McMICHEN, CLAYTON "PAPPY": *Singer, fiddler, songwriter, comedian, band leader. Born Allatoona, Georgia, January 26, 1900; died Battletown, Kentucky, January 4, 1970.*

Serious students of country music history know of the importance of "Pappy" McMichen to the field's development, but few modern fans have ever heard his name. In his heyday, though, not only was he one of the finest fiddlers in the United States but also an influence on the careers of many pivotal artists. In fact, Bob Shelton suggested, in a brief biography of McMichen for a Newport Folk Festival program, that if Jimmie Rodgers is known as the "Father of Country Music," McMichen should be called "The Uncle of Country Music." Among the reasons for that label were McMichen's pioneering work on radio before the *Grand Ole Opry* was in existence and the fact that he helped arrange the 1927 audition that a then-unknown Jimmie Rodgers had with Ralph Peer—the first step to stardom for the legendary "Singing Brakeman."

McMichen was born and raised in rural Georgia. The usual pattern of country music get-togethers, square dances, church socials, and the like brought an early interest in singing and performing. The fiddle was the main instrument for those affairs, which Clayton could play quite well by the time he was high school age—he already had a reputation as one of the top fiddlers in the region.

After World War I, McMichen began to perform with local groups in various parts of Georgia. In the early 1920s, he was featured on one of the pioneer country shows, on station WSB in Atlanta, long before the *Grand Ole Opry* was born. By the mid-1920s, he had settled in Atlanta and played with many of the top artists then in the city, including Gid Tanner and another great fiddler and long-time friend of Clayton's, Blind Riley Puckett. When Tanner formed his band, which gained fame as the Skillet Lickers, soon after Tanner made his first recordings in 1924 with Puckett, McMichen became a key member. The band used two fiddlers, Puckett and McMichen, after the latter joined. McMichen remained with the Skillet Lickers until 1931 as a featured performer, and his fiddling is a highlight of many of the band's recordings of such songs as "Sally Goodin'," "Wreck of the Old 97," and "Down Yonder." Later generations still were awed by his technique when some of the 1920s recordings were reissued on traditional folk music LPs in the post–World War II era.

For a long time, in fact, Pappy was the recognized fiddling champion of the United States. He fiddled his way to victory for the first time in 1926 and won the title repeatedly after that. He walked off with his last championship in 1952.

After leaving Tanner, McMichen formed his own groups in the 1930s and, between bands, played with other popular country bands of the period. By the end of the 1940s, he had moved to Louisville, Kentucky. Besides continuing his career as a country artist, he also had his own Dixieland jazz band. Called the Georgia Wildcats, the band was featured on radio and TV in Louisville in the late 1940s and the first part of the 1950s.

McMichen retired in 1954. However, a decade later the organizers of the 1964 Newport, Rhode Island, Folk Festival sought him out and convinced him to take part in the show. His playing that summer was warmly received by the relatively youthful audience. His performance was recorded by Vanguard Records and released as part of the album *Traditional Music at Newport, 1964, Part 2.*

MESSINA, JO DEE: *Singer, guitarist, songwriter, band leader (The Jo Dee Messina Band). Born Holliston, Massachusetts, August 25, 1970.*

The New England states haven't been known for spawning many hit country acts, though there have been a few, such as Maine's Dick Curless, who have won attention over the years. Massachusetts, its most urbane sector, has been more frequently a mecca for folk and rock standouts; yet the emergence of a performer like Jo Dee Messina suggests that such inroads might still be made.

Though rock and pop dominated the airwaves during her childhood, she emphasized that she had been a country fan almost her entire life. The fact that her parents had country favorites, Tammy Wynette in her father's case and Eddy Arnold in her mother's, might have had something to do with it. But the rural environment of her childhood, she explained to interviewers, had just as much to do with it. She told John Wirt of *Advocate* ("Enthusiastic Messina Living Her Dream," April 19, 1996), "I grew up in a real small farming town. It's not like Boston. It was so far away. . . . People had horses. A neighbor of mine had a bee farm. Somebody else would raise pigs or chickens. People had dairy cows."

She had started to listen to recordings by people like Dolly Parton, Loretta Lynn, Hank Williams, Jr., Patsy Cline, and the Judds before her teen years. She told Wirt, "I've always listened to [country music] . . . I guess I was in the minority. The majority was listening to pop. I'd hear that, too, growing up, going to school, etc., etc., but my heart was into country. That's what *my* radio was always on."

Before long she was singing along with some of the artists, and at thirteen started seriously considering trying for a career in music. At fourteen, she began to get opportunities to perform in local clubs and jamborees—with approval from her mother, who drove her

to each gig. At sixteen, she both got her license and formed her own band, which included her brother on drums and her sister on bass guitar. "We were an entirely country band. I relate a lot more to 'Leavin' on Your Mind' than to 'Hit Me with Your Best Shot.' My music is very country, but it's definitely a new breed of country." While her siblings performed in her band at weekend shows, they weren't in sync with Jo Dee's musical tastes. Later on, when their sister left for Nashville, both shifted to local rock groups.

After graduating from high school, Jo Dee toyed with the idea of going for a law degree in college, but decided she would rather devote her energies to making her singing dreams come true. She moved to Nashville, and for a time gained experience entering talent contests and singing on open-mike nights. The outlook took a turn for the better in the late 1980s, when she gained a spot on the *Live at Libby's* Saturday night program on a Kentucky station. Industry executive Byron Gallimore, vice president of the Pride Music Group in Nashville, heard her sing on the program and sought her out. He brought her into a Nashville studio to start making some demo tapes that could be shopped around to major record labels.

Among the people she met during those years was another aspiring, unknown performer named Tim McGraw. Each promised to help the other out if he or she gained industry recognition. As she told Deborah Evans Price of *Billboard* ("Stage Is Set for Jo Dee Messina," February 24, 1996), for a brief period it looked as though she would make the first breakthrough when her demos earned a deal with RCA. Before she could profit from the contact, though, the people who signed her at the label were replaced and nothing worked out with the new regime. "By the time I left RCA, everyone else that had offered us a deal had signed a female or two. When I first got my deal with RCA, Tim had said, 'When you make it big, don't forget me.' The funny thing is he made it big and didn't forget me. Tim never goes back on his word. He is such a good man."

Tim continued to praise her talents as his career prospered, but Jo Dee was continuing to try to bolster her career on her own. At Curb Records' 1994 Fan Fair segment, she approached a Curb executive, Phil Gernhard, asking for roster consideration. While the discussion went on, she recalled, they were joined by Nashville producer James Stroud, who told Gernhard he had heard her demos and they were excellent. After he listened to those tracks later on, Gernhard arranged for a contract with his label. Curb didn't try to rush things, taking some eight months to expose their new find to the major concert circuit while she, album co-producers Gallimore and McGraw, and Curb executives screened hundreds of possible songs before settling for a final selection of ten numbers. Curb Records arranged for a series of radio station visits during the fall of 1995 along with appearances as the opening act for nine concerts by Blackhawk and Tim McGraw. She also was featured at a special Curb showcase in the Bahamas.

Before the *Jo Dee Messina* disc was released on April 9, 1996, the first single, "Heads Carolina, Tails California" (written by Mark Sanders and Tim Nichols) came out early in the year. With good coverage by country DJs, the record soon appeared on the hit charts and rose steadily until peaking at number one in the *Gavin Report* and number two in *Billboard.* The video for the single reached number one on Country Music Television, and helped gain her selection by the network as one of the Rising Stars of 1996. The follow-up single, "You're Not in Kansas Anymore," also reached upper-chart levels, including a number seven spot in *Radio & Records.* Meanwhile, Messina continued to add to her concert credits from shows with Trisha Yearwood, Tracy Byrd, Alan Jackson, and a spring tour opening for Brooks & Dunn.

Her album also was well received by critics and record buyers, opening in the top 30 in *Billboard* and moving upward during the spring and summer. The reviewer in *USA Today* commented, "Who can't like Messina's radio perfet, get-out-of-town debut single, 'Heads Carolina, Tails California'? At times, this New Englander's vocals are loaded with muscle and passion not often heard in today's 'cool' country. The strongest tracks include 'You're Not in Kansas Anymore,' also dealing with the breakaway urge of deadended youths, as well as Messina's own 'On a Wing and a Prayer' [co-written with Walt Aldridge]."

Jo Dee continued to add new achievements to her résumé even as she began thinking about her second album project. In the spring of 1996 she performed on the Academy of Country Music TV Awards show. And in the voting for the Boston Music Awards, she gained four nominations, including one for Outstanding Act of the Year—the first time a country artist was nominated for that trophy.

MILLER, EMMETT: *Singer, vaudeville performer. Born Macon, Georgia, 1903; date of death uncertain, but likely in 1960s.*

The old adage "fame is fleeting," could have no better example than Emmett Miller, a talented minstrel-era star who carved a notable career for himself in the decades between the two World Wars and who had a profound influence on country and pop music, yet was almost completely unknown by the end of the 1950s. Belated research by music industry historians and the release of a retrospective CD in the mid-1990s demonstrated his impact on such seminal figures as Jimmie Rodgers, Bob Wills, and Hank Williams, Sr.

In his liner notes for the 1996 Columbia/Legacy album, *The Minstrel Man from Georgia—Emmett Miller,* Charles Wolfe described Miller as a bridge builder between "the old 19th century America to the new media-powered 20th century . . . merging the old and the new, the African American with the European. He fit none of our neat categories: he wasn't exactly blues, not quite country, not entirely pop, more than comedy. He recorded, in the same month with artists as diverse as Fiddlin' John Carson and tromboning and trumpeting Tommy Dorsey."

Miller was born and spent his youth in Macon, Georgia, where as he reached his teens he became tremendously interested in the patterns of speech and entertainment in the black community and spent many hours in that part of town. Not only could he mimic the way African-Americans of the region talked, he also had an excellent tenor voice that made him a good candidate for the still-flourishing minstrel field. In 1919, the sixteen-year-old Miller began his professional career with the Neil O'Brien Minstrels; when they ran into financial problems and disbanded, they were replaced by another troupe called the Dan Fitch Minstrels.

Over the next few years Miller became a leading member of that show, not only performing in traditional blackface skits, but also singing with a quartet called the Kings of Harmony that used no black makeup and wore formal tuxedos. It wasn't long before Miller gained attention as a soloist, where he demonstrated some unusual vocal patterns including, as Wolfe noted, "breaking into falsetto at odd, unexpected times and . . . adding to his lines an eerie, octave jumping break that was unlike anything anybody had ever heard."

The show not only played throughout the South, but also found enthusiastic audiences in Northern cities such as New York. This eventually gave Miller the chance to make his first recordings for Okeh in 1924, where his initial track was of a song that had become a signature tune in his stage work, "Anytime," backed by a blackface number, "The Pickaninny's Paradise." Much later, "Anytime" became a best-selling song for Eddy Arnold. (The song was written by Herbert Lawson in 1921; Miller essentially was a performer, not a songwriter).

In 1925, Miller left Fitch and settled for a time in Asheville, North Carolina, where he became a familiar figure on the local entertainment scene. In August 1925, Ralph Peer came to Asheville on one of his periodic trips to collect new record material and, after auditioning, Miller got the chance to make four new sides, including a number called "Lovesick Blues." He had picked that up from hearing other artists sing it and had made it an important part of his live act. The other recordings were "Big Bad Bill Is Sweet William Now," "I Never Had the Blues," and "You're Just the Girl for Me."

The following year, Emmett was back on the road again, this time as a featured member of the longtime top-ranked minstrel group the Al G. Field Minstrels. In 1928, he shifted to another show, the Dan Fitch Girls and Memories of Minstrels. With that assemblage or on his own, he spent a lot of time in New York in the late 1920s, recording thirty-one sides for Okeh. For some of them he was joined by Fiddlin' John Carson. On a majority of the tracks, he was backed by a band called the Georgia Crackers.

Ray Benson, leader of Asleep at the Wheel, who tracked down a bootleg tape of Miller's work after hearing about him from fiddler Johnny Gimble in the mid-1970s, recalled how amazed he was at the uniqueness of Miller's vocals and the members of his backing band. As he noted in December 1995 comments to Columbia/Legacy, listening to the tape was like finding "the Rosetta stone of Country Music, and western swing in particular. I mean, here was a record by a man largely unknown to most modern day musicians and singers, who was one of the original architects of modern Country and popular music." He remembered his feelings of awe at the roster of the Georgia Crackers, which included jazz and swing legends Jimmy and Tommy Dorsey, Gene Krupa, Eddie Lang, and Jack Teagarden. "This in and of itself would be enough to insure Mr. Miller a place in jazz history."

Those recordings soon had an effect on many now legendary artists. Jimmie Rodgers, "the father of modern country music," developed a style that contained many elements of Miller's. (Rodgers reportedly also did some blackface numbers in some of his stage appearances.) A notebook kept by Bob Wills in 1931, when he was doing a radio program in an early phase of his career in Texas with Herman Arnspringer, listed songs drawn from Miller's repertoire: "Right or Wrong," "Big Bad Bill," "Blues Singer from Alabam," "I Ain't Got Nobody," and "Lovin' Sam." A young country singer named Hank Williams fell in love with Miller's releases, and by the late 1940s had made "Lovesick Blues" his signature.

Miller continued to work with various minstrel shows in the early 1930s, but this form of entertainment was fading and the Depression also curtailed recording opportunities. By the mid-1930s he was calling Atlanta home base, and worked local venues with friends like Lasses White and Turk McGee. In 1936, he made some new recordings for the Bluebird label, which apparently were the last he completed. From the mid-1930s to the late 1940s, his career languished. He managed to find enough work to keep going, playing mostly third-rate venues in Southern cities, but fewer and fewer people knew who he was.

In 1949 and the early 1950s, he made a comeback of sorts, organizing a show with Turk McBee called *Dixiana,* or "the last great minstrel show." As a novelty act, it gained considerable press attention and drew sizable, curious crowds. Miller also got the chance to appear in the 1951 film *Yes, Sir, Mister Bones.* But the public interest in minstrels quickly wore off, and by 1952 Miller sank back into obscurity. As Wolfe noted, exactly what

he did with himself after that is open to question. There were suggestions he worked for a time in a Nashville-area club or that he went back to Macon where he eventually ran a vegetable stand. As of 1997, exactly when and where he died was still unknown, though sometime in the 1960s seems likely.

The Columbia/Legacy album of 1996, part of its Roots & Blues series, included twenty of his sides. The contents give some idea of his unusual singing skills, though also including a number of blackface skits and songs that might well have influenced the development of the *Amos & Andy* radio show. Besides most of the songs noted above (some recordings seem to have disappeared), the disc includes his treatment of such classics as "I Ain't Got Nobody," "St. Louis Blues," and even the old pop hit, "You're the Cream in My Coffee."

Though attention to Miller's own career received widespread impetus with that album release, a number of modern-day artists had previously shown their awareness of his contributions with albums based on his output. Merle Haggard recorded an album dedicated to Miller titled *I Love Dixie Blues,* George Strait made the charts with his version of "Right or Wrong," and the eclectic performer Leon Redbone issued a disc devoted to Miller material. Redbone also authored an article honoring Miller's life that appeared in *Le Monde,* Paris, France, on December 5, 1991.

MILLER, ROGER: *Singer, guitarist, banjoist, pianist, drummer, songwriter. Born Fort Worth, Texas, January 2, 1936; died Los Angeles, California, October 25, 1992. Elected to Country Music Hall of Fame in 1995.*

A free soul, as unpredictable in his way as the content of his many country standards, Roger Miller burst on the country and national audience in the mid-1960s to become one of the best-known singers and songwriters of the decade. He remained a popular figure in the music field in the 1970s, though without repeating his creative achievements of earlier years.

He was born Roger Dean Miller in Texas, but spent most of his youth in the small town of Erick, Oklahoma. He told an interviewer, "My father died when I was a year old. There were three little boys—I was the youngest—and my mother couldn't support us so she was going to put us in an orphanage. My father had three brothers and one lived in Arkansas, one in Oklahoma, and one in California. Each came and took a boy home and raised him. I went to Oklahoma."

His uncle and aunt were poor and Erick was hardly a metropolis. "Erick is so small that the city limits signs are back to back. Its population is 1,500, including rakes and tractors. The school I went to [a one-room school] had thirty-seven students, me and thirty-six Indians. One time we had a school dance and it rained for thirty-six straight days. During recess we used to play cowboys and Indians and things got pretty wild from my standpoint."

Roger's sense of humor served him well, for life was something less than affluent. As a boy he helped his uncle on the farm. "I hated it all, but I hated most of all on Saturdays cleaning out the chicken house. A lot of people who grew up on a farm will know why I said 'Lord, give me a guitar and let me get out of here and make something of the world.'"

He pinned his hopes on country music partly because that was the kind of music he heard all around him and partly because he admired country performer Sheb Wooley, who was an in-law of the Miller family. A friend later recalled Roger's uncle stating that "when the boy grows up he wants to be just like Sheb."

Once he'd made up his mind on his future career, young Roger spent many of his Saturday hours picking cotton to earn money to buy a guitar. It was one of the proudest days of his life when he finally could purchase a second-hand instrument. His schooling ended after the eighth grade, after which, hauling his guitar along, he wandered around Texas and Oklahoma for much of his teens working at an assortment of jobs. He worked as a ranch hand, herding cattle and dehorning them, among other things. He also spent some of his time riding Brahma bulls in rodeos. During those years, he not only learned many basic guitar chords, but picked up experience on banjo and piano as well.

Ordinarily you wouldn't think of entry into the Army as a fortunate turn, but for Roger it proved just that. When he joined up during the Korean War, it finally got him away from the back country and out into the world in general. It became a learning experience far better than his brief period in grade school. He noted, "When I got into the Army, I finally met some guys who really knew something about the guitar and they taught me and I learned what I could."

Part of his hitch was spent in Korea, his destination after basic training, where at first he drove a jeep. But his ability as a singer and musician got him into Special Services, where he became part of a country music band entertaining troops. Some of the songs he played were his own and the applause they received made him feel better about his chance for making it in music later on. Not only did he play guitar in that band, but also drums and fiddle.

He also thought some of the contacts he made would help. "When I was stationed in South Carolina, I met this sergeant who said he had a brother in the business, Jethro of Homer and Jethro. This sergeant could play the bass as well as Jethro could play the mandolin and we used to sit in the barracks and play. He was the one who really convinced me to go to Nashville after I got out of the Army. [Otherwise] I was probably going back to Oklahoma and work in a gas station."

The sergeant did arrange an audition for him at RCA after Roger got his discharge. "I just walked in and said to Chet Atkins, 'I want to audition, I'm a songwriter' and he said, 'Well, where's your guitar?' I said, 'I don't have one' and he said, 'You can use mine.' So there's Chet Atkins and I'm using his guitar and I sang in one key and played in another. It was a disaster."

Discouraged, he thought of doing something else for a time. One job he attempted was fire-fighter in Amarillo, Texas. He slept through the alarm of the second fire of his career and was fired after two months. He returned to Nashville determined to break into the music field this time. He first got a job as a bellhop at the Andrew Jackson Hotel, then spent his free time hanging around studios, meeting people in the music industry, trying out for jobs. Slowly he got work as a musician playing fiddle with Minnie Pearl and handling drums in Faron Young's backing group.

While all that was going on, he kept putting together new songs. Since he couldn't write music, he had to play or sing the song to someone else who would put it on paper. He made the rounds of music publishers and artists and finally began to attract some attention. After he joined the Ray Price show, Ray recorded one of his tunes, "Invitation to the Blues," and it made the charts. The song also was covered by Patti Page.

That success helped bring a full-time songwriting contract from the Faron Young organization. In the late 1950s and early 1960s, more and more artists recorded his material, examples being Ernest Tubbs's version of "Half a Mind" and Jim Reeves's recording of "Billy Bayou." Other hits Roger wrote for others included "You Don't Want My Love," "Hey, Little Star," "Lock, Stock and Teardrops," and "In the Summertime."

Roger wasn't satisfied with that. He longed to succeed as a performer too. "I had come to Nashville to be a singer, but I was unorthodox I guess. I'd sing songs for people and they'd say that would be good for someone else. I'd say what about me and they'd say, we'll get to you later . . . and it was quite a bit later when they got to me."

However, Roger finally did get a shot at recording for a major label when RCA took him on in the early 1960s. This led to his first top-10 hit, in 1961, "When Two Worlds Collide," cowritten with country star Bill Anderson. On most of his later hits, though, he wrote both words and music himself.

After that breakthrough, however, he couldn't buy a hit for the next two years. Disheartened, he moved to Hollywood to enroll in a dramatic acting course. He had started the course when his singing career suddenly caught fire. He had signed with Smash Records, and his releases on the label caught the ear of DJs around the United States. In 1964 he scored a top-10 country hit with "Chug-a-Lug" and a number-one success with "Dang Me." Both records also became favorites with pop fans. But 1964 was only a prologue to his sensational achievements of the next year. He turned out four best-sellers, one following on the heels of the other: "King of the Road," "Engine, Engine No. 9," "Kansas City Star," and "One Dyin' and a-Buryin'." Oddly, while all were top-10 country hits, none reached number one, whereas on pop charts, all reached the highest spot, earning Roger four gold-record awards. "King of the Road," of course, became his trademark song; by the 1970s, it had been recorded over 300 times by various artists and Miller's own single sold 2.5 million copies. During 1966, one of his songs, "In the Summertime," provided Andy Williams with a hit single that sold over 2 million copies.

This association inspired Andy to feature Roger on one of his NBC-TV programs in late 1965. Viewer reaction was so favorable that NBC asked Roger to host his own half-hour special, which was presented on January 19, 1966. That effort did well enough for Miller to do a fall weekly variety show that debuted on September 12, 1966. The ratings weren't healthy enough, however, and the show was canceled.

In the mid-1960s, Roger also appeared on many other variety shows, both pop and country, and was a favorite with live audiences. He performed in major venues from one end of the United States to the other. His engagement at Harrah's in Lake Tahoe brought out so many fans that additional performances had to be added.

Roger's output of 1964–65 won him an amazing total of eleven Grammy Awards. His 1964 trophies were for Best C&W Single ("Dang Me"); Best C&W Album (*Dang Me/Chug-a-Lug*); Best C&W Vocal Performance ("Dang Me"); Best C&W Song (writer's award, "Dang Me"); Best New C&W Artist of 1964. His 1965 awards were Best Contemporary (rock 'n' roll) Single ("King of the Road"); Best Contemporary Vocal Performance, Male ("King of the Road"); Best C&W Single ("King of the Road"); Best C&W Album (*The Return of Roger Miller*); Best C&W Vocal Performance, Male ("King of the Road"); Best C&W Song (writer's award, "King of the Road").

The two albums mentioned in the awards both rose to top-chart levels and won gold-record awards. Also earning gold-record awards in the mid-1960s were *Roger Miller/Golden Hits* and *Roger Miller, the Third Time Around.* His other 1960s LPs on Smash included *Words & Music* (1/67), *Walkin' in the Sunshine* (7/67); *Waterhole No. 3* (12/67), and *Roger Miller* (10/69). His other album credits in the 1960s included such RCA Camden releases as *Roger Miller* (12/64) and *One and Only Roger Miller* (9/65); *Amazing Roger Miller* on Nashville; and *Madcap Sensation* on Starday.

In the 1970s, Miller recorded for various labels, signing with Columbia Records for a while, among others. He started off the decade with an LP on Smash, *Roger Miller 1970,* and also had a collection on Columbia that year, *34 All-Time Great Sing-Along Selections* (12/70). His later Columbia releases included the album *Roger Miller Supersongs,* which spawned the single "I Love a Rodeo." Some of his other albums were *Country Side* on Starday and, on Mercury, *Best of Roger Miller* and *Trip in the Country.*

Although Roger continued to perform sporadically in the 1970s and occasionally was featured on network TV programs (including several appearances as a presenter on Grammy Award shows), he was much less in evidence than in the previous decade. He continued to write songs, some of which provided charted singles for other artists, and some that he placed on the charts himself. However, his own releases rarely made it past mid-chart levels. Among his charted singles in the decade were "Rings for Sale" on Mercury in 1972 and "I Believe in Sunshine" (late 1973–early 1974) and "Our Love" (1975) on Columbia. In the early 1980s, he gained a new recording alignment with Elektra Records; one result was the top-40 single "Everyone Gets Crazy Now and Then" in the fall of 1981.

His songwriting technique remained essentially the same even if it didn't bring the creative rewards of earlier times. "I write a line at a time, really. A line comes to me and then I sit down and sing it and then I write the next line and then I have two lines and I sing them. Then I do a third line and sing all three; then come up with the fourth. It's a line at a time, it's go back and come to it, it's like hitting a brick wall and each time you hit it, it gives a little. You find you've gotten the wall to give enough until you've written a whole song."

Despite his songwriting achievements, though, he stopped writing new songs in 1978, influenced in part by a feeling that his writing skills were not appreciated by others in the industry or by the general public. He was depressed that, aside from hits like "King of the Road" or novelties like "You Can't Rollerskate in a Buffalo Herd," little attention was given to his other songs, some of which he believed had greater artistic content.

His resistance to creating new material caused him at first to ignore a request from a former professor turned entrepreneur named Rocco Landesman that he compose the score for a musical based on Mark Twain's *Huckleberry Finn.* Landesman was persistent and finally persuaded Miller to take up the task in 1983 by suggesting that in so doing Roger could join the company of such greats as Cole Porter, Jerome Kern, and the like. Landesman told Samuel G. Freedman of the *New York Times* ("Journey of 'Big River' to Broadway Success," July 16, 1985), "Roger clearly thought it was mystifying that this ex-Yale professor would be quoting his lyrics." Miller commented, "I knew people liked my music, but I didn't think a scholarly person would be interested in it."

Roger finally came through with the score and, after tryouts, the show, called *Big River,* opened on Broadway and after a slow start became one of the hits of the season. It received thirteen Tony Award nominations and won seven of those, giving Roger the chance to bask in the nationwide spotlight as an overnight Broadway phenomenon.

He still treasured his country roots and was more

than a little pleased to accept the Academy of Country Music Pioneer Award in 1987. He continued to make sporadic concert and TV appearances in the 1980s and into the 1990s. His last performance was on the TNN TV special, "Hats off to Minnie Pearl." However, physicians had discovered a cancerous tumor beneath his vocal cords that failed to respond to therapy, which included a long series of radiation treatments. At the still young age of fifty-six, he succumbed to the disease in the fall of 1992.

Roger was voted into the Country Music Hall of Fame in 1995 and his induction was announced on the Country Music Association's TV awards program in October. By year-end, Mercury Records had released a three-disc package of Roger's work titled *King of the Road: The Genius of Roger Miller.*

MILSAP, RONNIE: *Singer, guitarist, pianist, songwriter. Born Robbinsville, North Carolina, January 16, 1944.*

By the end of the 1970s, Ronnie Milsap had won nearly every country-music award for which he was eligible. This might not seem so unusual, except that he only was involved with country music since 1973. Additionally, he became a top country star performing the music in an essentially traditional way, ignoring the progressive approach of people like Willie Nelson and Waylon Jennings despite his earlier grounding in classical music and rock 'n' roll. His emphasis has mainly been on slow to medium tempo country ballads that, while sometimes having more sophistication in music and lyrics than country songs of the past, and delivered in a vocal style with a little less of the characteristic "twang" of older artists, differed from typical country offerings of the 1940s to early 1960s only in degree.

It reflected the fact that, though his musical training took a different direction, his initial exposure as a small child had been to radio programs that featured what might be called "roots" country music. As he said when he signed as a country artist with RCA in early 1973, leaving what had been a promising career as a rock performer, "All I heard the first six years of my life was country music and it's hard to get away from your roots."

Those early years brought the boy more than his share of misfortunes, partly inherited. His father was a third-generation epileptic. Ronnie was not epileptic, but he was born blind. A previous child of his parents had been stillborn. Ronnie's mother had trouble dealing with those tragedies and left the family while Ronnie still was a baby, leaving him to be raised by his father's parents.

Until the age of five, Ronnie did not know he was blind. His grandparents never mentioned it, and his playmates didn't treat him like he was different. But at the age of five, he went to the North Carolina State School for the Blind at Raleigh rather than the local public school. Being so young and far from home scared him, but in the long run proved a boon to his career, for it was there that he was first exposed to musical instruments.

It soon became apparent that he was a prodigy. At the age of seven, he could play the violin like a professional; he mastered the piano at eight and the guitar at twelve. In his teens he picked up some woodwind and percussion instruments and demonstrated skill with them as well. His first training was in the classics, and even when he became a country star he still liked to play classical music for his own enjoyment. "My favorite composers are Mozart and Bach," he said. "I like Mozart's melodies and since I am a methodical minded Capricorn, Bach's complicated techniques appeal to me."

However, rock 'n' roll was his passion in his teens. While in high school he formed a rock group with three other blind musicians. They called themselves the Apparitions and performed at local clubs and dances.

While he loved music, young Milsap wasn't positive he could support himself as a musician. Thus he entered Young-Harris Junior College in Atlanta, Georgia, as a prelaw major. The first day of school, his two sighted roommates told him they didn't want to room with him because they didn't know how to act around a blind person. But when they all went down to the freshman orientation meeting held in a room with a piano, and Ronnie was seated by them on the piano bench, he couldn't resist the temptation to play. When the students heard him play his wild rock 'n' roll, he became the center of attention and the most popular student in the room. His roommates never again suggested he move out.

Ronnie completed two years at the junior college and was offered a full scholarship at Emory University Law School. But Ronnie had been performing steadily during his years at Young-Harris, and this eventually encouraged him to try to make a living playing music. He had become known for his instrumental abilities to performers and recording studio executives in Atlanta and was getting jobs as a backing artist at sessions and as a sideman for people like J.J. Cale. By the end of the 1960s, he had formed his own group, which became the house band at T.J.'s Club in Memphis, Tennessee, in 1969. In the late 1960s and early 1970s, Milsap and his group had recording agreements with several labels—Scepter, Chips Records, and Warner Brothers Records. Their output included the R&B hit "Never Had It So Good" and several other rock 'n' roll singles that had some chart action.

But Ronnie felt his career wasn't bringing him the satisfaction it should. His interest in country music had been rekindled when, in 1973, he picked up stakes and moved with his wife to Nashville. In April 1973, he signed with RCA Records country-music division and was soon in the studios working on his debut recordings. It didn't take long for him to make his presence felt in his new field. His first RCA single, "I Hate You," made the charts. At year end, his single "The Girl That Waits on Tables" was on the lists rising toward the top 10 in early 1974. He followed with such other 1974 top-10 bestsellers as "Pure Love," "Please Don't Tell Me How the Story Ends," and, at year end, "(I'd Be) a Legend in My Time," which went on to become a number-one hit in early 1974. Also on the charts from late 1973 and for much of 1974 was his album *Where the Heart Is.*

All of this translated into immediate recognition by his music industry peers as a major new talent. In the Country Music Association's voting for 1974, Milsap was named Male Vocalist of the Year. In Grammy polling, he was named winner of the Best Country Vocal Performance, Male, for 1974 for his single "Please Don't Tell Me How the Story Ends."

He continued to show his rapport with country fans in 1975 with such top-10 singles (besides "Legend in My Time") as "Too Late to Worry, Too Blue to Cry," "Daydreams About Night Things," and "She Even Woke Me Up to Say Goodbye." He also had the best-selling LPs *Night Things* and *Legend in My Time.* The latter won the CMA award for Best Album of the Year. Nor did he slow down during the next two years. His 1976 successes included the top-10 single "What Goes on When the Sun Goes Down" and what has become one of his trademark songs, "(I'm a) Stand by My Woman Man" (number one for several weeks in August and September) plus the hit LP *20-20 Vision.* For much of 1977, his LPs *Ronnie Milsap Live* and *It Was Almost like a Song* were on the charts (the latter remained on country lists more than a year and also was a pop chart hit), and his singles output included "It Was Almost like a Song," number one during the summer.

The honors he won for his 1976–77 work included being named CMA Male Vocalist of the Year both years and the 1976 Best Country Vocal Performance, Male, Grammy for "(I'm a) Stand by My Woman Man." He won two other CMA categories in 1977, making him the major winner of that year. Those were the most coveted honors of all, Entertainer of the Year and the Best Album of the Year for *Ronnie Milsap Live.*

Ronnie's 1978 hits included "Only One Love in My Life," number one most of July, and the bestseller, "Let's Take the Long Way Around the World." His album *Only One Love in My Life* was on upper-chart levels throughout the summer and still on the lists in 1979. The LP won the CMA Best Album of the Year award for 1978. Ronnie closed out the decade with still more hits. His 1979 best-selling singles included "Nobody Likes Sad Songs," "Back on My Mind Again/Santa Barbara," and "In No Time at All" and the album *Images.*

By the end of the 1970s, Milsap had become one of the most popular artists in country music, headlining concerts throughout the United States and the world.

Many of his recordings increasingly crossed over to pop charts and also often were on hit lists in other countries. In 1976, Ronnie became a regular cast member of the *Grand Ole Opry* and was still part of that revered institution in the early 1980s.

He began the 1980s with the hit single "Why Don't You Spend the Night," vying for number-one spot in March 1980. He followed with such other bestsellers as "Cowboys and Clowns" (which was issued on the Elektra Records label as part of the soundtrack from the movie *Bronco Billy*) and the number-one "My Heart/Silent Night (After the Fight)." At year end, *Billboard* magazine named him the Number One Country Music Singles Artist of 1980. Also on the charts in 1980 was a new RCA album, *Milsap Magic.* In December his LP *Ronnie Milsap's Greatest Hits* was on the charts, eventually moving to number one in January 1981. The single "Smokey Mountain Rain" was in the top 10 as 1980 drew to a close, remaining on the lists into 1981. His best-selling singles of 1981 included "Am I Losing You" and "I Wouldn't Have Missed It for the World."

Thus despite his handicap and with only a few years' experience in the field, Ronnie Milsap truly had become a legend in his time. Once asked whether blindness, rather than being a hindrance, had helped him become a success, he had replied, "It gains immediate attention, but acceptance is another story. You've got to work for that, son." He did agree that he probably could pick up sensations and gain an understanding of individuals better in some ways than sighted people. "Your ears becomes your eyes. . . . I try to look inside people."

Another of Ronnie's chart-making singles, "There's No Gettin' Over Me," earned him a Grammy in the 1981 voting for Best Country Vocal Performance, Male. That was the first of four victories in that category in the 1980s, the other being the 1985 award for the single "Lost in the '50s Tonight," the 1986 one for the album of the same title, and the 1987 trophy for a duet single with Kenny Rogers, "Make No Mistake, She's Mine." During that period, Ronnie was also a finalist a number of times in CMA voting, though he wasn't the eventual winner. Those nominations were for the 1981 Album of the Year for *Out Where the Bright Lights Are Glowing;* in 1982 and 1984 for Male Vocalist of the Year; for Entertainer of the Year in 1984; and for 1986 Album of the Year for *Lost in the '50s Tonight.*

While Ronnie didn't receive any new Grammy or CMA nods through the rest of the 1980s, he continued to add to his credits as a concert artist and guest on major TV programs. His albums and singles were rarely absent from the charts and he closed out the decade with such hit singles as "Don't You Ever Get Tired of Hurtin' Me," number one in *Billboard* the week of March 11, 1989, and "A Woman in Love," number two in *Radio & Records* the week of December 1, 1989.

He began the 1990s with another top-ranked single, "Stranger Things Have Happened," number one in

R&R the week of April 13, 1990. Other chart successes in the early 1990s included "Turn That Radio On," number three in *R&R* the week of January 31, 1992, and "All Is Fair in Love and War," number six in *R&R* the week of May 5, 1992. Late in 1992 the single "L.A. to the Moon" was on mid-chart levels. His RCA collection, *Greatest Hits, Volume 2,* was a best-seller in the early 1990s, passing the R.I.A.A., platinum-record level.

By the mid-1990s, like many long-established country stars, Milsap was finding it increasingly difficult to compete in record sales with the growing influx of a seemingly endless stream of new young performers, typically with movie-star looks and pop-music glamour. When his long association with RCA came to an end he briefly moved to Liberty, which released the single "True Believer," on the charts from July through the late fall of 1993. The single made the *Billboard* Top 40, but didn't come close to top-10 status.

One hang-up Ronnie never had was racial bias, and he always gave black artists their due. He described for Country Music Association *Close Up* magazine editor Teresa George ("Ronnie Milsap: Still Grinding out the Hits," July 1991) the cold shoulder he first received from white classmates when he started college compared to the warm reception given him by local black musicians. "Nobody wanted to room with me when I was in college until I sat and played the piano for my friends."

Once he began frequenting black nightclubs, he said, "All these black musicians would call me up and say, 'Come on down. We want you to sit in with us'. . . . Even as a kid growing up and listening to a lot of music, the early rock 'n' roll, the early black rock 'n' roll was always better—Little Richard, Little Willie John, and the list could go on and on of black entertainers in the fifties. Whether or not it's because I can't see or what, I can't understand racial prejudice."

One of the young artists he met at the time was future superstar Patti LaBelle. For his 1991 album, *Back to the Grindstone,* she flew to Nashville for a duet with Ronnie on the track "Love Certified." On another track he had the Harlem Boys Choir provide the backing vocals. He told Teresa George, "Kids have a whole lot harder time growing up today than I ever had. But as hard as mine was, and mine was awful, my adult life has been wonderful. It's been more of a Cinderella story."

In 1996, Ronnie was one of the first entertainers named to the Georgia Music Hall of Fame which opened in Macon on September 21.

MONROE, BILL: *Singer, guitarist, mandolinist, fiddler, songwriter, band leader (the Blue Grass Boys). Born Rosine, Kentucky, September 13, 1911; died Springfield, Tennessee, September 9, 1996. Elected to Country Music Hall of Fame in 1970.*

"It's got a hard drive to it. It's Scotch bagpipes and old time fiddlin'. It's Methodist and Holiness and Baptist. It's blues and jazz and it has a high lonesome sound. It's plain music that tells a good story. It's played from my heart to your heart, and it will touch you."

That's how Bill Monroe described bluegrass, "a music that I set out to have as my own. I never wanted to be known for copying any man. . . ." Although the elements that went into bluegrass were there before, in fact can be discerned in folk music going well back into the country's history, it was Monroe who blended them in a new way, particularly in his method of having the fiddle, mandolin, and banjo carry the lead in a format sometimes called "country music in overdrive." With his brother Charlie he spread the word of this new musical product of the border regions of the old South far and wide in the second half of the 1920s and early 1930s until he became known as the "Father of Bluegrass."

Monroe's love of country music, particularly country fiddling and mandolin playing, goes back to his earliest years growing up in the hills of Kentucky. Both his mother, Melissa, and uncle, Pen Vandiver, were excellent country fiddlers and Vandiver also was a fine mandolinist. As soon as he was old enough to handle a stringed instrument they helped start him on a path that was to lead to mastery of not only fiddle and mandolin but guitar as well. After a while, he could play guitar well enough that his uncle took him along as a backing musician while the older man set the pace at local dances. Later on Bill was to commemorate his uncle in the song "Uncle Pen."

Monroe was intensely curious about all kinds of music. Not only did he pay close attention to the traditional music he heard all around him as he grew up, he also recalled taking the opportunity of listening to the blues and gospel songs favored by local black artists. All of those influences found their way into the songs he was to write and the arrangements he made of both traditional and modern country material.

His older brother, Charlie, also was a fine instrumentalist, and another brother, Birch, played fiddle. The three brothers sometimes played together in local groups and, as time went on, became eager to form their own band. In the mid-1920s, the Monroe Brothers began to pick up a following in Kentucky and expanded their reputation with the advent of radio. They made their first broadcasts in 1927 and added more credits on various stations over the next decade. Their unique style of playing, dubbed "bluegrass" initially because of the connection with their home state, eventually made them favorites with country crowds over a steadily growing area. Gradually, from the end of the 1920s and into the early 1930s, audiences at country fairs and at local country shows in many parts of the Midwest and the South began to get enthused over

Charlie's "houn' dog guitar" and Bill's "potato-bug mandolin."

Many of the favorites of Monroe Brothers' fans of those years were assembled in a 1960s Camden LP. Among the songs included in the album, *Early Bluegrass Music by the Monroe Brothers,* were "New River Train," "No Home, No Place to Pillow My Head," "The Great Speckled Bird," "Once I Had a Darling Mother," "On the Banks of the Ohio," "Rosa Lee McFall," "Bringin' in the Georgia Mail," "Weeping Willow Tree," "Just a Song of Old Kentucky," "Don't Forget Me," and "Mother's Not Dead, She's Only Sleeping."

Many of those songs were bluegrass versions of traditional songs, some traceable back to Elizabethan times. But Bill Monroe was also adding new compositions of his own. In 1930, he achieved his first big hit with one of them, an instrumental called "Kentucky Waltz." Among his other compositions of those years that helped bring both bluegrass music and the Monroe Brothers' band to the top ranks of country bands active in the 1930s were "Get Up John," "Blue Grass Ramble," and "Memories of You."

In 1938, the Monroe Brothers decided to go separate ways. Charlie started a band named the Kentucky Pardners while Bill organized the first of dozens of Blue Grass Boys alignments. Though Charlie's group did reasonably well for over a decade, it was Bill's band that almost immediately gained widespread public attention. In 1939 they were invited to join the cast of the *Grand Ole Opry.* Monroe became a fixture on the show and was still on its roster more than fifty-eight years later.

Almost immediately the Blue Grass Boys became a training ground for other skilled artists. Among the early members of the troupe were Sam and Kirk McGee, who closed the group's road show with a twenty-minute old-time country & western songfest, and two young sidemen named Lester Flatt and Earl Scruggs, who were to go out on their own later in the 1940s to challenge the master for bluegrass leadership. Among other folk and country & western luminaries to be part of the Blue Grass Boys at some point in their careers were Clyde Moody, Howdy Forrester, Don Reno, Red Smiley, Jimmy Martin, Carter Stanley, Vassar Clements, Chubby Wise, Cedric Rainwater, Stringbean, and Byron Berline.

In the 1940s, Bill began to write lyrics as well as melodies. In many cases, he added words to existing songs—one of which brought Eddy Arnold a top-10 hit in 1951 with his release of "Kentucky Waltz." Among other Monroe originals that were recorded by both Bill and a number of other artists over the years were "Blue Moon of Kentucky," "I Hear a Sweet Voice Calling," "Along About Daybreak," "Cheyenne," "Memories of Mother and Dad," "Gotta Travel On," "On the Kentucky Shores," and "Scotland." One of the first songs

recorded by Elvis Presley in the early stages of his career was "Blue Moon of Kentucky."

During the mid-1940s, Monroe recorded for Columbia Records, in 1949 leaving to sign with Decca. Like many of Monroe's affiliations, the alignment proved a lasting one. He continued to record year after year for Decca and then on MCA, the label with which Decca merged. At the start of the 1980s, he remained on MCA's list with dozens of albums to his credit. Among his LPs on Decca were *Knee Deep* (8/58); *I Saw the Light* (10/58); *Mr. Bluegrass* (7/61); *All Time Favorites* (7/62); *Bluegrass Ramble, Bluegrass Special* (8/63); *Meet You in Church* (8/64); *Bluegrass Instrumentals* (1965); *High Lonesome Sound* (8/66); *Bluegrass Time* (8/67); *Voice from on High* (6/69); *Kentucky Bluegrass* (1970); and *Country Music Hall of Fame* (8/71). Some of his releases on other labels during the 1960s and early 1970s were *Bill Monroe and His Bluegrass Boys* (4/61, Harvard); *Father of Bluegrass Music* (10/62, Camden); *Songs with the Bluegrass Boys* (4/64, Vocalion); *Best of Bill Monroe* (7/64, Harvard); *Original Bluegrass Sound* (6/65, Harvard); *Bluegrass Style* (late 1960s, Vocalion); *16 All-Time Bluegrass Hits* (8/70, Columbia).

Over the years Monroe spent much of each year on the road. He gradually became a favorite with folk fans and during the folk music boom of the late 1950s and early 1960s, he often was featured on major folk concert tours and network TV shows. He and the Bluegrass Boys appeared at many major folk festivals during those years and later in the 1960s including a number of sets at the Newport Folk Festival. He remained a favorite of younger fans all through the 1970s and into the 1990s, when his itinerary included many stops on college campuses across the United States. His reputation also spread far beyond U.S. borders—in the 1960s and 1970s he was enthusiastically welcomed on several tours of Europe, Canada, and many Pacific nations, including Japan.

In 1970, the Country Music Association membership acknowledged his great contributions by electing him to the Country Music Hall of Fame in Nashville. By then Bill didn't have very far to go to visit his memorabilia in the Hall of Fame since he long since had become a resident of Tennessee, spending his time off the road handling chores on a 288-acre farm in Sumner County.

During the 1970s, bluegrass adherents were cheered by the establishment of an annual bluegrass festival with Monroe as the host in Bean Blossom, Indiana. MCA Records recorded some of the festivals, resulting in two live albums during the 1970s, the two-record *Bean Blossom* set in the mid-1970s and the single disc *Bean Blossom '79.* In the early 1980s, Monroe still was turning out new solo LPs on MCA, such as the 1981 *Master of Bluegrass.*

As of 1982, MCA maintained an extensive catalogue of Monroe's recordings. Besides the three albums mentioned above, still in print in 1982 were *Greatest Hits, Mr. Bluegrass, Bluegrass Ramble, Bluegrass Special, Bluegrass Instrumentals, The High Lonesome Sound of Bill Monroe, Bluegrass Time, Bill and Charlie Monroe, A Voice from on High, Kentucky Bluegrass, Country Music Hall of Fame, I'll Meet You in Church Sunday Morning, Father and Son* (with James Monroe), *Together Again* (with James Monroe), *Road of Life, Uncle Pen, I Saw the Light, The Weary Traveler, Bill Monroe Sings Bluegrass Body and Soul, Bluegrass Memories, Best of Bill Monroe, Bluegrass Style,* and *Bill Monroe Sings Country Songs.*

The elements of Bill's career changed very little as he remained a revered and inspiring individual for the rest of the 1980s and on into his seventh decade as a performer. In the mid-1990s, now in his eighties, he kept up his touring schedule with the Blue Grass Boys, drawing exuberant crowds of all ages to see him as a headliner in clubs, concert venues, or as a featured artist at major country/bluegrass and folk festivals. Over the years, he could be seen on various TV specials on major networks or the Public Broadcasting System.

He continued to record new material for MCA, and in the 1988 Grammy voting one of those albums, *Southern Flavor,* was named the Best Bluegrass Recording (Vocal or Instrumental). In 1993, the National Academy of the Recording Arts & Sciences, presenter of the Grammys, awarded him its Lifetime Achievement Award. He was given the Honor, NARAS stated, "For his pioneering artistry as the father of bluegrass; an influential singer, mandolinist, songwriter and band leader, he has made songs like 'Blue Moon of Kentucky' and 'Pike County Breakdown' an essential part of America's music heritage."

In citing him as one of the most important of its September 1994 list of "The 100 Most Important People in the History of Country," *Life* editors wrote that the music he helped make famous "was an American ideal, a harmonious blend of diverse influences, full of exuberance, enthusiasm and empathy. That's why Bill Monroe is more than just a great musician. He's a great American." They added that "Bill has always been the perfect gentleman."

Monroe albums listed in the Country Music Foundation catalog in the mid-1990s were such MCA releases as *Bill Monroe: Country Music Hall of Fame Series, Cryin' Holy Unto the Lord, Bean Blossom,* and *Bill Monroe/Celebrating 50 Years on the Grand Ole Opry* (a live performance album). Other albums in print included, on Columbia, *The Essential Bill Monroe 1947–1949* (two CDs or cassettes) and *Bill Monroe/Columbia Historic Edition;* on RCA, *Mule Skinner Blues;* and, on the German Bear Family label, *Bill Monroe/Bluegrass 1950–1958* (four CDs) and *Bluegrass/1958–1969* (four CDs). Rounder Records' 1995 catalog also offered the album *Bill Monroe with Lester Flatt & Earl Scruggs: The Original Bluegrass Band.* In 1995, bluegrass fiddler Byron Berline achieved a long-held dream by reuniting Monroe and Earl Scruggs, who hadn't performed together for decades, to record the track of "Sally Goodin" included on Byron's Sugar Hill album *A Fiddle & a Song,* issued in August 1995.

In 1995, Monroe was awarded the National Medal of the Arts. Through that year, Bill maintained his demanding concert schedule of some 200 dates a year and continued to perform until he was felled by a stroke in early 1996. He failed to recover from that and died in a hospice in Springfield, Tennessee, on Monday, September 9. On the following Wednesday, a 75-minute memorial service in his honor was performed by many country and bluegrass artists on the stage of the one-time home of the *Grand Old Opry,* the Ryman Auditorium in downtown Nashville. His mandolin was set on a spotlighted pedestal at mid-stage throughout the concert which opened with Vince Gill, Marty Stuart, and Ricky Skaggs singing "Working on a Building" after which they were joined by Emmylou Harris to do a bluegrass version of the old folk song, "Wayfaring Stranger." On Thursday, September 12, Monroe was laid to rest in his hometown of Rosine, Kentucky. It was estimated by record industry historians that during his lifetime Monroe sold over 50 million copies of his records.

MONROE, CHARLIE: *Singer, guitarist, songwriter, band leader (Kentucky Pardners). Born Rosine, Kentucky, June 4, 1903; died Reidsville, North Carolina, September 27, 1975.*

While Bill Monroe is justly honored as the "Father of Bluegrass Music," his older brother, Charlie, also had a hand in the development of the style. In the 1920s, in fact, it was Bill and Charlie's Monroe Brothers band, forerunner of Bill's Blue Grass Boys, that first excited country-music audiences with their new fast-paced blend of blues and traditional hill-country music.

Growing up in a rural area of Kentucky, Charlie and the other members of his family were part of a culture where music played an important role both as a leisure-time activity and, in the form of religious songs, an integral facet of churchgoing. Charlie, as did his younger brothers Birch and Bill, learned to sing many hymns through the old "shaped note" hymnals. Many members of their family were adept at various instruments, used for informal get-togethers and dances, and all the Monroe children started learning to play one or more of them early in life. In Charlie's case he took up guitar (as did his sister Bertha) while Birch practiced the fiddle and Bill eventually settled on mandolin, although reluctantly, since he liked guitar more. He was forced into it by his older siblings, who wanted a mandolin sound to blend with their contributions to the family band.

As they grew up, all of the children performed separately or in various combinations at local functions. In the mid-1920s, Charlie, Birch, and Bill formed a loose alliance that led to their debut on a local radio station in 1927. Still, music seemed more a hobby than a way of making a living, and in the late 1920s, Charlie and Birch left Kentucky to find work in the midwest factories. They first worked in the Detroit area, then moved on to jobs in oil refineries in Hammond and Whiting, on the East Chicago, Indiana, border. In 1929, Bill came north to join them. He found a position in the barrel house at the Sinclair refinery, where he remained on the payroll the next five years.

Once together again, the brothers resumed their musical association and picked up whatever work they could find in small clubs or, more usually, playing at local dances and house parties. In 1932, while the three Monroes and a friend, Tom Moore, were at a square dance in Hammond, Indiana, they were observed taking part in the dancing by a man named Tom Owens, who had a group that was part of the *WLS Barn Dance* tour. He approached the boys to join his troupe and they agreed; thus their first big break came as dancers, not musicians.

They remained with the *Barn Dance* tour for two years, primarily as dancers, but with opportunities to play their instruments as well. The relationship helped open some doors for them as musicians and they got the chance to work on station WAE in Hammond and later WJKS in Gary, Indiana. By 1934, Bill and Charlie were thinking seriously of trying for full-time careers in music. The die finally was cast when Charlie was asked by officials of Texas Crystals, a patent medicine, to go on a show sponsored by them on a Shenandoah, Iowa, station. Charlie asked his brothers to join him, but Birch had the chance for a new job in an oil refinery and demurred.

The Monroe Brothers, Charlie and Bill, were so well received in Iowa they were offered a spot on a larger station in Omaha. After that, Texas Crystals sponsored a move to Columbia, South Carolina, and later in 1935 to a daily program on WBT in Charlotte, North Carolina. The response to the brothers' music by listeners and audiences at their live performance dates helped increase their self-confidence and desire to reach still wider numbers of people.

That confidence was shaken a bit in 1936 when Texas Crystals dropped them, but almost immediately they were hired by the larger Crazy Water Crystal Company. The latter not only sponsored their daily program on WBT, but saw that they were featured on the Saturday night WBT *Crazy Barn Dance*. During those years, Charlie and Bill also were heard by audiences of station WFBC in Greenville, South Carolina, and WPTF in Raleigh, North Carolina.

Talent scouts from RCA became interested in them in the mid-1930s and, after several attempts, managed to get the Monroes into the studio in Charlotte to record a series of songs in February 1936 issued on the company's Bluebird label. Public response was good

enough that they recorded another series in a later session before the brothers went separate ways.

During that period, though Bill provided many excellent original songs, Charlie maintained his role as leader and Bill was restricted to a mainly secondary slot. Bill grew restless at that arrangement and in 1938 the two parted company. Bill organized a band called the Kentuckians soon after, which later changed its name to the Blue Grass Boys, while Charlie organized his Kentucky Pardners.

Charlie remained active with his band through the 1940s and he retained a sizable following over those years. Bill, desiring to make a complete break with the past, left RCA for Decca at the end of the 1930s, but Charlie remained on the RCA roster. He made many recordings for RCA, many of which remain important contributions to bluegrass history, but his achievements were overshadowed by the immense success of his brother.

In 1952, tired of the touring grind, Charlie broke up his band and went back home to spend his remaining years on his Kentucky ranch. *(See also Monroe, Bill.)*

MONTANA, PATSY: *Singer, guitarist, songwriter. Born Hot Springs, Arkansas, October 30, 1914; died San Jacinto, California, May 3, 1996. Inducted into Country Music Hall of Fame in October 1996.*

In the 1930s and 1940s, the *WLS Barn Dance* was probably the best-known country & western show in most of the country outside the South. One of the major attractions of the show was a dynamic western artist named Patsy Montana. Her stage name and her nickname of "The Yodeling Cowgirl" have a western ring to them, but her origins were a lot closer to the heartland of the *Grand Ole Opry* than to the Chicago-based *Barn Dance*.

As she told *Music City News* (August 1975, p. 20), "I grew up with 10 boys and no sisters around Hope and Hot Springs, Arkansas. [Her original name was Rubye Blevins.] My first exposure to country music would have been the old Jimmie Rodgers records and later on Gene Autry. I don't really remember a girl singer that I tried to follow. The only singer I remember in my early days out in California was Kate Smith."

Patsy attended both elementary and high school in Arkansas, graduating from Hope High School in the early 1930s. From there she went on to enroll in the University of Western Louisiana. She already had been enthusiastic about singing in her teens and by the time she went to college was spending more and more time perfecting her guitar playing and adding to her repertoire of country & western songs. Before long she cut short her educational efforts in favor of a show business career.

Recalling those early days, she noted, "I got my name from Monty Montana, who was the world's champion yodeler. I started to work with two other girls in a trio and the name automatically became the Montana Cowgirls. My real name is Rubye and one of the girls was named Ruthie. The names conflicted when they were announced over the air. At the time we were working with Stuart Hamblen and he named me, being more Irish than the others, Patsy, while we were on the air.

"I appeared in a couple of western movies with Gene Autry and did several appearances in what they called 'shorts' in those days. Coming back from California to go to the World's Fair in Chicago, I stopped to visit my folks in Hope, Arkansas. My mother, who listened to WLS, told me to say hello to some of the acts she heard on the radio if I got the chance."

One result of following that advice was a meeting with a group called the Prairie Ramblers. The members asked her to join and she accepted, a move that resulted in Chicago becoming home for many years thereafter. The Ramblers, whose members claimed they all were born in log cabins in Kentucky, comprised Chuck Hurt, Tex Atchison, Jack Taylor, and Salty Holmes. Patsy and the Ramblers graced stages all over the United States and in several other nations from 1934 through 1948. During that time, they were featured in almost every county fair in the country. Starting in 1935, Montana and the group were regulars on the *National Barn Dance,* for which Patsy remained a headliner into the 1950s. In 1934 she married Paul Rose, and, after a while, she found time to start raising a family. (Rose, an entertainment industry executive, managed an act called "Mac and Bob," and was also his wife's manager for many years.)

Montana began her long recording career in 1933, with such songs as "I Love My Daddy Too" and "When the Flowers of Montana Are Blooming." Her voice was heard on many different labels from then until the start of the 1960s, including Surf, Columbia, RCA Victor, Vocalion, and Decca. As of the mid-1970s, she estimated she had been represented by over 200 singles as well as dozens of albums. Some of her single releases of the 1930s were "The Wheel of the Wagon Is Broken," "I'm an Old Cowhand." "There's a Ranch in the Sky," "Singing in the Saddle," "A Cowboy Honeymoon," and "Montana." In 1935 she gained national attention with her single, "I Wanna be a Cowboy's Sweetheart," which sold over a million copies. That disc became the first million-selling recording by a female country artist. In later decades she turned out such songs as "Old Nevada Moon," "My Million Dollar Smile," "I Only Want a Buddy, Not a Sweetheart," "If I Could Only Learn to Yodel," "Little Sweetheart of the Ozarks," "Deep in the Heart of Texas," "Good Night Soldier," and "Leaning on the Old Top Rail." Most of her albums were collector's items by the 1960s, but in the mid-1960s Starday released some of her recordings in the LP *Sweetheart.*

Patsy wrote many original songs during her long career. Among her compositions were "My Baby's Lullaby," "Me and My Cowboy Sweetheart," "The Buckaroo," "Cowboy Rhythm," "I'm a Little Cowboy Girl," "The Moon Hangs Low," "My Poncho Pony," "A Cowboy Gal," and "I've Found My Cowboy Sweetheart."

In the late 1940s and during the 1950s, Montana kept a busy schedule on the concert circuit and on TV. During 1946–47 she had her own radio program on ABC called *Wake Up and Smile.* She also brought her family into the act for a while. As she recalled for *Music City News,* "At one time, my daughters and I were the only mother and daughters team around. Judy was about five and Beverly was about eight. We traveled as the Patsy Montana Trio."

In 1959, there were reports that she had retired briefly to sell real estate in Manhattan Beach, California, which Patsy later denied. Although her stage work was much more limited in the 1960s and 1970s, she still performed steadily. In the 1970s, she began to find growing interest about her among college-age fans and she did a number of shows on college campuses, where, besides western numbers, she sang such classic country songs as "Wabash Cannonball" and "Great Speckled Bird." She also took part in a number of the 1970s Nashville summer Fan Fair Reunions along with many other veteran country artists.

Comparing her years of intensive touring with the modern era, she said, "When we first started traveling on the road, we didn't have conveniences like hair dryers and air conditioning. I guess you don't miss something you never had. I just wonder how many miles I have slept cramped in a car with my head on the neck of that bass fiddle. I sometimes wonder if some of these younger artists could do what we did. You have to have endurance to be in this business. I feel sorry for these kids who go directly to the top, because they only have one way left to go and that's down."

Patsy sharply cut (but didn't abandon) personal appearances during the 1980s and settled down to semi-retirement in California. On June 27, 1987, she was inducted into the Cowgirl Hall of Fame in Hereford, Texas. She was nominated for the Country Music Hall of Fame several times, but as of 1995 had not received enough votes for induction. In the 1980s and 1990s, some of her old recordings were occasionally included with those of other artists in reissue collections. One of those in print in the mid-1990s was the *Time-Life* album *Country & Western Classics: The Women.*

In the mid-1990s she took part in an ABC-TV special called "Women in Country." The show's format honored veteran country performers like Patsy and Rose Maddox, while featuring members of the new crop of female stars of the 1980s and 1990s such as Pam Tillis and Michelle Wright. In 1996, Patsy again was nominated for the Country Music Hall of Fame, but before the final votes were taken, she died of heart failure at her home in San Jacinto, California. Soon after, it was announced she had finally received the requisite number of approvals and she was inducted into the Hall posthumously during the Country Music Association's televised awards show in October 1996.

MONTGOMERY, JOHN MICHAEL: *Singer, guitarist, songwriter, band leader (Early Times). Born Lexington, Kentucky, January 20, 1965.*

In the late 1980s and early 1990s, it seemed as if a new name was rising to the top of country charts almost weekly. The sudden surge of what seemed like overnight sensations caused some critics to compare modern country with the pop and rock fields, where callow artists in their teens and with limited experience often had one moment in the spotlight and then faded from view. But typical country "newcomers" had spent plenty of time in obscurity performing in out-of-the-way clubs and second-tier fairs before being discovered. In the case of John Michael Montgomery, for example, he was closing in on thirty before he became one of the hottest performers of the mid-1990s.

He had, in fact, been involved in music since his childhood. He grew up on a farm in the Lexington, Kentucky, region, but both his parents were stagestruck and worked local fairs and other events with a band that featured father Harold on vocals and lead guitar, and his mother on drums. When possible they brought their children into the act and John Michael made his stage debut at six. He recalled for *Entertainment* magazine (October 1, 1993) that his father "didn't always have the greatest band in the world, or the greatest P.A. system, or even the greatest music, but he knew how to stand on a stage and give people their money's worth."

Montgomery told Richard Cromelin of the *Los Angeles Times* ("A Rough Country Road," Calendar section, June 26, 1994), that his family "all lived around this big cravin' and that was music. We had musicians come over to our living room every night to play and practice. As a kid, at 2 and 3 o'clock in the mornin' I was allowed to sit there and watch 'em play and get up in the next mornin' and go to school.

"That's what they lived for, to be able to go out and play on the weekends. They would not work a job if it meant that they had to give up their music. If it meant takin' a cut in pay and goin' somewhere that wasn't too nice, then that's what happened."

But the years went by and the family group didn't score any breakthroughs while finances went from bad to worse. The strains finally led to his parents divorcing when he was in his late teens, which was a traumatic event for their children. Still, Harold Montgomery wouldn't give up. He had his son Eddie take over on drums and John Michael was given greater opportunity

to play more guitar parts and sometimes take over on lead vocals. Finally, however, his father also decided he would never realize his dreams and retired from the music field for a while. John Michael took the reins, among other things bringing in Tim Williams on bass guitar, a role Williams still was filling behind Montgomery in the mid-1990s.

The band took any work it could find on the fair and bar circuit in its home region. Then John and his group, called Early Times, entered a state band contest and took first prize. This led to a job as house band at the Austin City Saloon in Lexington. Before long, Montgomery parlayed his good looks—blue eyes, dimpled cheeks, lean, athletic 6'2" build—to set female fans' hearts throbbing. That, combined with his driving country-rock style, made him a local star. Word of his local celebrity status began to open some doors for him. He was courted by Estill Sowards, who became his manager, and Nashville booking agent John Dorris, who brought him to the attention of Rick Blackburn, president of Atlantic Nashville Records.

Blackburn saw Montgomery perform and was impressed, though he felt John Michael should shift from rock-flavored material to "power ballads." He told Cromelin, "I thought, 'As good lookin' as he is, if he can sing some power ballads, that's sure gonna make it interesting because that market is open.'"

Blackburn signed Montgomery in 1990 and set him up with record producer Wyatt Easterling to work on his debut recordings. John Michael soon showed he had a mind of his own. After he and Easterling argued over the project's direction, Montgomery stalked out and made a midnight call to Blackburn, who agreed to bring in a new producer. Montgomery told *Entertainment,* "I thought, 'It might be the end of your career, calling Rick up in the middle of the night,' but I didn't want to put out something I felt wasn't me."

The change proved worthwhile, however. He and the new producer, Doug Johnson, not only got along better, but Johnson was instrumental in bringing in three songs that became major hits, "Life's a Dance," which was chosen for the title track of Montgomery's debut album, the ballad "I Love the Way You Love Me," and "Beer and Bones." The album *Life's a Dance* came out in October 1992 and, buoyed by the success of its title single (which was in the top 4 in *Billboard* in January 1993) rapidly climbed the hit lists. It was still on the charts well into 1994, having easily exceeded R.I.A.A. platinum-award levels. "I Love the Way You Love Me," issued in early 1993, became one of the singles hits of the year, reaching number one in both *Radio & Records* and *Billboard* in May and staying at number one in the latter for almost a month. In the fall, "Beer and Bones" was in the top 15 in *Billboard* and by year-end another single, "I Swear," was in the top 20 on the way to number one in February 1994.

The honors weren't long in coming. As early as March 1993, *Country America* magazine had named him one of the new artists most likely to succeed. Later in the year he was one of the finalists for the Country Music Association's Horizon Award. At year-end, *Billboard* named him the Best New Male Country Artist of 1993.

There were some naysayers who suggested it was his matinee idol features and not his talent that made him a success. Montgomery responded by noting that "images have always been important in show business, especially when television becomes a part of it. . . . But looking good and presenting a certain image is not going to help sell a record that is bad. I don't think you're giving country fans much credit when you think they're gullible enough to buy something just because they like someone's look." ("Travelin' Man," *Tune-In,* Earl Dittman, August 1993.)

Montgomery gained many favorable critical comments from the country magazine field and in mainstream publications like *Stereo Review,* but was viewed less kindly by reviewers at some of the major media like *Rolling Stone* and the *Los Angeles Times.* The *Stereo Review* critic said Montgomery "turns in a first rate collection of traditional jukebox fare, and he sings it like he knows he's going to be the next guy to own Nashville." Typical of *Rolling Stone* feelings were Don McCleese's comments on Montgomery's second album, *Kickin' It Up:* "The power balladry of 'I Swear' suggests that contemporary country is in the midst of a full-blown Bread revival [referring to the soft rock group Bread of years past], while the up-tempo fare on this sophomore effort is just so much mechanical bull."

Country fans and most of Montgomery's country-music peers indicated they felt different. Released in early 1994, *Kickin' It Up* hit number three in *Billboard* in May and was platinum by summer. Academy of Country Music members voted him Best Male Vocalist and also called "I Love the Way You Love Me" Song of the Year as announced on the spring 1994 awards telecast.

Besides his album hit in 1994, Montgomery again did well with singles releases such as "Ropin' the Moon," a top-5 entry in *Billboard* in May, and "Be My Baby Tonight," number one in *Billboard, Radio & Records,* and other hit lists in August. In 1994 CMA voters again included him in the five finalists for the Horizon Award. He didn't win in that category, but "I Swear" earned him CMA Single of the Year honors. In accepting it on the October telecast, he paid emotional tribute to his father, who had recently passed away. He closed out 1994 with the hit single "If You've Got Love," number one in *Radio & Records* the week of November 25.

Oddly, during 1994, "I Swear" not only was a hit for Montgomery, but also provided a Rhythm & Blues best-seller for the soul quartet All-4-One. In the Grammy voting during 1994, both versions were nominated for Single of the Year in their respective categories. During the awards telecast on March 1, 1995, Montgomery joined with All-4-One to sing the number, which was written by Frank J. Myers and Gary Baker. During backstage interviews, Delious Kennedy of the soul group said it was really a coincidence that the two different singles came out, not a marketing ploy by Atlantic Records. "We both recorded it not knowing the other one had. We took our version to the record company president and he had Montgomery's version in his pocket. He listened to both and decided to release them."

Deciding not to give up on a good thing, both followed up by recording their versions of "I Can Love You Like That" for their next albums.

"I Swear" continued to be a good-luck charm for Montgomery, earning Single and Song of the Year nods from the ACM as announced in the May 10, 1995, awards TV show. The awards publicity helped keep his third album, *John Michael Montgomery,* at number one in *Billboard* throughout April and May of 1995. During May, the single "I Can Love You Like That" also reached number one in the magazine.

Offstage, Montgomery was not an extrovert and hoped his sudden stardom wouldn't prevent him from spending time with old friends or going to fast food restaurants or convenience stores without attracting a crowd. There was a time country artists could be "just folks," but the age of hype and TV exposure had changed that. A sign of the times was his experience with autograph seekers. Traditionally, country artists had always been able to talk with fans and sign autographs in a relaxed environment. Montgomery was shocked on one occasion to find that after signing his name countless times until he could hardly raise his hand, he got up to leave and had people still waiting in line start booing. He told Richard Cromelin, "It bears on my mind quite a bit. It's part of it that I just didn't realize."

As he commented in early 1994, "Being a country music star was never in my mind. It was beyond my dreams. I still look at it that way. All I want is to be able to go out and do my shows. As long as people are there and they enjoy what I'm doing, I'll be happy. It's that simple."

He also told interviewer Alanna Nash his achievements had helped make up for his father's disappointments. "My dad always wanted to be a [hit] act, but those dreams disappeared as he got older. So my success is his, too. It means he didn't waste all those years playing honky-tonks."

In the late spring of 1995, the album track "Sold (The Grundy County Auction Incident)," made the charts and gave him still another number-one singles success, reaching that spot in *Billboard* the week of July 1. Later in the year the single "No Man's Land" made the hit lists, peaking at number three in *Billboard.*

Country Music Association voters nominated him in two categories over the summer, for Album of the Year (*John Michael Montgomery*) and Male Vocalist of the Year. Academy of Country Music members failed to place him in the final five in any of the 1995 award categories, but he was a featured performer on the NBC-TV ACM Awards program on April 24, 1996. By then he had another single moving up the charts, "Long As I Live," which was vying for number one on several of them in May.

MORGAN, GEORGE: *Singer, guitarist, songwriter. Born Waverly, Tennessee, June 28, 1925; died Nashville, Tennessee, July 7, 1975.*

A country music "traditionalist," George Morgan never felt at home in the progressive country area of the 1970s. But a host of country fans and fellow performers looked fondly on his many years of stardom and his compositions like "Candy Kisses," which promised to become all-time country standards.

George spent his first two years in Waverly, Tennessee, but a tragic accident to his father that took place two weeks before his birth drastically affected family fortunes. Jack Morgan, who had a small farm and earned additional money by cutting cross-ties for the railroad, was walking across a stretch of railroad track while hunting groundhogs when his boot laces caught in a switchtrack. As luck would have it, a train was coming and, lacking a knife to cut the knotted lace, he had to fall back and break his leg to avoid being run over. The train cut off his leg.

As Morgan told Dixie Deen of *Music City News* (March 1967), "That put an end to his farming and cutting cross-ties days and when I was about two years old, after my brother Bill was born, my daddy had to move to Ohio to get work. . . . He got a job hauling coal with a horse and wagon."

By the time George was three, his father was able to send for the family. "He got a job with the Seiberling Rubber Company [in Barberton, Ohio] and he got a wooden leg around that time. I can remember times during the Depression that he would come home, take off that wooden leg, and the blood would be seeping out of that old stump stocking. These are not pleasant things," he told Deen, "but it is pleasant in my mind to know how much dad loved us to go through all this. I mean, he would work around the clock sometimes just to feed us."

Music, George recalled, was always one of the family's pleasures. "Every Saturday night, mom and dad both being from Tennessee, would tune in to the *Grand Ole Opry*. That was in the days of D. Ford Bailey, way before Roy Acuff and Minnie Pearl. I grew up listening to country music and my love for it was instilled because to my folks it was something from 'down home.'"

George went through grade school and entered high school in Barberton but dropped out in the eleventh grade to go to work. He agreed it wasn't the smartest move. "It wasn't because I had to go to work. We weren't all that poor and dad could have provided for me until I got through high school, but like so many foolish kids, I wanted to go to work." The job he took was in a Barberton restaurant, the first of a variety of occupations he essayed on the way to his music career.

During the mid-1940s, he interrupted his civilian chores to enlist in the Army. However, after three months he received an honorable discharge on medical grounds. After that, he put in time at a range of jobs, including working in a rubber plant, surveying in Oklahoma, and working in several restaurants in Ohio.

He had been playing guitar for some time and slowly was becoming more interested in the possibilities of the music field. In 1947, "we got a little band together and started working for peanuts, and sometimes not even for that."

When a small radio station opened in Wooster, Ohio, Morgan and his band auditioned for it and were hired. "There was no money in it. Our little country band opened up the station every morning for a couple of months, then the other guys in the band couldn't see any future in this and they all quit. I stayed on with my guitar."

While he was doing that, he came up with the song that was to prove his good luck charm, "Candy Kisses." He recalled for *Music City News,* "I was on the way to the station one morning and I was thinking about a girl and it occurred to me that my kisses meant less to her than the candy kisses my mother used to bring home had meant to me when I was a kid."

Meanwhile, he was finding favor with station audiences and his time slot was improved from an early morning one to a 5:00 P.M. period. He also began to have increased exposure on local shows and performed on station WAKR in nearby Akron. One of his disc jockey friends in Akron gave him his next move up by letting him know of an audition for one of the top country stations in the region, Wheeling, West Virginia's, WWVA. George went there, auditioned, and was hired. It was, he noted, "my first big money in radio when they paid me $40 a week. I worked there for a while and then, I don't know why, I got discouraged and decided to quit radio."

Fortunately, station manager Paul Myers loved "Candy Kisses" and persuaded Morgan to make a demonstration record of it, which he sent to RCA Victor's Nashville offices. Bob Ross of RCA happened to play the record for WSM executives just when they were looking for new talent. They soon picked up the phone and asked Morgan to come to Nashville for an audition. Ironically, RCA didn't sign him. Even as he was arriving in Nashville, Columbia artists & repertoire executive Art Satherly was back in Wheeling trying to find him. Satherly hurried back to Nashville, sought out Morgan, and soon had him signed to a recording contract.

Things swiftly fell into line for George in 1948. He joined *Opry* station WSM and soon found "Candy Kisses" a major hit. He had to share honors with several cover records; including his release, there were four top-10 versions of his song in 1948–49, though his was the number-one hit. (The others were by Cowboy Copas, Eddie Kirk, and Red Foley.) In 1949, he had four more top-10 hits: "Crybaby Heart," "Please Don't Let Me Love You," "Rainbow in My Heart," and "Room Full of Roses." He didn't have that volume of top-10 singles throughout the 1950s, though he did place many songs on lower-chart levels over the decade. His top-ranked singles of the period included "Almost" in 1952, a top-10 hit of his composition "I'm in Love Again" in 1959, and, in 1960, the top-10 single "You're the Only Good Thing."

After being a featured *Opry* star for the first part of the 1950s, Morgan left in 1956 to star on his own show on WLAC-TV in Nashville. He rejoined the *Opry* as a regular in 1959 and was still a show member in the 1970s. During the 1960s and 1970s, his TV credits included appearances on shows hosted by Bobby Lord, Porter Wagoner, the Wilburn Brothers, on *Hee Haw,* and on *Country Music Hall.* His personal appearances took him all over the United States and Canada and to audiences in Europe as well.

Among the other songs he recorded over the years were "Slipping Around," "You Loved Me Just Enough to Hurt Me," "You're Not Home Yet," "I'm Not Afraid," "A Picture That's New," "No Man Should Hurt as Bad as I Do," "You're the Only Star in My Blue Heaven," "Cheap Affair," "Cry of the Lamb," "Ever So Often," "Wheel of Hurt," "Lonesome Record," "Jesus Savior Pilot Me," "Little Pioneer," "Mansion over the Hilltop," "No One Knows It Better than Me," "Oh Gentle Shepherd," "Shot in the Dark," "Walking Shoes," and "Whither Thou Goest."

His Columbia albums included *Candy Kisses, Morgan, By George, Greatest Country & Western Hits, Slipping Around, Tender Loving Care, Red Roses for a Blue Lady, George Morgan* (issued 3/64); *George Morgan and Marion Worth* (issued 9/64).

The early impact of rock on the country field played a part in a decline in his recording volume in the early 1960s. This finally resulted in a closing out of his association with Columbia in 1966, ending an eighteen-year relationship. He moved over to Starday Records, and his debut LP on the label, *Candy Kisses,* came out in early 1967. This was followed soon after by the album *Hits by Candlelight.* Later releases on Starday included *The Best of George Morgan* and *The Real George Morgan.* He also was represented on the Nashville label in the early 1970s with *Room Full of Roses.*

During the 1970s, George recorded new material for a series of labels, including Step and MCA Records. During the last years of his career, he was on the Four Star label and was the master of ceremonies for that company's show during the summer of 1975 Fan Fair festivities in Nashville.

On May 26, 1975, Morgan suffered a heart attack while installing an antenna on the roof of his Nashville home. He recovered and resumed his music activities, but then found out he needed open heart surgery and entered Baptist Hospital in Nashville in early July for the operation. Unfortunately, complications arising from the surgery brought his illustrious career to a close—he died on July 7. Only a short time before going into the hospital he had made his last appearance on the *Opry.* It had been a joyous affair at a time when no one expected the tragedy of later weeks. His *Opry* friends had given him a cake in honor of his fifty-first birthday and George had proudly introduced his daughter, Lorrie, for her *Opry* singing debut.

MORGAN, LORRIE: *Singer, songwriter. Born Goodlettsville, Tennessee, June 27, 1959.*

With an illustrious country music last name and years of learning the fine points of the genre at the feet of many giants in the field—years that included a debut appearance on the *Grand Ole Opry* at age thirteen—it's not surprising that Lorrie Morgan finally became a star in her own right. But despite those advantages it wasn't an easy climb, and, for a while, it seemed as though she might have to be satisfied to bask in the reflected glow of George Morgan's accomplishments.

The year she was born, 1959, her father, after a hiatus of several years, had rejoined the *Opry* as a regular cast member, a position he occupied until his untimely death in 1975. From her earliest years, Lorrie spent many hours backstage at the *Opry* or on tour with her father and other country music luminaries. Her father naturally tutored her in stage presence and vocal skills, grooming her for her first chance to perform on stage at Opryland. This finally came in the 1970s, when she was either thirteen or fifteen (depending on which version is correct).

She recalled her first appearance as coming in her thirteenth year. "My little 13-year-old knees were absolutely knocking, but I saw dad standing there just bawling, and those people gave me a standing ovation. I thought, 'This is what I'm doing the rest of my life.' I thought it was going to be that easy. Little did I know."

It certainly might have gone easier if she could have remained under her father's wing a lot longer. But he was felled by a heart attack and died on July 7, 1975. After that, for several years she sought to keep the Morgan name in lights, touring with her mother or one other musician and using a club's house band or a pick-up group for instrumental support. She recalled it as a frustrating period where she was constantly on the road moving from venue to venue for one night stands or short engagements trying to match her vocals with bands that were often pretty shaky.

To get off that grind, she sought more regular working hours in Nashville, where her dad's friends could open some doors. "I started writing and got on as a writer at Acuff-Rose, and from there I went on to be their receptionist. I did a lot of demo sessions during my lunch hour and after work. Any time they asked me to do a demo, I would do it, and finally I was signed to Hickory Records which was owned by Acuff-Rose."

Hickory issued several albums and singles. Her album efforts didn't attract many followers, but a couple of singles made the charts. This work, coupled with intensive touring to promote her releases, helped win her a nomination from the Academy of Country Music as Best New Female Artist. But she didn't win the award, and her recording output didn't do well enough to keep her on the label. She sought another contract, but doors didn't open and for a time she considered giving up a performing career in favor of conventional jobs or domesticity. After an earlier failed marriage, she wed singer Keith Whitley in 1986, a union that resulted in the birth of a son, Jessie Keith. Whitley adopted her daughter, Morgan Anastasia, from the earlier marriage.

But it was difficult to give up on her dreams. She recalled, "I said to myself, 'This is the last time I'm going to try,'" as she worked on new material to place before record company A&R executives. "I was working the road, doing the Nashville Network, playing the *Grand Ole Opry* and still doing some demo sessions and writing, and I knew there would be one more opportunity for a record label to come my way."

The label turned out to be RCA (which later was acquired by Germany's Bertlesmann organization). "Had RCA not accepted that session, I wasn't sure what I was going to do, but I wasn't going to get turned down any more."

Her RCA debut album, *You Can Leave the Light On,* came out in 1989 and soon made the charts. It provided her with a series of chart hits including "Trainwreck of Emotion," "Dear Me," "Out of Your Shoes" (a number-one hit), and "He Talks to Me." A song she recorded with Keith Whitley also made the charts and was chosen as Vocal Event of the Year in the 1990 Country Music Association voting. In 1990, she was also a finalist for CMA's Female Vocalist of the Year and its Horizon Award. She also was nominated by TNN/*Music City News* voters for 1990 Female Artist of the Year and Star of Tomorrow. The latter poll in 1991 named her duet with husband Whitley as the Video Collaboration of the Year.

But by then she was still trying to recover her balance after tragedy had struck in May 1989, when Whitley had died of alcohol poisoning, leaving her to raise her two children as a single mother. Still stunned by the loss, she rushed into another, unfortunately short-lived marriage in the early 1990s.

She could take some solace from the fact that her career continued to prosper. Her second RCA album, *Something in Red,* issued in 1991, also became a run-

away success, reaching 130 weeks on the *Billboard* charts in the summer of 1993. The album, which exceeded platinum record levels, provided Lorrie with such singles hits as the title track, which rose to number seven on the *Radio & Records* chart the week of July 10, 1992; "We Both Walk"; "A Picture of Me Without You"; and "Except for Monday," number three in *R&R* the week of March 6, 1992.

Her next album, *Watch Me,* issued October 10, 1992, on BNA Entertainment (another Bertlesmann label), quickly made the hit lists and was still on *Billboard* charts in late June 1994 after eighty-three weeks. After reaching its peak position of number fifteen in *Billboard* it went on to earn Lorrie another platinum record from the R.I.A.A. The title track rose to number one in *R&R* the week of November 6, 1992, and was followed by the chart hits "What Part of Me" (number one in *R&R* the week of February 28, 1993), "I Guess You Had to Be There" (number ten in *R&R* the week of June 16, 1993), and "Half Enough" (number seven in *R&R* the week of November 29).

Lorrie's honors during 1991–92 included a 1991 CMA nomination for Female Vocalist of the Year and, from TNN/*Music City News,* nominations for Single of the Year (for "Till a Tear Becomes a Rose") and for Female Artist of the Year. She also received the last-named nomination in 1992. In 1992, she cohosted the Academy of Country Music nationally televised awards show (in which she was a finalist for Top Female Vocalist) with Clint Black and Travis Tritt.

During the first years of the 1990s she became a familiar figure to many TV viewers with guest spots on many shows including *48 Hours, Geraldo, The Tonight Show, TNN All-Star Salute to Ralph Emery, The 65 Years of the Grand Ole Opry, ABC-TV's New Year's Rockin' Eve, Hot Country Nights, Austin City Limits, Farm Aid,* and many others. Through the mid-1990s, she continued to add more TV credits to her resume while also headlining many concert events throughout the U.S. and in other parts of the world.

In the fall of 1993, BNA issued the album *Merry Xmas from London,* which reached top spots in *Billboard* late in the year. This was followed in May 1994 by the album *War Paint,* which was in the top 10 by June. The same month the single "If You Came Back from Heaven" (cowritten by Lorrie and record producer Richard Landis) made the charts, followed late in the summer by "Heart over Mind." Early in that year, she had received a Cable ACE nomination for Best Dramatic or Theatrical Special for her acting ability in the drama *Proudheart.*

While her career continued to thrive, her personal life remained difficult. Many gossip columnists had taken note of her pairing with Dallas Cowboys star quarterback, Troy Aikman. After a year of dating, she sadly noted in early 1994, it was just "another busted-up relationship." Her problems during the first part of the 1990s also had included a bankruptcy. Her health also had not been the best in late 1993 and early 1994, as she told Teresa George, Executive Editor of CMA's *Close Up.* "I've been very sick. I've had bronchitis and pleurisy. As a matter of fact, I still have pleurisy. It's not as bad as it was, or I wouldn't be here. I couldn't even walk a week ago."

She added, sadly, "I think to myself sometimes, 'Why does this happen to me? Why do the loves of my life go away?' There's a reason, and I know we don't always see the reason when it's happening, and I know a lot of people try and say, 'Well, it's to make you stronger, and it makes you sing with heart.' There's a time when it's like, 'Okay, enough is enough.' "

In the spring of 1995 her single "I Didn't Know My Own Strength" debuted on the charts and by early summer was in top levels. On June 27, 1995, BNA issued her *Greatest Hits* disc which peaked at number five in *Billboard* and remained in top chart rungs into 1996. On September 1, 1995, the R.I.A.A. presented her with a gold record award and by the spring of 1996 it had gone past platinum. In the fall of 1995 her single "Back in Your Arms Again" gained considerable airplay and rose to number four in *Billboard.* She maintained her hit singles pace into 1996 with the chart-makers "Standing Tall" and "By My Side," the last named a duet with rising newcomer Jon Randall.

MORRIS, GARY: *Singer, guitarist, songwriter, actor. Born Ft. Worth, Texas, December 7, c. mid-1950s.*

Texan Gary Morris had a strong impact on the 1980s country music scene, though that seemed to fade once the 1990s came along. However, in the meantime he had honed his acting skills, which promised to give him an anchor to windward if his country career failed to reignite.

In his hometown of Ft. Worth, Texas, he grew up in a musical environment that in the 1960s embraced a variety of genres from country to blues and rock. He listened to whatever happened to be dominating the radio waves during those years, but his main attention was on sports. An above-average athlete, he lettered in four sports in high school and starred in football, which earned him a scholarship to a Texas college. Once there, his interest in sports started to wane and, having a good voice and some talent on guitar, he formed a trio with two friends to play weekend dates in and around Abilene for $15 a night.

After his sophomore year in college, he dropped out and moved to Colorado, settling first in Colorado Springs, then moving to Boulder. He pursued country music in both places, playing small clubs nights and weekends while rounding out his income with various day jobs. His Boulder pursuits included construction work and some bar gigs, where his pay took the form of beer and cheeseburgers and any tips he could manage.

After a while he moved on to Denver, where he did some work writing advertising jingles for Coors Beer and Frontier Airlines commercials and honed his performing skills at the head of another trio, which gained house-entertainer status at Taylor's Supper Club.

Seeking wider exposure, he got his opportunity in 1976, when he was part of a trio hired to perform at campaign stops for presidential hopeful Jimmy Carter. After Carter became president, Morris's group was invited to play on a night when the Carters had asked members of the Country Music Association Board of Directors to be their guests. (In the mid-1980s, Morris himself became a CMA Board member.) Among the latter was Norro Wilson of Warner Brothers, who enjoyed the trio's work, though not enough to pull a contract from his pocket. But the acquaintance struck up between him and Morris eventually led to Gary's signing with the label in 1979.

Not long after Gary's debut recordings came out on Warner Brothers, his name began to show up on the country charts. In 1984, he placed the single "Wind Beneath My Sails" in top-chart positions, which brought Song of the Year Awards to writers Larry Henley and Jeff Silbar from both the Academy of Country Music and the CMA. CMA voters also nominated Gary for Male Vocalist of the Year. His 1985 output included the single and video of "Second Hand Heart," which received a CMA nomination for Music Video of the Year. In 1986, Gary received still another nomination in the latter category from the CMA for "100% Chance of Rain." The 1986 CMA voting also brought nominations for Male Vocalist of the Year and, for his recorded work with Crystal Gayle, Vocal Duo of the Year. The two artists also received CMA Vocal Duo of the Year nominations in 1987. During the spring of 1987, his album *Plain Brown Wrapper* was on the charts.

In 1985, Gary demonstrated acting talent in a somewhat unusual setting for a country star, as a featured performer in the Joseph Papp presentation of *La Bohème* in New York City. By then, he was also drawing the attention of TV soap opera fans for his role in *The Colbys.*

In the 1990s, Gary continued his activities in various parts of the entertainment spectrum. He didn't place any recordings on top-chart spots during the first half of the decade, but he remained a popular concert artist. Among his credits in the early 1990s was a 1991 command performance for the Queen of England, Elizabeth II, and her husband, Prince Philip, following the Governor's Dinner at the LBJ Library in Austin, Texas. His set in the 1990s usually included his composition "Somebody Lives There," a song about the homeless whose royalties were earmarked for the Habitat for Humanity, an organization whose objective was to help the homeless find permanent homes—a cause his original sponsor, Jimmy Carter, had been promoting for many years. In the fall of 1995, he completed work on a new live album which was issued by year-end.

MULLICAN, MOON: *Singer, organist, pianist, songwriter. Born Polk County, near Corrigan, Texas, March 27, 1909; died Beaumont, Texas, January 1, 1967.*

Aubrey "Moon" Mullican's family assumed that he would someday succeed to the management of his father's rich eighty-seven acre farm. But when Moon was eight, his father bought a pump-organ that was to change Moon's future. Within a few years, he had worked out a two-finger right-hand style of playing that was to provide the grounds for his claim to the title "King of the Hillbilly Piano Players."

Moon's skill in organ playing continued to improve. He played for his church when he was in his teens, and after a while, he branched out into playing piano for local dances. In Lufkin, Texas, in the late 1920s, he took home his first paycheck for a musical performance and decided to make music his occupation.

He moved to Houston, where he began accompanying local folk artists and eventually formed his own band, which played at clubs and on radio in many places in Louisiana and Texas during the 1930s. For a time, he was featured on station KPBX in Beaumont, Texas. During the decade, he also made the first of many records on such labels as Coral, Decca, and King. In 1939, he went to Hollywood for a role in the film *Village Barn Dance*. Audiences in California clubs were as impressed with his personal appearances as those in the Southwest.

In the 1940s, Mullican returned home to Texas. Part of the time, he owned his own nightclubs in Beaumont and Port Arthur. In the mid- and late-1940s, he began to move into the big time with his records of some of his own songs. In 1947, he had a number-one bestseller in "New Jole Blon," on the King label. The song placed second as Best Hillbilly Record of 1947 in polls conducted by *Cash Box* and the Juke Box Operators association. The following year, he had the third-ranked song in those polls, as well as a gold-record-seller in his composition "Sweeter than the Flowers." Moon hit the top-10 bracket on the charts with another King Records success in 1950, "Good Night Irene," and topped it that same year with the number-one "I'll Sail My Ship Alone." He had a third major hit in 1950 with "Mona Lisa." Then, in 1951, another Mullican composition (co-authored with W. C. Redbird) closed out his cycle of hits, "Cherokee Boogie."

For the rest of the 1950s and early 1960s, Mullican was active with tours that took him into all the states and overseas as well. He was featured on his own program on KECK, Odessa, Texas, and guested on such shows as *Grand Ole Opry*, ABC-TV's *Jubilee U.S.A.*, and the *Big D Jamboree*. Some of his other recordings of these and earlier years were "Columbus Stockade Blues," "Sugar Beet," "Jole Blon's Sister," "Early Morning Blues," "The Leaves Mustn't Fall," "Well Oh Well," "Sweeter than the Flowers No. 2," "Moon's Rock," "Pipeliner's Blues," "Jambalaya," "Every Which-Away," and "Moon's Tune."

Moon's long and illustrious career ended in 1967 when he was stricken with a fatal heart attack in Beaumont.

MURPHEY, MICHAEL MARTIN: *Singer, guitarist, record producer, songwriter. Born Dallas, Texas, early 1940s.*

Most artists in the 1960s and 1970s strongly resented being typecast musically. The best way to prevent that, of course, is to demonstrate capability in different stylings, something Michael Martin Murphey certainly did in his writing and performing efforts, at times turning out mainstream rock, at others country or folk-rock, and at still others, country. Thus he kept his career options open, though he also tended to keep possible fans off balance.

Murphey came by his country leanings naturally. Born and raised in Texas, he heard a mixture of country, rock, and pop throughout his formative years. A precocious child, he taught himself to play a plastic ukulele at six and began writing stories and poems at seven. His poetic bent later showed up in some classic songs, such as "Geronimo's Cadillac" from his debut solo LP on A&M in 1971 and the gold-record hit "Wildfire" in 1975.

Michael was performing a blend of folk, country, and rock during his early years in high school and had appeared in many small clubs and coffee houses in the Southwest by the time he got his diploma. By that time he had headed a band that was very successful with Dallas fans and on local TV and had gained other honors as well, including placing some of his poems in a national poetry anthology. He had an offer to appear on a national TV series in his late teens, but declined in favor of concentrating on in-person singing dates.

When he was twenty, he moved to Southern California, where he enrolled at the University of California at Los Angeles, taking courses in writing and poetry. Six months after he arrived in Los Angeles he had a songwriting contract with Sparrow Music and also was a regular at Randy Sparks's (of New Christy Minstrels fame) folk night-club, Ledbetter's, in West Los Angeles. Those activities brought a widening circle of friendships with other promising but still unknown artists, people the likes of Jackson Browne, Don Henley, and Glenn Frey (later founding members of the Eagles), Linda Ronstadt, and Jerry Jeff Walker.

At one point in the mid-1960s, it seemed that Murphey might beat all of them into the national spotlight. He organized a band called the Lewis and Clark Expedition that won a lot of attention in local showcase performances in Los Angeles. The group's debut LP, *I Feel Good, I Feel Bad,* made the national charts. He recalled, "It was an exciting time, one of incredible experimentation and cross-pollination of musical styles." But somehow things fell apart, partly because of management problems and partly due to personality clashes. Discouraged, for a time Michael withdrew from the industry treadmill to a remote haunt in the San Gabriel Mountains east of L.A. He wrote songs but mailed them in to his publishers, avoiding personal appearances.

In the late 1960s, he decided to go back to Texas, settling in Austin, where he took part in the movement that laid the groundwork for much of the progressive country trend in the 1970s. He assembled a new band that combined folk, country, and even some jazz, with rock elements. The group gained a local following and proved to be a springboard to his solo career. After record producer Bob Johnston heard Murphey perform in the Austin area, he offered Michael studio time, which resulted in an album that aroused the interest of a number of major record firms.

After considering various offers, Murphey chose A&M, which released his album label debut, *Geronimo's Cadillac,* in 1971 and followed it with *Cosmic Cowboy Souvenir* in 1973. *Geronimo's Cadillac* was called "brilliant" by the *Times* of London and brought an accolade from *Rolling Stone* magazine that called Murphey "the best new songwriter in the country" (though by then he'd been turning out originals for a long time, many of which had been included in other performers' albums). *Cowboy Souvenir* became a cult favorite, but never a major hit.

A somewhat disgruntled Murphey left A&M and a while later signed with Epic. He gave vent to some of his feelings when he took the stage at his first CBS sales convention and railed against industry overcontrol in "Nobody's Gonna Tell Me How to Play My Music." The song was included in his debut release on Epic in early 1974, *Michael Murphey.* In late 1974, he moved his family from Texas to Colorado, where he worked on material for his second Epic collection. Among the songs he recorded there at Caribou Ranch were "Wildfire" and "Carolina in the Pines," which became major singles hits in 1975 along with the album that contained them, *Blue Sky, Night Thunder.* In support of those releases, Murphey embarked on a highly successful cross country tour of the United States in 1975.

He continued to probe new musical and lyrical themes in succeeding albums with increasing emphasis on folk and country-styled material. He placed a number of songs on the singles charts in the second half of the 1970s, though none had the impact of "Wildfire." They included such songs as the rocker "Renegade" and country-oriented "Mansion on the Hill" from the late 1975 LP *Swans Against the Sun* and "Cherokee Fiddle" from the 1976 album release, *Flowing Free Forever.* His seventh solo album, *Lone Wolf,* came out at the start of 1978 and his eighth, *Peaks, Valleys, Honky Tonks and Alleys* in early 1978. The last named was one of the most heavily country-oriented albums in his career, having only a few dashes of rock on some tracks. The album included live updates of "Cosmic Cowboy" and "Geronimo's Cadillac," a fine rework of a 1972 song, "Backslider's Wine," and a new country-rock original (cowritten with Gary Nunn) titled "Years Behind Bars."

In 1978, Murphey moved to Taos, New Mexico, where he sought out influences in the Indian and Spanish cultures to add to his country & western background. After he had settled in, he signed a new recording contract with Liberty Records, which issued his debut on the label, *Michael Martin Murphey,* at the start of the 1980s. The album provided three top-10 singles, including "What's Forever For," which reached number one on some charts and helped bring him Best New Artist awards in the 1982–83 voting of both the Academy of Country Music and Country Music Association. He gained still more top-10 singles from succeeding albums such as the 1983 *The Heart Never Lies.* Those mid-1980s chartmakers included "Don't Count the Rainy Days," "Disenchanted," "What She Wants," "A Long Line of Love," "A Face in the Crowd" (a duet with Holly Dunn), and "I'm Gonna Miss You Girl."

His 1980s activities included completion of a number of successful videos, such as "Disenchanted," which won several awards, "A Long Line of Love," which was a finalist in several major video competitions, and "What She Wants." The last-named song and video dealt with the problem of teenage runaways and was one instance of Murphey's involvement in major causes. Among his concerns are Indian rights, environmental issues, and, at one point, lobbying the New Mexico state legislature in Sante Fe for passage of an emergency medical bill.

By the end of the 1980s, Murphey had joined the roster of Warner Brothers Records, where he sought to keep the western in Country & Western a viable force. He called his 1990 album, *Cowboy Songs,* "my most deeply felt work. This is the music of my people, my land, my culture and my own life.

"The cowboy is our Orpheus, or Ulysses. The history of the West is our Illiad and Odyssey, because it's the most dramatic clash of ideals and mores, values and morals that we've had in this country since the Revolutionary War. . . . This means to me what the blues meant to B. B. King, bluegrass means to Ricky Skaggs, jazz means to Wayne Shorter, and pop and rock means to Paul McCartney. It's really my roots, stuff I heard as a kid and want my children to hear."

To give expression to those concepts, Murphey organized the first WestFest in 1987, an event still going strong in the mid-1990s. After his initial recordings for Warners, he also helped persuade the company to establish the Warner Western label. The WestFest format comprised a series of sets over several days stressing country, western and Indian music, and related creative areas. As an example, the event held September 5–7, 1992, at Cooper Mountain, Colorado, featured country acts that included Vince Gill, Brooks & Dunn, Suzy Bogguss, the Texas Tornados, and others; Western performers that included Red Steagall, Don Edwards, Sons of the San Joaquin, Riders in the Sky, and cowboy poet Waddie Mitchell; and Native American entertainers Bearheart, Robert Mirabal, the Dennis Alley Wisdom Indian Dances, and Bill Miller.

Murphey played a set per day, covering styles from "cowboy rap" to C&W and introduced material planned for his 1993 album of songs about western outlaws. He was happy to point out that some of the West-Fest artists (Mitchell, Edwards, Sons of the San Joaquin) already had albums out on Warner Western with new ones by Mitchell, Steagall, and others planned for 1993–94. Interest in his WestFest concept continued to rise and total attendance at three concerts in 1994 topped 50,000. This caused him to add two more dates in addition to the main series at Copper Mountain in September 1994, an approach maintained into 1996. During the summer of 1995, Warner Western released his *Sagebrush Symphony* album, a live recording with the San Antonio Symphony.

MURPHY, DAVID LEE: *Singer, guitarist, songwriter, band leader (Blue Tick Hounds). Born Herrin, Illinois, January 7, c. early 1960s.*

In the "good-ol'-boy" country music tradition, it took David Lee Murphy more than a decade to savor his first major album release, the 1994 MCA *Out with a Bang.* Of course, he wasn't from the South, though he did grow up in the southern part of the midwest state of Illinois. Country music, of course, has always been strong in that area, and listening to "down home" recordings on the radio in the sixties and seventies helped inspire a belief in his potential in the field during his teenage years.

After working on his songwriting abilities and performing locally for some years, during the summer of 1983, Murphy decided the time was right to seek his fortunes in Nashville. He recalled, "From the day [in July 1983] that I pulled into town with the tarp flying on the back of my [pickup] truck, I tried to get recognition as a songwriter." His goal was to use his writing skills as a stepping stone to becoming a recording artist. He was a good enough performer to hold his own on the local bar scene, and late in 1983 managed to gain an opening act spot in a Nashville show headlined by Steve Earle. He felt confident he was on his way to the top of his field, but as he said later, it proved to be the first step in "the 10 year program" of "paying dues and scratching out a living."

From a performing standpoint, those years weren't easy, as he found whatever gigs he could in the honky-

tonk and nightclub circuit. For his act he assembled a four-piece band called the Blue Tick Hounds. "We played all the little bars in Nashville and every dive between here and Atlanta. We opened a few concerts. For all that we put into it, I guess we broke even."

As far as his songwriting side, he commented, "You move from club to club, from the never-done-anything club, to the finally got-a-song-cut club to the got-a-cut-by-a-major-artist club." Relatively speaking, the last-named goal didn't take all that long. In 1985, superstar Reba McEntire recorded his composition "Red Roses Won't Work Now." Before the end of the decade other artists had recorded his material, including Dobie Gray and Doug Stone. (Stone's recording was of "High Weeds and Rust.")

By the start of the 1990s, Murphy had a manager who, besides setting up bookings for the band, also shopped demo tapes to major record companies. In the fall of 1992 the latter played a tape for the assistant to MCA artists & repertoire executive Tony Brown. Brown, later listening to the material, not only decided to sign David Lee, but also chose the song "Just Once" from the demo for use on the soundtrack of the film *8 Seconds* (a movie starring Luke Perry as the late bull-riding champion Lane Frost). Released as a single in March 1994, "Just Once" (cowritten by Murphy and K. Tribble) provided Murphy with his first charted performance. The song spent many weeks on the charts, entering the *Billboard* Top 40 in June.

Meanwhile Murphy had completed work on an album, *Out with a Bang,* issued by MCA in April 1994. Despite its title, the album wasn't an immediate hit, but buoyed by success of a series of singles drawn from it, the disc debuted in *Billboard* the week of June 3, 1995, and reached the top 10 in November. The singles included "Fish Ain't Bitin'" (words and music by Murphy), on the charts in the fall of 1994; "Party Crowd" (written by Murphy and J. Henson) which made the top 20 in June 1995; and "Dust on the Bottle" (written by Murphy) which rose to number one in *Billboard* in the fall of 1995.

The album included a good share of what Murphy called his "Saturday-night-in-a-pickup-truck-with-the-windows-rolled-down-having-a-good-time-party-music," but also demonstrated his ability to write and sing material with different tempos and more somber insights. A somewhat unusual writing collaboration—with Minnie Pearl—provided the track "Why Can't People Just Get Along." In late 1995 the title track from the album, cowritten by Murphy and K. Tribble, was issued and rose to top chart positions in early 1996. In the spring he achieved another singles hit with his self-penned "Every Time I Get Around You."

MURRAY, ANNE: *Singer, ukulele player. Born Springhill, Nova Scotia, Canada, June 20, 1945.*

For someone who had to be persuaded to take her

first job as a performer, Anne Murray had come far indeed by the early 1980s. After a career that had it ups and downs in the 1970s, she came back strongly the latter part of the decade to become firmly established as one of the reigning stars of both pop and country music. Yet she had come close to making high school teaching her life profession.

The daughter of a rural physician, she grew up with five brothers in the coal mining town of Springhill, Nova Scotia. Although brought up in a middle-class home, Anne still was exposed to some of the rougher aspects of life. She told columnist Joan Sutton in 1978, "Living in a small town, that's pretty damned basic. Especially a coal mining town where every day these men flirt with death. Coal miners are pretty solid stock. They've had so many disasters in that town and they just bounce back. I've never seen anything like it. I'm sure that's got to have been an influence on me. Although I was never directly involved, all my friends' fathers were miners and there's a certain mentality, a certain very basic straight-ahead outlook on life."

Growing up in Springhill, Anne was exposed to country music, which was popular in Canada's rural areas, though she never thought of herself as a country singer until her career got under way. Her musical interests in high school tended more towards pop and folk. Still, it wasn't until she was halfway through college at the University of New Brunswick that she made her first halting move toward show business, auditioning for a job on the CBC-TV summer show *Sing Along Jubilee* in 1964.

William Langstroth, later to become her husband, was cohost and associate producer of the show at the time. He recalled for *Billboard* magazine (October 20, 1979) that Murray was one of eighty-five applying for work. "We auditioned the chorus first and I remembered she sat on a stool accompanying herself on a baritone ukulele, and led the others in 'Mary Don't You Weep,' which was a hot folk song of the sixties.

"After we were done there were only two of them left, Anne and another girl. But we couldn't hire her because we had all the altos we needed. I told her to keep in touch."

But she stuck in the mind of both Langstroth and his associate Brian Ahern. Two years later Langstroth wired and cabled the university trying to find her. When he did, she wasn't interested; she had decided she would take her B.A. and teach physical education in high school. "She gave me a lot of lip," Langstroth said. "I told her she should try again. She said, 'No way. I'm not coming to your stupid auditions.' But I kept talking and she showed up and we hired her." (She was on the show for four seasons.)

Even then, Anne was dubious about his and Ahern's suggestions that she devote full time to music. Ahern in particular was anxious to groom her for recording work. As she told Bob Allen for an article in *Country*

Music (July/August 1979), "I remember when I was still teaching [at a high school on Prince Edward Island], Brian Ahern sent me special delivery letters telling me to come on up to Toronto where he was learning to be a record producer. I thought he was crazy! In fact, when I did finally get there, I remember going down to the hock shop to get two of his guitars out of hock. That's how badly off he was. That was in the fall of '68."

Ahern persevered and got Murray the chance to record her first album, *What About Me,* on Arc Records, a small Canadian label. That, in turn, led to a recording contract with Capitol Records of Canada. One of the songs she recorded was "Snowbird." The single was released in the United States and became a major hit on both country and pop charts in 1970, as did her debut album on U.S. Capitol of the same title (issued in August 1970). The single earned her a gold record.

Capitol, which was based in Hollywood, California, brought her to the West Coast to try to give her the star treatment. Once in the United States, she guested on a number of TV shows, including many appearances on Glen Campbell's series. She also went out on intensive concert tours and recorded more material for Capitol. But it was something less than a halcyon time. For one thing, Anne felt ill at ease. She told a *Billboard* reporter (October 20, 1979), "I was plucked out of Springhill, Nova Scotia, and dropped on a Hollywood sound stage. I felt like Dorothy in Oz. Exactly like Dorothy, come to think of it. All I wanted to do was go home."

To add to her problems, there was a long relatively dry spell between major hits. She told Sutton, "The worst times was between 'Snowbird' and 'Danny's Song'—two and a half years waiting for that second song—that was really awful. Playing those dingy, terrible clubs all across the United States, for weeks and weeks and nobody cared. NOBODY! It was like beating your head against a stone wall. I learned nothing. It was a waste of time as far as I'm concerned. I gained nothing. I didn't make any money. I didn't do anything. A lot of people say you have to pay your dues and all that, but I don't think it was character building—I don't think it was anything but just rotten."

Murray did have a number of charted releases in the early 1970s, but for a long time none came close to the success of "Snowbird," a situation that causes industry people to begin to think of an artist as a one-hit phenomenon. Those interim singles were "Sing High—Sing Low" in 1970; "Talk It Over in the Morning," "A Stranger in My Place," and "Put Your Hand in the Hand" in 1971; and "Cotton Jenny" in 1972. Capitol also released a number of LPs over this period: *Anne Murray* (2/71); *Talk It Over in the Morning* (9/71); *Anne Murray/Glen Campbell* (11/71); *Annie* (4/72).

The turnaround came after Capitol issued Anne's single of the Kenny Loggins composition "Danny's Song" in 1973. The song made both pop and country upper-chart levels as did the LP of the title issued in April 1973. Other singles on both pop and country charts in 1973 were "What About Me," "Send a Little Love My Way," and "Love Song." "Love Song" was on the lists from late 1973 into early 1974, and the album of that title, issued by Capitol in February 1974, also did well. The year 1974 provided some singles that only made pop lists—"You Won't See Me," "Just One Look," and "Day Tripper." But it also provided Anne with two major country chart hits, "He Thinks I Don't Care," which rose to number one, and "Son of a Rotten Gambler," which made the country top 5. Anne also had two more LPs released in 1974, *Country* (8/74) and *Highly Prized Possession* (11/74).

Things seemed to be going well for Anne as 1975 began. Early in the year she was awarded the Grammy for Best Country Vocal Performance Female for the *Love Song* album. Murray's position as a concert attraction and desired TV guest artist had never been stronger. Once more she felt something was missing from her life. She told Bob Allen, "There were times when I just couldn't go on. It happened to me twice. The year after 'Snowbird' [1971] I didn't know what I was doing. It was a matter of stopping and saying, 'Look, I don't *have* to do anything.' Then again in 1975 I just said, 'Look, I just don't see any point to any of this.'"

What she felt was wrong was the lack of a meaningful private life. In 1975, she decided to give up the entertainment grind for a while and regain control over her personal activities. In June 1975 she married William Langstroth. Both of them wanted a family and a few months later Anne was carrying their first child. The baby, a boy named William Stewart Langstroth, Jr., was born in August 1976. (A few years later, the Langstroths added a girl, Dawn Joann, born April 20,1979.)

During Murray's absence from the music field in the mid-1970s, Capitol continued to release new recordings. Among them were the singles "Sunday Sunrise," "The Call," and "Uproar" in 1975; "Things" and "Golden Oldie" in 1976; and "Sunday School to Broadway" in 1977. LPs issued in the mid-1970s included *Together* (10/75) and *Keeping in Touch* (9/76). Most of those releases made the charts, but none was a massive success.

In 1978, after being out of the spotlight for several years, Anne decided to begin work as a singer again, but on her own terms. She intended to live and raise her family in Toronto (with occasional sojourns in her beloved Nova Scotia), record in Toronto studios, and only accept concert or TV engagements that suited her schedule. It was a matter, she told Bob Allen, of getting her priorities straight. "Someone can call me now and tell me there's a million dollar deal in Vegas and I'll say, well, what does this mean? Does that mean I have to work for six weeks? Does it mean I'll have to live in a hotel for six weeks? Because if it does, I'm not gonna do it.

"People wring their hands and tear out their hair at my attitude. But dammit, I just want it to be right y'know. I want it to be comfortable for me and my family, because they're the most important people. Nothing else is important anymore."

In late 1977, she went into the studios with producer Jim Ed Norman (her longtime association with Brian Ahern had ended amicably some time before) to work on a new LP. The result was the album *Let's Keep It That Way,* issued by Capitol in January 1978. From that came her first sizable pop hit single since 1974, a remake of the old Everly Brothers hit, "Walk Right Back." Her second single from the album, "You Needed Me," was a top-5 hit in both country and pop categories and was certified gold by the R.I.A.A. on November 1, 1978, for her second gold single. The album also was a bestseller with both pop and country fans, certified gold in October 1978 and reaching platinum in 1979.

Murray's 1978 efforts showed, as she said, "My career really took off." She earned three Grammy nominations for 1978 in the categories of Best Pop Vocal Performer, Female; Record of the Year; and Best Country Vocal Performance, Female. Her chart hits of 1979 were the singles "I Just Fall in Love Again," "Shadows in the Moonlight," and "Broken-Hearted Me" (number one on country charts in December) and the best-selling LP *New Kind of Feeling* (February 1979), which won a gold record by year end. She also turned out an excellent children's album in 1979, *Hippo in My Tub* (issued by Capitol in Canada and Sesame Street Records in the United States). She also served as 1979 Chairperson of the Canada Save the Children Fund and was honored by her country for adopting three foster children as part of her contribution to the program.

Anne started off the 1980s with another single on the charts, "Daydream Believer." As the year 1980 went by, she added such other top ranked singles as "Lucky Me," "I'm Happy Just to Dance with You," and "Could I Have This Dance," the latter number one on country charts in November 1980. During the year her charted albums included *I'll Always Love You, A Country Collection,* and *Anne Murray's Greatest Hits.* The last named was still in the top 5 in early 1981, by which time it had gone well past platinum-record levels, accounting for a worldwide sales total of over 3 million copies. In the early summer of 1981, her next LP, *Where Do You Go When You Dream* (April 1981) was on country lists. Among her charted singles of the year was the top-10 "It's All I Can Do."

During the late 1970s and early 1980s, while Murray's concert and TV work accounted for fewer days per year, it still represented more than a token effort. Her in-person appearances ranged from Las Vegas to Los Angeles's Greek Theater and New York's Carnegie Hall. Her radio credits included appearances on the

Grand Ole Opry and TV work included two guest spots on *Saturday Night Live;* host of *Solid Gold;* cohost of the *Mike Douglas* show for a week; *The Muppet Show;* Johnny Carson's *The Tonight Show;* and the *Merv Griffin* show; as well as a number of major specials with other major artists.

Murray's awards totals continued to mount in the early 1980s. In the Grammy competition, she won the nod for 1980 Best Country Vocal Performance, Female, for "Could I Have This Dance." She was top winner in the Canadian Juno Awards (Canada's equivalent of the Grammy) for 1980, winning in four categories. (That brought her career total of Juno trophies to sixteen). The Toronto *Sun* quipped that maybe the award should be renamed the "Annies."

In 1983, Anne was asked to cohost the Country Music Association award telecast with Willie Nelson. She wasn't up for any award at that time, though two years earlier she had been a finalist in the Female Vocalist of the Year category, and would be again in 1984 and 1986. In the 1983 Grammy voting her single, "A Little Good News," was a finalist for Best Country Vocal Performance, Female, and her victory was announced on that telecast February 28, 1984. The year 1984 was also a very good year for her with CMA voters, who made her a finalist not only for Female Vocalist, but also for Single and Album of the Year. She won in both latter classifications, for the LP *A Little Good News* and the title-track single. When those honors were announced on the October TV show, Anne became the first female artist to win the CMA Album of the Year trophy. In 1985 she added another CMA Award to her trophy cabinet, when she and Dave Loggins were named Vocal Duo of the Year.

In the mid- and late 1980s, Anne continued to add to her already substantial total of album sales. On June 11, 1985, the R.I.A.A. certified *Heart over Mind* gold. Two years later, *Anne Murray Country* went gold on March 17, 1987, followed by a platinum award for *New Kind of Feeling* on August 19 and a gold award for *Something to Talk About* on September 23, 1987. In 1986, she cohosted her second CMA Awards program, this time with Kris Kristofferson. In 1989, she was once more asked to fill that role, this time with Kenny Rogers. A feature on the telecast was Anne and Kenny's first live performance of their duet "If I Ever Fall in Love Again," included in Kenny's new album *Something Inside So Strong.*

The year 1989 also was a milestone for Anne's recording work, marking her twentieth anniversary with Capitol Records. Her successes on the label by then included four multiplatinum albums, eleven gold albums, two gold singles, and overall total record sales of over 20 million copies. On July 23, 1989, she helped christen the new Anne Murray Center in her home town of Springhill, Nova Scotia, which displayed memorabilia of her career.

In the early 1990s, Anne added to her gold record credits with R.I.A.A. certification of her *Christmas Wishes* album on November 22, 1991. During 1992, the Capitol Nashville label, then called Liberty, released her *Greatest Hits* album. It found a healthy sized audience and remained on the main *Billboard* country list for a long time before being transferred to its catalogue chart. It remained on the latter well into 1995 after accumulating multiplatinum sales of over 4 million copies.

She continued to be a featured artist on the concert circuit the first half of the 1990s and could often be seen on various country TV shows as well as major network TV programs. Her performance credits included a featured appearance with the Boston Pops Orchestra that also was telecast over the Public Broadcasting System. Starting in the mid-1990s, her recordings began to come out on SBK Records which issued the album *Groovin'* in early 1994 that spent several months on the country charts.

In late 1995, EMI Records released a three disc retrospective package, *Anne Murray, Now and Forever.* The contents include her first recorded number, the 1964 "Little Bit of Soap." Among the other 63 tracks were previously unissued versions of "Last Thing on My Mind," "Unchained Melody," and "Lonely But Only for You," an alternate take of "Snowbird," and a Spanish version of "Broken Hearted Me." During this period, Anne also announced establishment of the Leonard T. Rambeau Scholarship in honor of her late manager who died the previous April. The fund was to help students at the school he had attended, St. Mary's University in Halifax, Nova Scotia.

On March 10, 1996, she served as host for the 25th annual Juno Awards program in Copps Coliseum, Hamilton, Ontario. Over the years, she had been presented with 25 Junos, more than any other artist.

N

NELSON, WILLIE: *Singer, guitarist, songwriter, band leader (the Family), actor. Born Fort Worth, Texas, April 30, 1933. Elected to Country Music Hall of Fame in 1993.*

In the mid-1970s, Willie Nelson's name entered the consciousness of people the world over. Starting with *Red-Headed Stranger,* his albums regularly brought millions of dollars into the coffers of his record company, and his singles rose high on pop as well as country charts. By the end of the decade, he was acknowledged to be a superstar, not just of country music, but in every facet of popular music. He was still a dominant figure in pop and country music in the mid-1990s, though the intervening years had brought dry periods in his recording efforts and much personal pain, including the loss of a son through suicide and a long struggle to straighten out his tangled tax affairs. To those who knew him during his almost two decades of relative obscurity, when he played a steady succession of beer halls and honky tonks, to the countless singers who scored bestsellers with his compositions (his great song "Night Life" sold an estimated 30 million records for dozens of other artists), the only question was why it took so long.

Part of it was his personality—essentially shy and self-effacing, he preferred to avoid the glare of publicity; part was the inability of the country-music establishment of the 1950s and 1960s to understand the groundbreaking features of his material, grittier and more probing than much of the country music fare of those years. As time went by, however, he shed his self-consciousness and demonstrated a quiet strength in his abilities—and the music world also came to admire the progressive country approach of such "outlaws" as Willie, Waylon Jennings, and their like.

Willie's character was a natural extension of his upbringing. Though born in Forth Worth, he was raised during his formative years by his grandparents in the rural central Texas town of Abbott, from whence came the nickname Abbott Willie. He grew up loving the remoteness and peace of farm life and, like many farm boys, learned to play the guitar (both of his grandparents played) and took part in after-work sings with his friends. Many of the songs he sang were those he heard on radio from the *Louisiana Hayride* or *Grand Ole Opry.*

After leaving high school, Nelson spent a short time in the Air Force, then settled in Waco, Texas, at the start of the 1950s after getting married. He enrolled in Baylor University on a part-time basis with the thought of an eventual career in farming, but dropped out after two years. During that time he helped earn tuition money and money to support his family (which had grown to include a daughter, Lana) by a variety of jobs, including selling vacuum cleaners, encyclopedias, and Bibles. He gave that up when he found a job as a disc jockey on a San Antonio, Texas, radio station. A platter spinner for the next seven years on stations in Texas, Oregon, and California, he got restless and began to perform as a country artist whenever he could find dates on week nights or weekends. During that period he started to write songs of his own, such as "Family Bible" and "Night Life."

At the start of the 1960s, he moved to Nashville to try to make his mark on the larger country-music market. His main goal was to follow up on his songwriting skills; he didn't think of himself as a possible headline performer. One of the first to take note of his skills was Hank Cochran, who heard some of Willie's material in a set at Tootsie's Bar ("where," Cochran recalled, "those of us who were aspiring songwriters used to hang out"). He helped Willie get a writing contract with

Pamper Music. Ray Price was a part owner of Pamper at the time, and, after Willie and Ray became acquainted, Ray took Willie on as bass guitarist in Price's band.

While Willie worked as a sideman, his songs began to speak for him. Beginning in 1961, his reputation in the industry soared as a steady succession of his compositions made the hit lists. One of his first major credits was Patsy Cline's top-10 hit of "Crazy," followed in a short time by two other country hits for other artists. One of those was Ralph Emery's version of "Hello Fool" (cowritten by Willie and Jim Coleman) and Faron Young's single of "Hello Walls." In 1962, Young collaborated with Willie on another bestseller, "Three Days." In 1961, Willie wrote another classic, "Funny How Time Slips Away," which provided Patsy Cline with a top-10 hit in the early 1960s.

Like many songwriters, Nelson made demonstration records of his material to try and get others to record the songs. Sometimes such recordings cause record executives to decide the writer is the best one to make the record, but Willie's half-whispering style on demos didn't impress them. It was partly due to his psychological outlook, he decided later. He told Al Reinert for a *New York Times Magazine* article (March 26, 1978), "You know, I always thought I could sing pretty good. And I guess it kinda bothered me that nobody else thought so. I guess I was into a lot of negative thinking back then. I did a lot of bad things, got in fights with people, got divorced. All that stuff. My head was just pointed the wrong way, you know. Then I started to do a lot of reading. I got into [Kahlil] Gibran [author of *The Prophet*], got really into Edgar Cayce and his son, Hugh Cayce—books that had real positive attitudes.

"I was like a drunk that quit drinking. I kinda developed this real positive attitude toward my own life, got into my own life." But it took all of the 1960s before that happened.

Despite industry reservations about Willie's lifestyle and vocal skills, he didn't lack for recording opportunities. He was signed by Liberty Records even as he performed with Ray Price. The result was several chart-making singles, including two top-10 singles in 1962, the number-one ranked record of his composition "Touch Me," and a hit duet with Shirley Collie, "Willingly." For a time that success caused a flurry of personal appearances outside the small-club circuit, including a number of weeks in Las Vegas.

In late 1964, he was made a regular cast member of the *Grand Ole Opry.* He also left Liberty for RCA Records that year, remaining on the RCA roster into the early 1970s. As part of the growing Nelson legend, that part of his career is generally described in terms of abject failure, but in fact he had some moderate successes as a recording artist then. He placed a number of singles on the country charts, including "The Party's Over" and "Blackjack Country" in 1967 and "Little Things" in

1968. Some of his RCA albums also had reasonable sales, as well. Among his RCA LPs were *Country Willie, His Own Songs* (11/65), *Favorites* (6/66), *Willie Nelson Concert* (12/66), *Make Way for Willie Nelson* (5/67), *The Party's Over* (11/67), *Both Sides Now* (5/70), *Laying My Burdens Down* (12/70), *Columbus Stockade Blues* (12/70), *Willie Nelson and Family* (5/71), *Yesterday's Wine* (9/71), *Words Don't Fit the Picture* (3/72), and *The Willie Way* (8/72).

None of those efforts, however, did much toward gaining Nelson widespread recognition as a performer. He did have a following, but mainly among frequenters of small country bars and nightclubs where Willie could let down his hair and sing what he pleased how he pleased. In those years, he told Reinert, he just couldn't match his record efforts with his live act. "I'd get nervous. I just didn't feel comfortable in that kinda situation. You'd walk into the studio and they'd put six guys behind you who'd never seen your music before, and it's impossible to get the feel of it in a three-hour session. That was true for me, at least." So while he got comfortable royalties from discs of his songs made by others (among those who'd recorded his material by the early 1970s, besides almost every country star, were Frank Sinatra, Roy Orbison, Stevie Wonder, Al Green, Bing Crosby, Perry Como, Lawrence Welk, Aretha Franklin, Eydie Gorme, Timi Yuro, and dozens more), his career as an entertainer lagged.

To try to focus his thoughts and perhaps make a new start, he moved back to Texas from Nashville in 1972. The change did indeed effect a rebirth. In particular, he detected a latent interest in country music among younger fans. "I found that interest there and I also knew that they didn't have any place to go to listen to country music. . . . Their hair was too long to get into some of those places without getting into trouble . . . but I knew there was an audience there. . . . So I went down to the [rock-oriented] Armadillo World Headquarters and told them I wanted to play for their audiences and see if what I was thinking was right."

Willie laid the groundwork for his surge to stardom. During those years, he added to the impetus by opening his own club in Austin and, in the mid-1970s, organizing the annual rock-concert-style country festival Fourth of July picnics in Dripping Springs, Texas.

Willie, whose contract with RCA expired in 1971, next signed with Atlantic, just starting a new country section. He made three albums for that label, *Shotgun Willie*, *Trouble Maker*, and *Phases and Stages*, the last named, issued in early 1974, an unusual—for the country field—concept album describing the breakup of a marriage, one side from the woman's point of view, the other from the man's. The LPs did moderately well, but Atlantic disbanded the division in 1974 and Willie moved on to Columbia Records. In a crucial step, Columbia agreed to give Willie total creative control over his material. He produced his recordings and then gave

them to Columbia for distribution. (After the success of his first LP, he formed his own Lone Star label under a distribution agreement with CBS.)

The results were quick in coming. During the summer of 1975, Willie had his first top-10 single in years, "Blue Eyes Cryin' in the Rain." That success was dwarfed by the tremendous response, at home and abroad, to his debut Columbia LP, *Red-Headed Stranger*. This also was a concept album using songs by Willie and others to paint a picture of love and death in the days of "the old west." The LP reached number one on country lists in the fall of 1975 and even made the pop top 40. In concerts supporting the album, Willie found he could draw enthusiastic capacity crowds to medium-size halls and even large auditoriums, including many young fans, instead of the smaller clubs he appeared in before. Backing him on the tour was a band that included many sidemen who had been with him for decades. Its typical makeup in the mid-1970s was his sister Bobbie Nelson on piano, Jody Payne on guitar, Chris Ethridge on bass, Mickey Raphael on harmonica, and drummers Paul English and Rex Ludwig.

Red-Headed Stranger eventually went platinum, but even before it did, he was represented on another smash LP, *Wanted: The Outlaws*. Combining the talents of Willie, Waylon Jennings, Jessi Colter, and Tompall Glaser, the LP (a reissue by RCA of earlier recordings) was number one on country charts for many weeks in 1976 and a top-10 hit. The cross-country tour of the Outlaws backing the album remains one of the memorable live series in modern pop history. As a soloist, Willie continued to add to his laurels in 1976 with six top-10 singles: "Uncloudy Day," "I'd Have to Be Crazy," "Remember Me," "If You've Got the Money, I've Got the Time," and "Good-Hearted Woman," the last named a number-one hit. Willie also had a chart-making new Columbia LP in 1976, *Troublemaker*.

Nelson continued to consolidate his position as a superstar in succeeding years, turning out a stream of new material that sold millions of records demonstrating rare creativity and insight. And his concerts now vied with those of the most popular rock acts, drawing huge crowds to places like the Los Angeles Forum and New York's Madison Square Garden.

In 1977, Willie's tribute to the late Lefty Frizzell, *To Lefty from Willie*, was a best-seller, as were the singles "I Love You a Thousand Ways" and "Railroad Lady." In early 1978, he joined with Waylon Jennings for the LP *Waylon and Willie*, number one on country charts for weeks and arguably the finest country LP of the year. Several months after that came out, a new LP reflecting his interest in the pop music standards of earlier decades, *Stardust*, appeared and became a country and pop hit. It spawned such top-10 country singles as "Georgia on My Mind," "Stardust" (the Hoagy Carmichael classic), and "Blue Skies" (by Irving Berlin).

At the end of 1978, the LP *Willie and Family* was released and quickly took its place in upper country and pop chart brackets, where it remained well into 1979. (The "family" included notable musicians such as Johnny Gimble on fiddle and Grady Martin on guitar.) In early 1979, he teamed with Leon Russell for a series of memorable concerts that provided the basis for a midsummer live double LP, *One for the Road.* Later in the year, two more of his releases showed up on the album charts, *Willie Nelson Sings Kristofferson* and *Pretty Paper.* (In late 1979 and early 1980, Kristofferson toured a number of cities with Willie's show.) In August 1978, Willie also issued an LP of some of his early recordings, *Face of a Fighter,* on his own Lone Star Records label. All ten songs in the collection, originally recorded by Nelson in 1961, had never been recorded by other artists.

With his increasingly hectic schedule, Willie still found time to take a major supporting role (to Robert Redford and Jane Fonda) during 1979 in the movie *Electric Horseman.* His contributions included several vocals in the film score that took up one side of the soundtrack LP issued in 1980, including a new version of "Mamas Don't Let Your Babies Grow Up to Be Cowboys," which had been a singles hit in 1978 for Willie and Waylon.

In late 1979, Willie began work on another movie, *Honeysuckle Rose,* in which he costarred with Amy Irving and Dyan Cannon. When it was released by Warner Brothers in 1980, it was warmly received by almost all major critics, with considerable praise for Willie's acting contributions. The soundtrack album, issued by Columbia in the summer, was over platinum record levels by late fall. During the year, Willie had many other recording successes to add to an already astounding list. Early in 1980 his version of Kristofferson's "Help Me Make It Through the Night" was in the top ten and in February his single "My Heroes Have Always Been Cowboys" rose to number one on country charts. The following month his new version of his long-time hit composition "Night Life" (recorded with Danny Davis and the Nashville Brass) was in top-chart brackets followed a few months later with the hit single "Midnight Rider," and with Danny Davis, the top-10 "Funny How Time Slips Away." A little later in the year he had the bestseller "Faded Love" (with Ray Price), and a song he wrote for *Honeysuckle Rose,* "On the Road Again," was number one (September). Also on the charts was an RCA release of an old Nelson recording on that label, "Crazy Arms," and another Columbia single, "Family Bible." Along with many of his previously released LPs still on the charts in 1980, he added such new hits as *Danny Davis with Willie Nelson and the Nashville Brass* and *San Antonio Rose,* the latter a duet album with Ray Price that helped revitalize Ray's career.

Willie began 1981 where he left off the previous year, with still more hits. Early in the year he made top-chart levels with a duet with Ray Price, "Don't You

Ever Get Tired (of Hurting Me)" and the solo of the composition "Angel Flying Too Close to the Ground." He maintained an almost nonstop touring schedule in the early 1980s that took him across the United States several times and to many overseas venues as well, and he was featured on all manner of TV shows, from the PBS *Austin City Limits* program to many network and syndicated shows. The hectic pace caught up with him when he fell prey to physical problems during a tour stop in Hawaii in mid-1981, but after resting up for several months he was back to his normal routine by year end. By then, he had such other 1981 top-10 singles as "Somewhere over the Rainbow," "Mountain Dew," and "Heartaches of a Fool." Also high on both pop and country charts in late 1981 was his new Columbia release, *Willie Nelson's Greatest Hits and Some That Will Be.*

Meanwhile, from the mid-1970s on, more and more honors began to come Nelson's way. In the 1975 Grammy voting, he received the Best Country Vocal Performance, Male, award for the single "Blue Eyes Cryin' in the Rain," and in 1978 got the same award for "Georgia on My Mind" plus, with Waylon, for Best Country Vocal Performance, Duo or Group, for "Mamas Don't Let Your Babies Grow Up to Be Cowboys." In the Country Music Association voting for 1976, *Wanted: The Outlaws* was named album of the year and "Good Hearted Woman" single of the year. In 1978, *Waylon and Willie* was one of the five final nominees for album of the year as was *One for the Road* in 1979. Willie also was one of the five finalists for Male Vocalist of the Year in 1976, 1978, and 1979 and for Entertainer of the Year in 1976 and 1979. In 1979, he won that most prestigious CMA award, Entertainer of the Year. He added still another Grammy to his collection in early 1981 for "On the Road Again," voted the Best Country Song of 1980. The following year he was one of the finalists for the Grammy for Best Country Vocal Performance, Male, for his recording of the old movie standard "Somewhere over the Rainbow."

Discussing his feelings about American music in general and southern music in particular, Nelson was typically outspoken to interviewers in the late 1970s. Replying to Joe Bageant for an article for the *Rocky Mountain Musical Express,* he opposed musical categorizing. "Well, there really is no good reason to label music at all unless it helps to get the attention it deserves. I look at it all as just being American music, sound or whatever and, if you like it, you like it. It don't need a name to be enjoyable.

"Good music can be made anywhere as long as there are good people who enjoy making it, and recording anywhere so long as there is a good studio. But . . . there is something about the South which produces an awful lot of good music of all kinds . . . not just country. For one thing, there is so much more of it in general, and the people will go a long way out of their way to enjoy it. It's a strong point of pride with many of us and it gets kept alive."

To Bageant's description of the "ingredient" that makes Willie's style so distinctive as "honky soul," he replied, "Yeah, I know what you mean. What we are is a bunch of niggers really. White niggers playin' what comes natural for other white niggers to listen to!"

Willie began the 1980s with a series of excellent albums that included the duets with Ray Price on *San Antonio Rose* in 1980, *Greatest Hits (and Some That Will Be)* in 1981 and, in 1982, *In the Jailhouse Now* (with Webb Pierce) and *Always on My Mind*. The last-named, and his single of the title track, won Country Music Association Awards for both Single and Album of the Year. In 1983 he had a new album of duets with Merle Haggard out on Columbia's Epic label, and the two joined in a series of concerts that ranked among country's best of the period. In the 1983 CMA voting, the single "Pancho and Lefty" from the album was nominated for Single of the Year. Willie was also nominated by the CMA for Entertainer of the Year and Male Vocalist of the Year in 1983 as he had been in the first category in 1980 and 1982 and the second in the three previous years.

In 1984, though Willie continued to make hit charts with releases like his duet album with Spanish pop star Julio Iglesias (from which the single "To All the Girls I've Loved Before" won two CMA trophies for Single of the Year and Vocal Duo of the Year), he made the headlines for other reasons. The IRS had disallowed his real-estate tax shelters, and claimed he now owed them tens of millions of dollars. As the dispute dragged on, by 1990 the debt amounted to $32 million in taxes, interest, and penalties. As he told *People* magazine later ("Back in the Groove Again," Ann Maier and Steve Dougherty, 1993) at one point he found he was paying $5,000 a day in interest on the debt. He finally learned to laugh it off. "Here was this guitar player from Abbott, Texas, who started out making $8 a day. How did he get $32 million into these guys? Somebody missed a stitch."

Throughout the 1980s, as he tried to work things out, he received countless messages of support from friends, neighbors, and a great many strangers who loved his music and felt a kinship with his obviously generous spirit. In 1985, despite his other worries, he joined forces with rock star John Mellencamp to organize the Farm Aid concert to call attention to the difficulties assailing America's independent farmers. Farm Aid continued to be held intermittently into the 1990s, always featuring first-rank artists from country and rock. By the time of Farm Farm Aid V in 1992 (which featured, besides Mellencamp and Willie, such others as Alabama, Mary-Chapin Carpenter, and Neil Young), it was estimated that a total of over $10 million in concert proceeds had been distributed to help the farm community.

Willie's hectic schedule continued in the mid-1980s, encompassing his usual intensive concert work, new films, and even more new albums than usual to try to help pay his mounting tax tab. In 1985 he had such releases as *Brand on my Heart* (with Hank Snow) and *Me and Paul* as well as a landmark collection with Johnny Cash, Waylon Jennings, and Kris Kristofferson titled *Highwayman.* (The album title came from a song by Jimmy Webb, but the foursome called themselves the Highwaymen.) Besides all that, Willie also found time to record duet material with Ray Charles.

In the CMA voting for 1985, the single "Highwayman" was nominated for Single of the Year and Music Video of the Year and Willie and Ray Charles were nominated for Vocal Duo of the Year. The album *Highwayman* easily made the charts, eventually earning platinum-record certification from the R.I.A.A. In the 1986 CMA voting, Willie was nominated for Entertainer of the Year, and he and Waylon Jennings were finalists for Vocal Duo of the Year.

In October 1987, Willie's participation in a Costa Mesa, California, concert called the "Cowboys for Indians and Justice for Leonard Peltier" drew fire from FBI members and law-enforcement supporters. The concert, which also featured such artists as Kris Kristofferson, Joni Mitchell, and comedian Robin Williams, was part of a campaign to free Indian activist Peltier, who his adherents believed had been unjustly convicted in 1975 of killing two FBI agents. Among some twenty protestors outside the venue was state Senator William Campbell (R-Hacienda Heights), who complained to a reporter, "What about the wives, families and loved ones of the victims? When will Willie Nelson, Robin Williams and Kris Kristofferson hold a benefit concert for them?"

Concert organizer actor Peter Coyote commented, "We're sad. It's unfortunate. We're not gloating over anyone's death. To portray people coming here tonight as taking sides in that tragedy is not accurate or appropriate. We are here about something simple—due process. When you have 50 U.S. congressmen on your side, you can't be far from dead center."

During the late 1980s, though Willie had more new albums coming out on Columbia, they seemed weaker creatively than his earlier efforts, which isn't surprising considering the pressure he was under. Sales of his recordings fell off, but he remained as popular as ever with concert goers. Meanwhile, more and more of his assets were sold at auction by the IRS, some of which were bought by friends who held them in trust for Willie. In 1990, continued negotiations with the tax people improved things a bit, when the IRS agreed to cut his bill in half to only $18 million.

That year saw release of a second excellent Highwaymen album, *Highwayman II*, which, unlike *Highwayman I*, was supported by an extensive concert tour. As was the case with its predecessor, the new album rose high on the charts and earned gold and platinum R.I.A.A. awards. In mid-1991, a new album, *Who'll Buy My Memories—The IRS Tapes,* was issued specifically to help offset his tax debts. Initially only available through mail order, it did so well it was later released to record stores and provided some $1 million to turn over to the IRS. The year ended on a tragic note, however, when Billy Nelson, his thirty-three-year-old son from his first marriage, hanged himself at his Nashville-area home. In the wake of that news, Willie and his fourth wife, Anne-Marie (whom he met on the set of his 1986 film, *Stagecoach)* tried to shield their three- and four-year-old sons from the media.

In February 1992, his spirits were raised when his tax situation was finally resolved. By then he had managed to pay off $3.6 million of the bill, when the IRS agreed to reduce the amount due to a flat $9 million with no further interest or tax penalties. Questioned by Robert Hilburn of the *Los Angeles Times* ("Willie after the IRS and on the Road to 60," Calendar section, August 30, 1992) about whether he felt anger or humiliation about the situation, Nelson replied, "Oh, it was anger for sure—much more than humiliation or feeling sorry for myself." But the anger, he said, wasn't directed against the IRS, which he felt was just doing its job, but against the accounting firm of Price-Waterhouse. Asserting that organization had given him bad investment advice, he had filed a $45 million lawsuit in Dallas federal court.

Putting his reversals of fortune behind him, in early 1993 Willie could point to the release of his finest collection in many years, *Across the Borderline.* The record included three original songs by him plus guest appearances by Paul Simon, Bob Dylan, Bonnie Raitt and Sinead O'Connor. Later Dylan joined him in a series of concerts. In October Willie gained one of the most coveted honors in country music, election to the Country Music Hall of Fame. When he came on stage during the awards telecast to a standing ovation, he was dressed in more formal attire than his usual T-shirt and blue jeans. He quipped, "I really thought you had to die to get here. So I went out and dressed just in case." He also said he felt there were others just as deserving who hadn't been voted into the Hall yet, artists like Ray Price and Merle Haggard, but would he still accept the award? "You're damned right I will." Later, backstage, he commented, "I'm way ahead of the game. Country music has given a lot more to me than I've given to it. I get to do what I want to do, live the way I want to live."

Willie's career after that continued just about the way it always had except that in 1994 he ended his long association with Columbia and signed with Liberty Records. His debut on that label, *Healing Hands of Time,* came out in the fall and made both country and pop charts. Columbia meanwhile released the retrospective *Super Hits* album in mid-1994 that was still on the charts two years later after peaking at number thirty-four in *Billboard.* In early 1996, it achieved R.I.A.A. gold-record levels. Included in the nominations for the 37th annual Grammy Awards (for 1994), announced in January 1995, was one for Willie's version of "Moonlight Becomes You" in the Traditional Pop Vocal category. That single was the first release under a new contract arrangement with Justice Records.

His 1995 credits included doing one of Rodgers and Hammerstein's songs in a Public Broadcasting System special in tribute to Hammerstein and performing in May on the Academy of Country Music Awards TV program. (Also in 1995, his more than three decades of original lyrics were collected in the hardcover book, *Willie Nelson Lyrics 1957–1994.*) In July 1995, his first full album for Justice Records, *Just One Love,* was released. That same month, Rhino Records issued a boxed set titled *Willie Nelson: A Classic & Unreleased Collection.* Its contents included Willie's first single issued in 1957 on his own Willie Nelson label, twelve demos taped in the early 1960s to support hopes for a record deal, twelve previously unreleased or alternative tracks for the early 1970s *Shotgun Willie* and *Phases and Stages* sessions, and a series of swing numbers recorded with Merle Haggard's band.

In late 1995, Sony Legacy issued a multi-CD set called *Revolutions in Time . . . The Journey 1975–1993.* The package comprised 60 remastered songs, including a full disc of duets, and a 32 page booklet giving highlights of Willie's career. In June 1996, Nelson's new album, *Spirit,* debuted in the top 20 on national country charts.

NEVILLE, AARON: *Singer, soloist, and member of the Neville Brothers Band. Born New Orleans, Louisiana, c. 1940.*

Art Neville and the Neville Sound, the Meters, the Wild Tchoupitoulas, the Neville Brothers: collectively these names comprise a saga embracing some of the key elements of the post–World War II "New Orleans Sound." Essentially they represent the legacy of one family, the Nevilles, and the environment that gave birth to the solo career of Aaron Neville, he of the soaring unusual tremolo voice that charmed audiences with music that crossed most pop genres from rock to soul, R&B, and country. But some of his best performances were sublimated to the overall sound of the family group, in which he teamed with brothers Art, Charles, and Cyril.

As Steve Hochman noted in a review of a 1991 Neville Brothers concert ("Neville Brothers Lay Down an Irresistible Beat," *Los Angeles Times,* May 7, 1991), the one true star of all the Nevilles was the beat, "or, more accurately, the polyrhythmic beats. On this evening, even Aaron's indescribably angelic voice was subservient to the New Orleans 'second line' voodoo funk that the Nevilles have had custody of for more than 30 years as the Crescent City's musical first family. The only times the beats retreated was for Aaron's soul plea 'Tell It like It Is' and his encore of 'Amazing Grace.'"

Art, the oldest of the four brothers, was the first to gain attention from the New Orleans musical fraternity, with keyboard and vocal skills that made him one of the most highly regarded session players in the region. When he combined forces with three other top-ranked session artists to form the Meters (a name that supplanted an earlier version, Art Neville and the Neville Sound), he set in motion musical trends that impressed many of the most famous people in rock, pop, R&B, and soul, including the Rolling Stones, the Beatles, Patti LaBelle, and dozens of other major artists who incorporated some of the Neville Sound elements in their own music. Aaron wasn't part of the Meters, but the family kept in close touch and collaborated on various projects while Aaron concentrated on a solo career; when the Meters broke up, he became part of the Neville Brothers Band. (For more details, see the Meters' entry in *Stambler's Encyclopedia of Pop, Rock & Soul.*)

Aaron, the third of the four brothers (the family also included two sisters) demonstrated striking vocal talents in his preteen years and fortunately retained those powers when he reached maturity. He recalled being enthralled in elementary and high school not only with pop, soul, and jazz artists like Nat "King" Cole, Jackie Wilson, and Sam Cooke, but also by country and western performers, including Hank Williams, Sr., and Gene Autry.

Despite older brother Art's promising start in music, the family came from a poor neighborhood where there were plenty of dangerous temptations. Aaron was caught stealing an automobile as a teenager and spent two years in jail in the late 1950s. Once freed, he began to try to take advantage of his singing skills and in the early 1960s started to make local and then national charts with soul singles such as "Over You" and "Tell It like It Is." However, like many artists of the period, both black and white, he was shortchanged by his record companies to the point that he had to earn a living as a longshoreman in the mid-1960s while "Tell It like It Is" was rising up the soul charts.

By the end of the 1960s, Aaron was married with four children, but he also had a growing problem with heroin—a curse that was dragging him down in the early 1970s, when he left his family in Louisiana and moved to New York to perform in night spots in the region with brothers Charles and Cyril. Somewhere along the line, as his addiction grew worse, he realized he had a life-or-death decision to make and finally found the strength to combat his habit.

Discussing that period with Steve Pond ("Success Is All in the Family," *The New York Times,* May 16, 1993),

he said it was his Catholic faith that helped him. "I got through it because I wanted to do it. And also, I had faith in my prayers to God and my novenas to St. Jude, the saint of the impossible. He let me see something beyond all that. I was looking at friends and associates dropping, falling by the wayside. He let me see some ugly things and I said, 'Man, I don't want that for me.'"

He went back to New Orleans and his family in the mid-1970s and with their support and his religious faith, he managed to be drug-free by the time Art organized the Neville Brothers foursome with Cyril handling percussion and Charles saxophone. After their debut, *The Neville Brothers,* came out on Capitol, the band recorded a string of albums on other labels until they found an extended arrangement with A&M Records still going strong in the 1990s. Their album output included such superior releases as *Yellow Moon* in 1989, *Brothers' Keeper* in 1991, and *Family Groove* in 1992. Though by 1992 Aaron's solo career had soared, he told Pond, "I'm never going to neglect the Neville Brothers thing [whose concerts sometimes showcased other family members, such as Aaron's son Ivor] 'cause I am a Neville Brother and I don't feel I've made it until my brothers have made it."

The stimulus for that solo success was some duet recordings with Linda Ronstadt. One of those, "Don't Know Much," became a 1989 best-seller. Ronstadt then produced a new album of Aaron Neville vocals called *Warm Your Heart* (issued in 1991). The album contained a variety of stylings from soul to country, as did the follow-up album in 1993, *The Grand Tour,* in which Aaron presented his versions of songs written by people like Leonard Cohen, Bob Dylan, and George Jones.

In the Grammy Awards for 1989, announced on the February 24, 1990, telecast, Aaron and Linda Ronstadt won the trophy for Best Performance for a Duo or Group with Vocal for "Don't Know Much." At the same time, the Neville Brothers won in the Best Pop Instrumental Performance category for the track "Healing Chant" from *Yellow Moon.* The following year, Ronstadt and Neville again won Best Pop Performance for a Duo or Group with Vocal for the Elektra Entertainment single "All My Life." In the 1993 voting, the title track from *The Grand Tour* album earned a Grammy nomination for Best Male Country Record of the Year. At the close of 1993, the A&M single by Neville, "Don't Take Away My Heaven," was ranked number seven in *Radio and Records'* list of top country singles of the year.

One of the 1993–1994 projects Aaron was requested to join was the MCA Records concept album *Rhythm Country & Blues* which combined talents of country and R&B stars. One album track featured a duet between Aaron and Trisha Yearwood on the country standard "I Fall to Pieces." The album became a best-seller (passing R.I.A.A. platinum levels by the end of 1994) and the accompanying tour (in which Neville, Yearwood, and other record participants took part) drew sizable audiences across the U.S. In the 1994 Country Music Association voting the album was nominated for Album of the Year, and the Neville/Yearwood version of "I Fall to Pieces" for Vocal Event of the Year.

Besides doing solo tours, he continued to work with his brothers in the concert field, including annual appearances in the 1990s at the New Orleans Jazz and Blues Festival, which by the mid-1990s had become an internationally famous event. Aaron was in his fifties when he found himself suddenly a star with both country and pop fans while accruing a steadily growing string of hit records and videos and receiving major attention on network TV entertainment programs. It was a situation he might not have savored as much if it had come when he was in his twenties. And, of course, he still had the feeling his brothers hadn't yet received the recognition they deserved. But, as he told Steve Pond, that didn't mean he wasn't enjoying it.

"I remember, I used to hear cats on the radio singing and I'd sing along with them and I knew I sounded just as good. But a friend of mine called Skip, he always used to tell me, 'Aaron, patience is a virtue.' I wanted to say that when I won a Grammy, but I got choked up and forgot to say it. I wanted to say, 'Hey, Skip, patience *is* a virtue.'"

NEW GRASS REVIVAL: *Vocal and instrumental group. Original personnel 1972: Courtney Johnson, born Bareen County, Kentucky, December 20, 1939; Sam Bush, born Bowling Green, Kentucky, April 15, 1952; Curtis Burch, born Montgomery, Alabama, January 24, 1945; Ebo Walker. Walker left 1973, replaced first by Butch Robbins, then by John Cowan, born Evansville, Indiana, August 24, 1952. Group reorganized in 1981, comprised Bush; Cowan; Pat Flynn; Bela Fleck, born Kentucky.*

The blend of old-time bluegrass with more modern influences that sparked the revival of the music form in the 1970s sometimes was given the descriptive term "newgrass." Like many such terms, it tended to be used indiscriminately and was applied to a variety of groups with vastly different styles. However, one band that adopted it as its name went on to epitomize the best of modern bluegrass.

As charter member Sam Bush of the New Grass Revival told Ronni Lundy of *Bluegrass Unlimited* magazine (November 1978), "When we first started playing our music professionally, making our livings doing it . . . what we could do best [was] straight bluegrass. As we've gone on, we've learned to play other things, other instruments, other kinds of music. Hopefully our music has evolved into another kind of music that everybody will know comes from bluegrass, but is not straight bluegrass."

Appropriately, Bush and another founding member, Courtney Johnson, were born and raised in Bill Monroe's home state of Kentucky, the birthplace of blue-

grass. At an early age, thanks to his father's record collection, and later, influenced by the Flatt & Scruggs's TV show, he saved his money to buy a mandolin when he was eleven. His interest in bluegrass, though, really blossomed when he and a musician friend named Wayne Stewart attended the 1965 Roanoke Bluegrass Festival. During the 1960s, Sam also took up fiddling and was good enough to place fifth at the national fiddle contest in Weister, Idaho, on his first try. After that he came in first three years in a row.

He, Stewart, and Alan Munde formed a group that brought Sam's record debut on the album *Poor Richard's Almanac.* When Munde left the group, Courtney Johnson took over on banjo. Johnson, who grew up in western Kentucky, started his musical efforts on the guitar when he was seven. He told Ronni Lundy, "I was influenced by country then a lot, because my dad was into it and played that. I heard a lot of frailing type banjo too, when I was growing up, because we always went to dances. But I never really got into banjo until I was 25 years old. My brother traded for one and I just started tooling with it—learned how to play it. I just quit playing guitar then. My first influence, what I learned to play, was Ralph Stanley type."

Courtney was a friend of both Munde and Bush before they joined forces and was a natural to replace the former when he went on his way. In 1970, Bush and Johnson moved to a new band, the Bluegrass Alliance, whose other members included Lonnie Peerce on fiddle and Ebo Walker on bass. In 1971, that group was performing in Savannah, Georgia, when the members met guitarist and dobro player Curtis Burch.

Burch, born and raised in Brunswick, Georgia, was exposed to bluegrass from his early years; his father liked it and sang bluegrass accompanying himself on guitar. Curtis learned some guitar chords in his early years, but wasn't impelled too much toward a musical career until he heard his first live bluegrass band perform, Jim and Jesse and the Virginia Boys. Almost as soon as they opened the show, he recalled, "I came out of my seat ten feet high and I thought, 'That's where it's at.'" He played for his own enjoyment and with friends but wasn't making much progress in earning a living in music until he joined the Bluegrass Alliance in November 1971.

In 1972, Peerce and the other four members parted company and the latter took the new title of New Grass Revival. That lineup played at bluegrass festivals and on the folk club and college concert circuit for a while, but in 1973 faced a crisis of sorts when Ebo Walker left. He was replaced for a time by Butch Robbins, but Robbins, a skilled banjoist, chafed at having to concentrate on bass. After he departed, the group talked to several possible replacements, one of whom recommended they contact John Cowan.

Cowan, unlike the others, had no deep bluegrass roots. In fact, his early love was rock, particularly the

Beatles. He started out playing trumpet, later played bass fiddle in the school orchestra, and, at thirteen learned electric guitar. He played with various teenage rock bands during his high school years in Evansville, Indiana, and later worked with country-rock groups.

When Cowan auditioned, the others liked not only his bass technique but his fine singing voice, which he had employed initially in his church choir. As Bush told Lundy, they decided John's musical background could add a new element to the bluegrass fusion the band was seeking. "John has a different direction that he brought in with us. It was the kind of direction I think we were all looking for. We all liked to listen to the Allman Brothers and people who had really hot bass players and we'd go, 'God, if we just had somebody that could do stuff like that and give us some other things to do.'"

After Cowan joined in 1973, a good amalgam was reached. He quickly learned much of the basics of bluegrass from the others and before long was as devoted a bluegrass fan as they were. The new roster proved to be well suited to the evolving bluegrass environment of the 1970s. Playing in festivals across the country and in clubs and concert halls all over the United States in the mid-1970s, the group stamped itself as one of the most talented of the modern bluegrass movement.

Not only did the band develop its own style of progressive bluegrass, but demonstrated the ability to play everything from traditional bluegrass on out. Thus in the summer of 1977, they won plaudits for both their own sets and for complementing such diverse performers as John Hartford and Byron Berline at the Telluride, Colorado, festival and Norman Blake and Dan Crary at a festival in Winfield, Kansas. Some of the New Grass Revival offerings became classics in their own right to the point that other bands copied such New Grass favorites as "Great Balls of Fire."

In the mid-1970s, the band began its recording career with the LP *New Grass Revival,* issued initially on the Starday-King label and later reissued on Gusto Records. The band's recording efforts really made headway after it signed with Flying Fish Records. The first LP to come out was *Fly Through the Country.* This was followed in the late 1970s by *When the Storm is Over, Too Late to Turn Back Now,* and, in 1979, *Barren County.*

As the 1970s came to an end and the 1980s began, the New Grass Revival was well established as a major bluegrass institution. The band's commitments included occasional appearances on TV and radio and a touring schedule that kept it on the road forty-two weeks a year.

In 1980, the group teamed with Leon Russell for a wide-ranging concert tour that covered sixty-one dates in the United States and other shows in Australia and New Zealand. In their format, the New Grass Revival opened with its own set, then backed Leon for a rousing second half of the program. The series worked so well

that another group of concerts was undertaken in 1981. During one stop in the 1980 schedule, on May 15 at the Perkins Palace in Pasadena, California, both audio and video tapes were made. The video material was intended for the home TV market; the audio recordings were used to prepare the 1981 album (issued on Russell's Paradise Records label, distributed by Warner Brothers) *Leon Russell and the New Grass Revival, the Live Album.*

In 1981, a new alignment of the band took place with Bush and Cowan being joined by guitarist Pat Flynn and banjoist Bela Fleck. Fleck, already considered by some to be in a class with Earl Scruggs, was born in Kentucky, but spent his formative years in New York, where he focused on musical studies at the High School of Music and Art before pursuing a career as a professional performer. Flynn's previous experience included extensive session work in recording studios in Southern California, where he was noted for his excellent flat-picking acoustic guitar skills. By the time he joined the Revival, he had also demonstrated promising ability as a songwriter.

After winning favorable notices for performances in concert halls and bluegrass festivals in the early 1980s, the band received backing from the U.S. Information Agency for an overseas tour in 1984 that included stops in Turkey, Crete, Greece, Portugal, Spain, and Malta. That was so successful, the USIA set up another series in 1987 that included concerts in Egypt, Morocco, India, Bangladesh, and Nepal.

Bush told Judi Turner of the Country Music Association publication *Close Up,* "The USIA people told us they had never heard a better representation of all of America's music put into one style. On this kind of tour, 95% of the people had never heard of us before. . . . And some of them have heard very little American music." Cowan added, "It's responding totally to our music. They've had no indoctrination of any kind, so they're responding in a positive manner purely to the music. That's very gratifying."

In the mid-1980s, the band got the chance to sign with a major label, EMI Records, which issued its label debut in late 1986. The initial single release, "What You Do to Me," made the *Billboard* country list, but never got above the fifties level. With one exception, all the album tracks had vocals. The instrumental exception, "Seven by Seven," was nominated for a Grammy in the Best Country Instrumental category. By the end of 1987, the group completed work on a second EMI album.

Three of the four mid-1980s members had received major recognition from their musical peers. Fleck, who had won attention for a series of solo albums in previous years, scored five straight wins in the banjo category of *Frets* magazine, after which he was inducted into the publication's Gallery of Greats. During 1985–1986, Bush was twice named best mandolin player by *Frets* readers, while Flynn was chosen number one in the Guitar Jazz/Pop Flatpicking category two years in a row.

As was not unusual in bluegrass bands, all of the members found time for the other projects. During the 1980s and in the 1990s, their names were likely to appear on session credits for other artists. Flynn, for instance, worked on a number of Kathy Mattea's recordings, as well as on other artists' discs, while Fleck backed country stars like the Gatlins. Solo albums by Revival members in the mid-1980s included Sam Bush's *Late as Usual* on Rounder Records and John Cowan's release *Soul'd Out* on Sugar Hill. In the 1990s, Bela Fleck fronted his own band, Bela Fleck and the Flecktones.

NEWMAN, JIMMY C: *Singer, guitarist, songwriter. Born Big Mamou, Louisiana, August 27, 1927.*

Given the nickname "Mr. Alligator Man" in the 1960s for one of his hit songs of that decade, Jimmy Newman ranked with Doug Kershaw as one of the prime interpreters of Cajun music in the country field. In such routines as "Bayou Talk and Big Mamou," he always could captivate audiences with his singing and story telling in the Cajun accents of his home region of Louisiana. But over his several decades as a featured artist, he proved himself just as comfortable with country songs of all kinds.

As a boy of half-French origin, Jimmy grew up in the midst of Cajun culture and picked up many of its popular songs both at home and from local get-togethers. He learned to play guitar well by his mid-teens and was soon performing for friends and small gatherings. In his preteen years, he also gained pleasure from going to see western films; as a result, his first idol was Gene Autry, whose songs he often sang. In the 1960s, he also cited Jim Reeves, Tom T. Hall, and Glen Campbell as among his favorites.

When he was nineteen, in 1946, having decided on making music a career, he made his first move by singing with a band in Big Mamou, Louisiana. For several years he polished his act, heading his own band in small clubs and theaters in the South and Southwest.

He then got the chance to host his own show on KPLC Radio and TV in Lake Charles, Louisiana. He already had perfected the wailing Cajun signature, the electrifying "aieeee" call that prefaced many of his songs. That coupled with his strong voice soon won the attention of local audiences and paved the way for his advance to a major radio and TV show, the *Louisiana Hayride* in Shreveport. That kind of exposure not only helped make him a well-known performer beyond Louisiana borders, it also brought him a recording contract with Dot Records. In 1954, he gained national attention with the hit single of a song cowritten with J. Miller, "Cry, Cry, Darling." He followed with other chartmakers, such as "Seasons of My Heart," "Blue Darling," and "Day Dreaming." In 1956, he was

asked to join the cast of the *Grand Ole Opry*, and the next year he had his best-selling record up to that time, still one of his most-remembered songs, "Falling Star."

During the late 1950s, besides appearing regularly on the *Opry*, he performed throughout the United States, a pattern that still held true through the 1960s and 1980s. He switched to MGM at the end of the 1950s and had such top-level chart hits as "You're Making a Fool Out of Me" in 1958, "Grin and Bear It" in 1959, and "A Lovely Work of Art" in 1960. In the mid-1960s, he left MGM for Decca and soon had a new series of singles on national country charts. Among them were such Bayou-flavored songs as "Alligator Man," "Big Mamou and Bayou Talk," and "Louisiana Saturday Night." Other songs that became staple items in his repertoire during the 1960s were "D.J. for a Day," "Blue Lonely Winter," "Bring Your Heart Back Home," "Angel on Leave," "City of the Angels," and "Back in Circulation." He added two more top-10 singles to his credit in the mid-1960s: "Artificial Rose" in 1965 and "Back Pocket Money" in 1966.

Jimmy's album output in the 1950s included such Dot collections as *Crossroads, Fallen Star,* and *Cry, Cry Darling,* some of which were reissued in the 1960s. On MGM he had such releases as *Songs of Jimmy Newman* in 1962 and *Folk Songs of the Bayou* in 1963. His LP output for Decca included *Artificial Rose* in 1966, *World of Music* in 1967, *The Newman Way* in 1968, and *Country Time* at the start of the 1970s.

During the 1970s, Newman's recording career slowed down and his name didn't appear on hit charts very often. (Among the labels he recorded for in the 1970s were Shannon and Plantations.) However, he retained a strong following among country fans for his concerts and radio-TV work. He was a guest on many network or syndicated shows during those years and was still a major cast member of the *Grand Ole Opry*, often hosting as well as singing on one of the show's segments, a pattern continuing into the 1980s.

NEWTON-JOHN, OLIVIA: *Singer, actress, songwriter. Born Cambridge, England, September 26, 1947.*

There was some grumbling among country music diehards when Olivia Newton-John was named Country Music Female Vocalist of the Year for 1974. It didn't seem right, they suggested, for an artist from overseas who had primarily been known in England as a pop ballad and rock vocalist to suddenly gain such honors in her initial foray into the U.S. market. But most country-music people brushed that aside, noting that the U.S. audience had, in effect, validated Newton-John's credentials by buying her recordings in large numbers. Had she wanted to debate the matter, Olivia could have pointed out that the roots of country music lay in the centuries-old folk music of the British Isles and many a U.S. country star was descended from immigrants from her father's home region, Wales.

It was, in fact, folk music that first interested Olivia as a girl growing up in Australia. She was born in Cambridge, England, but her father, a college professor, had moved the family to Australia when Olivia was five to take an administrative post at a university. (Intellectual pursuits bulked large in Newton-John's family. Her grandfather was Nobel laureate Max Born.) When Olivia was in her late teens, she began to move away from folk toward the pop idiom.

Victory in a talent contest in Australia gained her a trip to England in the late 1960s, where her professional singing career began to accelerate rapidly. In the early 1970s she became one of the more successful young pop artists in Britain. As her reputation grew there, she naturally started thinking about the more affluent U.S. market, an idea matched by growing interest in her by American record firms. MCA Records offered a contract, and Newton-John began working on her initial recordings for the label in 1973. One of the first results was the single "Let Me Be There." The song proved acceptable to both pop and country listeners. Country fans liked it enough to move it onto the charts in late summer. The single moved steadily higher until it made the country top 10 by year's end and remained there into 1974.

Olivia proved it was no fluke with an even greater country hit, "If You Love Me (Let Me Know)," which became number one on country lists in the spring of 1974. With the pop volume added in, that effort earned a gold-record award, as did its predecessor. She showed her versatility by earning another gold record in the fall of 1974, this time for a pop single, "I Honestly Love You." Meanwhile, Newton-John also stormed the country album charts during 1974 with the gold record *Let Me Be There* in the spring and *If You Love Me,* on the charts in summer and still on them in early 1975.

With that kind of success, it's not surprising Olivia gained four Country Music Association Awards nominations for 1974, including Entertainer of the Year, Album of the Year, Single of the Year, and Female Vocalist of the Year. She came in number one in the last-named category.

She continued to be an almost perennial resident on the country charts throughout the 1970s. In 1975, her singles hits included "Have You Never Been Mellow," "Please, Mr. Please," and "Something Better to Do," and her album *Have You Never Been Mellow* made the top 10. In 1976, she came up with the number-one country chart hit "Come on Over" in May and the top-10 single "Don't Stop Believin'" in late summer. In late 1975 and early 1976 she placed the LP *Clearly Love* on upper-chart levels and soon after had the top-5 album *Come on Over.* Still going strong in 1977, she turned out the top-10 album *Making a Good Thing Better,* whose title track also rose high on the singles charts.

In 1978, Olivia stressed rock rather than country, starring opposite John Travolta in the film *Grease* and

having a featured part in the gold-record soundtrack album (issued by RSO Records). Her hit singles "You're the One That I Love," "Summer Nights," and "Hopelessly Devoted to You" were also issued by RSO. The first of those was certified platinum by the R.I.A.A.; the other two earned gold records. On the surface, it might have seemed she was turning strongly away from the country field, particularly when her next MCA solo album, *Totally Hot,* was issued in late 1978. However, a closer look at the album's contents showed that, despite its title, it still had several country-oriented numbers, such as "Dancin' Round and Round" and "Borrowed Time," the latter an original composition by Newton-John.

Her next album effort was a collaboration with the major rock band the Electric Light Orchestra, titled *Xanadu.* That 1979 release offered music from a mediocre movie of the same name; the film did poorly, but the LP was a bestseller, reaching platinum-record levels and spawning the gold-record single "Magic." Olivia's first solo album of the 1980s, *Physical,* was released by MCA Records in the fall of 1981 and was in the top pop chart brackets soon after. Several of the songs from the album were spotlighted by Newton-John in her late-1981 TV special.

The title track from *Physical* rose to number one on *Billboard*'s singles charts the week of December 18, 1981, and stayed there for nine more weeks. At the end of 1982, *Billboard* named "Physical" its number one single of the year.

Olivia supported the album with a wide-ranging tour, her first in five years. For many of the concerts, she was joined on stage by John Travolta. The series comprised a stunning success in which Olivia demonstrated more stage presence than at any previous time in her career. Near the end of the tour in late 1982, she told an interviewer, "I'm just more confident now. I can relax more and be myself on stage. I was always rigid. I was afraid to try new things, but I think I've gone through a lot of changes in the last few years."

Part of the problem stemmed from her growing-up years in Australia, she noted. "Where I come from, it wasn't considered proper for a woman to be considered ambitious. It had this sinister ring, as if you were someone who was trying to claw your way to the top. So I denied to myself for a long time that I had ambition. I'm more comfortable with that now because I realize that my drive isn't improper. I'm just out to improve myself."

Besides touring in 1982, Olivia had her fourth TV special, *Olivia Newton-John: Let's Get Physical.* Singles "Make a Move on Me" and "Heart Attack" made *Billboard*'s Top 10. Late in the year, MCA issued *Olivia's Greatest Hits, Volume 2,* which stayed on the LP charts into 1984, earning multiplatinum sales. Her projects included a new film with John Travolta, *Two of a Kind,* which unfortunately was another cinematic dud, though the soundtrack LP went platinum. The film score also brought her another top-10 single in early 1984, "Twist of Fate." During late 1985 and early 1986, she had another album on the charts, *Soul Kiss.*

In the late 1980s, Olivia signed with Geffen Records. Her label debut and her seventeenth album overall, *Warm and Tender,* was released on October 24, 1989. She pointed out that the album was inspired by the birth of her daughter, Chloe, on January 17, 1986. "It totally changed my life. It put it into perspective— that what's important is family and children and friends. I did the album for my daughter and my friends who have children and every parent and child." In general, though she continued to appeal to many in the pop field for most of the 1980s, her impact on that genre was fading by the start of the 1990s, in part because she increasingly devoted time to other interests such as running her own boutique operation. Nor did she hold the attention of the new generations of country fans of the 1980s and 1990s. While she liked country music, her approach to it had little in common with traditional artists, nor did it mesh with the creative efforts of the new wave of artists coming to the fore in the country field from the early 1980s on.

An unexpected thing happened in her pop career in 1996, when the *Grease* soundtrack album she had recorded in 1978 with John Travolta took on a new life, helped by the success of revivals of the musical. It had never been out of print, but in the fall of the year it suddenly became a hit again, rising to top levels on the national charts thanks to intensive radio coverage of three songs from the disc. With surprise, she recognized that she suddenly was popular with new generations of fans; suddenly, for the first time in years, people in their late teens or twenties were coming up to her asking for an autograph.

O

OAK RIDGE BOYS: *Vocal quartet with band backup (the Oak Ridge Band). Quartet personnel in mid-1980s, Duane Allen, born Taylortown, Texas, April 29, 1943; William Lee Golden, born Brewton, Alabama, January 12, 1939; Richard Sterban, born Camden, New Jersey, April 24, 1943; Joe Bonsall, born Philadelphia, Pennsylvania, May 18, 1948. Golden left 1987, replaced by Steve Sanders, born Richland, Georgia, September 17, 1952. Sanders left December 1995, replaced by William Lee Golden in January 1996.*

When the Oak Ridge Boys began to achieve national recognition in the country-music field in the late 1970s, they had already won four Grammy Awards and fifteen Dove Awards (the gospel-music equivalent of the Grammy). They already had headlined a Las Vegas show and opened for such top acts as Roy Clark and

Johnny Cash, had won awards in England and Sweden, and had toured the Soviet Union. By the mid-1970s, charter member Bill Golden noted, "We had reached the height of gospel success. We'd gone about as far as we could go." So the group turned to the secular field and soon eclipsed its gospel popularity.

Actually, by then no one in the group had been around when it first started. That had been during the World War II years. In the 1940s, a country quartet called the Country Cut-Ups formed in Knoxville, Tennessee, consisting of four singers and a piano accompanist, that often performed at the atomic energy research center in nearby Oak Ridge for workers not permitted to leave the facility for security reasons. After a while, the group became known as the Oak Ridge Quartet. Their most popular numbers proved to be gospel songs, so they gradually built their entire repertoire around southern-style gospel music.

After the war, the original group disbanded, but soon another foursome, based in Nashville, took over the name. From then until the current group stabilized in the mid-1970s, there were many changes in personnel over the decades. In all, including band members, about thirty performers have taken part in Oak Ridge efforts. Until he left in 1987, the member with the longest tenure was William Lee "Bill" Golden, who joined in 1964. He grew up in Brewton, Alabama, where he graduated from East Brewton High School in the 1950s. His first public performance came at age seven when he played guitar and sang with his sister on Brewton radio station WEBJ. Before joining the Oak Ridge group he was involved with his family farm and worked in a pulp mill.

Lead singer Duane Allen got the chance to join the group in 1966. Born and raised in Texas, he completed high school there and went on to earn a bachelor's degree in music from East Texas State University. His first public performance came at four when he sang in church with his family. For a while he sang baritone with the Southernaires Quartet in Paris, Texas, and also was a disc jockey for a time. A guitar player for many years before joining the Oaks, he was the only member of the quartet to play an instrument on stage as of the early 1980s. When the group moved into the secular field, he was the acknowledged leader.

New Jersey born and raised Richard Sterban became a quartet member in 1972. Like Allen, he had studied music in college, in his case Trenton State College. His first public performance came at seven when he sang a soprano solo in church. In later years, after his voice changed to a deep bass, he sang with such groups as the Keystone Quartet in Bristol, Pennsylvania, and the Stamps Quartet (which backed Elvis Presley) before joining the Oaks. Although strictly a singer with the quartet, he learned to play a number of instruments, including the trumpet, baritone horn, E-flat tuba, and sousaphone.

Last of the revamped 1970s foursome was tenor Joe Bonsall, who joined in 1973. He made his performing debut at the age of six on the Horn & Hardart amateur TV program in his native city of Philadelphia. While attending Frankford High School, he was a regular dancer on Dick Clark's *American Bandstand* TV program. His credits prior to joining the Oaks included singing with the local Faith Four group. His instrumental training was on the piano.

The Oak Ridge Quartet was already well known among gospel admirers before Golden and Allan joined in the mid-1960s, but its reputation was enhanced still further afterward. In the voting for the 1970 Grammys, the group won the award for Best Gospel or Other Religious Recording for the single "Talk About the Good Times" on the Heart Warming label. After Sterban and Bonsall joined, the quartet won that award three times more, in 1974 for "The Baptism of Jesse Taylor" (Columbia Records); in 1976 for "Where the Soul Never Dies" (Columbia); and in 1977 for "Just a Little Talk with Jesus" (album track, Rockland Records).

By the time the group picked up its fourth gospel Grammy, it already was moving in new directions, something that caused some bitterness in the gospel field. For instance, one gospel record executive told *People* magazine (May 28, 1979), "We're serious about Christian ideals and morals. The Oaks made it quite clear that religion was not their concern." *People* writer Dolly Carlisle, in the same article, quoted Allen's rejoinder suggesting that the record executive was being hypocritical. He told her that gospel acts onstage might come on "as the ministry, but backstage they look for who's going to pay the check. I feel less hypocritical about it now."

Joe Bonsall told Carlisle that even before the group broke away from the gospel field, it was being looked at askance. "We were always the subject of gossip. We were the first to wear long hair and beards, and when we added a rock drummer we were talked about for months. At one time, our only goal was to make gospel as prestigious as any other kind of music. The gospel establishment wouldn't let us do it, so we took our business elsewhere."

The group made its first attempt at crossing over into country and popular music in 1974, when they signed with Columbia Records. Their Columbia secular recordings sold poorly; they actually sold fewer albums than when they worked the gospel circuit. (In gospel, for instance, they typically sold $5,000 worth of records at one concert; on the gospel circuit the singers pitch their own records at their concerts.) For a while things became desperate. The group's income shrank from an annual gross of $250,000 to a fraction of that. Then Johnny Cash came to the rescue, offering them a loan and hiring them as opening act for one of his Las Vegas concerts. Another helpful step came in the form

of session work backing Paul Simon on what was to become a best-selling single, "Slip Slidin' Away."

Perhaps the most important move came when Jim Halsey, Inc., took over as manager of the group. He helped them assemble a country-music package and booked them as headliners at the Las Vegas Landmark Hotel in August 1975. In 1976 they opened with Roy Clark at the Frontier Hotel in Vegas and two weeks later left to tour the Soviet Union, performing in Riga, Moscow, and Leningrad.

All that was promising, but coming into 1977, the group remained better known for its gospel work than as a country or pop organization. In addition, the group had no major label affiliation. This was remedied in May 1977 when the Oaks signed with ABC Records. (Later, when ABC was acquired by MCA Records, the group remained on the new label roster.) This time success came almost immediately. Their debut LP, *Y'All Come Back Saloon,* spawned two number-one country singles on the way to becoming a chart hit itself: "Y'All Come Back Saloon" and a remake of the Bob Morrison tune "You're the One." They were guests on major TV variety shows, where their philosophy of "keep it happy, keep it exciting" stood them in good stead, for they were always interesting to watch as well as to listen to. They were named Top New Vocal Group of the Year for Singles in *Record World*'s 1977 Country Music Awards competition, won *Billboard*'s 1977 Breakthrough Award, and were named Best Vocal Group of 1977 by the Academy of Country Music.

The Oaks amplified these successes in 1978. Their second album, *Room Service,* was a bestseller, providing the hit singles "Crying Again" and "I'll Be True to You." They won a veritable cornucopia of awards for their work. All three major music trades lauded them: *Billboard* named them Number One Country Group; *Record World* called them the top Country Vocal Group—Singles and Albums; and *Cash Box* gave them the Singles Award for country vocal groups. In the Country Music Association voting for 1978, the quartet was named Vocal Group of the Year and the Oak Ridge Band the Instrumental Group of the Year. (The band, which then comprised four musicians, expanded to six at the start of the 1980s: lead guitarist Skip Mitchell, born Philadelphia, Pennsylvania; bass guitarist Don Breland, born House, Mississippi; keyboards, Garland Craft, born Kinston, North Carolina; drummer Fred Satterfield, born Los Angeles, California; rhythm & lead guitarist Pete Cummings, born Hendersonville, Tennessee; keyboards/rhythm guitarist Ron Fairchild, born Hendersonville, Tennessee.)

The group started off 1979 with another smash hit, the single "Come on In." Later they added such other bestsellers as "Sail Away" and "Dream On" (on MCA) and a Columbia release of older material, "Rhythm Guitar." Their MCA LP *The Oak Ridge Boys Have Ar-*

rived was on the charts most of the year after being released in March 1979. The group's awards for the year included the Country Vocal Group Singles Award from *Record World;* the Singles and Albums Award in that category from *Cash Box;* Best Vocal Group and Best Album honors from the Academy of Country Music; and nomination for Country Group or Duo of the Year in the American Music Awards. The group also was among the finalists in the *Music City News* Fan Awards for Vocal Group of the Year, Band of the Year, Single of the Year, and Album of the Year.

The Oaks began the 1980s in similar style. The year 1980 brought such singles hits as "Heart of Mine" and the number one hits "Leaving Louisiana in Broad Daylight" and "Trying to Love Two Women." Also on the charts much of the year was the LP *Together,* released in February 1980. The year 1981 provided such hits as "Beautiful You," the number-one "Fancy Free," and the blockbuster single "Elvira," number one on country charts and a major pop hit as well. At the Grammy Awards TV program in February 1982, the Oaks performed the song, which also won the Grammy for Best Country Performance by a Duo or Group with Vocal.

During the late 1970s and early 1980s, the Oaks became a major headline attraction on country and pop circuits at home and overseas. Typically the group was on tour 200 to 250 days a year. In the spring of 1979, the tandem tour of the Oaks and Kenny Rogers set the record as the largest grossing structured tour in the history of country music. The Oaks appearances during those years included capacity concerts at places like New York's Carnegie Hall and London's Royal Albert Hall as well as many other major venues around the world. The group also was a featured act at the International Jazz Festival in Montreaux, Switzerland. The Oaks TV appearances included *The Tonight Show, Don Kirschner Rock Concert, The Dukes of Hazzard, Hee Haw, Mike Douglas, Merv Griffin, Dinah!, The Midnight Special, "Lucy Comes to Nashville"* (special with Lucille Ball), and many others. The quartet also took part one year in Macy's Thanksgiving Day Parade in New York.

The group's singles releases in 1981 included the gold-record selling "Bobbie Sue" (issued in February) and the chart hit "Thank God for Kids" (issued October 28, 1982). Other 1982 singles were "I Wish You Could Have Turned My Head (and Left My Heart Alone)," and "So Fine." The last named, which was the first single not to reach top-chart levels since the group left gospel ranks, also was the first on which the Oaks made a video that was released in the U.S.

Allen recalled to Jack Hurst of the *Chicago Tribune,* "We couldn't even get our record label to have anything to do with the video—that's how excited they were about it—so we paid for it ourselves. It cost us about $45,000. And the record never got higher than no. 16.

"But the first video we ever did was in 1974 (which some credit as being the first video by a country act) on a song called 'Easy' from our first ABC Records (and first non-gospel) album. Few people ever have had the pleasure of even seeing that one, because nobody would play it, and we have yet to get any of our investment back on it. It never became a single in the U.S., but as a direct result of that video, it did become a no. 3 song in Australia—even though we had never been there and still haven't [as of 1985]."

The group had such chart singles during the mid-1980s as "American Made" (the title track from their 1983 album) and "I Guess It Hasn't Hurt to Hurt Sometimes" (issued February 1984). Some of their other releases, most of which made *Billboard* and other charts, included: "Make My Life with You" and "Everyday" in 1984; "Little Things" and "Touch a Hand, Make a Friend" in 1985; "Juliet" and "You Made a Rock out of a Rolling Stone" in 1986; and "It Takes a Little Rain (to Make Some Love Grow)," "This Crazy Love," and "Time In" in 1987.

During 1987, the country field was surprised by the announcement that veteran member Golden was departing, to be replaced by Steve Sanders, whose background ranged from rock to gospel. As a youngster called "Little Stevie Sanders," he had recorded pop and gospel material for MGM Records. He left music for a time, earning impressive credits as an actor including a role, as twelve-year-old Jody Baxter, in the Broadway musical *The Yearling,* and, at sixteen, a part in the movie *Hurry Sundown.* Rather than continue to pursue an acting career, he returned to his first love, music, working as a backing vocalist and guitarist with former gospel artist Mylon LeFevre and, in the UK, with rock star Steve Winwood and guitar great Albert Lee and as a member of the group Pyramid.

In 1977, he signed on as a writer for the Oaks' publishing firm, Silverline Music, and in time wrote or cowrote as number of songs in the group's repertoire. In 1982, he joined the quartet's band before being tabbed to take over the baritone parts of the Oaks' harmony in 1987.

The following year he could point to participation in another Oaks' top-10 hit, "Gonna Take a Lot of River." He also worked on his first Oaks album, *Heartbeat,* issued in September 1987, taking the lead vocal in the second verse of the opening track, "Come by Here." Other 1988 singles releases were "Time In" and "Bridges and Walls." These were followed in 1989 with "Beyond Those Years," "An American Family," and "No Matter How High."

In the first half of the 1980s, the quartet and their band rarely failed to win one or more nominations from Country Music Association voters. The foursome was nominated for Vocal Group of the Year every year from 1980 to 1986, and their album *Bobbie Sue* was nominated for 1982 album of the year. The boys were also finalists for Entertainer of the Year in 1981, 1982, and 1984. The band was nominated for Instrumental Group of the Year every year from 1980 through 1986 with the exception of 1985. During the decade, nominations and awards were given the group in many other awards polls besides the CMA's.

In the late 1980s, though the quartet continued to be a major concert draw, its recordings began to fall prey to country radio and TV's focus on new artists. By the start of the 1990s, the group's long affiliation with MCA Records ended and they moved to RCA. Their singles releases on that label in the early 1990s included "Lucky Moon," "Change My Mind," and "Baby on Board" in 1991 and "Fall" in 1992. None of those came close to the success of the releases of the late 1970s and early 1980s, nor did their next album make a dent on the charts. The RCA contract wasn't renewed and, for a while, the group was without a label home for the first time in decades. In late 1994, however, the quartet was signed by Liberty Records, with their first album for that label planned as a fall-1995 Christmas collection.

Oak Ridge fans were stunned when Sanders abruptly resigned from the group an hour before a concert in early December 1995, citing personal reasons for his departure. Duane Allen pressed his nineteen-year-old son, Dee, into service temporarily until the remaining members and their advisers could decide on what to do. Bill Golden, whose 1987 exit reportedly was the result of disagreement with Bonsall, Allen, and Sterban on his "mountain man" lifestyle, had resolved his differences with the others over the intervening years and was asked to rejoin, making his first reunion appearance in a show in Michigan on January 19, 1996. The revamped quartet continued to maintain an extensive tour schedule throughout the rest of the year.

O'CONNOR, MARK: *Instrumentalist (fiddle, guitar, mandolin, banjo, Dobro). Born Mount Terrace, Washington, August 5, 1961.*

It's been a given for more than a few years that when the Academy of Country Music or the Country Music Association announced their nominees for Musician of the Year, Mark O'Connor's name would be among them. While he could play many other instruments, the fiddle was always his claim to fame, an instrument he played with such passion and finesse as to amaze artists and record producers who heard him even before he reached his teens. In fact, he made his recording debut on a Rounder Records release in 1973 just after turning twelve.

Country music star Steve Wariner told the Country Music Association's *Close Up* (June 1991), "I met Mark when he was about 14 at [fiddler] Buddy Spicher's. Mark would pick up the fiddle and everyone's jaw would drop. I knew that Mark is one of those rare

people. . . . He's a natural genius. A lot of people throw that word around loosely, but I don't have a problem with tagging him with it. He really is unequaled."

O'Connor was born and spent his youth in the state of Washington. His family, and particularly his mother, indulged his interest in music, which began at an early age. Well before he reached his eleventh birthday he was playing guitar, mandolin, banjo, and dobro. As he recalled, "Johnny Cash was my favorite star, and I watched his TV show every week when I was eight years old. When Doug Kershaw took the stage, he had a very powerful impact on me—powerful enough for me to beg my parents for a fiddle for three years. I was already playing guitar, but the violin opened the door for me to be really inspired with music."

He told Janet Williams of *Close Up* that three weeks after he got his violin, he was already "playing a square dance. I was the fiddler, and all night I played three songs that I'd learned in three weeks. Then I started improvising. I remember what was going through my head. 'I'd like to change these tunes a little bit because I have to play them over and over.' I started doing alternate note choices and all." Between then and age thirteen, he added, he expanded his repertoire to over thirteen fiddle tunes.

Over the years he paid attention to a wide range of fiddle players, from Benny Thomasson and Jean-Luc Ponty to classical violinist Pinchas Zukerman. In the case of Zukerman, he pointed out, "My earliest experiences listening to music was with my mother's record collection, which was nearly all classical music. I first saw Pinchas Zukerman on public TV when I was a child. His genius was a great inspiration for me." Years later he recorded a duet with Zukerman of "Ashokan Farewell," the theme song from the Ken Burns *Civil Wars* special for PBS.

Thomasson was his biggest influence early on, though. "In 1973 I was 11 years old and living in Seattle, Washington. I attended the National Fiddler's Concert in Weiser, Idaho, that year, and I saw Benny Thomasson in a jam session with three other fiddlers. Upon hearing him play, I was truly inspired by music for the first time. Over the next couple of years, he became my mentor and friend. I devotingly place Benny Thomasson as the greatest old-time fiddler I have ever heard. Just his rhythmic feel of a two-bar phrase could be a life-long study for an accomplished musician, let alone his complete restructuring and development of an entire American fiddle tune repertoire."

Word of Mark's phenomenal talent began to spread through the folk and country field, and he had the chance to take part in many festivals around the U.S. during his teen years, years that brought him the opportunity to hear and sometimes perform with an array of luminaries on fiddle and other instruments including artists like Byron Berline, Vassar Clements, Buddy Spicher, Johnny Gimble, and Kenny Baker of Bill Monroe's Bluegrass Boys. Meanwhile, Mark was continuing to expand his experience in concert and recording work. From 1973 through the early 1980s, he was represented on some eight record releases, seven on Rounder Records and one for the Country Music Foundation. His concert and recording activities included work with the Dixie Dregs and as part of the David Grisman Quartet.

Record producers were eager to have his talent as a backing musician for many major performers. In 1983, he finally decided to settle in Nashville to take better advantage of those opportunities. For some six years he was one of the most in-demand session artists in the country field. His contributions can be heard on hundreds of albums by the greatest names in the business. While still doing session work, he signed a solo contract with Warner Brothers Records in the mid-1980s. The first product of that pact was *Meanings Of,* issued in 1986. It was followed in 1987 by *The Stone from Which the Arch Was Made* and in early 1988 by *Elysian Forest.* In 1986, the Academy of Country Music first named Mark Fiddler of the Year. After losing out to Johnny Gimble in 1987, he won that honor every year from 1988 through 1996. Country Music Association voters also nominated him for Musician of the Year every year from 1986 through the mid-1990s and awarded him the trophy from 1991 through 1994.

After completing the Warner Brothers' album *On the Mark,* issued in late 1989, O'Connor began thinking about an album that would feature almost a who's who of country performers. It was a project that ended up involving fifty-three instrumentalists of various kinds. To organize this project, Mark decided to give up regular session work. He told Janet Williams, "My musical career has taken on many different angles and doing sessions, which lasted six years, has been the longest I've ever done anything. I'm surprised I did it that long. Each phase of my career has been very interesting and I had a lot of attention and acclaim from my peers.

"The only difference was [that session work provided] my best living. It's really a comfortable living for a musician, so it took even more guts to quit, to go into the world of the unknown again. I feel like I'm on the cutting edge artistically, and I like living on the edge. I don't like to get too comfortable, because I want to keep on creating."

The fruits of that effort, the *Mark O'Connor & the New Nashville Cats* album came out on Warner Brothers in mid-1991. The first single, "Restless," featured, besides Mark, Steve Wariner, Vince Gill, and Ricky Skaggs. The album stayed on the charts for a number of months, peaking at number forty-four in *Billboard.* The album won Mark and friends Gill, Skaggs, and Wariner the 1991 Country Music Association Award for Vocal Event of the Year. In the 1991 Grammy voting it was chosen as the Best Country Instrumental Performance.

This was followed two years later by the album *Heroes,* in which Mark recorded duets with many fiddling greats including Doug Kershaw, Jean-Luc Ponty, and Charlie Daniels. The album peaked in *Billboard* in the fall of 1993 at number forty-six. Its sequel to Charlie Daniels's "The Devil Came Down to Georgia," titled "The Devil Comes Back to Georgia," was issued as a single and was on *Billboard* charts from the end of 1993 through early 1994. In the 1994 CMA members' poll, the disc, which featured, besides Mark and Charlie, Johnny Cash, Marty Stuart, and Travis Tritt, was nominated for Vocal Event of the Year. At the same time, CMA members named him Musician of the Year again, a trophy he also received in 1995 and 1996 for his fifth and six consecutive wins in this classification.

While not giving up his country activities, in the 1990s Mark increasingly carved a new career for himself in the classical field as a performer and composer. In 1993 he completed work on his "Fiddle Concerto for Fiddle and Orchestra" and played it in public for the first time. In 1995 the 45 minute Concerto was recorded with conductor Marin Alsop and the New York Concordia Orchestra for release on Warner Bros. By the end of 1996 he had performed the music with over 50 symphony orchestras in the U.S. and abroad.

Discussing the piece with Robert Hilburn of the *Los Angeles Times* ("The King of Crossover," Calendar section, October 27, 1996), he said his objective was "to explore the bridges between folk fiddling and classical music. [It] really is a journey, a travelogue. In the first movement it sets up a conversation between a violinist and a fiddler. Each of the two personas interpret the themes in their own style.

"But that's not enough. So in the second movement, the music goes back in time to the Baroque era, where it's possible that the violinist and the fiddler could have been the same person. Then there's a transition that hints at the present day. As the third movement takes off, the two styles are now completely in sync, meaning you cannot tell the difference between the modern-day classical violinist and the modern-day fiddler. I use an old, old dance form, the jig, that has traditions in both styles."

On the country side, he contributed to the concept album of Steve Wariner's titled *No More Mr. Nice Guy.* This disc, issued in early 1996, was an instrumental collection featuring dozens of the best musicians in country and other genres—O'Connor, Vince Gill, Chet Atkins, Bela Fleck, Leo Kottke, Lee Roy Parnell, and many more. He also agreed to appear in the Southern Jamboree closing ceremony at the Atlanta, Georgia, Olympic Games. In the event, presented on August 4, 1996, he and Faith Hill were featured as the country ambassadors to the world.

His classical concerts in 1996 include a series of trio appearances with classical stars Yo Yo Ma on cello and composer-bassist Edgar Meyer. With those artists he recorded the album *Appalachia Waltz* which debuted at number one on the *Billboard* classical chart in 1996. (After performing excerpts from that at a solo appearance on December 15, 1996, at the Ash Grove venue on the Santa Monica, California, pier, he said he had played it the day before at his sister's wedding. "And two months before my students played it at my wedding." He also played his composition "Song of the Liberty Bell," part of a score he was preparing for a 1997 PBS program on the Revolutionary War.) Scheduled for release in early 1997 was a new solo album whose tracks included six O'Connor-composed violin caprices as well as pieces for guitar and mandolin. During 1996, he also began recording his second fiddle concerto, the "Tennessee Concerto," supported by Marin Alsop and the St. Louis Symphony Orchestra, for release in 1997.

ORBISON, ROY: *Singer, guitarist, songwriter. Born Vernon, Texas, April 23, 1936, died, Hendersonville, Tennessee, December 6, 1988.*

Along with Elvis, Jerry Lee Lewis, and the Everly Brothers, a country-bred artist considered highly influential in the worldwide rise of rock 'n' roll was Roy Orbison, a man with whom the Beatles felt privileged to tour in 1963. Despite his tremendous achievements, by the time Elvis introduced Roy to the audience at the "Great One's" last Las Vegas show in 1977 as "the greatest singer in the world," it had been over a dozen years since his last major hit. A major reason for Orbison's decline had been a series of tragedies in the middle and late 1960s that might have shattered weaker people completely. But Roy hung in there while cover versions of some of his earlier songs brought hits for seventies artists (including Linda Ronstadt's number-one country hit of his "Blue Bayou"). In 1979, he began still another comeback attempt, starting with a new LP on Elektra, that eventually led to his first Grammy Award in the early 1980s. Later in the decade he was one of the first inductees into the newly established Rock and Roll Hall of Fame.

As might be expected of a boy growing up in Texas, his early influences were almost all country- and gospel-based. His father started teaching him how to play guitar when the boy was six and he was well versed in the instrument by the time he was a teenager. While attending high school, he was leader of his own country group, the Wink Westerners, and had a show on radio station KVWC in Vernon, Texas. When he was sixteen, he represented Texas at the International Lions Convention in Chicago, singing and accompanying himself on guitar.

At North Texas State College, he met another young artist with show-business ambitions, Pat Boone. Boone encouraged him to keep up with his music and Roy responded by organizing a new band that soon backed

him on a 1955 TV show presented on a Midland, Texas, station. His TV work and engagements at various venues with his group brought him in contact with many of the new rock-oriented country artists, including Jerry Lee Lewis, Elvis, and Johnny Cash. It was Cash who proved the main catalyst, suggesting that Roy make a demo tape of some of his material and take it to Sam Phillips, head of Sun Records in Memphis (the pioneer label in early rockabilly). It was a move that determined Roy's main musical direction from then on, pushing him into the rockabilly fold even though his main interests tended toward mainstream country.

As he told an interviewer: "I sent Phillips 'Oooby Dooby' because that was the kind of material Sun was releasing at the time. But I was really more interested in ballads. I hadn't felt comfortable doing rhythm & blues or rock. I got into [rock] by accident. We were working a dance on New Year's Eve and someone asked for 'Shake, Rattle and Roll.' I planned to do it at midnight, but started too soon so we had to keep doing it over and over. By the time midnight came, I was used to it and began to incorporate some rock numbers into our list of songs."

Actually, he almost struck out with Sun. After Phillips heard over the phone that Roy was recommended by Cash, the record executive snapped "Johnny Cash doesn't run my business" and hung up. But he eventually heard the tape and the resultant single became a major hit of 1956. (Credence Clearwater Revival later recorded it as well.)

After touring all over the U.S. with such artists as Cash, Lewis, and Carl Perkins, Roy responded to an invitation from Wesley Rose of Acuff-Rose music publishers to become a staff songwriter and departed from Sun in 1957. One of his first efforts was "Claudette," named after his wife, which was a chart hit. Jerry Lee Lewis also made the charts with Roy's "Down the Line" (redone decades later by the Blasters under its original title, "Go, Go, Go"). Buddy Holly too used some of Orbison's material in his repertoire.

Rose, who had also taken over as Roy's personal manager, arranged for a new recording contract with Fred Foster's Monument Records in 1959. The next year, Roy's "Only the Lonely," sold over 2 million copies. This was followed by a stream of best-sellers, most originals by Roy, a few from other writers. Among his *Billboard* Top 10 pop singles were "Running Scared" and "Cryin'" (backed with "Candy Man") in 1961, "Dream Baby" (1962), "In Dreams," and "Mean Woman Blues" backed with "Blue Bayou" (1963), and in 1964, "It's Over" and "Oh, Pretty Woman" (one of the most successful singles of the sixties, selling over 7 million copies worldwide). In all, Orbison placed twenty-seven straight records on the charts the first part of the sixties. One of the first rockabilly stars to use string sections, he often turned out lush country-pop rather than the raw, unleashed rock of Lewis and Presley.

He became a major international star in 1963, contracting to tour Britain with a rock group that at the time had much slimmer credentials than he did, the Beatles. It brought a close rapport between all of them and it also involved an accidental event that reshaped Roy's image. After his plane trip to England, he left his regular glasses in his seat and so had to wear his prescription "shades." Everyone liked the effect and from then on his combination of dark hair, dark glasses, and black suit became a personal trademark. After coheadlining with the Beatles, he returned to Europe in the mid-1960s for other tours with top groups, including several series with the Rolling Stones. He established a rapport with European fans that remained strong for decades. In the seventies when he was only vaguely remembered by many U.S. fans, he always could play before capacity houses overseas.

In 1965, after a half-decade of unparalleled success with Monument, he switched to MGM Records. His reasons were that "MGM offered access to motion pictures and television as well as records. It also provided financial security and that meant I would have all the time I needed to create." Soon after joining MGM, he made his first film, *Fastest Guitar Alive.* He also scored a mild hit with "Ride Away," but the sales fell far short of blockbusters such as "Oh, Pretty Woman."

Still, he had had dry spells before and there seemed no reason why he wouldn't be making top-chart levels again in due time. At that point, fate struck a devastating blow. His wife, Claudette, was killed as a result of a motorcycle accident. Stunned and disorganized, he sought escape in an ever more intensive concert schedule. As he told Robert Hilburn of the *Los Angeles Times:* "All I was doing was surviving. I was trying to work my way out of the turmoil. It takes time to get back on your feet. I just wasn't up to the demands of recording.

"I've got nothing against a performer who only sings, but it really puts a strain on someone who writes the songs, arranges them, and also sings. That's what I had been used to doing. For a while, I just couldn't pull it together."

In 1967, it seemed as though Orbison had ridden out the storm. He began to find it easier to write again. Plans for new recordings began. Then tragedy hit with redoubled force. A fire at his Nashville home killed two of his three children. After weeks of grief, he gave up writing in favor of the old concert-grind palliative.

Although he remained under contract to MGM, not much happened from a recording standpoint even when he was in the mood to work, mainly because the company was going through continuous upheavals in executive personnel. When Mike Curb took over at the start of the seventies, one of his first moves was to get Roy, whom he admired greatly, back in the studios. This resulted in some early 1970s albums and a few singles, but Roy's long absence from the record field in the U.S. seemed to have dissipated interest in him at home.

Still popular elsewhere, though, Roy brought his live act to other parts of the world and was rarely in evidence in the U.S. for much of the 1970s. He did appear in concert with Johnny Cash in 1973 and made a few other special engagements, but that was about it. As he noted: "I tended to fulfill commitments around the world, then come home and rest." He didn't lack for engagements. He made many tours of Europe and Australia in the 1970s. Typical of his schedule was the period in 1974 when he worked foreign venues seven months straight with only nine days off, including dates in Crete, Greece, and Taiwan. He did some recordings for Mercury in the mid-1970s after leaving MGM, but without any notable results. He did have some recording achievements during the decade, though, earning a gold record in Australia for a single release in 1974 and demonstrating his popularity with English fans with a reissue of some of his earlier material. *The Very Best of Roy Orbison* rose to number one in the UK in 1976.

Late in the decade, though, he and his work started to resurface at home. Linda Ronstadt scored a striking success with his "Blue Bayou," while his "Oh, Pretty Woman" became the theme for a series of TV commercials. He himself tried out the water in 1977 with a minitour of California venues. The results were positive. Almost all the shows were sold out and were critically acclaimed. His stature with fellow artists was indicated by the Eagles, Jefferson Starship, the Tubes, and Boz Scaggs's appearance in the audience at his Los Angeles date.

To add new impetus, he signed a recording contract with a new label, Elektra, during 1978. His debut on the label, *Laminar Flow* (May 1979), contained three new songs by him: two ballads and the fast-paced rocker "Movin'."

Among his albums over the years were such Monument collections as *Greatest Hits* (1962), *In Dreams* (1964), *Early Orbison and More Greatest Hits* (1964–65), *Orbisongs* (1965), and *Very Best of Roy Orbison* (1966). MGM LPs included *There Is Only One* (1966), *Roy Orbison Sings Don Gibson* (1967), *Great Songs, Hank Williams the Roy Orbison Way,* and *Roy Orbison Sings.* Sun reissued some of his earliest recordings in the LP *Original Sound.* In the 1980s, the two-disc *All-Time Greatest Hits of Roy Orbison* (Monument) and two-disc *In Dreams* (Virgin) kept his classics in print.

Though Roy kept active in the 1980s as a performer and writer, his main rewards came from successes achieved by other artists with some of his classic compositions. Those credits included top-10 hits scored by

Don McLean with "Crying" and Van Halen with "(Oh) Pretty Woman." During 1980, he recorded a duet with Emmylou Harris, "That Lovin' You Feelin' Again," for the soundtrack of the film *Roadie* on Warner Brothers Records. When the Grammy Award winners were announced on February 25, 1981, he and Emmylou won trophies for Best Country Performance by a Duo or Group with Vocal. That was the first Grammy Roy had ever received, an ironic situation considering his tremendous contributions to the rock and country fields over the decades.

In late 1986, officials of the Rock and Roll Hall of Fame announced that Roy would be one of the new inductees. At the ceremonies, held in New York's Waldorf Astoria in January 1987, he was introduced by Bruce Springsteen who said, in part, "Some rock 'n' roll reinforces friendships and community. Roy's ballads were always best when you were alone in the dark." The songs, he continued, "addressed the underside of pop romance—they were scary.

"When I went in to the studio to make [the album] *Born to Run,* I wanted to write words like Bob Dylan that sounded like Phil Spector, but with singing like Roy Orbison. But nobody sings like Roy Orbison."

Later in the year *A Night in Black and White: A Salute to Roy Orbison* was taped in Los Angeles for presentation as a Cinemax cable TV special. Paying respect to Orbison, who performed many of his hits on the program, were many of the superstars of both English and U.S. rock music, including Bruce Springsteen, Elvis Costello, and Tom Waits. The time also seemed ripe for a revival of Roy's recording and performing career. Soon after his Hall of Fame induction, he signed a new contract with British-based Virgin Records, and during 1988 he began work with producer T-Bone Burnett on his label debut. He also joined superstars Bob Dylan, George Harrison, Tom Petty, and Jeff Lynne in a group called the Traveling Wilburys that drew delighted and enthusiastic crowds to concerts across the U.S. and other parts of the world.

He recorded the album *Traveling Wilburys, Volume One* with the group, released in 1988 on the Wilbury/Warner Brothers label. The same year, Rhino Records released the "best of" CD, *For the Lonely: 18 Greatest Hits,* as well as a two-LP set called *For the Lonely: A Roy Orbison Anthology, 1956–1965,* that combined his Sun and Monument sessions.

Roy seemed well on the way to reestablishing himself as a star of the first rank when he was felled by a heart attack on December 6, 1988. After his death the *Wilburys* album reached number one on the *Billboard* pop chart. His Virgin album, *Mystery Girl,* maintained his high standards and was on album charts for many months in early 1989.

In the next few years, Roy received three posthumous honors from Grammy Awards voters. In the polling for 1988, whose results were announced on the February 24, 1989, telecast, his duet with k.d. lang on Virgin, "Cryin'," was named the Best Country Vocal Collaboration. In the 1989 voting, he shared the Best Rock Performance by a Duo or Group with the other Wilburys for their hit album. In the 1990 voting, his single version of his classic song, "Oh, Pretty Woman," a track from the Virgin album *A Black & White Night Live,* was selected for Best Pop Vocal Performance, Male.

After Roy's death, his widow, Barbara Orbison (they had two children, Roy Kelton and Alex), began working on a series of projects to keep Roy's contributions evergreen. The first was a tribute at the Universal Amphitheatre in Los Angeles on February 24, 1990, to benefit the homeless. Those taking part onstage or via video appearances included members of the original Byrds, B. B. King, Bonnie Raitt, John Fogerty, Emmylou Harris, and Johnny Cash.

Other things Barbara had in the works in the 1990s, besides memorial concerts, included completion of an autobiography Roy had started before his death, a documentary film of his career, and a possible movie based on his life. She also approved release of a video of Roy's only movie, *The Fastest Guitar Alive.*

She always emphasized her late husband's decency and humanity. For instance, with respect to homeless benefits, she told Steve Hochman of the *Los Angeles Times,* "Roy always said that inside every [pop musician] there's a homeless person, because you start out by sleeping on people's couches. Now Roy's music is actually helping people maybe to have a place to put their heads at night."

ORRALL, ROBERT ELLIS: *Singer, songwriter. Born Boston, Massachusetts, c. late 1950s.*

A performer born and bred in Boston seems an unlikely candidate for country-music success; yet over the years, more than a few country stars have come from places far afield from the U.S. South and West. For Robert Ellis Orrall, it did cause some mental reservations as he became more involved creatively in the field, which may have affected his performing aspirations. But while that avenue remained in doubt after the mid-1990s, his impact had been felt as supplier of challenging compositions to a fair number of country stars.

His interest in pop music went back to his elementary school days when he was already cajoling friends into forming bands with him. His focus on music based on pop and rock formats continued to grow stronger in his high school years when he first tried his skills as a songwriter. As he told Debbie Holley of *Billboard* ("RCA Focuses on Its Orrall Delivery," January 8, 1993), he assembled a band in the late 1970s to record some of his material. "I figured if I want to make a record, why don't I just make one. I didn't quite know what I was going to do with it."

He parlayed that experience with persistent pursuit

of club gigs to build up a following in the Boston area. With good review and interview articles in local papers, he gained the attention of executives at RCA's International Division, which signed him and issued three albums of his material in the U.S. and Europe in the 1980–84 time period. The pop/rock collections, he told Holley, "saw critical success. We got consistently great reviews and consistently poor sales." He did manage to score a top-40 single, a duet with Carlene Carter (before she returned to the country fold) titled "I Couldn't Say No."

Orrall realized as those years went by that many of his pop songs had a definite country flavor, which wasn't surprising since at that time he had literally developed a country alter ego. He told Mandy Wilson of the Country Music Association's *Close Up* magazine, "At the same time I had my pop deal with RCA, I also had a country band called 'The Sunny Cowboys.' It was really just two of us—Sunny Doug and Sunny Bob (that was me). So we called each other 'Sunny.' Doug Miller is a guy who was in a band with me in the fifth grade. So Sunny Bob and Sunny Doug would get together every Monday night and have 'Sunny Cowboy Night' when we'd write country songs. I actually sent tapes to Nashville trying to get a record deal for the Sunny Cowboys at the same time I had my pop deal.

"More and more as I sat down to write it seemed like my material was country. But because I was from Boston, I didn't feel like I could pursue it from an artist's point of view. I didn't think anyone would buy it. So I started writing songs for other people."

During the 1980s, Orrall was aligned for a number of years as a writer with such New York publishing firms as Zomba and BMG. He also earned sufficient songwriting credits to become a member of the writer's (and publisher's) representation group, ASCAP, an association that resulted in his traveling to Washington, D.C., in the mid-1980s to lobby on copyright matters with other ASCAP members. Among them were writers and publishing officials from Nashville, who suggested Orrall consider transferring there as a key career move.

He mulled it over for a time while demos of his songs were being sent to country performers. As interest in his song wares grew in Nashville with soloists and groups beginning to include them in recording sessions, he finally settled in Music City with his wife and children in 1990. Soon after he arrived, he was invited to a party hosted by the band Shenandoah in honor of achieving a number-one single with Orrall's song "Next to You, Next to Me." Other artists who included Orrall songs in their albums or who achieved chart hit singles with them were the Oak Ridge Boys, Dixiana, Vern Gosdin, Diamond Rio, Tom Wopat, Curtis Wright, Matthews Wright & King, and many others. He also collaborated with longtime friend Carlene Carter on "The Sweetest Thing" for her Warner Brothers album.

In the early 1990s, Orrall was doing well as a song writer, but he still hankered to savor the rewards of live audience response, and to hear his own performances on radio stations. He put together a band in 1991 for a showcase for record company officials at the Bluebird in Nashville. This produced an offer from RCA that he accepted, then set to work completing material for an album with writing friends Marcus Hummon, Billy Spencer, and Curtis Wright. The outlook seemed promising after the debut single, "Boom! It Was Over," made top-chart levels, peaking at number fifteen in *Radio & Records* the week of February 12, 1993.

RCA hoped that boded well for the album, *Flying Colors,* released February 23, 1993. The second single, "A Little Bit of Love" (cowritten by Orrall and L. Wilson), reached number thirty-one in *Billboard,* aided by substantial airplay. Orrall noted it was written about his two-year-old daughter. He told Mandy Wilson with pride, "When it comes on the radio, she goes nuts. She starts screaming 'Daddy! Daddy!' She knows that song."

However, the album proved a disappointment in terms of sales, and RCA didn't pick up an option for a second one. By late 1993, Orrall had formed a duo with Curtis Wright and the team got a contract from Giant Records. Their album, *She Loves Me like She Means It,* was released in the summer of 1994 preceded by a single of the title track (cowritten by Orrall, Billy Spencer, and Angelo), which made *Billboard* mid-chart levels. In October, the single "If You Could Say What I'm Thinking" (cowritten by Orrall and Wright) appeared briefly on lower-chart positions. By the end of 1994, Orrall was again focusing on his solo career, while also continuing to do some recording work with Wright. During the summer of 1995 when the Orrall & Wright single "What Do You Want from Me" was issued, Orrall was busy writing songs for a new solo album to be produced by Josh Leo.

Orrall's 1996 activities included leading ASCAP's 16th annual Country Songwriters Workshop at the organization's Nashville offices on April 3. He noted at the time he was developing material for a new album for his old label, RCA. When Reba McEntire's new album, *What Am I Gonna Do About You,* came out in October 1996, one of its more striking tracks was "What If It's You," cowritten by Orrall and Cathy Majeski. Though it wasn't the first single released, Reba emphasized she hoped it would be sent out later. "I'd love to see this one become a single. It's kind of a scary song, when you really think about it. You're married and you are looking at your spouse going, 'What if it's not you?' You find somebody at the grocery store. You look at them and go, 'Wow, I think I know you. Are we supposed to be together?' People marry the wrong people, sometimes. So I think this is a pretty dramatic story."

OSBORNE BROTHERS *Vocal and instrumental brother act. Bob Osborne, born Hyden, Kentucky, December 7, 1931; Sonny Osborne, born Hyden, Kentucky, October 29, 1937.*

Strong-willed individuals, the Osborne brothers went their own way over the years, often blazing new trails in bluegrass music, frequently to the dismay of the traditionalists. One of their heresies was to play the music with any sort of band makeup that suited their own tastes. If they felt like adding drums, for instance, they did so even if old-time bands didn't use the instrument. In the early 1960s, they also raised the hackles of many purists by using electric instruments in their stylings, an approach taken up by many bluegrass and country bands as the decade went by.

The brothers were weaned on bluegrass music growing up in Kentucky. The Osborne boys had learned to pick out country music on the five-string banjo, Sonny's favorite, and the mandolin, Bob's preferred instrument, by the time they were high school age. When younger brother Sonny was only sixteen, he and Bob made their radio debut on station WROL, Knoxville, Tennessee, with Bob singing high lead (tenor) and Sonny handling the baritone vocals.

The brothers left WROL for WJR, Detroit, in 1954 and received increasing attention during guest appearances in country shows around the Midwest. In October 1956, they became featured regulars on the *WWVA Jamboree* in Wheeling, West Virginia. That same year they signed their first major recording contract with MGM Records. In 1959, they expanded to a trio by adding Benny Birchfield (born Isaban, West Virginia, June 6, 1937), who played lead guitar and five-string banjo and also handled lead vocals.

The advent of the folk music boom in the late 1950s had focused new attention on bluegrass music, and artists such as Bill Monroe and Flatt & Scruggs became headliners at folk music concerts and festivals. The Osbornes created a considerable stir on the steadily expanding college folk music circuit with a memorable appearance at Antioch College, Ohio, in early 1959. After that, they became a major act in the college field, touring all over the United States in 1959 and throughout the 1960s.

The Osbornes varied their formats, sometimes working just as a duo, sometimes with Birchfield as a trio, other times adding a number of other instruments. This still held true during the 1970s, when the Osbornes played a part in the revival of bluegrass in that decade. The music had seemed to reach a peak with fans by the mid-1960s, then suffered a decline that lasted into the early 1970s. A resurgence began at that point with a slow but steady rise in bluegrass festivals, concerts, and clubs as the decade progressed. By the end of the 1970s, there were strong bluegrass movements all over the United States and in other countries and the Osbornes were much sought after for concert dates and appearances at annual festivals, including Bill Monroe's Bean Blossom event.

During the 1960s, the Osbornes were featured at several Newport Folk Festivals in Rhode Island. Discussing their importance in program notes for the 1964 Festival, Ralph Rinzler wrote, "[The Osbornes] made a strong impression on bluegrass music for several reasons: They developed a distinctive style of ultramodern trio harmony singing, the two harmony parts sometimes following the melody in parallel motion until reaching a final cadence when each part would move up successively to exchange notes (i.e., baritone to lead, lead to tenor and tenor to high baritone or else, on occasion, up a third at a time). The instrumental techniques (Sonny's banjo, Bob's mandolin) were original in sound and approach as was their material. This pair of young Kentuckians has always maintained its own distinctive niche in bluegrass. Their sound is immediately recognizable, strongly individualistic."

The Osbornes and Birchfield were featured as guests a number of times on the *Grand Ole Opry* starting in 1959. In 1964, they became regular cast members and still appeared regularly on the show during the 1970s and into the 1980s. During the 1960s and 1970s, they performed on many major TV shows and played country and folk clubs, festivals, fairs, etc., in all fifty states. They also made several tours of foreign countries. Among the songs associated with them over the years were numbers like "Each Season Changes You," "Banjo Boys," "Lovey Told Me Goodby," "Fair and Tender Ladies," "Ruby, Are You Mad," "Take This Hammer," "Once More," "Mule Skinner Blues," "Don't Even Look at Me," and a number of Boudleaux and Felice Bryant songs, including one that became the Osbornes' theme, "Rocky Top."

The Osbornes turned out a number of albums during their seven years on MGM, an association that came to a close in 1963 when they moved to Decca. Among the MGM LPs were *Bluegrass Music* (4/62), *Bluegrass Instrumentals* (12/62), *Cuttin' Grass* (11/63), *Osborne Brothers and Red Allen,* and in the late 1960s, *Osborne Brothers.* Their Decca albums included *Voices in Bluegrass* (8/65), *Up This Hill and Down* (8/66), *Modern Sounds* (8/67), *Up to Date & Down to Earth* (9/69), *Ru-Be-eeee, Osborne Brothers,* and *Country Roads* (last three, early 1970s).

In the mid-1970s, the Osbornes had a number of recordings on the MCA label, including a definitive two-record set, *The Best of the Osborne Brothers.* One of their MCA singles that made lower-chart levels was the 1976 release "Don't Let Smokey Mountain Smoke Get in Your Eyes." In the late 1970s, they were represented on the CMH label. In late 1977, they completed a two-disc set of Boudleaux and Felice Bryant songs titled *The Osborne Brothers: From Rocky Top to Muddy Bottom.* Besides their theme song, the LPs included such numbers as "Hey Joe," "All I Have to Do Is

Dream," "Love Hurts," and "Take Me as I Am (Or Let Me Go.)"

During the 1970s, the Osbornes were nominated for best band in the Country Music Association Awards competition on a number of occasions. Besides his performing activities, Sonny also found time in the late 1970s to write a column on banjo techniques and news of the bluegrass field for the *Banjo Newsletter.* In 1980, their CMH single "I Can Hear Kentucky Callin' Me" was on the charts.

Throughout the 1980s and into the 1990s, the Osborne Brothers group continued to be an important part of the bluegrass and folk festival circuit, though their rapport with the broader country market tended to diminish. They recorded new albums for independent bluegrass labels during those years, including *When the Roses Bloom in Dixieland* which was nominated for a Grammy in the Bluegrass Album of the year (for 1994) category.

Some of the group's classic recordings were packaged in two sets by Germany's Bear Family Records, both only available in the U.S. as import items. One of them, the 4 CD *The Osborne Brothers: 1956–1968,* included such hits as "Ruby," "Once More," "Rocky Top," and "The Kind of Woman I Got." The second set, *The Osborne Brothers: 1968–1974,* also comprising 4 CDs included such Decca/MGM tracks as "Tennessee Hound Dog," "Georgia Piney Woods" and the remake of "Ruby, Are You Mad."

OSLIN, K. T.: *Singer, keyboards player, songwriter. Born Texas, May 15, c. 1942.*

To say the least, K. T. Oslin was a "Katie come lately" in the country field, starting on the road to stardom at age forty-five in 1987. Many country artists scored career breakthroughs in their thirties, but, particularly among female artists, you can count those who found success in their mid-forties on the fingers of one hand.

She was born in Texas, but grew up mostly in Arkansas in an environment that was far from affluent. Her father died from leukemia at age thirty-eight, leaving her mother, Kathleen, to struggle to support two children, K. T., then two, and her four-year-old brother. Her mother earned a living as a lab technician and moved constantly, marrying and divorcing four times while the children were growing up. Oslin told Dolly Carlisle of *People* magazine ("K. T. Is Now O.K.," June 14, 1993), "I always looked at marriage as something where you're married for two years and then you divorce."

Considering her high-energy style on stage and the soaring effect of the vocals she belts out, it could come as a surprise to concertgoers that she always had self-doubts. She told Janet Williams of the Country Music Association's *Close Up* in August 1991, "As a little kid I was painfully shy. Then I discovered that I could make

people laugh, and I hid behind that for a long time. Once I got into plays I discovered that, yes, I have the ability to entertain. And it felt just fine to me.

"Kay Oslin is your everyday person and is as easily crushed by anything that anybody else is. I don't want attention brought to me, and I don't like to be stared at. But, when I get onstage and I know what I'm doing and I feel confident in my work, and if I'm presenting you with something that is worth your time, then I'm happy.

"But I still am shy. A lot of performers are. They just become another person. I put on the outfit, the high heels, the makeup, and I become 'K. T. Oslin.' She's a steamroller—nothing can stop that woman."

After finishing school, Oslin focused on an entertainer career. She kept at it persistently as a singer and sometime stage performer, appearing regionally around the country. For a time she lived in New York and found some work in Broadway shows. But the decades went by without any major moves upward. She made demos and sought to get them before record executives with minimum results until she finally pried the door open at RCA Nashville in the mid-1980s. Would she have kept striving for such an opening if that opportunity hadn't worked out? She told interviewers that might have happened; certainly someone in her mid-forties might begin to get panicky about whether life had passed her by.

Fortunately she didn't have to mull over the alternative. Her RCA debut album, *'80s Ladies,* featuring a title track written by her, became a chart hit. After two decades of "Oslin who?," she told Carlisle, in two months time she went "from being an obscurity to *The Tonight Show.*" While it might have been better "if I'd come out of the box a little slower," still it was better late than never.

All of a sudden things began happening fast. She got the chance to win over large numbers of fans with TV guest appearances and live performances. The voting for the 1987 Grammy Awards gave her the nod for Best Country Vocal Performance, Female, for " '80s Ladies." Released as a single, the song also reached top-chart levels. She followed up in 1988 with another first-rate album, *This Woman,* which provided her with another hit song, "Hold Me" (lyrics and music by Oslin), which earned her 1988 Grammys for Best Country Vocal Performance, Female, and Best Country Song. Other songs that became chart hit singles for her in the late 1980s were "Do Ya" and "I'll Always Come Back." Country Music Association voters in 1988 nominated "Do Ya" for Single of the Year.

By the start of the 1990s, Oslin had reached star status, able to draw large numbers of people to major venues around the U.S., Canada, and overseas. She kept up her standards with a fine third album issued by RCA in late 1990 called *Love in a Small Town.* It contained still more originals, including "Come Next Monday," which reached number one in *Radio & Records* the week of November 16, 1990.

A series of events, however, set emotional strains in motion that disrupted her career activities for a while. One came the day her doctor told the forty-nine-year-old artist that she was going through the change of life. After that, she told *People*'s Carlisle, "I cried for days." Though she hadn't had relationships where she'd considered marriage, she said, she'd daydreamed at times about having a family. "In the past I had chosen not to get pregnant. Now I didn't have the choice."

Other depressing occurrences included the passing of a beloved Staffordshite terrier in 1991 and the death of her mother from an aneurysm in 1992. Finally she decided to take off all of 1992. "I got tired," she said later. "I got bored and I got frustrated. I really did sort of go to Zombieland. I've been in this business a long time, and I think it just kind of caught up with me." Fortunately, she noted, she'd accrued enough money to be able to do that without having to worry about a wolf at the door.

Another factor that might also have contributed to a temporary retirement was concern about new material for another album. She took a long time to write new songs, and all but a few tracks on her first three collections had been self-penned. As of mid-1991, she only had written thirty numbers, twenty-seven of which had been recorded in the first three discs.

In any case, Oslin began to rouse herself for returning to action in early 1993. Besides beginning to think about a greatest-hits album, she accepted a role as a nightclub owner in the Peter Bogdanovich film *The Thing Called Love*, whose stars included the late River Phoenix and Trisha Yearwood. She also completed work on some new additions to the retrospective album, *Songs from An Aging Sex Bomb,* issued by RCA in the summer of 1993. Besides her earlier chart successes, it contained three new numbers, including, in particular, the excellent new Oslin composition "Feeding a Hungry Heart."

Describing her writing method to Janet Williams, Oslin said, "Mostly I write by myself. That's kind of lonesome, shutting yourself from everybody. But it's fun when it goes well. . . . When you're thinking of words, it's great fun, when you're not, it's agony. You just think, 'There are no other words, and there are no other notes, and if there are, I'm sure not gonna think of them.' And so you close the piano and you walk out and you see a weed and you pull it."

More than two years after her previous release, Oslin had a new album in stores in the fall of 1996. Entitled *My Roots Are Showing*, the RCA collection eschewed original compositions in favor of standards she considered among her long-time favorites, such as the traditional "Down in the Valley," the Delmore brothers' "Sand Mountain Blues," Charlie and Ira Louvin's "Baby Come Back," and the Webb Pierce-Wayne P. Walker "Pathway of Teardrops." An unusual track was K.T.'s performance of an obscure Irving Berlin number, "(I'll See You in) Cuba."

OSMOND, MARIE: *Singer, actress. Born Ogden, Utah, 1959.*

Although mostly known in the mid- and late 1970s as a pop and rock performer, the only woman in the Osmond family started her career with country material. In fact, her debut single was one of the best-selling country singles in 1973. While she joined brother Donny and other members of the large Osmond clan (the men in the brood total eight) in singing everything from sophisticated ballads to all-out rock in concerts and on the late 1970s Osmond TV show, she always included a country song in her repertoire now and then, some of which made the country hit lists.

Like all but one of the nine children, Marie was born in Ogden, Utah. (The exception is the youngest, Jimmy, who was born in Canoga Park, California.) The year she was born, the Osmond saga got under way when four of the boys started singing in church and rehearsing barber shop ballads. By the mid-1960s, the brothers had progressed to featured performers on the *Andy Williams Show,* later expanding to include brother Donny. So by the time Marie reached her teens, the Osmonds already were internationally known artists.

Her parents didn't want her to start in show business too young, though she demonstrated a good voice at an early age and curiosity about the entertainment field. Only when she was fourteen did the time seem propitious for her to pursue a singing career. She sang duets with brother Donny a few times during Las Vegas shows at the start of the 1970s, but it wasn't until a few years later that she really began to concentrate on performing.

She discussed plans for a recording effort with her brothers and family friend Mike Curb, previously president of MGM when the Osmonds became top disc stars on that label. The idea of starting out with country material arose from those sessions, including a suggestion from Curb that Sonny James produce the tracks. Marie signed with MGM early in 1973 and then flew to Nashville with her mother to start work with Sonny on the new project. A number of possible songs had been assembled, including one that had been a hit many years before called "Paper Roses." Marie admitted, "I'd never heard the song before they played it for me."

The single of the song was the first disc of Marie Osmond's released and it became a massive hit, riding not only to the top of the country charts but to pop charts around the world. The debut album that contained it also was a chart hit.

She told an interviewer in early 1974, "My voice isn't really a typical country twangy kind of voice, and I'm not strictly a country singer either, although my heart is now in country more than ever because everyone has been just so fantastic with me. I've really come to love country music and enjoy it. And I listen to a lot of country in order to keep up with what's going on."

In 1974, Osmond continued to stress country material, returning to Nashville to prepare a new album with Sonny James that was issued later in the year. She always had a certain amount of country content in albums she turned out after that, though increasingly the main elements were from other genres. In the mid-1970s, Marie teamed up with brother Donny as both a singing and recording team. In mid-1975, they made country charts with their version of "Make the World Go Away," issued on the Kolob label. In 1977, they included some country songs on their network *Donny and Marie* Show on ABC, a pattern that continued with the follow-up *Osmond Family* program.

In the 1980s, Marie began to stress her country material over more pop-oriented songs, a direction that seemed at odds with the efforts of some reviewers to describe her as "the Mormon Madonna." While she performed mainly in country shows in the first half of the 1980s, she didn't completely abandon her pop roots, taking part with her brothers, for instance, in the Osmonds' 25th Anniversary Special, which was telecast in September 1985, and doing a number of concerts with Donny Osmond.

She made top country-chart levels in the mid-1980s with a series of duet recordings with Dan Seals. Those resulted in receipt of the Country Music Association Award for Vocal Duo of the Year for 1986. The artists also were nominated in that category in 1987. She closed out the decade with a series of solo singles hits on Curb Records, which helped bring a nomination from the Academy of Country Music for Top Female Vocalist of 1989. She continued to add to her TV credits that year as she and Merle Haggard were featured in two sixty-minute TNN concert specials

The early 1990s resulted in several more charted singles, including the 1990 Curb release "Like a Hurricane." While still popular on the country concert circuit, she had no top-level hits during the first part of the decade. In the mid-1990s, she was signed to play the lead female role in a revival of the Rodgers & Hammerstein musical classic, *The Sound of Music,* that toured extensively throughout the U.S. Her performance received generally positive critical comparisons with the original star, Julie Andrews. In the fall of 1995 she was paired with actress-comedienne Betty White in a short-lived TV sitcom called *Maybe This Time.*

Despite the rigors and temptations of show business, Marie always seemed to keep her life on an even keel and her career in perspective. As she once told an interviewer, "People often say that nice people get walked on. I disagree. I'm a nice person, but I don't get walked on. I'm not easy."

OWENS, ALVIS EDGAR "BUCK": *Singer, guitarist, band leader, (the Buckaroos), TV show host (*Hee Haw*). Born Sherman, Texas, August 12, 1929. Elected to Country Music Hall of Fame in 1996.*

"It's hard to get started in this business," Buck Owens once told an interviewer, "but it's simple. You've got to be at the right place at the right time with the right product. I just did what everybody else did. I'd pick and sing for everybody I could, wherever I could, anytime I could. I'd keep learning, keep doing it, get all my ducks set up in a row. Then, when opportunity knocks, you're ready." Buck might also have used the word persistence as a key factor, because he was going on thirty when opportunity finally knocked with a vengeance, but he was ready and responded with a series of successes that made him one of the country superstars of the 1960s and 1970s.

He was born and spent his early years in Sherman, Texas, son of sharecropper parents. If the family didn't have much in the way of material comforts, there was closeness and love of music in the childhood of Alvis Edgar Owens, Jr. He recalled, "As long as I can remember, we always had a piano around the house and mama would sit and play the old hymns and we'd sing with her. She taught me most of 'em."

Like many families in the Southwest in the early 1930s, the Owenses were affected by the prolonged drought that led to the Dust Bowl era of the Depression years. Survival required trying to seek the family fortunes outside Texas. The promised land was California. Says Buck, "It was like *The Grapes of Wrath,* except that we didn't make it to California. We were all packed into a little car, five adults and five kids, with the mattress on top. We ended up in Arizona because the trailer broke down and we just couldn't go any farther."

The place that became home was Mesa, Arizona, where Buck got his first musical instrument, a mandolin his parents gave him on his thirteenth birthday. That year, to help out, Buck dropped out of school to go to work harvesting crops and hauling produce. "I was big enough and willing enough to do a man's work and I got a man's pay."

Meanwhile Owens was extending his musical abilities, teaching himself guitar and other instruments as well. "I was trying to learn to be a performer from anybody who would take the time to teach me." It paid off; he had his first radio show on a Mesa station when he was sixteen. One of the people who worked with him on radio and in a band called Mac's Skillet Lickers was a singer whom he married when he was seventeen, Bonnie Owens. When Buck was only eighteen, the Owenses had their first child.

Buck still had to keep busy at other tasks to support his family. One of his jobs involved hauling produce between Arizona and California's San Joaquin Valley. He was impressed with the region and also the fact that he had two uncles living in Bakersfield who were musicians and told him there was work in the area. Finally he decided to move his family there. He was twenty.

There were plenty of small country-music clubs in and around Bakersfield and, as his uncles said, jobs for good sidemen were available. Owens began playing with club bands, his main concern "trying to become a good guitarist." He did, indeed, impress the music fraternity with his skills in the early 1950s and, before long, he was earning session money backing many major country names. He often traveled down to Los Angeles to play guitar on recordings of such people as Tennessee Ernie Ford, Sonny James, and Tommy Sands.

At the time, he noted, he was satisfied with that niche. He didn't think of himself as a singer. He had a steady job in the house band at the Blackboard Club in Bakersfield. "I just wanted to be a picker and the boss told me to fill in for the singer who was gone that night. It was either sing or lose my job . . . so I sang." The crowd liked it, so he kept on singing. After a while, the band he was with left the club and, in fact, wanted to leave country music for different stylings. Buck remained true to country, going his own way to take Ferlin Husky's place as a member of Tommy Collins's band. His reputation grew, though his private life was troubled; by the mid-1950s his marriage to Bonnie ended in divorce. (She later married Merle Haggard.)

In the mid-1950s, the onset of rock and R&B had started cutting into country-music opportunities. Buck had to scramble to find enough engagements to keep going even as word of his ability was circulating around the country-music field. Finally he got a recording contract from Capitol Records on March 1, 1957. He cut some sides, providing a number of original songs for the sessions. Still, the first singles to come out hardly were blockbusters.

"It was 1958. I'd done some recording, worked several years at the Blackboard with Bill Woods, but I just didn't seem to be gettin' anywhere. So I left, went to Seattle because I had a chance to get on a station as a DJ, and I was there a year and a half. I'd already decided to give it up when 'Under Your Spell' caught on."

Now that the door had opened, Owens was quick to move on through. He went back to Bakersfield and commuted regularly between there and Los Angeles, working on new material. He scored two major hits in 1960s, "Excuse Me (I Think I've Got a Heartache")—a song he cowrote with Harlan Howard—and "Above and Beyond." During 1960, he also met Don Rich, a talented musician who later became lead guitarist of Buck's band, the Buckaroos, founded in 1962. In 1961, Buck collaborated with Harlan Howard again on the top-10 hits "Foolin' Around" and "Under the Influence of Love." He also teamed up with Rose Maddox in a series of duets that produced two more top-10 hits, "Loose Talk" and "Mental Cruelty." They were named top vocal team of the year in disc jockey polls.

Buck had a relatively lean year in 1962 with only one top-10 hit, "Kickin' Our Hearts Around," but it was only a temporary lull. In 1963 he had a banner year with hits like the number-one ranked "Love's Gonna Live Here" (written by him), "You're for Me," and "Act Naturally." The last named made the pop top 40 as well as country lists and was covered by no less a group than the Beatles. From 1963 on, Owens became one of the leaders of the 1960s in the country field. He placed twenty-six straight singles in the number-one position of one or another of the country charts and also had a dozen number-one albums.

Helping Owens achieve this was Jack MacFadden, who became his manager and close associate from the early 1960s on. "I met Jack when he was managing Judy Lynn," Buck told *Music City News* (October 1969). "We had talked about his managing me, but it was five months later before I hired him. I was a bit skeptical at first because Jack had had so many jobs of one kind or another, but it just goes to prove one thing. Whenever a person finds the job he is suited for, he will do a good job . . . and Jack has certainly done that for me. He is so very good with the financial end of the business."

There was plenty to keep Jack busy as the 1960s progressed. Concert business was good all across the United States and Canada and TV credits mounted as Owens was featured on programs ranging from country variety to Ed Sullivan. All the while, Buck kept hitting the top of the national country charts with new Capitol releases. In 1964, his output included best-selling singles of his compositions "I Don't Care," "My Heart Skips a Beat," and "Together Again." Also at the top of the charts in 1965 were the singles "Gonna Have Love," "Buckaroo," "Only You," "Before You Go," and "I've Got a Tiger by the Tail." The last named, which he cowrote with Harlan Howard, remains the one most often associated with him.

In 1966, he worked with Don Rich on the number-one single "Think of Me" and, with Rich and Nat Stuckey, cowrote another classic, "Waitin' on Your Welfare Line." He also wrote his third number-one single of 1966, "Open Up Your Heart." In 1967, he wrote or cowrote such winners as "Sam's Place," "Where Does the Good Times Go," and "Your Tender Loving Care." He was voted Top Country Male Artist for 1967 by *Billboard* magazine. By then he had other honors, as well. The Academy of Country & Western Music Awards in 1965 voted him Top Male Vocalist and Best Band Leader. During the next several years he again was named Best Band Leader, with the Buckaroos voted Best Band. In the first four Country Music Association polls, Buck Owens and the Buckaroos were selected as Instrumental Group or Band of the Year.

Buck finished the 1960s with still more charted singles. In 1968, he made the top 10 with "How Long Will My Baby Be Gone" and in 1969 achieved a country hit with his version of Paul Simon's "Bridge over Troubled Water."

By the end of the 1960s, Owens also had begun building a considerable investment empire. He bought radio stations in California and Arizona, had a booking agency with MacFadden (OMAC), owned a cattle ranch in Paso Robles, California, run by his father, had his own song publishing house, Bluebook Music, as well as other business interests. By then one of his two sons from his first marriage, Buddy Alan, was on the way to making a name for himself as a vocalist. (He and his second wife, Phyllis, had three children, Jack, Johnny, and Terry.)

In the late 1960s, Buck's live engagements included two tours of Europe, a region that also welcomed him back a number of times in the 1970s. One of his fondest memories was a performance given at the White House in 1968 by special invitation from President Lyndon Johnson. He also had his own syndicated TV show in the last years of the 1960s, but the major television opportunity came from another quarter in 1969. He was asked to take part in a summer show project that was to evolve into the extremely popular *Hee Haw* program. It actually began as a special, but after a while CBS-TV decided to expand it into a summer replacement show.

"To say that I was apprehensive isn't exactly right. I was afraid for the first one; then I was afraid for six. But when we found that we were to go for the summer I wasn't sure how I felt. Then as we got into a little more I felt we would make it.

"What *Hee Haw* is is just a country *Laugh-In* with a *Beverly Hillbillies* motif. It's a spoof of what life is like for a lot of hillbillies. But you notice we're careful to present the music dead serious, just like we've always done."

To everyone's surprise, *Hee Haw*, hosted by Buck and Roy Clark, went to number one on the national ratings. As a result, CBS ordered more segments for a regular version of the show that was first shown the next winter. As a prime-time program, it still was a hit, but CBS decided after a while the corn-pone humor didn't fit its hoped-for image. The show was canceled, but the *Hee Haw* organization refused to give up. It was revived as a syndication program and soon was doing as well or better with that approach than previously. In 1979, *Hee Haw* celebrated its first decade and seemed set to go on indefinitely. At the start of the 1980s, it was telecast regularly on over 200 stations all over the United States and Canada. During its tenure, Buck, Roy and other cast regulars welcomed just about every major country artist as *Hee Haw* guests at one time or another. As if working on *Hee Haw* wasn't enough of a task, Owens also hosted his own syndicated program, *Buck Owens Ranch Show*, which was syndicated in seventy markets as of 1980.

Nor did he neglect his recording career in the 1970s. He started out with such top-10 or top-20 hits the first part of the 1970s as "I Wouldn't Live in New York City (If They Gave Me the Whole Dang Town)" in late 1970, "I'll Still Be Waiting for You" and "Looking Back to See" (duet with Susan Raye) in 1972, "Big Game Hunter" (written by Owens) and "On the Cover of the Music City News" (Owens' version of Shel Silverstein's "On the Cover of the Rolling Stone") in 1974, and "Great Expectations" (written by Owens) and "Love Is Strange" (duet with Susan Raye) in 1975. Also on the charts in late 1975 was Buck's single of Jimmy Driftwood's "Battle of New Orleans."

In 1977, Buck's long association with Capitol came to an end and he signed with a new label, Warner Bros. After he left, Capitol leased his best early hits to Trip Records, which issued the definitive *16 Early Hits* album set. He started off relatively slowly on Warners with such moderate chart-making singles as "Nights Are Forever Without You" in early 1977 and "Do You Wanna Make Love" in early 1979. During the summer of 1979, though, he was once more in the top 10 with his duet with Emmylou Harris, "Play Together Again, Again" (cowritten by him with C. Stewart and J. Abbott). At year-end, he had another original, "Let Jesse Rob the Train," which moved to upper levels in early 1980. Later in the year his single of his composition "Love Is a Warm Cowboy" was a chart hit.

Over the years, Buck turned out dozens of albums, most of them on Capitol. Among his Capitol releases were *Buck Owens* (3/61), *Buck Owens Sings Harlan Howard* (8/61), *You're for Me* (10/62), *On the Band Stand* (6/63), *The Best of Buck Owens, Volume I* (6/64) (Volumes 2 and 3 came out later in the 1960s and Volume 4 in 1970), *Buck Owens Sings Tommy Collins* (11/63), *Together Again* and *My Heart Skips a Beat* (10/64), *I've Got a Tiger by the Tail* (5/65), *The Instrumental Hits of Buck Owens and His Buckaroos* (8/65), *Christmas Hits with Buck Owens and His Buckaroos* (late 1965), *Roll Out the Carpet* (3/66), *Dust on Mother's Bible* (6/66), *Carnegie Hall Concert* (9/66), *Most Wanted Band* (5/67), *In Japan* (6/67), *Open Up Your Heart* (12/67), *It Takes People like You to Make People like Me* (1/68), *Buck Owens in London* (7/69), *Close-up: Buck Owens* (7/69), and *Tall Dark Stranger* (12/69). Other Capitol LPs of the late 1960s and early 1970s were *A Night on the Town, Sweet Rosie Jones, Meanwhile Back at the Ranch, Christmas Shopping, We're Gonna Get Together, The Great White Horse* (with Susan Raye), *I've Got You on My Mind Again, Anywhere U.S.A., Big in Vegas, Bakersfield Brass, Boot Hill, Bridge over Troubled Water, Deluxe 3-Pack, Ruby, Rompin' and Stompin', The Kansas City Song, Under Your Spell Again, I Wouldn't Live in New York City, We're Gonna Get Together* (with Susan Raye), *Live at the White House,* and *Too Old to Cut the Mustard* (with Buddy Alan). During the 1960s and early 1970s, some of Buck's recordings also were released on the Starday and Hilltop label, the former including *Buck Owens*

(1962), *Fabulous Sound, County Hitmakers No. 1,* and *Sweethearts in Heaven,* and, on Hilltop, *If You Ain't Lovin'* and *You're for Me.* His debut album on Warner Bros. came out in the summer of 1976, titled *Buck 'Em.*

Besides his busy schedule of music industry activities, Owens also found time to help out charitable causes. One of his fund-raising operations for some years was the Buck Owens pro-celebrity invitational tennis and golf tournament. In 1977, he organized the Buck Owens Rodeo, which drew top cowboys from all over the United States to compete in Bakersfield each spring with proceeds going for such things as the Kern Community Cancer Center.

Looking back over his eventful career, Buck suggested that his success was due to a combination of planning and audience rapport. "There are singers and there are showmen. I know I'm no great singer, but I am a showman enough that I can communicate with the audience."

Buck continued to record new material on Warner Brothers until 1980, when his contract expired; already comfortable financially, he didn't seek to renew it or find another label. As the decade moved along, he focused more on his business activities in Bakersfield than on entertainment pursuits. Though he remained as cohost on *Hee Haw* until 1986, he made no new recordings and, by the late 1980s, almost none of his recordings remained in print. (*Hee Haw,* however, kept on going with Roy Clark as host into the 1990s.) Owens himself seemed to believe his day in the spotlight was over, and it was time to concentrate on behind-the-scenes activities.

As Mark Fenster noted in an article detailing the seminal years of Buck's career ("Under His Spell: How Buck Owens Took Care of Business," *The Journal of Country Music,* Volume XII, No. 3, 1989), "At the height of the Urban Cowboy boom of the early eighties, the name Buck Owens seemed to have as much relevance to contemporary music as Lawrence Welk. Owens was gladly ignored by Nashville's country music industry, to whom he had never endeared himself in the first place."

But more than a few of the new crop of young performers respected and have been influenced by his music. One rising star in particular, Dwight Yoakam, was a longtime Owens fan who believed Buck still had things to contribute to the field. One Friday afternoon in 1987, unannounced, he walked into Buck's Bakersfield office and talked him into taking part in Dwight's appearances at the Kern County Fair that night. Soon after, the two provided one of the highlights of the CMA 30th Anniversary TV show in January 1988 with a duet of "The Streets of Bakersfield." Their single of that number was a number-one hit on major charts.

This helped bring a recording contract for Buck with Capitol Records, whose first fruit was the album *Hot Dog* (which was followed in 1991 by *Kickin' In*).

Buck put together a new version of his band, the Buckaroos, and soon had nearly eighty bookings lined up for 1989. Buck's revitalized concert career continued in the 1990s, punctuated from time to time by guest appearances on TV programs in the U.S. and several other nations.

In the early 1990s, Rhino Records assembled the first comprehensive anthology covering his entire career, *The Buck Owens Collection 1959–1990.* Comprising three CDs or three cassettes, this included twenty of his number-one hits among its sixty-two selections and what Rhino considered the best of his duets with Yoakam, Emmylou Harris, and Beatles alumnus Ringo Starr. Besides a biography of its subject, the accompanying booklet included Buck's track-by-track commentary on the package's contents.

Just when things seemed to be going so well for him, with newfound attention from fans who weren't born yet when his career first took hold and with a personal fortune estimated at over $100 million (covering enterprises like radio stations in Bakersfield and in Phoenix, Arizona, plus various real estate holdings and other investments), in 1993 his doctors gave him the somber news that he had developed cancer of the throat. Buck took it stolidly and kept up a fierce struggle against the disease, despite operations that removed part of his tongue. Though he had some problems speaking in 1995 he was back in the studios recording new material while also making plans for orderly transfer of his estate to his two sons and for a new $5 million music museum in Bakersfield. While this was to be dedicated to country music in general, Buck didn't intend it to ignore its donor.

He told Herb Benham ("The Buck Stops in Bakersfield," *Los Angeles Times Magazine,* August 15, 1995) that when it opened in 1996 it would have "a 35-foot mural that's 19 feet high that's going to have vignettes in my life. They are going to be in black and white. It was either black or white in my life. Never gray. That's the way I was."

Health problems notwithstanding, he certainly didn't become a recluse. Rather he kept up his performing work in the mid-1990s, though not at a hectic pace. On June 16, 1995, for the first time in twenty-five years, he and Merle Haggard shared the same stage to the delight of their home town fans in Bakersfield. At the Academy of Country Music Awards telecast over NBC-TV on April 24, 1996, he served as one of the award presenters. During the Country Music Association Awards TV show in October 1996, he was inducted into the Country Music Hall of Fame. A few weeks later, on October 27, the Buck Owens Crystal Palace Museum and Theater formally opened in Bakersfield, containing, besides a collection of memorabilia from Buck's career, a huge dance floor and facilities for making TV productions. Among other things, a special car built for Buck by Nudie hangs on the wall behind a fifty foot bar.

Plans called for Buck and the Buckaroos to perform regularly at the venue.

PARNELL, LEE ROY: *Singer, guitarist, songwriter, band leader (The Hot Links). Born Abilene, Texas, December 21, c. mid 1950s.*

Like his early idol Bob Wills, Texan Lee Roy Parnell saw nothing wrong with exploring a wide range of popular music stylings while still considering himself in the country tradition. While Wills worked with elements of country, roots blues, and jazz in developing his seminal form of Western swing, Parnell worked in rock and soul in his arrangements to come up with a style more akin to the country approach given voice by the original Jimmie Rodgers than the pop swing bands of the 1930s, but he never forgot his debt to Wills.

As he recalled on the October 1994 Country Music Association Awards telecast as a nominee for the CMA Horizon Award, "When I was a kid in Texas growing up, my dad and Bob Wills were good friends. I guess when I was about six I sang with [Wills] on a radio show [on the Ft. Worth station WBAP with the two vocalizing on Wills's signature song, "San Antonio Rose"]. So if I win the Horizon Award tonight, Bob Wills is part of the reason."

As it happened, John Michael Montgomery won, but Parnell gave an impressive performance of his recording of "On the Road," and was also one of the stars who paid tribute to the Hall of Fame selection of 1994, Merle Haggard, by taking part in an extended version of Merle's "Working Man's Blues."

Parnell was born in Abilene, but grew up in Stephensville near Ft. Worth, where Bob Wills was a well-loved resident. The Parnell and Wills families were close, and Lee Roy's father exposed his son to Wills's music almost as soon as the child could walk and talk. Parnell said in the early 1990s, "Bob Wills was the big daddy. He was the one who inspired me to listen to music in the beginning and I still listen to his music religiously.

"When I got older I started listening to rock and roll. I loved the Allman Brothers because they blended blues with country. Dickie [Betts] and Duane [Allman] are the reason I play guitar the way I do. Then I began to delve into the great masters of country and blues like Jimmie Rodgers and Muddy Waters. Today if you asked me who's my favorite guitar player of all time, I'd say Jimmie Vaughn, and I'd say Merle Haggard is my favorite singer."

By the time Lee Roy was in high school he had developed a good slide-guitar style and performed with friends and local bands when the opportunities arose.

After high school, he had decided to seek his fortunes as an itinerant musician, finding gigs for a number of years with various club bands, a life story he outlined in songs like "I'm a Roads Scholar." In the mid-1970s he settled for a time in Austin, Texas, where he enjoyed the turbulent "outlaw country" movement and associated partying. He recalled, "Nobody in Austin made money. It was a great place to live, but we all starved to death."

Looking back, he told Teresa George, Executive Editor of the Country Music Association's *Close Up* magazine (July 1992), "I was a rebel without a clue. I was living the life of my heroes. My heroes were guys who rode on buses and motorcycles—fast—and drank a lot, lived hard. I got to be about 30 and I said, 'I've already outlived all of my heroes. They're all dead.' So there was a big change in my life about that time."

One of the changes was a divorce. Parnell had been married for several years and was the father of two small children when the marriage broke up in the mid-1980s. He also was acutely aware he was on the road to being an alcoholic. He told George, "I used to make promises to myself every day. I'd say, 'Well, I'm not going to do any drinking today.' But about 5 o'clock I'd drink."

In 1987 he made the decision to move to Nashville. His plan was to give up drinking while seeking to finally gain some financial security and artistic freedom. He recalled for *Close Up,* "Six months later, I had a publishing deal after beating on the doors and doing the two-step in front of everybody's offices. I came to town with nothing, and literally, it's a cliche now to say I had a one-room apartment, but I did."

He credited a newfound belief in God with giving him the willpower to stop his dependence on alcohol. Things were looking up as the 1980s came to a close. His songs were being placed with other artists and then, in 1989, he signed a recording contract with Arista Records. He was soon working on his debut album, *Lee Roy Parnell,* which was released on May 1, 1990. Hardly had that happened when a shock hit his system: Both his parents and his grandmother died within five weeks' time. Parnell noted that at one time he might have started bingeing, but this time he was able to face his problems and overcome them, even though the pain and sorrow took a while to fade.

The album and the singles drawn from it ("Crocodile Tears," "Oughta Be a Law," and "Family Tree") signaled the arrival of a promising new country voice, though they didn't set any sales records. The next album did better. Titled *Love Without Mercy,* it was released on April 28, 1992, and spawned four chart hits that rose to top positions on both *Billboard* and *Radio & Records* charts. The four were: "The Rock," in upper-chart levels the spring of 1992; "What Kind of Fool Do You Think I Am," number three in *R&R* the week of August 14; "Love Without Mercy," number seven in *R&R* the week of January 8, 1993; and "Tender Moment" (cowritten by Parnell, Cris Moore and Rory Bourke), number one in *R&R* the week of May 7, 1993.

His third Arista album, *On the Road,* was released on October 26, 1993, and the title track soon was a chart hit-single, reaching number four in *R&R* the week of November 11, 1993, and also achieving a top 10 *Billboard* status before year-end. This was followed by such chart singles as "I'm Holding My Own" (number one in *R&R* the week of April 8, 1994); "Take These Chains from My Heart" (number fourteen in *R&R* the week of July 22); and "The Power of Love."

By 1994 Parnell's circumstances had certainly improved from his first days in Music City. Back then, he shared quarters with songwriter Cris Moore. "We had no money. We had an eight-track [tape] machine and a green '76 Ford Torino. I really felt like I had to make it work or I was going to do something else."

Once he found a music publisher, the financial worries abated somewhat, and he began performing once a month on Monday nights at the Bluebird Cafe. The chance to move into the ranks of recording artists followed soon after. Lee Roy commented, "Things just kind of developed over time. I've always struggled, but the album deal was one thing in all my years of playing that just fell together, so I guess it was meant to happen."

In 1995, Lee Roy's schedule included a 110-city tour with Travis Tritt and Joe Diffie. This helped him score another number-one single on the Career label, "A Little Bit of You," which reached number one in *Cash Box* the week of August 19 and also made upper levels in *Billboard* and *Radio & Records. We All Get Lucky Sometimes,* the album from which that was drawn (recorded with his band, The Hot Links), was released by Career on August 1, 1995. After peaking at number twenty-six in *Billboard* that summer, it remained in upper chart levels well into 1996.

His 1995 output included a recording with Tex-Mex star Flaco Jimenez, "Cat Walk," that was nominated for a Grammy in the Best Country Instrumental Performance category. Along with many other top rank musicians, he contributed to the all-instrumental concept album produced by Steve Wariner, *No More Mr. Nice Guy,* released in the spring of 1996. In May 1996, his new single (cowritten with G. Nicholson) "Givin' Water to a Drownin' Man" debuted on the charts.

PARSONS, GRAM: *Singer, guitarist, songwriter, band leader. Born Winterhaven, Florida, November 5, 1946; died Joshua Tree, California, September 19, 1973.*

Immensely talented and dedicated, but haunted by personal demons that cut his life distressingly short, Gram Parsons never achieved the stardom that seemed his creative due. He did leave a legacy of original songs and influence on others that went a long way toward ultimately reaching his objective of uniting all segments of the pop music audience under the country/rock ban-

ner. As he outlined it at one point in the late 1960s, "We want the rock fans at the Whisky and the truck drivers at the Palomino to get together and talk to each other and understand each other."

Had he lived, he might have accomplished much of that and become a worldwide superstar. His musical heirs, however, including the Eagles and Emmylou Harris, contributed to bringing some of Parsons's dreams to pass.

Parsons was born in Winterhaven in the mid-1940s and grew up in the South, enamored, as he finished elementary school and moved into high school, of country, gospel, blues, and rockabilly. He showed talent as a musician at an early age, beginning piano lessons when he was only three. When he was thirteen, he decided to learn guitar "because Elvis played one." He had already become a Presley fan even when Elvis still was appearing as a country artist. "I can remember when Elvis first came down to town as second billing with Jimmie Dickens of the *Grand Ole Opry* Show. He was only about eighteen then, and they had it in the local high school gym and everybody came."

It didn't take Gram long to become proficient enough as a guitarist to be a key performer in a teen band called the Pacers. "We played Everly Brothers and attempted Ray Charles. That lasted for six months. At fourteen, I joined a band called the Legends—for six months—this time playing Everly Brothers and Chuck Berry. We worked all through Florida, did lots of club and TV work. This was about 1960–61."

He continued to play with various bands in his home region during the early 1960s. A good enough student to get accepted at Harvard University in 1965, he attended classes there briefly. "Acid was the major reason I dropped out—I had taken so much of it. Remember, I was interested in psychedelic trips, so I checked into them on my own and dropped out of Harvard."

He never had dropped out of music, so he formed a new band in Cambridge called the International Submarine Band. He moved the group to New York for a time in hopes of making it into the musical big time, then shifted again to Los Angeles. He did manage to record an LP for Lee Hazelwood's LHI label there, called *Safe at Home,* but that proved a commercial flop and the final alignment of the Submarine Band (which he reorganized several times) broke up. The LP demonstrated Parsons's continued love for both country and rock, with songs from such diverse sources as Merle Haggard, Waylon Jennings, Bob Dylan, and the Rolling Stones.

His next move was to the Byrds in 1968, where he had a kinship with another country-oriented member, Chris Hillman. The two helped persuade leader Roger McGuinn to go to Nashville to make a country-rock LP. The result was *Sweetheart of the Rodeo,* a compilation that included Byrds versions of songs by Haggard, the Louvin Brothers, Dylan, and two Parsons originals.

One of the latter, "Hickory Wind," is a haunting country song that was presented with great impact by Emmylou Harris in her 1979 album *Blue Kentucky Girl*. The lyrics express some of the disparate rural and city influences tugging at Parsons: "It's a hard way to find out that trouble is real/In a faraway city with a faraway feel/But it makes me feel better/Each time it begins/Calling me home, hickory wind."

In 1969, Hillman and Parsons left the Byrds to form their own band, the landmark country-rock group called the Flying Burrito Brothers (see separate entry). The band's first LP, *The Gilded Palace of Sin,* whose features included the Parsons-Hillman song "Sun City," came out on A&M that year and won strong critical praise, as did the band's concerts. Bob Dylan, among other major rock stars, called the group a favorite of his. Despite the band's great promise, it was a few years ahead of its time. The idea of combining country and rock was still anathema to most rock and country fans.

Still, things might have gone better if Gram hadn't been injured in a motorcycle accident in early 1970. After he recovered, he returned to the Burritos for a short time, but his musical ideas had changed somewhat during his recuperation, and he left to concentrate on solo work. His initial efforts came to naught in 1970, so he went to France for a while partly at the behest of Rolling Stones members, who esteemed his work. There were some discussions of a solo LP for him on their label, but again nothing happened.

Going back to Los Angeles, Parsons spent much of 1972 writing new material primarily in the country vein. This time he had record company interest, which led to release of his debut solo LP on Warner Brothers. Called *Gram Parsons,* it was heavily country-oriented, both in his original material and the other selections he sang. The album was flawed but showed promise. Warners approved a followup that was to come out in 1973 under the title *Grievous Angel.* Today, the LP is considered a major contribution to the melding of country and rock into a dynamic new music form, but it had little impact when it came out because by then Parsons was dead.

His death resulted from the problem he long had fought with varying degrees of success—drugs. On September 19, 1973, he was found unconscious on the floor of his room at Joshua Tree Inn. He was rushed to the Yucca Valley High Desert Hospital, but died soon after arrival. A strange incident took place in ensuing days. Still unknown individuals stole his coffin from the airport where it was awaiting transport back to his home and burned it near the Joshua Tree Monument.

Many who respected his ability mourned his passing, including close friend Emmylou Harris, who had done backing vocals on his solo albums and toured with his band briefly in his last months. She told a reporter later on, "Gram was a real pioneer. He cut straight through the middle with no compromises. He was never afraid to write from the heart, and perhaps that's why he was never really accepted. It's like the light was too strong and bright and people just had to turn away. They couldn't look at the light because it was all too painful. It could rip you up. Not many people can take music that real.

"If there's one thing in my life I really want to do it's get Gram's music out in the open where it should be. A lot of people who would've appreciated him never got to hear him. . . . I feel like I've glided in at a time when people are beginning to listen to country music. But what I'm trying to get them to realize is that they should look a little behind me to all that was going on before with Gram and the Burritos."

True to her word, Emmylou has had one or more Parsons's compositions on almost every solo album she has done. Thus on more than one occasion Parsons's name has appeared under songs ranked high on both pop and country charts in the mid and late-1970s as well as the 1980s.

Parsons continued to be remembered in various ways not only by Emmylou Harris, but by others both closely and remotely associated with him or his music. An annual memorial concert was established in California, usually held at the Palomino country music night club. Among the performers in the 1991 event were Johnny Cash's longtime pianist, Earl Poole Ball, vocalist Carla Olsen, and other rock and country acts including a group called She, whose roster included his daughter Polly Parsons as a backup singer. In 1986 an annual tribute concert to Gram and the late Clarence White was inaugurated in Nashville, Tennessee, with participants including the mid-1980s members of his onetime group the Flying Burrito Brothers.

In the spring of 1992, Polly Parsons made headlines when she filed a breach of fiduciary duties suit against the Byrds, Roger McGuinn, Sony Music Entertainment, and other individuals and music firms. The suit asserted that Polly "as the only living heir" had never been paid royalties from material in which her father had been involved. Among recordings in question were the Byrds albums *Sweetheart of the Rodeo* and *The Byrds,* a 1990 CD collection containing "lost" tracks featuring Parsons on vocals, as well as his solo albums *GP* and *Grievous Angel.*

In the late 1980s and in the 1990s, Parsons's name began showing up in ads and other material prepared by the Lawrence and Mayo advertising agency in Newport Beach, California. In a cellular phone ad with headlines about fictional carjackings and traffic snarls, one article quotes "Police spokesman Gram Parsons." In ads for a chain of print shops, office form examples included one with the heading "From the desk of Gram Parsons." As journalist Jim Washburn reported to the *Los Angeles Times,* these were the brainchildren of award-winning admen Bruce Mayo and Jon Gothold, who were long-time enthusiasts of Gram's recordings.

Mayo said, "Sometimes we might need something with a name on it, so why not his? To most people, it won't mean diddly. Jon and I do it for the 10 people who might notice, and it might amuse them."

He added, "Maybe one reason we chose Gram is part of me is pissed that Gram died, because I think the stuff he did was great. He had a big influence on a lot of people and didn't get recognized for much. I guess this is our little way of carrying on."

To the amazement of Dan and Evelyn Shirbroun, who had purchased the ten-room Joshua Tree Inn in 1988 where Parsons had died (in room 8), people were constantly checking in hoping to stay in that room. It took several years until they finally realized the cult status of Parsons with pop music fans; until then they hadn't even known who he was. Finally, in the fall of 1996, Parsons adherents arranged to set up what they hoped would be an annual event called the GramFest. The inaugural date was October 26, 1996, with Parsons's widow, Nancy, and daughter, Polly, in attendance. The concerts, held next door at Hi-Desert Playhouse, featured Polly, backed by the Calamity Twins duo from Nashville, singing some of her father's compositions.

PARTON, DOLLY: *Singer, guitarist, banjoist, actress, songwriter. Born Locust Ridge, Sevier County, Tennessee, January 19, 1946.*

Dolly Parton is a determined and knowing person. In the mid-1970s, then an acknowledged country star, she felt her career could go further. When she took steps to broaden her public following through some changes in musical direction and a wide-ranging public relations campaign orchestrated by a Los Angeles publicity firm, fans and country-music associates alike expressed alarm. She would destroy her career, they suggested, perhaps become a laughingstock by exposing herself to the comic barbs of interviewers like Johnny Carson. They reckoned without her inner strength and knowledge of her capabilities.

In part, some observers confused Parton's stage image with the actual person. The trademark large, fluffy blonde wig (she quipped to a Las Vegas audience in early 1981, "You'd be amazed how expensive it is to make a wig look this cheap"), well-developed chest, and Mae West–like figure suggested to some she was a dumb blonde. Those who met her knew otherwise: she was softspoken, attractive in a dignified way, and exuded both self-confidence and intelligence.

Those characteristics were evident in an interview with Robert Hilburn of the *Los Angeles Times* (Calendar Section, February 15, 1981, p. 66) when she recalled her important debut on Carson's *The Tonight Show* a few years earlier. "I didn't fear going on the [Carson] show because I work best one-to-one. I was a fan of Johnny Carson and I wanted people to notice me. I didn't care if it was for the right reasons or the wrong reasons at first. I felt I had a gift as a writer. I may not

be a great singer, but my voice is different. I'm secure in those areas.

"If I could get their [viewers] attention long enough, I felt they would see beneath the boobs and find the heart, and that they would see beneath the wig and find the brains. I think one big part of whatever appeal I possess is the fact that I look totally one way and that I am totally another. I look artificial, but I'm not."

Dolly always claimed that her optimistic outlook went back to her earliest years as a child growing up in rural Tennessee in the foothills of the Smoky Mountains. She was the fourth of a dozen children born to Lee and Avie Lee Parton. "I was born with a happy nature and a happy heart," she remarked. "I was born with the gift of understanding people and loving them and I've never been unhappy. I've always seen the light at the end of the tunnel."

Although she recalls her childhood with affection, it was anything but an affluent one. Her father hadn't been able to scratch enough income from the soil to support his growing family (which lived in a two-room shack with an upstairs attic) and had to do construction work to try to make ends meet. The children had few toys and their clothes mostly were hand-me-downs or made from bits and pieces of material. There are hints in some of Parton's later songs based on her early years, such as "Coat of Many Colors," that despite the warm family environment, the taunts of outsiders could cause pain.

Dolly started to sing almost as soon as she could talk. Before she could read or write, she would make up songs and ask her mother to write them down. When she was seven she began trying to learn guitar after making her first one from an old mandolin and two bass guitar strings. When she was eight an uncle gave her her first real guitar, a small Martin.

Even then she was thinking about a future in music. As she stated once about making music, "It's all I've ever known." She told Hilburn, "I knew I wanted to be a singer from the time I was 7 or 8 and learned my first chord on the guitar. I also wanted to be a star—the biggest in the world. I wanted pretty clothes and attention and to live in a big house and buy things for Mama and Daddy. Of course, I didn't have any better sense in those days.

"But as I got older, I didn't lose track of those dreams. I just thought, 'Well, why can't I do all that?' The secret was to take one step at a time. That's what I've done. I'm not saying everything has been wonderful. I've had bad times, but I've always tried to maintain a good outlook. I've had heartaches and disappointments, but never so great that it blocked my vision of the future."

As she grew into young womanhood, music remained her passion. She sang almost all the time, while she washed the dishes, hoed corn in the fields, or attended church. "I was brought up in the Church of

God," she said later. "It's a very free church. If anybody wanted to get up and sing or shout out an emotion, they would do it. There was a freedom there, so I came to know what freedom is, so I could know God and come to know freedom within myself."

Dolly didn't forsake a basic education. She completed elementary and high school. But at the age of eighteen, the day after she graduated from high school, she headed to Nashville, intent on pursuing her long-held dream. At first, she went to stay with the family of her uncle, Bill Owens. Owens had contacts with the music field and also was skilled at songwriting. He and Parton began to write some original songs, one of which, "Put It Off Until Tomorrow," finally was placed with country artist Billy Phillips and became a top-10 hit in 1966.

Almost as soon as Dolly reached Nashville, she met Carl Dean, an asphalt-paving contractor, whom she married two years later. She said in 1976, "My husband is a very home-based person. . . . He's good for me because he's so different in nature from me. We've been together twelve years, married ten, and we've never had an argument. There's nobody else like him and I know in my heart that there will never be another person for me."

Since arriving in Nashville, Parton had been doggedly working to get a hearing for her singing ability and songwriting talents. The success of the Bill Phillips single helped open more doors, and in late 1966 she signed a recording contract with Monument Records. Before long she had her first releases out on the label, including her debut album, *Hello, I'm Dolly,* in July 1967. Company president Fred Foster wrote in the liner notes, "Sometimes you just know . . . sometimes. And that makes up for all the times you had to guess. . . ." Monument soon issued a second LP, *As Long as Love.* The company released a number of singles by Dolly, two of which, "Dumb Blonde" and "Something Fishy," were chart hits in 1967.

Unfortunately for Monument, the firm didn't have long to savor the promise of its new-found artist. In 1967, major country artist Porter Wagoner was in need of a female vocalist to replace Norma Jean, who was leaving his show. Dolly's releases on Monument attracted his attention and one day he called her on the phone to ask if she'd join his troupe. The opportunity was too good to pass up. At the time, Porter was one of the most successful performers and band leaders. Beginning in the summer of 1967, Dolly began to appear in Wagoner's tour dates and on his syndicated TV show. Wagoner was on RCA Records and that label hastened to sign up his new vocalist. Over a decade and a half later, Dolly still was a mainstay of RCA's recording roster.

It didn't take long for Dolly to make her mark on RCA both as a duet partner with Wagoner and as a solo performer. Her 1968 output included the hit duet singles "Holding on to Nothing" and "The Last Thing on My Mind" and the solo best-seller "Just Because I'm a Woman." Also on country charts for many weeks was the LP with Wagoner, *Just Between Me and You.* In 1969, she and Porter collaborated on the hit singles "Your Love" and "Always Always" and hit album *Just the Two of Us.* During those years and in 1970, Parton had enough other solo and duet singles on the charts, including the 1970 number-one single "Mule Skinner Blues," for RCA to issue the first *Best of Dolly Parton* LP in late 1970.

During the first half of the 1970s, Dolly continued to add new entries to her list of classic recordings, and her intensive schedule of in-person dates impressed growing numbers of country fans with her finely tuned emotional control of her remarkable soprano voice. As her reputation continued to grow, she became restless at remaining under the aegis of the Wagoner show. In 1973 she left the show in favor of concentrating on her solo career, though Wagoner continued to produce her records until 1976. Among her singles successes of that period, mostly of her own compositions, were "Coat of Many Colors" in 1971; "Touch Your Woman" and "Washday Blues" in 1972; "Travelin' Man" in 1973; one of her trademark compositions, "Jolene," in 1973–74; "Please Don't Stop Loving Me" (duet, co-written with Wagoner) and "Love Is like a Butterfly" in 1974; "The Seeker" and "We Used To" in 1975; "Hey Lucky Lady," "All I Can Do," and "Is Forever Longer Than Always" (duet with Wagoner) in 1976. Her duet hits with Wagoner also included "Daddy Was an Old-time Preacher Man" and "If Teardrops Were Pennies and Heartaches Were Gold."

From the late 1960s through 1976, RCA issued one or more of Parton's albums each year, most of which made the charts. Among them were *Blue Ridge Mountain Bow* (1969); *Fairest of Them All, Real Live, Best of Dolly Parton* (1970); *Golden Streets of Glory, Joshua, Coat of Many Colors* (1971); *Touch Your Woman, My Favorite Songwriter, Porter Wagoner, The Right Combination / Burning the Midnight Oil* (with Wagoner) (1972); *Bubbling Over* (1973); *Jolene, Love Is like a Butterfly* (1975); *The Bargain Store, Best of Dolly Parton, Say Forever You'll Be Mine* (with Wagoner), *In Concert* (with Charley Pride, Ronnie Milsap, Jerry Reed, and Chet Atkins), *Dolly* (1975); and *All I Can Do* (1976). RCA also released some of her recordings on its Camden label, including *Just the Way I Am* and *Mine.* Also in print on Monument, besides the LPs noted earlier, was *In the Beginning.* Powerpak Records issued the LP *Release Me.*

By the mid-1970s, Dolly seemingly had accomplished all any country artist could desire. Her position as a soloist had been enhanced by the success of her new touring arrangements with her Traveling Family Band, composed mostly of her brothers, sisters, uncles, and cousins. She certainly didn't lack recognition from her peers. In 1968 she and Porter Wagoner had been voted Vocal Group of the Year by the Country Music Association, an honor they again won in 1971. In 1970, she was one of the final nominees in the Grammy competition for Best Country Vocal Performance, Female, for "Mule Skinner Blues." Increasingly in the 1970s she was ranked among the top ten female country soloists. In both 1975 and 1976, the CMA voted her Female Vocalist of the Year. All the major trade magazines—*Billboard, Record World,* and *Cash Box*—voted her the top female vocalist, country, of 1975.

But she was certain she still could scale new heights. In 1976, she decided to make the break, ending her recording association with Porter Wagoner, organizing a new backing band, and starting work on a new album aimed at having a more contemporary country sound than her previous work. Besides raising eyebrows in the country-music community in general, it brought a bitter reaction from Wagoner, triggering a lawsuit that engendered acrimony between the two artists for many years.

As it turned out, Dolly knew what she was doing. Her career did indeed develop from that of a country superstar to a reigning pop star and, at the start of the 1980s, a film star as well. The first step in this progression was the album *New Harvest . . . First Gathering,* released at the start of 1977 and soon on country charts. For a good part of the year it remained in the top 10, indicating that Dolly's country fans had not deserted her. Equally important, it made some inroads with the pop audience too. Late in the year, RCA issued another album that carried her star still higher, called *Here You Come Again.* The album was in the top 10 in country before 1977 was over and was still on the lists over a year later. Its title song became a major hit on both country and pop lists, showing up in late 1977 and staying on them into 1978. During 1978, she had such other singles hits as "Heartbreaker" and "Baby I'm Burning/I Really Got the Feeling." The album *Heartbreaker* was issued in late summer of 1978 and proved another best-seller. Dolly rounded out the decade with such other successes as the singles "You're the Only One" and "Sweet Summer Lovin'/Great Balls of Fire" and the album *Great Balls of Fire.* In October 1979, she signed a multimillion-dollar agreement with the Riviera Hotel in Las Vegas calling for six weeks of appearances per year from 1980 through 1982. Discussions also began for Parton's first featured movie role in the film *9 to 5,* costarring Jane Fonda and Lily Tomlin. By then, she had won the highest honor the Country Music Association could bestow, Entertainer of the Year, presented to her at the 1978 CMA awards telecast.

The movie industry took note of her new acting career by arranging for her first appearance as a presenter on the 1980 Academy Awards telecast on ABC-TV, April 14, 1980. The month before, RCA issued a new album, *Dolly Dolly Dolly,* which featured the single release "Starting Over Again." Both releases did well on country charts as did another 1980 single, "Old Flames Can't Hold a Candle to You." In February 1980, it was announced that after she completed work on *9 to 5* at 20th Century Fox, she would costar with Burt Reynolds in Universal Pictures' movie version of the stage play *The Best Little Whorehouse in Texas.* All of this didn't hurt her record sales; by early 1980 *Here You Come Again* had earned her her first platinum record and *Heartbreaker* had passed gold-record levels.

In November 1980, RCA issued her album *9 to 5 and Other Odd Jobs,* which featured as its title track the song Dolly wrote for her debut movie. The film was released December 1980 and won glowing reviews, including enthusiastic approval of Parton's acting efforts by critics from most major U.S. publications. In March 1981, her single "9 to 5" brought her still another number-one ranked country disc. At the 11th Annual American Guild of Variety Artists awards telecast in May, she was voted the Entertainer of the Year and Female Country Star of the Year. (She previously had been named Country Star of the Year by AGVA in 1978 and 1979.) By then she had made her debut at the Riviera in Las Vegas in a show which, though cut short by laryngitis, had been universally evaluated as a triumph, with several reviewers describing her work as "dazzling."

At the Grammy Awards in February 1982, Dolly was nominated in two categories for "9 to 5," Best Country Vocal performance, Female, and Best Country Song (songwriting award), and won the Grammys in both cases. Unfortunately, she couldn't accept them in person because she had to enter a hospital in Los Angeles for surgery. (The operation caused a major reshuffling of her schedules for the year.) Significantly, though she didn't win, she was one of five finalists in two noncountry categories, Song of the Year (for "9 to 5") and Best Album of Original Score Written for a Picture or TV Special (cowritten with Charles Fox. Soundtrack album, *9 to 5,* issued by 20th Century Fox Records).

Throughout the 1980s and into the 1990s, she remained among country's greatest stars. As Vince Gill commented in the 1990s, "Dolly Parton first came over my radio speakers twenty-five years ago, and still every time I hear that voice I'm astonished all over again." With the exception of a short-lived variety show on ABC-TV, almost everything she touched turned to financial gold, while her honors in all sorts of music polls proliferated. For instance, the Academy of Country Music, which had named her Entertainer of the Year in 1977, voted her Female Entertainer of the Year and her release "Islands in the Stream" Single of the Year in 1980, and in 1983 voted her work with Kenny Rogers as Vocal Duet of the Year. Later in the decade the ACM named the album *Trio* (a platinum-record winner recorded with Emmylou Harris and Linda Ronstadt) Album of the Year. (*Trio* also won the 1988 CMA Vocal

Event of the Year Award as well as the TNN/*Music City News* choice for Best Vocal Collaboration of 1988.) Her American Music Award honors comprised one for Favorite Country Album of 1978 (for *New Harvest . . . First Gathering*) and selection of the single "Islands in the Stream" as Favorite Country Single for both 1984 and 1985.

In the 1990s, recognition of her talent included presentation of the Gold Plate Award from the American Academy of Achievement and induction into the Academy's new Museum of Living History. The following year the single "Silver Threads and Golden Needles" (from the *Honky Tonk Angels* album recorded with Tammy Wynette and Loretta Lynn) was nominated by CMA voters in the Vocal Event of the Year category. The single didn't win the trophy, but the CMA named her its first Country Music Honors recipient.

Her 1980s recording successes included the album *Dolly Parton's Greatest Hits,* which earned a R.I.A.A. gold-record award in 1982 and *White Limozeen,* issued late in the decade on her new label, Columbia, which passed gold-record levels in 1989. Her number-one singles during the decade were: "But You Know I Love You" and "I Will Always Love You" in 1982; "Islands in the Stream" (with Kenny Rogers) in 1983; "Tennessee Homesick Blues" in 1984; "Real Love" (with Kenny Rogers) and "Think About Love" in 1985; and, after a gap of a few years, the hits "Why'd You Come in Here like That" and "Yellow Roses" in 1989. *Trio,* issued in 1987, was on the charts for many months in the late 1980s. Other 1980s album releases were, on RCA, *Heartbreak Express* and *Best Little Whorehouse in Texas* in 1982; *Burlap and Satin, The Great Pretender,* and *Rhinestone* in 1984; and *Real Love* in 1985; and her 1987 debut on Columbia, *Rainbow.*

Dolly continued her acting career from the mid-1980s into the 1990s with roles in the films *Rhinestone, Wild Texas Wind, Steel Magnolias,* and *Straight Talk.* In 1987 she took a new step in the entertainment field with the establishment of the Dollywood theme park in her home region of Tennessee in 1987. Over the years that followed, just about every name artist in the country field performed at the park one or more times. In 1988 she underscored her feelings as a concerned citizen by setting up the Dollywood Foundation for continuing education that uses proceeds from theme park events to support education in her native Sevier County.

Dolly moved into the 1990s with another excellent album on Columbia, *Eagle When She Flies,* issued in 1991, which demonstrated anew her position as one of country music's great stylists and writers. The album passed platinum sales-levels before that year was over, a year that provided another number-one single, "Rockin' Years," a duet with Ricky Van Shelton of a song written by her brother, Randy Parton. In 1993, besides the *Honky Tonk Angels* project, Dolly completed an excellent new solo album, *Slow Dancing with the Moon.* For that album, she wrote or cowrote eight of the twelve songs. The initial single release, "Romeo," comprised a duet by Dolly and Billy Ray Cyrus.

During 1993, pop singing star Whitney Houston recorded Dolly's composition "I Will Always Love You" (originally published by Dolly's Velvet Apple Music firm in 1973) for the soundtrack of the movie *The Bodyguard.* The single became a smash hit, entering the *Billboard* pop charts in late 1993 and going on to stay at number one for fourteen weeks, making it the longest-running number-one single in *Billboard* history to that point. It also helped boost the soundtrack album sales totals to over 28 million copies worldwide while the single amassed over 8 million copies sold on its own. At the forty-third annual Pop Awards dinner of the performing rights organization BMI in New York in May 1994, Parton's composition was named Song of the Year.

With some time out for plastic surgery, Dolly kept up a hectic touring schedule in the mid-1990s. In addition, she found time to work on a follow-up project to *Trio* with Emmylou Harris and Linda Ronstadt.

Her voice continued to enthrall audiences and critics the world over. She gave her own evaluation of it at one point to Leonard Pitts, Jr., pop music critic of *The Miami Herald* ("Dolly Parton Comes Full Circle," March 21, 1993). "My voice is very emotional and unique. . . . Like most stylists you either love it or you don't love it at all. Mine is more a throat voice. I'm not a trained singer. I don't know one note from another looking on paper [but in hearing it back], I know instantly if [I] hit a wrong note.

"I guess you'd call me a heart singer and a throat singer."

In the fall of 1995 her duet with Vince Gill of her composition "I Will Always Love You" was a country chart hit. Grammy Award voters nominated the single (which Gill included in his album *Souvenirs*) in the Best Country Collaboration with Vocals category. During the 1995 Country Music Association Awards TV show in October 1995, she joined with Willie Nelson, Marty Stuart, Dwight Yoakam, and Merle Haggard in performing some of the late Roger Miller's songs to honor his election to the Country Music Hall of Fame.

Her 1996 credits included the Columbia album *I Will Always Love You and Other Greatest Hits,* released in the spring, and the fall release on Rising Tide/Blue Eye Records of the album *Treasures.* First single drawn from the disc was a duet with Alison Krauss, "Just When I Needed You Most." The story of the album's preparation provided the basis for an hour long showcase program on CBS-TV on November 30, 1996. Meanwhile, Dolly could look ahead to the tenth anniversary of the all star concert series at Dollywood starting in May 1997. Artists making their first appearance in the series had their names placed in the park's Star Walk attraction.

PAUL, LES: *Singer, guitarist, songwriter, band leader, inventor. Born Waukesha, Wisconsin, June 9, 1915.*

When Les Paul made country-music history in the late 1970s through his memorable duets with Chet Atkins, many observers thought it was his initial exposure to the field. Les, after all, had become famous in the 1940s and 1950s for his superlative jazz and pop music output. In truth, he had actually been a major figure in the country field in his early years, and his pioneering work in electronic sound had helped revolutionize all phases of music from folk through rock after World War II.

Les showed an early musical flair as a child growing up in Wisconsin. (His original name was Lester William Polsfuss.) When he was nine, he took up both piano and harmonica. In those early years, he also demonstrated his inventive bent by experimenting with player piano rolls to make added sounds, building his own electric recorder with a wind-up motor and even considering the possibility during the 1920s of using radio components to amplify a guitar.

In the late 1920s he played in local speakeasies, Optimist and Lions clubs, and other local events under the pseudonym of Red Hot Red, the Wizard of Waukesha. During those years he made his radio debut on station WRJN in Racine, Wisconsin, and WHAD at Marquette University in Milwaukee; in 1928, he joined a cowboy band that worked station WLS in Chicago and also toured from Canada to Louisiana.

In the early 1930s, Paul became a local country star under the name "Rhubarb Red." But he also was becoming enamored of jazz and played under his own name with many major jazz artists in the Chicago area. He was making a princely sum for those days—$600 a week—as a country artist, with credits including a hit record for Montgomery Ward titled "Just Because." For a time he gave that up to play jazz piano for eight dollars a week. He formed his first trio then, but it got such poor response that in 1934 he resumed the Rhubarb Red phase on a variety of Chicago stations (WJJD, WIND, WBBM, and WLS, the home of the *National Barn Dance*) with joyous response from the audience.

He kept up his jazz work, though, and by the late 1930s the Les Paul Trio had become a feature on the Fred Waring network shows on NBC. His specialty by then wasn't piano but the electric guitar that he'd worked on for years to perfect. Les's credits of the time included doing the first TV broadcast with an orchestra in a show telecast by NBC in New York. In 1939, Les took the trio back to Chicago, where he served as musical director with stations WJJD and WIND and played with the Ben Bernie band on CBS. Still experimenting, in 1941 he built the first solid-body guitar, now a staple of pickers in rock, country, and even folk, with a pickup on it.

At the time Leo Fender was challenging for the honor, and some still argue about who was "first," but

Tom Wheeler, former editor of *Guitar Player*, told Mark Dery of *The New York Times* ("Les Paul: Once a Wunderkind, Still a Wizard," Arts & Leisure section, December 1, 1991) he felt it was really no contest. "Before Les, the people who were trying to amplify guitars had one idea, namely, to take an acoustic guitar and make it louder so that rhythm guitarists could be heard above horn sections. Les, in contemplating the electric guitar, saw an entirely new instrument."

During the 1940s, Paul moved to Hollywood, where he and his trio became one of the best-known pop acts in the nation. Things were going well in 1948, the year his first multiple recording, "Lover," was released, when an auto accident disabled him for two years. His right elbow never returned to normal, but he came back to team up with Mary Ford (for many years his wife) for one of the superstar combinations of the 1950s. Their hit records were legion, including such songs as "Tennessee Waltz," "Little Rock Getaway," "Mockin' Bird Hill," "How High the Moon," "The World's Waiting for the Sunrise," "Tiger Rag," and "Vaya con Dios." Some of those songs continue to turn up on country charts. In 1976, for instance, Freddy Fender had a hit with "Vaya con Dios."

Les continued to contribute new ideas to the recording art, such as a multiple-track recorder with one-inch-wide tape for eight tracks, called Sel Sync; flat response for both record and tape; and other innovations. The first time Les employed an eight-track system was in 1957, on a country & western song called "Fire." That step is now credited with being the breakthrough that led to the 16-, 24-, and 48-track formats on which recordings of recent decades are based.

In 1964, tired of the touring grind, Les decided to put his musical activities aside in favor of working on even more new ideas. His activities were hampered, though, when a friend accidentally broke his eardrum with a playful slap, an injury that required three operations. In 1967, Les and Gibson Guitar Co. announced production of a new line of guitars named after Paul. That family of instruments continues to be one of the most used by professional musicians.

After his long layoff, Les started to do some in-person appearances in 1974. That led to a suggestion that he team up with Chet Atkins, whose reputation as a guitarist matched Paul's. The two began recording tracks for a debut album in 1976, and, when the album appeared in 1977, called *Chester and Lester,* there was no doubt that it represented consummate instrumental artistry. Their performance provided new sound dimensions for the various country-based songs in the collection. The album won a Grammy Award, presented on the nationally telecast show in early 1978, which also featured a selection performed by the duo. In 1978, a second LP by Chester and Lester was released by RCA.

The National Academy of Recording Arts & Sciences recognized Paul's great accomplishments in several ways in the late 1970s and early 1980s. In 1979, his 1951 recording (with Mary Ford) of "How High the Moon" was added to the NARAS Hall of Fame. (Mary Ford died in 1971.) In 1983, Les was given a Lifetime Achievement Award "for his creative musicianship, his technical innovations, including the 8-track recording process and other multiple recording techniques, his invention of the solid body amplified guitar and his lifelong commitment to excellence in the recording arts and sciences."

In the mid-1980s, Les became a fixture at Fat Tuesday's jazz club in lower Manhattan, where he performed regularly on Monday nights for the balance of the 1980s; by 1996, he had moved his Monday-night venue uptown to a club called Iridium. Despite the fact his hands were crippled with osteoarthritis, which froze the fingers on his strumming hand, and, Dery noted, "that rendered most of the fingers on his fretting hand immobile," he could still do wonderful things with his chosen instrument.

Late in 1991, Capitol issued a retrospective of Paul's work called *The Legend and the Legacy,* which provided seventy-five recordings, some radio spots and included one disc containing thirty-four previously unreleased tracks from Capitol's vaults and Les's private collection. In 1992, Epic issued a tribute album featuring stars from many music genres including Jimmy Page, Jeff Beck, and Slash (of the rock group Guns 'n' Roses), Bootsy Collins, Maceo Parker, and others. Also available in 1992 was a video derived from the "Les Paul and Mary Ford at Home" TV program that ran from 1949–1958.

To celebrate the 20th anniversary of their *Chester and Lester* album, during the summer of 1996 Chet Atkins flew to New York to join Les in concert at the Iridium Club.

PAYCHECK, JOHNNY: *Singer, guitarist, band leader, songwriter. Born Greenfield, Ohio, May 31, 1938. (In Paycheck's 1960–70s bios he gave his year of birth as 1941.)*

In 1978, Johnny Paycheck's blockbuster singles hit, "Take This Job and Shove It," certainly struck home to anyone who worked for wages. In a way, it symbolized much of Paycheck's career in previous years. Flirting with possible superstar status several times during the preceding decade and a half, Johnny seemed intent on destroying his chances through personal excesses that perhaps reflected deep-seated self-doubts about his goals and abilities.

Paycheck (original name Donald Lytle), who grew up in the small town of Greenfield, near Chillicothe, Ohio, was attracted to country music from his boyhood, when he listened to country broadcasts on the radio. His parents gave him his first guitar when he was six, and within a few years he was a good enough musician to compete in local talent contests. By his early teens he had gained his first paying job as a singer and lap steel-

guitar player at the Club 28 in his hometown. He yearned to see more of the world, however, and at fifteen left home to bum his way around the U.S., hitching rides or hopping freight trains.

He earned some money along the way by picking up performing jobs when he could. He told an interviewer from *Country Song Roundup,* "I'd go into a town somewhere and not even have a guitar. I'd borrow one from whoever'd lend it. But, they'd say I was a little kid, so I didn't have too much trouble."

After a stint in the navy, which ended in a courtmartial for going AWOL, and time in a navy brig in Portsmouth, New Hampshire, he received a dishonorable discharge and returned to his itinerant musician ways in the late 1950s. Eventually, using the pseudonym Donny Young, he got his first major opportunity as a sideman with Porter Wagoner. After that brief tour assignment, he found a series of backing band spots in the late 1950s and early 1960s with stars like Faron Young (who used him for backing vocals and as an electric bass player), George Jones, and Ray Price. Meanwhile he was continuing to write new songs, which finally began to be picked up by an increasing number of country singers. More than a few charted tunes bore the "written by Donny Young" legend until that pseudonym was replaced by another one, Johnny Paycheck, which Lytle adopted from a rather unsuccessful boxer. As Donny Young, he also sought a solo career, recording four sides for the Decca label and two for Mercury from the late 1950s through the early 1960s, but they all flopped.

On some releases by other artists during those years, Johnny's (or Donny's) voice could be heard singing harmony. In fact, throughout the 1960s, he was asked to handle backing vocals for major artists whether or not he provided the song, because of the strong quality of his voice. Among those who employed his vocals to effect were Roger Miller, Ray Price, Faron Young, George Jones, Sheb Wooley, and Webb Pierce.

Despite that, no one tried to feature Paycheck until a record company artists & repertoire executive named Aubrey Mayhew happened to hear a demonstration recording Johnny made of one of his new songs. After Johnny's representative played it for Aubrey during the Country Music Association convention in November 1964, Mayhew sought Paycheck out and asked him to sign a management contract. A month later, Johnny's initial single was released, an original composition titled "Don't Start Countin' on Me." The record rose to upper country chart levels in early 1965 and was followed by an even more successful single, "The Girl They Talk About."

After that release began to pick up momentum, Mayhew arranged for Paycheck to join the package show headlined by George Jones and the Jones Boys. This time, instead of a backing musician, Paycheck was a featured performer. Between mid-1965 and mid-

1966, that association brought Paycheck into live shows in all fifty states plus a twenty-day tour of Europe. Paycheck also worked two *Jimmy Dean Television Shows* with Jones and appeared on a number of other network programs as well. In October 1965, he turned out a third single, "A-11," that rose to the top 20.

Encouraged by Johnny's 1965 success, Mayhew and Paycheck set up their own record label the following year called Little Darlin' Records. One of his early releases on that label, "The Lovin' Machine," became a top-10 hit in 1966. However, even as major success seemed on the horizon, Paycheck was beginning to show signs of strain. Before the 1960s were over, incidents involving drugs and alcohol had resulted in his leaving the Jones show under a cloud during a Los Angeles engagement.

For a time, Paycheck's name was anathema to record company executives, and important engagements often were hard to come by. Epic Records' producer Billy Sherrill finally agreed to sign Johnny if he would reform. The two went into the studios in Nashville in the early 1970s, and, before long, Johnny had a new string of recordings riding high on the charts. Among those were "Song and Dance Man," a top-10 hit in early 1974, and "My Part of Forever," high on the lists in May. He continued to have releases on the charts the next few years, such as "I Don't Love Her Anymore" and "All American Man" (cowritten with G. Adams) in 1975 and "Gone at Last" in early 1976, but things were beginning to turn sour again. Among other things, Johnny ran through all his earnings from his earlier efforts and was bankrupt financially and, to a considerable extent, emotionally.

However, he showed staying power. After hitting bottom for a time, he shook off his problems and persuaded Billy Sherrill he was ready for a sustained new effort. Once more they returned to the studios and, in a short time, Johnny was making greater inroads in the country market than ever before. In late summer his single of a song cowritten with Sherrill, "11 Months and 29 days," made the top 10 and was followed in mid-1977 with the top-10 hit "I'm the Only Hell (Mama Ever Raised)." He bettered both those offerings with "Slide Off Your Satin Sheets," which made it to number one.

Then at the end of 1977, he achieved his greatest success with his single of David Allan Coe's composition "Take This Job and Shove It," which reached number one in the United States in early 1978. The song not only dominated the country roster for a time, it also rose high on national pop charts. Later in 1978, he had another top-10 single, "Me and the IRS," and at year's end, his single "Friend, Lover, Wife" (co-written with Billy Sherrill) was well inside the top 10.

During 1978, Paycheck became one of the most sought-after artists for live concerts and major TV shows. His TV appearances included *The Midnight Special, Mike Douglas, Merv Griffin,* and the *Gong Show.* Besides playing many of the traditional country spots, he also was featured in such pop- or rock-oriented locales as New York's Bottom Line, The Boarding House in San Francisco, and the Roxy in Los Angeles.

Paycheck was one of the five finalists for the 1978 Grammy in the Best Vocal Performance, Male, category. He didn't win at that time, but he sang "Take This Job" on the nationally televised 1979 Grammy Awards program. Even as he did that, he had new recordings moving rapidly up country charts, one being a duet with George Jones of Chuck Berry's old hit, "Maybellene." At the same time, two of his Epic albums were on the hit lists, *Armed and Crazy* and *Johnny Paycheck's Greatest Hits, Volume II.*

The 1980s began auspiciously for Johnny with the single "Drinkin' and Drivin'" moving toward the top 20. Later on, he had such 1980 charted singles as "Fifteen Beers," "When You're Ugly like Us" (duet with George Jones), and "In Memory of a Memory" (co-written by Johnny and R. Pate). In early 1981, he and George Jones had the top-20 single "You Better Move On," and a few months later he teamed with Merle Haggard for the chart single "I Can't Hold Myself in Line."

However, despite the apparent career pinnacles and mass audience acclaim that followed his "Take This Job" fame, Johnny's private life started to drag him down. His wild living, hard-drinking, drug-taking excesses began to close more doors than had been opened. Negative headlines about alleged brawls and sexual abuses contributed to a slowdown in record sales that caused Epic to drop him from its roster in 1982.

He had always had a devil-may-care attitude, he indicated to Daniel Cooper ("Johnny Paycheck: Up from Low Places," *The Journal of Country Music,* Vol. 15, no. 1, 1992), but he'd carried it too far. "I've been rowdy all my life. I was wearing hat and fringe coats and everything in the fifties. Everybody thought I was an idiot back then, or anybody who did things like that. Not like, 'He's a ham,' but 'That guy's crazy, look how he's dressed.' Years later it became sort of the fad, so it wasn't like I was jumping into something new. I'd been like that all my life. So I fit in real good. The success is what I couldn't handle. And I don't care how long you've been in or who you are, you get involved in drugs, you're not gonna handle it. Drugs'll take you out."

Once he fell from grace with Epic and, particularly after his drug abuse problems increased, other major labels shunned him. He remained a major concert attraction and had some releases on small labels, such as one on AMI Record, "Everything Is Changing," that made lower-chart levels in late 1985. Just about that time, however, his world turned completely upside down. He was on his way back home for Christmas when he stopped off at a bar called the North High Lounge in

Hillsboro, Ohio, the night of December 19. He got into an argument with two men there, drew a .22 pistol and shot one in the head, fortunately inflicting only a grazing wound and no serious injury.

After treatment, the victim returned to the bar and confronted Paycheck, who quickly left the place and disposed of the gun before going to a friend's house to sleep it off. The authorities prosecuted him on two counts—attempted murder and disposing of the weapon—and he was found guilty on May 17, 1986. He had his attorney appeal the verdict, which took almost three years, while he continued to tour to help pay his legal bills. He finally exhausted his options and was sent to the Chillicothe Correctional Institute in February 1989 with a potential nine-year sentence.

Once in prison, he started to try to straighten his life out, realizing he had to try to overcome his addictions and work toward early release for good behavior. Among his accomplishments was completing studies for a high school equivalency diploma. Many of his friends in the music world kept in touch and, at one point, Merle Haggard joined him for a concert for the inmates that was both video- and audiotaped. The latter material was envisioned as the basis for a new album called *Behind the Wall*, but the project ran into financing roadblocks that kept it from being immediately released.

On January 10, 1991, Johnny's application for parole was approved by Ohio governor Richard Celeste with the proviso that Paycheck remain drug- and alcohol-abuse free and perform 200 hours of community service. To fulfill that requirement, Johnny lectured school children on the dangers of drugs and other mood-altering substances.

Again a free man, Johnny organized a new band and began touring once more. He also recorded enough tracks for a new album in the early 1990s which, however, had not found a label home by mid-decade. He also changed the form of his last name to read Pay-Check, which was the way it appeared on the credits for his minor role in the 1992 film *Paradise Park.*

Johnny remained highly regarded as an artist by his peers in the industry in the 1990s and he continued to perform at mainly smaller venues on the country circuit. He was in evidence at the Academy of Country Music Awards show on NBC-TV on April 24, 1996, where he was one of the awards presenters. In late 1996, the Country Music Foundation released the retrospective collection of Johnny's recordings of the mid-1960s titled *The Real Mr. Heartache* that demonstrated anew how much of a musical rebel he always had been. He wasn't afraid to write or perform songs whose lyrics in their way have more rapport with 1990s "Gangsta Rap" than the gloomiest subject matter of old time country traditionalists. For instance, the tracks included a song titled "(Pardon Me) I've Got Someone to Kill" and another called "You'll Recover in Time," the last

named about a couple whose divorce and its consequences caused them both to end up in straitjackets in a mental institution.

It was a period, as Ben Ratliff pointed out in reviewing the release in *The New York Times* ("Can Country Embrace This Rebel?" December 8, 1996), when many country producers were seeking a new blend of rock and country. Besides the darker lyric content, he noted, the sound structure changed, "and in the hands of the producer Aubrey Mayhew, who recorded Mr. Paycheck on his own independent label, Little Darlin,' the music literally became louder. 'The Little Darlin' sound, as Mr. Mayhew publicized it, was an aggressive blare. He encouraged spontaneity in a process that had become cut and dried, and he insisted on mastering the records 'hot,' pushing the [recording system] levels into the red; he wanted to create songs that would announce themselves on AM radio." It was an approach that certainly seemed to mesh with Paycheck's personality and, as the CMF package indicated, produced recordings that still retained freshness and impact 30 years after they were created.

PEARL, MINNIE: *Comedienne, singer. Born Centerville, Tennessee, October 25, 1912; died Nashville, Tennessee, March 4, 1996. Elected to Country Music Hall of Fame in 1975.*

"Howdeee!" For decade after decade that high-pitched greeting meant only one thing to country fans—Cousin Minnie Pearl was about to convulse them with laughter. For years she was recognized as the "Queen of Country Comedy," and in the mid-1990s she still reigned as the comedy star of the *Grand Ole Opry*. But she proved during her long and eventful career that her humor, "down home" though it might be in tone, was truly universal, equally laugh-provoking with urban as well as rural fans all over the world.

When she was born in Centerville, Tennessee, her parents gave her the name of Sarah Ophelia Colley. Although her home state long has been the hub of the country-music world, her upbringing certainly wasn't that of a farm girl. She was exposed to and enjoyed the classics, both literary and musical, and didn't pay too much attention to the country-music programs beginning to find their way onto southern radio stations. She told an interviewer, "Though my father used always to listen to the *Opry,* I didn't know too much about the singers until I began appearing on it. But once I started listening to them, I began to love the music. I've loved it ever since."

Actually, in her teens the pursuits that appealed most to young Sarah were teaching and the dramatic stage. Thus when she enrolled in fashionable Ward-Belmont College in Nashville in the late 1920s, she majored in stage technique. The art form that interested her most was dancing, at which she demonstrated considerable talent.

After completing college, Colley went on to teach dancing for two years. In 1934, she joined the Wayne P. Sewall Producing Company of Atlanta as a dramatic coach. For the next five years she toured throughout the southern states directing amateur plays, usually presented in local schools. During her travels, her natural flair for comedy began to assert itself as an accidental by-product of her work.

Sarah recalled how that occurred for Bob Hilburn of the *Los Angeles Times*. "Minnie Pearl was born during the Depression. I had a job traveling from town to small town in the South putting on plays for church and civic groups. It was a big thing at the time. There were hundreds of people doing that kind of work.

"To help publicize the show in each town, I would appear before the Lion's Club and other groups. In return for them letting me announce my show, I'd do a couple of minutes entertainment for them. I'd do an interpretation of a country girl, Minnie Pearl."

As she went from town to town, she mentally stored more material based on insights and impressions gained along the way. It was to provide the basis for extended routines later on. Some of the material went back to her home-town memories. For instance, as a child Sarah recalled walking three miles along the railroad tracks to a switching station called Grinder's Switch. Using that as her "home" instead of Centerville, she realized, had much more comic effect.

It actually was a tragic event that paved the way for making Minnie Pearl Colley's constant alter ego. After her father died in the late 1930s, she had to return to Centerville to take care of her mother. At first her main interest was teaching dramatics to local children. When she was asked to entertain at a local bankers' convention she revived Minnie Pearl. It went over so well that someone suggested it might go well on the *Grand Ole Opry*. She auditioned for *Opry* officials in Nashville and got mixed reactions. Everyone agreed it was funny, but some worried the audience might consider it a put-down of rural life. A compromise was reached. She was given a chance to perform, but well after the major artists had been on, at 11:05 on Saturday night. She was paid ten dollars for the effort. The fears quickly proved groundless: the audience loved her and fan mail began to arrive.

In 1940 Sarah was asked to become an *Opry* cast member. In the years that followed her homespun humor and unique costume became as much a part of the American comic tradition as Charlie Chaplin's tramp suit.

Discussing Minnie, the well-educated Colley said, "Minnie Pearl is uncomplicated. She's apple pie and clothes dried in the sun and the smell of fresh bread baking. I don't think people think of her so much as a show business act as a friend. When I'm on stage, I'm just plain Minnie Pearl wearing my battered old straw hat and battered shoes. The price tag on my hat seems to be symbolic of all human frailty. There's old Minnie Pearl standing on stage in her best dress, telling everyone how proud she is to be there and she's forgotten to take the $1.98 price tag off her hat."

From the 1940s into the 1990s, she played in theaters, on concert stages, and at county and state fairs across the United States and Canada. On several occasions she toured a number of overseas countries. Colley was featured again and again on major variety and talk shows on all three networks and major syndicated series, ranging from *The Today Show* and *Tonight* to *Dinah!* and *Hee Haw*. Over the years she was just as likely to turn up on a pop music program as a country one, with equally ecstatic response from theater crowds and TV viewers. In 1957, her national reputation was recognized by Ralph Edwards, who selected her as the subject for one of his most popular NBC-TV *This Is Your Life* segments. Other honors came Sarah's way over the decades, including selection as Nashville's "Woman of the Year" in 1965 and nomination for the Country Music Hall of Fame in 1968. Although she didn't receive the required number of votes for election at that time, her name was resubmitted by CMA members regularly until the total was achieved in 1975.

In 1967, Colley's outside interests included a new food franchise organization called "Minnie Pearl's Chicken System, Inc." Unfortunately, though it flourished for a few years, in the end competition from the other chicken franchise outlets was too much.

Colley's recording efforts over the years were not as widespread, naturally, as those of singers and instrumentalists. Still, she was represented by a number of LPs on various labels. Among her albums were several on RCA, including *Monologue* and *How to Catch a Man*. She had one on Everest Records issued *Lookin' for a Feller*. Some of her best offerings came out on Starday in the 1960s, including the albums *Cousin Minnie Pearl, America's Beloved,* and *Country Music Story*. One of her Starday singles, "Giddyup—Go Answer" made it into the country top 10 in 1966. Also in 1996 the Country Music Association voted her Country Music Woman of the Year.

When the Buck Owens/Roy Clark–hosted TV show *Hee Haw* went into syndication at the start of the 1970s, Minnie was a regular cast member. She continued to appear on the program for twenty years while continuing to be featured on the *Grand Ole Opry*.

In 1975, a bronze plaque in her honor was placed in the Country Music Hall of Fame in Nashville. The tribute read, in part, "Humor is the least recorded, but certainly one of the most important aspects of live country music. No one exemplified the values of pure country comedy more than Minnie Pearl. . . . Her trademarks, the dime store hat and shrill 'How-dee! I'm just so proud to be here,' made her the first country humorist to be known and loved worldwide."

Her career was put on hold for a time in the mid-

1980s when she was found to have breast cancer and had to undergo a double mastectomy. She soon bounced back, however, not only to star on the *Opry* and on the concert circuit, but also to do volunteer work for the American Cancer Society. In 1987, that organization presented her with its Courage Award. During an interview that year she stated, "I have no intention of retiring as long as I have my health. I'd like to go out with my hat on with the price tag."

In 1991, some fifty years after she joined the *Grand Ole Opry,* Minnie Pearl remained one of the brightest stars in the program's diadem. But she suffered a stroke in 1991 that essentially ended her performing work, though she kept active in various ways as much as possible. In 1992, she was among thirteen recipients of a National Medal of Art. In the mid-1990s, the Nashville Sound album *The Best of Minnie Pearl* was available in the Country Music Hall of Fame & Museum catalog. Also still in print was her self-penned book *Minnie Pearl Christmas at Grinder's Switch.* Some of her early work on the *Opry* was available in Volumes 6 and 8 of the *Grand Ole Opry Stars of the Fifties* video series. Among other videos in which she was included was *Grand Ole Opry Country Music Celebration.*

In late February 1996 she suffered another stroke and was admitted to Columbia Centennial Medical Center in Nashville. This time she was unable to recover, and died in the hospital on March 4.

PERKINS, CARL: *Singer, guitarist, band leader, songwriter. Born Ridgeley, Tennessee, April 9, 1932. Inducted into Rock and Roll Hall of Fame in 1987.*

Born the same year as his longtime close friend Johnny Cash, Carl Perkins's career tended to parallel that of Cash over the years. Both grew up in poverty, in Perkins's case his childhood was spent in a shack in Lake County, Tennessee, without electricity or running water. (Carl told interviewers he bartered a few dollars and a one-legged chicken named Peg with a black neighbor to get his first guitar.) Both Perkins and Cash started as country musicians, picked up on rock and became nationally known in that field in the mid-1950s and then moved back into the country market again in the 1960s and 1970s. Both also fought hard battles against drugs and other dangerous habits and won out. But in terms of level of artistic success, there's no doubt that Cash had a considerable edge.

Perkins's contributions to both progressive country and country-rock, however, should not be downplayed—they were considerable. His first and perhaps biggest accomplishment was his recording of his composition "Blue Suede Shoes" at Sam Phillips's Sun Studios in Memphis in late 1955. He was part of the wave of young country-bred artists who helped propel rock to its dominant status with material recorded by Sun, a group that included Jerry Lee Lewis, Cash, Elvis Presley, and Roy Orbison. In early 1956, Carl's single of

"Blue Suede Shoes" topped all three charts—pop, country, and R&B. He recalled for writer Tom Piazza in 1996, "Back in the days when that song was popular, somebody would always come up with a camera and want a picture of themselves stepping on the shoes. I used to carry a wire brush in my back pocket so I could reach down and brush them back to life. They sold the brush with the shoes."

Preparations were made for him to receive a gold record for the song on the *Perry Como* show. Perkins left a concert in Norfolk, Virginia, toward the end of March 1956, to drive to New York for the event. Early the next morning, he was almost killed in an accident outside of Wilmington, Delaware. He stayed in bed for a year recuperating, during which time Elvis Presley's hit version of "Blue Suede Shoes" eclipsed Carl's. Presley sent a note to Carl after his Ed Sullivan debut suggesting that Perkins might have been the superstar if the accident hadn't occurred.

Although Carl had some minor rock hits in the late 1950s, such as "Your True Love" on Sun and "Pink Pedal Pushers" and "Pointed Toe Shoes" on Columbia, his career languished after the accident. At one point in 1963, he had about decided to quit show business when his wife persuaded him to take an offer to tour England with Chuck Berry. While there, the Beatles gave a party in his honor and later demonstrated their esteem for him by recording three of his compositions, "Match Box," "Honey Don't," and "Everybody's Trying to Be My Baby."

Still, back home for a while, Carl's mental state went from bad to worse. Then, in the mid-1960s, as did Johnny Cash, Carl got his thinking straightened out and began to rebuild his life and career. Helping him achieve that was his long-suffering wife, Valda, whom he had married in 1953 and whom he always considered one of the true treasures of his life. In 1965, a bid from Cash for Perkins to join him for a two-day concert appearance in the South led to a decade of association. "We got there and John had me come up and do a couple of songs. That two-day tour lasted ten years. That's how long I played with John." During Cash's network TV show from 1969–1971, Perkins not only did backing work but generally had a solo spot during each show.

The TV exposure brought a new recording contract from Columbia that led to several LPs, including *Greatest Hits* and *On Top* in 1969 and *Boppin' the Blues* in 1970. Concentrating on the country field, Carl had several songs on the charts in the early 1970s, such as "Me Without You" in 1971 and "Cotton Top" and "High on Love" in 1972.

In 1976, Carl left the Cash tour to organize a new band of his own featuring his sons, Stan on drums and Greg on bass guitar. The boys were still part of the tour group when Perkins's debut album on a new label, Jet Records, came out in the fall of 1978. Called *Ol' Blue*

Suede's Back, it included country-rock versions of several Perkins songs, including the title track, plus such other familiar early rock numbers as "Maybellene," "Whole Lotta Shakin'," "Rock Around the Clock," and the Arthur Crudup song that started Elvis on the road to superstardom, "That's All Right Mama."

He remained active and was still performing in concerts and clubs through the 1980s and into the 1990s. He was featured in several long-form TV programs during those years typically presented over the Public Broadcasting System stations and also appeared in the 1985 film *Into the Night.* After 1986 National Academy of the Recording Arts & Sciences (NARAS) voting he was one of a group of rockabilly/country veterans to receive Grammy trophies (announced on the February 24, 1987, Grammy telecast) in the Best Spoken Word or Non-Musical Recording category. The award was for the American Record Corporation album, *Interviews from the Class of '55 Recording Sessions.* The title refers to the legendary 1955 Sun Records sessions. Honorees included, besides Carl, Sun owner Sam Phillips, Jerry Lee Lewis, Roy Orbison, Johnny Cash, Rick Nelson, and Chips Moman. Perkins also received a 1986 Grammy Hall of Fame Award for "Blue Suede Shoes."

The year 1987 was notable for Carl in more ways than one. Several weeks before the Grammy show he was one of the early inductees into the new Rock and Roll Hall of Fame in ceremonies at the New York Waldorf Astoria.

A collection that captured Carl's legacy in his early career phases available in the 1990s was the Bear Family Records box set *Carl Perkins: Classic!* The five CD set, available in the U.S. only as an import item, contained all of his Sun tracks, plus some unissued ones, his 1958–1962 Columbia recordings, and all of his tracks for Decca between 1963 and 1965.

In 1992, Columbia/Legacy issued the album *Carl Perkins/Restless* containing 18 songs from his two periods of affiliation with Columbia. The first 15 tracks covered a period from 1958 to 1962 starting with "Pink Pedal Pushers" (recorded February 3, 1956) and concluding with "Twister Sister" and "Hambone" (recorded June 27, 1962). The last three, recorded during 1968–69 were "Restless," "All Mama's Children" and "Just Coastin'."

By then Perkins was literally fighting for his life. While laying down some new tracks in a recording studio in 1991 he began to have problems singing. He sought medical help and was informed he had developed cancer of the throat. He underwent radiation treatment and after two years seemed to have his health back, something he called "a miracle" that he attributed in part to prayer and the strong support of his wife, Valda. By 1994 he resumed touring with his two sons, spending half the year on the road and the other half at his home in Jackson, Tennessee, relaxing and working

on new material. (As of 1996, he had lived in the same place for 50 years.)

His career, which had never brought him the massive following his creative achievements warranted, seemed to blossom anew in 1996. He had his autobiography, *Go, Cat, Go,* written with David McGee, on bookstore shelves and a new CD of the same title issued in October. It included duets with Johnny Cash; George Harrison, Paul McCartney, and Ringo Starr from the Beatles (who had been fans of his from the early 1960s); Tom Petty; Willie Nelson; Paul Simon; and John Fogerty (founder of Creedence Clearwater Revival).

Talking with Tom Piazza for a *New York Times* article ("The Lost Man of Rock-and-Roll Poised for a Revival," Arts & Leisure section, November 10, 1996), he indicated he was satisfied with his lot in life. "I'm not a society man. I don't go to the country clubs. I don't go to Nashville and hang out. I never fit in with that. My friends at home work at the service station. I like to go fishing. I like an old cotton field, and I like to spend time with Valda. I never get tired of her."

He added, while he never stopped enthusing about Elvis's achievements, "I never envied Elvis his mansion and all that. All these boys—Elvis, Jerry Lee, Roy Orbison—they all lost their wives, their families. People say, 'What happened to you, Carl? All of them went on to superstardom. Where'd you go?' I say, 'I went home.' And that's a good place to be."

PHILLIPS, SAM: *Entrepreneur, record company owner (Sun Records), record producer, disc jockey. Born Florence, Alabama, January 5, 1923.*

He wasn't a musician. He didn't work in any of the accepted centers of the recording industry in the post–World War II years. For a long time his main claim to fame seemed to be his transfer of the rights to Elvis Presley from his small Memphis-based operation to mighty RCA. But in retrospect in the 1980s and 1990s, people became aware of his enormous contributions to the development of pop music in the second half of the twentieth century. He had important influence not just on rock, but also R&B, soul, and country.

Grelun Landon, who, as vice president of the major music publishing firm Hill & Range in the 1950s, worked closely with Sam on a number of projects, recalled, "When I first met him in the mid-'50s he looked young, talked young—I thought he was a lot younger than he actually was. I talked to him before he had Elvis because Julian Aberbach of Hill & Range was responsible for a number of marketing arrangements with him. Part of the deal was that if H&R got any cover records of Sun material it would split the licensing fees with Sam.

"To me he was a genius. People either loved him or hated him. But he was always one of my favorite people in the field. Here he was this Southerner nobody ever heard of based in what to some seemed a backwater, and he was turning out some of the most unique music of the period. He was a power in Memphis, but no one else knew much about him. You might say he was a legend before he became a legend."

Sam's route to Memphis began in Alabama, where he was born and raised. He thought after his high school years he might seek a career in law, but his family needed financial help so he quit school and began looking for work. In 1942 he managed to sign on as a disc jockey with station WLAY in Muscle Shoals, Alabama, where he remained until the end of World War II. In 1946 he got a position as an announcer at station WREC in Memphis, Tennessee, a city rich in black blues traditions. It also was a time when a new evolution of the blues was coming to the fore, rhythm & blues, and Phillips took a strong interest in it.

In 1950, he opened the Memphis Recording Studio at 706 Union Avenue, which he hoped to build into a center for production of some of the emerging group of young blues and R&B artists. It took a while, but before long he was recording many artists who were to become legendary performers in later years, including B. B. King, Howlin' Wolf, Ike Turner, and Bobby "Blue" Bland. Most of the masters were then licensed to various labels, including Duke, RPM, and Chess. Landon recalled that one of Phillips's close ties during those years was with Syd Nathan, based in Ohio, who owned two separate labels, one for country and one for R&B. Nathan played a role in helping Sam set up his own record company, Sun Records.

Sam's first love remained R&B, but the turning point in his odyssey came in 1954 when the famous visit of Presley to the recording studio occurred. Elvis, then working as a truck driver, came in to record a song for his mother. Sam wasn't around, but his work impressed Phillips's secretary, Marian Keisker, who later passed a note to her boss suggesting he take a look at the young country artist. Eventually Sam did and the first major step toward the cultural explosion of rock 'n' roll was taken.

The initial five singles of Presley's stylings sparked industry interest in him and Sam took advantage of that to make a lucrative deal with RCA. The main inducement was his need to pay off certain bills, particularly money owed his record presser, and Phillips believed that money would put him in a position to promote other very talented performers like Johnny Cash, Carl Perkins, Roy Orbison and a bit later, Jerry Lee Lewis. One result was a series of classic recording sessions in 1955 that provided some of the most innovative country-rock type releases of the decade. The details of those times were recalled in the America Record Corporation 1985 *Class of '55* interview record which included interviews with all four of those artists plus Sam himself.

As it turned out, Phillips couldn't hold on to those

budding superstars either, again due in part to financial shortfalls. Landon recalled, "Some of that reportedly involved the extravagances of his brother, Judd Phillips, who handled promotional deals for Sun. The saying in the industry was that Sam would be cleaning up wheelbarrows full of money and Judd would lose it on the way to the bank. Judd and Sam argued a lot. In fact, they argued constantly, but it was a team that worked in terms of putting together excellent records and gaining attention for the artists."

Of course, another aspect was that Sam always had other projects to look after. He had owned a radio station in Memphis as early as the start of the 1950s and later bought more and also eventually invested in the mining industry and the Holiday Inn hotel chain.

In the late 1950s and early 1960s, Sam went to Nashville for a while to try and revive his recording industry prospects; when that didn't work out, he returned to Memphis. In 1969 he sold the rights to his Sun output to Shelby Singleton, and focused his attention on other ventures for the next two decades. As interest revived in the early years of rock in the second half of the 1980s and in the 1990s, Sam was sought out for interviews in major print media and guested on a number of major network talk shows.

There's no doubt that Phillips was a brilliant innovator and a visionary as well as a shrewd judge of talent. He didn't always come across promising new performers himself—people like Jack Clement and others in pop music sometimes recommended newcomers—but Sam was willing to listen. Some of the recording techniques developed in his studios also had great impact on the way pop music developed.

Landon noted, "Sam was good at recognizing new talent and anticipating demand. The radio stations mostly were owned by oldtimers who were unwilling to introduce new kinds of sound. Sam saw ahead and predicted that changes were coming and he was willing to back his ideas. Some of that insight came from the time in his career when he was booking acts. When they'd play school gyms with some of the new artists the kids responded with enthusiasm."

While other employees, particularly Jack Clement, did a considerable amount of the company's record production work in the mid-1950s, Landon recalled that Sam did quite a lot of production himself. "He helped create the 'Sun Sound.' It may have existed here and there in dribs and drabs, but the way he handled the board, the way he experimented with echo chambers, reverb and a lot of things not being done for that kind of music, if it was done at all, brought it all together in a new form. There were inputs from others at Sun at the time, but I think the main credit goes to Sam. It all seemed new and fresh in the fifties. Now if you talk about those ideas to young sound engineers they might say, 'So what? Everybody's doing that today.'"

PIERCE, WEBB: *Singer, guitarist, band leader, song-writer. Born near West Monroe, Louisiana, August 8, 1926; died Nashville, Tennessee, February 24, 1991.*

The name Webb Pierce strikes a responsive chord with Louisianans. Like former governor Jimmie Davis, he is considered as great a state asset as its industry or natural resources.

Born and raised in Louisiana, Webb achieved national fame in country music in his home state before moving on to the *Grand Ole Opry.* Brought up in a rural area, Webb could play excellent guitar in his teens. As he won notice for performing in local events, he gained his first radio job on station KMLB in Monroe. Encouraged by his reception, he moved on to Shreveport in the late 1940s to try to gain a wider audience. However, for a while he made little progress and had to earn his living as a salesperson for Sears, Roebuck. He continued to pick up performing jobs in his spare time and finally won the attention of Horace Logan, program director of station KWKH in Shreveport, sponsor of the new *Louisiana Hayride* show.

Pierce joined the cast, and before long was one of the featured performers. In the early 1950s, his band included many performers who went on to greatness on their own, including Faron Young, Goldie Hill, Jimmy Day, Tommy Hill, and Floyd Cramer. He began to achieve a wider reputation with his first records on the Four Star label. Some of the songs that made the charts were his own compositions.

In 1952, after signing with Decca, Pierce's name began to appear on the top rungs of the hit charts. He scored with two top-10 recordings of his own compositions, "That Heart Belongs to Me" and "Wondering," and had a number-one-ranked record in the hit "Last Waltz" with M. Freeman. He also had such other hits as "I'll Go on Alone," "I'm Walking the Dog," and "That's Me Without You," and two number-one-ranked hits, "It's Been So Long" and "There Stands the Glass." In 1952–53 he received the first of many awards, *Ranch and Farm* magazine's citation as Number-One Folk Singer and the Juke Box Operators award as Number-One Singer of 1953.

Along with his close friend Red Sovine, Webb moved to Nashville as an *Opry* regular. The hits continued to pour forth in 1954, such as the number-one-ranked "Slowly" (written with T. Hill), number-one-ranked "More and More," and top-10 "Even Tho" (written with W. Jones and C. Peeples), "Sparkling Brown Eyes," and "You're Not Mine Anymore" (written with the Wilburn Brothers). In 1955, Webb had three number-one songs, "In the Jailhouse Now," "Love, Love, Love," and "I Don't Care," the last cowritten with Cindy Walker. In 1956, he teamed with Red Sovine in two hit duets, "Why, Baby, Why" and "Little Rosa." He also hit with "Any Old Time" and "Teenage Boogie," both original compositions. In the late 1950s, he had such top-10 hits as "Bye Bye Love,"

"Holiday for Love" (coauthored with Wayne Walker and A. R. Peddy), "Honky Tonk Song," "I'm Tired" (1957); "Falling Back to You," "Tupelo County Jail" (written with Mel Tillis) (1958); and "A Thousand Miles Ago" (written with Mel Tillis) (1959).

By the start of the 1960s, Pierce had toured throughout the United States and Canada and guest-starred on such other network shows as Red Foley's *Jubilee U.S.A.* His successes of the 1960s included "Fallen Angel," "No Love Have I" (1960), "Let Forgiveness In," "Walking the Streets," "How Do You Talk to a Baby" (written with Wayne Walker), "Sweet Lips" (written with Wayne Walker and Davy Tubb) (1961); "All My Love," "Take Time," "Crazy Wild Desire" (written with Mel Tillis) (1962); "Sands of Gold" (written with Cliff Parman and Hal Eddy), "Those Wonderful Years" (written with Don Schroeder) (1963); and "Memory Number One" (1964). He hit the charts again in 1968 with the single "Luziana."

Through the mid-1960s, Pierce had compiled one of the best album sales totals of any popular music performer. His LPs on Decca included *Webb Pierce; Wondering Boy; Webb!* and *Just Imagination* (1958); *Bound for the Kingdom, Webb Pierce* (1959); *Webb with a Beat, Walking the Streets* (1960); *Golden Favorites, Fallen Angel* (1961); *Hideaway Heart, Cross Country* (1962); *I've Got a New Heartache, Bow Thy Head* (1963); *Sands of Gold, Webb Pierce Story* (two LP records) (1964); *Memory Number One, Country Music Time* (1965); *Sweet Memories, Webb Pierce Choice* (1966); *Where'd Ya Stay* (1967); *Merry-Go-Round World, Road Show* (late 1960s–early 1970s).

Pierce remained on Decca and its successor, MCA, into the mid-1970s. By 1977, he had moved to the Plantation Records roster.

By the early 1980s, Webb's days as a hitmaker had passed, and he retired from the entertainment sector in favor of concentrating on his business interests. In the late 1980s, he suffered from pancreatic cancer, which finally ended his life in February 1991. Summing up his career contributions, the Country Music Association noted that he had scored forty top-10 hits, including ten number-one singles. His total record sales, almost entirely on Decca/MCA, was estimated at over 68 million.

CMA also pointed out that Pierce "was one of the first singers to outfit himself and his band in rhinestones and one of the first non-western swing acts to use twin fiddles." He also laid claim to the honor of introducing the pedal steel guitar to country stylings.

Webb was nominated several times for the Country Music Hall of Fame, but as of 1996 he had not received sufficient votes to be elected. In naming him to its September 1994 roster of "The 100 Most Important People in the History of Country," the editors of *Life* magazine stated, "In his time [in the 1950s] he was as dominant as any country singer who ever lived." They cited the best available collection of Pierce's recordings to be *Sweet Memories/Sands of Gold* on the Mobile Fidelity label.

Another retrospective collection worth considering in the mid-1990s was the four CD boxed set produced by the Bear Family Records group of Germany. Called *Webb Pierce: The Wondering Boy 1951–1958*, the import item's 113 tracks included original versions of such songs as "Back Street Affair," "There Stands the Glass," "Slowly," "Honky Tonk Song," and "I'm Walking the Dog." Bear Family pointed out that 40 of the 113 songs presented made top chart levels in the U.S. trade press.

PIRATES OF THE MISSISSIPPI: *Vocal and instrumental group, Bill McCorvey, born Montgomery, Alabama, July 4 (lead vocals, songwriter); Rich Alves, born Pleasanton, California, May 25 (guitar, songwriter); Dean Townson (bass guitar); Pat Severs, born Camden, South Carolina, November 10 (pedal steel guitar); Jimmy Lowe, born Atlanta, Georgia, August 2 (drums).*

An accomplished band that combined elements of country rock with more traditional country stylings in their typically up-tempo fashion, the Pirates of the Mississippi tended to get more critical acclaim than mass audience approval. Not that the band didn't attract a following in the late 1980s and early 1990s that helped it make some inroads into the hit charts, but at least as of the mid-1990s, its hard-driving, good-time material fell short of the blockbuster success that might have given it the status of a superstar group like Alabama.

Thus in evaluating their well-conceived and generally highly praised fourth album, *Dream You*, the reviewer in *Country Fever* magazine cited them as "one of the most underrated acts in today's country music scene," and went on to list track after track that had notable impact. It was asserted that "What I Want and What I Get," cowritten by lead singer Bill McCorvey, "should be an anthem for everyone who's underpaid and overworked, and 'People My Age' [has a chorus that] sums up a lot of us in the words 'Most people my age are already grown/I'm caught between Willie and Waylon and the Rolling Stones.'"

The group came together in Nashville in the mid-1980s, with songwriters Bill McCorvey and Rich Alves as prime motivators. McCorvey had the vocal talents to front the group, backed by Alves on guitar, Dean Townson (at the time working in a factory) on bass guitar, pedal steel player Pat Severs (recruited from the ranks of session musicians), and drummer Jimmy Lowe (who was then getting his main income from computer programming). The band began performing on weekends at local clubs in the Nashville area, and word of mouth brought more and more fans to hear a group that described itself as a "North American redneck rock'n'roll party band." With its Nashville base, the band was well-positioned to gain record company interest and, after several years, it was signed to the Liberty label in 1989.

The band made an impressive debut on the national level with its first album, *Pirates of the Mississippi*, and the singles and videos drawn from it. The album came out in early summer of 1990 and won enough critical approval to place it on the *Billboard* country list, where it still remained some sixty weeks later in the fall of 1991 after peaking at number twelve. The album included an excellent version of Hank Williams's "Honky Tonk Blues" and such other chartmakers as "Feed Jake" and "Speak of the Devil" (cowritten by McCorvey, Alves, and D. Mayo). *Radio & Records* named the band Top New Group in its 1990 awards, and this was followed by its being cited by the Academy of Country Music's voters as Top New Vocal Group in 1991. The video of "Feed Jake" also won applause in 1991, earning the Best Video by a Group Award from *Music Row* magazine and receiving Top Overall Video honors in a poll of readers of *Nashville Scene*.

The band made the *Billboard* charts again with its second and third Liberty releases, *Walk the Plank* and *Street Man Named Desire*. The first of those was on the charts from late 1991 well into 1992. The main singles success with record buyers in 1992 was "Till I'm Holding You Again" (cowritten by McCorvey, Alves, and L. Gottlieb), a top-15 hit in *R&R* the week of May 1 and also on upper levels in *Billboard* and other music trades. In the fall the band had the single "Too Much" on the charts for many weeks.

The title song on *Street Man Named Desire* dealt with unemployment and homelessness. The song suggested an occasion for group members to discuss those problems on a number of local and national TV shows. They expressed their concern in more concrete form by performing at benefits to raise funds to help ease the problem. They also lent their talents to aid various charities devoted to raising money to help those in need.

Their fourth Liberty album, *Dream You*, was issued in August 1993 and certainly ranked creatively with their previous collections. It was still receiving excellent reviews well into 1994. Despite that, it had little impact on the charts, perhaps overwhelmed by the flood of new performers and record releases in the country field from labels with larger promotion budgets than Liberty. In any case, Liberty did not choose to keep the band on its roster thereafter. Before 1994 was over, however, the group was working on material for a new label.

POCO: *Vocal and instrumental group. Personnel in 1969, Richie Furay, born Dayton, Ohio, May 9, 1944 (vocals, guitar); Jim Messina, born Harlingen, Texas, October 30, 1947 (vocals, guitar); Rusty Young, born Long Beach, California, February 23, 1946 (vocals, steel guitar); Randy Meisner, born Scotts Bluff, Nebraska, March 6, 1946 (vocals, bass guitar). George Grantham, born Oklahoma, November 20, 1947 (drums), added by 1971. Meisner replaced by Timmy B. Schmit, born Sacramento, California,* *in the early 1970s. Messina replaced in 1971 by Paul Cotton, born February 26, 1943. Furay left in 1973, Grantham later in the 1970s. Rusty Young as only remaining original member added replacements to keep band active until 1984. Group re-formed in late 1988 with original members Young, Furay, Messina, Meisner, and Grantham.*

The reason why the Buffalo Springfield is considered one of the landmark groups in rock music is evident from the later careers of that relatively short-lived aggregation. Steve Stills and Neil Young became superstars as solo artists and as members of Crosby, Stills, Nash & Young. Two other onetime members of the "Herd," Richie Furay and Jim Messina, formed the nucleus of Poco, one of the more important rock bands of the early 1970s. While it never quite realized its full potential, Poco had a major influence on the country-rock of the seventies and eighties.

Furay, who was rhythm guitarist, vocalist, and contributor of original songs to the Buffalo Springfield, started to learn guitar at eight. During his college years, he moved from folk to rock because of his friendship with Steve Stills. While with the Herd, he became acquainted with Jim Messina, who took over as bassist with the group during its last seven months of existence in 1968.

Messina grew up in a country-music–oriented family. His father, a country musician, started Jim on guitar at an early age. At thirteen, Jim started playing in local bands in Colton, California, where his family had taken up residence. After high school, he worked as a producer with a small record company before moving on to employment as an engineer and producer in Hollywood recording studios. He supervised recordings of many major groups, including the Buffalo Springfield. After joining that group, he not only performed with them, but also produced their last album, *Last Time Around.*

Soon after this, he and Furay decided to found their own group, called Pogo at first. They added Rusty Young on pedal steel guitar, George Grantham on drums, and Tim (Timothy Bruce) Schmit on bass. All of the members were vocalists and all had originally proved themselves as songwriters.

Young, though born in California, spent most of his youth in Colorado. At age fourteen, he became the only male musician in an otherwise all-girl band. He dropped out of the University of Colorado after a year, to join a Denver group called Boenzye Creque. When it disbanded, he went to work as a studio musician in Los Angeles. One of the sessions was for the Springfield's last LP, on which he provided support for the song "Kind Woman." This led to an invitation from Furay and Messina to join their new band. He brought in George Grantham, born and raised in Oklahoma, from Boenzye Creque.

The original fifth member was bass guitarist Randy Meisner, but by the early 1970s he had departed the band and his place was taken by Timothy B. Schmit, who played with small bands while working for a degree in psychology at Sacramento State College. After coming within a few credits of his bachelor's degree, he decided he was more interested in pursuing a career in music. He moved to Los Angeles, and, hearing of a possible opening with Pogo, auditioned and soon became the band's bassist. (Around that time the group's name was changed from Pogo to Poco, to avoid legal problems with the copyright owners of the cartoon of that name.)

The group rehearsed for much of the summer and fall of 1968 before its first public appearance that November at the Troubadour in Los Angeles. Its sound was oriented toward country-rock, though its repertoire ranged from blues and blues-rock to experimental contrapuntal-type harmonies. The press was almost wholly positive toward the new group. Pete Johnson of the *Los Angeles Times* wrote: "Poco . . . is one of the tightest groups I have seen, a coordination which obviously stems from endless practice and good feelings within the combo. . . . The band seems the natural heir to the originality, diversity, and togetherness which marked the beginnings of the Byrds and the Buffalo Springfield, Southern California's two best folk-rooted rock groups so far."

The band's appearance with disc jockeys and fans started off reasonably well in 1969 when its debut LP, *Picking up the Pieces,* on Epic Records sold over 100,000 copies and appeared briefly on the charts. The group's second album, *Deliverin'* (1970), stayed on the charts from March into July. Similarly, the album *Poco* was on the charts for the entire summer. Two singles made the charts in 1970–71: "You Better Think Twice" and "C'mon."

In 1971, Jim Messina left to form a new band, Loggins and Messina, a first indication of some doubts about band direction among original members. His place was taken by Paul Cotton, who performed on the group's 1972 hit single "Railway Days." During that period, the band had a mild hit with its fourth Epic LP, *From the Inside* (late 1971). The band's June 1972 album, *A Good Feelin' to Know,* spent considerably more time on the charts, but still fell short of mass success.

After working on the 1973 album *Crazy Eyes,* Richie Furay left in favor of a solo career and Asylum Records head David Geffen's brief brainchild, the Souther, Hillman, Furay Band including J. D. Souther and former Byrd and Flying Burrito Brothers member Chris Hillman.

Poco then kept its core membership down to four. Without both of its founding members, the band seemed at a loss creatively as exemplified by one of its weakest offerings to that time, the 1974 release *Seven.* But it seemed to bounce back later that year with its eighth album, *Cantamas.*

Still, neither the remaining members nor Epic were

satisfied with the band's progress. It always had seemed on the verge of supergroup status in the early 1970s, but never achieved the hoped-for mass-audience approval. The band did build up a loyal following, but not enough to make the project economically attractive. One result was the band's departure from Epic in the mid-1970s. Epic, realizing the band still had many fans, continued to release earlier recordings on such LPs as *The Very Best of Poco* (1975), *Live* (1976), and *Ride the Country* (1979).

In 1975, the band signed with ABC Records, which issued its label debut, *Head over Heels,* in that year. The album suggested the group might be on the way to a fresh, exciting start. Unfortunately, the new creative surge proved temporary and such succeeding LPs as *Rose of Cimarron* (1976) and *Indian Summer* (1977) were disappointing. The departure of Timothy Schmit, who had become a central figure in the band, for a role in the Eagles, seemed the final blow. (Schmit's move had an element of déjà vu about it. He was replacing Randy Meisner.) The band did manage to make the singles charts with "Crazy Love" and "Heart of the Night" from its 1978 album *Legend,* but that appeared to be a last hurrah. After Poco's early 1980 *Under the Gun* on MCA (which had acquired ABC Records), the band's history, for all intents and purposes, was a closed book, although Rusty Young organized versions of Poco that remained active until 1984. Ironically, *Legend* was the only major commercial success under the Poco banner, and it came when everyone but Young from the 1969 aggregation had left and half of the band roster was made up of musicians from Britain.

After a hiatus of four years, some of the original members decided it was worth attempting to reunite. By then their outlook about personal artistic differences had mellowed, and all were essentially at loose ends careerwise. Supporting the idea of reforming the band was the rising pop star Richard Marx, who had been a fan of their music. Young told Mike Boehm of the *Los Angeles Times* ("Poco, Reunited After 20 Years, Has Richard Marx to Thank," July 13, 1990) that Richard Marx's agreement to write and produce a song for the proposed new Poco album was a key selling point in gaining a contract from RCA Records. Besides urging RCA to sign the band, Marx also agreed to meet the original song requirement.

Industry people in the main looked askance at the project, Young said. "People were saying, 'Can these guys still sing?' and 'These guys can't get along for five minutes!'" Despite the impressive post-Poco credentials of Messina, Furay, and Meisner, observers felt their glory days were well behind them, and wondered if they could find an audience for new recordings. The resulting album, *Legacy,* demonstrated that the performers retained much of their skills—and that they could still sell records. The album, which was issued in August 1989, had sold over 500,000 copies by the sum-

mer of 1990, a far better showing than the band was able to achieve in its heyday.

The evident interest in the group in the 1990s caused Columbia Records to reissue some of its previous collections. In mid-1995, the company's Legacy label released the album *Pickin' Up the Pieces,* followed soon after by *Poco* and *Crazy Eyes.*

POINTER SISTERS, THE: *Vocal group, all born Oakland, California. Ruth, born March 1946; Anita, circa 1948; Bonnie, circa 1953; June, circa 1954.*

At first glance, the Pointer Sisters might not be thought of as country artists; they are associated in most peoples' minds with jazz, pop, or R&B stylings. But the sisters made their mark in country as well, both as singers and as songwriters, a fact borne out by their nominations in country categories in both Grammy and Country Music Association competition in the mid-1970s.

The women, along with their two older brothers, began their musical careers as members of the choir of the West Oakland Church of God, where both their parents, Reverends Elton and Sarah Elizabeth Pointer, were ministers. As Ruth Pointer, oldest of the sisters, noted in biographical data for Planet Records in 1978, "Our parents naturally, as ministers, wanted to protect us from the bad lives people had led in the blues and jazz worlds. We weren't allowed to go to the movies or hear music other than gospel and TV soundtracks. [Later, as the women made their way successfully in the music world, their parents came around to being firm supporters.] In the beginning we had no one to imitate. We'd never heard of the Andrews Sisters or nostalgia. We started 'scatting' stuff." The situation, precluding any preconceived notions, later made all kinds of music seem interesting to them, including country. "We're a very country family," Ruth remarked.

The changing world helped make the elder Pointers relax their restrictions as the girls came of age. The three older sisters became enthusiastic about the idea of a singing career and sought work in the field while earning money in clerical jobs. Their initial attempts in 1969 met with no success, but a friendship with producer David Robinson finally led to session work as backup singers for Cold Blood's album *Sisyphus.* This was followed by more assignments, first with the Elvin Bishop group and then with artists like Dave Mason (who took them along on a European tour) and Taj Mahal. Finally they got their initial record contract in the early 1970s with Atlantic, which classified them as straight R&B singers. Two singles were released, which, according to the Pointers, "were heard only in our living room."

Then Robinson got them signed to ABC/Blue Thumb Records in 1973. That May, they made a sensational debut at Doug Weston's Troubadour in Los Angeles (by then, younger sister June had joined to make it a quartet), which led to appearances on major TV shows, including *Helen Reddy, The Tonight Show,* and *The Midnight Special.* In September, the sisters also were featured at the Monterey Jazz Festival. Their debut album on ABC, *The Pointer Sisters,* which included Willie Dixon's old Chicago blues song "Wang Dang Doodle," Allan Toussaint's "Yes We Can Can," and originals by the sisters, "Sugar" and "Jada," found favor with national audiences and was certified gold by the R.I.A.A. on February 7, 1974.

Their second album continued the momentum, receiving a gold-record award on July 25, 1974, only a short while after its release. The sister's country inclinations were emphasized during 1974 by the original song "Fairytale." At the early 1975 Grammy Awards program of the National Academy of Recording Arts and Sciences, the Pointers won the Grammy for 1974 Best Country Vocal Performance by a Duo or Group for the album track of "Fairytale." Anita and Bonnie, who penned the song, also were nominated for the songwriter's award, Best Country Song of 1974. The following year, the Pointers had another country-flavored song on the charts, "Live Your Life Before You Die." The song was one of the nominees for the 1975 Grammy Award for Best Country Vocal Performance by a Duo or Group at the early 1976 awards program. The sisters, of course, continued to find favor for other types of songs, such as the pop hit "How Long (Betcha Got a Chick on the Side)," a song from their 1976 album, *Steppin',* which was their fourth release on ABC/Blue Thumb, having been preceded by *Live at the Opera House.*

Meanwhile, despite audience approval, the sisters were unhappy. As June recalled, "We didn't read contracts in those days and we lived on the road and came home broke. But we enjoyed singing so much we just kept on." They also chafed at the typecasting of their record firm, which wanted to stress nostalgic songs with swing era feel, such as "Salt Peanuts" and "That's a Plenty" (which served as the title track for another ABC/Blue Thumb LP). "We weren't growing as singers. We didn't really know what our voices could do," June declared.

The girls were represented on two more ABC albums in the mid-1970s, *The Best of the Pointer Sisters* and, in 1977, *Having a Party.*

After the last album, which completed their contract agreement with ABC, the group broke up for a while. In 1978, though, three of the sisters, Ruth, June, and Anita, returned to action, joining a new label, Planet Records, which issued their debut LP, *Energy,* in November. The album was on the charts into 1979, for part of which it was joined by their second Planet LP (distributed by Elektra Records), *Priority.* During 1979, the trio had two major singles hits, "Fire" and "Happiness." *Energy* earned them their third gold-record album (the

second was for the ABC album titled *That's a Plenty*). The single "Fire" from *Energy* also brought the first R.I.A.A. certified gold single. In 1980, their next Planet album, *Special Things,* on the charts the last third of 1980 and into 1981, spawned their second gold single, "He's So Shy."

(Meanwhile, Bonnie had launched her solo career, signing with Motown Records. Her debut LP, *Bonnie Pointer,* was issued in late 1979 and was on the charts soon after, staying on them well into 1980. The album was the source of two 1980 hit singles for her, "Heaven Must Have Sent You" and "I Can't Help Myself.")

In mid-1981, Planet released the fourth album by Ruth, June, and Anita on the label, *Black and White.* In September, the album was certified gold. Earlier that month the single "Slow Hand" from the album also was certified gold. In late September 1981, the second single from *Black and White,* "What a Surprise," was released and soon was on the charts. It was an auspicious month for the girls in other ways: at the conclusion of *Billboard* magazine's Talent Forum in New York's Savoy Hotel, the trio was named R&B Group of the Year.

In the 1990s, the Pointers retained a strong following on the concert circuit and showed up in featured spots on TV talk and variety shows from time to time, but they had little impact on the hit charts, at least with solo material. In 1993, though, they were also to take part in the MCA Records project that sought to demonstrate the kinship of rhythm & blues and country. For their contributions, the Pointers collaborated with country superstar Clint Black for a version of Aretha Franklin's 1967 hit, "Chain of Fools."

The album, *Rhythm, Country & Blues,* issued at the start of 1994, rose to number one on country charts (and also did well in pop lists) and, by mid-year, had passed R.I.A.A. platinum-record levels. In the 1994 voting by members of the Country Music Association it was nominated for Album of the Year. During 1994, the Pointer Sisters joined with such other participating artists as Trisha Yearwood, Aaron Neville, Patti LaBelle, Marty Stuart, Sam Moore, and others in an extensive series of concerts called the Rhythm, Country & Blues Tour.

Clint Black commented, "When I'm playing to a country audience and I do something like 'Steamroller Blues' or break into some acoustic number of a folk song or something like that, I can feel the response. People out there, they are buying all the country records, but they're just like us. We've got all kinds of music in our collections."

Anita Pointer added, "When you see our show, we have country music too. We go from 'So Excited' to 'Slowhand.'" The last-named song had not only been a hit for them, but afterwards was also a country hit for Conway Twitty.

PRESLEY, ELVIS ARON: *Singer, guitarist, actor. Born Tupelo, Mississippi, January 8, 1935; died Memphis, Tennessee, August 16, 1977.*

When Elvis Presley died at the age of forty-two, the news shocked the world. Two days after he was found dead, his embalmed body, displayed in a casket in the foyer of his Graceland mansion in Memphis, Tennessee, drew thousands of mourners who stood patiently in long lines for the chance to get a last glimpse of the revered rock star. So many people lined up to see the body, in spite of sweltering heat, that dozens fainted from heat exhaustion. In the years that followed, throngs of fans made regular pilgrimages to Graceland to honor his memory.

Over a decade after his death, other performers were still doing big business as Elvis impersonators while a stream of new books and articles continued to keep alive the controversy about Presley's life and early death, admittedly from a heart attack induced by a drug overdose. He was, even after his death, the one and only king of rock 'n' roll and a country music superstar as well. A featured exhibit at the Country Music Hall of Fame in Nashville was his gold Cadillac, with Presley's first gold records embedded in its walls.

Some material on his career was even entered into the *Congressional Record.* A calculator would be in order to count the several hundred millions of recordings (both genuine copies and perhaps nearly as many counterfeit discs and tapes), T-shirts, and other franchised products purchased worldwide. There were also over thirty motion pictures. Even at the end of the 1980s, the image of Presley seemed ever present, which begs the question, "What sort of man was this?"

There was the singer, the performer-actor, and the individual. In the 1980s, the individual seemed to draw the most interest from a public yet to be sated in its compulsion to gain insight into what made Presley tick. Despite all the writings, that part of him remained an enigma. Perhaps publicist and author Bob Levinson summed it up best when he said, tongue in cheek, he was considering writing a book titled *I Never Knew Elvis.*

During the 1980s, a growing amount of analysis was devoted to Presley's voice and singing dynamics. Most overlooked was his ability as an actor. Elvis performed to an audience at all times, whether it was a solitary person or thousands of people. He played roles that said: "Notice me! Like me!" long before he went before Hollywood cameras, whether it was his all-black school outfits and sideburns days at Humes High School in Memphis or later, as he bought new cars by the six-pack to give away to friends. The roles were myriad and possibly a defense mechanism to keep others away from his personal self—a speculation at best, but one that helps explain the bafflement not only of authors of the many posthumous books about him, but also of his

associates going back to his pre-"Memphis Mafia" days. The man who understood this was his brilliant and canny manager, Colonel Thomas A. Parker, whose wavelengths are unique unto themselves; Elvis and the Colonel seemed to ride the same carrier band in their very special relationship.

Elvis was born in Tupelo, Mississippi, to Gladys and Vernon Presley. His twin brother, Jesse, was stillborn. It was during the Depression and both parents worked at whatever jobs were available. Elvis was brought up as part of a tight family unit—the three of them together—a bedrock that held even as some parts of his life crumbled around him later. He was influenced by country and gospel music, naturally, and by so-called race and middle-of-the-road pop songs. The traditional template for modern artists, the guitar, was a family gift that he came to cherish more than the hoped-for bicycle. His parents chose the guitar over the bicycle for their one remaining child because he couldn't get hurt with a guitar. The move from Tupelo to Memphis happened when he was thirteen years old.

Elvis's quick ear, remarked upon by musicians throughout his career, was augmented by a quick eye that seized upon detail sometimes more than the overall picture. Aside from his high school days—he never quite left them—he held jobs that included working as an usher in a movie theater. He seized upon some of the things he saw in the films as cues for actions in social and other situations—a finishing school away from home and regular school.

Elvis's recording career began in 1953, when he entered Memphis-based Sun Studios to make an acetate recording of two pop ballads as a birthday present for his mother. Sun staffer Marion Keisker brought him to the attention of owner Sam Phillips, who eventually set up formal taping sessions for his Sun Records, which also put out blues records. In addition, Phillips produced blues discs by Memphis-based artists such as B. B. King and Tuff Green for Bullet Records of Nashville. Bullet's principal, Jim Bullet, helped arrange financing and limited distribution for Sun, later selling his interest back to Phillips for $1,200. Though only in his twenties, Phillips was also involved with a radio station, WHER, and other projects. After adding Elvis to Sun's roster, he helped arrange for local disc jockey and booking agent Bob Neal to manage Presley and his band (Scotty Moore on guitar and Bill Black on stand-up bass).

Raw and untamed, Presley's 1954–55 tracks for Sun were the most exciting he ever recorded. His first release typified his rockabilly fusion of blues and hillbilly: bluesman Arthur "Big Boy" Crudup's "That's All Right (Mama)" backed with bluegrass founder Bill Monroe's "Blue Moon of Kentucky." Some Memphis disc jockeys refused to play a record with a "black" song on one side and a "white" song on the other, but local listeners' response to the polite young truck driver's debut disc was instant and overwhelming. Four more Sun singles followed, including a steamy remake of Roy Brown's 1947 R&B classic "Good Rockin' Tonight" and a haunting interpretation of bluesman Junior Parker's 1953 Sun hit "Mystery Train."

But Elvis wasn't Sun's only promising young artist. Besides, the label had money problems. Among other shortcomings, Sun product only was distributed in seven or eight states rather than nationally. When the opportunity came to sell Presley's contract to a major label, Phillips took it. Though Columbia and the newly formed ABC Records turned him down for various reasons, RCA bought Elvis for $35,000—an outrageous sum then. The money presented to Sun was used principally to pay off pressing debts (in both meanings of the word), especially to a record-manufacturing plant in Atlanta. This move gave Phillips the leverage needed to work other talent, including Johnny Cash and Carl Perkins. Also a catalyst in Presley's move to RCA was Colonel Parker, with whom Elvis signed for career management in mid-1955. (Still with one foot in the country field, Elvis was billed for some concerts booked by Parker as the "hillbilly cat.") Besides the RCA agreement, two music firms—Elvis Presley Music, Inc. (BMI) and Gladys Music, Inc. (ASCAP)— were formed with the New York publishing firm Hill & Range Songs, Inc. Under the arrangement, including a $5,000 advance, Elvis and Hill & Range each controlled 50% of the stock.

Much has been made of the assumption that Elvis was signed only as a songwriter to his own firms but, in fact, he was a coowner and it was only logical that whatever talents he might develop as a writer be assigned to his own companies. (In fact, almost all of Presley's songs over the years were written by others.) As always, he checked out the essence of all business deals negotiated by the Colonel, some of which he turned down, while for others he pressed for more favorable terms. The latter were rarities because Parker was very thorough in what often were precedent-setting arrangements later followed by others in the industry.

The Colonel studiously stayed away from the Presley personal life and Elvis's private investments, unless asked to advise either directly or by a surreptitious call from a concerned Vernon. The same applied to Elvis's performances, whether on stage, in the studio, or in movies. Even for Elvis's initial appearances on the Dorsey Brothers' network TV show, the Colonel remained in Madison, Tennessee, while Elvis, Scotty, and Bill were squired about by a talent agent from the William Morris Agency and a publishing-firm representative. It worked well until Elvis became such a celebrity that he lost the freedom to move about. The Colonel then organized a well-knit team to handle the star's safekeeping and his concert demands.

It was on guest appearances on several Dorsey shows and a "Milton Berle Show" that Presley performed his first national hit, "Heartbreak Hotel" (number one in *Billboard* for eight weeks starting April 21, 1956). The week of July 28, 1956, Elvis had "I Want You, I Need You, I Love You" atop the charts, followed in short order by "Don't Be Cruel"/"Hound Dog" (number one for eleven weeks starting August 18) and "Love Me Tender" (number one for five weeks starting on November 3). The Presley musical revolution had begun.

He added more *Billboard* number-one hits to his collection in 1957: "Too Much" (three weeks starting February 9), "All Shook Up" (April 13 and seven weeks after), "(Let Me Be Your) Teddy Bear" (seven weeks starting July 8), and "Jailhouse Rock"/"Treat Me Nice" (seven weeks starting October 21). He began 1958 with "Don't"/"I Beg of You" atop the charts for five weeks beginning February 10. But on March 24, his career was interrupted when he was inducted into the U.S. Army. During his two-year hitch (much of it in Germany), he only did one recording session for RCA, but that provided the hit "A Big Hunk of Love," number one in *Billboard* the weeks of August 10 and 17, 1959. (In July 1958, he also reached the top of the charts with the single "Hard Headed Woman," recorded before his induction but released after it.)

When Presley's army phase ended on March 1, 1960, he quickly returned to action both to record and to renew his film career that had begun with *Love Me Tender* and *Jailhouse Rock*. On April 25, 1960, his single "Stuck on You" hit *Billboard*'s number one for four weeks. Later in the year, he starred in his fifth movie, *G.I. Blues* (a Paramount release that included footage shot in Germany while Elvis was still in uniform). Before 1960 was over, his "It's Now or Never" made number one in *Billboard* for five weeks starting August 15 and "Are You Lonesome Tonight" for six weeks starting November 28. March 10 and 17, 1961, he had his next number-one success, "Surrender." In April 1962, he had another number-one single, "Good Luck Charm." That proved to be his last chart-topper for many years, a situation that reflected both the decline in the excitement of his music as it moved toward the middle of the road and his shift in career emphasis for most of the 1960s to movies rather than concert work. For four years after his 1965 "Crying in the Chapel" (a remake of the Orioles' 1953 R&B hit), he didn't even break the top 10.

The Hollywood years seemed like an answer to Presley's youthful fantasies. The fascination for film had been there since his days as a theater usher in Memphis and, for a long time, the chance to act in movies made him feel the same as a youngster let loose in a candy store. He tasted the off-screen delights of Hollywood with a bigger-than-life appetite and shared them with his friends. At one time, he had thirty-nine people on his own payroll, including those working in Graceland and his nearby Mississippi ranch. It was a substantial overhead that was whittled away only to rise again and again. He remained confident that the money machine would be greased well by his manager, who continued to come up with solutions to keep cash rolling in.

During the sixties, recording-contract requirements with RCA were met mainly by soundtrack material from mediocre movies, augmented by a rare recording session. It was a period when he was kept before a worldwide public by the Colonel's ingenuity and a dedicated staff.

By the late 1960s, most observers considered Elvis a has-been from a recording and concert standpoint. But his May 1, 1967, marriage to Priscilla Ann Beaulieu triggered a change in attitude and gave him a fresher outlook that made him more amenable to venture from his by then stifling Hollywood existence. Presley finally began to tire of his film chores and welcomed suggestions to renew his musical career. The decision to make the now-classic December 3, 1968, Singer TV special for NBC, followed a few months after the birth of his daughter, Lisa Marie, on February 1, 1968. The change in approach—as positive as the death of his mother in 1958 had been negative for him—and the reassuring success of the TV special opened his mind again to new challenges that the astute Colonel quickly channeled into the Las Vegas International Hotel opening on July 26, 1969, his first live appearance in eight years. The decision to tour had been made even before that show and the concerts proved all-out, exciting entertainment for an adoring America. By then, even recording sessions had recaptured his attention as evidenced by "U.S. Male" and "Guitar Man" (1968) and 1969's "In the Ghetto," "Don't Cry Daddy," and "Suspicious Minds" (number one in *Billboard* the week of November 1). Playing a strong role in many of the new releases was RCA-named producer Felton Jarvis.

More successes followed on both the recording and concert fronts, the latter including the Madison Square Garden Show in 1972—his first in that tough town—that won critical accolades including one dubbing him "prince of the heavens." Another milestone was the live concert telecast worldwide from Hawaii in January 1973 with all proceeds from ticket sales donated to charity and with the album *Aloha from Hawaii via Satellite* going instant platinum in the new quadraphonic format.

Meanwhile he placed new songs on the singles chart such as the 1970 "Kentucky Rain," "The Wonder of You"/"Mama Liked the Roses," and "You Don't Have to Say You Love Me." In 1971, he hit with "I Really Don't Want to Know"/"There Goes My Everything," "Where Did She Go, Lord"/"Rags to Riches," "I'm Leavin'," and "Life,"/"Only Believe." His 1972 chart makers were "Until It's Time for You to Go," "Separate Ways," and "It's a Matter of Time"/"Burning Love." In 1973 he scored with "Steamroller Blues"/"Fool" and "Raised on Rock"/"For Ole Times' Sake. Hits in subse-

quent years included "Moody Blue" and "(I'm So) Hurt."

Throughout his active career, Elvis turned out dozens of studio, live, and film soundtrack albums, most making pop and/or country charts for a harvest of gold and platinum awards. A sampling includes *Elvis Presley* and *Elvis* (mid-1950s); *Elvis' Golden Records* and *King Creole* (1958); *A Date with Elvis* and *For LP Fans Only* (1959); *Elvis' Golden Records Volume 2* and *Elvis Is Back!* (1960); *Something for Everybody* and *His Hand in Mine* (1961); *Pot Luck with Elvis* (1962); *Girls! Girls! Girls!, It Happened at the World's Fair*, and *Elvis' Golden Records Volume 3* (1963); *Roustabout* (1964); *Elvis for Everyone* (1965); *Spinout* (1966); *How Great Thou Art* (1967); *From Elvis in Memphis* (1969); *That's the Way It Is, Almost in Love, Let's Be Friends, Worldwide 50 Gold Award Hits, From Memphis to Vegas: Elvis in Person at the International Hotel Las Vegas, Nevada*, and *Elvis Back in Memphis* (1970); *Elvis Country, Love Letters from Elvis, The Other Sides—50 Gold Award Hits Volume 2*, and *You'll Never Walk Alone* (1971); *Elvis as Recorded Live at Madison Square Garden, Elvis Sings Burning Love and Hits from His Movies*, and *He Touched Me* (1972); *Raised on Rock/For Ole Times Sake* (1973); *Elvis: A Legendary Performer Volume I* and *Elvis Recorded Live on Stage in Memphis* (1974); *Elvis Today* (1975); and *A Legendary Performer Volume 2* and (resurrecting his earliest efforts) *The Sun Sessions* (1976).

In the mid-1970s, Elvis's comeback was accomplished fact and it seemed to outsiders his life couldn't be better—but it was an illusion. His divorce from Priscilla in 1972 had taken its traumatic toll and there were violent swings and excesses in both mood and appetite. He had proved it all, but what was it, what did it prove? There were more recording sessions (which, in most cases, he tried to avoid) and more appearance dates—Las Vegas and Lake Tahoe contracts where aborted shows became more common. He also was increasingly concerned over the health of his father, Vernon, who, aside from daughter, Lisa, was the last strong link to the private Elvis.

His remarkable constitution was taking a beating past the fail-safe point. His once quick energy and infectious sense of humor ebbed despite the efforts of close associates to turn things around. Hints of drug dependence circulated among his peer group and the industry as he secluded himself within Graceland or his Palm Springs home. A habit acquired years before, starting with "bennies" (an upper commonly used by country artists in those days in order to stay awake when driving to the next show date a hundred or more miles away) led to mid-1960s drug experimentation common to the Hollywood colony. Elvis always pushed the limit in everything.

His death in August 1977 shocked and saddened fans the world over who equated him with their own fantasies, a massive transference. Here was a man who loved his mother and father, served his country willingly, and embodied the young and restless spirit for all age groups. He was an American original who dispensed his gifts freely to all kinds of people, both in performing and in a personal way.

When Elvis died, he had a new album, *Moody Blue,* moving up the pop charts, as well as the chart single "Way Down." As soon as word got out about the music public's tragic loss, there was a literal rush on record stores as fans snapped up all his available recordings. RCA was soon releasing both old packages as well as new combinations of previously recorded material assembled by Joan Deary. Still, for over a year, record stores had trouble keeping his recordings in stock. By the end of 1977, half a dozen of his LPs were high on the charts. During 1978, his hit LPs included *Legendary Performer Volume 2* and *Elvis Sings for Children and Grownups Too.* In 1979, there were best-selling LPs *Legendary Performer Volume 3, Our Memories of Elvis, Our Memories of Elvis Volume 2,* and *Elvis: A Canadian Tribute.* In 1980, RCA put out an eight-LP boxed set *Elvis Aron Presley,* and in early 1981, the LP *Guitar Man* (whose selections, RCA announced, had been reengineered to reduce background sounds). The title track hit number-one single on country lists in March. As the decade went by, still more albums and singles posthumously made the hit list. The charted LPs included *The Elvis Medley* (1982) and *A Golden Celebration* and *Rocker* (both 1984). New discoveries of material from the early part of his career also continued to surface during the 1980s, such as *Elvis: The First Live Recordings* (Music Works/Jem Records, 1984) and Charly Records of England's releases of cuts from Elvis's legendary Sun jam sessions with Jerry Lee Lewis and Carl Perkins, the *Million Dollar Quartet* (mid-1980s) and *The Complete Million Dollar Session* (1988).

It was a situation where, in death, Elvis continued to share his largesse (especially to RCA Records, whose fortunes soared for many years). There were specials (e.g., *Elvis: One Night with You* and *Elvis Presley's Graceland,* both on HBO, 1985; and *Elvis and Me* (1988) a dramatization of Priscilla Presley's account of their marriage). Among the more sincere memorials was a chapel dedicated two years after his death by the Elvis Presley Memorial Foundation in his hometown of Tupelo and, of course, the Gold Cadillac display in Nashville visited by over 500,000 people annually.

The day of his funeral in Memphis, his producer, Felton Jarvis (for whom Elvis earlier had arranged a life-saving kidney transplant), met Sam Phillips at the crypt. Returning from the graveside service in a limousine with another longtime Elvis associate, Grelun Landon, Jarvis said in his soft Southern drawl, "You know, Grelun, it's the first time I met Sam and it feels right that his first and last producers should finally gather here."

The Elvis saga continued unabated into the 1990s with new TV specials, various retrospective album releases, and even new attention from academia. Boxed-sets released in the first part of the 1990s included an excellent one showcasing his early recorded work for Sun and RCA and a less consistent compilation, the five-CD RCA package, *From Nashville to Memphis: The Essential 60's Masters,* issued in the fall of 1993. In the summer of 1992, a soundtrack album for *Honeymoon in Vegas,* released by Epic Records, provided covers of twelve of Elvis's hits by rock and country stars including Dwight Yoakam, Travis Tritt, Billy Joel, and the rock band U2's lead singer, Bono. And in 1995 RCA completed their trilogy of box-set retrospectives with *Walk a Mile in My Shoes: The Essential '70s Masters,* which included extended takes of songs originally issued on the *Elvis Country* album.

In the mid-1990s, the U.S. Post Office had its own best-seller with an Elvis Presley stamp, while so many new books on Elvis were published they were almost a dime a dozen. Various authors argued about whether Elvis's death was due to an accidental drug overdose, suicide, or even murder. One volume that was definitely not run-of-the-mill was the first of a two-volume biography of Presley by noted writer Peter Guralnick, *Last Train to Memphis,* one of the major literary events of 1994.

Interest among Presley fans extended to his movies as well as his recordings. This inspired Fox Video to release eleven of his films from *Love Me Tender* to *Tickle Me* as part of a special collection with the individual film videos offered at $14.98 each.

By the time the University of Mississippi announced it would host a six-day meeting of international scholars in August 1995 called "In Search of Elvis: Music, Race, Religion, Art, Performance," the U.S. Library of Congress indicated its data files showed that since 1968 300 books in nine languages on Elvis had been published as well as over 30,000 articles. It remained to be seen how seriously the academic world would take "the King" in the future. Charles Noyes, a retired English professor at the University of Mississippi, told *The New York Times,* "If you assume that pop culture is a reasonable field of scholarly study, then I guess he is important. I personally am an 18th-century man, and I feel that if you can't write like Samuel Johnson or Alexander Pope, then you probably aren't worth studying. But seriously, Elvis is probably worth it, but he's not worth six days." And in that context, of course, the fact remains that Elvis was an interpreter of songs, not a writer.

Meanwhile, when the new Rock and Roll Hall of Fame building finally opened in Cleveland, Ohio, that summer, exhibits on Elvis's career were key elements of its contents. Colonel Parker died of complications from a stroke at age 87 in Las Vegas, Nevada, on January 21, 1997. *(See also Perkins, Carl; Phillips, Sam.)*— G.L.

PRICE, RAY NOBLE: *Singer, guitarist, band leader (Cherokee Cowboys), songwriter. Born Perryville, Texas, January 12, 1926. Elected to Country Music Hall of Fame in 1996.*

If you had looked at the top levels of the country hit charts in early 1979, you would have observed a song titled "Feet," recorded by Ray Price. It was the same Ray Price whose name often could be found in top-10 singles lists in 1952—and many other times in the intervening years. Few people in any area of country—or pop—music could match his consistency in maintaining a strong hold on a large segment of his audience for so many years. Changing with the times, demonstrating the ability to sing all kinds of songs, from folk music and traditional country to progressive country and sophisticated ballads, Price certainly ranks as one of the superstars of the modern country field.

Although his career reached its zenith when he lived in Tennessee, his roots were in Texas, where he spent his formative years. Ray was born in the small town of Perryville in rural Cherokee County in eastern Texas. He did plenty of farm chores as a youngster and also learned about horses and farm animals first hand, an interest he retained all his life. By the time he reached high school age, his family had moved to Dallas. He already had shown interest and talent in music by singing and performed in public at church festivals and other local events. By the time he finished high school, he had added to that experience, and also became proficient on the guitar.

He enrolled at North Texas Agricultural College in Abilene as a veterinary major, but his education was interrupted by World War II. He joined the Marines for what was to become a four-year tour of duty, including service in the Pacific Theater of operations. After receiving his discharge in 1946, Price returned to Abilene to resume his schooling. Once back on campus, he varied the routine of studies with a growing number of appearances as a country performer in local clubs. In 1948, "The Cherokee Cowboy" made his radio debut on the station KRBC (Abilene) *Hillbilly Circus*.

Still pursuing his degree with thoughts of making his livelihood as a rancher or farmer, Ray didn't at first think of music as more than a pleasant sideline. However, his performing career continued to move ahead in 1948 and 1949. When he was given the chance to join the cast of the prestigious *Big D Jamboree* broadcast over Dallas station KRLD, the matter was settled. His efforts during 1949 and 1950 began to make his name known to a steadily expanding number of fans. Parts of the program were broadcast nationally on the CBS network, with similar results as far as Ray was concerned. With that kind of exposure, a recording contract was in order; Price was signed to a regional label called Bullet. He made a number of singles for the label that made some inroads on several regional markets.

By 1952, he was ready to move up into the major leagues of country music. He signed with Columbia Records and before long had his first top-10 singles, "Talk to Your Heart" and "Don't Let the Stars Get in Your Eyes." During that year, he achieved the dream of all aspiring country artists, and joined the cast of the *Grand Ole Opry*. It made sense to relocate to Nashville, and Tennessee became his home state for several years before he returned to Texas.

Ray placed some songs on the charts in 1953, but didn't dent the top 10. However, he was back with a flourish in 1954 with three major hits: "Release Me," "I'll Be There," and "If You Don't Someone Else Will." Again he slacked off a bit in 1955, but had a banner year in 1956. His 1956 top-10 singles included "I've Got a New Heartache," "Wasted Words," and his first number-one national hit, "Crazy Arms." He sang that song to cheering audiences all over the United States that year, and it remained a key element of his stage show for decades afterward.

For the rest of the 1950s, Price's name rarely was absent from single charts (he had a number of charted albums as well). In 1957, he scored with the top-10 "My Shoes Keep Walking Back to You"; in 1958 he had the top-10 "Curtain in the Window" and his second number-one hit, "City Lights"; in 1959 he closed out the decade with still another number-one success, "Same Old Me," plus the top-10 hits "That's What It's Like to Be Lonesome," "Heartaches by the Number," and "Under Your Spell Again." His name often was at or near the top of major polls during those years; for 1959, almost all of the major music trade magazines named him Favorite Male Vocalist in the country & western category as well as honoring "Heartaches by the Numbers" as Best Record of the Year.

Some of the songs in Ray's repertoire by the early 1960s were original compositions, including such numbers as "Give Me More, More of Your Kisses," "I'm Tired," and the 1961 hit "Soft Rain." Although it was a new decade, with some changes in the kind of music favored by many listeners, Ray's career continued to prosper. In 1961, he made top-chart levels with "One More Time" and "I Wish I Could Fall in Love Today." In 1961, besides "Soft Rain," he made top-10 ranks with "Heart over Mind." Some of his other major singles of the 1960s included "Walk Me to the Door" and "Make the World Go Away" in 1963; "Please Talk to My Heart" and "Burning Memories" in 1964; "The Other Woman" in 1965; "A Way to Survive" and "Don't You Ever Get Tired of Hurting Me" in 1966; and a remake of the old folk classic "Danny Boy" in 1967.

Many of his recordings of the 1960s featured lush orchestral backing, which caused some criticism from country traditionalists. Price told an interviewer in 1967, "Strings are essential to my type of song. Most of my songs are ballads and the strings provide the soul for the ballad. There have been some who objected to the big violin sections that I use on the records, but it's mainly people who have made up their minds before really listening to the record. When they do listen, they usually like it." For a typical concert of the 1960s, Ray often took along a backing group that included as many as eight to ten violins, an unusual touch for a country artist. For his records, though, he sometimes employed as many as three dozen violinists.

As the 1970s drew nigh, the progressive country movement was having a strong impact on the field. Just as the onslaught of rockabilly in the 1950s and the British rock invasion in the 1960s didn't seem to tarnish Price's image, neither did the new trend. In fact, Ray seemed to recognize the quality of some of the new songs being written by newcomers like Kris Kristofferson. In mid-1970, he recorded Kristofferson's "For the Good Times," which soon became one of the most important events in Ray's career. The single rose to the top of both country and pop charts in the United States and also became one of the runaway international hits of the year. It rapidly went over the million mark and was to sell in multiples of that as the 1970s progressed. Price's album of that title, issued in September 1970, also was a tremendous success and was still on country charts over two years later. In late 1970 and early 1971, Price had another worldwide bestseller with Kristofferson's "For the Good Times" (the album came out in January 1971), adding another series of gold records (United States plus a number of foreign ones) to his collection. He couldn't keep that sensational pace up indefinitely, but he still had a respectable batting average over the next few years, placing such songs as "That's What Leaving's About/Lonesomest Lonesome" (1972) and "Storms of Trouble Times" (1974) on upper-chart levels.

In the mid-1970s, Ray ended his long association with Columbia and moved to ABC/Dot. (Later he was briefly affiliated with Myrrh Records.) Even as he made that move, though, he was entering semiretirement. He still made some recordings, but he wanted to get away from the grind of TV shows and far-flung touring to concentrate on his long-time love of animal husbandry. He passed up concert engagements and remained on his large horse ranch near Dallas, Texas, raising and selling horses.

Many people were hardly aware he had given up much of his music activity, since he still kept placing singles on the hit lists. Among those were "Roses and Love Songs" in early 1975 and "Farthest Thing from My Mind" in mid-1975, both on ABC/Dot. Columbia also released one of his singles, "If You Ever Change Your Mind," in late summer of 1975, and the song moved to the upper-chart reaches. In 1976, his ABC/Dot single "To Make a Long Story Short/We're Getting There" made the top 40. In late 1977, a Columbia release, "Born to Love Me," made the top 20.

At the end of 1978, Price decided to return to full-time status, signing a new contract with Monument Records. Guesting on *The Tonight Show* in early 1979 (in earlier years, he had been a frequent visitor on the show, as he had been on many other nationally telecast talk and variety shows during the 1960s and 1970s), Ray told Johnny Carson that he had enjoyed his nearly five-year absence from the spotlight, but he had begun to miss the excitement of the entertainment field. His fans appeared to welcome him back, keeping his debut single on Monument, "Feet," on the charts for over three months.

Ray had several more singles on Monument in 1979 that made the charts, such as "There's Always Me" and "Misty Morning Rain," but they didn't reach uppermost levels and he found himself without a label. He decided to seek the help of Willie Nelson, who once had been a sideman in Price's Cherokee Cowboys backing band. (Other alumni of that group include Roger Miller, Johnny Paycheck, and Johnny Bush.) He recalled, "I was having trouble getting a contract, so I went to Willie and said, 'Since you're doing albums with other people, how about doing one with me?'"

The result was the duet album *San Antonio Rose*, issued on Columbia in June 1980 and on the album charts soon after. Willie and Ray sang some of the songs from the album at Willie's annual Fourth of July picnic in Texas and won roaring approval from the large crowd. By fall the LP was at number three on the charts and was still in the top 40 in early 1981. The LP provided Ray and Willie with two hit singles, "Faded Love" in the fall of 1980 and "Don't You Ever Get Tired (Of Hurting Me)" in early 1981. In 1981, the twosome was among the final nominees in Academy of Country Music Awards voting for duet of the year and album of the year as well as finalists in *Music City News* polling for duet of the year.

In February 1981, Price signed a new recording contract with Dimension Records. During the year his charted singles on the label included "Getting Over You Again," "It Don't Hurt Me Half as Bad," and "Diamonds in the Stars." In early 1981, Columbia Records issued an album of some of his recordings on that label titled *A Tribute to Willie and Kris*. He also became involved in a talent scout project called Ray Price's Country Starsearch 1981, which called for him to appear at the finals in all fifty states as well as star in a TV presentation of the winners.

By the early 1980s, though Ray could hardly be classified as even semiretired—throughout the 1980s and into the mid-1990s he continued to make some 200 appearances a year at fairs, festivals, and concert halls—he definitely was taking a more laid-back attitude to the entertainment field. Starting in the mid-1970s he divided his time between show business and his thoroughbred horse ranch near Mt. Pleasant, Texas. He continued to record, winding up the 1980s, for instance, with a new album on Step One Records issued during August of 1989, but upper-chart levels eluded him.

One reason for that, of course, was the trend among top record labels and country radio to focus on newer artists with steadily decreasing attention to long-established veterans like Ray, Merle Haggard, and so many others. Price took it in stride. He told Chuck Phillips of the *Los Angeles Times* ("Ray Price: Celebrated Texas Tenor and the Good Times," May 19, 1989), "When I was young, I was like a wild horse running down the road. But as you get older, you find that you don't have to gallop so hard to win the race. That's when you learn to slow down and just do what you do best."

He reminisced about the influences on his career and cited Bob Wills as a primary force, not only for him but dozens of Texas-bred stars. "Everybody in Texas likes to dance and play. It's no big thing. Guys like me, Jim Reeves, Lefty [Frizell], George [Jones]—we were all serious about our music. But it was really Bob Wills. He was the one who got 'em all to dancing. Hell, we just kept 'em going."

While ranching was Ray's first love in the 1990s, he had no intention of ignoring his musical interests. As did many other country veterans, he built himself a theater in Branson, Missouri, where he performed regularly before typically sold-out houses. He maintained his contacts with longtime friends like Willie Nelson, many of whom strongly urged others in the country field to push for Ray's election to the Hall of Fame.

When Nelson was inducted during the Country Music Association's TV Awards program in October 1993, he stressed there were many others as deserving as he, including Merle Haggard (who was voted in the following year) and Ray. As of 1995, Ray hadn't made it, though he had many in the industry rooting for his eventual inclusion.

The number of Ray's albums in print in the mid-1990s was small considering his extensive output over some four decades. An excellent reissue available as of 1995 was the Columbia/Legacy collection, *The Essential Ray Price.* In 1995, the independent label Koch (distributed by Sony Music Special Products) reissued on CD Ray's album *San Antonio Rose: A Tribute to the Great Bob Wills,* which, on its original release 35 years before, has been the first tribute disc to Wills. Also available in the mid-1990s was a retrospective collection produced by Bear Family Records of Germany. That massive package, *Ray Price: The Honky Tonk Years,* encompassing 10 CDs, covered his recorded output from his first Bullet single in 1950 to "Danny Boy" in 1966. The tracks included hits like "City Lights," "Crazy Arms," "My Shoes Keep Walking Back to You," "Heartaches by the Numbers," "Night Life," "Release Me," and "I've Got a New Heartache."

On November 30, 1995, Ray was one of the featured artists who taped a TV special honoring the *Grand Ole Opry*'s 70th anniversary. The program was aired on CBS-TV in January 1996. At long last, in October 1996, Price was inducted into the Country Music Hall of Fame on the CMA Awards telecast.

PRIDE, CHARLEY: *Singer, guitarist, band leader (the Pridesmen). Born Sledge, Mississippi, March 18, 1938.*

Charley Pride is to country music as Jackie Robinson is to baseball. As Robinson did in sports, Pride broke the color barrier in a field where, on the prestige level, one had to be white to succeed. (Actually, Ray Charles had done well before Charley came along with country & western ballads, but Charles basically was a blues or pop type performer, whereas Pride was an all-out country artist.) Like Robinson, Pride was not just an adequate performer, he was a superstar, a fact recognized by the trade magazine *Cash Box,* which named Charley in 1980 as top male country artist of the decade (1970s).

Pride became interested in country & western music as a child in rural Mississippi. His choice was an unusual one for a black child in a region where the whites were country-music fans and most blacks preferred blues music. Of course, any kind of music was an escape from the drudgery of work in the cotton fields, the main occupation of his parents and Charley and his ten brothers and sisters as soon as each was old enough to contribute his or her meager earnings to the family coffers. He recalled that he was paid three dollars per hundred pounds of cotton picked from his childhood until he left home at seventeen.

He was the only one in his family who had any leaning toward music, blues or otherwise, spending his free time listening to country-music shows on the radio and singing the songs he heard for his own pleasure. One of his particular favorites from the late 1940s was Hank Williams. When Charley was fourteen, he got enough money together to buy a guitar and worked out his own method of playing from listening to various picking styles.

Although he could play pretty well by his late teens, he didn't consider music a likely career at the time. Strong and well built, he had natural athletic ability. Inspired by Jackie Robinson's breakthrough in professional baseball, Pride decided to try to make it in that field. His ability won him a place with the Memphis Red Sox of the Negro American League in the late 1950s and in time, after two years of military service, he moved up to a regular minor league assignment with the Helena, Montana, team. In 1960, he sang between innings of a ball game in Helena and won an ovation. He decided he wanted to sing more, and his landlady helped him get a job singing in a local country spot.

Pride still concentrated on baseball, spurred on by a brief tryout with the major league California Angels in 1961 as an outfield and pitching prospect. He had made Montana his home, working as a smelter for Anaconda Mining in the off season and finding nightclub work from time to time in local clubs. It was while singing in one of those spots in late 1963 that he was heard by country star Red Sovine. Red liked Charley's stylings and sought him out to offer him a recording audition. Pride held back for a time. A member of the New York Mets farm organization, he still had dreams of a successful big league career. Finally he decided it was worth taking Sovine up on his offer, and went to Nashville to audition for Chet Atkins. In 1964, Atkins agreed with Sovine that Pride had considerable promise and signed Charley to a contract with RCA Victor.

Pride cut his first record, "Snakes Crawl at Night," in August 1965, but it wasn't released until January 1966. In a short time it was a top-chart song, staying on the list for many weeks. Later in the year, he had another hit with "Just Between You and Me." In November 1966, his debut LP came out, *Country Charley Pride,* an album that made national country lists in 1967 and eventually earned him his first gold-record award.

After his sensational debut year in 1966, the doors began to open. In January 1967, he made his first appearance on the *Grand Ole Opry,* far from his last. Over the years, he often returned to the *Opry* stage, first at Ryman Auditorium and later at Opryland, as a guest on the *Opry* or on dozens of other shows recorded or taped (for TV) from there. On a number of occasions he was featured on the Country Music Association Awards telecasts as a performer, presenter, or award recipient.

He continued to add to his laurels the balance of the 1960s. In the nominating process for Grammy Awards for 1966, Pride was one of five finalists for Best Country & Western Vocal Performance, Male, for his single "Just Between You and Me." He had two hit singles in 1967 with "Does My Ring Hurt Your Finger" and "I Know One." In 1968, he had such best-selling singles as "The Day the World Stood Still" and "The Best Part's Over" and a top-rated album, *The Country Way* (issued January 1968), that later won another gold-record award. (It was his third release after *Pride of Country Music,* which came out in July 1967. Other 1968 albums were *Make Mine Country* and *Songs of Pride . . . Charley That Is.)*

Although country fans who came to his concerts for the first time in the late 1960s were surprised at his color—on records Charley didn't sound particularly "black"—they quickly accepted him as one of their own country stars. Year after year he added to his popularity as an in-person artist, headlining shows in places like the Playroom and Domino in Atlanta, Randy's Rodeo in San Antonio, Texas, and Panther Hall in Fort Worth, Texas. The last named provided the tapes for his first live album, *Charley Pride in Person at Panther Hall,* recorded in 1968 and issued in February 1969. The LP eventually went gold, as did his other two LPs released in 1969, *The Sensational Charley Pride* (7/69)

and *The Best of Charley Pride* (12/69). The latter moved to number one on U.S. country charts in early 1970.

Nor did Pride's momentum slow coming into the 1970s. With his band, the Pridesmen, and a show featuring both established and new artists, he regularly played to capacity audiences in all major country music venues at home and abroad. His face and voice regularly graced major TV music shows, both network and syndicated. And he continued to turn out albums that provided that rare combination of creative entertainment and commercial appeal. Of the nine albums issued from 1970 through 1972, six won gold-record awards and almost all appeared not only on country charts but pop lists as well. The gold-record offerings were *Just Plain Charley* (1970), *Charley Pride 10th Album* (8/70), *From Me to You* (3/71), *Did You Think to Pray* (6/71), *Charley Pride Sings Heart Songs* (12/71), and *The Best of Charley Pride, Volume 2* (4/72). (The others were *Christmas in My Home Town,* [1970]; *I'm Just Me,* [8/71]; *A Sunshiny Day with Charley Pride,* [11/72]; plus the Camden Records release, *Incomparable Charley Pride,* [11/72].)

Many of those efforts won nominations and awards in major competitions. Pride won two Grammys for 1971, one for Best Sacred Performance for the LP *Did You Think to Pray* and one for Best Gospel Performance for the single "Let Me Live." In 1972, he won a third Grammy for Best Country Vocal Performance, Male, for the album *Charley Pride Sings Heart Songs.* In addition, the CMA in the early 1970s voted him the group's most prestigious award, Entertainer of the Year, and also named him Best Male Country Vocalist of the Year. The Music Operators of America also named him Entertainer of the Year. Besides all that, he often was named the top male vocalist for country singles and/or albums by major music industry trade publications.

Through the rest of the 1970s, Charley continued to add to his already extensive plaudits. Each year his stage show played to in the neighborhood of a million fans. And his album and singles releases almost without exception made the charts, usually, in the case of albums, reaching the top 10, and the singles more often than not going as high as first, second, or third position.

His singles successes for the period included "Amazing Love," number one in late 1973 and still in the top 10 in early 1974; "We Could," in the top 10 in early summer 1974; "Then Who Am I?" number one in February 1975; "I Ain't All Sad," in the top 10 in the summer of 1975; "Hope You're Feelin' Me (Like I'm Feelin' You)," number one in October 1975; "The Happiness of Having You," number three in February 1976; "My Eyes Can Only See as Far as You," top 10 in May 1976; "A Whole Lotta Things to Sing About," top 10 early fall 1976; "I'll Be Leavin' Alone," number one in July 1977; "More to Me," number one in November

1977; "When I Stop Leavin' I'll Be Gone," number three in August 1978; and "Burgers & Fries," number one in December 1978 and still on the charts in early 1979. His 1979 hit singles included "You're My Jamaica," "Where Do I Put Her Memory," and, at year end, "Missin' You," which rose to number two on the charts in January 1980.

His charted LPs of the mid- and late 1970s included *Songs of Love by Charley Pride* (early 1973); *Sweet Country* (6/73); *Amazing Love* (issued early 1974); *Country Feelin'* (mid-1974); *Pride of America* (late 1974); *Charley* (summer 1975); *The Happiness of Having You* (late 1975); *Sunday Morning with Charley Pride* (early summer 1976); *She's Just an Old Love Turned Memory* (spring 1977); *I'm Just Me* (summer 1977); *Someone Loves You Honey* (early 1978); *Burgers & Fries/When I Stop Leavin' I'll Be Gone* (October 1979); and *You're My Jamaica* (mid-1979).

Charley started the 1980s in fine style with a tribute to Hank Williams, "I Got a Lot of Hank in Me." Released in early 1980, it rose to number one on U.S. country lists in May. Discussing the project earlier, he had noted "All the material in the album, except for one cut, will be Hank Williams's songs. The exception is the title song which I had especially written." He pointed out that it was a Williams song, "Lovesick Blues," that he was singing back in Helena that helped draw the attention of Red Sovine (and Red Foley).

"The whole country music business owes a lot to Hank Williams—he more or less invented the word 'crossover' when you apply it to country music. My album is a way of giving back what I've taken from the man, his talent and his music."

In his years of prominence, Charley himself had been a factor in other artists' careers. Touring with him had proven valuable for a number of performers, both new or experienced and looking for more recognition. Among those he helped to become stars in their own right were Gary Stewart, Dave and Sugar, Johnny Russell, Johnny Duncan, and Ronnie Milsap.

Charley's single of "Honky Tonk Blues" from the Hank Williams album reached number one on country charts in April 1980. During the summer his version of Hank's "You Win Again" was a top chart hit. Later in the year he had such other bestsellers as "Dallas Cowboys" and "You Almost Slipped My Mind." In early 1981, he had the singles success "Roll on Mississippi" and, in the fall, had another blockbuster with "Never Been So Loved," number one in October.

During the 1970s, Pride settled with his family in Dallas, Texas. In general, he was treated with respect by the community, but there still were incidents that unfortunately demonstrated that prejudice remained alive and sick in some individuals. Friends of his, knowing he was an avid golfer, proposed him for membership in the all-white Dallas Royal Oaks Country Club. After the vote was taken, he got a letter from the club informing him his application had been rejected because of vetoes from at least four persons. Pride remarked, "They gave me no reason, but the only one I can think of is that I'm black. . . . I'm not concerned—there are plenty of places I can play golf."

Charley's RCA albums in the late 1970s and early 1980s included *There's a Little Bit of Hank in Me, Roll on Mississippi, Charley Pride's Greatest Hits, Charley Pride Live, Country Classics, Night Games, Power of Love, Charley Pride's Greatest Hits Volume II,* and *The Best There Is.* Besides the chart hits "Mountain of Love" in 1981 and "You're So Good When You're Bad" in 1982, his singles releases of the early 1980s included "More and More," "Night Games," "Ev'ry Heart Should Have One," "Power of Love," "Missin' Mississippi," and "Down on the Farm."

As the 1980s went by, Charley remained an important figure in the country field, and a well-received performer at significant venues in the U.S. and other parts of the world. Like many veteran country artists, though, he found it increasingly difficult to get radio coverage for new record releases, which began to be reflected in diminished impact on the hit charts. By the mid-1980s this played a part in his departure from RCA. (His total album output for the label was 43.) He moved on to sign with 16th Avenue/Capitol, which issued the albums *After All This Time, Moody Woman,* and *I'm Gonna Love Her on the Radio* in the mid- and late 1980s. Singles on that label were "Have I Got Some Blues For You," "Shouldn't It Be Easier Than This," "Where Was I," "The More I Do," "Moody Woman," "If You Still Want a Fool Around," "I'm Gonna Love Her on the Radio," "White Houses," and "Amy's Eyes."

His importance as an artist was recognized by many honors during the decade, including the presentation of an honorary Doctor of Humanities from Wheeling College, West Virginia, in May 1985. During the ceremonies at the Jesuit school he sang "All My Children" as the benedictory song.

In the 1990s, besides a still sizable quota of concert appearances in many other locals, Charley joined the host of other country stars who claimed Branson, Missouri, as a second performing home. Starting in mid-1992 he became the regular Monday night attraction for much of the year at Mel Tillis's new theater. Later he was featured in his own Branson venue. In mid-decade he signed with a new record organization, Intersound, which released two albums of his material by 1995.

In the spring of 1996, during the Fourth Annual Trumpet awards program on the Turner Broadcasting System cable network, Charley was one of the award recipients. These awards were set up to salute achievements of African American men and women in the fields of education, medicine, literature, politics, sports, business, and entertainment. It was noted that by then

Charley had sold over 25 million albums and scored 36 number-one singles successes. About the same time, Honest Entertainment issued a new album of country and pop standards performed by Charley titled *Classics with Pride*.

PURE PRAIRIE LEAGUE: *Vocal and instrumental group, originally from Ohio. Original members, 1970: Craig Fuller, born Ohio; George Powell, born Salem, North Carolina; John David Call, born Waverly, Ohio; Jim Caughlin; Jimmy Lanham. In 1972, lineup included Fuller; Powell; Call; Billy Hinds, born Covington, Kentucky, September 17, 1946; Michael Connor, born Covington, Kentucky, December 7, 1949; Michael Reilly, born Fort Thomas, Kentucky. In the mid-1970s, Fuller replaced by Larry Goshorn, born Cincinnati, Ohio; Call replaced by Timmy Goshorn, born Cincinnati, Ohio. In August 1977, Goshorn brothers and Powell left. Vince Gill, born Oklahoma City, Oklahoma, April 1957, added in September 1978. Patrick Bolin, born Los Angeles, California, circa 1952, added in January 1979. Bolin replaced in 1980 by Jeff Wilson, born Los Angeles, California.*

The album symbol of Pure Prairie League (the name comes from the title of a women's temperance group in an old film that starred Errol Flynn) was a diminutive Norman Rockwellish cowboy called Luke, a fictional figure that somehow outlasted all the original band members. However, despite many changes during the 1970s, the band somehow maintained a thread of continuity from one alignment to the next and remained one of the more popular country-rock bands into the 1980s.

The two founding members were songwriter and rhythm guitarist George Powell and lead singer-guitarist Craig Fuller. Both grew up in Ohio (though Powell was born in North Carolina), as did a third original musician, guitarist John David Call, who was raised in Waverly and attended Ohio University as an engineering student and Ohio State University as a music major before joining Pure Prairie League. The other sidemen in the first band were Jim Caughlin and Jimmy Lanham. It was that group that worked on the original album *Pure Prairie League,* issued on RCA in March 1972.

As drummer Billy Hinds, who in 1979 had the most seniority, recalled, "The band originally started in Columbus, Ohio, and then ventured to Cincinnati where it played in a club called Billy's. I was working in another band at the same club and we got acquainted. I worked with them for a few months, then left. While I was gone, the others did the first album and first tour. After that, they asked me to come back and I helped record the group's second LP, *Bustin' Out* [issued in October 1972]."

When Hinds joined, he suggested that they might be interested in some of the people he'd worked with before, which soon resulted in pianist-keyboardist Michael Connor and bass guitarist Michael Reilly join-

ing up. Connor noted in 1979, "Michael [Reilly], myself, and Billy had played a lot together before that. I remember Michael and I were in England at the time when we got a call from Billy to come back."

At first, only Connor was added. States Billy, "The three of us worked together well, so I tried to get them into the project. [By then, in 1972, the group had shrunk to a core of Hinds, Fuller, and Powell.] But we already had a bass player for the recording sessions so Connor became a member and when we were ready to tour Reilly came aboard." The band's background prior to that was a blend of western country, some blues, and varied rock; Reilly, who was raised in Kentucky, expanded the influences to include bluegrass. The strong bluegrass influence is noticeable in his lead vocal efforts over the years.

Still, for a while it looked as though the newcomers might have joined a sinking ship. *Bustin' Out* didn't make much of an initial impact and RCA dropped the group. In late 1973, though, a strange thing happened. The song "Amy" from the first album began to get steadily increasing airplay, thanks to the song's discovery by a number of disc jockeys. That brought enough requests for a single to cause RCA to turn one out, which promptly made national charts. The sequence of events caused the record company to re-issue *Bustin' Out,* which also spawned another highly regarded single, George Powell's composition "Leave My Heart Alone."

The contract termination and other problems caused a hiatus of some eighteen months, during which no new recordings were made and another major reorganization took place. "One thing that hit us," says Hinds, "was the loss of Craig Fuller. He got into trouble on a draft evasion thing and left. He was replaced by Larry Goshorn." Goshorn, who took over on lead guitar and also contributed vocal and writing skills, was raised in Cincinnati, where he had been playing guitar in local rock bands since high school. He always had been an admirer of the Everly Brothers, whom he ranked as a prime influence on his performing and writing style.

The belated success of the 1972 releases had renewed RCA's interest in the band and led to a new contract in 1974. The result of that was the April 1975 album *Two-Lane Highway,* the first on which Reilly and Goshorn performed. The LP and its title track both made national charts, indicating that, at last, Pure Prairie League had established a foothold with the public at large. In support of the new recordings, the revamped band spent over 200 days on the road, playing major cities all over the United States. It was a pace the group kept up for the next few years, even though another long-time mainstay, John David Call, left to be replaced by Larry Goshorn's brother, Timmy.

Based partly on 1979 interview of Billy Hinds and Michael Connor by Irwin Stambler.

During that period, the group turned out a series of albums, most of which provided a single or two that showed up on the charts. These included "If the Shoe Fits," "Dance," and the group's first live album release, a two-record set titled *Live! Takin' the Stage* that came out in 1978. Also a 1978 release (in April) was another studio album, *Just Fly.*

By the time the last two albums were issued, Pure Prairie League had gone through still another drastic reshuffle. In August 1977, the last remaining founding member, Powell, departed, along with the Goshorns. "The Goshorns decided they could do better as a solo act, the Goshorn Brothers," Hinds said. "They sort of always wanted to do that," added Connor. "They have a younger brother who's also a musician, so the three of them decided to try a new group."

As to Powell's reason for leaving, Hinds noted, "George had a little girl and decided he wanted to be a father and husband and give up the tour grind to stay home. He got a farm in Williamsburg, Ohio, where he decided to concentrate on writing songs and doing demos."

After that, with home now in the Los Angeles area, Reilly, Hinds, and Connor set about to recruit new members. After auditioning a great many candidates, the first choice in September 1978 was multitalented Vince Gill, whose talents included vocals, songwriting, and such instruments as guitar, banjo, fiddle, dobro, and mandolin. Born and raised in Oklahoma City, he had a strong grounding in folk and country music as a boy and later played in a Kentucky-based bluegrass band called Boone Creek and traveled for close to three years with the Byron Berline group.

In February 1979, a fifth musician was added in the person of Los Angeles–born singer-songwriter-musician Patrick Bolin. Bolin provided such instrumental capabilities as saxophone and flute and an outlook more oriented toward mainstream rock. He also had been a member for a while of a Los Angeles bar band "who played Steely Dan type stuff."

The new alignment completed the eighth Pure Prairie League LP in early 1979, *Can't Hold Back.* Even before the RCA LP came out in late May 1979, the band was trying out some of its new songs before audiences across the country. The response seemed to be highly favorable whether the group headlined on college campuses or opened for such country rock groups as the Charlie Daniels Band and Marshall Tucker Band in larger venues. The impact of the newest members was obvious in the new release, *Can't Hold Back,* which included Bolin's composition "Goodbye, So Long," and such Gill originals as "Can't Hold Back," "I Can't Believe," "Misery Train," "I'm Going Away," and "Jelene."

By the start of 1980, the group had left RCA and signed with Casablanca Records. In January 1980, Bolin was replaced by singer-guitarist Jeff Wilson, who helped record the band's debut LP on Casablanca, *Firin' Up,* issued in 1980. His contributions included cowriting two songs on the album, "Too Many Heartaches in Paradise" and "Let Me Love You Tonight." The latter song provided a top-10 single, the band's first top-10 since "Amy." In April 1981, Casablanca released Pure Prairie League's second album, *Something in the Night.* Band members for the LP were Reilly, Hinds, Connor, Gill, and Wilson.

"The important thing," declared Connor, "is that though we keep expanding our musical directions, it still falls into a recognizable pattern. Even though we've had changes in personnel and in musical emphasis, Pure Prairie League still sounds like Pure Prairie League."

With Gill's departure in the early 1980s, however, the band's saga appeared at an end.

RABBITT, EDDIE: *Singer, guitarist, band leader (Hare Trigger), songwriter. Born Brooklyn, New York, November 27, 1944.*

Although country music is now popular all over the United States and in many foreign countries, the majority of country artists have been, and still are, from the southern regions of the nation. One notable exception is Eddie Rabbitt. He was born in Brooklyn, New York, to Irish immigrant parents. His family later moved to East Orange, New Jersey, where Eddie spent the remainder of his youth. He learned the love of music from his father, Thomas, who later was to play fiddle on Eddie's "Song of Ireland" in the album *Variations.* He learned to play guitar from his scoutmaster, Tony Schwickrath, who performed as a local country artist under the name Bob Randall. Eddie had only mastered two chords when Schwickrath moved out of town, but with those two chords and his voice he was able to win a talent contest at Kenettewapeck Summer Camp.

Eddie was now on his way to realizing the dream he had held since the age of five, to become a country-music singer. While still in high school, he won another talent contest, which enabled him to broadcast live from a Paterson, New Jersey, bar, one hour out of a regular Saturday night radio show. One night in 1964, when Rabbitt was celebrating his graduation from night school (he had dropped out of high school) in a New Jersey bar, the bar's piano player quit and Eddie convinced the owner to hire him. Following this stint, Rabbitt was able to find work in New Jersey and in some New York bars for twenty-five dollars a night. The area proved to be quite a hotbed of country-music activity, but Eddie finally decided that to succeed in the field he would have to head south. So he went to Nashville, hoping to become a star.

Eddie had beginner's luck. The first song he wrote in Nashville, "Working My Way up to the Bottom," was recorded by Roy Drusky, providing him with a hit. His luck did not continue, however, and in the next several months he was unable to sell any songs or to interest anyone in his singing. He started hanging out with such then-unknown talents as Kris Kristofferson, Billy Swan, and Larry Gatlin.

Eventually, Rabbitt's career picked up, and he was signed as a staff writer for the music publishers Hill and Range at a mere $37.50 a week. Many songs of his were recorded, some by major artists, but only a couple were hits.

At last Eddie won a recording contract on the basis of a song he wrote, "Kentucky Rain," but he found himself faced with a strange problem. Elvis Presley had heard the song and wanted to record it. Eddie had to decide between recording the song himself or letting Elvis have it. He decided to let Elvis record the song, hoping in that way to make some money and to bring some much-needed attention to himself. The song provided Elvis with his fiftieth gold record. The producer on Eddie's would-be recording contract, however, tore up the contract when he heard that the song had been given to Presley. Rabbitt recalls that the producer said, "If you're not interested enough in your own career to save your best song for yourself, then why should I care about your career? So let's just forget about the whole thing."

Nevertheless, Eddie's success continued to accelerate. In 1973 Ronnie Milsap recorded Eddie's composition "Pure Love," and it became a number-one hit. In 1974 Rabbitt signed a contract with Elektra Records and was at last able to sing his songs himself. His first single, "You Get to Me," reached number twenty-two nationally. After that, his solo career prospered with one hit after another.

Rabbitt had a major hit single with "Forgive and Forget," which led to his first album, *Eddie Rabbitt*. His second album, *Rocky Mountain Music* (1976), contained three hits, "Drinking My Baby off My Mind," "Two Dollars in the Jukebox," and the title song, "Rocky Mountain Music," which also crossed over to the pop charts. (Most of the songs were cowritten by Eddie and Even Stevens. The two still were writing most of Rabbitt's hits in the early 1980s, usually with a third collaborator, D. Malloy.) In 1977 Eddie scored hit singles with "I Can't Help Myself" and "We Can't Go on Living like This" from his album *Rabbitt*. His 1978-released LP, *Variations,* provided him with three hit singles, "Hearts on Fire," the smash hit "You Don't Love Me Anymore," and "I Just Want to Love You." In 1979, he had a number-one-ranked hit, "Every Which Way but Loose," from the Clint Eastwood movie of the same name. At year end, his single "Pour Me Another Tequilla" was in the top 10, where it remained into early the following year. In 1980, he had another num-

ber-one hit from a movie, "Driving My Life Away," from the motion picture *Roadie.*

His number-one hit single "Gone Too Far" reached that pinnacle in May 1980. Late in the year his single "I Love a Rainy Night" showed up on the charts, rising to the top of the lists in early 1981. In the fall of 1981 Rabbitt had still another number-one hit single, "Step by Step" (October 1981), and "Someone Could Lose a Heart Tonight" began moving toward the top levels as the year drew to a close. His 1979 LP release, *Loveline,* was on the charts into 1980. Also on the charts that year were his albums *Horizon* and the *Best of Eddie Rabbitt.* Both earned gold records and were still in upper-chart positions in 1981.

In addition to Eddie's proven songwriting skills, his good looks make him a favorite with women fans. His voice has a pleading tone that adds distinction to his pleasant tenor voice. His songs often deal with traditional country themes, but his style is relaxed, a soft pop sound with jazz and country undertones. By the beginning of the 1980s, it became clear that not only had country fans adopted this Yankee as one of their favorite performers, but that he was catching on in the wider pop music market. He served as guest host on the late-night television variety show *The Midnight Special* and also had his own highly acclaimed television special.

Rabbitt emphasized, however, that he never deliberately courted the pop market. As he told Tom Chester of *The Knoxville Journal,* "When you get out of the thing you do naturally, you lose it. We've had a lot of crossover things that have been getting good pop play. But I just do what I do, and it happens it does span more than the country market. . . . Country music is getting wider. People are getting into it and there's more acceptance of it. Since [President] Carter, people can be more proud of it. It seems like, though, country music is always five, six, or seven years behind the rock 'n' roll thing. Country is in the evolution stage of rock 'n' roll of seven years ago. But the pop scene is up against the wall as far as a new direction. Pop is stopped. It's been through the heavy metal and those scenes. Country music has moved up behind it. And the music is starting to flow into each other."

As the 1980s went by, Rabbitt's feeling about the pop field grew increasingly antagonistic. He told Janet Williams of the Country Music Association's *Close Up* publication (October 1991) that the way the pop field had developed made him glad not to be identified with it. He lashed out against companies and groups that sold "soft porn" to young listeners and record buyers. In particular he cited the NWA rap album that was number one in *Billboard* that June.

The album "has a gang rape song, lyrics like 'it's okay to kill a prostitute because they're all bitches anyway,' songs about abusiveness to women, all this nasty filthy language and it's the number one pop album in these United States! And who's buying them? Teenagers.

"Whatever happened to songs about love and romance? Sex is the thing now. Sex is great, but every song on the *Billboard* charts. . . . It's all 'I want your body, I want to sex you up! Every video you see is a bunch of girls with nothing on and a bunch of rock 'n' rollers singing about sex. I hate to see women degraded so that they are only sex objects. Women are beautiful, and they are the flowers in the garden. Men may be the weeds. To just take everything else away from them and just leave that as all a woman has claim to, that's ridiculous."

He emphasized he believed in family and marriage. His had been a lasting one that had survived its share of sadness. His career had been progressing nicely in the early 1980s and his spirits were buoyed still more when his wife, Janine, gave birth to a boy they named Timothy Edward Rabbitt on August 12, 1983. But the child proved sickly and required a liver transplant to try to save his life. Unfortunately, the boy died, due to transplant complications, at Minneapolis Hospital in Minnesota twenty-three months later. During the summer of 1986, a refurbished playroom they helped finance in the boy's memory was dedicated at the Vanderbilt Children's Hospital in Nashville.

The Rabbitts already had a daughter, Dimelza, born in the early 1980s, and added a son, Tom, in the late 1980s. Eddie had his career back in full swing by the time Tom came along. He remained a successful concert artist, though he kept his tour dates with band Hare Trigger to a lower annual total than the typical country star. His rapport with country fans was underscored by a poll taken by Survey Research, released in the summer of 1988, that showed two of Eddie's numbers were among the top-30 favorites of concert goers. One was "Drivin' My Life Away," which held number-four position, the other "You and I," at number twenty-eight, which had been a hit single in a duet with Crystal Gayle. His work with Crystal had earned them a CMA 1983 nomination for Vocal Duo of the Year.

Eddie began the 1990s with a flourish, placing three singles (on Capitol Records) high on the charts during 1990. These were "On Second Thought" (number one in *Radio & Records* the week of February 2); "Runnin' with the Wind" (number four in *R&R* the week of June 8); and self-penned "American Boy" (top 10 in *R&R* and *Billboard* late in the year). His 1991 chart singles included his composition "Hang Up the Pieces," drawn from his 1991 Capitol album release, *Ten Rounds*.

By the mid-1990s, Rabbitt's recording efforts were being overshadowed by the growing ranks of new artists, and his association with Capitol ended. He maintained his popularity as a concert performer and also guested on various TV programs presented on country music networks. His songwriting output brought him 1990s Broadcast Music, Inc. (BMI) honors for three million performances of "I Love a Rainy Night" and a two million one for "Kentucky Rain." Earlier he had received million-performance awards for "Drivin' My Life Away" and "Step By Step."

Eddie told Janet Williams while he loved making country music, his main thrills now came from his family. "I love my family a lot. If you marry a girl, I believe it's important to stay with her. Or don't. Don't be in between. Don't be on the road five times a week and expect a marriage to stay together. It won't—it's just not natural. I think men have to be sensitive to that. And don't have kids if you don't plan to be with them. I'm only out about a hundred days a year so I can be with my kids and family a lot. I wouldn't do any more than that. Usually I'm out for three or four days then home for three or four."

RANDOLPH, HOMER LOUIS "BOOTS," JR:
Saxophonist, trombonist, ukulele player. Born Paducah, Kentucky, June 3, circa 1927.

One of the staples of Boots Randolph's stage routine was to suddenly tell the audience "You're listening to the world's greatest hillbilly saxophone player" . . . pause for reaction . . . "Would you believe the world's ONLY hillbilly saxophonist." It's a bit of an exaggeration, because Randolph is a sophisticated instrumentalist who can play everything from jazz to classics on his sax, but there's no doubt about his ability to make country songs sound like they belonged naturally to his kind of instrument.

Randolph was born in Paducah, Kentucky, into a family that enjoyed playing music. As soon as Boots was old enough to learn an instrument, he was entrusted with a ukulele and became part of the family band, which comprised his father on fiddle, mother on guitar, sister Dorothy on bass, and older brothers Earl and Bob on banjo and mandolin. Initially the group played amateur talent contests, but as the Depression times of the mid-1930s increased the urgency of finding ways to make ends meet, the group took any engagements available, including clubs, auditoriums, and run-down theaters.

Randolph recalled, "It was pretty standard for us to come home from those talent contests with the old car loaded down with cans of corn and peas and boxes of macaroni, bacon, and bread. We didn't have much money—but boy, did we eat."

By that time, the family had moved to Cadiz, Kentucky, where Boots attended elementary school. The year before Boots was ready for high school, his father presented him with a trombone. "My dad picked it up in a trade. Would you believe he swapped a .38 caliber pistol for the trombone? Well he did. I learned the slide by ear. My first tunes were 'Tuxedo Junction' and 'Sweet Sue.'"

Boots played in the school band both in elementary school and at Central High School in Evansville, Indiana, where his family moved when the United States entered World War II. In his junior year, he switched to the saxophone because "It seems like a sax was easier to play while marching in the school band than a trombone." After his father bought him a tenor saxophone, he and brother Bob organized a six-person group (sometimes expanded to eight) that played at local Army bases.

In 1945, when Randolph was eighteen, he was drafted into the Army and took basic training at Camp Lee, Virginia, later joining the Army band based at Camp Kilmer, New Jersey. "Our band would stand on the pier and serenade the boys coming home or shipping out."

After his discharge he went home and tried to pick up where he had left off. However, he got married and, finding music jobs scarce in Evansville in 1948, got a job in a factory for a while. "I got this job at the American Fork and Hoe Company. They put me to work driving wedges into hammer heads. I hit my fingers and thumbs more often than I did the wedges. After four weeks I decided to quit. I reasoned that if I ever hoped to play the sax again I'd need my fingers and thumbs and that if I stayed with those wedges, I wouldn't have any left."

Randolph managed to find enough work as a sideman with various midwest combos to keep going. In 1954 he found steady employment at a night spot in Decatur, Illinois, where he remained for four years. He and an associate, James Rich, had written a tune called "Yakety Sax" at the time and they sent a tape of the country-oriented number to Chet Atkins, musical director at RCA Records' Nashville offices. The tape brought results. Atkins brought Boots to Nashville to do session work with major artists in both the pop and country fields and also signed him to a recording contract. Among those he supported were Al Hirt, Homer & Jethro, Perry Como, Roy Orbison, Teresa Brewer, Burl Ives, Eddy Arnold, Pete Fountain, and Elvis Presley.

However, his RCA recordings didn't have much impact on the public. After several years on the label, Boots left RCA and signed a new agreement with Monument Records. In a short time, his *Yakety Sax* album became a sensation with country fans. It was on the hit lists a good part of 1961, eventually passing gold-record levels in sales. From then on, Randolph became a familiar face on country shows throughout the 1960s, 1970s, and into the 1980s. He often was spotlighted on the *Grand Ole Opry* and appeared in almost every major country-music program. Besides TV and countless in-person headline appearances, he was in a number of series with country-music themes.

Meanwhile, Monument continued to turn out a succession of albums and singles in the 1960s and 1970s, most of which sold solidly, if not sensationally, with a number of them showing up on country charts. Among the singles were "Yakety Sax," "Windy and Warm," "Hey Mr. Sax Man," "Yodelin' Sax," "Miss You," "I Really Don't Want to Know," and "Baby, Go to Sleep." The album releases include such 1960s offerings as *Yakety Sax, More Yakety Sax, The Fantastic Boots Randolph, Sax Sational,* and *Boots with Strings.* Among the 1970s LPs were *Hit Boots 1970, Boots with Brass, Homer Louis Randolph* (issued 9/71); *Yakety Sax* (a two-record retrospective on Camden label); and *World of Boots Randolph* (9/72).

RAYE, COLLIN: *Singer, guitarist, band leader, songwriter. Born DeQueen, Arkansas, 1960.*

With a tenor voice that one critic described as "treacly" when employed in his first career-establishing hit, "Love, Me," but which later recordings demonstrated could be focused with power and passion on all kinds of material from traditional Waylon Jennings–style country songs to Rod Stewart rock classics, Collin Raye was poised to become a key force in shaping the country field of the 1990s. To reviewers who complained he seemed to cast his repertoire net too broadly, he emphasized that he felt the worst thing that could happen to any performer, particularly in modern country music, was to be typecast as one kind of artist or another.

"Every time an interviewer talks about my being a balladeer, I want people to know there's more to me than that. I'm a singer and I want to sing anything. So, as much as I love singing those ballads—and I do—I pride myself on being able to sing other kinds of songs just as hard, and mean it just as much.

"The problem is that when people pigeonhole you as one thing, you get the best of whatever kind of song your specialty is, which is great. But then a lot of times people won't pitch you a great up-tempo song, because they don't think it's your bag. I love to sing it all and to get out there and tear it up. So, that's been one of the challenges—and I think we did it."

Raye was born in Arkansas, but spent most of his growing up years in Texarkana, Texas. Later, when his career took off in the 1990s, he still called Texas home, living in Greenville and spending a lot of time in Dallas, where he and Cowboy football stars like Troy Aikman were friends.

He recalled being interested in music from an early age and demonstrating skill as a singer and guitar player in his early teens before making his professional debut at fifteen. His influences included rock and roll and such country singers as Buck Owens, Merle Haggard and, in particular, Waylon Jennings, whom he felt didn't get the credit he was due from the country audience. While he always included some rock material in his repertoire, he emphasized that country remained his foundation.

He commented, "It's real and it's loaded with heartfelt thoughts, emotions—the things that are so much a part of getting through the everyday grind. And country is homegrown stuff. To me, it's the basics for two or three other musical styles that grew into rock & roll. Lots of Texans helped shape that . . . and even Don Henley [of the Eagles] grew up on Bob Wills, Waylon Jennings and Buddy Holly. So there is room to grow."

From the late 1970s through the 1980s, Raye traveled widely and worked a variety of entertainment spots, either as a solo performer or in an act with his brother. In the 1980s, at one juncture, he and his brother were signed by Mercury Records, which led to the release of a few singles. Nothing much happened with those and the agreement lapsed. The brothers' act could be audience-pleasing, and for some years they did well in nightclubs and other venues in the Pacific Northwest. From time to time, Collin also found employment as a solo entertainer in Nevada clubs, appearing in both Las Vegas and Reno. He recalled periods when he sang five sets a night in Reno showrooms to pay his family's bills.

He told Kimmy Wix of *Music City News* ("Collin Raye Soars Beyond the Ballads," October 1992) that he had always made his living in that fashion. "I was never out of the business, but then again, I wasn't in the record business. I was in the live music business. That's where I, hopefully, learned whatever chops I've got, by playing a lot of the same places all the time and getting a lot of the same crowds. You have to try and be versatile and keep them coming back. The only way to do that is to play something different all the time and that's tough. Then again, it makes what I'm doing now much easier."

Like any country artist, Raye knew that achieving commercial success meant gaining a Nashville connection. It was not for lack of trying that his potential fell on deaf ears in Music City. But finally the chance arrived in the form of a hard-won contract from Epic Records and Collin was ready to take advantage of it. His debut album, *All I Can Be,* came out during the summer of 1991 and showed up on the *Billboard* chart at number sixty the week of September 14, 1991. In coming months it peaked at number seven and settled down for a long run. Except for one short period when it dropped from the magazine's top 75, it remained on the list for 114 weeks as of early 1994, earning a gold record from R.I.A.A. along the way. With over 900,000 copies sold in early 1994 it seemed certain to also capture a platinum award.

The title track, a Harlan Howard composition, was a singles-chart hit in the summer of 1991 and was followed by the second singles release, "Love Me," which became a number-one hit in December 1991. That ballad propelled Raye to star status, being cited in many country polls as one of the top-10 singles of the year.

In early 1992, the single "Every Second" began to move up the charts, reaching number two in *Radio & Records* the week of May 15. Later that year, Raye's second album, *In This Life,* was on the charts, peaking at number ten in *Billboard.* It remained on the list into 1994, earning another R.I.A.A. gold record for Collin. The title track, issued as a single, was also a hit, rising to number one in *R&R* the week of September 25, 1992, and the same position in *Billboard* a week later.

Raye began 1993 with the hit single "I Want You Bad (and That Ain't Good)," which reached number seven in *R&R* the week of January 8. It was followed by several more singles hits, "Somebody Else's Moon" (number four in *R&R* June 18); "That Was a River" (number two in *R&R* November 12); and "That's My Story," rising up the *Billboard* chart at year-end and in upper-chart levels in early 1994. Raye's third Epic album, *Extremes,* came out in early 1994 and peaked at number twelve in *Billboard* the week of February 12. It stayed on the list the rest of 1994, earning still another R.I.A.A. gold-record certification. Later in the year Collin added two more top-10 hits to his collection, "Little Rock" (number one in *R&R* June 24) and "Man of My Word" (number four in *R&R* the week of October 21).

Collin's recording success gave no sign of slacking off in 1995. By mid-year he had two additional top-10 singles, "My Kind of Girl" in March and "If I Were You" in June. Meanwhile, *Extremes* remained a bestseller, passing R.I.A.A. platinum levels early in the year.

At the same time, Raye was adding to his following with live concerts that were, to say the least, exuberant and usually unpredictable—except for the likelihood that at some point in the proceedings Raye would grab a water-filled machine gun and spray the audience. He told Kimmy Wix that he did sing some of his ballads with a relaxed, straightforward style but, besides that, "the show is 90 percent party atmosphere. I love to see people do outrageous things and to feel like they can do anything at one of my shows. I do stuff like that on-stage, too, so that they will feel comfortable."

Covering a Southern California concert for the *Los Angeles Times* ("Collin Raye, A Contemporary Guy Playing with Tradition," Calendar section, February 13, 1994), Dennis Hunt noted, "In concert, Raye can rock out on Rod Stewart's 'Hot Legs' or croon Elton John's melancholy 'Don't Let the Sun Go Down on Me.' The first single from the new album *(Extremes),* is 'That's My Story,' a frivolous Lyle Lovett song."

Raye told Hunt, "Critics jump on me for singing these non-country songs—asking how can a true country artist sing those songs. [But] country has changed so much in the past few years that a country artist can sing anything. Maybe he couldn't do it comfortably years ago, but he can now."

And he intimated it was important for a modern country artist to experiment, while not ignoring country's roots, to survive in what he saw as a field that was still facing limits in terms of overall potential audience size. "I don't think it's going to keep zooming. It's leveling off. Too many artists jumped into country. A lot of the artists who are around now won't be around in a year and a half. Tell you one thing: I wouldn't open a country honky tonk right now."

In August 1995, Raye's album *I Think About You* was issued and quickly reached upper chart positions. It peaked at number five in *Billboard* during the summer and received an R.I.A.A. gold record award on November 16. By year-end his single (and video) "Not That Different" was starting to move up the charts. Raye closed out the year by performing at two events on New Year's, appearing at the House of Blues in Los Angeles on December 31 in a show aired on CBS-TV and taking part in the Fiesta Bowl Block Party in Phoenix, Arizona. In early 1996, "Not That Different" continued to pick up momentum and in March reached number one on hit lists including those in *The Gavin Report* and on CMT. This was followed later in the year by the top-10 single of the album title track, "I Think About You."

REED, JERRY: *Singer, guitarist, songwriter, record producer, actor. Born Atlanta, Georgia, March 20, 1937.*

Patience, talent, a sense of humor—all those combined to make Jerry Reed one of country music's brightest stars of the 1970s, after an apprenticeship that lasted over two decades. Proud of his role as a family man, he made it to the top without the excesses that plagued the careers of many other artists. As he told writer Red O'Donnell, "I'm so normal it's sickening— really square. I've never been part of the drug or heavy booze scene. I get high on music. And I want to have a clear head when I write or perform that music."

Reed's love for music went back to his early years growing up in Atlanta, Georgia, working in the cotton mills. Like many other country musicians, music offered a way out of a working-class environment. He played guitar in grade school and began to appear at small clubs in and around Atlanta with country bands in his early teens.

When he was sixteen, a policeman friend extolled his guitar skills to Atlanta publisher-producer Bill Lowery, noting that Jerry also wrote promising songs. The result was a management contract. In 1955, Lowery obtained a writing and recording contract for Jerry with Capitol Records. The recording side didn't make any breakthroughs, but there was rising interest in his songs in the late 1950s and early 1960s. Among those who recorded some of them were Brenda Lee and Elvis Presley. One of Reed's numbers that Elvis put on vinyl in the 1960s was "Guitar Man."

Jerry moved to Nashville after a stint in the service to pursue his songwriting, supplementing his income with session work. In fact, during the first half of the 1960s, he gained a reputation as one of Nashville's best backing guitarists and was offered more assignments than he could handle. Besides playing behind most of

country and pop music's top names, he often accompanied major artists on concert tours.

Still hoping to move into the spotlight himself, he finally found encouragement in 1965. Another guitar wizard, Chet Atkins, RCA Nashville's artists & repertoire executive, signed Jerry with the company. Looking back, Reed told an interviewer from the Lexington (Kentucky) *Herald,* "I couldn't get a hit to save my life, and I'd been there [Nashville] three years. Then Chet Atkins began recording me for RCA records and we haven't been off the charts since. Chet just said, 'You're doing it wrong, Mr. Reed; let's try it this way,' and damned if he wasn't right."

The first result was the album *The Unbelievable Guitar and Voice of Jerry Reed.* Although it wasn't a smash hit after its release in 1967, RCA officials were satisfied with it. Their confidence was rewarded with the late 1960s LPs *Nashville Underground, Alabama Wild Man, Better Things in Life,* and *Jerry Reed Explores Guitar Country* (November 1969). Reed's following among fans increased, as did respect from his entertainment industry peers. Soon considered one of country and pop music's top writers, from 1956 to 1970 he won four BMI country awards (for "Misery Loves Company," "Remembering," "A Thing Called Love," and "U.S. Male") and two BMI pop awards (for "That's All You Gotta Do" and "Guitar Man"). Jerry appeared as a guest on two major TV programs, *Johnny Cash* and *The Glen Campbell Goodtime Hour* 1969 summer replacement show, as his performing career also advanced.

In 1970 everything finally came together to bring Reed national acclaim. He had three chart hit albums: *Cookin',* issued in March, *Me and Jerry,* a duet with Chet Atkins issued in midyear, and *Georgia Sunshine,* released in September. It was also the year he turned out one of his best-known singles, a song about a man who might be called the Paul Bunyan of the bayous, "Amos Moses." This song provided him with his first number-one country hit and also went high on the pop charts. For his year's work, he gleaned such honors as his first Grammy for Best Instrumental Performance *(Me and Jerry)* and a nomination for Best Country Male Performance and a BMI award, both for "Amos Moses." The Country Music Association in 1970 named him Instrumentalist of the Year.

Reed became a regular on *The Glen Campbell Goodtime Hour* on CBS-TV for the 1970–71 season, returning for the 1971–72 season. During the summer of 1971, he toured the United States with Campbell. Jerry's album releases in 1971 included the smash hit *When You're Hot, You're Hot,* issued in May, whose title song, "I'm Movin' On," became one of the year's best-selling singles (Harmony, 6/71), and *Ko-ko Joe* (10/71). Those efforts won him a second Grammy, Best Country Male Performance for "When You're Hot, You're Hot," and a second straight selection by the CMA as Instrumentalist of the Year. In the CMA competition, he also was among the finalists in six other categories, including Male Vocalist and Entertainer of the Year. On March 29, 1971, Reed was awarded a gold record from the R.I.A.A. for the single "Amos Moses."

Jerry's 1972 RCA LPs included *Smell the Flowers* (4/72), *Me and Chet,* with Atkins (6/72), *Best of Jerry Reed* (8/72), *Jerry Reed* (10/72), and, on Camden, *Oh What a Woman* (11/72). During the year he was part of the concert series called "Festival of Music," sharing top billing with Chet Atkins, Floyd Cramer, and Boots Randolph. He continued to add to his list of BMI songwriting awards, receiving honors for such early 1970s country efforts as "Georgia Sunshine," "Amos Moses," "Talk About the Good Times," "When You're Hot, You're Hot," "A Thing Called Love," and "Ko-ko Joe." He also was given BMI pop awards for "A Thing Called Love" and "Amos Moses." His charted singles in 1972 included "Alabama Wild Man," "Another Puff," and "Smell the Flowers."

During the summer of 1973, he was featured on the NBC-TV show *Music Country, U.S.A.* following the release of his chart-hit album *Lord Mr. Ford.* He also appeared on *Hee Haw* and won BMI country awards for "Alabama Wild Man" and "You Took All the Ramblin' Out of Me." In 1974, his TV credits included appearances on *Southern Sportsman, Hee Haw, Dinah!, Merv Griffin,* and Johnny Carson's *The Tonight Show,* and once again on *Music Country, U.S.A.* Jerry, who had left BMI for ASCAP, received ASCAP awards in 1974 for being artist and producer of the recordings "A Good Woman's Love" and "Uptown Poker Club."

A new career phase opened for Reed in 1974 when he joined the cast of Burt Reynolds's movie, *W.W. and the Dixie Dance Kings.* More than a few movie critics took favorable notice of his work in the film. In 1976, he worked with Reynolds again on the movie *Gator,* and the following year on the new Reynolds opus, *Smokey and the Bandit.* The film surprised the critics by becoming one of the unexpected hits of the cinema year. In 1978, Jerry started work on another movie project, this time a comedy starring Dom DeLuise. That film, titled *Hot Stuff,* was released during the summer of 1979. In 1980, he was part of the cast of *Smokey and the Bandit II.*

During the mid- and late-1970s, Jerry usually placed several singles on the charts each year, a situation that continued in the early 1980s. His charted RCA releases in 1980 were "Sugar Foot Rag," "Age/Workin' at the Carwash Blues," and "Texas Bound and Flying"; in early 1981, the single "Caffeine, Nicotine and Benzedrine (and Wish Me Luck)" was on lower-chart rungs. His charted albums in the early 1980s included *Jerry Reed Gets into Jim Croce* and *Texas Bound and Flying.*

In the 1980s, though Jerry continued to record new material and toured sporadically, he spent more time on films than other entertainment pursuits. During the 1984–85 time period, he worked on a film shot in and around Nashville whose stars included Arte Johnson, Ernest Dixon, and Esther Houston. The movie was released in the spring of 1985 under the title *What Comes Around.* A few years later he was a cast member of *BAT-21,* a production based on a true Vietnam occurrence that featured Gene Hackman and Danny Glover. After the picture was released in 1989, Jerry toured the South Pacific in mid-year to perform before U.S. servicemen stationed in the region. Besides those projects, Reed also was featured on commercials for Tennessee Food Market in 1989 and at the start of the 1990s. His career followed much the same pattern in the first half of the new decade. In the early 1990s he also recorded tracks for a new studio album with longtime friend Chet Atkins.

REEVES, DEL: *Singer, guitarist, songwriter, disc jockey, actor, TV show host. Born Sparta, North Carolina, July 14, 1933.*

Dubbed by some music commentators the "Dean Martin of country music" for his relaxed and easy stage manner, Del Reeves, like Martin, consistently retained the respect of a sizable audience during a long, eventful career. As a writer, performer, and TV personality, he had a strong impact on the country field from the 1950s into the 1980s.

Born and raised in North Carolina, Del was influenced by country music almost from the cradle. By the time he was in his teens he was performing many country & western songs in school shows and local functions. In the 1950s, he moved to California to further his musical career. Working in many local country-music events, he began to gain recognition for his abilities as a master of ceremonies, and by the late 1950s had his own TV show in the Southern California area. For four years, into the early 1960s, Del emceed the show and became acquainted with many of the most talented artists in the country field. With his wife, Ellen, he composed many songs that were recorded by such artists as Roy Drusky, Carl Smith, Rose Maddox, and Sheb Wooley.

His first recording contract with a major label came in the late 1950s when he joined Decca. In 1961, he gained his first top-10 hit when his single "Be Quiet Mind" became one of the year's most popular country releases. A few years later, he moved to United Artists and turned out two of the top country & western records of 1965, "The Belles of Southern Bell" and "Girl on the Billboard." The latter rose to number one and held that position for many weeks. During this period, Reeves turned out several hits that just missed top-10 status, such as "One Bum Town" and "Blame It on My Do

Wrong." In 1966, he made the top 10 again with the single "Women Do Funny Things to Me."

In that year, Reeves's status in the country field led to an invitation from the *Grand Ole Opry* to come to Nashville as a regular performer. He remained there as part of the honored *Opry* tradition into the 1990s. Beside appearing at the *Opry*, Del continued to tour widely, reaching audiences in all fifty states before the 1960s were over and performing in a number of foreign cities as well.

Through the late 1970s, Del remained a stalwart of United Artists' country efforts. His mid-1960s album releases included his debut on the label in October 1965, *Del Reeves, Doodle-Oo-Doo-Doo* (1/66), *Del Reeves Sings Jim Reeves* (3/66), *Special Delivery* (7/66), *Gettin' Any Feed* (10/66), *Struttin' My Stuff* (5/67), and *Six of One* (10/67). Some of his recordings were repackaged by Pickwick Records on the LP *Mr. Country Music*. His albums of the late 1960s and early 1970s on UA included *Best of Del Reeves, Volumes 1 and 2, Del Reeves Album, Big Daddy,* and *Friends and Neighbors*. Sun Records included tracks by him on such LPs as *Country Concert Live! Out in the Country,* and *Great Country Songs*. In 1972, Liberty issued an LP titled *Superpak*.

In the late 1960s and early 1970s, Reeves extended his list of major song hits to include "Landmark Tavern," "Philadelphia Phillies," "A Dozen Pair of Boots," and "The Best Is Yet to Come." He also had a modest hit in 1970 with "Right Back to Lovin' You." In the mid-1970s, the recording phase of his career slowed down. His singles hits were modest ones for the most part, showing up on the lower levels of the charts, as was the case with "Prayer from a Mobile Home" in 1974, "Puttin' in Overtime at Home" and "You Comb Her Hair" in 1975, and "I Ain't Got Nobody" in 1976. Things picked up, though, when he teamed up with another UA artist, Billy Jo Spears, for a series of singles successes that included "On the Rebound" and "Teardrops Will Kiss the Morning Dew" in 1976. In 1978, Del had a solo single on the charts, "Dig Down Deep." In the spring of 1980 his single "Take Me to Your Heart" on Koala Records was on lower-chart levels.

Del's talents brought him stardom in other fields as well. During the 1960s his film credits included appearances in *Gold Guitar, Forty Acre Feud, Cottonpickin', Chickenpickers,* and *Second Fiddle to a Steel Guitar.*

His entertaining activities continued to prosper in the 1970s and 1980s. Featured on major networks and syndicated TV shows as a guest during those years, he also starred for a time in a syndicated weekly variety show called *The Del Reeves Country Carnival* in the late seventies and early eighties. He continued to be a featured artist on the *Grand Ole Opry,* and in mid-October 1991 the other cast members duly honored his twenty-fifth anniversary on the show.

REEVES, JIM: *Singer, guitarist, band leader (the Blue Boys), songwriter. Born Panola County, Texas, August 20, 1924; died Tennessee, July 31, 1964. Elected to Country Music Hall of Fame in 1967.*

The bronze plaque in the Hall of Fame in Nashville reads: "The velvet style of Gentleman Jim Reeves was an international influence. His rich voice brought millions of new fans to country music from every corner of the world. Although the crash of his private airplane in 1964 took his life . . . posterity will keep his name alive . . . because they will remember him as one of country music's most important performers."

The last sentences have proved prophetic; for decades after Reeves's untimely passing, releases of previously unissued recordings, and reissues of early hits, kept his name on the charts even in the 1980s.

Born in rural Texas, James Reeves was more interested in sports than music as a boy. He was a first-string pitcher at the University of Texas in his sophomore year when he was drafted by the St. Louis Cardinals. Practicing on the Cardinals' farm team, he injured his leg sliding into second base. The leg did not heal properly and his doctors told him to forget baseball. He turned to entertainment as his only other skill.

Although he enjoyed playing the guitar and singing, Reeves did not think of a career as a musician right away. He had a good speaking voice and a knowledge of country music and used it to start working as an announcer. By the early 1950s he was a staff regular at station KWKH in Shreveport, home of the *Louisiana Hayride* country program. He performed occasionally in local clubs in his spare time and cut some records on the Abbott label. One of these, "Mexican Joe," caught on with the public. Jim, quite unexpectedly, found himself with a top-10 country hit.

Shortly afterward, he became a part of the *Hayride* cast. His stock went up some more when he scored a second top-10 success when his duet with Ginny Wright on Fabor Records, "I Love You," made the national charts in 1954. Also a chart hit that year was his single "Bimbo." Those accomplishments brought a contract offer from RCA Victor, a relationship that lasted for the rest of his career. "Yonder Comes a Sucker," his own composition, and his initial success for RCA, was a top-10 hit in 1955.

By the end of the 1950s, Reeves was a Nashville resident and a regular on the *Grand Ole Opry*. His first worldwide tour, accompanying a USO group to play for troops in Europe in 1954, preceded a string of four more tours for American troops throughout the world. In 1957, he was given his own daily show on ABC-TV, and was featured, during the late 1950s, on such programs as *The Ed Sullivan Show, The Steve Allen Show,* Dick Clark's *American Bandstand,* and *The Jimmy Dean Show,* among others. Jim continued his pattern in the early 1960s, traveling to all fifty states and throughout the world. In 1962, he received tumultuous welcomes from crowds throughout Africa and Europe, where he was immensely popular. In Norway alone he earned more than sixteen gold, silver, diamond, and platinum records through the late 1960s.

In his recording career in the United States, Reeves had scored more top-10 hits as of the early 1970s than any other country artist except Eddy Arnold and Webb Pierce. From 1955 to the end of the 1960s, he had one or more top-10 singles every year. Backing him on these efforts, from 1955 to the end of his life, was his band, the Blue Boys. His 1950s top-10 singles hits included "According to My Heart" and "My Lips Are Sealed" in 1956; his own composition, "Am I Losing You," and "Four Walls" in 1957; "Anna Marie," "Blue Boy," and number-one-ranked "Billy Bayou" in 1958; and his all-time bestseller, "He'll Have to Go" (a number-one hit), and "Home" in 1959.

Reeves continued with four top hits in 1960: "I Know One," "I Missed Me," "I'm Getting Better," and a reissue of "Am I Losing You." He turned out ten more top-10 hits between the start of 1961 and mid-1964: "The Blizzard" (1961); "Adios Amigo," "What I Feel in My Heart," "I'm Gonna Change Everything," "Losing Your Love" (1962); "Guilty," "Is This Me?" (1963); number-one-ranked "I Guess I'm Crazy," "Love Is No Excuse" (with Dottie West), and "Welcome to My World" (1964).

Naturally, Reeves was represented by many LPs in his lifetime, a number of which reached gold-record status. His initial LP was *Bimbo,* issued in 1955. This was followed by such albums on RCA/Camden as *Jim Reeves* (12/57), *Girls I Have Known* (8/58), *Warn the Heart* (9/59), *He'll Have to Go* (4/60), *According to My Heart* (6/60), *Intimate Side of Jim Reeves* (8/60), *To Your Heart* (11/61), *Tall Tales* (4/61), *Country Side* (4/62), *Touch of Velvet* (6/62), *We Thank Thee* (8/62), *Gentleman Jim* (3/63), *Good 'n' Country* (Camden, 12/63), *International Jim Reeves* (9/63), *Kimberley Jim* (4/64), and *Moonlight and Roses* (7/64).

In July 1964, returning home to Nashville from an engagement, Reeves was killed when his plane crashed during a thunderstorm. His voice was not stilled, however—under the direction of his widow, Mary, previously unreleased recordings enlarged her husband's legend. In the mid- and late-1960s, Jim was represented on the singles charts by many more bestsellers, a number of which reached number one on country charts. Among those were "I Won't Forget You," "Is It Really Over," and "This Is It," the last two ranked number one in 1965; number-one "Distant Drums" and "Snow Flake" in 1966; number-one "I Won't Come in While He's There" in 1967; and, in 1968, "That's When I See the Blue (In Your Pretty Brown Eyes)" and "I Heard a Heart Break Tonight."

His posthumously released albums included such gold-record successes as *Distant Drums* (1966) and *Touch of Sadness* (1968). Other LPs included *Best of Jim Reeves* (8/64), *Have I Told You Lately* (Camden, 12/64), *Jim Reeves Way* (3/65), *Best, Volume 2* (2/66), *Yours Sincerely* (12/66), *Blue Side of Lonesome* (6/67), *My Cathedral* (12/67), *Best, Volume 3* (8/69), *Writes You a Record* (3/71), *Something Special* (8/71), *God Be with You, Young & Country* (11/71), *Jim Reeves* (two discs, Camden, 6/72), *My Friend* (3/72), *Missing You* (11/72). In the early 1980s, a major best-selling album, *Don't Let Me Cross Over,* was released.

In the 1970s, Reeves's name continued to appear on country lists. Among his singles hits for the decade were "The Writing's on the Wall" and "Missing You" in 1972; "I'd Fight the World" (1974); "You Belong to Me" (1975); and "It's Nothing to Me," "Little Ole Dime" (1977).

As the decade came to a close, still another Reeves single, "Don't Let Me Cross Over," was moving up the charts, making it to the top 20 in early 1980. In January 1980, a second hit single made the charts, "Oh, How I Miss You Tonight," which rose into the national top 10 in mid-month. This was followed later in the year with electronically achieved "duet" singles with current performer Deborah Allen, which resulted in the hit "Take Me in Your Arms and Hold Me." Late in the year, his solo single "There's Always Me" rose to upper-chart levels, and the song served as the title cut for an album that was on the charts in late 1980 and early 1981.

As the 1980s went by, the presence of Reeves's name on the charts tapered off, but people still bought his recordings and his voice still could be heard occasionally on country radio. Many of his albums remained in print in the 1990s and were available on CDs, cassettes, or both formats as well as in some video releases. As of 1995 those included *Welcome to My World: The Essential Jim Reeves Collection; Jim Reeves; Gentleman Jim 1955–59; Four Walls: The Legend Begins; He'll Have to Go and Other Favorites; the Best of Jim Reeves;* and *Jim Reeves & Patsy Cline/Greatest Hits* (all on RCA). The last-named, besides containing joint recordings made by them while alive, also included a posthumous studio-made pairing.

Also available on the CAK label was *The Country Side of Jim Reeves.* A retrospective of some of Reeves's work on *Grand Ole Opry* broadcasts was assembled for the Country Music Foundation catalog titled *Jim Reeves/Live at the Opry.* A number of videos were on the market in the 1990s, including live footage of some of his performances such as the *Jim Reeves, Ray Price & Ernest Tubb* release, which included eight of his renditions. He was also represented on Volumes 3, 5, 9, and 12 of the Classic Country Club Collection of video material in *Grand Ole Opry Stars of the Fifties.*

Available as import items in the mid-1990s were two extensive collections assembled by the Bear Family Records group of Germany, *Jim Reeves: Gentleman Jim* (4 CDs) and *Jim Reeves: Welcome to My World* (16 CDs). The 16 CD set included all of Reeves's recordings for the Macy's, Fabor, Abbott, and RCA labels as well as all his known demos. Total contents of the package came to the hard-to-believe total of 447 songs plus a 126 page book about his background and career.

From 1965 on his wife, Mary, had presided over a number of Jim Reeves enterprises including a Jim Reeves Museum in Nashville. In failing health in 1996, she turned the reins over to long-time Reeves family friend Jim Ed Brown.

RESTLESS HEART: *Vocal and instrumental group. Original members, 1983: Larry Stewart, born Paducah, Kentucky, March 3, c. 1959 (lead vocals, guitar, keyboards); Dave Innis, born Bartlesville, Oklahoma, April 9 (guitar, songwriter); Paul Gregg, born Oklahoma (vocals, bass guitar); John Dittrich, born Union, New York, April 6 (vocal, drums); Greg Jennings, born Oklahoma City, Oklahoma, October 2 (vocals, guitar). Stewart left late 1991, Innis in 1992.*

The clash of egos in any band, rock, pop, or country, is always a danger and one that often becomes more severe the more successful a band becomes. The situation is usually exacerbated by the close contact between members during intensive touring, recording, and other demands that typically occupy up to 300 days or more a year. So it wasn't all that surprising after almost eight years of growth and many hit recordings that Restless Heart seemed to come apart at the seams in the early 1990s, a break confirmed by the departure of lead singer Larry Stewart and cofounder Dave Innis. Perhaps even more surprising was that the three remaining bandsmen managed to pick up the pieces and give signs of a resurgence of the group.

The moving force behind the organization of the band in the early 1980s was songwriter and record executive Tim DuBois, who later became president of Arista Records Nashville operation. He had been working with songwriter-musician Dave Innis to form a new band incorporating some of Innis's experienced musician friends who had originally been based in Oklahoma. Innis had formed a friendship with a songwriter-performer named Larry Stewart while both were students at Belmont College in Nashville. Innis had been impressed by Stewart's singing abilities, which were soon applied to demo tapes of Innis's songs. Innis also used the tapes to help persuade DuBois to include Stewart in the lineup of the new group that became Restless Heart. The other founding members were bass guitarist Paul Gregg, drummer John Dittrich, and guitarist Greg Jennings, who had previously been members of various other bands going back to their early teens.

The group soon signed with RCA Records and completed material for their debut album in 1984. Jennings pointed out that the band didn't yet have its final name when that album appeared. One of the songs on the first disc was "Restless Heart," and band members chose it

for their new name. RCA then decided to select eight songs for an extended-play album, titled *Restless Heart,* and released in 1985, that quickly caught the attention of radio programmers and, in turn, the country audience. During 1985 and 1986, it was a rare period when one of the tracks weren't on the hit charts. No less than four singles were best-sellers, with three going top 10: "I Want Everyone to Cry," "(Back to the) Heartbreak Kid," and "Till I Loved You."

The band's next album release, *Wheels,* did even better. Besides rising high on the hit charts itself to earn gold-record certification from the R.I.A.A., it provided four straight number-one hit singles. These were: "That Rock Won't Roll," "I'll Still Be Loving You," "Why Does It Have to Be (Wrong or Right)," and "Wheels." "I'll Still Be Loving You" not only did well on the country charts, but also crossed over to move high on pop charts as well, the first of a number of band releases to do that. It was good news from an economic standpoint, but in time caused major career direction difficulties for the group, with some of the country disc jockeys eventually questioning whether Restless Heart was a true country music representative.

By the time the third RCA album came out in 1988, Restless Heart was bracketed by some with the superstar country band Alabama. Reaction to the new album, *Big Dreams in a Small Town,* didn't change the assessment. It was another collection that featured well-meshed instrumental work and notable lead vocals by Stewart. The album provided two more number-one singles, "The Bluest Eyes in Texas" and "A Tender Lie," plus another two that rose high on country lists, "Say What's in Your Heart" and the title song. The group by then had moved from opening act in large venue tours to a bonafide headliner on its own.

The band started off the 1990s with another album success, *Fast Movin' Train,* issued in 1990, which earned their third straight R.I.A.A. gold record award. This time there was only one number-one singles success, but the band still placed a number of singles on the charts. The title track hit number one in *Radio & Records* the week of February 23, 1990, followed by the top-10 *R&R* song, "Dancy's Dream" (week of June 8, 1990) and "When Somebody Loves You," number twelve in *R&R* the week of November 19, 1990. In 1991, RCA issued the band's fifth album, *The Best of Restless Heart,* which, in addition to showcasing previous hits, spawned two new successes, "You Can Depend on Me" and "Familiar Rain."

On occasion, when a record company releases a "best of" album, it can be taken as an indication of mounting internal stresses in a group, or of the imminent departure of a band or solo artist from the label. In this case the most restless one was Larry Stewart, who announced he was opting for a solo career at the end of 1991, though he noted it was something that had been brewing in his thoughts for a year and a half.

As he told one interviewer, "They were great years, and there was a period when maybe we were even ahead of our time, but also the last couple of years we were not so on top of it. We hit a wall within our inner circle. After four albums and traveling the road together musically, a division was beginning. Five different individuals wanted to do different things, which is normal. Few bands last eight years and see eye to eye except maybe Alabama, and no one has ever done what they have done."

Stewart's leave-taking was amicable, but that wasn't the case with Innis, who was asked to leave not long after by the other three members. That trio asserted the problem was that Innis felt he had to do a lot more to make up for the loss of Stewart. Dittrich told Robert Baird of *New Country* magazine ("The Beat of a Restless Heart," June 1994), "He felt there was a need for someone to come forth and take over all those same responsibilities. I think the problem was that he didn't know what those responsibilities were. He decided he was going to be our savior, and that put him in a position he was unprepared to move into."

Meanwhile, the departure of Stewart caused other career ripples. Many radio programmers decided that without a lead singer the band was defunct and stopped scheduling its records and videos. Dittrich told Baird, "I'm sure everyone felt that if there was another voice in this band they'd have heard it. What they didn't know was that Paul and I had been lead singers in every band we'd ever been in. We just weren't given the opportunity here.

"The surprising thing is that our label didn't even know. I remember right after we had finished *Big Iron Horses* (the first album prepared by the remaining trio), we were in Seattle and a couple of big guys from our label came to see our live show. They came back afterward and were literally speechless. They were like, 'We didn't have any idea, any clue, that there was another lead singer in this band.' They were stunned."

The album confirmed there was life in the old band yet. Four more hit singles were added to the group's credits. These were "You Can Depend on Me," number two in *Radio & Records* the week of December 20, 1991; "When She Cries," number eight in *R&R* the week of December 4, 1992; "Mending Fences," number nine in *R&R* the week of March 25, 1993; and "We Got the Love," number seven in *R&R* the week of August 6, 1993. "When She Cries" proved a major favorite with many pop fans, crossing over to hit number one on trade publication adult contemporary charts. The song was the band's overall best-selling single ever and earned a Grammy nomination.

With that achievement, one might say Restless Heart was back, but some wondered exactly where that "back" was. Whether because of the band's desire to push the crossover position still further or because the label set up broadcast interviews that way, pop stations, now clamoring to talk to them, tended to get first call over country outlets around the nation. The band added to the country reviewers and broadcasters concerns with another 1993 crossover hit, "Tell Me What You Dream."

Those developments, Paul Gregg told Tom Wood of *The Tennesseean* ("Matters of the Heart: Restless Heart on Track with 3-Man Group," June 4, 1994), immediately caused the band to get "quite a bit of flak from some of the major weight-carrying radio stations across America. They've really got a burr under their saddle about Restless Heart, which I guess put a burr under my saddle. One thing we heard was that they really doubted our commitment to country music."

The bandsmen hotly disputed that assessment, Gregg asserted: "We've been making country records for 10 years and . . . for anybody to draw that kind of conclusion based on a record or two, it's stupid."

The trio also blamed RCA for some aspects of the situation, claiming label executives focused on the pop market to enhance sales, suggesting some steps were taken over their heads. This was disputed by RCA. Thom Schuyler, RCA's vice president and general manager, told Baird, "everyone is given a vote in the process. . . . There's no doubt that our contemporary division wanted [the band's A/C success] to happen. But the band members didn't register any unsettling concerns to me about what was taking place."

The label issued the group's seventh album, *Masters of the Heart,* in 1994, but the assertions by both sides may have damaged the creative relationship. In any case, by the fall Restless Heart and RCA had parted company. However, a contributing factor was likely the failure of the album and initial singles releases from it to have major chart impact. The debut single, "Baby Needs New Shoes," made hit lists in late spring, but never got past mid-chart levels. The album tracks seemed to deserve a better fate, but the problems with country deejays might have been taking effect.

Through all this, the band's core trio indicated they intended to stay together as a threesome, at least for awhile. They still enjoyed touring (augmented in 1994 concerts by Dwaine Rowe on keyboards and Chris Hicks on guitar and saxophone) and took pride in their roles as a brass band on a riverboat in the spring 1994 filming of *Maverick,* a vehicle that proved one of the top-grossing movies of the year.

Gregg joked with Baird that the group only had three different directions at this juncture. "We were arguing in the bus on our way here that eventually there will be one guy left. But which one?"

RICH, CHARLIE: *Singer, pianist, saxophone player, songwriter. Born Colt, Arkansas, December 14, 1932; died Hammond, Louisiana, July 25, 1995.*

The struggle for success in the music world is so brutal that among many industry people it breeds indifference to the fate of other aspirants. So it is a great tribute to Charlie Rich that his belated rise to stardom in 1973 was almost universally welcomed by those in his field. His renown was finally achieved primarily as a country-music performer, but his talent was such that he could easily have made it in rock 'n' roll, blues, or jazz.

As a child growing up on a small cotton plantation near Colt, Arkansas, Charlie was exposed to many types of music. He heard white gospel music at the Baptist church he and his parents faithfully attended; he heard blues from the black field hands who worked on the plantation; and he heard country on the radio listening to the *Grand Ole Opry.* Piano was the instrument he studied as a child, and, enamored of Stan Kenton and devoted to jazz, he played the tenor saxophone in his high school band.

After one year at the University of Arkansas, he joined the Air Force during the Korean War. In Enid, Oklahoma, where he was stationed, Charlie was playing in a jazz band and performing with a small combo in town when he married his high school sweetheart, Margaret Ann, the group's vocalist.

Rich tried farming for a year after his discharge for added financial security (his wife was soon to have their third child) before he returned to his music, with the encouragement of his wife.

During this time, Charlie became a regular performer in Memphis piano bars, while he and Margaret Ann wrote songs, sometimes together, sometimes individually. Margaret Ann, without telling Charlie, brought a tape of the songs to Bill Justis, artists and repertoire executive for Sun Records of Memphis. Justis listened to the songs; he liked them but he felt that they weren't commercial enough. He signed Rich as a session musician and told him to keep writing songs.

Charlie started out at Sun by backing performers such as Johnny Cash and Roy Orbison. He also wrote songs recorded by a number of other artists, including "The Ways of a Woman in Love," "Break Up," "I'll Make It All Up to You," and "I Just Thought You'd Like to Know." At the end of the 1950s, Sun started issuing some of Rich's own recordings. The third release included the song "Lonely Weekends," which was on the national charts from mid-March 1960 into August. Unfortunately, none of his follow-up records caught on, in large part because of a lack of sufficient support from Sun Records.

Rich switched to RCA Records and had a minor hit, "Big Boss Man." A few years later he switched labels again, to Mercury Records, and had a smash rock hit, "Mohair Sam," in 1965, but once again he failed to produce any follow-up hits. Again he returned to a life of engagements in small bars and clubs, mostly in the Midwest. His fall from the heights of success hit him very hard, and he reputedly turned to pills and liquor to try to boost his confidence. He moved to Hi Records in

the mid-1960s without any noticeable improvement in outlook and finally joined Epic, a subsidiary of Columbia Records, in 1968.

Charlie's move to Epic proved to be the turning point in his career. He was teamed with producer Billy Sherrill, a partnership that proved to be dynamic. Sherrill believed in Rich's talent and worked hard to win him the attention he deserved. Some of their earliest collaborations under the Epic label became regional hits but none made the upper levels of the charts. Those that made the lower rungs on the hit charts included the album *Big Boss Man* and the singles "July 12, 1939," "Nice 'n' Easy," and "Life's Little Ups and Downs" in 1970; the single "A Woman Left Lonely" in 1971; and the single "A Part of Your Life" in 1972. "Life's Little Ups and Downs," one of Charlie's favorites, is one of a number of songs written by his wife, Margaret Ann. For the most part, however, Rich's early years with Epic were disappointing and frustrating.

Finally, in 1972, Charlie achieved the breakthrough he needed. He recorded "I Take It on Home," written by Kenny O'Dell, and the song entered the country-music top 20. This song and another O'Dell composition that Charlie recorded, "Behind Closed Doors," impressed Bill Williams, a public relations executive who had just joined the Epic Nashville office. Williams gave Rich a great deal of publicity and arranged for him to make numerous personal appearances. His efforts paid off and "Behind Closed Doors" climbed to the number-one position on the country charts in 1973. The song also crossed over to the pop charts and sold over a million copies, earning a gold record and becoming one of the major hits of that year.

Rich's follow-up song, "The Most Beautiful Girl," did even better, selling more than 2 million copies to achieve platinum status. In 1973, he received many awards, including a Grammy as Best Country Male Vocalist and the Country Music Association's awards for Male Vocalist of the Year, Single of the Year, and Album of the Year for *Behind Closed Doors.* After nearly twenty years in the business, Charlie had finally achieved the success many people had felt he deserved all along. Some of his earlier recordings were released by RCA in 1973 in an album called *Tomorrow Night,* which did very well, ensuring that Rich's earlier output would not be forgotten.

The year 1974 was also extremely successful for Charlie Rich. That year, "the Silver Fox," as Rich came to be called because of his prematurely gray hair, was honored as Entertainer of the Year by the Country Music Association, probably the most coveted award in country music.

His hit singles from 1974 were "There Won't Be Anymore," "I Don't See Me in Your Eyes Anymore," "A Very Special Love Song," and "I Love My Friend" (number one in October). His 1975 successes on Epic were "My Elusive Dreams," "Everytime You Touch

Me," and "All Over Me." In 1976, his charted hits were "Road Song" and "Since I Fell for You," and in 1977, his Epic releases included the number-one hit (in August), "Rollin' with the Flow." In 1978, he had a charted single on United Artists label, "I Still Believe in Love," and, on Epic, the top-10 "Beautiful Woman" and the number-one duet (with Janie Fricke) of his composition "On My Knees" in September.

Charlie closed out the 1970s with his name often appearing on country charts with both new and old releases. His 1979 charted singles, for instance, were "The Fool Strikes Again," "Life Goes On," and "I Lost My Head" on UA, "Spanish Eyes" on Epic, and "I Wake You Up When I Get Home" on Elektra. He had, by then, severed his relationship with Epic and signed with Elektra. In 1980, his hit list singles were "You're Gonna Love Yourself in the Morning" on UA, "Even a Fool Would Let Go" on Epic, and "A Man Doesn't Know What a Woman Goes Through" on Elektra.

Charlie's albums in the late 1970s and early 1980s included *Rollin' with the Flow* and *Take Me* (Epic, both 1977); *Big Boss Man/Mountain Dew* (RCA, 1977); *Classic Rich* (Epic, 1978); *Classic Rich, Volume 2* (Epic, 1978); *Fool Strikes Again* and *Nobody But You* (U.S., both 1979); *Once a Drifter* (Elektra, 1980); *I Do My Swingin' at Home* (Epic, 1981). Also available during that period was the excellent collection of earlier gems in the Sun Records release of *Sun's Best of Charlie Rich.*

Many of Rich's recordings both on singles and albums from the mid-1970s on were far less satisfying than material he had made as he clawed his way to mass-audience success. For all that, his voice remained one of the most distinctive and easily identifiable ones in all of country music. His performing style at his best was a combination of all the musical influences in his life—gospel, blues, rock, country, and jazz. Perhaps, as his wife, Margaret Ann, suggested, the fact that he was so difficult to typecast was one reason success eluded him for so long. At the same time, once he scored his breakthrough, one difficulty he found it hard to overcome was the desire of record producers to try to pigeonhole him into certain kinds of pop-country arrangements.

The blending of all the elements in his musical persona with Charlie's deep, expressive voice led to a sound that many predicted would be of major importance to the future development of the genre and would also maintain Rich as a talent of legendary proportions. Unfortunately, that potential was largely thwarted, in part due to his continuing fight to overcome alcoholism and also an apparent feeling of inadequacy reflected in an inability to retain his once superb songwriting skills and his seeming acceptance of weaker material provided by others for his recording sessions.

Some of the creative insights of his pre-breakthrough period were shown by the inclusion of a 1972 demo tape of "Feel like Going Home" in the 1982 Columbia album *Rockabilly Stars*. The song styling presented a much darker and introspective tone, and a more compelling effect, than the upbeat version recorded for the 1975 *Silver Fox* album.

Though not completely out of sight from a performing standpoint, Charlie made no new recordings from the early 1980s into the start of the 1990s. That Rich still had things to say musically and lyrically was indicated by his first new album in more than a decade, the 1992 Sire Records release *Pictures and Paintings,* which included incisive renderings of some of his earlier offerings, such as a very effective remake of "Don't Put No Headstones on My Grave" (originally recorded for Sun) and two new songs by wife Margaret Ann. It was a collection that compared with the best he had ever done, though unfortunately not a best-seller. Still, it underscored the fact he remained indeed a talent of legendary proportions.

However, time ran out before he could further exploit that enormous potential. He and Margaret Ann stopped overnight at a motel in Hammond, Louisiana, in mid-summer 1995 on a trip to Florida, when he died from a blood clot on his lungs. Evaluating his career in the *Los Angeles Times* obituary on July 26, Robert Hilburn wrote, "Of all the great country and rock singers who followed Elvis Presley out of the South in the '50s, Charlie Rich came closest to matching the soulful purity of Presley's voice. . . . Despite the acclaim and sales, Rich never felt comfortable in the spotlight. If he weren't so shy and insecure, he surely would have been an even bigger commercial success. But maybe it was those inner tensions that gave his artistry such a warm and revealing edge."—*A. S.*

RICH, DON: *Singer, guitarist, fiddler, songwriter. Born Olympia, Washington, August 15, 1941; died 1974.*

Recognized as one of the best lead guitarists in country music, Don Rich played an important role in the rise of superstar Buck Owens, performing as lead musician of Buck's backing band, the Buckaroos. In fact, more than once Owens referred to him as "my right arm." Not only did Don meld the Buckaroos into one of the nation's most highly regarded country bands, he also achieved a number of hits of his own as a solo performer or in collaboration with Buck's son, Buddy Alan.

Rich was born and raised in Washington and recalled making his first efforts at playing guitar and singing when he was only three and a half. He progressed rapidly—in fact, at five he was already singing on local radio. When he was six, he took his first violin lessons and before long was fiddling with dance bands and playing violin on local radio shows. He continued to develop his skills and performing credits in his teens and, at fifteen, handled lead guitar for country artist Ted Mitchell.

In 1958, when he was seventeen, he met Buck Owens, who had moved to Washington state during the early phase of his career. Don worked with Owens at dances and on a TV show in the Tacoma area until the success of some of Owens's Capitol recordings caused Buck to return to California. Don stayed on in his home region, completing high school and enrolling in college as a music major with the objective of becoming a teacher.

However, by the end of 1959, Don decided he preferred a career as a musician. In January 1960, he headed south to join Buck on a full-time basis. By then, he could play enough different instruments to qualify as a one-man band, had he decided to do so. After a few years in which Don essentially organized pick-up bands to back Buck in various towns, they decided to form a permanent band that was given the name the Buckaroos. From the early 1960s on, Rich and the band backed Owens on hundreds of singles and dozens of albums, many of them top-10 successes. The band was also on the road as part of the Buck Owens Show several hundred days every year. Later, starting in 1969, Rich and the Buckaroos joined Buck on the *Hee Haw* TV show.

Besides backing Owens, Rich and the Buckaroos made a number of albums of their own from the mid-1960s to the 1970s. The band's debut LP, *The Buckaroos,* came out on Capitol in February 1966. It was followed by *The Buckaroos Strike Again!* (December 1967). Some of the group's other releases were *Rompin' and Stompin'* and *The Buckaroos Play the Hits.* The latter, issued in April 1971, was the first all-instrumental album by the band. On it, Don Rich played a variety of instruments—electric guitar, acoustic rhythm guitar, high third guitar, Dobro, gut string guitar, and fiddle. The other band members at the time were Jerry Wiggins (born Clinton, Oklahoma) on drums and percussion; Doyle Singer (born Danville, Arkansas) on bass guitar; and Jim Shaw on piano, organ, bass, harmonica, and synthesizer. Rich also had a solo LP in the early 1970s titled *That Fiddlin' Man* and recorded several songs with Buddy Alan that did well on the charts, including "Cowboy Convention," a top-20 single in 1970.

Don's career came to an end when he was killed in an auto accident in 1974.

RIDERS IN THE SKY: *Vocal and instrumental group, Fred Labour, born June 3, c. 1949 (vocals, songwriting); Douglas Bruce Green, born March 20, c. 1947 (vocals, guitar, songwriting); Paul Woodrow Chrisman, born Nashville, Tennessee, August 23, c. 1950 (vocals, fiddler, songwriting).*

In an era where there's not much open rangeland left and no one tries to make singing cowboy movies anymore, it's not surprising the "western" part of country & western music has been deemphasized. In fact, more

than a few artists and executives are only too happy to describe the field with the western reference omitted. Still, there remain cowboy elements in modern country songs and records, and one group, Riders in the Sky, in its own way keeps some of the once-popular western music genre alive, albeit typically using humor and a certain amount of satire to keep an audience spanning the age spectrum from preteens to adults more than a little entertained.

The trio was formed in the mid-1970s (the group's debut performance was on November 11, 1977) by Fred Labour (aka Too Slim) with Douglas Bruce Green (aka Ranger Doug) as the original members. Later, the original third member was replaced by Paul Woodrow Chrisman (aka Woody Paul). The three performers and sometime songwriters (whose repertoire includes more than a few self-penned numbers aimed at children, like Green's "One Little Coyote" and "The Cowboys A-B-Cs") have more than a few college years in their resumes, to say the least. Green earned a Master's degree in literature from Vanderbilt University, Labour a degree in wildlife management from the University of Michigan, and Chrisman a doctorate in nuclear engineering from Massachusetts Institute of Technology.

All of them had interests in folk music in general and western classics in particular going back to their teens, and some had fond memories of seeing cowboy films starring people like Gene Autry and Roy Rogers. While their concert, radio, and TV appearances from the late 1970s on featured takeoffs on western music perennials such as the "Mystery of the Lost Ozone" (a song whose lyrics pit good guy environmentalists against bad guys who pollute with things like aerosol sprays), at times they present excellent straight versions of songs like the Sons of the Pioneers' "Tumbling Tumbleweeds," Roy Rogers's "Happy Trails," and Gene Autry's "Back in the Saddle Again."

Looking back on the group's origins, Ranger Doug told Michael Bane of *Country Music* magazine ("20 Questions with Ranger Doug," January/February 1992), that he and Labour differed on whether their concept would succeed after their very first performance in late 1977. "Slim claims that the first night we played . . . it was so much fun. We laughed so hard, and we were laughing days later. He said he knew we had something people would want. I can't say that I had that feeling, honestly."

But Labour, Green, and later, Chrisman kept at it, and the idea blossomed into a show that built up a following throughout the U.S. and, after awhile, in many other countries. During the 1980s, the group gained wide audience recognition from its appearances on Garrison Keillor's National Public Radio program, *The Prairie Home Companion.* The trio also signed a recording contract with Rounder Records that resulted in twelve albums released on that label through the end of the 1980s. By then Riders in the Sky had moved to

MCA Records, which issued the album *Riders' Radio Theater* in 1988. The album title refers to the group's own radio show, which became a staple on NPR in the 1980s. During those years, the group also hosted the *Tumbleweed Theater* movie series for three seasons on the Nashville Network. They also appeared in two 1980s film releases, *Sweet Dreams* and *Wild Horses,* and continued intensive concert work, which totaled some 1,861 performances as of mid-January 1989.

The *Riders' Radio Theater* began on a Nashville-area station, but in 1990 moved to the Emery Theater in Cincinnati, Ohio, where programs were taped by station WVXU at the rate of two shows a night for two nights a month before live audiences. Linda Pender of *Cincinnati Magazine* in the article "Urban Cowboys" (August 1990), described one program where the Riders, after singing a happy birthday and commenting on Jesuit basketball prowess, "welcomed the rest of the company onstage. The Fair Roberta, stage manager. Big Zeno Clinker, sound effects, and Bix Bender, announcer. Radio personalities generally don't look like they sound. . . . So it should be noted that Texas Bix Bender, the Voice That Sold a Million Baby Chicks Over Border Radio, looks exactly like he sounds. Exactly.

"Fact is, everything about *Riders' Radio Theater* looks exactly like it sounds, right down to the ancient *applause* sign. The taping starts with the Riders' hallmark coyote howl, then proceeds on to music. They've warmed up with 'Down the Trail to San Antone' and 'Gold That Critter Down.' . . . Time for commercials; one featuring Woody Paul as Dr. Do-It-Yourself, one featuring Too Slim as Sidemeat (a grizzled cattle cook character), a standard issue western Geezer. A pigeon rises from the bowels of the Emery and escapes into the fly space. Big reaction from the audience, which mystifies the Riders, who can't see the bird. Ah, the charm of live radio."

In the early 1990s, the trio signed with a new record label, Columbia, which issued the album *Harmony Ranch,* aimed at young listeners, in mid-1991. The band had won laurels for an earlier release of that kind when they were on the Rounder roster. That album, *Saddle Pals,* was named Independent Children's Album of the Year in 1986. Woody Paul, the group's highly talented fiddler, commented, "I think there's an innocence about it that kids naturally identify with."

In 1991, the Riders were also featured on a new Saturday morning children's series, *Riders in the Sky,* aired on CBS-TV. Doug, the group's guitarist, said at the time, "There's gonna be three middle-aged, non-mutant singing cowboys on TV."

The group continued its frenetic activities into the mid-1990s with credits that included appearances on the *Grand Ole Opry,* various country music TV network programs, and as participants in the WestFest events organized by another strong supporter of a revival of interest in western music, Michael Martin Murphy. Doug Green and his associates kept stressing their goal was not just to entertain, but to help perpetuate an important part of the nation's musical heritage. As he had told Michael Bane of *Country Music* magazine earlier, ". . . a lot of people think we're making fun of the music; in the West, they understand. We're having fun with it, sharing a lot of laughs about something we all love.

"When we played a lot of colleges, people would ask what real cowboys thought of us, didn't they hate us making fun of them. But all the real cowboys, and people like the Sons of the Pioneers, they said, 'This is great! You're bringing it back with a sense of fun and anybody can understand it.' "

During 1993 they were asked to perform on the concept album being organized by Ray Benson and his band, Asleep at the Wheel, in which many country stars helped record some of the hits of western swing great Bob Wills. Along with such artists as Chet Atkins, Garth Brooks, Vince Gill, Dolly Parton, and others, the Riders helped prepare one of the better tribute albums of the period. The Liberty Records release, *Asleep at the Wheel Tribute to the Music of Bob Wills & the Texas Playboys,* was nominated for 1994 Album of the Year in both the CMA and Grammy Awards polls.

In 1995, the Riders returned to their original label home, Rounder Records, for their next album project. That disc, *Always Drink Upstream from the Herd,* won the trio the Wrangler Award for Outstanding Traditional Album. The trophy was presented to the group members and producer Joey Miskulin during the 35th Annual Western Heritage Awards program at the National Cowboy Hall of Fame in Oklahoma City on March 16, 1996. The Riders in the Sky also were among the acts featured in the Country Hall of Fame's third edition of "An Evening of Country Greats: A Hall of Fame Celebration" taped for telecast on TNN, The Nashville Network, on April 30, 1996. Their second Rounder Records album, *Public Cowboy Number One,* issued in 1996, was a tribute to Gene Autry.

In 1997, Warner Western issued a solo album by Ranger Doug containing 10 original cowboy tunes.

RIMES, LEANN: *Singer, songwriter. Born Jackson, Mississippi, August 28, 1982.*

There was a time when it wasn't unusual for artists in their early teens or even pre-teens to become headliners in the country field, though usually such young performers came from show business families. Yet after Tanya Tucker's sudden rise to stardom at thirteen, country went years without spawning stars of comparable youth—until 1995–96, when thirteen-year-old LeAnn Rimes's strong contralto voice brought her to national prominence. Though not born to show business parents, she showed precocious talent as a small child, and already had completed more than half a decade as a professional performer before her recordings started to show up in the charts in the summer of 1996.

She was born in Mississippi and spent her early years in the small Mississippi town of Flowood, near Jackson. Her parents were high school sweethearts. After they married Belinda Rimes worked as a receptionist while Wilbur Rimes sold equipment for an oil company. Both yearned to start a family, but for a long time it seemed that dream might never be realized. Then, after twelve years, Belinda became pregnant, giving birth to LeAnn in the summer of 1982. Under the circumstances, of course, the child was special to her parents, but she turned out to be even more special than they could have imagined.

Both the Rimeses liked music, yet they had no thoughts of making a career from it. Belinda often sang to her daughter and recalled being surprised, when LeAnn was eighteen months old, when the baby suddenly began to sing along on "Jesus Loves Me." Wilbur, who played guitar after a fashion, also sang to little LeAnn and before she was two she was handling some of the songs he played even better than he could. Before long he began to record her vocals. Listening to some of the old tapes, she told Calvin Baker of *People* magazine ("Rimes with Talent," September 2, 1996), she found them "Kind of cute—I could sing better than I could talk." As she told another interviewer, "My dad has tapes of me doing 'You Are My Sunshine,' 'Getting to Know You' (from the Rodgers and Hammerstein musical *The King and I*) and 'Have Mercy' by the Judds."

At age five, LeAnn performed "Getting to Know You" at a song-and-dance competition and took first place. Afterward, her parents remembered, she told them she wanted to pursue a show business career and try to become a star. With that in mind, the Rimes family relocated to Dallas, Texas, when the girl was six; in 1996, the three called a two-bedroom apartment in the Dallas suburb of Garland home. Hearing about an upcoming audition for the *Annie II* musical, her parents financed a trip to New York for a tryout. She didn't win the role, but when she was seven she made her stage debut in a Dallas musical production of Charles Dickens's *A Christmas Carol*, playing the lead role of Tiny Tim. A year later, in 1990, she got wider exposure when she won the TV *Star Search* competition two weeks in a row with her version of Marty Robbins's "Don't Worry About Me." The victories encouraged her to start thinking about writing original material, her first effort being the 1991 number "Share My Love."

Her early repertoire focused on songs associated with Barbra Streisand and Judy Garland, but after hearing some recordings by the late Patsy Cline she fell in love with Cline's brand of country music. By the start of the 1990s, her unchildlike way with country material earned her a regular place on the *Johnnie High Country Musical Review* staged in Arlington, Texas, and she was still a cast member in the mid-1990s. She told Calvin

Baker that the feeling she put into some of the adult lyrics didn't come from personal experience. "Dad would explain that it was a sad song, and I would sing it that way. I don't think I have to experience anything to sing it."

Besides her stage work, LeAnn added to her following with a series of a cappela performances of the "Star Spangled Banner" at major events. Those appearances included Dallas Cowboys football games, the Walt Garrison Rodeo, and the National Cutting Horse Championship in Forth Worth, Texas. Riding cutting horses, she noted in the mid-1990s, was one of her favorite nonmusical activities, which also included playing tennis, swimming, and attending concerts by other artists. She also opened a concert by Randy Travis at the Starplex in Dallas.

Negative fallout from her growing success came from fellow junior-high students, who subjected her to unwelcome hazing: While she had many friends, she recalled, there were four girls who scared her into leaving school and she continued her studies with a private tutor.

When she was eleven, she and her father felt she was ready to record her debut album. They decided to take the project to the studio in Clovis, New Mexico, where Buddy Holly and the Crickets had been recorded by Norman Petty years ago. Wilbur Rimes handled production chores, and LeAnn's talent so impressed Lyle Walker, who ran the studio, that he sought and gained co-management status with Wilbur. Meanwhile, other industry people had started to become aware of the promise of this young lady. After hearing her sing at a Cowboys game, Bill Mack, a songwriter and disc jockey on a Dallas station, dug out a song called "Blue" he had penned in the early 1960s for Patsy Cline. Before Cline could use it, she died in a plane crash; Mack had filed the song away because, until he heard LeAnn, he couldn't hear anybody but Patsy Cline doing it. (While Mack hadn't pushed it, "Blue" had been recorded earlier by Roy Drusky without much success.) He offered it to Rimes and she decided to include it in the new album. Wilbur at first rejected the song as being "too old" for his daughter. But, he told David Zimmerman of *USA Today* ("At 13, She's a Singing Star," June 11, 1996), "she said, 'No daddy, I love that song.' She put that little yodel lick in it and I said, 'That's it. She made it her own.'"

The debut album, *After All*, was issued on the independent Nor Va Jak label in 1994 and sold modestly on the regional market. LeAnn included many of the tracks in her concert sets, which by 1995 encompassed over 100 appearances either as an opening act or a headliner in small venues. The album wasn't a best-seller, but it attracted attention from a number of major record executives, including Mike Curb. He recalled, "Someone sent me her CD. I put it on and everyone just turned their heads and said, 'Who is that?'" Accompanied by his two teenage daughters, he tracked LeAnn down and signed her for his MCG/Curb label.

For her first Curb album it was decided to include a reworked version of "Blue," as well as another track from *After All*, "I'll Get Even with You." The disc included "Talk to Me," cowritten by LeAnn, Ron Grimes, and Jon Rutherford, and a duet with Eddy Arnold on his long-time standard, "Cattle Call." Rimes noted, "It was Mike Curb's idea to do the song. Eddy Arnold was great. He kind of adopted me as his granddaughter and then as his daughter."

Before the album came out, the thirteen-year-old faced the tough test of winning approval from some 24,000 people at one of the sessions of the annual Fan Fair event in Nashville. It turned out to be a triumph and fans, media members, and listeners to radio coverage of the concert expressed amazement at LeAnn's poise and vocal excellence. Some music industry members worried a little about what the future might hold for so young a performer. Songwriter Wayne Perry (writer of the Tim McGraw hit, "Not a Moment Too Soon") commented to reporter Miriam Longino, "I'm happy for her, but I hope she's careful. I've seen it so many times. I call it Fame and Misfortune. An artist works so hard to get to the top of the mountain, but things look really different once you're up there. I hope there's someone there to protect her."

Her parents told Zimmerman of *USA Today* they were aware of the pitfalls. Belinda said, "We want her to grow up and be a stable human being, and I hope we can take her through this and make that happen." Wilbur added, "Life's a struggle anyway you go at it. You just hope."

The first track issued from the album was "Blue," which the print media acclaimed as a striking example of LeAnn's abilities. Radio programmers were slow in using it, though it did manage to gain the top 10 on singles charts. But the disc did well enough for Curb to rush out a video version that June. The album, also called *Blue*, came out on July 9, 1996, and quickly gained not just the country charts, but the general hit lists. In fact, it debuted at number three on the *Billboard 200* on its way to gold record status and higher. In the summer and fall, many top country performers sought to have LeAnn on their concert rosters.

In the voting for the 1996 Country Music Association Awards, "Blue" was nominated for Single of the Year and LeAnn was a finalist for the Horizon Award. She didn't win either trophy, but her singing on the internationally televised awards show in October 1996 made millions of viewers agree they very likely were watching a major star of the future. And, in a remarkable moment, February of 1997 saw Rimes win a Grammy Award as Best New Artist of 1996: A rare accolade for a country performer, and a confirmation that, at the age of fourteen, LeAnn Rimes had arrived.

RITTER, TEX: *Singer, guitarist, actor, author, songwriter. Born Nederland, Texas, January 12, 1906; died Nashville, Tennessee, January 2, 1974. Inducted into Country Music Hall of Fame in 1964.*

The epitome of a man of the West, Tex Ritter achieved many firsts in his long career in entertainment. His credits as performer and writer covered almost every major phase of western lore from cowboy songs to a pioneering radio program, *The Lone Ranger.* Appropriately, he was one of the first five individuals voted into the new Country Music Hall of Fame in 1964, a year when he also was serving as president of the Country Radio Association (a post he also held in 1965).

Ritter was a true son of pioneer heritage. Born Maurice Woodward Ritter on a farm and ranch in Nederland, Panola County, Texas, he began to learn the basics of roping and riding from his earliest years. The land, settled by his great-grandfather in 1830, was a 400-acre homestead his forebears claimed when it still was part of Mexico. The youngest of six children born to James Everett and Elizabeth Matthews Ritter, Tex grew up in an atmosphere much like that re-created in countless western movies, with cattle roundups and ranch hands spinning tall stories or singing songs in their leisure time in the bunkhouse.

From an early age, he demonstrated a promising singing voice. However, when he graduated from high school in 1922 (with honors), he wasn't thinking about a show business career. Instead, he enrolled as a law major at the University of Texas. While there Tex impressed his classmates and instructors with his knowledge of Texas folklore and eventually worked out a combined singing and lecturing program.

Invitations to give his show, called *The Texas Cowboy and His Songs,* caused Ritter to wander farther and farther afield from the university. When one tour took him to Chicago, he settled there for a while and enrolled at Northwestern University to continue his law studies. He sang on local stations, where audience acceptance made him think of trying for bigger things in radio and theater. He left Chicago for New York in 1930.

One of the first things he did after arriving was to join the New York Theatre Guild. In 1931, this led to his appearing in the Broadway play *Green Grow the Lilacs,* a play by Lynn Riggs that gave graphic insight into the ranch country of Ritter's youth and provided the basis for the blockbusting Rodgers and Hammerstein musical *Oklahoma!*

Tex wanted to add to his radio credits, but many New York programmers doubted that eastern audiences would take to his strong Texas drawl. He persisted, and once he was on the air, the flood of favorable mail proved his point. Tex rapidly became an important factor in both regional and national radio fields. As a writer and performer, he played a key role in the original *Lone Ranger* series. During the 1930s, he performed on such major radio shows as *Death Valley Days, Tex Ritter's Camp Fire,* and *Cowboy Tom's Round-Up.* In 1933, he embarked on a recording career, signing with Columbia Records and turning out the first of hundreds of singles and albums.

With his background, Ritter was a natural for the burgeoning western film industry. In the mid-1930s, this prompted a move from New York to Hollywood. He first signed with Grand National Films in 1936 and completed his first movie, *Song of the Gringo,* the same year. In the years that followed, he made many more westerns, mostly from the mid-1930s through the mid-1950s, taking part in about eighty films in all. He worked for such studios as Monogram, Columbia, and Universal. When not making films, he toured the country coast-to-coast with his own company, playing to enthusiastic audiences at theaters, rodeos, and state fairs. Tex's personal magnetism continued to attract audiences all through his life, though he cut back sharply on in-person work by the second half of the 1960s.

In the 1950s and 1960s, he also was featured on many major TV shows, both general variety and country & western. After the western movie field slowed down with the advent of TV, Ritter left California for a new home in Nashville, where he soon was a regular on the *Grand Ole Opry.*

In the early 1970s, Ritter continued to be active in country-music industry affairs. He narrated the Country Music Association album *Thank You, Mr. President* and also presented it to then-president Richard Nixon. In 1971, Ritter was given the Founding President's award by the CMA and in 1971 headed the CMA United Nations overseas tour. In October 1973, Tex delivered a speech in tribute to members of the Hall of Fame at the Country Music Association Anniversary Banquet.

Ritter was Capitol Records' first country artist when he signed with that company in 1942. His association with the label extended over three decades, into the 1970s. His early work for Capitol included such albums as *Children's Songs and Stories by Tex Ritter, Cowboy Favorites by Tex Ritter, Tex Ritter and the Dinning Sisters,* and *Sunday School for Children.* Among his many singles releases (a number of which featured original songs by him) were "Someone," "There's a Gold Star in Her Window," "There's a New Moon over My Shoulder," "Jealous Heart," "You Two-Timed Me One Time Too Often," "One Little Tear Drop Too Often," "Have I Told You Lately That I Love You," "Rye Whiskey," "Boll Weevil," "Dallas Darlin'," "Deck of Cards," "Fort Worth Jail," "You Are My Sunshine," "Bad Brahma Bull," "I've Got Five Dollars, and It's Saturday Night," "Pledge of Allegiance," "The Fiery Bear," and "Blood on the Saddle."

Tex placed several dozen singles on country hit charts over the years, including a number of songs that reached the top 10. His first major success came in 1948 with his top-10 single of Al Dexter's "Rock and Rye Rag." In 1952, he had a major pop hit with his single "High Noon," the title song from the Gary Cooper film classic of the same name, that stayed in the top 10 on pop charts for months. In 1961, he scored a top-10 hit with "I Dreamed of a Hillbilly Heaven," a song he cowrote with Eddie Dean and Hal Sothern. In 1967, he once more graced upper-chart levels with "Just Beyond the Moon."

His Capitol albums included *Songs* (4/58), *Blood on the Saddle* (2/60), *Border Affair* (12/63), *Friendly Voice* (11/65), *Hillbilly Heaven* (12/65), *Best of Tex Ritter* (11/66), *Just Beyond the Moon* (9/67), *Sweet Land of Liberty* (6/67), *Green Green Valley* (late 1960s); *Super-countrylegendary* (early 1970s), and the three-record set, *The Legendary Tex Ritter* (11/73). He also was represented on Pickwick with *Tex Ritter Sings His Hits* (11/67) and *My Kinda Songs* (two discs, early 1970s) and on Hilltop with *Love You Big as Texas.*

During the second half of 1973, Tex completed a new single, a recitative written by Gordon Sinclair of Canada titled "The Americans (A Canadian's Opinion)," which was released by Capitol in early January 1974, a few days after Ritter's death. On January 2, 1974, he suffered a heart attack while visiting a friend. He was rushed to Baptist Hospital after first aid was administered, but could not be revived, and died at 7 P.M.

The bronze plaque in his honor at the Hall of Fame sums up his contributions. "One of America's most illustrious and versatile stars of radio, television, records, motion pictures, and Broadway stage. Untiring pioneer and champion of the country music industry, his devotion to his God, his family, and his country is a continuing inspiration to his countless friends throughout the world."

His album titles still in the active catalog of Capitol Records at the end of the 1970s were *An American Legend, The Best of Tex Ritter, Blood on the Saddle,* and *Hillbilly Heaven.*

During the 1980s and 1990s, few in the new generations of country & western fans knew who Tex was. His children didn't emulate his music interests, though John Ritter achieved much wider name recognition than his father from his work in films and as the star of the TV comedy sitcom *Three's Company* and a series of TV movies. Tex's voice could still be heard on TV reruns of some of the classic western films, like *High Noon,* for which he provided soundtrack material.

Collections of his recordings available in the mid-1990s included an album in Capitol Records' *Collector's Series* and an MCA Records anthology, *Tex Ritter: Country Music Hall of Fame Series,* included in the Country Music Foundation catalog and also offered by MCA as part of its Texas City Music catalog. Featured in the latter were some of his first recordings in the 1935–39 time period, including numbers like "Get Along

Little Dogies," "Lady Killin' Cowboy," and "Sing, Cowboy, Sing," the title song of one of his western films.

In *Life* magazine's September 1994 special issue, "The Roots of Country Music," Ritter was included in the editors' list of "The 100 Most Important People in the History of Country."

ROBBINS, HARGUS "PIG": *Pianist, keyboard musician, composer. Born Spring City, Tennessee.*

The session musicians, who play the instruments to back the singer or singers on a recording, are often extremely important to the sound of a particular record, but they seldom achieve star status. Hargus "Pig" Robbins, however, is one session musician who gained enough fame to become a soloist in his own right.

Hargus learned to play piano at the Tennessee School for the Blind in Nashville, which was where he went to school. He wanted to play country music but his instructors didn't teach country songs, so he taught himself to play in the country style he heard on the radio and on records. At age fifteen, he stopped the lessons and began to develop his own style.

After he graduated from high school, Hargus played in Nashville clubs and at parties. When he played piano for a friend's demo record, his playing attracted more attention than his friend's singing. Soon he decided to join the Musicians Union and become a session musician. A couple of years later he had already become one of the top keyboard session musicians in Nashville.

Robbins first attracted a great deal of attention when he played piano on George Jones's hit single "White Lightnin'" in 1960. Since that time, he has backed countless major country-music singers. He has also played piano for many rock musicians. He backed Bob Dylan on his album *Blonde on Blonde,* and he has backed Simon and Garfunkel, among others. In the 1950s he recorded his own rock 'n' roll album, for which he also did the vocals, under the name of Mel Robbins, but the LP failed to become a hit.

By the late 1970s, Hargus's musicianship had been honored through the receipt of some top awards. In 1976 he was named the Country Music Association's Instrumentalist of the Year. In 1977 he was accorded a similar honor by the Academy of Country Music. He was also voted Most Valuable Player by the Nashville chapter of the Recording Arts and Sciences in 1977. That year the NARAS Nashville chapter also named him Super Picker of the Year. In 1978, "Pig," as he is sometimes called, won a Grammy Award for Country Instrumentalist of the Year.

The honors he had been receiving enabled Robbins to embark on a solo recording career. In 1977 he signed with Elektra Asylum Records. His first album was entitled *Country Instrumentalist of the Year.* He produced the album himself, and he was accompanied by some of the finest Nashville musicians.

Hargus's second album was *Pig in a Poke.* Once again, he produced the LP himself and arranged all the songs. Again he was backed by some of the finest Nashville session musicians. The album featured a lot of old standard songs as well as an original composition, "Roamin' Round." He performed at the Wembley Country Music Festival in England in March 1978. In 1981, Hargus was again one of the five finalists for CMA Instrumentalist of the Year Award as was to be the case for the three following years.

For the balance of the 1980s and into the 1990s, Robbins continued to be a favorite keyboards player with Nashville record producers and performers. His name appeared on album credits for many stars of those years including some of Dolly Parton's mid-1990s releases and Johnny Rodriguez's 1996 disc, *You Can Say That Again.—A. S.*

ROBBINS, MARTY: *Singer, guitarist, pianist, songwriter, race car driver. Born Glendale, Arizona, September 26, 1925; died Nashville, Tennessee, December 8, 1982. Elected to Country Music Hall of Fame in 1982.*

One of the great names in modern country & western music, Marty Robbins seemed to epitomize the strengths and virtues of the legendary cowboy. Brought up in cowboy country, he became one of the most beloved interpreters of cowboy ballads and updated country-flavored pop variants. Survival against often sizable odds was his trademark, both as a performer and an individual. In the highly competitive modern C&W field, he remained a top-ranked writer and singer from the 1950s into the 1980s. In his personal life, he disregarded the dangers of high speed racing, continuing to compete despite several near fatal accidents; he also bounced back from a massive heart attack, keeping strong and active for many years thereafter before succumbing to a heart condition in late 1982.

Robbins's saga began in a rural area of Arizona in the small town of Glendale, where he was born and spent his first twelve years. One of a family of nine children (seven brothers and one sister), he recalls the lonesome atmosphere of the desert region his family called home, and the warm family life that centered around his father and grandfather. His father played the harmonica, one of the earliest musical influences on Marty, and his grandfather, who had worked as a traveling medicine man, was a teller of tales and singer of cowboy songs.

"His name was 'Texas' Bob Heckle. He had two little books of poetry he would sell. I used to sing him church songs and he would tell me stories. A lot of the songs I've written, with the exception of 'El Paso,' were brought about because of stories he told me. Like 'Big Iron' I wrote because he was a Texas Ranger. At least he told me he was."

Western movies were also an influence on young Marty. Gene Autry was a particular idol and Marty sometimes worked mornings picking cotton at a field ten miles away from home to earn enough to see the latest Autry film. He recalled sitting in the first row, "Close enough so I could have gotten sand in the eyes from the horses and powder burns from the guns. . . . I wanted to be the cowboy singer, simply because Autry was my favorite singer. No one else inspired me."

In 1937, the family moved to Phoenix, where Marty later attended high school. When he was nineteen, he signed up for a three-year hitch in the Navy, his first opportunity to see the world beyond Arizona. While he was stationed in the Pacific, he learned to play the guitar and, before long, was using it as an aid in writing his own songs. After he was discharged, toward the end of the 1940s, he went back home with some thoughts about a performing career. When a friend who had a local band gave him the chance to work with the group on occasion, Robbins snapped at it. As he gained experience, he began to seek more opportunities to do solo work, which led to more club dates in and around Phoenix. In between engagements, he sometimes earned money by working on construction projects.

While driving a brick truck one day, he listened to a local country show on radio station KPHO. He sought out the program director, told him he thought he could do better than the cowboy singer, and won a place on the program. KPHO-TV provided an opportunity for Marty to fill in for a nonshowing guest, which eventually led to hosting his own show, *Western Caravan*. Little Jimmy Dickens guested on the show one day and was so impressed by Robbins's ability that when he got to California, he suggested that his label, Columbia, look into the matter. A company official went to Phoenix, agreed with Dickens, and soon Robbins was a Columbia recording artist.

His first release on the label was "Love Me or Leave Me Alone." Neither this nor his second single was a blockbuster, but things changed sharply with the next release, "I'll Go It Alone," a top-10 hit, as was another original composition, "I Couldn't Keep from Crying." Soon after that, Fred Rose of Acuff-Rose Music Publishing flew to Phoenix to sign Marty as a writer. With that kind of interest and a growing list of credits for appearances in major western cities, it didn't take long before the *Grand Ole Opry* also beckoned. Within six months after *Opry* manager Harry Stone had arranged for Marty's initial guest appearance, Robbins was asked to become a regular (the year was 1953). He moved to Nashville, where, besides appearing on the Saturday night main *Opry* program, he did an early morning show on station WSM. Over a quarter of a century later, Robbins still was a mainstay on the *Opry*.

Things slowed a bit for Marty in 1954, when he failed to dent the country top 10, but in 1955 he was back again with the hit "That's All Right." In 1956, he achieved his first number-one-ranked song with "Singing the Blues," the beginning of a long string of such top hits. In fact, two of his three top-10 hits of 1957 made the uppermost rung—"Knee Deep in the Blues," "The Story of My Life," and "White Sport Coat." The latter, written by Marty, was a major hit in the pop field as well as country and made Robbins a national celebrity. His status continued for the remainder of the decade; he turned out such hits as his composition "She Was Only Seventeen" in 1958, "Stairway of Love" in 1958, and one of his all-time favorite compositions in 1959, "El Paso."

At the start of the 1960s, he had another major hit, "Big Iron," followed in later years with "Don't Worry (Like All the Other Times)" and "It's Your World," both in 1961; "Devil Woman" in 1962; number-one-ranked "Beggin' to You" in 1963; "One of These Days" and "The Cowboy in the Continental Suit" in 1964, all written by him. He also gained top-10 status for other writers' songs with such singles as "Ruby Ann" (number one) in 1962, "Ribbon of Darkness" (number one) in 1965, "The Shoe Goes on the Other Foot Tonight" in 1966, and "Tonight, Carmen" in 1967. During the 1960s, he received several awards, including a Grammy in 1960 for "El Paso," also named the Best Country & Western Recording. It was the first Grammy presented for a country song.

At the end of the 1960s, Robbins suffered a massive heart attack that shocked and worried his legions of fans. Tens of thousands of cards and letters of encouragement poured into the hospital where he underwent surgery and to his home, where he was recuperating. By the start of the 1970s, though, he was back in full swing, giving little indication of any undue concern or letup. Within a short time he had another major country hit with his composition "My Woman, My Woman, My Wife." The song earned him a second Grammy, this time for the Best Country Song of 1970.

Another love of Marty's that worried friends, family, and fans for many years was his infatuation with fast cars. During the 1960s, he started to indulge a longtime desire by racing stock cars on dirt tracks. He proved to be a cool and capable driver and, continuing even after his heart seizure, he progressed from local events to the big time, the National Association of Stock Car Auto Racing (NASCAR) Grand National Division, where he could compete against people like Richard Petty and Cale Yarbrough. In 1972, he did so well in one of his first efforts on major NASCAR tracks that he was named Rookie of the Southern 500. In July 1974, the racing fraternity held a Marty Robbins Night in honor of his contributions to the sport. However, the next year, three hair-raising crashes caused him to heed the pleas of close associates and concentrate on music. In one of those races, at Charlotte, North Carolina, he deliberately hit a concrete wall at over 145 mph to avoid slamming broadside into another driver's stalled car.

Over the decades as a recording artist, Robbins turned out over sixty albums. The first to earn him a gold record was *Gunfighter Ballads and Trail Songs,* issued by Columbia in September 1959, which included the song "El Paso." Other releases on the label included such LPs as *Singing the Blues* (1956, reissued on Harvard 9/69); *The Song of Robbins* (1957); *Song of the Islands* (2/58); *Marty's Greatest Hits* (1958); *Marty Robbins* (12/58); *More Gunfighter Ballads and Trail Songs* (9/60); *More Greatest Hits* (6/61); *Just a Little Sentimental* (10/61); *Portrait of Marty* (10/62); *Devil Woman* (11/62); *Hawaii's Calling Me* (8/63); *Return of the Gunfighters* (11/63); *Island Woman* (1964); *R.F.D.* (10/64); *Turn the Lights Down Low* (3/65); *What God Has Done* (3/66); *The Drifter* (9/66); *My Kind of Country* (5/67); *Tonight, Carmen* (9/67); *It's a Sin* (8/69); *Marty's Country* (11/69); *My Woman, My Woman, My Wife* (6/70); *Marty Robbins' Greatest Hits, Volume III* (6/71); *Marty Robbins Today* (9/71); *The World of Marty Robbins* (12/71); *Marty Robbins's All Time Greatest Hits* (9/72); and *Bound for Old Mexico* (11/72). Other Columbia titles are *I've Got a Woman's Love, Streets of Laredo, Marty Robbins Favorites, The Story of My Life, Saddle Tramp, The Bend in the River, Heart of Marty Robbins, From the Heart, Have I Told You Lately That I Love You, El Paso City, Adios Amigo, Alamo, Best of the Gold '50s, Vol. I, Best of the Gold '50s, Vol. II, Best of the Gold '60s, Marty After Midnight, By the Time I Get to Phoenix, Christmas with Marty Robbins, Country Hymns, Country Love, Vol. II and Vol. III, Country's Greatest Hits, Greatest C&W Hits, No Sign of Loneliness, 20 Years of Number One Hits, World of Country Giants,* and *World's Favorite Hymns.*

Marty also was represented by several albums on the MCA label. These included *This Much a Man, Marty Robbins,* and *Good and Country.*

Over the years his in-person appearances took him to all corners of the United States and Canada and made him a favorite with overseas audiences as well. During the 1970s, he made regular tours of England, Australia, and Japan as well as occasional swings through many other countries. Although his concerts numbered in the hundreds at some points in his career, by the end of the 1970s, he limited them to a still sizable average of eighty a year. His TV appearances could fill several pages as well. Beside guesting on many network shows, including, in the late 1970s, *Dean Martin's Music Country* and *The Midnight Special,* he had his own TV series for a number of years. In the occasional TV versions of the *Grand Ole Opry* (which remained primarily a radio show), he was always prominently featured. In addition, he took part in ten movies over the years, including a singing cowboy role in the film *Guns of a Stranger.*

As of the late 1970s, Robbins's achievements were among the more monumental ones of modern country music. By then he had written over 500 songs, won over twenty-five BMI awards for songwriting excellence,

had a top-10 record all but one year since 1959, had one or more chart records for nineteen straight years, and been on *Billboard* magazine charts 73 percent of the time over almost two decades. He also had been voted into the Nashville Songwriters Association Hall of Fame, with the CMA Hall of Fame election certain sometime in the future.

Robbins's singles hits in the early and mid-1970s included "Jolie Girl" in 1970; "Love Me/Crawlin' on My Knees" in 1973; "El Paso City" and "Among My Souvenirs" in 1976; and "I Don't Know Why, I Just Do" in 1977.

Marty finished the decade with one of his better years as a singles artist, having four releases in top-chart positions at various times: "Please Don't Play a Love Song," "Buenos Dias Argentina," "All Around Cowboy," and "Touch Me with Magic." In the early 1980s, he still did reasonably well, though the uppermost levels seemed to elude him. In 1980, his chart singles included "She's Made of Faith" and "An Occasional Rose"; in early 1981, "Completely out of Love" was in the top 50. "She's Made of Faith" and "Completely out of Love" were Robbins's compositions. In the early 1980s, he continued to be a featured artist on the *Grand Ole Opry.*

In 1982, when Marty was nominated for the Country Music Hall of Fame, the biography presented to CMA voters cited some of his many firsts. It was pointed out he was the first winner of a Grammy Award for a country song (1960 Best Country & Western Performance for "El Paso"; he won a second Grammy a decade later for "My Woman, My Woman, My Wife," named Best Country Song). He was also the first Nashville artist to be booked into Las Vegas and the first person to perform at the new Opry House in 1974.

As succeeding events demonstrated, he was fortunate in being elected to the Hall while he could personally savor the well-deserved honor on the October 1982 CMA Awards TV program. He also could enjoy another chart hit for the single "Some Memories Won't Die" before his heart gave out in early December.

In the years since then his memory has remained green as his hit recordings have continued to find airtime on radio stations at home and abroad. Tributes to his accomplishments continued to be made not only by artists who knew him personally, but also by generations of new stars. Many of his albums remained in print or were reissued during the 1980s and 1990s. Columbia/Legacy collections included *The Essential Marty Robbins 1951–82* and, in 1995, the first CD version of his classic *Song of Robbins* album, initially issued in 1957.

Besides *The Essential Marty Robbins,* the Country Music Foundation catalog in the mid-1990s offered five other Robbins collections. These were: *Marty Robbins/American Original, Marty Robbins/A Lifetime of Songs, Marty Robbins/Biggest Hits,* all on Columbia;

Marty Robbins/All Time Greatest Hits on Capitol; and, on the German Bear Family Country label, a five-CD boxed set titled *Marty Robbins Country 1951–1958.* Some of his music also was included in *Columbia Country Classics, Volume 2, Honky Tonk Heroes.*

Videos on the market in the mid-1990s included *Marty Robbins and Ernest Tubb* (featuring twelve Robbins live performances from 1954–56); *Marty Robbins: A Man and His Music;* and *The Best of the Marty Robbins Show* (culled from 1968–69 segments of his syndicated TV series). Some of his on-stage or TV renditions were also included in various video compilations.

The Bear Family Records group also had other compilations available as import items in the 1990s. These were *Marty Robbins: Country 1960–1966* and *Marty Robbins: Under Western Skies.* The last named, Bear Family stated, included the complete contents of his western albums offering such tracks as "El Paso," "Big Iron," and "The Cowboy in the Continental Suit." Each of these sets comprised four CDs. His albums still in the Columbia catalogue continued to sell as indicated by the R.I.A.A. certification of *Greatest Hits, Volume III* (originally issued on April 30, 1971) as gold on February 16, 1995.

ROBERTSON, DON: *Singer, instrumentalist (piano, organ, trumpet, trombone, tenor horn), arranger, composer, conductor. Born Peking, China, December 5, 1922.*

Few songwriters in the country & western field could claim as many successes as Donald Irwin Robertson. The greatest artists of the last forty years beat a path to his door for compositions for new song hits. His background as a skilled musician led to the development of several piano styles, including creation of the country style of piano, later popularized by Floyd Cramer, and an adaptation of the bluegrass banjo pickin' sound for the keyboard.

Don was introduced to music at the age of four by his mother, a talented amateur pianist and poet. The family was then living in China, where Don's father was head of the Department of Medicine at Peking Union Medical College. When Don was five, the family moved to Boston, then Chicago, where Dr. Robertson served as a professor at the University of Chicago. Young Don continued his piano lessons and began composing at seven. His first bent was classical music, particularly since his father often listened to symphonies in the evenings. Don also enjoyed singing hymns during these years in his church choir.

When Don was nine, the family began spending summer vacations at Birchwood Beach in Michigan, near the home of the Carl Sandburg family. The families became close friends and Robertson learned many folk and western ballads at Sandburg's knee as well as receiving instruction in guitar chording.

Don's interest in music continued when he entered high school. In order to join the school band, he learned

several brass instruments. Meanwhile, he began to play piano with local dance bands, becoming a professional musician at fourteen.

He also pursued his interest in writing poetry, prose, and short stories. This later provided a foundation for his lyric writing. His father hoped Robertson would follow in his footsteps, and Don did take a premed course at the University of Chicago. However, he finally resolved the conflict in favor of music and dropped out of college in his fourth year. Soon after, he was working as a music arranger at station WGN in Chicago.

In 1945 Robertson moved to Los Angeles, playing in nightclubs and augmenting his living by making demonstration records of new songs for publishers and songwriters. This eventually led to a job as a demonstration pianist with Capitol Records. Don had written many kinds of music up to this time, including symphonic and jazz compositions. Now he began to concentrate on folk and country material, reflecting the earlier influence of Carl Sandburg.

After writing dozens of songs, some in collaboration, and after many months of turndowns from singers and publishers, Don finally clicked with Hill and Range in 1953. The firm placed three of his songs with Rosemary Clooney, Eddy Arnold, and Frankie Laine, and one, "I Let Her Go," was a mild hit. In 1954, however, Don's career moved into high gear when Eddy Arnold scored a major hit with "I Really Don't Want to Know." The song became a country standard, providing Robertson with a BMI Award, a total of more than one hundred fifty versions by different recording artists, and sales of more than 5 million through 1969. Hank Snow also had a hit in 1954 with Don's "I Don't Hurt Anymore," which stayed on the charts for half a year.

Don had a string of smash successes for the balance of the 1950s. Those included "You're Free to Go" (Carl Smith); "Condemned Without Trial" (Eddy Arnold); "Unfaithful" (Hank Snow); "Go Back You Fool" (Faron Young); "Hummingbird" (Les Paul with Mary Ford); "Born to Be with You" (the Chordettes); "I'm Counting on You" (Elvis Presley, Kitty Wells); and "Please Help Me I'm Falling" (Hank Locklin). The latter, which gained Robertson an ASCAP Award, sold more than two million records.

In 1956, Don scored a major hit with his own recording of "The Happy Whistler," which reached number nine on the pop charts. Throughout his career Don provided piano or other instrumental backing for many top artists and groups, including Nat Cole, Elvis Presley, Waylon Jennings, Jessi Colter, Ann Margret, Al Martino, Ray Price, and Charley Pride. During these years he wrote twelve songs especially for Elvis Presley, including "Anything That's a Part of You," "There's Always Me," "Marguerita," "They Remind Me Too Much of You," "Love Me Tonight," "No More," and "I'm Yours."

During the 1960s, Robertson continued to turn out

hit compositions. These included "I Love You More and More Each Day" (Al Martino); "Does He Mean That Much to You" (Eddy Arnold); "Ninety Miles an Hour," "I Stepped over the Line," "The Queen of Draw Poker Town" (Hank Snow); "Wallpaper Roses" (Jerry Wallace); "Go Away" (Nancy Wilson); "Ringo" (Lorne Greene); "Longing to Hold You Again" (Skeeter Davis); "Outskirts of Town," "Watching My World Fall Apart" (the Browns).

RCA Victor issued an LP on which Don played a dozen of his hits, titled *Heart on My Sleeve.* In 1966 he signed a new contract with Victor for recordings under the supervision of A&R producer Chet Atkins.

When the Country Music Hall of Fame was opened in 1967, Robertson's name was one of those proudly displayed in the "Walkway of Stars."

Visitors to Disneyland in California, Disney World in Florida, and Tokyo Disneyland can hear Don (in his disguise as Gomer the computerized bear) featured at the piano playing his own composition, "Piano," in the opening number of the Country Bear Jamboree.

In 1972 Don was inducted into the Nashville Songwriters Association's Hall of Fame.

Some of Don's collaborators (usually mainly providing lyrics to his music) have been: Hal Blair, Howard Barnes, Jack Rollins, Lou Herscher, John Crutchfield, Sheb Wooley, Harold Spina, and Jack Clement. In the 1980s, Don wrote some songs with Billy Swan. He recalled, "Billy put out an album and some singles. Three of the singles got into the 20s and 50s [chart positions] on the charts. At one point, I played keyboards on stage for the Kris Kristofferson/Billy Swan show at the Greek Theatre in Los Angeles' Griffith Park." His song catalog continued to find favor with performers, both newcomers and veterans. Bob Dylan's 1988 album, *Down in the Groove,* included Robertson's "Ninety Miles an Hour (Down a Dead End Street)." In 1994–95, rising young country star John Berry included the song in two of his albums and it also was the B side of a number one single release of Berry's.

In the latter half of the 1980s, Don was relatively inactive as a songwriter or musician, but in the 1990s he picked up the pace in both areas. His activities in the early 1990s included playing piano for Hank Locklin on two occasions at the *Grand Ole Opry* when Locklin performed "Please Help Me I'm Falling." By the mid-1990s, Don had added many more performing credits to his resume and also started writing new songs in Nashville, mainly with longtime friend Jack Clement. "I also started working on some material with Hal Blair, who cowrote 'Please Help Me I'm Falling' with me and John Crutchfield, who cowrote [the Charley Pride hit] "'Does My Ring Hurt Your Finger'" with Jack Clement. It's been a lot of fun," he said in 1996. "I've been amazed at how much of my skills came back."

He demonstrated his performing skills with Clement and others on a number of occasions in 1995. He, Clement, and Joe Allen (writer of many hits by Gene Watson) performed at the Tin Pan South show in Nashville in April and in July he played keyboards in the band at the Chance Martin Benefit at the Wildhorse Saloon in Nashville "backing, among others, Johnny Cash, June Carter and Waylon Jennings. I also performed three times in 1995 at the Georgia Governor's mansion for Governor Zel Miller and the Georgia State Legislature. That included playing keyboards and singing harmony with Waylon, Jessi Colter and Jack on a Christmas TV special from the mansion."

Meanwhile, new recordings of some of his standards continued to appear. Anne Murray recorded "I Really Don't Want to Know" and "Born to Be with You" in her 1994 album, *Croonin'.* The latter song also was released as a single in Canada. That same year "Please Help Me I'm Falling" was in the soundtracks for two films, *A Perfect World* (with Kevin Costner and Clint Eastwood) and *Body Snatchers.* The song also was performed by Dolly Parton, Tammy Wynette, and Loretta Lynn in their 1993 album *Honky Tonk Angels* and in recordings by Sweethearts of the Rodeo.

Though Don was just beginning to resume his songwriting efforts in 1994–96 "getting into computer controlled methods to put together demos with a one man band," he was encouraged by the way his earlier songs seemed to find new life in the 1990s. "There seems to be a lot more interest among performers in the old standards. 'Please Help Me I'm Falling' is doing better now than when it first came out."

On November 1, 1994, when *Billboard* published a list of the 100 most popular country songs of all time, "Please Help Me I'm Falling" was number two. Looking back on the song's origins, Robertson recalled placing a grey metal desk and a filing cabinet ordered from Sears in 1955 in his living room in a small tract house in the San Fernando Valley as key items in his songwriting occupation. "One file drawer (now several) I devoted to creative fragments: titles, lyric phrases, melodic phrases on manuscript sheets, chord sequences, thoughts. I have always found that I have times when I have so many ideas I can hardly put them down fast enough, and other times when I haven't got an original thought in my head. When ideas are not forthcoming, I go through my files and try to find something interesting to work on and try to bring it to the next stage: organizing, developing, arranging.

"One day in 1959 I was with one of my frequent collaborators, Hal Blair. We began flipping through my fragment drawer. When something sparked his interest I pulled it out and set it aside as a possibility. As I recall, he picked out 2 or 3 that day. One was 'Please Help Me I'm Falling.' It had been in my file for more than a year. I had the title, the melody (complete, as I remember) and a few lines of lyric. Hal and I sequestered ourselves in an old rented house nearby, empty except for a piano and a couple of chairs and a working kitchen, and went to work [on the song]. I would hum and sing and play it over and over, working out the arrangement as I went along, and Hal would throw out lines and we would try out lines on each other, looking for ones that would work, lines that would sing well as well as carrying the emotional impact of our little musical scene. We worked on it pretty much non-stop for a couple of days until the song and the arrangement and my performance felt right to both of us."

They then presented the song to publisher Julian Aberbach (of the legendary Aberbach brothers who owned Hill & Range, Elvis Presley Music, etc.) at the company's Hollywood Boulevard office. "Julian said he was sure he could get a 'top country artist' to record it. A few days later I made a piano and voice demo at Gold Star recording studios in Hollywood and gave it to Julian along with a lead sheet. Julian, in turn, took it to RCA and it ended up in the hands of producer/musician Chet Atkins in Nashville. Chet liked it and, as I understand the sequence of events, at first presented it to Jim Reeves. Jim held it a few weeks and then turned it down. Chet then recorded it with Hank Locklin and it became one of the biggest country hits of 1960. I later met Jim Reeves at a DJ convention in Nashville and he laughingly told me turning the song down was not one of his best decisions."

Another collaboration with Blair illustrated some of the vagaries of record industry success. The time was the early 1960s and Robertson was closely involved with RCA, doing frequent sessions "sometimes as an artist and in other instances as piano sideman, arranger/conductor and/or songwriter." Staff producer Joe Reisman called on Robertson to write a couple of songs for an album planned for *Bonanza* star Lorne Greene, who had been signed to the label. Since singing wasn't one of Lorne's strong suits, Reisman suggested songs with a lot of talking and a minimum of singing would be desirable.

Don called for Hal Blair's help and the latter soon said he had some ideas. "I went over to his house in the Hollywood Hills. Hal had the title, 'Ringo,' and some opening lines. I thought it was great, so we began working out the story and putting lines together. We really didn't think about the music at that point, except that the meter and the rhythmic flow of the lyric was fundamental. I didn't think there'd be any problem working out the music once we got the story and lyric hammered out. So Hal and I did our think-tank number that we had done so many times before." Soon "Ringo" and another song, "Sand," were complete and turned over to Reisman, who planned to use both on the album on which he handled production as well as arranging/conducting chores.

The album, *Welcome to the Ponderosa,* came out in due course. Robertson said, "I don't remember the re-views, but I don't think they were very enthusiastic. It was a nice album, but probably not chart material. RCA had no plans for releasing singles, but apparently one of their branch distributors in Texas ordered custom singles. A local Texas DJ had been playing the 'Ringo' track (buried in the middle of side two of the album) and the distributor thought he could sell some singles. It then spread like wildfire from area to area around the country. To everyone's amazement the record shot up to number one on the *Billboard* pop Hot 100 in December of 1964. It also was translated into several other languages and recorded by local artists abroad. Canadian-born Lorne did a French version himself. At this writing, 'Ringo' (with parody voice) is running in two different Southwest Airlines TV and radio commercials featuring Jack Palance. Here it is 32 years later! Hal and I are indeed a couple of lucky songwriters."

Based partly on material from Robertson and interviews with Irwin Stambler.

ROBERTSON, A.C. "ECK": *Singer, fiddler, banjoist, band leader. Born Delaney, Arkansas, November 20, 1887; died Amarillo, Texas, February 15, 1975.*

Like many old-time rural fiddlers, Alexander Campbell "Eck" Robertson lived a long, eventful and sometimes troubled life. Considered one of the most skilled of the genre, he began his career at the turn of the century and after his career was interrupted by the Depression, was rediscovered for some last moments of glory in the mid-1960s.

Until recent decades, Robertson tended to be a shadowy, almost mythical individual, because for most of his life he lived in relative obscurity. Information about him available from the recording field was limited and, as it turned out, often inaccurate. This has been remedied through studies by folklorists who have provided more insight into his background and times. For instance, these efforts have strengthened his claim to have the first released commercial recording by a country musician. It also appears he was the first country artist to promote his or her recording on radio.

For many years it was accepted that he was born in Texas. Indeed, he spent most of his life in and around Amarillo. But it was later discovered he was born in Arkansas, the fifth of nine children in the family of preacher Joseph Robertson, who moved the family to Texas when Eck was three. As a youngster, Eck learned to play banjo and guitar and made his first move away from home to seek work as a musician in 1903. In 1906 he married fifteen-year-old Jeanette Belle "Nettie" Levy, who also had instrumental skills, playing guitar, mandolin, and piano. The two set up their own show to play theaters and open air tent shows in various places in the southwest. Over the years Nettie bore Eck ten children, eight girls and two boys, some of whom became part of a touring family group.

During the next decades, Eck continued to add to his credits as a fiddle player, performing in fiddle contests or providing background music for early movies. One of his innovations was to appear in full western costume. Some folklorists credit him with pioneering the wearing of western garb by country & western artists.

Civil War veterans' conventions also provided Robertson with employment. At a 1922 reunion in Richmond, Virginia, he met Oklahoma fiddler Henry Gilliland and the two decided to go to New York to try to make records. They managed to get a tryout with Victor for whom the duo recorded "Arkansaw Traveler" and "Turkey in the Straw" on June 30. The next day, Eck returned to record four more sides including "Sally Gooden" and "Ragtime Annie." After the two returned home, Eck to Vernon, Texas, RCA issued "Sally Gooden" and "Arkansaw Traveler" in April 1923. As Jeff Place of Smithsonian Folkways pointed out in liner notes for the planned fall 1997 reissue of the classic 1951 album *Anthology of American Folk Music* which included Robertson's "Brilliancy Medley," "In 1923, he played ['Sally Gooden'] over radio thereby becoming the first artist to advertise his recording over the new medium" (per Malone, *Country Music, U.S.A.*, p. 35).

Those were the last recordings he made for some time, though he maintained an active entertainment career playing small towns and some city venues in the south and southwest. As Blanton Owen wrote in *The Old Time Herald* ("Eck Robertson—'Famous Cowboy Fiddler,'" Fall 1992, pp. 21–25), "His 'act' took a definite shift toward popular entertainment and away from the strictly old-time and dance music. He booked his family into theaters as a vaudeville show - 'If You Don't Laugh We Will Call the Doctor'; 'Did You Ever Hear a Violin Actually Talk?'; and 'Novelty Music Entertainers' appeared regularly on their playbills. It is important to stress, however, that Eck never abandoned the old-time tunes."

Although Victor wanted to make more Robertson disks, they didn't know where to find him until Ralph Peer finally tracked him down late in the decade. In August 1929, Eck and his family recorded a number of tracks in a Dallas, Texas, studio, including "Texas Wagoner," and on October 11, 1929, the "Brilliancy Medley" was captured for vinyl. This might have launched a major recording career for Eck and The Robertson Family, but the Depression intervened. Gaining income for music was not easy in the 1930s, though Eck managed to find occasional performing dates for his family or for himself as a soloist. He also could fall back on his skill as a piano tuner for additional income.

In the mid-1930s, Eck was featured on a Dallas radio station. He was little known outside Texas, but he was in demand for local events in his home state throughout the 1930s and 1940s. He continued to be a major figure at fiddling contests throughout the South-

west and won prizes in many of them. In the 1950s, interest in Robertson revived nationally with the new folk music trend. The 1951 *Folkways Anthology* focused attention on Eck through inclusion of his "Brilliancy Medley." At about the time the record was released, Eck was going strong in still another Texas fiddling contest. In 1962, he traveled to Idaho for a contest and won first prize in the old-time fiddler's category.

Eck's virtuosity was emphasized by John Cohen of the New Lost City Ramblers in *Sing Out!* (April–May 1964, p. 57): "On the record of 'Sally Goodin,' one can hear more than a dozen variations on the simple theme. There are syncopated passages, single-string, double-string harmonies, blues notes, drone notes, short rapid grace notes which sound more like piping, and themes played entirely high up on the fingerboard as well as those in the first position."

Cohen and his fellow Ramblers, Mike Seeger and Tracy Schwarz, sought out Robertson in 1963. Eck's skills in the *Anthology* collection had caused excitement among many young performers in the folk boom of those years, including Bob Dylan, and those artists were eager to hear Robertson in person. This resulted first in Eck's appearance at a 1964 University of California at Los Angeles Folk Festival and an acclaimed set at the 1965 Newport Folk Festival.

Seeger and his friends queried Eck about his fiddle prowess including some of his special "tricks" that included throwing the fiddle or bow in the air, catching it and continuing to play the song without missing a beat, playing while lying on his back, and making his fiddle "talk." He described the last named technique to Mike Seeger, as quoted by Owen: "I could do it if I had my teeth. To touch the bridge of the fiddle with a piece of steel. . . . Well, you just put that piece of steel in your mouth. It's just like a cigar . . . You can take a pocketknife even, put it in your mouth; right shaped pocket knife, and do it. Anything that will kill the tone of the violin. You touch the bridge at intervals, and know how to pull your bow across the strings to make it do that."

After the 1965 exposure, Eck essentially faced diminishing opportunities in music. He continued to earn his living from tuning pianos for an Amarillo firm and repairing and reworking fiddles and other stringed instruments at a home shop. In the 1970s, after his home and shop were almost destroyed by a fire, he retired to a rest home where he died in 1975. He was buried in Fritch, Texas, his tombstone bearing the inscription "World's Champion Fiddler."

His extant, though limited, recordings in the 1990s provided a more lasting memorial. Jeff Place noted that a number of other performers had recorded versions of the "Brilliancy Medley," including Sam Bush, Mark O'Connor, and the British folk rock group Fairport Convention. On the original, included in the 1997 reissue, Eck's fiddle work was supported by Nettie on guitar, Daphne Robertson on guitar, and Dueron Robertson on banjo.

ROBISON, CARSON J.: *Singer, band leader (the Buckaroos, Pleasant Valley Boys), songwriter. Born Oswego, Kansas, August 4, 1890; died Pleasant Valley, New York, March 24, 1957.*

One of the most familiar voices on New York radio for many years belonged to Carson Robison. He helped build up a strong following for country & western music in the East, and his many pioneering efforts in the field made him a figure of national importance as well.

Robison was exposed to country and folk music from his early years in his home state of Kansas. He sang at local gatherings on many occasions during elementary and high school in the Oswego area. Carson moved to Kansas City in 1920 and was one of the first country & western singers ever to have his voice sent out on the radio.

Carson built up a strong reputation in the Midwest, which served as a basis for his next move, to New York in 1924. In the big city, he soon began his recording career for RCA Victor, initially as a whistler. Throughout the 1920s and early 1930s, he performed on radio and also was featured in vaudeville tours in the East and Midwest. Many of the audience favorites by then were songs he had written himself. In 1932, Robison formed his first group, the Buckaroos. The group accompanied him on radio shows, and during the 1930s toured England with him.

During the 1940s and 1950s, Robison made his base of operations Pleasant Valley, New York. He eventually named his group of those years the Pleasant Valley Boys. Many of his recordings made the hit brackets during the 1930s and 1940s. Probably his biggest success was his MGM top-10 1948 recording of his own composition "Life Gets Tee-Jus, Don't It?" The song provided hit records for many other artists in the decades that followed. Another Robison comic staple of the 1940s and 1950s was "I'm Going Back to Whur I Come From." He also was responsible for a western classic, "Carry Me Back to the Lone Prairie."

Some of Carson's other compositions are "Barnacle Bill the Sailor," "My Blue Ridge Mountain Home," "Left My Gal in the Mountains," "1942 Turkey in the Straw," "Home Sweet Home on the Prairie," "There's a Bridle Hangin' on the Wall," "The Charms of the City Ain't for Me," "Goin' Back to Texas," "Little Green Valley," "New River Train," "Wreck of the Number Nine," and "Settin' by the Fire."

Robison died on his beloved farm in Pleasant Valley, New York, in early 1957. He had remained active in music up to a short time before his death.

Robison was nominated for the Country Music Hall of Fame several times, but as of 1995 had not been elected. The brief biography assembled for the 1981 Hall of Fame voting pointed out that Carson ranked as Country Music's first professional songwriter and stated he had written over 300 songs during his career. It also noted his extensive work with another country music pioneer, the late Vernon Dalhart. Dalhart's name was also included among the 1981 nominees, but in his case there was enough voter support for his election.

RODGERS, JIMMIE (C.): *Singer, guitarist, songwriter. Born Meridian, Mississippi, September 8, 1897; died New York, New York, May 26, 1933. Elected to Country Music Hall of Fame.*

Generations of country-music fans and performers have looked back in awe at a figure they knew only from pictures or from records. The most revered name in country-music history, an acknowledged founding father of modern country & western patterns, Jimmie Rodgers achieved all this in just a few brief years in the national spotlight.

Rodgers was born and raised in rural Mississippi, where country music was a part of his environment, as was the country blues of the Negro field hands. Singing was one of the few pleasures that relieved the long hours of work for black and white alike (although Jimmie gave little thought to a music career).

In his teens, he worked briefly as a cowboy, but soon left wrangling for his first job on the railroad. Railroading, he felt, would be his life's work. For close to a decade, he worked on the roads as a brakeman, sometimes entertaining his fellow workers with popular country songs and sometimes with songs of his own on the guitar he had learned to play in his youth. His own compositions were a strangely moving blend of traditional country music, railroad songs, and country blues.

Jimmie might have remained a brakeman were it not for his failing health. He had contracted tuberculosis, and, by 1923–24, he no longer was fit for the rugged demands of railroading.

By then he was a family man with a wife and daughter to support. He had wooed Carrie Cecil Williamson, daughter of the Reverend J. T. Williamson, a Meridian minister, years before and won her hand on April 7, 1920. Their only surviving child, Carrie Anita, was born the following year. Jimmie's wife remained with him through rough periods and happy ones, helped nurse him in his battle with TB, and, after his death, played a role in preserving his contributions to country music and helping others continue the tradition he had started.

Rodgers decided to see if he could earn money as a performer. While Carrie worked as a clerk in a Meridian store, Jimmie toured as a blackface banjo player in a medicine show. Later he joined a tent show, where he performed in whiteface and managed to get enough money together to buy out the owners. Just when the outlook looked brighter, disaster struck. In 1925 the

The Marshall Tucker Band

Kathy Mattea

Reba McEntire

Roger Miller

Tim McGraw

(Peter Nash)

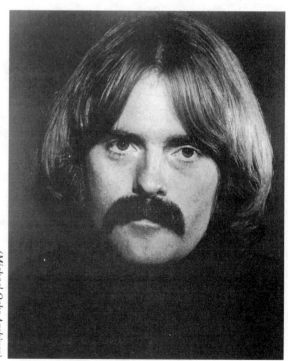

(Michael Ochs Archives)

The legendary Bill Monroe

Michael Murphy

Anne Murray

Willie Nelson

New Grass Revival

One of the many incarnations of the Nitty Gritty Dirt Band, whose roster over the decades ranged from quartets to sextets. Members in this picture are *(left to right):* Jeff Hanna, Jimmie Fadden, Al Garth, Merel Brigante, Richard Hathaway, and John McEuen

The Oak Ridge Boys in their 1970s heyday *(left to right):* William Lee Golden, Richard Sterban, Duane Allen, and Joe Bonsall

Mark O'Connor

(Peter Nash)

K. T. Oslin

Buck Owens

At the urging of Dwight Yoakam *(left)*, Buck Owens made a triumphant return to country concert performance in the late 1980s

Dolly Parton and Minnie Pearl at the
1977 CMA Awards show

Minnie Pearl

(Gary Glade)

Carl Perkins

Elvis Presley

Presley in the early part of his career

Eddie Rabbitt

Jim Reeves

Charlie Rich

Tex Ritter

Hargus "Pig" Robbins

The Original Jimmie Rodgers, father of modern
country music

Don Robertson, Waylon Jennings, and Jack Clement,
July 1995

tent and equipment were wiped out by a tornado. Jimmie turned to railroading again and almost killed himself doing it. Then a friend came to the rescue by finding him a job as a city detective in Asheville, North Carolina. The higher elevation of the town brought an improvement in his condition, and, by 1927, his wife and daughter joined him there.

Rodgers soon became bored with a detective's life. He formed a new act with three stringed-instrument artists; their first job was a free show in May 1927 on radio station WWNC for the Asheville Chamber of Commerce. The group, the Jimmie Rodgers Entertainers, slowly increased its appearances, and he talked the members into joining him on a summer tour north to Baltimore. After reading newspaper ads in July announcing that Victor Recording Company would hold field auditions in Bristol on the Tennessee–Virginia border in August, he changed the band's schedule.

He holed up in a cheap hotel across State Street from the hotel where Victor representative Ralph Peer was staying. His band, though, apparently bore a grudge against him and, unknown to him, went to Peer and asked that he record them separately under the name Tenneva Ramblers. When Jimmie went to see Peer, on August 4, 1927,* Peer didn't intend to record him, but Rodgers managed to persuade him to change his mind. Peer agreed, but only for one solo single. Jimmie cut two songs, "Sleep Baby Sleep" and "The Soldier's Sweetheart" and left with a payment of twenty dollars from Victor.

The Bristol session over, Jimmie and Carrie drove their old car to Washington, D.C., where Carrie worked as a waitress in a tearoom and Jimmie picked up whatever work he could find as a performer. His first single, he found out, was finding some acceptance, and he and Carrie pooled their meager resources so Jimmie could go to New York and see if Peer would let him make more records. Peer was willing, and, in November 1927, Rodgers recorded two more songs in Victor's Camden, New Jersey, studios: "Away Out on the Mountain" and a song tentatively called "T for Texas," replete with Jimmie's fanciest yodels. Issued as "Blue Yodel Number 1," the first of many "blue yodel" discs Rodgers was to make, it started slowly after its release, then really took off. By early 1928 it was a major hit and Jimmie was asked to return for more recordings.

In 1928, his output included "Blue Yodel Number 2" ("My Loving Girl Lucille"); "Blue Yodel Number 3" ("Evening Sun Yodel"); "Memphis Yodel"; "My Little Old Home Down in New Orleans"; and "Ben Dewberry's Final Ride." Almost every one of them exceeded a million copies sold a short time after issue. The story went that farmers all across the United States would go to the general store and order "A loaf of bread, a pound

of butter, and the new Jimmie Rodgers record." But his appeal wasn't rural only. He could appeal to all people, as was proven by the crowds that flocked to see him after Gene Austin added him to his show at the Earle Theater in Washington, D.C.

For the rest of his life, Jimmie Rodgers was one of the country's performing royalty. He toured the South and Southwest, where crowds fought to hear him, touch his clothes, or just get a brief glimpse of his frail form. His records continued to be avidly snapped up by his fans for the few years of life left to him. By early 1933, he had rolled up sales of almost 20 million records.

Beside releases noted above, his output included such hits as "Treasure Untold," "Lullaby Yodel," "The Sailor's Plea" (1928); "Hobo Bill's Last Ride," "Yodeling Cowboy Blues," "Mississippi River Blues," "The Land of My Boyhood Dreams," "That's Why I'm Blue," "Jimmie's Texas Blues," "Any Old Time" (1929); "The Mystery of Number Five," "Those Gambler's Blues," "I'm Lonesome Too," "For the Sake of Days Gone By" (1930); "Let Me Be Your Side Track," "My Good Gal's Gone Blues," "T.B. Blues," "The Wonderful City" (with the Carter Family), "When the Cactus Is in Bloom" (1931); "Gambling Barroom Blues," "Roll Along Kentucky Moon," "No Hard Times," "Down the Road to Home" (1932); "Somewhere Down Below the Dixon Line," "Mississippi Delta Blues," "Cowhand's Last Ride," and "Old Love Letters" (1933).

Among his other singles between 1927 and 1933 were "Mule Skinner Blues," "T for Texas," "Travelin' Blues," "One Rose That's Left in My Heart," "The Brakeman's Blues," "Daddy and Home," "My Time Ain't Long," and "Prairie Lullaby."

In addition to his personal appearances, Jimmie sang on several radio programs. He also made a movie short for Columbia pictures.

The money rolled in and Rodgers enjoyed spending it. He bought expensive cars and established a lavish home for himself and his family in Kerrville, Texas. He also was always willing to give funds to friends in need—or who said they were in need. That he always seemed to spend his income as fast as it came in wasn't too surprising. He knew his meteoric career had a time limit on it from the beginning. His health, always precarious, deteriorated badly in the winter of 1932–33, and he had to sell the remote Kerrville property and settle in San Antonio, Texas, where medical help was closer.

The bills kept piling up, and, feeling better in the spring of 1933, he was determined to try to complete another recording session up north. Accompanied by a trained nurse, he traveled to Galveston in a private train compartment, then embarked on a luxury cruise on the S.S. *Mohawk* to New York. Once there, he negotiated a lucrative new contract with Victor and began to make new recordings on May 17. But the improvement in

---

* *August 4 is the date given by RCA archivists: the date of August 1 also is given in the same report.*

health had proved deceptive. It soon was apparent he was in no shape to work.

Bob Gilmore, an assistant to Ralph Peer, recalled, "Jimmie was very ill . . . he had a nurse with him and a big Cadillac arranged so that he could lie down and rest. . . . In the recording studio he was propped up so that he could sing with the least expenditure of energy . . . and sometimes he would stop, in order to catch his breath."

Instead of the twenty-four songs he and Peer intended to make, he cut the list to twelve, completing the last group on May 24. He longed to return home, but was in no condition to travel. He spent his last days in New York's Taft Hotel, where he died on May 26, 1933. In all, between August 4, 1927, and May 24, 1933, he recorded 113 songs, all of which still were available on RCA long-playing records in the 1970s.

Artists still were making the hit charts with some of his compositions in the 1990s, as dozens of top performers had done over all the decades since his death. His influence spread from contemporaries like Gene Autry and Ernest Tubb to such others as Merle Haggard, Elvis Presley, and Charley Pride. Over the years, many songs were written in his memory, beginning with Bradley Kincaid's 1934 offerings, "The Death of Jimmie Rodgers" and "Jimmie Rodgers' Life," and continuing with Ernest Tubb's tributes in 1936, "The Last Thought of Jimmie Rodgers" and "The Passing of Jimmie Rodgers" on up to Elton Britt's country chartmaker of 1967–68, "The Jimmie Rodgers Blues," a biography of Rodgers made by combining the titles of most of his songs. He was the first member elected to the Country Music Hall of Fame, on November 3, 1961.

Countless musicians, from Ernest Tubb to artists of the 1990s, used guitar techniques developed by Rodgers. His methods were described as follows in *Golden Guitars, The Story of Country Music* (by Irwin Stambler and Grelun Landon, N.Y., Four Winds Press, 1971):

Rodgers' guitar phrasing often started with tuning the strings a half tone lower than is done conventionally. He then placed a capo next to the top fret, bringing it to tune and giving it a brighter voice because the strings were then tensed over metal rather than the ivory bridge. He played the bass strings with a straight pick on the neck of the guitar, above the acoustic hole, to accomplish a distinctive instrument voice blend. In pickups between choruses, or on sustained notes, he used to pick the same bass notes just above the bridge and below the acoustic hole to lead into the following vocal note.

These pickup runs and tight neck playing, along with some flicking finger strums across all the strings for accents, helped show the guitar's potential as a lead instrument. (The accepted practice of the day, used by such popular stars as Bradley Kincaid, was to apply the guitar in the background to chord along behind the mandolin, violin or other dominant front sounds.)

Rodgers also ended his songs by having the guitar play a bass sign-off signature. About the same time, Sara and Maybelle Carter of the Carter Family trio used bass runs to maintain the rhythm, an innovation for group playing.

Rodgers used "dirty blues" figures, but in the lower register, a technique often used by today's rock groups as well as old time boogie-woogie pianists. These figures, with the subthemes, were the basis for riffs used in the swing bands and were often converted for use as the melody line in popular big band songs of the 1930s and 1940s.

In the decades after Rodgers's death, RCA continued to reissue his recordings in various combinations. In the long-playing record era following World War II, the company always had a number of Rodgers's LPs in its active catalog. That list, as of the early 1980s, included the albums *Legendary Performer, Best of the Legendary Jimmie Rodgers, Country Music Hall of Fame: Jimmie Rodgers, Jimmie the Kid, My Rough and Rowdy Ways, My Time Ain't Long, Train Whistle Blues, This Is Jimmie Rodgers, Short but Brilliant Life of Jimmie Rodgers,* and *Never No Mo' Blues.*

Throughout the 1980s and into the 1990s, Jimmie continued to be revered by succeeding generations of performers, some of whom, like Merle Haggard, released tribute albums to him. An annual festival in his memory was established in his home town of Meridian, Mississippi, and the U.S. government printed a stamp in his honor. By the mid-1990s, his recordings were widely available on CDs and cassettes. Albums in those formats of his RCA recordings available from the Country Music Hall of Fame and Museum catalog or from Rounder Records comprise: *First Sessions 1927–28; The Early Years—1928–29; On the Way Up (1929); Ridin' High (1929–30); America's Blue Yodeler (1930–31); Down the Old Road 1931–32; No Hard Times, 1932;* and *Last Sessions, 1933.* Also available only as an import item in the U.S in the 1990s was a boxed set from Germany's Bear Family Records, *Jimmie Rodgers: The Singing Brakeman.* Bear Family claimed the six-CD package was "the only complete edition of Jimmie Rodgers work." The company added that it included a "newly researched bio and [previously] unpublished photos."

RODRIGUEZ, JOHN RAUL DAVIS "JOHNNY":

Singer, guitarist. Born Sabinal, Texas, December 10, 1952.

The enormous crossover success of Freddy Fender in 1975 made many people see him as the first Mexican-American country superstar. In actual fact, he followed in the footsteps of a young performer named Johnny Rodriguez, who erupted on the country scene a few years earlier and remained one of the major luminaries of the field into the early 1980s.

Rodriguez, like Fender, was born into a poor Texas family. He was the youngest of nine children living in a four-room shanty in Sabinal, a town ninety miles from the Mexican border. He hardly remembers his father, who died of cancer when Johnny was three, yet his memories of growing up in the rural town are surprisingly pleasant. As he told Bill Williams and Bob Kirsch of *Billboard,* "I know what struggling is. But I was always around music while I was growing up and I decided to sing country because that's what I am. My older brother, who has passed away, was a rodeo man and he'd sing a lot of country songs, often in Spanish. That's where I came up with the idea of doing some of my songs in English and half in Spanish."

He told Jerry Bailey of the *Country Music Beat* that his original opportunity came while he was a teenager jailed for goat rustling. His jailhouse singing enthralled a Texas Ranger who brought him to the attention of a promotor named Happy Shahan. Shahan, in turn, hired Johnny to perform in cowboy garb at the tourist attraction he ran called Alamo Village. Shahan, who took over as the youngster's manager, brought country star Tom T. Hall to hear him. Hall said he'd call on Rodriguez if an opening came up in his band.

Johnny waited a bit, then made his way to Nashville. "I had about eight dollars with me," he told Bailey. "I had this old guitar wrapped in a cellophane bag. I must have looked like a weirdo in downtown Nashville. I figured everybody saw me walking around and said 'Well, there's another squirrel.' I was too, boy. I was right in the middle of it all."

However, Hall, when contacted, agreed to pick him up. "Tom T. came by and picked me up in a black Cadillac he had back then. I never will forget it. I couldn't think anything but 'Wow!' So the next week I went to work for him playing lead guitar. Then I started fronting the band and eventually recorded 'Pass Me By.'"

The recording was Rodriguez's first single on Mercury Records, and it surprised even him by racing up the country charts to the number-four position. The next release, "You Always Come Back to Hurting Me," did even better, reaching the number-one position. His debut LP, *Introducing Johnny Rodriguez,* also was a hit, making the country top 10 soon after its release in 1972 and going to number one on all three major charts— *Billboard, Cash Box,* and *Record World.* Johnny showed that his success was no fluke with more recordings that verified his position as one of the most effective of the new country singers. His follow-up album was a top-10 hit in 1973 as was the next one, titled *My Third Album,* in the first half of 1974. The latter spawned the top-10 country hit single "Something."

During 1974, Rodriguez made his debut as a TV actor. He played a bit part in an *Adam-12* show that was shown on network TV in the fall. Encouraged by his performance, he agreed to accept a part in the western movie *Rio Diablo.*

His emphasis, however, remained on his country efforts both as a concert artist and recording star. Mercury released a *Greatest Hits* album in mid-1976 that rose to top-chart levels, as did his 1977 LP, *Practice Makes Perfect.* In 1978 he was represented in the top 20 by the album *Love Me with All Your Heart.* Among his chart singles in the late 1970s were "I Wonder If I Said Goodbye," number one in September 1976, "If Practice Makes Perfect," a top-20 hit in June 1977, and such fall chartmakers as "Eres Tu" and "Love Put a Song in My Heart."

In 1979, Johnny left Mercury and signed with Epic Records. His debut album on Epic, produced by Billy Sherrill, was titled *Rodriguez.* His first single on his new label was "Down on the Rio Grande." Late that year, his single "What'll I Tell Virginia" came out and made upper-charts levels. Also on the lists in late 1979 and early 1980 was a duet single with Charly McClain, "I Hate the Way I Love It." Other charted singles by Rodriguez in the early 1980s were "North of the Border" in the fall of 1980 and "I Want You Tonight" in early summer 1981.

By the late 1980s, though Johnny remained active as a performer, his recording career tapered off. After a long drought in new country albums, in the summer of 1996 he could point to a new release, *You Can Say That Again.* Backing him were a number of highly regarded studio musicians including Hargis "Pig" Robbins on piano, Sonny Garrish on pedal steel, Larry Paxton on bass, Jerry Kroon on drums, Stuart Duncan on fiddle, and producer Jerry Kennedy, who had worked with Rodriguez on some of his early hit albums, on guitar.

ROGERS, KENNY: *Singer, guitarist, songwriter. Born Houston, Texas, August 21, 1937.*

Certainly the phenomenon of country music, and pop music too, in the late 1970s and early 1980s was Kenny Rogers. With the huge success of his 1977 single "Lucille" and the 1978 album (and single) *The Gambler,* after twenty years of performing, he was on the way to bonafide superstardom. He maintained his momentum through much of the 1980s and, while his recording career brought diminishing returns in the 1990s, by then he continued to maintain a high profile with his acting activities and business investments, which included a theater in Branson, Missouri, and an expanding chicken restaurant franchise operation.

When Kenny made his mark in the country field in the 1970s and 1980s, some country purists looked on this development with less than all-out enthusiasm; though as a born and bred Texan, Kenny came from authentic country-music territory. His route to country music was by way of jazz, rock, and pop, a background that helped him record a single like "Lady," which made number one on pop, country, and soul charts in 1980. Despite the nay-sayers, though, country fans had no qualms about supporting him and his achievements, and in return, he played a major role in sustaining the country-music boom that got under way in the 1970s.

Rogers made it to the top from suitably humble beginnings. The fourth of eight children born to Edward and Lucille Rogers, he grew up in Houston under somewhat difficult circumstances. His parents were loving, but his father, a carpenter and shipyard worker (who also played the fiddle), had a hard time making ends meet in the Depression years and, worse still, was an alcoholic. As a child, Kenny spent a number of years with his family in a federal housing project and several rented houses.

His brother Randy told Sue Reilly and Kent Demaret of *People* magazine (December 1, 1980), "I think we felt a little bit like outsiders. We'd go to church in an old pickup truck and stoop down low in the seats because we didn't want anybody to see us. I think all that boosts Kenny in thinking, 'I just don't want to go back. There's nothing wrong with it, but I don't want to go back.'"

Kenny sang in the church choir and in a glee club as a boy and also started to learn to play instruments, including the piano. Recalling his guitar progress, his mother told *People,* "Kenny never had a guitar lesson, he just picked it up. On the weekends he was at one of the music stores, daylight until dark. He must have drove those people crazy, playing all the guitars they had down there. Oh gee, him and Mickey Gilley [another neighborhood boy at the time] used to come over to the house and Kenny would hammer on the guitar and Mickey on the piano. I thought they were going to run me out of the house."

In high school, Kenny formed his own rockabilly group, the Scholars, to play at dances and local events. He signed a recording contract while still in high school with Carlton Records and had a local hit with the 1958 single "That Crazy Feeling" (backed with "We'll Always Have Each Other"). His second single, "For You Alone," backed with "I've Got a Lot to Learn," was also issued in 1958. Carlton issued an LP, *One Dozen Goldies,* in 1959, the last solo release Rogers was to have for some years.

He briefly enrolled at the University of Houston, but dropped out in favor of playing bass and singing with a jazz group, the Bobby Doyle Trio. He toured nationally with the combo, and they had an album released on Columbia in 1962. He left them to work with the Kirby Stone Four, and in 1966 moved to Los Angeles and joined the New Christy Minstrels. He had a brief fling on Mercury Records in 1966, which resulted in one singles release ("Here's That Rainy Day," flip side "Take Life in Stride") and several unissued recordings: "He

Will Break Your Heart," "Please Send Me Someone to Love," "If You Don't Share Your Love," and "Rubber Soul."

In 1967, Rogers and Mike Settle, another Minstrel, decided to try their hand at rock music. They formed the group the First Edition with two other singers. The group later became a fivesome after a switch in personnel in which two of the original members, including founder Settle, left the group. The First Edition was a highly successful combo. It offered an alternative to the heavy metal, psychedelic sound popular in the latter half of the 1960s. In fact the group often sang country songs and fit in well in their frequent appearances on Johnny Cash's television show. Their hits included "Just Dropped in to See What Condition My Condition Was In," "Ruby, Don't Take Your Love to Town," "Something's Burning," "Reuben James," and "Heed the Call." They eventually came to be known as Kenny Rogers and the First Edition, as Kenny's voice seemed to be the most readily identifiable voice in the group. In 1971 the group hosted its own syndicated television variety show, *Rollin' on the River,* which was soon picked up by many United States and Canadian stations.

As the years passed, however, group members began to get bored with their act and also to wane in popularity. In 1975, Rogers decided to part from the First Edition and to try his luck on his own as a solo country artist. Although he signed a contract with United Artists (the name later was changed to Liberty) and had singles out on the label in 1975, at first the response was only nominal. Adding to his problems, his marriage of twelve years to Margo Gladys Anderson was winding up with considerable bitterness on both sides. (This was his third marriage.) He had close to two dry years as a performer; money was tight and he played small Las Vegas lounges and appeared on TV commercials selling quick and easy music lessons. He credits the love and support of his girlfriend and later fourth wife, Marianne Gordon (whom he met while guesting on the *Hee Haw* TV show on which she was a regular), with seeing him through those lean days.

Even when things were slow, he was confident the picture would brighten. He told Peter J. Boyer of the Associated Press, "I never had any doubt in my mind. I never felt I had a good voice, but I always knew that I had a very commercial voice. When I got this band together, I predicted that within one year I'd have a top-10 record. I always knew that with the right piece of material, I could pop with a record any given day."

Sure enough, in 1977, Kenny's recording of "Lucille" became a giant hit, soaring to the top of the country and pop charts. The song sold over 4 million copies. Kenny followed with another hit, "Sweet Music Man," which he wrote himself. The song has already become a standard and has been recorded by a number of other artists, both pop and country.

One day, Rogers ran into singer Dottie West in a

Nashville recording studio. On the spur of the moment, they recorded a song she was working on as a duet. "Every Time Two Fools Collide" became a top country hit in early 1978. Later in 1978, the duo had a hit with "Anyone Who Isn't Me Tonight." At the Country Music Association's awards in 1978, Kenny and Dottie were named the Top Vocal Duo of the Year.

Kenny continued to turn out his own solo hits. "The Gambler" became a number-one-ranked single in late 1978 and early 1979. In 1979 he had hits with "While She Waits" and "Coward of the County." (In fact, after "The Gambler" made the top 10, every single he released through the fall of 1981 also entered that charmed circle.) He had become one of the top performers in both pop and country fields and one of the most recognizable and well-liked celebrities in the United States.

During the late 1970s, Rogers complemented his recording efforts with intensive touring as well as many appearances on TV, including periods of hosting *The Tonight Show*. In 1980, he averaged 200 concerts a year, typically selling out major venues and often setting new attendance records. In 1981, with his position as a superstar well established and demands of TV movies increasing, he cut back to 100 or so appearances. Backing him on his live shows, as of the early 1980s, was a band (called Bloodline) led by drummer Bobby Daniels and including Eugene Golden on keyboards and vocals; Steve Glassmeyer on keyboards, flute, soprano sax, and vocals; Edgar Struble on keyboards and vocals; Randy Dorman and Rich Harper on guitars; and Chuck Jacobs on bass guitar.

Describing one of his concerts in Fort Worth, Texas, Roger Kaye of the Fort Worth *Star Telegram* wrote (1/12/81), "[Rogers] has the knack for making a large arena show seem like a much more intimate experience than it is, and that's due to his casual approach. Rogers talks to a crowd of 14,000 in the same way he might address a gathering of 14 or less. He makes it seem like it's all among friends."

In 1980, Kenny appeared in his first made for TV movie, *Kenny Rogers as the Gambler*. Telecast on the CBS network, it achieved the highest rating of any TV movie shown over the previous two years. Rogers also starred in three variety specials on the same network, "A Very Special Kenny Rogers," "Kenny Rogers and the American Cowboy," and "Kenny Rogers' America." In the fall of 1981, he was featured in his second TV movie, *Coward of the County*. Also in print in the early 1980s was a book he cowrote with music publicist Len Epand, published by Harper & Row, *Making It with Music*.

Rogers didn't slight the recording field in the early 1980s. The song that became the title of his second TV movie, "Coward of the County," was number one on singles charts in January 1980. In the spring, a new duet pairing, with singer/songwriter Kim Carnes, provided the bestselling single "Don't Fall in Love with a Dreamer." During the summer, he hit with "Love the World Away" and, in November, had "Lady" in number-one position on country charts. "Lady," written and produced by Lionel Ritchie of the Commodores vocal group, became his biggest seller to date, chalking up over 1.5 million copies sold by mid-1981. His albums had done equally well from the late 1970s into the early 1980s, with releases like *The Gambler* (1978) and *Kenny* (1979) reaching number one on country charts for many weeks and remaining on the lists into the 1980s, to be joined by such others as *Gideon* (whose songs all were written by Kim Carnes and her husband, Dave Ellingson), *Kenny Rogers Greatest Hits,* and *Share Your Love*. The *Greatest Hits* LP, issued in 1980, by the fall of 1981 had sold over 14 million copies. *Share Your Love,* released in the summer of 1981, had sales of over 2 million copies two months afterward. As of that time, Rogers's manager, Ken Kragen, estimated he had sold more than $200 million worth of records in three years.

A list of Rogers's record releases from his First Edition days to late 1981, compiled by Todd Everett, is as follows. His singles were, on Reprise, with the First Edition, "I Found a Reason" b/w "Ticket to Nowhere" (1967); "Just Dropped In" b/w "Shadow in the Corner of Your Mind," "Dream On" b/w "Only Me," "Look Around, It's Only Me" b/w "Charlie the Fer de Lance" (1968); "But You Know I Love You" b/w "Home Made Lies," "Ruby (Don't Take Your Love to Town)" b/w "Girl Get a Hold of Yourself," "Reuben James" b/w "Sunshine" (1969); "Something's Burning" b/w "Momma's Waiting," "Tell It All Brother" b/w "Just Remember You're My Sunshine," "Heed the Call" b/w "Stranger in My Place" (1970); "Someone Who Cares" b/w "Mission of San Nohero," "Take My Hand," "Where Does Rosie Go" b/w "What Am I Gonna Do?" (1971); and "School Teacher" b/w "Trigger Happy Kid" (1972). On the Jolly Roger label, Kenny and the First Edition were represented by the singles "Lady Play Your Symphony" b/w "There's an Old Man in Our Town," "(Do You Remember) the First Time" b/w "Indian Joe," "Today I Started Loving You Again" b/w "She Thinks I Still Care" (1972); "Lena Lookie" b/w "Gallo County Train," "What's She Gonna Do" b/w "Something About Your Song," and "Makin' Music for Money" b/w "Stranger in My Place" (1973). On United Artists, Rogers's singles were "Love Lifted Me" b/w "Home-Made Love," "A Home Made Love" b/w "There's an Old Man in Our Town" (1975); "While the Feeling's Good" b/w "I Would Like to See You Again," "Laura (What's He Got That I Ain't Got)" b/w "I Wasn't Man Enough" (1976); "Lucille" b/w "Till I Get It Right," "Daytime Friends" b/w "We Don't Make Love Anymore," "Sweet Music Man" b/w "Lyin' Again" (1977); "Every Time Two Fools Collide" b/w "We Love Each Other" (with Dottie West), "Love or Something like It" b/w "Starting Again," "Anyone Who Isn't Me Tonight" b/w "You and Me" (with Dottie West); "The Gambler" b/w "Momma's Waiting" (1978); "She Believes in Me" b/w "Morganna Jones," "All I Ever Need Is You" b/w "Won't You Play Another Somebody Done Somebody Wrong Song" (with Dottie West), "Till I Can Make It on My Own" b/w "Midnight Flyer" (with Dottie West), "You Decorated My Life" b/w "One Man's Woman," "Coward of the County" b/w "I Want to Make You Smile" (1979); "Don't Fall in Love with a Dreamer" b/w "Going Home to the Rock—Gideon Tanner" (with Kim Carnes), and "Love the World Away Saying Goodbye" b/w "Requiem—Going Home to the Rock" (1980). On Liberty Records, Kenny turned out "Lady" b/w "Sweet Music Man," "Lady" (Spanish version) b/w "Sweet Music Man" (1980); and "What Are We Doing in Love" b/w "Choosin' Means Losin'" (with Dottie West) (1981).

Album releases were, on Reprise, *First Edition* and *First Edition's Second* (1968); *First Edition '69, Ruby Don't Take Your Love to Town* (1969); *Something's Burning, Tell It All Brother* (1970); *Fools* (movie soundtrack), *Kenny Rogers and the First Edition's Greatest Hits, Transitions* (1971); and *The Ballad of Calico* (two records) (1972). Albums on Jolly Roger were *Back Roads, Monumental* (1972); and *Rollin'* (1973). United Artists solo albums were *Love Lifted Me* (1976); *Kenny Rogers/Lucille, Daytime Friends, Ten Years of Gold* (1977); *Every Time Two Fools Collide* (with Dottie West), *Love or Something like It* (title track written by Rogers with Steve Glassmeyer), *Convoy* (movie soundtrack), *The Gambler* (1978); *Kenny Rogers and Dottie West—Classics, Kenny* (1979); and *Gideon* (1980). On Liberty, he had the LPs *Kenny Rogers Greatest Hits* (1980); *Share Your Love* (1981); the duet "What Are We Doing in Love" on Dottie West's LP *Wild West,* and *Kenny Rogers' Christmas* (1981). Rogers also contributed the track "Love the World Away" included in the Elektra LP of the original *Urban Cowboy* soundtrack. Warner Brothers Special Products issued a two-record TV package, *Kenny Rogers and the First Edition,* released on the Lakeshore Music label.

One of the highlights of Kenny's activities in the early 1980s was collaboration with Dolly Parton on a series of recordings and an extensive concert tour that brought standing-room-only crowds to some of the largest arenas in the U.S. and Canada. During 1983, their singles releases "Islands in the Stream" and "Real Love" were chart hits. In the 1984 CMA Awards voting, "Islands in the Stream" was nominated for Single of the Year and Kenny and Dolly selected as finalists for Vocal Duo of the Year (as was the case in 1985 as well). They performed the song during the Awards telecast in October, which was hosted by Kenny. Their album output in the mid-1980s, besides *Islands in the Stream,* included the multiplatinum-selling *Once upon a Christmas.*

Rogers's audience extended to many other parts of the world, as shown by the response overseas to his greatest-hits releases. In early May 1986, for instance, *The Kenny Rogers Story, #3,* was number one on British country charts. His mid-1980s projects included a hit duet single with Ronnie Milsap, "Make No Mistake, She's Mine," and his 1988 recording of the official theme song for the U.S. Gymnastics team, "When You Put Your Heart in It," with proceeds from the last-named single going to the U.S. Gymnastics Foundation. Kenny also took the official team photo before the Seoul (South Korea) Olympics, reflecting his accomplishment in photography. By the mid-1990s he had completed two books showcasing his photographic skills (*Kenny Rogers America,* a compilation of scenic landscapes, and *Kenny Rogers: Your Friends and Mine,* a collection of celebrity portraits of people like Michael Jackson, Elizabeth Taylor, Elton John, George Burns, and others), and was working on a third involving country artists.

TV also continued to gain much of his attention in the 1980s and 1990s. By the end of the 1980s, he had completed three made-for-TV *Gambler* stories and was asked to do yet another. Before that, he portrayed an ambitious photographer alienated from his son in the 1989 TV drama *Christmas in America: A Love Story.* Costarring was his adult son, Kenny Rogers, Jr., and it was indicated that the script reflected to some extent actual experiences. The fourth *Gambler* episode, "The Luck of the Draw: The Gambler Returns," was presented as a miniseries on NBC in November 1991, with Reba McEntire handling the female lead. A fifth program, "Gambler V: Playing for Keeps," costarring Loni Anderson, Dixie Carter, and Bruce Boxleitner, aired on CBS the nights of October 2 and 4, 1994. In between the last two, Kenny hosted a 1992 Christmas special and starred with Naomi Judd and Travis Tritt in the western *Rio Diablo,* presented on CBS-TV on February 28, 1993.

If that wasn't enough, Rogers also contracted to play the detective lead in a new series of NBC-TV movies called *MacShayne.* The first was telecast on February 11, 1994, with Ann Jillian as costar and the second, costarring Maria Conchita Alonso and Michael McKean, on April 29, 1994. Good viewer response to his various TV projects was underscored by his signing in the mid-1990s production pacts worth $18 million with NBC and CBS. Meanwhile, Kenny also served as narrator for the Arts & Entertainment Network's highest rated series, *The Real West.*

Kenny's stage appearances in the 1990s included shows at the Grand Palace in Branson, Missouri, a venue owned by the Silver Dollar Corporation, of which he was a partner. The corporation also owned Silver Dollar City, White Water Raft Park, and other amusement attractions in Branson. That roster was expanded on April 13, 1995, by the opening of the Kenny Rogers Showboat *Branson Belle,* a riverboat set up for dining and entertainment. His entrepreneurial interests extended to the development with partner John Y. Brown (of Kentucky Fried Chicken fame) on the Kenny Rogers Roasters restaurant chain. The project was initiated in 1991, and by the end of 1993 a hundred were in operation, with plans to increase that to 700 in the U.S. before the end of the decade.

Despite all of his success in other areas, Kenny still longed for a solid rebirth of his country career. As he told Janet Williams of CMA's *Close Up* in April 1993, when his debut on a new label, Irving Azoff's Giant records, *If Only My Heart Has a Voice,* came out, he did understand the situation. "It's hard to get me played on country radio right now. And I understand that. Music is very cyclical, and I know that sooner or later will be a time when what I do is more [acceptable]. . . . Right now country music is much more country than I'm comfortable being.

"Basically, each radio station is trying to establish what in effect is an audio footprint for the station, so that when you go by, you go, 'Oh, that's KZLA.' If you don't do something that fits in this little small window of sound, they won't play it. I just have to keep throwing 'em out there and hope that I find one that *does* fall into that window of sound."

Not that Kenny's releases didn't get some record-buying attention. In 1990, his duet single with Dolly Parton, "Love Is Strange" (the title track of his third album for Reprise Records, which signed him in the late 1980s) peaked at number twelve in *Radio & Records* the week of September 28 and, in 1992, his single "If You Want to Find Love" on Reprise peaked at number eleven in *R&R* the week of February 21. Overall, though, he wasn't doing as well as in his halcyon days, which ended his association with Reprise and led to his Giant agreement. Reprise did issue the retrospective *Kenny (Great 20 Years) Rogers* in 1993. In 1994, he shifted gears creatively to record a new non-country album for Atlantic, *Timepiece: Orchestral Sessions with David Foster,* which provided his versions of songs by writers like the Gershwins, Rodgers and Hart, and Hoagy Carmichael.

Though Kenny reportedly had to deal with some serious health problems in the mid-1990s, they didn't seem to interfere with his musical activities. He continued to keep a variety of commitments in the concert and TV fields. In the spring of 1996, he signed a longtime multi-album recording agreement with Magnatone Records. Late in the year his high-profile projects included being featured in the Macy's Thanksgiving Day Parade and headlining another Christmas special, *Kenny Rogers: The Gift,* in December with Wynonna as guest star. Both also appeared on the *Opryland Country Christmas* program on CBS-TV. —*I. S./A. S.*

ROGERS, ROY: *Singer, guitarist, actor. Born Cincinnati, Ohio, November 5, 1911. Inducted into Country Music Hall of Fame as member of Sons of the Pioneers in 1980; elected as solo artist to Hall of Fame in 1988.*

The "King of the Cowboys" almost became the "King of the Bootmakers." Roy's father was a skilled shoemaker, and for a time Roy worked in a shoe factory. Luckily for movie audiences the world over, a cross-country trip in a beat-up jalopy helped launch Rogers (whose real name was Leonard Slye) on his fabled Hollywood career.

After seven years in Cincinnati, the family moved to a farm near Portsmouth, Ohio, where Roy learned to ride his first horse, a black mare that once raced at the county fair. Another favorite pastime of Roy's was the movies; on Saturday afternoons, he would go to see Buck Jones and Tom Mix films at the local cinema.

When he was a teenager, his family moved back to Cincinnati because of low finances. There Rogers met a man who owned a thoroughbred horse farm. He took a liking to Roy and gave him the chance to perfect his horsemanship. Around this time, Roy's family drove out to California to visit his newly married sister. When they returned to Portsmouth, Roy's dream was to return to California to work in the movies.

He bought a guitar and soon learned to play. In the late 1920s, he knew enough cowboy songs to sing and double as square-dance caller at local dances. In 1930, hearing that a distant relative was going to California, Rogers hitched a ride. His first jobs in Los Angeles were picking peaches and driving a sand and gravel truck. Roy became a favorite with his coworkers, entertaining them with his singing and guitar playing in the barracks at night. The excellent response made him think more seriously about a career as a musician.

He first joined a group of five other musicians called the Rocky Mountaineers. It was enjoyable, but not profitable, so he organized his own group, the International Cowboys. Still the results were not impressive. He broke up this group and soon joined a new one with two other young performers, Tim Spencer and Bob Nolan. They called their act the Sons of the Pioneers. Local audiences liked them, and before long they were making a respectable profit. They soon managed to gain a record date. When one of their first recordings became a major hit, the men were on their road to stardom.

The Sons of the Pioneers played more and more engagements in major western cities. They also were signed for a series of radio sketches. Roy branched out on his own in small singing roles in cowboy pictures. Hearing that Republic Studios was looking for a new cowboy lead, Roy applied for an audition. He was turned down, but sneaked in with a group of extras and got a hearing anyway.

The timing proved right. Gene Autry (whom the Sons of the Pioneers had backed in some films) had a falling out with the studio and walked out. Republic chief Herbert J. Yates promptly signed Rogers for the lead in the 1938 western *Under Western Skies.* From then on, Roy starred on one western after another, often accompanied in the singing segments by the Sons of the Pioneers. From that 1938 beginning through the 1951 movie *Spoilers of the Plains,* he made eighty-eight westerns in all, earning the title of "King of the Cowboys." His horse, Trigger, became as well known as the Lone Ranger's horse, Silver.

His leading lady for many of the 1940s films was Dale Evans. After Roy's first wife died in 1946, he married Dale. Rogers recalled for Bob Thomas of the Associated Press in January 1975, "That was 27 years ago and people said, 'We'll give 'em a year.'" Republic's Yates was so sure the public wouldn't accept Dale as Roy's girlfriend after the marriage that he dropped her from the series. Rogers told Thomas, "The studio got a jillion letters of protest and Yates had to put Dale back in the pictures."

After TV almost wiped out the movie western, Rogers and Evans started their own TV series, performing in 101 episodes through the late 1950s. In addition, the duo kept up busy recording sessions and traveled widely for in-person appearances in theaters and at rodeos and state and county fairs.

But the pressures of such a heavy schedule apparently caught up with Roy in 1958, when he developed a heart condition. The first signs appeared, he told Thomas, in 1975 when "I was hunting deer at 9,000 feet in Utah. I had just shot and cleaned one and the two fellows I was with put it on a carrier with a bicycle wheel to take it down the mountain. I had gone about 150 feet and my arms started hurting. I couldn't get air, but I thought it was the altitude."

After he returned home, though, those sensations continued. Finally going into a clinic for an examination, he found he had angina pectoris. For the next year, he had to sharply limit his activities. However, he stuck to the required regimen and rebuilt his health to the point that he could resume some, if not all, of his entertainment work in the 1960s. He still was in good shape in the mid-1970s, telling Thomas, "Now I can ride my motorcycle and do almost everything, except a rough-and-tumble fight in a film."

It turned out, however, that he was too optimistic. His health problems flared up again in 1978, and this time he required triple-bypass surgery and installation of a pacemaker. Fortunately he came through in good shape, and was able to resume most of his presurgery activities.

In the mid-1960s, Roy, Dale, and their family (which included children by previous marriages and a number of adopted children) settled in Apple Valley in California's Mojave Desert. One of the things they did there was to open the Roy Rogers Museum, whose exhibits include, beside career memorabilia, Roy's stuffed horse, Trigger. (Average annual tourist volume through the museum from the late 1960s through the start of the 1980s was about 100,000 people.)

Roy's other activities of the 1970s included providing his name for a string of fast-food restaurants and, in 1974–75, taping introductions for a syndicated TV series of old westerns, *Roy Rogers Presents the Great Movie Cowboys.*

His record releases included the 1974 single "Hoppy, Gene and Me" and later in the 1970s, on Capitol Records, the LP *The Country Side of Roy Rogers* and the charted single "Money Can't Buy Love."

During the heyday of his career in the 1940s and 1950s, most of his material was released through RCA Victor. His Victor albums included *Roy Rogers' Souvenir Album, Roy Rogers' Roundup, Skip to My Lou and Other Square Dances* (with Spade Cooley), and *Roy Rogers and Dale Evans.* Some of Roy's singles recordings were "You Can't Break My Heart," "Don't Blame It All on Me," "Rock Me to Sleep in My Saddle," "My Chickashay Gal," "Hawaiian Cowboy," "Dusty," "Home on the Range," "Old Fashioned Cowboy," "Stampede," "Smiles Are Made out of Sunshine," "Frosty the Snow Man," "I'm a-Rollin'," and "Yellow Bonnets and Polka Dot Shoes."

As the 1980s began, Roy was elected to the Country Music Hall of Fame along with other founding members of the Sons of the Pioneers. When this was announced on the October 1980 telecast of the CMA Awards program, Roy was the only surviving member of the group, Bob Nolan and Hugh Farr having died earlier in the year. In 1988 Roy was elected to the Country Music Hall of Fame as a solo performer, making him the only artist to receive that honor twice.

Throughout the 1980s into the 1990s, Rogers and Evans were still making occasional TV appearances, such as cohosting one of the NBC-TV *Nashville Palace* programs in the early 1980s and guesting on some of the CMA-sponsored TV events.

Roy and Dale also participated in various charity projects during those years and in special programs honoring cowboy films and western music at venues like Gene Autry's Western Heritage Museum in Los Angeles's Griffith Park, where they took part in several events with C&W artists young and old in the 1990s. Many of the new country stars were fans of Roy's, which led to recording sessions with Clint Black that brought a 1992 CMA nomination for Vocal Event of the Year. By then movie chroniclers reported that Roy had appeared in eighty-eight western films, thirty-five with Dale. In 1995, Roy collaborated with Rex Allen, Sr., and his son Rex Allen, Jr., on a new version of "Last of the Silver Screen Cowboys" included in the Allens' Warner Western Records album *The Singing Cowboys.* During that period, Roy and Dale published their joint autobiography, *Happy Trails.*

In October 1995, Roy, Dale, and son Roy Rogers,

Jr., announced plans for a new $45 million western theme park to be built around an upgraded Roy Rogers–Dale Evans Museum in Victorville, California (with an estimated museum renovation cost of $1 million). Incorporating educational facilities and entertainment venues, the park, they stated, would focus on presenting the story of the West from 1860 to 1960, giving visitors "the opportunity to relive the spirit of yesteryear." The schedule for RogersDale Park called for starting construction in 1996, leading to opening in 1997.

(See also Evans, Dale; Sons of the Pioneers.)

ROUSE BROTHERS: *Vocal and instrumental group, songwriting team. Ervin Rouse, Gordon Rouse, Earl Rouse, all born North Carolina.*

The Rouse Brothers separately and as a team played thousands of dates in country nightclubs from New York to Miami in a career that stretched from the 1930s to the 1970s. However, other than the people who saw their act, most country fans knew little about them because of their lack of recording success. Almost everyone was aware of their classic original fiddle tune, "Orange Blossom Special," though most thought it was a traditional song.

The boys were members of a large family, containing fifteen children all told, born and raised in rural North Carolina. Country music was an integral part of life, and quite a few of the Rouses learned one or more instruments and played in local groups. Ervin, Gordon, and Earl had the greatest persistence, and as the 1930s progressed managed to move from their home-town region to major cities on the East Coast.

Even before the brothers sallied forth from North Carolina, they were working up original material. One of their ideas for improving their position in the music field was to sell some of the songs to major publishers. It was rough going, as Ervin told Everett Corbin of *Music City News* (October 1969): "We walked all over New York and were turned down by all the music publishers. We were told that 'your music will never amount to anything.' We were discouraged and encouraged to 'stay out of the music business.'"

However, the Rouses had their musical skills to fall back on. If they couldn't sell their songs, they still could try to find work as performers, and eventually they began to get enough jobs to keep them going. In time they were able to do well enough to find bookings in such important clubs as New York's Village Barn and Miami's Royal Palm (where they shared one bill with Sophie Tucker).

It was while traveling from a New York engagement to another in Miami, Ervin told Corbin, that "Orange Blossom Special" was born. "We wrote it on the same day [in 1936] the Orange Blossom Special passenger train was christened at Miami. We were riding with our manager, Lloyd Smith, from Miami to New York and he

challenged us to write a song about the train. We took the challenge and it was completed by the time we got to Orlando." The tune, he noted, was cowritten by him and Gordon and was intended to be a combined "fiddling, singing, talking" song.

The Rouses copyrighted the song and initially sold the publishing rights to a New York firm whose copyrights later were acquired by Leeds Music. However, they didn't get the chance to record it for several years. In 1939, they finally signed with RCA's Bluebird label and recorded an album of country songs, including a number of other original compositions. During the early 1940s, the Rouses also made some recordings for ABC Records' country label, Melatone, but neither their RCA or Melatone efforts found a wide public response.

Meanwhile, though, "Orange Blossom Special" had a life of its own. More and more country artists included it in their repertoire and more and more recordings by major performers were released over the decades. A number of versions made the charts. In 1965, a single by Johnny Cash rose to the top 10 in the U.S. country lists and showed up on pop charts as well.

The Rouses continued to remain relatively anonymous, though they kept writing songs—particularly Ervin—and performing. Some of Ervin's other material was recorded by major artists. In 1945, he wrote "Sweeter than the Flowers," which provided chart hits for both Roy Acuff and Moon Mullican later in that decade. Mullican's release was a top-10 hit in 1948.

During one of Johnny Cash's network TV programs in 1969, he paid homage to the Rouses by having them perform "Orange Blossom Special" on the show. The brothers came up to Nashville for the program from their home in Miami, where they had been living for close to two decades. All were still working at the time, Earl handling vocals, guitar, and fiddle, Gordon, vocals and fiddle, and Ervin, vocals and fiddle.

RUSSELL, LEON: *Singer, pianist, trumpeter, guitarist, songwriter. Born Lawton, Oklahoma, April 2, 1942.*

Some people were surprised when Leon Russell, rock superstar, began turning out country-oriented albums in the 1970s, starting with *Hank Wilson's Back, Vol. 1* in late 1973. They shouldn't have been, considering Leon's exposure to folk and country material in his Oklahoma childhood and his early association with pioneers and the rockabilly era.

Still, his first training wasn't in a pop or country format, but in classical music. His father, a clerk for the Texas Company, and his mother both played the piano and started him on the instrument when he was three. He continued those studies until he entered high school. "I didn't really have the hands for classical stuff," he said, "and my teachers discouraged me from making up my own music."

He turned to the trumpet with the goal of becoming

a pop musician, formed a band (he had to lie about his age—fourteen—to get a job in a Texas nightclub), and performed in many concerts and dances in Oklahoma during 1956–57. These performances included sessions with Jerry Lee Lewis and a group called Ronnie Hawkins and the Hawks. Looking for broader horizons, in 1958 teenaged Leon moved to Los Angeles, where "I'd borrow a friend's ID to get a job, then I'd return the card and work until I was stopped by the police for being underage and out after curfew."

By the early 1960s, his talents on piano, trumpet, and a variety of other instruments earned him a glowing reputation in the music industry. He became one of the most sought-after session musicians in Los Angeles. One of the first producers to seek him out was Phil Spector, who employed Leon's talents on the 1963 LP *Ronnie and the Ronettes.* During the mid-1960s, Russell was particularly active with Gary Lewis & the Play-boys, contributing his ability in the form of sideman, arranger, and sometimes, songwriter on fourteen albums of Gary's. Among his other credits of those years was work on Herb Alpert's 1965 success, *Whipped Cream and Other Delights,* handling piano on the Byrds classic 1965 single "Mr. Tambourine Man," and doing similar session work for Frank Sinatra, Ike and Tina Turner, the Righteous Brothers, Paul Revere and the Raiders, and others.

One of his early solo efforts was the 1965 single on Dot Records, "Everybody's Talking 'Bout the Young," which didn't make much headway. He made a single, released in 1966, for A&M Records, which Leon says he would just as soon forget about.

In 1967, Russell dropped much of his outside work to concentrate on building his own studio. He still did some work with friends, including Delaney & Bonnie, performing with them on many dates in the late 1960s and early 1970s, including the network TV show *Shindig,* and backing them on a number of their recordings.

But Leon was eager to strike out on his own in the late 1960s, and, as one step toward that end, he teamed up with another young musician, Marc Benno. Calling themselves Asylum Choir, they made some tapes that earned them a contract from Smash Records in 1968, which led to the release of their debut LP in 1969, *Asylum Choir.* The LP got good reviews, but commercially was not successful. Meanwhile, through Delaney & Bonnie, Leon had become acquainted with blues/rock singer Joe Cocker and his manager Denny Cordell. Cordell asked Russell to work on Cocker's second LP and, impressed with Russell's skills, took him back to England to work up material for a solo LP. The collaboration resulted in the formation of a new label by the two, called Shelter Records, to handle Russell's product. The first album, originally titled *Can a Blue Man Sing the Whites,* later changed to *Leon Russell,* came out in early 1970, and, while it didn't challenge for top

spots, remained on the hit lists a respectable number of months. As the year went by, Russell bolstered his growing reputation by touring with Joe Cocker in the famous *Mad Dogs and Englishmen* series.

Russell's activities continued at a frantic pace in 1970–71 with session work on LPs by the Rolling Stones, Glen Campbell, Rita Coolidge, Delaney & Bonnie, and Dave Mason. He also took part in the landmark Concert for Bangladesh in New York's Madison Square Garden. His visibility contributed to the enormous success of his next release on Shelter, *Leon Russell and the Shelter People,* which was a bestseller for many months in 1971 and for much of 1972, earning him his first gold record.

Similar fortune awaited successive releases, such as *Carney* (which spawned his major hit "Tight Rope"), issued in 1972, and the three-record 1973 release *Leon Live* (featuring material made at the several concerts in which Leon played before tens of thousands of fans).

By the end of 1973, when *Hank Wilson's Back* came out, Russell was acknowledged as one of the brightest stars in pop music. This LP was a change of pace; it contained his treatment of such folk and country standards as "Battle of New Orleans," "Am I That Easy to Forget," "She Thinks I Still Care," and "Rollin' in My Sweet Baby's Arms." It was a fine offering, but it puzzled reviewers and fans alike and gained only a fair response from record buyers. One cut, however, "Rollin' in My Sweet Baby's Arms," rose high on country lists, indicating to Leon that he could find a following in the genre.

In 1974, Leon moved in still another direction musically with the LP *Stop All That Jazz,* which met with only lukewarm response. The same year, he backed a singer named Mary McCreary on her LP *Jezebel,* on Shelter. It was a harbinger of things to come—two years later she married him. In 1975, Russell proved he still had drawing power with the pop audience by turning out the gold-record LP *Will o' the Wisp.* At the time, Leon's relationship to Shelter Records was tenuous and he soon left to form a new company, Paradise Records, with distribution arranged through Warner Brothers Records.

His first release on the new label, appropriately, was a duet with Mary Russell in celebration of their marriage, called *The Wedding Album.* In 1977, the duo followed up with *Make Love to the Music* and, in 1979, Leon backed Mary on her solo collection *Heart of Fire.* From 1975 through 1977, he did some session work in addition to his work with Mary, but didn't complete any solo releases. He finally broke that silence with *Americana* in 1978, an album that was one of the weakest he'd done in his career.

Increasingly from the mid-1970s on, Russell had been including country-oriented material in his recordings. In 1979, he stressed that side of his musical interests more than ever, and it seemed to act as a catalyst in restoring his standing in pop music in general. In late 1978 and early 1979, he teamed up with a longtime friend, country giant Willie Nelson, for a series of concerts that since have become almost legendary with music buffs. In 1979, a two-record set taken from those appearances was issued on Columbia, titled *One for the Road,* presenting superb versions of all kinds of songs, from pop standards of the 1940s and 1950s to classic country and folk tunes. The album was nominated by the Country Music Association for Best Album of the Year and deservedly took top honors. During the same period, a new collection of Leon's came out on Paradise, titled *Life and Love,* that was as consistently strong in music and performance as *Americana* had been weak. The album presented both sides of Leon—several fine country and country rock tracks and a number of blues rockers that harked back to his work of the early 1970s. By the end of 1979, Russell could point to a banner year that included receiving a gold-record award for *One for the Road* and the rise of the single "Heartbreak Hotel" to number one on country charts.

For much of the late 1970s, Leon devoted most of his time developing his own videotaping facility, called Paradise Video (used by such people as former Eagle band member Randy Meisner and James Taylor). In early 1980, he formed a new musical alliance with the progressive bluegrass group New Grass Revival. From then through 1981, they performed a series of concerts across the United States and in Australia and New Zealand that rank with the best those artists have presented. In May 1980, one of those shows was taped by Paradise Records and some of the renditions (including bluegrass numbers; such Russell originals as "Stranger in a Strange Land," "One More Love Song," "Pilgrim Land," "Georgia Blues," and "Prince of Peace"; and versions of songs by the Beatles, Rolling Stones, and Hank Williams) were issued on the February 1981 LP, *Leon Russell and the New Grass Revival, the Live Album.* While it was a good album, it fell short of capturing the raw energy and chilling impact of the actual concerts.

SAWYER BROWN: *Vocal and instrumental group from Florida. Mark Miller born Dayton, Ohio, October 25, c. 1960 (lead vocals, songwriter); Gregg "Hobie" Hubbard (guitar, songwriter); Duncan Cameron (guitar, songwriter); Jim Scholten (bass guitar); Joe Smyth (drums).*

Sawyer Brown in the 1990s could lay claim to one of the longer tenures in country music. In a period when country bands seemed to spring up, become famous, and fade from view in four to five years' time, only a few bands besides Alabama could point to the kind of fan loyalty and recording success that could carry them for over a decade. In Sawyer Brown's case, the band began placing songs on top of the charts in the early 1980s and was still going strong both as a live concert act and hitmaker in the mid-1990s, while winning nominations in major awards polls year after year.

The group's origins go back to the late 1970s, when Mark Miller and Gregg Hubbard met while both were students at the University of Central Florida. Both had been involved in music projects in high school and already had tried their hands individually at songwriting before entering college. Both had been heavily influenced by the blend of rock 'n' roll and country, which was then flourishing in the Southeast through groups like the Allman Brothers and Lynyrd Skynyrd. Their goal was to find their own unique style of high-energy rock that still paid tribute to the traditional country sounds of their home region.

The rapport between the two was good, and they worked together as a duo and with other combinations of performers before deciding to try for more impressive achievements in Nashville. Their move to that city took place in 1981.

In Nashville they initially formed a group that included Jim Scholten on bass guitar and Joe Smyth on drums, musicians still part of the band makeup in the mid-1990s. It was a young, highly motivated band whose members were all in their early twenties. Lead guitar position changed hands a few times (Bobby Randall filled the role for a time) until Duncan Cameron came on board as the permanent fifth member. While Miller was the primary songwriter from early in the band's odyssey, many writing contributions over the years came from Hubbard and Cameron, though eventually Mac McAnally became Miller's main collaborator.

The first gig of what was to become Sawyer Brown was as the tour band for performer Don King. When that work ended, the musicians decided to remain together rather than disbanding, taking their name from a Nashville street. For a while the group found bookings in and around the Music City area with hopes, naturally, of gaining a record deal with a major label. But actual achievement of that goal required a roundabout route.

That saga began when the band got the opportunity to audition for the syndicated TV program *Star Search* in October 1983. The group put on an impressive set and was soon on its way to Los Angeles, where they soon were doing very well under the show's format. For five months in L.A., Sawyer Brown became frontrunners in the competition, winning the top position for twelve straight weeks and accumulating some $175,000 in prize money up to and including the finals, from which they emerged as Best New Star Musical Group. That success, in turn, earned a recording contract from Capitol/Curb and the chance to prepare the debut album, *Sawyer Brown.*

Soon the band was placing such singles on the charts as the mid-1980s releases "Used to Blue," "Leona," and "Step That Step," the last a Miller composition that gave Sawyer Brown its first number-one success. Buoyed by steady touring embracing several hundred engagements a year (in 1994 the band was still on the road for over 220 shows), the group drew an enthusiastic and rapidly growing following. During those years the band got the chance to work with many of the best-known country music stars including Kenny Rogers, Dolly Parton, Crystal Gayle, Eddie Rabbitt, and the Oak Ridge Boys. Its promise was recognized by others in the country field, who voted to present it with the Country Music Association's Horizon Award in 1985.

As the 1980s went by, the group was rarely absent from the hit charts with either singles or albums. (Their album output from its mid-1980s debut to the start of the 1990s came to seven releases.) During that period, year-end reports showed Sawyer Brown to rank regularly among the top-grossing concert acts in the country industry. There did seem to be a perceptible slowdown in its fortunes late in the 1980s, with record releases not moving as high on the hit lists as previously. Some industry observers wondered if the band's cycle was on the downward spiral becoming all too typical of the "modern" country era.

Fortunately it proved to be only a momentary lapse, as the group bounced back with even more vigor coming into the 1990s. Some reasons for the rebound might include a greater depth and meaning that the band had begun to bring to their new songs. Miller commented in early 1993, "I wrote 'Step That Step' when I was 23 years old. It's been more than 10 years now and I think we look at life differently. There's a much broader world view we bring to our writing now. I don't think that means you rock any less. I think we rock as hard as we ever did. It's just that we have something more to say."

The band started off the 1990s with their *Greatest Hits* album on the *Billboard* list, having peaked at number twenty-six. In early 1991, Curb Records issued a new collection, *Buick*, which stayed on the charts for many months after entering the *Billboard* Top 30 in the summer. However, the release that signaled a new leap forward for the band was that of Miller's composition "The Walk." The record peaked at number fifteen in *Radio & Records* the week of September 14, 1991, and did even better on other charts. The song examined the stages of life as seen through the eyes of a father and son, and was accompanied by a moving video that remained in top positions on the TNN and CMT video channels for many weeks. Many critics included the song on their best-of-the-year lists.

Miller commented, "That song was kind of an ace in the hole for us. We believed in it so much we put our heart and soul into promoting it. We knew it had the potential to strike some emotional chords with people."

It did that and also cleared the way for even more successful originals beginning with the title track from their next album, *The Dirt Road*. That song, written by Miller and Gregg Hubbard, shot to the top of the charts, peaking at number one in *R&R* the week of January 24, 1992. The album made the charts in early 1992 and, after peaking at number eighteen in *Billboard*, stayed on them through early 1993 on the way to gold-record certification by the R.I.A.A.

It was followed on the charts by "Some Girls Do," a single from the album that reached top position on all major charts, peaking at number one in *R&R* the week of May 8, 1992. Next to reach top-chart levels was the single "Cafe on the Corner" (written by respected Nashville songwriter Mac McAnally), the title song from the band's next album. The single peaked at number four in *R&R* the week of October 16, 1992. The album, issued in the fall of 1992, peaked at number eighteen in *Billboard* and stayed on its list through much of 1993 to earn another R.I.A.A. gold-record award.

Sawyer Brown started off 1993 with another hit from McAnally's pen, "All These Years," which peaked at number one in *R&R* the week of February 19. Soon after, the band had a *Billboard* Top 10 success with "Trouble on the Line" (at number ten and rising the week of May 29), cowritten by Miller and B. Shore. Next came the single "Thank God for You" (cowritten by Miller and McAnally) in upper *Billboard* levels in late summer, and "The Boys and Me," another Miller/McAnally collaboration, well within *Billboard*'s Top 10 by year-end.

During the fall of 1993, the band had another very listenable album climbing the charts, peaking at number thirteen in *Billboard* and staying on the magazine's lists through 1994 to win still another gold-record acknowledgment from the R.I.A.A. The band's hot streak continued through 1994 with more top-10 singles: "Hard to Say" (written by Miller) in the *Billboard* Top 5 in September and "This Time" (a Miller/McAnally song) high on hit lists by year-end.

In the first half of the 1990s, the band continued to be equally successful with videos of its hit songs, achievements recognized by Sawyer Brown's choice as Vocal Band of the Year in the TNN/*Music City News* Awards and Video Group of the Year by CMT voters. The band also received nominations in the 1992–93 time frame for Top Country Group in the American Music Awards poll and for Top Vocal Group in the Academy of Country Music member survey. In Country Music Association voting, the band was nominated for Vocal Group of the Year each year from 1991 through 1994.

The band continued its intensive tour schedule, with a performing intensity as good as or better than its mid-1980s work. Miller said, "I feel like when I go onstage now, I'm even more energetic because I know where to put the energy. It's like a ball player who's been in the league for ten years as opposed to the rookie just coming up. The younger guy may be a little quicker, but the veteran's still going to have the savvy to score more. The show is pretty spontaneous and we mix it up a lot. I like to think that if you come to us ten times, you'll get to see ten different shows."

The band had been spotlighted for so many years it was hard to realize the bandsmen had been pretty young when that first took place. In the mid-1990s, all the musicians were still in their early thirties. Miller noted, "Sometimes a newcomer will open for us and ask for advice, and he's a few years older than us. It's hard to throw your arm around him and start off by saying, 'Well, son . . .'"

In early 1995, the retrospective Curb album *Greatest Hits, 1990–1995* was on the charts. After peaking at number five in *Billboard,* it went past R.I.A.A. gold record levels by summer. The group scored another singles success during the first half of 1995 with "I Don't Believe in Goodbye," which peaked at number four in *Billboard* in early June. The band's charted singles in 1996 included "Treat Her Right" which made upper levels in the summer. The album *This Thing Called Wantin' and Havin' It All* was released in late 1995 and stayed on the charts well into 1996. The disc peaked at number ten in *Billboard.* Among Sawyer Brown's projects in 1996 was work on a track for a tribute album to the Beach Boys rock group.

SCRUGGS, EARL: *Singer, banjoist, guitarist, band leader (Foggy Mountain Boys, Earl Scruggs Revue), songwriter. Born Cleveland County, North Carolina, January 6, 1924. Elected to Country Music Hall of Fame (as part of Flatt & Scruggs team) in 1985.*

When the giants of modern country music are remembered, Earl Scruggs's name will be one of the first to come to mind. Apart from his many contributions as a songwriter and recording artist, his innovations in the art of the banjo created a revolution that affected the use of the instrument not only in country but in every facet of pop music. In fact, in a later—and controversial—phase of his career, Earl experimented with new blends of traditional and current styles, using an electrified banjo as part of his country, folk, and rock-oriented Earl Scruggs Revue.

Although he upset many country and folk purists with his innovations, he succeeded in attracting many new fans to the intricacies and delights of what has become known as the Scruggs Picking Style. The approach, based on the use of three fingers in the five-string banjo picking pattern, modifies the sound of the instrument with the Scruggs Tuner. The tuner allows the banjo player to achieve unusual warping of the strings for all kinds of distorted effects. These innovations, combined with Scruggs's intricate lead runs and background fills, caused Al Rudis of the *Chicago Sun-Times* to make the apt statement, "What Segovia is to the guitar, Earl Scruggs is to the five-string banjo."

Born and raised in North Carolina near the town of Selby, Earl first started teaching himself banjo at the early age of four and could play simple tunes on the instrument at the age of five. At ten he had already invented the three-finger picking style that was to become his trademark. Before long, he was a local celebrity, playing with a band on a local radio station when he was fifteen. To help himself financially, he worked at a textile mill for a while in his teens, but that demanding job only reinforced his desire to make his career in music. By the time he left Bolling Springs High School in 1942, his skills as a banjoist (he also learned to play excellent guitar by then) had matured to the point that band jobs were becoming available well outside his home section.

At one point, he worked for a time with the Morris Brothers (whose early recordings have sometimes been reissued on old-time folk music collections) on a Spartanburg, South Carolina, radio station. He retained fond memories of that period, and, in the 1970s, had the Morris Brothers take part in a Public Broadcasting System program titled "Earl Scruggs Family and Friends." (Also on the program were other famous names in country, folk, and rock, including Bob Dylan, Joan Baez, Roger McGuinn and the Byrds, and Doc and Merle Watson.)

Scruggs's first major milestone came in 1944, when he won the attention of Bill Monroe, the "Father of Bluegrass Music." Earl became a member of one of the most famous of Monroe's Blue Grass Boys lineups, a band whose other members included a dynamically talented young guitarist named Lester Flatt. Earl and Lester remained members of the Monroe troupe until 1948, appearing regularly with Bill on the *Grand Ole Opry* radio show and touring all over the country with his stage act.

But Flatt and Scruggs became restless working for someone else. In 1948, they left to form their own band, the group that was to become the legendary Foggy Mountain Boys. With the help of Flatt's friend Mac Wiseman, they gained a spot on the *Farm and Fun Time* program on station WCYB, Bristol, Virginia, the first of a series of stations they played all over the South and border states in the early 1950s. The exposure catapulted them to headliners of the *Opry* in 1953, where they remained featured *Opry* stars until the act broke up after over two decades of notable accomplishments.

Almost as soon as Flatt & Scruggs was formed, they gained a recording contract with Mercury that lasted until 1951. They switched to Columbia, the Flatt & Scruggs label throughout the rest of their career, turning out dozens of albums and singles, many of which not only made uppermost levels of country charts but often appeared on national pop lists too. During the 1950s and 1960s, when Flatt & Scruggs toured many foreign countries in addition to their regular 200 or more U.S. concerts, their recordings sometimes showed up on overseas hit lists as well.

Many of Flatt & Scruggs's most famous songs were written or cowritten by Earl. His compositions included "Flint Hill Special," named for his home community in North Carolina, "Randy Lynn Rag," in honor of his oldest son, later lead singer of the Earl Scruggs Revue, "Earl's Breakdown," "Foggy Mountain Breakdown" (the song that provided the name for the Flatt & Scruggs band), "Foggy Mountain Special," "Foggy Mountain Chimes," "Rocky Mountain Rock," and perhaps his most successful commercial effort, "The Ballad of Jed Clampett," the theme for the *Beverly Hillbillies* TV program. The Flatt & Scruggs single of that song was number one on both country and pop charts for a number of weeks in 1962. Among the songs that Scruggs cowrote with various other writers were "Shuckin' the Corn," "Crying My Heart Out over You," "Someone You Have Forgotten," "I Won't Be Hanging Around," and "Building on Sand."

In its over twenty years of existence, the Flatt & Scruggs team remained one of the most popular in the United States, much of the time having its own syndicated TV show aired all over the nation. Both separately and as part of the act, Flatt and Scruggs won all kinds of honors, including Grammy Awards.

However, even as early as 1960, internal strains were beginning to develop that eventually led to Flatt & Scruggs's breakup in 1969. Flatt loved the traditional, mainly acoustical approach to country and bluegrass, while Earl, influenced by his growing brood of talented young sons, was becoming restless with long-established ways. He traced some of his desire for a new direction to when, rehearsing for a TV show in 1960, he jammed with blues saxophonist King Curtis, who also was a guest on the program. "I saw where the banjo was more versatile than just straight bluegrass, and it sounded so good to me until I just couldn't get it off my mind."

As the 1960s went by, Earl wanted to work some amplified, sometimes rock-based material into the Flatt & Scruggs repertoire, but met with resistance from his partner. Finally the two split up and Scruggs started working up a new act in 1969 with his two sons, Randy and Gary. Randy, who started learning guitar before he was in his teens, had played on every record his father had made since Randy was thirteen. He took over on lead guitar in the new Revue and handled much of the arranging and a considerable amount of the songwriting in collaboration with older brother Gary.

Gary came to show business a little later than other family members. Although he also learned several instruments as a boy (his Revue chores, besides lead vocals, include electric bass, harmonica, and guitar), for a time he seemed headed toward another career. He enrolled in and graduated from Vanderbilt University in Nashville as a philosophy major, though with music as a minor. Before making the Revue his primary interest, he teamed with Randy to do two albums on the Vanguard label, *All the Way Home* and the *Scruggs Brothers.*

By the start of the 1970s, Earl and his family-based act were playing a variety of venues from small folk clubs to college auditoriums around the United States. For a time in the mid-1970s, the other band sidemen were Jody Maphis on drums and Jack Lee on piano. By 1978, it had become an all-family affair, with Randy's brother-in-law Taylor Rhodes (born Nashville) taking over from Maphis on drums (and also handling some rhythm guitar) and Steve Scruggs doing the keyboard work. Steve, youngest of Earl's boys (born 1958), had taken over on keyboards a few years earlier. Also multitalented, he could play a half dozen other instruments.

The Revue signed with Earl's longtime label, Columbia, and turned out one or more LPs every year for most of the 1970s. Another of the group's efforts was composing and performing the soundtrack for the movie *Where the Lilies Bloom;* Columbia released the soundtrack album in 1974. (In previous movie assignments, Earl Scruggs had played his "Foggy Mountain Breakdown" as the main background music for *Bonnie and Clyde.*) In 1975, the Revue joined with Earl in celebrating his twenty-fifth anniversary as a Columbia recording artist. That effort included a "super session," where support was provided by thirty-nine first-rank pop music stars, including Johnny Cash, Loggins and Messina, Alvin Lee, Dan Fogelberg, Tracy Nelson, Billy Joel, Michael Murphey, Leonard Cohen, and Buffy Sainte-Marie. The *Earl Scruggs Revue Anniversary Album Volume I* was issued in 1975 and *Volume II* in 1976.

Other 1970s albums by the Revue include *Family Portrait,* issued in 1976; *Live from Austin City Limits,* released in 1977; *Strike Anywhere,* issued in 1977; and *Bold & New,* issued in 1978. The latter was the first Revue LP produced by Chips Moman (Ron Bledsoe produced the earlier ones), who also coauthored with keyboardist Bobby Emmons one of the *Bold & New* songs, "The Cabin." Five of the songs in that album were cowritten by Gary and Randy Scruggs ("Take the Time," "Someone like You," "Louisiana Lady," "Found Myself a New Love," and "Our Love Is Home Grown"), who also had provided originals for many of the previous collections. The singles issued on Columbia in the mid- and late-1970s included "If I'd Only Come and Gone" in 1973; "Where the Lilies Bloom" in 1974; "Travelin' Prayer" in 1974; "Tall Texas Woman" in 1976; and "The Cabin" in 1978.

Earl Scruggs stated that he was happy with the way his career had gone since Flatt & Scruggs broke up. His new alignment gave him the freedom to have a drummer in the band, considered a heresy in traditional bluegrass groups. He felt that the heavier beat employed in typical Revue arrangements made even the more traditional numbers the band played sound better. "I remember back in the old days, when groups didn't even carry a bass fiddle," he told James Carrier of the Associated Press (January 2, 1976). "But the guitar player would take the deepest guitar that put out the fullest, deepest, bassiest sound for his vocal. And also they would stomp their feet quite a lot to add a beat to the group. So I thought that a good drummer and a set of drums would make a much better sound than a group of people pickin' and stompin' their feet against the floor.

"I didn't know how it would work, but it sounded too good not to try it. I just needed something to stimulate my feelings. I was getting bored and unhappy doing the same things for over 20 years.

"I feel I'm pickin' a better banjo now than I ever did. I feel I'm playing music with a much more exciting [flair] than I would be if I was playing back [with Flatt] because I wasn't mentally into it. There I just got to where I was not playing too good. I just got tired of playing the old routine.

"I just don't think you can stay with the same songs all your life without going along with the times. You've got to keep working on your material, doing them different ways or you just get out of the ball game, that's all."

But Earl didn't completely rule out getting back together with his old partner, at least on a limited scale. He recalled discussing the possibility with a not-too-well Flatt in 1979. "I went to see him in the hospital and he asked me if I'd like to do some shows with him. I showed interest in doing it, but my main concern, I told him, was for him to get his health back." Sadly, it didn't happen; a few months later Flatt died.

In 1982, Earl announced the breakup of the Earl Scruggs Revue. "Randy and Steve had a recording studio and they were really wanting to get off the road and start families. We had 11 or 12 real good successful and happy years together." Of course, that didn't mean that the boys and Earl wouldn't get together on various projects in years to come.

Earl toyed with the idea of retirement, but was soon working on a new album with Tom T. Hall. That led to the completion of *The Storyteller and the Banjoman,* coproduced by Randy Scruggs and John Thompson at the Scruggs Sound Studio in Nashville. That was followed by Earl's 1983 compilation, *Top of the World,* coproduced by the Randy Scruggs-John Thompson team. The album featured guest appearances by such Earl Scruggs fans as Ricky Skaggs, Lacy J. Dalton, the Burrito Brothers, and Rodney Dillard. The backing band, besides Skaggs on rhythm guitar and mandolin, had such top session players as Buddy Spicher on fiddle, Jerry Douglas on Dobro, and Gene Sisk on piano.

The initial single was the title track, "Sittin' on Top of the World," which Earl had cowritten with Rodney Dillard. Other tracks included two new instrumental numbers written by Earl, "Lindsey" and "Roller Coaster."

In 1985, the Flatt & Scruggs duo was elected to the Country Music Hall of Fame, a result that won a standing ovation from the audience when it was announced on the CMA Awards telecast in October. In the years that followed, Earl continued to delight fans both old and young with his still impeccable instrumental skills. As Rodney Dillard emphasized, "Earl Scruggs created a banjo style with no preconceptions of how it should be done, which gave him the freedom as an innovator and a true creative musician. Banjo styles post-Scruggs are only variations on a theme established by him. Earl is the father and the child of the five string banjo. For me, trying to describe Earl's playing would be very much like taking a black and white photograph of a rainbow."

In the fall of 1989, Scruggs was awarded the National Heritage Fellowship in Folk Arts honor by the National Endowment for the Arts for "his revolutionary style of banjo picking." (The early 1990s brought their share of sorrows, however, such as the death of Steve Scruggs in 1992.) Earl was still on the Columbia Records roster in 1995, some forty-five years since he first joined the label, though he hadn't recorded new material for the company for some years. He wasn't completely absent from the recording standpoint as indicated by the Grammy nomination of the single "Keep on the Sunny Side" as a finalist in the 1994 voting for Best Country Instrumental Performance. The single was recorded by Earl, son Randy, and Doc Watson. In 1995, Earl was again one of the finalists in that Grammy category for the track "Sally Goodin'" performed by him with Byron Berline and Bill Monroe.

In the mid-1990s the Country Music Foundation catalog offered ten albums of Flatt & Scruggs recordings. By that time, Bear Family Records had three extensive collections of tracks from the Flatt & Scruggs era in its catalog, covering all of their output from 1958 through 1969. The first of those, *Flatt & Scruggs 1948–1959,* was a four-CD set containing all of their Mercury recordings and their Columbia output from 1950–1959. Included is the original version of "Foggy Mountain Breakdown." The second package, covering 1959 through 1963 includes the theme from *The Beverly Hillbillies* and the album made from their Carnegie Hall concert of that period including nineteen previously unissued songs from the event. The third collection, comprising six CDs, covers the years 1964–1969 plus a Gordon Terry square dance album on which Flatt & Scruggs were backing musicians.

SCHLITZ, DON: *Songwriter. Born Durham, North Carolina, August 29, 1952.*

"The song is the thing," just about any artist in country music (or indeed just about every form of pop music) will tell you. Sometimes the performer will write his or her own material, and in fact more than a few country stars began as songwriters providing material for others. But even the most prolific writer/star performer will have to enlist the talents of a professional writer, either as a collaborator or supplier of ready-to-use hit-song candidates. As of the mid-1990s, Don Schlitz took both paths, cowriting hits with Mary-Chapin Carpenter while providing compositions to hit makers like Kenny Rogers and Randy Travis.

Schlitz was already becoming interested in songwriting as a teenager and, by the time he reached his early twenties, felt confident enough to move to Nashville in 1973 to seek a living at it. Fortunately, he had managed to become computer-proficient before getting there and was able to find a job as a computer operator at Vanderbilt University to help pay the bills while he sought to enlist interest in his writing talent from record firms and artists. It proved a more arduous task than his youthful exuberance had led him to expect. One year went by, then another, without a breakthrough in any direction. Finally, in 1978, he achieved his first published song, "The Gambler," which became a number-one hit in late 1978 and early 1979 for Kenny Rogers.

After that, Don never looked back. It was a rare period throughout the 1980s and up to the mid-1990s when his writing credentials weren't called out on chart-hit singles, often ones reaching the number-one spot on the hit lists. Artists reaping such rewards with his songs included the Judds with "Rockin' with the Rhythm of the Rain," the Nitty Gritty Dirt Band with "I Only Love You," John Conlee with "Old School," and such others as Randy Travis and Mary-Chapin Carpenter.

Schlitz's initial acquaintance with Randy Travis came in the mid-1980s when the fellow North Carolinian was just beginning to take his first steps toward stardom. The saga began when Schlitz was working on new material with songwriter and friend Paul Overstreet. They were putting together a song tentatively named "Greedy Heart" when Schlitz put forth a line that went "On the other hand . . ." and Overstreet followed up with "there's a golden band." Inspired by that wordplay, they went ahead and finished a song they titled "On the Other Hand."

They envisioned having a "name" artist like Merle Haggard or George Jones record the song, and were taken aback when informed it was to be recorded by a new artist they'd never heard of, a singer called Randy Travis. As Don Schlitz told an interviewer in the mid-1980s ("Don Schlitz, Success Never Sleeps," *Los Angeles Times,* March 6, 1988), the writers were initially disappointed. "But then we got a tape of Randy's version and it was good, *really* good. Then I saw Randy on TV and really liked him. I liked the fact that he was right there . . . no affectations."

Randy's single became a number-one hit, as did his follow-up release of a Schlitz/Overstreet song, "Forever and Ever Amen." In the 1987 Country Music

Association voting in which Travis swept five nominations, both songs were also nominated in the Song of the Year category. ("On the Other Hand" had also won for Song of the Year in 1986.) When winners were announced in the October 1987 telecast, "Forever and Ever Amen" brought more trophies for Schlitz and Overstreet.

Schlitz continued to pen chart hits for various artists in the years that followed, with his achievements reaching another peak in the mid-1990s when he collaborated with Mary-Chapin Carpenter on a series of songs for her best-selling albums of those years. One of these was the 1994 singles hit, "He Thinks He'll Keep Her," which was nominated for Song of the Year. (The recording also was nominated for Single of the Year.)

Looking back on his early struggles, Schlitz commented, "People come [to Nashville] with dreams and some of them come true, but it's the most competitive business I have ever seen . . . even at this point in my career, every time I write a song, it's like competing with 10,000 other songs.

"If I had a kid, I'd take a load of bricks and keep throwing them at him one at a time and ask him after each one if he wanted to be in the music business. If he went through all that, I'd say, 'O.K., maybe you are hard-headed enough.'"

SEALS, DAN: *Singer, guitarist, saxophone player, songwriter. Born McCamey, Texas, February 6, 1948.*

A born and bred Texan, Dan Seals first gained the notice of music fans in the 1970s as part of the England Dan and John Ford Coley duo. As Seals told the author, he assumed the pseudonym of England Dan to avoid confusion with his brother Jimmy Seals, part of the well known Seals & Croft soft-rock team. But the Seals clan had strong country music roots and one factor that contributed to the breakup of the England Dan and John Ford Coley partnership was Dan's desire to do more strongly country-oriented material.

Dan recalled that his father, a country musician and close friend of Ernest Tubb, schooled his sons in the basics of country by having the boys listen to recordings of people like Tubb, Jim Reeves, and Hank Williams, Sr. Dan could also look to incentives in that direction from the careers of other family members. His uncle, Chuck Seals, for instance, provided Ray Price with his 1956 song hit, "Crazy Arms," while cousin Troy Seals's songwriting output included successes like Ronnie Milsap's "Lost in the Fifties Tonight" and George Jones's "Who's Gonna Fill Their Shoes." In the 1990s, when the band Little Texas became a regular entry on country charts, its keyboards player was a distant cousin of Dan's, Brady Seals.

Though Dan began as a youngster playing in the family band, the popularity of rock and soul sidetracked him from traditional country to his eventual teaming with Coley to attain star status in the soft-rock domain.

Some of their 1970s hit singles, such as "I'd Really Love to See You Tonight," "Nights Are Forever Without You," and "Love Is the Answer," are still played often on radio oldies shows. After Dan went out on his own in the early 1980s, he signed with Capitol Records, which issued his initial recordings in the mid-1980s.

Dan placed several singles on lower-chart levels before hitting big with "God Must Be a Cowboy" in 1984, his first solo top-10 success. Two years later he had his first number-one single, "Bop," followed soon after by a number-one duet with Marie Osmond, "Meet Me in Montana." In the Country Music Association 1986 awards voting, "Bop" was named Single of the Year and the Osmond pairing Duet of the Year. Dan was also a finalist for CMA's 1986 Horizon Award. That year was a satisfying one for him in still another way: the number one single "Addicted" earned a Grammy nomination.

Before the 1980s were over, Seals had six more number-one singles: "Everything that Glitters," "You Still Move Me," "Three Time Loser," "I Will Be There," "One Friend," and "Big Wheels in the Moonlight." He also had such top-5 singles hits as "My Baby's Got Good Timing," "My Old Yellow Cart," and "They Rage On." As a songwriter, he received a number of BMI Citations for some of those compositions. He also made chart inroads with videos and albums, the latter including *Won't Be Blue Anymore,* which reached number one in the U.S. and earned a R.I.A.A. gold-record certification as well as a platinum award for Canadian sales. Another gold-record album was the greatest hits release, *Dan Seals—The Best,* issued at the end of the decade and still on *Billboard's* Top 75 list in mid-1992.

He began the 1990s with two more singles hits on Capitol, "Love on Arrival," which reached number one on some charts and number two in *Radio & Records* the week of April 13, 1990, and "Let the Good Times Roll" (number one in *R&R* for two weeks in July). His association with Capitol ended during that period and he was signed by Warner Brothers. One of his releases on that label was the album *Fired Up,* issued in June 1994. Later in the decade he moved to a new label, Intersound Entertainment.

From the mid-1980s into the 1990s he continued to be a popular concert act in the U.S., Canada, and overseas. His instrumental work featured, in particular, a specially strung nine-string guitar. Dan is lefthanded and sometimes performed using a righthanded guitar positioned upside down and backward. On occasion, he would also show off his skills as an alto and soprano saxophone player.

SELDOM SCENE: *Vocal and instrumental group. Original personnel: John Duffey, born Washington, D.C., March 4, 1934, died Arlington, Virginia, December 11, 1996; Ben Eldridge, born Richmond, Virginia, August 15, 1938; Tom Gray, born Chicago, Illinois, February 1, 1941; John Starling, born Durham, North Carolina, March 26,* *1940. Starling left in 1977, replaced by Phil Rosenthal, born Guilford, Connecticut, September 30, 1948. T. Michael Coleman, born c. early 1950s, joined 1987. Moondi Klein, born New York, New York, c. early 1960s, joined in late 1980s. Roster in early 1990s comprised Duffey, Auldridge, Eldridge, Klein, Coleman. Auldridge, Klein, and Coleman left in 1994 to form Chesapeake. Dudley Connell joined in 1995.*

The place is the Birchmere in the early 1980s, a bluegrass nightclub in Arlington, Virginia, across the Potomac from Washington, D.C. It is Thursday night of almost any week in the year. The lights have dimmed and the emcee has told the audience that there is to be no talking between the songs in the set. The band that walks on stage—the Seldom Scene—is familiar to much of the audience, many faithfully paying the admission fee week after week to see one of the premier bluegrass bands in the land—some critics have rated it the best bluegrass band currently active in the U.S.

The band, which celebrated its tenth anniversary on November 1, 1981, is comprised of five virtuoso musicians whose repertoire bridges the gap between traditional bluegrass and "newgrass," gospel, and popular music. The "Scene" is part of the reason that leader John Duffey (mandolin, guitar, vocals), who first made his mark with the Country Gentlemen, now can say facetiously, "Bluegrass is not pornography anymore. It's okay to say you enjoy it."

In 1971, he recalls, the members of the embryonic Seldom Scene "never expected the group to get much further than the living room." Duffey had quit the Country Gentlemen two years earlier and met up with the future members of the band while at a local get-together. The original five gathered in a corner and began to jam, quickly realizing that the combination was special. Soon after, they began playing at a little club in Washington, D.C., called the Rabbit's Foot, "for whatever we could make," as Duffey notes.

After six weeks they moved to another club, the Red Fox, in Bethesda, Maryland, where Emmylou Harris had gotten her start. (In fact, over the past decade such stars as Emmylou, Linda Ronstadt, and Bill Monroe have sat in with the Seldom Scene.) After six years at the Red Fox, now closed, the group moved to the Birchmere, where they played every Thursday night for years when not on tour.

"When we started playing the Red Fox," Duffey says, "a few calls came in. People were curious to see if I could still play. I had been out of commission for a while after I left the Gentlemen. We didn't expect it, but the Seldom Scene just sort of mushroomed into something."

The band received its name from Charlie Waller of the Country Gentlemen. At first he was doubtful that the group would get anywhere. He asked Duffey, "What are you going to call yourselves, the seldom seen?"

"We just changed the spelling around," Duffey remarks.

Duffey, who formed the Country Gentlemen in 1957 along with Charlie Waller and Bill Emerson, serves as the business manager for the Scene and states it finally has become a commercial success. One indication of this was the enthusiastic response they received on a six-city tour of California in 1981. Duffey reports that people were scalping tickets for the group's appearance at the Great American Music Hall in San Francisco.

One of the reasons for the band's rapport with the audience may be its ability to cut across musical genres and age differences. Duffey, who sports a flat-top haircut and was described by *The Washington Post* as looking like a bowler, notes that on some radio stations he has heard fifteen minutes of the Rolling Stones followed by fifteen minutes of the Seldom Scene.

As of early 1982, many of the band members still continued to work in side jobs. Ben Eldridge (banjo, guitar), a graduate of the University of Virginia, was employed as a mathematician at Tetra Tech in Arlington, an engineering firm working with the Navy on underwater acoustic research. Standup bass player Tom Gray worked as cartographer for *National Geographic*. Mike Auldridge, who graduated from the University of Maryland, not long before had given up working as a commercial artist, during which time he had served a stint at the *Washington Star*.

Initially, John Starling's profession affected the group's performing schedule. Duffey had to arrange dates to accommodate guitarist/vocalist Starling, an Army surgeon at Walter Reed Hospital and Fort Belvoir. "We wound up playing Thursday night," Duffey recalls, "because he operated on Thursday during the day. On Friday he just had to see if his patients were dead or not."

Starling left the group in 1977 to start a private practice in Montgomery, Alabama. "He decided after eleven and a half years as a surgeon that he wanted to be a doctor for a while." But Starling sometimes rejoins the group to perform on special occasions.

Phil Rosenthal (guitar, vocals), who describes the band arrangements and rehearsals as "very democratic," came to the group from a Connecticut band called Old Dog to replace Starling in 1977. The democratic nature of the group is evident in its harmonies. For instance, Rosenthal, a baritone, and Duffey, a tenor, trade off on lead vocals. Auldridge, better known for his Dobro licks, helps on the harmonies. Ben Eldridge and Tom Gray occasionally do likewise, most notably when banjoist Eldridge sings a three-beat solo in the Scene's rendition of Eric Clapton's "Lay Down Sally." Tom Gray, a former member of the Country Gentlemen, is known as perhaps the best bassist in bluegrass and the silent, shy Gray usually surprises the audience at least once a set with a flashy bass solo.

One of the group's hallmarks is Duffey's high, piercing voice. Occasionally soft and plaintive and a bit gravelly, his voice more typically has an almost electrifying impact on listeners when he does tunes like "Wait a Minute" or the original Jimmie Rodgers arrangement of "Mule Skinner Blues." Rosenthal takes the lead for some of the band's folk and country numbers, including the first song the band recorded, Steve Goodman's "City of New Orleans." The group made the recording in 1972 and Duffey says that the Seldom Scene, as well as Arlo Guthrie, received personal thanks from Goodman for recording the song.

Other songs that are crowd pleasers include: "A Small Exception of Me," "Rider," "After Midnight," "Georgia Rose," "Muddy Waters," and "What Am I Doin' Hangin' Round."

The group has an excellent reputation among its musical peers for its instrumental skills. Mike Auldridge, considered one of the best Dobro players in the country, has toured with Linda Ronstadt and played during the recording sessions for an album featuring Linda, Dolly Parton, and Emmylou Harris called *Trio*, released in 1987 by Columbia. In Seldom Scene concerts, Auldridge, a slim man with white hair, often contributes a tidy lick or solo. His metallic Dobro always permeates the group's sound. When he joins Rosenthal and Duffey to help out on the instrumental harmonies, he tucks his Dobro under his arm to avoid reverberation. Often, other members of the band take turns improvising on the jazzy patterns he sets. One such example is his unique arrangement of Benny Goodman's swing number "Stompin' at the Savoy," a favorite showpiece for the band's virtuosity.

Duffey has a major impact on the show's pacing with his comic antics and creative mandolin playing. "I play how I feel at a certain time," he says. "There are not many breaks that I play the same." As for his antics: "I'm the only one with enough nerve to put his ass on the line, I guess. Somebody has to do it."

The combination of first-rate musical skills and endearing showmanship have helped the Scene achieve its steadily growing reputation. According to Rosenthal, "Many bands work hard on the music, but when the band looks ill at ease or bored, that works against them. We are good entertainers on stage. We also seem to manage to come out with new material all the time."

During its quarter-century of existence, the Scene has honed that ability in many live performances as well as occasional TV appearances. They have played the White House—"The first time's kind of neat," Duffey says—and concert halls across the country. Now they usually go on tour from the end of April until October. But they always return to the Birchmere.

Duffey stresses that the band is "very choosy" about its material and that they have only recorded two songs on their albums that he is now sorry about. As of early

1982, nine Seldom Scene LPs had been issued (on Rebel Records): *Act I, Act II, Act III, Old Train, Live at the Cellar Door, The New Seldom Scene Album, Baptizing, Act IV,* and *After Midnight.* In addition, Mike Auldridge has recorded a number of instrumental albums, and Phil Rosenthal was working on a solo album called *Wild Flowers* in early 1982.

From the early 1980s into the 1990s, the group maintained its reputation as one of the best bluegrass bands in the world, touring widely as a festival attraction and headliner on the folk and bluegrass circuits. As of 1994, three founding members—Duffey, Auldridge and Eldridge—remained on board while Gray and Rosenthal's places were taken by Moondi Klein (lead vocals, banjo) and T. Michael Coleman (bass).

New Yorker Klein had begun a career in music at age seven when he was a member of the Metropolitan Opera Children's Chorus. He didn't pay much attention to bluegrass until his early teens, when his parents took the then fourteen-year-old to a bluegrass concert at the Original Carter Family Home in Hiltons, Virginia. The exposure inspired him to learn bluegrass banjo and, after attending college as a voice and music theory major, he moved to Washington, D.C., in 1984 and found gigs at local bluegrass oriented clubs. By the end of the decade he had joined one of his favorite bands, the Seldom Scene.

T. Michael Coleman was involved in bluegrass and folk music groups for many years before adding his talents to the Seldom Scene. For seventeen years he was part of the backing band for Doc Watson and also was active as a sideman and producer in Nashville. His session credits included work with such stars as Johnny Cash and Don Williams.

The band's association with the Rebel label ended in the mid-1980s. Following their departure, Rebel issued the album *The Best of the Seldom Scene, Volume I* in 1986. In 1988, the group's new record company, Sugar Hill, issued their label debut, *A Change of Scenery.* From 1988 into the mid-1990s, Rebel reissued Seldom Scene collections on CD, including, in 1988, *Live at the Cellar Door* and *Old Train; Baptizing* and *The New Seldom Scene Album* in 1989; *Act III* in 1990; *Act II* and *Act I* in 1993. In 1992, Sugar Hill issued the album *30th Anniversary Concert.* Though the group hadn't won a Grammy as of 1996, it was a finalist a number of times as was the case for its *Like We Used to Be* collection in the voting for 1994 Bluegrass Album of the Year. In September 1996, Duffey was inducted into the International Bluegrass Music Association's Hall of Fame.

In December 1996, John Duffey died of an apparent heart attack at his home in Arlington, Virginia. Dudley Connell, the band's lead singer at the time, told Reuters, that Duffey "was one of the half-dozen most important players ever in this industry. He helped redefine how people looked at bluegrass, made it acceptable to the urban masses by his choice of material and style of performance."*

SHAVER, BILLY JOE: *Singer, band leader, songwriter. Born Corsicana, Texas, August 16, 1941.*

One of the most original of the new breed of country songwriter that came to the fore starting in the late 1960s and early 1970s, Billy Joe Shaver established a reputation in the industry for his wild exploits as well as his creative talents. As he said about the former, "Sad to say, most of the stories you hear about me are true and then some. It use'ta be that no matter what I did, I jumped in all the way, with both feet in the trough. I always used to seem to be in the wrong place at the right time."

Billy Joe experienced a lot of hardships and saw much of the rougher side of life long before he decided to try for a place in the country music field. In fact, his troubles started before he was born; his parents separated before his birth in Corsicana, Texas, at the start of the 1940s and his mother placed him and his young sister in the care of their grandmother. (He told a Columbia Records interviewer in 1981, "My mother was actually a honky tonk girl, though she's a good Christian lady now and she prays for me a lot. She worked in honky tonks in Waco and Dallas.")

His grandmother had little money, but she cared for the children and encouraged her grandson's interest in music as he got a little older. "She would take me down to the grocery store down the road from us and every time she'd get a little behind on her credit she'd ask the woman if she would extend it. And [the woman] would say she would if she'd get that little boy to sing! They used to put me up on an old cracker barrel or somethin' and I'd sing my heart out." Most of the songs the boy picked up from listening to the radio, adding some lyrics of his own in some cases.

But as Billy Joe approached high school age, there wasn't much leeway for the luxury of continuing his education. He had to drop out of school after the eighth grade and go to work on farms run by several uncles. "I'd stay with one and then go on to another one and stay with him a while. I got passed around quite a bit."

Later on, he branched out to work at a variety of other jobs to increase his income. Among the occupations he tried in his teens and early twenties were bronc busting and bullriding, gas station attendant, a hitch in the U.S. Navy, and sawmill work. The last named proved very costly; as a result of a sawmill accident, he lost parts of four fingers on his right hand. He also sold cars for a time, "but I wasn't very good at it."

He was still interested in music, and, as time went on, he began to make an effort to move in that direction.

Based in part on personal interviews by Lyndon Stambler in the early 1980s.

Starting in the late 1960s, he made periodic trips from Texas to Nashville, making the trip either by hitchhiking or driving his old pick-up truck, to seek auditions from music publishers or artists & repertoire executives. Again and again the results were nil, but he persisted. Finally, he made his way to Bobby Bare's small publishing office. "At first Bobby told me he wasn't looking for any new writers, so I hung my head and started to walk out. Man, I must have looked pathetic, because he said, 'Aw, wait a minute! Where's your tapes?' I told him I didn't have any tapes, that my songs were all in my head. But he let me stay anyway and play him one song. Before I was through, he was drawing up the papers to sign me. I'll always admire Bobby for havin' such good taste."

At the beginning, Bare paid Shaver a small advance while the latter worked up new material and Bobby worked on getting word of Shaver's abilities around Nashville. The advance hardly allowed lavish living; to make ends meet, Billy Joe slept in Bare's office. But things soon began to change as a growing number of country artists recognized the promise of Billy Joe's compositions. One of the first to use this material, besides Bare, was Kris Kristofferson, who included Shaver's composition "Good Christian Soldier" in his 1971 *Silver Tongued Devil* LP. Another artist quick to recognize Shaver's potential was Tom T. Hall, who used Shaver's composition "Old Five and Dimers like Me" as a single as well as the title song for an album. In 1973, Waylon Jennings based an entire album, *Honky Tonk Heroes,* on Shaver material. As the 1970s went by, many other country stars recorded Billy Joe's songs, including Elvis Presley ("You Ask Me To"); Johnny Cash ("Old Chunk of Coal," "Jesus Was Our Savior," "Cotton Was Our King"); Bobby Bare and Johnny Rodriguez ("I Couldn't Be Me Without You"); the Allman Brothers Band ("Sweet Mama"); and such others as Jerry Jeff Walker, Tennessee Ernie Ford, and the Sons of the Pioneers. Billy Joe included some of those in his own performing repertoire, as well as such others as "Ain't No God in Mexico" and "I've Been to Georgia on a Fast Train."

Shaver began to record some of his own vocal renditions in the early 1970s, starting with some tracks made for MGM that were coproduced by Bobby Bare and Willie Nelson. Kris Kristofferson urged his own label of the time, Monument Records, to sign Billy Joe; the result was the 1973 LP *Old Five and Dimers like Me,* produced by Kris. The LP still ranks as one of the best country-music collections of the 1970s. In the mid-1970s, Shaver moved to Capricorn, completing two albums, *When I Get My Wings* and *Gypsy Boy.*

Unfortunately, Billy Joe's recording career was set adrift for a time when the Capricorn label went out of business. However, other performers continued to come to him for new material or turned out new versions of previous compositions, so he didn't have to worry about camping out in a publishing office again.

In late 1980, he signed a new recording contract with Columbia Records. His debut album on the label, *I'm Just an Old Chunk of Coal . . . But I'm Gonna Be a Diamond Someday,* was released in April 1981.

The title song of that 1981 album provided chart hits for others, but not for Shaver. He had two more albums issued on Columbia, the last being *Salt of the Earth* in 1987, but again stardom eluded him while longtime friends and supporters like Willie Nelson and Waylon Jennings continued to accrue rewards from recordings and the concert circuit. Billy Joe, however, didn't give up. He picked up club dates with a band that featured his son Eddy on lead guitar, and kept new demos circulating among recording industry executives.

But the drought in his recording career went on for more than a half dozen years before he finally got a new contract with the independent Nashville label Praxis. His label debut in 1993, *Tramp on the Street,* which, among other things, included two duet numbers with Waylon Jennings, showed he hadn't lost his skills as writer or performer. New media attention was focused on him in the mid-1990s with critical praise for his headline appearances at small clubs and concert halls around the country. He also augmented his following with opening act sets for a series of Willie Nelson and Waylon Jennings concerts.

While playing a date in the Los Angeles area in 1994, Shaver told Richard Cromelin of the *Los Angeles Times* that his career probably suffered from his reputation as sort of a loose cannon. "I guess sometimes I had a little too much fun. People think I'm unmanageable, which is not true. I don't look at myself as being that crazy. . . . It was mostly just fist fights. Everybody just blows my deal up, and I tried to get away from it, but it just would keep on comin'."

He was philosophical about the hard times he endured while friends rose to worldwide stardom, and emphasized he was happy for their achievements. "That's just the breaks. There's lots and lots of songs that I'm really fond of that more than likely I wouldn't have written if I hadn't gone down this hard road. And I wouldn't take anything for those songs. If I'd have went on and made a bunch of money and everything like that and seen somebody else writing songs like I'm writing, it would have broke my heart."

In 1996 he signed a multi-album contract with Texas-based Justice Records. His debut on the label, *Highway of Life,* was issued on August 6 of that year.

SHENANDOAH: *Vocal and instrumental group. Marty Raybon, born Sanford, Florida, December 8, 1959 (lead vocals, acoustic guitar); Stan Thorn, born Kenosha, Wisconsin, March 16, 1959 (vocals, keyboards); Mike McGuire, born Haleyville, Alabama, December 28, 1958* (drums, vocals); Ralph Ezell, born Union, Mississippi, June 26, 1953 (vocals, bass guitar); Jim Seales, born Hamilton, Alabama, March 20, 1954 (vocals, lead guitar). Ezell replaced in December 1995 by Rocky Thacker.

One of the most successful country bands in the late 1980s and 1990s (not to be confused with the folk group of the same name or several others laying claim to it in a series of lawsuits filed in the late 1980s), as more than one critic observed, seemed like a cat with nine lives. The group came back from bankruptcy and a series of label changes, appearing stronger than ever after each rebuff.

The band members, all of whom had years of experience as session musicians or members of various local groups, first got together in Muscle Shoals, Alabama, where they all still lived as of 1995. At the time, they were working as studio musicians while also seeking songwriting contracts. After playing together informally, they got a job as house band at a local club in 1985 and the following year were signed to the CBS label.

The question of what to call themselves then came up. At the time they were playing the MGM Club, but CBS rejected their picking the name MGM Band for legal reasons. Alternatives suggested were Rhythm Rangers or Shenandoah, both of which supposedly were free of entanglements. The group chose the latter for their debut album of 1987, titled Shenandoah. That album and the band's tour appearances sparked interest that blossomed with the next album release, the 1988 The Road Not Taken. The group's first charted singles releases, "Stop the Rain" and "They Don't Make Love," made the Billboard list, the former release peaking at number twenty-eight and the latter at number fifty-four. Their next singles showed better progress with "She Doesn't Cry Anymore," hitting number fourteen in the Gavin Report and "Mama Knows," reaching top-10 levels on all major charts in 1988, number three in Gavin, number seven in Radio & Records, and number five in Billboard.

Just when the future seemed bright, disaster struck. While getting ready for a 1988 performance, the band heard from a group in Kentucky threatening to have them arrested for unlawful use of that name. Hardly had a financial settlement been agreed on with the Kentucky group than another band in Las Vegas put in a claim, followed in short order by demands from three other "Shenandoahs." Soon Raybon, Seales, and company and their management were battling a series of lawsuits, even as the band was having a major impact on the charts with three straight singles hits, all of which reached number one on the charts during 1989, "Church on Cumberland Road," "Sunday in the South" (which stayed at number one in Billboard for two weeks in a row), and "Two Dozen Roses." In 1990, still more successes, typically written or cowritten by band members, appeared: "See If I Care," number seven in Billboard and number five in R&R in April, "Next to You, Next to Me," number one for three weeks in Billboard during the summer, and "Ghost in the House," number two in R&R and number five in Billboard in late fall. All of those reached number one on the Gavin chart in 1990.

Meanwhile, however, the band's legal troubles were becoming critical. As Marty Raybon told Robyn Flans of Country Fever ("Shenandoah," August 1994), "We went to the label and the production company and told them, 'We've got to have some help from y'all to pay these lawsuits, because it's taking everything we're making on the road. People who work with us have got to get a salary, and we have to have something to live on, too. Our show is not progressing because there are no funds to do it. We're not asking you to pay it all, just a third.'" Getting a negative label response, the band spokespersons asked the label to reconsider; otherwise Shenandoah would have to file for bankruptcy.

All the while, the band's popularity with country fans and music industry peers kept improving. In the 1989 TNN/Music City News poll the band was named Favorite Newcomer, and in 1991 Academy of Country Music voters named them the Vocal Group of the Year for 1991. The band placed more singles on the charts in 1991, "I Got You," number one in Gavin and three in R&R; "Moon Over Georgia" (number nine in Billboard, three in R&R, and one in Gavin); and "When You Were Mine" (respectively numbers thirty-eight, twenty-nine, and twenty-three).

Seeing no alternative, Shenandoah filed for bankruptcy, which automatically invalidated all its contracts, including the one with Columbia. Label officials claimed the step was taken to void the record agreement, and though Raybon, et al., maintained that that wasn't so and they wanted to stay on the label, no new agreement was made, and both CBS and the production company filed suits for damages. The band's last album on the label, Shenandoah's Greatest Hits, was issued in 1992.

To try to restart its career, the band signed with a new label, RCA, which issued the band's label debut, Long Time Comin', in the summer of 1992. The album made the Billboard Top 40 soon after and stayed for a number of months. The album provided the hit single, "Rock My Baby," which reached number two in both Billboard and R&R in August 1992 and number one in Gavin.

One of the band's key singles disappointments was the 1992, "Hey Mister (I Need This Job)," which was released on RCA soon after the success of "Rock My Baby." The naysayers suggested its failure to make any headway on country charts related to its representing a political statement in an election year. Raybon told Robert Germann of The Tennesseean, "To me, it was a song about compassion. I still think there is absolutely nothing wrong with that song, nothing wrong." He agreed the economic situation had an impact. "Well, yes, that did come into play; we thought about that. But we didn't make the economy." This was followed by "Leavin's a Long Time Comin," number nine in *Gavin* in early 1993, twelve in *R&R,* and nineteen in *Billboard.*

Shenandoah was nominated for Vocal Group of the Year in the 1992 Country Music Association voting, as it had been the previous two years. Its growing stature with fans was indicated by its move from primarily an opening act to one that could start to hold its own as a headliner in major venues. Still, RCA was somewhat disappointed with the debut album's sales. The band then completed work on its second RCA album, *Under the Kudzu,* which proved to be its second gold-record seller after its release in the summer of 1993. The album spawned four chart singles, three of which made top 10 or better on some or all of the major charts. The first, "Janie Baker's Love Slave," reached number eight in *Gavin* and number ten in *R&R* in August 1993. In early 1994, "I Want to Be Loved Like That" reached positions one, two, and three in, respectively, *R&R, Gavin,* and *Billboard.* A few months later, the group had one of the top singles hits of 1994, "If Bubba Can Dance (I Can Too)," cowritten by McGuire, Raybon, and Bob McDill.

Raybon told Tom Wood of *The Tennessean* ("Oh, Shenandoah, We Long to Hear You," May 27, 1994) the song evolved from seeing an infomercial by Melanie Greenwood about learning to do country line-dance. "We were at McDill's office one day, and the commercial came on. Bob thought it was great. McDill said, 'I don't know how to dance, but I could learn how to do that at home.' He went for a cup of coffee, came back and said, 'You know, if bubba can dance, I can, too,' and Mike and I just looked at each other. And I said, 'Man, that's what we're going to write today.' "

Under the Kudzu was the source of one more chart single, "I'll Go Down Loving You," but the highest it achieved was number twenty-four in *Gavin.* To the surprise of many in the industry, in August 1994 it was announced the band had left RCA and signed with Liberty Records. As part of the agreement, RCA turned the tapes for an almost-completed new album over to Liberty. The collection needed one more track to meet Liberty's typical format. The addition was "Somewhere in the Vicinity of the Heart," which featured a guest appearance by bluegrass star Alison Krauss. Besides becoming the title track, the single of the number went on to become a chart hit in early 1995. The album, released in November 1994, was preceded in October by the first single and video, "Darned if I Don't (and Danged if I Do)," a top-10 hit in July 1995.

When the Country Music Association Awards were announced on the October 1995 telecast, it was disclosed that Shenandoah and Krauss had won the trophy for Vocal Event of the Year. In early 1996, it was announced that "Darned if I Don't" was nominated for a 1995 Grammy in the Best Country Vocal by a Duo or Group with Vocal category. The band also received two other Grammy nominations—Best Country Collaboration with Vocals (for "Somewhere in the Vicinity of the Heart") and Best Southern Gospel, Country Gospel or Bluegrass Gospel Album (for its contributions to *Amazing Grace—A Country Salute to Gospel.*

At the end of December, Shenandoah reported that Rocky Thacker had replaced Ralph Ezell on bass guitar. Raybon told *Billboard,* "Ralph moved to Nashville to be a session player and there will be a lot of people continuing to hire him. He is going to do wonderful."

In early 1996, Shenandoah and its record label Capitol/Nashville (the new name for Liberty) announced plans to celebrate the band's tenth anniversary. This included release of the album *Now & Then* on April 2. For the collection, the band rerecorded some of its previous hits and also added some new songs with "All Over but the Shoutin'" picked as the first single. In early 1996, some of its singles issued in late December were on the charts: "Always Have, Always Will" and the top 20 success, "'Round Here." For most of 1996, the band toured in support of its new album while Raybon managed to work in some solo performances which included some songs due for release on a 1996 EMI/Sparrow gospel disc. Concert dates for Shenandoah included an appearance in the Dollywood Showcase of the Stars series.

The group's success was based on its secular material, but Raybon, for one, was never bashful about expressing his religious convictions and the desire to include gospel albums among future projects. McGuire told Robyn Flans, "He's a devoted family man and a good Christian man. I think he would have been a preacher if he weren't doing this." When not touring, in fact, Raybon often talked to churches in his home area. "I speak about faith, love, trying to be a good disciple and a good Samaritan, and I try to express my deep convictions about how I feel. And I take my family [wife and two children—he also has a son by a first marriage] with me."

SHEPPARD, T. G.: *Singer, guitarist, songwriter. Born Humboldt, Tennessee, July 20, 1944.*

Like many country artists, T. G. Sheppard (real name, Bill Browder) had to wait quite a few years before he became known to a sizable number of country fans. However, he was able to stick with it during many lean years of performing by earning a living in other phases of the business. He wasn't the first and certainly won't be the last entertainer to make his way from behind-the-scenes promotion work to the glare of personal stardom.

His saga began in the town of Humboldt, Tennessee,

where he was born and spent his early years. There was always music to be heard in his house—his mother was a gospel pianist and music teacher—and T. G. enjoyed gospel and country songs from his childhood on. He started to learn guitar before he was high school age and already was seeking opportunities to perform in his teens.

When he was sixteen in 1960, he moved to Jackson, Tennessee, where he was a sideman in several local country bands for a year. After that he packed up and headed to a larger locale, Memphis, where he joined the band headed by Travis Womack as a guitarist and backing vocalist. During those years, in addition to band work, Sheppard also added to his income by working as a recording session musician. Some demo tapes that he had made eventually brought him a recording contract from Atlantic Records. He made a number of singles for Atlantic, released under the pseudonym Brian Stacy, one of which, "High School Days," made upper-chart levels.

However, since his career as an entertainer wasn't making any phenomenal progress, it made sense to find a job in another segment of the business. This move, in the early 1960s, took the form of a position as promotion and advertising manager with Hot-Line Distributors in Memphis. He did well enough there to move, in time, to RCA Records as its southern region promotion executive. After some years with RCA, he decided to form his own independent company in Memphis, Umbrella Promotion, later called Umbrella Productions. He opened offices for his firm in a building that also housed the Onyx recording studios. After listening to the constant sound of recording sessions, he longed to get closer to the creative side of the field again. Before long he was doing some record producing of his own and singing professionally once more.

His involvement in the business side of music finally led to a contract for him with Melodyland Records. The song that helped bring that about was one brought to him during the summer of 1973 by a young writer named Bobby David, titled "Devil in the Bottle." Sheppard was enthusiastic about the song and, at first, tried to place it with some established country singers. However, no one accepted it, so he finally recorded it himself. The single came out in the fall of 1974 and soon made lower-chart levels. Helped by Sheppard's promotion efforts, it rose steadily higher until, in February 1975, it nestled in the number-one spot on U.S. country charts.

While in Memphis he became friendly with Elvis Presley. Elvis, delighted with T. G.'s success, gave him a new touring bus. He flew T. G. to Dallas in his private plane and simply handed him the keys to the bus once the plane touched down.

Analyzing his success, he told Bill Littleton of *Music City News* (February 1976), "Being in the promotion business probably had more to do with me hav-ing a hit the first time out with 'Devil in the Bottle' than anything else, except that 'Devil' was a hit quality song to begin with."

T. G. also proved successful in acquiring the services of Jack D. Johnson, who became his manager. Johnson had previously served in the same capacity for Ronnie Milsap and Charley Pride during the critical years of their professional lives.

"I knew what to expect and how to go about getting what I wanted—it wasn't like walkin' into the business cold and startin' from scratch. I feel sorry for kids who find themselves with hits without knowing enough about the business to keep the ball rolling."

T. G. certainly knew how to do that. He emphasized it with another major singles hit during the summer of 1975. The song, "Tryin' to Beat the Mornin' Home," which he cowrote with R. Williams and E. Kahanek, made it to number one at the end of June. In the fall, he had another top-10 hit with the single "Another Woman" and in early 1976, scored still another best-seller with "Motels and Memories."

By then, Sheppard was well on the way to becoming a concert favorite on the country circuit. From 1975 on, he maintained a heavy touring schedule that took him to all parts of the United States and Canada. He also was featured on major country broadcasts, including several appearances on the *Grand Ole Opry*.

During 1976, he changed labels, achieving a top-level hit with his version of Neil Diamond's "Solitary Man" in the summer. Later in the 1970s, he moved over to Warner/Curb Records, for whom he continued his series of chart-making singles and albums. He had a top-10 hit on Warner's in the summer of 1978 with "When Can We Do This Again" and matched that in the fall and winter with "Daylight," in the top 10 in November 1978. Among his charted singles in 1979 were "Happy Together," "Last Cheater's Waltz," and the top-10 hit "You Feel Good All Over." He started the 1980s in similar fashion with another number-one hit, "I'll Be Coming Back for More," and followed with such major successes as "Smooth Sailin'" in early summer and "Do You Wanna Go to Heaven?," number-one ranked in October 1980 on Warner/Curb. In 1981 he had such bestsellers as "I Feel like Loving You Again" and "I Loved 'Em Every One." His charted LPs on Warner/Curb included *3/4 Lonely* in 1979–80 and *Smooth Sailin'*, on the lists from late 1980 into 1981.

Though he enjoyed his status as a top country artist, he also admitted he had to try to cope with the changes it caused in his private life. He told Littleton, "The . . . 15 years [I was] involved in promotion, I would get up at eight or nine a.m. and go to work and be home at five or six p.m. And I would have Saturdays and Sundays off. Usually at night I would be out entertaining disc jockeys or have a client in town; we [he and his family] never really got to talk that much. But now, even being away from home so much, when I do get home we have so much to talk about, to get caught up on. When we find ourselves drifting apart, we sit down and talk. And we try to say, 'Well, now, why are we drifting apart? What's happening right now to make us do this? We usually pinpoint it and correct it right there.

"My wife and I are trying to stay close even though I am on the road. When I am out, I try to call home at least twice a day. I have a little boy . . . and the most important thing is keeping in contact with him."

In 1983, Sheppard achieved another number-one single with "Faking Love." With that, he established the impressive feat of placing ten of eleven singles, starting with the 1979 "Last Cheater's Waltz," at the number-one position for Warner Brothers. However, he felt the grass might be greener somewhere else, and in 1985 he signed with a new label, CBS. His album debut on CBS, *Livin' on the Edge,* came out that year followed by the 1986 collection, *It Still Rains in Memphis,* which yielded the number-one single "Strong Heart." In the summer of 1988, his third CBS album, *One for the Money,* reached the stores.

In the second half of the 1980s, Sheppard diversified his activities to include roles as hotelier and stock-car-racing supporter. In the first case, in 1988, he bought a 158-year-old log-house estate located on Moon Mountain between Pigeon Forge and Gatlinburg, Tennessee, and turned it into his own residence as well as a bed and breakfast called Moon Mountain Lodge. In 1985, he signed an agreement with Folgers Coffee to enter a race team on the NASCAR (National Association of Stock Car Auto Racing) Winston Cup circuit. The team was called the T. G. Sheppard Folgers Racing Machine. Besides often singing the national anthem at Winston Cup events, he also attended Folger's hospitality functions at various racing events. In the 1980s and early 1990s, the coffee firm also sponsored an annual T. G. Sheppard country music concert series.

SHERRILL, BILLY: *Pianist, saxophonist, songwriter, record producer, record industry executive. Born Phil Campbell, Alabama, November 5, circa 1938.*

Few people in the country music field have had the impact of Billy Sherrill. As a writer, as a selector of songs for specific artists, and as one of the most successful record producers in recent country music, Billy has been one of the most prolific starmakers in the industry. Among those who could credit much of the basis for their rise to prominence to Sherrill's contributions are superstars like David Houston, Charlie Rich, Johnny Duncan, and Johnny Paycheck. Legions of others could thank Sherrill for helping them achieve some of their most notable successes.

Music was a staple item in Billy's early life in Alabama—but not pop or even country. Gospels and hymns were the stylings stressed in his family, since his father was a traveling evangelist. When Billy became old enough to learn to play the piano he was pressed into service to help out at his parents' prayer meetings. After a while, though, his tastes changed and he switched from piano to saxophone and was soon working with bands that played honky-tonks all over the southern states.

Among the places Sherrill and his band worked in the late 1950s and early 1960s was the Jinmachi Club in Fort Campbell, Kentucky. The prayer-meeting atmosphere he was accustomed to was a thing of the past. The first night his group took the stage there, an altercation broke out and one man was killed.

After a while, he got tired of the life on the road and moved to Nashville to work in some of the other phases of the business. In addition to writing original material, he got a job working for the Nashville recording studios of Sam Phillips. Phillips had founded Sun Records in Memphis, whose alumni included such greats as Elvis Presley, Johnny Cash, and Jerry Lee Lewis. With Phillips's organization, Sherrill learned the ropes of recording and producing and before long his work attracted attention from other record operations. In the mid-1960s, he joined Epic Records and started an association that was to last for the rest of the 1960s and into the 1980s.

He was soon working with the relatively few country artists then on the Epic label. One of them was a promising newcomer from Louisiana named David Houston. Among the songs Billy suggested Houston record was one Billy had written with a friend named Glenn Sutton (who was still cowriting songs with him during the 1980s) called "Almost Persuaded." The number was recorded as the "B" side of an upcoming Houston single. The "B" side, though, turned out to be the winner, capturing a steadily growing number of airplays in 1966 and becoming one of the major country hits of the year. It made Houston a star and began a string of successes for Sherrill still going strong fourteen years later.

As the 1960s went by, Sherrill added more and more names to the artists whose production chores he handled. Among them was Barbara Mandrell, who made many noteworthy duets with David Houston, Andy Griffith, Charlie Walker, and, in the late 1960s, an artist whose career never had achieved the luster expected, Charlie Rich. For a number of years, although Sherrill and Rich kept striving for new, striking recordings, the stature of the Arkansas singer-pianist-songwriter remained relatively constant. Rich sometimes got discouraged, but Sherrill remained confident. Finally, in the early 1970s, Rich's fortunes started to take a turn for the better. Then Sherrill found Charlie a song titled "Behind Closed Doors" that became one of the major hits of 1974. The song reached number one on country charts and rose to top levels of the pop charts. The same thing happened to the *Behind Closed Doors* album Sherrill produced and the follow-up LP, *Very Special Love Song.* The title song from the latter album, written by Sherrill and Norro Wilson, was a top-10 hit in May 1974.

Even as Sherrill was helping to rejuvenate Charlie's career, he was working with a new young singer named Tanya Tucker. With the material he chose and his production expertise, Tanya soon was considered one of the top-10 female country singers even as Rich held similar honors among male artists.

As the mid- and late-1970s went by, it was rare that a song written or cowritten by Sherrill was absent from the hit charts. In 1976, for instance, Johnny Paycheck clicked with "11 Months and 29 Days," cowritten by Sherrill and Paycheck. Soon after, Tammy Wynette had a hit with "You and Me," in a top-chart position in September 1976 and cowritten by Billy and G. Richey. Other top-10 or top-20 chartmakers in the late 1970s were "Southern California," recorded by Tammy Wynette and George Jones and written by Sherrill, Richey, and R. Bowling (on the charts in the summer of 1977); "Baby, I Love You So," on the charts at the same time, recorded by Joe Stampley and written by Sherrill and Norro Wilson; "One of a Kind," top 10 for Tammy Wynette in November 1977, cowritten by Sherrill and S. Davis; "Beautiful Woman," by Sherrill, S. Davis, and N. Wilson, a hit for Charlie Rich in mid-1978; "Hello Mexico," top 10 for Johnny Duncan in September 1978 (by Sherrill, S. Davis, and Glenn Sutton); "Friend, Lover, Wife," top 10 for Paycheck in December 1978, by Sherrill and Paycheck; "Please Don't Play a Love Song," top 10 for Marty Robbins in late 1978, by Sherrill and S. Davis.

Among the well over a hundred other songs Sherrill arranged, wrote or cowrote over the years were "After Closing Time," "Already It's Heaven," "Another Lonely Song," "Baby's Come Home," "Brown Sugar," "Crying Steel Guitar," "The Day That Love Walked In," "Faith," "Gonna Go Down," "Good Lovin' Makes It Right," "Honey Let Me Be," "I Left Your Bags at the Honky Tonk," "I Wish I Had a Mommy like You," "Jamaica Blue," "Lighter Shade of Blue," "One More Chance," "Rock and Roll Teenager," "Rules of the Game," "Stand By Your Man," "Tia Maria," "Sugar Lips," "There's a Song on the Jukebox," "Tipsy," "The Ways to Love a Man," "Wonders of the Wine," and "Your Elusive Dreams."

In the mid-1970s, the artists produced by Billy included (besides Charlie Rich, George Jones, Tammy Wynette, and Johnny Paycheck) Barbara Fairchild, the late Bob Luman, Brenda Smith, Jody Miller, Troy Seals, and Steve Davis. Others he produced over the years included Freddy Weller, Gene Austin, Avant-Garde, Stan Hitchcook, Lois Johnson, Debbie Lori Kaye, Kris Kristofferson, Jim & Jesse McReynolds, Nashville Strings, Patti Page, Jimmy Payne, Peaches & Herb, the Poppies, Sandy Posey, Pozo Seco, Vivian Reed, Shel Silverstein, Jerry Vale, Bobby Vinton, Charlie Walker, Chuck Woolery, Otis Williams, Merle Kil-

gore, Nancy Ames, the Staple Singers, Ted Taylor, Goldberg Blues Band, Glenn Sutton, and Vicky Fletcher.

In the mid-1970s, Sherrill ranked as one of the most respected producers and innovators in the country field. His title at CBS Records by then was Vice President, Artists & Repertoire, Nashville office.

SILVERSTEIN, SHEL: *Singer, songwriter, poet, cartoonist. Born Chicago, Illinois, 1932.*

Looking something like a cross between Mr. Clean and a character from the Arabian Nights, Shel Silverstein is an unlikely candidate for country-music fame. Adding to the confusion are his many vocations—poet, author, and, prominently, cartoonist. Yet when he turned his attention to music, whether pop, folk, or country, he proved to be as deft as in his other activities.

He demonstrated an excellent talent as a humorist and artist in his youth and, when he went into the U.S. Army, soon became a staff artist for the service's *Stars and Stripes* magazine. Back in civilian life in the mid-1950s, he rapidly built up a reputation as a cartoonist, contributing to the pages of the first issues of *Playboy*, an association that lasted into the 1970s. His cartoons appeared in dozens of other publications from the early 1950s into the 1970s. One of his best-known series appeared in *Time* magazine starting in 1967, with the running title "Now Here's My Plan."

Creatively restless, he always was looking for other fields to conquer. When the folk boom came along, Silverstein took an active part as a singer and writer. In 1961, he completed an album called *Inside Folk Song* whose contents included a song still often played by folk artists, "The Unicorn Song." During the 1960s he turned out varied material, ranging from comic country songs like the Johnny Cash hit "A Boy Named Sue" to love ballads and satiric material. Some of his efforts were included in his Cadet LP, *Shel Silverstein,* released in August 1967.

He also was represented on book lists in the 1960s with such offerings as a collection of some of his cartoons, *Grab My Box,* and an illustrated children's book, *Uncle Shelby's ABC.* He was starting to lose interest in his artwork, though. As he told Chris Van Ness of the L.A. *Free Press* in 1972, "The drawing got painful. It just got to be no fun. When the thing you do best stops being fun, it just puts you through such terrible changes. I don't miss it; since it's no fun. I don't miss it. But you start thinking about what you are and who you are and you really have to look at yourself as a person rather than an artist."

Luckily he found the energy to try again. The result was the 1972 children's book classic, *The Giving Tree,* and other books as well. His 1960s and 1970s output, besides the titles noted above, included *Lafcadio, The Lion Who Shot Back, Uncle Shelby's Zoo, Don't Bump the Glump,* and *Where the Sidewalk Ends.*

At the start of the 1970s, Shel helped propel a previously unknown bar band called Dr. Hook and the Medicine Show to national attention. It proved an excellent association, since the country-rock-oriented Dr. Hook's members were as zany in their own way as Silverstein.

Recalling the way the relationship came about, Dr. Hook vocalist Dennis Locorriere said, "We were playing this bar in New Jersey and one time we gave a guy who said he had contacts a demo tape of two of our songs and one of Bob Dylan's. He met an acquaintance in an elevator in New York and told him, 'I've got this group in New Jersey who are too crazy for me' and gave him the tape. The other guy was music director of the movie *Who Is Harry Kellerman, and Why Is He Saying All Those Terrible Things About Me?* He liked us and fought to have us record the soundtrack. Shel was signed to do the score so that's how we got together."* (Silverstein previously had scored the film *Ned Kelly.*) One result was the fine soundtrack song "The Last Morning."

After that Silverstein provided all the songs for the group's early albums on Columbia. Those included such chartmakers as "Sylvia's Mother" and the 1973 smash, "Cover of the Rolling Stone." A takeoff on the song by Buck Owens with the title changed to "Cover of the Music City News" was a country chart hit as well. One of Shel's best songs for Dr. Hook was "Sing Me a Rainbow."

After Dr. Hook was well launched, Silverstein turned his sights on other efforts to a great extent, though he still turned out material with band members from time to time. As Ray Sawyer of Dr. Hook said in 1979, "For us, Shel will always be there." Locorriere added, "We write with him now when we see him, 'cause he travels a lot. Shel's the kind of guy who'll go to the bathroom saying 'I'll see you in a moment' and you won't see him until five years later."

During the 1970s, Silverstein continued to turn out solo albums from time to time, including *Freaker's Ball* on Columbia in 1972 and another LP in 1978. Many of his compositions were comic or satiric, as evidenced by such titles from *Freaker's Ball* as "Sarah Stout Won't Take the Garbage Out" and "Don't Give a Dose to the One You Love Most" (the latter a song used in several anti-VD campaigns).

All the while, though, he continued to turn out somewhat more conventional songs that found favor with country artists and audiences. Examples are "Queen of the Silver Dollar," the first big hit for Dave and Sugar in late 1975–early 1976, "The Winner," a top-20 success for Bobby Bare in the early summer of 1976, and the late summer 1976 hit for Dr. Hook, "A Couple More Years" (cowritten with Dennis Locorriere).

His association with Bobby Bare in the mid- and late-1970s was as close as his early years with Dr. Hook. The two collaborated on what was claimed to be "the first concept album in modern country music," the two-record 1975 release, *Bobby Bare Sings Lullabies, Legends and Lies.* Among the Silverstein compositions Bare placed on the singles charts were "Sylvia's Mother" (1972); "Daddy," "What If," and "Marie Laveau" (1973–1974); "Alimony" (1975); "The Winner," "Put a Little Lovin' on Me" (1976); and "Redneck Hippie Romance" (1977).

At the start of the 1980s, Shel was still pursuing his mixture of creative efforts. One of his projects was a new children's book, *A Light in the Attic,* issued by Harper & Row in the fall of 1981.

In the 1980s and 1990s, Shel worked on new children's books and other writing projects with less emphasis on music activities. More than a few of his songs continued to be recorded by artists in a variety of pop fields. In the mid-1990s, folksinger Bob Gibson, who had been a close friend—and sometime collaborator—of Shel's for decades, decided to record an album of songs written by Shel or cowritten by the two of them. Called *Makin' a Mess—Bob Gibson Sings Shel Silverstein,* the album, which Silverstein helped produce, was released by Asylum Records in late 1994. Songs in the collection included "I Hear America Singing," "Still Gonna Die," "Dying for Love" (about a mutual friend who died of AIDS complications); and "The Man Who Turns the Damn Thing On and Off" (a satirical commentary on the effects of modern technology).

SKAGGS, RICKY: *Singer, guitarist, mandolinist, fiddler, songwriter, band leader (Boone Creek, the Ricky Skaggs Band, Kentucky Thunder), record producer. Born Cordell, Kentucky, July 18, 1954.*

One of the promising "newcomers" to the country music scene at the start of the 1980s, Ricky Skaggs was hailed as a superstar by mid-decade. By the time he began to attract notice as a solo artist, though, he had already put in a long apprenticeship as a back-up musician and featured player.

He was born in Kentucky and grew up along Brushy Creek in Cordell. Both his parents were musicians, though his father took care of the family finances primarily through employment as a construction worker. By the time he was five, Ricky was already learning songs from his mother, while his father was tutoring him on the mandolin. He was a fast learner; by the time he was seven he was good enough to perform on a Flatt & Scruggs TV show. During these years he was strongly influenced by bluegrass music; in particular he was impressed by the music of Carter and Ralph Stanley, especially after attending a local appearance by the

---

* *From an interview with Irwin Stambler.*

In late 1996 HarperCollins published the newest in Silverstein's books, *Falling Up.* All of his earlier titles, *A Light in the Attic, When the Sidewalk Ends* and *The Giving Tree,* were still in print.

Stanley Brothers. Later on, when Ralph was reorganizing his band after his brother's death, Ricky—then a fifteen-year-old—was hired as a band member.

Ricky loved playing bluegrass, but the fortunes of that kind of music in the late 1960s and early 1970s were at a low ebb. After working for Ralph Stanley for a while, the constant touring, low pay, and meager public interest got to young Ricky. He decided to give up music and try for other kinds of work, moving to Washington, D.C., in the process.

The D.C. area was a hotbed of bluegrass activity and before long Skaggs had joined one of the region's longtime bellwether groups, the Country Gentlemen. After working with that band, he went on to play with J.D. Crowe & The New South and then formed his own band, Boone Creek. These activities kept him in the forefront of the "newgrass" movement of the 1970s that revived the fortunes of bluegrass music. He met—and was admired by—many important or soon to become important artists in rock, folk-rock, and country, including Linda Ronstadt, Lowell George, Rodney Crowell, Paul Craft, and Emmylou Harris. He also worked on six albums in those years, including two as one half of a duo with Keith Whitley.

In 1977, Emmylou Harris asked Skaggs to join her backing group, the Hot Band. Ricky toured widely with the group and also worked closely with Emmylou on several album projects, most notably the Dolly Parton/Linda Ronstadt/Emmylou Harris LP (which eventually provided the basis for the 1987 hit Columbia release, *Trio*) and Emmylou's *Roses in the Snow*. In the late 1970s and early 1980s, he found time for a variety of other projects, including production and engineering work on several albums by other artists, completion of a solo album on the Sugar Hill label, and a collaboration with Tony Rice on an "old-time" acoustic duet album.

At the start of the 1980s, Ricky signed a recording contract with Epic Records, which, he said, moved him from being a "harmony singer and handyman" with the Hot Band to a frontline performer. He recalled to Dan Forte of *Musician* magazine, "When I finally came to CBS after getting turned down by every other record company in town for being too country, [A&R man] Rick Blackburn wanted to know who produced what I'd been doing. I said, 'I did, and by the way, that's kind of one of the bargaining deals. I produce my own records.' That's been the case all along, I told him, 'I want to do this my way for now, because I really feel like I have something that people want to hear.' I wasn't bragging or boastful; I just felt I knew more about Ricky Skaggs than any other producer in town knew, as far as my limits and what I do best. I said, 'If we don't have hit records, then by all means I want to get a coproducer or producer. I'll just get in there and sing and pick.' "

His debut album on CBS's Epic label, *Waitin' for the Sun to Shine,* was released in May 1981 and soon appeared on the country charts, remaining there for almost a year. The LP spawned a number of chart singles, including two that made number one nationally, "Crying My Heart Out Over You" and "I Don't Care." Also a top hit was "Don't Get Above Your Raising." In 1982, his second Epic LP, *Highway and Heartaches,* a fine blend of traditional and modern-day country material also won favor with record buyers. That album and his Epic debut LP both went gold. The first single from the album, "Heartbroke," earned him a 1983 Grammy nomination for Best Country Vocal Performance.

Meanwhile, he was deluged with honors from publications and music-industry-award voters. In balloting for the 1982 Country Music Association Awards, he received five nominations and ended up winning two, Male Vocalist of the Year and the Horizon Award. (The other nominations were for Entertainer of the Year, single of the year for "Crying My Heart Out Over You," and for his group, the Ricky Skaggs Band, for Instrumental Group of the Year.) During the same period the Academy of Country Music voted him Top New Male Vocalist of 1981 and *Radio & Records* named him Best New Artist of 1982. Perhaps most satisfying of all, for someone who had always loved the *Grand Ole Opry* show, Ricky was made a regular cast member in June 1982 and was still a featured artist on the show going into the second half of the 1990s.

In the mid-1980s as he won a growing number of fans with his concert performances backed by his first-rate backing band, he continued to place new albums and singles on the charts. His album output included the gold-record-selling *Don't Cheat in Our Hometown* in 1983, *Country Boy* in 1984, *Favorite Country Songs,* and *Live in London* in 1985, *Love's Gonna Get Ya!* in 1986 and *Comin' Home to Stay* in 1988. His hit singles of the period included "Country Boy," whose hit video included cameo appearances by bluegrass scion Bill Monroe and New York City mayor Ed Koch; "Don't Cheat in Our Hometown," "Highway 40 Blues," and "Uncle Pen."

His accomplishments brought still more nominations and awards from the ACM, CMA, TNN *Music City News,* and major bluegrass organizations and publications. The CMA, for example, nominated him for Entertainer of the Year in 1983, 1985, and 1986 and selected him for the award in 1985. Its members also nominated him for Male Vocalist of the Year in 1983–85 and 1987 and selected his albums as finalists for three straight years (*Highways and Heartaches* in 1983, *Don't Cheat in Our Hometown* in 1984, and *Country Boy* in 1985). "Country Boy" was also nominated for Music Video of the Year in 1985, while the Ricky Skaggs Band was voted Instrumental Group of the Year three straight years from 1983 through 1985. Among other kudos, he won *Frets* magazine reader's approval in the multi-instrument class and *Guitar Player*'s poll named him best country guitarist in 1987 and 1988. He won two Grammy Awards in the mid-1980s, one in 1984 for Best Country Instrumental Performance on "Wheel Hoss" (a track from *Country Boy*), the other in 1986 for Best Country Instrumental Performance (Orchestra, Group or Solo) for "Raisin' the Dickens" (a track from *Love's Gonna Get Ya!*).

Besides producing his own releases, Ricky worked on material for other artists, particularly the Whites, whose members included his wife, Sharon. His work helped them become one of the more successful country groups in the mid-1980s. Ricky also recorded some material with his wife, which brought a CMA 1987 nomination for Vocal Duo of the Year.

One of Ricky's late 1980s projects was to produce a "comeback" album for Dolly Parton (who had first helped his career in 1983 by singing harmony on his *Don't Cheat in Our Hometown* disc). The album, issued in 1989, titled *White Limozeen,* did indeed reestablish her as a major country influence, and served as a major stepping stone for her later successes in the 1990s. Besides working with Dolly and his new Epic album in the late 1980s, he found time to guest on new releases by the Nitty Gritty Dirt Band, Kenny Rogers, Glen Campbell, and Jim and Jesse.

His 1989 album release was *Kentucky Thunder* and was a milestone in that for the first time he had decided to share the producing reins, with Steve Buckingham. He said he broke his long-standing rule of producing all his own sessions because "I felt like it was time for me to freshen up a little bit and get some different opinions and ideas from someone I could trust and buddy up with." The fact that other artists whose albums Steve had worked on, such as Ricky Van Shelton and Tammy Wynette, sang his praises, also helped in the decision, he indicated. The album resulted in three singles that made upper-chart positions in 1990, "Heartbreak Hurricane" (number nine in *R&R* the week of February 16), "Hummingbird" (number twelve in *R&R* the week of June 15), and "He Was on to Somethin'" (number fifteen in *R&R* the week of November 9).

In the early 1990s, Ricky also took part in a project organized by fiddle great Mark O'Connor called the New Nashville Cats, along with Steve Wariner and Vince Gill. In the 1991 Grammy voting (announced on the February 1992 awards telecast), Ricky, Steve, and Vince won trophies for Best Country Vocal Collaboration for their contributions to the Warner Brothers album *Mark O'Connor and the New Nashville Cats.*

During 1991–92, Skaggs was on the road backing his next album, *My Father's Son,* which was perhaps somewhat less effective overall than his earlier releases, but still contained excellent material such as the up-tempo debut single "Life's Too Long (to Live Like This)." By then Ricky had named his eight-piece backing group Kentucky Thunder. Key members included twenty-year-old lead guitarist Keith Sewell, bassist Jason Sellers, and drummer Keith Edwards. Still, the spotlight remained on Ricky's skills, which besides fiddle and mandolin included dazzling work on both acoustic and electric guitars.

As he told Forte of *Musician,* he had never tried to master electric guitar until the performer who handled electric lead for his band, Ray Flacke, left in 1985. "I was kind of forced into that. I couldn't afford who I wanted: Albert Lee." After auditioning possible replacements who didn't measure up to what he had in mind, he heeded his wife, Sharon's, advice and decided to learn to play lead himself. "So I sat down and learned Albert's solos in 'Honey' and 'Don't Cheat in Our Hometown,' and I learned as many of Ray's things as I possibly could. . . . I had about three days to woodshed before I started playing onstage in front of 15,000 people. I was scared to death when I walked onstage. But people were really encouraging, so I stayed with it."

Over the years Ricky increasingly took an evangelistic approach to his faith in his concert comments, which may have caused some falling off in his overall audience. In fact, during a July 1993 press conference held during the Jamboree in the Hills festival event in Morristown, Ohio, Ricky allowed that his zeal for promoting the views of his religion may have adversely affected his career. He agreed perhaps he had been a little overenthusiastic.

The *Billboard* "Nashville Scene" columnist applauded the action. "By its very nature, zealotry is unyielding and, thus, will always create more enemies than adherents. It wants to bypass the rules of evidence and debate and go straight for the unconnected conclusion. Most people sense the intellectual flaw and the political danger in that approach, They don't like single-cause lives, and they rightly feel threatened by those who insist they should. . . ." The columnist welcomed the fact that Ricky, while he emphasized he still held his religious beliefs as dearly as ever, "also makes clear that he now views himself as an artist who is Christian—not as a Christian artist."

Nothing, of course, could detract from Skaggs's greatness as a performer and contributions to the instrumental spectrum. Commenting on his multi-instrument approach to Forte, he said, "I play a lot of mandolin from a fiddle point of view, and since mandolin was my first instrument, I play a lot of fiddle with a mandolin left hand. I know I've caught myself playing acoustic guitar licks on the electric, but I've also caught myself playing electric guitar licks on the acoustic. And I play guitar licks on the Mandocaster [an electric mandolin], absolutely—especially electric guitar licks."

In the mid-1990s he continued to appear regularly on the *Grand Ole Opry* and maintained an intensive touring schedule at home and abroad. On November 30, 1995, he joined with other artists, including, among others, Alison Krauss, Vince Gill, Roy Clark, Emmylou Harris, George Jones, Loretta Lynn, Bill Monroe, Chet Atkins, and Marty Stuart, who taped a program in honor of the *Grand Ole Opry*'s 70th anniversary (which fell on November 28), presented on CBS-TV in January 1996. His chart singles of 1995–1996 included "Solid Ground," on the lists in late 1995 and early 1996, and his cover of the Harry Chapin song "Cat's in the Cradle," on the charts in the spring of 1996.

SMITH, ARTHUR: *Singer, guitarist, bandleader, songwriter, producer of package music shows, music publisher, business executive. Born Clinton, South Carolina, April 1, 1921.*

You might not think of the name Arthur Smith in connection with the 1973 movie hit *Deliverance* or its theme song, "Duelin' Banjos." In fact, the name escaped the people who incorporated the song into the project, but "Duelin' Banjos" didn't escape Smith's notice. Though it took two years of legal action, he proved that he and musician Don Reno had written the song and the court awarded him not only equitable royalties but the right to the award that named the tune Best Country Music Song of 1973. Of course, it wasn't the first time in a long and generally extremely successful career that Smith had fought for his rights and won. Over the years, with great energy and an iron will, he had carved out a niche for himself as performer, songwriter, and entertainment industry giant who, by the end of the 1970s had been one of the United States' largest producers of syndicated radio shows for many years.

Born in Clinton, South Carolina, his family moved to Kershaw when he was four. His father was a loom fixer in a textile mill, but his sparetime interest was in music. Smith recalled, "My father ran the town band and we always had a room full of instruments. I used to play trumpet when the band played in Kershaw on Sundays."

When only in eighth grade Arthur started a country band with two brothers, Ralph and Sonny, who after two years recorded some sides for a major record firm. Arthur, ever the spark plug, had opted for a music career after his high school graduation in the late 1930s, even though he was an A student (president and class valedictorian) with scholarship offers from Wofford College, the Citadel, and an appointment to the U.S. Naval Academy. Dixieland jazz was then his heart's calling and he didn't want to miss the chance to have a fifteen minute program on station WSPA in Spartanburg, South Carolina.

The group he assembled with his brothers, the Crackerjacks, found the going rough. "We nearly starved to death playing Dixieland," Smith noted. Still, it took World War II to end the program. His brothers joined the services and Arthur moved on, for a time, to a solo job on WBT in Charlotte. Arthur entered the Navy in 1944, serving with the Navy Band and working in the Personnel Bureau in Washington. He made those years pay off musically thanks to his continued effort at songwriting. His composition "Guitar Boogie," which he recorded on MGM Records, became a major hit, the biggest of his recording career. It eventually sold over 3 million copies. The resulting royalties helped him to "get going financially. Business has always intrigued me. I started out investing here and there in real estate and stocks and one thing led to another."

After the war, Arthur plunged into the music field, moving in several directions. Besides reorganizing his own act, he began to recruit others and soon was putting together variety shows for station WBT radio and WBT-TV in Charlotte, North Carolina. It was a logical step from there to packaging shows for live engagements throughout the South and for presentations on other radio and TV stations. Those shows, which rapidly became among the most popular grassroots music packages of the 1950s, blended traditional and popular country artists and material. Gospel and hymn singing was an integral part of the format, reflecting Arthur Smith's deep religious grounding. In 1947, he started teaching Bible classes and was still somehow finding time for that in his busy schedule decades later when his enterprises spread far beyond the music field.

Over the years, the format of the Arthur Smith Shows remained flexible, attracting all types of noted individuals. During the 1950s and 1960s, for instance, people from outside the country-music field who were guests included Richard Nixon, the Rev. Billy Graham, actor E. G. Marshall, and the sophisticated piano team of Ferrante and Teicher. Of course, almost every well-known country artist was presented, a situation which still held true into the 1970s when some of the stars included Johnny Cash, Charlie McCoy, Jimmy Dean, and Red Sovine, to name just a few. A feature of the 1970s was a segment called Bluegrass Corner, where the spotlight fell at one time or another on performers like the Osborne Brothers, Earl Scruggs, and Bill Monroe.

Not a few of the songs played on Smith's shows from time to time were his own. Among the credits were such numbers as "Banjo Buster," "I Saw a Man," "Feudin' Banjos" (of which more later), and "Shadow of the Cross." Writing religious songs always was a major interest of Smith and, of the more than 200 songs he had written or cowritten by the 1970s, over a quarter were hymns or gospels. His religious writings brought many awards from church organizations over the decades.

Smith, an accomplished instrumentalist on both guitar and mandolin, continued to be active as performer and recording artist in the 1950s and 1960s. His 1960s record releases included *Arthur Smith and the Crossroads Quartet* in 1962 on Starday, *Arthur Smith* on Hamilton (1964), and a number of recordings prepared in his own studios in Charlotte, including the single "Jet Set" in the mid-1960s issued on the Dot label. In the gospel field, the Crossroads Quartet, organized by Smith soon after his Navy hitch, ranked as one of the best. The group's recording efforts as of the late 1960s included three albums of favorite old hymns.

The name Crackerjacks was assumed by Smith's main secular group on his show, though it no longer was a Dixieland band. Among main members of the group were brother Ralph, instrumentalists Tommy Faile (added in 1950) and Wayne "Skeeter" Hass (added in 1953), and five-string banjo ace Carl "Happy" Hunt. Faile and Ralph Smith joined forces to do comedy sketches under such names as "The Radio Twins," "Brother Ralph and Cousin Fudd," and "The Counselors of the Airways."

Though his own show remained his prime concern, Arthur Smith and his organization produced many other major shows over the years. Among them were *Johnny Cash*, the *James Brown Show, Flatt & Scruggs,* and George Beverly Shea's *Hymntime*.

Smith's empire as of the late 1970s, besides the *Arthur Smith* television show, included the Arthur Smith Studio, where activities embraced production of records, radio shows, and commercials, a music publishing firm, Clay Music Co., and various other investments. Among his holdings were shares of Mutual Hardware Insurance Co., operating in nine southeastern states, of which he was a director and investment board member. At one stage of his career, he started the Arthur Smith Inns Corporation and a chain of supermarkets, though by the late 1970s he had sold those interests. The TV show's popularity had grown slowly but steadily over the years; by the mid-1970s it was being shown in 31 cities across the United States.

Shortly after the film *Deliverance* was released, Smith entered a legal action against Warner Brothers over the song "Duelin' Banjos." The number, he claimed, was actually a composition he and another musician, Don Reno, had devised in 1955. In that composition, called "Feudin' Banjos," Smith had played tenor banjo and Reno five-string banjo. "The whole idea was two banjos feuding." After a two-year battle, Smith won, the settlement awarding him close to $200,000, half of all future royalties from the *Deliverance* arrangement, and undisputed royalties for him and his publisher, Combine Music Corporation, on all future recordings of the song. Perhaps most rewarding for him was the conveyance of the 1973 award naming "Duelin' Banjos" Best Country Music Song of the Year.

SMITH, CAL: *Singer, guitarist, bandleader. Born Sabbiaw, Oklahoma, April 7, 1932.*

There might have been some confusion among casual country fans in the 1970s about whether Cal Smith was a misspelling of longtime star Carl Smith's name. But there was no doubt in the devoted country fan's mind that these were two individuals, alike in the fact that both were keystones of country music, but certainly different in style and approach. Cal Smith's deep-pitched voice wouldn't be mistaken for Carl's

higher register nor did Cal have the writing ability of Carl.

In fact, Cal realized relatively early in his career that he was an interpreter rather than originator. He told Sharon Rowlett of the *Rocky Mountain Musical Express* for a May 1978 article, "You know, a while back my wife was putting together pictures and clippings we've accumulated on the road. She ran across some papers and started reading. It was songs I'd started writing a long time ago. They were bad. I mean they were awful. I told her to throw them in the fireplace, but she said, 'No, papa, I want to keep them!' I found out I wasn't a songwriter so I just quit writing."

But he never gave up singing and playing country music, an obsession all his life. He told Rowlett that he had received support from his parents. "They knew I was going after music 'cause I've been crazy about music ever since I could walk. Momma and Daddy always supported me any way I wanted to go. The way they looked at it, they'd rather I be playing in a beer joint than out on the streets getting in trouble. 'Course I was a hot-headed little devil and I was into fights about half the time, but there I was less likely to be getting into jail. When I started in the music business, my folks was right with me."

Smith could play reasonably competent guitar before he was high school age and already had many hours as a working musician under his belt before he was out of his teens. His professional debut took place when he was fifteen, he told Rowlett, "in a little place called 'The Remember Me Cafe.' They served dinners. Actually, all it was was a beer joint, but they had a little old place off to one side where they served dinners. Most of the people around there worked in the vineyards and they'd be too tired to cook supper so they'd come down there at night and guzzle beer. When they got through eating, a boy named Jim Rice and me played music. [Their pay was $1.50 a night plus food.] Since we got $1.50, I had to make it up by eating."

That initial pay was symbolic of what was to be Smith's lot for many years. Throughout the 1950s, he worked as often as he could in music, but rarely could get enough income to support himself. To make ends meet, he worked at a wide variety of jobs including truck driver and steel mill worker. His first wife wanted him to give up music in favor of a steady living. "She gave me a choice of her or my music. I'm still playing my music." However, his second marriage in the late 1950s was going strong two decades later.

Cal also had some jobs as a disc jockey during the 1950s and spent a while in the U.S. armed forces. But no matter where he was, he kept singing and pickin' and, finally, things began to turn in his favor. Cal was performing in a group in the San Jose, California, area with a musician named Bill Drake, who had a brother, Jack, in Ernest Tubb's Texas Troubadours. When Tubb played San Jose, Cal got to meet Jack and Ernest, which led to his auditioning for the group. Soon Smith was touring the United States as a permanent member of that famous band. The Troubadours appeared not only on network radio and TV shows, but on the stage of the *Grand Ole Opry* in Nashville.

In the mid-1960s, he got the chance to sign with Kapp Records, which turned out such albums of his as *All the World, Goin' to Cal's Place* (issued in October 1967), and *The Best of Cal Smith*. He began to receive some attention from country fans in the late 1960s, though not enough to make him a household name. The Smith that often dominated the top-chart levels during those years was the one called Carl. By the start of the 1970s, he was represented on the Decca label, on which he had such releases as the 1972 charted single, "For My Baby."

Cal's long pursuit of artistic recognition finally paid off in the early 1970s after Decca merged with MCA Records. He turned out several promising releases before really hitting paydirt with a song called "Country Bumpkin" in 1974. The song (written by Don Wayne) rose to number one on country charts and, when it came time for Country Music Awards earned a nomination for Single of the Year, Song of the Year and, in the Album of the Year category, the LP of that title (also a best-seller) was included in the finalists. The LP honors went to Charlie Rich, but the other two awards were for Cal and Don Wayne.

For the next few years, Smith's name often showed up on country charts, often in the top levels. In early 1975, he had the top-10 single "It's Time to Pay the Fiddler." In June 1975, he again had a top-10 hit with "She Talked a Lot About Texas" and finished out the year with the hit single "Jason's Farm." In early 1976, he had the single "Thunderstorms" on the charts and in 1977 made the lists with "Helen" and "Throwin' Memories on the Fire." His charted MCA singles the last part of the decade included "Bits and Pieces of My Life" in 1978 and, in 1979, "The Rise and Fall of the Roman Empire." However, his MCA material no longer made upper-chart levels and, in the early 1980s, he and the label parted company.

SMITH, CARL: *Singer, guitarist. Born Maynardsville, Tennessee, March 15, 1927.*

One of the most successful country & western performers of the 1950s and 1960s, Carl Smith got his start cutting grass. At least, it was through the proceeds from this activity that young Carl was able to pay for his guitar lessons in his home town of Maynardsville. By the time he was thirteen, he felt he was ready to try his hand in an amateur talent contest; the crowd obviously felt the same way. It was then that Carl decided he wanted to become a country & western performer.

A few years later, he got his first big chance in Knoxville. One of the regular performers on station WROL needed a replacement and Carl subbed for him.

His work was good enough to win him a regular job on the station. After an interruption of eighteen months in the armed services, he got his discharge and returned to WROL in the late 1940s. For a while he decided to expand his horizons by appearing on other stations, including one in Augusta, Georgia, and another in Asheville, North Carolina.

In the end, though, WROL remained his good luck charm. He returned there to work with Mollie O'Day and Archie Campbell. Audience acceptance was strong, and Carl's reputation increased to the point of winning him a bid to join the *Grand Ole Opry*. His debut came in 1950, and within a short time he was one of the show's most popular personalities.

Along with the *Opry* job came a contract with Columbia Records. One of his first discs, "Let's Live a Little," was one of the major hits of 1951. For the next decade, it was a rare week when a Carl Smith record was not high on the charts. He added two more hits in 1951, "If Teardrops Were Pennies" and "Mr. Moon." His 1952 output included four major hits: the number-one-rated "Just Don't Stand There," "Are You Teasing Me," "It's a Lovely, Lovely World," and "Our Honeymoon." The following year, Carl gained number-one chart position for a second time with "Hey Joe." Other 1953 hits were "Satisfaction Guaranteed," "This Orchid Means Goodbye," and "Trademark." In 1954, Smith had best-sellers in "Love" and "Loose Talk." The latter was number one on the hit charts for more than thirty weeks. It won Carl *Billboard*'s Triple Crown award and *Down Beat* magazine's Best New Western Band of the Year award. Other major hits included "Kisses Don't Lie" and "There She Goes" (1955); "Why Why" (1957); "Your Name Is Beautiful" (1958); "Ten Thousand Drums" (1959); and "Foggy River" (1960).

Through the 1960s, Carl was featured in person and on TV and radio around the world. His tours took him to all states of the United States, all of Canada's provinces, and throughout Europe and the Far East. His TV guest spots included the *Porter Wagoner Show, Wilburn Brothers Show,* and the *Philip Morris Country Music Show*. In the mid-1960s, his weekly TV show— Carl Smith's *Country Music Hall*—was telecast coast-to-coast in Canada. During this period, he also appeared in two movies, *The Badge of Marshal Brennan* and *Buffalo Guns*.

In the 1960s, Smith and his talented wife, country songwriter Goldie Hill, resided with their three children on a large ranch near Nashville. As of the early 1980s Carl still called Nashville home. (Carl had previously been June Carter's husband from 1952–1957 and was the father of Carlene Carter. After he and June divorced, he married Goldie in September 1957.)

Smith's album output in the 1950s and early 1960s included *Great Country and Western Hits; Easy to Please; Sunday Down South; Let's Live; Smith's the Name; Carl Smith's Touch;* and *Kentucky Derby.*

Throughout the 1960s, he regularly turned out one or more LPs a year on Columbia, such as *Greatest Hits* (2/63); *Tall, Tall Gentleman* (12/63); *There Stands the Glass* (6/64); *I Want to Live and Love* (3/65); *Kisses Don't Lie* (11/65); *Man with a Plan* (7/66); *Gentleman Sings* (3/67); *Carl Smith Sings His Favorites* (9/67); and *Greatest Hits, Volume 2* (7/69). Carl also had several LPs on Harmony label in the 1960s, including *Best of Carl Smith* (10/64) and *Satisfaction Guaranteed* (6/67). Carl regularly placed singles releases on the charts all during the 1960s, though his percentage of top-10 successes didn't approach his 1950s output. In 1967, for instance, he had five singles on the charts, but none in the top 10. He finished up the decade in reasonably good style, making top-chart levels in 1968 with a remake of his 1960 hit, "Foggy River," and had two top-10 hits in 1969, "Faded Love and Winter Roses" and "Good Deal Lucille."

At the start of the 1970s, Carl wound up his twentieth year on Columbia Records, an event celebrated by release of the two-record *Anniversary Album,* issued in August 1970. Other Columbia LPs of the early 1970s included *I Love You Because* (3/70); *Carl Smith with Tunesmiths* (10/70); *Bluegrass* (5/71); *Don't Say You're Mine* (5/72); and *If This Is Goodbye.* He also was represented on the Harmony label with *Knee Deep in the Blues* (6/71). Among Carl's charted singles on Columbia in the early 1970s was "If This Is Goodbye" in the fall of 1972. It had a symbolic title, since Carl's long association with the label was coming to an end. He signed with Hickory Records and placed a number of singles on the charts, mostly on lower rungs, such as "The Way I Love My Mind" in 1975 and "If You Don't, Somebody Else Will" in 1976.

Though his recording status waned in the 1970s, Carl remained a popular figure on the country-music concert circuit and also continued to be active as a radio and TV performer.

By the 1980s, Carl was devoting more and more of his time to horse and cattle ranching at his spread near Franklin, Tennessee. He was nominated for the Country Music Hall of Fame several times, but as of 1996 had not received sufficient votes for induction. In the 1990s, some of his recordings were included in reissues or multiartist collections like *Columbia Country Classics, Volume 2, Honky Tonk Heroes.* Performances from his heyday were also available on several volumes of the *Grand Ole Opry Stars of the Fifties* video series including Volume 8 in which he was the featured artist. Besides that, some of his renditions were included in Volumes 2, 3, and 11.

SMITH, CONNIE: *Singer, guitarist. Born Elkhart, Indiana, August 14, 1941.*

From a large family and on her way to having a large one of her own (she eventually had four, two boys and two girls), Connie Smith gave in to the urging of friends in early 1963 and entered a country-music talent contest. That event changed her career from homemaker to entertainer. She eventually became one of country music's foremost female vocalists.

Connie's hometown was Elkhart, Indiana, where she was one of fourteen children. Her interest in country music went back to her early years. She recalled, "I was bashful as a kid, but I remember clear back when I was five years old I'd say, 'Someday I'm gonna sing on the *Grand Ole Opry.*' Of course, I said it with a laugh, because I didn't want anyone to know just how much I wanted to."

Later on, an accident gave her inspiration to take another step toward her eventual performing role (though she didn't envision such a future at the time). While Connie was mowing the lawn as her contribution to family chores, the blades uprooted a rock and sent it back against her leg like a shot. She suffered injuries so severe, there even was fear she might lose her limb. During the long weeks in the hospital, she began to learn to play guitar to pass the time. As she grew older, she combined her guitar and vocal talents to take part in local shows and even gain some TV exposure.

Still, the idea of succeeding in music seemed only a dream to her. After she got married and settled down to raise a family in a midwestern town, show business seemed even more unattainable. But her feelings about it changed after some friends persuaded her to enter a talent contest at a park called Frontier Ranch near Columbus, Ohio. Smith won the contest, and among those who had seen the show was country star Bill Anderson, who came over to congratulate her.

About six months later, she went to one of his performances and went backstage to renew acquaintances. He invited her to come to Nashville to sing on his show and, when she did, provided her with the music to his composition "Walk on Backwards." That, in turn, led to his asking her to help with some demonstration tapes he was making in May 1964. Connie returned home and, soon after, got a call from Bill, who was on tour in Minneapolis. He had played the tapes for top agent Hubert Long, who had then gotten Chet Atkins to listen to them. The result was an arrangement whereby Anderson provided some new songs and Atkins arranged for RCA to sign Smith to a recording contract. The first single, "Once a Day," was released by RCA in August 1964. After a slow start, it began to move and by November was number one on country charts, where it stayed an amazing two and a half months. When the year was over, *Billboard* named her "Most Promising Country Female Singer of 1964," an honor she won in 1965 as well.

During 1965, she added three more top-10 hits to her credits, "I Can't Remember," "If I Talk to Him," and "Then and Then Only." Her status was improving so rapidly that on June 13, 1965, she was asked to become a cast regular on the *Grand Ole Opry.* In 1966, she kept right on rolling with such top-10 hits as "Ain't Had No Lovin'" and "Nobody but a Fool" and in 1967 made top-chart levels with "I'll Come a-Runnin'." In 1968, she had the top-10 hits "Runaway Little Tears" and "Baby's Back Again" plus such hit albums as *Soul of Country Music* and *I Love Charley Brown*. At the end of 1968, *Billboard* ranked her third-best female vocalist of the year behind Loretta Lynn and Lynn Anderson.

During the mid- and late-1960s, Smith starred on almost every major country TV show and many general variety programs, including *The Jimmy Dean Show, American Swing Around, Singin' Country, Ralph Emery, Bobby Lord Show,* and *Lawrence Welk.* In concert tours, she was featured on bills having such stars as Loretta Lynn, George Jones, Bill Anderson, George Morgan, Rex Allen, Jimmy Dean, and Sonny James. She appeared in several country films, including *Road to Nashville, Las Vegas Hillbillies,* and *Second Fiddle to a Steel Guitar.*

Her debut album on RCA, *Connie Smith,* came out in May 1965. This was rapidly followed by a series of releases including *Cute'n'Country* (12/65), *Connie Smith Goes to Nashville* (5/66), *Born to Sing* (11/66), *In the Country* (Camden, 4/67), *Connie Smith Sings Bill Anderson* (7/67), *Downtown* (3/67), *Best of Connie Smith* (11/67), *Soul of Country Music* (2/68), and *I Love Charley Brown* (mid-1968). Demonstrating her religious feelings, she recorded several albums of that kind, including *Great Sacred Songs.* She was active in some of the Reverend Billy Graham's efforts, taking part in his programs at Expo '72.

Connie remained on the RCA Records roster into the early 1970s. Her singles hits included two top-10 singles in 1972, "Just What I Am" and "If It Ain't Love (Let's Leave It Alone)". Her early 1970s albums on RCA were *I Never Once Stopped Loving You* (10/70), *Where Is My Castle* (3/71), *Just One Time* (8/71), *Come Along and Walk with Me* (12/71), *City Lights, Country Favorites* (Camden, 4/72), *Ain't We Havin' Us a Good time* (6/72), and *If It Ain't Love* (8/72).

In 1973, Smith departed RCA and signed a new contract with Columbia Records. Late in the year she had her first singles hit on the new label, "Ain't Love a Good Thing," which entered the top 10 in early 1974. Later in the year, she had another chartmaker in "Dallas." She had many more charted singles on Columbia in the mid-1970s, including "Why Don't You Love Me" (top 15 in summer 1975), "The Song We Fell in Love To" (fall 1975), and, in 1976, "(Til) I Kissed You," "So Sad (To Watch Good Love Go Bad)," and "I Don't Wanna Talk It Over Anymore."

By 1977, Smith was recording for Monument Records, turning out such charted singles as "I Just Wanna Be Your Everything" in 1977 and "Smooth Sailin'" in 1978. Monument issued her album *New Horizons* in early 1978.

At the start of the 1980s she was still a regular cast member of the *Grand Ole Opry,* but through the mid-1980s she cut back on all other activities to focus on raising her family. By the late 1980s, she was again expanding her entertainment work, doing more concerts and seeking new recording opportunities. Her appearances in the 1990s included shows in the UK and Europe and in venues in Branson, Missouri. In 1993, she had a new album in print, *Live in Branson, Missouri.* On November 30, 1995, she was one of the stars who taped a TV program in honor of the *Opry*'s 70th anniversary that was presented on CBS in January 1996. Her credits in the mid-1990s included concerts at Dolly Parton's Dollywood theme park as part of the annual Showcase of Stars series. In the summer of 1996 she was in the studios preparing a new album.

SMITH, SAMMI: *Singer, songwriter. Born Orange, California, August 5, 1943.*

For a long time, Sammi Smith was known, unfairly, as a one-hit artist. The enormous success of her version of Kris Kristofferson's "Help Me Make It Through the Night" in 1971 propelled her into the spotlight so suddenly it seemed to obscure all that had gone before and much that came after. A combination of circumstances, personal and contractual, pushed her into the background for much of the 1970s until she began to be rediscovered at decade's end.

Sammi, whose father was a serviceman, was born in California, but moved constantly thereafter with her family in a disjointed childhood spread over Oklahoma, Texas, Arizona, and Colorado. She was, in fact, still a child when she moved into show business. "I don't know how I got started, but I was working at a club called Someplace Else [in Oklahoma City] six nights a week when I was eleven. When I first started I was singing rock 'n' roll; then I worked with big bands, doing pop material. I kind of drifted into country, but I like to mix it up. I wouldn't want to stick to just one thing."

Smith continued to sing in local bars and clubs during the mid-1960s, but there were stretches of time when she was on the sidelines. "I went to see a promoter about getting some work. He was doing a Johnny Cash show in Oklahoma City and somebody told Marshall Grant, Johnny's bass player, I was a singer and we got a tape and a few days later he called me and said he thought he could get me on a label, which he did."

The label was Columbia and resulted in her moving to Nashville in 1967. Sammi remained on the label until the start of the 1970s with limited success—only three minor hits. However, she met a janitor at the Columbia studio who was to prove an important friend—Kris Kristofferson. Later she became the first female vocalist with Waylon Jennings' band, touring with him for a year. Waylon suggested that RCA sign her when the Columbia contract ran out, but to no avail. She signed, instead, with a small Nashville label, Mega Records.

Her first single release, "He's Everywhere," didn't do badly, reaching the country top 30, but it was the next single that really took off. She'd made demo tapes of a number of Kristofferson songs, all of which became major hits, but only one of which she recorded. The song, of course, was "Help Me Make It Through the Night," which reached number one on country charts and the top 10 on national pop charts in 1971. In early 1972, the song earned Smith a Grammy as Best Female Country Vocalist for 1971.

One of Sammi's problems was that, despite the song's smash success, Mega remained an independent. This minimized the promotional and distribution backing for her followup songs. One might think her years with Mega after 1971 were ones of failure. Actually, she recorded seven albums, in all, for the label and from 1972 to 1976 placed sixteen other singles on country charts. These included "Today I Started Loving You Again" which reached number nine, "Then You Walk In," which rose to ten, and such others as "I've Got to Have You" (thirteen), "The Rainbow in Daddy's Eyes" (sixteen), "Long Black Veil" (twenty-six), and "For the Kids" (twenty-seven).

Mega went downhill financially, going out of business in 1976. That, plus Smith's desire to spend time with her family (as of 1978, she had four children of her own and had adopted twin Apache children) slowed down her career, despite the fact that her country-music peers had great regard for her talent. Kristofferson, for instance, commented, "She's blessed . . . with a voice that's somehow tough and tender and touchingly honest with the same sadness that haunted the songs of Edith Piaf. . . . She's one helluva writer, with a gift for lyrics and melody that makes a body want to smile. . . . And she sure ain't hard to look at."

Smith's writing ability was evinced with three songs on her first hit Mega album, including "When Michael Calls," B side of "Help Me Make It Through the Night." Many artists recorded her compositions during the 1970s, including such songs as "Cedartown, Georgia," a chart hit for Waylon Jennings, and "Sand-Covered Angels," a hit for Conway Twitty.

She became a close friend of Waylon Jennings and Willie Nelson, moving to a home near Dallas in 1973 as a result of her interest in the Austin, Texas, progressive country movement. In the mid-1970s, she moved from there to Globe, Arizona, where she became involved in programs to help the Indians on the San Carlos Apache Reservation (she is part Kiowa–Apache). This led to the organization of a country-music benefit show to help build a new school on the reservation and aid Apache education in general. Among those who donated their services for the first show, April 29 and 30, 1978, were Johnny Cash, Mickey Newbury, Johnny Rodriguez, and Steve Young.

After Mega folded, meanwhile, Sammi signed a new contract with Elektra. Her first album was released in 1976, the second one, *Mixed Emotions,* in 1977, and the third, *New Winds/All Quadrants,* in May 1978. Her husky, sultry voice showed to good advantage in all, and her career began to pick up momentum. Her debut single, "As Long as There's a Sunday" made the country top-50 and she followed with such other chart hits as "Loving Arms," "I Can't Stop Loving You," "Days That End in Y." The 1978 success, which had such other fine tracks as "Norma Jean" (about Marilyn Monroe), "I Ain't Got No Time to Rock No Babies," "Lookin' for Lovin'," and "It's Too Late," was the most interesting since her 1971 blockbuster.

Unfortunately, her arrangement with Elektra didn't work out as hoped for and she left the label. In 1980, she reappeared on the Sound Factory Label and had the single "I Just Want to Be with You" on the charts in late 1980 and early 1981 and "Cheatin's a Two Way Street" later in 1981.

SNOW, HANK: *Singer, guitarist, harmonica player, songwriter. Born Liverpool, Nova Scotia, Canada, May 9, 1914. Elected to Country Music Hall of Fame in 1979.*

For a country with only about a fifth the population of the United States and relatively far removed from the country-music heartland, Canada has contributed a surprisingly high percentage of performers to the field. Among them is one of the all-time modern country greats, Hank Snow, whose successes as recording artist and songwriter placed him in the top 10 on the U.S. country roster after World War II.

Snow's original interest in the music was stirred by a love of western movies. Tom Mix in particular was a favorite, though Mix, of course, was not a singer. As he recalled, "America . . . always I just loved the sound. I would go to any movie when I lived in Canada if it showed anything of America. Texas was always big on my mind." Later on, when Hank began to write C&W songs, the state still bulked large in his consciousness. "I wrote a lot of songs about Texas, you know. I'd read about these places, seen them in the movies."

Part of the youngster's infatuation with the relatively far-off glamour of the U.S. was based on a need to escape from an unhappy home life. "I was the victim of a broken home at the age of eight and inherited a very cruel stepfather." His stepfather, he claimed, often beat him and threw him out of the house. "I really didn't have any childhood. When you don't know where you are going to sleep for the night . . . or find food . . . you can't think with the mind of a child. You have to think with the mind of a man."

When other boys were getting ready for high school, Hank was earning a living at sea. To escape his stepfather's ire, he ran away, getting a job as a cabin boy. Off and on for much of his teens he worked at sea. "It was a bad situation, but a great education. It teaches you the hard realities of life." He had learned to play the harmonica and his shipmates welcomed the relief from boredom that Hank's playing provided.

In between voyages, Snow worked a variety of jobs, including selling newspapers, Fuller brushes, and being a stevedore. His earnings from a two-week job unloading salt from a freighter provided the money to buy his first guitar for $5.95. About that time he first heard recordings of the great Jimmie Rodgers, and he was soon spending his spare time trying to work out some of Rodgers' songs on the guitar. Still in his early teens, he began to perform in local bars or even in the streets, sometimes for a few dollars, often for no formal pay. "When I started unprofessionally in the entertainment field at about fifteen," he recalled, "I was encouraged by people who thought I had a bright future. That changed the whole picture for me."

After a while, he concentrated more and more on his performing work, gradually building up a following in the Halifax area. One of his first breakthroughs was the chance to have his own show on station CHNS in Halifax. He called himself Hank, the Singing Ranger, the name he was known by for well over a decade.

He still had his heart set on eventually cracking the U.S. market, acknowledging that it wouldn't be an overnight thing. He realized that he needed an affiliation with a major record company and managed to get an audition with RCA's Canadian branch in the autumn of 1936. He traveled from Halifax to Montreal with only enough money for round trip train fare, food, and a hotel. To conserve his funds, he walked five miles between studio and hotel. "They said they would audition me the next day and asked if I had my material prepared. I didn't know anything about having material prepared . . . but I said yes. I went back to the hotel and wrote two songs that night."

His audition went reasonably well and, in October 1936, he signed with RCA Victor, a relationship that was to last for nearly half a century. That alignment plus increased touring made him a featured artist throughout Canada over the next few years, but he remained virtually unknown in the United States. However, he was meeting many American artists in his travels, including a Texan who shared his love for Jimmie Rodgers, the now legendary Ernest Tubb. It was Tubb who arranged for Snow's U.S. debut in Dallas in 1944 and also urged others in the country to take note of the Canadian's talents. During the mid-1940s, Hank finally had the pleasure of seeing one of his recordings make inroads into the U.S. market, a single titled "Brand New Heart." However, almost until the end of the decade, though Hank performed increasingly in the United States, he remained primarily a Canadian artist, and RCA released his records only in that country.

In 1949, RCA finally changed the pattern, and the response among American fans was sufficient to make the company try releasing still more Snow discs in the United States. His 1949 singles, including the modest hit "Marriage Vows," still came out with the name Hank, the Singing Ranger. In 1950, he switched to his full name and soon had two smash hits, "Golden Rocket" and "I'm Movin' On," both written by Hank and both number-one successes on U.S. charts. By the time those were released, Hank already was a regular cast member of the *Grand Ole Opry*, which he had joined in January 1950. It was Ernest Tubb who had persuaded the *Opry* to add Hank and decades later, both Ernest and Hank continued to host major segments of the *Opry* Saturday night radio (and sometimes TV) program.

After 1950, Hank made the Nashville area home (at the start of the 1980s, he lived in nearby Madison, Tennessee) and became a U.S. citizen. He continued to grow in stature as a performer and individual, adding to his laurels almost every year from the 1950s through the 1970s with hit recordings, noteworthy concert tours, and a growing string of country music accolades.

In 1951, for instance, he placed four songs in the country top 10: "Bluebird Island," "Music Makin' Mama from Memphis," "Unwanted Sign on Your Heart," and "Rhumba Boogie." The latter reached number one on country charts and also was a hit in the pop field. His esteem with the U.S. country public was demonstrated when he suffered severe injuries in an auto accident. He received 22,000 get-well cards. Hank recovered and went on to turn out such 1950s and 1960s hits as "Fool Such as I," "Girl Who Invented Kissing," "I Went to Your Wedding," "Lady's Man" (1952); "Honeymoon in a Rocket Ship," "Spanish Fire Ball," "When Mexican Joe Met Jole Blon" (1953); "I Don't Hurt Anymore" (number one), "Let Me Go Lover" (1954); "Cryin', Prayin', Waitin', Hopin'," "Mainliner," "Yellow Roses" (1955); "Conscience, I'm Guilty," "Stolen Moments," "These Hands" (1956); "Tangled Mind" (1957); "Chasin' a Rainbow," "The Last Ride" (1959); "Miller's Cave" (1960); "Beggar to a King" (1961); "I've Been Everywhere" (number one, 1962); "Ninety Miles an Hour," "The Man Who Robbed the Bank at Santa Fe" (1963); "The Wishing Well" (1965); "I've Cried a Mile" (1966); "Down at the Pawn Shop" (1967); "The Late and Great Love of My Life" (1968); and "The Name of the Game Was Love" (1969).

Over the decades, Snow's album output was among the most prolific of any country artist. By the start of the 1980s, he had more than 100 LPs to his credit and still turned out one, two, or more new ones each year. Among the RCA titles from the late 1950s into the 1970s were *Country Classics, Country Guitar, Jamboree, Just Keep a-Movin', Sacred Songs* (1958); *When Tragedy Struck* (1959); *Songs of Jimmie Rodgers* (1960); *Souvenirs* (1961); *Sings with the Carters*

(1962); *I've Been Everywhere, Railroad Man* (1963); *Songs of Tragedy* (1964); *Favorite Hits* (1965); *Spanish Fire Ball, Christmas with Hank Snow* (1967); *Hits Covered, I Went to Your Wedding* (1969); *In Memory of Jimmie Rodgers, Cure for the Blues* (1970); *Tracks and Trains, Award Winners* (1971).

He also had a number of albums issued on RCA's Camden label over the years, including *Hank the Singing Ranger* (1960); *Southern Cannonball* (1961); *One and Only Hank Snow* (1962); *Last Ride* (1963); *Old and Great Songs* (1964); *I Went to Your Wedding* (1969); *Memories Are Made of This* (1970); *Wreck of the Old 97* (1971); and *Lonesome Whistle, Legend of Old Doc Brown* (1972).

One of the pleasantest memories for Snow went back to late 1953, when he went to Meridian, Mississippi, to dedicate a memorial to that town's famous son, Jimmie Rodgers. Over the years he almost never missed the annual celebration to Rodgers held there. In late 1954, he became the first guitarist to record duets with "Mr. Guitar," Chet Atkins. That same year, Hank's "I Don't Hurt Anymore" was named the best country record of the year in a *Cash Box* magazine poll, and in 1955, the poll indicated it was the most programmed record of the year. Almost a decade later, in 1963, another Snow classic, "I'm Movin' On," was voted the all-time favorite country music record by the nation's disc jockeys in a *Billboard* survey. This resulted in the magazine presenting Hank with its Award of Achievement.

Over the years, his contract with RCA was renewed steadily until an arrangement finally was concluded, extending through the year 1987. That agreement provided still another milestone for an illustrious career, permitting completion of a fifty-year affiliation between Hank and the label, the longest running association between an artist and a record company.

It was unfortunate for Hank that the Country Music Association Awards were not inaugurated until 1967. Had they been in effect in the 1950s and first half of the 1960s, Snow undoubtedly would have had a tidy share of nominations and more than a few victories to his credit. His peers recognized his important contributions to the field by inducting him into the Country Music Hall of Fame in 1979. He was recognized not only for considerable creative achievements, but also for his strength of character. Scandal was never associated with his name, and his charitable efforts included establishment of the Hank Snow Foundation for the Prevention of Child Abuse, intended to prevent others from suffering such traumas as he experienced as a child.

Hank's affiliation with RCA failed to last into the 1990s, but he was still a stalwart of the *Grand Ole Opry* in the mid-1990s, and he still made records and videos on smaller labels. He was among those included in the *Life* magazine list of "The 100 Most Important People in the History of Country" presented in its September 1994 special issue on "The Roots of Country Music."

Many of his recordings were available as of 1996 in the Country Music Foundation catalog or as import items from Germany's Bear Family Records. (Most of the multi CD albums listed in CMF were Bear Family sets indicated by the letters BCD.) That list included such RCA releases as *Hank Snow/Collector's Series, Volume 2; I'm Movin' On and Other Hits;* and, on the Bear Family label, *Hank Snow/The Singing Ranger, Volumes 1, 2, 3* and *4*. The first two volumes included 4 CDs each, *Volume 3* was presented on 12 CDs and *Volume 4* on 9 CDs. Also offered on BCD were *Hank Snow/The Thesaurus Transcriptions* and *Hank Snow/The Yodeling Ranger—The Canadian Years 1936–1947*. The *Thesaurus* package contains 140 recordings Hank made between 1950 and 1956 that had never been commercially available.

SONS OF THE PIONEERS: *Vocal and instrumental group. Founding members, early 1930s: Leonard Slye (Roy Rogers), born Cincinnati, Ohio, November 5, 1912; Bob Nolan, born New Brunswick, Canada, April 1, 1908, died Los Angeles, California, June 16, 1980; Tim Spencer, born Webb City, Missouri, July 7, 1908, died Apple Valley, California, April 26, 1976; Karl Farr (added 1934–35), born Rochelle, Texas, April 25, 1909, died West Springfield, Massachusetts, September 20, 1961; Hugh Farr (added 1934–35), born Llano, Texas, December 6, 1903, died Casper, Wyoming, March 17, 1980; Lloyd Perryman, born Ruth, Arkansas, January 29, 1917, died Colorado Springs, Colorado, May 31, 1977; Pat Brady (added 1937), born Toledo, Ohio. Original group elected to Country Music Hall of Fame in 1980 comprised Hugh and Karl Farr, Bob Nolan, Lloyd Perryman, Tim Spencer, and Roy Rogers.*

Even today, when anyone thinks of vocal groups in western music, one name stands out above all others: the Sons of the Pioneers. With different combinations of performers, the group has remained active from its inception in the early 1930s to the present day, though in its "golden years," roughly from the mid-1930s to the end of the 1940s, its makeup remained essentially stable, including for most of that period, Bob Nolan, Tim Spencer, the Farr brothers, Hugh and Karl, Lloyd Perryman, and Pat Brady. During those years, such songs as Bob Nolan's "Cool Water" and "Tumbling Tumbleweeds" and Tim Spencer's "Room Full of Roses" brought the group fame across the United States and in many other countries as well.

Appropriately for a group that brings to mind boots and saddles and the cowboy life of times past, one of the original members was a young, banjo-playing and singing performer named Leonard Slye, who went on to fame as Roy Rogers in western movies, where he gained the title "King of the Cowboys." Recalling the early days to Terry Atkinson of the *Los Angeles Times* (Calendar section, August 21, 1977), Rogers said the first step came in 1931 in Los Angeles, California, when, as a member of an all-instrumental group called the Rocky Mountaineers, he persuaded the others that having a singing group would boost audience interest. In response to an ad he placed in a local paper, Bob Nolan came on to form a duet with Roy. Nolan had been born in Canada to American parents and had moved first to Tucson and then Los Angeles. At the time, Nolan was working as a lifeguard on Venice Beach in Los Angeles.

Later, the group expanded to a trio with the addition of one of Nolan's Venice friends, Bill "Slumber" Nichols. Then, Rogers told Atkinson, "Bob decided to quit and went to caddy at the Bel-Air Country Club. So we put another ad in the paper and Tim Spencer answered." Recalling his route to that point in a letter to Grelun Landon (January 11, 1967), Spencer wrote, "I left Missouri and moved into New Mexico in 1915. Father and Mother homesteaded 360 acres of land there. Later the Spencer family moved to Oklahoma and then on to California in 1930. There I met Roy Rogers and Bob Nolan, which formed the nucleus of the Sons of the Pioneers."

Rogers continued, "Tim, Slumber and I worked together for a while. But eventually I joined the Texas Outlaws. Slumber hitched up with another group and Tim went back to work for Safeway."

Roy, however, remained confident that a western trio had a lot of potential and he soon began rehearsing a new one with some of his former associates. "Spencer, Nolan and I got a room in a little boarding house on Carlton Way just off Bronson [in Hollywood] and we rehearsed until our voices gave out." When they felt they were ready, they brought their act to the attention of the Texas Outlaws group and soon joined to become a part of the Outlaws' radio program on Los Angeles station KFWB from 1934 to 1936. The boys first called themselves the Pioneer Trio, Rogers noted, but an announcer accidentally introduced them as the Sons of the Pioneers and they were called that from then on. During those years, more personnel were added to the group. During 1934–35 instrumentalists Karl and Hugh Farr joined up, and, in 1936, tenor Lloyd Perryman was a new recruit. The group struck out on its own as members of the *Hollywood Barn Dance* on KHJ, and also started nibbling at the movie field individually and collectively. Some members contributed songs to western films and played roles in Columbia "B" westerns.

By the time Roy Rogers left to work as a featured performer in westerns for Republic Pictures, the Sons had become a six-member group consisting of Nolan, Spencer, Perryman, the Farrs, and singer-comedian Pat Brady, who joined in 1937. (Prior to Brady's addition, Rogers had been cast as the comic in many of the group's routines.) Though no longer officially a member, Roy never forgot the group, seeing to it that they sang and acted in many of his movies. (Brady, of course, was one of Roy's regular sidekicks and comedy contributors in movies and later in Rogers' long-running TV series.) However, that didn't take place right away. The Sons were obligated to work for Columbia Pictures as singers in westerns starring Charles Starrett from 1936 to 1940. In 1940, they signed with Republic and appeared in many films with Roy under a contract that ran until 1949.

From the late 1930s on, the Sons of the Pioneers established its own identity as a live performance group and as major recording artists. Nolan and Spencer were the main creative forces, each providing hundreds of original songs either for the group's repertoire or for use by others in western films or recording sessions. Nolan provided many memorable songs during the group's heyday, but, of course, is most often remembered for "Cool Water" and "Tumbling Tumbleweeds." The latter actually was first written as "Tumbling Leaves" from some of Nolan's sensations while looking at falling leaves one autumn day from his West Los Angeles apartment. Spencer's most successful offerings came somewhat later than Nolan's. He wrote Landon, "In 1946 I wrote the song entitled, 'Cigareets, Whuskey and Wild, Wild Women' which sold in excess of one million records. In 1949 I wrote the song entitled, 'Room Full of Roses,' which sold over a million recordings. I have written more than 250 western songs for motion pictures starring the Sons of the Pioneers and Roy Rogers."

The Sons' early recordings included work on Decca and Columbia labels. The main share of their output, though, came during a long-term alignment with RCA Victor that lasted until the late 1960s. Their Decca output included "Cool Water" and "There's a New Moon Over My Shoulder" and, on Columbia, "Open Range Ahead" and "The Devil's Great Grandson." Their contract with Columbia expired in 1939 and in 1940 they signed with RCA Victor. During the 1940s, they had many hit singles (and some best-selling albums) on Victor, including "Cool Water," "Tumbling Tumbleweeds," "Timber Trails," "Blue Shadows on the Trail," "Blue Prairie," "Pecos Bill," "Carry Me Back to the Lone Prairie," "Home on the Range," "Have I Told You Lately That I Love You," "Lie Low Little Doggies," "Cigareets, Whuskey," and "Room Full of Roses."

Besides appearing in an estimated 100 films from the late 1930s to the early 1950s, films that starred not only Roy Rogers but others like John Wayne, Bing Crosby, and Randolph Scott, the group kept up an active touring schedule that took it to rodeos, fairs, theaters, and night clubs across the United States. Their travels also took them to Canada and many other countries. In 1951, they were featured in a western concert at New York's Carnegie Hall.

By the early 1950s, though, some of the momentum began to go out of the group as it started to lose its primary writers. Bob Nolan stepped down from concert work in 1949. Roy Rogers said, "He's always been a loner. That's what made him retire in 1949 from touring. He just got tired of traveling." (However, Nolan continued to record with the group until 1957.) Tim Spencer wrote Landon, "I resigned from the Sons of the Pioneers as a singing member in 1952 and took over the management of the group through 1954. I then started a religious publishing company by the name of Manna Music. Since 1954, and to this date [1967], Manna Music has grown into a major publishing house. Our composition entitled 'How Great Thou Art' has in the past ten years, sold over one million copies of sheet music."

In the early 1950s, one of the new members of the group was Ken Curtis. His place was taken by Kentucky-born Dale Warren in 1952; Warren still was the lead singer of the group in the late 1970s.

With the departure of Spencer and Nolan, the amount of new material provided from within the group declined sharply. The Sons continued to maintain a sizable performing schedule, though, and had considerable TV guest appearance credits in the 1950s and 1960s and, to a lesser extent, in the 1970s. Among their 1960s TV credits were Johnny Carson's *The Tonight Show, Joey Bishop, Steve Allen, Merv Griffin,* and the *Kraft Music Hall.* Besides keeping up its concerts at rodeos and fairs from the mid-1950s through the early 1980s, the group had several overseas tours to such places as Japan, Australia, and Europe.

RCA continued to release new albums of the group's recordings (including some reissues) to the end of the 1960s. These included *Wagons West* (RCA Camden Records, 4/58); *Cool Water* (5/60); *Room Full of Roses* (7/60); *Lure of the West* (6/61); *Tumbleweed Trail* (4/62); *Good Old Country Music* (Camden, 12/62); *Our Man Out West* (2/63); *Cowboy Hymns* (5/63); *Trail Dust* (12/63); *Country Fare* (7/64); *Down Country Trails* (12/64); *Best of the Sons of the Pioneers* (2/66); *Songs of Bob Nolan* (7/66); and *Campfire Favorites* (4/67). Other label releases in the 1960s included *Tumbleweed Trails* (Vocalion, 5/64) and *Best of the Sons of the Pioneers* (Harmony, 7/64).

For a time, in the late 1960s, the Sons was a quartet composed of Perryman, Warren, Roy Lanham (guitarist, born Kentucky), and Billy Armstrong (fiddle). In the 1970s, Pat Brady returned to join Warren, Lanham, Perryman, and tenor Rusty Richards (born Orange County, California), for several years. At other times, the roster included Billy Leibert and Rome Johnson. When the Hollywood Chamber of Commerce decided to install a new star in the Walk of Fame honoring the Sons on September 24, 1976, the group members were Perryman, Warren, Richards, Lanham, and Leibert. Perryman remained active with the group up to shortly before his death in May 1977. His place was taken by Rome Johnson.

The group first was nominated for the Country Music Hall of Fame in the late 1960s, but did not receive enough votes from CMA members to be welcomed into the assemblage until 1980, the year that two of its earliest members, Nolan and Hugh Farr, died.

During the 1980s and into the 1990s, various combinations of performers continued to keep the group's traditions alive. Over the years some of the later members included an estimated two dozen relations of the founding members, including sons, grandsons, and cousins. Retrospective albums available in the mid-1990s included the *Sons of the Pioneers: Country Music Hall of Fame Series* on MCA Records, *Sons of the Pioneers/Cool Water* on RCA, and *Sons of the Pioneers/Columbia Historic Edition* on Columbia.

SOVINE, RED: *Singer, guitarist, bandleader (Echo Valley Boys), songwriter. Born Charleston, West Virginia, July 17, 1918; died Nashville, Tennessee, April 4, 1980.*

Esteemed for his acting almost as much as his singing, Red Sovine's deep baritone voice was used to good effect for straightforward country vocals as well as dramatic vignettes delivered against an instrumental backdrop. Although he could sing anything from uptempo songs to plaintive ballads as well as anybody in the country field in the post–World War II decades, it was his recitations that eventually gained him a unique niche in the country pantheon.

Woodrow Wilson "Red" Sovine was born and raised in Charleston, West Virginia, where he already was an accomplished guitarist and vocalist while in his teens in the 1930s. At seventeen, he became a member of a group called Jim Pike and the Carolina Tar Heels and performed with them regularly on the Friday night *Old Farm Hour Show* at radio station WCHS. An opportunity arose for them to move up to the prestigious WWVA station in Wheeling, where the group was featured on the famous Saturday night *WWVA Jamboree.*

In 1947, Sovine formed his own band, the Echo Valley Boys. They appeared for a time on WWVA, then moved to Shreveport, Louisiana, to join the cast of the KWKH *Louisiana Hayride,* whose star at the time was Hank Williams. When Hank left for the *Grand Ole Opry* on June 3, 1949, KWKH executives tabbed Red as the logical successor. Besides gaining the top spot on the *Hayride,* Red and his band fell heir to a fifteen-minute daily program of Hank's called the *Johnny Fair Syrup Show.*

While no one could completely fill the shoes of a giant like Williams, Red won the regard of *Hayride* fans in his own right. He remained a favorite of Louisiana fans into 1954 and won the approval of his musical peers. Among fellow *Hayride* cast members was singer-songwriter Webb Pierce, who became a close friend of Sovine's. The two often sang duets together and also co-wrote many songs. In 1954, both Webb and Red were given invitations to join the *Grand Ole Opry* and both accepted. Sovine settled in Nashville in the mid-1950s and remained a resident of Music City the rest of his life.

Both performers did well as *Opry* artists and rising recording stars in the mid-1950s. In 1956, they blended their vocal and instrumental talents on two major hit singles, "Why, Baby, Why" and "Little Rosa." The two turned out a number of other charted singles and original songs together in the late 1950s. In the 1960s, though, they tended to go separate ways.

Red continued to be a top-ranked country star in the 1960s and 1970s, turning out many singles and albums on a variety of labels. His biggest number of hits in those two decades was on Starday Records, though he had releases that made hit lists on such other labels as Decca and Chart. His biggest singles success in the 1960s was the Starday release "Giddyup Go," which rose to number one in the United States during 1965. His Starday albums of the 1960s included his label debut, *Red Sovine,* issued in October 1961, *Country Ballads of the '60s* (12/62), *Little Rosa, Giddyup Go* (1965), *Town & Country Action, Nashville Sound, I Didn't Jump the Fence, Phantom 309,* and *That's Truckdrivin'.* His Decca LPs included the late 1950s release *Red Sovine* and *Music Time,* reissued in May 1966. Other 1960s albums included *Giddyup Go* and *Dear John Letter* on Nashville Records, *Fine* on Somerset Records, and *Farewell, So Long,* issued by Metro (part of MGM Records) in August 1967.

Among his original compositions of the 1950s and 1960s were such offerings as "Don't Be the One," "Missing You," "Long Night," "Class of '49," "I Didn't Jump the Fence," "Too Much," and "I Think I Can Sleep Tonight." Pre-1970s chartmakers included, besides songs noted earlier, "You Used to Be My Baby," "Don't Drop It," "Don't Be the One," "I Hope You Don't Care," "I'm Glad You Found a Place for Me," "The Intoxicated Rat," "How Do You Think I Feel," "My New Love Affair," "I'm the Man," and "Best Years of Your Life."

By the end of the 1960s, Sovine's extensive in-person tours had taken him to all fifty states, many parts of Canada, and Europe. He was a familiar face to fans on the state and country fair and rodeo circuits, a situation that still held through much of the 1970s. He always kept his eye open for newcomers during his travels and helped alert Nashville to more than a few fine performers. His most notable discovery came in the early 1960s when he heard a ballplayer turned singer perform in a Montana club. He helped the artist get a record company audition, the opening phase of the career of Country Charley Pride.

Things slowed a bit for Red in the early 1970s, but in the mid-1970s, he found a new series of hits. In late summer of 1975, he made lower-chart levels with his emotionally charged single on Chart, "Daddy's Girl." Early the following year, he dipped into his earlier repertoire for a repeat singles hit with "Phantom 309"

on the Starday label. In the summer, he surged all the way to the top with another recitative offering, "Teddy Bear." Cowritten by Red with D. Royal, B. Burnette, and T. Hill, that Starday single reached number one in the United States in late July 1976. A month later, his album of the same title also moved into the number-one spot, capping one of Sovine's most notable years of his career. His achievements won him a number of awards, including a special category set up for him by *Cash Box* magazine in its annual poll—"Top Recitation Performer."

Red was still active and well regarded by country fans at the start of the 1980s, and still appearing on the *Opry* when his career was cut short by a fatal auto accident in Nashville on April 4, 1980. (Some obituaries suggested at the time that he died from a heart attack brought on by the crash.)

In the years that followed, some of Red's recordings were reissued in retrospective collections. In the mid-1990s, he was one of the artists represented on the Legends selection in Volume 12 of the *Grand Ole Opry Stars of the Fifties* video series. He was also included in Volume 4 of that series.

STAFFORD, JIM: *Singer, guitarist, banjoist, keyboards player, comedian, songwriter, actor. Born Eloise, Florida, January 16, 1944.*

Novelty songs always have had an important place in America's pop music idiom and, in the mid-1970s, Jim Stafford seemed to have almost a monopoly on the field. Taken by his wildly funny lyrics, the public sometimes overlooked his ability as a musician and his serious side as singer and actor.

As he noted, both sides of the coin were important in the environment in which he grew up. "You had to have a sense of humor to live in Eloise, Florida. It was built around a citrus plant. My people are country musicians from Tennessee. They just picked banjos, guitars, and fiddles . . . and when they came down here as migrant workers, they picked oranges, limes, and lemons." His father managed to avoid the picker's fate by going into the dry cleaning business.

The musical influence showed up in Jim (full name James Wayne Stafford) who started fooling around with the guitar early in life and could play well enough to perform at local events in his teens. When he started going to high school he had some thoughts of becoming a commercial artist or going into the ministry, but both those ideas paled for him when he became active in a rock group at fourteen.

He switched to the country field at twenty-one and moved to Nashville to try out on the *Opry* and develop a career as writer or soloist. He spent two years in Music City without making major progress, then moved to Atlanta where circumstances caused Stafford to combine his comic talent with music. "I was playing go-go clubs with a drummer friend. I'd play the bass pedals on the organ and the guitar at the same time and I'd talk out of necessity. I couldn't ad-lib my own name at first. Then the drummer quit and I was beside myself." He worked long hours in his spare time to develop a routine. This led to his writing novelty songs, since he felt his voice wasn't good enough for other kinds of material. An early effort was sparked by a go-go girl named Karen and came out as "I Ain't Sharin' Sharon."

The song didn't ring any bells, but his new act started to. In time it brought opportunities to perform in major venues around the United States in the late 1960s and early 1970s. Among the places he played were major Miami Beach hotels, the Cellar Door in Washington, D.C., Mr. Kelly's in Chicago, and the Bitter End in New York.

During that period he continued to write new material and, when the opportunity arose, tried to use it to further his writing or recording career. In 1973, Jim took one of his pieces, a song titled "Swamp Witch," to a high school friend, Kent LaVoie, who had become a recording success under the name Lobo. LaVoie was impressed with the song and so was his record producer, Phil Gernhard, who played a tape of it for MGM head Mike Curb. Curb was even more excited then Gernhard. He noted, "It had a special quality all its own. Jim Stafford reminded me of no one else around. He was no carbon copy, but an original artist."

Stafford was signed to MGM and soon had his debut LP, *Jim Stafford*, completed. The collection proved to be one of the happenings of 1974, spawning a series of hit singles that kept Stafford's name on the singles charts well into 1975. The first to earn a gold record was "Spiders and Snakes," which won the award from the R.I.A.A. on March 6, 1974. The other three were "Swamp Witch," "My Girl Bill," and "Wildwood Weed." Stafford was voted Top New Vocalist of 1974 by *Record World* and was ranked fourth as Top Male Vocalist behind Elton John, Stevie Wonder, and John Denver. Stafford's second album on MGM, *Not Just Another Pretty Foot*, was issued during 1975 and provided two more charted singles, "Your Bulldog Drinks Champagne" and "I Got Stoned and I Missed It."

During the mid-1970s, Stafford savored his new-won fame by appearing before all types of audiences, ranging from college crowds, state fairs, pop concerts, and a number of engagements in major hotels in Las Vegas, Reno, and Lake Tahoe. Among the artists he worked with on various bills were Charlie Rich, Tina Turner, and Olivia Newton-John. He was a guest on many network and syndicated TV shows in the mid- and late-1970s, including *Dinah! Merv Griffin, Sha Na Na, The Jim Nabors Show, Midnight Special, Rock Concert, Opryland USA, The Captain and Tennille,* and *Dick Clark's 25th Anniversary Special.* He also was cohost on several programs of the *Mike Douglas* show and, during the summer of 1975, was host of his own replacement variety show.

In the late 1970s, Stafford made his TV acting debut, playing the role of Sandy Duncan's husband in the "Lost and Found" episode of ABC-TV's sitcom series *The Love Boat.* During 1978–79, his TV activities including working with ABC on a possible future situation comedy and taping an hour-long special for syndication titled *Jim Stafford's Grand Central.* Making it easier for him to work on these projects was his move during the 1970s into a large house in the Hollywood hills. At the start of the 1980s, he was one of the cohosts of the TV program *Those Amazing Animals,* telecast on the ABC-TV network.

His musical projects in the late 1970s included writing and performing three songs for the score of the Disneyland animated film *The Fox and the Hound* (released 1981) and a return, after a hiatus, to album work. The album, slated for 1979 release, was prepared under the aegis of Mike Curb, who signed Jim for his Warner/Curb Records operation.

Commenting on his approach to crafting comedic songs, he said, "You have to construct it so people will stay with it and like it. It's like writing a little book. Humorous songs . . . well, they're so much harder to write. It's like telling a joke. You can't tell it blatantly. You do that—and you can do it once—and then it's all over."

Through the 1980s, Stafford's career included a steady diet of live performances with guest shots on many of the new country music network shows springing up in Nashville and other centers of pop music activity. He always put on an entertaining show, but he didn't add much to his list of record hits.

By the start of the 1990s he had become a featured artist in the rapidly growing country music mecca of Branson, Missouri. He became the headliner at the Star of the Ozarks theater and remained a top draw there until, by the mid-1990s, he was performing in his own 1,500-seat venue. He took part with other stars in the increasing number of Branson-originated TV programs such as the Family Channel's *Branson Music Hall,* which premiered on September 4, 1993, with a program that had such people, besides Stafford, as Johnny Cash, Mel Tillis, the Oak Ridge Boys, and Neal McCoy.

Stafford also helped prepare another show called *Neighbors,* an original wide-screen IMAX film first presented at the new ITEC Attractions Ozark Discovery IMAX Theater. In addition to performing in the film, Stafford also collaborated with bluegrass notable Rodney Dillard in writing and producing the soundtrack. Stafford commented, "We wanted to use music tradional to this area, so we used Albert Brumley's 'Let's Fly Away.' We also wanted something to represent Branson and used 'This Little Light of Mine, I'm Gonna Let It Shine,' because that's what's happening with Branson and its entertainment—Branson's star is shining."

STAMPLEY, JOE: *Singer, pianist, songwriter. Born Springhill, Louisiana, June 6, 1943.*

With an unusual consistency in song selection and performance, Joe Stampley established himself as one of the giants of country music in the 1970s. It was rare that any of his singles or albums failed to reach upper-chart levels, even rarer when any release failed to catch the public fancy at all. If there's a country-music heaven, it would have to bring a smile to the face of Hank Williams, who, appropriately, gave Stampley some of the first words of advice and encouragement when Joe was a small boy.

Stampley, born in Springhill, Louisiana, in June 1943, says, "I'm a wild and crazy Gemini. Except for seven years when I lived in Baytown, Texas, as a boy, Springhill's always been my home. It's in northern Louisiana near the Texas border and only about a mile from Arkansas. It's not Cajun country. They eat grits down south and we eat cornbread and taters up north."

His family loved country music and so did he, particularly the music of Hank Williams. "Got so I knew every song he recorded. I met him when I was about seven at a radio station in Baytown. It really was a thrill. I told him how much I liked his singing and that I tried to imitate him. He said, 'Just be yourself and act like yourself and later on it might pay off for you.'"

Taking the advice to heart, Joe kept on signing country songs as he moved toward his teens and also started working on some originals of his own. The piano was his instrument. "I musta been about eight years old when I started learning the piano, playing Hank Williams's songs mostly at the time. I never played the guitar. I can play a few chords, but nothing that amounts to anything. I can play the ukulele, though."

By the time Joe was in his midteens, he showed enough promise as a writer to attract the attention of Merle Kilgore, a disc jockey on a Springhill station. He was impressed enough by the fifteen-year-old Stampley's talents to collaborate on some songs with the boy. "Merle got me a record contract with Imperial Records in 1957–58. The record bombed, but it sold 500 copies in my little home town and I thought that was pretty good."

Undaunted, Joe kept preparing new material and keeping his eye open for opportunities. He had become increasingly involved in rock music during those years. "I got off onto rock when I was in high school and was a big fan of Little Richard, Elvis, Jerry Lee, a lot of R&B groups like the Miracles, and particularly the Impalas. The Impalas had a record called 'I Ran All the Way' that really knocked me out."

In 1961, Stampley made contact with Chicago-based Chess Records, which issued another single of his. Once more the recording sank almost without a trace. For a good part of the early and mid-1960s, Joe was involved with a rock group called the Uniques that played the Southern raunch 'n' roll circuit for a number of years. The group played in bars, clubs, and occasionally at college dances throughout the South and succeeded in building up a certain amount of following. The band was signed by Shreveport-based Paula Records in the mid-1960s and for a while it looked as though fate might smile more brightly than in the past on Joe. A single of a song he cowrote with Kilgore called "Not Too Long Ago" became a regional hit in 1966 and sold a half million copies. ("We also made regional charts with 'All These Things'; later on it was a big country hit for me on ABC/Dot in the 1970s.") However, the follow-up releases did poorly and Joe's performing career marked time at the end of the 1960s.

But when Joe returned to his first love, country, in the 1970s, everything finally came together for him. "The way that came about was that I started writing country songs about 1970 and began sending demos of them to Al Gallico [of Algee Music in Nashville]. He said 'You should be recording your own country stuff' and arranged for a contract with Paramount Records. [Gallico soon became Joe's manager.] The first country song I put out was 'Qounette McGraw from Smackover Arkansas.'"

By the time the next one was ready, Paramount had been bought by ABC/Dot. "My first real breakthrough came in 1972 when I did a single called 'If You Touch Me (You've Gotta Love Me).' [The song reached number one on country charts in September 1972.] Ever since then my releases have consistently been in or around the top ten and I've had a total of six number-one songs."

He had three other number-one singles during his stay with ABC/Dot, the other three being "Soul Song," "I'm Still Loving You," number one in early 1974, and "All These Things," number one in the summer of 1976. Among his other chart hits on ABC/Dot were his composition "How Lucky Can One Man Be," a chart hit in early summer of 1974, "Penny," a top-10 hit in early 1975, "Unchained Melody," on the lists in mid-1975, "Cry like a Baby," a chartmaker in the fall of that year, and "The Night Time and My Baby," a top-20 hit in September 1976. Stampley also turned out a series of LPs that made the country lists during the first half of the 1970s. ABC issued his *Greatest Hits, Volume I* in June 1975 and it moved into the top 20 soon after.

In 1975, Stampley switched to Epic Records, losing no momentum. His initial single release, produced by Norro Wilson, "Roll on Big Mama," became a number-one hit. His third single on Epic, "Bill Get Me a Woman" (after "Big Woman") was also a major hit, in the top 10 in November 1975. His last 1975 single was "She's Helping Me Get Over You," which was followed in early 1976 by another top-10 single, "Whisky Talkin'," in the summer. His other singles produced by Wilson included, in 1976, "Was It Worth It" and "There

She Goes Again"; and, in 1977, the top-10 hits "Baby I Love You So" and "Everyday I Have to Cry Some."

In 1978, Stampley's work for Epic enrolled a new producer, the equally accomplished Billy Sherrill. The first result of the new association was the early 1978 singles success "Red Wine and Blue Memories." This was followed by the top-10 September 1978 offering "If You Got Ten Minutes (Let's Fall in Love)," a Stampley original composition. In early 1979, the team made it three out of three with the top-5 single "Do You Ever Fool Around?"

Later in the year, he had two other top-selling releases, "Put Your Clothes Back On" and "I Don't Lie." In January 1980, his duet with Moe Bandy, "Holding the Bag," made the top 10. Other 1980 chart hits Stampley and Bandy collaborated on were "Tell Ole I Ain't Here" and "Just Good Ol' Boys." Stampley's solo hit singles in 1980 included his own composition "There's Another Woman," "After Hours," and "Haven't I Loved You Somewhere Before." His early 1981 successes included the solo "I'm Gonna Love You Back to Loving Me Again" and the Bandy duet, "Hey Joe (Hey Moe)," the latter from the album of the same title, issued in 1981.

After release of Joe's debut LP on Epic in 1975, every album through early 1979 made the charts. His second LP on the label, *Billy Get Me a Woman,* issued in late 1975, was still in the top 30 in early 1976. The next release, *The Sheik of Chicago,* in early summer of the year, made mid-chart levels and the next one, *All These Things,* rose to the top 5 in September 1976. His fifth album on Epic, *Saturday Night Dance,* showed up on hit lists in the summer of 1977 as did *Red Wine and Blue Memories* later in the year. In late 1979, Epic issued its first *Stampley Greatest Hits* LP, which moved up the lists at year end. In the fall of 1979, Stampley teamed up with Moe Bandy for another hit album, *Just Good Ol' Boys.*

Looking back on the 1970s, Stampley said in late 1979, "I've played in every state in the union and such other places as Bermuda, England, Sweden, Holland, and Canada. I've sold a lot of records. I haven't had a million seller, but I've had a number sell over 200,000 copies which is good in the country field. I had one called 'Soul Song' that crossed over into the top 30 on pop charts and sold about a half million. Songs like 'Roll on Big Mama' and 'You Ever Fool Around' sold over a quarter million each. I had about seventeen albums released on Epic and ABC during the decade.

"One of my greatest thrills was playing the *Grand Ole Opry* back when it was in the Ryman Auditorium and thinking about all the great artists who played on that stage. Overall I played the *Opry* six or seven times in the 1970s. And, of course, it's also a good feeling to know my name is on the sidewalk of the Country Music Hall of Fame in Nashville."

As the 1980s went by, Joe's career, like that of his friend and sometime collaborator Moe Bandy, was hampered by the focus of radio programmers basically on new, younger artists. In the early 1990s, little of his material was in print. In the mid 1990s this started to change as a growing number of small independents sought out agreements with major labels for reissue of recordings from the majors' vaults. In 1995, Razor & Tie Records issued a CD of Stampley tracks. Stampley also was represented on reissue discs from Varese Sarabande Records during that year.

* Based on an interview with Irwin Stambler, late 1979.

STANLEY BROTHERS (AND THE CLINCH MOUN-TAIN BOYS): *Vocal and instrumental group formed by Stanley brothers: Carter Glen Stanley, born McClure, Dickenson Country, Virginia, August 27, 1925, died Bristol, Virginia, December 1, 1966; Ralph Edmund Stanley, born Big Spraddle Creek near Stratton, Virginia, February 25, 1927. Clinch Mountain Boys personnel varied widely through group's more than five decades of activity.*

Fifty years, the big five-oh—that's what made the Stanley Brothers' appearance on August 24, 1996, at Ed Pearl's new Ash Grove on the Santa Monica, California, Pier special. It was an important stop on a tour celebrating leader Ralph Stanley's fiftieth year in show business. The group— all of whom were wearing white shirts, ties, and gray slacks—comprised Ralph on tenor vocals and banjo, his son Ralph Stanley II on rhythm guitar, a fiddler, mandolinist, upright bass player, and another young banjoist, Steve Sparkman.

Stanley Junior introduced his father, talking about Ralph's fifty years in bluegrass and about the honorary doctorate of arts he had received. (Stanley Senior egged him on: "Tell 'em about me. Brag on!") He talked about Ralph's nomination for a Grammy Award with Dwight Yoakam, and about his induction into the Bluegrass Hall of Fame; then, after describing Ralph as the best banjo player and tenor singer around, announced, "My father, Dr. Ralph Stanley." After which Ralph performed two old bluegrass standards, "Pretty Polly" and "Little Maggie." He sang some gospel songs, "I'll Answer the Call" and "Turn Back Ye Wayward Pilgrim." Before launching into "Pilgrim," he claimed to the audience that he was the first man in bluegrass music to do a capella singing onstage, and proceeded to perform the song in four-part harmony with the others. He also included two Stanley Brothers songs, "Sweethearts in Heaven" and Carter Stanley's composition, "The Lonesome River"—songs first introduced in 1949.

At one point Ralph talked about his son. "Ralph Stanley the second just turned 18. Are there any young single girls who want to be murdered? I mean married? Marriage is like murder. If you get murdered, you go quick. If you get married you ooze out over a long time." He also noted that two years earlier he had broken his leg and been temporarily confined to a wheelchair. They hired Steve Sparkman as the backup banjoist. "He was so good we had to keep him on. Besides me, he's the best banjoist in the world."

Despite the humor, there was no doubt that Ralph and his late brother Carter had contributed immeasurably to the development of bluegrass, as innovators themselves and as guiding heads, over the years, to many other future stars. Their odyssey began in childhood: Brought up in a musical family, with a father who was a fine singer and a mother who played excellent banjo, they were also influenced by the gospel singing at the Primitive Baptist Church their family attended. Ralph recalled that when he was eleven, his mother taught him to frail the banjo on the song "Rocky Island," a song he still kept in his repertoire. "People seem to enjoy it. Since that time I've recorded it and play it as much as I can, just like my mother taught me."

The brothers formed their first group, the Lazy Ramblers, as teenagers; the next year, working as a duo, they made their radio debut on station WJHL in Johnson City, Tennessee. Their careers were put on hold for a time when Ralph entered the U.S. Army for eighteen months in the mid-1940s. When he returned to civilian life, the brothers briefly joined Roy Sykes' Blue Ridge Mountain Boys, then assembled the first version of the Clinch Mountain Boys. They played local venues and then got radio exposure on WNVA in Norton, Virginia, before moving on to become regular cast members of the *Farm and Fun Time* show on station WCYB in Bristol, Tennessee. With Carter on lead vocals and guitar and Ralph on harmony vocals and banjo, with excellent support from three other bandsmen, the Stanleys soon were being mentioned by their peers in the same breath with Bill Monroe.

Ralph admitted in later years that he sometimes had doubts about achieving success in the music business. He told John Wright of the *Banjo Newsletter* ("Ralph Stanley Today," January 1984, pp. 5–10) that he didn't think he'd have continued if it wasn't for Carter's persistence. "Carter was a big influence on me. He—there's a hard—lot of hardships. This music business is a hard road to get started on, and I would have given up I guess several times if it hadn't been for him. He'd hold me right to it."

The brothers made their first recordings for the small Rich-R-Tone label in 1947 and then moved on a few years later to Columbia Records. That Columbia deal had immediate repercussions, as Ralph told Terry Atkinson of the *Los Angeles Times* ("Ralph Stanley Keeps on Pickin' in the Old Style," Part V, May 4, 1985, p. 2): Bill Monroe quit the label. He "told them there wasn't enough room for two [bluegrass acts]. So back at the first, there was some friction there. But since then we've become the best of friends. I've played a lot with him." The Stanleys completed several LPs for Columbia, but found it fiddicult to earn enough to keep the band going. (Some of their work on Columbia was packaged by Rounder Records in a 1980 reissue, *The Columbia Sessions, 1949–50*). In 1951 they broke up the group and both performed briefly with Bill Monroe, though Ralph's stay was cut short by an injury in an auto accident. Carter did stay long enough to perform on some tracks by the Blue Grass Boys. By 1952, the brothers had re-formed their band and soon had a new recording contract with Mercury Records; their tracks laid down for the label included a number of songs written separately or together by the Stanleys. Over the years, the brothers also recorded many numbers for the Starday/King organization.

Many of the tracks produced during Carter Stanley's lifetime remain among the most highly regarded bluegrass recordings ever made. Examples are "Rank Strangers," "Mountain Dew," "How Mountain Girls Can Love," "I'm a Man of Constant Sorrow," "Wildwood Flower," "It's Raining Here This Morning," "Little Maggie," and "Little Birdie."

The pressures of constant touring and trying to maintain an effective organization took their toll on Carter, who developed an alcohol addiction that finally led to his death in late 1966. The many albums recorded by the band under his aegis included: *Country Pickin' & Singin'* (1958); *The Stanley Brothers, Everybody's Country Favorites, Mountain Song Favorites,* and *Hymns & Sacred Songs* (all 1959); *Sacred Songs From the Hills* and *For the Good People* (both 1960); *Old Time Camp Meeting, The Stanley Brothers Sing Everybody's Country Favorites, The Stanley Brothers, The Stanley Brothers in Person, Sing the Songs They Like the Best,* and *Live at Antioch College—1960* (all 1961); *Award Winners at the Folk Song Festival, Good Old Camp Meeting Songs,* and *The Mountain Music Sound* (all 1962); *Five String Banjo Hootenanny, The World's Finest Five String Banjo, Just Because, Hard Times, Country-Folk Music Spotlight* and *Old Country Church* (all 1963); *Bluegrass Songs for You* and *Hymns of the Cross* (both 1964); *The Stanley Brothers - Their Original Recordings* (1965); and *The Angels Are Singing, Jacob's Vision, The Greatest Country & Western Show on Earth, A Collection of Original Gospel & Sacred Songs,* and *The Stanley Brothers Go to Europe* (all 1966).

Carter's loss, as might be expected, had a profound effect on Ralph, as reflected in his comments on the "Hills of Home" recording issued soon after his brother's passing. However, after some soul-searching, he decided to carry on, finding new performers to handle Carter's lead vocals and regrouping with longtime Clinch Mountain members Curly Ray Cline on fiddle and Jack Cooke on standup bass and harmony vocals. Amid a flood of reissues of pre-1966 material, Ralph and his band soon began putting together a series of excellent new albums—starting with the 1968 LPs *The*

Bluegrass Sound, Brand New Country Songs, and *Over the Sunset Hill.* Ralph's 1970 release was the album *Hills of Home,* followed in the early 1970s by *Cry From the Cross, Ralph Stanley Live in Japan, Something Old—Something New, Ralph Stanley Plays Requests, Old Country Church, The Stanley Sound Around the World,* and *Gospel Echoes of the Stanley Brothers.* Ralph and the band's releases in the mid- and late 1970s (with Ralph still using the Stanley Brothers joint name) included *A Man and His Music, Let Me Rest on a Peaceful Mountain, Live at McClure* (at the Carter Stanley Annual Bluegrass Festival, which Ralph inaugurated in 1970), *Old Home Place, Clinch Mountain Gospel,* and *Down Where the River Bends.*

Some of the recordings in the early 1970s were made by one of the most exciting bands Ralph put together. The roster included Curly Ray Cline, Jack Cooke, Roy Lee Centers, and two extremely talented musicians still in their teens, Keith Whitley and Ricky Skaggs. Ralph was so impressed with the talents of Whitley and Skaggs that he added them both to his band, despite the fact he already employed the classic five-man bluegrass lineup. During those years the Clinch Mountain Boys ranked with the very best bluegrass had to offer, and its key new artists went on to carve notable careers for themselves. A bright future was predicted for lead singer Centers, who was still with the band after Keith and Ricky left. When Roy Lee was shot to death at a party, though, Whitley returned to sing lead for Ralph for another four years. Alumni from later rosters who went on to assemble successful groups of their own included Larry Sparks and Charlie Sizemore.

During the first three years of the 1980s, Ralph and his group recorded a total of sixty cuts besides working with Curly Ray Cline on his own solo album. Releases during those years included *I'll Wear a White Robe, Hymn Time,* and *First Time Together* (an album of duets with Jimmy Martin) in 1980, *The Stanley Sound Today* (1981); *The Memory of Your Smile* (1982); *Bluegrass, Sings Traditional Bluegrass and Gospel, Live at the Old Home Place,* and *Child of the King* (all 1983). The last-named contained all new material, including several original numbers by Ralph and the band. Asked by John Wright about his source of new material, Ralph said, "Just here and there. Sometimes I write one, sometimes one of the Clinch Mountain Boys will write it. Or people all the time sending in songs and things. I guess I've got ten thousand that I'll probably never get to look at. Maybe a hit song buried, just laid up somewhere."

Album releases of Ralph and the band in the mid- and late 1980s included *Snow Covered Mound, Singing Sixteen Years, Shadows of the Past, Live in Japan, Lonesome & Blue, I'll Answer the Call,* and *Ralph Stanley and Raymond Fairchild.* The *Live in Japan* disc was a reissue by Rebel Records (which released a number of Ralph's albums in the 1970s) of an album originally available only in Japan on the Seven Seas label. From his several concert tours there, Stanley noted that he had found Japanese audiences particularly receptive to his bluegrass stylings, typically applauding after the concert was over for three or even four encores.

Ralph began the 1990s with such album releases as *(Clawhammer) The Way My Mamma Taught Me, Like Father Like Son,* and *Pray for the Boys.* The year 1992 proved significant in several ways. For one, the International Bluegrass Music Association inducted the Stanley Brothers into its Hall of Fame during the third annual IBMA Awards show in Owensboro, Kentucky. For another, Ralph enlisted the services of many of the greatest names in country and bluegrass for a new album project for Freeland Records. The project, he told Penny Parsons of *Bluegrass* magazine ("The Renaissance of Ralph Stanley," May 1995), grew out of a phone conversation with longtime friend Dick Freeland who had founded Rebel Records. In 1979, he called Stanley and said he wanted to come out of retirement and work on some new recordings with him. "So we met and sort of agreed on everything and that's when [this project] came up. I was wanting to record an album with just a couple or three country singers. He liked the idea and when we started contacting the entertainers, all of them were glad to do it, and so we got just 14 of them."

The all-star ensemble comprised Dwight Yoakam, Bill Monroe, Vince Gill, Patty Loveless, Emmylou Harris, Jimmy Martin, Charlie Sizemore, Ricky Skaggs, Alison Krauss, Charlie Waller, George Jones, Larry Sparks, Tom T. Hall, and Judy Marshall. The participants helped prepare thirty-one songs that made up a two-CD set, *Saturday Night/Sunday Morning,* issued on Freeland records in 1993. The compilation ranked as one of the best albums of its kind issued in the decade, winning praise from reviewers at home and abroad. At the 1993 IBMA Awards show, on which Ralph was a performer, he was presented with the award for IBMA Recorded Event of the Year for that release. In December 1993, IBMA also asked Ralph to serve as honorary chairman of its fundraising campaign (for which Ricky Skaggs served as chairman) for its bluegrass music museum. In the fall of 1993 and early 1994, the National Council for the Traditional Arts enlisted Ralph's participation in the Masters of the Five String Banjo tour.

The album sessions led to a close friendship between Ralph and Dwight Yoakam. Among other things, Dwight arranged for Ralph to be featured on the TNN *American Music Shop* show for which Dwight was host. It also brought about some studio work between the two, including a recording of Dwight's composition "Miner's Prayer" in tribute to his grandfather. Grammy voters nominated the song in the Country Duet category. At the same time, they provided Ralph with two other nominations, one for Best Bluegrass Album and another for Best Gospel Recording (for the *Sunday Morning* portion of the Freeland set). In 1994, Ralph and Dwight also performed together in a number of concerts.

Through the mid-1990s, Ralph and the Clinch Mountain Boys kept up a brisk tour schedule, while massive reissues from all phases of the Stanley Brothers saga continued to become available. In 1994, Germany's Bear Family Records issued a two-CD set, *The Stanley Brothers and the Clinch Mountain Boys 1953–59*. In 1995, Freeland Records issued a multidisc set of previously unreleased material recorded live in the early 1970s when Skaggs and Keith Whitley were band members. Rebel Records also issued a 4-CD boxed set containing five albums from 1971–73 plus *The Stanley Sound Around the World* (originally put out on the King Bluegrass label) and twelve tracks from an album recorded in Japan in 1971 that had never been released before in the U.S. Among the other material on the market in that period was a biography of Ralph Stanley by John Wright, *Traveling the High Way Home*, and an instructional videotape produced by Smithsonian Folkways Records and Homespun Tapes titled *The Banjo of Ralph Stanley from Old-Time to Bluegrass*. The latter, which included an interview of Ralph by Mike Seeger, also included a number of full-length renditions by Ralph and the Clinch Mountain Boys of some numbers. In the spring of 1996, Columbia Legacy came out with the CD reissue, *The Complete Columbia Stanley Brothers*.

Despite the upper thigh bone injury Ralph suffered in an accident at home in June 1994, he kept meeting performance dates, singing from his wheelchair while Steve Sparkman handled banjo lead. When he returned to full-time status for 1995–96 dates, the band comprised himself, Kentucky-born Sparkman, Ralph Stanley II, Jack Cooke on bass, Art Stamper on fiddle (replacing Curly Ray Cline, whose health problems required his retirement in 1992), Virginia-born Kenneth Davis on lead vocals, and James Alan Shelton (born in Tennessee) on lead guitar.

Ralph was known for his three-finger banjo picking style, and John Wright asked him why he decided to depend on it in addition to the clawhammer and two-finger picking techniques. Stanley replied, "Well, way back when I first started, you know, that was about all they had was the two finger, I mean the finger and thumb. But as the music advanced I thought I should advance with it. It was a better style and it was a better beat and all that."

As to how he developed it, he told Wright, "Well, I don't think I could put that in words. I just played it the way my fingers led me and I just—I really couldn't explain that, I don't guess. Couldn't play it any other way. Tried to copy a little bit here and there; I never could. And I'm proud that I didn't because what I do know is mine."

STATLER BROTHERS, THE: *Vocal quartet with backing band (Statler Brothers Band), Don S. Reid, born Staunton, Virginia, June 5, 1945; Harold W. Reid, born Augusta County, Virginia, August 21, 1939; Philip E. Balsley, born Augusta County, Virginia, August 8, 1939; Lew C. De Witt, born Roanoke County, Virginia, March 8, 1939, died mid-1980s. De Witt left group in early 1980s, replaced by Jimmy Fortune.*

Despite the name Statler Brothers, only two of the members of this vocal quartet are brothers and none of them is named Statler. Statler is actually the name of a regional brand of tissues. When the group was about to go to work touring with Johnny Cash, they were trying to think of a new name for themselves. Harold Reid saw a box of Statler Tissues across the room and said, "How about Statler? That's as good as anything." As group member Don Reid said, "We could just as easily be known as the Kleenex Brothers."

No matter what they might have called themselves, the original foursome probably could have succeeded, for the group featured a great deal of vocal talent as well as the considerable skills of the Reid brothers and, for many years, the late Lew C. De Witt.

All four of the "Brothers" grew up in rural Virginia. They first sang together in 1955 in Lynhurt Methodist Church in Staunton. They disbanded three years later, but then regrouped in 1960, calling themselves the Kingmen, singing primarily gospel music at local churches, banquets, and on local television shows. However, they all kept their day jobs.

In 1963 the quartet met Johnny Cash at a show in Roanoke, Virginia. Harold Reid persuaded the show's promoter to let him talk to Cash and he told him about the group. Cash asked them if they could get to nearby Berryville on Sunday. At Berryville Cash asked them to open the show for him, even though he had never heard them. After the show Cash told the group he liked them, so when they went home Harold persisted in calling the country superstar until Cash finally asked them to go on the road with him. Now officially renamed the Statler Brothers, the foursome toured with Cash for eight years. This exposure enabled them to win a recording contract with Columbia Records.

The Statler Brothers had their first national hit in 1966 with "Flowers on the Wall," which was written by De Witt. The single reached the top 10 on the country charts and the number-one spot on the national pop charts. The song also won two Grammy Awards for the group.

The quartet's affiliation with Johnny Cash continued. When Cash had his own television variety show in the late 1960s and early 1970s, the Statlers became a regular feature, often singing traditional gospel songs as well as their own material. In 1970 they ended their contract with Columbia Records and signed with Mercury Records.

The decade of the 1970s was phenomenally

successful for the Statler Brothers. They had numerous top-10 country singles. Among them were "Bed of Roses," on the charts in late 1970 and early 1971; "Do You Remember These?" and "The Class of '57" in 1972 (the latter won them a Grammy Award); "I'll Go to My Grave Loving You" and "I Was There" in 1975; "Some I Wrote" in 1977; and "The Official Historian of Shirley-Jean Burrell" in 1978. Other mid-1970s hits were "Whatever Happened to Randolph Scott" and "Do You Know You Are My Sunshine." In 1979 they made the top 10 with such singles as "Nothing as Original as You" and "How to Be a Country Star." Also in top chart positions during 1979 were "Who Am I to Say" and "Here We Are Again."

Many of their songs were written by Don and Harold Reid. The songs were unusual in that they often featured comedic touches, twists, and puns, while simultaneously dealing with poignant themes such as the dashed hopes of youth ("The Class of '57") and eternal devotion to one's mate ("I'll Go to My Grave Loving You," "Thank God I've Got You"). In 1978 the Statlers had a hit single with "Who Am I to Say," which was written by Harold's sixteen-year-old daughter, Kim.

The Statler Brothers' vocal style carried over from their gospel days, with traditional four-part arrangements. Don usually acted as emcee; Harold sang bass; Lew sang baritone, and Phil Balsey took the tenor role. In addition to their popular country recordings, the quartet continued to perform and record gospel music. In 1975 they recorded two gospel albums, *Holy Bible— Old Testament* and *Holy Bible—New Testament.* They had spent seven years researching this project and wrote fifteen of the twenty-two songs on the album.

For years the Statler Brothers were unrivaled as the top vocal group in country music. They won the Country Music Association Award for Top Vocal Group for an unprecedented seven years in a row. They yielded the title to the Oak Ridge Boys in 1978, only to come back and win this honor again in 1979. Their album *The Best of the Statler Brothers* remained on the country top 40 for over four years, the first LP in the history of *Record World* magazine to achieve that. The album was certified gold in July 1977, went platinum in June 1978, and, by early 1980, approached sales of 2 million, the double platinum level. Other of their best-selling LPs were *The Country America Loves* and *Short Stories,* both released in 1977.

In 1980, the group celebrated its tenth anniversary on Mercury Records. It started the year in good shape with the LP *The Statler Bros. Xmas Card* (issued in 1979) moving up the charts and, on the singles charts, "(I'll Even Love You) Better than I Did Then" moving toward top positions. Also on the hit lists for a while in early 1980 was a holdover from 1979, Don Reid's composition "Nothing as Original as You." Early in the year, the LP *The Best of the Statler Brothers Rides Again, Volume II,* came out and quickly showed up on the

charts to be joined in the summer by the *10th Anniversary* LP. The track "Charlotte's Web" from that album, issued as a single, made the top 10 in September 1980.

As of the Mercury anniversary date, it was announced, the group had released twenty albums and twenty-nine singles on the label, sold more than 10 million records, and been named Top Vocal Group in the *Music City News* Cover Awards (voted on by publication readers) every year from 1971 through 1980. Other statistics for the decade included: over 1,500 concerts performed before over 7 million people; distance traveled close to a million miles; 188 songs recorded, of which group members wrote 125. On July 4, 1980, the group also welcomed 60,000–70,000 people to its eleventh annual Happy Birthday U.S.A. concert in Staunton, Virginia, a day-long charity fund-raising event. The crowd at the first free concert had been about 6,000. (In 1981, the group gave its twelfth annual performance.) During the year, the Statlers played themselves in Burt Reynolds' *Smokey and the Bandit 2,* in which their song "Charlotte's Web" was part of the score. Their contributions included singing their 1970s number-one singles hit, "Do You Know You Are My Sunshine."

The group continued to add to its laurels in 1981, placing such singles as "Don't Forget Yourself" and "In the Garden" on best-seller lists.

The Statlers kept adding still more honors in the first half of the 1980s, receiving Country Music Association nominations for Vocal Group of the Year from 1981– 1983, then winning again in 1984. It continued its domination of that category in the *Music City News* poll, winning every year except for 1983 throughout the 1980s and for the first part of the 1990s. It received trophies in many other categories from *Music City News* voters during the decade: Album of the Year, 1979–81, 1985–86; Single of the Year, 1984, 1986–87, also winning in 1990; Country Special of the Year, 1984–85, 1987; Entertainer of the Year, 1985–87; Country Music Video of the Year, 1985–86, 1988; and Songwriter Award, 1982, 1985–87. The foursome also was named Comedy Act of the Year in 1980 and 1982–85 for its alter ego, Lester "Roadhog" Moran and the Cadillac Cowboys.

For the Cowboys, group members disguised themselves as characters named, besides Roadhog, Raymond "Wichita" Ramsey, Jr., Henry "Red" Vines, and "Wesley" W. Rexrode. Their first appearance was in 1974 and the act celebrated its twentieth anniversary in 1994 with a compilation titled *The Complete Lester "Roadhog" Moran and the Cadillac Cowboys* that included cuts from the only album issued to that date, *Alive at the Johnny Mack Brown High School* plus tracks from such recordings as "The Saturday Morning Radio Show," "Interview with Ralph Emery," and "Rainbow Valley Confidential Audition Tape."

In the early 1980s, the group lost one of its founding

members when Lew De Witt stepped down due to ill health. His place was taken by Jimmy Fortune, who was still performing with the other three original members in the mid-1990s.

From 1982 through 1989, the Statlers released twenty-two more singles on Mercury, along with eleven new albums from 1981–89. A sampling of the singles include "Whatever" and "Child of the Fifties" in 1982; "Guilty" and "Elizabeth" in 1983; "Atlanta Blue" in 1984; "My Only Love" and "Hello Mary Lou" in 1985; "Sweeter and Sweeter," "There Is Power in the Blood" and "Only You" in 1986; "I'll Be the One" in 1987; "The Best I Know" and "Am I Crazy" in 1988; and "More Than a Name on a Wall" and "A Hurt I Can Handle" in 1989. The album releases comprised: *Years Ago* (1981); *The Legend Goes On* (1982); *Today* (1983), gold record); *Atlanta Blue* (1984); *Partners in Rhyme* and *Christmas Present* (1985); *Four of the Show* and *Radio Gospel Favorites* (1986); *Maple Street Memories* (1987); *The Statlers Greatest Hits* (1988); and *Statler Brothers Live—Sold Out* (1989).

Coming into the 1990s, the Statlers continued to be concert favorites on the road and at home for their annual July 4th Happy Birthday U.S.A. festival, which was then attracting an average attendance of 100,000. They led off the new decade with the album *Music Memories of You* and the 1990 singles "It's a Small, Small World" and "Nobody Else." In 1991, Mercury issued the album *All American Country* plus four new singles, "Remember Me," "You've Been Like a Mother to Me," "There's Still Times" and "Put It on the Card." On October 21, 1991, the group premiered a new TV variety program, *The Statler Brothers Show,* on the TNN network, which went on to become one of the highest-rated programs in cable history and was still going strong half a decade later.

From 1992–95, the Statlers kept adding to their already substantial list of recorded releases starting with the 1992 album *Words and Music* and *Gospel Favorites* (offered only on TV) and singles "Nobody Loves Me Anymore" and "Same Way Everytime." In 1993 the group was represented by the album *Home* and in 1994 Mercury celebrated the Statler Brothers' thirtieth anniversary on the label with a three-record set incorporating sixty-two of the quartet's best sellers or top concert favorites plus a thirty-four-page booklet outlining the group's history and career highlights.

Called *The Statler Brothers 30th Anniversary Celebration,* the box set was offered through catalog and TV sales rather than record store outlets. On releasing the set, Mercury stated the group's total album sales at that point exceeded 15 million. Total albums issued on both Columbia and Mercury, including the box set, came to forty-seven with some seventy-three singles releases as of 1993.

On July 4, 1994, on the festival's twenty-fifth birthday, the group concluded its Happy Birthday U.S.A.

event. Harold Reid told Kimmy Wix of the *Music City News,* "After 25 years, what else can you do?" Jimmy Fortune added, "That's like a quarter of a century and we feel like we've given it our best shot. It's just getting so big. If a town holds 22,000 and you bring 90,000 people into town, it starts busting at the seams."—*I. S./A. S.*

STEAGALL, RED: *Singer, guitarist, songwriter, music publisher. Born Gainesville, Texas, December 22, c. late 1930s.*

Over the years, Red Steagall tried his hand at many things—rodeo riding, selling agricultural and chemical products, raising cattle. He did well at all of them, but in the end he went back to his first love, country music, and became a major figure in the field as a writer and performer.

As befits a man who could write songs like "Lone Star Beer and Bob Wills Music," Red spent a good part of his teen years at local Texas corrals trying his skills as a bronc buster and bull rider. Already an accomplished guitar player when he went to West Texas State University, he formed a country band that played clubs in and around the school to help pay his tuition. Some of his income was also used to take care of rodeo entry fees, where he proved one of the better bull riders.

After Steagall obtained his degree in agriculture, he got a job as a sales representative with an agrochemical company and traveled throughout the Southwest and mountain states in that capacity for most of the first half of the 1960s. After a while, he began to pick up occasional singing engagements at some of the towns he visited on his selling trips. He became particularly popular in the skiing resorts of Colorado and Utah.

In the mid-1960s, he got an offer he couldn't refuse. United Artists Music in Hollywood asked him to sign on as a record promotion executive. Being able to work full time in music and also spend time getting acquainted with disc jockeys around the country seemed more attractive to Red, who was increasingly enthusiastic about a music career. He was writing original music by then, and one of his songs was picked up by the great Ray Charles and turned into a rhythm & blues singles hit. With that credit under his belt, he left UA and started a new operation, establishing his own music publishing company and also acting as a West Coast representative for several Nashville publishers.

His songs began to find their way into more and more recording sessions of country artists. In 1968, this resulted in Red Saunders reaching high chart levels with his single of Steagall's "Beer Drinking Music." Soon after, Del Reeves had similar success with "Keep on Keepin'." Steagall, who had signed a recording contract with Dot Records, had some singles action of his own with "Walk All Over Georgia" and "A Dozen Pair of Boots." Red closed out his Dot affiliation for a while with another singles hit, "Alabama Woman."

One of Red's fonder memories of those years came

in 1974, when he played a key role in the formative career stages of an artist who was to become a superstar in the 1980s and 1990s. The discovery came while he was attending the National Rodeo Finals in Oklahoma City, Oklahoma, when his path crossed that of a young red-headed singer named Reba McEntire. He realized her great potential, helped her make her first demo tape and opened doors for her in Nashville.

As her talents became accepted by the country music industry, he continued to help her shape her career. "I stayed in a 'management' position for about seven years with Reba, but not as a paid manager. I just did it because I loved her and 'cause she is one of my dearest friends."

In the 1970s, Red moved his operation back to Nashville and signed a new recording agreement with Capitol Records. The result was another succession of chart singles and albums during the first part of the decade. Among his chart-making singles of that phase were "Party Dolls and Wine," "Somewhere My Love," "True Love," "The Fiddle Man," "I Gave Up Good Morning Darling," and "Finer Things in Life."

During the mid-1970s, Red headlined on major TV programs and in first-ranked clubs across the United States and Canada. Among his TV credits were appearances on the *Grand Ole Opry*, regular cast status on NBC's *Music Country, U.S.A.,* guest spots on the *Porter Wagoner Show, Hank Thompson Show, Wilburn Brothers Show,* and *Hee Haw.* In 1975, he played a role in the movie *Sing a Country Song.* His club appearances included a number of dates at Southern California's number-one country nightclub, the Palomino, similar action at the Western Place in Dallas, Panther Hall in Fort Worth, Stagecoach Inn in Stamford, Texas, the Brandin' Iron in San Bernardino, California, Knott's Berry Farm in Buena Park, California, and dozens of other venues of that order.

In the mid-1970s, Steagall returned to the label he'd first gained attention on, Dot, which by then was a part of the ABC Records organization. One of his early releases on ABC/Dot became a classic of the 1970s. Called "Lone Star Beer and Bob Wills Music," the single rose to top chart levels in the early spring of 1976. Along with the new interest in western swing generated by groups like Asleep at the Wheel and Commander Cody, the song sparked a revival of the old Wills band that led to several new album releases under the direction of Leon McAuliffe. Later in 1976, Steagall had another chart hit with his song "Truck Drivin' Man." In mid-1977, he was on the charts again with the single "Freckles Brown." By the end of the decade, Red had left ABC/Dot and signed with Elektra. That resulted in such 1980 charted singles as "3 Chord Country Song" (cowritten by Red and D. Steagall), "Dim the Lights and Pour the Wine," and "Hard Hat Days and Honky Tonk Nights."

With the income from his recordings and songs, Red could indulge his other love, agriculture. During the 1970s, he spent most of his leisure time on his large farm in Lebanon, Texas.

In the 1980s, Red continued to add to his catalog of original songs while also gaining a growing reputation as a "cowboy poet." By the early 1990s, some 200 songs of his had been recorded by other artists since the 1960s, including Ray Charles, Dean Martin, Nancy Sinatra, Johnny Duncan, George Strait, Del Reeves, and Roy Clark. In the mid-1980s, his recording years with Elektra having ended, he made his Texas ranch his permanent residence. He didn't retire from show business, though, maintaining a tour schedule of up to 250 dates a year throughout the 1980s and into the 1990s. He made a series of new albums on his own Ft. Worth label, RS Records, which he sold via mail order.

He continued to promote the "western" part of country & western, appearing at western music and arts festivals like the annual WestFest series organized by Michael Martin Murphy and also assembled events of his own. One example was the Cowboy Gathering & Western Swing Festival held October 25–27, 1991, in the Stockyards area of Ft. Worth, which became an annual event. The state legislature, which earlier had named Red the Cowboy Poet of Texas, at the same time declared October to be Cowboy Music Month.

In 1992 he was signed to Warner Brothers' new Warner Western label which issued his label debut, *Born to This Land,* in the spring of 1993. Sensing a resurgence of U.S. interest in cowboy lore, he commented that he thought "One reason why the cowboy image—and country music, as a whole—is so popular is because we have a whole generation of people who don't have any idea of where they came from. They grew up playin' with video games, and everything in their world is high-tech and computerized. They don't have any feeling for the land, or any sense of where they came from.

"The cowboy image has always exemplified independence and individualism and that's the thing that's made it endure, because everybody wants to feel independent. Everybody wants to feel individualistic, regardless of their walk of life."

Besides all of his other activities over the years, Red also managed to find time for movie and TV projects. He produced the film *Big Bad John,* and in 1991 he prepared a long-form video for Cabin Fever Entertainment, *Guts and Glory: The Legends of Rodeo.* He also worked on TV rodeo projects for ESPN and Bud Sports. Through 1996, he continued to appear regularly at Michael Martin Murphey organized events while hosting his own Ft. Worth festival every October, which typically drew some 25,000 people.

STEVENS, RAY: *Singer, pianist, songwriter, comedian, record producer. Born Clarksdale, Georgia, January 24, 1939.*

Combining an infectious sense of humor with fine musical skills, Ray Stevens created a unique niche for himself, first in the pop and rock field, then in country & western. Oddly, he was first known as a pop star though he made Nashville (the lodestone of country music) his home from the start of the 1960s. It was not until the 1970s that he was regarded as a full-fledged country star.

Ray, born Ray Ragsdale, was exposed to all forms of music in his Clarksdale, Georgia, home. He showed considerable promise in his early years as a classical pianist. In high school (Albany, Georgia), he formed his own R&B and blues band with school friends and played local clubs and dances. He also performed as a stand-up comedian between the group's sets. His musical favorites at the time were mainly R&B artists such as the Coasters, Drifters, and Midnighters. But as rockabilly artists like Elvis and Jerry Lee Lewis came to the fore, he turned his attention to that new format. Meanwhile, besides his band activity, teenage Ray also worked weekends as a disc jockey on a local station.

In 1956, the family moved to Atlanta, where Ray began taking some of his songs around to publishers. In 1957, he gained his first recording contract with a subsidiary of Capitol Records, an association that didn't turn out to be particularly productive. Ray, though, intended to continue his education. He enrolled at Georgia State University, majoring in classical piano and music theory, but also found time to perform with a small combo.

At the end of the 1950s, it looked as though his recording career might get into high gear when his single "Sergeant Preston of the Yukon" began moving up the charts in 1959. It sold well over 200,000 copies, then had to be withdrawn because of a lawsuit brought by a syndicate that owned the radio program rights to the title.

Stevens got his B.A. degree from Georgia State, then moved to Nashville in 1961. In 1962, he was back on pop hit lists again, this time with a composition that could well vie for a place in the Guinness Book of Records for title length: "Jeremiah Peabody's Polyunsaturated Quick Dissolving Fast Acting Pleasant Tasting Green and Purple Pills." He followed this with a string of many hits, the best known of which probably is "Ahab the Arab," in which he played the parts of Ahab and his camel, Clyde. Other comic gems of those years were "Freddie Feelgood" and "Hairy the Ape."

Stevens didn't want to become typecast as only a novelty songwriter, so he shifted gears from recording to behind the scenes work in the mid-1960s. For a number of years he made his living primarily as an arranger and record producer. Among those artists he was associated with were Patti Page, Brook Benton, Brenda Lee, Charlie Rich, and Ronnie Dove. In early 1966, he felt he was in a position to resume his recording career on his own terms, and he signed a new pact with Monument. From the beginning, the idea was that he could record serious songs as well as comic or satiric ones. As he noted, "I had built up a comedy image that was hard to break, but the lull between records had let the image die down. This made it possible for me to do something serious."

He soon showed he was capable of serious writing in 1968 with "Unwind" and "Mr. Businessman." The latter pointed to the shortcomings of a society where people ignored "the laughter of the children" while blindly pursuing economic success ("Tuesday evening with your harlot/and Wednesday it's your charlatan analyst . . ."). The widespread audience acceptance of the new material brought Ray the opportunity to perform in large auditoriums and concert halls around the United States. He also was featured on major talk shows, *The Ed Sullivan Show,* and many other network TV programs.

But his interest in humor was not abandoned, as evidenced by his massive 1969 hit, "Gitarzan," with lyrics that went, in part, "He's free as the breeze/He's always at ease/He lives in the jungle/And hangs by his knees/He swings through the trees/Without a trapeze/In his B.V.D.s." He followed that with another novelty hit, "Along Came Jones," then turned his hat around once more with the fine gold-record 1970 single, "Everything Is Beautiful." The single was number one on the *Billboard* pop chart for two weeks in a row in April 1970. The album of the same title also was a chart hit during 1970–71, as was the novelty single "Bridget the Midget." "Everything Is Beautiful" marked his move to a new label, Barnaby, with whom he remained until the mid-1970s.

Stevens was getting additional recognition for some of those efforts from the recording industry. "Gitarzan" received a Grammy Awards nomination for best male vocal performance of 1969 and "Everything Is Beautiful" not only received a nomination in 1970 but won Ray a Grammy.

During the 1969–70 TV season, Ray's guest appearances on the *Andy Williams Show* were so successful that he got the chance to host the summer replacement series in 1970. Joining him in hosting the show were Lulu and Mama Cass. Later, Ray made a number of additional appearances on the 1970–71 version of Williams' variety program.

He placed many other singles on the charts during the early 1970s on both Monument and Barnaby labels. The Monument chartmakers included "Have a Little Talk with Myself" and "Sunday Mornin' Comin' Down"; Barnaby successes included "America, Communicate with Me," "Sunset Strip," "All My Trials," "A

Mama and a Papa," and "Turn Your Radio On." Also on best-selling album lists in 1971 was the Barnaby LP *Greatest Hits.*

Signifying his closer ties with the country field in the early 1970s was the 1973 singles hit "Nashville." Ray also was featured on the NBC-TV show *Music Country, U.S.A.,* which began as a 1973 summer replacement and came back as a regular series in the spring of 1974. Throughout the 1970s, Stevens was a guest on many country-music network and syndicated shows and on a number of country-music TV specials.

In 1974, he placed the novelty single "The Streak" in the top 10 of both pop and country charts. The release became his top-selling single to that point, going well past platinum levels on the way to sales of over 4 million copies. The record was number one on the pop lists three weeks in a row in the spring. In the summer of 1975, he had great success with a new version of the old Errol Garner song "Misty." By the time "Misty" was placing the Barnaby banner in the country top 10, Ray had left that label in favor of Warner Brothers. Before 1975 was over, Ray had his first Warners single on the charts, "Indian Love Call." After the NARAS voting for the 1975 Grammy Awards, Ray was in possession of his second trophy, this time for his arranging skills on "Misty" in the category for Best Arrangement Accompanying Vocalists.

In 1976, Stevens' chart-making singles included "Young Love" early in the year, "You Are So Beautiful," in upper country chart levels in the summer, and "Honky Tonk Waltz," a chart hit in late summer-early fall. His debut album on Warner Brothers, *Just for the Record,* was issued in the spring of 1976. His second Warners' LP in 1977, titled *Feel the Music,* which he arranged and produced, included samples of both his serious and comic sides. One of the latter was a countrified version of "In the Mood," released as a single under the alias the Henhouse Five Plus Two. The latter made inroads on both pop and country charts. Also on the charts in 1977 was the single "Dixie Hummingbird."

In April 1979, his third LP for Warner Brothers, *The Feeling's Not Right Again,* was issued. The album was the fourteenth LP of his career. Among original compositions included in the 1979 release were "Get Crazy with Me," "Daydream Romance," "Feel the Music," "Be Your Own Best Friend," and his tongue-in-cheek "I Need Your Help Barry Manilow," the last named a top-10 singles hit for Ray in early 1979.

During 1979, Stevens left Warner Brothers and signed with RCA. In the spring of 1980, his single of his composition "Shriner's Convention" was on upper-chart levels for the new label. The album of that title also was on the charts in the summer. His other charted singles on RCA in the early 1980s included "Night Games" in 1980 and "One More Last Chance" in 1981.

Though Ray continued his writing and recording activities throughout the 1980s and through the mid-1990s, his singles offerings weren't as successful by and large as those of earlier decades, though he wasn't without charted releases. His album projects in the late 1980s included the 1987 MCA disc *Cracked Up,* whose contents included the zany comment on televangelists, "Would Jesus Wear a Rolex?" He remained very popular as a concert artist, and also made many appearances on TV programs during those years. By the 1990s, he had become a favorite with visitors to the thriving new center of country music entertainment, Branson, Missouri. His shows at his own venue there, the Ray Stevens Theatre, typically drew standing-room-only crowds.

Evaluating Ray's career in his Fifth Edition (1988) of *Top 40 Hits* (which covered the *Billboard* pop, not country charts), Joel Whitburn cited him as "The #1 novelty recording artist of the past 30 years." In the 1990s, Ray continued to earn new honors—for instance, in the 1993 TNN/*Music City News* Awards he was voted Comedian of the Year. As that indicated, Ray had established himself in the video as well as audio recording area. In the spring of 1993 Curb Home Video issued the *Ray Stevens Comedy Video Classics,* which packaged his performances of eight of his most successful songs. The album debuted at number two on the *Billboard* Top Music Video list and soon rose to number one. Later Stevens issued the *Ray Stevens Live* collection, which contained videos of twelve songs presented in his Branson show. In late 1993, Ray announced he was closing his Branson venue in order to have more time to work on songwriting, TV, and film projects.

STEWART, GARY: *Singer, guitarist, songwriter, bandleader. Born Kentucky, 1944.*

In private, Gary Stewart comes across as a soft-spoken, shy, introspective individual. That image isn't changed too much when he first comes onstage in his workaday-looking clothes and battered fedora, à la Hank Williams (whose songs he often sings). But once he starts singing and gets his guitar strings vibrating, he conveys a restless urgency that quickly establishes his authority with the audience and marks him as one of the major creative forces in modern country music.

Stewart's name generally is associated with his current home state of Florida, but his roots go back to Kentucky where he was born. His family, a large one ("I was one of eight or nine children—something like that"), was exposed to country music for the most part in the Blue Grass state. But when the clan moved to Florida, when he was twelve, the music heard on radios and records encompassed a much broader group of styles. As a result, in his teens, Gary became a rock musician for a time and toured with regional groups.

Tiring of the road, Gary relegated music to part-time status while he worked days at an aircraft factory near the Florida town of Okeechobee. He got a regular job singing and pickin' at a nightclub called the Wagon Wheel. His performances, which offered mostly well-known songs but included a few originals, caught the attention of Mel Tillis, who sometimes visited the Wagon Wheel when he returned to his home state from Nashville. Tillis suggested that Gary pursue his song-writing bent more diligently.

Acting on that advice, Stewart moved to Nashville and did get his writing operation under way. His output during that phase of his career included chart hits for Billy Walker ("When a Man Loves a Woman" and "She goes Walkin' Through My Mind") and Jack Green ("There's a Whole Lot About a Woman a Man Don't Know") as well as songs recorded by people like Nat Stuckey, Jim Ed Brown, Peggy Little, Roy Rogers, Cal Smith, Roy Drusky, and Jimmy Dean.

Gary made some stabs at doing his own recordings, but his characteristic self-doubts tended to hold him back, though he did make some sides for two record companies. "But the recording was kinda accidental. I enjoyed going into the studio and cutting records, but I really didn't have my heart in it. I just wanted to make a go of it as a songwriter."

Part of the problem also was Stewart's longing for the calmer environment of Florida. Eventually, he decided to move back to Florida. "I got homesick. I just needed to sit around in the sun and take it easy, which I did." Before going back, he made a demo tape that underscored his ability to sing a range of material. "We did a bunch of Motown songs—rhythm and blues things—and made 'em into country songs." The tape caught the ear of Roy Dea, then a producer for Mercury Records. Dea initially called Gary in Florida to recruit him for Mercury, but moved to RCA before anything happened. So it was that Stewart signed with RCA in 1973.

Gary's talents as an excellent pianist as well as guitarist (he had done some session work in Nashville) kept his phone ringing. Nat Stuckey called him to join his backing group. From that work, Stewart moved over to Charley Pride's band, the Pridesmen. Pride gave him the opportunity to do some of his own songs before the main act began, which started attracting a following for Gary from country audiences.

The first single issued by RCA was Gary's composition "Drinkin' Thing." The song was pulled out of circulation in favor of another single, "Ramblin' Man," which did reasonably well, but nowhere near as well as the reissue of "Drinkin' Thing." That song and another 1974 release, "Out of Hand," moved to top country chart levels and marked Stewart as an important new country influence.

His first album, *Out of Hand,* was one of the best debut albums of 1975 and was followed by an equally well-crafted collection, *Steppin' Out,* in 1976. Gary backed those releases with concerts throughout the United States with his own three- or four-piece group.

His following grew steadily, though not explosively, as the 1970s went by. Critics almost universally acclaimed him as a first-rank artist.

Stewart's albums and singles consistently made the charts, examples being the LP *Your Place or Mine,* a top-20 chartmaker in 1977, and *Little Junior* in 1978. His chart singles included "Ten Years of This" in 1977 and "Single Again" in 1978. His charted singles in the early 1980s included "Cactus and a Rose" and "Are We Dreamin' the Same Dream/Roarin'" in 1980 and "Let's Forget That We're Married" (cowritten with J. Lewis and S. Tackett) in 1981.

Making the charts is one thing, but failing to make the very top levels as Gary had done at the outset of his affiliation is another. For someone of his obvious creative abilities and high-voltage live concert potential, it seemed puzzling to many observers that his career appeared to stall at the end of the 1970s and begin to decline in the early 1980s. The answer, as is often the case with promising performers, was a self-destructive lifestyle that encompassed drug and alcohol abuse and more than a few domestic and legal problems.

He had also noted more than once that he wasn't sure he liked the idea of stardom. "I just never set out to be a country star or whatever it is," he said at one point. "I just don't have the itch to be a star." RCA took him at his word, since he didn't seem likely to make a new top-10, much less number-one recording, and dropped him from its roster. Rather than seek a new record company tie-in, Gary went back to Fort Pierce, Florida, and took only an occasional performing engagement to meet his living expenses.

In a "where are they now?" article for *The Journal of Country Music* in 1992 ("After the Flood," Volume 15, No. 1), Bob Allen pointed to a mid-1980s interview in which Stewart said, "I did all I could, pushed everything as young as I could." By then he was already a grandfather and had lived longer than he once thought possible. "I did a lotta livin' when I was young. I just wanted to get it all in there because the plane might go down any day, ya know."

In the late 1980s, he signed with the independent High Tone label, which issued two albums of newly recorded material, *Brand New* and *Battleground.* They proved above-average collections, but there were no threats to the top-chart levels. There was enough interest, though, for High Tone to obtain the rights from RCA for Gary's 1975 album, *Out of Hand,* which was reissued in the early 1990s.

By the mid-1990s, things had changed little for Stewart's lifestyle from the previous decade. His relatively few live dates were in Texas clubs and honky-tonks. He still could be a compelling performer, to which those who caught his shows attested. As he told Allen, "My voice has gotten lower and maybe I can't hit all those real high notes as I used to. I can't step as high as I used to, but I can still growl as high."

STEWART, LARRY: *Singer, guitarist, pianist, songwriter. Born Paducah, Kentucky, March 3, c. 1959.*

Perhaps taking a cue from the name Restless Heart, the band he fronted successfully as lead singer for almost a decade, Larry Stewart in 1991 decided it was time to move on to try to make it as a solo performer. As with any breakup of a popular group, people wondered whether all parties might lose ground, but as of the mid-1990s, it seemed there were now two star acts where previously there had been one.

Stewart was born and raised in Paducah, Kentucky, where he was encouraged to learn piano at any early age, particularly so he could eventually help his father's gospel career. He noted, "My father was a great singer. He sang gospel locally, never made the big time, though he knew a lot of people in Nashville. I've never known anyone who loved to sing as much as he did. He'd sing for anybody, anywhere. I'm not like that at all."

Though he had a certain amount of interest in music during those years, his main love was sports, an interest he still retained in his maturity, playing baseball whenever he could in the 1990s. He pointed out, "I've always been very shy, particularly when I was a kid. For one thing, I was obsessed with sports, especially baseball. (In his late teens, he recalled, he played on a community college team in Paducah that ended up sixth in its division in the entire United States.) Besides, being a singer was just really uncool in the crowd I ran with in Paducah.

"So I was very secretive about my music. I do remember lying in the foyer of our house, listening to the *Grand Ole Opry* on this funky old radio we had. Sometimes I'd lock the door to my bedroom, stand on the bed and pretend I was on stage singing—secretly, of course. The fact is, I actually ran from music the first 21 years of my life."

Larry's father kept urging his son not to overlook the possibilities of music. He was especially eager for Larry to go to Nashville and meet his friends and contacts in the country field to see about finding some kind of occupation in the industry. After his father died in 1978, Larry acceded to his wishes and moved to Nashville, enrolling in Belmont College as a business major. He already had a college sweetheart from his days at Paducah College, a pretty blond cheerleader at basketball games. She eventually moved to Nashville as well, working for the Country Music Association while Larry worked at the Country Music Hall of Fame until they got married and started a family.

Before that, Larry's residence was at the home of producer Jerry Crutchfield, a family friend. As Larry completed credits for a degree with a music business specialty, he still didn't think of performing as a career. "At that point, I was really more into the business side rather than the music side of the music business. All my life I'd seen gospel groups struggling to make ends meet and being away from home all the time living in these old buses, and I was really leery of that."

But gradually, as he became familiar with the secular aspects of country music, his views changed. It was an environment "where it was cool to be a singer, and I guess that's when I finally owned up to the fact that God had given me a talent and that I should use it." Before long, he was earning a fair amount of money making demo tapes for various songwriters.

While his demo work was prospering, he met a young performing hopeful named Dave Innis at the Belmont College recording studio. Innis also was a songwriter, and Stewart agreed to make some tapes for him. Their friendship blossomed, and Innis later introduced him to producer-songwriter Tim DuBois, who was involved with Innis in forming a new band. In time Stewart became an integral part of what soon became Restless Heart. The group recorded its first album in 1984 and was soon on the way to an eight-year saga with Stewart as lead singer that encompassed three gold-record albums, seven number-one singles, and awards of all kinds from country music organizations and publications.

Increasingly, however, as the years went by, Stewart was tempted to consider other career possibilities. One of the reasons, he told Linda F. Cauthen of *Country Fever* ("Larry Stewart Heads Down the Road on His Own," December 18, 1993), was the problem of keeping five individuals creatively content. "We had some great years and towards the end we realized that we were slipping a bit. When you get a certain amount of success, you have five guys with musical diversities that continue to grow and continue to change. Musically, we weren't on the same wavelength there towards the end. Something was missing. It wasn't a very good feeling to feel like we were slipping a little and needed a change."

He also felt he wanted more control over his personal life. He said in 1993, "I have two lovely children—Brittany and Brock [respectively, at the time, five and three] and a wonderful wife. Yet there I was spending most of my life on a bus with a bunch of guys, living with them more than my own family."

After finalizing the break at the end of 1991, Larry worked out a new agreement with RCA Records and went into the studios the next February to begin work on his first solo album. Most of the songs were written by others, but one song, "When You Come Back to Me," was cowritten by Stewart, Troy Seals, and Eddie Setzer. After almost one and a half years of recording and polishing the tracks, *Down the Road* was issued in the spring of 1993. It soon provided a hit single, "Alright Already," which rose to number four on the *Radio & Records* chart the week of May 21, 1993. The album also spawned some other chart singles such as "I'll Cry Tomorrow," on *Billboard* upper levels in late summer.

Larry's tenure with RCA, though, was short. He moved to Columbia Records for his 1994 album release, *Larry Stewart*. The first single from that, "Heart Like a Hurricane," was a chart hit in the fall in both audio and video versions. The tracks included the self-penned original, "I'm Not Through Loving You." Though not thought of by many observers as a writer, he had already accumulated some impressive credits. He had written several songs used by Restless Heart, including the hit "Long Lost Friend," and had provided Faith Hill with "But I Will" for her debut album. Pearl River also had released a single of his "Fool to Fall" and Mike Reid included Larry's "This Town" on his album *Twilight Town*.

Asked by Linda Cauthen about the musical differences between his solo and band work, Stewart responded that he believed the two differed in every way. "When you're in a band, your approach is totally different, because the focus is five guys. You still want great songs, but the songs have to lend themselves to a lot of things, like harmonies. Being a band with great musicians, you want material that has a style that each guy in the band wants to play, that feels natural. . . ."

As a soloist, he said, his desire was to take a simpler approach where the focus "is on the lyric, the songs. The production is more underproduced than overproduced. It's more traditional. The colors on the album are completely and totally different than any Restless Heart record we ever recorded because of the steel guitars and just the approach we took . . . I wanted it to be real. I wanted to sound like we were sitting in a room, or playing onstage and every instrument had its place. . . . So it's not stylized, more traditional."

(*See also Restless Heart.*)

STONE, CLIFFIE: *Singer, bandleader, bass violist, songwriter, disc jockey, record industry executive. Born Burbank, California, March 1, 1917. Elected to Country Music Hall of Fame in 1989.*

Clifford Gilpin Snyder, better known as Cliffie Stone, never ventured too far from his native California, but he made an indelible mark on the country-music field as a performer and entertainment field executive. He was particularly effective as a discoverer and manager of new talent, helping to forward the careers of such artists as Tennessee Ernie Ford, Molly Bee, Dallas Frazier, and many others.

His affinity for country music came naturally. His father, whose stage name was Herman the Hermit, was a successful comedian who played with many leading country stars in variety shows in California and elsewhere. (He later appeared on many of his son's TV shows.) Nonetheless, Cliffie's initial interest was in more pop-oriented material.

While attending Burbank High School in the 1930s, he was active in both music and acting events. He played trombone and bass fiddle, and performed for two seasons in comedies at the Pasadena Community Playhouse. The bass proved the most helpful later when he used it in a comedy routine he and Gene Austin put together for Ken Murray's Hollywood Blackouts.

In the mid-1930s, Stone played bass with such major dance bands of the period as Anson Weeks and Freddy Slack. After he started getting work as a country disc jockey in 1935, he swung away from the pop music of the period toward country & western. One of his first shows was the *Covered Wagon Jubilee* on KFVD. During the late 1930s and early 1940s he emceed the *Lucky Stars Show* on KFWB for seven years. In the 1940s he also led the band and was featured comedian on the CBS network *Hollywood Barn Dance* radio program. For many of those years his early morning show, *Wake Up Ranch,* was one of the most popular in the area. He also was an associate of songwriter-performer Stuart Hamblen in many activities. As one of the most popular people in Los Angeles-area radio, he was so much in demand during the mid-1940s that from 1943 to 1947 he often was master of ceremonies for as many as twenty-five to twenty-eight western radio shows a week.

In 1946, Capitol Records signed Stone in the dual role of head of country & western music and recording artist. He formed a new band for the latter effort and soon was turning out a steady stream of singles for the label. Among his releases of the 1940s and 1950s were "My Pretty Girl," "Spanish Bells," "When My Blue Moon Turns to Gold Again," "Christmas Waltz," "Blues Stay Away from Me," "Bryant's Boogie," and "Blue Canadian Rockies." He turned out several dozen albums during his long affiliation with Capitol, with some of the later releases including *Party's on Me* (1958), *Cliffie Stone Sing Along* (1961), and *The Great Hank Williams* (1964).

During those years and on into the 1960s, Cliffie wrote a number of originals, some of which made the hit charts in versions by him or other artists, in collaboration with people like Merle Travis, Eddie Kirk, and Leon McAuliffe. Among those compositions were "No Vacancy," "Divorce Me C.O.D.," "So Round, So Firm, So Fully Packed," "Steel Guitar Rag," and "Sweet Temptations."

In 1947, he met a fellow announcer from a Pasadena station named Ernie Ford. He quickly recognized Tennessee Ernie's potential and became his manager for ten years. Ford was one of the major additions to the Capitol roster. (Stone also was instrumental in bringing other important artists on board, including Hank Thompson.) Ford also became a regular in the early stages of a new TV program Cliffie organized called *Hometown Jamboree.* That program became one of the most eagerly awaited Saturday night variety shows in the Southern California area, one of the highest rated programs throughout its ten-year run.

Many of the best new talents in country music came to the fore on the *Jamboree,* which also showcased many established artists as guests or regulars. Among those featured on it over the years, besides Tennessee Ernie, were Polly Bergen, Merle Travis, Wesley Tuttle, Molly Bee, Bucky Tibbs, Tommy Sands, Joanie O'Brien, Billy Strange, Jeanne Black, Speedy West, Jimmy Bryant, Gene O'Quin, Ferlin Husky, Dallas Frazier, Harold Hensley, Billy Armstrong, and Billy Liebert. Also a regular was Cliffie's father, Herman the Hermit.

While keeping that show going, Stone also had a hand in Tennessee Ernie's mushrooming success. He produced Ford's show on ABC radio, CBS radio, NBC daytime TV, and later the highly ranked night-time TV series sponsored by Ford Motor Co. He handled production chores for that show for four years until a minor illness forced him to step down.

In the 1960s, Cliffie cut back on his performing chores in favor of management activities. His operations included some artist management work, a booking agency, and a number of music publishing firms. One of these, Central Songs, he sold to Capitol Records in 1969; another one, Snyder Music Corp., remained under his aegis into the 1970s. During the 1960s and early 1970s, he also continued his record production work, handling assignments for such labels as Tower and UNI. At the end of the 1960s, he still did some recording work for Capitol, commuting by then from his twenty-acre ranch in outlying Saugus, California.

A considerable amount of his time in the 1960s and 1970s was devoted to industry affairs. He served on committees and in executive capacities for both the Country Music Association in Nashville and the California-based Academy of Country & Western Music. In the 1970s, he served a term as president of the latter organization. As of the late 1970s, his main concern in a professional sense was directing the affairs of ATV Music Company. He also produced a number of bluegrass events in the late 1970s and in the 1980s.

His name was offered for inclusion in the Country Music Hall of Fame several times, resulting in his election in 1989. Though the pace of his activities was much less hectic as the 1980s drew to a close and the 1990s got underway, he kept in touch with goings-on in the field and remained involved in several show business enterprises.

In the fall of 1995 the board of directors of the Academy of Country Music named him the official historian and his new column, "Historically Speaking," debuted in the December 1995 issue of the ACM newsletter. He reported on some of his own activities in the column, noting his contributions to a TNN biography of his friend Tennessee Ernie titled *The Life and Times of Tennessee Ernie Ford.* For his insight into Ernie's career, program organizers interviewed him for three hours. He pointed out that his involvement with

Ford was outlined in Chapter 21, "The True Story About 16 Tons," in his book, *Everything You Always Wanted to Know About Songwriting.*

An example of his mid-1990s activities was his participation in Country Music Network's *Starfest 96* event at the Los Angeles County Fairplex in Pomona, California, in May 1996. Stone served as master of ceremonies on the main stage on one of the four days of the program and on Sunday performed with the original Riders of the Purple Sage group.

STONE, DOUG: *Singer, guitarist, drummer, bandleader, songwriter. Born Atlanta, Georgia, June 19, 1956.*

There are more than a few ironies in Doug Stone's path to country stardom. For example, his debut single was titled "I'd Be Better Off in a Pine Box," which caused *USA Today* to dub him a star of the future who was "bound for glory." Two years later those words seemed almost a premonition, when Stone was felled by a massive heart attack that almost ended his life as well as his career. Fortunately he survived, and in 1994 his upbeat song, "More Love," seemed a better description of his future.

He was born in Atlanta, Georgia, though he spent much of his early life in nearby Newman. Most of the incentive for his eventual focus on music came from his mother, an aspiring country singer/guitarist, who taught him to play the instrument at an early age. He made his stage debut at the age of seven, he recalled, when his mother pushed him onstage to join Loretta Lynn in a song.

His father was a mechanic who liked to tinker with odd inventions, and Doug and his siblings also came to find pleasure in working with their hands. In fact, when his parents separated when he was twelve and he went to live with his father and two brothers in a mobile trailer, he had to help with the cooking and the laundry. The falling-out between his parents centered around his father's new religious convictions, which conflicted with his mother's love for show business. As Doug told Dolly Carlisle of *People* magazine, "Daddy met the Lord in a mighty way. It didn't sit well with everybody. The whole family split up."

The situation failed to dim Doug's interest in music, though, and by the time he was fifteen he had left school in favor of performing. As he told Bob Allen of *Country Music* magazine, "I built my first studio when I was 16, around the time I had my first band. I bought my first mobile home and took out the front bedroom and built it there. I built about five other studios altogether. I kept building them in other people's homes and they'd either sell the house or their daddies would run us off for bein' too noisy. I finally got smart the last time and built one in a house I owned." Obviously, though Doug had moved in with his father, his outlook and objectives paralleled those of his mother.

He formed his first band with a close friend, and

Doug opened his professional career by playing at skating rinks for $5 a night. As he grew older his groups moved out, and began earning payoffs from local clubs and honky-tonks. Before he was out of his teens he was married, and by the end of the 1970s had two children to support. While music was his primary interest, he supported his family mostly by working days as a diesel mechanic, an occupation he maintained until an unexpected break gave him the chance to forgo a conventional blue-collar–type job.

Between his day and night activities (which *People* indicated included "some occasional straying with female fans") and the many hours spent in his recording studio, his first marriage soon came to an end. His wife gained custody of the children, and though Doug pursued his previous working schedule from 1979 until the early 1980s, he suffered a deep depression—a situation, he told *People*'s Carlisle, that left him with "a feeling of being so alone you don't care whether you're here or not."

It wasn't until 1982, when a friend set him up with photo lab worker Carie Cohen, that he began to regain his appetite for life. They began dating and soon married, and their relationship seemed not to suffer when he began to make a name for himself in country music late in that decade. In the mid-1990s he still pointed to the importance of his family support system—which, besides his wife, by then also included two more children, son Chanse and daughter Kala.

During the mid-1980s, he continued to hone his writing and performing skills while keeping up a steady string of local engagements. He hadn't thought much about gambling on a move to Nashville, until fate stepped in at the end of the decade. While he was appearing in a show at the local VFW hall, his act was observed by a Nashville-based management executive, Phyllis Bennett, who was impressed enough to ask Doug for some demo tapes. Along with her associates she shopped those around, and finally won him a recording contract from Sony Music in 1989.

His debut album, *Doug Stone*, was issued in the spring of 1990 and the first single, "I'd Be Better Off (In a Pine Box)," rapidly caught on with radio programmers and country fans, peaking at number four in *Radio & Records* the week of May 18, 1990, and also providing Doug with a number one video and a Grammy nomination. The album made top chart levels during the spring and summer and stayed on the *Billboard* list for years. It was still there after 172 weeks in mid-summer 1993, earning both gold and platinum R.I.A.A. awards. Four more hit singles were culled from it during 1990–91, including the number two hit "These Lips Don't Know How to Say Goodbye" and the number one singles "Fourteen Minutes Old" and "In a Different Light." His achievements brought a 1991 Country Music Association nomination for its Horizon Award, a nomination in the 1991 *Music City News* Awards for

Star of Tomorrow, and Academy of Country Music Awards nomination for 1991 Top New Male Vocalist.

Doug avoided the sophomore jinx with a second fine album, *I Thought It Was You*, which was in the *Billboard* Top 15 in September 1991 (peaking at number twelve) on its way to another R.I.A.A. gold record certification. The title track gave him another number one single during 1991, and he started 1992 with the chart-topping "A Jukebox with a Country Song," number one in *R&R* the week of January 17. A few months later, "Come In Out of the Pain" was number one on some charts and number two in *R&R* the week of May 29.

But by early 1992 another problem had surfaced: Doug was experiencing real physical pain. He was feeling tingling sensations in his chest that sometimes spread up an arm. They certainly suggested potential heart problems, but Doug found it difficult to believe he could be a heart-attack candidate at thirty-five. He figured it was just heartburn—a feeling reinforced by a medical examination that indicated no perceptible blockages. (Later it was revealed that he did indeed have major closures in arteries, including one in the main artery to his heart which was almost completely blocked.)

Doug maintained his tour schedule while also recording material for a new album, ironically entitled *From the Heart*. But he was close to death's door. After the first exams showed no significant physical problems, he told Dolly Carlisle of *People* ("This Heart of Stone's," July 20, 1992), "I went back on the road. The guys in the band didn't even know I was hurting. I came offstage and they said, 'What a great show! You must be feeling good.' I said, 'Hell no, I'm dying.'"

In late April, things came to a head during an appearance in Oregon. He recalled feeling "kind of disoriented. I didn't know if I was really here or I was just dreaming about it. That scared the hell out of me. The pain, it just kept getting worse and worse." He canceled a scheduled turn at the Academy of Country Music Awards TV show in Los Angeles and flew back to Nashville's Centennial Medical Center where a very concerned Carie awaited him. On April 29, a surgical team headed by Dr. Phillip Brown conducted an emergency operation that required a quadruple bypass procedure. It was literally a life-or-death situation, but fortunately the operation turned out well—so well, in fact, that five weeks later Stone was once more making live appearances in support of his new album.

The rest of 1992 was a rewarding one for him. *From the Heart* showed up on the *Billboard* chart almost as soon as it came out, and, after peaking at number nineteen, went past gold-record levels at the start of 1993. During the week of September 4, the single "Warning Labels" was a number three hit in R&R. The year also brought another nomination for Star of Tomorrow in the *Music City News* Awards poll, while he also received a Top Male Vocalist nomination from Academy of Country Music voters.

He started off 1993 with the hit single "Too Busy Being In Love," number one in *R&R* the week of January 22. As the year went by he added more singles successes to his credits: "Made for Lovin' You," number three in *R&R* the week of May 14; "Why Didn't I Think of That," number one in *R&R* the week of August 13; and "I Never Knew Love," top 10 in *Billboard* the week of December 18. He received another Top Male Vocalist nomination from the Academy of Country Music and also won the Star of Tomorrow Award in the TNN/*Music City News* poll.

At the end of 1993, Doug's fourth Sony album, *More Love*, was ready for release. In early 1994 it peaked at number twenty on the *Billboard* list and stayed on it into the fall, earning a gold record award from the R.I.A.A. in September. The title track, written by Stone and Gary Burr, rose to number six in *Billboard* the week of September 24. Late in 1994, Sony released the album *Doug Stone's Greatest Hits, Volume 1*, which peaked at number twenty-nine and remained on the charts for much of 1995. It was joined on the charts that April by the new album *Faith in Me, Faith in You*, whose title track reached number thirteen in *Billboard* in May. The *Greatest Hits* disc was certified gold by the R.I.A.A. on June 6, 1995. In late 1995, Doug had the single "Born in the Dark" in upper chart levels. He kept adding to his concert credits in 1995 and 1996, including a summer 1996 appearance at Dolly Parton's Dollywood theme park as part of the Showcase of Stars series.

STONEMAN FAMILY: *Vocal and instrumental group founded by Ernest V. "Pop" Stoneman, born Monarat, Carroll County, Virginia, May 25, 1893; died Nashville, Tennessee, June 14, 1968.*

In the years after World War II, much of traditional country music had been obscured by newer commercial versions. One family that still preserved much of the flavor and content of the old-time ballads and dance tunes was the renowned Stoneman clan.

The man who built the modern Stoneman musical dynasty was talented, rugged Ernest "Pop" Stoneman. Born in a log cabin in rural Virginia, he grew up in a family whose roots were deep in American history. His great, great, great, great-grandfather had come to America as a cabin boy from England (His mother's family, named Bowers, had originally emigrated from Germany.)

As in many rural homes, singing the old folk tunes and hymns, or variations of them, was a looked-for pleasure. Young Ernest enjoyed singing and performing from his early youth; he learned to play the harmonica and jew's-harp before he was ten and the banjo and autoharp by the time he was in his teens.

Continuing to improve his skills as he reached manhood, he played at local affairs but earned his keep in other ways. In the 1920s, the rise of the recording industry changed all this. Word of the collecting efforts of such record representatives as Frank Walker and Ralph Peer began to filter down to many rural artists.

As a result, Stoneman and Peer met and Pop's first record session was set up for the Okeh label. The session took place at the company's studios on September 24, 1924. (Later, Pop sometimes remembered the date, erroneously, as having been in 1925.) The songs were "The Sinking of the Titanic," "The Face That Never Returned," "Freckled Face Mary Jane," and "Me and My Wife." In 1926, Peer set up another session in which Stoneman and his group recorded "Sourwood Mountain." During those sessions, Pop added guitar playing to his talents.

During the balance of the 1920s, Pop toured widely, making personal appearances in many parts of the country. He also continued to turn out new recordings. He taught his wife to play fiddle and added other artists to his group, such as Uncle Eck Dunford. The Stonemans performed with many country-music greats from 1926 to 1931, including the Bailes Brothers, Riley Puckett, and Uncle Dave Macon. Among their songs were such titles as "When the Springtime Comes Again," "Say, Darling, Say," "The Black Dog Blues," "New River Train," "Hallelujah Side," "Cumberland Gap," "Hang John Brown," and "Bile Them Cabbage Down." Some of the songs were variations on traditional ballads or original compositions of Pop's.

The Depression had its effect on all country music in the early 1930s. With record dates few and far between and engagements hard to find, the Stonemans settled outside Washington, D.C. Pop got a job in a naval gun factory and, with his wife, concentrated on raising a family (twenty-three children were born, of whom thirteen survived to adulthood), playing occasional night dates when work was available.

As the children grew up, they learned instruments themselves and joined with their parents in working up song stylings. At the end of World War II, the Stoneman Family began to receive an increasing number of invitations to perform at concerts in many parts of the East and South. Some of the children married and left, but throughout the 1950s and 1960s Pop could always count on half a dozen or more for performing dates. The growth of interest in traditional country music in these decades resulted in new opportunities for the group. They played on many college campuses and at a number of major folk festivals. In 1962, the Stoneman Family made their debut on the *Grand Ole Opry* and returned several more times in the years that followed.

For a time, the group was persuaded by their managers to move to Los Angeles, California, to take advantage of the still flourishing folk movement. The move took place in April 1964, and led to guest appearances on such shows as *Shindig, The Steve Allen Show,*

The Meredith Wilson Special, The Jimmy Dean Show, and *The Danny Thomas Special.* The Stonemans also were featured at the Monterey Folk Festival.

During these years, new chances to record came from many different labels. In 1957, the group turned out *Banjo Tunes and Songs* for Folkways. Starday issued the LP *Ernest Stoneman and the Stoneman Family* in 1962, and another Stoneman Family album in 1964. World Pacific issued the LP *Big Ball in Monterey* in 1964. In the mid-1960s, the Stonemans were signed by Columbia Records.

As the mid-1960s went by, the fadeout of the folk boom and the resurgence of rock caused the group to reevaluate its position. By late 1965, the Stonemans found they weren't doing well enough in music to pay their bills. Jack Clement, then their comanager, suggested that Nashville might be a better base, so the group moved there in January 1966. Things seemed to pick up. They got more bookings in venues ranging from big city nightclubs to county fairs and were signed to turn out their own TV show, *Those Stonemans,* for the 1967–68 season. And Pop Stoneman and four of his children were voted top vocal group for 1967 by the Country Music Association. Pop, however, fell ill in early 1968 and died in Nashville in June.

Some of the family decided to reorganize and keep the Family going in the music field. Five banded together for this, Roni, Pattie, Donna, Van, and Jim Stoneman. All could sing and, between them, could play almost every instrument usually employed by a traditional country band, including Roni on banjo, Pattie on autoharp, Donna on mandolin, Van on guitar and dobro, and Jim on bass fiddle. Some of them, of course, were adept on several instruments. The decision to continue performing, it was noted by the CMA when Pop Stoneman was one of the nominees for the Country Music Hall of Fame in 1981, made the Stonemans "the longest continuous act in Country Music."

Jack Clement signed the group to MGM Records soon after they re-formed, which led to such releases as the charted single "Tupelo County Jail" (the first single issued on the label) and the LPs *The Stonemans* in 1966, and *Stoneman's Country* in 1967. In August 1969, the Stonemans left MGM and signed with RCA Victor. That alignment led to such recordings as the July 1970 LP *In All Honesty* and the LP *California Blues* (December 1971).

Later in the decade the group had several albums on the CMH label.

STRAIT, GEORGE: *Singer, guitarist, pianist, band leader (Ace in the Hole), record producer, actor. Born Poteet, Texas, May 18, 1952.*

When George Strait burst upon the scene in 1981, country music was in one of its periodic downturns, caused, some critics asserted, by recording companies' overemphasis on watered-down, crossover-type pop-country material. With his unassuming, relaxed style, Strait reminded country fans of the music's roots—though, backed by a superb band, Ace in the Hole, he didn't completely ignore some of the influences of the pop, rock, and jazz genres. In helping to restore the music's luster for country's core audience, he also contributed to the dramatic expansion of interest in new artists that fueled the boom period from the mid-1980s into the 1990s.

Strait was born in Poteet, Texas, but raised in Pearsall in a family headed by a father who initially was a junior high school math teacher before taking over the Strait family's cattle ranch. In that environment, George became an excellent rider and developed noteworthy skills at steer-roping, something he pursued for a while as a teenager and young adult and retained as a hobby during his show business career. Among his professional affiliations over the years was membership in the Professional Rodeo Cowboys Association.

Influenced by performers like Merle Haggard, George Jones, and Hank Williams, Sr., as a boy, he kept an interest in music in his high school years, teaching himself to play guitar along the way. Nonetheless, it seemed music would be a sideline, particularly after he eloped to Mexico during his senior year in high school to marry his high school girlfriend, Norma. (Later, to please their parents, they had a second church wedding in Texas.) Unlike many high school romances, this one proved lasting and they were still close companions in the 1990s while watching their son, George, Jr., grow up.

After graduating from high school, Strait enrolled in Southwest Texas State University at the start of the 1970s as an agriculture major before enlisting in the army. After completing basic training he was stationed in Hawaii, where he was joined by Norma. Hearing that the base commander was organizing a country band, he auditioned for lead singer and won the job, which remained his main military pursuit until his discharge a year later.

The Straits then returned to Texas, where George again took up his studies at Southwest Texas. He now wanted to pursue his musical activities, and put fliers up on campus trying to find a band that needed a singer. The group that was to become the Ace in the Hole responded, and soon Strait and the band were finding a variety of local engagements. Over the next six years, while Strait either attended classes or found day work, they played five nights a week at clubs, honky-tonks, and private parties within a 200-mile radius of the college campus in San Marcos. After George earned his B.A. in agricultural education in 1979, he worked as the full-time manager of a cattle ranch while performing with the band nights.

By the late 1970s, the group had progressed to where it got gigs as opening act for major artists on concert tours through the region. The grind of his daytime and evening activities began to wear on Strait and he started to think about making cattle ranching his only career. He recalled, "I was going to quit singing altogether because I didn't feel I was making the progress I should. I went to Nashville three times to do my own session, but nothing came of it. Still, I was trying as hard as I could."

He decided, after receiving strong support from his wife, to take another year to try for a record deal before giving up. The turning point came from a booking by the band in a club in San Marcos owned by Erv Woolsey. Woolsey liked what he heard and recalled Strait's work later when he left San Marcos to take an executive position with MCA Records in Nashville. He touted Strait to the label and brought George in to make some demos, which paid off in a contract in 1980. On April 23, 1980, Strait's first single, "Unwound," was released.

The single did surprisingly well, eventually making the charts, to clear the way for a veritable future avalanche of chart-topping singles and albums. Strait commented, "It's everybody's ambition who play[s] in local bands to be signed to a major label and be played on the radio. I hoped 'Unwound' would do well, but I didn't expect it to happen so fast."

Spurred by that release and such following singles as "Down and Out" and two straight number-one discs, "If You're Thinking You Want a Stranger" and "Fool Hearted Memory," his debut album, *Strait Country,* made the charts and proceeded to gain gold-record certification from the R.I.A.A. From then on through 1996, every album release won either gold or platinum records. His album releases through the mid-1980s included *Strait from the Heart* (gold); *Right or Wrong* (issued 1984, gold); *Does Ft. Worth Ever Cross Your Mind* (issued late 1984, platinum); *Greatest Hits, Volume 1* (issued 1985, platinum, still in the *Billboard* top 50 in late 1991); *Something Special* (gold); *#7* (issued 1986, gold); and *Merry Christmas Strait to You* (gold). *Does Ft. Worth* was voted Country Music Association Album of the Year for 1985, and in 1986 the Academy of Country Music named it Album of the Year.

After having a chart hit single with "Marina Del Rey," George had a run of six consecutive number-one successes during 1983–84, including "Amarillo by Morning," "A Fire I Can't Put Out," "You Look So Good in Love," "Right or Wrong," "Let's Fall to Pieces Together," and "Does Ft. Worth Ever Cross Your Mind."

Contributing to those successes was an intensive touring schedule of some 230 shows a year by Strait and Ace in the Hole. Audiences responded to the show, despite the fact that George didn't perform the wild antics or use the special effects of other concert artists. Terry Atkinson, reporting on a 1984 concert ("Strait Keeps up the Good Work," *Los Angeles Times,* May 25, 1984), wrote, "George Strait is so indistinctive that he's

distinctive. He sings country weepers just like George Jones and John Anderson do, but you don't believe for a minute he's had many heart-wrenching experiences. With his clean-cut good looks and easy smile, this Texan looks as if he never had a worry in his life. No one was going to mistake him for Waylon or Willie when he played the Palomino Monday night."

But he stressed not to underestimate Strait. "Though he writes little of his material, Strait chooses well, if cautiously. His tone is steady, rich and down-home without seeming overdone or phony."

Rick Mitchell of the *Houston Chronicle* ("Straight Shooter," July 5, 1990) characterized Strait's appearance as a national country performer in the first part of the 1980s as "a breath of fresh air. With Nashville pushing . . . pre-sweetened country-pop formulas in a misguided crossover movement, sales had entered a slump that lasted until mid-decade. They called it 'country without the twang.' Country without the twang is like jazz without swing, funk without the soul, rock without the roll. Who needs it?"

In any case, Strait's fans were happy with his approach, which continued to keep his recordings and concerts among eagerly awaited events. He had a slight "downturn" during 1985 when several singles made top-chart positions without reaching number one, but made up for that in remaining years of the decade with no less than eleven straight chart toppers. (His 1985 releases were "The Cowboy Rides Away," "The Fireman," number-one ranked "The Chair," and "You're Something Special to Me.") His number-one singles from 1985 to the start of the 1990s were: "Nobody in His Right Mind Would Have Left Her," "It Ain't Cool to Be Crazy About You," "Ocean Front Property," "All My Ex's Live in Texas," "Am I Blue," "Famous Last Words of a Fool," "Baby Blue," "If You Ain't Lovin' You Ain't Livin'," "Baby's Gotten Good at Goodbye," "What's Going on in Your World," and "Ace in the Hole."

Strait's late 1980s album releases, all of which made upper-chart levels, were: *Ocean Front Property* (gold, debuted at number one in *Billboard; Greatest Hits, Volume II* (issued 1988, platinum, still in *Billboard* Top 50 in spring 1991); *If You Ain't Lovin' You Ain't Livin'* (platinum); and *Beyond the Blue Neon* (platinum).

Although Strait had been nominated for the most coveted Country Music Association Awards, he didn't win the big one, Entertainer of the Year, until the 1989 voting. He told Rick Mitchell, "You try not to get excited or disappointed about these awards. But that night, I really wanted to win that thing. Being nominated for several years and coming away empty-handed was kind of discouraging."

He added that a major contributor to any success he had was the backing of the Ace in the Hole band, whose members as of 1991 were Rick McRae and Benny MacArthur on electric guitars, David Anthony on acoustic guitar, Terry Hale on bass guitar, Mike Daily on pedal steel guitar, Gene Elders on fiddle, Ronnie Huckaby on piano, and Phil Fisher on drums. The year 1989 also brought a Presidential Success Award presented to him by President George Bush in a White House Rose Garden ceremony.

In the early 1990s, some observers wondered whether Strait's long reign as a modern country idol might be imperiled by the onslaught of a wave of new personalities like Garth Brooks and Travis Tritt. However, as the decade progressed, he still seemed secure as a top attraction. On the concert circuit he continued to set new attendance records at many venues, for example selling 95,000 tickets in one day for a two-show engagement at the Houston Astrodome. He began the 1990s with the singles hit "Overnight Success," which reached number five in *Radio & Records* the week of February 9, 1990, and followed with "Love Without End, Amen," which spent five weeks at number one in *Billboard.* Then came "Drinking Champagne," number four in *R&R* the week of September 25, 1990, and "I've Come to Expect It of You," another five-weeks-long number-one hit late in the year. He added two more number-one hits in 1991, "If I Know Me" and "Chill of an Early Fall."

There were still more singles best-sellers achieved from 1992 through 1994. Those included "Gone As a Girl Can Get," which peaked at number six in *R&R* the week of June 12, 1992; "I Cross My Heart," number one in *R&R* the week of December 4, 1992, and number one for two weeks in *Billboard;* "Heartland," number one in *R&R* the week of March 19, 1993; "When Did You Stop Loving Me," number five in *R&R* the week of July 9, 1993; "Easy Come, Easy Go," number six in *R&R* November 26, 1993; "I'd Like to Have That One Back," number three in *Billboard* the week of February 26, 1994; "Lovebug," top 10 in *Billboard* May 1994; "The Man in Love with You," number four in *Billboard* in September 1994; and "The Big One," top 10 in *Billboard* in November 1994.

On the album side, George began the 1990s with *Livin' It Up,* issued in 1990 and later certified platinum. This was followed by *Chill of an Early Fall* (issued spring 1991, platinum); *Greatest Hits, Volume III* (issued December 1991); *Holding My Own* (1992, gold); *Pure Country* (issued late 1992 in conjunction with movie of that title, reached number one in *Billboard* and certified double platinum by the R.I.A.A.); and *Easy Come, Easy Go* (issued late 1993, peaked at number two in *Billboard,* platinum by year-end 1994). In late 1994, MCA issued his album *Lead On,* which hit number one in *Billboard* and was well past R.I.A.A. platinum in the spring of 1995. Among the singles drawn from the album was "You Can't Make a Heart Love Somebody," which reached number one in *Billboard* in March 1995.

His starring debut as a movie actor in the film *Pure Country* didn't do any harm to his recording career—the soundtrack album was the biggest seller of his career to then—nor did it detract from filmgoers' reception. The movie remained among the nation's top-10 grossing releases for some four weeks.

Despite his enormous success, Strait tried to keep it from radically affecting his private life. As much as possible he retreated to his Texas haunts to share time with his wife and son at their San Antonio home or Hill Country ranch. He told Ron Young of the *San Antonio Express-News* ("Shooting Straight with George," September 5, 1993), "Me and my wife have managed to keep it under control. I don't take the things about being a sex symbol too seriously. 'Cause whatever happens on-stage, it's not me when I'm offstage."

Young wondered whether the arrival of excellent new faces in the country field complicated the search for potential new hit songs. Strait replied, "It is difficult, but it's always been hard to find good songs. And I wouldn't say that right now it is any harder than any other time to find 'em. It's still tough, because you have to go through hundreds of tapes—thousands of songs. And as co-producer of my albums, I have to listen to the songs personally. I'm the one who's stuck with the song, ultimately, so I feel like it ought to be my choice when I do a song. And you never know when you're gonna find that song that's right for you."

During the balance of 1995 and throughout 1996, George demonstrated anew his great popularity with both hard-core country and pop music fans as his albums did well on both the country and pop lists. His single "Adalida" made the charts in the spring and peaked at number three in *Billboard* in June. In the summer the title track from his album *Lead On* was a best seller. Then in late fall he hit top positions with "Check Yes Or No," number one in *Billboard* several weeks in November-December. Even as that occurred, he had a new boxed set inside the top 10, *Strait Out of the Box.* It was certified gold on November 16 and by December 13, 1995, had gone past two million copies sold according to the R.I.A.A.

In early 1996, he had the single "I Know She Still Loves Me" high on the hit lists and in the spring, his next album, *Blue Clear Sky* showed he still could be counted on for quality recorded collections. The album opened at number one in *Billboard* the week of May 11, 1996. That same week the single of the title track was at number three in that magazine. Also debuting on the country hit lists the following week was his next release, the album cut "Carried Away."

The Academy of Country Music voters nominated him in three categories for 1995, Single Record of the Year (for "Check Yes Or No," Album of the year (for *Lead On*) and Top Male Vocalist. When the results were announced on the NBC-TV program on April 24, 1996, he was victorious in the Singles category. He did even better when the Country Music Association Awards were given out in October. *Blue Clear Sky* was named Album of the year, "Check Yes Or No" Single of the Year, and he was voted Male Vocalist of the Year.

STRINGBEAN: *Singer, banjoist, comedian. Born Annville, Kentucky, June 17, 1915; died Nashville, Tennessee, November 11, 1973.*

One of country music's finest banjo players, Stringbean carried on the tradition of the *Grand Ole Opry*'s first star, Uncle Dave Macon, in fine style. His blend of intricate picking and down-home humor remained popular with audiences for decades after Uncle Dave's passing and only a tragic incident ended that rapport in 1973.

Stringbean, born David Akeman, was raised on a farm near Annville, Kentucky, and developed an interest in the banjo almost from the cradle. His father was an expert banjo-picker, and David and his four brothers and three sisters enjoyed listening to him play and often joined in sing-alongs. When he was fourteen, his dreams finally came true when his father gave him a banjo. He had, of course, picked up basics on his father's banjo, but with his own he was able to progress even faster. Before long he was good enough to entertain at local dances, barn raisings, and other events.

At eighteen, by then a tall gangling six feet two inches, he started playing professionally in the Lexington, Kentucky, region. In two years' time he was working on station WLAP in Lexington. As the late 1930s went by, he continued to increase his reputation with fans and other country artists, touring or performing with Lew Childre, Bill Monroe, Ernest Tubb, Red Foley, and Uncle Dave Macon.

He gained a particularly close friendship with Uncle Dave, who taught him much of his own technique. In recognition of their close relationship, Uncle Dave willed his "godchild," whose nickname was "The Kentucky Wonder," one of his banjos upon his death in 1952. Beginning in 1942, Stringbean was a regular cast member on the *Opry* and remained a featured performer on both the radio and occasional TV versions of the show up to his death. A feature of his act was his comic costumes, usually consisting of a loud shirt that extended almost to his knees and pants that seemed to start where the shirt ended. As did fellow musician and comic Grandpa Jones, Stringbean used his banjo skills as a change of pace from his humorous sketches and routines. In the years after World War II, he not only starred on the *Opry,* but performed on Red Foley's ABC programs for a dozen years.

His considerable talent came through more on records, where he was a noted exponent of the old-time country banjo sound. He turned out many singles and albums on several labels from the 1940s into the 1970s. Among his best-known single releases of the 1950s and 1960s were "Run Little Rabbit Run," "I Wonder Where Wanda Went," "Short Life and Trouble," "Train Special 500," "Barnyard Banjo Picking," "Crazy Viet Nam War," "20¢ Cotton and 90¢ Meat," "Hey Old Man," "John Henry," "Big Ball in Nashville," and "Pretty Little Pink." His LPs on the Starday label included *Kentucky Wonder* (2/62), *Stringbean* (10/62), *Salute to Uncle Dave Macon* (5/63), *Old Time Banjo Picking and Singing,* and *Way Back in the Hills of Kentucky* (2/64). In the early 1970s he was represented on the Nugget label with the LP *Me and My Old Crow.*

When the *Hee Haw* TV program started on the CBS network in 1969, Stringbean was one of the original cast members. Besides taking part in many of the comedy sketches, he sometimes joined in banjo band numbers with Grandpa Jones, Roy Clark, Buck Owens, and other cast members.

In late 1973, his associates on the program were shocked to learn of the brutal killing of Stringbean and his wife, Estelle. They both were found shot to death in their home in the Nashville area. Apparently they had returned home after Stringbean's appearance on the *Opry* on November 11 to surprise a burglar, or burglars, who killed them and fled.

STUART, MARTY: *Singer, mandolinist, guitarist, songwriter, band leader (Hot Hillbilly Band, Rock & Roll Cowboys), record producer. Born Philadelphia, Mississippi, September 30, 1958.*

On his way to becoming a major star in the 1990s, Marty Stuart could look back to only a handful of years before when he'd become so discouraged he seriously considered leaving the music field. It wasn't that he'd shown no talent; after all, he'd been a sideman with some of the greatest artists in country music. But his hoped-for solo career had stalled and much less capable performers were topping the charts. On careful consideration, though, he realized music had been his life—he'd been a professional bandsman when he was thirteen—and, fortunately for him, he changed his mind and, before long, his goal was within his grasp.

As a child growing up in Philadelphia, Mississippi, he early realized he cared about traditional country music more than any of the other material on radio or TV. He also learned at an early age that he had a flair for instrumental skills, and could pick out complex tunes on the guitar or mandolin long before his teens. His musical interests were whetted by his immediate family. His grandfather, he recalled, was an old-time fiddle-player, an uncle was a Johnny Cash fan, and his father liked to play records by Flatt & Scruggs and country string bands. When a cousin offered him a Beatles album, he turned him down flat.

He got his first guitar at age nine and over the next few years learned to play that instrument quite well and the mandolin even better. When he was twelve he got the chance to tour with the Sullivan Family gospel string band, and performed with them at Pentecostal church revivals and bluegrass festivals. His travels took him to Bill Monroe's Bean Blossom Festival, where his path first crossed that of his idol, Lester Flatt. He told Colin Escott ("The Gospel According to Marty," *The Journal of Country Music,* June 1992), "I stood by his bus all afternoon waiting for him. It was a walk of an eighth or a quarter of a mile from his bus to the stage, and I walked behind him, studying him. I knew I belonged in that world."

When that golden summer ended, Marty really had to grit his teeth to return to school. But fate intervened and he didn't stay long. He told Karen Schoemer of *The New York Times* ("Marty Stuart Doesn't Need a Big Hat to be Country," July 12, 1992), "Nobody in my school knew who Bill Monroe was, or Lester Flatt and Earl Scruggs, and barely Johnny Cash. Nobody spoke that language. I proceeded to get myself kicked out. The thing that broke it all down was that I was reading a country music magazine inside my history book. The history teacher came up behind me. She slapped it out of my hand and said, 'If you get your mind off the trash and get it onto history, you might make something of yourself.' To which the genius here replied, 'I'm more interested in making history than I am learning about it.'"

Helped by Roland White, then with the Flatt group (and previously a founding member of the Kentucky Colonels) Marty got the chance to demonstrate his mandolin dexterity for Lester, who offered the then-thirteen-year-old a job. With his parents' grudging approval, Stuart became a regular with the band in 1971 and stayed with it until Flatt's death in 1979. (Later his family relocated to Nashville to be closer to their precocious son.)

The years with Flatt shaped Marty's future approach to his music. He recalled, "One show in particular made a mark on my career. We were playing Michigan State. The opening act was Gram Parsons and Emmylou Harris, then Lester, then the Eagles. That showed me you could play country music and just stand and do what you do. We were Martians to this audience, but they loved us."

As he noted to Chris Gill of *Guitar Player* ("21st Century Rock & Roll Cowboy," April 1994), "That night I saw that country music and rock & roll were the same thing. I'd heard 'Blue Moon of Kentucky,' and I thought that the tempos we played at in a bluegrass band were just as fiery as 'Jumpin' Jack Flash.' But I knew it was going to be a long time before I ever saw that whole thing come into focus. I saw what was trying to go on, and that's the track I've always stuck with. It's what I believe in."

After Lester Flatt's death, Johnny Cash was one of the artists Marty called to help in a tribute to his mentor. The phone call triggered an acquaintance that led to Johnny's asking Stuart to join his backing band, which Marty did from 1980 to 1986. At the same time, Stuart was trying to develop a solo career. In 1979, his first ef-

fort was an album released on his own label that had little or no impact. He followed that in the early 1980s with a more ambitious project, where he gained musical support from Doc and Merle Watson, Earl Scruggs, and Cash. That album, *Busy Bee Cafe,* was released on the Sugar Hill label in 1982. An excellent collection, it won praise from fellow artists, but few sales. (It was reissued on CD a decade later, when Stuart's solo career was on the upswing).

Besides touring with Cash, Stuart's activities as a sideman included appearances in the early 1980s with other legendary figures in country history. Those he performed with included Doc and Merle Watson (whose concerts, he said, gave him the most fun in his life onstage) and fiddling virtuoso Vassar Clements.

In 1986, Marty left the Cash band to apply all his energies to his career. His prime goal was a major-label contract, and he finally won one from Rick Blackburn of Columbia Records. His debut on Columbia, *Marty Stuart,* came out in 1986 and produced a chart hit, "Arlene," but had only mediocre sales. Marty was abruptly dropped and company officials decided not to release the second album (*Let There Be Country*) he'd been working on. He never concealed his bitterness about the incident.

By the time he'd signed with the label, he told Colin Escott, the company philosophy had changed from the days when Cash, Flatt & Scruggs, and the like were the bellwethers. "There weren't any creative geniuses and there wasn't any loyalty. If you're selling, you're selling—if you ain't, you're out. They gave me a quarter million dollars to learn the record industry, so I don't have any real regrets, though I wish they'd stood beside me through at least one more record. It was a good cold shower." He noted that there were five songs in the unreleased collection that in time became hits for other performers.

After his Columbia experience, Marty felt creatively and emotionally spent. At one point in 1987, he told Chris Gill, "I wanted to say, 'Done.' I tried everything. If I'd had 'Achy Breaky Heart' with 'Your Cheatin' Heart' on the flipside, I couldn't have gotten arrested in this town. I told my mom, 'I quit.' She let me go through my whole speech and said, 'Right. What are you going to do?' I thought about it and said, 'I'd better get back to work.'"

As always, he had no lack of requests to do session work and he did back many of the major projects of the period, including Highwaymen tracks and the reunion of Sun artists Roy Orbison, Carl Perkins, Jerry Lee Lewis, and Johnny Cash, but he still had a lingering feeling of depression in 1988. The turning point this time, he said, was finding an old Sullivan Family album he'd bought eighteen years before and hadn't played for some time. The album cheered him up and, surprisingly, Jerry Sullivan called to ask if Marty could suggest a mandolin player for a weekend concert. Marty volunteered himself and went on to produce a new album for the group, *A Joyful Noise,* that was eventually issued in 1991.

By then, Marty had signed a new major label agreement, this time with MCA Records. His debut album, *Hillbilly Rock,* came out in 1990. It sold moderately well and provided three singles that made the charts, the title song, "Cry Cry Cry," and "Western Girls." His next release in 1991, *Tempted,* did even better, selling more album copies and providing four charted singles, the title track, "Little Things," "Til I Found You," and "Burn Me Down," the last a 1965 Eddie Miller song updated with some new lyrics and music by Marty. With the heartfelt approval of his country music peers, by then Marty had finally earned his place in the entertainment spotlight. Besides being featured on major TV programs and talk shows, he embarked on a phenomenally successful tour with Travis Tritt in 1992 called the "No Hats Tour." Their duet of "This One's Gonna Hurt You (for a Long, Long Time)," the title track from Marty's third album, helped propel it to upper *Billboard* chart levels on the way to earning him his first gold-record award from the R.I.A.A. (The single peaked at number six in *Radio & Records* the week of July 24, 1992. Earlier Marty's solo single, "Burn Me Down," went to the same position.)

In the 1992 Country Music Association Awards voting, Stuart and Tritt were nominated for Vocal Event of the Year. Later, Marty wound up one of his most satisfying career years with another hit single, "Now That's Country," in top-chart positions in November.

During 1993, Marty joined with other major country artists in recording the Ray Benson album project, *Asleep at the Wheel Tribute to the Music of Bob Wills & The Texas Playboys,* which was nominated by the CMA for 1994 Album of the Year. The album also received notices in other polls including the Grammy Awards. Marty also participated in another concept project, MCA's *Rhythm, Country & Blues,* a best-selling release in 1993–94 and also a CMA nominee for 1994 Album of the Year. Marty also took part in the nationwide concert tour for the last-named release, which showcased duets between country stars and major performers in the soul and R&B genres.

Stuart's fourth MCA collection, *Love and Luck,* co-produced by Marty and Tony Brown, was issued in early 1994. It included the original Stuart composition, "That's What Love's About," another song, "Oh What a Silent Night," cowritten with Harlan Howard, and a compelling blend of other ballads and up-tempo material, but it wasn't the major seller his third album had been. In early 1995, MCA issued the greatest-hits album, *The Marty Party Hit Pack,* which appeared in the *Billboard* Top 40 soon after.

Though his career prospered in the 1990s, Marty realized he was still fighting an uphill battle because of

his belief in maintaining the true roots of his favorite type of music. As he commented to Karen Schoemer, "Why is country so big these days? It's the reason Long John Silver sells more fish than the catfish house on the edge of town; they've succeeded in making fish taste not so much like fish. It's the same with country. I hear some authentic country music on the radio today, but most of it's glossed-over pop. It takes more than that to really sustain in country music."

On November 30, 1995, Marty was one of the artists featured in the taped tribute to the Grand Ole Opry's 70th anniversary, telecast on CBS in January 1996. A few months later, Marty performed on the Academy of Country Music's NBC-TV awards show on April 24. During those months, Marty and Travis Tritt prepared a new music video (and single) of "Honky Tonkin's What I Do Best" for MCA and worked out plans for a major concert series in the summer and fall called the Double Trouble tour. Their collaboration on the song earned them a nomination from CMA Awards voters for Vocal Event of the Year.

STUCKEY, NAT: *Singer, guitarist, songwriter. Born Cass County, Texas, December 17, 1938; died Nashville, Tennessee, August 24, 1988.*

In general terms, some of the major early milestones in Nat Stuckey's career could be compared to those of the late Jim Reeves. Both came from east Texas, both first won attention as disc jockeys on station KWKH in Shreveport, Louisiana, and as performers on the network country show *Louisiana Hayride.* However, the similarities stop there. Stuckey, very much his own man, made a conscious effort to insure that his vocal style differed from Reeves. As he said, "I always felt complimented when people told me I sounded like Jim Reeves, but that's also why I had to change my style." And, of course, Stuckey's career blossomed years after the fatal plane crash that claimed Reeves' life.

Stuckey, whose formal name is Nathan Wright Stuckey II, grew up in Cass County, where country & western was revered by most of his family and friends. "An uncle taught me most of what I know about playing the guitar and the rest I sort of picked up myself. I've never had any formal training. I had a semester of voice at Arlington State College where I took the two-year course leading to an associate degree in radio and television."

After completing the course, he naturally strove to get into the radio/TV industry, which led to his ultimately joining KWKH in the 1960s. His experience performing at small clubs and with local bands back home gave him an in to a spot on the *Louisiana Hayride.* In the mid-1960s, he gained a recording contract from Shreveport-based Paula Records, a relationship which quickly bore fruit for both parties.

For Paula, he soon proved both a regional and national success. During 1967 and 1968, Nat placed six singles on the charts, including one that made the national top 10. These included "Oh Woman" and "All My Tomorrows" in 1967 and "My Can Do Can't Keep Up with My Want To" in 1968. He also had a charted album for Paula in 1967, *Nat Stuckey Sings*. Some of his other Paula hits were "Leave This One Alone" and one of his compositions most covered by other artists, "Sweet Thing." Among his other often-recorded compositions of the 1960s and early 1970s were "Pop a Top," "Don't You Believe Her," "Waitin' in Your Welfare Line," "Adorable Woman," and "The First Day."

Stuckey took another page from Reeves' book in 1968 when he signed a new recording contract with RCA and moved to Nashville. He rewarded his new label with chart hits on his debut single, "Plastic Saddle" and "Joe and Mabel's 12th Street Bar and Grill." RCA, which had bought up some of his material from Paula, released his debut LP *Nat Stuckey Sings* in late 1968. This was followed by a string of album releases such as *Sunday Morning with Nat Stuckey and Connie Smith* (3/70); *Old Man Willis* (5/70); *Country Fever* (10/70); *She Wakes Me with a Kiss* (4/71); *Only a Woman Like Me* (8/71); and *Forgive Me for Calling You Darling* at year end. During those years he placed a number of singles on the country lists, including "She Wakes Me Every Morning" in late 1970 and early 1971.

In the late 1960s and early 1970s he also became one of an increasing number of country artists who brought their talents to the attention of European audiences. His fourth tour to Europe in the fall of 1970 was made in company with Dottie West and Hank Snow.

In the mid-1970s, Nat switched to MCA Records and placed a sizable number of albums and singles on the charts for that organization. The singles included "The Way He's Treated You" in the summer of 1976; "That's All She Ever Said Except Goodbye" in the fall of 1976; "Buddy I Lied" in the summer of 1977; "I'm Going Home to Face the Music" in late 1977; and, in 1978, "The Days of Sand and Shovels."

Nat's performing career was affected in the 1980s by the trends away from "traditional" country inspired by a growing contingent of young rock-influenced country artists. Stuckey earned much of his income in that decade by working on commercial jingles. Still only in his fifties, he was diagnosed with lung cancer in July 1988 and died barely a month later. His recording credits by then included thirty-five hit singles and some of his compositions continued to be recorded by new performers while also showing up on retrospective albums of the careers of artists who had top-10 successes with some of his material such as Buck Owens ("Waitin' in Your Welfare Line"); Ray Price ("Don't You Believe Her"); Jim Ed Brown ("Pop a Top"); and Loretta Lynn and Ernest Tubb, who had a best-selling duet of Nat's "Sweet Thing."

SUPERNAW, DOUG: *Singer, guitarist, songwriter. Born Bryan, Texas, c. 1959.*

As a member of what might be called "The New Faces of the 1990s," a development that included such new stars as John Michael Montgomery, Martina McBride, Brooks & Dunn, Tim McGraw, and others, Doug Supernaw played a role in an upheaval that had radical impact on country music. The onrush of dynamic young performers pushed many long-established stars into the background and simultaneously helped expand the field to new heights of financial, if not necessarily creative, success.

Supernaw himself wasn't necessarily overjoyed at the field's new directions. He said at one point, "I made a commitment to country when I was born. I like country to be country, pop to be pop, blues to be blues—the main thing is, I like music if it's got heart and soul. I love tear-jerkin' music—George Jones, Vern Gosdin, Keith Whitley, Gene Watson."

His devotion to country music came from his mother, an Illinois coal miner's daughter who loved it from her childhood. His father, an Oklahoma-born oil research scientist who worked for companies like Texaco, strongly favored classical music and later wasn't too enthusiastic about his son's eventual career choice. That mix of influences, Doug said, caused him to call himself "a sophisticated redneck."

He was born in Bryan, Texas, but his family moved to Houston when he was five. He told *Radio & Records* that he had a passing interest in music as a child. "I wrote my first song at seven, but I never really learned to play any instruments when I was young. In the band in seventh grade, they gave me one of those kettle drums you had to hit twice. I had two notes—boom and boom."

During those years the family emphasis was on sports. Supernaw played golf, football, basketball, and baseball while still in elementary school, and continued with considerable ability in his high school years. His father was an avid golfer and Doug noted, "I lived on a golf course from the time I was 10."

His golf prowess got him a golf scholarship to the University of St. Thomas in Houston. However, he had resumed songwriting in earnest during his high school years, an interest that became more important than hitting a little white ball with a variety of slender clubs. Doug reminisced, "My economics class was good for about 20 songs. I sat right in the front row. They thought I was taking notes."

He hadn't been in college for an extended time when he decided to enter a singing contest at a local club. He won second place, but stayed up so long he overslept the next morning and missed a golf team meeting. He was thrown off the team and had to quit school. It was 1979 and he found work with a local group called the Occasions. He was lead vocalist for that band for two years, and also assembled a band of his own.

By itself, performing didn't earn him enough money to keep body and soul together. After enrolling briefly in Texas Tech, he got a job working on an oil rig near Dime Box, Texas. In the course of that two-year stint, he said, "I wrote a lot of good songs on the rig; that's where I first started to get serious about my guitar playing." For a while, Doug worked as a booking agent for the Arena Theater in Houston, and that later led to a job as producer of Ricky Van Shelton's first East Texas tour. Among artists he booked in the mid-1980s were Willie Nelson and Reba McEntire.

He didn't abandon his performing hopes, and made his first foray to Nashville in 1984. He told *R&R*, "At that time in '84, the singers in Nashville were older and I don't think I looked the part. They were almost afraid of you if you were younger, so I just went back to Texas and kept booking shows and playing on weekends."

He became more confident in 1987 and returned to Nashville to see if he could place some of his songs. He made several trips between Texas and Music City before he felt he might be ready to focus fully on big-time prospects and in 1988 took up residence in Tennessee. But he suffered further frustrations. For instance, at one point he was offered a recording contract, with the proviso that he change his name. He turned it down, because, as he said later, he was "proud of my name and had no intention of performing under a pseudonym."

In 1989, he again went back to Houston, where he organized a new band that began to attract attention among country adherents in the region. Interest in the group became strong enough that it gained a Coors Light Beer company concert sponsorship, even though the band had no label agreement. Word of this began to filter back to Nashville, and this time when Supernaw sent out demo tapes offers began to come in. He finally signed with BNA Entertainment in 1992, which released his first single, "Honky Tonkin' Fool," in early 1993 and his debut album, *Red and Rio Grande* in April 1993. The album contained two tracks written or cowritten by Doug, the title song and "Carousel."

Backed by Doug's extensive touring as opening act or guest band at honky-tonks around the U.S., the album made the *Billboard* list during the summer of 1993, peaking at number twenty-seven and still on them a year later in June 1994. The single "Reno" peaked at number four in *R&R* the week of August 20, 1993. Later that year BNA released the single "I Don't Call Him Daddy," a poignant story of a divorced father's relationship with his son, and it soon became one of the year's major successes. It reached number one in both *Billboard* and *R&R* in December 1993. In 1994, the album spawned other chartmakers, such as the title song and "State Fair." The latter two stayed on the charts a number of months without making topmost

levels. During the first half of 1995, he had another hit single "What'll You Do About Me."

Supernaw was enthusiastic about his newfound success, and left no doubt that he was enjoying every minute of it. As he told Teresa George of CMA's *Close Up* magazine (March 1994), one of his pet peeves was star performers complaining about the stresses of the music business. "We don't have it hard. I mean that's a crock. Hard was my bass player working 10 hours a day for HL&P (Houston Light & Power) reading meters and then going to play for four hours and then getting up at six in the morning and going to read meters. That was hard. That's what all the bands out there that are not signed do. What we do is get on the bus and play for an hour and a half. Yeah, we're away from our family and stuff, but it's easy."

He also promised to keep in mind the importance of the public to a performer's success (though whether he could continue to be as available if he reached superstar status was something he didn't yet have to address). He told Teresa George, "I did a tire store in Wyoming and there were 700 or 800 people. When we started getting toward the end of the line, people started thanking me for signing autographs. I said, 'I've been here for three hours. That guy has been there changing lug nuts for 18.' What would I rather be doing? Maybe I'll piss every other artist off, but I don't buy that. I don't think it's a chore."

In late 1995 and early 1996, Doug had the single "Not Enough Hours in the Night" moving up the charts. His next album, *You Still Got Me*, came out at the start of 1996 and was on the charts for several months, but never reached upper positions.

SWEETHEARTS OF THE RODEO, THE: *Vocal and instrumental duo, Janis Gill, born Torrance, California, March 1, 1954 (vocals, guitar, songwriter); Kristine Arnold, born California, October 28, c. mid-1950s (vocals, guitar).*

For a number of years Vince Gill was better known as the husband of Janis Gill, one half of the very successful 1980s sister bluegrass act, the Sweethearts of the Rodeo. Then in the 1990s the tables suddenly turned, as Vince moved toward superstar status and the Sweethearts' fortunes seemed to decline. Still, the sister team could look back on a substantial body of record successes and the possibility that new creative accomplishments might lie ahead.

Janis Oliver and her younger sister were born and bred in the South Bay region of Los Angeles, California, and spent their formative years in Manhattan Beach, just below the site of Los Angeles International Airport. That part of the U.S. has never been closely identified with country music, although it always had a number of country music clubs and well-attended festivals in outlying areas that featured folk and bluegrass performers.

However, the main emphasis in the late 1960s and early 1970s, when the girls were in their teens, was on rock and roll. Janis recalled that a lot of high school classmates were involved in rock groups, but she and her sister, who learned to play proficient guitar, focused on country and bluegrass (with an ear for folk/country groups like the Byrds). The first incentive for avoiding the rock format, Janis said, was the desire to do "anything to stand out. The funny thing is, we realized after a while that we thoroughly enjoyed it."

After high school in the mid-1970s, they gained performance experience on the West Coast folk and bluegrass circuit. Like other hopefuls, they made demo tapes and tried to get L.A.-based record company executives interested, but to no avail. But working the bluegrass circuit brought other rewards; it was there Janis met her husband-to-be.

Oklahoma-born Vince Gill had been playing with a Kentucky based bluegrass band when he accepted a bid to move to Los Angeles to join Sundance, a group led by the excellent bluegrass fiddle player Byron Berline. One night in 1977 at a show in a Redondo Beach, California, venue where Sundance was the headliner, the Sweethearts were the opening act. Gill told *People* magazine ("Vince and Janis Gill," June 10, 1991) that they passed each other on the way to the stage. "I caught her eye, and she caught my eye, but I don't think she liked my eye as much as I liked hers."

For almost three years afterward, he said, he asked her to date on several occasions, but without success. "I guess I was a pretty big hillbilly to her." One stumbling block, Janis said later, was the fact that Vince was three years younger than she was; moreover, he already had a steady girlfriend, and she had a beau as well. But by 1980, both those relationships had ended, and when Vince asked her hand in marriage she agreed. By then Kristine had also married, her husband being songwriter Leonard Arnold.

That was one reason the sisters retired from music in the early 1980s. The other, Kristine said, was that "Janis and I had been beating down doors trying to get somebody interested in our music in L.A. for years and we frankly were burned out, and we thought, 'I don't want to do this anymore. I want to have my family.'" In the Gills' case their early 1980s addition was a daughter named Jenny who in the 1990s was playing keyboards and sometimes singing with Vince on TV.

In 1983, the Gills moved to Nashville as Vince sought new career opportunities. He did find work as a bandsman and sometime recording-session musician, but the main breakthrough came for the sisters. The Nashville scene had an exciting impact on Janis. "There was so much going on in this town at that time. It just blew me away. Everybody was writing, everybody was producing. And I got so enthusiastic about the whole thing, I thought it would have been cheating ourselves out of a chance not to try it again."

Kristine noted, "Janis called me up after a few months and said, 'I think you should move out here. I think that if we ever had a chance, this is where it's going to be.' It didn't take any convincing."

Soon after being reunited, the Sweethearts of the Rodeo (a name taken from a Byrds album) were entered in the Wrangler Country Showdown, the largest country music talent contest. They survived the early rounds and reached the regional finals in Nashville, knowing the audience would include many important Music City record industry executives. Kristine remembered Janis told her the night before, "Kristine, I have this feeling, if we become state champs, we're gonna win this thing."

They did win, singing an original by Janis, "Gotta Get Away," and before the week was out were signed by Columbia. Their initial single, a remake of the Everly Brothers' "Hey Doll Baby," became a top-20 chart hit. This encouraged Columbia to issue their debut album, *Sweethearts of the Rodeo,* which spent some time on the charts and provided more hits like "Chains of Gold," "Midnight Girl/Sunset Town," and "Since I Found You." The duo also turned out their first three videos while soon keeping busy with TV appearances and intensive live appearances. Among artists they performed with were George Jones, Los Lobos, Bob Dylan, and the Fabulous Thunderbirds. Kristine expressed satisfaction "that the Sweethearts are able to get in front of a George Jones crowd and please those people and get in front of a Bob Dylan crowd and please those people." Their popularity also transcended national boundaries as Britain's *Country Song Roundup* named them the Most Promising New International Act.

Their second album, *One Night, One Time,* came out in the late 1980s and, besides making the charts itself, spawned more singles hits, including the title song, a cover of a Los Lobos number. The collection provided three top-10 hits, one a remake of the Beatles' "I Feel Fine." The others were "Satisfy You" and "Blue to the Bone."

While Janis's career blossomed, Vince was singing backing vocals for many top artists and making some inroads as a songwriter. His wife naturally worried about the pressures on their marriage. Janis told *People* the fact her career took off so quickly caused her to be "pulled in a million different directions, and it was tough getting into the rhythm and the rhyme of a life like that. That's upsetting to a household, especially when your husband is trying to do the same thing."

She said she used to pray for his career to advance, partly because she felt he deserved it and partly because she felt it would help their marriage. Vince said, "I was never bitter toward her for her success and never will be. I was probably frustrated for lack of my own and that might have got perceived by her and other people as not taking it as I should."

He told *USA Today* later, when he was an established star ("Fame Calls Gill's Name," September 29, 1993), "People were naturally looking for me to be upset. But she's my best pal in the world, and she was a singer and a guitar player long before I met her." The Sweethearts' third Columbia album, *Buffalo Zone,* came out at the start of the 1990s and provided the hit single "This Heart," a fast-paced recording that reached number fifteen in *Radio & Records* the week of March 23, 1990. A unique aspect of the song, Kristine said, was her lead vocal. "In the past we always went in together and sang lead and harmony at the same time. This time I went in and sang the song the way I felt it should be sung and then Janis came in with the harmony." A similar pattern was followed on the other tracks, she added, "So the songs are freer, they're not so structured." In 1991, they added to their list of charted singles with "Hard Headed Man."

However, overall, the album didn't have the impact on the critics or charts as the duo's previous releases. Their next album, *Sisters,* issued in 1992, was even less successful and proved to be their farewell collection for Columbia. In reviews of that album, some writers did take note of Janis's playful take on her husband in the track "Man of My Dreams" whose lyrics, as Steve Pond noted in *US* (January 1993), went, in part, "He won't pick up his clothes or wash the car/But he sure can sing and play guitar/He can watch TV for hours and hours/He never thinks of bringing flowers/He's the man of my dreams."

Pond asked Vince whether he'd taken the hint about bouquets to which Gill replied, "Afraid not. I just never think of all that good stuff. But I'm taking her to Hawaii tomorrow. That's being a pretty good guy."

The respect the duo had from the country music community was shown by its repeated nominations for Country Music Association Vocal Duo of the Year. The first nomination came in 1988 and the girls were finalists in that category every year from then through 1996.

Outwardly, the marriage of Janis and Vince Gill appeared an idyllic relationship, but apparently over the years strains built up between the two. In any case, in early 1997 Janis filed for divorce, requesting custody of their daughter.

TANNER, GID: *Fiddler, singer, bandleader (the Skillet Lickers). Born Thomas Bridge, near Monroe, Georgia, June 6, 1885; died Dacula, Georgia, May 13, 1960.*

One group a country & western fan of the 1920s and 1930s was sure to know was Gid Tanner and his Skillet Lickers. Tanner organized his band soon after becoming one of the first recorded artists in the country field,

and before it disbanded in the 1930s, the group had made 565 records. Few of these are available today, but those that are stand the test of time surprisingly well. This is evident, for example, from Skillet Licker renditions of "Ida Red" and "On Tanner's Farm" on the RCA Victor LP *Smoky Mountain Ballads.*

Like many country greats, James Gideon Tanner was born on a farm, maintaining his chicken farm in Georgia right up to his death. Young Gid fell in love with local fiddle music almost as soon as he could do chores on his parents' farm. At fourteen, when an uncle died and left him a fiddle, he lost no time in learning how to play it. In his teens he was already making a reputation for himself playing at local dances and fairs. In the 1920s he began to branch out, taking part successfully in several of the famous fiddle contests of Fiddlin' John Carson.

Thus when a Columbia Records' talent scout moved through the area looking for artists to make the firm's first country records, Tanner was a name that he heard much about. He asked Gid to come to New York, and Gid took George Riley Puckett with him. The two made their first records on March 7, 1924. The recordings were well enough received that Tanner's name became known across the South. Soon after, he formed his Skillet Lickers. Puckett (born Alpharetta, Georgia, 1890; died College Park, Georgia, July 13, 1946) became lead singer of the band.

Through the late 1920s and the early 1930s, the group was one of the most popular in country music. From 1926 to 1929 it included, besides Tanner and Puckett, Clayton McMichen and Tanner's brother Arthur. McMichen remained with Tanner until 1931. Various other musicians played with the band in the 1930s, including Tanner's son, Gordon, and Jimmie Tarleton. In the 1930s, the Skillet Lickers were featured on radio stations in many parts of the United States, including Covington, Kentucky; Cleveland, Ohio; Chicago; and Atlanta.

The top hit of the Skillet Lickers was "Down Yonder." Other hits included "The Wreck of the Southern Old 97" and "Sally Goodin'."

A typical arrangement of Tanner's group was described in *Who's Who in Country Music** as follows: "[The band used] two fiddles, often doubling each other at the unison for lead, a back-up guitar and a banjo. All four members sang and Puckett usually took the lead." *(See also McMichen, Clayton.)*

---

* *1965–66 edition, published by Thurston Moore, Colorado.*

TARLETON, JIMMIE: *Singer, guitarist, banjoist, harpist, songwriter. Born Chesterfield County, South Carolina, May 8, 1892; died 1973.*

An amazingly gifted musician, Jimmie Tarleton provided American folk and country music with a legend and some of the most famous songs in the folk-country repertoire. Those who heard him play never forgot it, even those who attended some of his performances in the mid-1960s, when he came out of a long, enforced retirement. Had Tarleton been born twenty years later, he might have become wealthy and famous in his lifetime. As it was, he settled for a flat fee of seventy-five dollars for his most famous compositions, "Columbus Stockade Blues" and "Birmingham Jail."

Johnny James Rimbert Tarleton was born on a farm near the Pedee River in Chesterfield County, South Carolina. His father played a homemade banjo and taught Jimmie to play when he was six (he was also studying the French harp). His mother sang many old hill-country ballads, including such songs as "Barney McCoy," "Kitty Wells," "Lowe Bonnie," and "Wish I Was a Single Girl Again." Jimmie learned these and sang and recorded them later in life. By the time he was nine, he had also mastered the guitar. Jimmie enjoyed the evening family sing-alongs, and as he grew up, he performed at local dances, barn raisings, and other events.

By the time Jimmie was in his teens, he had decided to try to play professionally, moving north during the World War I decade and working at odd jobs while performing nights in bars and cafes in New York and nearby Hoboken. After several years of this, he headed west, working as a textile mill hand in Texas, Oklahoma, and Arkansas. In his spare time, he picked up whatever he could in the way of dates at local honky-tonks.

In the early 1920s, things were looking up a little for country performers, who were in demand for rural fairs and traveling medicine shows. The mid-1920s found him playing with groups in the Columbus, Georgia, region. In 1926, he teamed up with singer-guitarist Tom Darby (who grew up in Columbus, Georgia, and was the same age as Tarleton). The record industry was beginning to find a market for country music and was looking for new artists. This opened the door to Tarleton and Darby, who gained a record date with Columbia Records, and on April 5, 1927, they recorded "Down on Florida on a Hog" and "Birmingham Town." They were asked to come back several more times that year. On November 10, they recorded "Columbus Stockade Blues" and "Birmingham Jail," both written by Jimmie, who had composed the latter some years earlier after spending time in the jail for moonshining. The boys were offered a royalty agreement, but Darby talked Tarleton into settling for seventy-five dollars for both songs.

Tarleton continued to record for several labels over the next few years, including Columbia (1927–30), RCA Victor in 1932, and American Record Corp. in 1933. Tarleton's output on RCA was solo; his recordings on the other two labels were made with Darby. He recorded more than seventy-five songs, many of which were made into major hits by others. During the 1920s

and early 1930s he toured the country with many major artists, including Gid Tanner and the Skillet Lickers, Arthur Smith, the Delmore Brothers, and Jimmie Rodgers.

Life was far from easy, though. In 1932, he was caught riding the rods home from a recording session in New York for RCA Victor. A short term in an Atlanta jail resulted in the song "Atlanta Prison Blues." In 1931, he had to work at odd jobs, including a short period as a mill hand in East Rockingham, North Carolina, where he worked with the Dixon brothers. All three artists traded song material and instrumental techniques.

Since the Depression had ruined much of the country-music market, Tarleton retired from an active music career in 1935. For the next twenty years he worked at various jobs, finally ending up in Phoenix City, Alabama, in the mid-1960s. There he was discovered by folk music collectors who wanted to discuss some of his great early country recordings. One collector, Gene Earle, taped some of Tarleton's music in December 1963 for a proposed LP. This, in turn, led to an invitation from the owner of the Ash Grove in Los Angeles. In August 1965, at his week's engagement in Los Angeles, Tarleton showed cheering audiences that he was still a superlative artist.

In the mid-1960s, besides performing at a number of venues on the folk circuit, he also made several appearances at the Newport Folk Festival. His new solo recordings finally came out on a Testament Records release. Some of his earlier work with Darby was reissued during that period on the Old Timey label. However, as the folk music boom began to be edged aside by the rise of rock bands like the Beatles and Rolling Stones and the impact of the soul movement, opportunities for Tarleton began to decline again. His death in 1973 was preceded by that of his longtime partner two years earlier.

TEXAS TORNADOS: *Vocal and instrumental group, Freddy Fender, born San Benito, Texas, June 4, 1937 (vocals, guitar); Doug Sahm, born San Antonio, Texas, November 6, 1941 (vocals, guitar); Flaco Jimenez, born Central Texas, March 11, 1939 (vocals, accordion); Augie Meyers, born St. Hedwig, Texas c. late 1930s (vocals, guitar, keyboards, bajo sexto). Group disbanded in 1994, reassembled in 1996.*

For an all-too-brief time, four unique and first-rate talents joined together to form a band whose music summed up all the elements of Texas styles, blending country, blues, rock, and homegrown Tex-Mex. The band might have seemed a little long in the tooth, with a combined age of over 200 years, but their music, for those fortunate to catch one of their live performances, provided a freshness and joie de vivre matching any of the younger audience favorites of the early 1990s.

Freddy Fender, born Baldemar Huerta in a Rio Grande Valley town, became one of the relatively few

Mexican-Americans to make it big in country music. He had plenty of hard times battling personal problems like drugs, alcohol, and national racist stereotyping, but he overcame those difficulties to score a string of country hits in the 1970s before again being waylaid by the excesses of stardom. Still, he slowly rebuilt his life and career in the 1980s and was ready for the opportunities of becoming part of a new all-star group.

The combination of Fender and Doug Sahm might have seemed a bit odd to some observers; Sahm was best known as a successful rocker with his sixties group the Sir Douglas Quintet, while Fender was normally thought of as a more traditional country artist. But Sahm had excellent country credits from his youth, and Fender had some rock and blues background.

In Sahm's case, he had been engrossed by country music as a child and had learned to play excellent steel guitar before he was in his teens. When only twelve, known as "Little Doug," his reputation extended well beyond Texas, and he was invited to exhibit his steel-guitar prowess on the *Grand Ole Opry* when he was thirteen. Among his early memories was sitting on Hank Williams, Sr.'s, knee during the country legend's last public performance in 1953.

Fender had played just about every type of music in his early dues-paying period, performing in dance halls and bars in the Louisiana-Texas area. He recalled using his tenor voice for lead vocals in a band that played black clubs in those still-segregated years. "We did go play at a few black clubs," he said. "It was easier for me to get into their places than it was for them to get into ours." He recalled being called "El Bebop Kid" by friends and fans around McAllen, Texas.

Flaco Jimenez became one of the most noted practitioners of one strain of Tex-Mex music in the world from the start of the 1980s on. As a child growing up in the San Antonio, Texas, region he heard his father Santiago and two friends, Valerio Longola and Narcisco Martinez, pioneer a style that combined Mexican Norteno music with polkas and waltzes preferred by German and Czech immigrants who settled in the central Texas hill country. The style became known as conjunto, and Jimenez played a major role in expanding its scope of interest not only across the U.S., but in many other parts of the globe.

He already had a regional hit with "Haste La Vista" in the 1950s, accompanying himself with a diatonic accordion, and went on to achieve the respect of fellow musicians that eventually brought him a Grammy Award for his 1986 Arhoolie Records album, *Ay Te Dejo en San Antonio,* chosen for Best Mexican-American Performance. In the mid-1970s, he became part of Ry Cooder's Chicken Skin Revue and played on the album of *Chicken Skin Music.* Cooder also had Jimenez play on the soundtrack for Jack Nicholson's 1982 movie, *The Border,* and he had a similar assignment for the movie *Extreme Prejudice.* His 1970s credits included an appearance in the 1974 documentary *Chula Fronteras* and during that and following decades performances on various TV shows included NBC's *Saturday Night Live* and Public Broadcasting System's *Austin City Limits.*

Augie Meyers credited his focus on singing and playing an instrument to the struggles of his youth, when his physical movements were sharply limited. "I had polio. I didn't walk until I was ten." When he was thirteen he began taking guitar lessons, employing the chord patterns to gain effective use of his left hand. Around that time, a black gospel pianist got him started on playing keyboards.

In his teens he began working with local acquaintances in various band combinations as was another local resident named Doug Sahm. Sahm became friends with Augie from going with his parents to shop at a grocery store run by Meyers's mother. Their exchanges, Meyers said, went something like, "Doug would say, 'Yeah, I got a band' and I'd say I got a band I'm working with. He was always on one side of town and I was on the other." After some years they became band mates in the Sir Douglas Quintet, and Meyers shared in the glory of hits like "She's About a Mover" and "Mendocino."

Though both went separate ways after the Sir Douglas Quintet broke up, with Meyers fronting his own band, the Western Headband, and Sahm doing solo work at times and assembling other bands at other times, they kept in touch. This eventually led to their becoming half of the Texas Tornados at the end of the 1980s.

The Tornados signed with Reprise Records' Texas office, which issued its debut album, *Texas Tornados,* in the summer of 1990. The album made the *Billboard* chart and stayed on through fall and winter, reaching the top 20 at one point. The single "Who Were You Thinking Of" made country charts, and "Adios Mexico" made Latin ones. The band played venues, mostly smaller ones, in all parts of the U.S. and Canada, winning appreciative response from their audiences. In the 1990 Grammy voting, announced on the February 20, 1991, awards telecast, the group received the Best Mexican-American Performance trophy for the album track "Soy De San Luis."

Follow-up recordings continued to provide very listenable and instrumentally challenging contents. The 1991 collection, *Zone of Our Own,* provided a single that made the top 20 in Mexico, "La Mucura." One problem, though, in an era of prearranged playlists was getting sufficient airplay to reach a broader cross-section of U.S. music fans. Steve Ciabottini, reviewing their 1993 Reprise release *Hangin' On by a Thread* in the *CMJ New Music Report,* enthused about the material, but worried about exposure.

As for the album, he wrote, "As old as each of them is . . . it's hard to believe the Texas Tornados are just getting warmed up. And while we're sure there's dozens of groups with graying temples playing similar material in the sawdust-floor clubs of Texas night after night, we'd bet our last cent that any of those bands would undoubtedly give the Tex nod to the Texas Tornados as the band to beat. The reason? With each new record, the Tornados create a batch of 'new' classics which makes you feel as if you're witnessing the birth of both rock 'n' roll and the Tex-Mex tumbleweeds ballad as the be-all and end-all of popular music."

Addressing radio programmers of album-oriented rock (part of the readership of this publication), he urged them, as they held the Tornados album in their hands "trying to figure out what they're supposed to do with it, here's your chance to turn folks (young and old) onto a band so damn cool, your audience just might insist you replace that *Grateful Dead Hour* with *Le Hora Del Tornados.*"

Yet, such appeals didn't change any fixed formats and, while far less deserving artists scored blockbuster successes, the Tornados remained a band with a devoted following, but not an enormous one. Whether it was for economic reasons or the desire to get away from the constant demands of touring, the group hung up its instruments in 1994 (though all four continued solo careers) but fortunately left behind a superb body of recorded work from their pre-1994 collaboration. Each also worked on separate recording efforts, one example being the Arista Texas release in the fall of 1994, *Flaco Jimenez.* Joining him on that disc were Raul Malo of The Mavericks, Lee Roy Parnell and Radney Foster. The album contained country and R&B type material, but still maintained the main focus on Jimenez's conjunto sound.

In late 1995, the four Tornados decided to get back together again and signed a new recording contract with Reprise Records Burbank, California, Division. The new album, *Four Aces,* prepared in studios in Austin, Texas, was released in June 1996 with the initial single Doug Sahm's composition "Little Bit Is Better Than Nada." Sahm also wrote the title track. Fender's contributions included the self-penned "In My Mind" and "Amor De Mi Vida."

THOMPSON, HANK: *Singer, guitarist, harmonica player, bandleader (Brazos Valley Boys). Born Waco, Texas, September 23, 1925. Elected to Country Music Hall of Fame in 1989.*

If anyone was heir to the mantle of Bob Wills in the post-World War II decades, it was Hank Thompson, whose big band sound played a prominent role in country & western music of the 1950s and 1960s. Thompson's stylings, though, were wider ranging, incorporating many of the new country sounds that came along from the late 1940s on thanks to such artists as Hank Williams, Sr. and Elvis. Although Thompson and his Brazos Valley Boys could play Wills' style "Western

swing," they were equally adept at honky-tonk music and "down home" country songs too.

As a boy growing up in Waco, Texas, in the early 1930s, Hank was influenced by everything from the then-popular Jimmie Rodgers 78s to the *Grand Ole Opry.* His first love instrumentally was the harmonica. Inspired by the growing number of western movies where the singing hero often strummed a guitar, he began to play that instrument as well. Gene Autry was a particular favorite.

In response to his request for a guitar, his parents finally bought a four-dollar model for him as a Christmas present. With that treasured instrument, Hank spent hours figuring out chord patterns and trying to emulate the guitar runs of some of the country & western stars of the day. This finally paid off in the early 1940s when he got a job performing in a Saturday morning youth program at a local theater that was broadcast on station WACO. A flour company liked him and sponsored him on a show called *Hank the Hired Hand.* After six months, and having gained his high school degree in January 1943, Hank enlisted in the U.S. Navy, where he remained for three years on a tour of duty that included extensive voyages throughout the South Pacific.

After his discharge he attended Princeton University in New Jersey for a time. (His college experience also included studies at Southern Methodist University and the University of Texas at Austin). After getting his fill of higher education, he returned to home base in Waco to do a noon show on station KWTX. Response to his efforts was so good, he put together his own band, named the Brazos Valley Boys. They soon became a popular attraction in shows and dances all over central Texas. Hank had written a number of original songs by then, some while in the Navy, and in 1946 recorded two of them on the local Globe Records label. The two releases, "Whoa Sailor" and "Swing Wide Your Gate of Love," did well, and he began to gain a following in other parts of the country. A number of country artists also recorded another of his compositions, "A Lonely Heart Knows."

Tex Ritter was one of Thompson's most enthusiastic listeners. He arranged an introduction for Hank to Capitol Records officials, who signed him in 1948, the beginning of an association that lasted until 1966 (though Capitol kept releasing Hank's LPs several years after that) and encompassed dozens of major hit recordings. In his first year on Capitol, Thompson turned out two major successes, "Humpty Dumpty Heart," a top-10 single, and "Today." In 1949, he had two more top-10 hits, a remake of "Whoa Sailor" and a new composition, "Green Light."

In the early 1950s, Hank had a number of records that made the charts, but none that gained the highest levels. His fortunes changed in 1952 with the top-10 hit "Waiting in the Lobby of Your Heart," cowritten with the long-time Brazos Valley Boys lead singer Billy

Gray. The same year, he achieved his first number-one-ranked record with "Wild Side of Life." In 1953, he had the top-10 hits "Wake Up Irene" and "No Help Wanted." He followed with a banner year in 1954, when he placed five singles in the country top 10: "Breakin' the Blues" (cowritten with Billy Gray and A. Blasingame), "Honky Tonk Girl" (cowritten with C. Harding), "New Green Light" (by Hank), "We've Gone Too Far (cowritten with B. Gray), and "You Can't Have My Love" (cowritten with Gray, Harding, and M. Roberts). The last-named record featured a duet between Billy Gray and a new vocalist soon to be a star in her own right, Wanda Jackson.

By the time those songs were being played on stations across the United States, Thompson had moved band headquarters from Texas to Lake Tenkiller in eastern Oklahoma. It was the same year (1953) that he and the band helped set attendance records at the Texas State Fair. The engagement became an annual event, and decades later Hank and his group still returned to headline there. During the 1950s and 1960s, the group performed at many other major fairs and rodeos across the nation and usually had extended appearances at Nevada hotels each year. The band also was featured on many TV shows over the years, including *The Jimmy Dean Show, The Tonight Show* with Johnny Carson, *American Swing Around,* NBC-TV's *Swingin' Country,* and the WGN *Barn Dance.* From the mid-1950s into the late 1970s, Hank often was on the road a good part of the year. In the mid-1960s, the band typically averaged 240 personal appearances annually, a pace that slowed somewhat in the 1970s. Those shows took Hank and the band to all fifty states, many major Canadian cities, and on a number of tours of the Far East and Europe.

On occasion, Thompson flew from one U.S. engagement to the next in his own plane. A licensed pilot, he had logged many flying hours by the late 1970s, when he owned a twin engine Cessna 310. It was sometimes his mode of transportation on hunting and fishing trips from his home in Sand Springs on the Keystone Reservoir in Oklahoma.

From the early 1950s to the early 1960s, Hank had one or more top-10 singles every year on Capitol except for 1957. Those included such originals as "Don't Take It Out on Me," and "Wildwood Flower" in 1955; "I'm Not Mad, Just Hurt" in 1956; "I've Run Out of Tomorrows" in 1959 (cowritten with L. Compton and V. Mizi); and "A Six Pack to Go" (cowritten with J. Lowe and D. Hart) in 1960. He also had top-10 hits by other writers: "Squaws Along the Yukon" in 1958 and "Oklahoma Hills" in 1961.

Hank was represented by many albums on Capitol from the late 1940s to late 1960s. Among his early and mid-1950s LPs were *Songs of the Brazos Valley, North of the Rio Grande, All Time Hits,* and *Hank.* In the late 1950s, releases included *Hank's Dance Ranch* (6/58),

Favorite Waltzes (2/59), and *Breakin' In* (4/59). He led off the 1960s with the album *Most of All* (5/60) and followed with *This Broken Heart* (1/61), *Old Love Affair* (9/61), *At the Golden Nugget* (11/61), *No. 1* (7/62), *Cheyenne Days* (1/63), *Best* (5/63), *State Fair of Texas* (10/63), *Golden Hits* (5/66), *Luckiest Heartache* (4/66), and *Breakin' the Rules* (10/66). Although he left Capitol in 1966, there were still plenty of recordings left for a number of new releases, including *Best* (3/67), *Countrypolitan Sound* (4/67), *Gold Standard Collection* (5/67), and *Just an Old Flame* (10/67).

By the time Thompson signed with Warner Bros. in 1966, he had rolled up record sales on Capitol of over 30 million albums and had placed around 100 records on the hit charts. For most of his tenure with Capitol, the Brazos Valley Boys were ranked number-one country band in many important polls. The group held that position on both *Billboard* and *Cash Box* magazine lists thirteen consecutive years, from 1953 to 1966.

He still had pulling power in the mid-1960s even though country swing bands were generally losing favor. His first single on Warner Bros., for instance, made national charts, as did the LP of that title, *Where Is the Circus.* However, the new association didn't prove comfortable for the parties involved, and in 1968 he signed with ABC/Dot. This alignment still held firm over a decade later.

Thompson was on the ABC/Dot roster when he celebrated his twenty-fifth year as a recording artist in 1971. In honor of that landmark, ABC issued a two-record set, *Hank Thompson's 25th Anniversary Album.* Other releases on the label in the late 1960s and early 1970s included *Hank Thompson Sings the Gold Standards, (Hank Thompson) On Tap, in the Can, or in the Bottle, Smokey the Bar, Hank Thompson Salutes Oklahoma, Hank Thompson's Brazos Valley Boys, Next Time I Fall in Love (I Won't),* and *Cab Driver.* His mid- and late-1970s LPs included *Hank Thompson's Greatest Hits, Volume 1, Kindly Keep It Country, A Six Pack to Go, Hank Thompson Sings the Hits of Nat King Cole, The Thompson Touch,* and *Doin' My Thing.*

While almost all his material came out on ABC or Capitol, some of his recordings were presented on releases (mostly reissues) on other labels. Among those were *Country Greats* on Paramount, *New Rovin' Gambler* on Pickwick, and *You Always Hurt the One You Love* on Hilltop.

Although Hank wasn't the dominant force in country music in the late 1970s that he'd been a decade or two earlier, he still commanded the respect of musical peers and a sizable number of country fans as well. Among other honors that came his way in the second half of the 1970s was his selection by *Country Music Magazine* as the reigning country "King of Swing."

By the end of 1970s, ABC had been absorbed by MCA, and Thompson's releases at the start of the 1980s appeared on that label. In early 1980, he had the chart-hit single "Tony's Tank-Up, Drive-In Cafe" on MCA and, in August, was represented by a new LP, *Take Me Back to Tulsa.* As of that release date, MCA estimated that Hank had achieved in his career over 100 charted singles, including two dozen that had made *Billboard's* top 10.

As the 1980s went by, although Thompson continued to record new material on MCA for a time and then on other labels, the hit charts increasingly were dominated by a new group of artists. Some of them whose styles were in the country-rock vein cited Thompson's western-swing blend of twin fiddle and steel guitar with the two-step sound of honky-tonk as having an important influence on their own careers. Through the 1980s into the 1990s, Hank remained active on the concert circuit while also appearing many times on the various regional and national country music TV shows.

After being a finalist in the voting for the Country Music Hall of Fame on several occasions, he was finally elected in 1989. After his induction, the Country Music Foundation released a package of his hits, mainly from the 1960s and 1970s, titled *Hank Thompson Country Music Hall of Fame Series.* The tracks included "Smoky the Bar," "Mutiny on the Monotony," "Just an Old Flame," "Time Wounds All Heels," and "Swing Wide Your Gate of Love." As of 1995, the Country Music Hall of Fame and Museum catalog also offered three other Thompson albums: *Here's to Country Music, Hank Thompson/20 Greatest Hits,* and *Hank Thompson/All Time Greatest Hits.*

TILLIS, MEL: *Singer, guitarist, songwriter, bandleader (the Statesiders), actor, music publisher. Born Pahokee, Florida, August 8, 1932.*

"One reason I'm here tonight is to d-d-dispel those rumors going around that Mel Tillis has quit st-st-stuttering. That's not true. I'm still stuttering and I'm making a pretty good living at it t-t-too!"

That typical audience greeting reflects the strength of an individual who can take a problem like a major speech defect and turn it into an asset by making maximum use of his natural-born talents. Certainly that is true of Mel Tillis, who has been a premier country-music songwriter for decades, bringing him the highest Country Music Association accolade in 1977, Entertainer of the Year.

As to why Tillis developed his trademark stutter, he once told a reporter, "When I was three in Pahokee, Florida, I caught malaria and stuttered ever since. Some people said it was an emotional problem and would go away. I felt embarrassed and sensitive about it as a youngster, but it didn't go away." As he grew up, he went to a number of university speech clinics to try to solve the problem. "I had been unable to meet people, was afraid to get up in front of an audience. I even had a fear of answering the telephone. But let me tell you, it's much better to face the problem head on." The clinics hadn't been able to eliminate the stammer, but Mel had learned to live with it.

Tillis had learned to play guitar while growing up in Florida, but hadn't decided on how he'd earn a living when he enlisted in the Air Force at the start of the 1950s. He got out in 1955, spent two semesters at the University of Florida before dropping out in 1956, then went home to work at all sorts of odd jobs, from truck driver to strawberry picker. As he told John T. Pugh from *Music City News* (May 1970), "It was then that I wrote a song entitled 'I'm Tired.' Webb Pierce recorded it. It was a number-one hit and I got the hell out of that strawberry patch in a hurry."

It was part of a pattern of lucky breaks that paved the road to Nashville. He told Pugh, "I was having a hard time. I was down to my last couple of bucks when a singer in the Duke of Paducah band had to have an operation. I was asked to fill in. So I went on the road with them and made enough to live on for awhile.... And for the first couple of years, 1956 and 1957, this is pretty much how it went. My wife, Doris, and I would go down to our last few dollars but every time our prayers were answered and something would break for us so we could keep going."

At the time, despite his initial writing success, Mel wanted to emphasize a performing career. Although he stuttered in conversation, his voice came through loud and clear when he sang. "Singing is a kind of mechanical helper. With the various instruments playing along, the rhythm and everything moving, my voice just seems to flow with it . . . like following the bouncing rubber ball."

He actually cut his first record in 1956, his version of the folk classic "It Takes a Worried Man." But industry people suggested that he needed original material, either his own or from another writer, to succeed as a vocalist. Since a newcomer's access to professional material can be limited, he turned his attention to writing and penned an estimated 350 songs during his first six years. The Tillis touch caught the fancy of the country-music field, and a stream of new recordings of his material by a who's who of the industry issued forth from the late 1950s into the 1960s. In 1963, the trend reached its first peak with Bobby Bare's recording of "Detroit City," a top-10 hit in the country field and a strong entry on the pop side too. By the end of the decade it had become a classic, recorded 115 different times for a sales total of 4.5 million records. Among the many other chartmakers from Mel's pen in the 1960s was "Ruby, Don't Take Your Love to Town," which was recorded by many country artists but earned a gold record in the pop version by Kenny Rogers and the First Edition.

Mel, however, still had his sights set on performing success. He recorded a number of his songs for Columbia Records in the late 1950s and mid-1960s, but none was a massive hit, though a fair number made the charts. (His Columbia chartmakers included "The

Violet and the Rose," "Walk on By," "Georgia Town Blues," and "Sawmill.") After his switch to Decca he made the charts with "How Come Your Dog Don't Bite Nobody But Me," cowritten with Webb Pierce, plus several other releases that made lower-chart levels. He was still seeking at least a top-20 or top-30 success when he switched to Ric in the mid-1960s, then Kapp. He finally did achieve that initial breakthrough, not with one of his own songs but one provided by Harlan Howard, "Life Turned Her That Way." Later, he scored his biggest singles hit of the decade with "These Lonely Hands of Mine," written by Lamar Morris.

As the 1960s went by, things kept looking brighter for Tillis the entertainer. With his band, the Statesiders, he became one of the major attractions on the country music circuit, starring in clubs, auditoriums, and country fairs across the United States. It was a pattern that continued throughout the 1970s to even greater effect, since Mel began to frequent the upper levels of both singles and album charts with his many releases of the decade. (As of the late 1970s, the makeup of the Statesiders included the relatively unusual combination of three fiddle players along with guitar, drum, and keyboards. Throughout the 1970s, Mel and the band averaged about 250 concerts a year.)

Starting in the late 1960s, Tillis became increasingly visible on national TV. Besides being featured on many *Grand Ole Opry* shows and specials telecast from *Opry* facilities in Nashville throughout the 1970s, he also appeared on such shows as *Tony Orlando and Dawn, AM America, Dinah!, Match Game, Merv Griffin, Hollywood Squares, The American Sportsman*, Johnny Carson's *The Tonight Show, Good Morning America, The Midnight Special*, as a regular cast member of *Glen Campbell's Goodtime Hour, Love American Style*, and the *Ian Tyson Show* in Canada. In the summer of 1977, he also cohosted his own summer replacement on ABC titled *Mel and Susan Together.*

Mel extended his acting roles when he accepted movie parts. In the movie *W.W. & The Dixie Dance Kings*, released in the mid-1970s (starring Burt Renolds) he played a dual role—himself and a service station attendant. He also had a small part in the 1979 TV movie *Murder in Music City.*

A familiar face on the Country Music Association Awards Show from its inception in 1967, he performed on a number of the programs and also was nominated in one category or another on several occasions. In the 1975 awards, for instance, he and Sherry Bryce were nominated as best vocal duo. In 1977, of course, he was nominated and won in the voting for Entertainer of the Year.

In the late 1960s, Mel signed a recording contract with MGM Records, which released such albums as *Arms of a Fool/Commercial Affection, Mel Tillis at Houston Coliseum with the Statesiders, Living and Learning/Take My Hand* (with Sherry Bryce and the Statesiders), *One More Time, Very Best of Mel Tillis,* and *World to End.* Mel had a good share of singles on the charts under the MGM banner during the first half of the 1970s, either solo vocals or duets with Sherry Bryce. Among the duets were "Let's Go All the Way Tonight," "You Are the One," and "Mr. Wright and Mrs. Wrong," the first two in 1974 the other in 1975. Solo chart singles included "Woman in the Back of My Mind." (All those songs, it might be added, were handled by Sawgrass Music, the publishing firm Mel established in the late 1960s.) By 1976, Mel had moved again, this time to MCA. He made even greater inroads on the country hit lists than in the first part of the 1970s. In 1976, he had a number one hit on MCA with "Good Woman Blues" and did well with the single "Love Revival," a top-20 entry; in 1977, he had such hit songs as "Burning Memories" and "I Got the Hoss." In 1978, he placed "I Believe in You" in the top 5 in the summer and repeated the trick in the late fall with "Ain't No California," still on the charts in 1979. Other best-selling 1979 singles on MCA were "Send Me Down to Tucson/Charlie's Angel" and "Coca Cola Cowboy." His 1979 MCA charted LPs were *Mr. Entertainer, Are You Sincere,* and *I Believe in You.*

In 1979, Tillis left MCA for Elektra/Asylum Records. His first single release for that label, "Me and Pepper," came out in October. His debut LP on Elektra/Asylum came out in May 1980, titled *Your Body Is an Outlaw.* The title track, issued as a single, quickly made upper-chart levels. His 1980 singles on Elektra included "Lying Time Again," on the charts early in the year; "Your Body Is an Outlaw," a summer hit; and "Steppin' Out" on upper-chart positions late in the year. (MCA also issued a new LP in early 1980, *M-M-Mel Live.*) At the end of 1980, Elektra released the single "Southern Rains," which rose to number one in February 1981. In the summer of 1981, Mel had another bestselling single for Elektra with "A Million Old Goodbyes."

Mel's career continued to proceed along the same general path for the rest of the 1980s. He had a devoted following who filled the clubs and concert halls or the stands at state and county fairs to enjoy his repertoire of by-now classic country songs and his relaxed humor. His recording success, though, tapered off during the decade, caused partly by country radio's decreasing coverage of material by longtime veteran entertainers.

Not that those years were uneventful. In December 1984, for instance, his biography, *Stutterin' Boy,* written by Walter Wager, was published. In 1985 he completed a movie with Roy Clark called *Uphill All the Way* and also took part in the multistar "Bakersfield to Chicago Farm Aid" journey. From the mid-1970s his concert schedule had included stops at the small town of Branson, Missouri. As the town started to become a new mecca for country fans in the late 1980s, Mel played a major role in helping that happen. After testing the water by appearances at Roy Clark's venue during 1987–88, he bought a home in Branson and leased a theater, where he soon drew capacity crowds to his two-shows-per-day, six-days-a-week routine. In 1990, at the height of the tourist season in early fall, he met fan demand by working seven days a week.

As he told an interviewer, "I make more money here than I can on the road. And it's easier. Some people say, 'Why do you have two shows a day?' Well, have they ever worked on a milk truck from house to house and door to door? This is like a vacation for me."

In 1992, Mel opened his own 2,000-seat venue in Branson, while Willie Nelson became the headliner at Mel's former Ozark Theater location. As of the mid-1990s, Mel's Branson operation was still thriving though, as always, he found time for concert work and occasional TV guest spots outside his Branson headquarters.

During the 1990s, as Mel's chart status diminished, daughter Pam's career took on increasing luster. The two were so closely connected in people's minds, though they maintained separate careers (while occasionally performing or recording some material together), that the editors of *Life* magazine's "Roots of Country Music" special issue in September 1994 included them as a single entry in their list of "The 100 Most Important People in the History of Country."

In the mid-1990s, examples of Mel's recordings in print included the album *Mel Tillis's Greatest Hits* on the Curb label and as one of the artists on the *Country Gold* video.

TILLIS, PAM: *Singer, pianist, songwriter. Born Nashville, Tennessee, c. 1957.*

As the oldest daughter of a living legend, Pam Tillis had to fight the usual battles a child in that position encounters. But after a few false starts, she proved she deserved major audience attention in her own right, something attested to by her country music peers who voted her Female Artist of the Year in the 1994 Country Music Association poll. As she said in accepting the trophy on the October Awards telecast, "I love what I do. I love it so much and I want to share it with the world. Thank you so much, M-M-M-Mel Tillis."

Growing up in a family environment where people like Willie Nelson, Webb Pierce, and Chet Atkins were likely to drop by the house and the *Grand Ole Opry* was practically a home away from the family's Florida home, there was no way Pam could escape the influence of "down home" music. Her father had fond memories of a little girl who waved at him when he went onstage, and sometimes fell asleep in his guitar case. Before she was in her teens she gave evidence of talent, beginning to try her skills at songwriting, somewhat awkwardly, when she was only eleven.

Still, like any child of the times, she was well aware of the other formats in the spotlight in the 1960s and

1970s, including pop, rock, and R&B. Like her classmates as she reached her teens, she tended to focus on that material rather than country. She had learned to play the piano, which, she told interviewer Holly Gleason, came in handy at that time. "I was real, real shy and really nerdy—so when you've got one thing you can do real well, it gives you self-esteem. Sitting down at the piano and singing a song at a party was something I could do that the head cheerleader and the homecoming queen couldn't, and it made me special."

Before long she was branching out to other entertainment endeavors. She made her public debut performing at a talent night in Nashville's Last Chance Saloon in the mid-1970s and was soon gaining experience at a number of well-known local clubs like the Exit/In. She kept that up as a soloist or a member of various bands when she finished high school and became a college student at the University of Tennessee in Knoxville.

While she didn't ignore country, most of her material was in the pop or rock vein. She stressed, "I grew up in old Nashville; I know what real country music is and I have a real love for it. But I've always been open to all kinds of music. I love to sing everything, including things that might seem kind of progressive or experimental. I like being on both sides of that fence and bringing it all to the table."

In the early 1980s, having gone past her college years, she sought to make her name in the rock-and-roll sector. She signed with Warner Brothers Records in 1983 and the one and only album on the label, *Beyond the Doll of Cutie,* was released in 1984. The album made little headway with record buyers and, while some of the five singles culled from it made the charts, they stayed on lower levels. By 1987, when Pam left the label, she was already finding her way back to her country roots as she began to gain some attention from country performers for her songwriting ability. Besides providing chart hits for a number of artists, her songwriting activities brought her in contact with the top writer Bob DiPiero, whom she married in 1991. (She had previously been married to painter Rick Mason in the late 1970s and early 1980s and bore him a son, Ben, in 1979.)

She continued to try to keep her performing career alive, this time with a blend of pure-country material and country-rock stylings. In 1989 she finally signed with a Music City–based label, Arista's Nashville division, which led to the release of her label album debut, *Put Yourself in My Place,* in early 1991. It made the *Billboard* list soon after and was still on them in the fall of 1992, having peaked at number ten the previous year. The album went on to earn a gold-record award from the R.I.A.A.

The title track made the *Billboard* Top 30 by the fall of 1991 and was followed in upper-chart levels by the single "Don't Tell Me What to Do." The latter provided

Pam with her first number-one hit, which reached that pinnacle exactly ten years after her father had similar success with "Southern Rains."

As she built up her following opening on tour dates for artists like Alan Jackson, country fans continued to boost her new singles to chart success. She began 1992 with the single "Maybe It Was Memphis" peaking at number two in *Radio & Records* the week of January 31 while also making the *Billboard* Top 10. Next came the top-15 release, "Blue Rose Is . . ." and "Shake the Sugar Tree," number two in *R&R* the week of October 3, 1992.

Late in 1992, her second Arista album, *Homeward Looking Angel,* came out and once more presented a dynamic song selection, some cowritten by Pam. The album was on high chart levels in late 1992 and early 1993 and by July had gained another gold-record certification for her. The single "Let That Pony Run" was moving up the charts at the start of 1993, peaking at number four in *R&R* the week of March 19, 1993, and the *Billboard* Top 5 the same month. Before the year was over, Pam had two more top-10 singles, "Cleopatra, Queen of Denial" (cowritten by her, Bob DiPiero, and J. Buckingham) and "Do You Know Where Your Man Is?"

In the spring of 1994, Pam's third Arista album, *Sweetheart's Dance,* was released, one that indicated continued growth by Pam as both performer and writer. The first single from the album, "Spilled Perfume," (cowritten by Pam and D. Dillon) was near the top of the *Billboard* chart in June, by which time the album was also in the *Billboard* Top 10, on the way to surpassing gold-record levels by November. Before 1994 was over, Pam had two more hit singles from that collection, a spirited update of Jackie DeShannon's early 1960s composition "When You Walk in the Room" and the wild "Mi Vida Loca (My Crazy Life)."

Commenting on the inspiration that led her to write the Tex-Mex flavored number, she told a *TV Guide* reporter it came from Geraldo Rivera's TV talk show. "I was watching Geraldo and he was doing a show on girl gang members. One of them had a tattoo on her wrist that said, 'Mi Vida Loca.' Geraldo asked her what it meant and she said, 'It's Spanish for "my crazy life."' I thought, 'That's beautiful!' The songwriter bell went off and 'Mi Vida Loca' ended up on the album."

The album showcased Pam's versatility still further with her buoyant version of a bluegrass/gospel number, "Till All the Lonely's Gone." Joining her on that track were her father, three sisters and a brother, and bluegrass originator Bill Monroe (who provided a mandolin solo). Other cuts on the album found Pam's vocals being supported by such other 1990s notables as Vince Gill and Mary-Chapin Carpenter.

Comparing the Nashville scene in the 1990s with the situation when her father was making his reputation, she noted that where there were only a handful of songwriters back then, now good writers seemed to be everywhere. She told *People* magazine, "There's gotta be 50,000 writers in this town." Also, she added, "Dad's fans stayed loyal. Nowadays, to stay in the top 5, I gotta work my butt off, because there's always someone else coming along." Her father commented that he thought it was good to have fresh blood coming into the field, which he thought was "gettin' kinda stale," to which his daughter responded, "I don't know if we need as many as we got."

In the mid-1990s, though, country artists and fans thought they were lucky to have Pam emerge as a potential future superstar. Preceding her CMA Best Female Artist award, she had received other nominations from Grammy voters, American Music Award poll participants, and members of the Academy of Country Music. Meanwhile, she was extending her activities into other entertainment areas, trying her acting skills in an episode of *L.A. Law* for TV; in the Peter Bogdanovich film, *This Thing Called Love;* and in a Brandon Tartikoff made for TV opus *XXX's and OOO's.*

One of her prime interests aside from her career, she told Holly Gleason, was women's rights. "As a woman in the '90s I deal with lots of anger. We are not free. Our personal freedoms are so limited by the state of the world in which we live. I'd like to write a song about that, about the fact that a woman's not safe to go walking in the park alone in the middle of the day. About the fact that my son can't play in the creek at my mother's house that I played in because it's polluted.

"I'm thankful the ceilings are being raised, that women are getting more chances. Every time one succeeds, that's room for more . . . but I don't want to lose the balance. And with country music being such a competitive, controlled format, there's a lot of things I can't say that I want to."

In the spring of 1995, her single "I Was Blown Away" moved into upper chart positions . . . in the summer she had the chart hit single "In Between Dances." Her next Arista album, *All of This Love,* came out in late 1995 and stayed on the charts for much of 1996. It didn't reach top rungs, though, peaking at 25 in *Billboard* at the end of 1995. The single "Deep Down" from the album won fan attention, however, staying on most major lists from late 1995 into early spring and peaking at number six in *Billboard.* In the Academy of Country music voting for 1995, she was a finalist in the Top Female Vocalist category and won a similar nod from Country Music Association voters for 1996. Her credits for 1996 included completing a video and single for "The River and the Highway" during the summer and singing the title track from the *All of This Love* album on the Family Films Awards show on CBS-TV in the fall.

TIPPIN, AARON: *Singer, guitarist, songwriter, bandleader. Born Pensacola, Florida, July 3, c. late 1950s.*

Aaron Tippin doesn't have a great voice, but like any good pop or country performer he knows how to bend and shape it to reflect the emotions inherent in a song. His gritty, rough-hewn style, in the tradition of Merle, Waylon, and the Williamses senior and junior, proved effective both with sad blue-collar ballads and raucous honky-tonk music. In a period when many of his traditionalist idols tended to get short shrift from TV and radio opinion makers, Tippin was able to get the exposure he needed to attract a large following in spite of the domination of the 1990s country scene by cookie cutter newcomers.

He was born in Florida but grew up in South Carolina, where his father established an air-service business. Besides operating a maintenance facility for light planes, the operation eventually also offered air-taxi service. Growing up around airplanes, Aaron naturally became interested in flying, and in his teen years earned money from employment in family airplane operations as well as local farm work to pay for flying lessons. He also found another interest, country music, and was taking part in local music events in his high school years.

Like many teenagers, he had plenty of wild oats to sow and had his share of escapades, including buzzing his high school after he'd earned his pilot's license. Talking about the single "I Miss Behaving" from his second album with the *Music Express* of Toronto, Canada, in May 1992, he commented, "That was written with two of my pals, Mark Collie and Charlie Craig. It was the day after a party and we were sitting around about half hung-over, and the last thing we wanted to think about was writing a song. We got to talking about when we were 18 and 19 and we could drink and party all night, take a shower at 6 A.M. and go on to work. It was a case of 'Why can't we do that anymore?' and then Mark came up with the title. People love it, because they remember."

After high school, Tippin became a good enough flier to get a job as a corporate pilot. Between flight assignments, he continued to try to write new songs and follow what was going on in the country music field. He was torn between the two career possibilities and finally decided he had to see if he could succeed as a musician. He recalled for Earl Dittman of *Tune-In* magazine ("The Return of the Hillbilly Terminator," September 1993), "I had a damn good career as an aviator. But one day I said, 'This doesn't work. Look out! I'm going to jump off a cliff.' And I did; I turned right around and did it. In two day's time my life changed. One day I was flying, the next day I wasn't.

"I walked in the office and turned in my wings and said, 'Here boys, I'm done with these.' Then I went up into the woods, got the guys together and said, 'Let's play some honky tonks. . . .' "

Tippin, who had assembled his first band when he was twenty-two, then focused on gaining as much experience as he could in gigs all over the Southeast. Like most aspiring musicians, he had to supplement performing income with earnings from whatever day jobs he could find. He said later, "I did mostly manual labor to support my musical career, and that's what led to this blue-collar feel in my songs."

In the mid-1980s he took the bull by the horns and moved to Nashville. His initial goal was to try to place some of his songs with other performers and his work was good enough to get him a job as staff songwriter with the prestigious Acuff-Rose publishing company. Once assured of a steady income, he tried to enhance his status by singing at local venues and preparing demos of his material for submission to record firms. Five years went by without much progress in that direction, but at the end of the 1980s he finally got a positive response from RCA Records, which led to the release of his debut single, "You've Got to Stand for Something," issued in September 1990. That song, cowritten by Tippin, became a hit in 1991, peaking at number five in *Radio & Records*.

It was the title song for his debut album, which RCA released in January 1991. The record made the *Billboard* chart, peaking at number twenty-three, and was still in the top 30 in the fall, eventually accumulating total sales of 400,000 copies. It provided two more chart singles, "I Wonder How Far It Is For You," issued in February 1991 with a peak *Billboard* position of number twenty-six, and "She Made a Monkey Out of Me," which peaked at number thirty-five. Videos of all three were released with the latter song reaching number nine on the CMT channel.

The widespread airplay given those recordings, coupled with extensive touring by Tippin, paved the way for even greater results with his second album, *Between the Lines,* issued by RCA in March 1992 and on the charts soon after. It was preceded by the single "There Ain't Nothin' Wrong with the Radio" (cowritten by Tippin and B. Brook), issued in December 1991 and number one in *Radio & Records* the week of April 17, 1992. By then the album was in *Billboard* Top 10 enroute to being certified gold in July 1992 and platinum the year after (August 1993). The album's first single also rose in video form to number one on both CMT and TNN channels, eventually placing as the number-seventy-eight overall video release of 1992 on CMT. The second single from the album, "I Wouldn't Have It Any Other Way," was released in May 1992 and reached number three in *R&R* the week of August 28, 1992. Its video placed number one on both CMT and TNN.

The other two singles from the album were "I Was Born with a Broken Heart," issued on November 11, 1992, and peaking later at number twenty-seven and "My Blue Angel" (cowritten by Tippin), released in January 1993 to peak at number seven in *R&R* the week of April 16, 1993. The video of the latter song rose to number four on CMT and number one on TNN.

Aaron's third album, *Call of the Wild* (with all tracks cowritten by him), came out in August 1993, preceded by its first single, "Working Man's Ph.D." Both were soon high on the charts in both *Billboard* and *R&R* as well as other trade magazines. The single, penned by Tippin with Bobby Boyd, peaked at number six in *R&R* the week of April 27, 1993, and the album, after rising to number six in *Billboard,* went on to be certified gold by the R.I.A.A. in December 1993. Tippin's audience rapport was recognized by his Country Music Association peers who nominated him for the 1993 CMA/RSO New Touring Artist of the Year Award.

Two new chart singles were culled from the collection, the title track, which reached number fourteen in *R&R* the week of January 7, 1994, and "Honky Tonk Superman." All of the album singles releases were also taped for videos with the one for "Working Man's Ph.D." reaching number one on TNN and number five on CMT. Commenting on the song, which stresses the worth and dignity of common labor, Tippin stressed he didn't mean to put down education "because I think everybody should be as educated as possible, but somewhere down the line, we decided if you weren't a brain surgeon or an astronaut you didn't have any reason not to be proud of who you are and what you do. That's really all the song does. It says that no matter what you do for a living, take great pride in it."

Tippin seemed eager to be a country "traditionalist" in other ways than as a singer. For instance, at least through the mid-1990s, he followed the old fan-friendly approach, including acceding to almost every request for an autograph. He told Dittman, "Me, a star? That's a shameful misuse of the term. . . . I always tell my 15-year-old daughter that all of this doesn't make us anybody special. We're just normal folks like everybody else. I tell her, 'The only thing different about me, honey, is a God-given talent. All I have done is work with it. Past that, we're no different.'

"For instance, last night we got through eating supper at this very ordinary restaurant and a few folks asked for autographs, which suits me just fine. After that, we went over to a go-cart track. I stood in line behind about 20 people and waited my turn just like everybody else. I think we all must realize that sometimes the lights and the smoke make things bigger than they really are."

Another time he also pointed out the importance of feedback. A performer, he argued, "should be the most in-touch person there is. . . . [on stage] he hears the audience scream when he does a good song, and he hears them clap politely when he does a bad one. If he signs autographs—like I do—the fans will come through the line and tell you what they like. They'll do it every night. And the funny thing is, they know exactly what they like. All you have to do is be smart enough to listen."

A look at the credits for Tippin's albums through 1994 showed he had a part in just about every song. (His fourth RCA album, *Lookin' Back at Myself,* came out in the fall of 1994 and was on the charts well into 1995.) He commented, "I used to think that being a singer/songwriter was a whole lot tougher than just being a singer. But I've found out that even though writing is more work, it's a whole lot easier when you're getting ready to put an album together. You don't have to scan all over town, hunting for songs that will say something just like you want to say."

His approach to developing an album, he added, was to pick out those songs that provided what he felt was an appropriate package. "I'll pick subjects and write four or five songs about them and let the strongest ones surface. I wrote 34 songs to get the 10 for *Call of the Wild.* I had the idea in mind the year before of what I wanted to say and do in that project. That was already there. It was just a matter of filling in the holes. I'm always searching for that idea that will lead me to a great song."

In early 1995 Aaron had the single "She Feels Like a Brand New Man Tonight" (cowritten by Tippin and M.P. Heeney) on the charts. On May 15, 1995, R.I.A.A. certified *Lookin' Back at Myself* as gold and on August 10 presented a similar plaque to him for *You've Got to Stand for Something.* In the fall of the year he had a new album, *Tool Box,* on the charts. It peaked at number twelve in *Billboard* and continued in upper chart positions into 1996. The first single, "That's As Close As I'll Get to Loving You," which preceded the album, provided Tippin with another number one hit. In early 1996, the single "Without Your Love" made its appearance on the charts. He wasn't up for an award in the Academy of Country Music 1995 poll, but he was one of the featured performers on the NBC-TV telecast on April 24, 1996.

TOMPALL AND THE GLASER BROTHERS:
Vocal and instrumental trio, all born in or near Spalding, Nebraska. Tompall Glaser, September 3, 1933; Charles "Chuck" Glaser, February 27, 1936; James "Jim" Glaser, December 16, 1937.

The number of country-music superstars to come out of Nebraska is almost infinitesimal. But any state that can lay claim to the birthplace of such talents as the three Glaser brothers must be considered an important link in the progress of country music. Both as a group and as individuals, the Glasers left their mark on the field, not only as performers and writers but as discoverers and developers of other major artists.

The boys' love for music was inspired by their father Louis, a skilled guitarist who saw to it that his sons learned the instrument at early ages. The oldest, Tompall, gave his first performance at seven and later was joined by Chuck and Jim, when they were old enough, in an act that gained experience at PTA meetings, class picnics, and other local functions.

They loved country music from the start, though their father had some doubts at one point, Jim Glaser told John Pugh of *Music City News* (December 1971). "At first our dad didn't want us in the business because there was no place in Nebraska to play country music except dives and honky-tonks. When we were singing country music, it wasn't the 'in' thing it is now, and we were looked down on, even out there. But we never considered quitting or changing. We just knew we had to get to Nashville."

The boys persisted in their efforts to make a music business career. In their teens in the mid-1940s, they had their own TV show in Holdredge, Nebraska. In the mid-1950s, hearing that an *Arthur Godfrey's Talent Scouts* unit was going to be in Omaha, the Glasers traveled the 180 miles from Holdredge to audition. They did so well they were presented on Godfrey's nationally televised show.

Still looking for a chance to break into the country field, in 1957 they managed to get past the door guardian at a Marty Robbins concert to meet him. This led to their first chance as professional recording artists on his label, Robbins Records. Their debut single, written by Chuck, was "Five Penny Nickel." The record was far from a blockbuster, but the experience encouraged the brothers to move to Nashville in January 1958.

Jim told John Pugh, "Growing up in the middle of Nebraska like we did, we were so far out, we never had a chance to see anybody, or learn from anyone, or be influenced by anyone or anything we ever saw. So we came [to Nashville] pretty primitive, I'm afraid. Not one of us even knew how to dress. And country music was still looked down upon—especially here. In fact, Nashville has probably been one of the last places in the country to accept country music. But we were in the country music colony, so we weren't aware of it. We loved the music community, and eventually grew up to love all of Nashville."

Once in Nashville, the brothers renewed their acquaintance with Robbins and got the chance to work with him. As Tompall recalled "He asked us to go out on the road as his back-up group, and we were with him for almost two years. But it became obvious we were going to have to act as a main act, or always be typed as a back-up group."

Being in Nashville brought exposure to major record firms, and, in 1959, the Glasers got a contract from Decca as Tompall and the Glaser Brothers. The Glasers also picked up much needed extra income by working as recording session musicians.

Their session credentials from those years are impressive. They backed Marty on his classic hit "El Paso" and also supported Claude King on his bestseller, "Commancheros." Besides working with Robbins, the band toured with some other well-known people, including Johnny Cash, with whom they appeared at New York's Carnegie Hall.

Hoping to make it big, they left Robbins, but at first the going was slow. "After we left Marty, we still didn't have any hit records," Jim recalled. "Then Johnny Cash called us for his back-up vocal group. We told him we didn't want that image, and he always presented us as talents in our own right, like he does with the Statler Brothers."

That association with Cash, which lasted for three years until the Glasers felt they really were ready to headline on their own, undoubtedly played an important part in gaining widespread audience acceptance. But also contributing was work with the *Grand Ole Opry*. The Glasers first were featured on the show in 1960. Then, in 1962, they were signed as regulars and still maintained that status with the show over a decade afterward.

An indication that things were moving forward was the appearance of many of their recordings on national charts as the 1960s progressed. Among the chart-making singles on Decca written by one or more of the brothers were "She Loves the Love I Give Her," "A Girl Like You," and "Let Me Down Easy." Other Decca hits were "Teardrops 'Til Dawn," "Odds and End," and "Baby They're Playing Our Song." The vocal blend the trio used on most of those releases was the same one they generally employed whenever they appeared together in later years with Tompall handling lead, Jim tenor, and Chuck baritone.

In the mid-1960s, the Glasers became dissatisfied with their Decca Records association and switched to MGM in 1966. Before long, they had two new hit singles on the new label, "The Last Thing on My Mind" and "Gone, on the Other Hand." With the now legendary Jack Clement handling most of the production chores, they added many more chart hits during the late 1960s and early 1970s. Their debut MGM LP, *Tompall and the Glaser Brothers,* was issued in June 1967 and was followed by such other LPs as *Award Winners* and *Rings and Things.* During those years, the brothers topped many polls as the best vocal group in country music. From the mid-1960s into the early 1970s, they gained that designation from the *Music City News* on four occasions, in *Billboard* polls two times, *Cash Box* three times, and, in 1970, won the Best Vocal Group award in the Country Music Association voting.

They achieved equally important successes in other parts of the music industry. In the songwriting end, for instance, all the brothers wrote songs that put other artists' names on country charts. Jimmy Glaser's catalogue included such often covered songs as "Thanks a Lot for Trying Anyway" and "Sitting in an All Night

Cafe." Tompall wrote "Stand Beside Me," a major hit for Jimmy Dean in the mid-1960s, and, with Harlan Howard, penned "The Streets of Baltimore," a smash success for Bobby Bare in 1966. Another performer who scored with a Tompall composition was Jimmy Newman, who made top levels with "You're Making a Fool Out of Me."

The Glasers also became very active in music publishing, record production, and other aspects of the business side of music. Glaser Productions was set up to handle booking and artist guidance. By the end of the 1960s, the brothers also owned three music firms, Glascap (ASCAP), Glaser Publications (BMI), and Glace (SESAC). Most of their original songs were published under those banners, including "History Repeats Itself," "All Night Cafe," "Streets of Baltimore," "A Taxpayer's Letter," "Stand Beside Me," and "You Take the Future."

Some of the Glasers' efforts went into production. Chuck, in particular, signed with Decca in the mid-1960s and produced sessions of people like Jimmy Payne, Leon McAuliffe, Gordon Terry, and John Hartford. Hartford, in fact, was a Glaser discovery. When he came to the Glaser offices with his great song "Gentle on My Mind," it had been turned down by almost every major music firm in Nashville.

The brothers still were doing most of their performing work together in the early 1970s, though increasingly they were turning their gaze toward more individual work. Jimmy had signed with Monument Records for some solo recordings in the late 1960s and Tompall also had already started to do a lot of solo appearances by the end of the decade. The brothers still could make the hit charts as a group, as was indicated by such early 1970s hits as "Faded Love" and "California Girl and the Tennessee Square."

At the end of the 1960s, Chuck and Tompall also became increasingly committed to the progressive country movement spearheaded by people like Waylon Jennings and Willie Nelson. When they opened their own recording operation, Glaser Studios, in 1969, it became Nashville headquarters for many so-called country-music outlaws, including people like Jennings, Nelson, Steve Young, Kinky Friedman, Mickey Newbury, and many others, and continued as a progressive mecca well into the 1970s.

The pressure of this and other outside activities plus the individualistic outlook of the Glasers began to affect their performing work. Although they continued to be one of the most popular groups in country music at the start of the 1970s, their relationship became difficult. As Jim Glaser said in 1981, "We tried to be too involved. We had too much going on, running publishing companies and staying on the road all the time. Things got to be very hectic and the tension just mounted until it peaked in 1973." Tompall added, "It was all personalities. Nobody would compromise."

Thus, although each had done some separate work prior to 1973, after their final falling-out over group activities, all three decided to go off on their own full time. They sold their publishing companies to Famous Music and got rid of most of their other joint enterprises. Tompall intended to concentrate on performing, though he did some production work, including coproducing Waylon Jennings' 1973 LP *Honky Tonk Heroes*. Jim also went in that direction, turning out solo recordings on MGM and MCA and touring widely throughout the United States and abroad, including several very successful tours of England. He placed a number of singles on the charts, including one cowritten with Jimmy Payne, "Woman, Woman (Have You Got Cheatin' on Your Mind)," that made upper-chart levels. Chuck opted for behind-the-scenes work, continuing his production work with a number of artists, including Kinky Friedman and the Texas Jew Boys, a group he also managed. He also headed his own booking agency, called Nova.

Chuck's efforts came to an abrupt halt for a while after he suffered a massive stroke in 1975. It affected the left side of his body, and his doctors thought its effects might prevent him from ever singing or walking again. However, he refused to give up, and doggedly went through rehabilitation for several years to recover his lost faculties.

Meanwhile Tompall continued to work hard on the concert circuit and as a recording artist. During the mid-1970s his material was issued on MGM and ABC labels. He placed a number of singles on the charts, the most successful of which was "Put Another Log on the Fire," issued in the spring of 1975.

It was his work with progressive country friends Willie Nelson, Waylon Jennings, and Jessi Colter that brought him a lot of attention in the mid-1970s. Some of his stylings were included in the RCA 1975 collection, *Wanted: The Outlaws,* one of the biggest-selling albums in pop music history and the most successful album to that point in country music. The album won a gold record on March 30, 1976, and went on to exceed double-platinum levels later on, the first country LP ever to achieve that. In connection with the album, Tompall made several major tours with the others to venues all across the United States and Canada and in a number of overseas countries.

In 1978, Louis Glaser became very ill and his sons returned to Nebraska to be with him over Christmas. Chuck recalled in an interview for Elektra/Asylum Records in 1981, "It was the first time we three had been together longer than ten minutes in more than six years. We decided we didn't hate each other after all. We fooled around with some tunes [Chuck having regained use of his singing voice] and realized our musical tastes had come together again. When we got back to Nashville, I found a Tim Henderson song called

'Maria Consuela' and played it for Tompall. He called Jim and we decided to record it in our studio."

The single was released on Elektra/Asylum and made the charts. This was followed by more new Tompall and the Glaser Brothers singles, including the hit single "Lovin' Her Was Easier. . . ." In late 1981, the brothers had their first LP ready for release on Elektra/Asylum.

As the 1980s went by, the Glaser activities in the performing field slowed down. By the 1990s, Tompall's concert work mainly consisted of occasional appearances in Europe. In 1996, Tompall was happy about RCA's decision to issue a special 20th anniversary edition of the *Outlaws* album. The package contained the original eleven songs in the album plus nine "lost" tracks recorded by some of the artists in that time frame. It also included a new track of a Steve Earle and Reno Kling song, "Nowhere Road," recorded by Waylon Jennings and Willie Nelson.

Looking back on the project's origins in the mid-1970s, Glaser told Deborah Evans Price of *Billboard* (May 18, 1996) the album was intended as a protest against trends of the period in the country field. "Waylon and I were disgusted with the way radio was handling country music. There was a logjam like it gets every once in a while where everything gets repetitious and labels are too much in charge. We were just trying anything we thought might break it."

TRACTORS, THE: *Vocal and instrumental group, Steve Ripley, born Boise, Idaho, January 1, 1950 (lead vocals, guitar, drums); Walt Richmond, born McAllister, Oklahoma, April 18, 1947 (bass vocals, keyboards, horns, accordion, clarinet); Ron Getman, born Fairfax, Oklahoma, December 13, 1948 (high harmony vocals, guitar, steel guitar, dobro, mandolin); Casey Van Beek, born Leiden, Holland, December 1, 1942 (low harmony vocals, bass guitar); Jamie Oldaker, born San Francisco, California, September 5, 1959 (drums, percussion).*

On the Country Music Association Awards telecast in October 1994, the showstopper was a group almost none of the global audience had ever heard of called the Tractors. Were these fresh-faced newcomers straight out of high school? Anything but; the five-member quintet whose uninhibited country-boogie-rock music almost had people dancing in the aisles were grizzled veterans who had learned their craft through years of performing in bars, backing bands, and some recording sessions as well.

A typical story is that of Steve Ripley, with Walt Richmond the band's primary songwriting member, who, though born in Idaho, was performing with local bands in Oklahoma honky-tonks beginning in his teen years. Over the two decades from the late 1960s to the late 1980s, his credits included working with legendary artists like Leon Russell, J. J. Cale, and Bob Dylan.

With Dylan, besides serving as lead guitarist in one of Bob's road bands, he also played on the album *Shot of Love*. He also learned record-production skills, among other things producing western swing tracks by Johnny Lee Wills. To add to all that, he designed a guitar that won wide acceptance in the industry, finding favor with people like rock stars Eddie Van Halen (of Van Halen), Steve Luthaker (of Toto) and country-pop mainstay Jimmy Buffett.

Native Oklahoman Walt Richmond, who also gained some insight into various musical blends through his acquaintance with Leon Russell, played keyboards with a number of Southwest groups and later backed folk-rock star Bonnie Raitt, who guested on the Tractors debut album. Richmond, also with production experience, coproduced that collection with lead vocalist Ripley.

The other three members had also been picking up performing know-how since their teens and could also point to career associations with household-name artists. Multitalented instrumentalist Ron Getman had provided vocal and instrumental support for Janis Ian and Leonard Cohen, among others. Casey Van Beek played bass guitar in support of Linda Ronstadt and the Righteous Brothers, while drummer-percussionist Jamie Oldaker worked with superstar English guitarist Eric Clapton.

Active in the Tulsa, Oklahoma, area as the 1980s drew to a close, the five musicians eventually got together in a new band project that took shape at the recording studio called the Church. Built in 1932 as the Tulsa Evangelical United Brethren Church, it was eventually acquired by Leon Russell, who converted it into a studio. At the end of the 1980s, an audition call went out for a new group and there was no lack of applicants.

Ripley recalled in 1994, "When this thing started four years ago, people swarmed this building wanting to be a Tractor. And the joke got to be, 'If you didn't learn to play "Johnny B. Goode" when it was a hit for Chuck Berry, then you're too young.'" Those selected for the band got a lot older before the project reached fruition. The tracks for the first album slowly took shape in the early 1990s, with much of the material written by Ripley or cowritten by him and Walt Richmond. Demo tapes were passed around and finally brought a contract from Arista Records which issued the debut disc, *The Tractors*, during the summer of 1994. The tracks covered a variety of styles from blues and barrelhouse boogie to honky-tonk and down-and-dirty country.

Ripley emphasized band members' interests didn't recognize any specific genre boundaries. "We're trying to look at it the way people did before it was so specifically categorized—rock and roll, rockabilly, country, country rock, modern country, new country, rockin' country. Back then no one knew what it was—they just did what they felt—and look what came out! People weren't trying to copy anything, they were just making music they loved."

Print media response was almost unanimously favorable. The *USA Today* critic raved in July 1994, "The group . . . can play just about anything. The album preserves spontaneous ad-libs and mistakes, plus some great music laced with the happy contentment of '60s survivors who stuck to their musical guns. Call it neo-Dixie or rockin' country. Old pal Bonnie Raitt helps out on slide guitar." More to the point, the up-tempo exuberant renditions on the album caught fire with country radio, which in recent years had seemed somewhat less than eager to play material offered by veteran entertainers.

The songs on the album were ear-catching and the vocal and instrumental mix generally first-rate, but the lyrics took aim at some of the problems confronting many people. Ripley commented, "You get to a point where you feel a freedom from the culture, where you just punch through the other side and you have this freedom to write what you want to express. If it's an undisguised straight-out attack on politics and corporate America, or 'C'mon baby, let's dance' . . . poetry or cosmic debris gibberish. It doesn't make it or keep it from being art. . . . Of course, the art of 'dumbing out' is always something we're going for."

As for life for the average person, he commented, "Hey, it's a game, a big game—but there's a lot at stake, too. We don't live in a perfect world. Whether you're on the poor side of town or the $100,000-a-year, two-income family, everyone has the same stress: how are we going to pay the mortgage? Whether it's a $2,000 mortgage or $200, it's the same stress. . . . 'How are we going to pay those bills?'

"So this record reflects that. It's filled with noises, first takes, knee-jerk reactions—we rolled tape and we'd leave it. Sure there are mistakes, but we kept those imperfections and tried to massage it into something people will identify with."

Still, he stressed, "This isn't about depression. This is party music, dance music, because we're all in the same boat—and that's something we can identify with. That's what all those blues songs are about, and those are some of the happiest songs there are."

The Tractors album quickly caught on with record buyers and moved rapidly up *Billboard* charts, peaking at number two in the fall and passing R.I.A.A. platinum levels by December. The first single, "Baby Likes to Rock It" (written by Ripley and Richmond) was a top 15 hit in both *Radio & Records* and *Billboard* in the November/December 1994 period. Early in 1995, the band had another single on the charts, "Tryin' to Get to New Orleans" (co-written by Ripley, Richmond and Tim DuBois). It toured widely during the year, playing at major concert venues and also performing at Michael Martin Murphy's WestFest event in September. Just after returning from an early fall tour of Europe, band

members were elated to find that their song "Baby Likes to Rock It" had been named Music Video of the Year by the CMA. Steve Ripley and Jamie Oldaker were on hand at the awards telecast in October to receive the award.

The band closed out 1995 with their album *Have Yourself a Tractors Christmas* riding high on the hit lists. Soundscan, the organization which compiles data on actual record dealer sales, reported that during the first week of release of the Tractors' disc, the album outsold all other Christmas collections by almost two to one. The single "Santa Claus Boogie" was a top rated entry on TNN, CMT and other video outlets.

TRAVIS, MERLE: *Singer, guitarist, banjoist, fiddler, songwriter. Born Ebenezer, Kentucky, November 29, 1917; died October 20, 1983. Elected to Country Music Hall of Fame in 1977.*

One of the more important songwriters as well as performers in country music for many years, Merle Travis was also an innovator in the field. He originated a method of guitar playing called "Travis-style" that has been adopted by countless performers since Merle started using it decades ago. In addition, he also is credited with an early version of the solid body guitar, a concept that became the basis for the electric guitars favored by all rock musicians as well as an increasing number of folk and country performers since the 1960s.

Born and raised in Kentucky, Merle Robert Travis knew the state's mining towns well and often wrote of the troubles and sorrows of digging coal, though he himself managed to stay out of the mines. He told Irby M. Maxwell in an interview for *Guitar Player* magazine (June 1969), "I was born in Southwest Kentucky in a little place called Ebenezer in Muhlenberg County. Once I made a record called 'Nine Pound Hammer' and there's a verse in it called 'It's a long way to Harlan, it's a long way to Hazard,' and when I tell them I am from the other side of the state why they say, 'Well, you've sung about Harlan and Hazard,' and I would tell them, 'I've sung about heaven all my life, and nobody's ever accused me of being there.' "

Merle's father relaxed after work by playing the five-string banjo. Young Merle loved the music and tried to play the banjo himself. His father gave him an old one when he was six and Merle could play it fairly well in a few years. Several years later, his brother made him a homemade guitar. Merle's unusual way of playing the guitar, the famed Travis style, resulted from his applying banjo technique to the new instrument. He used his thumb as an accompaniment while the forefinger played the melody on the higher pitched strings. Merle told Maxwell, "I was about 12 when I started to learn some little old chords [on the guitar]. The first instrument I began to play with was a five-string banjo. I was always fascinated by string instruments and I learned to fiddle a little bit. Very little."

After finishing grade school, Merle quit formal education and earned money playing for square dances, fish fries, and "chitlin' rags." He improved his guitar playing by observing many Kentucky performers, including Mose Rager and Ike Everly, the latter the father of the Everly Brothers. "They used to play at parties and little get-togethers on Sunday afternoon or just anywhere that there were two guitars." Their style, he noted, was similar to what he uses. "A thumb pick, and one little ole finger. I seldom use anything but my thumb and index finger, but on some things I use three fingers. My usual is to thumb pick and no pick on my third finger of my right hand."

For a while in his teens, he worked for the Civilian Conservation Corps. As soon as he earned enough to buy a thirty-dollar Gretsch guitar, he joined a friend hitchhiking around the country. They played on street corners and slept in train stations, parked cars, or on park benches. His wanderings eventually took him to Evansville, Indiana, in 1935, where he sang on a marathon broadcast on a local station. A group called the Tennessee Tomcats heard the broadcast and asked him to join them. For some months he toured the Midwest with them and was paid the princely sum of thirty-five cents a day. At times his path crossed that of fiddler and band leader Clayton McMichen. McMichen liked Merle's playing and one day sent Travis a telegram to join his band, the Georgia Wildcats. Travis joined in 1937 and toured widely with the group, playing fairs, local shows, and fiddling contests, where McMichen sometimes matched skills with fiddlers like Natchez the Indian and Curly Fox.

It was with the Georgia Wildcats that Travis debuted on radio station WLW in Cincinnati in the late 1930s. After a while he had a featured spot on the show and progressed to more important roles on network radio programs. He played such well-known shows of the period as the *Plantation Party* and *National Barn Dance* and was a cast regular for a number of years on the *Boone County Jamboree,* which later became known as the *Midwestern Hayride,* on WLW. During his six years on that station, he shared bills with many of the most famous names in country music. For a time, he was part of a quartet (The Brown's Ferry Four) whose other members were Grandpa Jones and the Delmore Brothers, Alton and Rabon.

Travis' career was interrupted by World War II, when he enlisted in the Marines and spent several years as a leatherneck. After receiving his discharge, he settled in Southern California, where he worked with such performers as Cliffie Stone, Tex Ritter, and Wesley Tuttle. He was a cast regular for a number of years on Stone's *Hometown Jamboree TV* program and also appeared on many other country radio and TV programs originating in the Los Angeles area.

Merle, of course, had been writing original material for some time and now he had the chance to record some of it (as well as songs by other writers) on a major label, Capitol. He had good success with such singles as "No Vacancy," "Divorce Me C.O.D," "So Round, So Firm, So Fully Packed," and "Cincinnati Lou." His first Capitol album in 1947, *Folk Songs of the Hills,* included his composition "Sixteen Tons." Not much happened with the number at the time, but some years later, Tennessee Ernie Ford recorded it and the song became one of the major hits of 1955 and went on to be one of the top-selling singles of all time. Other hit songs written by Merle are "Smoke, Smoke, Smoke That Cigarette," "Dark as a Dungeon," "Sweet Temptation," and "Old Mountain Dew."

It was during the late 1940s that Merle came up with his solid body guitar idea. He told Maxwell, "As far as I know, I had the first solid body that you play Spanish style. I got an idea when I heard a steel player playing and thought, with electric pickups, why have the hollow body. I bet a solid body would be good and the sustainability would be much better. I drew a picture on the back of a program sheet (the layout including having all the tuning pegs on one side) in a show we were doing over in Pasadena called *Hometown Jamboree*. . . . I asked a friend of mine, Paul Bigsby, if he could make it. He said, 'Sure, I'll build it.' I still have it." He recalled that a friend named Leo Fender saw him play it, asked if he could borrow it to build a similar instrument "and as far as I know that was the first Fender guitar."

During the 1950s, Travis was featured on both local and national TV shows telecast from the West Coast. He also headlined country concerts all over the United States. With the advent of the folk boom, he often was featured at major festivals both in the United States and other countries. His wide-ranging live appearances continued in the 1960s when he moved to Nashville, where he was a popular regular cast member of the *Grand Ole Opry.* During the 1960s and 1970s, he performed before audiences in every state in the union, every province of Canada, and in major nations throughout Europe and the Pacific Basin. He remained a Capitol Record recording artist from the mid-1940s to the late 1960s. His albums during his last decade with Capitol included *Back Home* (12/57), *Walkin' the Strings, Travis!* (3/62), *Songs of the Coal Miners* (9/63), and *Best of Merle Travis* (3/67). A collection of his recordings also came out on Pickwick Records in the mid-1960s, *Our Man from Kentucky.*

Travis continued to be active in the 1970s, though not on as hectic a schedule as previous years. He continued to appear on the *Opry* and guested on various televised country shows, and concerts. He was nominated for the Country Music Hall of Fame several times during the decade and finally was voted onto that distinguished roster in October 1977.

Merle died in 1983, but his musical achievements, particularly his instrumental innovations, seemed likely to influence both country and pop artists well into the future. In including him on its list of "The 100 Greatest Guitarists of the 20th Century" in the February 1993 issue of *Musician* magazine, the publication's editors noted, "Chet Atkins could have sworn he was listening to two guitarists the first time he heard Merle Travis playing on the radio. Atkins went on to perfect his three-finger style to emulate what Travis was doing with just his thumb and index finger."

In including Merle in the *Life* magazine list of "The 100 Most Important People in the History of Country" in a special September 1994 issue, the list preparers cited both his writing and performing contributions. They cited some of his lyrics, as "country wit at its finest" while "The Kentuckian's brilliant fingering— widely imitated . . . was so infectious he never required a rhythm section and is now regarded as one of the greatest guitarists in history. Any genre."

Albums still in print of his work, as of 1996, included *The Best of Merle Travis* on Rhino Records and *The Merle Travis Story—24 Greatest Hits* on the Country Music Hall of Fame label. Travis also was represented in various collections such as CMH's compilation of *50 Years of Bluegrass Hits*. Also available as an import item was the German Bear Family Records 5 CD boxed set *Guitar Rags and a Too Fast Past*. The set contained all his Capitol recordings from 1946–1955 and previously unavailable recordings on a number of small labels such as King and Bel-Tone. The tracks covered his major hits such as "Divorce Me COD," "Steel Guitar Rag," "No Vacancy," and "Cincinnati Lou" plus the contents of some guitar-only albums.

TRAVIS, RANDY: *Singer, guitarist, bandleader, songwriter, actor. Born Hendersonville, North Carolina, May 4, 1959.*

It might be said that country music literally saved Randy Travis's life, or at least that it assured a life of success and comfort rather than one spent behind bars. On the other hand, it could also be said Randy returned the compliment by helping, with his neotraditional, straightforward singing style, to put new life into a country music industry whose fortunes were sagging considerably in the early 1980s.

Randy (original name Randy Traywick) was born and raised in North Carolina, son of a horse trainer whose activities also inspired an interest in riding and nurturing such animals from Randy's early years. Travis also recalled that the environment engendered his interest in all things western, from movie "oaters" to learning gun tricks as he grew older. However, he was a troubled boy who became increasingly difficult to deal with as he reached his teens. About his only saving grace was a deep interest in country & western music, an interest he pursued when he wasn't taking part in wild escapades that soon got him in trouble with the law.

Among other things, Randy was into drugs and also

was building up a criminal record in his midteens for fighting, several car thefts, driving under the influence, and other such offenses. He was in danger of being sent to jail for five years in 1976 when he auditioned for a singing job at a nightclub in Charlotte, North Carolina, run by Lib Hatcher and her husband, Frank. She was bowled over by the youngster's ability and decided to try to straighten him out. She went to court and got the judge to agree to parole Randy into her custody.

Hatcher told *People* interviewers for an article for a special issue on country stars ("The Aloha Cowboy," fall 1994), "I didn't know anything about managing, but I realized he was good and that it would be a shame to see that talent go to waste."

Soon after she began to shape her protégé's career, Randy took up residence with her and her husband. He recalled for *People*, "It was pretty awkward, living part-time with a woman and her husband who you weren't sure how he felt about you. Sometimes I wondered whether or not I'd wake up in the morning."

Hatcher began to line up dates for Traywick at other places besides her club and started to plan for the logical steps to winning a record deal. Meanwhile, relations between Lib and Frank continued to deteriorate, and by the start of the 1980s they had separated, and she and Randy moved to Nashville to shop demos around the recording industry. For years they only got turndowns, but in the meantime romance came to the couple, even though she was some nineteen years older.

Randy commented, "I think we discovered how much we needed each other. Her marriage had been bad, and I was a total wreck. Plus, we shared an ambition to make it in the music business and worked night and day to make it happen. Our lives were inseparable."

Their break finally came in 1984 when they won a contract from Warner Brothers Records, which resulted in the release of his debut album, *Storms of Life*, in 1985. His down-home, nongimmicky sound proved a breath of fresh air for the country field and the album, along with several singles drawn from it, made major chart inroads. By the end of 1986, the album had passed R.I.A.A. platinum-record levels and Randy had his first best-selling single, "On the Other Hand." The fact that what had been considered good sales totals for country albums at the time typically fell far short of gold-record levels, much less platinum, opened country industry eyes to what might be gained from supporting new artists who until then had been banging on record company doors in Nashville with minimum response.

Randy's talents were quickly recognized by fellow artists, resulting in his first major award, the 1985 Academy of Country Music choice for Top New Male Vocalist. ACM followed up the next year by naming *Storms of Life* Album of the Year, "On the Other Hand" Best Single, and Randy Top Male Vocalist. In 1986 voting by Country Music Association members he was selected for the Horizon Award. That he was no one-hit wonder was demonstrated in 1987 when his second album, *Always and Forever,* proved just as fine a collection as his debut release. The album stayed at number one on the *Billboard* charts for ten months. It was voted Album of the Year for 1987 by the CMA, which also named his single "Forever and Ever, Amen" Single of the Year. In the 1987 Grammy Awards voting, *Storms of Life* was named Best Country Vocal Performance, Male. Those represented just a few of the honors Travis received for his records, videos, and concert work from the late 1980s into the 1990s.

Randy bolstered his status with the music public with intensive touring, totaling some 250 shows year after year, and many appearances on radio and TV. His albums, singles, and videos continued to make upper-chart levels. His 1988 album release, *Old 8 × 10,* was a best-seller and also won him a second Grammy and his next album, *Heroes and Friends,* arrived at number one in *Billboard* the week of November 24, 1990. His 1990 singles hits were "Hard Rock Bottom of Your Heart," number one in *Radio & Records* two weeks in a row in March, "He Walked on Water," number one in *R&R* the week of July 13, and "A Few Ole Country Boys" (a duet with George Jones), number five the week of October 19.

One of the requests from Warner Brothers when Randy was signed was that his relationship with Lib Hatcher be kept under wraps. After saying they were "just friends" for years, they finally resolved the matter by marrying in 1991. The situation had little impact on his career, which continued to prosper despite increasing competition to traditional-style performers from rock- and folk-influenced newcomers. *Heroes and Friends* went past platinum in 1991 and Randy placed singles like "Point of Light" on the charts. In the early 1990s, the Travis couple's desire for privacy caused them to spend an increasing part of their spare time at their ranch or beach house in Maui, Hawaii (hence the reference to "The Aloha Cowboy"), though they sometimes could be found on a 200-acre estate near Nashville.

Randy started to cut back on his entertainment activities for a while, giving up touring for several years because, he told *People,* "I just burned out waking up in a different town every day." However, he still did selected appearances on TV and began accepting parts in movie westerns and TV dramas such as *Matlock* and *Down Home.* He began to realize his childhood dreams of acting in western movies, taking a series of roles in the mid-1990s including a small part in *Young Guns* and more extensive parts that included playing a gambler in the 1994 hit film *Maverick* and a homeless man in *At Risk.* Other films in which he appeared were *The Legend of O. B. Taggart, Dead Man's Revenge* (which starred Bruce Dern), and the Rob Lowe vehicle, *Frank and Jesse.*

About those experiences, Travis commented, "It's been fun doing these westerns. I spent all my life practicing quick draw and riding horses, teaching 'em tricks. I thought, 'Boy, I spend a lot of time doing things that do me no good whatsoever.' It finally paid off."

Of course, though avoiding touring for a while allowed Travis to indulge his acting desires, he didn't abandon his bread-and-butter occupation. He completed his first one-hour special focusing on the music of the American West called *Wind in the Wire,* which first aired on ABC-TV on August 25, 1993. That was also the title of a soundtrack album issued by Warner Brothers the same month.

His name continued to appear on top singles-chart levels as well from 1992–1995. In 1992, for instance, his hits included "Better Class of Losers," number one in *Radio & Records* the week of February 21, "I'd Surrender All," number thirteen in *R&R* the week of May 15, and "I Didn't Have You," number one for two weeks in *R&R* in the early fall. His 1993 chartmakers included "Look Heart, No Hands," number eleven the week of January 15, and "An Old Pair of Shoes," number twelve the week of June 11. During 1993, Randy also earned a gold record for the album *Greatest Hits, Volume 2* (*Volume 1,* issued a few years earlier, also was a best-seller.)

In 1994, Randy had a new album on the charts, *This Is Me,* released in April. It peaked at number ten in *Billboard* during the spring and was still on the lists in early 1995, having earned him another R.I.A.A. gold-record award. Randy demonstrated he was still a strong favorite with country fans with not only steady album sales, but still more hit videos and singles. His 1994 chart successes included the singles "Before You Kill Us All," number one in *R&R* the week of May 6; "Whisper My Name," number one in *R&R* the week of August 26; and "This Is Me," number ten in *R&R* the week of November 25.

In early 1995 he had another top 10 single with "The Box." In August of that year the R.I.A.A. certified both *Volume 1* and *Volume 2* of his *Greatest Hits* compilations as platinum sellers. His fans gained more insight into his life in the summer of 1996 when he was the subject of a lengthy interview by Ralph Emery telecast over TNN.

TREVINO, RICK: *Singer, guitarist, pianist, clarinetist, songwriter. Born Austin, Texas, May 16, 1971.*

The early 1990s were a time of explosive growth in country music rosters, when almost every month seemed to provide several new names on the hit lists. On closer examination, most of the "new faces" had been paying dues off the beaten paths and were more likely to be in their thirties or even forties than in the first blush of young adulthood. Rick Trevino was an exception, a performer discovered at twenty-one and a chart success at twenty-two. He was also somewhat unique in being a country artist who could record hit songs in either English or Spanish.

Michael Corcoran, country music critic of the

Dallas Morning News ("Columbia Bets It Has a Future Superstar in Austin's Rick Trevino," October 7, 1993), suggested he might be tagged as a "Hispanic Garth Brooks" or a "Tex-Mex Ricky Van Shelton." But the third generation Mexican-American responded, "It's a little strange to me to be referred to as the Mexican this or the Hispanic that because it was never an issue growing up. I'm proud of my heritage, but I lived in a mostly Anglo environment, so I was never hit with 'Oh you can't do that.' I was just one of the guys."

His interest in music went back to his early childhood, he recalled. "From the moment I saw my father performing Tejano music with Neto Perez and the Originals in the clubs in Houston, I remember thinking, 'I want to be just like my dad.' I was three years old and I *knew*."

Oddly, though, his initial prime exposure was to classical music. His parents started him on piano lessons when he was five, and at six he performed in his first recital playing the main theme from the *Star Wars* movie score. He told *Radio & Records* that, in those preteen years, "I had to practice every afternoon before I could go out and play. Sometimes I'd get upset, but within a few years I started getting good, and began to see that I was different from everybody else and could do something no other kid could do as well."

In junior high school, his interest began to be affected by his peer group. He always liked sports and was beginning to show prowess as a baseball player. He also paid increasing attention to pop music, including rock and country, and soon picked up skills on other instruments, such as the guitar. He also formed a band called True Illusions that was soon finding favor at high school dances and other events. The group was better than an average teen-age band—good enough to have been chosen to open for an Austin concert by Gloria Estefan and the Miami Sound Machine.

While rock was popular in the Austin area, there was plenty of country music coverage on radio, and Austin, of course, was a hotbed of the modern country movement. Among performers that won Trevino's interest were Elvis, Merle Haggard, George Jones, and George Strait. A number of sidemen in Strait's backing band, Ace in the Hole, were Austin residents, and Rick became friendly with them and received comments about the fine points of performing and which records could aid in his artistic development. When Rick's career began to blossom, some of them played in his band.

Trevino was also scoring athletic points in high school. As he noted, "In high school, I chose the thing I feared the most, which was baseball, because music came too easily to me." Once involved, though, his nervousness evaporated and he eventually became a starter. "I went as far as I could with baseball, which was farther than I expected, so I wasn't disappointed. And music was always something I was doing along the way, playing churches, weddings, playing with local bands, whatever.

"I was lucky, because my father didn't get to play baseball on nice fields with good coaches or go to schools with the best teachers. He didn't have those things. But he was always there to provide the opportunities he didn't have; he gave us the opportunities, then we decided what we wanted to do."

Rick's ballplaying was good enough to bring him an offer of a partial scholarship to Memphis State University, but he decided to stay closer to home and try his luck as a walk-on at Texas A&M in College Station. He kept up with his classes, but didn't make the team, which made him decide to expend more energy on music. Besides doing weekend gigs in his home area, he also entered a singing contest at a local club. He didn't win the contest in his first attempt, but returned during his sophomore year and was named top artist. After that, he decided to drop out of school and add to his performing experience. (His mother served as his manager during that period.)

His discovery as a promising artist is attributed to a storm-induced change of plans by a record industry executive named Paul Jarosik. Jarosik was driving toward Austin when the trip was halted near Lake Travis by the news that roads were washed out between there and Austin. Jarosik had intended to eat dinner in Austin, but now had to settle for a place called the Thirsty Turtle near the lake. Trevino performed there on weekends, and the walls had clippings from local papers that enthusiastically praised his abilities. Restaurant personnel also gave him glowing reports, and Jarosik decided to ask Trevino to send him a demo tape. Rick did that, and Jarosik liked it enough to pass it on to Sony Records producer Steve Buckingham.

The tape convinced Sony Records officials there was something exciting about the young singer-songwriter. The song was one Rick had written in honor of his grandfather shortly after the old man's death. Rick told Corcoran, "He was always asking me if I knew 'San Antonio Rose,' the Bob Wills song, and I kept putting it off. Then one day my grandfather passed away and I realized that I'd never played the song for him and never would be able to. So I went home and wrote, 'Here's My San Antonio Rose to You.'"

Buckingham flew to Texas to sign Rick and soon had him in the studio working on debut material, both in English and Spanish. His debut single, "Just Enough Rope," came out in the summer of 1993 and was on the *Billboard* chart from September through the end of the year. His first Spanish effort, the album *Dos Mundos,* came out in the fall and a *Billboard* reviewer enthused in the November 6, 1993, issue, "Trevino's delightful outing is the first straight-up Spanish language record in many moons, and it works on every count."

Trevino commented, "With the ballads, when you sing it in Spanish, it's twice as romantic because the lyric seems to go to its extreme of expression. It's a big part of who I am. Everything I write originates in English, but what comes from my heart is Spanish." (However, his initial English-language singles chart hits were written by others.)

In early 1994, he had the single "Honky Tonk Crowd" on the charts. It became a *Billboard* Top 40 entrant later in the year. His debut album in English, *Rick Trevino*, made the *Billboard* list in early 1994 and stayed on it for most of the year, peaking at number twenty-three. During the summer of 1994, his hit single "She Can't Say I Didn't Cry" became one of the year's top sellers, peaking at number one in *R&R* the week of September 2 and going to number three in *Billboard* the following week. In March 1995, he had another single moving up the charts, "Looking for the Light," the title song for his second album, which debuted on the charts the same month. In the summer of 1995, his single "Bobbie Ann Mason" made it to the top 20. On September 5, 1995, the R.I.A.A. certified his debut album as gold.

TRITT, TRAVIS: *Singer, guitarist, bandleader, songwriter, actor. Born Marietta, Georgia, February 9, c. 1963.*

One of the brightest new stars of the 1990s, outwardly Travis Tritt seemed the personification of the "outlaw" image of performers like Hank Williams, Jr., and Waylon Jennings. And, indeed, he identified with them on certain levels. However he indicated he didn't intend to pursue some of the wilder aspects sometimes associated with honky-tonk music.

In fact, it was because of his family's fears about what a show business career might do to him that for a long time they took a dim view of such an outcome. Travis's interest in music went back to his childhood. He sang in the children's choir at the Assembly of God Church his family attended in his hometown of Marietta, Georgia, and recalled the impact singing lead vocals on Ray Stevens's "Everything Is Beautiful" had on him. He began to teach himself to play guitar at the age of eight, and when he was fourteen wrote his first song. As he progressed through his teens, he began to think seriously about making a living as a country artist, but his parents were not happy about the idea.

As he told Lisa Smith of *The Gavin Report* ("Travis Tritt: It Just Keeps Getting Better," November 22, 1991), they opposed him because "They didn't want me to end up like Elvis. When I was a kid, it seemed like everything you read about people in the music industry was bad. George Jones was arrested for shooting at Tammy Wynette, Merle Haggard showed up drunk at a concert, Elvis was suspected of drug abuse. My parents were scared—any parent that cares about their kids would be. So I suppressed the urge, but I knew what I wanted to do since I was four years old."

Tritt finished high school in 1981 and got married at about the same time. He had been gaining experience as a singer in local venues, and his father kept asking, "When the hell are you going to get a real job?" With that pressure plus having a wife to support, he did get a job with a heating and air-conditioning wholesale company. He remained with the firm for four years, starting out loading trucks and moving up the ladder to a management position. But he felt ill at ease as a company man, wondering whether he had the ability to succeed in music. His marriage having ended—and realizing he didn't want to wake up years later thinking he "could have been a contender"—he resigned his job and sought as many gigs as he could find at local clubs while also spending much of his free time songwriting.

It did not sit well at home, he told Lisa Smith. "My parents went berserk. My mother cried a lot, and it got to the point where I didn't talk to my dad for several months. . . . I didn't understand it at the time, but they just didn't want their son turning into a lowlife."

Tritt persevered with his new career objective and his path crossed that of Danny Davenport, a local representative of Warner Brothers Records. Initially, Davenport's main idea was to help place some of Tritt's original compositions. Then he heard Tritt perform before a local audience and decided Travis also had potential as a singer. He suggested they put together an album using his home studio, a project that required Tritt's making a $10,000 investment in the work. Tritt recalled that his family feared he was only being taken to the cleaners by a shrewd operator. After two years, they were satisfied with the product, and Davenport took the tapes to play for his Warner Brothers superiors in Los Angeles, Lenny Waronker and Mo Ostin.

Their verdict was favorable and they forwarded the material to Warner Brothers/Nashville for further consideration. The Nashville people didn't react right away, which didn't help Travis's blood pressure, but at long last they agreed to what amounted to a tryout—a contract for three singles. The pact was signed in 1987 and Travis finally went into the studios the following year to lay down candidates for the releases. By late 1988, Davenport and Tritt felt they had a good combination of material for an album, but the record company said any album would have to wait on public reaction to the singles. The initial release, "Country Club," came out in August 1989, and did surprisingly well for the first effort by an unknown performer. It soon became the title track for Tritt's debut album, issued in March 1990.

Everything seemed coming up roses for Travis at the end of 1989. Warner's had approved the new album, and his successes had healed the breach between him and his parents. But suddenly he had a soul-shaking scare. He was giving a concert in Tulsa, Oklahoma, in December 1989 when halfway through the show he lost his voice. A local doctor diagnosed it as laryngitis, which didn't sound that worrisome, but at the next stop in Pine Bluff, Arkansas, his throat felt even worse. He took a plane back to Nashville to consult with experts at the Vanderbilt clinic. They reported he had burst a blood vessel, which caused a polyp on his vocal chords. To heal it, they said, meant not using his voice in any way for three months.

He didn't savor that, but decided to follow orders since the physicians said if he didn't he might never be able to sing again. Fortunately, he recovered and in the spring was able to perform in support of his debut album either as a soloist in small clubs or an opening act for established performers. *Country Club* made the *Billboard* list, the start of a multiyear sojourn on it that eventually resulted in a platinum-record award from the R.I.A.A. Accompanying the album in 1990 were a series of hit singles, beginning with "Help Me Hold On," number one in *Radio & Records* for two weeks in April. After that came "I'm Gonna Be Somebody," number one in *R&R* the week of August 10. Late in the year "Put Some Drive in Your Country" was inside the *Billboard* Top 30. In the Country Music Association Awards voting for 1990, Travis was nominated for the Horizon Award. He didn't win that time, but he was nominated again in 1991 and this time was victorious.

His next album, *It's All About to Change,* was issued by Warner Brothers in the summer of 1991 and quickly rose up the charts, peaking at number two in *Billboard* on the way to achieving platinum sales-levels in 1992. Still on the list in 1993, its R.I.A.A. totals had gone past double platinum. Late in 1991, his duet single with Marty Stuart, "The Whiskey Ain't Workin'," came out and rose to number one in *R&R* in late January 1992. During the year exuberant audiences welcomed Stuart and Tritt at venues across the U.S. in what was called the "No Hats Tour."

In the spring, Travis had the solo hit "Nothing Short of Dying" which peaked at number one in *R&R* the week of May 15. In the summer, he and Stuart had another chart single "This One's Gonna Hurt You" (written by Stuart) and Travis wound up after that with the single "Lord Have Mercy on the Working Man," which rose to number two in *R&R* the week of October 30. He also had two more albums to his credit before the end of 1992, *T-R-O-U-B-L-E,* and *A Travis Tritt Christmas: Loving Time of the Year.* Both easily made the charts with *T-R-O-U-B-L-E* passing R.I.A.A. gold levels by January 1993 and rising past platinum in the spring. On the CMA Awards telecast in October 1992, it was announced that Tritt and Marty Stuart had won the award for Vocal Event of the Year. Tritt had also been nominated for the songwriter's award for "Here's a Quarter (Call Someone Who Cares)" and for Male Vocalist of the Year.

Tritt started off 1993 with the hit single (written with S. Harris) "Can I Trust You With My Heart," number one in *R&R* for two weeks in January. Later the single "T-R-O-U-B-L-E" (written by J. Chesnutt) rose to number eleven in *R&R* the week of May 14 followed by

"Looking Out for Number One" (cowritten by Travis and Troy Seals), number seven in *R&R* the week of September 10. During the year he joined with several other stars in a George Jones & Friends album project that included the track "I Don't Need Your Rockin' Chair." This was chosen as 1993 Vocal Event of the Year by the CMA.

But that wasn't the only multiartist project he was involved in. Executives at Giant Records had the idea of doing a tribute album to the Eagles as a benefit effort to help preserve Walden Woods. Tritt was one of the first artists contacted. He told Lyndon Stambler, "I was told the Eagles were not going to be involved in the recording of any of the songs on the album. In fact, they were not. . . . They wanted each artist to donate his personal proceeds to the Walden Woods project. I said I don't have a problem with any of that. I was just proud to be part of an album of this magnitude involved with the Eagles name. These are some of the greatest songs I grew up with, some of the most influential songs of my career, and songs that I've played, probably like every other artist on the album, over and over in bars and clubs when I was being a human jukebox, basically, and trying to get a deal."

He originally thought of doing "Desperado," but Clint Black had opted for that, so he chose "Take It Easy." This was planned to be the only single release from the collection, and the Giant people asked Travis to do a video also. "I said, 'If I'm going to do a video, the only way I'm going to do a video is if we get the Eagles back together.' They sort of laughed. Everybody kind of chuckled and got a big kick out of it, because nobody thought it could happen. . . . Nobody thought this would happen because every time either Glenn Frey or Don Henley had been interviewed prior to that and they were asked about Eagles' reunions, they would kind of go, 'Yeah, when hell freezes over.' I read an article where Don Henley was asked point blank, 'Are the Eagles going to ever get back together?' and he said, 'No, there is no way I see this is going to happen because Glenn Frey and I hate each other.'"

Undaunted, Tritt asked his management to contact the two and also discussed the idea with Giant Records president Irving Azoff, the Eagles' former manager. To everyone's surprise, they finally got an okay from the two. Tritt thought he might see the two prime movers end up in a fistfight, but nothing like that occurred. Instead of that, he told Lyndon Stambler, "when the video happened, it was just the opposite. I saw a bunch of guys who got together and really seemed to realize that they didn't hate each other as bad as they thought they did. . . . The whole thing was set up around, basically it was just Travis Tritt and the Eagles hanging out in a bar, shooting pool, performing together, etc. I got to be an Eagle for a day."

The end result, of course, was an Eagles reunion tour with an accompanying live album called *The Hell*

Freezes Over Tour, one of the premiere concert events of the mid-1990s. The tribute album, *Common Thread: Songs of the Eagles,* was named Album of the Year in 1994 CMA voting. (Tritt also contributed to another multiartist album nominated in that CMA category, MCA's *Rhythm, Country & Blues.*)

As if all that wasn't enough, Tritt began writing his autobiography and worked on recording tracks for a new album to accompany the book's release in the spring of 1994. The book and album both were titled *Ten Feet Tall and Bulletproof,* as was the long-form video issued at the same time by Warner Brothers. (Other projects Tritt was involved in at this time included serving as host for VH-1's *Country Countdown,* recording the theme song for the film *The Cowboy Way,* in which he also had a role as a rodeo participant, and a 110-city tour with Joe Diffie and Lee Roy Parnell.) The album made the *Billboard* chart almost as soon as it was issued and, after peaking at number three, went past gold and platinum R.I.A.A. totals by year-end. The week of July 8, his self-penned single "Foolish Pride" rose to number one in *R&R* and later the title track of the album, which he also wrote, was a chart hit. Late in 1994, his single "Between an Old Memory and Me" showed up on *Billboard*'s list and made the top 20 in early 1995. In the summer of 1995, "Tell Me I Was Dreaming" (cowritten by Tritt and B. R. Brown) rose to number two in *Billboard* and number one elsewhere.

One of the tracks on the 1994 album, "Outlaws Like Us," paid homage to two of his most-admired performers, Hank Williams, Jr., and Waylon Jennings. Both agreed to join him on the track. Tritt defined his definition of "outlaw" for Richard McVey of *Cash Box* ("Travis Tritt: A Mere Ten Feet Tall and Bulletproof," May 7, 1994): "To me it simply means one thing and that's doing things your own way regardless of what the 'establishment' tries to tell you is 'commercial.' That means you're going to have constant battles with your record labels and constant battles with the powers that be. . . . But it also gives you a tremendous amount of personal satisfaction in knowing that someone came up to you and said, 'that will never work,' and you go out and make it. Unfortunately, the term 'outlaw' tends to be applied to your personality and not just the music [where people tend to say] 'Travis Tritt is an asshole . . . he's hard to work with . . . he's moody . . . he's got a huge ego,' but the fact of the matter is none of those things are true."

One of his problems in writing his life story, he told McVey, was his relatively untroubled upbringing. He asked himself initially, "What in the world am I going to write about? . . . I wasn't abused as a child, I haven't tried to commit suicide, I haven't been in any rehab centers. . . . As I thought about it, the only thing I could think of, or angle I could come up with, is showing people what really goes on behind the scenes."

Ten Feet Tall and Bulletproof, which had peaked at number three in *Billboard* soon after its release, was still in upper chart levels in 1995, having passed platinum sales levels the year before. On September 12, 1995, Warner Bros. issued the restrospective *Greatest Hits—From the Beginning.* The album, which rose to number three in *Billboard,* was certified gold by the R.I.A.A. on November 16, 1995. That same month, Tritt had the top-10 single on the charts, "Sometimes She Forgets" (written by Steve Earle). In early 1996, his single "Only You (and You Alone)" was on the hit lists followed later in the year by his duet single and video with Marty Stuart, "Honky Tonkin's What I Do Best." During the summer and fall of 1996, the two took off on an intensive concert series called the Double Trouble Tour.

TUBB, ERNEST: *Singer, guitarist, composer, bandleader (the Texas Troubadours), publisher. Born Crispo, Texas, February 9, 1914; died Nashville, Tennessee, September 6, 1984. Founding member of the Country Music Association in 1958. Elected to Country Music Hall of Fame in 1965.*

Ellis County, Texas, is about forty or fifty miles south of Dallas. It was picture-book cottonwoods ranch country when young Ernest Tubb stretched his growing frame and dreamt of becoming a cowboy movie star. A mail-order guitar and self-instruction book were still in his future at that point, although he did some singing with the string bands that played dances, mostly square dances, around the country.

At eighteen, in the Depression year of 1932, Tubb got a paying job in San Antonio as a soda jerk. By then he could play guitar, though not as well as he desired. Two years later, still in San Antonio, he talked himself into a singing and picking job at KONO and married Lois Elaine Cook. The year 1935 was a decisive one; he met Carrie, the gracious widow of Jimmie Rodgers. Ernest had never met Rodgers, but the Singing Brakeman's recordings had long ago convinced Tubb to give up his boyhood cowboy star notions. Jimmie became Ernest's ideal as the young Texan copied Rodgers' phrasing for a time and absorbed the already substantial Rodgers lore. Also in the hot summer of 1935, Ernest's first son, Justin, was born on August 20th.

By 1936, Carrie Rodgers and the Tubbs had become close friends. She not only gave Ernest the original Jimmie Rodgers guitar, but also obtained an RCA Victor recording contract for him. She arranged a theater personal appearance tour and acted as his manager for a short time. He recorded at the old Texas Hotel in San Antonio, making cuts of "The Passing of Jimmie Rodgers" and "Jimmie Rodgers' Last Thoughts." These were released on RCA Victor's Bluebird label. Things were looking up, but life still consisted of the grind of one-night stands and spells of unemployment.

Sadness also was part of these years. A second son, Rodger Dale, was born and died in 1938. Tubb wrote

"Our Baby's Book" in his memory; the song remained one of the most requested ones in his repertoire. In 1939, Violet Elaine, "Scooter Bill," was born.

The start of one of the industry's longest and most successful recording affiliations came in 1940 when Tubb was signed by Decca Records. In San Antonio, Texas, on April 4, he recorded two songs he had written, "Blue Eyed Elaine" and "I'll Get Along Somehow." They sold records, enough at any rate for a twenty-dollar-a-week job at KGKO in Fort Worth. This job, in turn, soon gave him the chance to become identified with a commercial sponsor.

He became known as "The Gold Chain Troubador," for the Gold Chain Flour Company, earning a full seventy-five dollars a week. But things were discouraging for Tubb and he seriously considered giving up his career for a defense job, where the pay was steady and certain. Things suddenly turned around when he decided to record a song he had been playing around with. It has become his all-time hit, a gold-record-seller, "Walking the Floor Over You." The song started opening doors, even those to Hollywood.

He made two western movies in 1942. Charles Starrett was the established star in both, and both can still be seen in those very late television showings under the original titles of *Fighting Buckaroo* and *Ridin' West*. Hollywood was not exactly shaken by this. But the effort did help gain him a guest appearance late in the year on the *Grand Ole Opry*. *Opry* audiences and executives were impressed with him. In 1943 he became a regular and was still a fixture on the *Opry* in the year of his death, 1984. The following year he appeared in another motion picture, *Jamboree*, and in 1947, in the film *Hollywood Barn Dance*. Along with better-paying personal appearances and thousands of miles of traveling each month, Tubb set a precedent by appearing at Carnegie Hall.

The money was easier and he started expanding business interests, working out a music firm arrangement with Jean and Julian Aberbach of Hill and Range Songs, Inc. He also founded the Ernest Tubb Record Shop in Nashville in 1947, later relocated to 417 Broadway near the original *Opry*. Another milestone was the arrangement with WSM for broadcasting the *Midnight Jamboree*, immediately following the *Opry* broadcast each Saturday night. Among those who credited opportunities to perform on that show with paving the way to future stardom were Loretta Lynn, Johnny Cash, Patsy Cline, the Wilburn Brothers, and Bobby Helms.

Although Ernest had three songs on the *Billboard* Top-10 charts in 1948, it was a bittersweet year; he and Elaine were divorced. He continued having one hit after another in 1949, with a final count of seven songs on the top 10 and one a near miss. The latter was "My Tennessee Baby" dedicated to Olene Adams Carter, who soon married him. The others were "Blue Christmas," "Don't Rob Another Man's Castle," "Have You Ever

Been Lonely," "I'm Bitin' My Fingernails and Thinking of You," "Slippin' Around," "Tennessee Border No. 2," and "Warm Red Wine."

Tubb and Red Foley recorded a duet in 1950, "Goodnight Irene," which gained the top honors for the year. Tubb continued his grueling round of appearances by airplane, car, train, and bus, covering more than 100,000 miles a year, playing concerts, honky-tonks, parks, everywhere he could be booked with his band, the Texas Troubadors. Daughters Erlene Dale and Olene Gayle were born in 1951 and 1952 before his first Korean and Japanese tour with Hank Snow.

Foul weather and exhaustion brought on a lingering illness that made him leave the *Opry* until November 1954. Three more children, Ernest Dale Tubb, Jr. (1956), Larry Dean (1958), and Karen Delene (1960), joined the Tubb home at a time when Tubb was successfully recuperating between his still hectic schedules of road trips. His traveling in the 1960s was in his own bus, outfitted for mileage comfort.

His recordings of "Thanks a Lot" in 1963, the duet with Loretta Lynn on "Mr. and Mrs. Used to Be" in 1964, and the millionth sale of "Walking the Floor Over You" in 1965, showed his continued popularity. This was acknowledged in 1965 by his election to the coveted Country Music Association's Hall of Fame.

Close to 200 single records were released by Tubb over the years to 1981, along with numerous albums. Other hits include "Rainbow at Midnight," "It's Been So Long, Darling," "You Nearly Lose Your Mind," "Women Make a Fool Out of Me," "Take Me Back and Try Me One More Time," "Tomorrow Never Comes," and "Thanks a Lot."

His 1960s LP credits include several on the Vocalion label, such as *Texas Troubadours* (1960) and *Great Country* (12/69). His many Decca albums include such titles as *Ernest Tubb Favorites; Daddy of 'Em All; Importance of Being Ernest; Story of Ernest Tubb* (two LPs, 1959); *Record Shop* (1960s); *Golden Favorites, All Time Hits* (1961); *On Tour* (1962); *Just Call Me Lonesome, Family Bible* (1963); *Thanks a Lot* (8/64); *Country Dance Time, My Pick of the Hits* (both issued 8/65); *Mr. & Mrs. Used to Be* (9/65); *Hittin' the Road* (1/65); *Stand By Me* (6/66); *Hits Old and New* (11/66); and *Singin' Again* (8/67). His Decca album releases of the late 1960s and early 1970s included *Greatest Hits, Volume 2; One Sweet Hello;* and *Good Year for the Wine*.

While Ernest didn't have much impact on the hit charts in the 1970s, he continued to be very active and much revered and honored by performers old and new and by countless fans, particularly those who came to applaud his segment of the *Grand Ole Opry*, broadcast by then from the new *Opry* headquarters in Opryland. Throughout the 1970s and into the 1980s, he continued to host his *Midnight Jamboree* radio show broadcast live from the Ernest Tubb Record Shop Number 2 next door to Opryland. Throughout the decade and in the early 1980s, he kept up his hectic touring schedule, still averaging 200 working days as of 1981. Although nominally still on the Decca roster at the end of the 1970s, his output tapered off to zero on the label. By the start of the 1980s, only three titles remained in the active album catalogue of MCA (which had absorbed Decca): *Ernest Tubb's Golden Favorites, Ernest Tubb's Greatest Hits,* and the two-record set *The Ernest Tubb Story.*

On February 9, 1979, coinciding with Tubb's sixty-fifth birthday, a tribute LP came out on Cachet Records titled *Ernest Tubb: The Legend and the Legacy.* Among the stars whose contributions were overdubbed on Tubb's renditions by producer Pete Drake (Tubb was not aware of this until the album was completed) were Willie Nelson, Waylon Jennings, Charlie Daniels, Loretta Lynn, Conway Twitty, Justin Tubb, Charlie Rich, Cal Smith, Merle Haggard, Johnny Paycheck, George Jones, Marty Robbins, the Wilburn Brothers, Vern Gosdin, Ferlin Husky, and many more. Also issued in early 1979 was a single from the album, "Waltz Across Texas," featuring Ernest, Willie Nelson, Charlie Daniels, and Charlie McCoy.

Fittingly, the LP rose to upper-chart levels and was one of the top-50 best-selling LP releases of the year.

Ernest continued to be active on the *Opry* and on concert tours with his band, the Texas Troubadours, into the 1980s, though by then he was battling the emphysema that finally claimed his life in September 1984.

Tubb continued to record new material for Decca and its successor label, MCA, into the mid-1970s. Overall it was estimated that his forty-four-year association with Decca/MCA resulted in sales of some 35 million records. After that, he recorded for several other labels: First Generation, Award, Sound Factory, Soundwaves, and Elektra/Curb. Over the years, during his lifetime and afterward, reissues came out on a variety of labels. Besides MCA, those appeared on Bear Family Records (a German company), Rhino Records, Rounder Records, the Franklin Mint Record Society, Time-Life Records, and Columbia.

Among extant records as of 1995 was a best-of collection published by MCA, which included material covering twenty-five years of Tubb's career, from the 1941 "Walking the Floor Over You" to the 1965 classic, "Waltz Across Texas." Another available LP in the mid-1990s was Rhino Records' *Ernest Tubb Live 1965.* Material available from the Country Music Foundation catalog in the mid-1990s included the SCR CD (or cassette) *Ernest Tubb Collection* and the BCD package of his early work titled *Ernest Tubb/Let's Say Goodbye Like We Said Hello.* The last named was a five-CD set containing over 100 tracks recorded between March 1947 and the end of 1953.

Tubb's tremendous recorded output could be seen from discographies like those compiled by Ronnie

Pugh, head of reference for the Country Music Foundation library. His compilation just for the years 1958–1982 took up fifteen pages in the *Journal of Country Music,* Volume 11, no. 1 issue. (Pugh's discography of Tubb's recordings from 1936–57 was presented in *JCM,* Volume 9, no. 1, 1981.)

In including Tubb in its choice of the "100 Most Important People in the History of Country" (September 1, 1994), *Life* magazine editors cited the time in 1941 when Ernest had his guitar player plug in an electrified instrument. They noted Tubb wasn't the first to use such an instrument, "but he developed a wholly unique style perfectly in keeping with country spirit." It was probably not something that traditionalists, who accepted Tubb's great creative contributions to the development of the country genre, liked to recall.

TUBB, JUSTIN: *Singer, guitarist, songwriter. Born San Antonio, Texas, August 20, 1935.*

A great deal of entertainment magic seems to go with the name Tubb. It's a magic that carried over from one generation to the next as Justin Wayne Tubb proved a worthy heir to the mantle worn by his Country Music Hall of Fame father, Ernest.

Justin naturally was steeped in country-music lore from the cradle. He spent some of his boyhood years in San Antonio before attending Castle Heights Military School at Lebanon, Tennessee, 1944–48. During his high school years in San Antonio, Justin already showed his potential playing a mean guitar and singing at school events.

He enrolled at the University of Texas at Austin for the 1952–53 session. But the pull of country music was too great and he left for a disc jockey job at WHIN in Gallatin, Tennessee, during 1953–54. Besides spinning platters, he entertained his audience by singing; many of the songs in his repertoire were his own compositions. It didn't take long before he signed with Decca in 1953 and had a number of records receiving plays across the nation, including his own compositions "Ooh-La-La" and "The Story of My Life."

In 1954, Tubb joined with Goldie Hill on a top-10 hit, "Looking Back to See." He also turned out such records as "Something Called the Blues," "I'm Lookin' for a Date Tonight," "I Miss You," "Sure Fire Kisses," "Fickle Heart," and his own song "Sufferin' Heart." By now his name was well known nationally and he was asked to become a *Grand Ole Opry* regular in 1955. He sang such new songs that year as "I Gotta Go Get My Baby," "Chuga-Chuga, Chica-Mauga," "My Heart's Not for You to Play With," "I'm Sorry I Stayed Away So Long," "All Alone," "Within Your Arms," "Who Will It Be?" and "Pepper Hot Baby." His 1956 output included his own "I'm Just a Fool Enough" and such other records as "You Nearly Lose Your Mind," "Lucky, Lucky Someone Else," and "It Takes a Lot of Heart."

Some of his other recordings of the 1950s included his own "I'm a Big Boy Now" and "The Life I Have to Live"; "Miss the Mississippi and You," "Desert Blues," "The Party Is Over," and "If You'll Be My Love" (1957); "Sugar Lips" and his own "Rock It Down to My House" and "Almost Lonely" (1958); and two of his compositions, "I Know You Do" and "Buster's Gang" (1959). Decca also issued an LP of Tubb's work in 1958 called *Country Boy in Love.*

Tubb left Decca in 1959 and signed with Starday for 1960–62. (He also turned out one release for Challenge during this period.) In 1962, he went with RCA Victor. During the 1960s, many top performers sang Justin's compositions, including his father, the Wilburn Brothers, Faron Young, Webb Pierce, Patsy Cline, Jim Reeves, Mac Wiseman, Skeeter Davis, Cowboy Copas, Red Sovine, Teresa Brewer, Ray Price, and Hank Snow. A number of these were top-10 hits, including Hawkshaw Hawkins' version of "Lonesome 7-7203," a number-one-rated hit of 1963; Faron Young-Margie Singleton with "Keeping Up with the Joneses," and Jim Reeves-Dottie West with "Love Is No Excuse" in 1964.

Justin continued to turn out hit records of his own, such as "Take a Letter Miss Gray" in 1963 and "Dern Ya" in 1964. He also had great success with his LPs in the 1960s, including the 1962 Starday releases *Modern Country Music Sound of Justin Tubb* and *Justin Tubb, Star of the Grand Ole Opry.* In the mid-1960s, he was represented on RCA Victor with such albums as *Justin Tubb* (3/65); *Where You're Concerned* (9/65); *The Best of Justin Tubb* (1965); *Together and Alone* (8/66); and *That Style* (8/67). At the end of the decade he had some recordings come out on the Paramount label, including the album *Things I Still Remember.*

His personal appearances during the 1960s took him to almost all of the states and the Canadian provinces. He also toured Germany. His TV guest spots included the *National Barn Dance* and *WWVA Jamboree.*

From a recording standpoint, the 1970s weren't very rewarding for Tubb, whose traditional approach to the music, like that of his father's, suffered under the combined inroads of country-rock and progressive country. He complained during a backstage interview at the *Opry* in the late 1970s (during a nationally televised TV show) that the problem for traditional artists was getting any kind of coverage for record releases on country radio programs. He told the interviewer he was sure there was a large audience for the kind of music he believed in, but that without radio coverage there was no way for those people to know about new songs in that style.

Meanwhile, though recording opportunities were sparse in the 1970s and early 1980s, Justin didn't lack for work. He toured steadily, guested on many country TV shows and continued to be a fixture on the *Grand Ole Opry.*

TUCKER, TANYA: *Singer. Born Seminole, Texas, October 10, 1958.*

At the end of the 1970s, a blurring of the edges in country music gave rise to many hybrid forms that helped bring across-the-board pop interest to many country artists. Still, country audiences, while fiercely loyal to favorite performers, tend to look askance at any changes in style, as Tanya Tucker found out in the late 1970s. However, with her vibrant voice and dynamic stage presence, it seemed reasonable to assume she might attract a broader following, as 1970s stars Dolly Parton and Crystal Gayle had done.

Tucker was only in her twenties at the time, but she had been a country star for most of the decade, having achieved her first top-10 country single in her early teens. Her parents had encouraged her musical interests when she was a small child, the youngest of three children of construction worker Beau Tucker and his wife, Juanita. After the family moved to Phoenix in 1967, the girl's attraction to country music was fostered by her father, who took her to concerts by such artists as Ernest Tubb, Mel Tillis, and Leroy Van Dyke.

By the time the family moved again, this time to St. George, Utah, Tanya's singing efforts made her parents decide that she could succeed in the entertainment field. When the film *Jeremiah Johnson* was being shot on location in Utah, Juanita Tucker took her daughter to audition for a major part. Tanya missed out on that, but did earn some money as a bit player.

Convinced of Tanya's abilities, the Tuckers later moved to Las Vegas, Nevada, hoping to make connections with entertainment industry executives. They had Tanya cut a demonstration tape that caught the ear of songwriter Dolores Fuller, who brought her to the attention of Billy Sherrill, artists & repertoire head of Columbia Epic Records in Nashville. Billy liked what he heard and signed Tucker for Epic. In March 1972, Tanya and her father went to Nashville for her first recording session, where she taped the song "Delta Dawn." Released as a single, it became one of the major country hits of the year, reaching the top 10 on the charts of all three major music industry trade magazines. The debut album, also titled *Delta Dawn,* became a country best-seller.

Another track from that album, "Jamestown Ferry," provided another singles hit, actually a double hit, since the reverse side, "Love's the Answer," also moved high on the charts. In 1973, Tanya, then only fourteen, proved her debut was no fluke by coming out with a well-crafted second album, *What's Your Mama's Name.* Not only did the album reach the top rungs of the charts, but the title song rose to number one on the national country lists. During 1973 and 1974, Tucker achieved a series of other hit singles on Columbia, including such number-one successes as "Blood Red and Going Down," "Would You Lay with Me (in a Field of Stone)," and "The Man Who Turned My Mother On."

Tanya and her advisers decided not to remain with Columbia and when her contract expired, in late 1974, she moved over to MCA. Her debut on that label proved that her popularity remained strong: *Tanya Tucker* rose into the country top 10 on most charts. Her 1975 singles hits included "San Antonio Stroll" and "Lizzie and the Rainman," the latter number one on U.S. country charts in July 1975. In early 1976, she made the charts with the album *Lovin' and Learnin'* and the single "You've Got Me to Hold Onto." Later in the year, Columbia released one of her previous recordings, "Here's Some Love," and it moved up to the top rungs. In 1977, she had a top-10 single, "It's a Cowboy Lovin' Night" and the hit album *Ridin' Rainbows.*

Through the mid-1970s, she was featured on almost every important network TV show, including the *Grand Ole Opry.* Her name generally appeared on lists of the best five or ten country female vocalists, including a number of nominations over the years in the Country Music Association Awards. In 1974 and 1975, for instance, she was one of the five finalists for Female Vocalist of the Year.

In 1978, Tucker decided to move from conventional country toward the country fusion end of the spectrum. The change included assembling a new band with more rock flavor and moving back to Columbia for her new album, *TNT.* The debut of the "new" Tanya took place during a show at the *Grand Ole Opry* on November 1, 1978, with perhaps a predictable result. When she started singing a series of songs in country-rock fashion including "Heartbreak Hotel," Buddy Holly's "Not Fade Away," and "Texas (When I Die)," some of the audience booed lustily. Still, by the time the set was over she apparently had won over most, if not all, of the audience.

Her manager, Steve Gold, said afterward, "She wasn't the pure-as-country little girl they'd come to know and love and some just couldn't take the reality of change. We won't change anything because of a handful of dissidents. They're probably the same kind of people who booed Bob Dylan when he stepped out and played that amplified guitar of his years ago."

TNT was one of the top-selling LPs of 1979 and Tucker also had the best-selling single "Texas (When I Die)." Her LP *Tear Me Apart* was on the country top 50 from late 1979 into early 1980. By the time her duet with close companion Glen Campbell ("Dream Lover," MCA) showed up on the singles charts in September 1980, it was apparent that Tanya was backtracking somewhat from her recent pop image. Later that fall, she had a hit with "Pecos Promenade," in the top 10 in November. The same month her new LP *Dreamlovers* was on country charts. In early 1981 she had a top-10 hit with the single "Can I See You Tonight" on MCA and later in the year reached upper-chart levels with "Lovin' What Your Lovin' Does to Me," a duet with Glen Campbell issued on his label, Capitol.

In early 1982 she was signed by Arista Records, including sessions in the Nashville studios produced by the rising hitmaker/producer, David Malloy.

Coming into the 1980s, Tanya was almost as well known among industry insiders for her wild lifestyle, which encompassed almost nonstop partying and a series of liaisons with both music industry stars and less publicized individuals. Besides her relationship with Campbell, which cooled off at the end of the 1980s, her reputed partners included, at one time or another, Merle Haggard, Andy Gibb, and TV star Don Johnson. For a long time her personal foibles didn't appear to affect her career, but eventually, as she admitted to Vincent Coppola for a *Redbook* magazine article ("Country Singer Tanya Tucker Has Survived Several Heartbreaking Relationships and a Hard-drinking, Hell-raising Past to Find Peace and Purpose in Motherhood," September 1993), it caught up with her in the 1980s.

When she couldn't seem to fight off her alcohol and drug-abuse demons, she realized she might not last out the decade. At one point, she made a list of famous people most likely to wake up dead. She placed Keith Richards at the top of her list (fortunately a prediction that didn't come true). "I wasn't as bad as Keith," she told Coppola, "but several people said I'd never make it past thirty."

Despite that, she managed to keep her career going. In 1985 she signed with a new label, Capitol Records, which issued her label debut, *Girls Like Me,* in early 1986. It was a worthy effort, which prompted *Country Music* magazine's Patrick Carr to call it "a piece of work which far exceeds any other she has ever made in terms of depth and personal meaning." The album made the *Billboard* Top 20 and provided the number-one single "Just Another Love."

This was followed in 1987 by the album *Love Me Like You Used To,* which spawned several chart hits, including the single "I Won't Take Less Than Your Love." The latter, which she recorded with its writers, Paul Overstreet and Paul David, was nominated for the Country Music Association Vocal Event of the Year.

In 1988, Tanya found a new love, a former football quarterback at West Virginia University and aspiring actor named Ben Reed. She met him at a concert in Tulsa, Oklahoma, and hired him to perform on one of her music videos. They became an item, which led to her announcing later in the year that she was pregnant (though she didn't identify the father at the time). By the time her daughter, Presley, was born, however, they'd had an argument and (temporarily) parted. (The breakup, she recalled, had been on her thirtieth birthday during Country Music Awards week.)

She credited her impending motherhood with helping her decide to overcome her substance-abuse problem once and for all. That included signing herself in for months to the Betty Ford Clinic in Southern California. In 1993, by then the mother of another child (of whom Ben Reed was also the father), she told Coppola, her old "empty" feeling had been replaced by the challenges of parenthood. "Now my life revolves around my kids. . . . It's a gradual process. You don't have a baby and the next day you're different. The more you're with a child, the more you think about things you've never thought of before. It sounds corny, but I worry about the environment, school, drugs, things every mother worries about." But she added she doubted she'd ever be a typical mother, since "my lifestyle is so different."

Amid all these things, Tanya's career flourished as never before. She steadily placed new singles and albums on the charts in the later 1980s and into the 1990s and her total of nominations from the CMA, Academy of Country Music, various video polls, and the Grammy Awards continued to mount. She was nominated for CMA Female Vocalist of the Year in 1989 and 1990 and, with T. Graham Brown, for 1990 CMA Vocal Event of the Year. She had four best-selling singles in 1990, all on Capitol, "My Arms Stay Open All Night" (number one in *Radio & Records* the week of January 19); "Walking Shoes" (number one in *R&R* the week of May 25); "Don't Go Out" (with T. Graham Brown, number four in *R&R* the week of August 17); and "It Won't Be Me" (number nine in *R&R* the week of November 30).

In 1991, a year in which she was reunited with Ben Reed, she was represented on album charts with another superb album, *Tennessee Woman*. The body of work it encompassed together with audience response to her concerts, TV appearances, and videos, helped bring a third straight CMA nomination for Female Vocalist of the Year. This time she won, but when that victory was announced on the TV awards show in October, Tanya was in the hospital giving birth to son Beau.

It didn't take long for her career to be in full swing again. She opened 1992 with the singles hit "(Without You) What Do I Do with Me" (number two in *R&R* the week of January 10). That came out on Liberty Nashville, to which Capitol had assigned its country roster, as did the follow-up hits "Some Kind of Trouble" (number three in *R&R* the week of April 17); "If Your Heart Ain't Busy Tonight" (number four in *R&R* the week of August 7); and "Two Sparrows in a Hurricane," a number-one hit on all major charts. Also a chart hit was the Liberty album *Can't Run from Yourself*, which eventually went well past R.I.A.A. platinum-record levels.

"Two Sparrows in a Hurricane," written in tribute to her parents' fiftieth wedding anniversary, was not only a hit single, but also spawned a number-one video, which was voted the ACM Video of the Year. Besides Tanya, the video also featured her two children as well as their father, Ben Reed. The single was also nominated for 1993 CMA Single of the Year.

Her 1993 credits included a new album, *Soon,* as well as a R.I.A.A. platinum award for the earlier release *What Do I Do with Me.* Her singles releases included "It's a Little Too Late" (number one in *R&R* the week of March 12); "Tell About It" (a duet with Delbert McClinton, number five in *R&R* the week of July 2); and "Soon" (number four in *R&R* the week of November 26). She continued to draw capacity crowds to shows in arenas, civic centers, and fairs with some 250 appearances in the mid-1990s billed as the "Black Velvet Lady Tour" sponsored by the Black Velvet product firm. That company also supported her participation in the "Black Velvet Smooth Steppin' Showdown," a national amateur two-step dance contest. During that period, CMA voters continued to recognize her achievements, again nominating her for Female Vocalist of the Year in 1992 and 1993 and including her duet with Delbert McClinton among Vocal Event of the Year finalists. During 1993, Tanya also issued an exercise video, *Tanya Tucker Country Workout.*

In 1994, she teamed with rock legend Little Richard on one of the tracks ("Somethin' Else") in the MCA Records' *Rhythm, Country & Blues* album project. The album became a best-seller and was nominated for CMA Album of the Year. The album didn't win, but Tanya and Little Richard's steamy rendition of their vocal collaboration was one of the highlights of the October 1994 TV Awards show. During the year, Tanya added two more singles to her list of hits, "We Don't Have to Do This" (number six in *R&R* the week of April 8) and "Hangin' In" (number four in *R&R* the week of August 12).

In early 1995, she placed the single "Between the Two of Them" on the charts. Soon after she had a new album, *Fire to Fire,* and single, "Find Out What's Happenin' " on hit lists. These were on Capitol/Nashville, the new label name for the Liberty country roster. Many of her older albums were still in print as shown by the R.I.A.A. awards she received during the year. On February 16, two Columbia albums from the early 1970s, *What's Your Mama's Name* and *Would You Lay With Me (In a Field of Stone),* were certified gold. On the following day, three of her Liberty albums were certified gold—*Greatest Hits, Strong Enough to Bend* and *Tennessee Woman*—and a fourth, *Greatest Hits 1990–1992*—platinum.

TURNER NICHOLS: *Vocal and instrumental duo; Zack Turner, born Greenville, South Carolina (vocals, guitar, piano, songwriting); Tim Nichols, born Portsmouth, Virginia (vocals, guitar, songwriting).*

The saga of many latter-day country music combinations—duos, trios, and so forth—is a saga of songwriters as well as singers. In an era when Nashville thronged with young, talented original tunesmiths, who also often had vocal and instrumental credentials, it was inevitable that more than a few would combine a writing affinity with a desire to gain the gratification of audience applause. It was a far cry from earlier days of country music when you could almost count the number of successful writers on the fingers of both hands. It was an environment in which Zack Turner and Tim Nichols, among others, found purchase.

Their backgrounds, while not identical, were similar in many ways. Both cited among important influences Merle Haggard, Waylon Jennings, and Elvis. (Turner added George Jones, while Nichols cited Johnny Cash.) Both learned to play guitar at fairly young ages (Turner also took lessons on piano as a boy), and both demonstrated writing potential before being out of their teens.

Turner grew up in Greenville, South Carolina, in an environment where country music was a major interest of the entire family. While his mother had a day job as a hairdresser and his father was a truck driver, both loved to play and sing country music and performed in local clubs weeknights and weekends whenever possible. By age fourteen, he was performing onstage with his father and at eighteen formed his own band, which worked the club and honky-tonk circuit throughout the Southeast. When not onstage, Zack kept writing new material, which he tried to put before publishing companies in Nashville. In 1986 he signed his first contract with Ten Ten Music before moving over to the Coburn Music operation.

Nichols grew up in Portsmouth, Virginia, but when he was a high school sophomore his father moved the family to Springfield, Missouri. His mother was a homemaker while his father ended up being a jack of many trades. At one point, like Zack's dad, he drove a truck, but other times he worked as a fireman, policeman, barber, and salesman. Tim recalled loving the idea of performing even in his preteen years. Sometimes he stood in front of a mirror, singing into a hairbrush. Unlike Zack's, Tim's parents weren't performing hopefuls, though they did take him to Springfield country concerts, where he got the chance to talk briefly to artists like Johnny Cash and Ronnie Milsap.

Nichols loved playing music in his teens, but he felt insecure about pursuing a performing career. Instead, when he finished high school he enrolled in college with a vague idea of using a college education as a stepping stone to a position in broadcasting. He didn't particularly enjoy his classes and left school to try to earn a living as a factory worker. He moonlighted as a musician and, finding factory operations overly demanding, finally decided to gamble on working full-time as an entertainer. He thought the best way to start out would be to become a contract songwriter and went to Nashville with that goal in mind.

Once there, however, he fell in with a "song shark" who made lofty promises and took his money but opened no doors. This experience was later played out on a CBS-TV 60 Minutes segment. The TV exposure helped gain him jobs with country bands in which he picked up experience in many club dates throughout the Midwest.

In 1984 he again made his bid for a songwriting job, now considerably wiser about possible pitfalls. This time he met with success, signing a publishing deal with Ronnie Milsap's publishing company. Later on he became a contract writer at Coburn Music.

In the mid-1980s, many songwriters, established or hopeful, frequented the Bluebird Cafe, where it was possible for a writer to get onstage and showcase some of his or her songs. One evening in October, Zack Turner performed new material at a time when Tim Nichols was in the audience. They didn't know each other, but a mutual publishing friend introduced them and both decided to meet at another time to see if two heads might prove better than one in devising new songs.

The two had a daytime meeting in a publishing company office. Tim recalled, "We talked and we just tried to get to know each other until we decided to go out to lunch. We really had a lot in common: the way we were raised—we're both the oldest kids in our families, we're both from blue-collar, working class families, and our ideals and upbringing were similar. We had the work ethic instilled in us and the belief that we could do anything we wanted to do if we were willing to make the necessary sacrifices. And on top of all that, we were both Merle Haggard fans. After lunch we came back and wrote a song called 'You Can't Hurt Me Anymore.'" (The song was included on their debut album.)

The new writing team's first song to be cut by a major artist was "I'm Over You," recorded by Keith Whitley, but not issued until after Whitley's untimely passing. The two cowriters went on to place songs with many other country entertainers, including stars like Alan Jackson, Travis Tritt, and Doug Stone. The two had also written with others before and continued to do so after they initiated their collaboration. The first cut for Nichols was Ronnie Milsap's recording of "This Time Last Year," cowritten by Tim with Jon Vezner.

After writing together for several years, in which time they made joint demos and live showcase performances, the duo began to focus on doing their own recordings for a major Nashville label. Turner said, "A record deal was the obvious next step." Tim added, "When we started doing writer's night together, we wanted to relate to people and to entertain. I think we succeeded, and we think we can relate to 10,000 people just as we would to one."

Executives at BNA Records liked their efforts and signed them to a record contract in 1992. Their first album, *Turner Nichols*, was released on October 26, 1993, preceded by the initial single, "Moonlight Drive-In" released July 13, 1993. The single made the *Billboard* chart in the fall and made midchart levels before year-end. The genesis of the song gives some insight into the way the creative process can work.

Nichols remembered, "Zack, Billy Kirsch [who cowrote the number with them] and I were going to

New York City to play a reception for the Chairman of Pepsico. We decided we didn't want to fly up there, so we rented a Mercury Marquis. . . . When we got to Bristol [on the Tennessee border], we were inspired when we looked off the interstate and saw the Moonlight Drive-In. We thought it was a great songwriting idea and started talking about our drive-in adventures and stories. By the time we got to Allentown [Pennsylvania], we had finished the song and put it down on a hand-held recorder."

TWAIN, SHANIA: *Singer, songwriter. Born Windsor, Ontario, Canada, August 28, 1965.*

A major candidate for new country-music star of the second half of the 1990s, Ms. Twain, of part Indian, part Anglo heritage, certainly had the right first name. Pronounced shu-NYE-uh, it translates from Ojibway (the Indian tribe of her father) as "I'm on my way." She surely seemed headed in the right direction in 1995, with several singles hits and one of the more notable albums from the "class of '95," a group of relative newcomers that included such other promising performers as Ty Herndon, Rhett Akins, and Chely Wright.

Shania's family was dirt poor, and when her parents realized they had a daughter whose talents might someday ease their economic straitjacket, they sought to point her toward the stage. She recalled making her public debut, of sorts, at age three in her hometown of Timmins, Ontario. Her mother, she said, "would put me up on restaurant counters, where I'd sing along with the jukebox for the people on the stools."

The good reception those events received inspired her parents to seek even more outlets for their precocious child. By the time she was eight, she had taken part in talent contests, sung at carnivals, and also had some TV exposure. As she said later, the concern of her family, including younger siblings, in fostering her singing opportunities had become something of an obsession, particularly for her mother. She told *Cash Box* in 1995, "My mother lived for my career. We were extremely poor . . . and my mother was often depressed with five children and no food to feed them. She knew I was talented and she lived with the hope that my abilities were my chance to do something special."

Looking back, she felt it had deprived her of a normal childhood. "My parents forced me to perform, which in the long run was the best thing, because I was naturally quite a recluse. If not for my parents, I'd still be singing in my bedroom and be quite content, mind you." But, she also stressed, she knew they cared for her and she did grow up in a loving family.

By the time she was ten, she was singing professionally. "My mother would take me to the occasional club and I'd get up and sing." By the time she entered high school, she had regular band engagements that kept her occupied up to four nights a week, a situation she said little about to her school friends.

She said, "They never knew that side of me. I've always been very quiet about myself that way. Even my schoolmates never knew I was a singer. It was just something I did for myself, something I was very private about. A friend of mine in high school asked me once, 'Is it true that you play in a band at night and that you went to do the Tommy Hunter Show [a Canadian talk/variety program] in Toronto?' I said, 'Yes, it's true.' It was like I had to make this confession. I said, 'I've got to tell you, I'm a singer,' and she said, 'Well, I just don't believe you. I've known you all this time, and I don't believe you're a singer.'"

But she was a singer and a good one, who proved versatile enough to handle many different stylings. Her family had always loved country, so she was exposed to that early on. When her parents had money they drove the 500 miles to Toronto so she could take vocal and music lessons, which included some classical training and exposure to musical comedy material.

Upon graduating from high school, she left home to settle in larger urban areas of Ontario. For the next few years she added to her experience, not only singing with bands in nightclubs, but even taking opportunities like opening for musical theater star Bernadette Peters with the Toronto Symphony Orchestra. However, she always made sure her schedule allowed her to work with forest crews part of the year along with her father.

"From spring through fall, I'd work with my father in the bush. I was foreman with a 13-man crew, many of whom were Indians. I'd run the crew and we'd plant millions of trees through the summer. We'd get up between 4 and 6 in the morning, live on beans, bread and tea, walk up to an hour to the site and work there all day with no shelter in rain, snow or sunshine, in the middle of the bush, hours from civilization. I did that for five years. It was very hard work, but I loved it. Then, after a summer of northern exposure, from the treacherous June blackflies to an August hailstorm, I'd go back to Toronto and slip into my sequined gown again. I come from two completely different worlds, and I fit comfortably in both."

That situation changed abruptly when she was twenty-one. When both her parents were killed in an automobile accident, she had to take over as surrogate mother to her brothers and sisters. In short order she got a job singing regularly at the Deerhurst resort in Northern Ontario, an arrangement that resulted in her performing as a soloist and a cast member in various musical productions, doing material ranging from Gershwin scores to versions of some of Andrew Lloyd Webber's shows.

After three years, her brothers and sisters were able to go out on their own and she decided it was time for a more definitive career approach. She consulted with friend and one-time performer Mary Bailey, who became her manager and agreed to help Shania make contacts in the country music field, which Twain had decided was her real musical calling. In 1991, Bailey arranged for Shania to contact Nashville attorney Dick Frank, who in turn helped set up preparation of a demo tape by producer-songwriter Norro Wilson and Mercury Nashville A&R executive Buddy Cannon. Cannon took the tape to Mercury senior vice president Harold Shedd, who quickly agreed she should be signed to the label.

Her label debut, *Shania Twain,* was released in late 1992 and included material written or cowritten by Twain. As she said at the time, "The album is very diverse, but all of it is me. I've always sung country, but it didn't take me long as a teenager to begin enjoying different kinds of music. I had a lot of classical vocal lessons that let me realize the range I had and the fun I could have with my voice, so I explored everything from rock and R&B to Christian music, and I tried to bring all of those elements into my writing as that developed."

The album showcased what obviously was a performer with great potential. It received some attention, though it was far from a major seller and placed singles on lower chart levels such as "What Made You Say That" in the spring of 1993. It was a very different story with her second album, *The Woman in Me,* which was released by Mercury in early 1995. Tracks from the collection quickly became favorites of country programmers and the first single from it, "Whose Bed Have Your Boots Been Under" (cowritten by Twain and record producer John "Mutt" Lange) made the top 10 on several charts. This was followed by a second hit single, "Any Man of Mine" (also by Twain and Lange). The album entered *Billboard*'s Top 10 soon after release and by mid June was in the number-three position with a gold record certification from R.I.A.A. already achieved. On June 22 it was certified platinum and also had risen to number one on the charts where it stayed for some weeks staying in upper chart positions for the rest of the year before returning to the number one spot in January 1996. The album received a two-million-copy award from the R.I.A.A. on August 14, 1995, one for three million on November 7, for four million on December 15 and moved past 5 million in early 1996.

Meanwhile, Shania kept on placing a string of singles on the charts. In the fall of 1995 the title track was a hit and in February 1996 "(If You're Not In It for Love) I'm Outta Here" reached number one in *Billboard.* In May 1996, "You Win My Love" reached number one and soon after "No One Needs to Know" was a chart hit. Except for "You Win My Love," where words and music were by Lange, the others all were cowritten by Twain and him. Her music video of "The Woman in Me" was certified gold by the R.I.A.A. on December 5, 1995.

CMA Awards voters nominated her in three categories for 1996, Song of the Year (with Lange for "Any Man of Mine"); Female Vocalist of the Year; and Horizon Award. In early 1996, she received the Best New Country Artist designation in the American Music and Blockbuster Entertainment Award voting. Other trophies included the Grammy for Country Album of the Year for *The Woman in Me,* the Canadian Juno Award for Best Country Female Vocalist and the Levi's Entertainer of the Year Award based on phoned in votes from fans. Her nominations in the Academy of Country Music 31st Annual Awards poll were Album of the Year (*The Woman in Me*), Single Record of the Year ("Any Man of Mine") and Top New Female Vocalist. When the results were announced on the April 24, 1996, telecast over NBC, she took home Album of the Year and Top New Female Vocalist honors.

TWITTY, CONWAY: *Singer, guitarist, songwriter, bandleader (the Lonely Blue Boys, the Twitty Birds), record producer. Born Friars Point, Mississippi, September 1, 1933*; died Springfield, Missouri, June 5, 1993.*

In country music, the golden touch is relatively rare compared to pop music. Many first-rank country artists whose recordings constantly appear at the top of the charts go years without reaching gold-record levels. But one performer who had the golden touch was Conway Twitty, who proved a major favorite first in rock 'n' roll and then in country, winning R.I.A.A. gold-record citations on many occasions in both career phases.

Twitty was born and raised in country-music country. His real name was Harold Lloyd Jenkins, and he was the son of a Mississippi ferryboat captain. His birthplace was Friars Point, Mississippi, but when he was ten his family moved to Helena, Arkansas.

Jenkins was an early country bloomer and formed a band when he was ten, the Phillips County Ramblers. The group proved competent enough after a short time together to gain its own radio show on station KFFA in Helena. Although music continued to be an important part of Jenkins' life as he progressed into his teens, he considered going into the ministry while a high school student. He also was a star on his high school baseball team and was offered a contract from the Philadelphia Phillies when he graduated.

The time was the mid-1950s, and the military draft was still in effect. The U.S. Army called Harold to the colors, and he spent several years in uniform. While stationed in Japan, he formed a group called the Cimarrons that played in service clubs around that nation.

When he got out of the Army, he already was aware of the new sound coming to the fore, rock 'n' roll. Influenced by the music of people like Elvis and Jerry Lee Lewis, Jenkins joined the floodtide of young Southern-based artists coming into the field. He decided Harold Jenkins lacked the flair needed for a pop career and picked a pseudonym, taking his first name from the

* Twitty's birthplace was initially indicated as Helena, Arkansas, in bio material.

town of Conway, Arkansas, and his last from Twitty, Texas. It didn't take long for his new name to catch on. With his rock band, which performed many original compositions by Conway, he stormed the top of the national charts in 1958 with the single of his composition "It's Only Make Believe." The song easily went past the million-copy mark for Twitty's initial gold-record breakthrough.

He kept up the pace during the late 1950s and early 1960s with a string of singles and albums on MGM Records that made the charts. He had another gold-record award hit in 1960 with "Lonely Blue Boy" and had many other releases that sold well over a half million copies each. With his group he toured widely, playing before capacity crowds in all fifty states as well as cities in Canada, Europe, and other foreign locales. He was featured on many major network TV showcases, including a number of appearances on Dick Clark's *American Bandstand* and *The Ed Sullivan Show.* Between 1958 and the mid-1960s, his rock releases sold over 16 million copies. During those years he also appeared in six movies, for three of which he supplied title songs and/or scores: *Platinum High, Sex Kittens Go to College,* and *College Confidential.*

By the mid-1960s, things were slowing down for Conway in the pop arena and he shifted back to his first love, country & western. He chose Oklahoma City, Oklahoma, as operations base and assembled his first country band, the Lonely Blue Boys. Several friends put him in touch with Decca record producer Owen Bradley, who signed him on the label and had him in the studio for his initial sessions in 1965. It was the start of a recording alignment still going strong a decade and a half later. Also on the label was an already established female country vocalist, Loretta Lynn, and not long after Conway joined Decca, discussions of possible duet efforts were under way.

Back in Oklahoma City, Conway and the Lonely Blue Boys were building a strong local following. When the first UHF-TV country station went on the air on June 1, 1966, the *Conway Twitty Show* was announced as a weekly feature. In a short time, the show, taped by KLPR-TV, was seen in other parts of the country in syndication. But it soon became apparent that for the kind of exposure Twitty needed, Oklahoma City was off the beaten path. By the late 1960s, Twitty had moved to the Nashville area and his name soon became known in the country field. His records began to play throughout the United States as he became a featured performer on the *Grand Ole Opry* and such other major country TV shows of the period as *Johnny Cash* and *Hee Haw.*

In 1968, he made pop chart levels with "Next in Line" and "Image of Me." In 1969, he added two more major hits, "To See My Angel" and "I Love You More Today." He topped all those in 1970 with the blockbuster single "Hello Darlin'." The song not only rose to

number one on country charts, it crossed over to pop lists, as indeed did many of his recordings of the 1970s. It ended up the sixth best-selling single in the country field for the year. Later in the decade it was requested by a team of U.S. astronauts and Russian cosmonauts circling the globe in a joint space mission. Also a top-10 hit in the 1970s was the single "That's When She Started to Stop Loving Me."

In 1971, he made the charts with such singles as "I Wonder What She'll Think About Me Leaving" and "What a Dream." But the year was equally impressive for his collaboration with Loretta Lynn. Their output included several top chart hits, including the eighth-best seller for the year "After the Fire Is Gone." Their album *We Only Make Believe* was one of the fifty best-selling LPs for 1971. (Twitty had three solo LPs on that select list, *I Wonder What She'll Think, How Much More Can She Stand,* and *Fifteen Years Ago.*) At year's end, the Country Music Association voted Loretta and Conway the best country duo, an award they won the next three years in a row.

Both as a soloist and with Lynn, Conway's pace hardly slackened as the 1970s went by. In 1972, his hits included "She Needs Someone to Hold Her," "I Can't See Me Without You," "I Can't Stop Loving You/(Lost Her Love On) Our Last Date," and, with Loretta, "Lead Me On." All but the first were title songs on chart hit LPs. In 1973, Conway's releases started coming out under the MCA imprint (MCA owned Decca) and included such successes as "Baby's Gone," "Louisiana Man," "You've Never Been This Far Before," and, with Loretta, "Mississippi Woman." The last two were title songs on hit LPs.

In 1974, Conway scored with the single "I'm Not Through Loving You Yet" (cowritten with L. E. White). The following year he had top-10 singles hits of his compositions "Linda on My Mind" and "Don't Cry Joni/Touch the Hand" and his duet with Lynn, "Feelin's." In 1976, his composition "After the Good Is Gone" provided him with a number-one country hit. Also in the top 5 or better that year were the duet "The Letter" (cowritten by Conway and C. Haney) and "The Game That Daddies Play." In 1977, his original "I've Already Loved You in My Mind" rose to the top 10 and his duet with Loretta, "I Can't Love You Enough," was a number-one success. Late in the year he had another top-10 single with a remake of the Little David Wilkins song "Georgia Keeps Pulling on My Ring." In 1978, he and Loretta made top-chart levels with "From Seven Till Ten/You're the Reason My Kids Are Ugly"; his solo releases "Boogie Grass Band" and "Your Love Had Taken Me That High" made the top 5.

In the 1970s, Twitty changed the name of his backing group from Lonely Blue Boys to the Twitty Birds. As of 1978, band members were John Hughey on steel guitar, Gene Hughey on bass, Tommy "Pork Chop" Markham on drums, Al Harris on piano, Charlie Archer on guitar, and Jack Hicks on harmonica and banjo. Throughout the 1970s, Conway and his group averaged over 200 engagements a year.

By the end of the 1970s, Twitty's activities covered a spectrum of businesses and organizations. He owned several music publishing firms: Hello Darlin' Music, Neverbreak Music, and Twitty Bird Music (the latter coowned with Tree International). In addition, he and Lynn jointly owned United Talent Agency, which in the late 1970s booked over $5 million in talent out of Nashville. In another direction, he also was part owner in the late 1970s of the Nashville Sounds baseball team, a member of the Southern League.

Besides the four CMA Awards credited to Conway and Loretta, he had many other awards as of 1978. These included twenty-two CMA nominations, a Grammy in 1971, four American Music Awards, six Academy of Country Music Awards, fourteen *Music City News* Awards, thirteen *Billboard* Awards, and two Truckers' Awards.

As the 1970s ended and the 1980s began, there seemed no slackening in the popularity of Conway as a soloist or of the Twitty-Lynn duet team. In singles during 1979, Conway had three major solo hits, "Your Love Has Taken Me That High," "Don't Take It Away," and "I May Never Get to Heaven." He had two solo LPs on the charts much of the year, *Conway* and *Cross Winds*, and *The Very Best of Loretta Lynn and Conway Twitty* was on the charts from mid-1979 well into 1980. For much of that time, their LP *Diamond Dust* also was on the lists. In late December 1979, his single "Happy Birthday Darlin' " rose to number one.

In January 1980, Conway and Loretta had the top-10 single "You Know What Your Lovin' Does to Me/The Sadness of It All." A few months later, Conway had the top-10 single "I'd Love to Lay You Down" and in April placed the LP *Heart and Soul* in the country top-10 album list. In early summer, he and Loretta had the single "It's True Love" in upper-chart levels. In the latter part of the year, Twitty had the chart-hit single "A Bridge That Just Won't Burn" and the LP *Rest Your Love on Me*. The solo single "Rest Your Love on Me/I Am the Dream (You Are the Dream)" and duet "Love What Your Lovin' Does to Me" both came out early in 1981 and were in the top 10 in April. His collaborations with Loretta won CMA nominations for Vocal Duo of the Year from 1980 through 1982.

By then Conway was serving as his own record producer, having taken over that role during 1979 from veteran producer Owen Bradley. Having made that decision, he left MCA and signed with Elektra Records in 1980. Though Bradley had helped Twitty gain a series of number-one hits, Conway continued to add to his totals as his own producer in the 1980s. By 1981, his number-one credits included thirty-eight releases, and in 1985 his hit Elektra single "Don't Call Him a Cowboy" raised the total to fifty. (His debut album on Elektra, *Southern Comfort,* was issued in early 1982.) One of his 1982 projects was opening Twitty City, a nine-acre tourist complex in Hendersonville, Tennessee, a suburb of Nashville. Home base for Conway and his family until his death, Twitty City tourist attractions include a museum covering highlights of Conway's career.

A key reason for leaving Decca/MCA, he told Dennis Hunt of the *Los Angeles Times* ("Conway Twitty: Seeking His Just Desserts as Music Star," May 27, 1982, Part VI, page 2), was that after sixteen years on the label he didn't feel he had gained the recognition he thought was warranted an artist who had achieved more number-one singles than any other country star.

He also emphasized his pride in his rapport with female fans. "When I'm writing," he told Hunt, "I think about women first. They're the ones who buy most of my records. I try to write songs that say something women want to hear. I also try to write songs that say what men want to say to women but don't know how.

"I'm not a Romeo or anything like that. I just understand women. They're not like other folks, you know. They're different. It's hard for men to understand them sometimes. But I do. I know how they think and what they think and why they think certain things. I'm not bragging. It's just a gift I have."

During Twitty's Elektra years, MCA issued an album stressing Conway's achievements as a songwriter that included such originals as "Hello Darlin'," "Linda on My Mind," and "You've Never Been This Far Before." In 1987, Conway returned to MCA Nashville, which remained his recording home for the rest of his life. One of his first single releases after rejoining the label was another number-one hit, "Julia." He closed out the 1980s with still more singles hits such as "Still in Your Dreams" and the 1989 number-one disc, "Saturday Night Special."

Throughout the 1980s and into the 1990s, Twitty remained a major draw on the concert circuit and often guested on TV shows, both major network variety specials and programs presented on country based outlets like the Nashville Network. By the start of the 1990s, Conway was also one of the stars who regularly appeared at Branson, Missouri, events. Helping out as coproducer of his new recordings by then was his third wife, Dee Henry. During 1990, his album *Crazy in Love* was on the charts late in the year and the title track single was in the number-three spot in *Radio & Records* and number two in *Billboard* in late November. MCA also issued two major retrospective albums in 1990, *Conway Twitty's Greatest Hits, Volume III*, and the *Silver Anniversary Collection,* the latter collection containing twenty-five of Twitty's hits covering a twenty-five-year period.

Conway commented that while those two albums gave him "a sense of accomplishment," he believed in looking forward, not backward. "What you have done means nothing. Only what you do next means something to me. Once I've done it, it doesn't mean anything to me anymore. It's that love for what I do, and it's that next song. It's that challenge."

Looking back over his career transitions from rock to straight country to a more contemporary blues-tinged sound in the 1980s, he added, "I'm an artist who's always tried to change before the changes come. It keeps me fresh, too, as an artist, when I don't sing the same old thing all the time. One of the reasons I've survived in this business for so long, is that I am aware of what's going on. I stay, to the best of my ability, right on top of things. I think singers in my position, they lose it between the ears before they lose it in their vocal cords. If I can stay on top of it between my ears, I think I can handle the vocal part."

Conway's next album, *Even Now,* issued in August 1991, produced the chart hit "She's Got a Man on Her Mind," which did not, however, add to his total of over fifty number-one singles. In 1992, Conway was back in the studios working on a new solo album and with soul singer Sam Moore (of the old team of Sam and Dave) on contributions to the multiartist MCA album *Rhythm, Country & Blues.*

In the early summer of 1993, Twitty was in the midst of a solo tour with plans later on to take part in a series of concerts with other artists from the *Rhythm, Country & Blues* project. He completed a matinee show at the Jim Stafford Theater in Branson on June 4 and got on his tour bus to go back to Nashville. An hour on the road the bus pulled into a truck stop in Springfield, Missouri, when Twitty fell ill. His wife, Dee, found him doubled over in the bathroom complaining of abdominal pains. He was rushed to nearby Cox Medical Center South, where surgeons discovered he had ruptured a blood vessel in his abdomen. They performed a seemingly successful repair, but twelve and a half hours later Twitty suffered a fatal heart attack.

One of the first to register shock and disbelief was Twitty's longtime duet partner, Loretta Lynn, whose husband, Mooney, was recovering from heart surgery at the same hospital. She told *People* magazine, "I've lost not only a great singing partner but a great friend." Vince Gill commented, "He was strictly about music, not about the bells and whistles that go with it."

After his death, MCA released his last studio album, *Final Touches,* which was on the charts from late summer of 1993 into early 1994. Record buyers also sought out his greatest hits collections and in the fall, three were on the *Billboard* Hot Recurrents list, *Very Best of Conway Twitty, Best of the Best of Conway Twitty,* and *Conway Twitty's Greatest Hits, Volume III.* The first of those was still on the charts in 1994 after sixty weeks with sales well past R.I.A.A. platinum levels. There also was increased interest in his video material, which included the two-tape boxed set listed in the Country Music Foundation catalog that comprised

Conway Twitty's #1 Hits and *Conway Twitty King of Hits.*

In the 1994 CMA voting, nominations were given to the *Rhythm, Country & Blues* album and to Conway and Sam Moore for Vocal Duo of the Year. During the star-studded concert series in support of that album (which sold well past platinum-record levels) Moore gave a heartfelt tribute to his late duet partner's memory. Not surprisingly, the editors of the *Life* magazine special issue on country music in September 1994 included Conway in their list of "The 100 Most Important People in the History of Country."

TYLER, T. TEXAS: *Singer, guitarist, bandleader, songwriter. Born Mena, Arkansas, circa 1916; died Springfield, Missouri, January 23, 1972.*

With his best-selling recitative single "Deck of Cards" in 1948, T. Texas Tyler helped set a pattern that still was carried on in the 1970s by country stars like Red Sovine and Jimmy Dean. His composition, which was about a soldier's pack of cards representing major points in the gospels, heralded a pattern in Tyler's later life as he became increasingly engrossed with religion.

Born in Arkansas and raised in Texas, Tyler learned to play the guitar before he was in his teens and at sixteen started to perform locally. During the 1930s, determined to further his musical career, he went east, gaining a spot on the *Major Bowes Amateur Hour* and also joining a radio show in Newport, Rhode Island. Late in the decade, he started moving westward. En route to Los Angeles he picked up experience with a variety of country & western groups, including the Ozark Ramblers, Dixie Melody Boys, and Oklahoma Melody Boys.

His career was interrupted by service in the U.S. Army during World War II, a period that provided material for several of his most successful songs. After receiving his discharge in 1946, Tyler returned to L.A. and settled in Hollywood, where he organized a band that was to become a major factor in the country & western field in the late 1940s and the 1950s. He also signed a recording contract with a small label, Four Star Records, whose producer and record executive, Don Pierce, was to play a major role in Tyler's rise to star status.

Tyler already was on the Four Star roster when Pierce bought a partial interest in the firm. Going on the road as a salesman, Pierce found that the only Four Star artist dealers were interested in was Tyler. Pierce took a closer look at the performer's potential and developed a close working relationship. One of the first results was two major hits in 1948, "Deck of Cards" and "Dad Gave My Dog Away," the latter cowritten by Tyler. The two joined forces on a number of other hits in succeeding years, including "Remember Me," "Filipino Baby," "Divorce Me C.O.D.," and "Bummin' Around," the last named a top-10 hit in 1953.

In the late 1940s and early 1950s, T. Texas had his own show on Los Angeles TV called *Range Round Up.* In 1950, the magazine *Country Song Roundup* voted the program Best Country Music Show of the year. Tyler also made a number of western films, including *Horsemen of the Sierra* for Columbia Pictures in 1949. That same year, he was featured in a country & western concert held at New York's Carnegie Hall.

During the 1950s and 1960s, Tyler headlined shows in all parts of the United States and appeared on many radio and TV programs, including several guest spots on the *Grand Ole Opry.* During the 1950s, he signed with Pierce's new label, Starday. Among his singles were "Oklahoma Hills," "Home in San Antone," "Honky Tonk Girl," "Beautiful Life," "The Old Country Church," "In the Sweet By and By," "Follow Through," and "Fairweather Baby." For much of the 1960s, most of Tyler's releases came out on the King Records label, though there also were releases on various others, including Starday, Pickwick, and Capitol.

One of his Starday albums was the 1964 *Sensational New Hits of T. Texas Tyler,* which provides an indication of his repertoire at the time. The album songs included "Dear Souvenirs" and "Crawdad Town" (both written by Tyler), "Texas Boogie Woogie," "Invitations," "My Talk About Leaving," "Just Like Dad," "Injun Joe," "Morning Glory," "It's a Long, Long Road Back Home," "Sunset Years of Life," and "Little Piece of Life."

Some of his other LPs extant in the 1960s were *T. Texas Tyler* (11/59); *Great Texas, T. Texas Tyler, T. Texas Tyler Sings Sacred Country Songs,* all on King; *Favorites,* Wrangler Records (7/62); *Hits of T. Texas Tyler,* Capitol (10/65); *Great Hits,* Pickwick.

Long known as a devout man, during the 1960s Tyler's interest in religion reached the point that he decided to give up performing in favor of the ministry. It was a career he seemed eminently suited for in view of his long-time reputation in the entertainment field as "the man with a million friends." In the early 1970s he contracted cancer and died in 1972 in Springfield, Missouri.

$\mathcal{V}$

VAN SHELTON, RICKY: *Singer, guitarist, bandleader. Born Grit, Virginia, January 12, c. early 1960s.*

Ricky Van Shelton certainly doesn't have the best baritone voice in country music, nor is his singing style particularly unique, but some indefinable aspect of his approach to his material and his personality combined to propel him to stardom in his chosen profession. Of course, the fact that the slim, well-proportioned performer is handsome didn't hurt. As one of the "country hunks" that helped widen the ranks of country music's female adherents, he played a role in the financial boom the field experienced in the late 1980s and early 1990s.

He traced his desire to stand out back to early childhood growing up in rural Virginia. "When I was about five years old, I told my mom I wanted to sing and draw pictures. I never changed my mind and I never stopped believing that it would come true. I've got this desire in me. Even when I was small, I didn't give up. If you wonder, that's doubt and when there's doubt, it ain't gonna happen."

At five or even quite a few years after, Ricky didn't consider country music as his likely mode of expression. But when he was in his early teens, by which time he had learned to play pop guitar, his older brother had a country band he wanted the then-fourteen-year-old Ricky to join. Ricky recalled that his brother offered to let him drive his Fairlane 289 automobile if Ricky would oblige. The bribe worked and Ricky's career direction had been established, though he continued to pay attention to trends in rock and pop genres.

By the time Ricky was through with high school, his interest and competence in country music had become dominant, and he was accepting performing engagements in ever-widening circles from his home area. For several years, Van Shelton made the rounds of local clubs, county fairs and honky-tonks, slowly improving his stage presence, which tended to be a little stiff. Even in the early 1990s he seemed a little less relaxed on stage than other headliners, even though by then he had become one of the best-selling record and video artists in modern country. It was something many reviewers remarked about even as they noted his improvements in the mid-1990s.

Commenting on a performance at the Universal Amphitheatre, for instance, Steve Hochman of the *Los Angeles Times* expressed approval of a segment of the show in which Ricky and his six-piece band traced the musical roots of modern country with a series of songs by the Beatles, Buddy Holly, Jerry Lee Lewis, and Roy Orbison. Not only was that intriguing, he wrote, "But more than that, the once-uptight-seeming Shelton was clearly having fun, something that continued in a really loose encore in which he went way out to left field with a rocking version of Los Angeles rockabilly veteran Ray Campi's 'Rockabilly Rebel,' a song (he told the crowd, 'We found in a truck stop') and a silly [version of] 'Long Tall Texan.' "

During the 1980s, Ricky's periodic appearances in Nashville caught the attention of Steve Buckingham, vice president of artists & repertoire for Columbia Records. Buckingham recalled, "I remember being struck by the fact that he had a voice that was so well suited to two very distinct styles: the energetic early rockabilly/rock & roll and those traditional country ballads. And he has such a respect for the traditions that comprise country music. If there's one thing about

Ricky Van, he knows where music comes from and he appreciates its roots to the point where he wants to insure its survival in its most pristine form."

He soon had Ricky in the studio working on material for his label debut album, *Wild-Eyed Dream,* released in February 1987. Aided by the success of the single "Crime of Passion," the album rapidly rose to top brackets in *Billboard,* where it stayed for more than a year, earning both gold and platinum R.I.A.A. certifications. The impact of his initial recordings and videos also paid off in a series of honors in 1988 such as the Country Music Association Horizon Award, Academy of Country Music's Top New Male Vocalist choice, TNN Viewers Choice Awards selection as Favorite Newcomer, and *Music City News* citing as Star of Tomorrow.

With more singles and videos gracing hit charts in 1987 and 1988, still more victories came his way in 1989. These included CMA voters naming him Male Vocalist of the Year; three TNN Viewers' Choice trophies for Favorite Male Vocalist, Favorite Singles, and Favorite Video Artist; and four prizes from *Music City News* Awards voters for Male Artist of the Year, Single of the Year, Video of the Year, and Album of the Year. The last-named award was for his second Columbia album, *Loving Proof,* released in September 1989 and on the *Billboard* list soon after, where it still could be found in late 1990 after accumulating 119 weeks on the chart and R.I.A.A. platinum certification. The title track was a top-20 hit as well.

Ricky kept his album success string intact with the release of *RVS III* in January 1990, which passed platinum levels before year-end after peaking at number one in *Billboard.* It spawned a number of charted singles, including "Life's Little Ups and Downs," a top-20 success in November. In the 1990 TNN/*Music City News* poll he was named Entertainer of the Year and Male Artist of the Year, awards he won again in 1991.

His 1991 output included the album *Backroads,* released in May, which stayed on the charts well into 1992 and whose title track became a top-20 singles hit. The album peaked at number three in *Billboard* in the summer of 1991. During 1992, he was represented on album charts with the somewhat tepid gospel album, *Don't Overlook Salvation,* issued by Columbia in May, and the *Greatest Hits Plus* album released in August. Both of those exceeded R.I.A.A. gold-record totals. His chart hit singles during the year included a duet with Dolly Parton titled "Rockin' Years," "After the Lights Go Out," and a remake of an Elvis Presley number, "Wear My Ring Around Your Neck," which was used on the soundtrack for the film *Honeymoon in Vegas.*

In the 1992 TNN/*Music City News* Awards voting, the duet with Dolly Parton earned Vocal Collaboration of the Year and Video of the Year honors. During 1992, a different facet of Van Shelton's persona surfaced with the publication of the children's book, *Tales from a Duck Named Quacker,* which its publisher reported in 1993 had sold over 60,000 copies, an impressive figure for such a book. In the fall of 1993, another Van Shelton book, *Quacker Meets Mrs. Moo,* came off the presses.

At the end of 1992, the single "Wild Man" appeared on the *Billboard* list on the way toward top-10 ranks in early 1993. It was followed on the charts in March by the single "Just As I Am," which reached *Billboard*'s Top 30 in May. In August of 1993, Ricky's first new secular album in two and a half years, *A Bridge I Didn't Burn,* was issued by Columbia and stayed on the hit lists into 1994, peaking at number seventeen in *Billboard.* Chart singles drawn from the album included "Where Was I" in the *Billboard* Top 40 in February 1994, and "Wherever She Is," a top-30 entrant in the fall.

Besides the aforementioned titles, Ricky had many other charted singles during the late 1980s and early 1990s. These included: "From a Jack to a King," "Don't We All Have the Right," "Life Turned Her That Way," "Somebody Lied," "I'll Leave the World Loving You," "I Meant Every Word He Said," "I've Cried My Last Tear Over You," and "Statue of a Fool." In late spring of 1995 Columbia/Sony issued the retrospective album *Super Hits* that stayed on lower chart levels for most of the year.

W

WAGONEERS: *Vocal and instrumental group from Austin, Texas: Monte Warden, born Texas, c. 1968 (lead vocals, guitar); Brent Wilson (vocals, guitar); Craig Pettibone (bass guitar); Tom Lewis.*

The Wagoneers came along when more than a few bands in the country field incorporated a certain amount of rock flavor in their offerings, and the Austin-based quartet followed suit. Still, they retained a strong enough traditional sound to appeal to a younger generation of Texas fans. They established a respectable following in the Lone Star state, sufficient to make them the first choice of A&M Records executives when they decided to establish a new country roster in the late 1980s. (The label hadn't featured country groups since the period of the Flying Burrito Brothers' fame, over a decade before.)

The band members were all well thought of in the Austin area, where Monte Warden initially built up a reputation for himself as a teen performer. Warden, the primary songwriter as well as lead singer of the Wagoneers, recalled writing his first songs when he was eleven. By the time he was fifteen, he was lead singer of a group called Whoa! Trigger, voted the city's best new band of 1983 by readers of the *Austin Chronicle.* Before joining forces with Warden, the other three musicians had picked up experience in local bands, sometimes working as backing-band members for solo performers. Lewis and Wilson, for instance, toured in support of regional star Sleepy LaBeef. Lewis told Kelly Gattis of the Country Music Association's *Close Up*, "Playing with Sleepy was like going to the Berklee School of Music on the road."

The group came together in the mid-1980s and, after winning approval from Austin fans, began expanding their club and honky-tonk gigs to other parts of the state. In the summer of 1987, they felt they were ready to gain wider industry attention. The band started playing new songs by Warden at a series of showcase performances that were attended by representatives from such Nashville music firms as Almo-Irving, Screen Gems, and Dick James Music. Word of mouth then aroused interest among country record labels, which culminated in their A&M signing in November 1987. Soon after that the band's debut album, *Stout and High*, was released in 1988 and A&M started lining up concert engagements, including the chance to serve as opening act for Willie Nelson. (Others with whom the band toured in the late 1980s were Emmylou Harris, George Strait, k.d. lang and Randy Travis.)

Discussing the band's style, Warden told Gattis, "I'm a country singer. I'm a country songwriter. And I play a Martin guitar. Period. But the guys that I play with like rock 'n' roll and that's where our unique sound comes in. We don't consciously put an edge on our music, but I don't think those guys could or would want to play 'Sally Gooden,' and I know I wouldn't want to play [Led Zeppelin's] 'Stairway to Heaven,' so somewhere in the middle comes the Wagoneers."

On tour the band proved to be a solid-sounding foursome that play high energy, listenable material, but seemed to need something to set them apart from their competition. Commenting on some of their appearances with Willie Nelson, for instance, Robert Hilburn of the *Los Angeles Times* ("Wagoneers Roll Within Modest Boundaries," November 28, 1988) wrote, "You won't find the culture clash of the Flying Burrito Brothers' blend of country sentimentality and rock commentary in the '60s, or the maverick heroism of the 'outlaw' brigade in the '70s.

"Within more narrow and modest boundaries, however, the Wagoneers serve up enough winning songs to earn themselves a few choice spots on any good country jukebox. 'I Wanna Know Her Again'—from the band's just-released A&M album—is a medium tempo tune about reestablishing contact with a loved one that stands up to anything Randy [Travis], Dwight [Yoakam] or, yes, Willie [Nelson], has given us lately."

The band's material certainly made inroads with country fans beyond U.S. borders. The group was well received during a number of late 1980s dates in Canada and also gained a following in Europe. Warden recalled for Gattis the band's initial experiences in the U.K.

"They [A&M] threw us over in England [in June 1988] and we played our first show to 20 people, 10 of them being from A&M. Our second show was before about 150 people, our third to about 400 and by the time we got to our fourth and fifth shows we had sold out a 600-seat hall with people lined around the block." In the fall the band made another swing of European cities that earned good audience response and critical reviews.

During the summer of 1989, A&M issued the band's second album on the label, *Good Fortune*. Like the earlier one, it gained some attention but did not become a best-seller. Coming into the 1990s, the group had demonstrated it had potential and, with an average age of twenty-four, its members still had the time to challenge for country music's upper levels.

WAGONER, PORTER: *Singer, guitarist, songwriter, bandleader (the Wagonmasters). Born West Plains, Missouri, August 12, 1930.*

American network TV executives looked down their noses at country music after World War II. But the viewing public thought differently, as indicated by the dozens of syndicated shows by top artists in country music that flourished throughout the 1960s and 1970s. Among the most popular of those was Porter Wagoner's, whose vocal talents and showmanship resulted in a program that was still finding favor long after most top-rated network shows were only memories. At the end of the 1970s, the program was fast coming up on the twenty-year mark with a weekly exposure of more than 100 stations having a total audience of over 45 million people.

It was an achievement that perhaps embodied the traits of levelheadedness and persistence usually attributed to people from Porter's home state of Missouri. The show's content reflected Wagoner's lifelong love affair with country music, which began when he was a farm boy growing up near the small town of West Plains in Missouri. When Porter wasn't occupied with farm chores or schooling, he liked to listen to country programs on the radio. While still a preteenager, he learned to play guitar and often played and sang along with country songs broadcast over local stations.

In 1944, young Porter got a job as a clerk in a West Plains market to help out his family's limited finances. He often took his guitar along and, when business was slow, entertained customers and the store owner by singing and picking. After a while, the idea came to use the boy's talent as an advertising device. The market owner sponsored him on a fifteen-minute program on local radio. Both show and store prospered in the late 1940s and Wagoner's stylings came to the attention of E. E. "Si" Siman of radio station KWTO in Springfield, Missouri. Siman signed Porter to perform on a weekly show on the station in the fall of 1951.

That proved to be the right place and the right time for the aspiring singer. The now legendary Red Foley was in the process of organizing his *Ozark Jamboree* for origination from Springfield. He added Wagoner to the cast and also spent some time schooling the young man in some of the finer points of interpreting country material. Before long the pupil had progressed so well that he became a featured artist on the *Jamboree,* which by then had achieved national TV coverage.

About the same time, RCA executive Steve Sholes signed Porter to a recording contract. Though Sholes stayed with Wagoner for almost four years, Porter's recordings struck no spark with country fans. That all changed in 1955 when Porter's single "Satisfied Mind" became a top-10 national hit. From then through 1982, it was a rare year when Porter's name didn't show up on the charts. After he made hit lists with "Eat, Drink and Be Merry" in late 1955 and "What Would You Do (If Jesus Came to Your House)" the following year, his reputation as one of the fastest rising newcomers in the field was solidified. His status was recognized in 1957 by the *Grand Ole Opry,* which invited him to join the regular cast.

In 1960, Porter signed to do his own syndicated show originating from Nashville, where he lived by then. In its first year of existence, the show was telecast on eighteen stations. By the late 1960s the number had grown to eighty-six and in the 1970s went over the 100 mark. Cast regulars over the years included many people who went on to individual stardom. This was particularly true of the female singers Wagoner recruited for the show. In the mid-1960s, he was joined by Norma Jean, who sang both solo numbers and duets with Porter. In the late 1960s, that role fell to another highly gifted artist, Dolly Parton. Between 1968 and 1975, Porter and Parton almost always were among the five finalists in CMA voting for Best Vocal Duo of the Year. Also a crowd pleaser on the TV program was Porter's band, the Wagonmasters.

The regulars as well as guest artists generally accompanied Wagoner on intensive in-person tours of the United States and Canada, which averaged 230 days on the road in the late 1960s and hardly less than that in the 1970s.

Porter kept adding new hits to his repertory every year in the 1960s, starting with "Your Old Love Letters" in 1960. That was joined by such other chart successes as "Cold Dark Waters Below" and "Misery Loves Company" in 1961; "I've Enjoyed as Much of This as I Can Stand" in 1963; "Sorrow on the Rocks" in 1964; "Green Green Grass of Home" in 1965; "Skid Row Joe" in 1966; "The Cold Hard Facts of Life" in 1967; and "Be Proud of Your Man" in 1968. In 1968, he also reached top-chart levels with two duets with Dolly Parton, "Holding on to Nothing" and "The Last Thing on My Mind." Through the end of 1968, he ranked among the top twenty singles artists of the post-World War II years, with thirteen top-10 singles and one number-one song ("Misery Loves Company)" to his credit.

Throughout his career, Porter also loved to sing gospel music. In the mid-1960s, he made a number of gospel recordings with the Blackwood Brothers that were among the best of that genre released in the decade. Those efforts brought him three Grammy Awards for religious albums from the National Academy of the Recording Arts and Sciences. In 1966, the award was for the Best Sacred Recording (*Grand Ole Gospel*), in 1967 for Best Gospel Performance (*More Grand Old Gospel*), and in 1969 for Best Gospel Performance (*In Gospel Country*).

From the mid-1950s through the end of the 1970s, Porter was represented by dozens of album releases on RCA, many of which made country charts. In the 1960s, five of his albums were top-10 hits. Among his releases were *Porter Wagoner* (3/62); *Duets with Skeeter Davis* (7/62); *Porter Wagoner Show* (5/63); *Satisfied Mind* (12/63); *Y'All Come* (12/63); *In Person* (7/64); *Blue Grass Story* (3/65); *Thin Man* (8/65); *Old Log Cabin for Sale* (4/65); *Grand Old Gospel* (2/66); *On the Road* (5/66); *Your Old Love Letters* (3/66); *Confessions* (10/66); *Best of Porter Wagoner* (10/66); *I'm Day Dreamin'* (Camden, 2/67); *Soul of a Convict* (3/67); *Cold Hard Facts* (6/67); *More Grand Gospel* (10/67); *Green Grass of Home* (Camden, 2/68); *Just Between You and Me* (2/68); *Feeling* (Camden, 7/69); *Always, Always* (with Dolly Parton, 9/69); *Me and My Boys* (9/69); *Skid Row Joe Down in the Alley; Howdy Neighbor* (Camden, 1970); *Best of Porter Wagoner, Volume 2* (7/70); *Down in the Alley* (12/70); *Porter Wagoner and Dolly Rebecca* (with Parton, 5/70); *Once More* (with Parton); *Simple as I Am* (6/71); *Best of Porter Wagoner and Dolly Parton* (8/71); *Porter Wagoner Country* (Camden, 7/71); *You Gotta Have a License* (2/70); *Two of a Kind* (with Parton, 4/71); *Porter Wagoner Sings His Own Songs* (10/71); *Blue Moon of Kentucky* (11/71); *Right Combination/Burning the Midnight Oil* (with Parton, 3/72); *What Ain't to Be* (3/72); and *Ballads of Love* (8/72).

As the LP *Sings His Own* indicates, Porter made the charts with more than a few of his original writings, though he always was happy to use good material wherever he could find it. When he teamed with Dolly Parton, the alignment brought together two individuals who were first-rate writers as well as entertainers. Thus the 1975 top-10 duet single "Say Forever You'll Be Mine" was a Parton composition while their top-10 1976 single "Is Forever Longer than Always" was a Wagoner song (cowritten with F. Dycus). Porter also had several solo hits with Dolly's compositions, an example being "Carolina Moonshine" in early 1975. Among other Wagoner singles that made the charts in the mid- and late 1970s were "George Leroy Chickashea" in early 1974; "Tore Down/Nothing Between" in late 1974; "I Haven't Learned a Thing" in late 1977; and "Ole Slew Foot/I'm Gonna Feed 'Em Now" the end of 1978.

Porter ended the 1970s and opened the 1980s with a minor hit on RCA, the single of his composition "Hold on Tight." In the summer, he had the single "Is It Only 'Cause You're Lonely" on lower-chart levels. In the fall, RCA began to release material that Porter and Parton had previously recorded in the years they had been a duet team. The first of these, the single "Making Plans," was a top-10 hit in late September and, at year end, their "If You Go, I'll Follow You" made upper levels. Also high on the album charts in the fall was the album *Porter and Dolly.*

Lawsuits followed Dolly's departure from the Wagoner organization in the mid-1970s, but were eventually resolved as each went their own way. She later told interviewers her years with Porter comprised "seven of the best years of my life and seven of the worst." In February 1988, though, the two performed together for the first time since their breakup. By then, however, while Parton had eclipsed Wagoner in terms of public favor, Porter still retained a core of faithful adherents and was able to remain a good concert draw in the U.S. and abroad through the 1980s into the 1990s. Though unable to top the charts in the post-1970s years, he still kept active as a recording artist in the mid-1990s and also remained an important part of *Grand Ole Opry* programs.

In naming Porter one of "The 100 Most Important People in Country" in the *Life* magazine special issue of September 1994, Charles Hirshberg and Robert Sullivan asserted that, while Wagoner was "Too often thought of as Dolly's porter, it was Wagoner and not the women who sang with him (Norma Jean before La Parton) who had fans flocking to the *Opry* in the late '60s." The best album available of Wagoner's material as of 1994, they added, was the Pair Records' *Sweet Harmony.*

An extensive and well-documented biography was issued by the Rutledge Hill Press of Nashville in 1992 (*A Satisfied Mind: The Country Music Life of Porter Wagoner,* by Steve Eng). In a generally approving review in *The Journal of Country Music,* Nolan Porterfield did his own evaluation of Wagoner's career. "As long as 'honesty' remains country music's magic ingredient, Wagoner can pack 'em in. And if one thing doesn't work, he'll try something else, with a repertoire that has stretched from hard country to disco and hit all points in between—bluegrass, gospel, r&b, rockabilly, pop ditties, dying baby songs, morbid recitations and homeless wino laments. He's surely one of country music's more flexible, if not versatile, performers, always willing to change, experiment, push at the edge and still hang on to his image as a Nashville fixture, Nudie suit, *Opry* slot and all."

As quoted by Eng at one point, Wagoner suggested that, all things being equal, he'd just as soon go fishing. "I have shared the stage of the *Grand Ole Opry* with Roy Acuff, sung duets with Dolly Parton, and I've been in a movie with Clint Eastwood, but none of those thrills measure at all, compared to sitting on this long skinny point in this beautiful moonlight, throwin' for smallmouth bass."

One of the most comprehensive collections of Porter's work in print as of 1996 was the German Bear Family Records boxed set, *Porter Wagoner: The Man From West Plains.* Besides re-issues of Porter's major hits, such as "Satisfied Mind" and "Company's Comin'," the package included 20 sides that had never been released before.

WALKER, CINDY: *Singer, guitarist, songwriter. Born Mexia, Texas, c. late 1920s.*

To 99.9 percent or more of the U.S. population, the only response to the name of the town of Mexia, Texas, would be "Where?" To professionals in country & western music for many years the word brought instant recognition as the home of Cindy Walker, one of the most creative writers in the field.

Songwriting ran in her family. Her grandfather, Professor F. L. Eiland, was a noted hymn writer whose "Hold to God's Unchanging Hands" became widely used in American churches. Cindy naturally heard cowboy ballads and country music programs from her earliest years. She showed talent almost as soon as she could talk, and at seven had her first professional work, singing and dancing in the Toy Land Review. She became increasingly interested in show business as she grew older, perfecting her dancing and also learning to play the guitar.

She went on to a career as a dancer, working at Billy Rose's Casa Manana in Forth Worth, Texas. Already interested in songwriting, she penned a theme for the show that met with enthusiastic approval when she presented it to the manager. Eventually it was played by Paul Whiteman's band on a national hookup.

In 1942 her father, a cotton buyer, made a business trip to Los Angeles on which Cindy and her mother went along. She had decided this was her opportunity to try to break into the movies, and over the next five years she did find work as a performer and gained minor roles in several films. She continued to write new songs and sought to place them with publishers or record companies. At one point, she recalled building up courage to talk her way past the receptionist in the offices of Bing Crosby's enterprises to play a song for Bing's brother, Larry. Larry liked it enough to ask her to make a demo that he could give to Bing. The latter agreed to record the song, "Lone Star Trail," on Decca and record company executive Dave Kapp liked the demo well enough to give Cindy a recording contract.

Cindy's recording career didn't fare very well, but she remained optimistic about her writing potential. During her early Hollywood years she didn't attempt to do much with the country field, particularly since most C&W artists were based elsewhere. A turning point in her career, she later told interviewers, came when she passed a tour vehicle on a Hollywood street with the name of fellow Texan Bob Wills on its side. "I knew he had to be in Hollywood," she recalled, and sought him out. Wills was impressed with her work and ended up recording more than fifty of her songs in decades to come.

In 1947 she decided to concentrate on writing for the country market and quit her other chores. The choice paid off as more and more artists recorded her material. One of the first to hit upper brackets in the C&W field was Eddy Arnold's top-10 version of her "Take Me in Your Arms and Hold Me" in 1950. In 1952, Hank Snow provided another top-10 credit with "Gold Rush Is Over," and in 1953 she worked with Porter Wagoner on the song "Trademark" that gave Carl Smith a national best-seller.

About this time, Cindy had grown tired of Hollywood and longed for her own home territory. In 1954 she picked up stakes and moved back to Mexia. From then on, she worked even longer hours as a writer, sending most of her completed songsheets to top artists by mail. The year 1955 provided music fans with a song that was number one in the nation for many weeks. The hit recording was made by her coauthor on "I Don't Care," Webb Pierce. Among Cindy's other top-10 hits of the next decade were "You Don't Know Me," recorded by Eddy Arnold, Stonewall Jackson's version of "Leona" (1962), and two posthumous hits for Jim Reeves, "This Is It" (1965) and "Distant Drums" (1966).

By the mid-1960s, Cindy had more than 400 published songs to her credit. Among those were such other major hits as "China Doll," "I Was Just Walking Out the Door," "Bubbles in My Beer," "Blue Canadian Rockies," "Thank You for Calling," "In the Misty Moonlight," and "The Night Watch."

Cindy became the first female writer elected to the Nashville Songwriters Association's Songwriters Hall of Fame in 1970. Her output of new material tapered off as the years went by, but through the 1970s and 1980s she was often represented on hit charts or album credits by new versions or reissues of her older songs or releases of new compositions by major country artists.

She was included in the list of "The 100 Most Important People in the History of Country" compiled by the editors of *Life* magazine in a September 1994 special issue on country music. The editors called her "The greatest female songwriter in the history of country music." The total of her published compositions by then had gone well past 500.

WALKER, CLAY: *Singer, guitarist, songwriter. Born Beaumont, Texas, c. 1970.*

For someone who wasn't much enthralled with country music for much of his early life, Clay Walker had much to thank country audiences for in the 1990s. Growing up in a mostly black section of Beaumont, he was strongly influenced by the R&B and soul favorites of the community. As he told interviewers later, he wasn't a country music enthusiast at first because, "It was too sad for me. My all-time favorite artist isn't even country, it's Lionel Richie." Still, combining some of the R&B flavor with a voice that has a close resemblance to country legend George Jones may account for Walker's positive impression on listeners.

Walker himself didn't feel his offerings were that unique, however. He told Dennis Hunt of the *Los Angeles Times* ("Clay Walker—After the Victory at That Talent Show," Calendar section, January 30, 1994), "When people say I sound like certain singers, they're right. When you're young, you fall in love with the style of singers and you imitate them. [Besides Jones and some R&B artists, he named James Taylor and Bob Seger as important influences.] That's the way it is. I'd love to be an original, but I'm not. I'd hardly call myself a great singer either. I've had to make do with the talent I have—and I've done OK."

His father was a devoted country fan who had been playing guitar for years and had achieved some performing credits. He gave his son a guitar when Clay was nine and inspired him to develop singing and playing skills. Clay wrote his first songs at fifteen and has been keeping at it ever since. Once he reached high school age, he began competing in talent contests, which proved a logical route to eventual success.

One major challenge was his participation in a Beaumont high school contest where he was the only white entry from a mostly black student body. "To make things even tougher, I was singing a country song and I knew most of the kids didn't like country music, because they'd kid me about it." But, despite the odds, he won the contest after receiving a standing ovation from his schoolmates. "It's a feeling of triumph I can't really describe. But it was an instant addiction. I wanted to experience it again and again. Ever since then a singing career is all I've cared about."

Actually, he might have tried for a different vocal career if it weren't for the fact that his father kept pressure on him to take the country path. His father had no objections to Clay's accepting gigs in local clubs at sixteen and getting a short engagement at George Jones's theme park at seventeen. About the latter, he told *Radio & Records,* "But when that ended, reality set in and I realized that now I had to play in bars. At Jones Country, I had a captive audience—they were able to see the big stars and they'd scream for me, too. But I had to gain my own fame."

After that, he followed the typical musician's path

of combining day jobs with night and weekend appearances. "I worked on the maintenance crew in a Goodyear rubber plant to save money to go on the road. I had to wear a hard hat and steel toe boots every day. When I traveled around, I would hang that hard hat inside the trailer and put those boots in the corner. Every time I thought I didn't want to do another gig, I looked at that hard hat and those boots—and got my butt out on that stage."

He continued his touring and local bar efforts in the late 1980s and early 1990s while trying unsuccessfully to obtain that all-important recording opportunity. He told Hunt, "It was frustrating that I wasn't getting a contract, but I never doubted I'd eventually get one from somebody. That's because my father taught me something else too—to have incredible confidence in myself."

The "somebody" turned out to be Irving Azoff's Giant Records company, which signed him in 1992 and released his first single, "What's It to You," in mid-1993, just ahead of his debut album. The single made the charts that summer, rising surprisingly fast in all of them and reaching number one in *R&R* the week of October 10, 1993. The album, *Clay Walker,* appeared on the *Billboard* list in the fall and eventually rose to number eight in early 1994, having surpassed R.I.A.A. gold-record levels. It remained on the hit charts through 1994, picking up a platinum certification from R.I.A.A. along the way.

By the end of 1993, Walker had another single, written by him, "Live Until I Die," in the *Billboard* Top 15. It was still on the list when his next self-penned song, "Where Do I Fit in the Picture," debuted on it in early 1994. The latter also became a hit, peaking at number eight in *R&R* the week of May 6. By then Clay had accumulated many more hours of live appearances in clubs and as an opening act for others, but this time in prestigious venues. In the summer of 1994, his single, "Dreaming with My Eyes Open" (written by T. Arata) was on the charts, rising to number one in *Billboard* the week of August 27, having reached the same spot in *R&R* a week earlier. A few weeks later it was joined on the charts by still another Walker single, "If I Could Make a Living," which reached number one in *R&R* the week of November 11.

That single was the title track from his second album, issued in the fall of 1994 and on the charts from then well into 1995. By then the album, which peaked at number four in *Billboard,* had earned another platinum record award from the R.I.A.A., presented on May 4, 1995. In early 1995, the single "This Woman, This Man," from the album was winning good listener response, rising to number one in the spring. Another single from that album, "My Heart Will Never Know," reached top chart positions in midsummer. By the end of the year he had another album, *Hypnotize the Moon,* on the best-seller lists, where it remained for most of 1996. After peaking at number ten in *Billboard,* it went past gold record levels in the spring and was the recipient of a platinum record award by year-end. The single "Who Needs You Baby" from the album peaked at number two in *Billboard* in November 1995 and the next single release of the title track also rose to that position in early 1996.

WALKER, JERRY JEFF: *Singer, guitarist, songwriter, bandleader (Four-Man Deaf Cowboy Band, Lost Gonzo Band, Gonzo Compadres). Born Catskill Mountains, New York, March 16, 1942.*

For years Jerry Jeff Walker was known almost solely for writing the classic folk-flavored song "Mr. Bojangles." But in the mid-1970s, having completed the circuit from folk to rock to country, he gained new luster as one of the foremost writers and performers of the progressive country movement.

Although he became an exponent of the so-called Austin sound in the 1970s, he was a transplanted Texan. Born and raised in upstate New York in a family where music was almost a way of life, Jerry was exposed to a range of influences, since his grandparents were members of a square dance band and his mother and sister were part of an "Andrews Sisters-type trio." Still, though he sang a lot as a youngster, he also took up other pursuits. He was a starting forward on his high school basketball team, which won the New York championship, and he wanted to become an astronaut.

But he hadn't ignored singing and had also taken up the guitar. Always restless, at sixteen he quit high school to wander around the country for a while, including a stay in New Orleans, earning money by singing in bars and passing the hat. He returned home after a while to complete his high school education, graduating in 1959. By then he was an ardent fan of the folk movement and sang songs written by such people as Pete Seeger, Woody Guthrie, and the original Jimmie Rodgers.

At the start of the 1960s Walker was singing in small clubs and coffee houses in the East. But before long the wanderlust caught hold again and he was off to the far reaches of the United States, booked for appearances in coffee houses and on college campuses throughout the West and Southwest. On one of those tours in the mid-1960s, he met songwriter-musician Bob Bruno while working in Austin, Texas, a city that he fell in love with. The two formed a folk-rock band called Circus Maximus that they brought to New York and won a recording contract with Vanguard Records in 1967. Their debut album, *Circus Maximus,* was issued in December of that year. The band won a local reputation playing in New York area clubs for the next few years.

Walker had been writing original material for some time, including what was to become the famous "Mr. Bojangles," a song about an old street dancer Jerry Jeff had met one time in a New Orleans drunk tank. One day in the late 1960s, Jerry Jeff and folk artist David Bromberg visited New York station WBAI-FM in Greenwich Village and sang "Bojangles." The disc jockey, Bob Fass, taped it and played it many times thereafter. The exposure brought the song to the attention of other singers, which led to hit cover versions by Nilsson and the Nitty Gritty Dirt Band. It also helped convince Jerry Jeff to go out as a solo artist again. He signed with Atlantic Records, which released his version of the song. Ironically, it fell flat. It was not until he included a new version on a mid-1970s album that he had a hit of his own.

The Atlantic alignment proved nonproductive. Three LPs came out on the label (*Mr. Bojangles* and *Five Years Gone* in 1969 and *Being Free* in 1969), but little happened with them. Jerry Jeff had some well-received solo engagements in places like the Bitter End in Manhattan, then faded from view for a while, at least as far as the general public was concerned. He stayed for a while in Key West, Florida, then regrouped in the early 1970s, moving to Austin, where he bought some land in the hills near the town and built a house. He signed a new recording contract with MCA and recorded an album with some friends and a portable tape recorder that was released in 1973 as *Jerry Jeff Walker*. He called his band of those years the Four-Man Deaf Cowboy Band. With them he began to gain new attention from folk and country fans in 1973, making the charts with the single "L.A. Freeway" (a song written by his friend Guy Clark) and the album *Viva Terlingua*, which was on national pop charts the end of 1973 and early in 1974.

Viva Terlingua was recorded in one of Walker's favorite spots of the mid-1970s, the ghost town of Luckenbach. It had been bought by a grizzled Texan named Hondo Crouch, who had become almost a second father to Jerry Jeff. Luckenbach, of course, later was made nationally famous in the hit song performed by Waylon Jennings.

On the album Jerry's voice was more grainy and "craggy" than the pure, pleasant voice of his earlier performing years. Typifying his hard driving life of the mid-1970s, the feeling and intensity he put into a song, particularly in personal appearances, overcame the limitations of range of the new voice and often seemed to impart more meaning to the material.

The peccadilloes that had produced those changes, of course, became part of his mystique. Audiences often came to his concerts in part to see if he showed up and in what condition. Legends aside, Jerry pointed out that he couldn't have achieved the output he did if he did everything reputed about him. As he told John Morthland of *Country Music* magazine, "I've broken in some journalists. Meaning they've exaggerated the point. Being loose when I'm performing is something I've always tried for. I think music should be performed and played as if we were not too uptight about it."

Walker also stressed that he got to almost all his concerts, because he owed it to fans and because he gets pleasure from entertaining. A favorite statement of his over the years was that he got many personal returns from the "pure joy of playing."

In the mid-1970s, Jerry Jeff continued to expand his following all over the country with a steady stream of new albums backed by a tight country-rock group called the Lost Gonzo Band. Those releases included his third MCA LP, *Collectibles,* recorded live in Austin and issued in 1974, followed by *Ridin' High, It's a Good Night for Singing* (on the charts in 1975), and *A Man Must Carry On,* a chartmaker in 1976. The last named was a live album recorded on the road in five U.S. cities. While Jerry Jeff was mixing it he heard that Crouch had died, and converted the album into a tribute to him, including a rendition of one of Hondo's poems. Talking about Crouch fondly, he reminisced to Morthland, "He just made magic. I never been anyplace he was where there wasn't magic."

After that album, the Lost Gonzo Band decided to try to make it on its own, though MCA did issue another album in 1978 of Walker and Gonzo Band material called *Contrary to Ordinary.*

By that time, Jacky Jack (as Walker was called by close friends), had moved on to another record company, Elektra/Asylum. His debut LP on that label, *Comfort and Crazy,* came out in November 1978. The title song was a Guy Clark composition and the album included a Jerry Jeff original, "Good Loving Grace." However, the Elektra association didn't work out as hoped for, and, by 1981, Jerry Jeff was back with MCA, which released the album *Reunion* in May 1981. (Prior to that, MCA issued the 1980 retrospective LP, *The Best of Jerry Jeff Walker.*)

Talking about his work, he said, "You see these gray hairs? I been pickin' a long time, man, and I'm going to play the way I always played and there's going to be a little of something you just picked up on and there may be something here I sang ten years ago, but it's all going to be mixed in here. . . . It's a picture of life. I like to have people come up to me and say thank you for the night that you came into our room. Me and my wife were just kinda layin' around by the fire or something and your music, it felt like you were talkin' to us and we enjoyed it. That's great!"

In the rest of the 1980s through the mid-1990s, Walker continued to personify the laid-back style of the artist doing what he felt moved to do while experimenting with all kinds of musical combinations. His blends included country, folk, honky-tonk, reggae, rock, Tex-Mex, blues, and whatever else captured his fancy at one time or another. He regularly performed in Austin clubs and on tour (with a backing band in the mid-1990s dubbed the Gonzo Compadres) at mostly smaller venues, often featuring songs in his concerts by close friends from various Austin periods like Guy Clark and Ray

Wylie Hubbard. His credits included appearances on the Public Broadcasting System's *Austin City Limits* TV show.

In the mid-1990s, MCA included reissues of some of his classic albums in its Texas City Music catalog. These were *Viva Terlingua, Ridin' High* (and a twin-pak cassette of both of those) and *A Man Must Carry On*. In the spring of 1996, a new live album, *Night After Night,* was released on the independent Tried & True label.

WARINER, STEVE NOEL: *Singer, guitarist (lead, bass and steel), banjoist, drummer, songwriter. Born Noblesville, Indiana, December 25, 1954.*

As a musician's musician, Steve Wariner didn't always get the respect he deserved from industry officials or the country music public at large. It took a little while for him to gain the ear of the public when he first signed with a major label in the mid-1970s, but once he did he became one of the consistent favorites of country fans in the 1980s and 1990s.

Like many successful country performers over the years, he came from a show business background. His father, Roy Wariner, was a professional singer and instrumentalist and helped Steve learn the rudiments of guitar while the boy was growing up in Indiana. By the time Steve was ten he was performing in live concerts, and before long was also gaining credits for singing and playing on local radio and TV shows. He didn't focus on music to the exclusion of other youthful pursuits—he liked sports and played on some high school teams—but music was his favorite activity, particularly since not only did he enjoy doing it, but also earned money from some of his gigs.

His instrumental skills were above average (and he showed prowess on a wide variety of them), which led to his first big career milestone, his selection as bass guitarist in the band of country star Dottie West. That helped influence a move to Nashville, where he did session work in the mid-1970s while also touring with such country standouts as the late Bob Luman and Chet Atkins. The appreciation of his guitar talents continued to grow to the point where some people even spoke his name in the same breath as Atkins.

As he said later on, "I get a lot of guitar players who come out to the show telling me how much I've influenced them. It seems kind of odd because I don't look at myself that way. Those are the kinds of things I still say to Chet Atkins. I'm not technical at all. I just play what I feel. I'd rather play something off the top of my head and just feel it than to try to read what someone else wants me to play."

With Atkins' support, he was signed by RCA Records in the summer of 1977. He recalled being a bit puzzled by all the people thronging RCA facilities when he went for his initial studio work. "I was so excited on the days of my first recording session. But there were all these TV crews, CBS, NBC newsmen all around clamoring to talk to Chet and the other Nashville studio pickers. It was the day after Elvis died! So there I was, just a kid, huddled back in the corner."

He might have felt like a kid, but by then he was twenty-two years old. In those years, of course, older performers dominated the country field and it was expected that artists in their twenties still had plenty of dues to pay before reaching top rungs, a situation that was to change markedly in coming decades.

The industry mindset tended to limit media coverage of newcomers, and Steve's recording career got off to a relatively slow start. His initial releases in the late 1970s didn't do much, but things began to change at the beginning of the 1980s. He scored his first top-10 single in 1980 with "Your Memory," followed in 1981 by the top-10 single "By Now" and the number-one release, "All Roads Lead to You." In 1982 his RCA album debut, *Steve Wariner,* appeared, followed in 1983 by *Midnight Fire.* In 1983 he had another top-10 singles hit with the title track of the 1993 album.

Steve had more top-10 chart singles in 1984 with "Lonely Women Make Good Lovers" and "Why Goodbye," but his association with RCA was winding up. RCA issued a *Greatest Hits* album in 1985, but by then he had signed with MCA Records, which issued his label debut album the same year titled *One Good Night Deserves Another.* Before the year was over he had a second MCA album in the stores, *Life's Highway.* (He still had a backlog of material at RCA, which issued the album *Down in Tennessee* in 1986.) Wariner continued to have his name on singles charts in 1985 with two top-10 releases, "What I Didn't Do" and "Heart Trouble" plus the number-one success, "Some Fools Never Learn."

Wariner's association with MCA proved to be a rewarding one for more than a half dozen years. He continued to expand his concert activities both in the U.S. and other countries, while steadily adding to his list of hit singles and album discography. From the mid-1980s on he also kept sharpening his songwriting skills. His new albums on MCA in the late 1980s increasingly featured songs written or cowritten by Steve. Among his cowritten numbers were "You Can Dream of Me" with John Hall, leader of the group Orleans, "Baby I'm Yours" with Guy Clark, and "Precious Things" with Mac MacAnally. Among other hit songs he wrote or cowrote were "Hold On," "Where Did I Go Wrong," "When I Could Come Home to You," and "I Should Be With You."

His 1986 output included the number-one singles hits "You Can Dream of Me" and "Life's Highway" and the top-10 successes "Starting All Over Again" and "That's How You Know That Love's Right." The last one, a duet with Nicolette Larson, was nominated for a Country Music Association Award. His 1987 credits included three number-one singles—"Small Town Girl," "The Weekend" and "Lynda"—and a top-10 duet with Glen Campbell, "The Hand That Rocks the Cradle."

The duet single was nominated for a Grammy Award. Wariner also had two albums on the charts during the year, *It's a Crazy World* and *Greatest Hits*. His 1988 chart singles comprised the top-10 disks "Baby I'm Yours" and the Wariner-penned "Hold on a Little Longer" and the number one "I Should Be With You" (also a Wariner composition). The last-named was the title track for his fifth MCA album.

Steve closed out the next decade with two more number-one singles, "Where Did I Go Wrong" and "I Got Dreams." At year end his cowritten single "When I Come Home to You" was on the charts, peaking at number four in *Radio & Records* the week of January 12, 1990. His 1989 MCA album release was *I Got Dreams*. During 1990 he made top-chart levels with the singles "The Domino Theory," number four in *R&R* the week of May 25, and "Precious Thing," number four in *R&R* the week of September 21. Releases in 1990 included *Laredo* and *Greatest Hits, Volume 2*. Still, from an album standpoint, things seemed to be slowing down for Steve, and his stay on MCA was coming to an end. In 1991 he left that label for Arista Records, providing his new label with the singles hit "Leave Him Out of This," number three in *R&R* the week of December 28, 1991.

Wariner's debut album on Arista, *I Am Ready*, came out in 1991 and provided his first number-one single for his new affiliation, "The Tips of My Fingers," which hit the top spot in *R&R* the week of April 3, 1992. Later he had a number seven *R&R* song, "A Woman Loves," the week of August 14. During 1991 he joined forces with other Nashville notables as part of a band organized by fiddler Mark O'Connor called the New Nashville Cats. The group, which also included Vince Gill and Ricky Skaggs, won the Grammy Award for the Best Country Vocal Collaboration. The award was for the single "Restless," drawn from the Warner Brothers album *Mark O'Connor & the New Nashville Cats*. Meanwhile his Arista debut album entered the *Billboard* chart the end of 1991 and stayed on it for most of 1992 to achieve the best sales total of any Wariner collection to that time. Steve placed more singles on the charts in 1992, including "Crash Course in the Blues" late in the year, cowritten by Steve with J. Jarvis and Don Cook.

Charted singles for Wariner in 1993 included "Like a River to the Sea" early in the year, "If I Don't Love You," number seven in *R&R* the week of October 1, 1993, and "Drivin' and Cryin'," moving up the charts at year-end. In June of 1994, the single "It Won't Be Over You" was in upper chart levels, peaking at number fifteen in *R&R* the week of June 17, and in September the title track from his second Arista album, *Drive*, made the lists.

After completing work on that album Wariner said, "I'm real comfortable with my little place in the music world. But you know what? There is still fire there. I still practice guitar every day in the year. This time I wanted to have a more driving, upbeat album, have some songs that would lend themselves to dance or clubs. I think this album has the most variety of anything I've done. It covers the spectrum, from straight country to some rocking-edge tracks."

He also could still count on his dad for support. "He's not one to show emotion. But when I won a Grammy he wrote me a note that said, 'When you were a little boy, I always knew that this would happen someday. You sure deserve it. And I love you.' I started to bawl when I read it."

His 1996 activities included serving as an award presenter on the Academy of Country Music's 31st Annual Awards Show aired on NBC-TV the night of April 24. By then he had completed work on his concept album, *No More Mr. Nice Guy*, an all-instrumental disc featuring world class musicians from many segments of pop music from country to blues and jazz. Artists taking part include Vince Gill, Larry Carlton, Chet Atkins, Leo Kottke, Mark O'Connor, Richie Sambora, Carl Jackson, Bela Fleck, Sam Bush, Mac MacAnally, Lee Roy Parnell, Jimmy Olander, Randy Goodman, Nolan Ryna, Ron Gannaway, Bryan White, Derek George, Bryan Austin and Jeffrey Steele.

WELCH, GILLIAN: *Singer, guitarist, pianist, drummer, songwriter. Born Los Angeles, California, October 2, 1967.*

Few of the new artists of 1996 received encomiums to rival those Gillian Welch garnered from the critical community. Her debut album, *Revival*, on the Almo Sounds label was without a doubt one of the finest collections of original material to grace record-store shelves in some time. In style a folk-country collection, the release deservedly won enthusiasm from reviewers across much of the pop music spectrum. Noting the ease with which Welch moved from performing a song like "Paper Wings," "an ode to the smoldering pop-country style of Patsy Cline, to the rock-accented tension of 'Tear My Stillhouse Down,'" Robert Hilburn of the *Los Angeles Times* suggested that "At every turn, she demonstrates a spark and commitment that should endear her to anyone, from country and folk to adult pop and rock and roll fan, who appreciates imagination and heart."

In her appearance and choice of clothing styles, she reminded onlookers of the distraught Appalachian women caught in WPA photographs of the 1930s. The lyrical and musical content of her songs seemed to reflect a childhood in the downtrodden rural areas of parts of the U.S., yet her background couldn't have been more different. She had grown up in an affluent section of West Los Angeles, the daughter of Ken and Mitzi Welch, songwriters and arrangers whose credits included years of work on music for the *Carol Burnett* TV show.

Her parents made sure she was given good instrumental grounding, including piano lessons at seven and guitar at ten. She also learned to play the drums and ukelele.

She recalled being exposed to her father and mother's work with Carol Burnett. "Every Friday we used to go to the tapings. We were good friends with Carol and her family." She was well acquainted with cast members on the programs such as Harvey Korman and Tim Conway. At home, with all kinds of instruments available, she added, "We would do the hootenanny thing. My parents loved the standards, like Rodgers and Hart and Irving Berlin, and we had those huge books of music called 'Greatest Hits of '60s and '70s' and we would sit around and play songs like 'Bad, Bad Leroy Brown.' The first stuff that I bought when I started buying records was acoustic, like James Taylor, and all the Beatles records. My dad was a big Randy Newman fan, so that stuff was already around the house. Towards the end of high school in 1984, I discovered R.E.M. and thought they were it."

She still wasn't sure about her basic tastes in music when she entered the University of California at Santa Cruz in 1985. After a while, she started attending a place called Sluggo's Pizza on Tuesday nights to listen to a bluegrass group called the Harmony Grits. As she told *Request* magazine in May 1996, "That band was my first serious exposure to bluegrass, and I just loved it. It made a lot of sense. I thought, 'Oooh, I can play this stuff.'" She became friends with the band and began borrowing records from their collection; studying them carefully, she began to introduce some of the elements she heard into her own guitar playing. She was impressed by many artists, past and present, from the Blue Sky Boys and the Delmore Brothers to Bill Monroe, but her particular favorites were the Stanley Brothers.

She graduated from college in 1989 with a degree in photography, but soon realized she loved music more. With her parents' approval, she moved to Boston in 1990 and enrolled in the Berklee College of Music to study songwriting. Apart from her studies, she built up her performing experience by playing, as she later said, "this backwards mountain music in clubs and coffeehouses." During her last year at Berklee, she became friends with another bluegrass fan and aspiring musician and songwriter, David Rawlings, whom she met at a tryout for the school's country music ensemble. The two soon formed a writing and performing partnership, and in July 1992 first Gillian and then David relocated to Nashville to further their musical careers. Once there, Welch noted, "we arranged the songs that I had written for acoustic guitar and lead and baritone vocals" and began performing at open-mike sessions and writers nights at local clubs.

In the fall, with support from other Berklee alumni,

Gillian made contact with Denise Stiff, at the time a staff member of a local music industry firm and also Alison Krauss's manager; Stiff helped her put together demo tapes and other material to submit to music publishers. Most of the twenty-odd publishers who examined the package said they liked the music but didn't know what to do with it, but some expressed more serious interest—which led to a contract as a staff writer with Almo Irving Music. Before long Nashville artists like Tim and Mollie O'Brien, the Nashville Bluegrass Band, Trisha Yearwood, and Emmylou Harris began to record some of her material. Emmylou included her version of Gillian's "Orphan Girl" in her acclaimed *Wrecking Ball* album.

Gillian, though, aspired to record her songs herself, as she kept telling publishing company official David Conrad. He finally sent a tape of her stylings to Jerry Moss at Almo Sounds in Los Angeles. Almo was founded by Moss and Herb Alpert (who previously had started A&M Records). In the summer of 1994, she went to L.A. to audition for Moss, a trip that resulted in a recording contract. With T-Bone Burnett, whom she had met earlier, as producer, she prepared ten tracks for her debut album, four of which were solo duets with David Rawlings's session musicians joined in on the other tracks. Three of the songs were completely written by Gillian, including "Orphan Girl" and "Tear My Stillhouse Down"; the remainder were cowritten by her and Rawlings. The latter included such excellent songs as "Paper Wings" ("Paper wings, all torn and bent/But you made me feel like they were heaven sent"), "Barroom Girls," and "Acony Bell."

When the album, entitled *Revival*, came out in 1996, it revealed a new country music voice—an excellent one that demonstrated how the basic qualities of the art form could still be relevant in the age of technology. Writing in *CMJ* magazine (April 8, 1996, James Lien commented, "*Revival* is so powerful and moving, so simple and full of grace, you become convinced you're in a remote prairie cabin, pensively pacing over wooden floors, so much so that you can feel the wind in the window cracks and the thunderheads rolling overhead . . . with sturdy acoustic guitars, standup bass, old-fashioned harmony singing and Welch's high, clear voice, *Revival* is a triumph of traditional American roots music that will stand the ages."

Jay Orr of the *Nashville Banner* ("Gillian's Island," April 11, 1996, Section C, p. 14) noted that Welch's subjects "include orphans, death, desitution, poverty, crime, drunkenness, loneliness. Though the list of them looks dreary on paper, Welch's treatment never gets heavy-handed."

Gillian responded, "This is the stuff that appeals to me. I'm a big fan of those darker, Appalachian murder tunes. For lack of a better word, they're so gnarly. They don't pull any punches."

WELLS, KITTY: *Singer, guitarist, songwriter. Born Nashville, Tennessee, August 30, 1919. Elected to Country Music Hall of Fame in 1976.*

For longer than any other performer, Kitty Wells reigned as unofficial "Queen of Country Music." While she would have to add "emeritus" to the title from the 1970s on, she still ranked as one of the most respected performers in the country field even if her name only showed up occasionally on the hit charts in comparison to the many top-10 successes of the 1950s and 1960s. (From 1952 through 1969, she had twenty-five top-10 songs, almost twice the total of the nearest female country singer of those years.)

Wells, whose real name was Muriel Deason, grew up in Nashville, but had to go much further afield to establish a reputation as an up-and-coming country artist. She sang along with country music on the radio as a girl. By the time she was fifteen she could play the guitar and began to perform at the local dances in the Nashville area. A few years later, in 1936, she made her radio debut on station WSIX in Nashville.

In 1938, she married Johnny Wright of the Johnnie and Jack country duo. She was featured on their show and traveled widely with the troupe. She got her stage name of Kitty Wells courtesy of her husband. During this period, her voice reached country listeners via appearances on a great many radio stations, such as WCHS, Bluefield, West Virginia; WNOX, Knoxville, Tennessee; WPTF, Raleigh, North Carolina; and WEAS, Decatur, Georgia. At the time, the country field was dominated by male artists. Still, she might have become a nationally recognized star then except for the fact that she concentrated part of her time on raising a family.

As her children got a little older, Wells began to expand her singing efforts. In 1947, she was given a guest spot on the *Grand Ole Opry.* That same year, she, her husband, and coworker Jack Anglin, plus their band, the Tennessee Mountain Boys, signed on as regular cast members of the *Louisiana Hayride,* broadcast from Shreveport. All of them gained an increasingly wider reputation across the United States from their work on the show from 1947 to 1952 and from a series of successful recordings, initially by Johnny and Jack, then by Kitty. Her breakthrough came in 1952 with her single "It Wasn't God Who Made Honky Tonk Angels." Issued on Decca, it was number one on U.S. country charts for many weeks, selling some 800,000 copies. During ensuing years, it sold at a slower pace, but steadily, until, by the 1970s, it had gone past the million-copy mark.

With Wells, her husband, and Jack Anglin all having top-10 hits to their credits, it wasn't long before the *Grand Ole Opry* came after them. During 1952, they agreed to join the premier country radio program and moved to Nashville, which was still Kitty and Johnny's home in the 1990s. In 1953, though she didn't have a blockbuster the equal of "Honky Tonk Angels," she still placed several singles on the charts, including a top-10 hit, "I'm Paying for That Back Street Affair."

She shifted into high gear in 1954–55 with such hits as "One by One" and "As Long as I Live," both duets with Red Foley, and "Making Believe" and "Lonely Side of Town." In 1956, she hit the top 10 with "Searching Soul" and in 1957 scored with "I'll Always Be Your Fraulein" and "Repeating." She rounded out the decade with such national successes as "I Can't Stop Loving You" (1958) and "Amigo's Guitar" (cowritten by Kitty and John Loudermilk) and "Mommy for a Day" (1959). Decca recognized her importance to the company by signing her to a lifetime contract in 1959, an agreement still in effect in the 1970s after Decca had become MCA Records.

She continued to hold sway at the top of the hit lists as the 1960s progressed, starting off with a big 1960 bestseller, "Left to Right." In 1961, she turned out another number-one hit, "Heartbreak U.S.A.," and had a big year in 1962 with such top-10 singles as "Day into Night," "Unloved, Unwanted," "We Missed You," and "Will Your Lawyer Talk to God?" She missed the top 10 a few times in 1963, but came back in 1964 with "Password" and "The White Circle on My Finger" and made the top 10 in 1965 with "You Don't Hear." In 1967, she made upper-chart levels with the single "Love Makes the World Go Round." While she fell short of top-10 honors the last few years of the decade, she still was one of the most successful country recording artists, placing four singles on the bestseller lists in 1968 and several more in 1969. Some of her 1960 releases were duets with such artists as her husband, Johnny Wright, Webb Pierce, and Roy Drusky.

Among Wells' other best known songs were "Cheatin's a Sin," "I Don't Claim to Be an Angel," "God Put a Rainbow in the Cloud," and "How Far to Heaven?"

She also completed many albums for Decca during the 1950s and 1960s, many of which were high on the album charts. Among her LPs were *Lonely Street* (10/58), *After Dark* (7/59); *Dust on the Bible* (9/59); *Kitty's Choice* (5/60); *Kitty Wells* (mid-1950s); *Seasons of My Heart* (1960); *Golden Favorites* (4/61); *Heartbreak U.S.A.* (7/61); *Queen of Country Music* (4/62); *Singing on Sunday* (1963); *Especially for You; Kitty Wells Story* (two records, 10/63); *Country Music Time* (10/64); *Burning Memories* (4/65); *Lonesome, Sad and Blue* (8/65); *Family Gospel Sing* (11/65); *Songs Made Famous by Jim Reeves* (4/66); *All the Way* (8/66); *Kitty Wells Show* (1/67); *Loves Makes the World Go Round* 6/67); *Together Again,* with Red Foley (9/67); *Queen of Honky Tonk* (12/67); on Vocalion Records, *Kitty Wells* (1/67) and *Heart* (8/69). Her album releases of the late 1960s and early 1970s included such Decca collections as *Bouquet of Country Hits, Singing 'Em Country, Your Love Is the Way, They're Stepping All Over My Heart,* and *Pledging My Love.*

Kitty's chartmakers in the late 1960s and early 1970s included "They're Stepping All Over My Heart," "Sincerely" (on the charts in the spring of 1972), and "Easily Persuaded," a hit in mid-1973. At the time the last named was released, MCA Records reported that during her years on the Decca/MCA roster she had turned out a total of 461 singles and forty-three albums.

From the mid-1950s through the end of the 1970s, Kitty's in-person appearances took her around the world several times. By the start of the 1980s, besides having performed in all fifty states, she also had traveled to all Canadian provinces, Germany, France, Italy, Holland, and England. In 1969, she and her husband began a syndicated TV show called *The Kitty Wells/ Johnny Wright Family Show,* which remained a staple for viewers all over the United States and Canada for many years. Their son, Bobby Wright, joined them on the program and in the concert package they took to major cities and county and state fairs. Wells often was featured on other TV programs, including, in the 1950s and 1960s, *The Ozark Jamboree, Jimmy Dean Show, Nightlife* and Carl Smith's *Country Music Hall.* In the 1970s, she appeared on Johnny Carson's *The Tonight Show* and *Hee Haw,* among others. She also was one of the country artists featured in the film *Second Fiddle to a Steel Guitar.*

Over the years, Wells received many honors. From 1953 to 1968, various polls voted her the number-one female country singer. In 1954, Governor Frank Clement of Tennessee presented her with a citation as Outstanding Tennessee Citizen, and she was honored with various tributes from other states in later years. In 1976, she received the greatest honor of all for a country performer, election by her peers to the Country Music Hall of Fame in Nashville.

In addition to all her other activities, she also assembled several books, including *Favorite Songs and Recipes,* published in 1973.

Through the 1980s into the 1990s, Kitty continued to hold a quietly favored position in the country pantheon, revered by many older fans and held in high esteem by country artists old and young. In the mid-1990s she remained a regular performer on the *Grand Ole Opry* and did some touring, but not at the breakneck pace of her early years. She was one of the honored veteran artists on the ABC-TV *Women in Country* special and also gained new attention from reviewers who approved of her vocal contributions to the title track of the Loretta Lynn/Dolly Parton/Tammy Wynette 1993 album *Honky Tonk Angels.*

The title track, "It Wasn't God Who Made Honky Tonk Angels," was designed, of course, as a tribute to Kitty's career. Lynn recalled her early emulation of Kitty's style, and why she had to change it, in several interviews. She told Beverly Keel of the *Nashville Banner* (September 28, 1993), "I always sang just like Kitty till some old drunk stumbled up to the stage one night and said, 'Hey, little girl, there's already been one Kitty Wells, now sing something else.'"

In including Kitty in the *Life* list of "The 100 Most Important People in the History of Country," the magazine's editors noted that her recording of "Honky Tonk Angels" in 1952 provided a song "every bit as bold in its day as anything Patsy, Willie and other 'revolutionaries' would come up with later." That number and others in her repertoire put her in the unique position for that time of being a woman telling men off.

In 1995 her albums in print included: *Kitty Wells: Country Music Hall of Fame Series* on MCA; *Kitty Wells, Greatest Hits, Volume 1* and *Kitty Wells/Greatest Hits, Volume 2,* both on the SOR label; *Kitty Wells/20 Greatest Hits* on Deluxe; and *Kitty Wells/Country Spotlight* on Dominion. Some of her renditions were included in Volumes 2 and 10 of the *Grand Ole Opry Stars of the Fifties* video series. In the 1990s, Germany's Bear Family Records came out with a CD edition of its previous LP set of Kitty's recordings in her most productive period from 1949–1958. Titled *Kitty Wells: The Queen of Country Music,* the 4 CD package contained a number of tracks not included in the vinyl set as well as a rewritten booklet including "photos from Kitty's personal scrapbook." Naturally the package incorporated her best known numbers from those years such as "It Wasn't God Who Made Honky Tonk Angels," "Makin' Believe" and "I'm Paying for That Back Street Affair."

Kitty continued to perform at country venues in the mid-1990s, including concerts at Dolly Parton's Dollywood theme park as part of the Showcase of Stars series.

WEST, DOTTIE: *Singer, guitarist, songwriter. Born McMinnville, Tennessee, October 11, 1932; died September 4, 1991.*

Dottie West might be called the "Queen of Duets," because in her long and eventful career she recorded notable material with four different singing partners: Jim Reeves, Don Gibson, Jimmy Dean, and Kenny Rogers. Still, her career is even more remarkable for her solo work, both as a performer and a songwriter.

Looking back over her singing collaborations in June 1979, she told Mark Lundahl of the *San Bernardino* (California) *Sun,* "My first duet was with Jim Reeves. At that time he saw me as a new artist and songwriter and he wanted to help get my name around.

"I think the chemistry really worked for Don Gibson and me. But we only recorded one album because he didn't want to go on the road. He was too interested in just writing songs, so that teaming fell by the wayside. You can't just be recording and stay at home. Your fans want to see you."

And of her late 1970s pairing with Kenny Rogers, which brought her career to new heights, "Recording with Kenny has broadened my audience. He's kind of a unique crossover artist because he's gone from the pop field to country. Singing for his crowd is kind of like singing for the folks that Elvis drew. There are all ages and all types of people."

But those events and the many others that made her a country-music superstar were far from the mind of the little girl growing up as a member of a low-income farm family in Tennessee. The oldest of ten children, Dottie was burdened with her share of responsibilities: chopping cotton, working in sugar cane fields, and sometimes cooking for her huge family. But it wasn't all hard physical work. Her parents loved country music and saw to it that their children were exposed to it, as well as to the activities at the nearby Southern Baptist Church, where Dottie eventually sang in the choir. As a child, Dottie began learning guitar from her father, Hollis March, whom she said "could play anything with strings on it." But there were some less savory aspects of their relationship, indicated in later reports of childhood sexual abuse.

A string of part-time jobs in her teens helped finance her music lessons and her future college education. Her dream came true at the start of the 1950s, when she enrolled at Tennessee Technological University in Cookeville as a music major. (In recognition of her achievements, in 1966 that school established the Dottie West Music Scholarship.)

During her first week on campus, she met a boy named Bill West, who shared her love for country music (though in her courses she explored all musical forms). His goal was to get an engineering degree, but he could play excellent steel guitar and was soon accompanying Dottie at school events. Before long, they decided to marry, an alliance that lasted through many years on the road and four children before ending in divorce in 1969.

Both Wests graduated, Bill with an electronics degree and Dottie as a music major. Bill quickly got a job with a Cleveland electronics company and they moved to Ohio. For five years he persevered at engineering while they supplemented their income by appearing as a country music team. One show they appeared on regularly was Gene Carroll's *Landmark Jamboree* TV show in Cleveland. In 1959, after Dottie gained a recording contract from Starday Records, the time was ripe for a move to Nashville.

Nothing dramatic happened right away, but it didn't take long for the Wests to become friends with many other struggling young artists, many of whom were to become top names in the future, such as Willie Nelson, Hank Cochran, and Roger Miller. It was from informal get-togethers with people like that, Dottie recalled, that she discovered her talent as a songwriter.

"It was through guitar-pulling sessions that I really became a writer," she told James Albrecht of *Country Style* magazine (July 1978). "When I first went to Nashville, Patsy Cline was my best friend. I had idol-ized her singing before that, and we became good friends. . . . She never wrote songs. But she really got me into going to what we called guitar pullings at the time. We'd sit with one guitar in the room and we'd pass the guitar around and everybody would sing the song they had written that day and try to knock each other out. So it really kept you on your toes and you wrote a lot of songs that way. I learned a lot from Willie Nelson, Hank Cochran, and Roger Miller."

The first complete song she came up with in those years was "Is This Me?" written in 1961. The song was recorded by Jim Reeves and became a hit for him. It also earned Dottie a BMI Writer's Award. That success coupled with Jim Reeves' recommendation of her singing potential to Chet Atkins led to a long-term contract with RCA Records in 1962. (Prior to the RCA alignment, Dottie had left Starday and worked briefly with Atlantic Records.) Soon after the RCA deal, the Wests were given a songwriting contract by Tree Publishing Company.

It took a little while for the momentum to build up, but in 1964, Dottie West moved from relative obscurity to country-music prominence. Helping to bring that about was the Wests' composition "Here Comes My Baby." Soon after the single came out, it was nestling in the country top 10 and was covered by pop artists like Perry Como. Since then over 100 artists in both country and pop have released their own versions of the song, an accepted perennial standard.

West made her initial mark as a duet artist teaming with Jim Reeves on a top-10 version of Justin Tubb's "Love Is No Excuse." The promising pairing was brought to an abrupt end with Reeves' tragic death in a plane crash. It was an event that took much of the pleasure away from Dottie's selection as a regular cast member of the *Grand Ole Opry,* an association still firm to the end of her life. "Here Comes My Baby" was nominated for a Grammy Award, the first of sixteen such nominations West was to attain through 1979. (It also was her only winner over that period, bringing her the Award for Best Country Vocal Performance for 1964.)

Dottie followed with a string of charted songs, including such major hits as "Would You Hold It Against Me?" in 1966, "Paper Mansions" in 1967, "Rings of Gold" (number one as a single and as title song of an album) with Don Gibson in 1968, and "I Was Born a Country Girl" (written with Red Lane) in 1969. Other charted singles of those years were "Gettin' Married Has Made Us Strangers," "What's Come Over My Baby?" and, with son Dale, "Mommie Can I Still Call Him Daddy?"

In the mid- and late-1960s, West's personal appearances covered all fifty states, Canada, and Europe. Her guest spots on TV included *The Jimmy Dean Show,* Carl Smith's *Country Music Hall,* and a regular slot on the *Faron Young Show.* She also appeared in two movies, *Second Fiddle to a Steel Guitar* and *There's a Still on the Hill*. On July 10, 1965, her home town of McMinnville honored her with "Dottie West Day."

In 1970, West accepted an offer from the Coca-Cola Company to write a commercial based on her song "I'm a Country Girl," an alliance that was to prove more important than she might have predicted. The commercial featuring the song did so well that in 1972 the company offered her a lifetime contract to write advertising numbers. (As of the end of 1979, she had provided fifteen such commercials.) The first results of the agreement was a 1973 song, co-written with Coke commercial producer Billy Davis, called "Country Sunshine." From its advertising use, the song won Dottie a Clio Award for best commercial of the year, the first such honor ever given a country artist. Perhaps more important, her single of it became a hit, helping to restore her musical fortunes, which sagged a bit in the early 1970s, possibly due to the trauma of her breakup with Bill West. (In the mid-1970s, she married drummer Byron Metcalf, who, as Bill had been, was a member of her tour group.) "Country Sunshine" later became Dottie's theme song.

Her activities in the mid-1970s included repeated tours of Europe, which brought such accolades as being voted Top American Female Vocalist (country) in England in 1972 and 1973. In 1976, she also changed record companies, joining United Artists. The immediate result was the single "When It's Just You and Me," the biggest-selling single of West's career to that point, but the move led as well to her phenomenally successful work with Kenny Rogers.

She had known Rogers before signing with UA as a solo artist. As she told Janet Martineau of *The Saginaw News* (July 21, 1979), "I love to sing harmony and Kenny and I have been friends for a long time. He and Marianne [his wife] are just friendly, nice people, and they would come to our home to visit and spend the night when they were in Nashville."

So there already was a rapport when the two coincidentally were slated to have successive recording sessions for UA one night. "He came by my sessions and watched me record while he was waiting. Then he decided to come in and help me record a song called 'Every Time Two Fools Collide.' It was to have been a single for me and I had already cut the track—the music was in my key, so that's why Kenny hit some high notes in there he had never hit before."

The single turned out to be a hit. "We all felt the magic and the chemistry was right. And the company said, 'Hey, you guys have got to do an album.'" The result was an album titled *Every Time Two Fools Collide,* which moved to the top of the country charts and was a crossover into pop as well. As of late 1979, it had exceeded 550,000 copies sold, for a gold record award. In 1979, they followed with another LP called *Classics* that did even better (565,000 copies as of fall 1979), for a second gold-record success.

In November 1979, UA issued another album by Dottie titled *Special Delivery,* her thirty-third LP (including duets) to come out over two decades. Among those LPs were *Sensational Dottie West* on Starday (early 1960s), *I Fall to Pieces* on Nashville, and some tracks on the Starday LP *Queens of Country Music.* Her 1960s RCA releases included *Here Comes My Baby* (7/65), *Dottie West Sings* (2/66), *Suffer Time* (8/66), *With All My Heart* (2/67), *Sacred Ballads* (8/67), *Sound of Music* (Camden, 9/67), *I'll Help You* (12/67), and *World of Music.* Among her 1970s LPs on RCA were *Country & West* (7/70), *Forever Yours* (with the Jordanaires, (11/70), *Legend in My Time* (3/71), *Careless Hands* (5/71), *Have You Heard* (11/71), and *I'm Only a Woman* (7/72).

The West-Rogers duet brought opportunities to perform in some of the largest concert halls in the United States and in other countries. Dottie also made her debut as a guest on Johnny Carson's *The Tonight Show* in the late 1970s and was featured on many other network and syndicated talk shows. In October 1979, the twosome won the Country Music Association award for Vocal Duo of the Year, an honor they also were given in 1978.

During 1979, Dottie and Kenny's LPs *Classics* and *Every Time Two Fools Collide* remained on the charts most of the year. They also had the singles hits "Anyone Who Isn't Me Tonight," "Til I can Make It on My Own," and "All I Ever Need Is You." The whirlwind success of this duet work seemed to have had a depressing impact on her UA solo releases for a time. But after she changed producers (from Larry Butler to Brett Maher and Randy Goodrum) that situation improved. First fruits of that collaboration included the LP *Special Delivery* and the 1980 top-10 single "A Lesson in Leavin'." Other solo singles hits in 1980 and 1981 included "You Pick Me Up (and Put Me Down)," "Leavin's for Unbelievers," and "Are You Happy Baby?" which reached number one in 1981. Also on upper-chart levels in 1981 was her solo album *Wild West.*

During 1980, West's marriage to Byron Metcalf had broken up. She told *Country Style* writer Jim Albrecht (May 1981), "Byron was an alcoholic. And I had lived with this. But the harder our schedule became, the worse it was for him. And that really was the problem.

"This is the first time I've said this, but I don't think he'd mind because since then he talks about it. He went to the hospital and has not had a drink since. But it was too late for our relationship. . . ."

Her schedule, of course, was backbreaking. In 1980 she made personal appearances totaling 320 shows, according to her management firm, Kragen & Company, with no letup in 1981. Besides TV appearances with such artists as Kenny Rogers, Mel Tillis, Larry Gatlin, Eddie Rabbitt, and the Oak Ridge Boys, and hundreds of concerts, she also made most of the major talk shows and hosted her own cable-TV special.

During the mid- and late 1980s, she continued to perform regularly on the *Grand Ole Opry* in between extensive tours. In the 1984 and 1985 Country Music Association voting, her duet work with Kenny Rogers brought more nominations for Vocal Duo of the Year. She also made top-chart levels with the single "What Are We Doin' in Love" and placed other releases on lower-chart rungs.

She remained a favorite of concert goers across the U.S., but was a particular favorite in Las Vegas. In her stage appearances, she demonstrated boundless energy and enthusiasm throughout the 1980s. But things turned sour at the start of the next decade, as Dottie made headlines not for her musical accomplishments, but for her troubles with the Internal Revenue Service, which claimed she owed them some $1.5 million in back taxes. In 1990 the IRS began taking steps to make her meet those bills by auctioning off her ranch, home, and many of her other assets. Undaunted, she expressed confidence she would spring back, increasing her concert commitments and making plans to complete a new album of duets in 1991.

But this was not her decade. On August 30, 1991, she was a passenger in a car en route to a performing date on the *Grand Ole Opry* when it overran an exit ramp and crashed. On September 4, as she underwent surgery to correct some of those injuries, her heart gave out. After her death it was estimated she had written over 400 songs, had more than 40 albums released as well as over 100 singles.

In January 1995, Michelle Lee portrayed Dottie in the made-for-TV film, "Big Dreams & Broken Hearts: The Dottie West Story." The well-crafted show combined dramatized segments with comments by such longtime associates as Chet Atkins, Willie Nelson, and Loretta Lynn. In the recreation of Dottie's duet work with Kenny Rogers, Rogers played himself. While presenting the high points of Dottie's career, the film didn't ignore her private life demons. Reviewing the film in the *Los Angeles Times*, Lynn Heffley referred to the "tabloid touch" of the script, "as the specter of sexual abuse by her father hangs over West's troubled life here—her divorces, her penchant for young men, her drinking and her compulsive overspending."

In the summer of 1996, a reissue of some of her most successful recordings was made by RCA as part of its Essential Series.

WEST, SHELLY: *Singer, songwriter. Born Cleveland, Ohio, May 23, c. late 1950s.*

One of the premiere duos of the first half of the 1980s combined the talents of two artists with illustrious family names in the annals of post–World War II country music. Shelly West was the daughter of performer-songwriter superstar Dottie West and steel-guitar exemplar Bill West. Her singing partner, Dave Frizzell, was the brother of Country Music Hall of Famer Lefty Frizzell. As a team they placed a series of singles and albums on the hit charts, but in the second half of the decade focused on solo careers with mixed results. Initially, Shelly did quite well on her own in the mid-1980s, but seemed to lose momentum from a recording standpoint later in the decade.

Shelly, of course, grew up in the aura of her parents' musical achievements and saw the backstage workings of major shows like the *Grand Ole Opry* and the less opulent settings of the honky-tonks and small clubs that often made up the country concert circuit. During 1975–76, she got the taste of the stage environment as a backup singer on her mother's shows. After that, she decided to strike out on her own, moving to California where she got the opportunity to team up with David Frizzell. Their rapport was good, and by the start of the 1980s they had begun to attract the attention of industry executives and fans alike.

Their debut album, *Carryin' on the Family Names,* and the three that followed, spawned a series of singles that made upper-chart levels. The one that established them as important country entertainers was "You're the Reason God Made Oklahoma," a number-one hit that was followed by such best-sellers as "Texas State of Mind," "Husbands and Wives," "I Just Came Here to Dance," and "Silent Partners." The last named was the first of their songs to be made into a video and gained wide exposure on country TV programs in the mid-1980s. In the 1981 Country Music Association voting, the team was nominated for the Horizon Award and the Vocal Duo of the Year. CMA members also nominated them for Vocal Duo of the Year in 1982 and 1983. The duo also received awards and nominations from many other places, including a Grammy nomination, the Academy of Country Music and Music City News polls and editorial boards from *Billboard, Radio & Records,* and *Cash Box.* In the mid-1980s, Shelly and Dave also had cameo roles as a duo auditioning for the *Grand Ole Opry* in the Clint Eastwood film *Honky Tonk Man.*

Starting in the mid-1980s, while not completely ending their duet work, both team members sought to expand their solo credentials. For the Warner Brothers/Viva label, Shelly turned out the label debut *West by West* in 1983, which provided the number-one country single "Jose Cuervo." *Billboard* later reported that it had been the magazine's number-one charted song for 1983 and that release also was nominated for Song of the Year in Academy of Country Music voting. In October 1983, her second solo album, *Red Hot,* came out and spent a number of months on the charts. Shelly could point to two more chart singles by early 1984, the top-10 "Another Motel Memory" and "Somebody Buy This Cowgirl a Beer." During 1984, her third collection, *Don't Make Me Wait on the Moon,* was released, from which four singles were culled: the title track, "If I Could Sing Something in Spanish," "I'll Dance the Two-Step," and the top-20 chartmaker, "Now There's You."

As a solo performer, Shelly worked with many top country stars in the mid- and late 1980s, including Merle Haggard, Mickey Gilley, John Anderson, Loretta Lynn, Lee Greenwood, Kenny Rogers, and Conway Twitty. She was a featured guest on many TV programs over those years, such as *The Tonight Show* and *Merv Griffin,* and also did a number of concerts in European nations. She continued to appear at many major country venues in the 1990s, but as of 1996 hadn't been able to recapture the recording success of earlier years.

WHITE, BRYAN: *Singer, guitarist, drummer, songwriter. Born near Oklahoma City, Oklahoma, February 17, 1974.*

Becoming a star or reaching the threshold of stardom in one's teens isn't very unusual in rock and roll, but the typical country artist must accrue a lot more experience as a performer in small venues or years of demo-tape rejections before becoming a headliner. Bryan White defied the odds, successfully climbing the ramparts of Nashville fresh out of high school in Oklahoma. Though he felt confident he would eventually make it in the field, even he was surprised at gaining hit singles and a gold album before he was twenty-two. "I really didn't expect for half of this to happen to me in the amount of time that it did. We were hoping to have one hit record in two or three years. It just seemed like everything we did took it up to a different level."

In his early years, Bryan shuttled between his father's and mother's places. They divorced while he was a child, but, he said, it was not a bitter breakup. Both liked country music, and he heard a lot of it as he spent time with one parent or the other. He showed an aptitude for music early on, starting to play drums at five and performing on stage initially in his preteen years. At seventeen, he decided to focus on playing guitar, and started writing original songs with the idea in the back of his mind of moving to Music City after he graduated from high school.

As he noted, "Mowing lawns and fishing were the only two options I could think of besides music. It was pretty scary to make the move at the time, but when you are that young, I think you feel invincible to a certain extent. Everybody is full of hopes when they first move to Nashville—and those hopes are so strong that nothing can discourage you. When I set my mind to do something and say I'm gonna do it, I just have to do it. I knew I wanted to sing; I knew I wanted to play; I knew I wanted to write. I didn't think about anything else. I just packed up and left. For the first year I had to have my family wire me money every month."

For all that, the eighteen-year-old's career reached its first key milestone only three months after he found his way to Tennessee. He gained the attention of people at Glen Campbell Music and became a staff songwriter while also gaining a management deal with GC Management. Besides writing and taping some of his own songs, he was soon in demand to make demos for other writers, including some of the most successful in Nashville. He also built up performing experience in small local venues, which helped bring a recording contract from Asylum Records in 1994. Album session tracks, produced by Asylum president Kyle Lehring and Billy Joe Walker, Jr., quickly spawned the chart single "Eugene You Genius," which made the *Billboard* Top 40 in late 1994. That was followed by the early 1995 top-20 hit, "Look At Me Now."

His advisers set up a performing schedule that added to his forward career momentum, including a well-received appearance at the spring 1995 Country Radio Seminar and opening dates for established artists like Pam Tillis, Tracy Lawrence, and Diamond Rio. During 1995 he performed at some 200 concerts across the U.S. and Canada, typically doing the opening set using only his voice and acoustic guitar with no band backing. He recalled, "It was tough. There was no one to hide behind and no one to catch me if something went wrong. I learned a lot and I think the experience made me a much better player and singer."

The exposure helped. His debut album, *Bryan White,* was on the charts by the summer of 1995, and the single "Someone Else's Star" rose to number one in *Billboard* by early fall. He added another number one single with "Rebecca Lynn," on the charts in late 1995, rising to number one the week of January 6, 1996. Both those number-one singles were written by others, but Sawyer Brown's single of "I Don't Believe in Goodbye," which Bryan cowrote, was a major hit. *Bryan White* earned a gold record award from the R.I.A.A. by the end of 1995. Recognition of his achievements came from Country Music Television's poll which named him Rising Video Star of the Year.

White's activities during 1995 included performing contributions to a number of worthy causes. In April he organized a benefit in his home state that raised over $60,000 to provide scholarships for children injured or orphaned in the infamous bombing of the Oklahoma City Federal building. He also took part in benefits for cerebral palsy, cystic fibrosis, AIDS "Country CARES," the Native American Clothing Drive, Buddies of Nashville, St. Jude's Children's Hospital, and Boys and Girls Clubs of America.

In early 1996, Bryan completed his second album for Asylum, *Between Now and Forever,* which made the charts soon after its release. Bryan cowrote four of the ten tracks: "Blindhearted" (with Randy Goodrum); "So Much for Pretending" (with Derek George and John Tirro); the title track (with George Teren and Don Pfrimmer); and "On Any Given Night" (with Allison Mellon and Jeff Ross).

When the winners of the Academy of Country Music's 1995 awards were announced on the TV special in late April 1996, Bryan won the trophy for Top New Male Vocalist. As he told reporters backstage at the Universal Amphitheatre in Los Angeles, "I couldn't be happier. I don't even have a mantel. I have a dresser; that's where it's going until I get a house with a mantel."

Soon after that, Bryan had another top-10 single, "I'm Not Supposed to Love You Anymore." He continued to pursue an active touring schedule, including a concert at Dolly Parton's Dollywood theme park as part of the Showcase of Stars series. His 1996 recorded output included doing his version of "When You Wish Upon a Star" (from the animated Disney film *Pinocchio*) for the *Disney Country* album.

WHITE, JOY: *Singer, guitarist, songwriter. Born Turrell, Arkansas, c. early 1960s.*

By late 1994, Joy White still hadn't broken through to the rank and file of country music followers, though by all rights she should have been on the way to country prominence. Her strong, vibrant voice reflected touches of Emmylou Harris, Linda Ronstadt, and one or two other superstars, yet it retained an individual style and brashness that set her apart from the others. Critics and her country music peers who heard her debut recordings felt certain she was destined to become a radiant addition to the modern country pantheon, yet those releases gained relatively little public response.

Still, it seemed likely she would at the least become a cult favorite and surely worthy of notice among those taking the longer view of country music history. As for Joy, she remained hopeful, aware that more than a few major forces in the field took a little longer and paid a few more dues before claiming a position in the spotlight. She told Clark Parsons of the *Nashville Scene*, "I think there's going to be longevity for me. I never figured my career would be like, wham. Everything I've ever done, I crawled for it. I hope I won't have to be crawling long."

She was born in the small farming town of Turrell, Arkansas, but moved to Mishawaka, Indiana, the place she grew up in, when she was three. "My dad's a guitarist," she noted in discussing early influences, "and he and my mom could sing real good together." Joy also exhibited vocal ability as a child and made her audience debut in church, when at four she was placed on the altar to sing gospel music. The congregation loved it, and she began singing a few songs every Sunday. Later she became part of a family gospel group called the Whites (a not uncommon name among gospel groups).

She was aware of what was going on in secular music, although she leaned toward rock and pop rather than country. "Country radio was playing in our house all the time, but really I didn't like it much back then. A lot of country in the '70s was very watered down, and they were slammin' out two albums a year! It's just not like that now."

She credited a Linda Ronstadt country-flavored recording of "Silver Threads and Golden Needles" with changing her attitude a lot. The song styling and particularly the pedal steel guitar background support, she recalled, "really was what changed my mind about country music. I was in the car with my mom—I wasn't old enough to drive yet—when I heard that on the radio and remember saying, 'God, this is great! Steel guitar!'" During those years, though, she also was attracted to recordings by Emmylou Harris, Neil Young, and even some of the blues-tinged discs of the original Jimmie Rodgers.

Often at home she sang along with recordings or radio performances by various artists. "Singing is like a fix for me. I'd say 'I gotta go home and sing for awhile' and head home to sing along with about three albums. Then I'd be fine."

A lot of the records she sang along with were from rock and roll, and when Joy got to high school she became engrossed in helping organize rock bands with friends and acquaintances. She told John Bonner of *The Country Gazette* ("Joy White—Red Hair, Red Lips, Sass and Fire," December 1992) her teenage performances embraced "some pretty wild stuff. I'd do anything from Heart to Linda Ronstadt to Fleetwood Mac, Pat Benatar, John Mellencamp, ZZ Top, Bonnie Raitt— we did a lot of stuff like that."

Things went pretty well for her career locally, she recalled. She derived a decent income from her band work and for doing commercial jingles in studios in Ft. Wayne, Indiana. "I graduated high school half a year early [at 17] because I had so much going on; I was doing commercial jingles and had my band. But it seemed I was screaming and I did not want to ruin my voice."

Gradually her desire to slow things down a bit, and a renewed interest in what was happening in Nashville, caused her to shift musical gears and focus on country. She liked the idea of having a solo career and exploiting her writing talents when she moved to that city in the early 1980s, initially moving in with a sister who lived in nearby Columbia, Tennessee. Her early efforts included making demo recordings for Nashville songwriters. She told Clark Parsons, "When I first came to town, everybody used me for ballads, then country songs, then rowdy songs." By 1986 it was virtually a full-time job; she was making some ten demos per week.

"For girl [singers] it's a lot," she said. "People that do a lot of demos are technically good. If they're bad, it's gonna show. You learn different ways to sing, how to sing songs softer, how to sing harmony."

But her goal remained getting her own record affiliation. She achieved one milestone when a performance at a local nightclub's "open mike night" brought a meeting with industry executive Russ Sanjek, who provided some contacts. She did achieve an abortive agreement with Capitol Records in the late 1980s, but that fell apart due to company personnel changes. Meanwhile she looked on as one young performer after another moved upward. She told *Radio & Records,* "When I first came to town, it was hard watching people get these record deals and not knowing how they were doing it. A lot of them had backers with a lot of money and they would get signed because of it. Luckily, that's changed. Now it seems a lot of the artists getting signed have spent time doing demo work."

She commented to Parsons that when she first got to Nashville, "I was very young. I did things always backwards, putting my foot in my mouth, partying too much." Before she hit her stride in the demo field she worked at various jobs, including waitressing and briefly shining shoes in a hotel. At one point she shined the shoes of George Jones and took the liberty of putting a demo tape in them, though she never heard back about it.

At the end of the 1980s she was finally in position to do demo tapes of her own songs after gaining a contract with Tree Publishing. At least one of her compositions got on an album, "Big City Bound," recorded by Highway 101 for their *Bing Bang Boom* release.

The tables really seemed to turn in her favor in June 1991 when she performed an exciting thirty-minute set in Nashville Entertainment Association's first Extravaganza showcase. The set was so striking that four labels sought to sign her—RCA, BNA, SBK, and Sony. Marty Stuart had already alerted Steve Buckingham of Columbia/Sony to her impressive talent and Stuart's interest (as well as that of her boyfriend, Larry Marrs, a member of Stuart's band) likely played a role in her opting for Sony.

Her debut album, *Between Midnight and Hindsight,* came out on the Columbia label in the fall of 1992, along with the first single, "Little Tears." The single made only a brief appearance on the charts, even though most reviewers were ecstatic about the album and its contents (which included such White originals as "Bittersweet End" and "It's Amazing"). Jack Hurst, country music critic of the *Chicago Tribune,* wrote that her voice "exhibits a kick and fire that suggest the imminent arrival of a female Dwight Yoakam. Her dominant sound is that of a raucous rebelliousness. It's hard to remember when a country female has dared to be quite this traditional and at the same time, this bold." Neil Pond of *Country America* called her "Nashville's most lively new contender for the crown of hillbilly queen." And Dan DeLuca said that Joy was "One of the brightest new faces to come out of Nashville this year."

In the *Dallas Morning News* of January 10, 1993, Michael Corcoran cited her as an artist who deserved more fame from country fans in 1993. While the audience didn't react as hoped for that year or next, industry figures continued to hope that it was only a temporary delay in an important country music saga.

WHITE, LARI: *Singer, songwriter, actress. Born Dunedin, Florida, May 13, 1965.*

Another of the country music "overnight successes" of the 1990s, Lari (pronounced "Laurie") White accumulated a wealth of experience as a performer in such diverse fields as rock, jazz, and gospel before she decided to make her mark in the country music she had heard all around her as a child in Dunedin, Florida. She also demonstrated talent as an actress during one career phase, but fortunately for the country field she opted to focus her writing and singing talents on the Nashville scene.

Lari was exposed to a wide musical spectrum from an early age, though she listened to more country music at the homes of friends and relatives than at home. She recalled first demonstrating childish singing skills in her grandmother's living room at two-and-a-half, but she made her real performing debut with her parents two years later. She said, "Both my parents were public school teachers, but music was such a part of the family that I was probably singing harmony out of the womb. And it was all different kinds of music. We had classical records and atonal modern music right next to Ray Charles and John Denver albums."

Her public debut, she told *Tune In* magazine ("Rising Stars: Lari White," March 1993) came at the Crystal Community Center as part of a trio with her parents. "I became the third part of a trio with my mom and dad, who had sung in different groups when they were younger and even performed as a duo for a while. At the show I sang 'Somewhere Over the Rainbow.' I was totally enamored with the *Wizard of Oz* [from which the song was drawn]. I always wanted to lean against a haystack and sing."

After that, though, her main singing activities weren't aimed at secular audiences, but at churchgoers like the ones who attended services conducted by her grandfather, a Primitive Baptist preacher. With the addition of her younger brother and sister, her parents organized the White Family Singers, who performed at churches throughout the region as well as at festivals, community center events, and art shows. There was a segment of their program, though, in which the youngsters performed a medley of hits by Elvis Presley and rock stars of the period.

Once in high school, Lari felt certain she wanted to make a future career as a writer, musician, and entertainer. During those teen years she did solo performances as well as working in school rock bands. She also competed in talent shows, which eventually helped earn her a full academic scholarship at the University of Miami, where she majored in Music Engineering with a minor in voice principles.

While pursuing her degree, she also did a lot of outside work, which both provided money to help meet living expenses and experience in many facets of the music business. She said, "At night I'd sing in top 40 bands, jazz bands and big bands and days I'd be in a studio doing background vocals and jingles. I even sang salsa sessions and did a Toyota Corolla commercial in Spanish."

She told *Tune In* one of her stranger experiences was her first club gig at a Jewish-Cuban wedding. "We did a 'pre-heat' (playing background music) at 6:30. They served dinner at 8:30 and we kept playing. We were the Big Band and we alternated with the Salsa band. We did that until three in the morning. At four they started serving breakfast. So my first club gig was a 12-hour job, and I decided then and there it was the career for me."

During her last six months in college, she began writing in earnest. Despite her years of performing rock, pop, and jazz material, she gravitated to country songs. "They were more acoustic oriented, not very pop, but with pop influence. Then I went to Los Angeles, Chicago and New York to check out their music scenes. When I came to Nashville to audition for a talent show, I simply fell in love with the town and the whole creative community."

The time was spring, 1988, and the show TNN's "You Can Be a Star." She walked off with first prize, which provided her with enough money to take up residence in Music City. It also brought an opportunity to make a recording on Capitol Records. Capitol issued the single, "Flying Above the Rain," in 1989. The disc made some regional inroads, but faded quickly. However, Lari stressed it gave her considerable insight into the workings of the music business.

During 1988 and 1989, she continued to write new songs and prepare demo tapes for submission to publishing companies and artists. In time this led to an arrangement with Ronnie Milsap's publishing firm and resulted in several songs being recorded by top rank artists. Shelby Lynne, for one, made the charts with Lari's "What About the Love We Made," and Tammy Wynette recorded her "Where's the Fire."

Besides that, Lari started taking acting classes with the idea of improving her stage presence, but the approach took on a life of its own. "I originally wanted to get more comfortable onstage, but then I started auditioning, and for the next year and a half I worked in plays and musicals like *Crimes of the Heart* and *Fiddler on the Roof* for the Tennessee Repertory Theatre and the Barn Dinner Theatre. I became a much better songwriter because I studied acting—I learned about creating characters and telling stories, and that you can't make anything real for someone else unless it's real for you."

Some of her friends foresaw good prospects for her in the musical theater, but after tasting local success on the stage, she decided she really wanted to carve out a career in the country field. One tentative step was to audition for the group Highway 101, which was seeking a replacement for vocalist Pauline Carlson. That didn't work out, she said, partly because it seemed they wanted someone with a more traditional country vocal sound.

Lari continued to look for avenues to gain attention for her talent and one way was to return to talent showcases. At one show hosted by ASCAP, things broke her way. A cousin of Rodney Crowell, who was a member of the songwriting and publishing association, was very impressed and suggested she might meet the backup singer qualifications for Crowell's upcoming summer tour. The audition for Rodney earned her the job as well as, later on, an important supporter for her solo career efforts.

She told *Radio & Records,* "We hit it off right from the start. He'd been a hero of mine for a long time as a writer and producer. He knew I'd been getting some label attention and he suggested we do my first album as a team." When she decided to sign with RCA Records in January 1992, Rodney and guitarist Stuart Smith got the production assignment. The result was her debut album, *Lead Me Not,* issued at the start of 1993, which included in its ten tracks eight songs written or cowritten by Lari. The first single release, "What a Woman Wants," was cowritten by Lari and Chuck Cannon.

The debut single made the *Billboard* charts in February 1993 and stayed at mid-chart levels for several months. The title song, a gospel flavored number written by Lari, was on the *Billboard* list from early May through mid-summer. The album itself won high praise from reviewers across the spectrum from *Billboard* and *Country America* to *Rolling Stone.*

Lari's second RCA album, *Wishes,* came out in the summer of 1994 and stayed on *Billboard* charts well into 1995. It produced two chart hit singles in 1994, "That's My Baby" (cowritten by Lari and Cannon), which made *Billboard*'s Top 15 in July while peaking at number nine in *R&R* the same month, and "Now I Know," which peaked at number nine in *R&R* the week of November 25, 1994. In early 1995, another single moved up the *Billboard* list to top-10 ranks, "That's How You Know (When You're in Love)," another collaboration between Lari and Chuck Cannon.

In early 1996, she made the charts with "Ready, Willing and Able," followed in late spring and summer by "Wild at Heart" (cowritten by her and A. Anderson). She prepared a video of the last named song, but ran into unexpected trouble when TNN and CMT began to show it. In the video, Lari is seen as a patient in a mental hospital who persuades others to begin to dance to the song. The idea, she later indicated, was to symbolize how feelings of confinement and frustration could be eased by finding exuberant, joyful outlets. Representatives of the Alliance for the Mentally Ill complained that the script, in fact, tended to reinforce negative images about mental health patients. White stated she had not realized how the video's message might be misinterpreted and requested the TV stations to remove it from their playlist.

White meanwhile was working on tracks for her next album, titled *Don't Fence Me In.* She was joined in recording the title track of the old pop song by Trisha Yearwood and Shelby Lynn.

WHITES, THE: *Vocal and instrumental group, Buck White, born Texas (vocals, mandolin, guitar, piano), Cheryl White, born Arkansas, c. early 1950s (vocals, bass), Sharon White (Mrs. Ricky Skaggs), born Arkansas, c. early 1950s (vocals, guitar).*

One of the finest bluegrass ensembles active from the 1960s to the 1990s, the Whites first gained attention on backing Emmylou Harris in many of her concerts before focusing on succeeding on their own. They did so well during the mid-1980s that, as Neil Pond noted in the *Music City News,* some people in the industry "started referring to the Whites as 'the new first family of country music,' a tag that harkens back to the musical purity and personal integrity of no less than Mother Maybelle and the venerable Carter family."

Group organizer Buck White grew up in Texas and developed considerable skill on various instruments, particularly mandolin and piano, before he met and married wife Pam, who also loved country, bluegrass, and gospel music. After their two daughters, Cheryl and Sharon, reached their teens, the Whites formed a group called Down Home Folks in the early 1960s and began to try out their bluegrass styles at small clubs and at various festivals. They also pursued the gospel circuit, as Cheryl recalled for interviewer Thomas Goldsmith. "We sang in lots of churches when we were kids in Arkansas. At one point there were no boundaries between country and gospel music."

In 1967, the band became a threesome and took the name the Whites, with Buck handling vocals, mandolin, guitars, and piano; Cheryl, vocals and bass; and Sharon, guitar and vocals. The trio expanded their touring efforts and also started thinking about getting the opportunity to record material on a major label. To further that objective, in 1971 they moved to Nashville. For a time their record company goal eluded them, but they continued to be well received on the bluegrass trail while also finding work as backing band for various artists, including Emmylou Harris. Ricky Skaggs, for some years a member of her Hot Band, became a friend and in time proposed marriage to, and was accepted by, Sharon.

In the late 1970s they were able to record a single for Capitol Records that showcased their talents quite well, but not much happened afterward. In the early 1980s, they signed with Curb Records, which resulted in a chart-making debut album on Warner/Curb. The first single release from that collection, "You Put the Blue in Me," became a top-10 hit in 1982. This was followed by a series of chart singles in the mid-1980s such as "I Wonder Who's Holding My Baby Tonight," "Hangin' Around," "Give Me Back That Old Familiar Feeling," "Home Town Gossip," and "Pins and Needles."

Their achievements brought more than a few honors from their country peers during those years. In 1983, for example, Country Music Association voters nominated them for Vocal Group of the Year and the Horizon Award. In 1985, CMA again nominated them for Vocal Group of the Year and included the Whites in the finalists for Instrumental Group of the Year. They didn't win the last-named award, but it was kept in the family, going to the Ricky Skaggs Band. In 1987 the trio celebrated its twentieth anniversary with the album *Ain't No Binds.*

After moving to MCA Records late in the decade, the Whites' releases failed to gain upper chart-levels and they found themselves between labels. In a sense, they went back to their roots by signing to do a gospel album for Word Records. Buck pointed out that while they usually had at least one gospel song on their previous albums, they hadn't been able to interest their former labels in releasing an all-gospel disc. Their new album, *Doing It By the Book,* was coproduced by the Whites and Ricky Skaggs, and did well in the religious market in the early 1990s.

In interviews Cheryl emphasized she felt you didn't have to be a deeply devout Christian to gain something from the album. She told Goldsmith, "There's some kind of strife that everybody has, whether it's in their home life or whatever. Just because we're Christians we're not immune to it."

Though they weren't vying for secular chart hits by then, group members stressed they didn't mind the respite. (Of course, they had become regular cast members of the *Grand Ole Opry* in years past and still had the national exposure their show appearances provided in the mid-1990s.) Buck observed to Goldsmith, "It's a whole lot less pressure on us because we're not in the chart race."

Cheryl recalled, "Our whole mood would depend on where we were on the chart that week." Sharon added, "We've all been through some changes, but it's been healthy for us . . . you get caught up in that wheel. We've been riding the tail end of that whirlwind for a while."

In the summer of 1996, Step One Records issued a new Whites album, *Give a Little Back.*

WHITLEY, KEITH: *Singer, guitarist, songwriter. Born Sandy Hook, Kentucky, July 1, 1955; died Nashville, Tennessee, May 9, 1989.*

Conventional street drugs like heroin or cocaine often played major roles in the destruction of careers or lives of rock and R&B artists, but liquor has tended to be the addictive substance associated with tragic endings of country artists. Not that country performers over the years ignored other drugs, but, as spelled out in many country hits over the decades, alcohol was the major failing of performers who far too often closed out promising careers when the future seemed limitless.

And so it was with the star-crossed life of Keith Whitley. His addiction not only ended his life prematurely, but also was a traumatic setback for his wife, singer Lorrie Morgan, and their young children.

Whitley was born in eastern Kentucky in 1955, where bluegrass and traditional country music were dominant forms even as rock and roll enthralled young generations of fans. Keith recalled that his mother loved the then-new breed of country artists, people like Lefty Frizzell and Hank Williams, Sr., and their recordings often provided background sounds during his early years. He was far more familiar with their styles than with bluegrass as he made his first efforts to sing and play guitar in his preteens. He proved adept enough to make his radio debut on a West Virginia station when he was nine.

Keith continued to add to his professional experience, playing with other family members or school friends as he moved into his teens. The pivotal milestone in his professional music development came when he was fifteen and met another artist in the same age bracket, Ricky Skaggs. Skaggs reminisced for Don Forte of *Musician* magazine ("Ricky Skaggs Moonshine Lightning," January 1990), "I was playing fiddle with my dad and we went to this talent show in Estill, Kentucky, where Keith and his brother and a little band were playing. Neither one of us won; some girl with a dog and pony did—whoever got the biggest applause. But we were practically the same age and we met in the basement of this old high school, and we got to talking about who we liked and listened to.

"A lot of his past was like mine, so we just started singing something together, and it was really fun. Sounded like we'd been singing together forever. I invited him to my house the next week. The friendship and the music grew, and we started working with Ralph Stanley right after that. Ralph was late for a show one night, and the club owner asked Keith and me to get up and sing. People loved it and then Ralph came strolling in about midway through our show. He set his banjo down and just pulled up a stool and watched us! We were freakin' out. It was a real thrill to be touring with one of my idols—and people 30 and 40 years my senior."

The two teenagers became members of Stanley's bluegrass group in 1970 and recorded with him for much of the decade. As members of Stanley's Clinch Mountain Boys they helped record thirteen albums on the Plantation label, including the award-winning *Cry from the Cross.* In 1973, Skaggs and Keith performed on a duo collection, *Second Generation Bluegrass.* In the mid-1970s, Ricky left to join J. D. Crowe's New South band, but Keith stayed with Stanley until 1979, when he also moved over to Crowe's group, Skaggs meanwhile having left to try for a solo career. Keith stayed with Crowe through the early 1980s, performing on several Rounder Records albums including the 1982 *Somewhere Between.*

By the time Whitley moved to Nashville in 1984 to seek his own recording contract, he already had a reputation as a heavy drinker. Still, he was a very effective performer, as indicated on some of his demo tapes, like his recording of "Does Fort Worth Ever Cross Your Mind." It got some attention from company artists & repertoire people, but eventually became a number-one single for George Strait, not Whitley. To add insult to injury, critics derided his 1985 extended-play release, *A Hard Act to Follow,* as a seeming copy of Strait's stylings.

The initial release of his debut full length album, *L.A. to Miami,* didn't do very well either. However, a revamped version issued in 1986 began to find an audience for his music, and provided three singles that made the charts, including "Homecoming '63" and "Ten Feet Away."

After that, Keith's life and career seemed to take a turn for the better. He acknowledged to himself and to others that he'd had a severe drinking problem since his childhood. This new insight appeared to improve his outlook and his creative possibilities as a songwriter and performer. He seemed to be helped as well by his romance with Lorrie Morgan, the talented daughter of country legend George Morgan. They married in 1986, and in 1987 she bore him a son. He also adopted her daughter by an earlier marriage.

In the late 1980s his career moved strongly forward with a series of chart hit singles and albums, beginning with the 1988 album *Don't Close Your Eyes.* Over the years, Keith had always cited Lefty Frizzell as one of his prime influences, and a song in that album was particularly structured to emphasize that affinity. The song, "I Never Go Around Mirrors," had been cowritten and recorded by Lefty and Whitey Shafer. Keith persuaded Shafer to add new lyrics. The story goes that Whitley sought out Frizzell's grave and read the new lines over it before going back to the studio to do the new recording on which Lefty's brother, Allen Frizzell, sang backup.

That track made the charts, as did the title track, which reached number one. Other top-chart hits for him in the late 1980s were "When You Say Nothing at All," "No Stranger to the Rain," and "I Wonder What You Think of Me." The last-named was the title track for the last album he completed before his death. The album, like the single, was a chart hit.

His record company, RCA, was beginning to think of release dates for that last album when Keith was found dead of alcohol poisoning in his Nashville home. As Mark Coleman noted in *The Journal of Country Music* ("No Stranger to the Rain," Vol. 13, No. 2), the post-mortem showed his body to contain "an incredible 0.477 blood alcohol level. It was estimated that Whitley, known to be a binge drinker, had ingested the equivalent of 100-proof liquor in just two hours."

Coleman continued, "Yeah, Keith Whitley's timing was lousy, no question, but another question lingers. Simply put, is a honky tonk singer compelled, by definition, to live out the words of his song? Does it always have to happen this way?" And he answered himself, "The easy answer is, maybe it does and the evidence presented by Keith Whitley's bumpy ascent and brief, brilliant heyday would seem to support that. Reduced to a rock & roll cliche, you gotta pay your dues if you wanna sing the blues."

Coleman also concluded that Whitley wouldn't be quickly forgotten and, if the first part of the 1990s was any harbinger, Coleman was right. There seemed to be an increasing awareness among country fans in the U.S. and abroad of what had been lost as Keith's recording and videos appeared consistently on upper-chart levels.

His last album and several singles culled from it were top-chart entries during 1989 and 1990. A duet single with his wife was named Vocal Event of the Year in the 1990 Country Music Association voting. Their vocalizing also was named 1991 Video Collaboration of the Year in the TNN/*Music City News* poll. In late 1991, his duet single with Earl Thomas Conley, "Brotherly Love," was a chart hit in the fall. (Their collaboration earned a CMA 1992 nomination for Vocal Event of the Year.)

Besides that, a *Greatest Hits* album issued by RCA Records in 1991 was still on the *Billboard* chart 110 weeks later on October 3, 1992, having gone well past R.I.A.A. gold-record totals, and it continued selling after that until it went past platinum levels. (That album peaked at number-five in *Billboard*.) From the fall of 1991 through the first part of 1992, Keith had another album sharing the charts with *Greatest Hits* called *Kentucky Bluebird*. Also a chart hit during the first half of 1992 was the single "Somebody's Doin' Me Right," which peaked at number fifteen in *Billboard* and number thirteen in *R&R* during March.

In the mid-1990s, six Whitley albums were available from the Country Music Hall of Fame & Museum Catalog: *Don't Close Your Eyes, Greatest Hits, I Wonder Do You Think Of Me, A Hard Act to Follow* and *Kentucky Bluebird* (all on RCA) and, on Rebel, with Ricky Skaggs, *Second Generation Bluegrass*. His *Greatest Hits* album remained on the *Billboard* Top Country Catalog chart for years and by mid-1996 had gone past platinum sales levels. In late 1994, BNA Records issued *Keith Whitley: A Tribute Album* containing covers of his hits by major country artists. The collection remained on the charts well into 1995.

WHITMAN, SLIM: *Singer, guitarist, songwriter. Born Tampa, Florida, January 20, 1924.*

Examining the biographies of country-music stars, one can see in more than a few cases that sports' loss was music's gain. In the case of Slim Whitman, during his teenage and young adult years, he focused on baseball except during World War II, when he enlisted in the Navy and learned to play guitar from his shipmates. He had been a promising pitcher, with good hitting capability.

Otis Dewey Whitman, Jr., born and raised in Tampa, Florida, with four brothers and sisters, was a star pitcher on his high school baseball team. After his discharge from the Navy in 1945, he returned to baseball and signed a contract in 1946 with the Plant City Berries of the Orange Belt League. His pitching record the following year was a cool 11-1 and his hitting a hot .360. To bring in extra income, he turned to performing music in local clubs.

The exposure led to the chance to sing on station WDAE in Tampa in 1948. As his reputation grew with country fans, he expanded his efforts in the field. In 1949, he made a major step forward when he got a recording contract with RCA Victor through the recommendation of Col. Thomas A. Parker who, at that time, was managing the career of Eddy Arnold. One of his first songs for the label, "Casting My Lasso to the Sky," won some national attention. He began to get more impressive performing credits, including a 1949 appearance on a Mutual network show with The Light Crust Doughboys. Soon after, he moved to Shreveport to become a regular on the KWKH *Louisiana Hayride*. The show was broadcast over many other stations, helping to greatly increase his following among U.S. country fans.

Still, Slim's recordings on RCA didn't make much headway on the best-seller lists. In 1952, he signed with a West Coast independent, Imperial Records, a move that soon paid big dividends. His first year on the label, he achieved a top-10 hit with the single "Keep It a Secret," the first of many such successes in the 1950s and 1960s. In 1953, he had a top-10 hit with "North Wind" and in 1954 he had two, "Secret Love" and "Rose Marie." The last two, country versions of, respectively, a pop song and a musical comedy standard, were the beginning of a trend that lasted the rest of his career. Some other chart makers between the early 1950s and the mid-1960s were "Love Song of the Waterfall," "The Bandera Waltz," "Amateur in Love," "China Doll," and "Indian Love Call." In 1965, he had the top-10 single "More than Yesterday" and in 1968 equaled that with the single "Rainbows Are Back in Style."

Many of these recordings rose to upper-chart levels throughout Europe, as well as in Canada, Japan, Australia, Taiwan, and South Africa. This was underscored by strong audience response to his concerts in those areas in the 1960s and 1970s. In fact, in the 1970s, his popularity in some overseas nations probably exceeded that in his homeland. When Slim's chart-making releases in the United States were sparse, he still could make strong inroads on hit lists abroad. Thus, in a major English music poll, he was voted the number-one international star for four different years in the 1970s.

From the mid-1950s into the 1970s, Whitman made dozens of albums for Imperial Records and for successor labels (Imperial was acquired by Liberty, which later became part of United Artists.) Among these were the following (on Imperial unless otherwise noted): *Slim Whitman Favorites* (two discs, mid-1950s); *Slim Whitman Sings* (issued 11/58); *My Best to You* (10/59); *Million Record Hits; Just Call Me Lonesome; Once in a Lifetime; Annie Laurie; Forever; Slim Whitman; Songs of the Old Waterwheel; I'll Never Stop Loving You; Cool Water; Heart Songs & Love Songs; I'm a Lonely Wanderer; Yodeling; Irish Songs* (all early 1960s); *All Time Favorites* (4/64); *Country Songs/City Hits* (10/64); *God's Hand in Mine; Love Song of the Waterfall* (5/65); *Reminiscing* (11/65); *More than Yesterday* (4/66); *Birmingham Jail* (Camden Records, 6/66); *Unchain Your Heart* (Sun Records, 6/66); *Travelin' Man* (10/66); *Time for Love* (1/67); *15th Anniversary* (4/67); *Lonesome Heart* (Sun, 7/67); and *Memories* (1/68).

Late 1960s and early 1970s LPs included *Million Sellers* (Liberty Records); *Slim!* (Liberty); *Ramblin' Rose* (Sun); *Slim Whitman* (Sun, 12/69); *Great Country* (Sun); *Tomorrow Never Comes* (United Artists Records); *Guess Who* (UA); *It's a Sin to Tell a Lie* (UA); *Best of Slim Whitman* (UA, 1972); and *Superpak* (Liberty).

During the 1970s, Whitman had several charted singles on the UA label, including "It's All in the Game" in the spring of 1974. At the start of the 1980s, he had a new album out titled *All My Best*, which included his versions of such old standards as "Una Paloma Blanco," "Vaya con Dios," "Rose Marie," "Red River Valley," and "Have I Told You Lately That I Love You." That album was a "TV package," marketed by means of TV commercials rather than sold in record stores. The results were phenomenal; by the fall of 1980 *All My Best* had sold an amazing 2 million copies. That kind of impact didn't go unnoticed by U.S. record firm executives. When Slim came to give a performance at the Cleveland Richfield Coliseum, Steve Popovich, president of Cleveland International Records, met with him and started discussions leading to Whitman's signing with the firm. He arranged for distribution through Epic Records, and in the fall Slim's debut single on Epic/Cleveland was issued. In a short time, "When" was in upper-chart levels. Soon after, his initial Epic/Cleveland LP, *Songs I Love to Sing,* was on record store racks. In the spring of 1981, his single "I Remember You" was on the country charts and in August 1981, his second Epic/Cleveland LP, *Mr. Songman,* was issued.

At that time, Epic pointed out, Slim's credits included over fifty albums recorded on various labels with combined sales of more than 50 million worldwide. In the late 1970s, his overseas highlights included having a single of "Rose Marie" number one on British pop charts for eleven consecutive weeks, something

even the Beatles had never accomplished; the same single at the start of the 1980s still held the Australian record for all-time best-selling 45 rpm disc. His career to then had provided over thirty top-50 singles and nineteen gold-record level releases.

As of 1982, Whitman and his wife, Jerry, lived in Middleberg, Florida. On the road for his many concerts worldwide, he was backed by a six-piece band fronted by his twenty-three-year-old son, Byron.

As the 1980s went by with surging ranks of newcomers vying for recording and concert opportunities, veterans like Slim were increasingly hard-pressed to find ways of placing their names before the public. In the 1980s and 1990s, some of Whitman's recordings were repackaged in albums offered for sale only on TV promotions. A major favorite with European fans, Slim still toured at home and abroad as of 1996 performing with his son, Byron. His record sales by then exceeded a total of 65 million copies.

WIGGINS(ES), THE: *Vocal and instrumental duo, Audrey Wiggins, born Waynesville, North Carolina, December 26, 1967; John Wiggins, born Nashville, Tennessee, October 13, 1962.*

It took a number of false starts, but by the mid-1990s the brother and sister team of John and Audrey Wiggins were bidding fair to become one of the best-regarded family teams to grace the country scene. In their own way, they had carried out their father's life-long dream of country music success, though ruing the fact that an accident ended his life scant months before he could have had the pleasure of hearing their first major label release played on radio stations in Nashville and across the U.S.

Radio programmers and disc jockeys were properly impressed. Larry Daniels of KNIX in Phoenix commented in 1994, "Has anyone noticed? The void in country music caused by the departure of the Judds is beginning to be filled by the new brother and sister act, John and Audrey Wiggins. That same real quality Naomi and Wynonna possessed as a team is manifest in the Wiggins's music and on-stage performance."

Their father, Johnny Wiggins, came from the Appalachian Mountains town of Waynesville, North Carolina, where he had played guitar and sung since his early youth. In 1960, he and his wife, Judy, moved to Nashville, where Johnny hoped to make his musical skills pay off in fame and fortune. He already knew how to work with his hands and took a job as a mechanic while seeking to make the necessary industry contacts. His first opportunity wasn't as a performer, but a job as mechanic and driver for the tour bus of Ernest Tubb and his Texas Troubadours. He was part of the Tubb retinue when son John was born in 1962. (The family already had a two-year-old girl, Leighanne.)

Wiggins senior began to make forward moves in his career, thanks to his association with Tubb, who became aware of Wiggins's excellent voice and gave him an opening spot on his concerts as "The Singing Bus Driver." Johnny also got the chance to record three albums on Tubb's Troubadour label. But Johnny began to realize that the almost yearlong dates on the road were endangering his family life. John recalled, "They were gone so long that me and my older sister didn't recognize him when he came off the road. We ran from him. That got to him."

Finally, Johnny decided to quit his job and move the family back to Waynesville, where Audrey was born in 1967. But he made sure music remained a part of the home environment. (He also kept in touch with Ernest Tubb and some of his other associates from Nashville.) Audrey commented, "Mama said that when we first started talking, we started singing too. They saw something in us from the time we were little bitty and nurtured that. We would sing in churches, at folk festivals, at parties."

John actually made his stage debut at four when he sang "Honky Tonk Man" with Tubb's band. Before he reached his teens he had learned the guitar rudiments and formed his own bluegrass band while in the sixth grade. His father had established a paving business, and as a teenager son John shoveled asphalt on business jobs. He kept up his music with his parents' encouragement, and was earning money on weekends at local clubs. Audrey was also making progress with her performing abilities. Ernest Tubb again helped out, having her sing "Lovesick Blues" with his group during a *Grand Ole Opry* show when she was twelve.

By the time she was in junior high school, she and her brother had worked up an act that was featured at Waynesville's End of the Trail country music club. The siblings also recorded an album they offered for sale at their performances titled *Live at the End of the Trail: John and Audrey Wiggins with Their Cross-Country Band.* John noted, "We sang it in a studio in Asheville and added pretaped applause. It sold pretty good. But I don't think anybody came back for seconds after they wore the first one out."

Up to then, Audrey's main contributions took the form of yodeling, but in 1979, after hearing Ricky Skaggs and Emmylou Harris blend their voices on the song "Everytime You Leave," they decided to become a full-fledged duet team. They practiced their version of the song and used it to win first prize at the North Carolina Folk Festival. They also made the acquaintance of talented fiddle player Clinton Gregory, who joined their act and played with it until 1987. With Gregory as part of the team, the Wigginses got a chance to become the house band (in 1981) at the Stampin' Ground Music Barn at Maggie Valley, North Carolina, a town that claimed the title of "The Clogging Capitol of the World."

During their six years at the club, John said, "We were workin' seven nights a week, so we went back to that same little studio and recorded a lot of instrumental stuff for people to clog to. We did 'Wake Up Little Susie,' 'Freight Train,' 'Cool Water.' Daddy sang the 'Tennessee Waltz.' It was a cute record, better than the first one. We had a little picture of us made and we'd go out there between shows doing autographs. I thought we had made the big time. . . . But we still didn't have a clue."

Their father knew it was only the ground floor and that for a breakthrough a presence in Nashville was all-important. In 1984 he took his children to Nashville to record a 45-rpm disc. Audrey remembered, "We came down and did a Pam Tillis song called 'Some Mistakes Cost More Than Others' and on the flip was 'Twilight Time.' He even took us to this video production company and we made low-budget videos of those two songs. I hope to God nobody ever sees them."

Nothing sprang from that, and the family members returned home. Three years later John, Audrey, and Clinton Gregory moved to Nashville full-time. They found day jobs while looking for an opening to the music industry. Audrey got a position at the Music Valley Wax Museum, while John found a series of jobs at the Music Valley Car Museum, with a construction firm, and, following in his father's footsteps, as a bus driver for rock guitarist Henry Lee Summer. Audrey noted, "We had no idea how to get in and where the networking is. We didn't know hardly anybody in town. We did a showcase at the Nashville Palace and nobody came."

But it proved a good move for Gregory, who found work in Suzy Bogguss's backup band. Later he was able to become a name artist himself, signing with Polydor Records and placing a number of records on the charts in the 1990s. As for John and Audrey, they once more returned dejectedly to their home area to work at local venues while John sought to improve his songwriting abilities.

The Wigginses were anything if not persistent. At the start of the 1990s, Johnny, John, and Audrey again took up residence in Nashville. They found an apartment on Music Row and Audrey became a tour guide at the Country Music Hall of Fame. They made more demos, some of which they played for a neighbor who was an attorney in the music field, who, in turn, set up a meeting with well-known record producers Jim Cotton and Joe Scaife. This time luck was on their side. Cotton and Scaife made professional demos, which brought a series of record company auditions and finally a contract offer from Mercury.

John said it turned out to be a bittersweet milestone. "One great thing was getting to call daddy and say, 'Daddy! We got the deal, the full-blown deal with Mercury Records.' And he was really excited. But he never got to hear the last session." Ironically, considering Johnny Wiggins's long association with automotive vehicles, he was killed in a car accident in January 1993.

In early 1994, the duo's Mercury debut album was released. In June they had a single on the *Billboard* chart, "Falling Out of Love" (written by John) and in October they had a top-30 single, "Has Anybody Seen Amy." In the Country Music Association voting for its 1995 awards, the duo was nominated for Vocal Duo of the Year as was also the case for 1996. Their next album, *The Dream*, came out on Mercury in April 1997.

WILBURN, TEDDY AND DOYLE (WILBURN BROTHERS): *Vocal duo, guitarists, songwriters, music publishers. Both born Thayer, Missouri, Virgil Doyle, July 7, 1930; died October 16, 1982; Thurman Theodore "Teddy," November 30, 1937.*

Many groups or duos in the music field go under the name of "brothers" without the slightest relationship. The Wilburns, though, are authentically titled. In fact, until 1951, the act was known as the Wilburn Family and included two older brothers, Leslie (born Thayer, Missouri, October 13, 1925) and Lester (born Thayer, Missouri, May 19, 1924). Also part of the Wilburn family group was Vinita Geraldine Wilburn, born Thayer, Missouri, June 5, 1927.

The Wilburns grew up in rural Missouri, where the boys were performers at very early ages. In 1938, they began by singing on street corners in Thayer. In a short time, they progressed to more professional performances, appearing in shows in many parts of Missouri, then extending their activities to neighboring states. Their audience rapport was excellent, and the older artists with whom they appeared soon spread the word that the Wilburns were rising stars.

In 1941, the Wilburn Family was asked to join the *Grand Ole Opry*. The boys quickly attracted a national following in the next few years. World War II interfered with their careers, but afterward, they once more starred on the *Opry*. In 1948, the group moved to Shreveport for a featured spot on the KWKH *Louisiana Hayride*. They remained until 1951, when the act was once more broken up, this time by the Korean War.

When the act resumed in 1953, it consisted of Teddy (Thurman Theodore) and Doyle (Virgil Doyle). They returned to the *Opry* and remained regular cast members. Through the mid-1950s, they toured the country and turned out many records that chalked up respectable sales. Their lists of credits during this period included first place in the *Arthur Godfrey's Talent Scouts* TV show. In 1956, they provided Decca Records with a top-10 hit, *Go Away with Me*. From then on, Wilburn Brothers songs were on the bestseller lists regularly. As their reputation increased, the brothers diversified into other parts of the music business. In the late 1950s, all four brothers helped form a new music publishing firm, Sure-Fire Music. The music turned out by the company included a number of songs written by the Wilburns. The brothers had three major hits in 1959, "A Woman's Intuition," "Somebody's Back in Town," and "Which One Is to Blame," the first two of which bore the Sure-Fire imprint.

The 1960s proved even more successful for the brothers than earlier decades. In 1962, they had one of the top hits in the country, "Trouble's Back in Town." The following year, they had many hits, including two in the top 10, "Roll Muddy River" and "Tell Her So." Their mid-1960s top-10 score included "It's Another World" (1965) and "Someone Before Me" (1966). Decca Records recognized their worth, signing them to a "life" contract in the mid-1960s.

Some of their other recordings during the 1950s and 1960s were "Knoxville Girl," "I Can't Keep Away from You," "Mister Love," "Look Around," "Deep Elem Blues," "Cry, Cry, Darling," "Always Alone," "You Will Again," and "I'll Sail My Ship Alone." The brothers' songwriting activity included "That's When I Miss You," "I Know You Don't Love Me Anymore," "Need Someone," and "Much Too Often."

During the 1960s, the men toured all fifty states. They starred on Australian TV for thirty-nine weeks as part of the Roy Acuff *Open House* show. They were also featured on guest spots on *American Bandstand* and *Jamboree U.S.A.* They added to their business enterprises by establishing the Wil-Helm Talent Agency. The agency, formed in conjunction with country artist Smiley Wilson, became one of Nashville's top booking firms. By the mid-1960s, it represented such stars as Loretta Lynn, Jay Lee Webb, the Osborne Brothers, Harold Morrison, Jean Shephard, Martha Carson, Slim Whitman, and Charlie Louvin.

The Wilburn Brothers turned out many successful LPs during the 1950s and 1960s. These included *Carefree Moments* on Vocalion (1962) and several dozen albums on Decca. Among the latter were *Wilburn Brothers; Wilburn Brothers Sing Folk Songs; Big Heartbreak; Take Up the Cross; Side by Side* (1959); *Sing, Lovin' in God's Country* (1961); *City Limits* (1962); *Trouble Back in Town* (1963); *Never Alone* (1964); *Country Gold* (1965); and *Two for the Show* (1967).

The Brothers remained on Decca and its successor, MCA Records through the mid-1970s. At the start of the 1980s, they remained active on the concert circuit and still were *Grand Ole Opry* cast members.

Their collaboration came to an end with Doyle's death in the fall of 1982. Teddy, however, carried on the Wilburn tradition thereafter, and some of the duo's recordings slowly became available on reissue collections.

WILLIAMS, DON: *Singer, guitarist, songwriter. Born Floydada, Texas, May 27, 1939.*

When Don Williams accepted his award for the Country Music Association's Male Vocalist of the Year in October 1978, he wore what he usually wears— faded blue jeans, denim jacket, and a worn-out hat that was designed for him when he appeared in the Burt Reynolds movie *W.W. and the Dixie Dancekings.* He was being honored for his music, which sounds as simple and relaxed as the way he dresses.

The son of a mechanic, Don's family traveled frequently when he was young. His mother taught him to play guitar at the age of twelve. He listened mostly to country music but also enjoyed listening to Elvis Presley, Chuck Berry, and other early rock figures. After awhile, his family settled in Corpus Christi, Texas, where Don went to high school.

After graduating from high school, Don spent two years in the Army. During this time he also met and married his wife, Joy. After he left the army, he held odd jobs, such as driving a bread truck and working in the oil fields of Texas. He worked on music evenings with his friend Lofton Kline and they began singing at local bars. They called themselves the Strangers Two. In 1964 they met Susan Taylor when she was on the same bill with them at a college dance. She joined forces with Kline and Williams and they became known as the Pozo Seco Singers. They had a top-10 national hit in 1965 with their recording "Time." They had a few minor hits after that and eventually wound up playing in lounges and rowdy dance halls, which Williams grew to detest. The group disbanded in 1971.

His experience with that group was the major cause for his intense dislike of promotion campaigns that invaded his privacy and the basis of his newfound desire to maintain creative independence. He told Jim Jerome for a *Playboy* article (March, 1978), "It was real canned—the song order, what I said, how the others reacted. It just cut the heart out of it for me. I swore I'd never paint myself into that corner again."

After Pozo Seco disbanded, Williams decided to quit the music business and opened a furniture store with his father-in-law. But by the next year, he was longing to get back to making music. He went to Nashville, primarily to become a writer. He looked up some of the contacts he had made while he was a Pozo Seco singer and connected with Allen Reynolds of the Jack Clement organization, which included JMI Records and Jack Music Publishing. Don was hired by them to try to get other artists to record his songs and other songs from the publishing company's catalogue. Some of his compositions were recorded, but they were different enough for that time to cause many artists to think twice about recording them.

However, Williams believed strongly in his songs, and he decided to record them himself. With Allen Reynolds producing, he turned out *Don Williams, Volume One* on the JMI label. The album included the now-classic hits "Amanda" and "In the Shelter of Your Eyes," the latter on country charts in 1972. At that time, most Nashville songs featured elaborate instrumental backings; nevertheless, Williams's gentle, subdued music caught on. Williams and Reynolds teamed up again for *Don Williams, Volume Two.*

Soon afterward, JMI Records folded, and Don signed with ABC/Dot Records and began to produce his own recordings. His first ABC album was *Don Williams, Volume Three,* on hit lists in 1974, followed in 1975 by the top-10 hit LPs *You're My Best Friend* and *Don Williams' Greatest Hits.* In 1976 and 1977, he had more album releases on top-chart levels: *Harmony, Visions,* and *Country Boy,* the last named staying on into 1979. His LP *Expressions,* issued in 1978, was his last release on ABC/Dot before that organization was absorbed by MCA Records, which remained his label into the 1980s. From these albums came a long string of country hit singles, many of which made number one on U.S. charts. Those include "You're My Best Friend," "Some Broken Hearts Never End," "Till the Rivers All Run Dry," "Louisiana Saturday Night," "Say It Again," "I Wouldn't Want to Live if You Didn't Love Me," "Country Boy," "She Never Knew Me," "The Ties That Bind," "Rake and Ramblin' Man," and "Tulsa Time." "Tulsa Time" (written by Danny Flowers, guitarist of Don's backup band) was named single record of the year in 1979 by the Academy of Country Music.

Although Williams's records sold very well, for a time he seemed to be more of a star in Great Britain than in the United States. In 1975, he was named both Male Country Singer of the Year and Country Performer of the Year by the Country Music Association of Great Britain, and his LP *You're My Best Friend* was named Album of the Year. In 1976, six of his albums were in the top 20 on Great Britain's year-end charts; four of his albums were in the top 5. He attracted the admiration of English rock guitarist-singer Eric Clapton, and they later shared a concert bill in Nashville.

In July 1977, Williams scored a major concert triumph when he appeared at New York's Carnegie Hall and received three standing ovations from the crowd. To reproduce the sound from his albums as closely as possible on stage, Williams used only two musicians other than himself, Danny Flowers on harmonica and guitar and David Williamson on bass. After being nominated several times for the Country Music Association's Male Vocalist of the Year Award, he finally won that honor in October 1978.

Many of Williams's hits from the mid-1970s on were by other writers, particularly Bob McDill and Wayland Holyfield. However, Don always loved to write new songs of his own. Describing his writing style, Jennifer Bolch of the *Dallas Times Herald* (May 28, 1979) noted that Williams told her he usually wrote the music first, then added the lyrics. "The music comes first, typically a flowing, gentle hummable tune with its backbone hiding in the hypnotic rhythm. Then the lyrics. 'I just sit down and fool around with the guitar, and when I get something that seems to set a mood, the words start to come,' he explained."

Much has been written about Don's quiet lifestyle. He lives on a ranch outside Nashville with his wife and two sons and does much of the ranch work himself. He is a regular Sunday churchgoer; he doesn't drink or use drugs. He is basically a quiet, unassuming family man, who doesn't go out of his way to call attention to himself.

Don's music, however, has gained plenty of attention; his style has been described by critics as "restrained, unadorned, even dignified" and "so smooth and mellow it's almost conservative." Williams himself calls his music "intensely simple," but he says, "It's the hardest music I've ever made. It seems like it would be simple but it takes more time than anything I've ever done because I try and make every sound count!"

Many observers marveled at the fact that Williams managed to gain a massive following without engaging in large scale "hype" campaigns or going in for flashy costumes or headline-catching exploits. Asked about this by Linda Luoma for *Music City News* (June 1979, p. 13), he replied, "I really don't try to make any accounting for my success except to say that I try to do what I honestly believe in—and I've never done anything because I thought I was better than other people.

"Classically speaking, I don't think I've ever wanted to talk about the same things that other country artists want to talk about in their music. I try not to be taken in by whatever the going gimmick is. The main things I've always been concerned with in my music and my songwriting, more than anything else, are people's feelings for each other, rather than triangle situations or sittin' down in a bar to drink your blues away.

"To me, country music is not a form of music that deals with things that are extremely controversial or profane or anything else that would make it a radical, extremist form of music. My idea of country music is as a family form of entertainment. I just try to make country music the way I like to hear country music."

He told Jim Jerome, "As many people know me as an artist as I can really care about. It'd be a real compliment to my music—and to writers like Bob [McDill] and Wayland [Holyfield]—if we reached a broader market. I'd be a fool to be hard-nosed and unreasonable, if it's s'posed to happen. But you can get buried in promotion and manipulation out there. Greed does strange things to people. I never want to get so filthy stinkin' rich that I become a hermit who can't go out on the street."

At any rate, Don's approach continued to pay off with best-selling singles and LPs for his new MCA label. In 1979, besides "Tulsa Time," he had such best-selling chart singles as "Lay Down Beside Me" and "It Must be Love." His LP *Expressions* stayed on the charts in 1979 and into 1980, as did the MCA *Best of Don Williams Volume II* release. In 1980, his singles hits included "I Believe in You," "Good Ole Boys Like Me," "Love Me Over Again," and "It Must Be Love." He also had two new albums on upper-chart levels, *Portrait* (issued in late 1979) and *I Believe in You*. In the spring of 1981, he had another top-10 single, "Falling Again."

"The Gentle Giant," as Don was called by others in the music field, continued to gain the respect of rising new stars in the 1980s as also was the case with country veterans both male and female. He was nominated for Country Music Association Male Vocalist of the Year in both 1980 and 1981. In 1980, CMA voters also nominated his single "Good Ole Boys Like Me" for Single of the Year and in 1981 made a finalist of his MCA album *I Believe in You* (issued August 1980) in the Album of the Year category. His other 1980s MCA albums were *Especially for You* (issued June 1981); *Listen to the Radio* (issued April 1982); *Yellow Moon* (April 1983); *The Best of Don Williams, Volume III* (February 1984); *Cafe Carolina* (May 1984); and *Greatest Hits, Volume IV* (October 1985).

Don left MCA for Capitol in 1985, and his new label debut, *New Moves,* came out in January 1986. It was followed by *Traces* in October 1987 and *Prime Cuts* in January 1989.

In the mid-1980s, Don's chart singles included duets with Emmylou Harris, which earned them a 1984 CMA nomination for Vocal Duo of the Year. Though he could draw large audiences on the country concert circuit, he scheduled considerably fewer dates than other performers, an approach he kept up throughout the decade. And once off the road, he never tarried long in Nashville but hurried to his home in Ashland. Once there, as his wife, Joy, noted in 1992 when they were enjoying their thirty-second year of married life, he avoided making the forty-five minute trip to Music City unless it was absolutely necessary.

Don himself told Mandy Wilson of CMA's *Close Up* magazine, "Apart from whatever needs I to have to care of, I try to spend as little time as possible in the music business. Because when I'm working, I give it everything I've got, and when I'm home I try to give my family my undivided attention.

"But the music itself keeps me in this business. It's the only thing I have done in my life as far as work is concerned that I have never really felt blase about. I really do believe if I ever get to that point I'll just hang it up. There are times when I work on the road that I get hard-pressed to feel what I'm doing. When that happens, I am always left with the idea that I have cheated everybody. It just doesn't feel honest. I wanna feel honest about what I'm doing, so as a result I don't do a lot of road work."

At the end of the 1980s, Williams moved from Capitol to RCA and for a time made greater inroads into the country charts than in the mid-1980s. In late 1989 he had the hit single "I've Been Loved By the Best" on the charts, drawn from his May 1989 RCA album *One Good Well.* It peaked at number three in *Radio & Records* the week of December 1. In 1990, he had three more best-sellers, "Just As Long As I Have You," which reached number four in *R&R* the week of March 16;

"Maybe That's All It Takes" (number thirteen in *R&R* August 3); and the number-one hit late in the year, "Back In My Younger Days." His second RCA album, *True Love,* (issued October 1990) also spent several months on the hit lists. Among his 1991 chartmakers was "Lord Have Mercy on a Country Boy," a top-20 *Billboard* success in late summer. His 1992 output on RCA included the album *Currents* (issued in March) and the single "Standing Knee Deep in a River (Dying of Thirst)."

His new string of chart successes began to taper off in the mid-1990s, though his concerts always were well attended. He worried increasingly about the problems of unemployment or underemployment he increasingly observed in his travels, as well as the rising lawlessness. He told Mandy Wilson he believed it all "goes back to losing respect for yourself because you can't make a living. People lose hope and think that anything goes."

Speaking out about the need for more concern and action by Washington to solve the problems, he acknowledged, was out of character. "I've never believed in mixing platforms, because the way I see it, most people have paid their money to hear the songs. And for me to use the stage to air out religious or political views could be very compromising."

During 1993 Don changed record affiliation again, this time switching from RCA to American Harvest. His first release on that label was taken from a concert given in England in March 1993. The album, *An Evening with Don Williams Best of Live,* came out in June 1994. During that year he restricted his live performances mainly to the Charley Pride Theatre in Branson, Missouri. He commented he was thinking of establishing his own venue there. "I've never really sat in one place like that," he said. "I've got to sort through some things and see if that's really gonna be good for me, and everybody with me."—I. S./A. S.

WILLIAMS, HANK, JR.: *Singer, guitarist, banjoist, songwriter, bandleader (the Cheatin' Hearts, The Bama Band). Born Shreveport, Louisiana, May 26, 1949.*

Unlike many other sons of famous fathers, Hank Williams, Jr., was immensely talented. If his name hadn't already been famous, he undoubtedly would have made it so both as performer and writer. Having to compete with the towering legend of his father presented the almost insoluble challenge of coming to terms with the benefits and limitations of his position.

Hank Jr. was born in Shreveport, where his father, already an established star on the *Louisiana Hayride,* was readying himself for the next major step—to be a featured artist on the *Grand Ole Opry.* When the child was three months old, the family moved to Nashville, where Hank Jr. grew up and attended elementary and high school. He was only three years old when his father died.

Hank Jr. showed a flair for music at an early age; he began to play guitar before he was in his teens. He also was a fine athlete, playing on such varsity teams in high school as football, basketball, boxing, and swimming. By then, however, he already was beginning to follow in his father's footsteps, with increasing exposure to country-music audiences. By the time he was fourteen, he was accompanying his mother, Audrey Williams, with her Caravan of Stars show when school was out. Record companies were showing a marked interest in this promising performer with a trademark name, but Mrs. Williams took her time in agreeing to such an alignment for the boy.

Finally, in 1964, both she and Hank Jr. felt the time was right for such a move. They moved to California and signed him with MGM Records. While he started recording his debut material, he continued his high school work with a private tutor and also enrolled in a Hollywood professional school. As expected, the emergence of a new scion of the Williams family interpreting the classic songs of his father intrigued country fans. His debut album, *Hank Williams, Jr., Sings,* issued by MGM in May 1964, started selling briskly soon after its release. In a short time, he had his first top-10 hit with his single of his father's "Long Gone Lonesome Blues," an impressive success for a fifteen-year-old. In December 1964, his next LP came out, titled *Your Cheatin' Heart.* The title song became his theme song and the name of his four-man backing band. (Later he changed his backing band's name to The Bama Band.)

Young Hank's rapport with country audiences continued to grow throughout the mid-1960s. His albums and singles continued to do well and by the late 1960s, he was giving 200 or more live shows a year, often to record-breaking crowds. Among his credits for those years were appearances on such national TV shows as *The Ed Sullivan Show, The Tonight Show, Mike Douglas, Shindig, Kraft Music Hall,* and countless fairs, rodeos, and festivals. He also was featured in several MGM films, including the 1967 *A Time to Sing.*

His album releases in the mid-1960s included a concept album combining some of his performances with those of his father (issued 6/65); *Ballads of Hills and Plains* (11/65); *Blues Is My Name* (5/66); *Shadows* (8/66); *My Own Way* (6/67); and *Best of Hank Williams Jr.* (12/67). He scored a second top-10 singles hit in 1966 with his father's "Standing in the Shadows." Although much of his repertoire was made up of Hank Sr.'s writings, Hank Jr. also wrote original material. He received BMI Songwriter Awards for some of them; one he was awarded at sixteen made him the youngest person ever to receive the honor.

In both large and small venues, he drew huge audiences. One of the most impressive occasions occurred on May 4, 1969, when he and Johnny Cash drew a capacity crowd at Cobo Hall in Detroit. The concert gross, reported as $83,000 for tickets and $100,000 when programs and album sales were added in, was the highest ever for a country concert to that point.

In his part of the show, supported by the Cheatin' Hearts, whose lead musician was Lamar Morris, and members of his father's Drifting Cowboys, he held the stage for over an hour to wild acclaim from the audience. His program, much of which was recorded and released in October 1969 in the MGM LP *Hank Williams, Jr., Live at Cobo Hall in Detroit,* included "Detroit City," a solo on the five-string banjo of "Foggy Mountain Breakdown," "Standing in the Shadows," "Jambalaya," "I'm So Lonesome I Could Cry," "You Win Again," "Games People Play," "She Thinks I Still Care," "Darling, You Know I Wouldn't Lie," "Your Cheatin' Heart," and "I Saw the Light."

In the late 1960s and early 1970s, Hank was represented on record racks by a veritable flood of LPs. They included the MGM releases *Sunday Morning, Greatest Hits, Volume I, Greatest Hits, Volume II, Roy Orbison Way, Removing the Shadow* (with L. Johnson), *Hank Williams, Jr., All for the Love of Sunshine, I've Got a Right to Cry, Sweet Dreams* (with the Curb Congregation), *Songs of Johnny Cash,* and *11 Roses.*

He didn't lack for singles hits in the first part of the 1970s. Among his charted releases were "So Sad (To Watch Good Love Go Bad)," a duet with Lois Johnson that made the top 10 in late 1970; "Send Me Some Lovin'," another duet with Johnson in the spring of 1972; "Pride's Not Hard to Swallow," on hit lists in the fall of 1972; "The Last Love Song," top 5 in early 1974; "Rainy Night in Georgia," top 10 in early summer 1974; and "The Same Old Story," a chartmaker in mid-1975.

During the early 1970s, Hank, only in his early twenties, reevaluated his goals in life, his relationship to his father and his generation. As he wrote in his autobiography, *Living Proof* (issued by G. P. Putnam's Sons in October 1979), "I'd been singing Daddy's songs almost every night for the past fifteen or sixteen years and I thought I knew everything there was to know about it. What I'd forgotten was that knowing is not the same as feeling. I knew my father, but I had let his soul slip away from me, and a lot of other people had found it. . . ."

He also commented, "They were polarized times, and the music was (and still is) the cutting edge of the times. If you listened to country music, you were a redneck asshole, and if you listened to rock and roll, you were a hippie freak. So what happened to the Allman Brothers in Macon, Georgia, was of no concern to the pickers in Nashville, Tennessee, a couple of hundred miles up the road. But it was important to me, because those Georgia boys were trying to tell me something."

During that period, Hank had fits of depression that led to a suicide attempt in 1974 that fortunately failed. He also indulged excessively in drugs and alcohol. He

later credited the blunt words of his doctor with causing him to reevaluate his life. He recalled that the doctor told him, "You've been taught to act like, walk like and talk like Hank Williams all your life and if you don't get your act together, you're going to die like him, too, only you'll get there before he did."

Determined to modernize his musical outlook, he moved from Nashville to the small town of Cullman, Alabama. He spent time talking to the musicians and studio operators in Muscle Shoals, where much of the new blends of country and rock were being brought to recorded life. The result of that was the album *Hank Williams, Jr., and Friends,* the friends including people like Charlie Daniels, Allman alumnus Chuck Leavell, and Toy Caldwell of the Marshall Tucker Band. The album was confusing to many of the long-time Williams' family adherents, though it has since become something of a progressive country classic.

Hank was sure he was on the right path, but his efforts were suddenly interrupted by a near fatal mishap. Taking a short vacation before returning to the music wars, he went hiking in the Rockies in Montana during August 1975. While making his way at 11,000 feet, a snowfield collapsed and catapulted him down the mountain some 500 feet. He hit a boulder and, though badly injured, survived. After being rescued by helicopter, he spent long periods in the hospital and at home convalescing.

After recuperating for a long period of time, Hank began to resume his career, though his backlog of recordings was such that his name rarely was absent from hit charts very long. Thus MGM had a singles hit in early summer 1975 with one of Hank Jr.'s original compositions, "Living Proof," even as Hank was on the move to a new label. (That song provided the title for his autobiography, on which he started working in the late 1970s.)

Mike Curb, who had been president of MGM for a number of years when Williams, Jr., was on that label, had set up his own company, Curb Records, and Hank Jr. went along. He turned out a number of charted singles for the Warner/Curb organization, including "One Night Stands," on hit lists in 1977, and "I Fought the Law" in late summer and early fall of 1978. He also completed two LPs for Warner/Curb, *One Night Stands* (issued 4/77) and *The New South* (10/77), both reissued on Elektra/Curb in August 1981.

In 1979, the record affiliation moved laterally when Hank joined several other Curb country artists on the Elektra roster. (Elektra and Warner's both are part of Warner Communications Co.) The first result of that was his spring 1979 album on Elektra/Curb, *Family Traditions,* which included several of Hank's new compositions based on some of the incidents in his life, such as "I Just Ain't Been Able," "Paying on Time," and "I've Got Rights." The title song from the album was nominated for a Grammy for Best Country Vocal Performance, Male, for 1979 and also brought Hank a BMI Writer's Award, the first he'd received since the 1974 BMI honor for "The Last Love Song."

Hank's career took a strong upward turn after his move to Elektra. He turned out a string of fine albums that ranked among the best progressive country collections of the early 1980s. These included *Whiskey Bent and Hell Bound* (10/79); *Habits Old and New* (7/80); *Rowdy* (1/81); and *The Pressure Is On* (8/81). From his Elektra LPs came such notable singles as "To Love Somebody," "Family Tradition," "Whiskey Bent and Hell Bound" (a number-one hit), and "Women I've Never Had"—all released in 1979; "Kaw-Liga" and "Old Habits" in 1980; and the number-one 1981 hits, "Texas Women," "Dixie on My Mind," and "My Rowdy Friends." When the last named (from *The Pressure Is On)* made number one in October 1981 it marked his twenty-fifth top-10 single and sixth number-one hit. He backed those releases with a series of impressive live appearances, backed by his tour group, The Bama Band, whose members as of 1981 were Cliff Pippin on drums, Joe Hamilton on bass, Eddie Long on steel guitar, Dixie Hatfield on keyboards, Lamar Morris on lead guitar, and Wayne Turner on rhythm guitar.

Williams's career really boomed in the 1980s, with record after record and video after video making bestseller lists and annual awards coming in by the dozens, particularly in the second half of the decade. New or reissued albums from the 1977–81 time period stayed on the charts until 1982 when they were joined by the new Elektra/Curb LPs *High Notes* (issued April 1982, later earned a gold record) and *Hank Williams Jr.'s Greatest Hits, Volume 1* (issued September 1982, double platinum). With those and seven others (*One Night Stands, The New South, Family Tradition, Whiskey Bent, Habits Old and New, Rowdy,* and *The Pressure Is On*), on October 23 and 30, 1982, he had nine albums on *Billboard* charts at one time. As of 1997, no other living artist had equaled that feat.

At the end of 1982, Hank won *Billboard* awards for Top Male Artist, Top Album, and Top Singles Artist. He received three BMI Writer's Awards "All My Rowdy Friends (Have Settled Down)," "Dixie On My Mind," "Texas Woman"), to join five earlier BMI songwriting honors ("Standing in the Shadows," 1966; "Cajun Baby," 1970; "The Last Love Song," 1974; "Family Tradition," 1980; and "Old Habits," 1981.) In 1983, he received another BMI Award for "A Country Boy Can Survive" and in 1984 for "Gonna Go Huntin' Tonight" and "Leave Them Boys Alone."

In the mid-1980s, he turned out a string of albums that went gold or better. These included *Strong Stuff* (issued on Elektra/Curb, January 1983) and, on Warner/Curb, *Men of Steel* (issued September 1983); *Major Move* (May 1984); *Five-O* (April 1985); *Hank Williams Jr.'s Greatest Hits, Volume II* (October 1985, platinum); *Montana Cafe* (June 1986); *Hank "Live"*

(January 1987); and *Born to Boogie* (July 1987, platinum). Warner/Curb also released the album *The Early Years* in October 1986. Those albums provided more singles hits, most notably "All My Rowdy Friends Are Coming Over Tonight," "Born to Boogie," and "Young Country." Also worth noting is the single "Mind Your Own Business," released in September 1986, whose flip side was the song "My Name Is Bocephus," the latter highlighting the nickname Hank has enjoyed for many years.

"All My Rowdy Friends Are Coming Over Tonight" won both the Academy of Country Music and Country Music Association Awards for Video of the Year and also was voted Favorite Country Video, Male, in the American Music Awards. During 1985, Hank received two more BMI Writing Awards for "Attitude Adjustment" and "Man of Steel." In 1986, a year in which Hank moved his home and business operations from Alabama to Paris, Tennessee (the move was completed on July 3), Hank was also named Composer/Performer of the Year by *Cash Box* magazine.

Until the mid-1980s, Hank had not received much consideration from voters in major music award competitions, but that began to change, thanks in part to a stronger promotional campaign orchestrated by Hank's longtime friend and manager Merle Kilgore. In 1985 and 1986, Hank was a finalist for CMA Male Vocalist of the Year. That preceded a breakthrough year when he was voted Entertainer of the Year by both the ACM and CMA, honors again accorded him in 1988. In the 1987 CMA voting, he also received the Video of the Year Award for "My Name Is Bocephus." He also was a 1987 CMA nominee for Male Vocalist of the Year.

Hank closed out the 1980s with still more successes as a recording artist, TV guest on many network shows, and country music concert attraction. Unlike most country stars of the time, his live performances typically incorporated striking visual effects that rivaled the presentations of rock 'n' roll superstar acts. His bestselling albums at the end of the 1980s on Warner/Curb were *Wild Streak* in 1988 and *Greatest Hits, Volume III*. The first of those went gold, the second exceeded platinum.

In 1989, thanks to the wonders of modern electronics, he was able to record a series of duets with his father that resulted in a hit album and several best-selling singles. One of the singles, "There's a Tear in My Beer," earned a 1989 Grammy (announced on the February 1990 Awards telecast) for Best Country Collaboration. It also won Video of the Year from both the ACM and CMA and was named Vocal Event of the Year by the CMA. The recordings also helped Hank, Jr., win another Entertainer of the Year Award from the ACM. The Music Operators of America also selected the father-and-son release Record of the Year.

Hank began the 1990s with still more achievements, including his "All My Rowdy Friends" commercial, which formed the new theme for ABC-TV's Monday Night Football show. The football game intro won the Sport Emmy for 1990, a feat repeated from 1991–93. This made him the first country music artist ever to win an Emmy. His 1990 award collection also included the International Film & TV Festival of New York's Gold Medal for Best Commercial Video, a TNN/*Music City News* Video of the Year Award for his duet with Hank, Sr., and the Music Operators of America CD of the Year Award for *Greatest Hits, Volume III.*

Hank's two 1990 album releases, both of which went gold, were *Lone Wolf* and *America* (*The Way I See It*). He made the singles charts with "Ain't Nobody's Business," number six in *Radio & Records* the week of April 4, and "Good Friends, Good Whiskey, Good Lovin'," number seven in *R&R* the week of July 6, 1990. Other singles releases in 1990 were "Man to Man," "Don't Give Us a Reason," and "I Mean I Love You."

After the release of *Pure Hank* on Warner/Curb in April 1991, Hank switched to a new label, Curb/Capricorn. Three releases came out on it, *Maverick* in February 1992; *The Hank Williams Jr. Collection* (*Bocephus Box Set*) in November 1992; and *Out of Left Field* in March 1993. All made the charts, but their sales pace was slower than previous album releases. After a two-year hiatus, a new release, *Hog Wild,* was issued on the MCG/Curb label in February 1995 and made the *Billboard* Top 15 soon after.

His Monday Night Football lead-in wasn't renewed for the 1994 season, but public complaints about the change caused ABC to sign Williams to a new three-year contract through 1997. On January 29, 1995, he won a rousing ovation from spectators at Joe Robbie Stadium in Miami when he performed shortly before opening kickoff at Super Bowl XXIX.

By 1995, Hank could point to a career that encompassed ten number-one singles, thirteen number-one albums, twenty gold and five platinum singles, and one double platinum LP (*Greatest Hits, Volume I*). Among the performers he had recorded with over the years were Ray Charles, Willie Nelson, John Lee Hooker, Johnny Cash, Reba McEntire, Huey Lewis, Tom Petty, Waylon Jennings, Travis Tritt, George Jones and George Thorogood. During 1995 his MCG/Curb album *Hog Wild* was on the charts for a number of months, peaking at no. 14 in *Billboard* early in the year. In the spring and summer of 1996, his album *A.K.A. Wham Bam Sam* was on the hit lists.

WILLIAMS, HANK, SR.: *Singer, guitarist, bandleader (the Drifting Cowboys), songwriter. Born Georgiana, Alabama, September 17, 1923; died West Virginia, January 1, 1953. Elected to Country Music Hall of Fame (one of the three first selections) in 1961.*

In his short, troubled lifetime, Hank Williams inspired millions with his music, though he was unable to translate his talent to an inner happiness for himself. Along the way, the creative standards he set posed a challenge that only the best efforts of talented writers and performers could come close to matching. His impact on country music has been as great as another troubadour who died too young, the original Jimmie Rodgers.

Born in the small town of Georgiana, Alabama, a rural farming area, he was the son of a railroad engineer, and his mother played the organ for services and gospel sings at the local church. She began to teach young Hiram Hank Williams gospels and hymns as soon as he could talk, and, by the time he was six, he was one of the youngest members of the church choir. On his eighth birthday, he was given a guitar as a present. Although he didn't receive guitar lessons, he picked up whatever he could from experimenting and, whenever possible, watching others play. For a while, he learned several chords from trailing after an old black street musician named Tee-Tot.

The idea of earning a living in music came to him slowly. He had an intuitive feel for melody, but for a time music to the boy was mainly something one did in church, or performed for the fun of it with family or friends. But by the time he reached his teens, he was copying some of the songs he heard on radio or records and sitting in with local groups. When he was fourteen, he organized his own band and started looking for opportunities to play at local hoedowns and other events. When he could, he went to country-music shows by established artists passing through the area. Roy Acuff recalled later that Hank was like many of those small town aspirants who often could be found hovering on a street corner with a Sears, Roebuck-type guitar, hoping to be discovered. He remembered Hank in the late 1930s as a shy, skinny, nervous boy in his mid-teens.

But young Hank wasn't ready for a step up yet. He had years to spend in run-down dance halls and honky tonks in his home state before he was to achieve stardom, although he was not without home area accomplishments. Soon after he organized his first band the group auditioned for the manager of station WSFA in Montgomery, Alabama, and came out with a job. The group, which was the initial incarnation of his Drifting Cowboys, remained as regulars on WSFA for over a decade. The first musician who was to become a charter member of the Drifting Cowboys of Williams' glory years was steel guitarist Don Helms, who joined in 1943 in Alabama and remained with Hank almost all the time until Williams' death.

Still, Hank might never have become more than a regional performer if it hadn't been for his early marriage to Audrey Williams. Strong-willed and confident of Hank's talent, she became a combination booking agent, road manager, and drum beater for her husband. Although Hank and his band still played in seedy bars and at country fairs, she was instrumental in increasing the number of those dates and extending the locations to many other states besides Alabama. Both Audrey and Hank constantly began looking for contacts and opportunities to move up in the music world. Hank already was writing some of the original songs that were to make him famous, and one goal was to link up with a publisher and, hopefully, a recording company.

The place to go was Nashville, where, in 1946, the contact with Fred Rose, cofounder with Roy Acuff of the Acuff-Rose publishing house, was finally made. With Audrey urging the exceedingly tense Hank on, he sang five songs for Rose. The songs impressed Fred, but it was hard for him to associate the quality in them with the ill-at-ease country bumpkin sort of fellow who presented them.

Rose claimed throughout his life that he decided on a test, telling Hank to go into another room and "Write some kind of a song right here on the spot as proof!" Fifteen minutes later, according to Rose, Williams came back with "Mansion on the Hill," still a classic song that is often rerecorded not only by country but by pop artists like John Denver and Michael Murphey. Williams was signed by Acuff-Rose and, in the next half a decade, became the firm's most important writer. Not only did the company publish Hank's material, Rose collaborated with Williams on some of his later efforts.

The next important step in establishing Williams's credentials was a record contract. In 1947, this fell into place when veteran music executive Frank Walker signed him for the newly established MGM Records label. In August 1948, Hank took another step forward when he became a regular on the KWKH *Louisiana Hayride* in Shreveport, for many years second only to the *Grand Ole Opry* for country variety show honors. It was during this period that his son Hank Williams, Jr., was born (in May 1949). Hank and the Drifting Cowboys began to make their mark rapidly. A short time after joining the *Hayride,* they had their first disc on country hit lists, "Move It on Over." People began to talk about some of the other remarkable new songs Hank was singing and officials of the *Grand Ole Opry* started to take notice. As more of Hank's singles showed up on country charts the first part of 1949, the *Opry* decided he should be asked to join. He accepted joyfully and moved his band and family to Nashville. (He made his *Opry* debut on June 11, 1949.) From then on, Williams dominated the country-music field with half a dozen or more hit records every year. By the early 1950s, his genius was becoming apparent to the pop music field in general, and renditions of some of his songs by pop artists were selling in the millions throughout the world.

His successes in 1949 included the number-one-rated "Love Sick Blues." Other top-10 songs that year included his compositions "Mind Your Own Business" and "You're Gonna Change," plus "My Bucket's Got a Hole in It," and "Wedding Bells." All four of his gold records for 1950 were his own songs, "I Just Don't Like This Kind of Livin'," "Long Gone Lonesome Blues," "Moaning the Blues," and "Why Don't You Love Me?" Both "Long Gone Lonesome Blues" and "Why Don't You Love Me?" reached number one on country charts. The same was true of his seven top-10 hits of 1951, "Baby, We're Really in Love," "Crazy Heart," "Dear John," "Hey, Good Lookin'," "Howlin' at the Moon," "I Can't Help It," and "Cold, Cold Heart." During the year, Tony Bennett's version of "Cold, Cold Heart" became a multimillion-selling hit, the first indication that Hank was more than "just" a country star.

Williams scored in 1952 with such songs as the number-one hit "I'll Never Get Out of This World Alive"—all too immediately prophetic; his all-time standard composition "Jambalaya,"; "Half as Much"; "Honkey Tonk Blues"; and "Settin' the Woods on Fire." Although he died at the start of 1953, his records continued to dominate the singles charts that year with titles like "Kaw-Liga," "I Won't Be Home No More," "Weary Blues from Waitin'," and "Your Cheatin' Heart" (all written or cowritten by him) and a number-one hit of a Rose-Heath song, "Take These Chains from My Heart." Besides the top-10 hits listed above, Hank recorded and/or wrote dozens of other songs of equal quality that made lower-chart levels or provided major hits in later years for other artists.

Even as his reputation as a writer and recording artist soared, Williams's life was unraveling. The seeds of destruction already had been sown before he made the big time. He had been drinking steadily as a teenager and was an alcoholic before he was out of his teens. As the years went by and the pressures mounted, he tried other crutches, working his way through various pills until, at the end, he was as much a drug addict as an alcoholic. The victim of many phobias, including fear of the dark, he also became increasingly jealous and suspicious of his wife and friends. His life with Audrey became a series of fights, recriminations, and reconciliations. Things finally reached a breaking point, however, and they separated and divorced in the early 1950s.

His inner turmoil spilled over into his performing work. Increasingly undependable, he would show up for concerts in a drugged state, often incoherent, and sometimes he would fail to show up at all. Buck Moon, writing in the *Rocky Mountain Musical Express,* recounted talking to people who had seen such appearances in the later stages of Williams's career. One said, "Up to a point, liquor and pills just made him sing better and better. Then, all of a sudden, he'd just cave in. Sometimes he'd get real mean. You never knew which way he was going to go."

Another stated, "Oh, I don't think he was so much a hateful guy inside. It was more like he would be burned . . . or burned out as they call it. Blind crazy drunk and nothin' mattered."

When not completely wrapped in an alcoholic haze, *Opry*'s Minnie Pearl recalled, he could be a commanding figure onstage. She reported Williams "had a real animal magnetism. He *destroyed* the women in the audience."

His relationship with the *Opry* naturally disintegrated. After several warnings, he was suspended, a move that his son and his legion of fans still consider uncalled for. It was an event Hank felt deeply, though whether his staying on the *Opry* would have materially changed his downhill slide is doubtful.

Williams continued to attempt to keep going. He made some sincere efforts at rehabilitation, but instead of going to medical or psychiatric experts, he consulted several people considered "quacks." Some of the treatments he was given probably contributed to the physical decline that resulted in his death.

In September 1952, he married again, this time to a nineteen-year-old named Billie Jean Jones, who later wrote a biography of him. The marriage took place on an auditorium stage and people paid fifty cents apiece to watch the ceremony. Before and after, Hank kept on performing wherever he could, though without his band. The Drifting Cowboys declined to go back on the road with Williams because of the growing problems in dealing with him the last half-year of his life. He was sleeping in the back seat of a Cadillac driving through West Virginia during a series of one-night stands when he died on New Year's Day of 1953.

As often happens, he was honored more in his passing than in his lifetime. To a great extent, the true measure of his greatness didn't begin to appear until after his death. Members of the Drifting Cowboys note that while they were doing all those memorable songs with Hank they had little awareness that something unusual was taking place. Hank himself probably didn't think of his achievements as anything representing that much of a departure from the general country field. One writer commented, "Hank Williams was never quite aware of the true measure of his contribution. His life, like those of his fellow country-music performers of his own time and of today, was that of an itinerant musician, traveling the tank towns with his band, returning to Nashville long enough to make a new recording and hitting the road again."

In six years, he managed to compress what would have been a lifelong achievement for others. He completed enough recordings for a sizable number of new releases after his death and his overall catalogue has been packaged and repackaged year after year since then. Some have been reworked with the addition of whole orchestras as background in some cases or in electronically achieved duets with son Hank, Jr., who hardly knew his father.

New LPs of his work were constantly coming out in the 1950s, 1960s, 1970s, and 1980s. Among the MGM LPs were *Honky Tonkin'* (issued in the 1950s); *Lonesome Sound* (3/60); *Wait for the Light to Shine* (10/60); *Greatest Hits* (2/61); *Hank Williams' Spirit* (8/61); *On Stage* (3/62); *Greatest Hits, Vol. 2* (7/62); *Beyond the Sunset* (6/63); *Very Best* (11/63); *Greatest Hits, Vol. 3* (3/64); *Very Best, Vol. 2* (7/64); *Lost Highway* (10/64); *Hank Williams' Story* (four discs, 1964); *Kaw-Liga* (7/65); *Hank Williams* (Metro, 2/65); *Mr. & Mrs. Metro* (2/66); *Movin' On* (8/66); *Legend Lives Anew* (9/66); *Again,* with Hank Williams, Jr. (11/66); *More Hank Williams,* with strings (2/67); *Immortal Hank Williams* (Metro, 6/67); *I Won't Be Home No More* (9/67); *Essential Hank Williams* (9/69); *Life to Legend* (early 1970s); *24 Greatest Hits* (early 1970s). Others include *Unforgettable; Wanderin' Around; First, Last & Always; Hank Williams; Hank Williams, Vol. 2; I Saw the Light; I'm Blue Inside; Let Me Sing a Blue Song;* and *Hank Williams Lives Again.*

At the start of the 1980s, LPs of Hank's still in MGM's current catalogue included *Hank Williams Live at the Grand Ole Opry; Hank Williams Sr.'s Greatest Hits; Home in Heaven; I Saw the Light; 24 of Hank Williams' Greatest Hits; 24 Greatest Hits, Vol. 2;* and *Very Best of Hank Williams.*

In 1961, the newly established Country Music Hall of Fame dedicated the first bronze plaques of selectees. One of those was for Hank Williams, the other two, appropriately, for the original Jimmie Rodgers and Fred Rose. His plaque reads, in part, "Performing artist, songwriter . . . Hank Williams will live on in the memories of millions of Americans. The simple, beautiful melodies and straightforward, plaintive stories in his lyrics of life as he knew it will never die. His songs appealed not only to the country music field, but brought him great acclaim in the 'pop' music world as well."

Indeed, by the time that plaque was mounted, Hank already was legendary and became even more in succeeding years. Anyone who ever came in contact with him (and many who never met him) had favorite stories of his life and times, some true, most apocryphal. His songs flourished, not only in his own recordings, but in countless new versions by major artists. Almost every year, some well-known country, pop, or rock star completed an album of Hank's compositions. He also was blessed with a worthy heir in his namesake, Hank Williams, Jr., who became the premier interpreter of his father's material, though not before waging a fierce struggle to escape the blanket of his father's reputation and achieve success on his own terms.

Many tributes were paid to Hank on radio and TV, including a 1979 tribute to his memory that interspersed performances of some of his songs by various artists, including Hank, Jr., with episodes from his life. Hank, Sr.'s, songs still could provide major hits for others in the 1980s, as shown by Charley Pride's top-10 single "Honky Tonk Blues" and best-selling LP *There's a Little Bit of Hank in Me.*

For the millions of people familiar only with Hank Williams' songs, it's hard to equate the insight, sensitivity, and, in some cases, exuberance with the tormented image of the man, particularly in his last years. Probably the variance is due to the fact that Hank was a very sick man at a time when few people recognized his addiction as a form of illness. In all likelihood, the true essence of the man comes through in his creative legacy.

Far from being diminished in the 1980s and 1990s, Hank's legacy to country music in particular and pop music in general shone even more brightly. His son continued to burnish his memory, making a spectacular use of advanced technology to sing duets with his father in recordings that topped the charts and won new awards. Posthumous honors accrued to Hank, Sr., from the Grammy voters and members of the Country Music Association and Academy of Country Music.

The National Academy of the Recording Arts & Sciences, sponsor of the Grammys in 1983 inducted "Your Cheating Heart" into the NARAS Hall of Fame. In 1987, NARAS voters awarded the Academy Lifetime Achievement Award to Hank, Sr., the citation reading, "A pioneering performer, who proudly sang his songs so honestly and openly, capturing the joys and sorrows and essence of country life, and whose compositions helped create successful careers for various singers who followed him."

The first records issued by the Country Music Foundation, operator of the Country Music Hall of Fame in Nashville, were two long-playing albums of Hank's demonstration recordings including several songs (such as "Pan American") made in Alabama before he made his first tracks for Sterling Records in 1946. The first of those discs, *Just Me & My Guitar,* came out in 1985, followed in 1986 by *The First Recordings.* In 1987, Polydor Records (part of the Mercury organization), which held the rights to all the material Hank recorded for MGM, issued a massive eight-volume vinyl collection containing 169 songs by him, including material recorded under his pseudonym, Luke the Drifter, and duets with Audrey Williams.

Oddly, none of Hank's material was available on compact discs until 1988, when Polydor released *Hank Williams/40 Greatest Hits* on two CDs. In 1991, Polydor issued *The Original Singles Collection . . . Plus* on three CDs containing eighty-four songs. The latter comprised all sixty-one singles released in his lifetime, plus four posthumous releases and nineteen rarities including a 1942 recording Hank made at Griffin's Radio Shop in Montgomery, Alabama. In 1991, the CMF repackaged its two demo collections into a twenty-four song CD titled *Rare Demos: First to Last.*

Hank's life continued to serve as the inspiration, directly or indirectly, for several film projects including the 1982 Canadian-developed movie, *Hank Williams— The Show He Never Gave.* In 1989 he was the subject of a play by Randal Myler and Mark Harelik called *Lost Highway* that premiered at the Mark Taper Forum in Los Angeles during the summer.

The year 1989 also might be cited as the year Hank Williams, Jr., brought his father back to life in a musical sense by recording a series of duets that resulted in a best-selling album. One of the tracks, "There's a Tear in My Beer," prepared as both a single and a video, became a hit in both formats. In the 1989 CMA voting, the Curb/Warner Brothers release was nominated for both Single of the Year and Music Video of the Year and won in the latter category. In the Grammy voting in 1989, the duet won Hank, Sr., his first-ever Grammy as part of the Best Country Vocal Collaboration. Similar acclaim met the release in Academy of Country Music polling where it was selected as finalist in five categories including top song, record and video.

In January 1993, on the fortieth anniversary of his death, the songwriter's lyrics were published in hardcover as *Hank Williams: The Complete Lyrics.* And that summer, still another facet of Hank Williams's work became available to the general public when Mercury Records issued the *Health and Happiness Shows* album, a compilation of eight fifteen-minute radio programs performed in 1949 by Hank and Audrey Williams and the Drifting Cowboys. The programs were sponsored by the patent medicine company Hadacol and used the Sons of the Pioneers' "Happy Roving Cowboys" as theme song.

On one program, Hank preceded a performance of "Lovesick Blues" with the comments, "There's a lot of suffering in this song. . . . We hope you never have to go through nothing like this. . . . We have to go through it quite often, though." Audrey laughed at the words but, in fact, the awkward statement reflected the simple truth of Hank's life.

During 1994, a book titled *Hank Williams: The Biography* won the Ralph J. Gleason Music Book Award. In the summer of 1996, an abridged version called *The Legend of Hank Williams: Audio Book with Music* was released. Country artist Sammy Kershaw handled the audio book reading assignment. Thirteen songs were in the package including "Move It On Over," "Your Cheatin' Heart," "I'm So Lonesome I Could Cry" and "Cold, Cold Heart." Also incorporated were two rare recordings of spoken material by Hank: one a taped apology for missing a 1951 New Year's Eve concert in Baltimore, Maryland, the other a commercial. The apology was for the need for his wife and the Drifting Cowboys to handle the performance due to his inability to be there because of back surgery he had to undergo that month.

WILLIAMS, TEX: *Singer, guitarist, banjoist, harmonica player, bandleader (Western Caravan), actor. Born Ramsey, Fayette County, Illinois, August 23, 1917; died Newhall, California, October 11, 1985.*

Although Nashville remains the unofficial capital of country & western music, there has long been a strong contingent of artists who called the West Coast home.

One of those who played an important role in making that section an important part of the national country & western scene was Tex Williams, whose firsts included posting the first million-selling record for Hollywood-based Capitol Records and serving as first president of the Academy of Country and Western Music.

Although Sol Williams's nickname is Tex, he was born and raised in rural areas of southern Illinois. Considering that he was to become a movie cowboy, his bout with polio when he was only one or two years old was a major challenge. As he told Lee Rector of *Music City News* (August 1975), the illness "left me with a slight limp. I figured that there was no use in even thinking about making pictures."

But music didn't seem that unlikely, particularly since he was born into a family where playing instruments and singing were taken as a natural part of life. "How I got into the business of making music," he told Rector, "was after supper we got the banjos and fiddles and guitars out and played for a couple of hours. We listened to the *Grand Ole Opry* every night on an old Atwater-Kent radio."

Tex's skills were considerable when he was in his teens. At thirteen, he got his own program on station WJBL in Decatur, Illinois. "I was what you might call a one man band. I played a five string banjo and harmonica as I sang sad cowboys songs." When he was fourteen, he moved his act to station WDZ, Tuscola, Illinois, and played at many functions during his high school years.

However, it was more of a hobby than a job until Tex was out of high school. At nineteen, he went west to the state of Washington to join his brother. Once there, he got a job playing with a professional group called the Reno Racketeers. Two years later, he headed south to Los Angeles to seek more rewarding opportunities.

Once there he became acquainted with Tex Ritter and worked with that now legendary figure in a western called *Rollin' Home to Texas*. This was the first of many films in which he appeared from the late 1930s into the 1950s. His companions in some of them were Charles Starrett, Buster Crabbe, and Judy Canova. In the late 1940s and early 1950s, he was under contract to Universal International, taking part in twenty-four features until the inroads of TV caused the phasing out of westerns.

When he wasn't working on movies, Williams had plenty to do as a musician. One of his first efforts in that field was to join the Spade Cooley band as sideman and lead vocalist. At the first recording session with Cooley in 1943, Tex sang the vocal on "Shame on You," which was a major C&W hit of the mid-1940s. He remained with Cooley during the war years, then decided to go on his own in 1946, forming a twelve-piece band, the Western Caravan, and signing a recording contract with Capitol Records. In a short time, he established himself

as one of the label's major artists. His initial release, "The Rose of the Alamo," sold over 250,000 copies. Several releases later, he topped that with his single of the Tex Ritter-Merle Travis song "Smoke, Smoke, Smoke." The song became a tremendous success in both country and pop fields, the first million-seller issued by Capitol. Some of Williams's other well-received singles of the period were "California Polka," "Texas in My Soul," and "Leaf of Love."

In the late 1940s and early 1950s Tex played to capacity audiences in such places as the Aragon Ballroom in Chicago, Orpheum Theater in Los Angeles, and Oriental Theatre in Chicago. During those years, he also turned out a steady string of singles and albums on Capitol, working with such stars as Jo Stafford, Roberta Lee, Dinah Shore, and Tennessee Ernie Ford. In the 1950s, he also had his own local TV show on KRCA in Hollywood.

Williams and his band kept up a hectic schedule during those years. At one point, when he wasn't touring with his group, the band was appearing five nights a week at the Riverside Rancho in the Southern California area or headlining the show at Tex's own club, the Tex Williams Village in Newhall. Throughout the 1950s up to the time the group was disbanded in 1965, it was often featured on major radio and TV programs, including the *Grand Ole Opry, Spike Jones Show, Jo Stafford Show, National Barn Dance, Swingin' Country* (NBC), *Gene Autry's Melody Ranch, The Jimmy Dean Show, Midwestern Hayride,* and *Porter Wagoner Show.* Tex also starred for a time on his own NBC network program, *Riverside Rancho.*

Tex stopped using a regular band, he told Rector, when he sold his club in 1965. "After that, I really had no use for a band. As a matter of fact, I couldn't maintain a band. When you have a band, you have to keep those guys working. It had reached a point where I really didn't care to work that much. You've got to work four or five nights a week to keep those kids up. They've all got families too."

Not that Williams gave up performing himself. He was still doing personal appearances over a decade later. "Now when I go to Las Vegas or Reno or somewhere in Nevada, where you do four or maybe eight weeks, I take a local group that I've worked with."

During the 1960s, Tex recorded for several labels, including Decca and Boone. His Decca albums included the early 1960s *Tex Williams,* issued in December 1962. One of his singles on Decca, "Deck of Cards," was still in the catalogue in the 1970s. He was represented by several LPs on Liberty and Imperial in the mid-1960s, such as *Tex Williams Live at the Mint* (the Mint Club in Las Vegas) (1963) on Liberty and *Voice of Authority* on Imperial (June 1966). In January 1967, Sun Records issued an LP titled *Tex Williams.* In the late 1960s, he recorded material for Kentucky-based Boone Records, including two releases that remained on national charts for thirty weeks. Boone also released the LP *Two Sides of Tex Williams.*

Tex recorded a number of records in Nashville in the early 1970s, but by mid-decade was back in Los Angeles studios working for Granite Records. He was signed to that label by longtime friend Cliffie Stone, who had originally signed him for Capitol in 1946. His debut on Granite was an album issued in 1974 and four singles, including a remake of the Nat "King" Cole hit "Lazy Hazy Days of Summer," issued during 1974–75. Those releases did well enough for Cliffie and Tex to begin work on additional singles and a second album.

Through the 1970s into the early 1980s, Tex continued to be active in the entertainment field, though his performance opportunities were considerably less frequent than in his heyday. He was among the founders of the Academy of Country & Western Music (later the Academy of Country Music) in the mid-1960s and became its first president in 1967. His recording career extended into the 1980s, with one of his last projects being completion of the 1981 release *California Express Featuring Tex Williams.* In 1983, his early years in westerns filmed in the Santa Clarita Valley were remembered with the addition of his name to the Newhall Western Walk of Fame.

Williams gave his last performance on New Year's Eve, December 31, 1984, before he was sidelined by the ravages of cancer. First signs appeared in his bladder, which was removed by doctors at Newhall Community Hospital during the summer of 1985. However, the disease spread to his liver, and he died at the hospital the night of Friday, October 11, of kidney failure.

WILLIS, KELLY: *Singer, songwriter. Born Virginia, c. 1969.*

A surprising number of successful performers are lacking in self-confidence and have to overcome severe self-doubts before making in-person appearances. In many cases, an individual sheds his or her fears by, in effect, becoming another personality on stage. Most make that move before they're past high school age, but Kelly Willis was a late bloomer and required an outside influence to help her make her mark in the entertainment field.

Born and raised in Virginia, she took an interest in country music in her preteen and teen years, when most of her friends doted on rock 'n' roll. As she later told interviewers, she was a shy child who avoided anything, including singing, that would require getting up in front of an audience whether family, friends, or schoolmates. As she grew older, though, she became acquainted with musicians who realized that she did have potential as a vocalist.

In particular, drummer Max Palermo took her under his wing. As she told staffers at the Country Music Association's *Close Up* magazine (October 1991), "He convinced me that I didn't need to be afraid of singing too loud. I wasn't really secure enough to sing the way I sing. When I finally got the nerve to sing in front of his whole band [Radio Ranch], it was like that was what I was going to do. I was so reserved and quiet that it was handicapping me in all areas of my life. Just being able to sing a song was really all I needed."

Before long the once-shy girl was gaining attention for her strong, high-powered vocal stylings, which helped her and her backing group get a contract from RCA Records. Her 1990 debut on the label, *Well-Traveled Love,* was a worthy effort that won enthusiastic reviews, as did her next album, *Bang Bang,* issued during 1991. By then, besides headlining at small clubs, she was opening for country superstar Dwight Yoakam. Despite excellent critical support, her recordings, which included several singles releases, did only moderately well from a sales standpoint. She told *Close Up,* "I try not to live and die by my reviews, but it's really important to me that people think it's a good work, rather than whether or not it's going to be a top-10 single."

When the movie *Thelma and Louise* was released in mid-1991, it featured some material by Kelly. She commented, "I was really lucky. They called and wanted to use the video for 'I Don't Want to Love You But I Do' in a bar scene. Instead they used the song. We were recording *Bang Bang* at the time and thought we'd throw some other things their way. We gave them 'Little Honey,' which we would have put on the album if they didn't want it. We thought it would fit in good with the story after reading the script. I was really proud to be associated with it, because it's such a strong woman's film."

In the early 1990s, Kelly began branching out into songwriting, turning out songs with various collaborators including the audience favorite "Baby Take a Piece of My Heart." By then Kelly called Austin, Texas, home, a city known for its innovative "outlaw" country sound. She acknowledged that setting up residence in Nashville might help her career, but she stressed her love for the Texas capital city. "Being away from the business and the glamour keeps me in line with why I started doing music."

WILLS, BOB: *Fiddler, bandleader (the Texas Playboys). Born Hall County, Texas, March 6, 1905; died Fort Worth, Texas, May 13, 1975. Inducted into Country Music Hall of Fame in 1968.*

Bob Wills' considerable contributions to country music were recognized by his election to the Country Music Hall of Fame in 1968. By then, he had mellowed a good deal or he might have objected to the honor. He certainly didn't take kindly to the gradual elimination or the shortening of the descriptive phrase "country & western" to just "country." He was, after all, the pioneer of "western swing." Beyond that innovation, he never liked being known as a rural artist; his conscious musical taste leaned strongly to jazz and blues. In truth, however, it was his marriage of those elements with the folk music traditions of his native Texas (black, Spanish, and white) that made him a major innovator in mid-twentieth century popular music.

He didn't have to look far for musical inspiration as a child. His father, John Wills, was an excellent country fiddler. During Bob's early years, though, the family was very poor and got by eking a living from agricultural field work and whatever John Wills could earn for his fiddle playing. When the family moved from Bob's natal area in East Texas to a new location 500 miles to the northwest, the then-eight-year-old had to help out by picking cotton along with his father and other family members. The migrant camps the Wills clan stayed in en route (in a journey made in a covered wagon) were shared by other poor workers, black, white, and Mexican. Those weren't the pleasantest surroundings, but in retrospect, they proved important by exposing young Bob to black blues and other ethnic music.

Before Bob was ten, he already was introduced to a musical instrument, but not the fiddle. He started to learn to play the mandolin, encouraged by his father, who wanted Bob to be able to provide backup for John's fiddle playing. Wills later told the story of learning to play the fiddle at ten because of a cousin's difficulties in learning a tune. Bob said he could learn it faster and he proved his point. After that, he borrowed his cousin's fiddle until he had worked up about half a dozen fiddle tunes.

According to Charles R. Townsend, professor of history at West Texas State University, in his late 1970s biography of Wills (*San Antonio Rose,* University of Illinois Press), Bob made his first solo appearance as a fiddler at ten. Townsend writes that the event took place in 1915 near the town of Turkey in west Texas. Bob had gone on ahead to await his father, who was to play for a dance on a local ranch. To silence the increasingly restless crowd when his father didn't show up on time, the boy finally picked up his dad's fiddle and played the tunes he knew. He did so well that even when Wills Sr. arrived, having been busy "frequenting the corn-liquor wagons," Bob continued to hold the spotlight until the dance was over.

As the years went by, Bob continued to increase his repertoire and performing skills, playing with his family part of the time and with various local bands during his teens. Although he sometimes worked at other jobs when he needed spare income, once he reached adulthood he had pretty well committed himself to a musical career.

Although he had always loved music, growing up in the "Bible Belt" he had sometimes had doubts about going down that path. In fact, for a time he considered giving up the entertainment field in favor of entering the ministry. Later on, that part of his life returned to cause misgivings about his chosen occupation. He once mused,

"I see a big crowd dancing. Here I am up here making the music, and they're out there, and some of them might be drinking and all of this and that. I feel like I'm sinning, or causing other people to sin."

Wills had been a professional musician for a long time when he made the moves that were to start him on the route to stardom at the beginning of the 1930s. Renowned steel guitarist Leon McAuliffe recalled, "Bob Wills in about 1931 came to Forth Worth [Texas], just himself and a guitar player. He met a singer named Milton Brown and they went on radio KFJZ as the Wills Fiddle Band. They got their show sponsored by Aladdin Lamp Company. Called themselves the Aladdin Laddies. They were so popular they got themselves sponsored on a network of radio stations called the Texas Quality Network. That was WBAP, Fort Worth, and also WFAA, and KPRC in Houston, and WOI in San Antonio. The company sponsoring them was the Burris Mill and Elevator Company that manufactured Light Crust Flour. That's where the Light Crust Doughboys [see separate entry] came from."

Bob stayed with the Doughboys for a while, then moved on. According to McAuliffe, "Milton and Bob went separate ways. Bob went to Waco and called his band Bob Wills and the Playboys. In the summer of 1933, he moved to Oklahoma City for a short stay and then on to Tulsa in February 1934 where his band became the Texas Playboys. At that time it included Bob; Tommy Duncan; two brothers, June and Kermit Whelan; Bob's brother, Johnny Lee Wills; and a cousin Em Lansford. When they'd been in Waco they had an announcer named Everett Stover who played trumpet. Stover quit his job and went with them to Oklahoma. Also they met a fella who had a department head position with Cities Service Oil in Waco, O. W. Mayo, who quit his job and joined them and became business manager.

"The band went on station KVOO in Tulsa. They all lived in the basement of the building. They'd been in Tulsa, played on KVOO every day for a couple months, then booked a job (at a ballroom) in another Oklahoma town. They had packed houses, so they made money for the first time. They were playing some original tunes. Bob hadn't written 'San Antonio Rose' yet, but there were things like 'She's Killin' Me,' 'Fan It,' and 'Take Me Back to Texas,' which later was called 'Take Me Back to Tulsa.' Also did some Stuart Hamblen tunes: 'My Mary,' 'Brown Eyed Texas Rose.'"

From then on, as Bob's reputation continued to grow in Tulsa and the Southwest, he gave a lot of thought to improving his band. For the almost ten years before World War II brought a close to that phase of the Playboys saga, he steadily expanded and refined the group. In the early years, noted McAuliffe, "Most of the guys were relatives, but not as good musicians as he wanted. Also he wanted to add other instruments like more horns and drums." [Those instruments were anathema to the traditional country & western acts of the period, but Wills always had his own ideas. He once noted, "I've loved horns since I was a little boy."]

"As Bob began to make changes, the first thing he added was the drums. Then his bass player Kermit Whelan left—Kermit had played steel guitar a little bit, but not full time—and he added me in March 1935. Smokey [drummer William Eschol 'Smokey' Dacus] had come on a few months earlier. Meantime he added a saxophone and decided on a piano. He'd had a couple of piano players. Tommy Duncan, when he wasn't singing, played piano some. He wanted a good piano player because he'd been signed by Columbia to record in September. He knew Al Strickland in Fort Worth and sent for him. Joe Ferguson didn't come in until January 1937. Joe won a singing contest in Tulsa so Bob let him do a guest shot on the show and hired him and had two singers. He put Joe to playin' tenor sax and that didn't work out too well. Bob and his cousin Em didn't get along too well, so Em left and Bob taught Joe to play bass.

"Eldon [Shamblin] joined in early 1937. The style of rhythm guitar he played and the chords he knew really was a boost to the band.

"Bob added trombones starting in 1935 with his first record session. He kept going from there with more brass instruments, and with other changes from time to time."

The second half of the 1930s and the early 1940s amounted to a golden era for the Playboys. Once his recordings began to come out on Columbia, Wills began to achieve a national reputation. By the early 1940s, he was becoming one of the best-selling record artists and his music was being broadcast to all parts of the United States on network radio. His cries of "Ah, ha! San Antone" and "Take it away, Leon" became national catchwords.

Bob's star was on the ascendant just before the United States entered World War II. McAuliffe stated, "The band reached a point in 1941–42 when we began to get more contracts. We had 'San Antonio Rose' for a hit. Originally it was an instrumental, but we came back with words in 1941–42. By the early 1940s, we had added four saxes, three trumpets and two trombones. We were playing a lot of pop tunes. By then Bob had kinda phased out most of the original band. While it was good, it was limited in what it could do and he wanted to play all kinds of music."

Through that period, the Playboys recorded regularly for Columbia and were featured in major venues throughout the West and Southwest. It also became part of the movie scene, performing in ten western films. But the war brought things to a halt. Recalled McAuliffe, "My time with Bob ended in December 1942. World War II was here and everybody began to get draft notices or take defense jobs. Bob went into the service too. He didn't stay very long. He shouldn't have gone in

the first place because he was thirty-eight years old when he went in."

In his years with Columbia, Wills recorded the songs that still are the ones primarily associated with his name. Besides "San Antonio Rose," he had such other major hits as "Steel Guitar Rag," "Faded Love" (cowritten with his father), "Texas Playboy Rag," "Mexicali Rose," "Take Me Back to Tulsa," "New Worried Mind," and "Yellow Rose of Texas." His original compositions numbered in the hundreds. In addition to songs like "San Antonio Rose" and "Texas Playboy Rag," his credits include numbers like "Texas Two Step," "Wills Breakdown," "Lone Star Rag," and "Betty's Waltz."

A few more of his relatively successful Columbia singles are "Cotton Eye Joe," "Bob Wills Special," "Oozlin' Daddy Blues," "Ida Red," "Osage Stomp," "Oklahoma Rag," "Bob Wills Boogie," "Ten Tears," and "Steel Guitar Stomp."

While Bob was in the service, he had given what was left of his band and his radio show and dance schedule to his brother, Johnny Lee Wills. After his discharge he went to California to organize a new Playboys group. He remained in California well into the 1950s, changing his base of operations several times, including a stay in Sacramento. The band had some success, but the musical fabric of the country was changing and Wills wasn't able to return to the heights he had enjoyed in the early 1940s.

The group recorded for MGM Records in the 1950s, though never achieving hits of the "San Antonio Rose"—"Steel Guitar Rag" era. Among the singles issued on MGM were "Spanish Fandango," "Little Cowboy Lullaby," "Cotton Patch Blues," and "Blues for Dixie."

In the late 1950s, Wills decided to return to the scene of his early triumphs, his band makeup still changing either through attrition or his search for a better sound. It was during this period that Leon Rausch joined. He noted, "I started with him in 1958. I took Tommy Duncan's brother's place. He left him in California and he picked me up on the way back. I stayed with him until 1961. He went back to horns and back to fiddles. We had eleven people in the band the second I was with them.

"We showed real bad when we came to Tulsa in 1958. Bob couldn't figure out why he couldn't be king of the hill again. But it had been fifteen years and he'd hardly played Oklahoma for that time. But we did sell well in Vegas. We played the Showboat in 1959 for the first time and the band sold real well. So finally the boys from downtown came and gave him a little more money to play the Golden Nugget four weeks in a row. In 1960 we decided we could move there and book in and out of Vegas a month at a time.

"During that time, Tommy Duncan came back and they did an album on Liberty, *Together Again*. Personal problems were a difficulty. The album sold reasonably well, but couldn't recapture the old thing. All in all we did three albums in 1960–61."

The pattern remained essentially the same after Rausch left. Wills kept hoping for a new breakthrough, but it seemed an increasingly lost cause as rock 'n' roll dominated the music picture. Wills's albums continued to be available for most of the 1960s on either Liberty or Harmony labels, though his new output was meager. His Liberty titles included *Living Legend, Mr. Words and Mr. Music,* and *Bob Wills Sings and Plays.* On Harmony, he was represented by titles like *Bob Wills Special* and *Home in San Antone.* The decade was marked, though, by Wills's election to the Country Music Hall of Fame in 1968.

By the start of the 1970s, western swing seemed relegated to the pages of musical history books. Most of the veteran Playboy artists were playing part time, working at other jobs, or were in retirement. But a new generation of musicians began to rediscover the art form as the decade went by, typified by the essentially East Coast, college-spawned band, Asleep at the Wheel. And artists like Merle Haggard continued to pay tribute to Wills in some of their new recordings.

Wills himself was confident that his music had lasting qualities and in 1973 conceived the idea of handpicking a band of some of the best musicians who'd played in the Playboys over the years for a greatest hits collection. The result was the multidisc *For the Last Time* set that came out on United Artists in the mid-1970s. The band members were Smoky Dacus on drums, Al Stricklin on piano (Stricklin wrote a book called *My Years with Bob Wills,* published by Naylor Press in 1976), Leon McAuliffe on steel guitar, Leon Rausch on bass and vocals, Joe Ferguson on bass, Eldon Shamblin on electric guitar, and Keith Coleman and Johnny Gimble on fiddles (both first joined Wills in 1949).

Before the sessions were completed, Wills suffered a stroke and was confined to a rest home in Fort Worth, Texas. After a series of strokes, he died there in May 1975, aware, however, that interest in his music was reviving. After his death, Leon McAuliffe and Leon Rausch took over as coleaders of the re-formed band. With the approval of Bob's widow, Betty, the band began to do a series of stage and TV appearances. It also signed with Capitol for a new series of LPs, starting with *The Late Bob Wills' Original Texas Playboys,* issued in March 1977. (In August 1976, Capitol also released an LP based on tapes of earlier Bob Wills's radio broadcasts, *Bob Wills and His Texas Playboys in Concert.*) In January 1978, a second LP by the McAuliffe-Rausch aggregation appeared, *Live and Kickin'.* In the CMA voting for 1977 Instrumental Group of the Year, the Original Texas Playboys was named the winner.

At the start of the 1980s, besides the LPs just noted, many other Wills LPs were in the active catalogue of several companies. On Columbia was the title *Bob Wills*

Anthology and Remembering. . . . MCA offered *Bob Wills and His Texas Playboys, Bob Wills in Person, Bob Wills Plays the Greatest String Band Hits, King of the Western Swing, Living Legend, The Best of Bob Wills and His Texas Playboys,* and *Time Changes Everything.* Liberty had *Bob Wills Sings and Plays,* Epic provided *Fathers and Sons,* and RCA marketed *Western Swing Along.*

It seemed, as Waylon Jennings said in 1975, "It doesn't matter who's in Austin, Bob Wills is still the King."

As the 1980s turned into the 1990s, Wills's posthumous popularity, if anything, seemed to grow with each passing year. Many established stars who had been active while Wills was still alive and younger performers who recalled listening to his radio shows or recordings in the formative years paid tribute to his influence in interviews or by recording their versions of some of his songs. An album that was a finalist for the Country Music Association 1994 Album of the Year Award was assembled by Wills' disciple Ray Benson, leader of the band Asleep at the Wheel. That Liberty collection, *Asleep at the Wheel Tribute to the Music of Bob Wills & the Texas Playboys,* enlisted the talents of such stars as Chet Atkins, Garth Brooks, Brooks & Dunn, Vince Gill, Johnny Gimble, Lyle Lovett, Merle Haggard, Dolly Parton, Riders in the Sky, Johnny Rodriguez, George Strait and Marty Stuart, plus Texas Playboys' alumni Leon Rausch and Eldon Shamblin.

At the October 1994 Award telecast, Lyle Lovett and Asleep at the Wheel performed the "Blues for Dixie" track from the album. Later that song was nominated for a Grammy Award as was the album. When the winners were announced on the Awards TV show in February 1995, "Blues for Dixie" was named the Best Country Performance by a Duo or Group with Vocal.

More than a few artists over the years recorded covers of songs written by Wills, who was voted into the Nashville Songwriters Association's Songwriter Hall of Fame in 1970. But there was no lack of Wills's own recordings in the 1990s. As was its practice, the Country Music Foundation strove to keep important recordings of Hall of Famers in print. In the mid-1990s, its catalog listed such collections as the *Bob Wills: Country Music Hall of Fame Series* album on MCA and others like *The Essential Bob Wills* on Columbia Country Classics; *Bob Wills/Columbia Historic Edition; Bob Wills/21 Golden Hits* on High Tone; *Bob Wills Greatest Hits* on Curb; and *Bob Wills/24 Greatest Hits* on Sony. Also available in record stores or by mail was Rhino Records' *Bob Wills & His Texas Playboys Anthology 1935–73,* a two-CD or two-cassette set presenting Wills' main recordings on Vocalion, Okeh, Columbia, MGM, Liberty, plus some Tiffany radio transcriptions.

Also offered by the MCA-organized Texas City Music operation, besides the Hall of Fame Series edition, were The Best of Bob Wills, culled from his only

Nashville sessions in the late 1960s, and The King of Western Swing/Bob Wills & His Texas Playboys.

McAuliffe and Rausch quotes based on 1979 interviews with Irwin Stambler.

WISEMAN, MAC: *Singer, guitarist, songwriter, producer, disc jockey. Born Crimora, Virginia, May 23, 1925.*

In concert in the 1980s and 1990s, a big, heavyset man with a graying beard and (usually) smiling, round face, Malcolm B. "Mac" Wiseman looked like the archetypal veteran folk-country music star. It was a proper designation, for Wiseman is an important figure in country music in general and bluegrass in particular in a career that, in the early 1990s, rounded out its fifth decade.

As Mac told Everett Corbin of *Music City News* (October 1973, p. 30), he was born into a family of modest means, but one where "we were always blessed with music, mostly country and mountain style.

"My daddy owned one of the first hand-wound phonographs in our little rural community and owned the first battery powered radio in our area. I recall that people came from several miles distance on Saturday night to listen to the *Opry* and the *WLS Barn Dance,* often staying until the wee hours of the morning or sometimes all night, then having breakfast and going home."

He told Corbin that he started to play the guitar when he was about twelve, "never thinking or dreaming it would lead to anything in the music world."

As Mac grew up, his interest in music intensified and he went on to study at the Shenandoah Conservatory of Music in Dayton, Virginia. After graduation, he began his entertainment industry career as a newscaster and disc jockey for radio station WSVA in Harrisburg, Virginia. While he held this job, he also found time to perform with local country bands. He found performing to his liking and joined Bill Monroe and the Blue Grass Boys for a short time, cutting several of the all-time great bluegrass debuts with Monroe.

In 1947, he was host of the highly popular *Farm and Fun Time* program on WCYB, Bristol, Virginia. He had become friends with two young bluegrass artists in Monroe's Blue Grass Boys band, Earl Scruggs and Lester Flatt. When the latter decided to leave the band in 1948, they moved over to become regular performers on WCYB. With Wiseman, they formed the since legendary Foggy Mountain Boys, with whom Mac worked for several years, including featured spots on station WROL in Knoxville, Tennessee, in 1949 and on the WRVA *Old Dominion Barn Dance* in Richmond, Virginia.

In 1951, Mac decided to work as a solo artist. That year he starred on the *Louisiana Hayride* in Shreveport and was also offered a recording contract with Dot Records. He had a string of hit recordings, such as "Shackles and Chains," "'Tis Sweet to Be Remembered," "Ballad of Davy Crockett," "Love Letters in the Sand," and "Jimmy Brown the Newsboy," which remained on the national charts for thirty-three weeks.

For a time, Mac devoted a lot of his time to working behind the scenes in the record industry. From 1957 to 1961 he served as artists & repertoire executive for Dot Records and he ran the company's country-music department. In 1961, he left Dot for Capitol Records as a performer and producer, though Dot continued to release albums by him after his departure. He returned to Dot in 1966 as a recording artist, but only for a short time, completing material for three albums, one of which featured old standards backed with heavy string orchestral arrangements and one that was folk-oriented. His album credits on Dot after those were completed included *Mac Wiseman* (issued 1/58); *12 Great Hits* (9/60); *Keep on the Sunnyside* (12/60); *Fireball Mail* (3/62); *This is Mac Wiseman* (5/66); *Bluegrass* (10/66); and *Master at Work* (11/66). He also had material on the Hilltop label in the 1960s, such as the LP *Mac Wiseman,* and, on Hamilton Records, *Songs of the Dear Old Days* (11/66).

From the mid-1960s on, he was a frequent performer at the steadily growing number of bluegrass festivals that came into existence in the United States and in other countries. He was a featured artist at one of the first of the large bluegrass events, staged in 1965 by Carlton Haney. The attendance was small, but the festival was the forerunner of the future, when crowds of 100,000 were not unusual.

In 1969, Wiseman signed a new recording contract with RCA, which issued several of his albums in the early 1970s, including one he cut with old friend Lester Flatt. The debut LP on RCA was titled *Johnny's Cash and Charlie's Pride* and came out in June 1970. RCA also released a single of the title track.

During the 1970s, though his career as a recording artist was relatively uneventful, Mac was in the forefront of the decade's bluegrass revival. While he continued to perform traditional bluegrass rather than the progressive formats of new artists, he achieved excellent rapport with college students, who admired his flowing vocal style and superb guitar playing. As he told Corbin in 1973, "A good fifty percent of my work now is on the college circuit, and some ninety to ninety-five percent of the requests are for the older, traditional songs.

"I think it is the unbelievable interest shown by these college students which is making bluegrass music so popular, and I think it is just on the threshold of what it is going to do. I base this on factual information on attendance at college concerts and the big bluegrass festivals."

One thing he also could point to: at least one of his early LPs, the 1956 Dot *'Tis Sweet to Be Remembered,* found strong new sales response in the 1970s, thanks to his concert work.

In April 1973, Wiseman also brought the bluegrass message overseas as the only U.S. bluegrass artist invited to appear at England's prestigious Wembley Festival. Over the next two decades he continued to be a familiar figure on the bluegrass festival, club and concert hall circuit at home and overseas.

Through the years, Mac was often cited as an important member of the bluegrass pantheon in various polls and award competitions. One example was the 4th Annual International Bluegrass Music Association Awards, announced in September 1993, which named Wiseman as one of the Instrumental Performers of the Year. During the 1980s and 1990s he recorded new material on smaller labels while some of his previously recorded work was included in reissue compilations of bluegrass artists such as the 1994 Country Music Foundation Records album, *Great American Train Songs,* which featured Mac, Grandpa Jones, and the late Merle Travis.—A. S.

WOOLEY, SHEB: *Singer, guitarist, songwriter, actor, comedian. Born Erick, Oklahoma, April 10, 1921.*

Diversification doesn't work for everyone, but it paid off for Sheb Wooley. In his long career, he achieved considerable success in a variety of entertainment field occupations, including those of country singer and comedian, songwriter of both pop and country hits, movie and TV actor, and music executive. Carrying diversification a step further, for many years he was as well known under his comic pseudonym of Ben Colder as under his own name.

Sheb, who grew up on a farm in Oklahoma, heard country music from his earliest years. He was a pre-teenager when he got his first musical instrument. He told an interviewer, "I persuaded my dad to swap a shotgun for a guitar. He showed me a few chords." Sheb took it from there and while he was in high school formed a band that played for local dances and was given a twice-a-week radio show on a local station.

After leaving high school, he worked for a time as a pipe welder in an oil field until he decided there had to be a better way to make a living. "One day I threw away my helmet and came to Nashville."

He told Audrey Winters of *Music City News,* "In Nashville [in the mid-1940s] I worked at WLAC radio and would guest frequently on [the WSM show] *Noontime Neighbors* and I cut a couple of records for Bullet Records." He stayed for a year in Music City, then moved to Fort Worth, Texas, where his musical career took a major step forward, starting with a show on station WBAP in 1946.

"I fell into a deal similar to the *Light Crust Doughboys* radio show, only this was a show sponsored by Calumet Baking Powder. The show was on twenty-five major radio stations. I emceed the show, wrote the commercials and created the Chief [the Indian chief the company featured on its product label]. We toured all the southwestern states and the show lasted three years."

At the end of the 1940s, Wooley headed west, settling in Los Angeles, where he sought to combine careers in movies and records. He achieved the latter goal, signing a recording contract with MGM Records, an association that lasted into the 1970s. To bolster his acting hopes he lined up a Hollywood agent and also spent three months as a student at the Jack Koslyn School of Acting. In 1949, he began work in movies and on TV while continuing to add to his experience as a singer and songwriter.

His first big film break occurred when he successfully auditioned for a part in the movie *Rocky Mountain,* a film in which he played the "heavy" while Errol Flynn and Patrice Wymore portrayed the hero and heroine parts. Throughout the 1950s and on into the 1960s, he had plenty of movie work, performing in such films as *Man Without a Star* with Kirk Douglas, *Little Big Horn* with John Ireland, and in such classics as *High Noon* (where Wooley played Ben Miller, the man seeking to gun down hero Gary Cooper) and *Giant.* All in all, Wooley appeared in over forty films.

His face became equally well known to TV viewers for parts in a number of western programs. His most famous role was that of Pete Nolan in the long-running network TV series *Rawhide,* which was on the air regularly for seven years in the late 1950s and early 1960s. Wooley was with the show for five years of its seven-year run.

Meanwhile, many of Sheb's compositions, not a few of them wildly funny, kept on embellishing the repertoires of country & western pop singers. In 1953, his parody of two hit songs, "When Mexican Joe Met Jolie Blon," provided a top-10 hit for Hank Snow. While on location for the movie *Giant,* he wrote a song called "Are You Satisfied" that sold a fair number of records when he recorded it for MGM, but provided a best-selling disc for Rusty Draper. In the late 1950s, Sheb wrote a new novelty song called "Purple People Eater" and this time his single was the blockbuster, eventually selling over 3 million copies in both the pop and country markets.

"After 'Purple People Eater'," he told Winters, "every song I wrote would go pop, such as 'Sweet Chile' and 'Star of Love.' But in 1961 I wrote 'That's My Pa' [a number-one-ranked country hit on MGM in 1962] and this put me back into country music. Also it was my first MGM session in Nashville.

"Jim Vianneau, A&R man for MGM, farmed me out for a while to Jack Clement. This was when I recorded 'Almost Persuaded #2' [a top-10 single in 1966] and 'Son, Don't Go Near the Eskimos.' The pseudonym Ben Colder was originated then. We made an album of this type song and kept doing it regularly afterward."

The first Ben Colder LP came out in October 1963 and was followed later in the 1960s by such albums as

Big Ben Strikes Again (1/67), *Wine, Women & Song* (9/67), *Have One On* (9/69), and, in the early 1970s, by *Best of Ben Colder, Wild Again,* and *Live & Loaded.* Under his own name, Wooley's LP output included *Very Best of Sheb Wooley* (5/65) and *It's a Big Land* (2/66). The Colder imprint appeared on a series of hit singles at the end of the 1960s, such as "Purple People Eater #2" in 1967, "Tie the Tiger Down" in 1968, "The Lincoln's Parked at Margie's Again," and "Carroll County Accident." Wooley closed out the 1960s with a best-selling cover version of "Harper Valley P.T.A.," which went over the 300,000 copy mark.

During the 1960s, the Wooley/Colder act delighted audiences all over the world. Sheb was featured on almost every major country TV program that came along during the decade and also had his own set a number of times on the *Grand Ole Opry.* His contributions were acknowledged by the Country Music Association, which voted him best comedian of 1968. In 1969, he was asked to join the cast of the new CBS network country show, *Hee Haw,* remaining a member of the cast of that highly popular show into the 1970s.

Although his recording activities slowed down in the 1970s, Wooley remained a concert attraction and still was maintaining a busy in-person performing schedule at nightclubs and fairs in the early 1980s. Over the next decade, Sheb's notable activities involved other facets of the entertainment field than music. For instance, in 1986, he was a costar in the basketball movie *Hoosiers,* filmed in Indiana, along with such established film names as Gene Hackman, Barbara Hershey, and Dennis Hopper. He also became a familiar figure to TV viewers from his work in western-based dramas.

His TV appearances earned him accolades from top journalists in Japan in 1991, who named him the number-one celebrity they would most like to feature in future stories about U.S. movie stars. This high regard by writers and the Japanese public was based on his role in the series *Rawhide,* which had been the number-one program in that country for seven years. Sheb didn't completely abandon his live act, appearing as a featured artist in clubs across the U.S. from time to time, including places like New York's Bottom Line in the early 1990s.

WRIGHT, JOHNNY: *Singer, guitarist, fiddler, songwriter. Born Mount Juliet, Tennessee, May 13, 1914.*

One of the royal families of country music, the Johnny Wright clan provided country enthusiasts with many great moments for more than three decades. Johnny's wife, Kitty Wells, won the title "Queen of Country Music Singers" while Johnny starred as an individual performer and as half of the team of Johnnie and Jack.

The musical tradition of the Wright family went back several generations. Johnny's grandfather was a champion old-time fiddler in Tennessee, and his father was a gifted five-string banjoist. Thus he was exposed to many country-music performances during his youth in Mount Juliet and was tutored on several instruments.

He sometimes performed for school events during his public school days. After finishing school, he began to perform in the region. In 1936, he began his first radio engagement on station WSIX, Nashville. One of the members of his show was a talented young singer named Muriel Deason. Johnny decided she needed a new stage name and chose Kitty Wells from a popular song, "I'll Marry Kitty Wells." Two years later, they married.

The WSIX show was the beginning of a long career as a radio performer that included appearances on WCHS, Charleston, West Virginia; WHIS, Bluefield, West Virginia; WNOX, Knoxville; WEAS, Decatur, Georgia; WPTF, Raleigh, North Carolina; and WAPI, Birmingham, Alabama. For most of these engagements, he starred with Jack Anglin, with whom he formed the team of Johnnie and Jack in 1938. With their supporting group, the Tennessee Mountain Boys, they toured widely in the next few years and the period after World War II.

In 1947, the Wrights and Jack Anglin joined the cast of the KWKH *Louisiana Hayride* in Shreveport. In 1951, Johnnie and Jack scored two major national hits, "Crying Heart Blues" and "Poison Love." The team was given the high sign in 1952 from the *Grand Ole Opry* and moved to Nashville. Johnnie and Jack had a big year in 1954 with such top-10 national hits as "Beware of It," "Goodnight, Sweetheart, Goodnight," and "I Get So Lonely." Two other top hits were "South of New Orleans" and "The Moon Is High and So Am I." Many of the audience favorites were songs written by Wright and Anglin. During their twenty-five year association, they wrote more than 100 songs, many of which were bestsellers for other major artists. Their LP output included *Hits of Johnnie and Jack* on RCA Victor (1960) and *Johnnie and Jack* (1963) and *Sincerely* on Camden.

The team came to an end on March 8, 1963, when Jack was killed in a car crash near Madison, Tennessee. Johnny reorganized the Tennessee Mountain Boys, adding Kitty Wells and their daughter Ruby, and Bill Phillips. The new troupe was acclaimed on a cross-country tour, the forerunner of many appearances around the United States during the 1960s. In 1965, Johnny scored another top-10 hit with his recording of "Hello Viet Nam." The song provided the title for a successful LP. Johnny's credits in the 1960s included two other LPs, *Saturday Night* and *Country Music Special.* Besides appearing in all fifty states during this period, the Johnny Wright group also traveled to Canada, the Far East, and many parts of Europe.

Some of the other songs recorded by Wright over the years are "I Get So Lonely," "Sailor Man," "Leave

Our Moon Alone," "Lonely Island Pearl," "That's the Way the Cookie Crumbles," "Sweetie Pie," "Humming Bird," "Baby, It's in the Making," "All the Time," "Pleasure Not a Habit in Mexico," "What Do You Know About Heartaches," "You Can't Divorce My Heart," "Banana Boat Song," "I Want to Be Loved," "I Love You Better Than You Know," "Love, Love, Love," "Live and Let Live," "Keep the Flag Flying," "Nickels, Quarters and Dimes," "Dear John Letter," "I Don't Claim to Be an Angel," "You Can't Get the Country Out of a Boy," and "Three Ways of Knowing."

Johnny also appeared in a movie, *Second Fiddle to a Steel Guitar.* During the 1970s, he and his wife co-hosted their own syndicated *Kitty Wells–Johnny Wright* TV show.

Kitty and Johnny continued their activities into the 1980s, but at a somewhat slower pace. In the mid-1990s, an extensive collection from Wright's Johnnie and Jack years was available from the Country Music Foundation. On the German Bear Family Records label, that comprised six CDs containing 181 tracks originally released in the 1947–1962 period. The set included cuts from their Apollo, RCA, and Decca sessions plus a discography and session notes. Some of Wright's performances with Kitty also were available in the mid-1990s on cassettes and CDs listed in the CMF catalogue. (*See also* Wells, Kitty.)

WYNETTE, TAMMY: *Singer, guitarist, accordionist, pianist, songwriter. Born Itawamba County (near Tupelo), Mississippi, May 5, 1942.*

From a tar-paper shack in Mississippi to worldwide acclaim as top female vocalist in country music (a French critic called her The Edith Piaf of country America) describes the spectacular saga of Tammy Wynette. Overcoming many obstacles, she fought her way to stardom and set new standards for country singers in the 1960s and 1970s.

Tammy's vicissitudes began before she had any understanding of the world around her. She was only eight months old when her father, guitarist William Hollis Pugh, died. Her mother had to go to Birmingham, Alabama, to earn a living in an aircraft factory, leaving Tammy in the care of her grandparents (whom she lived with until she was thirteen). Her early years on her grandparents' farm in Mississippi, she recalled, were much like the life described in the song "Ode to Billy Joe." When she was old enough she picked and chopped cotton and baled hay along with the hired hands. The fact that her grandfather paid her the going pay rate, which served as an allowance, gave her a spirit of independence that served her well in later years.

"Our property crossed the state line," Tammy (original name Virginia Wynette Pugh) recalled, "so I tell people my top half comes from Mississippi and my bottom half from Alabama, and if they're not happy, turn me around."

After World War II, her mother returned to help bring her up. By that time, Tammy had had her first taste of music, singing Sacred Harp religious songs. (In this form of singing, notes were sung instead of words.) She also picked up some country songs as a child. "The first song I ever learned to sing," Tammy told Dixie Dern of *Music City News,* "was 'Sally Let Your Hands Hang Down' and I remember my grandfather, one of the greatest people in the world, used to get such a kick out of hearing me sing that. Then I learned a song that Kitty Wells and her daughter, Ruby, had out called 'How Far Is Heaven.' Mother asked me to learn that. . . . It was so close to home, you see, Daddy being dead."

She recalled singing "Sally" for company as a little girl. "My granddaddy would wink and say 'come here, Nellie Belle (he always called me Nellie Belle), come here and sing "Sally" for me.' Then they would all get such a kick to see me—I was just about five years old—play the piano and sing that song. My grandmother hated it! She didn't think it was a nice song at all."

As she grew older, she became interested in learning to play some of the instruments left her by her father. The collection included guitars, accordion, piano, mandolin, and bass fiddle. Her mother let Tammy take music lessons, but tried to persuade her daughter to use music only as a hobby. The lessons went on for five years, ending before Tammy was in her teens.

Wynette's youthful desire to become a performer was strong. In her teens, she loved to entertain. As she told Deen, "I remember in high school whenever the bell would ring for a fifteen- or twenty-minute recess . . . I might go for a Coke or doughnut, but then I always headed to the auditorium and the piano. That is where I spent all my extra time in school. A whole gang would come in and sit around and play and sing and that was every day, every single day I was in school. Every time there was a chapel program they always called me to round up people to do it. They knew that was my interest."

However, just before finishing high school she traded her music dreams for marriage, and settled in Tupelo, Mississippi, with her husband. After a few months, they returned to the rural environment, taking up residence near her grandparents' home, about fifty miles from Tupelo. After her first daughter was born, Tammy learned hairdressing. She worked for a time in a beauty shop in Tupelo and then switched to a job as a chiropractor's receptionist.

Her working career was interrupted by new additions to her family. She had a second daughter and was carrying a third when her marriage broke up.

Wynette moved to Birmingham, Alabama, and worked in a beauty shop until her next child was born. The baby girl was born prematurely and developed spinal meningitis soon after Tammy brought her home. She nursed the child, helped by her relations, until the baby was sufficiently on the way back to recovery for her to go back to work to support her family and also attempt to pay off over $6,000 in bills incurred during her baby's illness. She needed some way of augmenting her income. In the back of her mind she always had thought about doing something with her musical skills and now necessity forced her to. She persisted in seeking work as an entertainer and finally managed to get a performing role on the *Country Boy Eddie Show* on WBRC-TV in Birmingham.

She also sang in clubs in several southern cities, including Memphis, and began writing songs with Fred Lehner of station WYAM in Birmingham. Doors began to open for her in the music field, and after she took part in a Porter Wagoner package show and he asked her to perform with the show in several local towns, she felt confident that she could earn a full-time living as an entertainer.

Her prime need was a recording contract, and she began to make the rounds of recording companies. Wynette traveled to Nashville and auditioned first for United Artists, then for Hickory and Kapp. Each visit resulted in a little more interest, but no contract. Her Kapp reception was so good she returned to Birmingham expecting a call or letter any day. But several months went by and nothing happened. She went up to Nashville again, partly to try other companies and partly to try to place some songs with Epic that a friend of hers had written with one of the label's major artists in mind.

Not much happened with the songs, but Epic executives were impressed with her potential, and the long-sought recording contract finally materialized. Soon after signing with Epic in 1966, Wynette recorded a single of Johnny Paycheck's composition "Apartment #9." The record became a big hit in 1967 and, when she followed with an even greater number, the top-10 hit, "Your Good Girl's Gonna Go Bad," her position as one of the most promising newcomers was secure. Adding weight to that was the choice of another 1967 hit, "I Don't Wanna Play House," by members of the National Academy of the Recording Arts & Sciences as the Best C&W Solo Vocal Performance, Female, of 1967. She had still another top-10 hit in 1967 in a duet with David Houston, "Elusive Dreams."

Proving that 1967 was no one-time phenomenon, Tammy turned out equally impressive recordings during the closing years of the 1960s, including such country classics as "D-I-V-O-R-C-E" and "Take Me to Your World" in 1968 and "Stand By Your Man," a number-one hit in 1969. The last-named song earned her a second Grammy for Best Country Vocal Performance, Female, of 1969. By late 1969, she had enough legitimate successes for Epic to issue her *Greatest Hits, Volume 1* LP, which did so well with country fans that it was certified gold by the Recording Industry Association of America, the first album by a female country vocalist to do that.

During the 1960s, Tammy became one of the most popular concert artists on the country-music circuit, playing before enthusiastic crowds throughout the United States. She also was a guest on major network TV programs and, in 1969, signed on as a regular cast member of the *Grand Ole Opry,* an affiliation still in effect at the start of the 1980s.

The 1970s proved to be as rewarding for Wynette in terms of record success as the late 1960s had been. Besides turning out her usual quota of solo hit singles, she teamed up with George Jones in the early 1970s for one of the top-ranked duets in the country field. The two became husband and wife in the early 1970s, a highly publicized merger that later turned into a highly publicized marital break-up. Among the hit singles Tammy achieved by herself or with George the first half of the 1970s were "The Wonders You Perform" in 1970; "The Cere-money" (with Jones) and "My Man" in 1972; "Another Lonely Song" (cowritten with Billy Sherrill and N. Wilson) in 1974; and "I Still Believe in Fairy Tales" in 1975. Some of her other hit songs of the late 1960s and early 1970s were "I'll See Him Through," "Run, Woman, Run," "We Sure Can Love Each Other," "Good Lovin'," and "Bedtime Story."

In the late 1960s and early 1970s, many honors and awards came Tammy's way. She was almost always one of the three finalists in the *Music City News* poll for Top Female Vocalist and came in first several times. She also regularly made the top five finalists in Country Music Association voting for Female Vocalist of the Year and three times won the award.

Her name continued to show up regularly on the top rungs of national country charts in the second half of the 1970s. Among her singles bestsellers were "'Til I Can Make It on My Own" (early 1976), "Golden Ring" (number one in August 1976), "You and Me" (fall 1976), "Southern California" (with George Jones, summer 1977), "One of a Kind" (late 1977), and "Womanhood" (fall 1978).

Besides her achievements as a singles artist, Wynette also had an unusually good track record as an album artist. Most of her LPs made the country charts, with many of them entering the top 10. Her debut on Epic, *Tammy Wynette,* came out in June 1967. This was followed by such late 1960s albums as *Your Good Girl's Gonna Go Bad, D-I-V-O-R-C-E, Inspiration,* and the first volume of her *Greatest Hits.* At year end, she had three LPs on the country lists, *The World of Tammy Wynette, Tammy's Touch,* and *Greatest Hits.* In early 1970, she made the charts with the albums *First Songs of the First Lady* and *Ways to Love a Man* (issued 3/70). In 1971, her albums included *We Sure Can Love Each Other* (7/71) and *Greatest Hits, Volume 2* (10/71). Also issued during 1971 was a duet album with George Jones, *We Go Together,* which made upper-chart levels in early 1972. Also a chart hit in the spring of 1972 was

Tammy's *Bedtime Story.* In the fall, she and George teamed up again for the top-10 album *Me and the First Lady.* Among Tammy's other chart-making LPs of the 1970s were *Another Lonely Song* (top 10, May 1974), *We're Gonna Hold On* (with George Jones, top 20, May 1974), *Woman to Woman* (late 1974–early 1975), *Til I Can Make It on My Own* (number three in May 1976), *Golden Ring* (with George Jones, top 10, fall 1976), *Let's Get Together* (top 20, early 1977), *Womanhood* (top 20, August 1978), and *Tammy Wynette's Greatest Hits, Volume IV* (top 10, late 1978).

During the 1970s, Wynette's stage appearances took her to many overseas nations in addition to her concerts all over the United States and Canada. Her popularity in Europe was particularly high; in 1976 she was named Number One Female Vocalist of Great Britain in an English poll. By the end of the 1970s, worldwide sales of her recordings approached the 20 million mark, and her total of number-one-ranked singles and albums was thirty-five.

On July 6, 1978, Tammy married longtime friend George Richey. It was her fifth marriage and one that finally seemed to last. The two still were married in the mid-1990s, in a relationship where Richey, a record producer and songwriter, had an important impact on her career while also helping her spring back from a variety of seizures, and occasionally life-threatening health problems.

In the fall of 1979, her autobiography (as told to Joan Dew), *Stand by Your Man,* was published by Simon and Schuster. During the year, her 1978 albums *Womanhood* and *Greatest Hits, Volume IV* were on the charts for long periods. Her 1979 release, *Just Tammy,* also made the lists. In 1980, she teamed up with George Jones once more. The pain of their earlier relationship, she asserted, had faded into the background. She said, "George and I never lost respect for each other. Our marriage didn't work, but that was the only thing that didn't work for us. We've always worked well professionally." This seemed borne out by the success of their 1980 duet single, "Two Story House," that rose to number two on the charts in May 1980. A few months later, Tammy had a hit solo single with "He Was There (When I Needed You)." In the fall, Tammy and George had the single "A Pair of Old Sneakers" on the charts for a number of months. In the spring of 1981, she had a new album, *You Brought Me Back,* from which the single hits "Cowboys Don't Shoot Straight (Like They Used To)" was culled.

Starting in 1981, Richey took over record production chores from Sherrill, working with Tammy on three new albums. These were *Soft Touch,* released in May 1982; *Good Love and Heartbreak,* issued in November 1982; and *Even the Strong Get Lonely,* issued in June 1983. During 1982 Tammy had the top-10 single "Another Chance." While many of her albums did quite

well in the 1980s and early 1990s, that proved to be her last country top-10 single as of the mid-1990s.

Meanwhile, Tammy continued to battle daunting illnesses, which involved, among other things, several abdominal operations. By the mid-1980s, surgical treatment not only hadn't achieved the desired cure, but also left her with a dependency on painkilling drugs. The problems sometimes caused her to cancel or fail to show up at concerts. She commented, "The pain was just unreal. It was always either take a pain pill and go perform or call the producer and hear him say, 'I'm sorry, this is the second time you've been sick. I'll have to sue because I can't refund these tickets.' I was trying to be macho woman. I was trying to be supergirl, and I couldn't."

In November 1986, she entered a four-week program at the Betty Ford Center in California to try to overcome her addiction. The third week, however, she became desperately ill and had to be hospitalized, finally becoming a patient of eleven weeks at the Mayo Clinic in Minnesota. There she underwent some fifteen hours of surgery over that period, including removal of part of her stomach. That seemed at last to provide physical relief and the counseling of the Betty Ford Center helped her solve some of her addictive problems.

In 1987 she completed an excellent new album, *Higher Ground,* in which she performed a series of duets with such stars as Rodney Crowell, the O'Kanes, Vern Gosdin, and Emmylou Harris. During 1988 and 1989 she hosted and starred in the General Motors' Truck Division's Great American Music Tour, organized by husband Richey. Joining her on that concert series were the rising new stars Randy Travis and the Judds. During the 1989 tour segment, Tammy had a new album in the stores, her fifty-first on Epic, *Next to You.* The producer was the veteran Norro Wilson and the tracks included a song cowritten by Tammy and Richey, "When a Girl Becomes a Wife." Randy Travis also included a duet with Tammy, "We're Strangers Again," on his best-selling *Heroes and Friends* album.

Tammy entered the 1990s with her career in good shape, and her momentum continued with various innovative projects to mid-decade. In 1991 her album *Best Loved Hits* won critical acclaim not only in the U.S., but also in many other nations. During the year she was presented with the Living Legend Award at the TNN/ *Music City News* Country Music Awards program. In late 1991, she went off on a completely new tangent by agreeing to work with Bill Drummond and Jimmy Cazuty of the British rap/funk dance group KLF on a new single and video. The audio version was recorded in Nashville and she then flew to London to make the video.

The song, she said, "Doesn't make a whole lot of sense to me. . . . It was so far from what I normally do."

But the project was challenging and a lot of fun. She told David Zimmerman of *USA Today* that in the video she stood on top of a huge platform dressed in a skintight "turquoise mermaid outfit with a bustier like Madonna wears. And I had this crown on. I don't know what the meaning of that was.

"These guys are crazy," she said of her KLF friends. In the video, Drummond and Cazuty wore "robes and hoods with rhinoceros tusks" and when she appeared with them on Britain's *Tops of the Pops* TV program "they were dressed as 12-foot ice-cream cones." The single and video, released in January 1992, proved a huge international hit. The releases reached number one in eighteen countries (including five weeks in Israel) and also did well on pop charts in the U.S.

During 1992, Tammy started work on a new album project with Dolly Parton and Loretta Lynn while Epic prepared a major retrospective honoring her twenty-five years on the label. The last-named project resulted in a boxed set of three CDs or three cassettes, called *Tears of Fire,* containing sixty-seven songs, including all her classic recordings. In the midst of the 1992 presidential campaign, though, a flap arose when Hillary Clinton, whose husband was running for president, was quoted as saying, "I'm not sitting here, some little woman standing by her man like Tammy Wynette."

Wynette bristled, demanded an apology, and got it. She told Michael Bane of *Country Music* magazine, "And, you know, I had just gotten my two millionth play award for 'Stand By Your Man.' It's been played on the radio two million times. I was really feeling proud of it and thinking this song had really been good to me, and she comes up with a statement like that. It just hurt my feelings is all. I'll get over it." In fact, after Hillary's apology, the two got together and pledged future friendship.

As for the Parton/Lynn/Wynette collaboration, Tammy noted, "Dolly came by and got me one day and took me to her house. She said, 'We've got to do this before we get too damn old to sing.'" Released by Columbia in 1993, *Honky Tonk Angels* proved one of the best country collections of the year. It found favor with record buyers, eventually exceeding platinum sales levels, and was also nominated for the Country Music Association Album of the Year Award. On the awards telecast in October 1993, the three country superstars sang "Silver Threads and Golden Needles" from the album.

Everything seemed coming up roses for Tammy when once more health problems intervened. On December 28, 1993, she was rushed to a Nashville hospital in critical condition. The illness was diagnosed as a bile-duct infection caused by scar tissue from a previous operation. She was placed on a respirator while physicians and friends feared for her life. But once more she pulled through. Just after New Year's Eve she issued a statement, "I don't remember a lot, but I feel wonderful to be alive and want to thank everyone for their prayers. I just thank God that I'm alive."

In succeeding months she regained strength and completed still another album, *Without Walls,* issued in the fall of 1994. Joining her on this collection were a diverse group of artists ranging from Wynonna and Lyle Lovett from country ranks to pop-rock stars Sting and Elton John. After that, she got together with George Jones to work on their first joint album in fifteen years. That recording, called *One,* was issued by MCA in the summer of 1995 and proved again what consummate artists these once romantically linked individuals were. It deservedly received careful consideration as one of the year's best in many award competitions. (In February 1995, Epic/Legacy issued the long out of print debut album of Tammy's, *Your Good Girl's Gonna Go Bad,* on CD).

At the MCA showcase at Fan Fair 1995 in Nashville, Jones and Wynette appeared on stage together for the first time in 17 years. Shortly after, on June 9, 1995, at Tupelo, Mississippi, they performed in the first of a series of 30 concerts that took them to a number of U.S. cities as well as venues in the UK, Ireland and Switzerland. In the Country Music Association 1996 awards voting, Jones and Wynette were nominated in the Vocal Event of the Year category for *One.*

WYNONNA: *Singer, guitarist. Born Ashland, Kentucky, May 31, 1964.*

Breaking up always is hard to do, but after an eight-year success saga with mother Naomi as the Judds (see separate entry) that scaled the heights in country and, to some extent, pop music, realizing that an onstage relationship going back almost a decade was coming to an end must have been a particularly somber time for Wynonna Judd. Together the Judds had accumulated twenty-three top-10 hits, eight Country Music Association awards, four Grammys, and over 11 million copies in worldwide album sales; now, in 1991, Wynonna felt she had to practically reinvent herself as a solo artist. Despite nagging insecurities and doubts, she proceeded to do just that, dropping her last name Madonna-style and turning out a series of recordings that marked her as a potentially seminal force in redirecting the future of country.

Some of Wynonna's fears may have stemmed from the always-traumatic effects of a divorce in the family. Born Christine Claire Ciminella in Ashland, Kentucky, she moved to California at four; four years later, her father and mother went separate ways. As of the 1990s, Michael Ciminella lived in Florida, where he earned his living making videos of thoroughbred horses.

When Wynonna was ten she, her mother, and sister Ashley returned to Ashland, where she remained through elementary and some years in high school before the family moved again to Franklin, Tennessee. The sometimes lonely, introverted girl began learning the guitar before she was a teenager, and focused on a variety of performers as touchstones. It was after coming back to Kentucky, she said, "when I discovered music. My influences—I thank God for this now—were records from the old record shops, the used bins. Bluegrass was my first influence, and the mountain harmonies, the mountain soul of Hazel and Alice, the harmonies of the family from the Delmore Brothers, the Stanley Brothers and the Louvin Brothers.

"And then I started listening to Bonnie Raitt. She's been one of the biggest influences of my vocal style. Instead of top 40 I was listening to big bands, and I was listening to the stuff that my grandparents were going dancing to on the weekends. I was pretty eclectic."

As she entered her high school years, music became almost all-encompassing for Wynonna. She recalled, "I didn't have a TV, telephone or Nintendo to occupy my time, so I had to play guitar to keep busy." Naomi didn't discourage her daughter's interest in music, but she became increasingly disturbed about Wynonna's retreat from the world at large. "I wanted to be in music more than anything in the whole world," Wynonna stated later. "Instead of worrying about me going out and drinking and driving, mom was worried about me [not] getting out of the house and getting a real job."

She told *People* magazine ("Farewell Judds, Hello Wynonna," July 13, 1992), "She'd try to cow-prod me to get out and do things, and I rebelled against that. It was frustrating for her to work double shifts, come home and see me doing nothing but music."

On two occasions, the two temporarily split. Once, after an argument, Wynonna went off and stayed with a friend in Franklin. Another time her mother sent her to stay for a while with her father. Tensions remained until Wynonna managed to graduate from high school, but then the two found rapport in singing together and the new stage act that evolved brought them into the country spotlight in the early 1980s. In deciding on stage names, Wynonna settled on one of the places named in the pop hit "Route 66."

Before the onset of hepatitis that forced her mother to abandon the hectic demands of touring and recording, Wynonna had developed a womblike view of life, in which her mother was the organizer and shield against the onslaught of public popularity. Thrust on her own after the extensive series of "farewell" concerts that ended in December 1991, she pondered whether she could go through with a solo concert series after her first solo album, *Wynonna,* came out on Curb/MCA in the spring of 1992. She told *People,* "I go between one minute feeling like I can conquer the world and the next wanting to call my mom and have her come and get me."

She made her solo debut performing the first single from her new collection, "She Is Her Only Need," on the American Music Awards TV program. Public reaction to that song should have given her instant reassurance. It soared to number one on all major charts, peaking at that position in *Radio & Records,* for instance, the week of March 27, 1992. Similar success followed for her two other 1992 single releases, "I Saw the Light," number one in *R&R* the week of June 26, and "No One Else On Earth," number one the week of October 30. The album also became a blockbuster, making the *Billboard* list soon after release and, after peaking at number one, staying in the top 10 for months. By fall it had passed platinum levels and it went on to go past the three million mark, the first multiplatinum album by a female country singer in decades. The album did well as a crossover hit as well, peaking at number four in the *Billboard* Hot 200 during 1992.

It was an excellent collection, with striking stylistic diversity and moving delivery by the singer. It won almost universal praise across a spectrum from the major media to the trade press. David McGee wrote in *Rolling Stone,* "Its cohesiveness—and the depth of its themes—marks it as a key document in the ongoing redefinition of country music's mainstream, as surely as does the confluence of blues, rock & roll, country and pop styles that crop up in various combinations throughout. It's easily the most important release by a country artist so far this decade."

James Hunter of the *New York Times* concurred ("Wynonna Judd Stands Alone," May 24, 1992). "*Wynonna* is a faultless '90s country album. More than any record since Randy Travis and Dwight Yoakam steered country music in a new direction in 1986, it demonstrates that a country performer can explore vibrant pop, deep gospel and straightforward rock and still make sense even to country traditionalists."

There were a few naysayers. The *Los Angeles Times* reviewer felt her song choices reflected timidity to go outside the boundaries set by most 1980–1990s albums, but the paper gave a much more positive stamp of approval to her follow-up album, *Tell Me Why,* released in April 1993.

Before that came out, though, Wynonna had managed to get rid of most of the butterflies both from a recording and concert standpoint. (By the time the second album came out, she had a fourth number-one single from *Wynonna,* "My Strongest Weakness," at the top of the *R&R* list the week of February 12, 1993.) She commented, "With the first album I felt devastated. I had to get up in the morning and go, 'Wynonna, I am, I can, I will.' I had to talk to myself, have a lot of meetings with myself. With this album I felt energized and excited. The first album was—I'm moving from home, but I'm still going back for meals. With this album—I've got my own apartment, it's all furnished and I'm staying up real late, and I'm drinking out of the milk carton."

The second album was arguably on a par with the first one, perhaps even a bit more innovative in some

Sawyer Brown

Earl Scruggs Revue

The mid-1960s version of the Sons of the Pioneers, including *(front, left to right)* Pat Brady, Lloyd Perryman, Ray Lanham; *(back, left to right)* Rusty Richards and Dale Warren

Bluegrass great Ralph Stanley at McCabe's Guitar Shop in Santa Monica, California, February 1992

This group photo of a Los Angeles area–based country group in 1938 shows later Country Music Hall of Famer Cliffie Stone (*far right, with standup bass*) standing near his father, bearded Herman the Hermit

The Stoneman Family (mid-1960s) with the late Ernest V. "Pop" Stoneman seated center with his autoharp. After his passing, the family continued to keep the group's traditions alive

After founder Bob Wills's death in 1975, Leon McAuliffe *(second from left, between* Al Stricklin *and* Smoke Dacus) and Leon Rausch *(standing, with arm on shoulder of producer* Tommy Allsup) assembled a group of Texas Playboys veterans that had recording and concert success in the late 1970s. Other members shown are *(front)* Bob Kiser, Johnny Gimble, Jack Stidham, and *(rear)* Keith Coleman

George Strait

Hank Thompson

Hank Thompson *(standing, center)* and his Brazos Valley Boys in the mid-1960s

Mel Tillis

Aaron Tippin

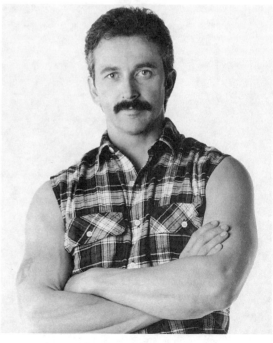

Merle Travis

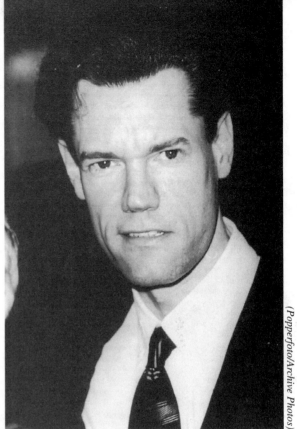

Randy Travis

Travis Tritt

Ernest Tubb

Loretta Lynn and Conway Twitty

Shania Twain

A young Dolly Parton first attracted attention from country music fans in the mid-1960s when she performed with Porter Wagoner and his band

Conway Twitty

Jerry Jeff Walker

(Elektra/Scott Newton)

Doc Watson

(Vanguard/Dan Seeger/Michael Ochs Archives)

Hank Williams

Hank Williams, Jr.

(©/TM 1997 Estate of Hank Williams, Sr., c/o CMG Worldwide, Inc. www.cmgww.com)

Bob Wills

Tammy Wynette and George Jones

Dwight Yoakam

Tammy Wynette

numbers. It also peaked at number one in *Billboard,* reaching that pinnacle during 1993 and staying on the lists through 1994, picking up an R.I.A.A. platinum-record award along the way. It also made the pop charts. Still, it scored a little less heavily with record buyers. During 1993, the title track peaked at number two in *R&R* the week of May 21. The next single, "Only Love," gave her a fifth number-one hit, peaking at that spot in *R&R* the week of September 24, 1993. The third single, "Is It Over Yet," was her first to miss the top 10 in *R&R,* peaking at number fifteen the week of November 26, 1993, but it rose to top 10 on other lists. Two more chart hits were drawn from the album in 1994, "Girls With Guitars" and "Rock Bottom."

Meanwhile, Wynonna was continuing to demonstrate growing skills as an in-person solo performer. During 1993 she teamed with Clint Black in the "Black and Wy" (Wy is her nickname among friends) show, in which she impressed many veteran critics with her capabilities. Rick Mitchell of the *Houston Chronicle* noted after a November date at a major Houston venue that her albums "only hint at the power of Wynonna's live performances. Backed by three harmony singers and a three-piece horn section, she brought a bonafide funkiness to tunes such as 'Let's Make a Baby King' and 'Mama He's Crazy.'"

In her show she combined Memphis soul, blues-tinged numbers, and foot tapping honky-tonk. Mitchell observed, "She has the voice to sing it all, but can she break down the musical walls without losing the country core of her audience?"

Wynonna indicated that she wasn't planning to change her approach. "If I hear a song that affects me I do it. To me there's two kinds, good and bad.

"In my personal life I have friends that are diverse. I have friends that are responsible and have real jobs. I have real creative, strange friends, and I have friends who are farmers and don't know anything about a Grammy Award. I try to do everything I can to represent those people and what they have to do with my life. I find myself in a lot of different situations in life, and maybe I'm speaking out about those situations through my music."

One unexpected situation she found herself in during 1994 was becoming pregnant. She said she had no plans to marry the man she was living with at that time, but did intend to have the child. In one of life's strange twists, she had once said that she'd never expected her mother to retire—that if anything broke them up, it would be Wynonna's own desire to leave the road and have children. Of course, she had no plans of leaving the entertainment field permanently, but starting a family did make her put it aside for a while. The child, a son named Elijah, was born in 1995. By then she and the boy's father, Arch Kelley III, had decided to marry and on June 21, 1996, at a Nashville hospital they added a girl, named Patricia Grace, to their family.

By then Wynonna had completed the first phase of a planned two year series of concerts in support of her new MGM/Curb album, the first completed in almost three years, *Revelations.* The single "To Be Loved By You" preceded the album and earned a number one ranking on the charts in the spring of 1996. The album, released in March, peaked at number two in *Billboard* and already was certified platinum by May.

Y

YEARWOOD, TRISHA: *Singer, guitarist, songwriter. Born Monticello, Georgia, September 19, 1964.*

Like Wynonna, the performer she was most often compared with in the 1990s (some critics saw them vying for the unofficial title of Queen of Country Music), Trisha Yearwood came from a middle-class rather than a blue-collar background. But with her fine vocal ability and an insight into the roots of country that went back to childhood years, she could deliver with authority a sophisticated ballad at one moment and a sawdust-tinged honky-tonk rouser the next.

Kathy Mattea told an interviewer from *The Journal of Country Music* ("Trisha Yearwood Gets Serious," Paul Kingsbury, Vol. 15, No. 1), "I remember the first time I heard Trisha on a demo. She just broke my heart. I didn't even care about the song. It was like, 'Who is this, tell me who this is!' It also doesn't surprise me in the least. She just sings. She's just got heart. Her voice is just amazing. There's only been a handful of women that I felt that way about since I moved to town. One was her, one was Wynonna, and Mary-Chapin Carpenter."

Trisha was born and raised in the small town of Monticello in North Georgia. Both parents had professional occupations, though she stressed, "I'm basically a country girl. My mom and dad have real jobs, but we lived on a farm." In her father's case, he served as city manager of Monticello after working as a banking executive for twenty-five years. Her mother was a school teacher.

Her earliest influence she recalled, was Elvis Presley, going back to when she was five or six and a neighbor gave her some used Elvis albums. She listened to them constantly, usually singing along. At the time, she recalled, "I was going to marry Elvis."

Besides that, she told Kingsbury, "my parents always had the radio on to country music, so I was exposed immediately to George Jones and Tammy Wynette and Hank Williams. Then when I was a young teenager, and old enough to start forming my own tastes and buying my own records, I got into kind of folky, country-rock: Carole King and Linda Ronstadt (who was probably my biggest musical influence), James

Taylor—stuff that's now played on country radio. Real lyric oriented kind of stuff, considered rock and roll at the time, but lyric oriented."

Trisha started college in Georgia, but in 1985 she moved to Nashville to complete her studies at Belmont College. Her degree program was in music business and her goal was to fashion some kind of career in the country field. It took her a little while to get used to big city life, though. "I wasn't used to going to a gas station and not have somebody ask me about my grades or how my mom and dad were. I wasn't used to going into the grocery store and not having to plan on staying to catch up with everybody and tell them how you were doing. Music Row's kind of like a small town, though. It's taken a while, but I think I've gotten to know everybody."

Before receiving her college degree, she gained entry into the music industry by getting an intern position at MTM Records. "I worked in publicity. It should have been enough to send me home, to realize how a label really works. Then when I graduated I worked the front desk answering the telephones. I met a lot of people and it really lit a fire under me to get out there and get session work."

In the late 1980s she found increasing work as a demo artist and also began to gain assignments to do background vocals in recording sessions. She became friends with other demo singers awaiting the chance to be discovered. One of them was Garth Brooks, who was impressed by her vocal ability; when he began to reach the first rungs of stardom, he sought her out to contribute to one of his recordings. She was given the opportunity to provide backing vocals on his No Fences album.

Indirectly this association cleared the way for her to move from demo to solo artist. Brooks's record producer' introduced her to another producer, Garth Fundis, who took her under his wing and helped set up a showcase for record company executives that led to a record deal from MCA that she signed in January 1991. By the end of that year she had shot from anonymity to embryonic stardom with a series of spectacular record and video successes. The debut single, "She's in Love with the Boy," issued in advance of the album, reached number one in Billboard and other major charts, staying atop the Billboard list two weeks in a row. The album, Trisha Yearwood, quickly caught the public fancy (aided by strong reviews), peaking at number two in Billboard in August 1991 and going on to gain a platinum-record award from the R.I.A.A. before the end of 1992. She quickly scored two more top-10 singles hits with "That's What I Like About You" and "Like We Never Had a Broken Heart," the latter a duet with Garth Brooks.

During 1991, she added to her following by opening for Brooks on a major concert tour. His support of her career gave rise to rumors in the tabloids about a possi-

bly closer relationship, something she vehemently denied. She told Dennis Hunt of the Los Angeles Times ("Yearwood: This Success Belongs to Her," February 8, 1992), "I hear movie stars and performers screaming about the tabloids all the time. But until they zero in on your life and involve you in some scandal, you don't really know how horrible it feels.

"It's no fun to have to defend yourself against nasty rumors or hear people saying that you rode somebody's coattails to get where you are. OK, I probably wouldn't have made it as quickly without Garth, but I would have made it somehow. I do have talent."

Yearwood continued to improve her status in 1992 with still more chart hits. The week of June 12, the single "The Woman Before Me," reached number one in Radio & Records. In the fall she scored with "The Wrong Side of Memphis," the initial single release from her next album, number four in R&R the week of October 2. That second MCA album, Hearts in Armor, was issued in August and proved as good or better than her debut collection. It was in the Billboard Top 20 in September and had surpassed R.I.A.A. platinum levels by May 1993. At year-end, the single "Walkaway Joe" from the album was rising on the charts, reaching Billboard's Top 4 in early January of 1993 and peaking at number two in R&R the week of January 6, 1993. Her 1992 work included recording a duet with Raul Malo of the Mavericks of the old Elvis song, "Devil in Disguise," for the soundtrack of the movie Honeymoon in Vegas. When the results of Academy of Country Music members' voting were announced on the April 29, 1992, telecast, Yearwood was named Top New Female Vocalist.

In 1993, Trisha had two more hits from her second album, "You Say You Will," number ten in R&R the week of April 23, and "Down on My Knees," number fourteen in R&R the week of August 6. Late in the year her third album, The Song Remembers When, was released preceded by a single of the title track. The single peaked at number seven in R&R the week of November 26 and the album rose to number seven in Billboard in mid-December, going on to earn a gold-record certification from the R.I.A.A. in the spring of 1994.

She began 1994 with another single moving up the charts, "Better Your Heart Than Mine," and later scored a still bigger success with the single "XXX's and OOO's (An American Girl)," which rose to number one in Billboard the week of September 10, staying in that position through September 17. The song had originally been written by Matraca Berg and Alice Randall for a hoped-for TV series that never materialized. Originally it had been written for Wynonna, but when she fell ill the writing and production team turned to Yearwood.

Before doing that project, Trisha completed work on a Christmas album, The Sweetest Gift, in May for release during the latter months of the year.

It was a busy year for Trisha in other ways, as she toured with other country and R&B stars who worked on the MCA album project *Rhythm, Country & Blues.* Her contribution to the album, which hit number one in *Billboard* during 1994 and went past R.I.A.A. platinum levels before year-end, was a duet with Aaron Neville on the country standard, "I Fall to Pieces." In the CMA 1994 voting, the album was nominated for Album of the Year and the duet for Vocal Event of the Year. Trisha was also one of the finalists in the Female Vocalist of the Year category.

Because all of Trisha's releases through 1994 were based on material written by others, some critics assumed she didn't write songs. She told Paul Kingsbury that wasn't true. She had done some originals before her career took off, including two recorded by other artists. One of those, cowritten with Mark Sanders, "If I'm Ever Over You," was recorded by Michelle Wright; the other, "How Do I Break It to My Heart," had been cut by Kenny Rogers. The Rogers track, she emphasized, had been laid down before his manager, Ken Kragen, also became her manager.

Having top-rank artists record her compositions, she said, encouraged her to try her hand again. "I felt like the songs [they recorded] were good songs. The hard part for me has been to write a song that would be a great song for me to record. But so far, either musically it's not exactly right, or lyrically it's not quite strong enough for what I want to say. But it's very encouraging that other artists find value in it and it definitely is an inspiration to write for me."

On February 14, 1995, her intriguing MCA Nashville album, *Thinkin' About You,* came out and quickly made top 10 chart levels. It was preceded by the single "You Can Sleep While I Drive" which spent many weeks on the hit lists in the spring and early summer. The album, a gem of a collection, won rousing support from the critics. The *Rolling Stone* reviewer called it "a near-perfect example of the country-pop genre" while *Country Music*'s critic described it as "a work in which the separate traditions of Nashville country-folk and California country-rock have been fused into a genuinely superior pop album." Record buyers agreed with those evaluations, resulting in a gold record award from the R.I.A.A. on April 26, 1995, and a platinum one the following December 13. In the fall she had two more singles from the disc on the charts, "I Wanna Go Too Far" and the Gretchen Peters composition, "On a Bus to St. Cloud." In the Grammy Awards voting for 1995, *Thinkin' About You* was nominated for Country Album of the year.

Besides her own work, Trisha joined Linda Davis and Martina McBride in helping Reba McEntire record the track "On My Own" for her 1995 album *Starting Over.* Later she and Shelby Lynne helped Lari White record the old pop western tune "Don't Fence Me In," the title track from Lari's 1996 album release.

In August 1996, MCA Nashville issued her next studio album, *Everybody Knows,* which soon was on the charts. The first single drawn from the collection was "Believe Me Baby (I Lied)," written by Kim Richey.

YOAKAM, DWIGHT: *Singer, guitarist, songwriter, actor. Born Pikeville, Kentucky, October 23, 1957.*

With his oversized, buff-colored cowboy hat pulled almost to eye level and his skintight pants, Dwight Yoakam onstage looks like a cross between a rodeo cowboy and a glam-rocker. Though his home base from the later 1970s on was way out West in Los Angeles, cowboy touches typically didn't surface in his song stylings, mostly self-penned compositions, though elements of rockabilly and honky-tonk certainly did.

Dwight was born in Kentucky, but was raised in Columbus, Ohio, where his family moved when he was two. (His father earned a living there by running a gas station.) Country music was the staple musical influence his parents had been brought up on and, Dwight remembered fondly, so had other members of his extended family. He told Karen Schoemer of *Rolling Stone* magazine ("Big Time," September 30, 1993), "I listened to records with my mother and father and aunt and uncle. One of my earliest musical memories is sitting in a den. They had a stereo. They were all sitting on the couch just singing on Saturday night with records, singing along with Patsy Cline and Leroy Van Dyke's 'Walk On By.' My dad's parents both died when I was young. My mother's parents—he was a coal miner who lived till he died in Kentucky. We sat around and sang hymns at the kitchen table."

Though he grew up in Ohio, Dwight recalled regularly going back on weekends to visit relations in Kentucky. "I used to call us taillight babies, because the process was that, on the weekends, those people who had come north to work in the factories would take their kids and ride back to Kentucky, West Virginia." The Yoakams' path to Kentucky was on Route 23, an image that eventually cropped up in one of Dwight's songs, "Readin', Rightin', Rt. 23."

He loved country music from his early years, but was also affected by the rock revolution, a particularly strong memory being of his first exposure to the Beatles on the Ed Sullivan TV show. The music seemed very strange to his ears, but the preteener tried out some of their patterns on the new guitar he'd received as a Christmas present. As an eight year old, he amazed a neighbor when he played and sang an original song of his in the Yoakams' living room.

Through his elementary school years and into his teens, Dwight spent more and more of his spare time closeted in his room practicing guitar and making up new songs. He wasn't a recluse; he did come out to play his material for family and school friends. In high school he became a member of several bands, including a high-intensity rockabilly group. But he didn't enjoy the classroom, often cutting school to work on his music or do his studying in the local library. His approach to his adolescent years was odd in some ways, but his focus on musical creativity did help him stay clean of alcohol and drugs.

He did manage to get sufficient credits to earn his high school degree and was accepted as a student at Ohio University, but he dropped out in his sophomore year when he decided he wanted to make music his vocation. Instead of moving to Nashville, in 1977 he headed west to Southern California, where he lived hand to mouth for several years while he slowly gained experience and contacts playing in local clubs and honky-tonks. For a time he shared a tiny apartment with record producer Pete Anderson, a habitat comprising a kitchen, bath, and laundry room that also served as Dwight's bedroom.

He took that environment to heart in later years in his views about the problems of homelessness. He told Brad Hogue of *Cash Box* ("Dwight Yoakam: *This Time Bigger Than Ever*," May 15, 1993), "We've got to do something to make available not only living space on a tenancy basis, but living space that's available and affordable to own. Property ownership is paramount and critical to our continued existence as a democracy. If you and I can't envision ourselves owning a dwelling place, it robs us of one of the most basic aspects of the emotion of hope. . . . Most people can't afford it because it's been put out of reach by the way our society has functioned in the past 25 years."

The major change in the Yoakam persona, the acquisition of his trademark cowboy hat (which soon also concealed his baldness) came in 1979. He had a gig at a Hollywood night spot when he happened to walk by a tailor shop run by Manuel, known for his work on spangled outfits for Nudie's clients. Dwight told Karen Schoemer, "It was long before I'd made any records. I couldn't afford his jackets. At that time I couldn't afford anything." But he tried a cowboy hat on and liked the way it felt. He then proceeded to redesign it with Manuel's help.

"It was an old R.C.A. crown—that stands for the Rodeo Cowboy Association. They had different titles for the blocks. And the brim was what we call a bullrider block, where it comes down real far on the front and low in the back. So I had him combine those. He'd steam some more, bring it out, and I'd go, 'Break it down a little lower.' He'd take it back out, I'd look at it, say, 'Naw, that ain't it.'" Finally Yoakam was satisfied and paid around $75, a substantial sum for him in those days.

The hat seemed to serve as a talisman that imbued its owner with new confidence in his stage work and writing skills. Still, there was no overnight change in his fortunes. He had several more years of dues-paying, of slowly gaining a foothold as a promising newcomer on the country scene whose demos began to gain more

attention from record executives. His early 1980s efforts included work with other local artists more concerned with folk-rock and country-rock than Dwight's rock-tinged down home stylings. Among those with whom he shared concert stages in that period were Los Lobos, the Blasters, and Lone Justice (featuring the dynamic Maria McKee on lead vocals).

In 1984, he made his first inroad in the recording sector with a six-song extended play (EP) collection on a small independent label titled *Guitars, Cadillacs, Etc. Etc.* The EP drew praise from several influential critics and enough sales to arouse the interest of the Burbank-based Reprise organization. Reprise Records (part of the Warner Brothers Records group) bought rights to the album and, after adding four more tracks by Dwight, reissued it in 1986. The album quickly showed up on national charts on the way to Dwight's first R.I.A.A. gold-record certification. On that album and many of the later collections, some of the material reflected Yoakam's love for the kind of country music spawned by Bakersfield performers Buck Owens and Merle Haggard. (Among other influences particularly cited by Dwight are Johnny Horton, Hank Williams, Sr., Hank Locklin, and the Louvin Brothers.)

In 1987, he helped one of his idols, Buck Owens, return to active performing and recording. In Bakersfield for a gig at the Kern County Fair, Dwight went to Owens's business office unannounced and talked Buck into joining him onstage that night. The crowd reaction was so enthusiastic that Buck decided to take Yoakam's advice and become active in entertaining once more. In January 1988 their duet of "The Streets of Bakersfield" was one of the high points of the CMA 30th Anniversary TV special. Their single of the song was a number-one hit on major country charts.

Dwight swiftly followed up his debut album success with a string of collections that went gold or platinum. Those included *Hillbilly Deluxe* in 1987; *Buenos Noches from a Lonely Room* (1988); and *Just Lookin' for a Hit* (1989). He started off the 1990s with the album *If There Was a Way*, which peaked at number seven in *Billboard* and stayed in upper levels for years, having gone well past platinum sales totals after 150 weeks on the list in the summer of 1992.

In 1992 he had such singles hits as "It Only Hurts When I Cry" (number six in *Radio & Records* the week of March 28) and "The Heart That You Own" (number nine in *R&R* the week of July 10). Besides hit albums and singles, Dwight could also point to a number of successful video releases. By then Dwight had become one of the nation's top-grossing concert acts, drawing huge crowds to major venues in the U.S. and many other nations. He also could often be seen performing on network TV shows, including various award telecasts.

Though cowboy songs were not part of Yoakam's concert repertoire, he did join with guitar expert Ry

Cooder in performing such western fare as "Streets of Laredo" in a salute to filmdom's singing cowboys held at the Gene Autry Western Heritage Museum in Los Angeles' Griffith Park in May 1992.

In 1993, he led off with the self-penned hit single, "Ain't That Lonely Yet," which rose to number twelve in *R&R* and stayed there for two weeks in March and also was at number twelve in *Billboard* the end of May. His next Reprise album, *This Time,* came out in March and by May was at number four in *Billboard,* eventually going past R.I.A.A. platinum levels by year-end. Two more Yoakam originals became top hits in 1993, "A Thousand Miles From Nowhere," number one in *R&R* the week of September 3, and "Fast As You," number two in *R&R* the week of December 17.

In early 1994, the single "Try Not to Look So Pretty" was in upper-chart levels, followed during the summer by "Pocket of a Clown" (both written by Dwight). Both songs were among those included in a new long-form video, *Pieces of Time,* issued by Reprise in September 1994. The video also included the Grammy winning "Ain't That Lonely Yet," as well as Dwight's version of Elvis's hit "Suspicious Minds," which had been included in the soundtrack for the 1993 film *Honeymoon in Vegas.*

Yoakam's mid-1990s activities included contributions to projects of other artists. That included his version of "Truckin'" on the Grateful Dead tribute album *Deadicated*; taping of the song "Common Day Man" as part of the soundtrack for the film *Falling from Grace* (rock star John Mellencamp's directing debut); and vocals on Warren Zevon's composition "Carmelite" included in the Flaco Jimenez solo album *Partners.* Others he recorded songs with included Patty Loveless, k.d. lang, Maria McKee, and the Indigo Girls.

In the mid-1990s Dwight also began to accumulate acting credits, starting with a small part in the 1991 Dennis Hopper/Nicolas Cage film that went on to become a cult classic, *Red Rock West.* In 1993, he made his stage debut in Los Angeles in the play *Southern Rapture* and also signed for another film role in a Peter Fonda project titled *Gingersnaps.* In 1996, he starred as a rodeo clown in the film *Painted Hero.*

Yoakam was always one who treasured his privacy, harking back to his youthful writing and reading habits. He commented to Brad Hogue on the inroads on privacy caused by fame: "We have a culture that's infatuated with celebrity. It's a double-edged sword because on the one hand, I make my living on people being infatuated to some degree with my public performance. The other edge to that sword is the one that puts too much importance on the indulgence of that infatuation."

This Time stayed on the country charts well into 1995, having received certification from the R.I.A.A. earlier for over two million copies sold. During the year, Reprise records issued the album *Dwight Live!*

taped during Yoakam's final performance of the *This Time* tour at the Warfield Theater in San Francisco. (Grammy voters nominated *Dwight Live!* for Best Country Album of 1995). His next album project was *Gone,* released at the end of 1995 and containing eight songs written by him and two cowritten with Kostas. The first single from it was "Nothing," by Yoakam and Kostas, which made top 20 ranks in December 1995. This was followed on the hit lists by Dwight's self-penned "Gone (That'll Be Me)," in upper levels in the spring. As its sale tapered off, the single "Sorry You Asked," written by Yoakam, was moving up the charts. By summer of 1996, *Gone* had gone past gold record levels.

YOUNG, FARON: *Singer, guitarist, actor, songwriter, bandleader (the Country Deputies), music publisher, newspaper publisher (Music City News). Born Shreveport, Louisiana, February 25, 1932; died Nashville, Tennessee, December 10, 1996.*

One of Faron Young's hit records of the mid-1950's began "Live fast . . . ," a motto that could be used to describe several aspects of his life. One of those included an intense devotion to country music that made him a top star in his early twenties and one of the most diverse operators in the field a decade later.

Although city-born, Faron moved to the country as a child when his father bought a small dirt farm outside Shreveport. While still in public school he received his first guitar and spent many hours figuring out chords and fingering. When Faron entered Fair Park High School in Shreveport, he could sing many of the top country hits, providing his own guitar accompaniment. It wasn't long before he formed his own band and played at school affairs as well as local fairs and hoedowns.

At the start of the 1950s, Faron entered Centenary College of Louisiana. For a while he tried to continue to combine studies with part-time musicianship. However, he had become well known in the region as an exciting performer and the offers of musical advancement were too tempting. He joined station KWKH and soon moved over to the cast of the *Louisiana Hayride.* Another rising star, Webb Pierce, also was on the *Hayride.* Pierce took Young on as a featured vocalist for tours over the entire southern region.

In 1951, Young was signed by Capitol Records. He quickly turned out two hit recordings, "Tattle Tale Tears" and "Have I Waited Too Long." In 1953, he became a regular cast member of the *Grand Ole Opry.* His meteoric rise was delayed by the Korean War: he entered the Army in the fall of 1952. No sooner did he finish basic training than he won an Army talent show on ABC-TV. Between 1952 and 1954, he toured the world entertaining troops and was starred on the Army's radio recruiting show.

Even before his discharge, Faron was making a dent

in the national ratings. In 1953, he had a top-10 recording of his own composition "Goin' Steady" on Capitol. In 1954, he returned to Nashville to rejoin the *Opry*. He received a royal welcome from a rapidly growing number of fans and soon had another top-10 hit, "If You Ain't Lovin'." He hit his stride in 1955 with such national successes as "Go Back You Fool," "It's a Great Life," and "Live Fast, Love Hard and Die Young." He was voted "America's Number One Artist of 1955" by *Southern Farm and Ranch* magazine.

There were very few months in the years that followed when Young was not represented on the national hit charts. In 1956, he had top-10 hits in "I've Got Five Dollars and It's Saturday Night" and "Sweet Dreams." In 1957, he scored with "I Miss You Already." He rounded out the 1950s with such hits as "Alone with You" and "That's the Way I Feel" in 1958 and the number-one ranked "Country Girl" in 1959. During the 1950s, besides touring widely, Faron made his acting debut in several movies, including the 1958 *Country Music Holiday* with Ferlin Husky and Zsa Zsa Gabor. He was also featured in *Daniel Boone* and *Hidden Guns*.

Faron began the 1960s with two top-10 hits he coauthored, "Face to the Wall" (with Bill Anderson) and "Your Old Used to Be" (with Hilda Yoimd). In 1961, he coauthored a hit—"Backtrack"—with Alex Zanetis. He also turned out another number-one-rated song, "Hidden Walls." He was represented in 1962 with "The Comeback" and "Three Days" (coauthor, Willie Nelson) and in early 1963 with "Down by the River."

In 1963, Faron switched labels from Capitol to Mercury. He continued to provide his new company with national hits, including, "The Yellow Bandana" in 1963, "You'll Drive Me Back" in 1964, "Walk Tall" in 1965, "I Guess I Had Too Much to Dream Last Night" in 1967, "She Went a Little Farther" in 1968, and "I've Got Precious Memories" and "Wine Me Up" in 1969.

Young's output of LPs by the mid-1960s was well over the two dozen mark. The titles on Capitol included *Sweethearts or Strangers; This is Faron Young* (1958); *Talk About Hits* (1959); *Best of Faron Young, Fan Club Favorites* (1961); *All Time Great Hits* (1963); and *Memory Lane* (1964). His Mercury LPs included *This is Faron; Faron Young Aims at the West* (1963); *Songs for Country Folks, Dance Favorites* (1964); *Songs of Mountains and Valleys* (1965); *Faron Young's Greatest Hits* and *Faron Young Sings the Best of Jim Reeves* (1966); *Unmitigated Gall* (4/67); and *I've Got Precious Memories* (7/69).

During the 1960s, Young toured all the states and made several trips to Germany, France, Mexico, and England. By the mid-1960s, he had many other flourishing projects, including his own music publishing firm, Vanadore Music, and his own monthly paper, *Music City News*. Long an ardent auto racing driver and fan, he was also owner of Sulphur Dell auto track in

Nashville. Among his souvenirs was a letter from President Johnson thanking Young for playing at a number of the President's speaking engagements during the 1964 campaign.

Faron started off the 1970s with the charted album *Wine Me Up* on Mercury. He continued to turn out a series of new LPs on the label during the first half of the decade, including *Occasional Wife/If I Ever Fall in Love, Step Aside, It's Four in the Morning,* and *This Little Girl of Mine*. His early 1970s singles output included such top-10 discs as "It's Four in the Morning" and "This Little Girl of Mine" in 1972 and "Some Kind of Woman" in 1974. "It's Four in the Morning" was voted Best Single of 1972 by the Country Music Association of Great Britain. In the mid-1970s, his charted singles included "Another You" and "Here I Am in Dallas" in 1975, "Feel Again" and "I'd Just Be Fool Enough" in 1976, and "Crutches" in 1977. Though he placed many singles on the charts in the first half of the decade, his recording career slowed down markedly as the 1970s went by, perhaps because of the pressures of his nonperforming activities. He left Mercury for MCA Records in the late 1970s and turned out some material for them, including the 1979 LP *Chapter Two,* but nothing that resembled his hits of earlier years. By the start of the 1980s that association ended.

Meanwhile, he retained a strong following for his concert work and remained a cast regular of the *Grand Ole Opry,* still featured on the show during the 1980s. He appeared on many country TV specials throughout the 1970s and into the 1980s, including the 1979 Hank Williams, Sr., memorial show. He continued to serve as publisher of the *Music City News,* still one of the country-music field's major trade papers and influences in the early 1980s.

Faron also accumulated some credits in films including a role in *Hidden Guns* that earned him the nickname "the Singing Sheriff." Other movie works included *Raiders of Old California* and *Daniel Boone*.

During the 1980s, Young's association with the *Music City News* phased out, but he continued with other business activities. He was nominated several times for the Country Music Hall of Fame, but as of 1996 had not moved past that phase to election. Some of his recorded work was available in audio or video retrospective collections in the mid-1990s, one example being his inclusion in the video *Greats of the Grand Ole Opry "The Song Masters, Volume 4."* In the mid-1990s, his old label, Mercury, had begun to achieve good results with reissues of some of its archival recordings. In January 1995, the record company announced it would release a group of albums under its American Essentials line of catalog collections including a package of a dozen or so of Faron Young hits.

Three albums of his work were available in the 1990s from the Country Music Hall of Fame & Museum catalog: *Faron Young/All Time Greatest Hits* on Curb

Records and, on the SOR label, *Faron Young/ Greatest Hits Volume 1* and *Greatest Hits Volume 2*. In 1995, the Country Music Foundation introduced a one CD reissue of some of Faron's recordings. Also available as an important item in the mid-1990s was the multi-CD package produced by Bear Family Records of Germany, *Faron Young: The Classic Years 1952– 1962*. The five CDs contained all of his Capitol recordings including such hits as "I've Got Five Dollars and It's Saturday Night," "If You Ain't Lovin' You Ain't Livin'," "Die Young," "Alone With You," and "Hello Walls."

In the mid-1990s, Faron (who for much of his life struggled with alcohol abuse) was suffering from nagging health problems including emphysema and the need for prostate surgery. All of that contributed to a deep feeling of depression that culminated in a suicide attempt on December 9, 1996. A friend found him at home unconscious and bleeding from a self-inflicted gunshot wound and summoned help. (Police reported Faron also had left a note stating his intention of committing suicide). Young was rushed to the Columbia Summit Medical Center in Nashville where attempts to save him failed and he died of his injuries on December 10.

AWARDS

RECORDING INDUSTRY ASSOCIATION OF AMERICA* (RIAA)

Gold, Platinum and Multiplatinum Recording Awards

Artist	Title	Company	Date
1959			
Elvis Presley	Hard Headed Woman (S)	RCA Victor	Aug. 11
1960			
Ernie Ford	*Hymns*	Capitol	Feb. 20
1961			
Jimmy Dean	Big Bad John (S)	Columbia	Dec. 14
Ernie Ford	*Spirituals*	Capitol	Oct. 10
Elvis Presley	*Elvis Golden Records*	RCA Victor	Oct. 17
Elvis Presley	*Blue Hawaii*	RCA Victor	Dec. 21
1962			
Ray Charles	I Can't Stop Loving You (S)	ABC-Paramount	July 19
Ray Charles	*Modern Sounds in Country & Western Music*	ABC-Paramount	July 19
Ernie Ford	*Star Carol*	Capitol	Mar. 12
Ernie Ford	*Nearer the Cross*	Capitol	Mar. 22
Elvis Presley	Can't Help Falling in Love (S)	RCA Victor	Mar. 30
1963			
Elvis Presley	*G.I. Blues*	RCA Victor	Mar. 12
Elvis Presley	*Elvis Christmas Album*	RCA Victor	Aug. 13
Elvis Presley	*Girls, Girls, Girls*	RCA Victor	Aug. 13
1964			
Johnny Horton	*Johnny Horton's Greatest Hits*	Columbia	Nov. 2
Roy Orbison	Oh, Pretty Woman (S)	Monument	Oct. 30
1965			
Johnny Cash	*Ring of Fire*	Columbia	Feb. 11
Roger Miller	King of the Road (S)	Smash	May 19

*Awards listed are only for country & western and country rock categories or recordings associated with artists included in the book. (S) indicates a single record as opposed to an album. Initially certifications were based on records only, but as other formats (tapes and compact discs—CDs) became available, the totals included them.

RIAA requires a minimum of one million copies sold for gold record (not gold music video) certification of a single. The platinum category was created in 1976 with two millions copies sold required for single certification. For gold-record album certification, prior to 1976 sales totaling $1 million were required. From 1975 on this was changed to 500,000 unit sales having a minimum dollar value of $1 million based on 33⅓ of the list price of each record or tape sold. A platinum album certification was predicated on sales of at least one million copies, and later, when a multiplatinum category was added, two million units or more sold were required for certification.

Artist	Title	Company	Date
Roger Miller	*Return of Roger Miller*	Smash	Sept. 1
Marty Robbins	*Gunfire Ballads & Trail Songs*	Columbia	Sept. 21

1966

Artist	Title	Company	Date
Eddy Arnold	*My World*	RCA	May 12
Johnny Horton	Battle of New Orleans (S)	Columbia	Dec. 20
Roger Miller	*Golden Hits*	Smash	Feb. 11
Roger Miller	*Dang Me*	Smash	Aug. 4
Roy Orbison	*Roy Orbison's Greatest Hits*	Monument	Mar. 24
Elvis Presley	*Elvis Presley*	RCA	Nov. 1
Elvis Presley	*Elvis' Golden Records, Vol. 2*	RCA	Nov. 1
Elvis Presley	*Elvis' Golden Records, Vol. 3*	RCA	Nov. 1
Jim Reeves	*The Best of Jim Reeves*	RCA	July 20

1967

Artist	Title	Company	Date
Johnny Cash	*I Walk the Line*	Columbia	July 14
Bobbie Gentry	Ode to Billie Joe (S)	Capitol	Sept. 11
Bobbie Gentry	*Ode to Billie Joe*	Capitol	Oct. 9
Boots Randolph	*Yakety Sax*	Monument	Feb. 7

1968

Artist	Title	Company	Date
Eddy Arnold	*The Best of Eddy Arnold*	RCA	Mar. 28
Glen Campbell	*By the Time I Get to Phoenix*	Capitol	Oct. 17
Glen Campbell	*Gentle on My Mind*	Capitol	Oct. 17
Glen Campbell	*Wichita Lineman*	Capitol	Nov. 18
Johnny Cash	*Johnny Cash at Folsom Prison*	Columbia	Oct. 30
Ray Charles	*Modern Sounds in Country & Western Music*	ABC	April 6
Ray Charles	*Greatest Hits*	ABC	April 6
Ray Charles	*A Man and His Soul*	ABC	Aug. 16
Bobby Goldsboro	Honey (S)	United Artists	April 4
Bobby Goldsboro	*Honey*	United Artists	Nov. 27
Jim Nabors	*Jim Nabors Sings*	Columbia	Jan. 5
Buck Owens	*Best of Buck Owens*	Capitol	March 6
Elvis Presley	*How Great Thou Art*	RCA Victor	Feb. 16
Elvis Presley	*Loving You*	RCA Victor	April 9
Jim Reeves	*Distant Drums*	RCA Victor	Feb. 26
Jeannie C. Riley	Harper Valley PTA (S)	Plantation	Aug. 26
Jeannie C. Riley	*Harper Valley PTA*	Plantation	Dec. 20

1969

Artist	Title	Company	Date
Gene Autry	Rudolph the Red-Nosed Reindeer (S)	Columbia	Nov. 10
Glen Campbell	*Hey Little One*	Capitol	Jan. 10
Glen Campbell	Wichita Lineman (S)	Capitol	Jan. 22
Glen Campbell	*Galveston*	Capitol	April 16
Glen Campbell	*Glen Campbell—Live*	Capitol	Sept. 19
Glen Campbell	Galveston (S)	Capitol	Oct. 14
Johnny Cash	*Johnny Cash's Greatest Hits*	Columbia	July 24
Johnny Cash	*Johnny Cash at San Quentin*	Columbia	Aug. 12
Johnny Cash	A Boy Named Sue (S)	Columbia	Aug. 14
Bobbie Gentry & Glen Campbell	*Gentry/Campbell*	Capitol	Jan. 29
Buddy Holly & the Crickets	*Buddy Holly Story*	Decca	Dec. 24

Artist	Title	Company	Date
Buddy Holly & the Crickets	That'll Be the Day (S)	Coral	Dec. 30
Elvis Presley	*His Hand in Mine*	RCA Victor	April 9
Elvis Presley	In the Ghetto (S)	RCA Victor	June 25
Elvis Presley	*Elvis TV Special*	RCA Victor	July 22
Elvis Presley	Suspicious Minds (S)	RCA Victor	Oct. 28
Elvis Presley	*From Vegas to Memphis*	RCA Victor	Dec. 12
Boots Randolph	*Boots with Strings*	Monument	Dec. 18
Soundtrack	*How the West Was Won*	MGM	June 11
Ray Stevens	Gitarzan (S)	Monument	June 16
B. J. Thomas	Hooked on a Feeling (S)	Scepter	Feb. 24
B. J. Thomas	Raindrops Keep Falling on My Head (S)	Scepter	Dec. 23
Hank Williams, Sr.	*Hank Williams Greatest Hits*	MGM	June 11
Hank Williams, Sr.	*Your Cheatin' Heart*	MGM	June 11

1970

Artist	Title	Company	Date
Glen Campbell	*Try a Little Kindness*	Capitol	Feb. 19
Johnny Cash	*Hello, I'm Johnny Cash*	Capitol	Jan. 29
Merle Haggard	*Okie from Muskogee*	Capitol	Oct. 2
Loretta Lynn	*Don't Come Home A-Drinkin' (with Lovin' on Your Mind)*	Decca	April 13
Anne Murray	Snowbird (S)	Capitol	Nov. 16
Jim Nabors	*Jim Nabors' Christmas Album*	Columbia	Dec. 4
Elvis Presley	*From Elvis in Memphis*	RCA Victor	Jan. 28
Elvis Presley	Don't Cry Daddy (S)	RCA Victor	Feb. 21
Elvis Presley	The Wonder of You (S)	RCA Victor	Aug. 14
Charley Pride	*The Best of Charley Pride*	RCA Victor	Jan. 19
Ray Stevens	Everything Is Beautiful (S)	Barnaby	June 26
B. J. Thomas	*Raindrops Keep Falling on My Head*	Scepter	July 22
Tammy Wynette	*Tammy's Greatest Hits*	Epic	April 16

1971

Artist	Title	Company	Date
Lynn Anderson	*Rose Garden*	Columbia	Feb. 25
Lynn Anderson	Rose Garden (S)	Columbia	Feb. 3
Johnny Cash	*The World of Johnny Cash*	Columbia	Mar. 25
Merle Haggard	*The Fightin' Side of Me*	Capitol	Mar. 11
Freddie Hart	Easy Loving (S)	Capitol	Nov. 29
Elvis Presley	*On Stage February 1970*	RCA Victor	Feb. 23
Ray Price	*For the Good Times*	Columbia	Mar 3
Charley Pride	*Charley Pride's 10th Album*	RCA Victor	Feb. 23
Charley Pride	*Just Plain Charley*	RCA Victor	Feb. 23
Charley Pride	*Charley Pride in Person*	RCA Victor	Feb. 23
Jerry Reed	Amos Moses (S)	RCA Victor	Mar. 29

1972

Artist	Title	Company	Date
Glen Campbell	*Glen Campbell's Greatest Hits*	Capitol	May 15
Mac Davis	Baby Don't Get Hooked on Me (S)	Columbia	Sept. 20
Dr. Hook	Sylvia's Mother (S)	Columbia	Aug. 2
Donna Fargo	Happiest Girl in the Whole U.S.A. (S)	Dot	Aug. 23
Merle Haggard	*The Best of Merle Haggard*	Capitol	Nov. 2
Freddie Hart	*Easy Loving*	Capitol	Oct. 23
Loretta Lynn	*Loretta Lynn's Greatest Hits*	Decca	Jan. 18
Rick Nelson	Garden Party (S)	Decca	Nov. 24

Artist	Title	Company	Date
Elvis Presley	*Elvis as Recorded at Madison Square Garden*	RCA Victor	Aug. 4
Elvis Presley	Burning Love (S)	RCA Victor	Oct. 27
Charley Pride	*Charley Pride Sings Heart Songs*	RCA Victor	Feb. 15
Charley Pride	Kiss an Angel Good Mornin' (S)	RCA Victor	May 8
Charley Pride	*The Best of Charley Pride*	RCA Victor	Oct. 19
Leon Russell	*Leon Russell & the Shelter People*	Shelter	Feb. 3
Leon Russell	*Carney*	Shelter	Sept. 19
Conway Twitty	*Hello Darlin'*	Decca	May 15

1973

Artist	Title	Company	Date
Mac Davis	*Baby, Don't Get Hooked on Me*	Columbia	May 7
Dr. Hook	The Cover of Rolling Stone (S)	Columbia	Apr. 4
Donna Fargo	Funny Face (S)	Dot	Jan. 4
Donna Fargo	*The Happiest Girl in the Whole U.S.A.*	Dot	Jan. 29
Kris Kristofferson	Why Me (S)	Monument	Nov. 8
Kris Kristofferson	*The Silver Tongued Devil & I*	Monument	Nov. 9
Kris Kristofferson	*Jesus Was a Capricorn*	Monument	Nov. 29
Anne Murray	*Snowbird*	Capitol	Dec. 21
Nitty Gritty Dirt Band	*Wm. E. McEuen Presents Will the Circle Be Unbroken*	United Artists	May 25
Marie Osmond	Paper Roses (S)	Kolob	Dec. 7
Elvis Presley	*World Wide 50 Gold Award Hits, Vol. 1*	RCA Victor	Feb. 13
Elvis Presley	*Elvis—Aloha from Hawaii Via Satellite*	RCA Victor	Feb. 13
Elvis Presley	*Elvis—That's the Way It Is*	RCA Victor	June 28
Charley Pride	*The Sensational Charley Pride*	RCA Victor	June 14
Charley Pride	*From Me to You*	RCA Victor	June 14
Charley Pride	*The Country Way*	RCA Victor	June 14
Charlie Rich	Behind Closed Doors (S)	Epic	Sept. 4
Charlie Rich	*Behind Closed Doors*	Epic	Nov. 27
Charlie Rich	The Most Beautiful Girl (S)	Epic	Dec. 10
Kenny Rogers	*Kenny Rogers & The First Edition Greatest Hits*	Reprise	Mar. 27
Leon Russell	*Leon Live*	Shelter	June 26

1974

Artist	Title	Company	Date
Mac Davis	*Stop & Smell the Roses*	Columbia	Sept. 23
Eagles	*Eagles*	Asylum	Jan. 22
Eagles	*On the Border*	Asylum	June 5
Eagles	*Desperado*	Asylum	Sept. 23
Merle Haggard	*The Best of the Best of Merle Haggard*	Capitol	Apr. 30
Kris Kristofferson	*Me & Bobby McGee*	Monument	Dec. 18
Lynyrd Skynyrd	*Second Helping*	MCA	Sept. 20
Lynyrd Skynyrd	*Pronounced Leh-nerd Skin-nerd*	MCA	Dec. 18
Jim Nabors	*The Lord's Prayer*	Columbia	Jan. 15
Olivia Newton-John	Let Me Be There (S)	MCA	Feb. 8
Olivia Newton-John	If You Love Me (Let Me Know) (S)	MCA	June 26
Olivia Newton-John	*If You Love Me (Let Me Know)*	MCA	Sept. 9
Olivia Newton-John	I Honestly Love You (S)	MCA	Oct. 9
Olivia Newton-John	*Let Me Be There*	MCA	Oct. 14
Donnie & Marie Osmond	I'm Leaving It (All) Up to You (S)	MGM	Sept. 20
Pointer Sisters	*The Pointer Sisters*	Blue Thumb	Feb. 7
Pointer Sisters	*That's A-Plenty*	Blue Thumb	July 25
Charlie Rich	*Very Special Love Songs*	Epic	April 22

Artist	Title	Company	Date
Charlie Rich	*There Won't Be Anymore*	Epic	Oct. 23
Jim Stafford	Spiders & Snakes (S)	MGM	March 6
Ray Stevens	The Streak (S)	Barnaby	Aug. 24
Billy Swan	I Can Help (S)	Monument	Dec. 2

1975

Artist	Title	Company	Date
Glen Campbell	Rhinestone Cowboy (S)	Capitol	Sept. 5
Glen Campbell	*Rhinestone Cowboy*	Capitol	Dec. 31
Eagles	*One of These Nights*	Asylum	June 30
Freddy Fender	Before the Next Teardrop Falls (S)	Dot	May 22
Freddy Fender	Wasted Days & Wasted Nights (S)	Dot	Sept. 18
Kris Kristofferson & Rita Coolidge	*Kris & Rita Full Moon*	A&M	Oct. 20
Lynyrd Skynyrd	*Nuthin' Fancy*	MCA	June 27
Marshall Tucker Band	*The Marshall Tucker Band*	Capricorn	Aug. 14
Marshall Tucker Band	*Where We All Belong*	Capricorn	Nov. 7
Michael Martin Murphy	Wildfire (S)	Epic	July 21
Michael Martin Murphy	*Blue Sky-Night Thunder*	Epic	Nov. 17
Olivia Newton-John	*Have You Never Been Mellow*	MCA	Feb. 26
Olivia Newton-John	Have You Never Been Mellow (S)	MCA	March 5
Olivia Newton-John	Please Mister Please (S)	MCA	Sept. 16
Olivia Newton-John	*Clearly Love*	MCA	Sept. 29
Donnie & Marie Osmond	*I'm Leaving It All Up to You*	MGM	Feb. 21
Elvis Presley	*Elvis—A Legendary Performer, Volume I*	RCA Victor	Jan. 8
Charley Pride	*Did You Think to Pray*	RCA Victor	Jan. 9
Charley Pride	*(Country) Charley Pride*	RCA Victor	Jan. 9
B. J. Thomas	Another Somebody Done Somebody Wrong Song (S)	ABC	May 23

1976 (gold)

(Until 1976, R.I.A.A. only provided gold record awards, but starting that year, coverage was extended to platinum sales totals. Later categories were added for multiplatinum recording sales and for music videos.)

Artist	Title	Company	Date
Glen Campbell	*That Christmas Feeling*	Capitol	Dec. 10
Mac Davis	*All the Love in the World*	Columbia	May 21
Jimmy Dean	I.O.U. (S)	GRT	May 20
Dr. Hook	Only Sixteen (S)	Capitol	May 17
Eagles	*Eagles—Their Greatest Hits 1971–1975*	Asylum	Feb. 24
Eagles	*Hotel California*	Asylum	Dec. 13
England Dan & John Ford Coley	*Nights Are Forever*	Big Tree	Dec. 1
Waylon Jennings, Jessi Colter, Willie Nelson, Tompall Glaser	*The Outlaws*	RCA Victor	Mar. 30
Lynyrd Skynyrd	*One More (for) from the Road*	MCA	Oct. 26
Marshall Tucker Band	*Searchin' for a Rainbow*	Capricorn	Feb. 4
Willie Nelson	*Red Headed Stranger*	Columbia	Mar. 11
Olivia Newton-John	*Come On Over*	MCA	Apr. 27
Olivia Newton-John	*Don't Stop Believin'*	MCA	Dec. 8
Pure Prairie League	*Bustin' Out*	RCA Victor	Mar. 16
Leon Russell	*Will O' the Wisp*	Shelter	Mar. 9
Leon Russell	*The Best of Leon Russell*	Shelter	Dec. 29
Red Sovine	Teddy Bear (S)	Gusto	Nov. 16
Conway Twitty	*You've Never Been This Far Before*	MCA	Apr. 29

Artist	Title	Company	Date
1976 (platinum)			
Eagles	*Eagles—Their Greatest Hits 1971–1975*	Asylum	Feb. 24
Eagles	*Hotel California*	Asylum	Dec. 15
Jennings/Colter/ Nelson/Glaser	*The Outlaws*	RCA Victor	Nov. 24
Lynyrd Skynyrd	*One More (for) from the Road*	Capricorn	Dec. 30
1977 (gold)			
Jimmy Buffett	*Changes In Latitude, Changes in Attitudes*	ABC	June 20
Glen Campbell	Southern Nights (S)	Capitol	Apr. 20
Glen Campbell	*Southern Nights*	Capitol	Oct. 5
Johnny Cash	The Johnny Cash Portrait/ His Greatest Hits Volume 2	Columbia	Oct. 25
Rita Coolidge	*Anytime . . . Anywhere*	A&M	Aug. 18
Rita Coolidge	Your Love Has Lifted Me (Higher & Higher) (S)	A&M	Aug. 30
Eagles	New Kid in Town (S)	Elektra/Asylum	Mar. 21
Eagles	*Hotel California*	Elektra/Asylum	May 12
Crystal Gayle	*We Must Believe in Magic*	United Artists	Nov. 14
Waylon Jennings	*Dreaming My Dreams*	RCA	Mar. 24
Waylon Jennings	*Ol' Waylon*	RCA	June 14
Waylon Jennings	*Are You Ready for the Country*	RCA	Aug. 1
Marshall Tucker Band, The	*Carolina Dreams*	Warner/Reprise	June 2
Marshall Tucker Band, The	*A New Life*	Warner Bros.	Aug. 16
Ronnie McDowell	The King Is Gone (S)	GRT	Sept. 8
Rick Nelson	Travelin' Man (S)	UA/Imperial	Aug. 10
Olivia Newton-John	*Greatest Hits*	MCA	Oct. 21
Ozark Mountain Daredevils	*Ozark Mountain Daredevils*	A&M	Sept. 6
Dolly Parton	*Here You Come Again*	RCA	Dec. 27
Elvis Presley	Way Down (S)	RCA	Sept. 12
Elvis Presley	*Pure Gold*	RCA	Sept. 12
Elvis Presley	*Welcome to My World*	RCA	Sept. 30
Elvis Presley	*From Elvis Presley Boulevard, Memphis, Tennessee*	RCA	Oct. 7
Elvis Presley	*Elvis—A Legendary Performer, Vol. 2*	RCA	Oct. 25
Elvis Presley	*Elvis Sings the Wonderful World of Christmas*	RCA	Nov. 4
Elvis Presley	*His Hand in Mine*	RCA	Dec. 1
Elvis Presley	*Elvis Country*	RCA	Dec. 1
Kenny Rogers	Lucille (S)	United Artists	June 22
Kenny Rogers	*Daytime Friends*	United Artists	Dec. 15
The Statler Bros.	*The Best of the Statler Brothers*	Phonogram/Mercury	Mar. 10
Jerry Jeff Walker	*Viva Terlingua*	MCA	Dec. 16
Hank Williams, Sr.	*24 Greatest Hits*	Polydor/MGM	Mar. 1
1977 (platinum)			
Jimmy Buffett	*Changes in Latitudes, Changes in Attitudes*	ABC	Dec. 14
Rita Coolidge	*Anytime . . . Anywhere*	A&M	Oct. 19
Waylon Jennings	*Ol' Waylon*	RCA	Oct. 7
Kris Kristofferson/ Barbra Streisand	*A Star Is Born*	Columbia	Jan. 21
Lynyrd Skynyrd	*Street Survivors*	MCA	Dec. 12

Artist	Title	Company	Date
Olivia Newton-John	*Greatest Hits*	MCA	Dec. 15
Elvis Presley	*Moody Blue*	RCA	Sept. 12
Elvis Presley	*In Concert*	RCA	Oct. 14
Elvis Presley	*Elvis Sings the Wonderful World of Christmas*	RCA	Dec. 1

1978 (gold)

Artist	Title	Company	Date
Jimmy Buffett	*Son of a Son of a Sailor*	ABC	Apr. 5
Jimmy Buffett	*You Had to Be There*	ABC	Nov. 10
Rita Coolidge	*Love Me Again*	A&M	June 21
Rita Coolidge	We're All Alone (S)	A&M	Feb. 2
Dr. Hook	Sharing the Night Together (S)	Capitol	Dec. 26
Exile	Kiss You All Over (S)	Curb	Oct. 4
Exile	*Mixed Emotions*	Warner Bros.	Oct. 10
Crystal Gayle	*When I Dream*	United Artists	Sept. 15
Emmylou Harris	*Elite Hotel*	Reprise	July 27
Waylon Jennings	*Waylon Live*	RCA	Jan. 13
Waylon Jennings	*I've Always Been Crazy*	RCA	Sept. 26
Waylon Jennings/ Willie Nelson	*Waylon & Willie*	RCA	Feb. 3
Kris Kristofferson	*Songs of Kristofferson*	Columbia	Nov. 9
Lynyrd Skynyrd	*Skynyrd's First and . . . Last*	MCA	Sept. 8
Marshall Tucker Band, The	*Together Forever*	Capricorn	May 2
Marshall Tucker Band, The	*The Marshall Tucker Band's Greatest Hits*	Capricorn	Oct. 30
Ronnie Milsap	*It Was Almost Like a Song*	RCA	Feb. 10
Ronnie Milsap	*Only One Love in My Life*	RCA	Oct. 13
Anne Murray	*Let's Keep It That Way*	Capitol	Oct. 12
Anne Murray	You Needed Me (S)	Capitol	Oct. 26
Willie Nelson	*The Sound in Your Mind*	Columbia	May 5
Willie Nelson	*Stardust*	Columbia	July 20
Olivia Newton-John/ John Travolta	You're the One That I Want (S)	RSO	Apr. 12
Olivia Newton-John/ John Travolta	Summer Nights (S)	RSO	Aug. 31
Olivia Newton-John	Hopelessly Devoted to You (S)	MCA	Aug. 31
Olivia Newton-John	*Totally Hot*	MCA	Nov. 15
Dolly Parton	Here You Come Again (S)	RCA	Feb. 1
Dolly Parton	*The Best of Dolly Parton*	RCA	June 12
Dolly Parton	*Heartbreaker*	RCA	Aug. 16
Johnny Paycheck	*Take This Job & Shove It*	Epic	Dec. 18
Elvis Presley	*Elvis—A Legendary Performer, Vol. 3*	RCA	Dec. 18
Kenny Rogers	*Ten Years of Gold*	United Artists	Feb. 15
Kenny Rogers	*Love or Something Like It*	United Artists	Sept. 15
Kenny Rogers	*The Gambler*	United Artists	Nov. 30
Statler Brothers	*Entertainers . . . On and Off the Record*	Mercury	Dec. 19
Bonnie Tyler	It's a Heartache (S)	RCA	June 16

1978 (platinum)

Artist	Title	Company	Date
Jimmy Buffett	*Son of a Son of a Sailor*	ABC	May 10
Crystal Gayle	*We Must Believe in Magic*	United Artists	Feb. 15
Waylon Jennings/ Willie Nelson	*Waylon & Willie*	RCA	Apr. 11
Lynyrd Skynyrd	*Skynyrd's First and . . . Last*	MCA	Nov. 10

Artist	Title	Company	Date
Marshall Tucker Band, The	*Carolina Dreams*	Capricorn	May 23
Anne Murray	*Let's Keep It That Way*	Capitol	Dec. 19
Willie Nelson	*Stardust*	Columbia	Dec. 26
Olivia Newton-John/ John Travolta	You're the One That I Want (S)	RSO	July 18
Olivia Newton-John	*Totally Hot*	MCA	Dec. 5
Dolly Parton	*Here You Come Again*	RCA	Apr. 28
Kenny Rogers	*Ten Years of Gold*	United Artists	July 20

1979 (gold)

Artist	Title	Company	Date
Charlie Daniels Band	*Million Mile Reflections*	Epic	June 28
Charlie Daniels Band	The Devil Went Down to Georgia (S)	Epic	Aug. 21
Dr. Hook	When You're in Love with a Beautiful Woman (S)	Capitol	Aug. 22
Dr. Hook	*Pleasure & Pain*	Capitol	Sept. 11
Waylon Jennings	*Greatest Hits*	RCA	May 16
Anne Murray	*New Kind of Feeling*	Capitol	Feb. 5
Willie Nelson	*Willie & Family Live*	Columbia	Feb. 13
Willie Nelson & Leon Russell	*One for the Road*	Columbia	Aug. 2
New Riders of the Purple Sage	*Adventures of Panama Red*	Columbia	Nov. 19
Olivia Newton-John	A Little More Love (S)	MCA	Feb. 12
Dolly Parton	*Great Balls of Fire*	RCA	Nov. 13
Poco	*Legend*	MCA	Apr. 12
Pointer Sisters	Fire (S)	Elektra	Feb. 5
Pointer Sisters	*Energy*	Elektra	Feb. 13
Kenny Rogers & Dottie West	*Classics*	United Artists	July 2
Tanya Tucker	*TNT*	MCA	Feb. 23

1979 (platinum)

Artist	Title	Company	Date
Charlie Daniels Band	*Million Mile Reflections*	Epic	Aug. 16
Waylon Jennings	*Greatest Hits*	RCA	Sept. 7
Kenny Rogers	*The Gambler*	United Artists	Feb. 27

1980 (gold)

Artist	Title	Company	Date
Dr. Hook	Sexy Eyes (S)	Capitol	Aug. 10
Eagles	*The Long Run*	Asylum	Feb. 1
Eagles	Heartache Tonight (S)	Asylum	Feb. 1
Larry Gatlin	*Straight Ahead*	Columbia	June 6
Crystal Gayle	*Miss the Mississippi*	Columbia	Jan. 10
Crystal Gayle	*Classic Crystal*	United Artists	Mar. 7
Waylon Jennings	*What Goes Around*	RCA	Mar. 3
Waylon Jennings	*Music Man*	RCA	Aug. 22
Waylon Jennings	Theme from *The Dukes of Hazzard* (S)	RCA	Dec. 9
Johnny Lee	Lookin' for Love (S)	Full Moon	Nov. 18
Lynyrd Skynyrd	*Gold & Platinum*	MCA	Mar. 25
Anne Murray	*I'll Always Love You*	Capitol	Feb. 7
Anne Murray	*Greatest Hits*	Capitol	Nov. 10
Willie Nelson	*Willie Nelson Sings Kristofferson*	Columbia	Mar. 6
Willie Nelson & Family	*Honeysuckle Rose* (soundtrack)	Columbia	Oct. 15
Olivia Newton-John	Magic (S)	MCA	July 16

Artist	Title	Company	Date
Olivia Newton-John & ELO	*Xanadu* (soundtrack)	MCA	Aug. 19
Oak Ridge Boys	*Y'All Come Back Saloon*	MCA	Mar. 21
Oak Ridge Boys	*The Oak Ridge Boys Have Arrived*	MCA	Aug. 29
Oak Ridge Boys	*Together*	MCA	Oct. 10
Pointer Sisters	*He's So Shy* (S)	Elektra	Nov. 25
Eddie Rabbitt	*Horizon*	Elektra	Oct. 24
Eddie Rabbitt	*The Best of Eddie Rabbitt*	Elektra	Oct. 24
Kenny Rogers	*Kenny*	Capitol	Jan. 16
Kenny Rogers	Coward of the Country (S)	United Artists	Mar. 7
Kenny Rogers	*Gideon*	United Artists	May 28
Kenny Rogers	Lady (S)	United Artists	Nov. 25
Kenny Rogers	*Greatest Hits*	Liberty	Dec. 2
Rossington/ Collins Band	*Anytime, Anyplace, Anywhere*	MCA	Aug. 19
Soundtrack (various artists)	*Urban Cowboy*	Asylum	July 14
Don Williams	*Best of Don Williams, Volume 2*	MCA	Oct. 7
Don Williams	*I Believe in You*	MCA	Dec. 2

1980 (platinum)

Artist	Title	Company	Date
Charlie Daniels Band	*Full Moon*	Epic	Nov. 7
Eagles	*The Long Run*	Asylum	Feb. 1
Lynyrd Skynyrd	*Gold & Platinum*	MCA	Apr. 18
Anne Murray	*Greatest Hits*	Capitol	Nov. 26
Willie Nelson	*Willie Nelson & Family Live*	Columbia	Mar. 6
Willie Nelson & Family	*Honeysuckle Rose* (soundtrack)	Columbia	Nov. 12
Olivia Newton-John & ELO	*Xanadu* (soundtrack)	MCA	Aug. 19
Kenny Rogers	*Kenny*	Capitol	Jan. 16
Kenny Rogers	*Gideon*	United Artists	May 28
Kenny Rogers	*Greatest Hits*	Liberty	Dec. 2
Soundtrack (various artists)	*Urban Cowboy*	Asylum	July 24

1981 (gold)

Artist	Title	Company	Date
Charlie Daniels Band	*Saddle Tramp*	Epic	Sept. 4
Mac Davis	*It's Hard to Be Humble*	Casablanca	Mar. 4
Eagles	*Live*	Asylum	Jan. 7
Larry Gatlin	*Greatest Hits*	Columbia	Sept. 9
Emmylou Harris	*Luxury Liner*	Warner Bros.	Feb. 11
Emmylou Harris	*Blue Kentucky Girl*	Warner Bros.	Feb. 18
Emmylou Harris	*Profile—Best of Emmylou Harris*	Warner Bros.	Feb. 18
Emmylou Harris	*Roses in the Snow*	Warner Bros.	Apr. 1
Emmylou Harris	*Evangeline*	Warner Bros.	Oct. 9
Waylon Jennings/ Jessi Colter	*Leather & Lace*	RCA	Sept. 15
George Jones	*I Am What I Am*	Epic	Sept. 18
Loretta Lynn	*Greatest Hits, Volume II*	MCA	Oct. 29
Lynyrd Skynyrd	*Gimme Back My Bullets*	MCA	Jan. 20
Barbara Mandrell	*The Best of Barbara Mandrell*	ABC	Jan. 26
Ronnie Milsap	*There's No Gettin' Over Me*	RCA	Dec. 8
Ronnie Milsap	*Greatest Hits*	RCA	Feb. 12
Anne Murray	*Where Do You Go When You Dream*	Capitol	June 29
Willie Nelson	*Somewhere over the Rainbow*	Columbia	May 5

Artist	Title	Company	Date
Willie Nelson	*Willie Nelson's Greatest Hits (& Some That Will Be)*	Columbia	Nov. 3
Juice Newton	*Juice*	Capitol	Aug. 13
Juice Newton	Angel of the Morning (S)	Capitol	July 1
Juice Newton	Queen of Hearts (S)	Capitol	Sept. 2
Olivia Newton-John	Physical (S)	MCA	Dec. 3
Olivia Newton-John	*Physical*	MCA	Dec. 16
Oak Ridge Boys	*Oak Ridge Boys Greatest Hits*	MCA	Feb. 4
Oak Ridge Boys	Elvira (S)	MCA	June 16
Oak Ridge Boys	*Fancy Free*	MCA	July 23
Dolly Parton	*9 to 5* (S)	RCA	Feb. 19
Dolly Parton	*9 to 5 and Odd Jobs*	RCA	Mar. 6
Pointer Sisters	Slowhand (S)	Planet	Sept. 2
Pointer Sisters	*Black & White*	Planet	Sept. 16
Eddie Rabbitt	I Love a Rainy Night (S)	Elektra	Mar. 10
Eddie Rabbitt	Drivin' My Life Away (S)	Elektra	Mar. 25
Eddie Rabbitt	*Step by Step*	Elektra	Nov. 5
Kenny Rogers	*Share Your Love*	Liberty	Aug. 28
Statler Brothers	*The Best of the Statler Brothers Rides Again, Volume 2*	Mercury	Feb. 25
Statler Brothers	*The Originals*	Mercury	June 26
Thirty-Eight Special	*Wild-Eyed Southern Boys*	A&M	June 10
Conway Twitty	*Greatest Hits, Volume 1*	Decca	Oct. 29
Conway Twitty & Loretta Lynn	*Lead Me On*	Decca	Oct. 29
Hank Williams, Jr.	*Whiskey Bent & Hell Bound*	Curb	Nov. 2

1981 (platinum)

Artist	Title	Company	Date
Alabama	*Feel So Right*	RCA	Sept. 15
Eagles	*Eagles Live*	Elektra	Jan. 7
Ronnie Milsap	*Greatest Hits*	RCA	July 14
Willie Nelson	*Somewhere over the Rainbow*	Columbia	Aug. 13
Olivia Newton-John	*Physical*	MCA	Dec. 16
Oak Ridge Boys	*Fancy Free*	MCA	July 29
Eddie Rabbit	*Horizon*	Elektra	Feb. 23
Kenny Rogers	*Share Your Love*	Liberty	Aug. 28

1982 (gold)

Artist	Title	Company	Date
Alabama	*Mountain Music*	RCA	Apr. 29
Charlie Daniels Band	*Windows*	Epic	Nov. 19
Glen Frey	*No Fun Aloud*	Asylum	Dec. 8
Don Henley	*I Can't Stand Still*	Asylum	Dec. 8
Kendalls, The	*Heaven's Just a Sin Away*	Churchill	Nov. 30
Johnny Lee	*Lookin' for Love*	Full Moon	May 12
Barbara Mandrell	*Live*	MCA	Feb. 22
Anne Murray	*Christmas Wishes*	Capitol	Oct. 25
Willie Nelson	*Always on My Mind*	Columbia	Apr. 30
Willie Nelson	*Pretty Paper*	Columbia	Nov. 22
Juice Newton	*Quiet Lies*	Capitol	July 16
Olivia Newton-John	*Olivia's Greatest Hits, Volume II*	MCA	Nov. 15
Oak Ridge Boys	*Bobbie Sue*	MCA	Apr. 6
Oak Ridge Boys	*Christmas*	MCA	Dec. 27
Ray Price	*All Time Greatest Hits*	Columbia	Dec. 28
Marty Robbins	*All Time Greatest Hits*	Columbia	Dec. 28
Kenny Rogers	*Christmas*	Liberty	Jan. 5

Artist	Title	Company	Date
Kenny Rogers	*Love Will Turn You Around*	Liberty	Aug. 30
Soundtrack	*Coal Miner's Daughter*	MCA	Jan. 11
Statler Brothers	*Christmas Card*	Mercury	Oct. 20
Thirty-Eight Special	*Special Forces*	A&M	July 2
Hank Williams, Jr.	*The Pressure Is On*	Elektra	Apr. 13

1982 (platinum)

Artist	Title	Company	Date
Alabama	*Mountain Music*	RCA	Apr. 29
Alabama	*My Home's in Alabama*	RCA	June 30
Crystal Gayle	*When I Dream*	Liberty	May 11
Willie Nelson	*Always on My Mind*	Columbia	June 15
Willie Nelson	*Willie Nelson's Greatest Hits (& Some That Will Be)*	Columbia	June 15
Juice Newton	*Juice*	Capitol	Jan. 5
Olivia Newton-John	Physical (S)	MCA	Jan. 5
Olivia Newton-John	*Olivia's Greatest Hits, Volume II*	MCA	Nov. 29
Oak Ridge Boys	Elvira (S)	MCA	Mar. 8
Oak Ridge Boys	*The Oak Ridge Boys Greatest Hits*	MCA	Apr. 16
Kenny Rogers	*Christmas*	Liberty	Jan. 5
Thirty-Eight Special	*Wild-Eyed Southern Boys*	A&M	Feb. 24

1983 (gold)

Artist	Title	Company	Date
Alabama	*The Closer You Get*	RCA	May 3
John Anderson	Swingin' (S)	Warner Bros.	June 14
Rosanne Cash	*Seven Year Ache*	Columbia	Jan. 6
David Allan Coe	*Greatest Hits*	Columbia	Nov. 7
Eagles	*Eagles Greatest Hits, Volume II*	Asylum	Jan. 7
Merle Haggard	*Big City*	Epic	July 11
Merle Haggard & Willie Nelson	*Poncho & Lefty*	Epic	July 11
Don Henley	Dirty Laundry (S)	Asylum	Mar. 28
Buddy Holly & the Crickets	*20 Golden Greats*	MCA	Nov. 14
Waylon Jennings/ Willie Nelson	*WW II*	RCA	Mar. 21
Loretta Lynn	*Coal Miner's Daughter*	MCA	June 15
Willie Nelson & Ray Price	*San Antonio Rose*	Columbia	Oct. 3
Oak Ridge Boys	*American Made*	MCA	Apr. 3
Oak Ridge Boys	*Room Service*	MCA	Apr. 13
Dolly Parton	*Dolly Parton's Greatest Hits*	RCA	Oct. 31
Elvis Presley	I Got Stung (S)	RCA	Apr. 15
Elvis Presley	Are You Lonesome Tonight (S)	RCA	Apr. 15
Elvis Presley	Don't (S)	RCA	Apr. 15
Elvis Presley	Return to Sender (S)	RCA	Apr. 15
Elvis Presley	It's Now or Never (S)	RCA	Apr. 15
Elvis Presley	A Fool Such As I (S)	RCA	Aug. 3
Elvis Presley	Wear My Ring Around Your Neck (S)	RCA	Aug. 3
Kenny Rogers & Dolly Parton	Islands in the Stream (S)	RCA	Oct. 18
Kenny Rogers	*We've Got Tonight*	Liberty	Dec. 21
Ricky Skaggs	*Waitin' for the Sun to Shine*	Epic	Mar. 7
Ricky Skaggs	*Highways & Heartaches*	Epic	Oct. 3
Conway Twitty	*The Very Best of Conway Twitty*	MCA	Dec. 8
Bonnie Tyler	*Faster Than the Speed of Night*	Columbia	Oct. 3

Artist	Title	Company	Date
Bonnie Tyler	Total Eclipse of the Heart (S)	Columbia	Oct. 3
Hank Williams, Jr.	*Family Tradition*	Elektra	Dec. 23

1983 (platinum)

Artist	Title	Company	Date
Alabama	*The Closer You Get*	RCA	May 3
George Jones	*I Am What I Am*	Epic	Dec. 29
Elvis Presley	*Welcome to My World*	RCA	Jan. 14
Kenny Rogers	*Eyes That See in the Dark*	RCA	Oct. 31
Kenny Rogers & Dolly Parton	Islands in the Stream (S)	RCA	Dec. 7
Kenny Rogers	*20 Greatest Hits*	Liberty	Dec. 21
Thirty-Eight Special	*Special Forces*	A&M	Feb. 4
Bonnie Tyler	*Faster Than the Speed of Night*	Columbia	Nov. 7

1984 (gold)

Artist	Title	Company	Date
Alabama	*Roll On*	RCA	Apr. 2
John Anderson	*Wild & Blue*	Warner Bros.	May 15
Lee Greenwood	*Somebody's Gonna Love You*	MCA	Feb. 24
Willie Nelson	*Without a Song*	Columbia	Jan. 9
Willie Nelson	*City of New Orleans*	Columbia	Dec. 18
Olivia Newton-John/ John Travolta	*Two of a Kind* (soundtrack)	MCA	Jan. 16
Oak Ridge Boys	*Deliver*	MCA	June 15
Oak Ridge Boys	*Oak Ridge Boys Greatest Hits 2*	MCA	Nov. 21
Pointer Sisters	*Break Out*	Planet	June 1
Kenny Rogers	*What About Me*	RCA	Dec. 3
Kenny Rogers & Dolly Parton	*Once Upon a Christmas*	RCA	Dec. 3
Ricky Skaggs	*Don't Cheat in Our Home Town*	Epic	Oct. 5
Thirty-Eight Special	*Tour De Force*	A&M	Jan. 31
Hank Williams, Jr.	*Hank Williams Jr.'s Greatest Hits*	Curb	Aug. 21

1984 (platinum)

Artist	Title	Company	Date
Alabama	*Roll On*	RCA	Apr. 2
Merle Haggard & Willie Nelson	*Poncho & Lefty*	Epic	Aug. 7
Olivia Newton-John/ John Travolta	*Two of a Kind* (soundtrack)	MCA	Jan. 16
Pointer Sisters	*Break Out*	Planet	Oct. 4
Kenny Rogers	*What About Me*	RCA	Dec. 3
Kenny Rogers & Dolly Parton	*Once Upon a Christmas*	RCA	Dec. 3
Hank Williams, Jr.	*Hank Williams Jr.'s Greatest Hits*	Curb	Aug. 21

1985 (gold)

Artist	Title	Company	Date
Alabama	*40 Hour Week*	RCA	Apr. 1
Alabama	*Alabama Christmas*	RCA	Nov. 15
Patsy Cline	*Greatest Hits*	MCA	July 31
Charlie Daniels Band	*A Decade of Hits*	Epic	Nov. 1
Glenn Frey	*The Allnighter*	MCA	Aug. 6
Lee Greenwood	*You've Got a Good Love Comin'*	MCA	Feb. 15
Lee Greenwood	*Greatest Hits*	MCA	Nov. 7
Don Henley	*Building the Perfect Beast*	Geffen	Jan. 29
The Judds	*Why Not Me*	RCA	Apr. 4

Artist	Title	Company	Date
Ronnie Milsap	*Greatest Hits Volume 2*	RCA	Oct. 2
Anne Murray	*A Little Good News*	Capitol	Mar. 15
Anne Murray	*Heart over Mind*	Capitol	June 11
Pointer Sisters	*Contact*	RCA	Sept. 3
Kenny Rogers	*Heart of the Matter*	RCA	Dec. 5
George Strait	*Does Fort Worth Ever Cross Your Mind*	MCA	Apr. 8
George Strait	*George Strait's Greatest Hits*	MCA	Nov. 22
Hank Williams, Jr.	*Major Moves*	Warner Bros.	Jan. 10
Hank Williams, Jr.	*Men of Steel*	Warner Bros.	Jan. 29
Hank Williams, Jr.	*Rowdy*	Curb	May 31
Hank Williams, Jr.	*Five-O*	Warner Bros.	Oct. 29

1985 (platinum)

Artist	Title	Company	Date
Alabama	*40 Hour Week*	RCA	Jan. 1
Alabama	*Alabama Christmas*	RCA	Nov. 15
Don Henley	*Building the Perfect Beast*	Geffen	Apr. 9
Pointer Sisters	*Contact*	RCA	Sept. 3

1986 (gold)

Artist	Title	Company	Date
Alabama	*Alabama's Greatest Hits*	RCA	Mar. 31
Bellamy Brothers	*The Bellamy Brothers Greatest Hits*	MCA	Oct. 10
John Conlee	*John Conlee's Greatest Hits*	MCA	Nov. 6
The Everly Bros.	*The Very Best of the Everly Brothers*	Warner Bros.	Apr. 17
Lee Greenwood	*Inside Out*	MCA	Nov. 6
Emmylou Harris	*Pieces of the Sky*	Reprise	Oct. 13
Waylon Jennings/ Willie Nelson/ Johnny Cash/ Kris Kristofferson	*The Highwayman*	Columbia	Feb. 10
The Judds	*Rockin' with the Rhythm*	RCA	Feb. 12
Willie Nelson	*The Troublemaker*	Columbia	Dec. 16
Elvis Presley	Crying in the Chapel (S)	RCA	Mar. 31
George Strait	*Something Special*	MCA	Feb. 4
George Strait	*#7*	MCA	Sept. 18
Thirty-Eight Special	*Strength in Numbers*	A&M	July 7
Randy Travis	*Storms of Life*	Warner Bros.	Oct. 10
Hank Williams, Jr.	*Strong Stuff*	Warner Bros.	Jan. 22
Hank Williams, Jr.	*High Notes*	Warner Bros.	Apr. 7
Hank Williams, Jr.	*Greatest Hits—Volume 2*	Warner Bros.	May 13
Hank Williams, Jr.	*Montana Cafe*	Warner Bros.	Dec. 22

1986 (platinum)

Artist	Title	Company	Date
Alabama	*Alabama's Greatest Hits*	RCA	Mar. 31
Lynn Anderson	*Rose Garden*	Columbia	Nov. 21
Johnny Cash	*Johnny Cash's Greatest Hits*	Columbia	Nov. 21
Johnny Cash	*Johnny Cash at San Quentin*	Columbia	Nov. 21
Johnny Cash	*Johnny Cash at Folsom Prison*	Columbia	Nov. 21
Mac Davis	*Baby, Don't Get Hooked on Me*	Columbia	Nov. 21
Johnny Horton	*Johnny Horton's Greatest Hits*	Columbia	Nov. 21
The Judds	*Rockin' with the Rhythm*	RCA	Oct. 7
The Judds	*Why Not Me*	RCA	Apr. 25
Willie Nelson	*Red Headed Stranger*	Columbia	Nov. 21
Dolly Parton	*Greatest Hits*	RCA	Oct. 7
Charlie Rich	*Behind Closed Doors*	Epic	Nov. 21

Artist	Title	Company	Date
Marty Robbins	*Gunfighter Ballads & Trail Songs*	Columbia	Nov. 21
Hank Williams, Jr.	*The Pressure Is On*	Warner Bros.	Apr. 7

1986 (multiplatinum)

Artist	Title	Company	Date
Alabama	*My Home's in Alabama* (2 M)	RCA	Aug. 20
Johnny Cash	*Johnny Cash's Greatest Hits* (2 M)	Columbia	Nov. 21
Johnny Cash	*Johnny Cash at San Quentin* (2 M)	Columbia	Nov. 21
Johnny Cash	*Johnny Cash at Folsom Prison* (2 M)	Columbia	Nov. 21
Charlie Daniels Band	*Million Mile Reflections* (2 M)	Columbia	Nov. 24
Ronnie Milsap	*Greatest Hits* (2 M)	RCA	Apr. 25
Willie Nelson	*Red Headed Stranger* (2 M)	Columbia	Nov. 21
Willie Nelson	*Willie Nelson's Greatest Hits (& Some That Will Be)* (2 M)	Columbia	Dec. 8

1987 (gold)

Artist	Title	Company	Date
Alabama	*The Touch*	RCA	Jan. 6
Patsy Cline	*Sweet Dreams* (soundtrack)	MCA	Apr. 2
The Judds	*Heartland*	RCA	Apr. 9
Reba McEntire	*Greatest Hits*	MCA	Dec. 8
Reba McEntire	*What Am I Gonna Do About You*	MCA	Apr. 21
Reba McEntire	*Whoever's in New England*	MCA	Jan. 28
Anne Murray	*Country*	Capitol	Mar. 17
Anne Murray	*Something to Talk About*	Capitol	Sept. 28
Willie Nelson	*Half Nelson*	Columbia	Apr. 6
Dolly Parton/ Linda Ronstadt/ Emmylou Harris	*Trio*	Warner Bros.	July 14
Dan Seals	*Won't Be Blue Anymore*	EMI	Feb. 6
Ray Stevens	*He Thinks He's Ray Stevens*	MCA	Feb. 26
George Strait	*Greatest Hits, Volume II*	MCA	Nov. 16
George Strait	*Ocean Front Property*	MCA	Aug. 16
George Strait	*Strait From the Heart*	MCA	Feb. 26
Randy Travis	*Always & Forever*	Warner Bros.	July 14
Hank Williams, Jr.	*Hank Live*	Warner Bros.	Aug. 11
Hank Williams, Jr.	*Born to Boogie*	Curb	Sept. 18
Dwight Yoakam	*Guitars, Cadillacs, Etc., Etc.*	Reprise	Jan. 21
Dwight Yoakam	*Hillbilly Deluxe*	Reprise	Oct. 21

1987 (platinum)

Artist	Title	Company	Date
Alabama	*The Touch*	RCA	Jan. 6
Patsy Cline	*Greatest Hits*	MCA	Nov. 16
Lynyrd Skynyrd	*Nuthin' Fancy*	MCA	July 21
Lynyrd Skynyrd	*Pronounced Leh-nerd Skin-nerd*	MCA	July 21
Lynyrd Skynyrd	*Second Helping*	MCA	July 21
Anne Murray	*Christmas Wishes*	Capitol	Aug. 19
Anne Murray	*New Kind of Feeling*	Capitol	Aug. 19
Dolly Parton/ Linda Ronstadt/ Emmylou Harris	*Trio*	Warner Bros.	July 14
George Strait	*George Strait's Greatest Hits*	MCA	Feb. 26
George Strait	*Ocean Front Property*	MCA	Dec. 1
Randy Travis	*Always & Forever*	Warner Bros.	July 14
Randy Travis	*Storms of Life*	Warner Bros.	Feb. 10

Artist	Title	Company	Date

1987 (multiplatinum)

Artist	Title	Company	Date
Lynyrd Skynyrd	*Pronounced Leh-nerd Skin-nerd* (2 M)	MCA	July 21
Lynyrd Skynyrd	*Second Helping* (2 M)	MCA	July 21
Lynyrd Skynyrd	*Street Survivors* (2 M)	MCA	July 21
Lynyrd Skynyrd	*Gold & Platinum* (3 M)	MCA	July 21
Lynyrd Skynyrd	*One More (for) from the Road* (3 M)	MCA	July 21
Anne Murray	*Greatest Hits* (3 M)	Capitol	Oct. 16

1988 (gold)

Artist	Title	Company	Date
Alabama	*Alabama Live*	RCA	Aug.
Alabama	*Just Us*	RCA	Sept. 9
Emmylou Harris	*Quarter Moon in a Ten Cent Town*	Warner Bros.	Mar. 23
The Judds	*The Judds Greatest Hits*	RCA	Oct. 5
Reba McEntire	*The Last One to Know*	MCA	Apr. 20
Reba McEntire	*Reba*	MCA	Dec. 13
K. T. Oslin	*'80s Ladies*	RCA	Mar. 22
K. T. Oslin	*This Woman*	RCA	Dec. 21
Elvis Presley	*Roustabout*	RCA	May 20
George Strait	*Strait Country*	MCA	Apr. 18
George Strait	*If You Ain't Lovin' (You Ain't Livin')*	MCA	Apr. 22
Randy Travis	*Old 8x10*	Warner Bros.	Sept. 18
Conway Twitty	*Conway Twitty's Greatest Hits, Vol. II*	MCA	Nov. 29
Conway Twitty	*Number Ones*	MCA	Nov. 29
Conway Twitty & Loretta Lynn	*The Very Best of Conway Twitty & Loretta Lynn*	MCA	Nov. 29
Conway Twitty & Loretta Lynn	*We Only Make Believe*	MCA	Nov. 29
Ricky Van Shelton	*Wild-Eyed Dream*	Columbia	Apr. 11
Ricky Van Shelton	*Loving Proof*	Columbia	Dec. 2
Hank Williams, Jr.	*Wild Streak*	Warner Bros.	Aug.

1988 (platinum)

Artist	Title	Company	Date
Elvis Presley	*Aloha From Hawaii Via Satellite*	RCA	May 20
Elvis Presley	*Elvis as Recorded at Madison Square Garden*	RCA	May 20
Elvis Presley	*Elvis' Golden Records*	RCA	May 20
Elvis Presley	*Pure Gold*	RCA	May 20
George Strait	*Greatest Hits, Volume II*	MCA	June 28
Randy Travis	*Old 8x10*	Warner Bros.	Sept. 13
Hank Williams, Jr.	*Born to Boogie*	Warner Bros.	Feb. 23

1988 (multiplatinum)

Artist	Title	Company	Date
Elvis Presley	*Aloha From Hawaii Via Satellite* (2 M)	RCA	May 20
Elvis Presley	*Elvis Sings the Wonderful World of Christmas* (2 M)	RCA	May 20
Randy Travis	*Always & Forever* (2 M)	Warner Bros.	Jan. 28
Randy Travis	*Always & Forever* (3 M)	Warner Bros.	Aug.
Randy Travis	*Storms of Life* (2 M)	Warner Bros.	Apr. 8
Hank Williams, Jr.	*Hank Williams, Jr.'s Greatest Hits* (2 M)	Warner Bros.	Oct. 18

1989 (gold)

Artist	Title	Company	Date
Alabama	*Southern Star*	RCA	Apr. 4
Clint Black	*Killin' Time*	RCA	Sept. 24

Artist	Title	Company	Date
Earl Thomas Conley	*Greatest Hits*	RCA	July 26
Merle Haggard	*His Epic—The First Eleven—To Be Continued*	Epic	Aug. 7
Don Henley	*The End of the Innocence*	Geffen	Sept. 6
George Jones	*Anniversary—Ten Years of Hits*	Epic	Sept. 11
The Judds	*Christmas Time with the Judds*	RCA	Sept. 24
The Judds	*Rivers of Time*	RCA	June 9
Reba McEntire	*Sweet Sixteen*	MCA	Aug. 22
Willie Nelson	*Take It to the Limit*	Columbia	Sept. 18
Roy Orbison	*Mystery Girl*	Virgin	Mar. 29
Roy Orbison	*In Dreams: Greatest Hits*	Virgin	July 11
Johnny Paycheck	*Greatest Hits, Volume II*	Epic	Sept. 11
Ray Stevens	*I Have Returned*	MCA	July 9
George Strait	*Beyond the Blue Neon*	MCA	Apr. 29
Thirty-Eight Special	*Flashback*	A&M	Apr. 24
Keith Whitley	*Don't Close Your Eyes*	RCA	July 25
Hank Williams, Jr.	*Greatest Hits, Volume III*	Warner Bros.	Apr. 11
Dwight Yoakam	*Buenas Noches From a Lonely Room*	Reprise	Jan. 4

1989 (platinum)

Artist	Title	Company	Date
David Allan Coe	*Greatest Hits*	Columbia	Sept. 18
Charlie Daniels Band	*A Decade of Hits*	Epic	Jan. 23
The Judds	*Heartland*	RCA	Jan. 25
The Judds	*The Judds Greatest Hits*	RCA	May 23
Reba McEntire	*Greatest Hits*	MCA	May 16
Ronnie Milsap	*Greatest Hits, Volume 2*	RCA	May 5
Willie Nelson	*Pretty Paper*	Columbia	Sept. 18
Roy Orbison	*Mystery Girl*	Virgin	May 29
K. T. Oslin	*'80s Ladies*	RCA	May 23
Ricky Van Shelton	*Wild-Eyed Dream*	Columbia	July 24
Tammy Wynette	*Tammy's Greatest Hits*	Epic	June 9
Dwight Yoakam	*Guitars, Cadillacs, Etc., Etc.*	Reprise	May 10

1989 (multiplatinum)

Artist	Title	Company	Date
Alabama	*40 Hour Week* (2 M)	RCA	Oct. 25
Alabama	*Alabama's Greatest Hits* (3 M)	RCA	Oct. 25
Alabama	*Roll On* (3 M)	RCA	Oct. 25
Patsy Cline	*Greatest Hits* (2 M)	MCA	July 24
Don Henley	*Building the Perfect Beast* (2 M)	Geffen	Apr. 11
Kenny Rogers & Dolly Parton	*Once Upon a Christmas* (2 M)	RCA	Oct. 26

1990 (gold)

Artist	Title	Company	Date
Alabama	*Pass It on Down*	RCA	
Garth Brooks	*No Fences*	Capitol	Oct.
Garth Brooks	*Garth Brooks*	Capitol	
Rodney Crowell	*Diamonds & Dirt*	Columbia	1st Q
Charlie Daniels Band	*Simple Man*	Epic	June
Vince Gill	*When I Call Your Name*	MCA	Oct.
Vern Gosdin	*Chiseled in Stone*	Columbia	1st Q
Highway 101	*Highway 101*	Warner Bros./Sire	1st Q
Alan Jackson	*Here in the Real World*	Arista	Sept.
Kentucky Headhunters	*Pickin' on Nashville*	Mercury	May
k. d. lang	*Absolute Torch & Twang*	Warner Bros./Sire	Mar.
Kathy Mattea	*Willow in the Wind*	Mercury	July 24

Artist	Title	Company	Date
Reba McEntire	*Live*	MCA	July 11
Reba McEntire	*Rumor Has It*	MCA	Nov. 5
Ronnie Milsap	*Lost in the Fifties Tonight*	RCA	April 19
Lorrie Morgan	*Leave the Light On*	RCA	April 19
Restless Heart	*Big Dreams in a Small Town*	RCA	August 2
Kenny Rogers	*Something Inside So Strong*	Reprise	July 23
George Strait	*Livin' It Up*	MCA	
Randy Travis	*Heroes & Friends*	Warner Bros.	Nov. 30
Travis Tritt	*Country Club*	Warner Bros.	Sept. 19
Ricky Van Shelton	*RVS III*	Columbia	March 14
Keith Whitley	*I Wonder Do You Think of Me*	RCA	July 20
Keith Whitley	*Greatest Hits*	RCA	Nov. 7
Don Williams	*Best of Don Williams, Volume III*	MCA	Nov. 27
Hank Williams, Jr.	*Lone Wolf*	Warner Bros.	April 3

1990 (platinum)

Artist	Title	Company	Date
Clint Black	*Killin' Time*	RCA	Jan. 23
Garth Brooks	*Garth Brooks*	Capitol	Oct. 1
Garth Brooks	*No Fences*	Capitol	Oct. 30
Kentucky Headhunters	*Pickin' on Nashville*	Mercury	Oct. 17
Randy Travis	*No Holdin' Back*	Warner Bros.	Jan 17
Conway Twitty	*The Very Best of Conway Twitty*	MCA	May 14
Don Williams	*I Believe in You*	MCA	Nov. 27
Hank Williams, Jr.	*Greatest Hits, Volume 2*	Warner Bros.	March 7

1990 (multiplatinum)

Artist	Title	Company	Date
Clint Black	*Killin' Time* (2 M)	RCA	Oct. 29
Garth Brooks	*No Fences* (2 M)	Capitol	Nov. 30
Willie Nelson	*Willie & Family Live* (2 M)	Columbia	Aug. 22
Willie Nelson	*Stardust* (4 M)	Columbia	Jan. 9
Randy Travis	*Always & Forever* (4 M)	Warner Bros.	July 30

1990 (music videos—gold)

Artist	Title	Company	Date
Alabama	*Pass It on Down*	RCA	July 26
The Judds	*Great Video Hits*	RCA	June 26
Reba McEntire	*Reba*	MCA	March 9
Ronnie Milsap	*Great Video Hits*	RCA	July 26
Kenny Rogers	*Great Video Hits*	RCA	June 26
Various artists	*RCA Great Video Hits, Volume I*	RCA	Nov.
Keith Whitley	*I Wonder Do You Think of Me*	RCA	March 2
Don Williams	*Don Williams—Live*	RCA	July 26
Hank Williams, Jr.	*Full Access*	Cabin Fever	June 15

1990 (music videos—multiplatinum)

Artist	Title	Company	Date
Alabama	*Pass It on Down*	RCA	July 26

1991 (gold)

Artist	Title	Company	Date
Clint Black	*Put Yourself in My Shoes*	RCA	Jan. 8
Garth Brooks	*Ropin' the Wind*	Capitol	Nov. 8
Mark Chestnutt	*Too Cold at Home*	MCA	Sept. 24
Mac Davis	*Greatest Hits*	Columbia	Aug. 9
Vince Gill	*Pocket Full of Gold*	MCA	Aug. 7
Mickey Gilley	*Encore*	Epic	June 20

Artist	Title	Company	Date
Alan Jackson	*Don't Rock the Jukebox*	Arista	July 19
The Judds	*Love Can Build a Bridge*	RCA	Mar. 8
Kentucky Headhunters	*Electric Barnyard*	Mercury	June 5
Patty Loveless	*Honky Tonk Angel*	MCA	Apr. 9
Kathy Mattea	*Collection of Hits*	Mercury	Aug. 21
Reba McEntire	*My Kind of Country*	MCA	Aug. 7
K. T. Oslin	*Love in a Small Town*	RCA	Feb. 25
Dolly Parton	*Eagle When She Flies*	Columbia	July 2
Restless Heart	*Fast Movin' Train*	RCA	June 11
Dan Seals	*The Best of Dan Seals*	Capitol	May 30
Shenandoah	*The Road Not Taken*	Columbia	Jan. 22
Doug Stone	*Doug Stone*	Epic	Sept. 13
George Strait	*Chill of an Early Fall*	MCA	May 21
Randy Travis	*High Lonesome*	Warner Bros.	Oct. 31
Travis Tritt	*It's All About to Change*	MCA	Aug. 7
Ricky Van Shelton	*Backroads*	Columbia	July 16
Trisha Yearwood	*Trisha Yearwood*	MCA	Apr. 10
Dwight Yoakam	*If There Was a Way*	Reprise	Sept. 12
Dwight Yoakam	*Just Lookin' for a Hit*	Reprise	June 7

1991 (platinum)

Artist	Title	Company	Date
Clint Black	*Put Yourself in My Shoes*	RCA	Jan. 8
Garth Brooks	*Ropin' the Wind*	Capitol	Nov. 8
Vince Gill	*When I Call Your Name*	MCA	Oct. 4
Lee Greenwood	*Greatest Hits*	MCA	Apr. 11
Alan Jackson	*Don't Rock the Jukebox*	Arista	Oct. 25
Alan Jackson	*Here in the Real World*	Arista	Mar. 12
Reba McEntire	*Rumor Has It*	MCA	Apr. 1
Willie Nelson	"Always on My Mind" (S)	Columbia	Oct. 7
Statler Brothers	*Best of the Statler Brothers*	Mercury	Oct. 28
George Strait	*Beyond the Blue Neon*	MCA	Aug. 2
George Strait	*If You Ain't Lovin' (You Ain't Livin')*	MCA	Aug. 27
George Strait	*Livin' It Up*	MCA	Jan. 1
Randy Travis	*Heroes & Friends*	Warner Bros.	July 24
Travis Tritt	*Country Club*	MCA	July 30
Travis Tritt	*It's All About to Change*	MCA	Nov. 13
Ricky Van Shelton	*RVS III*	Columbia	Apr. 8

1991 (multiplatinum)

Artist	Title	Company	Date
Clint Black	*Put Yourself in My Shoes* (2 M)	RCA	Oct. 1
Garth Brooks	*No Fences* (3 M)	Capitol	Apr. 2
Garth Brooks	*No Fences* (4 M)	Capitol	July 3
Garth Brooks	*No Fences* (5 M)	Capitol	Oct. 24
Garth Brooks	*Garth Brooks* (2 M)	Capitol	May 29
Garth Brooks	*Ropin' the Wind* (4 M)	Capitol	Nov. 8
Patsy Cline	*Greatest Hits* (3 M)	Decca/MCA	Sept. 13
Anne Murray	*Greatest Hits* (4 M)	Capitol	May 30
Anne Murray	*Christmas Wishes* (2 M)	Capitol	Nov. 22
George Strait	*Greatest Hits* (2 M)	MCA	Sept. 19

1991 (music videos—gold)*
* (gold = 50,000 units sold; platinum = 100,000)

Artist	Title	Company	Date
Clint Black	*Put Yourself in My Shoes*	RCA	Feb. 25
Patsy Cline	*The Real Patsy Cline*	Cabin Fever	Mar. 1

Artist	Title	Company	Date
Alan Jackson	*Here in the Real World*	Arista	Mar. 26
The Judds	*Love Can Build a Bridge*	RCA	Feb. 7
Kentucky Headhunters	*Pickin' on Nashville*	PolyGram	Mar. 29
K. T. Oslin	*Love in a Small Town*	RCA	Mar. 20
Ricky Van Shelton	*To Be Continued*	Sony	Jan. 8

1991 (music videos—platinum)

Lee Greenwood	*God Bless the USA*	MCA	May 21
The Judds	*Love Can Build a Bridge*	MPI Home Video	Feb. 7
Hank Williams, Jr.	*Full Access*	Cabin Fever	Mar. 1

1991 (music videos—multiplatinum)

Garth Brooks	*Garth Brooks*	Capitol Nashville	Oct. 2

1992 (gold)

Alabama	*Greatest Hits, Volume II*	RCA	Mar. 27
Alabama	*American Pride*	RCA	Nov. 6
Clint Black	*The Hard Way*	RCA	Sept. 18
Suzy Bogguss	*Aces*	Liberty	Sept. 14
Garth Brooks	*Beyond the Season*	Liberty	Nov. 9
Garth Brooks	*The Chase*	Liberty	Nov. 19
Brooks & Dunn	*Brand New Man*	Arista	May 26
Mary-Chapin Carpenter	*Shooting Straight in the Dark*	Columbia	Apr. 8
Mark Chestnutt	*Long Necks and Short Stories*	MCA	Oct. 22
Billy Ray Cyrus	*Some Gave All*	Mercury	July 20
Billy Ray Cyrus	Achy Breaky Heart (S)	Mercury	July 7
Diamond Rio	*Diamond Rio*	Arista	Mar. 24
Vince Gill	*I Still Believe in You*	MCA	Nov. 6
George Jones	*Super Hits*	Epic	Feb. 13
Sammy Kershaw	*Don't Go Near the Water*	Mercury	Aug. 25
Hal Ketchum	*Past the Point of Rescue*	Curb	June 2
k. d. lang	*Shadowland*	Sire	Jan. 16
Tracy Lawrence	*Sticks and Stones*	Atlantic	July
Lyle Lovett	*Lyle Lovett and His Large Band*	Curb/MCA	Aug. 3
Gary Morris	*Why Lady Why*	Warner Bros.	Jan. 16
Collin Raye	*All I Can Be*	Epic	Apr.
Ray Stevens	*Greatest Hits*	MCA	Sept. 16
Doug Stone	*I Thought It Was You*	Epic	June 9
George Strait	*Ten Strait Hits*	MCA	July 20
George Strait	*Holding My Own*	MCA	June 23
George Strait	*Pure Country*	MCA	Nov. 18
Pam Tillis	*Put Yourself in My Place*	Arista	June 16
Aaron Tippin	*Read Between the Lines*	RCA	July 22
Randy Travis	*An Old Time Christmas*	Warner Bros.	Feb. 18
Travis Tritt	*T-R-O-U-B-L-E*	Warner Bros.	Oct. 20
Ricky Van Shelton	*Greatest Hits Plus*	Columbia	Nov. 6
Wynonna (Judd)	*Wynonna Judd*	MCA	June 5
Trisha Yearwood	*Hearts in Armor*	MCA	Nov. 4

1992 (platinum)

Clint Black	*The Hard Way*	RCA	Sept. 18
Garth Brooks	*Beyond the Season*	Liberty	Nov. 9

Artist	Title	Company	Date
Garth Brooks	*The Chase*	Liberty	Nov. 19
Brooks & Dunn	*Brand New Man*	Arista	Aug. 17
Glen Campbell	*By the Time I Get to Phoenix*	Capitol	Jan. 8
Glen Campbell	*Wichita Lineman*	Capitol	Feb. 12
Billy Ray Cyrus	*Some Gave All*	Mercury	July 20
Billy Ray Cyrus	Achy Breaky Heart (S)	Mercury	July 7
Charlie Daniels Band	*Fire on the Mountain*	Epic	Jan. 22
Tennessee Ernie Ford	*The Star Carol*	Capitol	Apr. 1
Tennessee Ernie Ford	*Hymns*	Capitol	Feb. 5
Vince Gill	*Pocket Full of Gold*	MCA	Jan. 8
Vince Gill	*I Still Believe in You*	MCA	Nov. 6
Lorrie Morgan	*Something in Red*	RCA	Aug. 28
Willie Nelson	*Willie Nelson Sings Kristofferson*	Columbia	Mar. 10
Dolly Parton	*Eagle When She Flies*	Columbia	Aug. 4
Ricky Skaggs	*Highways and Heartaches*	Epic	Jan. 3
George Strait	*Does Fort Worth Ever Cross Your Mind*	MCA	Jan. 13
George Strait	*Chill of an Early Fall*	MCA	Jan. 16
George Strait	*Pure Country*	MCA	Nov. 18
Tanya Tucker	*What Do I Do With Me*	Liberty	Sept. 16
Wynonna	*Wynonna*	MCA	June 5
Trisha Yearwood	*Trisha Yearwood*	MCA	Mar. 26

1992 (multiplatinum)

Artist	Title	Company	Date
Garth Brooks	*Garth Brooks* (3 M)	Liberty	Jan. 15
Garth Brooks	*Garth Brooks* (4 M)	Liberty	July 29
Garth Brooks	*No Fences* (6 M)	Liberty	Jan. 15
Garth Brooks	*No Fences* (7 M)	Liberty	Mar. 11
Garth Brooks	*No Fences* (8 M)	Liberty	June 17
Garth Brooks	*No Fences* (9 M)	Liberty	Sept. 23
Garth Brooks	*Ropin' the Wind* (6 M)	Liberty	Jan. 15
Garth Brooks	*Ropin' the Wind* (7 M)	Liberty	Mar. 30
Garth Brooks	*Ropin' the Wind* (8 M)	Liberty	July 29
Garth Brooks	*Beyond the Season* (2 M)	Liberty	Nov. 9
Garth Brooks	*The Chase* (5 M)	Liberty	Nov. 19
Glen Campbell	*Wichita Lineman* (2 M)	Capitol	Feb. 12
Patsy Cline	*Greatest Hits* (4 M)	MCA	July 22
Billy Ray Cyrus	*Some Gave All* (3 M)	Mercury	July 24
Billy Ray Cyrus	*Some Gave All* (4 M)	Mercury	Sept. 22
Billy Ray Cyrus	*Some Gave All* (5 M)	Mercury	Nov. 12
Charlie Daniels Band	*A Decade of Hits* (2 M)	Epic	Aug. 11
Alan Jackson	*Don't Rock the Jukebox* (2 M)	Arista	Aug. 26
The Judds	*Why Not Me* (2 M)	RCA	July 22
The Judds	*The Judds Greatest Hits* (2 M)	RCA	Jan. 15
Reba McEntire	*For My Broken Heart* (2 M)	MCA	July 20
Willie Nelson	*Honeysuckle Rose* (2 M)	Columbia	May 11
Willie Nelson	*Greatest Hits (& Some That Will Be)* (3 M)	Columbia	Mar. 10
Randy Travis	*Storms of Life* (3 M)	Warner Bros.	Feb. 18
Travis Tritt	*It's All About to Change* (2 M)	Warner Bros.	July 15

1992 (music videos—gold)

Artist	Title	Company	Date
Garth Brooks	*This Is Garth Brooks*	Liberty	Aug. 18
Vince Gill	*I Still Believe in You*	MCA Music Video	Nov.
Alan Jackson	*Here in the Real World*	Arista	Jan. 22
The Judds	*Their Final Concert*	MPI Home Video	Aug. 3

Artist	Title	Company	Date
Reba McEntire	*For My Broken Heart*	MCA Music Video	Apr. 15
Reba McEntire	*Reba in Concert*	MCA	Jan. 6
Randy Travis	*Forever and Ever*	Warner Music Video	Apr. 2

1992 (music videos—platinum)

Artist	Title	Company	Date
Garth Brooks	*This Is Garth Brooks*	Liberty	Aug. 18
The Judds	*Their Final Concert*	MPI Home Video	Aug. 3
Reba McEntire	*For My Broken Heart*	MCA Music	Nov. 16

1992 (music videos—multiplatinum)

Artist	Title	Company	Date
Garth Brooks	*Garth Brooks* (300,000 units)	Liberty	Jan. 15
Garth Brooks	*Garth Brooks* (400,000 units)	Liberty	April 24
Garth Brooks	*This Is Garth Brooks* (400,000 units)	Liberty	Aug. 18
Billy Ray Cyrus	*Billy Ray Cyrus* (200,000 units)	PolyGram Music Video	Oct. 5
Billy Ray Cyrus	*Billy Ray Cyrus* (300,000 units)	PolyGram Music Video	Nov. 2

1993 (gold)

Artist	Title	Company	Date
Suzy Bogguss	*Voice in the Wind*	Liberty	Oct. 12
Garth Brooks	*In Pieces*	Liberty	Oct. 28
Brooks & Dunn	*Hard Workin' Man*	Arista	Apr. 27
Mark Chestnutt	*Almost Goodbye*	MCA	Oct. 20
Patsy Cline	*Patsy Cline Collection*	MCA	May 27
Confederate Railroad	*Confederate Railroad*	Atlantic	May 28
Billy Ray Cyrus	*It Won't Be the Last*	Mercury	Sept. 13
Billy Dean	*Fire in the Dark*	Liberty	Oct. 12
Joe Diffie	*Honky Tonk Attitude*	Epic	Dec. 28
Exile	*Greatest Hits*	Epic	Jan. 7
Vince Gill	*Best of Vince Gill*	RCA	Mar. 8
Vince Gill	*Let There Be Peace on Earth*	MCA	Nov. 16
Alan Jackson	Chattahoochie (S)	Arista	Dec. 1
The Judds	*Collector's Series*	RCA	June 1
The Judds	*Wynonna & Naomi*	RCA	June 1
Toby Keith	*Toby Keith*	Mercury	Dec. 14
Sammy Kershaw	*Haunted Heart*	Mercury	Oct. 13
Tracy Lawrence	*Alibis*	Atlantic	Apr. 20
Chris LeDoux	*Whatcha Gonna Do with a Cowboy*	Liberty	Feb.
Little Texas	*Big Time*	Warner Bros.	Dec. 1
Patty Loveless	*Only What I Feel*	Epic	Oct. 19
Lyle Lovett	*Pontiac*	MCA	Nov. 15
Reba McEntire	*It's Your Call*	MCA	Feb. 19
Reba McEntire	*Merry Christmas to You*	MCA	July 8
Reba McEntire	*Greatest Hits, Volume II*	MCA	Dec. 1
John Michael Montgomery	*Life's a Dance*	Atlantic	Apr. 28
Lorrie Morgan	*Watch Me*	BNA	Jan. 14
Nitty Gritty Dirt Band	*20 Years of Dirt: Best of the Nitty Gritty Dirt Band*	Warner Bros.	Dec. 3
Dolly Parton	*Slow Dancing With the Moon*	Columbia	Apr. 19
Collin Raye	*In This Life*	Epic	Feb. 18
Kenny Rogers	*Christmas in America*	Reprise	Jan. 6
Sawyer Brown	*The Dirt Road*	Curb	Jan. 6
Statler Brothers	*Holy Bible—New Testament*	Mercury	July 13
Statler Brothers	*Today*	Mercury	July 13

Artist	Title	Company	Date
Doug Stone	*From the Heart*	Epic	Dec. 17
George Strait	*Easy Come, Easy Go*	MCA	Dec. 1
Marty Stuart	*This One's Gonna Hurt You*	MCA	Jan. 12
Pam Tillis	*Homeward Looking Angel*	Arista	June 6
Aaron Tippin	*Call of the Wild*	RCA	Dec. 17
Randy Travis	*Greatest Hits, Volume Two*	Warner Bros.	Jan. 27
Tanya Tucker	*Greatest Hits 1990–1992*	Liberty	Dec. 17
Various Artists	*Common Thread: Songs of the Eagles*	Giant	Dec. 17
Clay Walker	*Clay Walker*	Giant	Dec. 17
Wynonna	*Tell Me Why*	MCA	July 16
Trisha Yearwood	*The Song Remembers When*	MCA	Dec. 29
Dwight Yoakam	*This Time*	Reprise	May 25

1993 (platinum)

Artist	Title	Company	Date
Alabama	*Southern Star*	RCA	June 24
Alabama	*Pass It on Down*	RCA	June 24
Alabama	*American Pride*	RCA	June 24
Alabama	*Alabama Live*	RCA	Nov. 3
Garth Brooks	*In Pieces*	Liberty	Oct. 28
Brooks & Dunn	*Hard Workin' Man*	Arista	Apr. 27
Mary-Chapin Carpenter	*Come On, Come On*	Columbia	Jan. 19
Confederate Railroad	*Confederate Railroad*	Atlantic	May 28
Billy Ray Cyrus	*It Won't Be the Last*	Mercury	Sept. 13
Diamond Rio	*Diamond Rio*	Arista	Mar. 24
The Judds	*Christmas Time with the Judds*	RCA	Oct. 11
The Judds	*Love Can Build a Bridge*	RCA	July 19
Tracy Lawrence	*Alibis*	Atlantic	Aug. 31
Reba McEntire	*Sweet Sixteen*	MCA	Jan. 7
Reba McEntire	*Reba*	MCA	Feb. 9
Reba McEntire	*It's Your Call*	MCA	Feb. 19
Reba McEntire	*Whoever's in New England*	MCA	July 6
Reba McEntire	*Greatest Hits, Volume II*	MCA	Dec. 1
John Michael Montgomery	*Life's a Dance*	Atlantic	Aug. 27
Lorrie Morgan	*Leave the Light On*	BNA	Sept. 1
Lorrie Morgan	*Watch Me*	BNA	Dec. 7
Dolly Parton	*Slow Dancing with the Moon*	Columbia	Oct. 5
Ray Stevens	*Greatest Hits*	MCA	Feb. 10
Doug Stone	*Doug Stone*	Epic	Mar. 1
George Strait	*Easy Come, Easy Go*	MCA	Dec. 1
Aaron Tippin	*Read Between the Lines*	RCA	July 19
Travis Tritt	*T-R-O-U-B-L-E*	Warner Bros.	Mar. 10
Various Artists	*Common Thread: Songs of the Eagles*	Giant	Dec. 17
Keith Whitley	*Greatest Hits*	RCA	June 24
Wynonna	*Tell Me Why*	MCA	July 16
Trisha Yearwood	*Hearts in Armor*	MCA	Apr. 15
Dwight Yoakam	*If There Was a Way*	Reprise	Jan. 6
Dwight Yoakam	*This Time*	Reprise	Oct. 26

1993 (multiplatinum)

Artist	Title	Company	Date
Garth Brooks	*In Pieces* (3 M)	Liberty	Oct. 28
Garth Brooks	*Garth Brooks* (5 M)	Liberty	Sept. 21
Garth Brooks	*No Fences* (10 M)	Liberty	May 4
Brooks & Dunn	*Brand New Man* (3 M)	Arista	June 23
Brooks & Dunn	*Hard Workin' Man* (2 M)	Arista	Dec. 15

Artist	Title	Company	Date
Billy Ray Cyrus	*Some Gave All* (6 M)	Mercury	Jan. 15
Billy Ray Cyrus	*Some Gave All* (7 M)	Mercury	May 3
Vince Gill	*I Still Believe in You* (2 M)	MCA	Sept. 29
Alan Jackson	*A Lot About Livin' (and a Little 'Bout Love)* (2 M)	Arista	Aug. 11
Alan Jackson	*A Lot About Livin' (and a Little 'Bout Love)* (3 M)	Arista	Dec. 1
Waylon Jennings	*Greatest Hits* (4 M)	RCA	Nov 2.
Reba McEntire	*Rumor Has It* (2 M)	MCA	Apr.
Reba McEntire	*It's Your Call* (2 M)	MCA	June 16
Reba McEntire	*Greatest Hits, Volume II* (2 M)	MCA	Dec. 15
George Strait	*Pure Country* (2 M)	MCA	Feb. 2
Statler Brothers	*Best of the Statler Brothers* (2 M)	Mercury	July 13
Various Artists	*Common Thread: Songs of the Eagles* (2 M)	Giant	Dec. 17
Wynonna	*Wynonna* (3 M)	MCA	Aug. 6

1993 (music videos—gold)

Artist	Title	Company	Date
Billy Ray Cyrus	*Live on Tour*	PolyGram Music Video	Jan. 15
Reba McEntire	*Greatest Hits*	MCA Music Video	Dec. 15
Ray Stevens	*Comedy Video Classics*	Curb Home Video	Dec. 23
Travis Tritt	*It's All About to Change*	Warner Music Video	June 7

1993 (music videos—platinum)

Artist	Title	Company	Date
Billy Ray Cyrus	*Live on Tour*	PolyGram Music Video	Jan. 15
Vince Gill	*I Still Believe in You*	MCA Music Video	Apr. 21
Reba McEntire	*Reba in Concert*	MCA Music Video	Jan. 12
Ray Stevens	*Comedy Video Classics*	Curb Home Video	Dec. 23

1993 (music videos—multiplatinum)

Artist	Title	Company	Date
Garth Brooks	*This Is Garth Brooks* (500,000 units)	Liberty	Jan. 7
Billy Ray Cyrus	*Live on Tour* (200,000 units)	PolyGram Music Video	Jan. 17
Ray Stevens	*Comedy Video Classics* (300,000 units)	Curb Home Video	Dec. 23

1994 (gold)

Artist	Title	Company	Date
Alabama	*Cheap Seats*	RCA	Jan. 27
John Anderson	*Greatest Hits*	Warner Bros.	June 14
John Anderson	*Solid Ground*	RCA	June 14
David Ball	*Thinkin' Problem*	Warner Bros.	Aug. 17
John Berry	*John Berry*	Liberty	Oct. 26
Clint Black	*No Time to Kill*	RCA	Jan. 13
Clint Black	*One Emotion*	RCA	Dec. 7
BlackHawk	*BlackHawk*	Arista	Sept. 19
Brooks & Dunn	*Waitin' on Sundown*	Arista	Dec. 1
Jimmy Buffett	*Fruitcakes*	MCA	June 26
Mary-Chapin Carpenter	*State of the Heart*	Columbia	Mar. 15
Mary-Chapin Carpenter	*Stones in the Road*	Columbia	Dec. 6
Rosanne Cash	*King's Record Shop*	Columbia	Oct. 3
Patsy Cline	*Heartaches*	MCA	Oct. 20
Confederate Railroad	*Notorious*	Atlantic	Apr. 21
Billy Dean	*Young Man*	Liberty	Aug. 23

Artist	Title	Company	Date
Diamond Rio	*Close to the Edge*	Arista	Jan. 26
Joe Diffie	*Third Rock from the Sun*	Epic	Oct. 26
Joe Diffie	*Regular Joe*	Epic	Dec. 28
Jeff Foxworthy	*You Might Be a Redneck If . . .*	Warner Bros.	Oct. 18
Crystal Gayle	*Crystal Gayle's Greatest Hits*	Columbia	Dec. 27
Crystal Gayle	*These Days*	Columbia	Dec. 27
Vince Gill	*When Love Finds You*	MCA	Aug. 17
Vern Gosdin	*10 Years of Greatest Hits (Newly Recorded)*	Columbia	Dec. 27
Faith Hill	*Take Me As I Am*	Warner Bros.	May 11
Alan Jackson	*Honky Tonk Christmas*	Arista	Jan. 18
Alan Jackson	*Who I Am*	Arista	Aug. 30
George Jones	*Walls Can Fall*	MCA	Oct. 4
George Jones	*Wine Colored Roses*	Epic	Dec. 6
Toby Keith	*Boomtown*	Polydor	Nov. 29
Sammy Kershaw	*Feeling Good Train*	Mercury	Dec. 17
Tracy Lawrence	*I See It Now*	Atlantic	Nov. 10
Little Texas	*First Time for Everything*	Warner Bros.	Mar. 3
Little Texas	*Kick a Little*	Warner Bros.	Dec. 14
Patty Loveless	*When Fallen Angels Fly*	Epic	Nov. 18
Lynyrd Skynyrd	*The Boxed Set*	MCA	Dec. 19
Kathy Mattea	*Time Passes By*	Mercury	June 8
Kathy Mattea	*Lonesome Standard Time*	Mercury	Nov. 23
Kathy Mattea	*Untasted Honey*	Mercury	Nov. 29
The Mavericks	*What a Crying Shame*	MCA	Aug. 22
Martina McBride	*The Way That I Am*	RCA	Sept. 7
Neal McCoy	*No Doubt About It*	Atlantic	Aug. 11
Reba McEntire	*Best of Reba McEntire*	Mercury	Apr. 15
Reba McEntire	*Read My Mind*	MCA	June 28
Tim McGraw	Indian Outlaw (S)	Curb	Apr. 11
Tim McGraw	*Not a Moment Too Soon*	Curb	May 27
Tim McGraw	Don't Take the Girl (S)	Curb	June 28
John Michael Montgomery	I Swear (S)	Atlantic	Aug. 12
John Michael Montgomery	*Kickin' It Up*	Atlantic	Aug. 14
Lorrie Morgan	*War Paint*	RCA	Sept. 16
Neville Brothers	*Yellow Moon*	A&M	July 12
Dolly Parton/ Tammy Wynette/ Loretta Lynn	*Honky Tonk Angels*	Columbia	Jan. 5
Dolly Parton	*Home for Christmas*	Columbia	Dec. 27
Collin Raye	*Extremes*	Epic	July 13
Restless Heart	*Big Iron Horses*	RCA	Apr. 6
Marty Robbins	*Biggest Hits*	Columbia	Dec. 27
Marty Robbins	*Marty's Greatest Hits*	Columbia	Dec. 27
Sawyer Brown	*Outskirts of Town*	Curb	Oct. 27
Ricky Van Shelton	*A Bridge I Didn't Burn*	Columbia	Feb. 1
Ricky Van Shelton	*Don't Overlook Salvation*	Columbia	Feb. 3
Ricky Van Shelton	*Ricky Van Shelton Sings Christmas*	Columbia	Sept. 20
Shenandoah	*The Extra Mile*	Columbia	Jan. 14
Ricky Skaggs	*Country Boy*	Epic	Nov. 9
Ricky Skaggs	*Live in London*	Epic	Nov. 9
Soundtrack	*Maverick*	Atlantic	July 20
Statler Brothers	*Partners in Rhyme*	Mercury	Apr. 15
Statler Brothers	*Holy Bible—Old Testament*	Mercury	May 2

Artist	Title	Company	Date
Statler Brothers	*10th Anniversary*	Mercury	Dec. 27
Statler Brothers	*Atlanta Blue*	Mercury	Dec. 27
Doug Stone	*More Love*	Epic	Aug. 19
Doug Supernaw	*Red and Rio Grande*	RCA	July 8
Pam Tillis	*Sweetheart's Dance*	Arista	Sept. 21
The Tractors	*The Tractors*	Arista	Oct. 26
Randy Travis	*This Is Me*	Warner Bros.	July 6
Travis Tritt	*Ten Feet Tall and Bulletproof*	Warner Bros.	July 13
Tanya Tucker	*Soon*	Liberty	May 16
Tanya Tucker	*Love Me Like You Used To*	Liberty	Aug. 25
Conway Twitty	*The Very Best of Conway Twitty*	MCA	Sept. 26
Various Artists	*Rhythm, Country & Blues*	MCA	May 3
Various Artists	Rudolph the Red-Nosed Reindeer (S)	Disney	Mar. 25
Various Artists	*Skynyrd Friends*	MCA	Dec. 29
Steve Wariner	*I Am Ready*	Arista	Nov. 29

1994 (platinum)

Artist	Title	Company	Date
Clint Black	*No Time to Kill*	RCA	Jan. 13
Brooks & Dunn	*Waitin' on Sundown*	Arista	Dec. 1
Jimmy Buffett	*Fruitcakes*	MCA	Dec. 19
Mary-Chapin Carpenter	*Stones in the Road*	Columbia	Dec. 6
Mary-Chapin Carpenter	*Shooting Straight in the Dark*	Columbia	Dec. 13
Mark Chestnutt	*Almost Goodbye*	MCA	Oct. 27
Mark Chestnutt	*Longnecks and Short Stories*	MCA	Nov. 23
Mark Chestnutt	*Too Cold at Home*	MCA	Nov. 23
Joe Diffie	*Honky Tonk Attitude*	Epic	Dec. 5
Eagles	*Eagles Greatest Hits, Volume II*	Elektra	Aug. 17
Vince Gill	*When Love Finds You*	MCA	Aug. 17
Vince Gill	*Let There Be Peace on Earth*	MCA	Oct. 18
Alan Jackson	*Who I Am*	Arista	Aug. 30
George Jones	*Super Hits*	Epic	Feb. 3
Toby Keith	*Toby Keith*	Polydor	Oct. 25
Sammy Kershaw	*Don't Go Near the Water*	Mercury	July 22
Sammy Kershaw	*Haunted Heart*	Mercury	Nov. 17
Little Texas	*Big Time*	Warner Bros.	Apr. 12
Patty Loveless	*Only What I Feel*	Epic	Dec. 5
Kathy Mattea	*A Collection of Hits*	Mercury	Nov. 17
Reba McEntire	*Read My Mind*	MCA	June 28
Tim McGraw	*Not a Moment Too Soon*	Curb	May 27
John Michael Montgomery	*Kickin' It Up*	Atlantic	Mar. 14
Willie Nelson	*City of New Orleans*	Columbia	Oct. 7
Willie Nelson	*Without a Song*	Columbia	Nov. 14
Aaron Neville	*The Grand Tour*	A&M	Jan. 19
Collin Raye	*All I Can Be*	Epic	Dec. 5
Ray Stevens	*He Thinks He's Ray Stevens*	MCA	Nov. 14
Doug Stone	*I Thought It Was You*	Epic	Dec. 28
The Tractors	*The Tractors*	Arista	Nov. 29
Travis Tritt	*10 Feet Tall and Bulletproof*	Warner Bros.	Dec. 19
Tanya Tucker	*Can't Run from Myself*	Liberty	Nov. 29
Ricky Van Shelton	*Greatest Hits Plus*	Columbia	Dec. 27
Various Artists	*Rhythm, Country & Blues*	MCA	May 3
Clay Walker	*Clay Walker*	Giant	Aug. 31

Artist	Title	Company	Date
Hank Williams, Jr.	*24 Greatest Hits*	Polydor	Mar. 4
Trisha Yearwood	*The Song Remembers When*	MCA	Dec. 19
Dwight Yoakam	*Hillbilly Deluxe*	Warner Bros.	Apr. 12
Dwight Yoakam	*Just Lookin' for a Hit*	Reprise	Nov. 16

1994 (multiplatinum)

Artist	Title	Company	Date
Clint Black	*Killin' Time* (3 M)	RCA	Sept. 13
Garth Brooks	*In Pieces* (4 M)	Liberty	Jan. 26
Garth Brooks	*In Pieces* (5 M)	Liberty	Nov. 29
Garth Brooks	*No Fences* (11 M)	Liberty	Sept. 21
Garth Brooks	*Ropin' the Wind* (10 M)	Liberty	Nov. 16
Garth Brooks	*Garth Brooks* (6 M)	Liberty	Nov. 29
Brooks & Dunn	*Hard Workin' Man* (3 M)	Arista	Nov. 29
Brooks & Dunn	*Brand New Man* (4 M)	Arista	Nov. 29
Jimmy Buffett	*Boats, Beaches, Bars & Ballads* (2 M)	MCA	Oct. 27
Mary-Chapin Carpenter	*Come On, Come On* (2 M)	Columbia	Mar. 1
Mary-Chapin Carpenter	*Come On, Come On* (3 M)	Columbia	Dec. 13
Billy Ray Cyrus	*Some Gave All* (8 M)	Mercury	Nov. 17
Eagles	*Hotel California* (10 M)	Elektra	Aug. 12
Eagles	*Eagles Live* (2 M)	Elektra	Aug. 12
Eagles	*Eagles Greatest Hits, Volume II* (3 M)	Elektra	Aug. 17
Vince Gill	*I Still Believe in You* (3 M)	MCA	Aug. 1
Vince Gill	*Pocket Full of Gold* (2 M)	MCA	Dec. 19
Alan Jackson	*Here in the Real World* (2 M)	Arista	Aug. 10
Alan Jackson	*A Lot About Livin' (And a Little 'Bout Love)* (4 M)	Arista	Sept. 13
Alan Jackson	*Don't Rock the Jukebox* (3 M)	Arista	Nov. 29
Reba McEntire	*Greatest Hits* (2 M)	MCA	Mar. 4
Reba McEntire	*Greatest Hits, Volume II*	MCA	Nov. 23
Reba McEntire	*Read My Mind* (2 M)	MCA	Nov. 23
Reba McEntire	*It's Your Call* (3 M)	MCA	Dec. 19
Tim McGraw	*Not a Moment Too Soon* (2 M)	Curb	May 27
Tim McGraw	*Not a Moment Too Soon* (3 M)	Curb	Sept. 8
John Michael Montgomery	*Kickin' It Up* (2 M)	Atlantic	Aug. 11
Willie Nelson	*Always on My Mind* (4 M)	Columbia	Oct. 21
Statler Brothers	*The Best of the Statler Brothers* (3 M)	Mercury	Apr. 15
George Strait	*Pure Country* (3 M)	MCA	Jan. 24
George Strait	*Greatest Hits, Volume II* (2 M)	MCA	July 19
George Strait	*Easy Come, Easy Go* (2 M)	MCA	Nov. 23
Various Artists	*Common Thread: Songs of the Eagles* (3 M)	Giant	June 27
Trisha Yearwood	*Trisha Yearwood* (2 M)	MCA	Dec. 19
Dwight Yoakam	*This Time* (2 M)	Reprise	Aug. 31

1994 (music videos—gold)

Artist	Title	Company	Date
Billy Ray Cyrus	*The Video Collection*	PolyGram Music Video	Feb. 22
Alan Jackson	*Livin', Lovin,' and Rockin' That Jukebox*	Arista/West Home Video	Oct. 5
The Judds	*Naomi & Wynonna—The Farewell Tour*	MPI Home Video	Feb. 4
Tim McGraw	*Indian Outlaw*	Curb	June 9
John Michael Montgomery	*Kickin' It Up*	Atlantic	July 20

Artist	Title	Company	Date
1994 (music videos—gold)			
Various Artists	*Smoky Mountain Hymns—The Video*	Brentwood	Apr. 7
Various Artists	*Smoky Mountain Hymns Video, Volume 2*	Brentwood	Apr. 7
1994 (music videos—platinum)			
Patsy Cline	*The Real Patsy Cline*	Cabin Fever	Aug. 18
Billy Ray Cyrus	*The Video Collection*	PolyGram Music Video	June 20
Alan Jackson	*Livin,' Lovin,' and Rockin' That Jukebox*	Arista/West Home Video	June 21
Various Artists	*Smoky Mountain Hymns—The Video*	Brentwood	Apr. 7
1994 (music videos—multiplatinum)			
Billy Ray Cyrus	*Billy Ray Cyrus* (400,000 units)	PolyGram Home Video	Feb. 25
1995 (gold)			
Alabama	*Greatest Hits, Volume III*	RCA	Jan. 31
John Berry	*Standing on the Edge*	Capitol	Nov. 15
BlackHawk	*Strong Enough*	Arista	Nov. 14
Suzy Bogguss	*Something Up My Sleeve*	Capitol	Sept. 28
Garth Brooks	*The Hits*	Liberty	Feb. 17
Garth Brooks	*The Garth Brooks Collections*	Liberty	Mar. 7
Jimmy Buffett	*Barometer Soup*	MRG	Nov. 5
Tracy Byrd	*No Ordinary Man*	MCA	Jan. 31
Tracy Byrd	*Love Lessons*	MCA	Sept. 21
Johnny Cash	*The Johnny Cash Show*	Columbia	Feb. 16
Rosanne Cash	*Greatest Hits 1979–1989*	Columbia	Feb. 16
Mark Chesnutt	*What a Way to Live*	Decca	Mar. 14
Jerry Clower	*Mouth of the Mississippi*	Decca	Jan. 31
Jerry Clower	*From Yazoo City (Mississippi Talkin')*	MCA	Mar. 31
Billy Ray Cyrus	*Storm in the Heartland*	Mercury	Jan. 23
Charlie Daniels Band	*Midnight Wind*	Epic	Feb. 10
Diamond Rio	*Love a Little Stronger*	Arista	Apr. 5
Eagles	*Hell Freezes Over*	Geffen	Jan. 13
Jeff Foxworthy	*Games Rednecks Play*	Warner Bros.	Sept. 21
Faith Hill	*It Matters to Me*	Warner Bros.	Nov. 13
George Jones & Tammy Wynette	*Greatest Hits*	Epic	Sept. 12
Alison Krauss	*Now That I've Found You*	Rounder	May 1
Neal McCoy	*You Gotta Love That*	Atlantic	Aug. 8
Reba McEntire	*Have I Got a Deal For You*	MCA	Feb. 27
Reba McEntire	*Starting Over*	MCA	Dec. 5
Tim McGraw	*All I Want*	Curb	Dec. 7
John Michael Montgomery	*John Michael Montgomery*	Atlantic	Aug. 8
Lorrie Morgan	*Greatest Hits*	BNA	Sept. 1
David Lee Murphy	*Out with a Bang*	MCA	Dec. 1
Collin Raye	*I Think About You*	Epic	Nov. 16
Marty Robbins	*Greatest Hits, Volume III*	Columbia	Feb. 16
Kenny Rogers	*20 Great Years*	Reprise	Nov. 13
Sawyer Brown	*Greatest Hits 1990–1995*	Curb	Apr. 5
Doug Stone	*Greatest Hits*	Epic	June 6

Artist	Title	Company	Date
George Strait	*Lead On*	MCA	Jan. 13
George Strait	*Strait Out of the Box*	MCA	Nov. 16
Aaron Tippin	*You've Got to Stand for Something*	RCA	Mar. 10
Aaron Tippin	*Lookin' Back at Myself*	RCA	May 15
Rick Trevino	*Rick Trevino*	Columbia	Sept. 5
Travis Tritt	*Greatest Hits—From the Beginning*	Warner Bros.	Nov. 16
Tanya Tucker	*What's Your Mama's Name*	Columbia	Feb. 16
Tanya Tucker	*Would You Lay with Me*	Columbia	Feb. 16
Tanya Tucker	*Strong Enough to Bend*	Liberty	Feb. 17
Tanya Tucker	*Greatest Hits*	Liberty	Feb. 17
Tanya Tucker	*Tennessee Woman*	Liberty	Feb. 17
Shania Twain	*The Woman in Me*	Mercury	May 31
Shania Twain	"Whose Bed Have Your Boots Been Under" (S)	Mercury	Aug. 8
Various Artists	*Keith Whitley: A Tribute Album*	RCA	Aug. 17
Clay Walker	*If I Could Make a Living*	Giant	Feb. 9
Lari White	*Wishes*	RCA	May 15
Tammy Wynette	*Greatest Hits, Volume II*	Epic	Feb. 10
Trisha Yearwood	*Thinkin' About You*	MCA	Apr. 26

1995 (platinum)

Artist	Title	Company	Date
Alabama	*Greatest Hits, Volume II*	RCA	July 31
Alabama	*Greatest Hits, Volume III*	RCA	Nov. 21
David Ball	*Thinkin' Problem*	Warner Bros.	Mar. 16
John Berry	*John Berry*	Capitol	Sept. 21
Clint Black	*One Emotion*	RCA	Dec. 22
BlackHawk	*BlackHawk*	Arista	Mar. 9
Suzy Bogguss	*Aces*	Liberty	Feb. 17
Garth Brooks	*The Hits*	Liberty	Feb. 17
Garth Brooks	*The Garth Brooks Collections*	Liberty	Mar. 7
Tracy Byrd	*No Ordinary Man*	MCA	Apr. 26
Johnny Cash	*The Johnny Cash Portrait*	Columbia	Feb. 16
Confederate Railroad	*Notorious*	Atlantic	Jan. 4
Diamond Rio	*Love a Little Stronger*	Arista	Nov. 22
Joe Diffie	*Third Rock From the Sun*	Epic	Jan. 13
Eagles	*Hell Freezes Over*	Geffen	Jan. 13
Jeff Foxworthy	*You Might Be a Redneck If . . .*	Warner Bros.	Jan. 5
Jeff Foxworthy	*Games Rednecks Play*	Warner Bros.	Sept. 21
Larry Gatlin	*Straight Ahead*	Columbia	Feb. 16
Vince Gill	*Best of Vince Gill*	RCA	Feb. 1
Faith Hill	*Take Me As I Am*	Warner Bros.	Jan. 5
Alison Krauss	*Now That I've Found You*	Rounder	May 23
Tracy Lawrence	*Sticks and Stones*	Atlantic	Jan. 4
Tracy Lawrence	*I See It Now*	Atlantic	Aug. 8
The Mavericks	*What a Crying Shame*	MCA	Feb. 16
Martina McBride	*The Way That I Am*	RCA	May 15
Neal McCoy	*No Doubt About It*	Atlantic	Oct. 18
Reba McEntire	*Reba McEntire Live*	MCA	Aug. 25
Reba McEntire	*The Last One to Know*	MCA	Aug. 11
Reba McEntire	*Starting Over*	MCA	Dec. 5
Tim McGraw	*All I Want*	Curb	Dec. 7
John Michael Montgomery	*John Michael Montgomery*	Atlantic	Aug. 8
Johnny Paycheck	*Take This Job and Shove It*	Epic	Feb. 10
Collin Raye	*Extremes*	Epic	June 6
Collin Raye	*In This Life*	Epic	July 7

Artist	Title	Company	Date
Dan Seals	*The Best of Dan Seals*	Liberty	Feb. 17
George Strait	*Lead On*	MCA	Jan. 13
George Strait	*Strait Out of the Box*	MCA	Nov. 16
Pam Tillis	*Homeward Looking Angel*	Arista	Apr. 5
Pam Tillis	*Sweetheart's Dance*	Arista	Apr. 26
Randy Travis	*Greatest Hits, Volume I*	Warner Bros.	Mar. 6
Randy Travis	*Greatest Hits, Volume II*	Warner Bros.	Mar. 6
Tanya Tucker	*Greatest Hits 1990–1992*	Liberty	Feb. 17
Shania Twain	*The Woman in Me*	Mercury	June 22
Clay Walker	*If I Could Make a Living*	Giant	May 4
Trisha Yearwood	*Thinkin' About You*	MCA	Dec. 13
Dwight Yoakam	*Buenas Noches From a Lonely Room*	Reprise	Mar. 22

1995 (multiplatinum)

Artist	Title	Company	Date
Alabama	*Greatest Hits* (4 M)	RCA	July 31
John Anderson	*Seminole Wind* (2 M)	RCA	June 1
Brooks & Dunn	*Brand New Man* (5 M)	Arista	April 5
Brooks & Dunn	*Hard Workin' Man* (4 M)	Arista	April 5
Brooks & Dunn	*Waitin' on Sundown* (2 M)	Arista	May 30
Garth Brooks	*No Fences* (13 M)	Liberty	Feb. 17
Garth Brooks	*Ropin' the Wind* (11 M)	Liberty	Feb. 17
Garth Brooks	*The Chase* (6 M)	Liberty	Feb. 17
Garth Brooks	*The Garth Brooks Collections* (3 M)	Liberty	Mar. 7
Garth Brooks	*The Hits* (5 M)	Liberty	Feb. 17
Garth Brooks	*The Hits* (6 M)	Liberty	June 23
Garth Brooks	*The Hits* (7 M)	Liberty	Aug. 14
Garth Brooks	*The Hits* (8 M)	Liberty	Sept. 28
Garth Brooks	*Beyond the Season* (3 M)	Liberty	Nov. 15
Patsy Cline	*Greatest Hits* (6 M)	Decca/MCA	Feb. 2
Charlie Daniels Band	*Million Mile Reflections* (3 M)	Epic	Jan. 13
Eagles	*Eagles Greatest Hits, Volume II* (7 M)	Elektra	June 5
Eagles	*Eagles—Their Greatest Hits 1971–1975* (22 M)	Elektra	June 5
Eagles	*Hell Freezes Over* (4 M)	Geffen	Jan. 13
Eagles	*Hell Freezes Over* (5 M)	Geffen	Apr. 6
Eagles	*Hotel California* (14 M)	Elektra	June 5
Jeff Foxworthy	*You Might Be a Redneck If . . .* (2 M)	Warner Bros.	Aug. 10
Vince Gill	*When Love Finds You* (3 M)	MCA	Dec. 13
Alan Jackson	*Who I Am* (2 M)	Arista	Feb. 14
Alan Jackson	*Who I Am* (3 M)	Arista	May 30
Alan Jackson	*A Lot About Livin' (And a Little 'Bout Love)* (5 M)	Arista	Apr. 5
Alan Jackson	*A Lot About Livin' (And a Little 'Bout Love)* (6 M)	Arista	July 14
Alan Jackson	*Don't Rock the Jukebox* (4 M)	Arista	Apr. 5
Kentucky Head-hunters	*Pickin' on Nashville* (2 M)	Mercury	Jan. 10
Tracy Lawrence	*Alibis* (2 M)	Atlantic	Aug. 8
Reba McEntire	*For My Broken Heart* (3 M)	MCA	Aug. 11
Reba McEntire	*Greatest Hits* (3 M)	MCA	Aug. 11
Reba McEntire	*Greatest Hits, Volume II* (4 M)	MCA	Aug. 11
Reba McEntire	*Read My Mind* (3 M)	MCA	Aug. 11

Artist	Title	Company	Date
Tim McGraw	*Not a Moment Too Soon* (4 M)	Curb	Apr. 5
Tim McGraw	*All I Want* (2 M)	Curb	Dec. 7
John Michael Montgomery	*Life's a Dance* (2 M)	Atlantic	Jan. 4
John Michael Montgomery	*Life's a Dance* (3 M)	Atlantic	Aug. 8
John Michael Montgomery	*Kickin' It Up* (3 M)	Atlantic	Jan. 4
John Michael Montgomery	*John Michael Montgomery* (2 M)	Atlantic	Aug. 8
George Strait	*Pure Country* (5 M)	MCA	Dec. 13
George Strait	*Strait Out of the Box* (2 M)	MCA	Dec. 13
The Tractors	*The Tractors* (2 M)	Arista	Nov. 22
Shania Twain	*The Woman in Me* (2 M)	Mercury	Aug. 14
Shania Twain	*The Woman in Me* (3 M)	Mercury	Nov. 7
Shania Twain	*The Woman in Me* (4 M)	Mercury	Dec. 15
Wynonna	*Wynonna* (4 M)	Curb/MCA	Jan. 20

1995 (music videos—gold)

Artist	Title	Company	Date
Eagles	*Hell Freezes Over*	MCA/Geffen Home Video	Jan. 28
Jeff Foxworthy	*You Might Be a Redneck If . . .*	Warner/Reprise Video	Apr. 20
Shania Twain	*The Woman in Me*	Polygram Music Video/ Mercury	Dec. 5

1995 (music videos—platinum)

Artist	Title	Company	Date
Eagles	*Hell Freezes Over*	MCA/Geffen Home Video	Jan. 28
Eagles	*Hell Freezes Over* (200,000)	MCA/Geffen Home Video	June 19
Jeff Foxworthy	*You Might Be a Redneck If . . .*	Warner/Reprise Video	Apr. 20
Reba McEntire	*Greatest Hits*	MCA/Music Video	Feb. 28
Elvis Presley	*The Lost Performances*	MGM/UA Home Video; Turner Entertnmt.	Apr. 19

1996 (gold)

Artist	Title	Company	Date
Alabama	*In Pictures*	RCA	Jan. 11
Clint Black	*Greatest Hits*	RCA	Dec. 1
Brooks & Dunn	*Borderline*	Arista	July 30
Garth Brooks	*Fresh Horses*	Capitol/Nashv.	Feb. 21
Jimmy Buffett	*Banana Wind*	MCA	Aug. 7
Jimmy Buffett	*Christmas Island*	Margaritaville	Dec. 11
Mary-Chapin Carpenter	*A Place in the World*	Columbia	Dec. 20
Deana Carter	*Did I Shave My Legs for This?*	Capitol/Nashv.	Nov. 8
Terri Clark	*Terri Clark*	Mercury/Nashv.	Apr. 5
Charlie Daniels Band	*Super Hits*	Epic	May 9
Billy Dean	*Greatest Hits*	Capitol/Nashv.	July 22
Diamond Rio	*Diamond Rio IV*	Arista	Sept. 13
Joe Diffie	*Life's So Funny*	Epic	July 3
Steve Earle	*Copperhead Road*	Uni	May 1
Jeff Foxworthy	*Crank It Up—The Music Album*	Warner Bros.	Nov. 18
Vince Gill	*Souvenirs*	MCA	Jan. 29
Vince Gill	*High Lonesome Sound*	MCA	Oct. 4

Artist	Title	Company	Date
Don Henley	*Actual Miles—Don Henley's Greatest Hits*	Geffen	Mar. 26
Alan Jackson	*Greatest Hits Collection*	Arista	Jan. 3
k. d. lang	*All You Can Eat*	Warner Bros.	Jan. 8
Tracy Lawrence	*Time Marches On*	Atlantic	Mar. 12
Little Texas	*Greatest Hits*	Warner Bros.	Dec. 6
Lone Star	*Lone Star*	RCA	Oct. 28
Patty Loveless	*The Trouble With the Truth*	Epic	Aug. 1
Kathy Mattea	*Walking Away a Winner*	Mercury/Nashv.	Oct. 18
The Mavericks	*Music for All Occasions*	MCA	Apr. 4
Martina McBride	*Wild Angels*	RCA	Feb. 23
Mindy McCready	*Ten Thousand Angels*	BNA	Aug. 27
John Michael Montgomery	*What I Do the Best*	Atlantic	Nov. 6
Willie Nelson	*Super Hits*	Columbia	Apr. 17
Aaron Neville	*Tatooed Heart*	A&M	Mar. 12
Nitty Gritty Dirt Band	*More Great Dirt: The Best of the NGDB, Volume 2*	Warner Bros.	Aug. 8
Jim Reeves	*The Legendary Jim Reeves*	RCA	Sept. 20
Statler Brothers	*Gospel Favorites*	Polygram Special	Aug. 13
George Strait	*Clear Blue Sky*	MCA	July 30
Marty Stuart	*Tempted*	MCA	Apr. 25
Aaron Tippin	*Tool Box*	RCA	Apr. 8
Shania Twain	*Shania Twain*	Mercury/Nashv.	Oct. 30
Various Artists	*Academy of Country Music— 101 Greatest Country Hits*	K-Tel	May 16
Various Artists	*Amazing Grace: A Country Salute to Gospel*	Sparrow	June 20
Various Artists	*Smoky Mountain Hymns, Volume I*	Brentwood	Aug. 19
Clay Walker	*Hypnotize the Moon*	Giant	Mar. 22
Wynonna	*Revelations*	MCA	Apr. 18
Dwight Yoakam	*Gone*	Reprise	Jan. 8
Dwight Yoakam	*Dwight Live*	Reprise	Feb. 27

1996 (platinum)

Artist	Title	Company	Date
Alabama	*In Pictures*	RCA	Sept. 20
Alabama	*Cheap Seats*	RCA	Sept. 26
Clint Black	*Greatest Hits*	RCA	Dec. 1
Brooks & Dunn	*Borderline*	Arista	July 30
Garth Brooks	*Fresh Horses*	Capitol Nashv.	Feb. 21
Deana Carter	*Did I Shave My Legs for This?*	Capitol Nashv.	Nov. 21
Vince Gill	*Souvenirs*	MCA	Jan. 29
Faith Hill	*It Matters to Me*	Warner Bros.	Feb. 27
Alan Jackson	*Greatest Hits Collection*	Arista	Jan. 3
Tracy Lawrence	*Time Marches On*	Atlantic	Oct. 23
Patty Loveless	*When Fallen Angels Fly*	Epic	Apr. 11
Marshall Tucker Band	*The Marshall Tucker Band's Greatest Hits*	AJK Music	Dec. 9
Neal McCoy	*You Gotta Love That*	Atlantic	Feb. 29
Mindy McCready	*Ten Thousand Angels*	BNA	Dec. 16
Reba McEntire	*Merry Christmas to You*	MCA	Sept. 19
Lorrie Morgan	*Greatest Hits*	BNA	Mar. 15
Collin Raye	*I Think About You*	Epic	Sept. 11
George Strait	*Holding My Own*	MCA	Sept. 19
George Strait	*#7*	MCA	Sept. 19
George Strait	*Merry Christmas Strait to You*	MCA	Sept. 19

Artist	Title	Company	Date

1996 (multiplatinum)

Artist	Title	Company	Date
George Strait	*Something Special*	MCA	Sept. 19
George Strait	*Ten Strait Hits*	MCA	Sept. 19
George Strait	*Blue Clear Sky*	MCA	Sept. 19
Travis Tritt	*Greatest Hits—From the Beginning*	Warner Bros.	May 2
Clay Walker	*Hypnotize the Moon*	Giant	Sept. 11
Wynonna	*Revelations*	MCA	Apr. 18
Alabama	*Greatest Hits* (5 M)	RCA	Apr. 1
Alabama	*Alabama Christmas* (2 M)	RCA	July 11
Alabama	*The Closer You Get* (4 M)	RCA	Sept. 30
Blackhawk	*Blackhawk* (2 M)	Arista	July 24
Garth Brooks	*Fresh Horses* (3 M)	Capitol Nashv.	Feb. 21
Garth Brooks	*Fresh Horses* (4 M)	Capitol Nashv.	May 14
Garth Brooks	*Garth Brooks* (7 M)	Capitol Nashv.	Mar. 8
Garth Brooks	*The Hits* (9 M)	Capitol Nashv.	Oct. 30
Patsy Cline	*Greatest Hits* (7 M)	MCA	Sept. 19
Billy Ray Cyrus	*Some Gave All* (9 M)	Mercury	July 16
Eagles	*Hell Freezes Over* (6 M)	Geffen	Jan. 17
Jeff Foxworthy	*Games Redneck Play* (2 M)	Warner Bros.	Jan. 18
Jeff Foxworthy	*You Might Be a Redneck If . . .* (3 M)	Warner Bros.	June 14
Vince Gill	*When I Call Your Name* (2 M)	MCA	Sept. 19
Vince Gill	*I Still Believe in You* (4 M)	MCA	Sept. 19
Faith Hill	*Take Me As I Am* (2 M)	Warner Bros.	Aug. 8
Alan Jackson	*Greatest Hits Collection* (2 M)	Arista	Jan. 3
Alan Jackson	*Greatest Hits Collection* (3 M)	Arista	Apr. 17
Alison Krauss	*Now That I've Found You* (2 M)	Rounder	Mar. 1
k. d. lang	*Ingenue* (2 M)	Sire	May 1
John Michael Montgomery	*John Michael Montgomery* (3 M)	Atlantic	Feb. 29
John Michael Montgomery	*Kickin' It Up* (4 M)	Atlantic	June 13
Kenny Rogers	*Eyes That See in the Dark* (2 M)	RCA	Nov. 8
George Strait	*Strait Out of the Box* (3 M)	MCA	Feb. 23
George Strait	*Greatest Hits* (3 M)	MCA	June 24
George Strait	*Greatest Hits, Volume II* (3 M)	MCA	Sept. 19
George Strait	*Ocean Front Property* (2 M)	MCA	Sept. 19
Randy Travis	*Always & Forever* (5 M)	Warner Bros.	Aug. 7
Randy Travis	*No Holdin' Back* (2 M)	Warner Bros.	Aug. 8
Travis Tritt	*Country Club* (2 M)	Warner Bros.	June 7
Travis Tritt	*It's All About to Change* (3 M)	Warner Bros.	June 7
Travis Tritt	*T-R-O-U-B-L-E* (2 M)	Warner Bros.	June 7
Shania Twain	*The Woman in Me* (5 M)	Mercury Nashv.	Feb. 7
Shania Twain	*The Woman in Me* (6 M)	Mercury Nashv.	Mar. 20
Shania Twain	*The Woman in Me* (7 M)	Mercury Nashv.	May 23
Shania Twain	*The Woman in Me* (8 M)	Mercury Nashv.	Sept. 13
Dwight Yoakam	*This Time* (3 M)	Reprise	Aug. 8

1996 (music videos—gold)

Artist	Title	Company	Date
Various Artists	*Smoky Mountain Christmas Video* (longform)	Brentwood	Aug. 19

1996 (music videos—platinum)

Artist	Title	Company	Date
Shania Twain	*The Woman in Me* (longform)	Polygram Music	Apr. 5

NASHVILLE SONGWRITERS ASSOCIATION, INTERNATIONAL

Awards and Presentations*

SONGWRITER OF THE YEAR

1967	Dallas Frazier
1968	Bobby Russell
1969	Merle Haggard
1970	Kris Kristofferson
1971	Kris Kristofferson
1972	Tom T. Hall
1973	Kris Kristofferson
1974	Don Wayne
1975	Ben Peters
1976	Bob McDill
1977	Roger Bowling and Hal Bynum
1978	Sonny Throckmorton
1979	Sonny Throckmorton
1980	Bob Morrison
1981	Kye Fleming and Dennis Morgan
1982	Kye Fleming
	Dennis Morgan
1983	Jeff Silbar
	Larry Henley
1984	Kenny O'Dell
1985	Bob McDill
1986	Paul Overstreet
1987	Don Schlitz
1988	Bob McDill
1989	Kostas
1990	Jon Vezner
1991	Pat Alger
1992	Gary Burr (tie)
	Susan Longacre
1993	Dennis Linde
1994	Gary Burr
1995	Mark D. Sanders

SONGWRITER/ARTIST OF THE YEAR
(begun in 1989)

1989	Clint Black
1990	Vince Gill
1991	Alan Jackson
1992	Garth Brooks (tie)
	Alan Jackson
1993	Clint Black
1994	Vince Gill
1995	Vince Gill

SONG OF THE YEAR
(begun in 1978, this award was initially presented to the writer as Songwriter of the Year through 1977)

1978	"You Needed Me"/Randy Goodrum
1979	"She Believes in Me"/Steve Gibb
1980	"He Stopped Loving Her Today"/Bobby Braddock and Curly Putman
1981	"You're the Reason God Made Oklahoma"/Larry Collins and Sandy Pinkard
1982	"Always on My Mind"/Johnny Christopher, Wayne Carson (Thompson), Mark James
1983	"Holding Her And Loving You"/Walt Aldridge, Tommy Brasfield
1984	"Mama He's Crazy"/Kenny O'Dell
1985	"Baby's Got Her Blue Jeans On"/Bob McDill
1986	"On the Other Hand"/Don Schlitz, Paul Overstreet
1987	"Forever and Ever, Amen"/Don Schlitz, Paul Overstreet
1988	"Chisled in Stone"/Max D. Barnes, Vern Gosdin
1989	"If Tomorrow Never Comes"/Garth Brooks, Kent Blazy
1990	"Where've You Been"/Jon Vezner, Don Henry
1991	"Somewhere in My Broken Heart"/Richard Leigh, Billy Dean
1992	"Achy Breaky Heart"/Don Von Tress
1993	"The Song Remembers When"/Hugh Prestwood
1994	"I Swear"/Frank J. Myers, Gary Baker
1995	"I Can Love You Like That"/Jennifer Kimball, Steve Diamond, Maribeth Derry

SONGWRITERS HALL OF FAME MEMBERS

Year Inducted	Name
1978	Joe Allison
1975	Bill Anderson
1970	Gene Autry
1992	Max D. Barnes
1976	Carl Belew
1982	Chuck Berry
1991	Charlie Black

*NSAI is an organization based in Nashville, Tennessee, whose goal is "to advance, promote, foster, and benefit composers and authors of musical compositions," primarily in the country & western field. The Songwriter of the Year (established 1967) and Song of the Year (established 1978) awards are based on the vote of NSAI membership.

Those elected to the Hall of Fame are presented with a bronze sculpture called The Manny. Since 1977, the maximum number of songwriters that can be inducted annually is limited to four.

Year Inducted	Name	Year Inducted	Name
1986	Otis Blackwell	1970	Bob Miller
1970	Johnny Bond	1975	Eddie Miller
1989	Rory Michael Bourke	1973	Roger Miller
1981	Bobby Braddock	1971	Bill Monroe
1990	Sue Brewer	1976	Moon Mullican
1970	Albert Brumley	1973	Steve & Ed Nelson
1972	Boudleaux & Felice Bryant	1973	Willie Nelson
1971	Smiley Burnette	1980	Mickey Newbury
1988	Hoagy Carmichael	1971	Bob Nolan
1971	Jenny Lou Carson	1995	Kenny O'Dell
1970	A. P. Carter	1987	Roy Orbison
1971	Wilf Carter	1995	Buck Owens
1977	Johnny Cash	1971	Tex Owens
1989	Maggie Cavender	1986	Dolly Parton
1995	Jerry Chestnutt	1970	Leon Payne
1973	Jack Clement	1985	Carl Perkins
1971	Zeke Clements	1980	Ben Peters
1974	Hank Cochran	1976	Curly Putman
1991	Sonny Curtis	1972	Jack Rhodes
1970	Ted Daffan	1971	Tex Ritter
1970	Vernon Dalhart	1975	Marty Robbins
1984	Hal David	1972	Don Robertson
1971	Jimmie Davis	1971	Carson J. Robison
1971	Alton & Rabon Delmore	1970	Jimmie Rodgers
1971	Al Dexter	1970	Fred Rose
1975	Danny Dill	1994	Bobby Russell
1979	Rev. Thomas A. Dorsey	1993	Don Schlitz
1994	Jerry Foster & Bill Rice	1988	Troy Seals
1976	Stephen Foster (special award)	1989	Sanger D. "Whitey" Shafer
1976	Dallas Frazier	1984	Billy Sherrill
1972	Lefty Frizzell	1983	Beasley Smith
1973	Don Gibson	1978	Hank Snow
1970	Rex Griffin	1979	Joe South
1977	Woody Guthrie	1971	Tim Spencer
1977	Merle Haggard	1980	Ray Stevens
1978	Tom T. Hall	1970	Redd Stewart
1970	Stuart Hamblen	1971	Gene Sullivan
1983	W. C. Handy	1987	Sonny Throckmorton
1990	Ted Harris	1976	Mel Tillis
1982	William J. "Billy" Hill	1970	Floyd Tillman
1994	Buddy Holly	1970	Merle Travis
1992	Wayland Holyfield	1970	Ernest Tubb
1971	Vaughn Horton	1993	Conway Twitty
1973	Harlan Howard	1971	Jimmy Wakely
1971	Bradley Kincaid	1970	Cindy Walker
1970	Pee Wee King	1975	Wayne Walker
1977	Kris Kristofferson	1971	Wiley Walker
1993	Red Lane	1978	Don Wayne
1980	Hudie "Leadbelly" Ledbetter	1990	Jimmy Webb
1994	Richard Leigh	1981	Ray Whitley
1976	John D. Loudermilk	1975	Marijohn Wilkin
1979	Charlie & Ira Louvin	1970	Hank Williams, Sr.
1983	Loretta Lynn	1970	Bob Wills
1970	Vic McAlpin	1995	Norro Wilson
1985	Bob McDill	1971	Scotty Wiseman
1979	Elsie McWilliams		

SONGWRITERS HALL OF FAME

Inducted in 1970

Gene Autry
"Back in the Saddle Again" (C)
"Goodbye Little Darlin' Goodbye"
"Silver Haired Daddy of Mine"
"Be Honest with Me"
"Here Comes Santa Claus" (C)

Johnny Bond
"Tomorrow Never Comes"
"Cimmaron"
"I Wonder Where You Are Tonight"
"Ten Little Bottles"

Albert Brumley
"I'll Fly Away"
"I'll Meet You in the Morning"
"Turn Your Radio On"
"Jesus, Hold My Hand"

A. P. Carter
"Wildwood Flower"
"Wabash Cannon Ball"
"Will the Circle Be Unbroken"
"Keep on the Sunny Side"

Ted Daffan
"Born to Lose"
"No Letter Today"
"Worried Mind"
"Truck Driver's Blues"

Vernon Dalhart
"Prisoner's Song"
"Wreck of the Old 97"
"Death of Floyd Collins"

Rex Griffin
"Just Call Me Lonesome"
"The Last Letter"
"I Told You So"
"Won't You Ride in My Little Red Wagon"

Stuart Hamblen
"It Is No Secret (What God Can Do)"
"Texas Plains"
"My Mary"
"This Ole House"
"Remember Me, I'm the One Who Loves You"

Pee Wee King
"Tennessee Waltz" (C)
"Slowpoke" (C)
"Bonaparte's Retreat" (C)

Vic McAlpin
"To My Sorrow"
"Standing at the End of the World"
"God Walks These Hills with Me"
"Almost"
"What Locks the Door"

Bob Miller
"Rockin' Alone in an Old Rocking Chair"
"Seven Years with the Wrong Woman"
"Little Red Caboose Behind the Train"
"In the Blue Hills of Virginia"

Leon Payne
"I Love You Because"
"You've Still Got a Place in My Heart"
"Lost Highway"
"Empty Arms"
"Fools Rush In"

Jimmie Rodgers
" 'T' for Texas"
"Mother, the Queen of my Heart"
"Waitin' for a Train"
"Train Whistle Blues"

Fred Rose
"Red Hot Mama"
"Hang Your Head in Shame"
"Foggy River"
"Blue Eyes Crying in the Rain"
"Take These Chains From My Heart"

Redd Stewart
"Tennessee Waltz" (C)
"Slowpoke" (C)
"Bonaparte's Retreat" (C)

Floyd Tillman
"I Love You So Much It Hurts Me"
"Slippin' Around"
"It Makes No Difference Now"

Merle Travis
"Nine Pound Hammer"
"Smoke, Smoke, Smoke"
"Sixteen Tons"
"I Am a Pilgrim"

Ernest Tubb
"Walkin' the Floor Over You"
"It's Been So Long Darlin' "
"Try Me One More Time"
"Soldier's Last Letter"

Cindy Walker
"Distant Drums"
"You Don't Know Me"
"In the Misty Moonlight"

Hank Williams
"Your Cheatin' Heart"
"Lovesick Blues"
"Cold, Cold Heart"
"Jambalaya"

Bob Wills
"Faded Love"
"Take Me Back to Tulsa"
"Maiden's Prayer"
"San Antonio Rose" (C)
"Texas Two Step"

Inducted in 1971

Smiley Burnette
"Ridin' Down the Canyon"
"Mama Don't Allow No Music"
"My Home Town"
"It's My Lazy Day"

Jenny Lou Carson
"Let Me Go, Lover"
"Jealous Love"
"Don't Rob Another Man's Castle"

Wilf Carter
"I'm Thinking Tonight of My Blue Eyes"
"The Fate of Old Strawberry Roan"

Zeke Clements
"Just A Little Lovin' (Will Go a Long Way)"
"Why Should I Cry"
"Smoke on the Water"

Jimmie Davis
"You Are My Sunshine"
"Nobody's Darlin' But Mine"

Delmore Brothers (Alton and Rabon)
"Blues Stay Away from Me"
"Brown's Ferry Blues"

Al Dexter
"Pistol-Packin' Mama"
"Down at the Roadside Inn"
"Wine, Women and Song"
"Rosalita"
"Too Late to Worry (Too Blue to Cry)"
"Guitar Polka"

Vaughn Horton
"Mockin' Bird Hill"
"Address Unknown"
"Teardrops in My Heart"

Bradley Kincaid
"Legend of Robin's Redbreast"

Bill Monroe
"Blue Moon over Kentucky"
"Kentucky Waltz"
"Uncle Pen"

Bob Nolan
"Cool Water"
"Tumblin' Tumbleweeds"
"NE-HAH-NEE (Clear Water)"

Tex Owens
"Cattle Call"
"Give Me a Home on the Lone Prairie"

Tex Ritter
"Boll Weevil Song"
"Green Grow the Lilacs"
"Rye Whiskey"
"High, Wide and Handsome"

Carson J. Robison
"My Blue Ridge Mountain Home"
"Life Gets Teejus, Don't It"
"Wreck of the Number Nine"

Tim Spencer
"Room Full of Roses"
"Cigarettes, Whiskey, and Wild, Wild Women"
"Timber Trail"

Gene Sullivan
"Live and Let Live"
"I Might Have Known"

Jimmy Wakely
"Those Gone and Left Me Blues"
"Too Late"
"I'll Never Let You Go, Little Darling"
"You Can't Break the Chains of Love"

Wiley Walker
"When My Blue Moon Turns to Gold Again"

Scotty Wiseman
"Have I Told You Lately That I Love You"
"Remember Me"
"Mountain Dew"

Inducted in 1972

Boudleaux and Felice Bryant
"Rocky Top"
"Dream, Dream, Dream"

"Bye, Bye Love"
"Wake Up Little Suzy"

Lefty Frizzell
"If You've Got the Money (I've Got the Time)"
"Always Late"
"Mom and Dad Waltz"

Jack Rhodes
"Satisfied Mind"
"Conscience, I'm Guilty"
"Beautiful Lies"

Don Robertson
"Please Help Me, I'm Falling"
"I Really Don't Want to Know"
"I Don't Hurt Anymore"
"Does My Ring Hurt Your Finger"

Inducted in 1973

Jack Clement
"Just a Girl I Used to Know"
"I Know One"
"Just Between You and Me"
"Miller's Cave"
"Guess Things Happen That Way"

Don Gibson
"Oh, Lonesome Me"
"I'd Be a Legend in My Time"
"I Can't Stop Loving You"

Harlan Howard
"Heartaches by the Number"
"Pick Me up on Your Way Down"
"The Chokin' Kind"
"She Called Me Baby"
"Busted"

Roger Miller
"King of the Road"
"Dang Me"
"When Two Worlds Collide"
"Husbands and Wives"
"Engine, Engine Number Nine"

Steve Nelson and Ed Nelson, Jr.
"Bouquet of Roses"
"Frosty the Snowman"
"With This Ring I Thee Wed"

Willie Nelson
"Hello Walls"
"Funny How Time Slips Away"
"Crazy"

"Night Life"
"Healing Hands of Time"

Inducted in 1974

Hank Cochran
"Make The World Go Away"
"Don't Touch Me"
"Little-Bitty Tear"

Inducted in 1975

Bill Anderson
"City Lights"
"Still"
"Po' Folks"
"Tips of My Fingers"

Danny Dill
"Detroit City" (C)
"Partners"
"Let Me Talk to You"
"The Long Black Veil" (C)
"The Comeback"
"Sweet Lips"
"A Pain a Pill Can't Locate"
"So Wrong"
"Esther"
"Why Don'tcha Come Home"
"Old Courthouse"
"Who Rides with Billy"

Eddie Miller
"Release Me"
"There She Goes"
"Thanks a Lot"

Marty Robbins
"El Paso"
"White Sport Coat"
"You Gave Me a Mountain"
"My Woman, My Woman, My Wife"

Wayne Walker
"Burning Memories"
"All the Time"
"I've Got a New Heartache"
"Are You Sincere"

Marijohn Wilkin
"Waterloo"
"Long Black Veil" (C)
"One Day At A Time" (C)
"Scars in the Hands of Jesus"

Carl Belew
"What's He Doing in My World"
"Am I That Easy to Forget"
"That's When I See the Blue"
"Lonely Street"
"Stop the World"

Dallas Frazier
"There Goes My Everything"
"All I Have to Offer You Is Me" (C)
"Hickory Holler Tramp"
"Ain't Had No Loving"
"Alley Oop"
"Mohair Sam"

John D. Loudermilk
"Abilene" (C)
"Talk Back Trembling Lips"
"Waterloo"
"Bad News"
"Break My Mind"

Moon Mullican
"You Don't Have to Be a Baby to Cry"
"Sweeter Than the Flowers"
"Moon's Tune"
"I'll Sail My Ship Alone"
"Cherokee Boogie"
"I Was Sorta Wondering"
"Pipe Liner Blues"

Curly Putman
"Green, Green Grass of Home"
"Elusive Dreams" (C)
"Blood Red and Going Down"
"Set Me Free" (C)
"D-I-V-O-R-C-E" (C)

Mel Tillis
"Detroit City" (C)
"Ruby, Don't Take Your Love to Town"
"I Ain't Never" (C)
"Heart Over Mind"
"One More Time"
"Mental Revenge"
"Memory Maker"

Special Award—1976—Stephen Foster

Johnny Cash
"I Walk the Line"
"Don't Take Your Guns to Town"
"Folsom Prison Blues"
"San Quentin"
"Understand Your Man"

Woodie Guthrie
"Oklahoma Hills"
"This Land Is Your Land"
"So Long, It's Been Good to Know You"
"This Train Is Bound For Glory"

Merle Haggard
"Okie from Muskogee"
"My Mother's Hungry Eyes"
"If We Make It Through December"
"Sing a Sad Song"
"Today I Started Loving You Again"

Kris Kristofferson
"For the Good Times"
"Help Me Make It Through the Night"
"Why Me"
"One Day At A Time" (C)

Joe Allison
"Teen Aged Crush"
"He'll Have To Go"
"Live Fast, Love Hard, Die Young"
"I'm a Lover, Not a Fighter"
"It's a Great Life"
"Rock City Boogie"
"He'll Have To Stay"

Tom T. Hall
"I Washed My Face in the Morning Dew"
"Harper Valley PTA"
"Old Dogs, Children, and Watermelon Wine"
"I Love"
"Country Is"
"I Like Beer"

Hank Snow
"I'm Movin' On"
"Rhumba Boogie"
"Golden Rocket"
"Bluebird Island"
"Brand on My Heart"
"Music Makin' Mama from Memphis"

Don Wayne
"Saginaw Michigan"
"The Belles of Southern Bell"
"Country Bumpkin"

The Reverend Thomas A. Dorsey
"Peace in the Valley"
"Take My Hand, Precious Lord"

The Louvin Brothers (Charles and Ira)
"Born Again"
"If I Could Only Win Your Love"
"Satan Lied to Me"
"When I Stop Dreaming"
"The Family Who Prays"
"Are You Teasing Me"

Elsie McWilliams
"For Jimmie Rogers"
"Sailor's Plea"
"My Old Pal"
"Mississippi Moon"
"I'm Lonely & Blue"

Joe South
"(I Never Promised You) a Rose Garden"
"Walk a Mile in My Shoes"
"Games People Play"
"No Man Is An Island"
"Down in the Boondocks"

Inducted in 1980

Hudie "Leadbelly" Ledbetter
"Good Night Irene"

Ben Peters
"Kiss an Angel Good Morning"
"That Was Before My Time"
"Daytime Friends and Nighttime Lovers"

Ray Stevens
"Ahab the Arab"
"Mr. Businessman"
"Everything Is Beautiful"
"The Streak"

Mickey Newbury
"She Even Woke Me up to Say Goodbye"
"Sweet Memories"
"American Trilogy"
"San Francisco, Mabel Joy"

Inducted in 1981

Bobby Braddock

Ray Whitley
(Note: Until 1981, NSAI listed a few of the more notable songs of each new Hall of Fame inductee; this was discontinued after 1980.)

Inducted in 1982

Chuck Berry
William J. "Billy" Hill

Inducted in 1983

W. C. Handy
Loretta Lynn
Beasley Smith

Inducted in 1984

Hal David
Billy Sherrill

Inducted in 1985

Bob McDill
Carl Perkins

Inducted in 1986

Otis Blackwell
Dolly Parton

Inducted in 1987

Roy Orbison
Sonny Throckmorton

Inducted in 1988

Hoagy Carmichael
Troy Seals

Inducted in 1989

Rory Michael Bourke
Maggie Cavender
Sanger D. "Whitey" Shafer

Inducted in 1990

Sue Brewer
Ted Harris
Jimmy Webb

Inducted in 1991

Charlie Black
Sonny Curtis

Inducted in 1992

Max D. Barnes
Wayland Holyfield

Inducted in 1993

Don Schlitz
Conway Twitty
Red Lane

Inducted in 1994

Richard Leigh
Bobby Russell
Jerry Foster & Bill Rice
Buddy Holly

Inducted in 1995

Jerry Chestnutt
Kenny O'Dell
Buck Owens
Norro Wilson

ACADEMY OF COUNTRY MUSIC

The Academy of Country Music (originally called the Academy of Country and Western Music) was founded in Los Angeles, California, in 1964 in response to the needs of the industry and fans in the western and southwestern United States. The geographical distance from Nashville precluded active participation on a regular basis of many artists, songwriters, music publishers, and record companies with the acknowledged hub of country music in Nashville. From the outset, the Academy was oriented toward a broad service thrust, embracing considerations of fans as well as industry personnel rather than being strictly a trade organization as is the Nashville-based Country Music Association. While many CMA stalwarts, like Cliffie Stone, Johnny Bond, and Bill Boyd, maintained a visible Nashville presence, they also devoted much time and effort on behalf of the Academy.

Initially regional in character, over the years the Academy has expanded its scope toward national impact. This is reflected in the shift of its awards show (first presented in 1965) from a local event to one that is telecast nationwide and to other countries as well. The Academy's program (on NBC-TV in the 1980s through the mid-1990s) was produced by Dick Clark and reflects a more "Hollywood" presentation, where media stars join country music artists for gala presentations, a format eschewed by the CMA telecast.

Providing continuity in Academy activities from its early years to the 1990s has been executive secretary, Fran Boyd.

ACADEMY OF COUNTRY AND WESTERN MUSIC AWARDS*

1965

Man of the Year: Roger Miller
Top Male Vocalist: Buck Owens
Top Female Vocalist: Bonnie Owens
Best Vocal Group: Merle Haggard and Bonnie Owens
Best Band Leader: Buck Owens
Most Promising Male Vocalist: Merle Haggard
Most Promising Female Vocalist: Kaye Adams
Best Songwriter: Roger Miller
Best TV Personality: Billy Mize
Best Radio Personality: Biff Collie
Best Producer/A&R Man: Ken Nelson
Best Music Publisher: Central Songs, Inc.
Best Nightclub: Palomino Club (Los Angeles)
Best Talent Management: Jack McFadden
Best Publication: Billboard

Sidemen:

Best Steel Guitar: Red Rhodes
Best Fiddle: Billy Armstrong
Best Lead Guitar: Phil Baugh
Best Bass: Bob Morris
Best Piano: Billy Liebert
Best Drums: Muddy Berry

1966

Man of the Year†: Dean Martin
Top Male Vocalist: Merle Haggard
Top Female Vocalist: Bonnie Guitar
Top Vocal Group: Bonnie Owens and Merle Haggard
Band Leader/Band: Buck Owens Buckaroos
Most Promising Male Vocalist: Billie Mize
Most Promising Female Vocalist: Cathy Taylor
Most Promising Vocal Group: Bob Morris and Faye Hardin
Best TV Personality: Billy Mize
Best Radio Personality (tie): Biff Collie/Bob Kingsley
Best Producer/A&R Man: Ken Nelson
Best Music Publisher: Central Songs, Inc.
Best Country Nightclub: Palomino Club
Best Talent Management/Booking Agent: Jack McFadden
Song of the Year: "Apartment #9" (Bobby Austin/Fuzzy Owen/Johnny Paycheck)

Sidemen:

Lead Guitar: Jimmy Bryant
Steel Guitar (tie): Tom Brumley/Ralph Mooney
Drums: Jerry Wiggins
Bass: Bob Morris

---

*Awards are determined by vote of the Academy membership except for the Pioneer Award and the Jim Reeves Memorial Award, both of which are chosen by the Board of Directors. The Pioneer Award, created in 1968, is "for the recognition of outstanding and unprecedented achievement in the field of country music." It is not necessarily an annual award and has had more than one recipient in a year. The Jim Reeves Memorial Award, created in 1969, is "presented annually to an individual, not necessarily a performing artist, who had made substantial contributions toward furthering international acceptance of country music during the preceding calendar year."
†Award based on contributions to advancing country music.

1966 (cont.)

Fiddle: Billy Armstrong
Piano: Billy Liebert

1967

Man of the Year: Joey Bishop
Top Male Vocalist: Glen Campbell
Top Female Vocalist: Lynn Anderson
Top Vocal Group: Sons of the Pioneers
Top Duet: Merle Haggard/Bonnie Owens
Band Leader/Band: Bucky Owens Buckaroos
Most Promising Male Vocalist: Jerry Inman
Most Promising Female Vocalist: Bobbie Gentry
Best TV Personality: Billy Mize
Best Radio Personality: Bob Kingsley
Best Country Nightclub: Palomino Club
Song of the Year: "It's Such a Pretty World Today"
(Dale Noe/Freeway Music)
Album of the Year *and* Single Record of the Year:
Gentle on My Mind (Glen Campbell/A&R: Al De-
Lorey)
Sidemen:
Lead Guitar: Jimmy Bryant
Steel Guitar: Red Rhodes
Drums: Pee Wee Adams
Bass: Red Wooten
Fiddle: Billy Armstrong
Piano: Earl Ball

1968

Man of the Year: Tom Smothers
Directors' Award: Nudie
Pioneer Award: "Uncle Art" Satherly
Most Promising Female: Cheryl Poole
Most Promising Male: Ray Sanders
Top Female Vocalist: Cathie Taylor
Top Male Vocalist: Glen Campbell
Album of the Year: Glen Campbell and Bobbie Gentry
Single Record of the Year (Award to Artist): "Little
Green Apples"/Roger Miller
Song of the Year (Award to Composer): "Wichita
Lineman"/Jim Webb
Top Vocal Group: Johnny & Jonie Mosby
Band of the Year (Club): Billy Mize's Tennesseans
Band of the Year (Touring): Buckaroos
Radio Personality (Regional): Tex Williams
Radio Personality (Los Angeles): Larry Scott
TV Personality: Glen Campbell
Country Nightclub (Regional): Golden Nugget
Country Nightclub (Metropolitan): Palomino
Steel Guitar: Red Rhodes
Piano: Earl Ball
Lead Guitar: Jimmy Bryant
Fiddle: Billy Armstrong
Drums: Jerry Wiggins
Bass: Red Wooten

1969

Man of the Year: John Aylesworth—Frank Peppiatt
Pioneer Award: Bob Wills
Jim Reeves Memorial Award: Joe Allison
Man of the Decade: Marty Robbins
Specialty Instrument: John Hartford
Rhythm Guitar: Jerry Inman
Comedy Act: Roy Clark
Most Promising Male Vocalist: Freddy Weller
Most Promising Female Vocalist: Donna Fargo
Top Female Vocalist: Tammy Wynette
Top Male Vocalist: Merle Haggard
Album of the Year: *Okie from Muskogee*/Merle Hag-
gard
Single Record of the Year: "Okie from Muskogee"
Song of the Year: "Okie from Muskogee"
Top Vocal Group: Kimberlys
Band of the Year: Merle Haggard's Strangers
Disc Jockey: Dick Haynes
TV Personality: Johnny Cash
Nightclub: Palomino Club
Steel Guitar: Buddy Emmons
Piano: Floyd Cramer
Lead Guitar: Al Bruno
Fiddle: Billy Armstrong
Drums: Jerry Wiggins
Bass: Billy Graham

1970

Man of the Year: Hugh Cherry
Jim Reeves Memorial Award: Bill Boyd
Pioneer Award: Tex Ritter, Patsy Montana
Entertainer of the Year: Merle Haggard
Top Male Vocalist: Merle Haggard
Top Female Vocalist: Lynn Anderson
Album of the Year: *For the Good Times*/Ray Price
Single Record of the Year: "For the Good Times"
Song of the Year: "For the Good Times"
Top Vocal Group: Kimberlys
Most Promising Male Vocalist: Buddy Alan
Most Promising Female Vocalist: Sammi Smith
Country Nightclub: Palomino Club
TV Personality: Johnny Cash
News Publication: Billboard
Radio Station: KLAC, Los Angeles
Disc Jockey: Corky Mayberry, KBBQ
Comedy Act: Roy Clark
Band of the Year (Non-Touring): The Tony Booth
Band
Band of the Year (Touring): The Strangers
Steel Guitar: J. D. Maness
Piano: Floyd Cramer
Lead Guitar: Al Bruno
Fiddle: Billy Armstrong
Drums: Archie Francis
Bass: Billy Graham & Doyle Holly

1971

Man of the Year: Walter Knott
Jim Reeves Memorial Award: Roy Rogers
Pioneer Award: Bob Nolan, Stuart Hamblen, Tex Williams
Entertainer of the Year: Freddie Hart
Top Male Vocalist: Freddie Hart
Top Female Vocalist: Loretta Lynn
Album of the Year: *Easy Lovin'*/Freddie Hart
Single Record of the Year: "Easy Lovin'" Freddie Hart
Song of the Year: "Easy Lovin'"
Top Vocal Group: Conway Twitty/Loretta Lynn
Most Promising Male Vocalist: Tony Booth
Most Promising Female Vocalist: Barbara Mandrell
Country Nightclub: Palomino Club
TV Personality: Glen Campbell
Radio Station: KLAC, Los Angeles, Ca.
Disc Jockey: Larry Scott (KLAC)
Comedy Act: Roy Clark
Band of the Year (Non-Touring): Tony Booth Band
Band of the Year (Touring): Strangers
Steel Guitar: J. D. Maness
Piano: Floyd Cramer
Lead Guitar: Al Bruno
Fiddle: Billy Armstrong
Drums: Jerry Wiggins
Bass: Larry Booth

1972

Man of the Year: Lawrence Welk
Jim Reeves Memorial Award: Thurston Moore
Pioneer Award: Cliffie Stone, Gene Autry
Entertainer of the Year: Roy Clark
Top Male Vocalist: Merle Haggard
Top Female Vocalist: Donna Fargo
Album of the Year: *Happiest Girl*/USA
Single Record of the Year: "Happiest Girl/USA"— Donna Fargo
Song of the Year: "Happiest Girl/USA"
Top Vocal Group: Statler Brothers
Most Promising Male Vocalist: Johnny Rodriquez
Most Promising Female Vocalist: Tanya Tucker
Country Nightclub: Palomino Club
TV Personality: Roy Clark
Radio Station: KLAC, Los Angeles, California
Disc Jockey: Larry Scott
Band of the Year (Non-Touring): Tony Booth Band
Band of the Year (Touring): Strangers
Steel Guitar: Buddy Emmons
Piano: Floyd Cramer
Lead Guitar: Al Bruno
Fiddle: Billy Armstrong
Drums: Jerry Wiggins
Bass: Larry Garner (Booth)

1973

Song of the Year: "Behind Closed Doors"/Kenny O'Dell
Entertainer of the Year: Roy Clark
Single of the Year: "Behind Closed Doors"/Charlie Rich
Top Female Vocalist of the Year: Loretta Lynn
Top Male Vocalist of the Year: Charlie Rich
Album of the Year: *Behind Closed Doors*/Charlie Rich
Most Promising Female Vocalist: Olivia Newton-John
Most Promising Male Vocalist: Dorsey Burnette
Top Vocal Duet or Group of the Year: Brush Arbor
Country Nightclub: The Palomino
Band of the Year (Non-Touring): Sound Company/Ronnie Truhett
Band of the Year (Touring): Brush Arbor
Steel Guitar: Red Rhodes
Piano: Floyd Cramer
Lead Guitar: Al Bruno
Fiddle: Billy Armstrong
Drums: Jerry Wiggins
Bass: Larry Booth
Jim Reeves Memorial Award: Sam Oouvello
Pioneer Award: Hank Williams
Disc Jockey of the Year Award: Craig Scott, WJJD, Chicago
Radio Station of the Year: KLAC, Los Angeles

1974

Bass Guitar: Billy Graham
Drums: Jerry Wiggins
Fiddle: Billy Armstrong
Lead Guitar: Al Bruno
Piano: Floyd Cramer
Steel Guitar: J. D. Maness
Country Disc Jockey of the Year: Larry Scott
Country Radio Station of the Year: KLAC
Band of the Year (Touring): Strangers
Band of the Year (Non-Touring): The Palomino Riders
Country Nightclub of the Year: Palomino Club
Most Promising Female Vocalist: Linda Ronstadt
Most Promising Male Vocalist: Mickey Gilley
Top Vocal Group of the Year: Loretta Lynn/Conway Twitty
Album of the Year: *Back Home Again*/John Denver
Male Vocalist of the Year: Merle Haggard
Female Vocalist of the Year: Loretta Lynn
Single of the Year: "Country Bumpkin"/Cal Smith
Entertainer of the Year: Mac Davis
Song of the Year: "Country Bumpkin"/Don Wayne
Jim Reeves Memorial Award: Merv Griffin
Pioneer Award: Merle Travis/Tennessee Ernie Ford/Johnny Bond

1975

Bass: Billy Graham
Drums: Archie Francis
Fiddle: Billy Armstrong
Lead Guitar: Russ Hansen
Piano: Jerry Lee Lewis
Steel Guitar: J. D. Maness
Rhythm Guitar: Jerry Inman
Country Radio Station of the Year: KLAC, Los Angeles, Ca.
Country Disc Jockey of the Year: Billy Parker, KVOO, Tulsa, Oklahoma
Country Music Nightclub of the Year: Palomino
Band of the Year (Touring): Strangers (Merle Haggard)
Band of the Year (Non-Touring): Palomino Riders (Jerry Inman)
Most Promising Female Vocalist: Crystal Gayle
Most Promising Male Vocalist: Freddy Fender
Top Vocal Group: Conway Twitty/Loretta Lynn
Album of the Year: *Feelings* (Loretta Lynn/Conway Twitty)
Male Vocalist of the Year: Conway Twitty
Female Vocalist of the Year: Loretta Lynn
Single Record of the Year: "Rhinestone Cowboy" (Glen Campbell)
Entertainer of the Year: Loretta Lynn
Song of the Year: "Rhinestone Cowboy" (Glen Campbell)
Jim Reeves Memorial Award: Dinah Shore
Pioneer Award: Roy Rogers

1976

Bass: Curtis Stone
Fiddle: Billy Armstrong
Drums: Archie Francis
Lead Guitar: Danny Michaels
Piano: Hargus "Pig" Robbins
Steel Guitar: J. D. Maness
Rhythm Guitar: Jerry Inman
Radio Station: KLAC, Los Angeles
Disc Jockey: Charlie Douglas, WWL, New Orleans
Nightclub: Palomino
Band of the Year (Touring): Red Rose Express
Band of the Year (Non-Touring): Possum Holler
Most Promising Female Vocalist: Billy Jo Spears
Most Promising Male Vocalist: Moe Bandy
Top Vocal Group: Conway Twitty/Loretta Lynn
Album of the Year: *Gilley's Smoking*/Mickey Gilley
Male Vocalist of Year: Mickey Gilley
Female Vocalist of Year: Crystal Gayle
Single Record of the Year: "Bring It on Home"/Mickey Gilley
Entertainer of the Year: Mickey Gilley
Song of the Year: "Don't the Girls Get Prettier at Closing Time"/Mickey Gilley

Jim Reeves Memorial Award: Roy Clark
Pioneer Award: Owen Bradley

1977

Bass: Larry Booth
Drums: Archie Francis & George Manz
Fiddle: Billy Armstrong
Keyboard: Hargus "Pig" Robbins
Lead Guitar: Roy Clark
Steel Guitar: Buddy Emmons
Specialty Instrument: Charlie McCoy
Radio Station: KGBS, Los Angeles
Disc Jockey: Billy Parker
Country Nightclub: Palomino
Band of the Year (Touring): Asleep at the Wheel and Sons of the Pioneers
Band of the Year (Non-Touring): Palomino Riders
Top New Female Vocalist: Debby Boone
Top New Male Vocalist: Eddie Rabbitt
Top Vocal Group: Statler Brothers
Album of the Year: *Kenny Rogers*/Kenny Rogers
Top Male Vocalist: Kenny Rogers
Top Female Vocalist: Crystal Gayle
Single Record of the Year: "Lucille"/Kenny Rogers
Entertainer of the Year: Dolly Parton
Song of the Year: "Lucille"/Kenny Rogers
Career Achievement: Johnny Paycheck
Jim Reeves Memorial: Jim Halsey
Pioneer Award: Sons of Pioneers

1978

Bass: Rod Culpepper
Drums: Archie Francis
Fiddle: Johnny Gimble
Keyboard: Jimmy Pruett
Lead Guitar: James Burton
Steel Guitar: Buddy Emmons
Specialty Instrument: Charlie McCoy
Radio Station: KVOO, Tulsa, Oklahoma
Disc Jockey: Billy Parker
Country Nightclub: Palomino
Band of the Year (Touring): Original Texas Playboys
Band of the Year (Non-Touring): Rebel Playboys
Top New Female Vocalist: Cristy Lane
Top New Male Vocalist: John Conlee
Top Vocal Group: Oak Ridge Boys
Album of the Year: *Ya'll Come Back Saloon*/Oak Ridge Boys
Top Male Vocalist: Kenny Rogers
Top Female Vocalist: Barbara Mandrell
Single Record of the Year: "Tulsa Time"/Don Williams
Entertainer of the Year: Kenny Rogers
Song of the Year: "You Needed Me"/Anne Murray
Jim Reeves Memorial: Joe Cates
Pioneer Award: Eddie Dean

1979

Bass: Billy Graham
Fiddle: Johnny Gimble
Drums: Archie Francis
Guitar: Al Bruno
Keyboard: Hargus "Pig" Robbins
Steel Guitar: Buddy Emmons
Specialty Instrument: Charlie McCoy (Harmonica)
Band of the Year (Non-Touring): Midnight Riders
Band of the Year (Touring): Charlie Daniels Band
Radio Station of the Year: KFDI, Wichita, KS
Disc Jockey of the Year: King Edward IV, WSRC, Roanoke, VA
Country Nightclub of the Year: Gilley's, Pasadena, TX
Top New Female Vocalist: Lacy J. Dalton
Top New Male Vocalist: R. C. Bannon
Top Vocal Group: Moe Bandy/Joe Stampley
Album of the Year: *Straight Ahead* (Larry Gatlin)
Top Male Vocalist: Larry Gatlin
Top Female Vocalist: Crystal Gayle
Single Record of the Year: "All the Gold in California"/Larry Gatlin
Entertainer of the Year: Willie Nelson
Song of the Year: "It's a Cheatin' Situation"/Moe Bandy
Country Music Movie of the Year: *Electric Horseman*
Jim Reeves Memorial Award: Bill Ward (Metro Media)
Pioneer Award: Patti Page
Artist of the Decade: Loretta Lynn (1969–1979)

1980

Bass: Curtis Stone
Fiddle: Johnny Gimble
Drums: Archie Francis
Guitar: Al Bruno
Keyboard: Hargus "Pig" Robbins
Steel Guitar: Buddy Emmons/J. D. Maness
Specialty Instrument: Charlie McCoy (Harmonica)
Band of the Year (Touring): Charlie Daniels Band
Band of the Year (Non-Touring): Palomino Riders
Radio Station of the Year: KLAC, Los Angeles
Disc Jockey of the Year: Sammy Jackson
Nightclub of the Year: Palomino Club/Gilley's Club
Top New Female Vocalist: Terri Gibbs
Top New Male Vocalist: Johnny Lee
Top Vocal Group: Alabama
Top Vocal Duet: Moe Bandy/Joe Stampley
Album of the Year: *Urban Cowboy*/Soundtrack
Top Male Vocalist: George Jones
Top Female Vocalist: Dolly Parton
Single Record of the Year: "He Stopped Loving Her Today"/George Jones
Entertainer of the Year: Barbara Mandrell
Song of the Year: "He Stopped Loving Her Today"/George Jones

Country Music Movie of the Year: *Coal Miner's Daughter*
Jim Reeves Memorial Award: Ken Kragen
Pioneer Award: Ernest Tubb
Special Achievement: George Burns

1981

Bass: Joe Osborn/Curtis Stone
Fiddle: Johnny Gimble
Drums: Buddy Harmon
Guitar: James Burton
Keyboard: Hargus "Pig" Robbins
Steel Guitar: Buddy Emmons
Specialty Instrument: Charlie McCoy (Harmonica)
Band of the Year (Touring): Strangers (Merle Haggard)
Band of the Year (Non-Touring): Desperados (Johnny & Jonie Mosby)
Radio Station of the Year: WPLO/Atlanta, Georgia
Disc Jockey of the Year: Arch Yancey/KNUZ
Country Nightclub: Billy Bob's Texas
Top New Female Vocalist: Juice Newton
Top New Male Vocalist: Ricky Skaggs
Top Vocal Group: Alabama
Vocal Duet: David Frizzell & Shelly West
Album of the Year: *Feels So Right* (Alabama)
Top Male Vocalist: Merle Haggard
Top Female Vocalist: Barbara Mandrell
Single Record of the Year: "Elvira" (Oak Ridge Boys)
Entertainer of the Year: Alabama
Song of the Year: "You're The Reason God Made Oklahoma"/David Frizzell & Shelly West
Jim Reeves Memorial Award: Al Gallico
Pioneer Award: Leo Fender
Tex Ritter Award (Country Motion Picture): *Any Which Way You Can*

1982

Album of the Year: *Always on My Mind*/Willie Nelson/Chips Moman/Columbia
Bass: Red Wooten
Club: Gilley's
Disc Jockey: Lee Arnold
Drums: Archie Francis
Entertainer: Alabama
Female Vocalist: Sylvia
Fiddle: Johnny Gimble
Guitar: Al Bruno
Jim Reeves Memorial Award: Jo Walker-Meador
Keyboard: Hargus "Pig" Robbins
Male Vocalist: Ronnie Milsap
New Female Vocalist: Karen Brooks
New Male Vocalist: Michael Martin Murphey
Non-Touring Band: Desperados
Pioneer Award: Chet Atkins
Radio Station: KIKK (Houston, TX)

1982 (cont.)

Single Record of the Year: "Always on My Mind"/Willie Nelson/Chips Moman/Columbia

Song of the Year: "Are the Good Times Really Over" Merle Haggard

Specialty Instrument/Dobro: James Burton

Steel Guitar: J. D. Maness

Tex Ritter Award: "The Best Little Whorehouse in Texas"

Touring Band: Ricky Skaggs Band

Vocal Duet: David Frizzell/Shelly West

Vocal Group: Alabama

1983

Album of the Year: *The Closer You Get*/Alabama/Harold Shedd/Alabama/RCA

Bass: Joe Osborn

Club: Gilley's

Disc Jockey: Rhubarb Jones

Drums: Archie Francis

Entertainer; Album of the Year: Alabama

Female Vocalist: Janie Fricke

Fiddle: Johnny Gimble

Guitar: Reggie Young

Keyboard: Floyd Cramer

Male Vocalist: Lee Greenwood

New Female Vocalist: Gus Hardin

New Male Vocalist: Jim Glaser

Non-Touring Band: The Tennesseans

Pioneer Award: Eddy Arnold

Radio Station: KRMD (Shreveport, LA)

Single Record of the Year: "Islands in the Stream"/Kenny Rogers/Dolly Parton/Karl Richardson/Barry Gibb/Albhy Galuten/RCA

Song of the Year: "The Wind Beneath My Wings"/Gary Morris

Specialty Instrument/Harmonica: Charlie McCoy

Steel Guitar: J. D. Maness

Tex Ritter Award: "Tender Mercies"

Touring Band: Ricky Skaggs Band

Vocal Duet: Dolly Parton & Kenny Rogers

Vocal Group: Alabama

1984

Album of the Year: *Roll On*/Alabama/Harold Shedd/Alabama/RCA

Bass: Joe Osborn

Club: Gilley's

Disc Jockey: Don Hollander/Small Market; Billy Parker/Medium Market; Coyote Calhoun/Large Market

Drums: Larrie Londin

Entertainer; Album of the Year: Alabama

Female Vocalist: Reba McEntire

Fiddle: Johnny Gimble

Guitar: James Burton

Keyboard: Hargus "Pig" Robbins

Male Vocalist: George Strait

New Female Vocalist: Nicolette Larson

New Male Vocalist: Vince Gill

Non-Touring Band: The Tennesseans

Pioneer Award: Roy Acuff

Radio Station: WMC/Memphis, TN (Large); WLWI/Montgomery, AL (Small); KVOO/Tulsa, OK (Medium)

Single Record of the Year: "To All the Girls I've Loved Before"/Willie Nelson/Julio Iglesias/Richard Perry/Columbia

Song of the Year: "Why Not Me"/The Judds

Specialty Instrument/Mandolin: Ricky Skaggs

Steel Guitar: Buddy Emmons

Tex Ritter Award: "Songwriter"

Touring Band: Ricky Skaggs Band

Video: John Goodhugh/Hank Williams, Jr.

Video of the Year: "All My Rowdy Friends Are Comin' over Tonight"/Hank Williams, Jr.

Vocal Duet; Song of the Year: The Judds

Vocal Group: Alabama

1985

Album of the Year: *Does Ft. Worth Ever Cross Your Mind*/George Strait/Coproducer Jimmy Bowen/George Strait/MCA

Bass: Joe Osborn

Club: Billy Bob's/Ft. Worth, TX

Disc Jockey: Eddie Edwards

Drums: Archie Francis

Entertainer: Alabama

Female Vocalist: Reba McEntire

Fiddle: Johnny Gimble

Guitar: James Burton

Keyboard: Glen Hardin

Male Vocalist: George Strait

New Female Vocalist: Judy Rodman

New Male Vocalist: Randy Travis

Non-Touring Band: Nashville Now Band

Pioneer Award: Kitty Wells

Radio Station: WAMZ (Louisville, KY)

Single Record of the Year: "Highwayman"/Willie Nelson, Waylon Jennings, Kris Kristofferson, Johnny Cash/Chips Moman/Columbia

Song of the Year: "Lost in the Fifties (In the Still of the Night)"/Ronnie Milsap

Specialty Instrument/Dobro: James Burton

Steel Guitar: Buddy Emmons

Tex Ritter Award: "Sweet Dreams"

Touring Band: Ricky Skaggs Band

Video of the Year: "Who's Gonna Fill Their Shoes"/George Jones/Kitty Moon

Vocal Duet: The Judds

Vocal Group: Alabama

1986

Album of the Year: *Storms of Life*/Randy Travis/Kyle Lehning/Warner Bros.

Album of the Year; Single of the Year: Kyle Lehning/A: Producer S: Coproducer w/Keith Steagall

Bass: Emory Gordy, Jr.

Club: Crazy Horse Steak House & Saloon/Santa Ana, CA

Disc Jockey: Chris Taylor

Drums: Larrie Londin

Entertainer: Hank Williams, Jr.

Female Vocalist: Reba McEntire

Fiddle: Mark O'Connor

Guitar: Chet Atkins

Individual Award/Career Achievement: Carl Perkins

Keyboard: John Hobbs

Male Vocalist: Randy Travis

New Female Vocalist: Holly Dunn

New Male Vocalist: Dwight Yoakam

Non-Touring Band: Nashville Now Band

Pioneer Award: Minnie Pearl

Radio Station: KNIX (Tempe, AZ)

Single Record of the Year: "On the Other Hand"/Randy Travis/Keith Steagall/Kyle Lehning/Warner Bros.

Song of the Year: "On the Other Hand"/Randy Travis

Specialty Instrument/Dobro: James Burton

Steel Guitar: J. D. Maness

Touring Band: Ricky Skaggs Band

Video of the Year: "Whoever's in New England"/Reba McEntire/Jon Small

Vocal Duet: The Judds

Vocal Group: Forester Sisters

1987

Album of the Year: *Trio*/Dolly Parton, Emmylou Harris, Linda Ronstadt/George Massenburg/Warner Bros.

Bass: Emory Gordy, Jr./David Hungate David Hungate/Emory Gordy, Jr.

Club: Crazy Horse Steak House & Saloon/Santa Ana, CA

Disc Jockey: Jim Tabor/WMC Memphis, TN

Drums: Archie Francis

Entertainer: Hank Williams Jr.

Female Vocalist: Reba McEntire

Fiddle: Johnny Gimble

Guitar: Chet Atkins

Keyboard: John Hobbs/Ronnie Milsap

Male Vocalist: Randy Travis

New Female Vocalist: K. T. Oslin

New Male Vocalist: Ricky Van Shelton

Non-Touring Band: Nashville Now Band

Pioneer Award: Roger Miller

Radio Station: KNIX (Tempe, AZ)

Single Record of the Year: "Forever and Ever, Amen"/Randy Travis/Kyle Lehning/Warner Bros.

Song of the Year: "Forever and Ever, Amen"/Randy Travis

Specialty Instrument/Mandolin: Ricky Skaggs

Specialty/Dobro: Jerry Douglas

Steel Guitar: J. D. Maness

Touring Band: The Strangers

Video: Jack Cole/K. T. Oslin

Video of the Year: "80's Ladies"/K. T. Oslin/Marc Ball

Vocal Duet: The Judds

Vocal Group: Highway 101

1988

Album of the Year: *This Woman*/K. T. Oslin/Harold Shedd/RCA

Bass: Curtis Stone

Club: Crazy Horse Steak House & Saloon/Santa Ana, CA

Disc Jockey: Dandalion/Jon Conlon

Drums: Steve Duncan

Entertainer: Hank Williams, Jr.

Female Vocalist: K. T. Oslin

Fiddle: Mark O'Connor

Guitar: Al Bruno

Keyboard: John Hobbs

Male Vocalist: George Strait

New Female Vocalist: Suzy Bogguss

New Male Vocalist: Rodney Crowell

Non-Touring Band: Nashville Now Band

Pioneer Award: Buck Owens

Radio Station: WSIX (Nashville, TN)

Single Record of the Year: "Eighteen Wheels and a Dozen Roses"/Kathy Mattea/Allen Reynolds/Mercury

Song of the Year: "Eighteen Wheels and a Dozen Roses"/Kathy Mattea

Specialty Instrument/Harmonica: Charlie McCoy

Steel Guitar: J. D. Maness

Touring Band: Desert Rose Band

Video: Preacher Ewing/Bill Fishman/Hank Williams, Jr.

Video of the Year: "Young Country"/Hank Williams, Jr./Brent Bowman

Vocal Duet: The Judds

Vocal Group: Highway 101

1989

Album of the Year: *Killin' Time*/Clint Black/James Stroud/Mark Wright/RCA

Bass: Michael Rhodes

Club: Crazy Horse Steak House & Saloon/Santa Ana, CA

Disc Jockey: Jon Conlon

Drums: Steve Duncan

Entertainer: George Strait

Female Vocalist: Kathy Mattea

Fiddle: Mark O'Connor

Guitar: Brent Rowan

1989 (cont.)

Keyboard: Skip Edwards

New Female Vocalist: Mary-Chapin Carpenter

New Male Vocalist; Male Vocalist; Album of the Year; Single of the Year: Clint Black

New Vocal Duet or Group: Kentucky Headhunters

Non-Touring Band: Nashville Now Band

Radio Station: WSIX (Nashville, TN)

Single Record of the Year: "Better Man"/Clint Black/James Stroud/Mark Wright/RCA

Song of the Year: "Where've You Been"/Kathy Mattea

Specialty/Dobro: Jerry Douglas

Steel Guitar: J. D. Maness

Touring Band: Desert Rose Band

Video: Joanne Gardner/Hank Williams, Sr. & Jr.

Video of the Year: "There's a Tear in My Beer"/Hank Williams, Jr./Joanne Gardner

Vocal Duet: The Judds

Vocal Group: Restless Heart

1990

Album of the Year: *No Fences*/Garth Brooks/Allen Reynolds/Capitol/Nashville

Bass: Bill Bryson

Club: Crazy Horse Steak House & Saloon/Santa Ana, CA

Disc Jockey: Gerry House

Drums: Steve Duncan

Entertainer; Male Vocalist; Album of the Year; Song of the Year; Single of the Year; Video: Garth Brooks

Female Vocalist: Reba McEntire

Fiddle: Mark O'Connor

Guitar: John Jorgenson

Keyboard: John Hobbs

New Female Vocalist: Shelby Lynne

New Male Vocalist: Alan Jackson

New Vocal Group or Duet: Pirates of the Mississippi

Non-Touring Band: Boy Howdy Band

Pioneer Award: Johnny Cash

Radio Station: WSIX, Nashville

Single Record of the Year: "Friends in Low Places"/Garth Brooks/Allen Reynolds/Capitol Nashville

Song of the Year: "The Dance"/Garth Brooks

Specialty/Dobro: Jerry Douglas

Steel Guitar: J. D. Maness

Touring Band: Desert Rose Band

Video of the Year: "The Dance"/Garth Brooks/Marc Ball

Vocal Duet: The Judds

Vocal Group: Shenandoah

1991

Album of the Year: *Don't Rock the Jukebox*/Alan Jackson/Scott Hendricks and Keith Steagall/Arista

Bass: Roy Huskey, Jr.

Disc Jockey: Gerry House/Nashville, TN

Drums: Eddie Bayers

Entertainer; Male Vocalist: Garth Brooks

Female Vocalist: Reba McEntire

Fiddle: Mark O'Connor

Guitar: John Jorgenson

Keyboard: Matt Rollings

New Female Vocalist: Trisha Yearwood

New Male Vocalist; Song of the Year: Billy Dean

Nightclub: Crazy Horse Steak House & Saloon, Santa Ana, CA

Pioneer Award: Willie Nelson

Radio Station: WAMZ (Louisville, KY)

Single Record of the Year: "Don't Rock the Jukebox"/Alan Jackson/Keith Steagall and Scott Hendricks/Arista

Song of the Year: "Somewhere in My Broken Heart"/Billy Dean

Specialty/Dobro: Jerry Douglas

Steel Guitar: Paul Franklin

Video of the Year: "Is There Life Out There"/Reba McEntire/Robin Baird Beresford

Vocal Duet; New Vocal Duet or Group: Brooks & Dunn

Vocal Group: Diamond Rio

1992

Album of the Year: *Brand New Man*/Brooks and Dunn/Scott Hendricks & Don Cook/Arista

Bass: Glenn Worf

Club: Billy Bob's Texas/Fort Worth, TX

Disc Jockey: Jon Conlon

Drums: Eddie Bayers

Entertainer: Garth Brooks

Female Vocalist: Mary-Chapin Carpenter

Fiddle: Mark O'Connor

Guitar: John Jorgenson

Keyboard: Matt Rollings

Male Vocalist: Vince Gill

New Female Vocalist: Michelle Wright

New Male Vocalist: Tracy Lawrence

New Vocal Duet or Group: Confederate Railroad

Pioneer Award: George Jones

Radio Station: KNIX (Phoenix, AZ)

Single Record of the Year: "Boot Scootin' Boogie"/Brooks & Dunn/Scott Hendricks & Don Cook/Arista

Song of the Year: "I Still Believe in You"/Vince Gill

Specialty Instrument/Dobro: Jerry Douglas

Steel Guitar: J. D. Maness

Tex Ritter Award: "Pure Country"/George Strait/Jerry Weintraub

Video of the Year: "Two Sparrows in a Hurricane"/ Tanya Tucker/Brent Hedgecock

Vocal Duet; Album of the Year; Single of the Year: Brooks & Dunn

Vocal Group: Diamond Rio

1993

Album: *A Lot About Livin' (And a Little About Lovin')*/Alan Jackson
Single Record: "Chattahoochee"/Alan Jackson
Song: "I Love the Way You Love Me"/John Michael Montgomery
Video: "We Shall Be Free"/Garth Brooks
Guitar: Brent Mason
Vocal Duet: Brooks & Dunn
Pioneer Award: Charley Pride
Drums: Eddie Bayers
New Female Vocalist: Faith Hill
Entertainer: Garth Brooks
New Vocal Group or Duet: Gibson Miller Band
Bass: Glenn Worf
Steel Guitar: J. D. Maness
Career Achievement Award: John Anderson
New Male Vocalist: John Michael Montgomery
Radio Station: KNIX (Phoenix, AZ)
Vocal Group: Little Texas
Fiddle: Mark O'Connor
Keyboard: Matt Rollings
Talent Buyer/Promoter: Mr. Bill Presents/Phoenix, AZ
Specialty—Percussion/Harmonica: Terry McMillan
Disc Jockey: Tim Hattrick & Wally D. Loon
Club: Toolies Country/Phoenix, AZ
Male Vocalist: Vince Gill
Female Vocalist: Wynonna

1994

Entertainer of the Year: Reba McEntire
Album of the Year: *Not a Moment Too Soon*/Curb/Tim McGraw/James Stroud/Byron Gallimore
Top Vocal Duet: Brooks & Dunn
New Male Vocalist: Tim McGraw
Top Female Vocalist: Reba McEntire
New Female Vocalist: Cheryl Wright
Guitar: Brent Mason

Radio Station of the Year: WSIX (Nashville, TN)
Specialty Instrument (Harmonica): Terry McMillan
Keyboard: Matt Rollings
Bass: Glenn Worf
Steel Guitar: Paul Franklin
Fiddle: Mark O'Connor
Drums: Eddie Bayers
Pioneer Award: Loretta Lynn
Disc Jockey of the Year: Gerry House (WSIX)
Jim Reeves Memorial Award: Garth Brooks
Nightclub of the Year: Billy Bob's Texas/Ft. Worth, TX
Video of the Year: "The Red Strokes"/Garth Brooks/Jon Small/Steven Carter

1995

Album of the Year: *The Woman in Me*/Shania Twain
Bass: Glenn Worf
Drums: Eddie Bayers
Entertainer of the Year: Brooks & Dunn
Female Vocalist: Patty Loveless
Fiddle: Rob Hajacos
Guitar: Brent Mason
Keyboard: Matt Rollings
Male Vocalist: Alan Jackson
New Female Vocalist: Shania Twain
New Male Vocalist: Bryan White
New Vocal Duet or Group: Lonestar
Pioneer Award: Merle Haggard
Single Record of the Year: "Check Yes or No"/George Strait
Song of the Year: "The Keeper of the Stars"/Tracy Byrd
Special Achievement: Jeff Foxworthy
Specialty Instrument/Harmonica: Terry McMillan
Steel Guitar: Paul Franklin
Video of the Year: "The Car"
Vocal Duet: Brooks & Dunn
Vocal Group: The Mavericks

THE COUNTRY MUSIC HALL OF FAME

The Country Music Hall of Fame elections are conducted under the auspices of the Country Music Association. Hall of Fame inductees are selected each year by an anonymous panel of 200 electors, each of whom has participated actively in the music business for at least fifteen years and has made a significant contribution to the industry. These electors vote by secret ballot and the results are tallied by a national accounting firm, Deloitte & Touche LLP. Winners are traditionally announced on the televised CMA Awards Show in October.

The Hall of Fame building is located in Nashville's Country Music Hall of Fame and Museum, which was opened in 1967, and is operated and maintained by the Country Music Foundation, where each year more than 500,000 visitors enjoy its exhibits.

COUNTRY MUSIC HALL OF FAME MEMBERS*

1961*

(Original members in 1961 limited to deceased)
JIMMIE RODGERS, born Meridian, Mississippi, September 8, 1897; died New York, New York, May 26, 1933
FRED ROSE (publisher, songwriter, singer, pianist), born Evansville, Indiana, August 24, 1897; died Nashville, Tennessee, December 1, 1954
HIRAM KING "HANK" WILLIAMS (SR.), born Mount Olive, Alabama, September 17, 1923; died January 1, 1953

1962

ROY CLAXTON ACUFF, born Maynardsville, Tennessee, September 15, 1903; died Nashville, Tennessee, November 23, 1992

1964

WOODWARD MAURICE "TEX" RITTER, born Panola County, Texas, January 12, 1906; died Nashville, Tennessee, January 2, 1974

1965

ERNEST DALE TUBB, born near Crisp, Texas, February 9, 1914; died Nashville, Tennessee, September 6, 1984

1966

RICHARD EDWARD "EDDY" ARNOLD, born near Henderson, Tennessee, May 15, 1918
JAMES RAE DENNY (manager, publisher, talent booker), born Buffalo Valley, Tennessee, February 28, 1911; died Nashville, Tennessee, August 27, 1963
GEORGE DEWEY HAY (The Solemn Old Judge, emcee, Grand Ole Opry), born Attica, Indiana, November 9, 1895; died Virginia Beach, Virginia, May 9, 1968
DAVID HARRISON "UNCLE DAVE" MACON, born Smart Station, Tennessee, October 7, 1870; died Readyville, Tennessee, March 22, 1952

1967

CLYDE JULIAN "RED" FOLEY, born near Berea, Kentucky, June 17, 1910; died Ft. Wayne, Indiana, September 19, 1968
JOSEPH LEE "JOE" FRANK (promotion manager), born Limestone County, Alabama, April 15, 1900; died May 4, 1952

*Year members elected.

STEPHEN HENRY "STEVE" SHOLES (record company executive) born Washington, D. C., February 12, 1911; died Nashville, Tennessee, April 22, 1968

1968

JAMES ROBERT "BOB" WILLS, born Limestone County, Texas, March 6, 1905; died Ft. Worth, Texas, May 13, 1975

1969

ORVON GENE AUTRY, born near Tioga, Texas, September 29, 1907

1970

WILLIAM SMITH "BILL" MONROE, born near Rosine, Kentucky, September 13, 1911; died Springfield, Tennessee, September 9, 1996
THE CARTER FAMILY "original" Carter Family—Alvin Pleasant Delaney "A. P." Carter, born Maces Spring, Virginia, December 15, 1891; died Maces Spring, Virginia, November 7, 1960
Sara Dougherty Carter Bayes, born Wise County, Virginia, July 21, 1899; died Lodi, California, January 8, 1979
Maybelle Addington "Mother Maybelle" Carter, born Nickelsville, Virginia, May 10, 1909; died October 23, 1978

1971

ARTHUR EDWARD "UNCLE ART" SATHERLEY (record industry executive), born Bristol, England, October 19, 1889; died February 6, 1986

1972

JIMMIE HOUSTON DAVIS, born Beech Grove, near Quitman, Louisiana, September 11, 1904

1973

CHESTER BURTON "CHET" ATKINS, born Luttrell, Tennessee, June 20, 1924
PATSY CLINE (Virginia Patterson Hensley), born Winchester, Virginia, September 8, 1932; died Camden, Tennessee, March 5, 1963

1974

OWEN BRADLEY (pianist, bandleader, record company Artists & Repertoire man), born Westmoreland, Tennessee, October 21, 1915
FRANK "PEE WEE" KING (Frank A. Kuczynski), born Abrams, Wisconsin, February 14, 1914

1975

MINNIE PEARL (Sarah Ophelia Colley, comedienne), born Centerville, Tennessee, October 25, 1912; died Nashville, Tennessee, March 4, 1996

1976

KITTY WELLS (Muriel Deason), born Nashville, Tennessee, August 30, 1919
PAUL COHEN (record company executive), born Chicago, Illinois, November 10, 1908; died April 1, 1970

1977

MERLE ROBERT TRAVIS, born Rosewood, Muhlenberg County, Kentucky, November 29, 1917; died October 20, 1983

1978

LOUIS MARSHALL "GRANDPA" JONES, born Henderson County, Kentucky, October 20, 1913

⌐ERT LONG (manager, booking agent), born Poteet, Texas, December 3, 1923; died Nashville, Tennessee, September 7, 1972
CLARENCE EUGENE "HANK" SNOW, born Liverpool, Nova Scotia, May 9, 1914

1980

JOHN R. "JOHNNY" CASH, born Kingsland, Arkansas, February 26, 1932
CONNIE B. GAY (impresario, broadcaster, music industry executive), born Lizard Lick, North Carolina, August 22, 1914; died December 4, 1989
ORIGINAL SONS OF THE PIONEERS (Roy Rogers, Bob Nolan, Tim Spencer, Karl Farr, Hugh Farr, Lloyd Perryman)

1981

VERNON DALHART (Marion Try Slaughter), born Jefferson, Texas, April 6, 1883; died September 15, 1948
GRANT TURNER (radio announcer), born Baird, Texas, May 17, 1912; died October 19, 1991

1982

WILLIAM ORVILLE "LEFTY" FRIZZELL, born Corsicana, Texas, March 31, 1928; died Nashville, Tennessee, July 19, 1975
ROY HORTON (music publisher), born Pennsylvania, November 5, 1914
MARTIN DAVID "MARTY" ROBBINS, born Glendale, Arizona, September 26, 1925; died Nashville, Tennessee, December 8, 1982

1983

"LITTLE" JIMMY DICKENS, born Bolt, West Virginia, December 19, 1920

1984

RALPH SYLVESTER PEER (record company executive, music publisher), born Independence, Missouri, May 22, 1892; died January 19, 1960
FLOYD TILLMAN, born Ryan, Oklahoma, December 8, 1914

1985

FLATT & SCRUGGS, Lester Flatt, born Overton, Tennessee, June 19, 1914; died Nashville, Tennessee May 11, 1979; Earl Scruggs, born Cleveland County, North Carolina, January 6, 1924

1986

BENJAMIN FRANCIS "WHITEY" FORD (comedian), born DeSoto, Missouri, May 12, 1901; died June 20, 1986
WESLEY H. ROSE (music publisher, first board chairman of Country Music Association in 1958), born Chicago, Illinois, February 11, 1918; died April 26, 1990

1987

ROD BRASFIELD (comedian), born August 22, 1910; died September 12, 1958

1988

LORETTA LYNN, born Butcher Holler, Kentucky, April 11, 1935
ROY ROGERS (Leonard Slye), born Cincinnati, Ohio, November 5, 1911

1989

JACK STAPP, born December 8, 1912; died December 20, 1980
CLIFFORD "CLIFFIE" STONE, born Burbank, California, March 1, 1917
HANK THOMPSON, born Waco, Texas, September 3, 1925

1990

ERNEST "TENNESSEE ERNIE" FORD, born Bristol, Tennessee, February 13, 1919, died Reston, Virginia, October 17, 1991

1991

BOUDLEAUX & FELICE BRYANT (songwriting team), Boudleaux born Shellman, Georgia, February 13, 1920; died June 25, 1987. Felice born Milwaukee, Wisconsin, August 7, 1925

1922

GEORGE JONES, born Saratoga, Texas, September 12, 1931
FRANCES WILLIAMS PRESTON (music industry executive), born August 24, 1934

1993

WILLIE NELSON, born Fort Worth, Texas, April 30, 1933

1994

MERLE HAGGARD, born Bakersfield, California, April 6, 1937

1995

JO WALKER-MEADOR (former CMA executive), born Orlinda, Tennessee, February 16, 1924
ROGER MILLER, born Ft. Worth, Texas, January 2, 1936; died Los Angeles, California, October 25, 1992

1996

PATSY MONTANA, born Hot Springs, Arkansas, October 30, 1914; died San Jacinto, California, May 3, 1996
ALVIS EDGAR "BUCK" OWENS, born Sherman, Texas, August 12, 1929
RAY PRICE, born Perryville, Texas, January 12, 1926

NATIONAL ACADEMY OF RECORDING ARTS & SCIENCES GRAMMY AWARDS*

The National Academy of Recording Arts & Sciences is a nonprofit organization composed of more than 4,500 members nationwide representing the entire spectrum of creative people in the phonograph recording field. It was formed, in 1957, to advance the arts and science of recording, and to foster creative leadership for artistic, cultural, educational, and technical progress in the recording field. The organization is also known as the "Recording Academy" or by its initials, NARAS.

The Recording Academy is best known for its annual Grammy Awards, which are given for outstanding artist and/or technical achievements during each award's eligibility year to those deemed by their voting peers to be most worthy of the honor. The Grammy Awards are presented on nationwide television in late February or early March. The program reached over 55 million viewers throughout the world each year in the early 1980s, a number that increased several fold by the mid-1990s.

Best Country Song

1964 DANG ME, Roger Miller, composer
1965 KING OF THE ROAD, Roger Miller, composer
1966 ALMOST PERSUADED, Billy Sherrill, Glen Sutton, composers
1967 GENTLE ON MY MIND, John Hartford, composer
1968 LITTLE GREEN APPLES, Bobby Russell, composer
1969 A BOY NAMED SUE, Shel Silverstein, composer
1970 MY WOMAN, MY WOMAN, MY WIFE, Marty Robbins, composer
1971 HELP ME MAKE IT THROUGH THE NIGHT, Kris Kristofferson, Fred Foster, composers
1972 KISS AN ANGEL GOOD MORNIN', Ben Peters, composer
1973 BEHIND CLOSED DOORS, Kenny O'Dell, composer
1974 A VERY SPECIAL LOVE SONG, Norris Wilson & Billy Sherrill, composers
1975 (HEY WON'T YOU PLAY) ANOTHER SOMEBODY DONE SOMEBODY WRONG SONG, Chips Moman & Larry Butler, composers
1976 BROKEN LADY, Larry Gatlin, composer
1977 DON'T IT MAKE MY BROWN EYES BLUE, Richard Leigh, composer
1978 THE GAMBLER, Don Schlitz, composer
1979 YOU DECORATED MY LIFE, Bob Morrison, Debbie Hupp, composers
1980 ON THE ROAD AGAIN, Willie Nelson, songwriter
1981 9 TO 5, Dolly Parton, songwriter
1982 ALWAYS ON MY MIND, Johnny Christopher, Wayne Carson, Mark James, songwriters

1983 STRANGER IN MY HOUSE, Mike Reid, songwriter
1984 CITY OF NEW ORLEANS, Steve Goodman, songwriter
1985 HIGHWAYMAN, Jimmy L. Webb, songwriter
1986 GRANDPA (TELL ME 'BOUT THE GOOD OLD DAYS), Jamie O'Hara, songwriter
1987 FOREVER AND EVER, AMEN, Paul Overstreet & Don Schlitz, songwriters
1988 HOLD ME, K. T. Oslin, songwriter
1989 AFTER ALL THIS TIME, Rodney Crowell, songwriter
1990 WHERE'VE YOU BEEN, Jon Vezner & Don Henry, songwriters
1991 LOVE CAN BUILD A BRIDGE, Naomi Judd, John Jarvis & Paul Overstreet, songwriters
1992 I STILL BELIEVE IN YOU, Vince Gill & John Barlow Jarvis, songwriters
1993 PASSIONATE KISSES, Lucinda Williams, songwriter
1994 I SWEAR, Gary Baker & Frank J. Myers, songwriters
1995 GO REST HIGH ON THAT MOUNTAIN, Vince Gill, songwriter
1996 BLUE, Bill Mack, songwriter

Best Country Vocal Performance, Female

1964 HERE COMES MY BABY, Dottie West
1965 QUEEN OF THE HOUSE, Jody Miller
1966 DON'T TOUCH ME, Jeannie Seely
1967 I DON'T WANNA PLAY HOUSE, Tammy Wynette
1968 HARPER VALLEY P.T.A., Jeannie C. Riley
1969 STAND BY YOUR MAN, Tammy Wynette
1970 ROSE GARDEN, Lynn Anderson

*Country, western, country rock awards, or awards related to *Encyclopedia* entries only.

1971 HELP ME MAKE IT THROUGH THE NIGHT, Sammi Smith
1972 HAPPIEST GIRL IN THE WHOLE USA, Donna Fargo
1973 LET ME BE THERE, Olivia Newton-John
1974 LOVE SONG, Anne Murray
1975 I CAN'T HELP IT (IF I'M STILL IN LOVE WITH YOU), Linda Ronstadt
1976 ELITE HOTEL, Emmylou Harris
1977 DON'T IT MAKE MY BROWN EYES BLUE, Crystal Gayle
1978 HERE YOU COME AGAIN, Dolly Parton
1979 BLUE KENTUCKY GIRL, Emmylou Harris
1980 COULD I HAVE THIS DANCE, Anne Murray
1981 9 TO 5, Dolly Parton
1982 BREAK IT TO ME GENTLY (single) Juice Newton
1983 A LITTLE GOOD NEWS (single) Anne Murray
1984 IN MY DREAMS (single) Emmylou Harris
1985 I DON'T KNOW WHY YOU DON'T WANT ME (single) Rosanne Cash
1986 WHOEVER'S IN NEW ENGLAND (single) Reba McEntire
1987 '80s LADIES (track from *'80s Ladies*) K. T. Oslin
1988 HOLD ME (track from *This Woman*) K. T. Oslin
1989 ABSOLUTE TORCH & TWANG (album) k.d. lang
1990 WHERE'VE YOU BEEN (single) Kathy Mattea
1991 DOWN AT THE TWIST AND SHOUT (single) Mary-Chapin Carpenter
1992 I FEEL LUCKY (single) Mary-Chapin Carpenter
1993 PASSIONATE KISSES (single) Mary-Chapin Carpenter
1994 SHUT UP AND KISS ME (single) Mary-Chapin Carpenter
1995 BABY NOW THAT I'VE FOUND YOU (single), Alison Krauss
1996 BLUE (single) LeAnn Rimes

Best Country Vocal Performance, Male

1965 KING OF THE ROAD, Roger Miller
1966 ALMOST PERSUADED, David Houston
1967 GENTLE ON MY MIND, Glen Campbell
1968 FOLSOM PRISON BLUES, Johnny Cash
1969 A BOY NAMED SUE, Johnny Cash
1970 FOR THE GOOD TIMES, Ray Price
1971 WHEN YOU'RE HOT, YOU'RE HOT, Jerry Reed
1972 CHARLEY PRIDE SINGS HEART SONGS, Charley Pride
1973 BEHIND CLOSED DOORS, Charlie Rich
1974 PLEASE DON'T TELL ME HOW THE STORY ENDS, Ronnie Milsap
1975 BLUE EYES CRYING IN THE RAIN, Willie Nelson

1976 (I'M A) STAND BY MY WOMAN MAN, Ronnie Milsap
1977 LUCILLE, Kenny Rogers
1978 GEORGIA ON MY MIND, Willie Nelson
1979 THE GAMBLER, Kenny Rogers
1980 HE STOPPED LOVING HER TODAY, George Jones
1981 (THERE'S) NO GETTIN' OVER ME, Ronnie Milsap
1982 ALWAYS ON MY MIND (single) Willie Nelson
1983 I.O.U. (single) Lee Greenwood
1984 THAT'S THE WAY LOVE GOES (single) Merle Haggard
1985 LOST IN THE FIFTIES TONIGHT (IN THE STILL OF THE NIGHT) (single) Ronnie Milsap
1986 LOST IN THE FIFTIES TONIGHT (album) Ronnie Milsap
1987 ALWAYS & FOREVER (album) Randy Travis
1988 OLD 8X10 (album) Randy Travis
1989 LYLE LOVETT & HIS LARGE BAND (album) Lyle Lovett
1990 WHEN I CALL YOUR NAME (single) Vince Gill
1991 ROPIN' THE WIND (album) Garth Brooks
1992 I STILL BELIEVE IN YOU (album) Vince Gill
1993 AIN'T THAT LONELY YET (single) Dwight Yoakam
1994 WHEN LOVE FINDS YOU, Vince Gill
1995 GO REST HIGH ON THAT MOUNTAIN (single), Vince Gill
1996 WORLDS APART (single) Vince Gill

Best Country Vocal Performance By a Duo or Group

1967 JACKSON, Johnny Cash, June Carter
1969 MACARTHUR PARK, Waylon Jennings and the Kimberlys
1970 IF I WERE A CARPENTER, Johnny Cash and June Carter
1971 AFTER THE FIRE IS GONE, Conway Twitty and Loretta Lynn
1972 CLASS OF '57, The Statler Brothers
1973 FROM THE BOTTLE TO THE BOTTOM, Kris Kristofferson, Rita Coolidge
1974 FAIRYTALE, The Pointer Sisters
1975 LOVER PLEASE, Kris Kristofferson, Rita Coolidge
1976 THE END IS NOT IN SIGHT (THE COWBOY TUNE), Amazing Rhythm Aces
1977 HEAVEN'S JUST A SIN AWAY, The Kendalls
1978 MAMAS DON'T LET YOUR BABIES GROW UP TO BE COWBOYS, Waylon Jennings & Willie Nelson
1979 THE DEVIL WENT DOWN TO GEORGIA, Charlie Daniels Band
1980 THAT LOVIN YOU FEELIN' AGAIN, Roy Orbison & Emmylou Harris

RA, Oak Ridge Boys
TAIN MUSIC (album) Alabama
LOSER YOU GET (album) Alabama
A HE'S CRAZY (single) The Judds
Y NOT ME (album) The Judds
GRANDPA (TELL ME 'BOUT THE GOOD OLD DAYS) (single) The Judds
1987 TRIO (album) Dolly Parton, Linda Ronstadt & Emmylou Harris
1988 GIVE A LITTLE LOVE (track from *Greatest Hits*) the Judds
1989 WILL THE CIRCLE BE UNBROKEN VOLUME 2 (album) Nitty Gritty Dirt Band
1990 PICKIN' ON NASHVILLE (album) Kentucky HeadHunters
1991 LOVE CAN BUILD A BRIDGE (single) The Judds
1992 EMMYLOU HARRIS & THE NASH RAMBLERS AT THE RYMAN (album) Emmylou Harris & the Nash Ramblers
1993 HARD WORKIN' MAN (single) Brooks & Dunn
1994 BLUES FOR DIXIE (track from *Tribute to the Music of Bob Wills & the Texas Playboys*) Asleep at the Wheel, with Lyle Lovett
1995 HERE COMES THE RAIN (single), The Mavericks
1996 MY MARIA (single) Brooks & Dunn

Best Country Instrumental Performance

1968 FOGGY MOUNTAIN BREAKDOWN, Flatt and Scruggs
1969 THE NASHVILLE BRASS FEATURING DANNY DAVIS PLAY MORE NASHVILLE SOUNDS, Danny Davis and The Nashville Brass
1970 ME & JERRY, Chet Atkins and Jerry Reed
1971 SNOWBIRD, Chet Atkins
1972 CHARLIE McCOY/THE REAL McCOY, Charlie McCoy
1973 DUELING BANJOS, Eric Weissberg, Steve Mandell
1974 THE ATKINS-TRAVIS TRAVELING SHOW, Chet Atkins, Merle Travis
1975 THE ENTERTAINER, Chet Atkins
1976 CHESTER & LESTER, Chet Atkins & Les Paul
1977 COUNTRY INSTRUMENTALIST OF THE YEAR, Hargus "Pig" Robbins
1978 ONE O'CLOCK JUMP, Asleep at the Wheel
1979 BIG SANDY/LEATHER BRITCHES, Doc & Merle Watson
1980 ORANGE BLOSSOM SPECIAL/HOEDOWN, Gilley's "Urban Cowboy" Band
1981 COUNTRY—AFTER ALL THESE YEARS, Chet Atkins
1982 ALABAMA JUBILEE (album track) Roy Clark
1983 FIREBALL (album track), the New South (Ricky Skaggs, Jerry Douglas, Tony Rice, J. D. Crowe, Todd Phillips)

1984 WHEEL HOSS (track from *Country Boy*), Ricky Skaggs
1985 COSMIC SQUARE DANCE (track from Chet Atkins album *Stay Tuned*), Chet Atkins & Mark Knopfler
1986 RAISIN THE DICKENS (track from *Love's Gonna Get Ya*) Ricky Skaggs
1987 STRING OF PARS (track from *Asleep at the Wheel*) Asleep at the Wheel
1988 SUGARFOOT RAG (track from *Western Standard Time*) Asleep at the Wheel
1989 AMAZING GRACE (track from *Will the Circle Be Unbroken, Volume 2*) Ricky Skaggs
1990 SO SOFT, YOUR GOODBYE (track from *Neck and Neck*), Chet Atkins & Mark Knopfler
1991 THE NEW NASHVILLE CATS (album), Mark O'Connor
1992 SNEAKIN' AROUND (album) Chet Atkins & Jerry Reed
1993 RED WING (single) Asleep at the Wheel featuring Eldon Shamblin, Johnny Gimble, Chet Atkins, Vince Gill, and Reuben "Lucky Oceans" Gosfield
1994 YOUNG THING (track from *Read My Licks*) Chet Atkins
1995 HIGHTOWER (single), Asleep at the Wheel
1996 JAM MAN, Chet Atkins G.G.P.

Best New Country and Western Artist°

1964 ROGER MILLER
1965 THE STATLER BROTHERS

Best Country and Western Album°

1964 DANG ME/CHUG-A-LUG, Roger Miller, producer, John Kennedy
1965 THE RETURN OF ROGER MILLER, Roger Miller

Best Country and Western Recording (Single)°

1958 TOM DOOLEY, The Kingston Trio
1959 THE BATTLE OF NEW ORLEANS, Johnny Horton
1960 EL PASO, Marty Robbins
1961 BIG BAD JOHN, Jimmy Dean
1962 FUNNY WAY OF LAUGHIN', Burl Ives
1963 DETROIT CITY, Bobby Bare
1964 DANG ME, Roger Miller; producer: Jerry Kennedy
1965 KING OF THE ROAD, Roger Miller
1966 ALMOST PERSUADED, David Houston
1967 GENTLE ON MY MIND, Glen Campbell

Best Country Vocal Performance, Duet

1987 MAKE NO MISTAKE, SHE'S MINE (single) Ronnie Milsap and Kenny Rogers

°Categories discontinued, first two after 1965, third after 1967

Best Country Vocal Collaboration

1988 CRYING (single) Roy Orbison & k. d. lang
1989 THERE'S A TEAR IN MY BEER (single) Hank Williams, Jr., and Hank Williams, Sr.
1990 POOR BOY BLUES (single) Chet Atkins & Mark Knopfler
1991 RESTLESS (single) Steve Wariner, Ricky Skaggs, Vince Gill (from the *Mark O'Connor & The New Nashville Cats* album)
1992 THE WHISKEY AIN'T WORKIN' (single) Travis Tritt & Marty Stuart
1993 DOES HE LOVE YOU (single) Reba McEntire and Linda Davis
1994 I FALL TO PIECES (single) Aaron Neville and Trisha Yearwood
1995 SOMEWHERE IN THE VICINITY OF THE HEART (single), Shenandoah with Alison Krauss
1996 HIGH LONESOME SOUND (single), Vince Gill featuring Alison Krauss and Union Station

Best Bluegrass Recording (Vocal or Instrumental)

1988 SOUTHERN FLAVOR (album) Bill Monroe
1989 THE VALLEY ROAD (track from *Will the Circle Be Unbroken, Volume 2*) Bruce Hornsby and the Nitty Gritty Dirt Band
1990 I'VE GOT THAT OLD FEELING (album) Alison Krauss
1991 SPRING TRAINING (album) Carl Jackson & John Starling (& the Nash Ramblers)
1992 EVERY TIME YOU SAY GOODBYE (album) Alison Krauss and Union Station
1993 WAITIN' FOR THE HARD TIMES TO GO (album) The Nashville Bluegrass Band
1994 THE GREAT DOBRO SESSIONS (album) Jerry Douglas & Tut Taylor producers
1995 UNLEASHED (album), The Nashville Bluegrass Band
1996 TRUE LIFE BLUES: THE SONGS OF BILL MONROE (album) various artists

Best Country Album

1994 STONES IN THE ROAD, Mary-Chapin Carpenter
1995 THE WOMAN IN ME, Shania Twain
1996 THE ROAD TO ENSENADA, Lyle Lovett

Best Gospel or Other Religious Recording

1961 EVERYTIME I FEEL THE SPIRIT, Mahalia Jackson
1962 GREAT SONGS OF LOVE AND FAITH, Mahalia Jackson
1963 DOMINIQUE, Soeur Sourire; (The Singing Nun)
1964 GREAT GOSPEL SONGS, Tennessee Ernie Ford and the Jordanaires

1965 SOUTHLAND FAVORITES, George Beverly Shea and the Anita Kerr Singers
1966 GRAND OLD GOSPEL, Porter Wagoner and the Blackwood Brothers
1967 MORE GRAND OLD GOSPEL, Porter Wagoner and the Blackwood Brothers
1968 THE HAPPY GOSPEL OF THE HAPPY GOODMANS, Happy Goodman Family
1969 IN GOSPEL COUNTRY, Porter Wagoner and the Blackwood Brothers
1970 TALK ABOUT THE GOOD TIMES, Oak Ridge Boys
1971 LET ME LIVE, Charley Pride
1972 L-O-V-E, Blackwood Brothers
1973 RELEASE ME (FROM MY SIN), Blackwood Brothers
1974 THE BAPTISM OF JESSE TAYLOR, Oak Ridge Boys
1975 NO SHORTAGE, Imperials
1976 WHERE THE SOUL NEVER DIES, Oak Ridge Boys
1977 SAIL ON, Imperials
1977 JUST A LITTLE TALK WITH JESUS, Oak Ridge Boys
1978 WHAT A FRIEND, Larry Hart
1978 REFRESHING, The Happy Goodman Family
1979 HEED THE CALL, Imperials
1979 LIFT UP THE NAME OF JESUS, The Blackwood Brothers
1980 WE COME TO WORSHIP, Blackwood Brothers
1980 THE LORD'S PRAYER, Reba Rambo, Dony McGuire, B. J. Thomas, Andrae Crouch, the Archers, Walter & Tremaine Hawkins, Cynthia Clawson

Best Traditional Gospel Performance

1981 THE MASTER V, J. D. Summer, James Blackwood, Hovie Lister, Rosie Rozell, Jake Hess
1982 I'M FOLLOWING YOU (album) Blackwood Brothers

Best Contemporary Gospel Performance

1982 AGE TO AGE (album) Amy Grant

Best Gospel Performance by a Duo or Group
(Choir or Chorus added in 1987)

1983 MORE THAN WONDERFUL (single) Sandi Patti & Larnelle Harris
1984 KEEP THE FLAME BURNING (track from Debby Boone *Surrender*) Debby Boone & Phil Driscoll
1985 I'VE JUST SEEN JESUS (track from *I've Just Seen Jesus*) Larnelle Harris & Sandi Patti
1986 THEY SAY (track from *So Glad I Know*) Sandi Patti & Deniece Williams
1987 CRACK THE SKY (album) Mylon LeFevre & Broken Heart

1988 THE WINANS LIVE AT CARNEGIE HALL (album) The Winans
1989 THE SAVIOR IS WAITING (track from *Our Hymns/Various Artists*)

Best Pop Gospel Album

1990 ANOTHER TIME . . . ANOTHER PLACE, Sandi Patti
1991 FOR THE SAKE OF THE CALL, Steven Curtis Chapman
1992 THE GREAT ADVENTURE, Steven Curtis Chapman

Best Inspirational Performance

1967 HOW GREAT THOU ART, Elvis Presley
1968 BEAUTIFUL ISLE SOMEWHERE, Jake Hess
1969 AIN'T THAT BEAUTIFUL SINGING, Jake Hess
1970 EVERYTHING IS BEAUTIFUL, Jake Hess
1971 DID YOU THINK TO PRAY, Charley Pride
1972 HE TOUCHED ME, Elvis Presley
1973 LET'S JUST PRAISE THE LORD, Bill Gaither Trio
1974 HOW GREAT THOU ART, Elvis Presley
1975 JESUS, WE JUST WANT TO THANK YOU, Bill Gaither Trio
1976 THE ASTONISHING, OUTRAGEOUS, AMAZING, INCREDIBLE, UNBELIEVABLE DIFFERENT WORLD OF GARY S. PAXTON, Gary S. Paxton
1977 HOME WHERE I BELONG, B. J. Thomas
1978 HAPPY MAN, B. J. Thomas
1979 YOU GAVE ME LOVE (WHEN NOBODY GAVE ME A PRAYER), B. J. Thomas
1980 WITH MY SONG I WILL PRAISE HIM, Debby Boone
1981 AMAZING GRACE, B. J. Thomas
1982 HE SET MY LIFE TO MUSIC (album) Barbara Mandrell
1983 HE'S A REBEL (track) Donna Summer
1984 FORGIVE ME (track from *Cats Without Claws*) Donna Summer
1985 COME SUNDAY (track from *Say You Love Me*) Jennifer Holliday

Best Gospel Performance, Female

1983 AGELESS MELODY (single) Amy Grant
1984 ANGELS (track from *Straight Ahead*) Amy Grant
1985 UNGUARDED (album) Amy Grant
1986 MORNING LIKE THIS (album) Sandi Patti
1987 I BELIEVE IN YOU (track from *Water Under the Bridge*) Deniece Williams
1988 LEAD ME ON (album) Amy Grant
1989 DON'T CRY (track from *Heaven*) CeCe Winans

Best Gospel Performance, Male

1983 WALLS OF GLASS (album) Russ Taff
1984 MICHAEL W. SMITH (album) Michael W. Smith
1985 HOW EXCELLENT IS THY NAME (track from *I've Just Seen Jesus*) Larnelle Harris
1986 TRIUMPH (album) Philip Bailey
1987 THE FATHER HATH PROVIDED (album) Larnelle Harris
1988 CHRISTMAS (album) Larnelle Harris
1989 MEANTIME (track from *Heaven*) BeBe Winans

Best Pop/Contemporary Gospel Album

1993 THE LIVE ADVENTURE, Steven Curtis Chapman
1994 MERCY, Andrae Crouch

Best Southern Gospel Album

1990 THE GREAT EXCHANGE, Bruce Carroll
1991 HOMECOMING, the Gaither Vocal Band
1992 SOMETIMES MIRACLES HIDE, Bruce Carroll

Best Southern Gospel, Country Gospel, or Bluegrass Gospel Album

1993 GOOD NEWS, Kathy Mattea
1994 I KNOW WHO HOLDS TOMORROW, Alison Krauss and the Cox Family
1995 AMAZING GRACE—A COUNTRY SALUTE TO GOSPEL, Various Artists
1996 I LOVE TO TELL THE STORY—25 TIMELESS HYMNS, Andy Griffith

Record of the Year

1974 I HONESTLY LOVE YOU, Olivia Newton-John; producer John Farrar
1977 HOTEL CALIFORNIA, the Eagles; producer Bill Szymczyk

Album of the Year

1968 BY THE TIME I GET TO PHOENIX, Glen Campbell; producer Al de Lory

Song of the Year

1959 THE BATTLE OF NEW ORLEANS, Jimmy Driftwood, composer
1968 LITTLE GREEN APPLES, Bobby Russell, composer

Best Arrangement Accompanying Vocalists

1967 ODE TO BILLY JOE, Bobbie Gentry; arranger Jimmy Haskell
1975 MISTY, Ray Stevens; arranger Ray Stevens

Best Arrangement for Voices (Duo, Group or Chorus)

1977 NEW KID IN TOWN, the Eagles; arrangers, the Eagles

Best Album Notes

1968 JOHNNY CASH AT FOLSOM PRISON, Johnny Cash, annotator
1969 NASHVILLE SKYLINE, Bob Dylan; Johnny Cash, annotator
1972 TOM T. HALL'S GREATEST HITS, Tom T. Hall, annotator
1974 FOR THE LAST TIME, Bob Wills & His Texas Playboys; Charles R. Townsend, annotator

Best Pop Vocal Performance by a Duo or Group

1965 FLOWERS ON THE WALL, Statler Brothers (Best Contemporary Vocal Group)
1975 LYIN' EYES, the Eagles
1984 JUMP FOR MY LOVE (single), the Pointer Sisters
1989 DON'T KNOW MUCH (single) Linda Ronstadt and Aaron Neville
1990 ALL MY LIFE (single) Linda Ronstadt and Aaron Neville

Best Pop Vocal Performance, Female

1967 ODE TO BILLY JOE, Bobbie Gentry (Best Contemporary Vocal Performance, Female)

1974 I HONESTLY LOVE YOU, Olivia Newton-John
1978 YOU NEEDED ME, Anne Murray
1992 CONSTANT CRAVING (single) k. d. lang

Best Pop Vocal Performance, Male

1960 GEORGIA ON MY MIND, Ray Charles
1969 GENIUS OF RAY CHARLES, Ray Charles (Best Performance, Album)
1965 KING OF THE ROAD, Roger Miller (Best Contemporary Vocal Performance, Male)
1967 BY THE TIME I GET TO PHOENIX, Glen Campbell (Best Contemporary Vocal Performance, Male)
1970 EVERYTHING IS BEAUTIFUL, Ray Stevens
1990 OH PRETTY WOMAN (track from *A Black & White Night Live*) Roy Orbison

Best Pop Vocal Performance by a Duo or Group

1984 JUMP (FOR MY LOVE) (single) the Pointer Sisters

Best Rock Vocal Performance, Male

1985 THE BOYS OF SUMMER (single) Don Henley

Best Spoken Word or Non-Musical Recording

1986 INTERVIEWS FROM THE CLASS OF '55 RECORDING SESSIONS (album) Carl Perkins, Jerry Lee Lewis, Roy Orbison, Johnny Cash, Sam Phillips, Rick Nelson, and Chips Moman

COUNTRY MUSIC ASSOCIATION

The Country Music Association (CMA) was formed in 1958 in Nashville, Tennessee, by industry members primarily as a response to the overwhelming rock 'n' roll wave then sweeping the United States. It was a period when radio stations defected to rock in a swelling wave that threatened to throttle exposure of efforts by country performers, songwriters, and disc jockeys in both recordings and personal appearances. To counteract this, CMA enlisted the energies and combined talents of industry people throughout the United States in programs to preserve and advance country music. CMA's efforts have played a major role in reviving recognition of the art form and elevating it to its present influential status in popular music at home and abroad.

CMA has emerged as the world's largest trade organization and, in 1982, opened its first overseas office in London, England. CMA initiated its own awards show in 1967 and has been a leader in the drives to stop record counterfeiting and piracy, assist country radio stations (grown from around 80 in 1961 to about 1,500 in 1982) in all areas and, in the 1980s was involved in supporting home taping legislation. Jo Walker-Mendor, Executive Director for many years, was active since CMA's inception in the development of the organization.

COUNTRY MUSIC ASSOCIATION AWARDS

Annual winners by categories

Category 1

ENTERTAINER OF THE YEAR

1967	Eddy Arnold
1968	Glen Campbell
1969	Johnny Cash
1970	Merle Haggard
1971	Charley Pride
1972	Loretta Lynn
1973	Roy Clark
1974	Charlie Rich
1975	John Denver
1976	Mel Tillis
1977	Ronnie Milsap
1978	Dolly Parton
1979	Willie Nelson
1980	Barbara Mandrell
1981	Barbara Mandrell
1982	Alabama
1983	Alabama
1984	Alabama
1985	Ricky Skaggs
1986	Reba McEntire
1987	Hank Williams, Jr.
1988	Hank Williams, Jr.
1989	George Strait
1990	George Strait
1991	Garth Brooks
1992	Garth Brooks
1993	Vince Gill
1994	Vince Gill
1995	Alan Jackson
1996	Brooks & Dunn

Category 2

SINGLE OF THE YEAR

1967	"There Goes My Everything"/Jack Greene
1968	"Harper Valley P.T.A."/Jeannie C. Riley
1969	"A Boy Named Sue"/Johnny Cash
1970	"Okie From Muskogee"/Merle Haggard
1971	"Help Me Make It Through the Night"/Sammi Smith
1972	"The Happiest Girl in the Whole U.S.A."/Donna Fargo
1973	"Behind Closed Doors"/Charlie Rich
1974	"Country Bumpkin"/Cal Smith
1975	"Before the Next Teardrop Falls"/Freddy Fender
1976	"Good Hearted Woman"/Waylon Jennings & Willie Nelson
1977	"Lucille"/Kenny Rogers
1978	"Heaven's Just a Sin Away"/The Kendalls
1979	"The Devil Went Down to Georgia"/Charlie Daniels Band
1980	"He Stopped Loving Her Today"/George Jones
1981	"Elvira"/Oak Ridge Boys
1982	"Always on My Mind"/Willie Nelson
1983	"Swingin'"/John Anderson
1984	"A Little Good News"/Anne Murray
1985	"Why Not Me"/The Judds
1986	"Bop"/Dan Seals
1987	"Forever And Ever, Amen"/Randy Travis
1988	"Eighteen Wheels and a Dozen Roses"/Kathy Mattea
1989	"I'm No Stranger to the Rain"/Keith Whitley
1990	"When I Call Your Name"/Vince Gill

1991   "Friends in Low Places"/Garth Brooks
1992   "Achy Breaky Heart"/Billy Ray Cyrus
1993   "Chattahoochee"/Alan Jackson
1994   "I Swear"/John Michael Montgomery
1995   "When You Say Nothing at All"/Alison Krauss and Union Station
1996   "Check Yes or No"/George Strait

Category 3

ALBUM OF THE YEAR

1967   There Goes My Everything/Jack Greene
1968   Johnny Cash at Folsom Prison/Johnny Cash
1969   Johnny Cash at San Quentin Prison/Johnny Cash
1970   Okie from Muskogee/Merle Haggard
1971   I Won't Mention It Again/Ray Price
1972   Let Me Tell You About a Song/Merle Haggard
1973   Behind Closed Doors/Charlie Rich
1974   A Very Special Love Song/Charlie Rich
1975   A Legend in My Time/Ronnie Milsap
1976   Wanted—The Outlaws/Waylon Jennings, Jessi Colter, Willie Nelson, Tompall Glaser
1977   Ronnie Milsap Live/Ronnie Milsap
1978   It Was Almost Like a Song/Ronnie Milsap
1979   The Gambler/Kenny Rogers
1980   Coal Miner's Daughter/Original Motion Picture Soundtrack
1981   I Believe in You/Don Williams
1982   Always on My Mind/Willie Nelson
1983   The Closer You Get/Alabama
1984   A Little Good News/Anne Murray
1985   Does Fort Worth Ever Cross Your Mind/George Strait
1986   Lost in the Fifties Tonight/Ronnie Milsap
1987   Always and Forever/Randy Travis
1988   Born to Boogie/Hank Williams, Jr.
1989   Will the Circle Be Unbroken Vol. II/Nitty Gritty Dirt Band
1990   Pickin' on Nashville/Kentucky Headhunters
1991   No Fences/Garth Brooks
1992   Ropin' the Wind/Garth Brooks
1993   I Still Believe in You/Vince Gill
1994   Common Thread: The Songs of the Eagles/John Anderson, Clint Black, Suzy Bogguss, Brooks & Dunn, Billy Dean, Diamond Rio, Vince Gill, Alan Jackson, Little Texas, Lorrie Morgan, Travis Tritt, Tanya Tucker, and Trisha Yearwood
1995   When Fallen Angels Fly/Patty Loveless
1996   Blue Clear Sky/George Strait

Category 4

SONG OF THE YEAR

1967   "There Goes My Everything"/Dallas Frazier
1968   "Honey"/Bobby Russell
1969   "Caroll County Accident"/Bob Ferguson
1970   "Sunday Morning Coming Down"/Kris Kristofferson
1971   "Easy Loving"/Freddie Hart
1972   "Easy Loving"/Freddie Hart
1973   "Behind Closed Doors"/Kenny O'Dell
1974   "Country Bumpkin"/Don Wayne
1975   "Back Home Again"/John Denver
1976   "Rhinestone Cowboy"/Larry Weiss
1977   "Lucille"/Roger Bowling, Hal Bynum
1978   "Don't It Make My Brown Eyes Blue"/Richard Leigh
1979   "The Gambler"/Don Schlitz
1980   "He Stopped Loving Her Today"/Bobby Braddock, Curly Putman
1981   "He Stopped Loving Her Today"/Bobby Braddock, Curly Putman
1982   "Always on My Mind"/Johnny Christopher, Wayne Carson, Mark James
1983   "Always on My Mind"/Johnny Christopher, Wayne Carson, Mark James
1984   "Wind Beneath My Wings"/Larry Henley, Jeff Silbar
1985   "God Bless the USA"/Lee Greenwood
1986   "On the Other Hand"/Paul Overstreet, Don Schlitz
1987   "Forever and Ever, Amen"/Paul Overstreet, Don Schlitz
1988   "80's Ladies"/K. T. Oslin
1989   "Chiseled in Stone"/Max D. Barnes, Vern Gosdin
1990   "Where've You Been"/Jon Vezner, Don Henry
1991   "When I Call Your Name"/Vince Gill, Tim DuBois
1992   "Look at Us"/Vince Gill, Max D. Barnes
1993   "I Still Believe in You"/Vince Gill, John Barlow Jarvis
1994   "I Swear"/John Michael Montgomery
1995   "Independence Day"/Gretchen Peters
1996   "Go Rest High on That Mountain"/Vince Gill

Category 5

FEMALE VOCALIST OF THE YEAR

1967   Loretta Lynn
1968   Tammy Wynette
1969   Tammy Wynette
1970   Tammy Wynette
1971   Lynn Anderson
1972   Loretta Lynn
1973   Loretta Lynn

FEMALE VOCALIST OF THE YEAR

1974	Olivia Newton-John
1975	Dolly Parton
1976	Dolly Parton
1977	Crystal Gayle
1978	Crystal Gayle
1979	Barbara Mandrell
1980	Emmylou Harris
1981	Barbara Mandrell
1982	Janie Frickie
1983	Janie Frickie
1984	Reba McEntire
1985	Reba McEntire
1986	Reba McEntire
1987	Reba McEntire
1988	K. T. Oslin
1989	Kathy Mattea
1990	Kathy Mattea
1991	Tanya Tucker
1992	Mary-Chapin Carpenter
1993	Mary-Chapin Carpenter
1994	Pam Tillis
1995	Alison Krauss
1996	Patty Loveless

Category 6

MALE VOCALIST OF THE YEAR

1967	Jack Greene
1968	Glen Campbell
1969	Johnny Cash
1970	Merle Haggard
1971	Charley Pride
1972	Charley Pride
1973	Charlie Rich
1974	Ronnie Milsap
1975	Waylon Jennings
1976	Ronnie Milsap
1977	Ronnie Milsap
1978	Don Williams
1979	Kenny Rogers
1980	George Jones
1981	George Jones
1982	Ricky Skaggs
1983	Lee Greenwood
1984	Lee Greenwood
1985	George Strait
1986	George Strait
1987	Randy Travis
1988	Randy Travis
1989	Ricky Van Shelton
1990	Clint Black
1991	Vince Gill
1992	Vince Gill
1993	Vince Gill
1994	Vince Gill
1995	Vince Gill
1996	George Strait

Category 7

VOCAL GROUP OF THE YEAR

1967	The Stoneman Family
1968	Porter Wagoner & Dolly Parton
1969	Johnny Cash & June Carter
1970	The Glaser Brothers
1971	The Osborne Brothers
1972	The Statler Brothers
1973	The Statler Brothers
1974	The Statler Brothers
1975	The Statler Brothers
1976	The Statler Brothers
1977	The Statler Brothers
1978	The Oak Ridge Boys
1979	The Statler Brothers
1980	The Statler Brothers
1981	Alabama
1982	Alabama
1983	Alabama
1984	The Statler Brothers
1985	The Judds
1986	The Judds
1987	The Judds
1988	Highway 101
1989	Highway 101
1990	Kentucky Headhunters
1991	Kentucky Headhunters
1992	Diamond Rio
1993	Diamond Rio
1994	Diamond Rio
1995	The Mavericks
1996	The Mavericks

Category 8

VOCAL DUO OF THE YEAR
(Introduced in 1970)

1970	Porter Wagoner and Dolly Parton
1971	Porter Wagoner and Dolly Parton
1972	Conway Twitty and Loretta Lynn
1973	Conway Twitty and Loretta Lynn
1974	Conway Twitty and Loretta Lynn
1975	Conway Twitty and Loretta Lynn
1976	Waylon Jennings and Willie Nelson
1977	Jim Ed Brown and Helen Cornelius
1978	Kenny Rogers and Dottie West
1979	Kenny Rogers and Dottie West
1980	Moe Bandy and Joe Stampley
1981	David Frizzell and Shelly West
1982	David Frizzell and Shelly West

VOCAL DUO OF THE YEAR (cont'd.)

1983 Merle Haggard and Willie Nelson
1984 Willie Nelson and Julio Iglesias
1985 Anne Murray and Dave Loggins
1986 Dan Seals and Marie Osmond
1987 Ricky Skaggs and Sharon White
1988 The Judds
1989 The Judds
1990 The Judds
1991 The Judds
1992 Brooks & Dunn
1993 Brooks & Dunn
1994 Brooks & Dunn
1995 Brooks & Dunn
1996 Brooks & Dunn

Category 9

INSTRUMENTAL GROUP OF THE YEAR
(Discontinued in 1987)

1967 The Buckaroos
1968 The Buckaroos
1969 Danny Davis & the Nashville Brass
1970 Danny Davis & the Nashville Brass
1971 Danny Davis & the Nashville Brass
1972 Danny Davis & the Nashville Brass
1973 Danny Davis & the Nashville Brass
1974 Danny Davis & the Nashville Brass
1975 Roy Clark and Buck Trent
1976 Roy Clark and Buck Trent
1977 The Original Texas Playboys
1978 The Oak Ridge Boys Band
1979 Charlie Daniels Band
1980 Charlie Daniels Band
1981 Alabama
1982 Alabama
1983 The Ricky Skaggs Band
1984 The Ricky Skaggs Band
1985 The Ricky Skaggs Band
1986 The Oak Ridge Boys Band

Category 10

VOCAL EVENT OF THE YEAR
(Introduced in 1988)

1988 Trio—Dolly Parton, Emmylou Harris, Linda Ronstadt
1989 Hank Williams, Jr., Hank Williams, Sr.
1990 Lorrie Morgan, Keith Whitley
1991 Mark O'Connor & The New Nashville Cats (featuring Vince Gill, Ricky Skaggs and Steve Wariner)
1992 Marty Stuart, Travis Tritt
1993 George Jones & Friends—"I Don't Need Your Rockin' Chair" (with Vince Gill, Mark Chesnutt, Garth Brooks, Travis Tritt, Joe Diffie, Alan Jackson, Pam Tillis, T. Graham Brown, Patty Loveless, Clint Black)
1994 Reba McEntire with Linda Davis, "Does He Love You"
1995 Shenandoah and Alison Krauss, "Somewhere in the Vicinity of the Heart"
1996 Dolly Parton with special guest Vince Gill, "I Will Always Love You"

Category 11

MUSICIAN OF THE YEAR
(Changed from Instrumentalist of the Year in 1988)

1967 Chet Atkins
1968 Chet Atkins
1969 Chet Atkins
1970 Jerry Reed
1971 Jerry Reed
1972 Charlie McCoy
1973 Charlie McCoy
1974 Don Rich
1975 Johnny Gimble
1976 Hargus "Pig" Robbins
1977 Roy Clark
1978 Roy Clark
1979 Charlie Daniels
1980 Roy Clark
1981 Chet Atkins
1982 Chet Atkins
1983 Chet Atkins
1984 Chet Atkins
1985 Chet Atkins
1986 Johnny Gimble
1987 Johnny Gimble
1988 Chet Atkins
1989 Johnny Gimble
1990 Johnny Gimble
1991 Mark O'Connor
1992 Mark O'Connor
1993 Mark O'Connor
1994 Mark O'Connor
1995 Mark O'Connor
1996 Mark O'Connor

Category 12

COMEDIAN OF THE YEAR
(Discontinued in 1971)

1967 Don Bowman
1968 Ben Colder
1969 Archie Campbell
1970 Roy Clark

MUSIC VIDEO OF THE YEAR
(Initiated in 1985, Not Awarded in 1988)

1985 "All My Rowdy Friends Are Comin' over Tonight"/Hank Williams, Jr./Warner Bros. Records
1986 "Who's Gonna Fill Their Shoes"/George Jones/Epic Records
1987 "My Name Is Bocephus"/Hank Williams, Jr./Warner Bros. Records
1989 "There's a Tear in My Beer"/Hank Williams, Jr./Warner Bros. Records
1990 "The Dance"/Garth Brooks/Capitol Nashville
1991 "The Thunder Rolls"/Garth Brooks/Capitol Nashville
1992 "Midnight in Montgomery"/Alan Jackson/Arista Records
1993 "Chattahoochee"/Alan Jackson/Arista Records
1994 "Independence Day"/Martina McBride
1995 "Baby Likes to Rock It"/The Tractors
1996 "My Wife Thinks You're Dead"/Junior Brown

HORIZON AWARD*
(Added 1981, requirements listed below)

1981 Terri Gibbs
1982 Ricky Skaggs
1983 John Anderson
1984 The Judds
1985 Sawyer Brown
1986 Randy Travis
1987 Holly Dunn
1988 Ricky Van Shelton
1989 Clint Black
1990 Garth Brooks
1991 Travis Tritt
1992 Suzy Bogguss
1993 Mark Chesnutt
1994 John Michael Montgomery
1995 Alison Krauss
1996 Bryan White

*The HORIZON AWARD is awarded to that artist, whether individual or a group of two or more, who has demonstrated, in the field of country music, the most significant creative growth and development in overall airplay and record sales activity, live performance professionalism, and critical media recognition during the eligibility period. No act shall be eligible for the HORIZON AWARD which has previously won that award or which has been a final ballot nominee for any other Country Music Association annual award as an individual or as a group 75% or more of whose members comprise the act.

Nominations for the HORIZON AWARD shall be made by the Board of Directors and officers of the Country Music Association, as they may from time to time determine, and shall be submitted to the membership of the Association upon the second round of the voting for the annual Country Music Association Awards pursuant to the rules and regulations governing the balloting on such annual awards. The HORIZON AWARD is an annual award.

BIBLIOGRAPHY

Adamson, Dale. "John Conlee," *Houston Chronicle,* 17 June 1979.

———. "Guy Clark's Got an Album Out, But He's Not Sure If It's His First," *Houston Chronicle,* 4 January 1976.

Albrecht, Jim. "Dottie West," *Country Style,* May 1981.

Allen, Bob. "After the Flood" [Moe Bandy, Gary Stewart], *The Journal of Country Music* 15, no. 1 (1992), pp. 48–55.

———. "Anne Murray, A New Kind of Feeling," *Country Music,* July 1979.

———. "Cheatin' Heart Special: Hank Williams, Jr.," *Rolling Stone,* 17 January 1974, p. 20.

Anonymous. "The Original Hippies, Homer and Jethro," *Gibson Gazette* 2, no. 1 (1971).

———. "Roy Acuff: After All These Years, Still Number One," *Country Song Roundup,* November 1978, pp. 15–17, 38.

———. "Scruggs Talks Through Banjo," *Music City News,* October 1969, p. 34A.

———. "Johnny Bond," CMA *Close Up,* March 1975, pp. 1, 7.

———. "Jim Ed Brown," *CMA Close Up,* October 1979, pp. 1, 3.

———. "Pee Wee King," *CMA Close Up,* May 1976, 1, 3.

———. "Charley Pride," *CMA Close Up,* March 1974, 1, 3.

———. "Porter Wagoner," *CMA Close Up,* August 1975, 1, 7.

———. "Rising Stars: Lari White," *Tune In,* March 1993.

———. "The 100 Greatest Guitarists [of the Twentieth Century]," *Musician,* February 1993.

———. "The Aloha Cowboy" [Randy Travis] *People* (special issue on country stars), fall 1994, p. 36.

Anthony, Michael. "Twitty Remains Loyal to Country Music," *Minneapolis Tribune,* 25 July 1979.

Armor, Jerry C. "Linda Davis," *Country Song Roundup,* May 1994.

Arolick, Carrie. "Bobbie Cryner—Hear Her Road," *Country Song Roundup,* December 1993.

Atkinson, Terry. "Western Rock: Son of the Sons of the Pioneers," *Los Angeles Times,* 27 August 1977, Calendar section, pp. 32, 34–35.

———. "Strait Keeps up the Good Work," *Los Angeles Times,* 25 May 1984.

Bailey, Jerry. "Johnny Rodriguez: 'Sometimes I Get Lonesome,'" *Country Music Beat,* January 1975.

Baird, Robert. "The Beat of a Restless Heart," *New Country,* June 1994.

Bane, Michael. "Eddie Rabbitt: Our New Entertainer of the Year," *Country Music,* January 1978.

———. "20 Questions with Ranger Doug" [Riders in the Sky], *Country Music,* January/February 1992.

Benham, Herb. "The Buck Stops in Bakersfield" [Buck Owens], *Los Angeles Times Magazine,* 15 August 1995.

Billboard (weekly), Billboard Music Group, New York, NY, various issues.

Blount, Roy Jr., "Wrasslin' with This Thing Called Willie Nelson," *Esquire,* August 1981, pp. 78–80, 83–87.

Boehm, Mike. "The Skies Are Rosy Again for Country's Boy Howdy," *Los Angeles Times,* 31 January 1994.

———. "Poco Reunited After 20 Years, Has Richard Marx to Thank," *Los Angeles Times,* 13 July 1990.

Bonner, John. "Joy White—Red Hair, Red Lips, Sass and Fire," *The Country Gazette,* December 1992.

Bowman, Rob. "O. B. McClinton: Country Music, That's My Thing," *The Journal of Country Music* 14, no. 2 (1992), pp. 23–29.

Brokaw, Sanford. "Vern Gosdin—Success and the Grand Ole Opry the Second Time Around," *Country Song Roundup,* 1978.

Brown, James. "Other Things to Do—Phil Everly," *Los Angeles Times,* Part IV, January 3, 1974.

Buchalter, Gail. "Tanya Tucker Grows up into New Music Image," *Los Angeles Herald-Examiner,* 20 November 1978.

Burk, Bill E. "For Juice Press of Success Has Sweet Flavor" [Juice Newton], *Memphis Press-Scimitar,* 22 May 1981.

Cabot, Christopher. "Apostle of Nashville Sound" [Chet Atkins], *Los Angeles Times,* 13 September 1974.

Cackett, Alan. "Johnny Rodriguez," *Country Music People,* July 1974.

Caldwell, Carol. "Listen to Rosanne Cash," *Esquire,* July 1981.

Caliguiri, "Iris DeMent," *CMJ New Music Roundup,* 30 May 1994.

Campbell, Bob. "The Oak Ridge Explosion" [Oak Ridge Boys], *Country Music,* June 1979.

Carlisle, Dolly. "Gospel's Oak Ridge Boys Find a New Energy Source," *Country People,* 28 May 1979.

———. "Vince and Janis Gill," *People,* 10 June 1991.

———. "K. T. Is Now O.K." [K. T. Oslin], *People,* 14 June 1993.

Carr, Patrick. "Johnny Cash's Freedom," *Country Music,* 25 April 1977.

Carrier, James. "Scruggs Plugs in to the New Sound," *Associated Press,* 2 January 1976.

Carter, Walter. "Moe & Joe Make Good Ol' Boy Music" [Moe Bandy and Joe Stampley] *Tennessean,* 3 October 1979.

Cash Box magazine, New York, NY, various issues, 1970s through 1996.

Cash, Johnny. *Man in Black.* City: Zondervan, 1975.

Cauthen, Linda F. "Larry Stewart Heads Down the Road on His Own," *Country Fever,* 18 December 1993.

Cherry, Hugh. "Johnny Cash—The Man Behind the Mask," *Family Weekly,* 16 August 1970.

Ciabottini, Steve. "Texas Tornados," *CMJ New Music Report,* 1992.

Claypool, Bob. "Daniels Mirrors His Music" [Charlie Daniels]. *Houston Post,* 22 May 1977, p. 42.

———. "Van Zandt—No Average Tourist on Life's Road," *Houston Post,* 1 June 1977.

Coe, David Allan. *Just for the Record,* Big Pine Key, Florida: Dream Enterprises, 1978.

Cohen, John. "Fiddlin' Eck Robertson," *Sing Out,* April–May 1964, pp. 55–59.

Cohen, Norman, and Anne Cohen. "The Legendary Jimmy Tarleton," *Sing Out,* September 1966, pp. 16–19.

Coleman, Mark. "No Stranger to the Rain" [Keith Whitley], *The Journal of Country Music* 13, no. 2, pp. 44–46.

Coppola, Vincent. "Country Singer Tanya Tucker Has Survived Several Heartbreaking Relationships and a Hard-drinking, Hell-raising Past to Find Peace and Purpose in Motherhood," *Redbook,* September 1993.

Corbin, Everett. "It's a Long Way from Chester County" [Eddy Arnold], *Music City News,* October 1969, p. 3B.

———. "Uncle Dave Macon, First Feature Star of the Grand Ole Opry," *Music City News,* October 1973, pp. 24-C, 26–27-C.

———. "Mac Wiseman: Getting Back to Country Roots," *Music City News,* October 1973, pp. 30-C, 31-C.

———. "Rouse Brothers Have Claim to Fame, Write 'Orange Blossom Special,'" *Music City News,* October 1969, p. 38-B.

Corcoran, Michael. "No Trace of Doubt, Tracy Lawrence Makes It Clear That He's Star Material," *Dallas Morning News,* 31 May 1993.

———. "Columbia Bets It Has a Future Superstar in Austin's Rick Trevino," *Dallas Morning News,* 7 October 1993.

Country Music Hall of Fame & Museum, published for Country Music Foundation by Rosebud Books.

Cromelin, Richard. "Dedicated to Just Plain Folks" [Vince Gill], *Los Angeles Times,* 25 September 1994, Calendar section.

———. "For k.d. lang, It's Bye-Bye Patsy—Hello 'Ingenue,'" *Los Angeles Times,* 2 August 1992.

———. "Look out for the Turbo-Tonker" [Tim McGraw], *Los Angeles Times,* 5 June 1994.

Cronin, Peter. "Arista's BlackHawk Rises Through Ranks of Radio," *Billboard,* 15 January 1994.

———. "Vince Gill: Pickin' and Grinnin'," *Musician,* September 1991.

Cusic, Don. *Randy Travis: The King of the New Country Traditionalists,* New York: St. Martin's Press, 1990.

Dane, Michael. "Roy Clark," *Country Music,* June 1978.

Deen, Dixie. "Purely . . . Porter Wagoner," *Music City News,* March 1967, pp. 3–4.

Deford, Frank. "To Conway Twitty, Who's Been a Star of Both, Country Is a Higher Art Than Rock 'n'Roll," *People,* 3 September 1979.

Delmore, Alton. *The Delmore Brothers: Truth Is Stranger Than Publicity* [paperback reissue available from Country Music Hall of Fame & Museum].

Dery, Mark. "Les Paul: Once a Wunderkind, Still a Wizard," *The New York Times,* 1 December 1991, Arts & Leisure section.

Dew, Joan. "Freddie Hart: Pumping Out Great Music," *Country Music,* October 1976.

———. "Guess Who Lives Next Door to the Governor? Mrs. Sarah Ophelia Colley Cannon, That's Who" [Minnie Pearl], *Country Music,* November 1974.

———. "Tammy Wynette: Heroine of Heartbreak," *Cosmopolitan,* April 1978.

Dittman, Earl. "A Cowboy's Heart" [Chris LeDoux], *Tune In,* January 1994.

———. "The Return of the Hillbilly Terminator" [Aaron Tippin], *Tune In,* September 1993.

Dorfman, Marilyn. "Lone Star Sippin'—The Country Honkytonks Are Still Home for Michael Murphey," *Unicorn Times,* August 1979.

Edwards, Joe. "Country Singer Eddy Arnold Has Reclaimed Fine Voice," Associated Press, May 1991.

Ehler, Jay. "Waylon Jennings," *Country Life,* March/April 1973, pp. 4–5.

Eipper, Laura. "Conway Twitty—Making Changes These Days," *Tennessean,* 13 May 1979.

———. "Sharing Laughter with the Whole World" [Minnie Pearl], *Tennessean,* 1978.

Eng, Steve. *A Satisfied Mind: The Country Music Life of Porter Wagoner,* Nashville: Rutledge Press, 1992.

Escott, Colin. "The Gospel According to Marty" [Marty Stuart], *The Journal of Country Music,* June 1992.

———. "Teenage Idyll: An Everly Brother Looks Back," *The Journal of Country Music* 15, no. 2 (1993): pp. 18–23.

Eskow, John. "Hank Williams, Jr., The Son Also Rises," *New Times,* 29 May 1978.

Everett, Todd. "Dwight Yoakam: Not Just Another Hat," *The Journal of Country Music* 15, no. 3 (1993): pp. 11–15.

Fenster, Mark. "Under His Spell: How Buck Owens Took Care of Business," *The Journal of Country Music* 12, no. 3 (1989): p.

Flans, Robyn. "Shenandoah," *Country Fever,* August 1994.

Fong-Torres, Ben. "Leon Russell," *Rolling Stone,* 2 December 1970, pp. 33–37.

Forrest, Rick. "The Kenny Rogers Touring Machine," *On Stage,* 1981.

Forte, Don. "Ricky Skaggs Moonshine Lightning," *Musician,* January 1990.

Freedman, Samuel G. "Journey of 'Big River' to Broadway Success" [Roger Miller], *New York Times,* 16 July 1985.

Fulton, E. Kaye. "The New Improved Anne Murray, Happier, Richer Than Ever," *Odyssey* 1, no. 2 (1979).

Gattis, Kelly. "Playing with Sleepy Was Like Going to the Berklee School of Music on the Road" [Wagoneers], *Close Up,* September 1989, pp. 6–7.

Gentry, Linnell. *History and Encyclopedia of Country, Western and Gospel Music.* Nashville: McQuiddy Press, 1961.

George, Teresa. "John Berry," CMA *Close Up,* October 1994.

———. "Hank Cochran," CMA *Close Up,* September 1989, p. 12.

———. "Radney Foster," CMA *Close Up,* May 1994, p. 28.

———. "Ronnie Milsap: Still Grinding out the Hits," *CMA Close Up,* July 1991, p. 2.

———. "Lee Roy Parnell," CMA *Close Up,* July 1992, p. 8.

———. "Doug Supernaw," CMA *Close Up,* March 1994, p. 8.

Gill, Chris. "21st Century Rock & Roll Cowboy" [Marty Stuart], *Guitar Player,* April 1994.

Gleason, Holly. "A Megastar for Everyone," [Garth Brooks], *New York Times,* 26 September 1993, Arts & Leisure section.

———. "Martina McBride—Beautiful Woman, Beautiful Music," *Bone,* January 1994.

Green, Douglas B. "Barbara Mandrell, Picker/Singer," *Pickin',* September 1978.

———. Notes for jacket of album *Roy Acuff Greatest Hits, Volume 1,* Elektra Records, September 1978.

Greifinger, Marv. "Linda Davis, No Overnight Sensation," *Country Fever,* August 1994.

Guralnick, Peter. "Ernest Tubb, Still the Texas Troubadour," *Country Music,* 1977.

———. "Mickey Gilley's Piano Roll Blues," *Country Music.*

———. *Last Train to Memphis* [Elvis Presley], 1994.

Gutterman, Jimmy. *Jerry Lee Lewis—Rockin' My Life Away,* Nashville: Rutledge Press, 1991.

———. Liner notes for *The Jerry Lee Lewis Anthology—All Killer No Filler!,* Rhino Records, 1993.

———. "Songs That Tell a Story" [Charlie Louvin], *The Journal of Country Music* 12, no. 2 (1989): pp. 36–43.

Hansen, Valeria. "Bobbie Cryner Facing Her Fears," *Country Post,* January/February 1994.

Hardesty, Will. "The Pride of Paw Paw, West Virginia: Asleep at the Wheel," *Rocky Mountain Musical Express,* August 1977, p. 15.

Hedy, Judy. "Mel Tillis—It's a Long Way from Detroit City," *Country Song Roundup,* February 1977.

Henstell, Bruce. "How the King of Western Swing Reached the End of His Rope" [Spade Cooley], *Los Angeles Magazine,* June 1979, pp. 126–136.

Hilburn, Robert. "Dazzling Vegas Debut for Dolly Parton," *Los Angeles Times,* 23 February 1981, Calendar section.

———. "George Jones—Back from the Brink," *Los Angeles Times,* 8 March 1981, pp. 72, 74.

———. "Gram Parsons—Straight Home to Us," *Los Angeles Times,* 2 November 1975, pp. 62–63.

———. "Nelson Avoids the Country Bland Wagon," *Los Angeles Times,* 23 November 1976, p. 68.

———. "Wagoneers Roll Within Modest Boundaries," *Los Angeles Times,* 28 November 1988.

———. "Johnny Cash Looks Back with a Smile," *Los Angeles Times,* February 2, 1992, Calendar section.

———. "Hail to the Real King" [Lefty Frizzell], *Los Angeles Times,* 9 May 1993.

———. "This Guy Sounds Just Like Merle Haggard" [Merle Haggard], *Los Angeles Times,* February 10, 1991.

———. "Heartaches by the Score" [Harlan Howard], *Los Angeles Times,* 14 June 1992.

———. "I Couldn't Be Happier" [Lyle Lovett], *Los Angeles Times,* 22 July 1993, p. F1.

———. "Willie After the IRS and on the Road to 60," *Los Angeles Times,* 30 August 1992.

———. "The King of Crossover" (Mark O'Connor), *Los Angeles Times,* Calendar section, 27 October 1996.

Hirshberg, Charles and Robert Sullivan. "The 100 Most Important People in the History of Country," *Life,* September 1994.

Hochman, Steve. "Neville Brothers Lay Down an Irresistible Beat," *Los Angeles Times,* 7 May 1991.

Hoelzli, Cyndi. "The Father of Western Beat—Jimmy Dale Gilmore," *The Gavin Report,* 27 September 1991.

———. "George Jones," *The Gavin Report,* 24 January 1992.

Hogue, Brad. "Dwight Yoakam, This Time Bigger Than Ever," *Cash Box,* 15 May 1993.

Horak, Terri. "Fiddles, Songs and Friends on Berline's Sugar Hill Set," *Billboard,* 15 July 1995, p. 30.

Hume, Martha. "Crystal Gayle, At Home in the Middle of the Road," *Rolling Stone,* 19 May 1977.

Hunt, Dennis. "Alabama Loves Southern Rock," *Los Angeles Times,* 4 June 1981, Calendar section.

———. "Conway Twitty: Seeking His Just Desserts As a Music Star," *Los Angeles Times,* 27 May 1982, Part VI, p. 2.

———. "Brooks & Dunn," *Los Angeles Times,* 3 January 1993. Calendar section.

———. "Collin Raye, A Contemporary Guy Playing With Tradition," *Los Angeles Times,* 13 February 1994.

———. "Gatlin Goes for the Gusto," *Los Angeles Times,* 30 November 1980.

———. "Olivia Newton-John: Just Another Pretty Voice," *Los Angeles Times,* Part IV, pp. 1, 12.

———. "Clay Walker—After the Victory at That Talent Show," *Los Angeles Times,* January 30, 1994, Calendar section.

———. "He Engineered Success of Confederate Railroad" [Danny Shirley], *Los Angeles Times,* 21 May 1994.

Hunter, Glenn. "Stoney Edwards, the Case of Country Music's Number Two Black Star," *Country Music,* March 1976.

Hunter, James. "Beaumont Blues: Mark Chesnutt Hails Honky Tonk," *LA Weekly,* April 24/30, 1992.

———. "Wynonna Judd Stands Alone," *The New York Times,* 24 May 1992.

Hurst, Jack. "Barbara Mandrell Tries Not to Mix Music, Politics," *Chicago Tribune,* 3 January 1979, Section 4.

———. "Hank Williams, Jr. Is Alive and Well and That's Very Close to Being a Miracle," *Chicago Tribune Magazine,* 12 February 1978.

———. "Mandrell on the Move," *Chicago Tribune Magazine,* 22 April 1979.

———. "Willie Nelson, Country Music's Gentleman Outlaw," *Chicago Tribune Magazine,* 18 November 1979.

———. "New Dawn Awaits 'Make It Through the Night' Singer" [Sammi Smith], *Chicago Tribune,* 23 March 1978.

———. "Thompson, Echo from the Past, Still Finds a Place on the Charts" [Hank Thompson], *Chicago Tribune,* 12 September 1979.

———. "Three Men and an Attitude," [BlackHawk], *Chicago Tribune,* 6 February 1994.

———. "Back to the Future, Bobbie Cryner's Fiery Sound Is Straight out of Yesterday," *Chicago Tribune,* 22 August 1993.

———. "Arriba Reba!" [Reba McEntire], *Chicago Tribune,* 26 September 1993.

Jennings, Dana Andrew. "Bluegrass, Straight and Pure, Even If the Money's No Good" [Del McCoury Band], *New York Times,* Arts & Leisure section.

Jerrold, Jan. "The Del McCoury Band," *British Bluegrass News,* May 1993.

Johnson, Jared. "Eddie Rabbitt Prove Country-Pop Crossover Capabilities," *Denver Post,* 9 September 1979.

Jones, Grandpa, with Charles Wolfe. *Everybody's Grandpa—Fifty Years Behind the Mike.* Knoxville: University of Tennessee Press, 1984.

Keil, Karen. "A Touch of Pride," [Charley Pride], *Folk & Country* 1, no. 3 (May 1968): p. 5.

Kening, Dan. "So Long Cinderella," [Suzy Bogguss], *Country Post,* January/February 1994.

King, Bill. "On the Road With the Oak Ridge Boys," *Atlanta Journal & Constitution,* 16 February 1980, Weekend, pp. 34–36.

Kingsbury, Paul. "Trisha Yearwood Gets Serious," *The Journal of Country Music* 15 no. 1, 1993 pp. 12–19.

Kingsley, Michelle Pelick. "Wanted: Byron Berline," *Frets,* June 1979, pp. 34–36.

Koppel, David. "Jessi Colter and Her Big Grey Bus," *Chicago Sun Times,* 6 August 1978.

Lightfoot, William. "Belle of the Barn Dance: Reminiscing with Lulu Bell Wiseman Stanley" [Lulubelle and Scott], *The Journal of Country Music,* 12 no. 1 (1987): pp. 2–15.

Littleton, Bill. "T. G. Adjusts to Success" [T.G. Sheppard], *Music City News,* February 1976, p. 19.

Lloyd, Jack. "Asleep at the Wheel Plays More Than Western Swing," *Philadelphia Enquirer,* 9 December 1977.

Maier, Ann, and Steve Dougherty. "Back in the Groove Again" [Willie Nelson], *People,* 21 June 1993, p. 53.

Mann, Roderick. "Kristofferson: A Star Is Reborn," *Los Angeles Times,* 10 January 1982, Calendar section, p. 18.

Mansfield, Brian. "Angel Eyes" [Emmylou Harris], *Request,* October 1993.

Mariani, John. "The Fighting Side of Merle Haggard," *Saga,* November 1979, p. 41.

Marsh, Dave, and John Swenson. *New Rolling Stone Record Guide.* New York: Random House/Rolling Stone, 1983.

McCall, Michael. Liner notes for *Skynyrd Frynds,* MCA Records, 1994.

McVey, Richard. "Chris LeDoux Goes Haywire over His New Album," *Cash Box,* 17 September 1994.

———. "Travis Tritt: A Mere Ten Feet Tall and Bulletproof," *Cash Box,* 7 May 1994.

Millard, Bob. "Mark Chesnutt: Child of the Honky Tonks," *Country Music.*

Mitchell, Rick. "Straight Shooter" [George Strait], *Houston Chronicle,* 5 July 1990.

Modderno, Craig. "Lady's Man" [Kenny Rogers], *US,* 9 December 1980.

Moon, Buck. "Tribute to a White Trash Saint" [Hank Williams, Sr.], *Rocky Mountain Musical Express,* March 1977, p. 20.

Moore, Mary Ellen. "Watch This Face: Mel McDaniel," *Country Music,* January 1977.

Moore, Thurston. *Country Music Who's Who,* Denver, Colorado: Heather Publications, various editions.

Morthland, John. "Jerry Jeff Rides Again" [Jerry Jeff Walker], *Country Music,*

———. "Jersey's Country Boy" [Eddie Rabbitt], *Newsday,* 18 September 1977.

Music City News. Nashville, Tennessee, various issues.

Neff, James. "Freddy Fender Bares All," *Country Style,* 11 August 1977.

Nelson, Paul, and Jon Pankake. "Uncle Dave Macon—Country Immortal," *Sing Out!,* summer 1963, pp. 19–21.

Oermann, Robert. "Mark Chesnutt: A Country Classic," *Tennessean,* 18 December 1993, Living section.

———. "Dirt Band Gets Down to Nitty Gritty 'Acoustic'," *Tennessean,* 17 June 1994.

O'Meara, Sheri. "Billy the Kid Comes of Age" [Billy Dean], *Hot Country Headlines,* January 1994.

Orr, Jay. "Home Town Girl Makes Good" [Mary-Chapin Carpenter], *Request,* August 1992.

———. "Gibson, Miller Hit It Off," *Nashville Banner,* 12 January 1993.

Pender, Linda. "Urban Cowboys" [Riders in the Sky], *Cincinnati Magazine,* August 1990.

Phillips, Chuck. "Ray Price: Celebrated Texas Tenor and the Good Times," *Los Angeles Times,* 19 May 1989.

———. "Country Song Draws Ire of Feminists" [Holly Dunn], *Los Angeles Times,* 26 July 1991.

Piazza, Tom, "The Lost Man of Rock-and-Roll" [Carl Perkins], *The New York Times,* 10 November 1996 Arts & Leisure section, pp. 14, 19.

Pitts, Jr., Leonard. "Dolly Parton Comes Full Circle," *The Miami Herald,* 21 March 1993.

Pond, Steve. "Success Is All in the Family" [Aaron Neville], *New York Times,* 16 May 1993.

Pugh, John T. "Mel Tillis—From a Strawberry Patch to National Stardom," *Music City News,* May 1970, p. 22.

Radio & Records (weekly). Los Angeles, California, various issues.

Rassenfoss, Joe. "A Couple Weeks, That's a Long Time" [Delbert McClinton], *Birmingham Post-Herald Kudzu,* 31 October 1980, p. 4.

Record World (weekly). Record World Publishing Co., New York, various issues.

Rector, Lee. "Oak Ridge Boys Set High Energy Levels for Career, Today and Tomorrow," *Music City News,* November 1979, pp. 14–15.

Reid, Dixie. "Wisdom Road" [Tracy Lawrence], *The Sacramento Bee,* 30 September 1992.

Reinert, Al. "King of Country" [Willie Nelson], *The New York Times Magazine,* 26 March 1978.

Ridley, Jim. "Shooting for the Moon—Linda Davis Grabs the Spotlight," *New Country,* June 1994.

Roberts, Frank M. "Life's a Bed of Roses for the Statler Brothers," *Charlotte News,* 17 January 1980.

Robinson, Lisa. "Rogers Is a Big Star" [Kenny Rogers], *New York Times Feature Syndicate,* 14 September 1981.

Roden, Jim. "Bandy Revives a New Old Sound," *Dallas Times Herald,* 6 February 1976.

Ross, Richard. "Cactus Brothers," *Los Angeles Reader,* 1 October 1993.

Rowlett, Sharon. "Cal Smith," *Rocky Mountain Musical Express,* May 1978, p. 17.

Satterfield, La Wayne. "Johnny Rodriguez, New Heartthrob of Country Music," *Music City News,* October 1973, p. 37-A.

———. "Melba Wraps Herself in Song" [Melba Montgomery], *Music City News,* October 1973, p. 16-A.

———. "O. B. Doesn't Mind Being 'The Other One'," *Music City News,* October 1973, pp. 3-C, 37-C.

Scherman, Tony. "Once a 'Fiddlin' Teen', She's Now in Demand" [Alison Krauss], *New York Times,* 26 April 1994, Arts & Leisure section, p. 1.

Schoemer, Karen. "Marty Stuart Doesn't Need a Big Hat to Be Country," *The New York Times,* 12 July 1992.

———. Big Time" [Dwight Yoakam], *Rolling Stone,* 30 September 1993.

Shibley, Jeff. "Kansas Gal Martina McBride," *The Note,* November 1993.

Smith, Lisa. "Travis Tritt: It Just Keeps Getting Better," *The Gavin Report,* 22 November 1991.

Sowienski, Dick. "Hollywood Is a Nine-Letter Word," [Clint Black] *Country America,* April 1993.

Stambler, Irwin. *Encyclopedia of Pop, Rock & Soul,* New York: St. Martin's Press, 1974, 1977, 1989.

Stambler, Irwin, and Grelun Landon. *Encyclopedia of Folk, Country & Western Music,* New York: St. Martin's Press, 1969, 1983.

———. *Golden Guitars, The Story of Country Music,* New York: Four Winds Press, 1971.

Tritt, Travis. *Ten Feet Tall and Bulletproof,* spring 1994.

Turner, Judi. "New Grass Revival," CMA *Close Up,* March 1987, pp. 3–5.

Wager, Walter. *Stutterin' Boy* [Mel Tillis], 1984.

Whitburn, Joel. *The Billboard Book of Top 40 Hits,* New York: Billboard Publications, 1992.

———. *Top Country Records* [based on *Billboard* charts], Menomenee Falls, Wisconsin: Record Research, various editions.

Wiggins, Gene, *Fiddlin' Georgia Crazy* [Fiddlin' John Carson], Chicago: University of Illinois Press, 1987.

Williams, Don. "The Private World of Don Williams" (as told to Kelly Delaney), *Country Style,* September 1980.

Williams, Hank Jr. with Bane, Michael, *Living Proof, Autobiography of Hank Williams, Jr.,* New York: Putnam, 1979.

Williams, Janet E., "Carlene Carter," CMA Close Up,
———. "Russell Smith," CMA *Close Up,* July 1991, pp. 18–19, 25.
———. "Joe Diffie," CMA *Close Up,* March 1992, p. 3.
———. "Faith Hill," CMA *Close Up,* June 1994, p. 8.
———. "Tracy Lawrence," CMA *Close Up,* June 1993, p. 28.
———. "Mark O'Connor," CMA *Close Up,* June 1991, p. 10.
———. "K. T. Oslin," CMA *Close Up,* August 1991, p. 6.
———. "Kenny Rogers," CMA *Close Up,* June 1993, p. 4.
Willman, Chris. "Interior Dialogue" [Rosanne Cash], *Los Angeles Times,* 31 March 1991, Calendar section.
———. "Lovett Country" [Lyle Lovett], *Los Angeles Times,* 31 May 1992, pp. 1, 54.
Wilson, Mandy. "Charlie Daniels," CMA *Close Up,* July 1993, p. 28.
———. "Holly Dunn," CMA *Close Up,* September 1992, p. 10.
———. "Ira Louvin," CMA *Close Up,* March 1992, p. 18.
———. "Eddie Rabbit," CMA *Close Up,* October 1991, p. 8.

Winbush, Don. "The Color of Country" [Steve Earle], *Time,* 8 September 1986.
Winters, Audrey. "Buck Owens: A Career Built on Careful Planning," *Music City News,* October 1969, p. 40-A.
Wix, Kimmy. "Collin Raye Soars Beyond the Ballads," *Music City News,* October 1992.
Wolfe, Charles K. "The White Man's Blues, 1992–40," *The Journal of Country Music* 15, no. 3 (1993): pp. 38–44.
Wood, Tom. "Matters of the Heart, Restless Heart on Track with 3-Man Group," *Tennessean,* 4 June 1994.
———. "Oh, Shenandoah, We Long to Hear You," *Tennessean,* 27 May 1994.
Wright, John. "Ralph Stanley Today," *Banjo Newsletter,* January 1984, pp. 5–10.
Young, Jon. "Charlie Daniels' Million-Dollar Miles," *Rolling Stone,* 1 November 1979.
Young, Ron. "Shooting Straight with George" [George Strait], *San Antonio Express-News,* 5 September 1993.
Zimmerman, David. "Bogguss' Varied 'Voices'," *USA Today,* 4 November 1992.

INDEX OF ARTISTS

INDEX OF
ALBUM AND SONG TITLES

He Touched Me (Tennessee Ernie Ford), 164
"He Walked on Water," 497
He Walks with Thee, 162
"He Was on to Somethin'," 442
"He Was There (When I Needed You)," 558
"He Will Break Your Heart," 418
Head over Heels, 377
"Head to Toe," 12
"Headache Tomorrow (Or a Heartache Today), A," 184
"Heads Carolina, Tails California," 310
"Healing Chant," 338
Healing Hands of Time, 337
Health and Happiness Shows, 547
"Heard It in a Love Song," 284
Heart (Kitty Wells), 524
Heart and Soul, 511
"Heart Attack," 342
Heart Full of Love, 145
"Heart Full of Love, A," 17
"Heart Like a Hurricane," 467
Heart Never Lies, The, 328
Heart of Fire, 424
Heart of Marty Robbins, 409
"Heart of Mine," 345
Heart on My Sleeve, 411
"Heart Over Mind," 325, 383
Heart Over Mind, 332
Heart Songs & Love Songs (Slim Whitman), 536
"Heart Strings," 17
"Heart to Heart," 88
Heart to Heart (Lee Clayton), 89
Heart to Heart (Reba McEntire), 303
"Heart That You Own, The," 564
"Heart Trouble," 521
"Heart Won't Lie, The," 182, 304, 305
"Heartache," 41
Heartache Begins, 94
"Heartache Tonight," 147
"Heartaches and Flowers," 2
Heartaches and Tears, 224
"Heartaches by the Number," 209, 210, 219, 383, 385
Heartaches by the Number, 224
"Heartaches of a Fool," 335
Heartbeat, 345
"Heartbeat in the Darkness," 11
"Heartbreak Ahead," 215
Heartbreak Express, 365
"Heartbreak Hotel," 380, 425, 505
"Heartbreak Hurricane," 442
"Heartbreak Kid." *See* "(Back to the) Heartbreak Kid"
"Heartbreak Mountain," 223
"Heartbreak Street," 107
"Heartbreak USA," 210
"Heartbreak U.S.A.," 524
Heartbreak U.S.A., 524
"Heartbreaker," 364
Heartbreaker, 364
"Heartbroke," 87, 441
Heartland, 473
Heartland, 229
"Hearts Are Gonna Roll," 237
"Hearts Are Lonely," 259
Hearts in Armor, 562

"Hearts of Stone," 162
"Hearts on Fire," 390
Hearts on the Line, 161
"Heartstrings," 241
"Heat of the Night," 377
"Heaven In My Woman's Eyes," 61
"Heaven Must Have Sent You," 378
"Heaven Says Hello," 217
"Heaven Was a Drink of Wine," 194
"Heed the Call," 418, 419
"Helen," 445
"Hell and High Water," 54
Hell Freezes Over, 148
Hell Freezes Over Tour, The, 500–501
"He'll Have to Go," 397
He'll Have to Go, 397
He'll Have to Go and Other Favorites, 397
Hello, I'm Dolly, 363
Hello, I'm Johnny Cash, 77
"Hello, This Is Anna," 297
"Hello Darlin'," 510, 511
"Hello Fool," 333
"Hello Mary Lou," 461
Hello Operator . . . This Is Country Gazette, 109
"Hello Texas," 59
"Hello Viet Nam," 555
"Hello Walls," 333, 567
"Help Me," 243
"Help Me Hold On," 500
"Help Me Make It Through the Night," 208, 243, 335, 447, 448
"Help the Cowboys Sing the Blues," 219
Help Yourself, 173
"Henrietta," 302
Hemingway Hideaway," 34
"Hep Cat Baby," 17
"Her First Mistake," 267
"Her Name Is . . . ," 225
"Here, There and Everywhere," 200
"Here Comes Heaven," 17
Here Comes Honey Again, 217
"Here Comes My Baby," 526
Here Comes My Baby, 527
"Here Comes Santa Claus," 25
"Here Comes the 80s," 113
"Here Comes the Hurt Again," 184
"Here Comes the Rain," 288
"Here Comes the Rain Baby," 17
"Here I Am," 264
"Here I Am Again," 271
"Here I Am Drunk Again," 28
Here I Am Drunk Again, 28
"Here I Am in Dallas," 566
Here in the Real World, 212
Here in the Real World, 212
"Here We Are," 6
"Here We Go Again," 82, 460
Here You Come Again, 364
"Here's a Quartet (Call Someone Who Cares)," 500
Here's a Toast to Mama, 261
Here's Charly McClain, 293
"Here's My San Antonio Rose," 498
Here's Patsy Cline, 94

"Here's Some Love," 505
"Here's That Rainy Day," 418
Here's What's Happening, 112
Heroes (Cash/Jennings), 78, 220
Heroes (Mark O'Connor), 234
Heroes and Friends (Randy Travis), 497, 558
"He's a Heartache (Looking for a Place to Happen)," 169
"He's Back and I'm Blue," 129
"He's Everywhere," 448
"He's Living My Dreams," 293
"He's My Rock," 251
"He's Out of My Life," 169
"He's So Shy," 378
"Hey, Good Lookin'," 545
"Hey, Little Star," 312
"Hey Baby," 295
"Hey Cinderella," 41
"Hey Doll Baby," 479
"Hey Good Lookin'," 141
"Hey Joe," 56, 352, 445
"Hey Joe, Hey Moe," 28, 57, 456
Hey Joe, Hey Moe, 28
Hey Little One, 64
"Hey Lucky Lady," 363
"Hey Mister (I Need This Job)," 435
"Hey Mr. Sax Man," 392
"Hey Old Man," 474
"Hey Porter," 76
Hi Fi in Focus, 23
"Hickory Wind," 46, 361
"Hidden Walls," 566
"Hide and Seek," 139
Hideaway Heart, 374
"Hiding in My Heart," 257
"High Blood Pressure," 254
"High Cotton," 6
High Cumberland Jubilee, 59
"High Fashion Queen," 160
High Lonesome, 1997, 118
"High Lonesome Sound," 183
High Lonesome Sound (Bill Monroe), 317, 318
High Lonesome Sound (Vince Gill), 183
"High Noon," 406
High Notes (Hank Williams, Jr.), 543
High on a Hilltop (Sing a Sad Song/High on a Hilltop), 193
"High on Love," 371
High on the Mountain, 299
"High Power Love," 202
"High Rollin'," 179
"High School Confidential," 251
"High School Days," 437
"High School Romance," 197
High Tech Redneck, 226
High Time, 172
"High Weeds and Rust," 329
Higher Ground, 558
Highly Prized Possession, 331
Highway and Heartaches, 441
"Highway 40 Blues," 441
Highway of Life, 434
"Highway Patrol," 56, 79
"Highwayman," 203, 244
Highwayman, 64, 87, 203, 220, 244, 336
Highwayman 2, 72, 78, 90, 203, 220, 244, 336-37
Hillbilly Boogie, 131, 132

Hillbilly Deluxe (Dwight Yoakam), 564
"Hillbilly Fever," 132
Hillbilly Heaven, 406
"Hillbilly Hell," 33
Hillbilly Jazz, 92, 93
Hillbilly Rock, 476
Hills of Home, 457
Hills of Home, 458
Hindsight 20/20, 70
Hippo in My Tub, 331
Hi-Res, 152
"His Hand in Mine," 381
His Own Songs (Willie Nelson), 334
"History Repeats Itself," 492
Hit Boots (Boots Randolph), 392
"Hit Me with Your Best Shot," 309
Hit Sound (Everly Brothers), 155
"Hit the Ground Running," 103
"Hit the Road Jack," 82
Hits (Floyd Cramer), 112
Hits, The (Garth Brooks), 51
Hits, Hits, Don Gibson Way, 177
Hits by Candlelight (George Morgan), 324
Hits Covered (Hank Snow), 450
Hits from Hee Haw (Grandpa Jones), 228
Hits from the Heart (Hank Cochran), 96
Hits of Country Cousins (George Jones), 224
Hits of Johnnie and Jack, 555
Hits of T. Texas Tyler, 513
Hits Old and New (Ernest Tubb), 502
Hittin' the Road, 502
"Hobo Bill's Last Ride," 415
Hog Wild, 544
"Hold Back the Dawn," 59
"Hold Me," 280, 353
"Hold On," 81, 113, 521
Hold On, 137
"Hold on a Little Longer," 522
"Hold on Tight," 517
"Hold That Critter Down," 403
"Hold Thou My Hand," 162
"Hold to God's Unchanging Hands," 517
"Hold What You've Got," 217
"Holdin' a Good Hand," 191–92
"Holdin' Heaven," 61
"Holding Her and Loving You," 104
Holding My Own, 473
"Holding on to Nothing," 363, 516
"Holding the Bag," 28, 456
Holding the Bag, 28
"Holiday for Love," 374
Holly, Holly, Holly, 164
Holly Dunn, 144
Hollywood, Tennessee, 175
"Hollywood Waltz," 147
Holy Bible—New Testament (Statler Brothers), 460
Holy Bible—Old Testament (Statler Brothers), 460
"Holy One," 157
"Home," 134, 213, 271, 397

GENERAL INDEX